# Maths for Scientists

Fourth Edition

PEARSON
Custom Publishing

We work with leading authors to develop the strongest educational materials bringing cutting-edge thinking and best learning practice to a global market.

Under a range of well-known imprints, including Financial Times/Prentice Hall, Addison Wesley and Longman, we craft high quality print and electronic publications which help readers to understand and apply their content, whether studying or at work.

Pearson Custom Publishing enables our customers to access a wide and expanding range of market-leading content from world-renowned authors and develop their own tailor-made book. You choose the content that meets your needs and Pearson Custom Publishing produces a high-quality printed book.

To find out more about custom publishing, visit www.pearsoncustom.co.uk

A Pearson Custom Publication

# Maths for Scientists

## Fourth Edition

Compiled from:

*Modern Engineering Mathematics*
Fourth Edition
by Glyn James, David Burley, Dick Clements, Phil Dyke, John Searl and Jerry Wright

*Mathematics for Physics with Calculus*
by Biman Das

*Engineering Mathematics: A Foundation for Electronic, Electrical, Communications and Systems Engineers*
Third Edition
by Anthony Croft, Robert Davison and Martin Hargreaves

*Calculus: A Complete Course*
Seventh Edition
by Robert A. Adams and Christopher Essex

PEARSON
Custom Publishing

Pearson Education Limited
Edinburgh Gate
Harlow
Essex CM20 2JE

And associated companies throughout the world

*Visit us on the World Wide Web at:*
www.pearsoned.co.uk

First published 2006


Taken from:

*Modern Engineering Mathematics* Fourth Edition
by Glyn James, David Burley, Dick Clements, Phil Dyke, John Searl and Jerry Wright
ISBN 978 0 13 239144 3


*Mathematics for Physics with Calculus*
by Biman Das
ISBN 978 0 13 191336 3


*Engineering Mathematics: A Foundation for Electronic, Electrical, Communications and Systems Engineers* Third Edition
by Anthony Croft, Robert Davison and Martin Hargreaves
ISBN 978 0 13 026858 7


*Calculus: A Complete Course* Seventh Edition
by Robert A. Adams and Christopher Essex
ISBN 978 0 321 54928 0


ISBN 978 1 84959 865 1

Printed and bound by in Great Britain by Antony Rowe.

# Contents

THE UNIVERSITY OF
WARWICK

# INTRODUCTION

**Mathematics for students on the first year of an honours degree course in physics.**

A sound knowledge of certain areas of mathematics is essential for the successful study of physics at university level. However, students' mathematical knowledge coming to university varies considerably. The aim of this textbook and the module it accompanies is to revise relevant parts of the A-level or pre-university syllabus, to provide students with sufficient mathematical knowledge to undertake first year physics modules, to help them gain fluency in using that knowledge and, finally, to prepare them for further mathematics and physics modules later on in the physics course.

Ideas in physics are developed by application of mathematics and it is therefore important for physics students to be comfortable with using a range of mathematical techniques as well as merely understanding the concepts behind them. We have therefore compiled this customised textbook by selecting sections from a number of established mathematics textbooks which not only explain the key techniques and demonstrate them from examples relevant to physics and engineering applications but which also have a useful bank of exercises (with solutions) for students to practise on. We therefore recommend that students read the relevant sections in the textbook as that material is lectured and attempt at least 1 or 2 suitable exercises per lecture.

# Vectors

# 4 Vector Algebra

| Chapter 4 | Contents |
| --- | --- |

## 4.1 Introduction

Much of the work of engineers and scientists involves forces. Ensuring the structural integrity of a building or a bridge involves knowing the forces acting on the system and designing the structural members to withstand them. Many have seen the dramatic pictures of the Tacoma bridge disaster (see also Section 10.10.3), when the forces acting on the bridge were not predicted accurately. To analyse such a system requires the use of Newton's laws in a situation where vector notation is essential. Similarly, in a reciprocating engine periodic forces act, and Newton's laws are used to design a crankshaft that will reduce the side forces to zero, thereby minimizing wear on the moving parts. Forces are three-dimensional quantities and provide one of the commonest examples of vectors. Associated with these forces are accelerations and velocities, which can also be represented by vectors. The use of formal mathematical notation and rules becomes progressively more important as problems become complicated and, in particular, in three-dimensional situations. Forces, velocities and accelerations all satisfy rules of addition that identify them as vectors. In this chapter we shall construct an algebraic theory for the manipulation of vectors and see how it can be applied to some simple practical problems.

The ideas behind vectors as formal quantities developed mainly during the nineteenth century, and they became a well-established tool in the twentieth century. Vectors provide a convenient and compact way of dealing with multi-dimensional situations without the problem of writing down every bit of information. They allow the principles of the subject to be developed without being obscured by complicated notation.

It is inconceivable that modern scientists and engineers could work successfully without computers. Since such machines cannot think like an engineer or scientist, they have to be told in a totally precise and formal way what to do. For instance, a robot arm needs to be given instructions on how to position itself to perform a spot weld. Three-dimensional vectors prove to be the perfect way to tell the computer how to specify the position of the workpiece of the robot arm and a set of rules then tells the robot how to move to its working position.

Computers have put a great power at the disposal of the engineer; problems that proved to be impossible 50 years ago are now routine. With the aid of numerical algorithms, equations can often be solved very quickly. The stressing of a large structure or an aircraft wing, the lubrication of shafts and bearings, the flow of sewage in pipes and the flow past the fuselage of an aircraft are all examples of systems that were well understood in principle but could not be analysed until the necessary computer power became available. Algorithms are usually written in terms of vectors and matrices (see Chapter 5), since these form a natural setting for the numerical solution of engineering problems and are also ideal for the computer. It is vital that the manipulation of vectors be understood before embarking on more complex mathematical structures used in engineering computations.

Perhaps the most powerful influence of computers is in their graphical capabilities, which have proved invaluable in displaying the static and dynamic behaviour of systems. We accept this tool without thinking how it works. A simple example shows the complexity. How do we display a box with an open top with 'hidden' lines when we look at it from a given angle? The problem is a complicated three-dimensional one that must be analysed instantly by a computer. Vectors allow us to define lines that can be projected on to the screen, and intersections can then be computed so that the 'hidden' portion can be eliminated. Extending the analysis to a less regular shape is a formidable vector problem. Work of this type is the basis of CAD/CAM systems, which now assist engineers in all stages of the manufacturing process from design to production of a finished product. Such systems typically allow engineers to manipulate the product geometry during initial design, to produce working drawings, to generate toolpaths in the production process and generally to automate a host of previously tedious and time-consuming tasks.

The general development of the theory of vectors is closely associated with coordinate geometry, so we shall introduce a few ideas in the next section that will be used later in the chapter. The comments largely concern the two- and three-dimensional cases, but we shall mention higher-dimensional extensions where they are relevant to later work such as on the theory of matrices. While in two and three dimensions we can appeal to geometrical intuition, it is necessary to work in a much more formal way in higher dimensions, as with many other areas of mathematics.

## 4.2 Basic definitions and results

### 4.2.1 Cartesian coordinates

Setting up rectangular cartesian axes O$xyz$ or O$x_1x_2x_3$, we define the position of a point by **coordinates** or **components** $(x, y, z)$ or $(x_1, x_2, x_3)$ as indicated in Figure 4.1(a). The indicial notation is particularly important when we consider vectors in many dimensions $(x_1, x_2, \dots, x_n)$. The axes O$x$, O$y$, O$z$, in that order, are assumed to be right-handed in the sense of Figure 4.1(b), so that a rotation of a right-handed screw from O$x$ to O$y$ advances it along O$z$, a rotation from O$y$ to O$z$ advances it along O$x$ and a rotation from O$z$ to O$x$ advances it along O$y$. This is an accepted convention, and it will be seen to be particularly important in Section 4.2.9 when we deal with the vector product.

The length of OP in Figure 4.1(a) is obtained from Pythagoras' theorem as

$$r = (x^2 + y^2 + z^2)^{1/2}$$

The angle $\alpha = \angle$POA in the right angled triangle OAP is the angle that OP makes with the positive $x$ direction as in Figure 4.2. We can see that

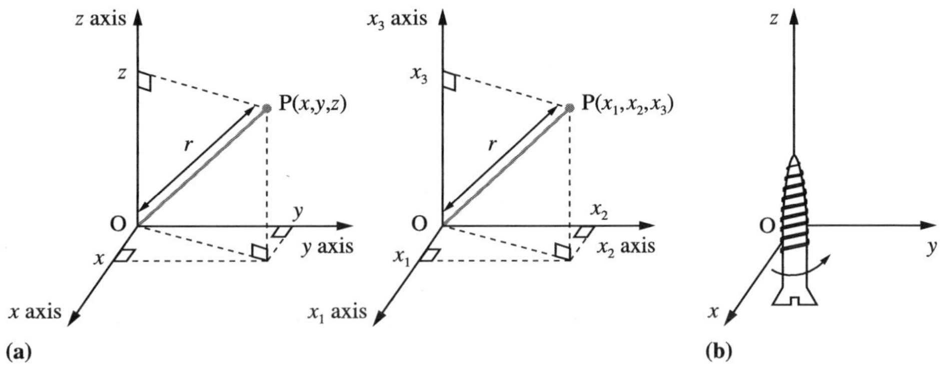


**Figure 4.1**
(a) Right-handed coordinate axes.
(b) Right-hand rule.

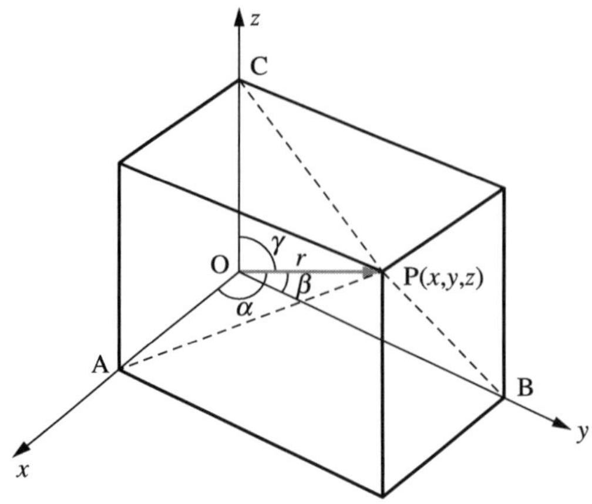


**Figure 4.2** Direction cosines of OP, $l = \cos\alpha$, $m = \cos\beta$, $n = \cos\gamma$.

$$l = \cos\alpha = \frac{x}{r}$$

Likewise, $\beta$ and $\gamma$ are the angles that OP makes with $y$ and $z$ directions respectively, so

$$m = \cos\beta = \frac{y}{r}, \quad n = \cos\gamma = \frac{z}{r}$$

The triad $(l, m, n)$ are called the **direction cosines** of the line OP. Note that

$$l^2 + m^2 + n^2 = \frac{x^2}{r^2} + \frac{y^2}{r^2} + \frac{z^2}{r^2} = \frac{x^2 + y^2 + z^2}{r^2} = 1$$

**Example 4.1**

If P has coordinates (2, −1, 3), find the length OP and the direction cosines of OP.

**Solution**

$OP^2 = (2)^2 + (-1)^2 + (3)^2 = 4 + 1 + 9$, so that $OP = \sqrt{14}$

The direction cosines are

$$l = 2\sqrt{\tfrac{1}{14}}, \quad m = -\sqrt{\tfrac{1}{14}}, \quad n = 3\sqrt{\tfrac{1}{14}}$$

**Example 4.2**

A surveyor sets up his theodolite on horizontal ground, at a point O, and observes the top of a church spire, as illustrated in Figure 4.3. Relative to axes O$xyz$, with O$z$ vertical, the surveyor measures the angles $\angle TOx = 66°$ and $\angle TOz = 57°$. The church is known to have height 35 m. Find the angle $\angle TOy$ and calculate the coordinates of T with respect to the given axes.

**Solution**

The direction cosines

$$l = \cos 66° = 0.406\,74 \quad \text{and} \quad n = \cos 57° = 0.544\,64$$

are known and hence the third direction cosine can be computed as

$$m^2 = 1 - l^2 - n^2 = 0.537\,93$$

Thus, $m = 0.733\,44$ and hence $\angle TOy = \cos^{-1}(0.733\,44) = 42.82°$. The length $OT = r$ can now be computed from the known height, 35 m, and the direction cosine $n$, as

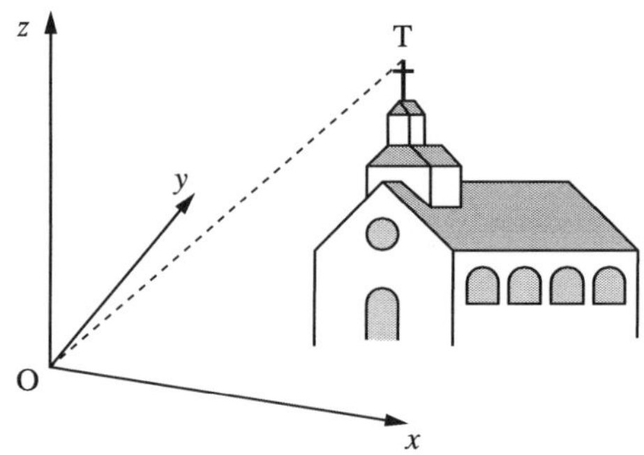


**Figure 4.3**
Representation of the axes and church spire in Example 4.2.

$$\cos 57° = 35/r, \quad \text{so} \quad r = 64.26 \text{ m}$$

The remaining coordinates are obtained from

$$x/r = \cos 66° \quad \text{and} \quad y/r = \cos 42.82°$$

giving $x = r\cos 66° = 26.14$ and $y = r\cos 42.82° = 47.13$

Hence the coordinates of T are (26.14, 47.13, 35).

---

### 4.2.2 Scalars and vectors

Quantities like distance or temperature are represented by real numbers in appropriate units, for instance 5 m or 10°C. Such quantities are called **scalars** – they obey the usual rules of real numbers and they have no direction associated with them. However, **vectors** have both a magnitude and a direction associated with them; these include force, velocity and magnetic field. To qualify as vectors, the quantities must have more than just magnitude and direction – they must also satisfy some particular rules of combination. Angular displacement in three dimensions gives an example of a quantity which has a direction and magnitude but which does not add by the addition rules of vectors, so angular displacements are *not* vectors.

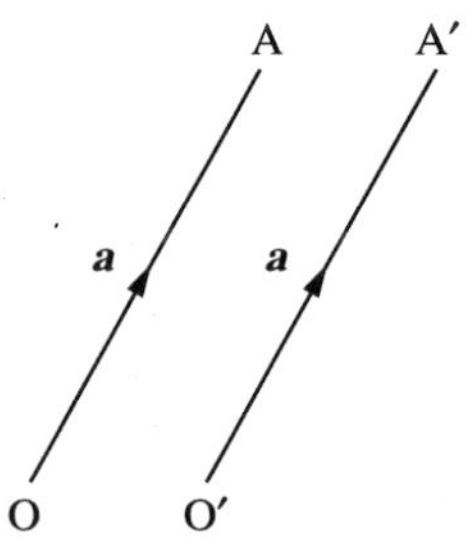


**Figure 4.4**
Line segments representing a vector ***a***.

We represent a vector geometrically by a line segment whose length represents the vector's magnitude in some appropriate units and whose direction represents the vector's direction, with the arrowhead indicating the sense of the vector, as shown in Figure 4.4. According to this definition, the starting point of the vector is irrelevant. In Figure 4.4, the two line segments OA and O′A′ represent the same vector because their lengths are the same, their directions are the same and the sense of the arrows is the same. Thus each of these vectors is equivalent to the vector through the origin, with A given by its coordinates $(a_1, a_2, a_3)$ as in Figure 4.5. We can therefore represent a vector in a three-dimensional space by an ordered set of three numbers or a 3-tuple. We shall see how this representation is used in Section 4.2.4.

We shall now introduce some of the basic notation and definitions for vectors. The vector of Figure 4.5 is handwritten or typewritten as $\underset{\sim}{a}$, $\underline{a}$, $\overrightarrow{OA}$. On the printed page bold-face type ***a*** is used. Using the coordinate definition, the vector could equally be written as $(a_1, a_2, a_3)$. (Note: There are several possible coordinate notations; the traditional one is $(a_1, a_2, a_3)$, but in Section 5.2.1 of Chapter 5 on matrices we shall use an alternative standard notation.)

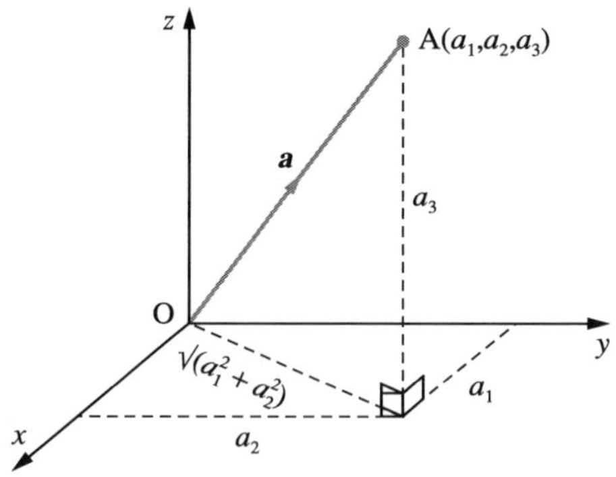


**Figure 4.5**
Representation of the vector ***a*** by the line segment OA.

Some basic properties of vectors are:

*(a) Equality*

As we considered earlier, two vectors ***a*** and ***b*** are equal if and only if they have the same modulus and the same direction and sense. We write this in the usual way

$$\mathbf{a} = \mathbf{b}$$

We shall see in Section 4.2.4 that in component form, two vectors $\mathbf{a} = (a_1, a_2, a_3)$ and $\mathbf{b} = (b_1, b_2, b_3)$ are **equal** if and only if the components are equal, that is

$$a_1 = b_1, \quad a_2 = b_2, \quad a_3 = b_3$$

*(b) Multiplication by a scalar*

If $\lambda$ is a scalar and the vectors are related by $\mathbf{a} = \lambda \mathbf{b}$ then

if $\lambda > 0$, ***a*** is a vector in the same direction as ***b*** with magnitude $\lambda$ times the magnitude of ***b***;

if $\lambda < 0$, ***a*** is a vector in the opposite direction to ***b*** with magnitude $|\lambda|$ times the magnitude of ***b***.

*(c) Parallel vectors*

The vectors ***a*** and ***b*** are said to be **parallel** or **antiparallel** according as $\lambda > 0$ or $\lambda < 0$ respectively. (Note that we do not insert any multiplication symbol between $\lambda$ and ***b*** since the common symbols · and × are reserved for special uses that we shall discuss later.)

*(d) Modulus*

The **modulus** or **length** or **magnitude** of a vector ***a*** is written as $|\mathbf{a}|$ or $|\overrightarrow{OA}|$ or $a$ if there is no ambiguity. A vector with modulus one is called a **unit vector** and is written $\hat{\mathbf{a}}$, with the hat (^) indicating a unit vector. Clearly

$$\mathbf{a} = |\mathbf{a}|\hat{\mathbf{a}} \quad \text{or} \quad \hat{\mathbf{a}} = \frac{\mathbf{a}}{|\mathbf{a}|}$$

*(e) Zero vector*

The **zero** or **null vector** has zero modulus; it is written as $\mathbf{0}$ or often just as 0 when there is no ambiguity whether it is a vector or not.

**Example 4.3** A cyclist travels at a steady 16 km/h on the four legs of his journey. From his origin, O, he travels for one hour in a NE direction to the point A; he then travels due E for half an hour to point B. He then cycles in a NW direction until he reaches the point C, which is due N of his starting point. He returns due S to the starting point. Indicate the path of the cyclist using vectors and calculate the modulus of the vectors along BC and CO.

**Solution** The four vectors are shown in Figure 4.6. If $\hat{\boldsymbol{i}}$ and $\hat{\boldsymbol{j}}$ are the unit vectors along the two axes then by property (b)

$$\overrightarrow{AB} = 8\hat{\boldsymbol{i}} \quad \text{and} \quad \overrightarrow{CO} = -L\hat{\boldsymbol{j}}$$

where $L$ is still to be determined. By trigonometry

$$DB = 8 + 16 \sin 45° = 8 + 8\sqrt{2}$$

and hence the modulus of the vector $\overrightarrow{BC}$ is

$$|BC| = \frac{DB}{\cos 45°} = 8\sqrt{2} + 16$$

The modulus $L$ of the vector $\overrightarrow{CO}$ is

$$L = |\overrightarrow{CO}| = CD + DO = (8 + 8\sqrt{2}) + 16 \cos 45° = 8 + 16\sqrt{2}$$

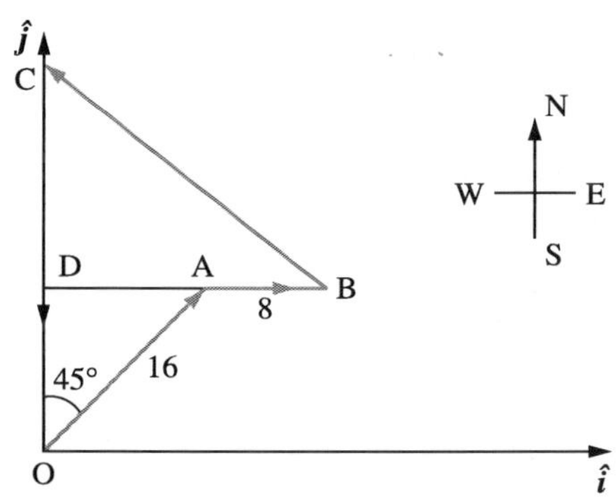


**Figure 4.6** Cyclist's path in Example 4.3.

## 4.2.3 Addition of vectors

Having introduced vectors and their basic properties, it is natural to ask if vectors can be combined. The simplest form of vector combination is addition and it is the definition of addition that finally identifies a vector. Consider the following situation. The helmsman of a small motor boat steers his vessel due east (E) at 4 knots for one hour. The path taken by the boat could be represented by the line OA, or **a**, in Figure 4.7. Unfortunately there is also a tidal stream, **b**, running north-north-east (NNE) at $2\frac{1}{2}$ knots. Where will the boat actually be at the end of one hour?

If we imagine the vessel to be steaming E for one hour through still water, and then lying still in the water and drifting with the tidal stream for one hour, we can see that it will travel from O to A in the first hour and from A to C in the second hour. If, on the

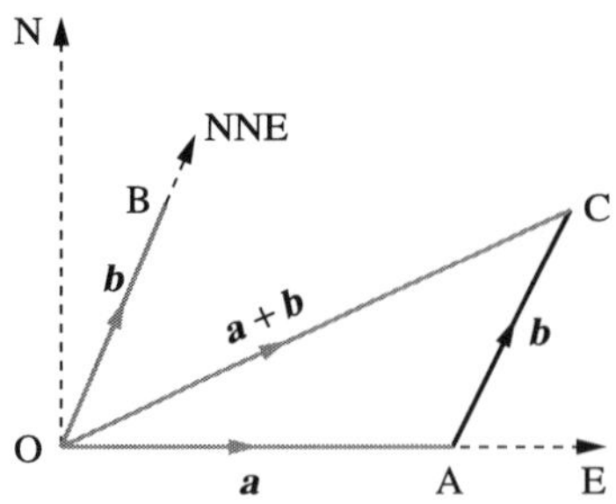


**Figure 4.7**
Addition of two vectors.

other hand, the vessel steams due E through water that is simultaneously moving NNE with the tidal stream then the result will be to arrive at C after one hour. The net velocity of the boat is represented by the line OC. Putting this another way, the result of subjecting the boat to a velocity $\overrightarrow{OA}$ and a velocity $\overrightarrow{AC}$ simultaneously is the same as the result of subjecting it to a velocity $\overrightarrow{OC}$. Thus the velocity $\overrightarrow{OC} = \mathbf{a} + \mathbf{b}$ is the sum of the velocity $\overrightarrow{OA} = \mathbf{a}$ and the velocity $\overrightarrow{AC} = \mathbf{b}$.

This leads us to the **parallelogram rule** for vector addition illustrated in Figure 4.8 and stated as follows:

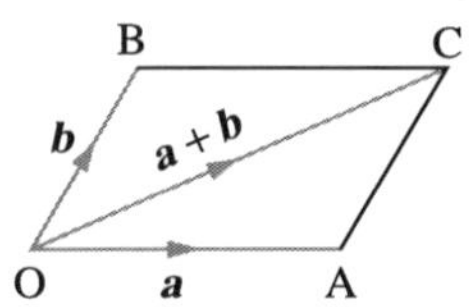


**Figure 4.8**
Parallelogram rule for addition of vectors.

> The sum, or resultant, of two vectors $\boldsymbol{a}$ and $\boldsymbol{b}$ is found by forming a parallelogram with $\boldsymbol{a}$ and $\boldsymbol{b}$ as two adjacent sides. The sum $\boldsymbol{a} + \boldsymbol{b}$ is the vector represented by the diagonal of the parallelogram.

In Figure 4.8 the vectors $\overrightarrow{OB}$ and $\overrightarrow{AC}$ are the same, so we can rewrite the parallelogram rule as an equivalent **triangle law** (Figure 4.9), which can be stated as follows:

> If two vectors $\boldsymbol{a}$ and $\boldsymbol{b}$ are represented in magnitude and direction by the two sides of a triangle taken in order then their sum is represented in magnitude and direction by the closing third side.

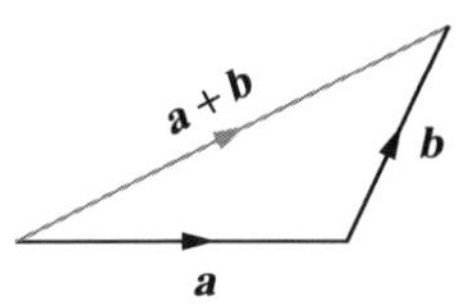


**Figure 4.9**
Triangle law for addition of vectors.

The triangle law for the addition of vectors can be extended to the addition of any number of vectors. If from a point O (Figure 4.10), displacements $\overrightarrow{OA}$, $\overrightarrow{AB}$, $\overrightarrow{BC}$, ... , $\overrightarrow{LK}$ are drawn along the adjacent sides of a polygon to represent in magnitude and direction the vectors $\boldsymbol{a}$, $\boldsymbol{b}$, $\boldsymbol{c}$, ... , $\boldsymbol{k}$ respectively then the sum

$$\boldsymbol{r} = \boldsymbol{a} + \boldsymbol{b} + \boldsymbol{c} + \ldots + \boldsymbol{k}$$

of these vectors is represented in magnitude and direction by the closing side OK of the polygon, the sense of the sum vector being represented by the arrow in Figure 4.10. This is referred to as the **polygon law** for the addition of vectors.

We now need to look at the usual rules of algebra for scalar quantities to check whether or not they are satisfied for vectors.

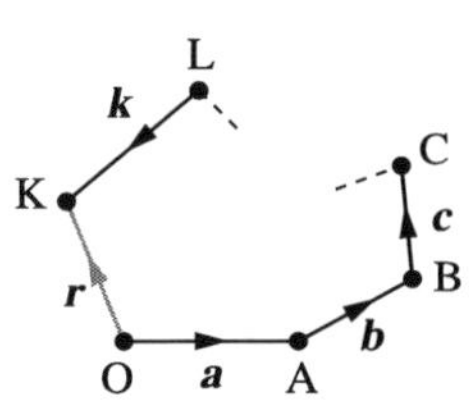


**Figure 4.10**
Polygon law for addition of vectors.

### *(a) Commutative law*

$$\boldsymbol{a} + \boldsymbol{b} = \boldsymbol{b} + \boldsymbol{a}$$

This result is obvious from the geometrical definition, and says that order does not matter.

### (b) Associative law

$$(\boldsymbol{a} + \boldsymbol{b}) + \boldsymbol{c} = \boldsymbol{a} + (\boldsymbol{b} + \boldsymbol{c})$$

Geometrically, the result can be deduced using the triangle and polygon laws, as shown in Figure 4.11. We see that brackets do not matter and can be omitted.

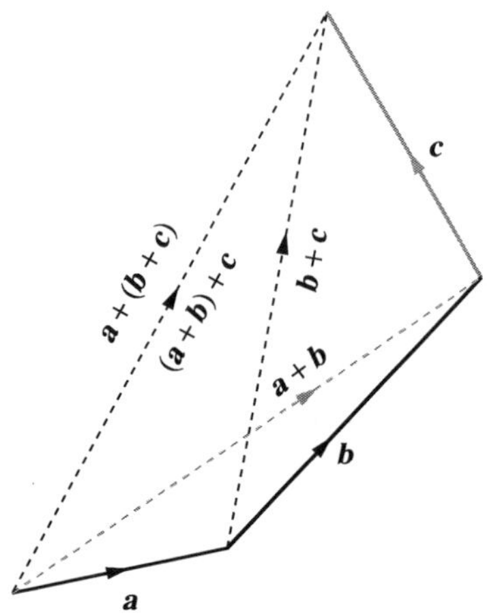


**Figure 4.11** Deduction of associative law.

### (c) Distributive law

$$\lambda(\boldsymbol{a} + \boldsymbol{b}) = \lambda\boldsymbol{a} + \lambda\boldsymbol{b}$$

The result follows from similar triangles. In Figure 4.12 the side O′B′ is just $\lambda$ times OB in length and in the same direction so $\overrightarrow{O'B'} = \lambda(\boldsymbol{a} + \boldsymbol{b})$. The triangle law therefore gives the required result since $\overrightarrow{O'B'} = \overrightarrow{O'A'} + \overrightarrow{A'B'} = \lambda\boldsymbol{a} + \lambda\boldsymbol{b}$. This result just says that we can multiply brackets out by the usual laws of algebra.

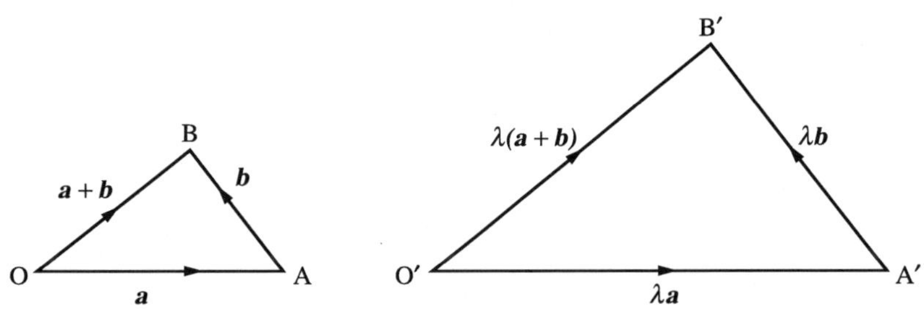


**Figure 4.12** Similar triangles for the proof of the distributive law.

### (d) Subtraction

We define subtraction in the obvious way:

$$\boldsymbol{a} - \boldsymbol{b} = \boldsymbol{a} + (-\boldsymbol{b})$$

This is illustrated geometrically in Figure 4.13. Applying the triangle rule to triangle OAB gives

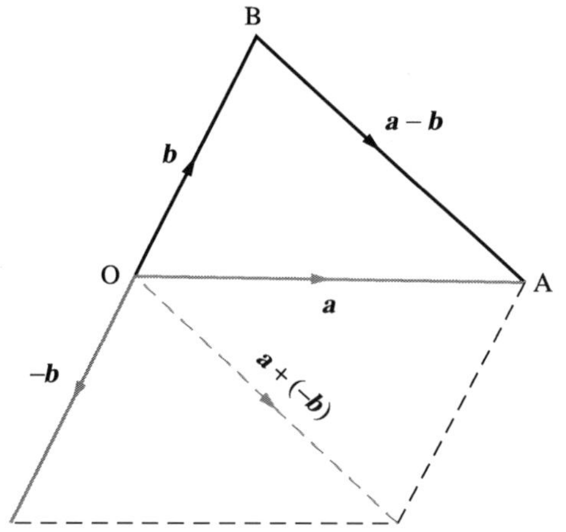


**Figure 4.13**
Subtraction of vectors.

$$\overrightarrow{BA} = \overrightarrow{BO} + \overrightarrow{OA} = \overrightarrow{OA} + \overrightarrow{BO}$$
$$= \overrightarrow{OA} - \overrightarrow{OB} \quad \text{since} \quad \overrightarrow{BO} = -\overrightarrow{OB}$$

from which the important result is obtained, namely

$$\overrightarrow{BA} = \overrightarrow{OA} - \overrightarrow{OB}$$

**Example 4.4**

From Figure 4.14, evaluate

***g*** in terms of ***a*** and ***b***, ***f*** in terms of ***b*** and ***c***

***e*** in terms of ***c*** and ***d***, ***e*** in terms of ***f***, ***g*** and ***h***

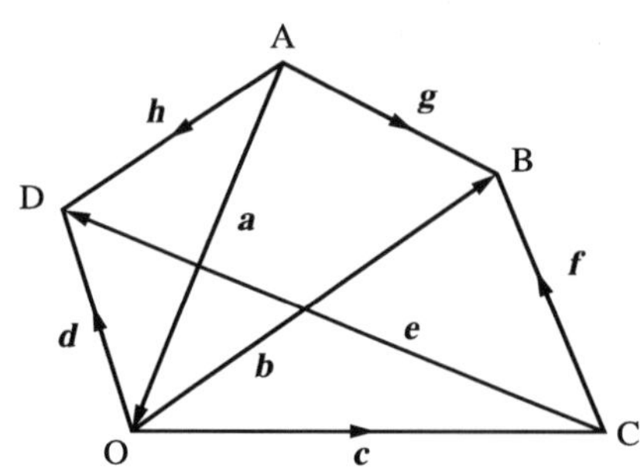


**Figure 4.14**
Figure of Example 4.4.

**Solution** From the triangle OAB: $\overrightarrow{AB} = \overrightarrow{AO} + \overrightarrow{OB}$ and hence $\boldsymbol{g} = \boldsymbol{a} + \boldsymbol{b}$

From the triangle OBC: $\overrightarrow{CB} = \overrightarrow{OB} - \overrightarrow{OC}$ and hence $\boldsymbol{f} = \boldsymbol{b} - \boldsymbol{c}$

From the triangle OCD: $\overrightarrow{CD} = \overrightarrow{OD} - \overrightarrow{OC}$ and hence $\boldsymbol{e} = \boldsymbol{d} - \boldsymbol{c}$

From the quadrilateral CBAD the polygon rule gives

$\overrightarrow{CD} + \overrightarrow{DA} + \overrightarrow{AB} + \overrightarrow{BC} = 0$ and hence $\boldsymbol{e} + (-\boldsymbol{h}) + \boldsymbol{g} + (-\boldsymbol{f}) = \boldsymbol{0}$ so $\boldsymbol{e} = \boldsymbol{f} - \boldsymbol{g} + \boldsymbol{h}$

**Example 4.5** A quadrilateral OACB is defined in terms of the vectors $\overrightarrow{OA} = \boldsymbol{a}$, $\overrightarrow{OB} = \boldsymbol{b}$ and $\overrightarrow{OC} = \boldsymbol{b} + \frac{1}{2}\boldsymbol{a}$. Calculate the vector representing the other two sides $\overrightarrow{BC}$ and $\overrightarrow{CA}$.

**Solution** Now as in rule (d)

$$\overrightarrow{BC} = \overrightarrow{BO} + \overrightarrow{OC} = -\overrightarrow{OB} + \overrightarrow{OC}$$

so

$$\overrightarrow{BC} = \overrightarrow{OC} - \overrightarrow{OB} = (\boldsymbol{b} + \tfrac{1}{2}\boldsymbol{a}) - \boldsymbol{b} = \tfrac{1}{2}\boldsymbol{a}$$

and similarly $\overrightarrow{CA} = \overrightarrow{OA} - \overrightarrow{OC} = \boldsymbol{a} - (\boldsymbol{b} + \frac{1}{2}\boldsymbol{a}) = \frac{1}{2}\boldsymbol{a} - \boldsymbol{b}$

**Example 4.6** A force $\boldsymbol{F}$ has magnitude 2 N and a second force $\boldsymbol{F}'$ has magnitude 1 N and is inclined at an angle of 60° to $\boldsymbol{F}$ as illustrated in Figure 4.15. Find the magnitude of the resultant force $\boldsymbol{R}$ and the angle it makes to the force $\boldsymbol{F}$.

**Solution** (i) Now, from Figure 4.15 we have $\boldsymbol{R} = \boldsymbol{F} + \boldsymbol{F}'$, so we require the length OC and the angle CON.

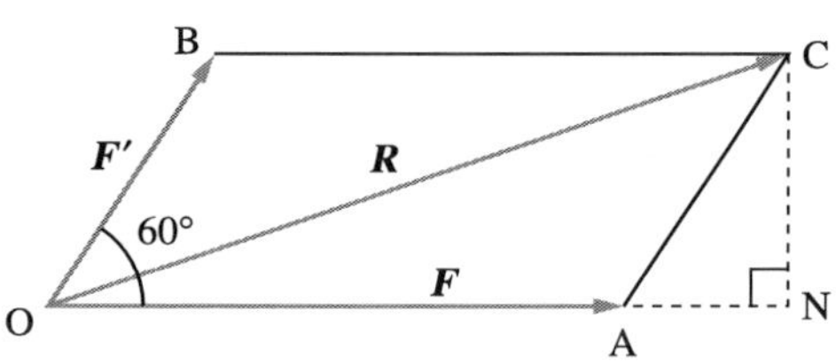


**Figure 4.15**
Figure of Example 4.6.

(ii) We first need to calculate CN and AN using trigonometry. Noting that $|\boldsymbol{F}'| = OB = AC = 1$ we see that

$$CN = AC \sin 60° = \tfrac{\sqrt{3}}{2} \text{ and } \quad AN = AC \cos 60° = \tfrac{1}{2}$$

(iii) Noting that $|\boldsymbol{F}| = OA = 2$ then $ON = OA + AN = \frac{5}{2}$. Thus using Pythagoras' theorem

$$OC^2 = ON^2 + CN^2 = \left(\tfrac{\sqrt{3}}{2}\right)^2 + \left(\tfrac{5}{2}\right)^2 = 7$$

and hence the resultant has magnitude $\sqrt{7}$.

(iv) The angle CON is determined from $\tan CON = \dfrac{CN}{ON} = \frac{\sqrt{3}}{5}$ giving angle CON = 19.1°.

**Example 4.7** An aeroplane is flying at 400 knots in a strong NW wind of 50 knots. The plane wishes to fly due west. In which direction should the pilot fly the plane to achieve this end, and what will be his actual speed over the ground?

**Solution** The resultant velocity of the plane is the vector sum of 50 knots from the NW direction and 400 knots in a direction $\alpha°$ north of west. In appropriate units the situation is shown in Figure 4.16(a). The vector $\overrightarrow{OA}$ represents the wind velocity and $\overrightarrow{OB}$ represents the aeroplane velocity. The resultant velocity is $\overrightarrow{OP}$, which is required to be due W. We wish to determine the angle $\alpha$ (giving the direction of flight) and magnitude of the resultant velocity (giving the ground speed).

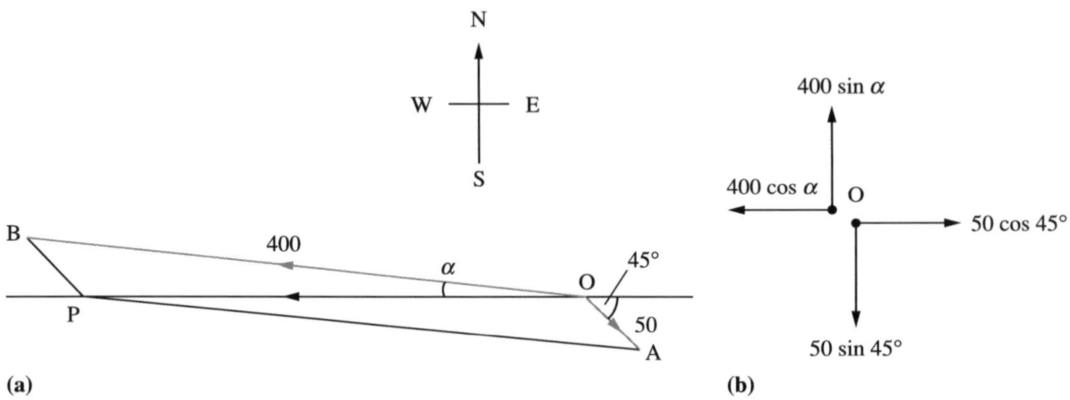


**Figure 4.16** (a) The track of the aeroplane in Example 4.7. (b) Resolving the velocity into components.

Resolving the velocity into components as illustrated in Figure 4.16(b) and recognizing that the resultant velocity is in the westerly direction, we have no resultant velocity perpendicular to this direction. Thus

$$400 \sin \alpha° = 50 \sin 45°$$

so that

$$\alpha = 5.07°$$

The resultant speed due west is

$$400 \cos \alpha° - 50 \cos 45° = 363 \text{ knots}$$

**Example 4.8** If ABCD is any quadrilateral, show that $\overrightarrow{AD} + \overrightarrow{BC} = 2\overrightarrow{EF}$, where E and F are the midpoints of AB and DC respectively, and that

$$\overrightarrow{AB} + \overrightarrow{AD} + \overrightarrow{CB} + \overrightarrow{CD} = 4\overrightarrow{XY}$$

where X and Y are the midpoints of the diagonals AC and BD respectively.

**Solution** Applying the polygon law for the addition of vectors to Figure 4.17,

$$\overrightarrow{EF} = \overrightarrow{EA} + \overrightarrow{AD} + \overrightarrow{DF}$$

and

$$\overrightarrow{EF} = \overrightarrow{EB} + \overrightarrow{BC} + \overrightarrow{CF}$$

Adding these two then gives

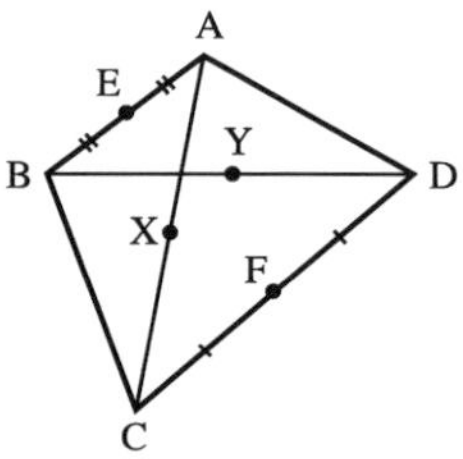


**Figure 4.17** Quadrilateral of Example 4.8.

$$2\overrightarrow{EF} = \overrightarrow{EA} + \overrightarrow{AD} + \overrightarrow{DF} + \overrightarrow{EB} + \overrightarrow{BC} + \overrightarrow{CF}$$
$$= \overrightarrow{AD} + \overrightarrow{BC} + (\tfrac{1}{2}\overrightarrow{BA} + \tfrac{1}{2}\overrightarrow{CD} - \tfrac{1}{2}\overrightarrow{BA} - \tfrac{1}{2}\overrightarrow{CD})$$

since E and F are the midpoints of AB and CD respectively. Thus

$$2\overrightarrow{EF} = \overrightarrow{AD} + \overrightarrow{BC}$$

Also, by the polygon law for addition of vectors,

$$\overrightarrow{XY} = \overrightarrow{XA} + \overrightarrow{AB} + \overrightarrow{BY}$$

and

$$\overrightarrow{XY} = \overrightarrow{XC} + \overrightarrow{CB} + \overrightarrow{BY}$$

Adding and multiplying by two gives

$$4\overrightarrow{XY} = 2\overrightarrow{XA} + 2\overrightarrow{AB} + 2\overrightarrow{BY} + 2\overrightarrow{XC} + 2\overrightarrow{CB} + 2\overrightarrow{BY}$$
$$= 2\overrightarrow{AB} + 2\overrightarrow{CB} + 4\overrightarrow{BY} \qquad (\text{since } \overrightarrow{XA} = -\overrightarrow{XC})$$
$$= 2\overrightarrow{AB} + 2\overrightarrow{CB} + 2\overrightarrow{BD} \qquad (\text{since } \overrightarrow{BD} = 2\overrightarrow{BY})$$
$$= \overrightarrow{AB} + \overrightarrow{CB} + (\overrightarrow{AB} + \overrightarrow{BD}) + (\overrightarrow{CB} + \overrightarrow{BD})$$

so that

$$4\overrightarrow{XY} = \overrightarrow{AB} + \overrightarrow{CB} + \overrightarrow{AD} + \overrightarrow{CD}$$

---

### 4.2.4 Cartesian components and basic properties

In Section 4.2.2 we saw that vectors could be written as an ordered set of three numbers or 3-tuple. We shall now explore the properties of these ordered triples and how they relate to the geometrical definitions used in previous sections.

In Figure 4.18, we denote mutually perpendicular unit vectors in the three coordinate directions by $\boldsymbol{i}$, $\boldsymbol{j}$ and $\boldsymbol{k}$. (Sometimes the alternative notation $\hat{\boldsymbol{e}}_1$, $\hat{\boldsymbol{e}}_2$ and $\hat{\boldsymbol{e}}_3$ is used.) The notation $\boldsymbol{i}, \boldsymbol{j}, \boldsymbol{k}$ is so standard that the 'hats' indicating unit vectors are usually omitted.

Applying the triangle law to the triangle OXM, we have

$$\overrightarrow{OM} = \overrightarrow{OX} + \overrightarrow{OY} = x\boldsymbol{i} + y\boldsymbol{j}$$

**Figure 4.18** The component form of a vector.

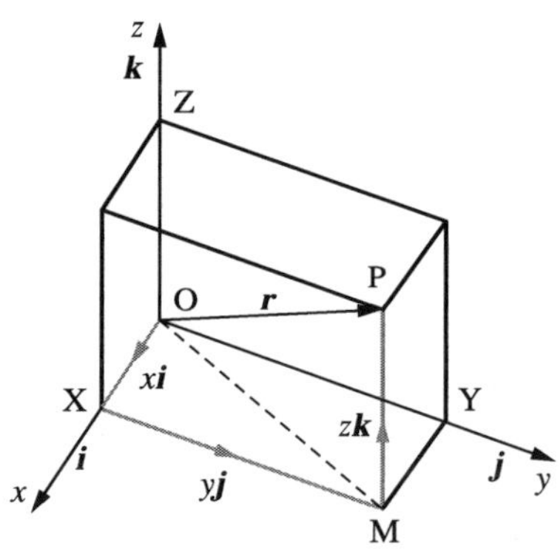

Applying the triangle law to the triangle OMP then yields

$$\overrightarrow{OP} = \overrightarrow{OM} + \overrightarrow{MP} = x\boldsymbol{i} + y\boldsymbol{j} + z\boldsymbol{k} \quad \textbf{(4.1)}$$

The analysis applies to any point, so we can write any vector $\boldsymbol{r}$ in terms of its **components** $x$, $y$, $z$ with respect to the unit vectors $\boldsymbol{i}, \boldsymbol{j}, \boldsymbol{k}$ as

$$\boldsymbol{r} = x\boldsymbol{i} + y\boldsymbol{j} + z\boldsymbol{k}$$

Indeed, the vector notation $\boldsymbol{r} = (x, y, z)$ should be intepreted as the vector given in (4.1). In some contexts it is more convenient to use a suffix notation for the coordinates, and

$$(x_1, x_2, x_3) = x_1\hat{\mathbf{e}}_1 + x_2\hat{\mathbf{e}}_2 + x_3\hat{\mathbf{e}}_3$$

is interpreted in exactly the same way. It is assumed that the three basic unit vectors are known, and all vectors in coordinate form are referred to them.

The **modulus** of a vector is just the length OP so from Figure 4.18 we have, using Pythagoras' theorem,

$$|\boldsymbol{r}| = (x^2 + y^2 + z^2)^{1/2}$$

The basic properties of vectors follow easily from the component definition in (4.1).

### *(a) Equality*

Two vectors $\boldsymbol{a} = (a_1, a_2, a_3)$ and $\boldsymbol{b} = (b_1, b_2, b_3)$ are **equal** if and only if the three components are equal, that is

$$a_1 = b_1, \quad a_2 = b_2, \quad a_3 = b_3$$

### *(b) Zero vector*

The zero vector has zero components, so

$$\mathbf{0} = (0, 0, 0)$$

### *(c) Addition*

The addition rule is expressed very simply in terms of vector components:

$$\boldsymbol{a} + \boldsymbol{b} = (a_1 + b_1, a_2 + b_2, a_3 + b_3)$$

The equivalence of this definition with the geometrical definition for addition using the parallelogram rule can be deduced from Figure 4.19. We know that $\overrightarrow{OB} = \overrightarrow{AC}$, since

**Figure 4.19**
Parallelogram rule, $x$ component.

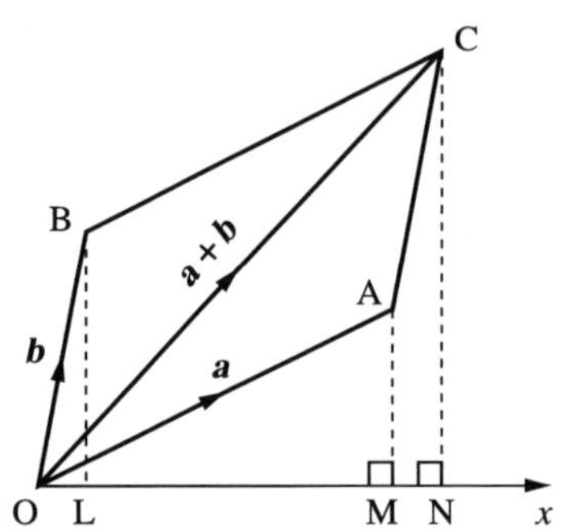

they are equivalent displacements, and hence their $x$ components are the same so that we have OL = MN. Thus if we take the $x$ component of $\boldsymbol{a} + \boldsymbol{b}$

$$(\boldsymbol{a} + \boldsymbol{b})_1 = \text{ON} = \text{OM} + \text{MN} = \text{OM} + \text{OL} = a_1 + b_1$$

the $y$ and $z$ components can be considered in a similar manner, giving $(\boldsymbol{a} + \boldsymbol{b})_2 = a_2 + b_2$ and $(\boldsymbol{a} + \boldsymbol{b})_3 = a_3 + b_3$.

### *(d) Multiplication by a scalar*

If $\lambda$ is a scalar and the vectors are related by $\boldsymbol{a} = \lambda\boldsymbol{b}$ then the components satisfy

$$a_1 = \lambda b_1, \quad a_2 = \lambda b_2, \quad a_3 = \lambda b_3$$

which follows from the similar triangles of Figure 4.12.

### *(e) Distributive law*

The distributive law in components is simply a restatement of the distributive law for the addition of numbers:

$$\begin{aligned}\lambda(\boldsymbol{a} + \boldsymbol{b}) &= \lambda(a_1 + b_1, a_2 + b_2, a_3 + b_3)\\ &= (\lambda(a_1 + b_1), \lambda(a_2 + b_2), \lambda(a_3 + b_3))\\ &= (\lambda a_1 + \lambda b_1, \lambda a_2 + \lambda b_2, \lambda a_3 + \lambda b_3)\\ &= (\lambda a_1, \lambda a_2, \lambda a_3) + (\lambda b_1, \lambda b_2, \lambda b_3)\\ &= \lambda\boldsymbol{a} + \lambda\boldsymbol{b}\end{aligned}$$

### *(f) Subtraction*

Subtraction is again straightforward and the components are just subtracted from each other:

$$\boldsymbol{a} - \boldsymbol{b} = (a_1 - b_1, a_2 - b_2, a_3 - b_3)$$

The component form of vectors allows problems to be solved algebraically and results can be interpreted either as algebraic ideas or in a geometrical manner. Both these interpretations can be very useful in applications of vectors to engineering.

In MATLAB a vector is inserted as an array within square brackets so, for example, a vector $\boldsymbol{a} = (1, 2, 3)$ is inserted as `a = [1 2 3]` or `a = [1,2,3]`, where in the latter commas have been used instead of spaces. It is inserted as `a := array([1,2,3]);` in MAPLE, where it is usually necessary to invoke the *linalg* package first. The operations of addition, subtraction and multiplication by a scalar are represented by `+`, `-` and `*` respectively. The magnitude or length of a vector $\boldsymbol{a}$ appears in MATLAB as `norm(a)` and in MAPLE as `norm(a,2)`.

**Example 4.9**

Determine whether constants $\alpha$ and $\beta$ can be found to satisfy the vector equations

(a) $(2, 1, 0) = \alpha(-2, 0, 2) + \beta(1, 1, 1)$

(b) $(-3, 1, 2) = \alpha(-2, 0, 2) + \beta(1, 1, 1)$

and interpret the results.

**Solution** (a) For the two vectors to be the same each of the components must be equal, and hence

$$2 = -2\alpha + \beta$$
$$1 = \beta$$
$$0 = 2\alpha + \beta$$

Thus the second equation gives $\beta = 1$ and both of the other two equations give the same value of $\alpha$, namely $\alpha = -\frac{1}{2}$, so the equations can be satisfied.

(b) A similar argument gives

$$-3 = -2\alpha + \beta$$
$$1 = \beta$$
$$2 = 2\alpha + \beta$$

Again, the second equation gives $\beta = 1$ but the first equation leads to $\alpha = 2$ and the third to $\alpha = \frac{1}{2}$. The equations are now not consistent and no appropriate $\alpha$ and $\beta$ can be found.

In case (a) the three vectors lie in a plane, and any vector in a plane, including the one given, can be written as the vector sum of the two vectors (–2, 0, 2) and (1, 1, 1) with appropriate multipliers. In case (b), however, the vector (–3, 1, 2) does not lie in the plane of the two vectors (–2, 0, 2) and (1, 1, 1) and can, therefore, never be written as the vector sum of the two vectors (–2, 0, 2) and (1, 1, 1) with appropriate multipliers.

**Example 4.10** Given the vectors $\boldsymbol{a} = (1, 1, 1)$, $\boldsymbol{b} = (-1, 2, 3)$ and $\boldsymbol{c} = (0, 3, 4)$, find

(a) $\boldsymbol{a} + \boldsymbol{b}$ (b) $2\boldsymbol{a} - \boldsymbol{b}$ (c) $\boldsymbol{a} + \boldsymbol{b} - \boldsymbol{c}$

(d) the unit vector in the direction of $\boldsymbol{c}$

**Solution** (a) $\boldsymbol{a} + \boldsymbol{b} = (1 - 1, 1 + 2, 1 + 3) = (0, 3, 4)$

(b) $2\boldsymbol{a} - \boldsymbol{b} = (2 \times 1 - (-1), 2 \times 1 - 2, 2 \times 1 - 3) = (3, 0, -1)$

(c) $\boldsymbol{a} + \boldsymbol{b} - \boldsymbol{c} = (1 - 1 + 0, 1 + 2 - 3, 1 + 3 - 4) = (0, 0, 0) = \boldsymbol{0}$

(d) $|\boldsymbol{c}| = (3^2 + 4^2)^{1/2} = 5$, so

$$\hat{\boldsymbol{c}} = \frac{\boldsymbol{c}}{5} = (0, \tfrac{3}{5}, \tfrac{4}{5})$$

**Example 4.11** Given $\boldsymbol{a} = (2, -3, 1) = 2\boldsymbol{i} - 3\boldsymbol{j} + \boldsymbol{k}$, $\boldsymbol{b} = (1, 5, -2) = \boldsymbol{i} + 5\boldsymbol{j} - 2\boldsymbol{k}$ and $\boldsymbol{c} = (3, -4, 3) = 3\boldsymbol{i} - 4\boldsymbol{j} + 3\boldsymbol{k}$

(a) find the vector $\boldsymbol{d} = \boldsymbol{a} - 2\boldsymbol{b} + 3\boldsymbol{c}$;

(b) find the magnitude of $\boldsymbol{d}$ and write down a unit vector in the direction of $\boldsymbol{d}$;

(c) what are the direction cosines of $\boldsymbol{d}$?

**Solution** (a) $\boldsymbol{d} = \boldsymbol{a} - 2\boldsymbol{b} + 3\boldsymbol{c}$

$$= (2\boldsymbol{i} - 3\boldsymbol{j} + \boldsymbol{k}) - 2(\boldsymbol{i} + 5\boldsymbol{j} - 2\boldsymbol{k}) + 3(3\boldsymbol{i} - 4\boldsymbol{j} + 3\boldsymbol{k})$$
$$= (2\boldsymbol{i} - 3\boldsymbol{j} + \boldsymbol{k}) - (2\boldsymbol{i} + 10\boldsymbol{j} - 4\boldsymbol{k}) + (9\boldsymbol{i} - 12\boldsymbol{j} + 9\boldsymbol{k})$$
$$= (2 - 2 + 9)\boldsymbol{i} + (-3 - 10 - 12)\boldsymbol{j} + (1 + 4 + 9)\boldsymbol{k}$$

that is, $\boldsymbol{d} = 9\boldsymbol{i} - 25\boldsymbol{j} + 14\boldsymbol{k}$.

(b) The magnitude of $\boldsymbol{d}$ is $d = \sqrt{[9^2 + (-25)^2 + 14^2]} = \sqrt{902}$
A unit vector in the direction of $\boldsymbol{d}$ is $\hat{\boldsymbol{d}}$, where

$$\hat{\boldsymbol{d}} = \frac{\boldsymbol{d}}{d} = \frac{9}{\sqrt{902}}\boldsymbol{i} - \frac{25}{\sqrt{902}}\boldsymbol{j} + \frac{14}{\sqrt{902}}\boldsymbol{k}$$

(c) The direction cosines of $\boldsymbol{d}$ are $9/\sqrt{902}$, $-25/\sqrt{902}$ and $14/\sqrt{902}$.

Check that in MATLAB the commands

```
a = [2 -3 1]; b = [1 5 -2]; c = [3 -4 3];
d = a - 2*b + 3*c
```

return the answer given in (a) and that the further command

```
norm(d)
```

gives the magnitude of $\boldsymbol{d}$ as 30.0333. Here MATLAB gives the numeric answer; to obtain the answer in the exact form then the calculation in MATLAB must be done symbolically using the Symbolic Math Toolbox. To do this the vector $\boldsymbol{d}$ must first be expressed in symbolic form using the `sym` command. Since the command `norm` does not appear to be available directly in the Toolbox, use can be made of the `maple` command to access the command in MAPLE. Check that the commands

```
d = sym(d);
maple('norm',d,2)
```

return the answer `902^(1/2)` given in (b).

**Example 4.12**

A molecule $XY_3$ has a tetrahedral form; the position vector of the X atom is $(2\sqrt{3} + \sqrt{2}, 0, -2 + \sqrt{6})$ and those of the three Y atoms are

$$\overrightarrow{OY} = (\sqrt{3}, -2, -1), \quad \overrightarrow{OY'} = (\sqrt{3}, 2, -1), \quad \overrightarrow{OY''} = (\sqrt{2}, 0, \sqrt{6})$$

(a) Show that all of the bond lengths are equal.

(b) Show that $\overrightarrow{XY} + \overrightarrow{YY'} + \overrightarrow{Y'Y''} + \overrightarrow{Y''X} = \boldsymbol{0}$

**Solution** (a) $\overrightarrow{XY} = \overrightarrow{OY} - \overrightarrow{OX} = (-\sqrt{3} - \sqrt{2}, -2, 1 - \sqrt{6})$ and the bond length is

$$|\overrightarrow{XY}| = [(-\sqrt{3} - \sqrt{2})^2 + (-2)^2 + (1 - \sqrt{6})^2]^{1/2} = 4$$

$\overrightarrow{YY'} = \overrightarrow{OY'} - \overrightarrow{OY} = (0, 4, 0)$ and clearly the bond length is again 4.

The other four bonds $\overrightarrow{XY'}$, $\overrightarrow{XY''}$, $\overrightarrow{Y'Y''}$, $\overrightarrow{Y''Y}$ are treated in exactly the same way, and each gives a bond length of 4.

(b) Now $\overrightarrow{Y'Y''} = \overrightarrow{OY''} - \overrightarrow{OY'} = (\sqrt{2} - \sqrt{3}, -2, \sqrt{6} + 1)$ and $\overrightarrow{Y''X} = \overrightarrow{OX} - \overrightarrow{OY''} = (2\sqrt{3}, 0, -2)$ so adding the four vectors gives

$$\overrightarrow{XY} + \overrightarrow{YY'} + \overrightarrow{Y'Y''} + \overrightarrow{Y''X}$$

$$= (-\sqrt{3} - \sqrt{2}, -2, 1 - \sqrt{6}) + (0, 4, 0) + (\sqrt{2} - \sqrt{3}, -2, \sqrt{6} + 1) + (2\sqrt{3}, 0, -2)$$

$$= \mathbf{0}$$

and is just a verification of the polygon law.

**Example 4.13** Three forces, with units of newtons,

$\boldsymbol{F}_1 = (1, 1, 1)$

$\boldsymbol{F}_2$ has magnitude 6 and acts in the direction $(1, 2, -2)$

$\boldsymbol{F}_3$ has magnitude 10 and acts in the direction $(3, -4, 0)$

act on a particle. Find the resultant force that acts on the particle. What additional force must be imposed on the particle to reduce the resultant force to zero?

**Solution** The first force is given in the usual vector form. The second two are given in an equally acceptable way but it is necessary to convert the information to the normal vector form so that the resultant can be found by vector addition. First the unit vector in the given direction of $\boldsymbol{F}_2$ is required

$$|(1, 2, -2)| = (1 + 2^2 + (-2)^2)^{1/2} = 3$$

and hence the unit vector in this direction is $\frac{1}{3}(1, 2, -2)$. Since $\boldsymbol{F}_2$ is in the direction of this unit vector and has magnitude 6 it can be written $\boldsymbol{F}_2 = 6(\frac{1}{3}, \frac{2}{3}, -\frac{2}{3}) = (2, 4, -4)$

Similarly for $\boldsymbol{F}_3$, the unit vector is $\frac{1}{5}(3, -4, 0)$ and hence $\boldsymbol{F}_3 = (6, -8, 0)$. The resultant force is obtained by vector addition.

$$\boldsymbol{F} = \boldsymbol{F}_1 + \boldsymbol{F}_2 + \boldsymbol{F}_3 = (1, 1, 1) + (2, 4, -4) + (6, -8, 0) = (9, -3, -3)$$

Clearly to make the resultant force zero, the additional force $(-9, 3, 3)$ must be imposed on the particle.

**Example 4.14** Two geostationary satellites have known positions $(0, 0, h)$ and $(0, A, H)$ relative to a fixed set of axes on the earth's surface (which is assumed flat, with the $x$ and $y$ axes lying on the surface and the $z$ axis vertical). Radar signals measure the distance of a ship from the satellites. Find the position of the ship relative to the given axes.

**Solution** Figure 4.20 illustrates the situation described with R $(a, b, 0)$ describing the position of the ship and P and Q the positions of the satellites.

The radar signals measure PR and QR which are denoted by $p$ and $q$ respectively. The vectors

**Figure 4.20**

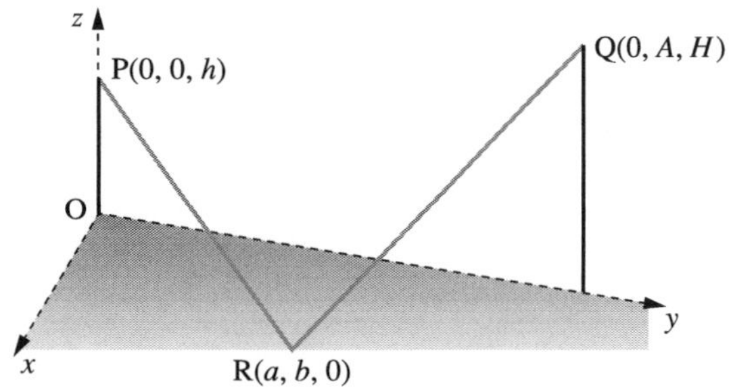


$$\overrightarrow{PR} = \overrightarrow{OR} - \overrightarrow{OP} = (a, b, 0) - (0, 0, h) = (a, b, -h)$$

$$\overrightarrow{QR} = \overrightarrow{OR} - \overrightarrow{OQ} = (a, b, 0) - (0, A, H) = (a, b - A, -H)$$

are easily calculated by the triangle law. The lengths of the two vectors are

$$p^2 = |\overrightarrow{PR}|^2 = a^2 + b^2 + h^2 \quad \text{and} \quad q^2 = |\overrightarrow{QR}|^2 = a^2 + (b - A)^2 + H^2$$

Subtracting gives

$$p^2 - q^2 = A(2b - A) + h^2 - H^2$$

and hence

$$b = (p^2 - q^2 - h^2 + H^2 + A^2)/2A$$

Having calculated $b$ then $a$ can be calculated from

$$a = \pm\sqrt{(p^2 - b^2 - h^2)}$$

Note the ambiguity in sign; clearly it will need to be known which side of the $y$ axis the ship is lying.

*Comment* In practice the axes will need to be transformed to standard latitude and longitude and the curvature of the earth will need to be taken into consideration. Can the same calculation be used for aircraft? The speed of the ship has been neglected in the calculation above but is the speed of the aircraft important?

## 4.2.5 Complex numbers as vectors

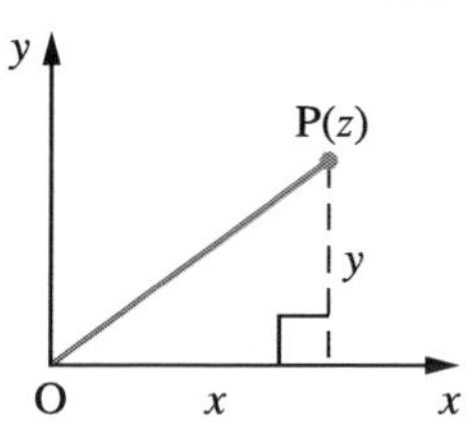


**Figure 4.21** Argand diagram representation of $z = x + jy$.

We saw in Chapter 3, Section 3.2, that a complex number $z = x + jy$ can be represented geometrically by the point P in the Argand diagram as illustrated in Figure 4.21. We could equally well represent the point P by the vector $\overrightarrow{OP}$. Hence we can express the complex number $z$ as a two-dimensional vector

$$z = \overrightarrow{OP}$$

With this interpretation of a complex number we can use the parallelogram rule to represent the addition and subtraction of complex numbers geometrically as illustrated in Figures 4.22(a, b).

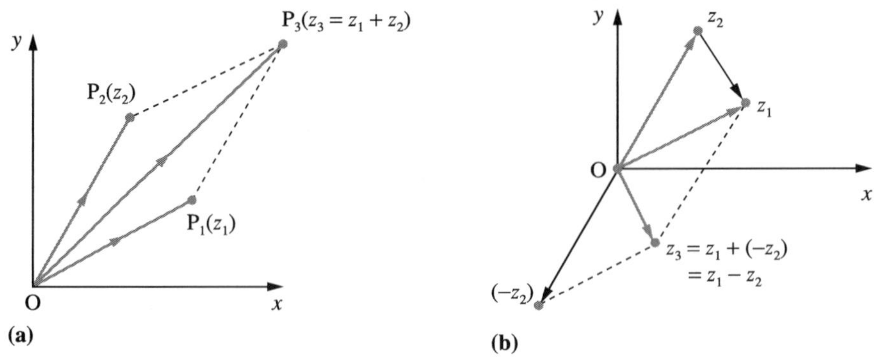


**Figure 4.22**
(a) Addition of complex numbers.
(b) Subtraction of complex numbers.

**Example 4.15**

A square is formed in the first and second quadrant with OP as one side of the square and $\overrightarrow{OP} = (1, 2)$. Find the coordinates of the other two vertices of the square.

**Solution**

The situation is illustrated in Figure 4.23. Using the complex form $\overrightarrow{OP} = 1 + 2j$ the side OQ is obtained by rotating OP through $\pi/2$ radians, then

$$\overrightarrow{OQ} = j(1 + 2j) = -2 + j$$

The fourth point R is found by observing that $\overrightarrow{OR}$ is the vector sum of $\overrightarrow{OP}$ and $\overrightarrow{OQ}$, and hence

$$\overrightarrow{OR} = \overrightarrow{OP} + \overrightarrow{OQ} = -1 + j3$$

The four coordinates are therefore

$$(0, 0), (1, 2), (-2, 1) \text{ and } (-1, 3)$$

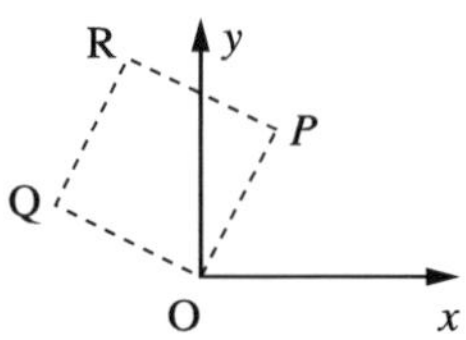


**Figure 4.23**
Square of Example 4.15.

**Example 4.16**

M is the centre of a square with vertices A, B, C and D taken anticlockwise in that order. If, in the Argand diagram, M and A are represented by the complex numbers $-2 + j$ and $1 + j5$ respectively, find the complex numbers represented by the vertices B, C and D.

**Solution**

Applying the triangle law for addition of vectors of Figure 4.24 gives

$$\begin{aligned}\overrightarrow{MA} &= \overrightarrow{MO} + \overrightarrow{OA} \\ &= \overrightarrow{OA} - \overrightarrow{OM} \\ &\equiv (1 + j5) - (-2 + j) \\ &= 3 + j4\end{aligned}$$

Since ABCD is a square,

$$MA = MB = MC = MD$$

$$\angle AMB = \angle BMC = \angle CMD = \angle DMA = \tfrac{1}{2}\pi$$

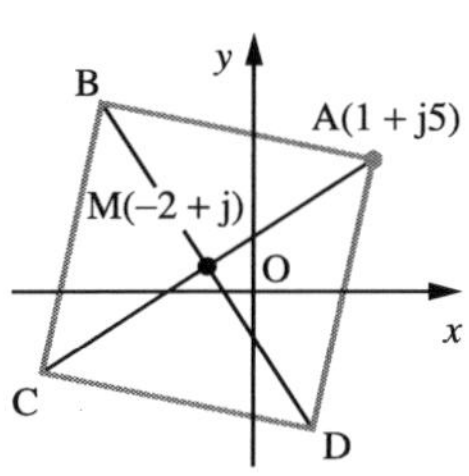


**Figure 4.24**
Square of Example 4.16.

Remembering that multiplying a complex number by j rotates it through $\frac{1}{2}\pi$ radians in an anticlockwise direction, we have

$$\overrightarrow{MB} = j\overrightarrow{MA} \equiv j(3 + j4) = -4 + j3$$

giving

$$\overrightarrow{OB} = \overrightarrow{OM} + \overrightarrow{MB} \equiv (-2 + j) + (-4 + j3) = -6 + j4$$

Likewise

$$\overrightarrow{MC} = j\overrightarrow{MB} \equiv j(-4 + j3) = -3 - j4$$

giving

$$\overrightarrow{OC} = \overrightarrow{OM} + \overrightarrow{MC} \equiv -5 - j3$$

and

$$\overrightarrow{MD} = j\overrightarrow{MC} \equiv j(-3 - j4) = 4 - j3$$

giving

$$\overrightarrow{OD} = \overrightarrow{OM} + \overrightarrow{MD} \equiv 2 - j2$$

Thus the vertices B, C and D are represented by the complex numbers $-6 + j4$, $-5 - j3$ and $2 - j2$ respectively.

## 4.2.6 Exercises

Check your answers using MATLAB or MAPLE whenever possible.

1 Given $\boldsymbol{a} = (1, 1, 0)$, $\boldsymbol{b} = (2, 2, 1)$ and $\boldsymbol{c} = (0, 1, 1)$, evaluate

(a) $\boldsymbol{a} + \boldsymbol{b}$ (b) $\boldsymbol{a} + \frac{1}{2}\boldsymbol{b} + 2\boldsymbol{c}$ (c) $\boldsymbol{b} - 2\boldsymbol{a}$

(d) $|\boldsymbol{a}|$ (e) $|\boldsymbol{b}|$ (f) $|\boldsymbol{a} - \boldsymbol{b}|$

(g) $\hat{\boldsymbol{a}}$ (h) $\hat{\boldsymbol{b}}$

2 If the position vectors of the points P and Q are $\boldsymbol{i} + 3\boldsymbol{j} - 7\boldsymbol{k}$ and $5\boldsymbol{i} - 2\boldsymbol{j} + 4\boldsymbol{k}$ respectively, find $\overrightarrow{PQ}$ and determine its length and direction cosines.

3 A particle P is acted upon by forces (measured in newtons) $\boldsymbol{F}_1 = 3\boldsymbol{i} - 2\boldsymbol{j} + 5\boldsymbol{k}$, $\boldsymbol{F}_2 = -\boldsymbol{i} + 7\boldsymbol{j} - 3\boldsymbol{k}$, $\boldsymbol{F}_3 = 5\boldsymbol{i} - \boldsymbol{j} + 4\boldsymbol{k}$ and $\boldsymbol{F}_4 = -2\boldsymbol{j} + 3\boldsymbol{k}$. Determine the magnitude and direction of the resultant force acting on P.

4 If $\boldsymbol{a} = 3\boldsymbol{i} - 2\boldsymbol{j} + \boldsymbol{k}$, $\boldsymbol{b} = -2\boldsymbol{i} + 5\boldsymbol{j} + 4\boldsymbol{k}$, $\boldsymbol{c} = -4\boldsymbol{i} + \boldsymbol{j} - 2\boldsymbol{k}$ and $\boldsymbol{d} = 2\boldsymbol{i} - \boldsymbol{j} + 4\boldsymbol{k}$, determine $\alpha$, $\beta$ and $\gamma$ such that

$$\boldsymbol{d} = \alpha\boldsymbol{a} + \beta\boldsymbol{b} + \gamma\boldsymbol{c}$$

5 Prove that the vectors $2\boldsymbol{i} - 4\boldsymbol{j} - \boldsymbol{k}$, $3\boldsymbol{i} + 2\boldsymbol{j} - 2\boldsymbol{k}$ and $5\boldsymbol{i} - 2\boldsymbol{j} - 3\boldsymbol{k}$ can form the sides of a triangle. Find the lengths of each side of the triangle and show that it is right-angled.

6 The vector $\overrightarrow{OP}$ makes an angle of 60° with the positive $x$ axis and 45° with the positive $y$ axis. Find the possible angles that the vector can make with the $z$ axis.

7 Given the points P(1, −3, 4), Q(2, 2, 1) and R(3, 7, −2), find the vectors $\overrightarrow{PQ}$ and $\overrightarrow{QR}$. Show that P, Q and R lie on a straight line and find the ratio PQ:QR.

8 A cyclist travelling east at 8 kilometres per hour finds that the wind appears to blow directly from the north. On doubling his speed it appears to blow from the north-east. Find the actual velocity of the wind.

9 Relative to a landing stage, the position vectors in kilometres of two boats A and B at noon are

$$3\boldsymbol{i} + \boldsymbol{j} \quad \text{and} \quad \boldsymbol{i} - 2\boldsymbol{j}$$

respectively. The velocities of A and B, which are constant and in kilometres per hour, are

$$10\boldsymbol{i} + 24\boldsymbol{j} \quad \text{and} \quad 24\boldsymbol{i} + 32\boldsymbol{j}$$

Find the distance between the boats $t$ hours after noon and find the time at which this distance is a minimum.

10 If the complex numbers $z_1$, $z_2$ and $z_3$ are represented on the Argand diagram by the points $P_1$, $P_2$ and $P_3$ respectively and

$$\overrightarrow{OP_2} = 2\text{j}\overrightarrow{OP_1} \quad \text{and} \quad \overrightarrow{OP_3} = \tfrac{2}{5}\text{j}\overrightarrow{P_2P_1}$$

prove that $P_3$ is the foot of the perpendicular from O on to the line $P_1P_2$

11 ABCD is a square, lettered anticlockwise, on an Argand diagram, with A representing $3 + \text{j}2$ and B representing $-1 + \text{j}4$. Show that C lies on the real axis and find the complex number represented by D and the length of AB.

12 A triangle has vertices A, B, C represented by $1 + \text{j}$, $2 - \text{j}$ and $-1$ respectively. Find the point that is equidistant from A, B and C.

13 Given the triangle OAB, where O is the origin, and denoting the midpoints of the opposite sides as O′, A′ and B′, show vectorially that the lines OO′, AA′ and BB′ meet at a point. (Note that this is the result that the medians of a triangle meet at the centroid.)

14 Three weights $W_1$, $W_2$ and $W_3$ hang in equilibrium on the pulley system shown in Figure 4.25. The pulleys are considered to be smooth and the forces add by the rules of vector addition. Calculate $\theta$ and $\phi$, the angles the ropes make with the horizontal.

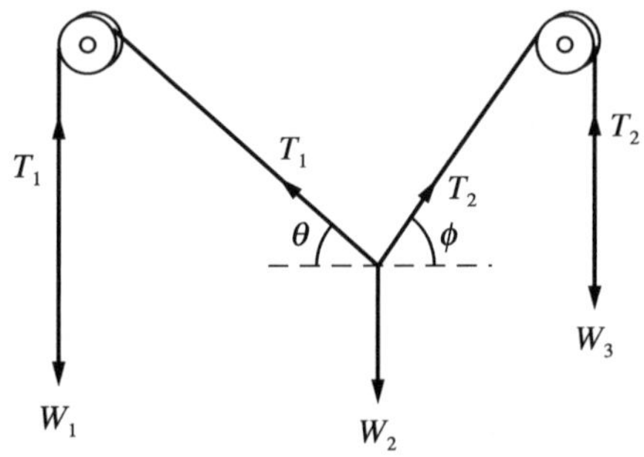


**Figure 4.25** Pulley system in Question 14.

15 A telegraph pole OP has three wires connected to it at P. The other ends of the wires are connected to houses at A, B and C. Axes are set up as shown in Figure 4.26. The points relative to these axes, with distances in metres, are $\overrightarrow{OP} = 8\boldsymbol{k}$, $\overrightarrow{OA} = 20\boldsymbol{j} + 6\boldsymbol{k}$, $\overrightarrow{OB} = -\boldsymbol{i} - 18\boldsymbol{j} + 10\boldsymbol{k}$ and $\overrightarrow{OC} = -22\boldsymbol{i} + 3\boldsymbol{j} + 7\boldsymbol{k}$. The tension in each wire is 900 N. Find the total force acting at P. A tie cable at an angle of 45° is connected to P and fixed in the ground. Where should the ground fixing be placed, and what is the tension required to ensure a zero horizontal resultant force at P?

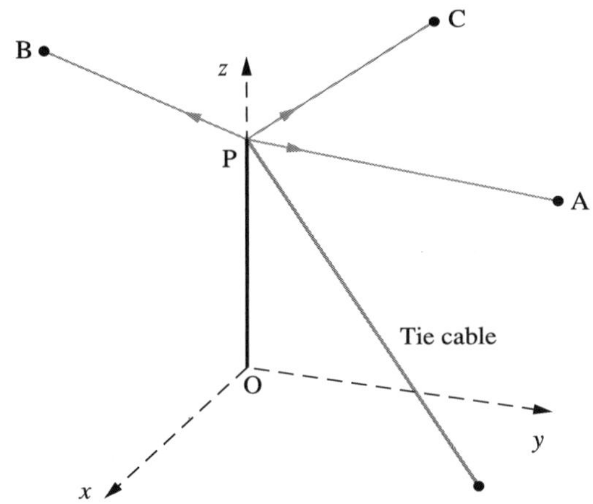


**Figure 4.26** The telegraph pole of Question 15.

16 A boom OB carries a load $\boldsymbol{F}$ of magnitude 500 N and is supported by cables BC and BD as shown in Figure 4.27 where the dimensions of the system are given. Determine the tensions in the cables so that equilibrium is maintained and the resultant force at the point B is along OB.

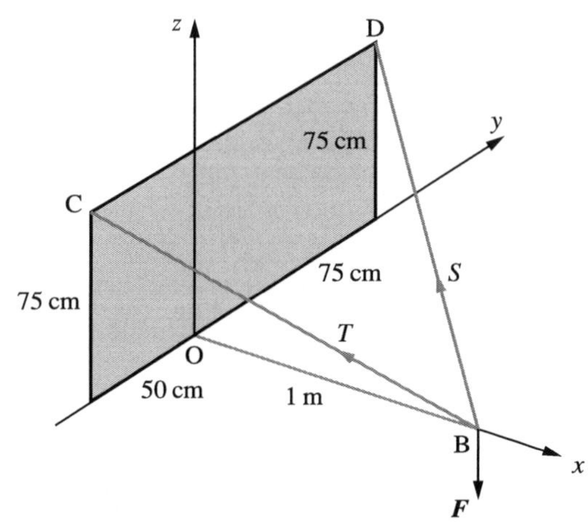


**Figure 4.27** Boom supported by cables in Question 16.

## 4.2.7 The scalar product

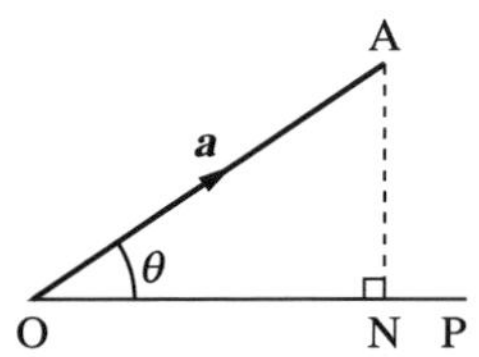


**Figure 4.28** The component of $\boldsymbol{a}$ in the direction OP is ON $= |\boldsymbol{a}|\cos\theta$.

A natural idea in mathematics, explored in Chapter 1, is not only to add quantities but also to multiply them together. The concept of multiplication of vectors translates into a useful tool for many engineering applications, with two different products of vectors – the 'scalar' and 'vector' products – turning out to be particularly important.

The determination of a component of a vector is a basic procedure in analysing many physical problems. For the vector $\boldsymbol{a}$ shown in Figure 4.28 the component of $\boldsymbol{a}$ in the direction of OP is just ON $= |\boldsymbol{a}|\cos\theta$. The component is relevant in the physical context of work done by a force. Suppose the point of application, O, of a constant force $\boldsymbol{F}$ is moved along the vector $\boldsymbol{a}$ from O to the point A, as in Figure 4.29. The component of $\boldsymbol{F}$ in the $\boldsymbol{a}$ direction is $|\boldsymbol{F}|\cos\theta$, and O is moved a distance $|\boldsymbol{a}|$. The work done is defined as the product of the distance moved by the point of application and the component of the force in this direction. It is thus given by

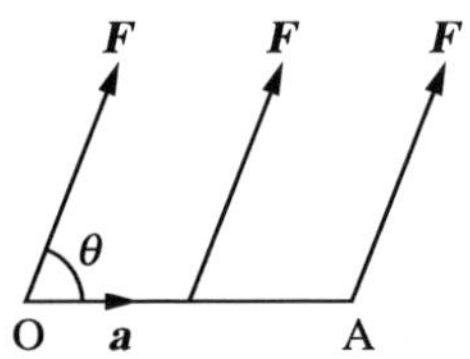


**Figure 4.29** The work done by a constant force $\boldsymbol{F}$ with point of application moved from O to A is $|\boldsymbol{F}||\boldsymbol{a}|\cos\theta$.

$$\text{work done} = |\boldsymbol{F}|\,|\boldsymbol{a}|\cos\theta$$

The definition of the scalar product in geometrical terms takes the form of this expression for the work done by a force. Again there is an equivalent component definition, and both are now presented.

### Definition

The **scalar** (or **dot** or **inner**) **product** of two vectors $\boldsymbol{a} = (a_1, a_2, a_3)$ and $\boldsymbol{b} = (b_1, b_2, b_3)$ is defined as follows:

**In components**

$$\boldsymbol{a}\cdot\boldsymbol{b} = a_1b_1 + a_2b_2 + a_3b_3 \tag{4.2a}$$

**Geometrically**

$$\boldsymbol{a}\cdot\boldsymbol{b} = |\boldsymbol{a}|\,|\boldsymbol{b}|\cos\theta,$$ where $\theta$ $(0 \leqslant \theta \leqslant \pi)$ is the angle between the two vectors

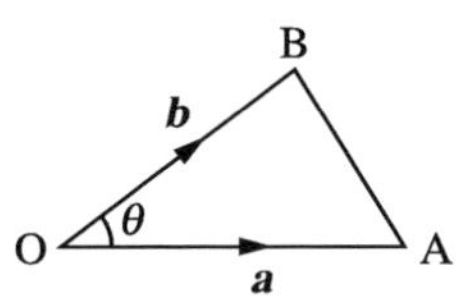


**Figure 4.30** Cosine rule for a triangle; equivalence of the geometrical and component definitions of the scalar product.

Both definitions prove to be useful in different contexts, but to establish the basic rules the component definition is the simpler. The equivalence of the two definitions can easily be established from the cosine rule for a triangle. Using Figure 4.30 the cosine rule (2.16) states

$$AB^2 = OA^2 + OB^2 - 2(OA)(OB)\cos\theta$$

which in appropriate vector or component notation gives

$$(a_1 - b_1)^2 + (a_2 - b_2)^2 + (a_3 - b_3)^2 = (a_1^2 + a_2^2 + a_3^2) + (b_1^2 + b_2^2 + b_3^2) - 2|\boldsymbol{a}|\,|\boldsymbol{b}|\cos\theta$$

Thus expanding the left-hand side gives

$$\begin{aligned} &a_1^2 - 2a_1b_1 + b_1^2 + a_2^2 - 2a_2b_2 + b_2^2 + a_3^2 - 2a_3b_3 + b_3^2 \\ &= a_1^2 + b_1^2 + a_2^2 + b_2^2 + a_3^2 + b_3^2 - 2|\boldsymbol{a}|\,|\boldsymbol{b}|\cos\theta \end{aligned}$$

and hence

$$\boldsymbol{a} \cdot \boldsymbol{b} = a_1 b_1 + a_2 b_2 + a_3 b_3 = |\boldsymbol{a}|\,|\boldsymbol{b}| \cos\theta \tag{4.2b}$$

Two important points to note are: (i) the scalar product of two vectors gives a **number**. (ii) the scalar product is only defined as the product of two vectors and *not* between any other two quantities. For this reason, the presence of the dot $(\cdot)$ in $\boldsymbol{a} \cdot \boldsymbol{b}$ is essential between the two vectors.

### Basic rules and properties

The basic rules are now very straightforward to establish.

#### *(a) Commutative law*

$$\boldsymbol{a} \cdot \boldsymbol{b} = \boldsymbol{b} \cdot \boldsymbol{a}$$

This rule follows immediately from the component definition (4.2a), since interchanging $a_i$ and $b_i$ does not make any difference to the products. The rule says that 'order does not matter'.

#### *(b) Associative law*

The idea of associativity involves the product of three vectors. Since $\boldsymbol{a} \cdot \boldsymbol{b}$ is a scalar, it cannot be dotted with a third vector, so the idea of associativity is not applicable here and $\boldsymbol{a} \cdot \boldsymbol{b} \cdot \boldsymbol{c}$ is not defined.

#### *(c) Distributive law for products with a scalar λ*

$$\boldsymbol{a} \cdot (\lambda \boldsymbol{b}) = (\lambda \boldsymbol{a}) \cdot \boldsymbol{b} = \lambda(\boldsymbol{a} \cdot \boldsymbol{b})$$

These results follow directly from the component definition (4.2a). The implication is that scalars can be multiplied out in the normal manner.

#### *(d) Distributive law over addition*

$$\boldsymbol{a} \cdot (\boldsymbol{b} + \boldsymbol{c}) = \boldsymbol{a} \cdot \boldsymbol{b} + \boldsymbol{a} \cdot \boldsymbol{c}$$

The proof is straightforward, since

$$\begin{aligned}\boldsymbol{a} \cdot (\boldsymbol{b} + \boldsymbol{c}) &= a_1(b_1 + c_1) + a_2(b_2 + c_2) + a_3(b_3 + c_3) \\ &= (a_1 b_1 + a_2 b_2 + a_3 b_3) + (a_1 c_1 + a_2 c_2 + a_3 c_3) \\ &= \boldsymbol{a} \cdot \boldsymbol{b} + \boldsymbol{a} \cdot \boldsymbol{c}\end{aligned}$$

Thus the normal rules of algebra apply, and brackets can be multiplied out in the usual way.

#### *(e) Powers of* a

One simple point to note is that

$$\boldsymbol{a} \cdot \boldsymbol{a} = a_1^2 + a_2^2 + a_3^2 = |\boldsymbol{a}|\,|\boldsymbol{a}| \cos 0 = |\boldsymbol{a}|^2$$

in agreement with Section 4.2.4. This expression is written $\boldsymbol{a}^2 = \boldsymbol{a} \cdot \boldsymbol{a}$ and, where there is no ambiguity, $\boldsymbol{a}^2 = a^2$ is also used. No other powers of vectors can be constructed, since, as in (b) above, scalar products of more than two vectors do not exist. For the standard unit vectors, $\boldsymbol{i}, \boldsymbol{j}$ and $\boldsymbol{k}$,

$$\boldsymbol{i}^2 = \boldsymbol{i} \cdot \boldsymbol{i} = 1, \quad \boldsymbol{j}^2 = \boldsymbol{j} \cdot \boldsymbol{j} = 1, \quad \boldsymbol{k}^2 = \boldsymbol{k} \cdot \boldsymbol{k} = 1 \tag{4.3}$$

### *(f) Perpendicular vectors*

It is clear from (4.2b) that if $\boldsymbol{a}$ and $\boldsymbol{b}$ are perpendicular (orthogonal) then $\cos\theta = \cos\frac{1}{2}\pi = 0$, and hence $\boldsymbol{a} \cdot \boldsymbol{b} = 0$, or in component notation

$$\boldsymbol{a} \cdot \boldsymbol{b} = a_1b_1 + a_2b_2 + a_3b_3 = 0$$

However, the other way round, $\boldsymbol{a} \cdot \boldsymbol{b} = 0$, *does not* imply that $\boldsymbol{a}$ and $\boldsymbol{b}$ are perpendicular. There are three possibilities:

$$\text{either } \boldsymbol{a} = 0 \quad \text{or} \quad \boldsymbol{b} = 0 \quad \text{or} \quad \theta = \tfrac{1}{2}\pi$$

It is only when the first two possibilities have been dismissed that perpendicularity can be deduced.

The commonest mistake is to deduce from

$$\boldsymbol{a} \cdot \boldsymbol{b} = \boldsymbol{a} \cdot \boldsymbol{c}$$

that $\boldsymbol{b} = \boldsymbol{c}$. This is only one of three possible solutions – the other two being $\boldsymbol{a} = 0$ and $\boldsymbol{a}$ perpendicular to $\boldsymbol{b} - \boldsymbol{c}$. The rule to follow is that *you can't cancel vectors in the same way as scalars.*

Since the unit vectors $\boldsymbol{i}, \boldsymbol{j}$ and $\boldsymbol{k}$ are mutually perpendicular,

$$\boldsymbol{i} \cdot \boldsymbol{j} = \boldsymbol{j} \cdot \boldsymbol{k} = \boldsymbol{k} \cdot \boldsymbol{i} = 0 \tag{4.4}$$

Using the distributive law over addition, we obtain using (4.3) and (4.4)

$$\begin{aligned}(a_1, a_2, a_3) \cdot (b_1, b_2, b_3) &= (a_1\boldsymbol{i} + a_2\boldsymbol{j} + a_3\boldsymbol{k}) \cdot (b_1\boldsymbol{i} + b_2\boldsymbol{j} + b_3\boldsymbol{k}) \\ &= a_1b_1\boldsymbol{i} \cdot \boldsymbol{i} + a_1b_2\boldsymbol{i} \cdot \boldsymbol{j} + a_1b_3\boldsymbol{i} \cdot \boldsymbol{k} + a_2b_1\boldsymbol{j} \cdot \boldsymbol{i} + a_2b_2\boldsymbol{j} \cdot \boldsymbol{j} \\ &\quad + a_2b_3\boldsymbol{j} \cdot \boldsymbol{k} + a_3b_1\boldsymbol{k} \cdot \boldsymbol{i} + a_3b_2\boldsymbol{k} \cdot \boldsymbol{j} + a_3b_3\boldsymbol{k} \cdot \boldsymbol{k} \\ &= a_1b_1 + a_2b_2 + a_3b_3\end{aligned}$$

which is consistent with the component definition of a scalar product.

Perpendicularity is a very important idea, which is used a great deal in both mathematics and engineering. Pressure acts on a surface in a direction perpendicular to the surface, so that the force per unit area is given by $p\hat{\boldsymbol{n}}$, where $p$ is the pressure and $\hat{\boldsymbol{n}}$ is the unit normal. To perform many calculations, we must be able to find a vector that is perpendicular to another vector. We shall also see that many matrix methods rely on being able to construct a set of mutually orthogonal vectors. Such constructions are not only of theoretical interest, but form the basis of many practical numerical methods used in engineering (see Chapter 6 of the companion text *Advanced Modern Engineering Mathematics*). The whole of the study of Fourier series (considered in Chapter 12), which is central to much of signal processing and is heavily used by electrical engineers, is based on constructing functions that are orthogonal.

In MATLAB the scalar product of two vectors $\boldsymbol{a}$ and $\boldsymbol{b}$ is given by the command `dot(a,b)`. In MAPLE it is given by `innerprod(a,b)`.

**Example 4.17** Given the vectors $\boldsymbol{a} = (1, -1, 2)$, $\boldsymbol{b} = (-2, 0, 2)$ and $\boldsymbol{c} = (3, 2, 1)$, evaluate

(a) $\boldsymbol{a}\cdot\boldsymbol{c}$ (b) $\boldsymbol{b}\cdot\boldsymbol{c}$ (c) $(\boldsymbol{a}+\boldsymbol{b})\cdot\boldsymbol{c}$

(d) $\boldsymbol{a}\cdot(2\boldsymbol{b}+3\boldsymbol{c})$ (e) $(\boldsymbol{a}\cdot\boldsymbol{b})\boldsymbol{c}$

**Solution** (a) $\boldsymbol{a}\cdot\boldsymbol{c} = (1\times 3) + (-1\times 2) + (2\times 1) = 3$

(b) $\boldsymbol{b}\cdot\boldsymbol{c} = (-2\times 3) + (0\times 2) + (2\times 1) = -4$

(c) $(\boldsymbol{a}+\boldsymbol{b}) = (1, -1, 2) + (-2, 0, 2) = (-1, -1, 4)$ so that

$$(\boldsymbol{a}+\boldsymbol{b})\cdot\boldsymbol{c} = (-1, -1, 4)\cdot(3, 2, 1) = -3 - 2 + 4 = -1$$

(note that $(\boldsymbol{a}+\boldsymbol{b})\cdot\boldsymbol{c} = \boldsymbol{a}\cdot\boldsymbol{c} + \boldsymbol{b}\cdot\boldsymbol{c}$)

(d) $\boldsymbol{a}\cdot(2\boldsymbol{b}+3\boldsymbol{c}) = (1, -1, 2)\cdot[(-4, 0, 4) + (9, 6, 3)]$

$$= (1, -1, 2)\cdot(5, 6, 7) = (5 - 6 + 14) = 13$$

(note that $2(\boldsymbol{a}\cdot\boldsymbol{b}) + 3(\boldsymbol{a}\cdot\boldsymbol{c}) = 4 + 9 = 13$)

(e) $(\boldsymbol{a}\cdot\boldsymbol{b})\boldsymbol{c} = [(1, -1, 2)\cdot(-2, 0, 2)](3, 2, 1) = [-2 + 0 + 4](3, 2, 1)$

$$= 2(3, 2, 1) = (6, 4, 2)$$

(note that $\boldsymbol{a}\cdot\boldsymbol{b}$ is a scalar, so $(\boldsymbol{a}\cdot\boldsymbol{b})\boldsymbol{c}$ is a vector parallel or antiparallel to $\boldsymbol{c}$)

Check that in MATLAB the commands

```
a = [1 -1 2]; b = [-2 0 2]; c = [3 2 1];
dot(a,c), dot(b,c), dot(a + b,c), dot(a,2*b + 3*c),
dot(a,b)*c
```

return the answers given in this example.

**Example 4.18** Find the angle between the vectors $\boldsymbol{a} = (1, 2, 3)$ and $\boldsymbol{b} = (2, 0, 4)$.

**Solution** By definition

$$\boldsymbol{a}\cdot\boldsymbol{b} = |\boldsymbol{a}|\,|\boldsymbol{b}|\cos\theta = a_1b_1 + a_2b_2 + a_3b_3$$

We have in the right-hand side

$$(1, 2, 3)\cdot(2, 0, 4) = 2 + 0 + 12 = 14$$

Also

$$|(1, 2, 3)| = \sqrt{(1^2 + 2^2 + 3^2)} = \sqrt{14}$$

and

$$|(2, 0, 4)| = \sqrt{(2^2 + 0^2 + 4^2)} = \sqrt{20}$$

Thus, from the definition of the scalar product,

$$14 = \sqrt{(14)}\sqrt{(20)} \cos \theta$$

giving

$$\theta = \cos^{-1}\sqrt{\tfrac{7}{10}}$$

**Example 4.19**

Given $\boldsymbol{a} = (1, 0, 1)$ and $\boldsymbol{b} = (0, 1, 0)$, show that $\boldsymbol{a} \cdot \boldsymbol{b} = 0$, and interpret this result.

**Solution** $\boldsymbol{a} \cdot \boldsymbol{b} = (1, 0, 1) \cdot (0, 1, 0) = 0$

Since $|\boldsymbol{a}| \neq 0$ and $|\boldsymbol{b}| \neq 0$, the two vectors are perpendicular. We can see this result geometrically, since $\boldsymbol{a}$ lies in the $x$–$z$ plane and $\boldsymbol{b}$ is parallel to the $y$ axis.

**Example 4.20**

The three vectors

$$\boldsymbol{a} = (1, 1, 1), \quad \boldsymbol{b} = (3, 2, -3) \quad \text{and} \quad \boldsymbol{c} = (-1, 4, -1)$$

are given. Show that $\boldsymbol{a} \cdot \boldsymbol{b} = \boldsymbol{a} \cdot \boldsymbol{c}$ and interpret the result.

**Solution** Now $\quad \boldsymbol{a} \cdot \boldsymbol{b} = 1 \times 3 + 1 \times 2 - 1 \times 3 = 2$

and $\quad \boldsymbol{a} \cdot \boldsymbol{c} = 1 \times (-1) + 1 \times 4 + 1 \times (-1) = 2$

so the two scalar products are clearly equal. Certainly $\boldsymbol{b} \neq \boldsymbol{c}$ since they are given to be unequal and $\boldsymbol{a}$ is non-zero so the conclusion from

$$\boldsymbol{a} \cdot (\boldsymbol{b} - \boldsymbol{c}) = 0$$

is that the vectors $\boldsymbol{a}$ and $(\boldsymbol{b} - \boldsymbol{c}) = (4, -2, -2)$ are perpendicular.

**Example 4.21**

In a triangle ABC show that the perpendiculars from the vertices to the opposite sides intersect in a point.

**Solution** Let the perpendiculars AD and BE meet in O as indicated in Figure 4.31, and choose O to be the origin. Define $\overrightarrow{OA} = \mathbf{a}$, $\overrightarrow{OB} = \boldsymbol{b}$ and $\overrightarrow{OC} = \mathbf{c}$. Then

AD perpendicular to BC implies $\boldsymbol{a} \cdot (\boldsymbol{b} - \mathbf{c}) = 0$

BE perpendicular to AC implies $\boldsymbol{b} \cdot (\mathbf{c} - \mathbf{a}) = 0$

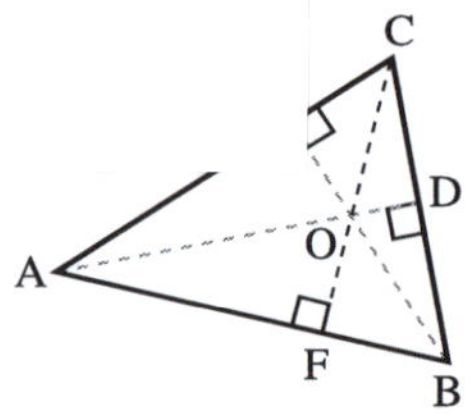


**Figure 4.31**
The altitudes of a triangle meet in a point (Example 4.21).

Hence, adding,

$$\boldsymbol{a}\cdot\boldsymbol{b} - \boldsymbol{a}\cdot\boldsymbol{c} + \boldsymbol{b}\cdot\boldsymbol{c} - \boldsymbol{b}\cdot\boldsymbol{a} = 0$$

so

$$\boldsymbol{b}\cdot\boldsymbol{c} - \boldsymbol{a}\cdot\boldsymbol{c} = \boldsymbol{c}\cdot(\boldsymbol{b} - \boldsymbol{a}) = 0$$

This statement implies that $\boldsymbol{b} - \boldsymbol{a}$ is perpendicular to $\boldsymbol{c}$ or AB is perpendicular to CF, as required. The case $\boldsymbol{b} - \boldsymbol{a} = 0$ is dismissed, since then the triangle would collapse. The case $\boldsymbol{c} = 0$ implies that C is at O; the triangle is then right-angled and the result is trivial.

**Example 4.22**

Find the work done by the force $\boldsymbol{F} = (3, -2, 5)$ in moving a particle from a point P to a point Q having position vectors $(1, 4, -1)$ and $(-2, 3, 1)$ respectively.

**Solution**

Applying the triangle law to Figure 4.32, we have the displacement of the particle given by

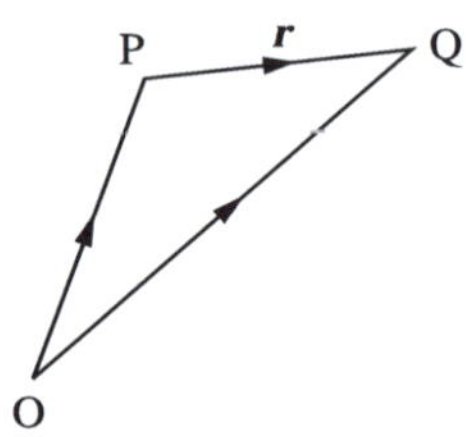


**Figure 4.32**
Triangle law for Example 4.22.

$$\boldsymbol{r} = \overrightarrow{PQ} = \overrightarrow{PO} + \overrightarrow{OQ} = \overrightarrow{OQ} - \overrightarrow{OP}$$
$$= (-2, 3, 1) - (1, 4, -1) = (-3, -1, 2)$$

Then the work done by the force $\boldsymbol{F}$ is

$$\boldsymbol{F}\cdot\boldsymbol{r} = (3, -2, 5)\cdot(-3, -1, 2) = -9 + 2 + 10$$
$$= 3 \text{ units}$$

---

The **component** of a vector in a given direction was discussed at the start of this section, and, as indicated in Figure 4.28, the component of $\boldsymbol{F}$ in the $\boldsymbol{a}$ direction is $|\boldsymbol{F}|\cos\theta$. Taking $\hat{\boldsymbol{a}}$ to be the unit vector in the $\boldsymbol{a}$ direction,

$$\boldsymbol{F}\cdot\hat{\boldsymbol{a}} = |\boldsymbol{F}||\hat{\boldsymbol{a}}|\cos\theta = |\boldsymbol{F}|\cos\theta$$
$$= \text{the component of } \boldsymbol{F} \text{ in the } \boldsymbol{a} \text{ direction}$$

**Example 4.23**

Find the component of the vector $\boldsymbol{F} = (2, -1, 3)$ in

(a) the $\boldsymbol{i}$ direction

(b) the direction $(\frac{1}{3}, \frac{2}{3}, \frac{2}{3})$

(c) the direction $(4, 2, -1)$

**Solution**

(a) The direction $\boldsymbol{i}$ is represented by the vector $(1, 0, 0)$, so the component of $\boldsymbol{F}$ in the $\boldsymbol{i}$ direction is

$$\boldsymbol{F}\cdot(1, 0, 0) = (2, -1, 3)\cdot(1, 0, 0) = 2$$

(note how this result just picks out the $x$ component and agrees with the usual idea of a component).

(b) Since $\sqrt{(\frac{1}{9}+\frac{4}{9}+\frac{4}{9})}=1$, the vector $(\frac{1}{3},\frac{2}{3},\frac{2}{3})$ is a unit vector. Thus the component of $\boldsymbol{F}$ in the direction $(\frac{1}{3},\frac{2}{3},\frac{2}{3})$ is

$$\boldsymbol{F}\cdot(\tfrac{1}{3},\tfrac{2}{3},\tfrac{2}{3})=\tfrac{2}{3}-\tfrac{2}{3}+2=2$$

(c) Since $\sqrt{(16+4+1)}\neq 1$, the vector $(4, 2, -1)$ is not a unit vector. Therefore we must first compute its magnitude as

$$\sqrt{(4^2+2^2+1^2)}=\sqrt{21}$$

indicating that a unit vector in the direction of $(4, 2, -1)$ is $(4, 2, -1)/\sqrt{21}$. Thus the component of $\boldsymbol{F}$ in the direction of $(4, 2, -1)$ is

$$\boldsymbol{F}\cdot(4,2,-1)/\sqrt{21}=3/\sqrt{21}$$

## 4.2.8 Exercises

Where appropiate check your answers using MATLAB or MAPLE.

**17** Given that $\boldsymbol{u}=(4,0,-2)$, $\boldsymbol{v}=(3,1,-1)$, $\boldsymbol{w}=(2,1,6)$ and $\boldsymbol{s}=(1,4,1)$, evaluate

(a) $\boldsymbol{u}\cdot\boldsymbol{v}$ (b) $\boldsymbol{v}\cdot\boldsymbol{s}$

(c) $\hat{\boldsymbol{w}}$ (d) $(\boldsymbol{v}\cdot\boldsymbol{s})\hat{\boldsymbol{u}}$

(e) $(\boldsymbol{u}\cdot\boldsymbol{w})(\boldsymbol{v}\cdot\boldsymbol{s})$ (f) $(\boldsymbol{u}\cdot\boldsymbol{i})\boldsymbol{v}+(\boldsymbol{w}\cdot\boldsymbol{s})\boldsymbol{k}$

**18** Given $\boldsymbol{u}$, $\boldsymbol{v}$, $\boldsymbol{w}$ and $\boldsymbol{s}$ as for Question 17, find

(a) the angle between $\boldsymbol{u}$ and $\boldsymbol{w}$

(b) the angle between $\boldsymbol{v}$ and $\boldsymbol{s}$

(c) the value of $\lambda$ for which the vectors $\boldsymbol{u}+\lambda\boldsymbol{k}$ and $\boldsymbol{v}-\lambda\boldsymbol{i}$ are perpendicular

(d) the value of $\mu$ for which the vectors $\boldsymbol{w}+\mu\boldsymbol{i}$ and $\boldsymbol{s}-\mu\boldsymbol{i}$ are perpendicular.

**19** Find the work done by the force $\boldsymbol{F}=(-2,-1,3)$ in moving a particle from the point P to the point Q having position vectors $(-1, 2, 3)$ and $(1, -3, 4)$ respectively.

**20** Find the resolved part in the direction of the vector $(3, 2, 1)$ of a force of 5 units acting in the direction of the vector $(2, -3, 1)$.

**21** Find the value of $t$ that makes the angle between the two vectors $\boldsymbol{a}=(3,1,0)$ and $\boldsymbol{b}=(t,0,1)$ equal to 45°.

**22** For any four points A, B, C and D in space, prove that

$$(\overrightarrow{DA}\cdot\overrightarrow{BC})+(\overrightarrow{DB}\cdot\overrightarrow{CA})+(\overrightarrow{DC}\cdot\overrightarrow{AB})=0$$

**23** If $(\boldsymbol{c}-\frac{1}{2}\boldsymbol{a})\cdot\boldsymbol{a}=(\boldsymbol{c}-\frac{1}{2}\boldsymbol{b})\cdot\boldsymbol{b}=0$, prove that the vector $\boldsymbol{c}-\frac{1}{2}(\boldsymbol{a}+\boldsymbol{b})$ is perpendicular to $\boldsymbol{a}-\boldsymbol{b}$.

**24** Prove that the line joining the points $(2, 3, 4)$ and $(1, 2, 3)$ is perpendicular to the line joining the points $(1, 0, 2)$ and $(2, 3, -2)$.

**25** Show that the diagonals of a rhombus intersect at right-angles.

**26** (a) A batch of bricks weighing 10 N is lifted from storage, taken to be the point $(0, 0, 0)$, against gravity to a point on the first floor of the building with coordinates $(0, 4, 5)$ m. Gravity acts in the $(-z)$ direction and the $x$, $y$ directions are at ground level. Calculate the work done in raising the bricks.

(b) A straight wall is to be built with $p$ bricks in each layer. The weight of each brick is $W$ newtons and it has thickness $h$ m. Neglecting the thickness of the mortar, estimate the work done in raising the bricks from ground level to build a wall of height $nh$ m. Show that the work done increases linearly with $p$ but as the square of $n$.

27 Find the equation of a circular cylinder with the origin on the axis of the cylinder, the unit vector $\boldsymbol{a}$ along the axis and radius $R$.

28 A cube has corners with coordinates (0, 0, 0), (1, 0, 0), (0, 1, 0), (1, 1, 0), (0, 0, 1), (1, 0, 1), (0, 1, 1) and (1, 1, 1). Find the vectors representing the diagonals of the cube and hence find the length of the diagonals and the angle between the diagonals.

29 A lifeboat hangs from a davit as shown in Figure 4.33 with the $x$ direction, the vertical part of the davit and the arm of the davit being mutually perpendicular. The rope is fastened to the deck at a distance $X$ from the davit. It is known that the maximum force in the $x$ direction that the davit can withstand is 200 N. If the weight supported is 500 N and the pulley system is a single loop so that the tension is 250 N, then determine the maximum value that $X$ can take.

30 A simple derrick is constructed as in Figure 4.34 with axes set up as indicated. The wires AP and BP are in tension, and the arm of the derrick, PC, is loaded with a weight $W$ at C. The $x$ and $y$ components of the forces at P are always in equilibrium. Determine the range of the angle $\theta$ that will ensure that the tensions $T_1$ and $T_2$ are always positive and hence the wires will not slacken.

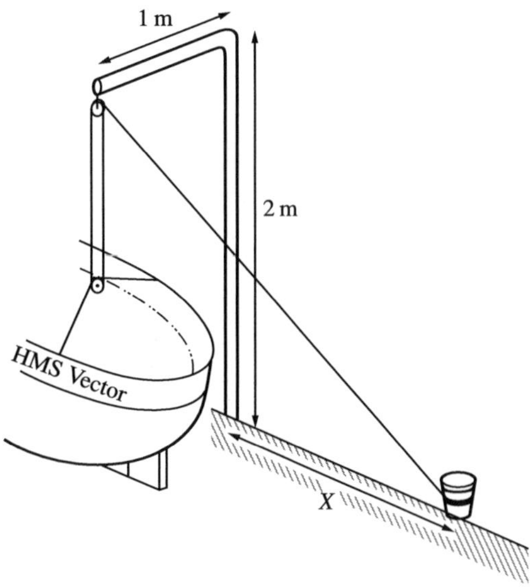


**Figure 4.33** Davit in Question 29.

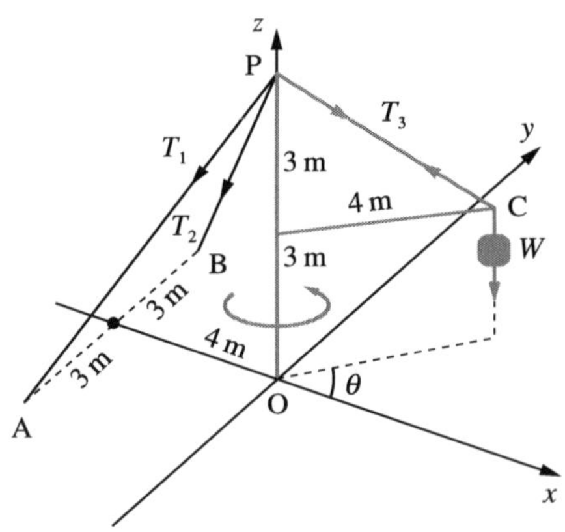


**Figure 4.34** Simple derrick in Question 30.

### 4.2.9 The vector product

The **vector** or **cross product** was developed during the nineteenth century, its main practical use being to define the moment of a force in three dimensions. It is generally only in three dimensions that the vector product is used. The adaptation for two-dimensional vectors is of restricted scope, since for two-dimensional problems, where all vectors are confined to a plane, the direction of the vector product is always perpendicular to that plane.

#### *Definition*

Given two vectors $\boldsymbol{a}$ and $\boldsymbol{b}$, we define the vector product geometrically as

$$\boldsymbol{a} \times \boldsymbol{b} = |\boldsymbol{a}|\,|\boldsymbol{b}| \sin\theta\, \hat{\boldsymbol{n}} \tag{4.5}$$

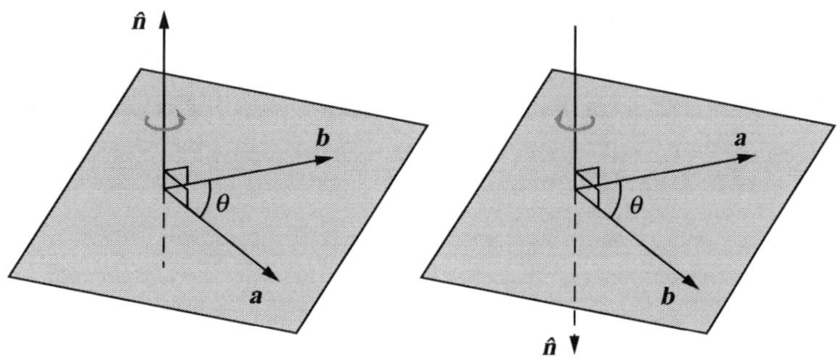


**Figure 4.35**
Vector product $\boldsymbol{a} \times \boldsymbol{b}$, right-hand rule.

where $\theta$ is the angle between $\boldsymbol{a}$ and $\boldsymbol{b}$ ($0 \leqslant \theta \leqslant \pi$), and $\hat{\boldsymbol{n}}$ is the unit vector perpendicular to both $\boldsymbol{a}$ and $\boldsymbol{b}$ such that $\boldsymbol{a}$, $\boldsymbol{b}$, $\hat{\boldsymbol{n}}$ form a right-handed set – see Figure 4.35 and the definition at the beginning of Section 4.2.1.

It is important to recognize that the vector product of two vectors is itself a vector. The alternative notation $\boldsymbol{a} \wedge \boldsymbol{b}$ is also sometimes used to denote the vector product, but this is less common since the similar wedge symbol $\wedge$ is also used for other purposes (see e.g. Chapter 6, Section 6.4.2).

There are wide ranging applications of the vector product.

### Motion of a charged particle in a magnetic field

- If a charged particle has velocity $\boldsymbol{v}$ and moves in a magnetic field $\boldsymbol{H}$ then the particle experiences a force perpendicular to both $\boldsymbol{v}$ and $\boldsymbol{H}$, which is proportional to $\boldsymbol{v} \times \boldsymbol{H}$. It is this force that is used to direct the beam in a television tube.
- Similarly a wire moving with velocity $\boldsymbol{v}$ in a magnetic field $\boldsymbol{H}$ produces a current proportional to $\boldsymbol{v} \times \boldsymbol{H}$, see Figure 4.36, thus converting mechanical energy into electric current, and provides the principle of the **dynamo**.
- For an **electric motor** the idea depends on the observation that an electric current $\boldsymbol{C}$ in a wire that lies in a magnetic field $\boldsymbol{H}$ produces a mechanical force proportional to $\boldsymbol{C} \times \boldsymbol{H}$, again see Figure 4.36. Thus electrical energy is converted to a mechanical force.

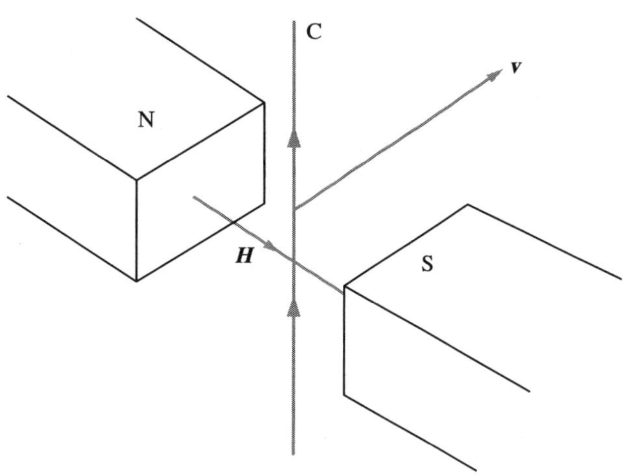


**Figure 4.36**
In a magnetic field $\boldsymbol{H}$, (i) motion of the wire in the $\boldsymbol{v}$ direction creates a current in the $\boldsymbol{H} \times \boldsymbol{v}$ (dynamo), (ii) a current $\boldsymbol{C}$ causes motion $\boldsymbol{v}$ in the $\boldsymbol{C} \times \boldsymbol{H}$ direction (electric motor).

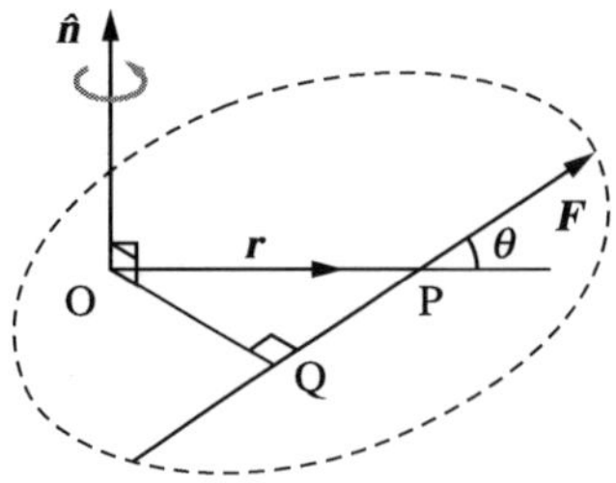


**Figure 4.37**
Moment of a force.

## Moment of a force

The moment or torque of a force $\boldsymbol{F}$ provides the classical application of the vector product in a mechanical context. Although moments are easy to define in two dimensions, the extension to three dimensions is not so easy. In vector notation, however, if the force passes through the point P and $\overrightarrow{OP} = \boldsymbol{r}$, as illustrated in Figure 4.37, then the moment $\boldsymbol{M}$ of the force about O is simply defined as

$$\boldsymbol{M} = \boldsymbol{r} \times \boldsymbol{F} = |\boldsymbol{r}||\boldsymbol{F}| \sin \theta \, \hat{\boldsymbol{n}} = \mathrm{OQ}|\boldsymbol{F}|\hat{\boldsymbol{n}} \tag{4.6}$$

This is a vector in the direction of the normal $\hat{\boldsymbol{n}}$, and moments add by the usual parallelogram law.

## Angular velocity of a rigid body

A further application of the vector product relates to rotating bodies. Consider a rigid body rotating with angular speed $\omega$ (in rad s$^{-1}$) about a fixed axis LM that passes through a fixed point O as illustrated in Figure 4.38. A point P of the rigid body having position vector $\boldsymbol{r}$ relative to O will move in a circular path whose plane is perpendicular to OM and whose centre N is on OM. If NQ is a fixed direction and the angle QNP is equal to $\chi$ then

$$\text{the magnitude of angular velocity } = \frac{\mathrm{d}\chi}{\mathrm{d}t} = \omega$$

(Note that we have used here the idea of a derivative, which will be introduced in Chapter 8.) The velocity $\mathbf{v}$ of P will be in the direction of the tangent shown and will have magnitude

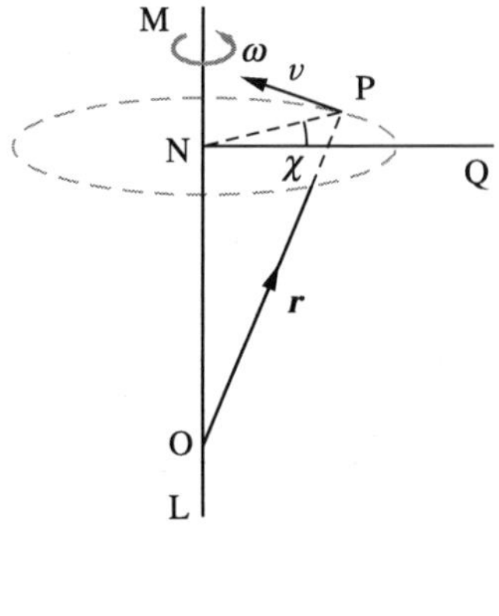


**Figure 4.38**
Angular velocity of a rigid body.

$$v = \text{NP}\frac{d\chi}{dt} = \text{NP}\omega$$

If we define $\boldsymbol{\omega}$ to be a vector of magnitude $\omega$ and having direction along the axis of rotation, in the sense in which the rotation would drive a right-handed screw, then

$$\boldsymbol{v} = \boldsymbol{\omega} \times \boldsymbol{r} \tag{4.7}$$

correctly defines the velocity of P in both magnitude and direction. This vector $\boldsymbol{\omega}$ is called the **angular velocity** of the rigid body.

### Area of parallelogram and a triangle

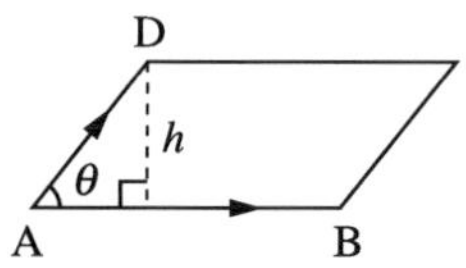


**Figure 4.39** Representation of a parallelogram.

Geometrically we have from Figure 4.39 that the area of a parallelogram ABCD is given by

$$\text{area} = h|\overrightarrow{\text{AB}}| = |\overrightarrow{\text{AD}}|\sin\theta|\overrightarrow{\text{AB}}| = |\overrightarrow{\text{AD}} \times \overrightarrow{\text{AB}}|$$

Note also that the area of the triangle ABD is $\frac{1}{2}|\overrightarrow{\text{AD}} \times \overrightarrow{\text{AB}}|$, which corresponds to the result

$$\text{area of triangle ABD} = \tfrac{1}{2}(\text{AD})(\text{AB})\sin\theta$$

We now examine the properties of vector products in order to determine whether or not the usual laws of algebra apply.

### Basic properties

#### *(a) Anti-commutative law*

$$\boldsymbol{a} \times \boldsymbol{b} = -(\boldsymbol{b} \times \boldsymbol{a})$$

This follows directly from the right-handedness of the set in the geometrical definition (4.5), since $\hat{\boldsymbol{n}}$ changes direction when the order of multiplication is reversed. Thus the vector product does not commute, but rather anti-commutes, unlike the multiplication of scalars or the scalar product of two vectors. Therefore the order of multiplication matters when using the vector product. For example, it is important that the moment of a force is calculated as $\boldsymbol{M} = \boldsymbol{r} \times \boldsymbol{F}$ and *not* $\boldsymbol{F} \times \boldsymbol{r}$.

#### *(b) Non-associative multiplication*

Since the vector product of two vectors is a vector, we can take the vector product with a third vector, and associativity can be tested. It turns out to *fail in general*, and

$$\boldsymbol{a} \times (\boldsymbol{b} \times \boldsymbol{c}) \neq (\boldsymbol{a} \times \boldsymbol{b}) \times \boldsymbol{c}$$

except in special cases, such as when $\boldsymbol{a} = 0$. This can be seen to be the case from geometrical considerations using the definition (4.5). The vector $\boldsymbol{b} \times \boldsymbol{c}$ is perpendicular to both $\boldsymbol{b}$ and $\boldsymbol{c}$, and is thus perpendicular to the plane containing $\boldsymbol{b}$ and $\boldsymbol{c}$. Also, by definition, $\boldsymbol{a} \times (\boldsymbol{b} \times \boldsymbol{c})$ is perpendicular to $\boldsymbol{b} \times \boldsymbol{c}$, and is therefore in the plane of $\boldsymbol{b}$ and $\boldsymbol{c}$. Similarly, $(\boldsymbol{a} \times \boldsymbol{b}) \times \boldsymbol{c}$ is in the plane of $\boldsymbol{a}$ and $\boldsymbol{b}$. Hence, in general, $\boldsymbol{a} \times (\boldsymbol{b} \times \boldsymbol{c})$ and $(\boldsymbol{a} \times \boldsymbol{b}) \times \boldsymbol{c}$ are different vectors.

Since the associative law does not hold in general, we never write $\boldsymbol{a} \times \boldsymbol{b} \times \boldsymbol{c}$, since it is ambiguous. Care must be taken to maintain the correct order and thus brackets must be inserted when more than two vectors are involved in a vector product.

*(c) Distributive law over multiplication by a scalar*
The definition (4.5) shows trivially that

$$\boldsymbol{a} \times (\lambda \boldsymbol{b}) = \lambda(\boldsymbol{a} \times \boldsymbol{b}) = (\lambda \boldsymbol{a}) \times \boldsymbol{b}$$

and the usual algebraic rule applies.

*(d) Distributive law over addition*

$$\boldsymbol{a} \times (\boldsymbol{b} + \boldsymbol{c}) = (\boldsymbol{a} \times \boldsymbol{b}) + (\boldsymbol{a} \times \boldsymbol{c})$$

This law holds for the vector product. It can be proved geometrically using the definition (4.5). The proof, however, is rather protracted and is omitted here.

*(e) Parallel vectors*
It is obvious from the definition (4.5) that if $\boldsymbol{a}$ and $\boldsymbol{b}$ are parallel or antiparallel then $\theta = 0$ or $\pi$, so that $\boldsymbol{a} \times \boldsymbol{b} = 0$, and this includes the case $\boldsymbol{a} \times \boldsymbol{a} = 0$. We note, however, that if $\boldsymbol{a} \times \boldsymbol{b} = 0$ then we have three possible cases: either $\boldsymbol{a} = 0$ or $\boldsymbol{b} = 0$ or $\boldsymbol{a}$ and $\boldsymbol{b}$ are parallel. As with the scalar product, if we have $\boldsymbol{a} \times \boldsymbol{b} = \boldsymbol{a} \times \boldsymbol{c}$ then we cannot deduce that $\boldsymbol{b} = \boldsymbol{c}$. We first have to show that $\boldsymbol{a} \neq 0$ and that $\boldsymbol{a}$ is not parallel to $\boldsymbol{b} - \boldsymbol{c}$.

*(f) Cartesian form*
From the definition (4.5), it clearly follows that the three unit vectors, $\boldsymbol{i}, \boldsymbol{j}$ and $\boldsymbol{k}$ parallel to the coordinate axes satisfy

$$\begin{aligned} &\boldsymbol{i} \times \boldsymbol{i} = \boldsymbol{j} \times \boldsymbol{j} = \boldsymbol{k} \times \boldsymbol{k} = 0 \\ &\boldsymbol{i} \times \boldsymbol{j} = \boldsymbol{k}, \quad \boldsymbol{j} \times \boldsymbol{k} = \boldsymbol{i}, \quad \boldsymbol{k} \times \boldsymbol{i} = \boldsymbol{j} \end{aligned} \tag{4.8}$$

Note the cyclic order of these latter equations. Using these results, we can obtain the cartesian or component form of the vector product. Taking

$$\boldsymbol{a} = (a_1, a_2, a_3) = a_1\boldsymbol{i} + a_2\boldsymbol{j} + a_3\boldsymbol{k}$$

and

$$\boldsymbol{b} = (b_1, b_2, b_3) = b_1\boldsymbol{i} + b_2\boldsymbol{j} + b_3\boldsymbol{k}$$

then, using rules (c), (d) and (a),

$$\begin{aligned} \boldsymbol{a} \times \boldsymbol{b} &= (a_1\boldsymbol{i} + a_2\boldsymbol{j} + a_3\boldsymbol{k}) \times (b_1\boldsymbol{i} + b_2\boldsymbol{j} + b_3\boldsymbol{k}) \\ &= a_1b_1(\boldsymbol{i} \times \boldsymbol{i}) + a_1b_2(\boldsymbol{i} \times \boldsymbol{j}) + a_1b_3(\boldsymbol{i} \times \boldsymbol{k}) + a_2b_1(\boldsymbol{j} \times \boldsymbol{i}) + a_2b_2(\boldsymbol{j} \times \boldsymbol{j}) \\ &\quad + a_2b_3(\boldsymbol{j} \times \boldsymbol{k}) + a_3b_1(\boldsymbol{k} \times \boldsymbol{i}) + a_3b_2(\boldsymbol{k} \times \boldsymbol{j}) + a_3b_3(\boldsymbol{k} \times \boldsymbol{k}) \\ &= a_1b_2\boldsymbol{k} + a_1b_3(-\boldsymbol{j}) + a_2b_1(-\boldsymbol{k}) + a_2b_3\boldsymbol{i} + a_3b_1\boldsymbol{j} + a_3b_2(-\boldsymbol{i}) \end{aligned}$$

so that

$$\boldsymbol{a} \times \boldsymbol{b} = (a_2b_3 - a_3b_2)\boldsymbol{i} + (a_3b_1 - a_1b_3)\boldsymbol{j} + (a_1b_2 - a_2b_1)\boldsymbol{k} \tag{4.9}$$

The cartesian form (4.9) can be more easily remembered in its determinant form (actually an accepted misuse of the determinant form)

$$\boldsymbol{a} \times \boldsymbol{b} = \begin{vmatrix} \boldsymbol{i} & \boldsymbol{j} & \boldsymbol{k} \\ a_1 & a_2 & a_3 \\ b_1 & b_2 & b_3 \end{vmatrix} = \boldsymbol{i}\begin{vmatrix} a_2 & a_3 \\ b_2 & b_3 \end{vmatrix} - \boldsymbol{j}\begin{vmatrix} a_1 & a_3 \\ b_1 & b_3 \end{vmatrix} + \boldsymbol{k}\begin{vmatrix} a_1 & a_2 \\ b_1 & b_2 \end{vmatrix}$$

$$= (a_2b_3 - b_2a_3)\boldsymbol{i} - (a_1b_3 - b_1a_3)\boldsymbol{j} + (a_1b_2 - b_1a_2)\boldsymbol{k} \tag{4.10}$$

This notation is so convenient that we use it here before formally introducing determinants in the next chapter.

An alternative way to work out the cross product, which is easy to memorize, is to write the vectors $(a, b, c)$ and $(A, B, C)$ twice and read off the components by taking the products as indicated in Figure 4.40.

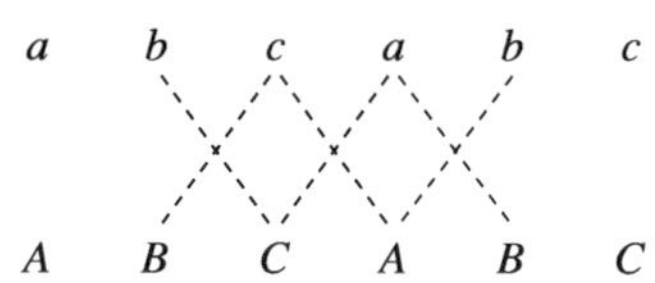


**Figure 4.40** Gives the three components as $bC - cB$, $cA - aC$, $aB - bA$.

In MATLAB the vector product of two vectors $\boldsymbol{a}$ and $\boldsymbol{b}$ is given by the command `cross(a,b)`. In MAPLE it is given by `crossprod(a,b)`.

**Example 4.24**

Given the vectors $\boldsymbol{a} = (2, 1, 0)$, $\boldsymbol{b} = (2, -1, 1)$ and $\boldsymbol{c} = (0, 1, 1)$, evaluate

(a) $\boldsymbol{a} \times \boldsymbol{b}$ (b) $(\boldsymbol{a} \times \boldsymbol{b}) \times \boldsymbol{c}$ (c) $(\boldsymbol{a} \cdot \boldsymbol{c})\boldsymbol{b} - (\boldsymbol{b} \cdot \boldsymbol{c})\boldsymbol{a}$

(d) $\boldsymbol{b} \times \boldsymbol{c}$ (e) $\boldsymbol{a} \times (\boldsymbol{b} \times \boldsymbol{c})$ (f) $(\boldsymbol{a} \cdot \boldsymbol{c})\boldsymbol{b} - (\boldsymbol{a} \cdot \boldsymbol{b})\boldsymbol{c}$

**Solution**

(a) $\boldsymbol{a} \times \boldsymbol{b} = \begin{vmatrix} \boldsymbol{i} & \boldsymbol{j} & \boldsymbol{k} \\ 2 & 1 & 0 \\ 2 & -1 & 1 \end{vmatrix} = \boldsymbol{i}\begin{vmatrix} 1 & 0 \\ -1 & 1 \end{vmatrix} - \boldsymbol{j}\begin{vmatrix} 2 & 0 \\ 2 & 1 \end{vmatrix} + \boldsymbol{k}\begin{vmatrix} 2 & 1 \\ 2 & -1 \end{vmatrix} = (1, -2, -4)$

(b) $(\boldsymbol{a} \times \boldsymbol{b}) \times \boldsymbol{c} = \begin{vmatrix} \boldsymbol{i} & \boldsymbol{j} & \boldsymbol{k} \\ 1 & -2 & -4 \\ 0 & 1 & 1 \end{vmatrix} = \boldsymbol{i}\begin{vmatrix} -2 & -4 \\ 1 & 1 \end{vmatrix} - \boldsymbol{j}\begin{vmatrix} 1 & -4 \\ 0 & 1 \end{vmatrix} + \boldsymbol{k}\begin{vmatrix} 1 & -2 \\ 0 & 1 \end{vmatrix} = (2, -1, 1)$

(c) $(\boldsymbol{a} \cdot \boldsymbol{c})\boldsymbol{b} - (\boldsymbol{b} \cdot \boldsymbol{c})\boldsymbol{a} = 1\boldsymbol{b} - 0\boldsymbol{a} = (2, -1, 1)$
(Note that (b) and (c) give the same result.)

(d) $\boldsymbol{b} \times \boldsymbol{c} = (-2, -2, 2)$

(e) $\boldsymbol{a} \times (\boldsymbol{b} \times \boldsymbol{c}) = (2, -4, -2)$
(Note that (b) and (e) do not give the same result and the cross product is *not* associative.)

(f) $(\boldsymbol{a} \cdot \boldsymbol{c})\boldsymbol{b} - (\boldsymbol{a} \cdot \boldsymbol{b})\boldsymbol{c} = 1\boldsymbol{b} - 3\boldsymbol{c} = (2, -4, -2)$
(Note that (e) and (f) give the same result.)

Check that in MATLAB the commands

```
a = [2 1 0]; b = [2 -1 1]; c = [0 1 1];
cross(a,b)
cross(cross(a,b),c)
```

return the answers to (a) and (b).

**Example 4.25** Find a unit vector perpendicular to the plane of the vectors $\boldsymbol{a} = (2, -3, 1)$ and $\boldsymbol{b} = (1, 2, -4)$.

**Solution** A vector perpendicular to the plane of the two vectors is the vector product

$$\boldsymbol{a} \times \boldsymbol{b} = \begin{vmatrix} \boldsymbol{i} & \boldsymbol{j} & \boldsymbol{k} \\ 2 & -3 & 1 \\ 1 & 2 & -4 \end{vmatrix} = (10, 9, 7)$$

whose modulus is

$$|\boldsymbol{a} \times \boldsymbol{b}| = \sqrt{(100 + 81 + 49)} = \sqrt{230}$$

Hence a unit vector perpendicular to the plane of $\boldsymbol{a}$ and $\boldsymbol{b}$ is $(10/\sqrt{230}, 9/\sqrt{230}, 7/\sqrt{230})$.

**Example 4.26** Find the area of the triangle having vertices at P(1, 3, 2), Q(−2, 1, 3) and R(3, −2, −1).

**Solution** We have seen in Figure 4.39 that the area of the parallelogram formed with sides PQ and PR is $|\overrightarrow{PQ} \times \overrightarrow{PR}|$ so the area of the triangle PQR is $\frac{1}{2}|\overrightarrow{PQ} \times \overrightarrow{PR}|$. Now

$$\overrightarrow{PQ} = (-2 - 1, 1 - 3, 3 - 2) = (-3, -2, 1)$$

and

$$\overrightarrow{PR} = (3 - 1, -2 - 3, -1 - 2) = (2, -5, -3)$$

so that

$$\overrightarrow{PQ} \times \overrightarrow{PR} = \begin{vmatrix} \boldsymbol{i} & \boldsymbol{j} & \boldsymbol{k} \\ -3 & -2 & 1 \\ 2 & -5 & -3 \end{vmatrix} = (11, -7, 19)$$

Hence the area of the triangle PQR is

$$\tfrac{1}{2}|\overrightarrow{PQ} \times \overrightarrow{PR}| = \tfrac{1}{2}\sqrt{(121 + 49 + 361)} = \tfrac{1}{2}\sqrt{531} \approx 11.52 \text{ square units.}$$

**Example 4.27**

Four vectors are constructed corresponding to the four faces of a tetrahedron. The magnitude of a vector is equal to the area of the corresponding face and its direction is the outward perpendicular to the face, as in Figure 4.41. Show that the sum of the four vectors is zero.

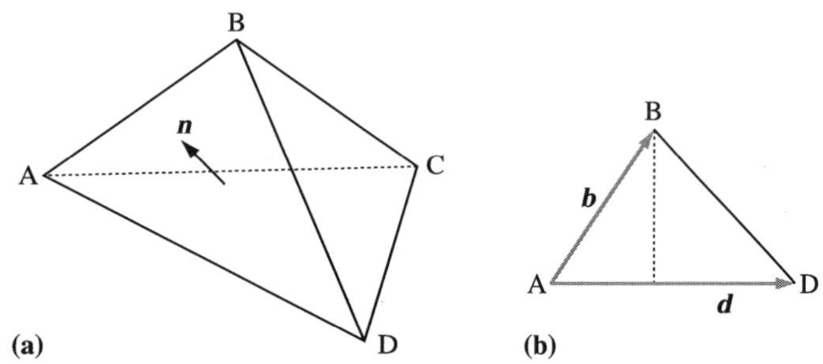


**Figure 4.41** (a) Tetrahedron for Example 4.27; (b) triangle from (a).

**Solution** In Figure 4.41(a) let $\overrightarrow{AB} = \boldsymbol{b}$, $\overrightarrow{AC} = \boldsymbol{c}$ and $\overrightarrow{AD} = \boldsymbol{d}$. The outward perpendicular to triangle ABD is parallel to

$$\boldsymbol{n} = \overrightarrow{AD} \times \overrightarrow{AB} = \boldsymbol{d} \times \boldsymbol{b}$$

and the unit vector in the outward normal direction is

$$\hat{\boldsymbol{n}} = \frac{\boldsymbol{d} \times \boldsymbol{b}}{|\boldsymbol{d} \times \boldsymbol{b}|}$$

From Figure 4.41(b) the area of triangle ABD follows from the definition of cross product as

$$\text{area} = \tfrac{1}{2}\text{AD}(\text{AB} \sin \theta) = \tfrac{1}{2}|\boldsymbol{d} \times \boldsymbol{b}|$$

so the vector we require is

$$\boldsymbol{v}_1 = \text{area} \times \hat{\boldsymbol{n}} = \tfrac{1}{2}\boldsymbol{d} \times \boldsymbol{b}$$

In a similar manner for triangles ACB and ADC the vectors are

$$\boldsymbol{v}_2 = \tfrac{1}{2}\boldsymbol{b} \times \boldsymbol{c} \quad \text{and} \quad \boldsymbol{v}_3 = \tfrac{1}{2}\boldsymbol{c} \times \boldsymbol{d}$$

For the fourth face BCD the appropriate vector is

$$\boldsymbol{v}_4 = \tfrac{1}{2}\overrightarrow{BD} \times \overrightarrow{BC} = \tfrac{1}{2}(\boldsymbol{d} - \boldsymbol{b}) \times (\boldsymbol{c} - \boldsymbol{b}) = \tfrac{1}{2}(\boldsymbol{d} \times \boldsymbol{c} - \boldsymbol{d} \times \boldsymbol{b} - \boldsymbol{b} \times \boldsymbol{c})$$

Adding the four vectors $\boldsymbol{v}_1$, $\boldsymbol{v}_2$, $\boldsymbol{v}_3$ and $\boldsymbol{v}_4$ together gives the zero vector.

**Example 4.28**

A force of 4 units acts through the point P(2, 3, –5) in the direction of the vector (4, 5, –2). Find its moment about the point A(1, 2, –3). See Figure 4.42.

What are the moments of the force about axes through A parallel to the coordinate axes?

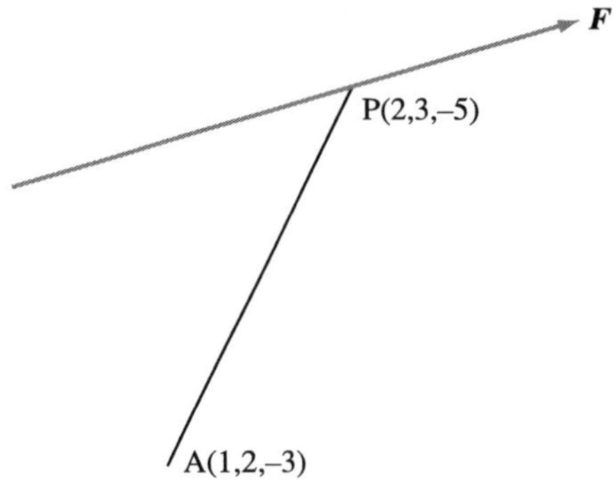


**Figure 4.42**
Moment of the force ***F*** about the point A in Example 4.28.

**Solution** To express the force in vector form we first need the unit vector in the direction of the force.

$$\frac{4\boldsymbol{i} + 5\boldsymbol{j} - 2\boldsymbol{k}}{\sqrt{(16 + 25 + 4)}} = \frac{1}{\sqrt{45}}(4, 5, -2)$$

Since the force ***F*** has a magnitude of 4 units

$$\boldsymbol{F} = \frac{4}{\sqrt{45}}(4, 5, -2)$$

The position vector of P relative to A is

$$\overrightarrow{\mathrm{AP}} = (1, 1, -2)$$

Thus from (4.6) the moment ***M*** of the force about A is

$$\boldsymbol{M} = \overrightarrow{\mathrm{AP}} \times \boldsymbol{F} = \frac{4}{\sqrt{45}}\begin{vmatrix} \boldsymbol{i} & \boldsymbol{j} & \boldsymbol{k} \\ 1 & 1 & -2 \\ 4 & 5 & -2 \end{vmatrix}$$

$$= (32/\sqrt{45}, -24/\sqrt{45}, 4/\sqrt{45})$$

The moments about axes through A parallel to the coordinate axes are $32/\sqrt{45}$, $-24/\sqrt{45}$ and $4/\sqrt{45}$.

**Example 4.29** A rigid body is rotating with an angular velocity of 5 rad s$^{-1}$ about an axis in the direction of the vector (1, 3, –2) and passing through the point A(2, 3, –1). Find the linear velocity of the point P(–2, 3, 1) of the body.

**Solution** A unit vector in the direction of the axis of rotation is $\frac{1}{\sqrt{14}}(1, 3, -2)$. Thus the angular velocity vector of the rigid body is

$$\boldsymbol{\omega} = (5/\sqrt{14})(1, 3, -2)$$

The position vector of P relative to A is

$$\overrightarrow{\mathrm{AP}} = (-2 - 2, 3 - 3, 1 + 1) = (-4, 0, 2)$$

Thus from (4.7) the linear velocity of P is

$$v = \omega \times \overrightarrow{AP} = \frac{5}{\sqrt{14}}\begin{vmatrix} i & j & k \\ 1 & 3 & -2 \\ -4 & 0 & 2 \end{vmatrix}$$

$$= (30/\sqrt{14}, 30/\sqrt{14}, 60/\sqrt{14})$$

**Example 4.30** A trapdoor is raised and lowered by a rope attached to one of its corners. The rope is pulled via a pulley fixed to a point A, 50 cm above the hinge as shown in Figure 4.43. If the trapdoor is uniform and of weight 20 N, what is the tension required to lift the door?

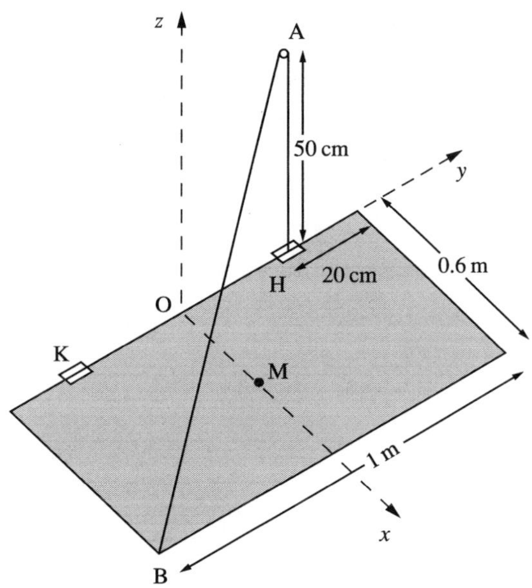


**Figure 4.43** Trapdoor in Example 4.30.

**Solution** From the data given we can calculate various vectors immediately.

$$\overrightarrow{OA} = (0, 30, 50), \quad \overrightarrow{OB} = (60, -50, 0), \quad \overrightarrow{OH} = (0, 30, 0)$$

If M is the midpoint of the trapdoor then

$$\overrightarrow{OM} = (30, 0, 0)$$

The forces acting are the tension $\boldsymbol{T}$ in the rope along BA, the weight $\boldsymbol{W}$ through M in the $-z$ direction and reactions $\boldsymbol{R}$ and $\boldsymbol{S}$ at the hinges. Now

$$\overrightarrow{AB} = \overrightarrow{OB} - \overrightarrow{OA} = (60, -80, -50)$$

so that $|\overrightarrow{AB}| = 112$, and hence

$$\boldsymbol{T} = -T(60, -80, -50)/112$$

Taking moments about the hinge H, we first note that there is no moment of the reaction at H. For the remaining forces

$$\begin{aligned} \boldsymbol{M}_{\mathrm{H}} &= \overrightarrow{\mathrm{HM}} \times \boldsymbol{W} + \overrightarrow{\mathrm{HB}} \times \boldsymbol{T} + \overrightarrow{\mathrm{HK}} \times \boldsymbol{R} \\ &= (30, -30, 0) \times (0, 0, -20) + (60, -80, 0) \times (60, -80, -50)(-T/112) + \overrightarrow{\mathrm{HK}} \times \boldsymbol{R} \\ &= (600, 600, 0) + T(-35.8, -26.8, 0) + \overrightarrow{\mathrm{HK}} \times \boldsymbol{R} \end{aligned}$$

Since we require the moment about the $y$ axis, we take the scalar product of $\boldsymbol{M}_{\mathrm{H}}$ and $\boldsymbol{j}$. The vector $\overrightarrow{\mathrm{HK}}$ is along $\boldsymbol{j}$, so $\boldsymbol{j} \cdot (\overrightarrow{\mathrm{HK}} \times \boldsymbol{R})$ must be zero. Thus the $\boldsymbol{j}$ component of $\boldsymbol{M}_{\mathrm{H}}$ must be zero as the trapdoor just opens; that is,

$$0 = 600 - 26.8T$$

so

$$T = 22.4 \text{ N}$$

---

## 4.2.10 Exercises

Check your answers using MATLAB or MAPLE whenever possible.

31 Given $\boldsymbol{p} = (1, 1, 1)$, $\boldsymbol{q} = (0, -1, 2)$ and $\boldsymbol{r} = (2, 2, 1)$, evaluate

(a) $\boldsymbol{p} \times \boldsymbol{q}$ (b) $\boldsymbol{p} \times \boldsymbol{r}$

(c) $\boldsymbol{r} \times \boldsymbol{q}$ (d) $(\boldsymbol{p} \times \boldsymbol{r}) \cdot \boldsymbol{q}$

(e) $\boldsymbol{q} \cdot (\boldsymbol{r} \times \boldsymbol{p})$ (f) $(\boldsymbol{p} \times \boldsymbol{r}) \times \boldsymbol{q}$

32 Show that the area of the triangle ABC in Figure 4.44 is $\frac{1}{2}|\overrightarrow{\mathrm{AB}} \times \overrightarrow{\mathrm{AC}}|$. Show that

$$\overrightarrow{\mathrm{AB}} \times \overrightarrow{\mathrm{AC}} = \overrightarrow{\mathrm{BC}} \times \overrightarrow{\mathrm{BA}} = \overrightarrow{\mathrm{CA}} \times \overrightarrow{\mathrm{CB}}$$

and hence deduce the sine rule

$$\frac{\sin A}{a} = \frac{\sin B}{b} = \frac{\sin C}{c}$$

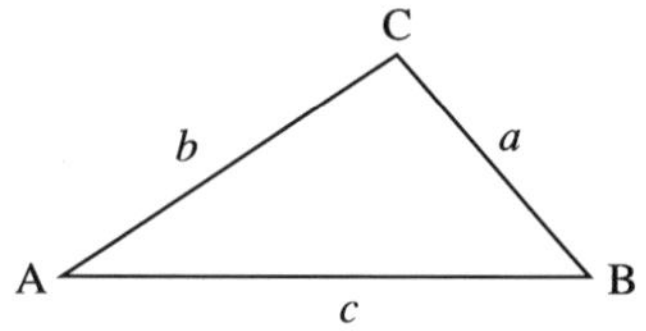


**Figure 4.44**
Sine rule: Section 2.6.1.

33 Prove that

$$(\boldsymbol{a} - \boldsymbol{b}) \times (\boldsymbol{a} + \boldsymbol{b}) = 2(\boldsymbol{a} \times \boldsymbol{b})$$

and interpret geometrically.

34 The points A, B and C have coordinates (1, −1, 2), (9, 0, 8) and (5, 0, 5) relative to rectangular cartesian axes. Find

(a) the vectors $\overrightarrow{\mathrm{AB}}$ and $\overrightarrow{\mathrm{AC}}$

(b) a unit vector perpendicular to the triangle ABC

(c) the area of the triangle ABC.

35 Use the definitions of the scalar and vector products to show that

$$|\boldsymbol{a} \cdot \boldsymbol{b}|^2 + |\boldsymbol{a} \times \boldsymbol{b}|^2 = \boldsymbol{a}^2\boldsymbol{b}^2$$

36 If $\boldsymbol{a}$, $\boldsymbol{b}$ and $\boldsymbol{c}$ are three vectors such that $\boldsymbol{a} + \boldsymbol{b} + \boldsymbol{c} = 0$, prove that

$$\boldsymbol{a} \times \boldsymbol{b} = \boldsymbol{b} \times \boldsymbol{c} = \boldsymbol{c} \times \boldsymbol{a}$$

and interpret geometrically.

37 A rigid body is rotating with angular velocity 6 rad s$^{-1}$ about an axis in the direction of the vector (3, −2, 1) and passing through the point A(3, −2, 5). Find the linear velocity of the point P(3, −2, 1) on the body.

38 A force of 4 units acts through the point P(4, −1, 2) in the direction of the vector (2, −1, 4). Find its moment about the point A(3, −1, 4).

39 The moment of a force $\boldsymbol{F}$ acting at a point P about a point O is defined to be a vector $\boldsymbol{M}$ perpendicular to the plane containing $\boldsymbol{F}$ and the point O such that $|\boldsymbol{M}| = p|\boldsymbol{F}|$, where $p$ is the perpendicular distance from O to the line of action of $\boldsymbol{r}$. Figure 4.45 illustrates such a force $\boldsymbol{F}$. Show that the perpendicular distance from O to the line of action

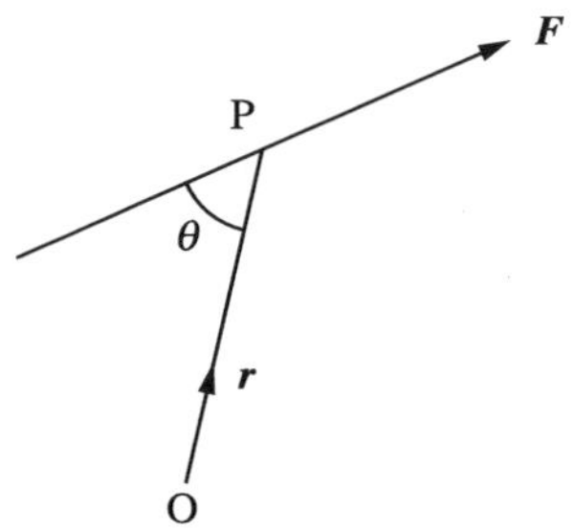


**Figure 4.45**
Moment of force $\boldsymbol{F}$ about O.

of $\boldsymbol{F}$ is $|\boldsymbol{r}|\sin\theta$, where $\boldsymbol{r}$ is the position vector of P. Hence deduce that $\boldsymbol{M} = \boldsymbol{r} \times \boldsymbol{F}$. Show that the moment of $\boldsymbol{F}$ about O is the same for any point P on the line of action of $\boldsymbol{F}$.

Forces (1, 0, 0), (1, 2, 0) and (1, 2, 3) act through the points (1, 1, 1), (0, 1, 1) and (0, 0, 1) respectively:

(a) find the moment of each force about the origin;

(b) find the moment of each force about the point (1, 1, 1);

(c) find the total moment of the three forces about the point (1, 1, 1).

40 Find a unit vector perpendicular to the plane of the two vectors (2, −1, 1) and (3, 4, −1). What is the sine of the angle between these two vectors?

41 Prove that the shortest distance of a point P from the line through the points A and B is

$$\frac{|\overrightarrow{AP} \times \overrightarrow{AB}|}{|\overrightarrow{AB}|}$$

A satellite is stationary at P(2, 5, 4) and a warning signal is activated if any object comes within a distance of 3 units. Determine whether a rocket moving in a straight line passing through A(1, 5, 2) and B(3, −1, 5) activates the warning signal.

42 The position vector $\boldsymbol{r}$, with respect to a given origin O, of a charged particle of mass $m$ and charge $e$ at time $t$ is given by

$$\boldsymbol{r} = \left(\frac{Et}{B} + a\sin(\omega t)\right)\boldsymbol{i} + a\cos(\omega t)\boldsymbol{j} + ct\boldsymbol{k}$$

where $E$, $B$, $a$ and $\omega$ are constants. The corresponding velocity and acceleration are

$$\boldsymbol{v} = \left(\frac{E}{B} + a\omega\cos(\omega t)\right)\boldsymbol{i} - a\omega\sin(\omega t)\boldsymbol{j} + c\boldsymbol{k}$$

$$\boldsymbol{f} = -a\omega^2\sin(\omega t)\boldsymbol{i} - a\omega^2\cos(\omega t)\boldsymbol{j}$$

For the case when $\boldsymbol{B} = B\boldsymbol{k}$, show that the equation of motion

$$m\boldsymbol{f} = e(E\boldsymbol{j} + \boldsymbol{v} \times \boldsymbol{B})$$

is satisfied provided $\omega$ is chosen suitably.

### 4.2.11 Triple products

In Example 4.24 products of several vectors were computed: the product $(\boldsymbol{a} \times \boldsymbol{b}) \cdot \boldsymbol{c}$ is called the **triple scalar product** and the product $(\boldsymbol{a} \times \boldsymbol{b}) \times \boldsymbol{c}$ is called the **triple vector product**.

#### Triple scalar product

The triple scalar product is of interest because of its geometrical interpretation. Looking at Figure 4.46, we see that

$$\begin{aligned}\boldsymbol{a} \times \boldsymbol{b} &= |\boldsymbol{a}|\,|\boldsymbol{b}|\sin\theta\boldsymbol{k} \\ &= (\text{area of the parallelogram OACB})\boldsymbol{k}\end{aligned}$$

Thus, by definition,

$$\begin{aligned}(\boldsymbol{a} \times \boldsymbol{b}) \cdot \boldsymbol{c} &= (\text{area of OACB})\boldsymbol{k} \cdot \boldsymbol{c} \\ &= (\text{area of OACB})|\boldsymbol{k}||\boldsymbol{c}|\cos\phi \\ &= (\text{area of OACB})h \quad (\text{where } h \text{ is the height of the parallelepiped}) \\ &= \text{volume of the parallelepiped}\end{aligned}$$

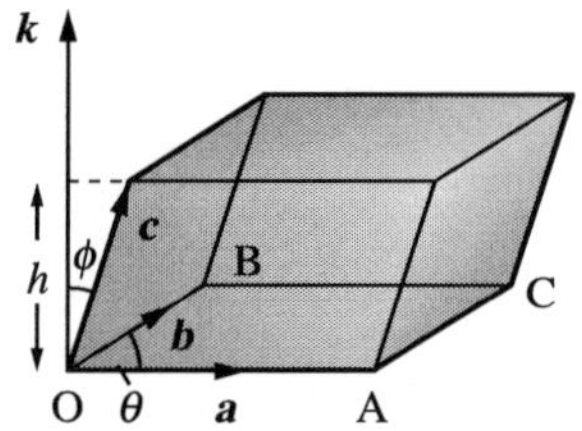


**Figure 4.46**
Triple scalar product as the volume of a parallelepiped.

Considering $(\boldsymbol{a} \times \boldsymbol{b}) \cdot \boldsymbol{c}$ to be the volume of the parallelepiped mounted on $\boldsymbol{a}$, $\boldsymbol{b}$, $\boldsymbol{c}$ has several useful consequences.

(a) If two of the vectors $\boldsymbol{a}$, $\boldsymbol{b}$ and $\boldsymbol{c}$ are parallel then $(\boldsymbol{a} \times \boldsymbol{b}) \cdot \boldsymbol{c} = 0$. This follows immediately since the parallelepiped collapses to a plane and has zero volume. In particular,

$$(\boldsymbol{a} \times \boldsymbol{b}) \cdot \boldsymbol{a} = 0 \quad \text{and} \quad (\boldsymbol{a} \times \boldsymbol{b}) \cdot \boldsymbol{b} = 0$$

(b) If the three vectors are coplanar then $(\boldsymbol{a} \times \boldsymbol{b}) \cdot \boldsymbol{c} = 0$. The same reasoning as in (a) gives this result.

(c) If $(\boldsymbol{a} \times \boldsymbol{b}) \cdot \boldsymbol{c} = 0$ then either $\boldsymbol{a} = 0$ or $\boldsymbol{b} = 0$ or $\boldsymbol{c} = 0$ or two of the vectors are parallel or the three vectors are coplanar.

(d) In the triple scalar product the dot $\cdot$ and the cross $\times$ can be interchanged:

$$(\boldsymbol{a} \times \boldsymbol{b}) \cdot \boldsymbol{c} = \boldsymbol{a} \cdot (\boldsymbol{b} \times \boldsymbol{c})$$

since it is easily checked that they measure the same volume mounted on $\boldsymbol{a}$, $\boldsymbol{b}$, $\boldsymbol{c}$. If we retain the same cyclic order of the three vectors then we obtain

$$\boldsymbol{a} \cdot (\boldsymbol{b} \times \boldsymbol{c}) = \boldsymbol{b} \cdot (\boldsymbol{c} \times \boldsymbol{a}) = \boldsymbol{c} \cdot (\boldsymbol{a} \times \boldsymbol{b}) \tag{4.11}$$

(e) In cartesian form the scalar triple product can be written as the determinant

$$\begin{aligned} \boldsymbol{a} \cdot (\boldsymbol{b} \times \boldsymbol{c}) &= \begin{vmatrix} a_1 & a_2 & a_3 \\ b_1 & b_2 & b_3 \\ c_1 & c_2 & c_3 \end{vmatrix} \\ &= a_1 b_2 c_3 - a_1 b_3 c_2 - a_2 b_1 c_3 + a_2 b_3 c_1 + a_3 b_1 c_2 - a_3 b_2 c_1 \end{aligned} \tag{4.12}$$

**Example 4.31** Find $\lambda$ so that $\boldsymbol{a} = (2, -1, 1)$, $\boldsymbol{b} = (1, 2, -3)$ and $\boldsymbol{c} = (3, \lambda, 5)$ are coplanar.

**Solution** None of these vectors are zero or parallel, so by property (b) the three vectors are coplanar if $(\boldsymbol{a} \times \boldsymbol{b}) \cdot \boldsymbol{c} = 0$. Now

$$\boldsymbol{a} \times \boldsymbol{b} = (1, 7, 5)$$

so

$$(\boldsymbol{a} \times \boldsymbol{b}) \cdot \boldsymbol{c} = 3 + 7\lambda + 25$$

This will be zero, and the three vectors coplanar, when $\lambda = -4$.

**Example 4.32** In a triangle OAB the sides $\overrightarrow{OA} = \boldsymbol{a}$ and $\overrightarrow{OB} = \boldsymbol{b}$ are given. Find the point P, with $\boldsymbol{c} = \overrightarrow{OP}$, where the perpendicular bisectors of the two sides intersect. Hence prove that the perpendicular bisectors of the sides of a triangle meet at a point.

**Solution** Let $\hat{\boldsymbol{k}}$ be the unit vector perpendicular to the plane of the triangle; the situation is illustrated in Figure 4.47.

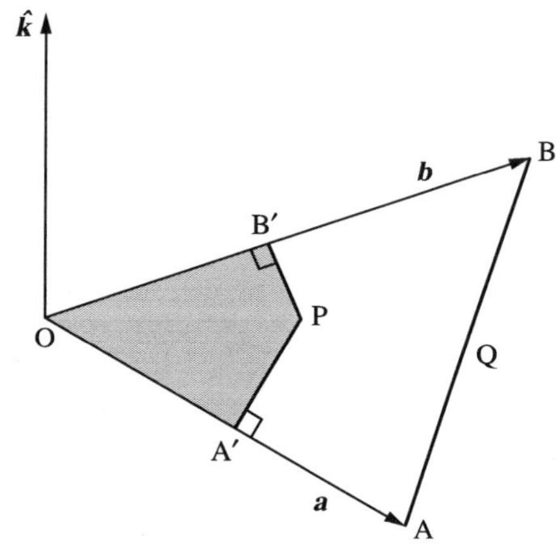


**Figure 4.47** Perpendicular bisectors in Example 4.32.

Now

$$\overrightarrow{OP} = \overrightarrow{OA'} + \overrightarrow{A'P} = \tfrac{1}{2}\boldsymbol{a} + \alpha\hat{\boldsymbol{k}} \times \boldsymbol{a}$$

for some $\alpha$, since the vector $\hat{\boldsymbol{k}} \times \boldsymbol{a}$ is in the direction perpendicular to $\boldsymbol{a}$. Similarly

$$\overrightarrow{OP} = \overrightarrow{OB'} + \overrightarrow{B'P} = \tfrac{1}{2}\boldsymbol{b} + \beta\hat{\boldsymbol{k}} \times \boldsymbol{b}$$

Subtracting these two equations

$$\tfrac{1}{2}\boldsymbol{a} + \alpha\hat{\boldsymbol{k}} \times \boldsymbol{a} = \tfrac{1}{2}\boldsymbol{b} + \beta\hat{\boldsymbol{k}} \times \boldsymbol{b}$$

Take the dot product of this equation with $\boldsymbol{b}$, which eliminates the final term, since $\boldsymbol{b} \cdot (\hat{\boldsymbol{k}} \times \boldsymbol{b}) = 0$, and gives

$$\tfrac{1}{2}\boldsymbol{b} \cdot (\boldsymbol{b} - \boldsymbol{a}) = \alpha\boldsymbol{b} \cdot (\hat{\boldsymbol{k}} \times \boldsymbol{a})$$

Hence $\alpha$ has been computed in terms of the known data, so assuming $\boldsymbol{b} \cdot (\hat{\boldsymbol{k}} \times \boldsymbol{a}) \neq 0$

$$\overrightarrow{OP} = \tfrac{1}{2}\boldsymbol{a} + \frac{\tfrac{1}{2}\boldsymbol{b} \cdot (\boldsymbol{b} - \boldsymbol{a})}{\boldsymbol{b} \cdot (\hat{\boldsymbol{k}} \times \boldsymbol{a})}\hat{\boldsymbol{k}} \times \boldsymbol{a}$$

We now need to check that PQ is perpendicular to AB:

$$\overrightarrow{AB} = \overrightarrow{OB} - \overrightarrow{OA} = \boldsymbol{b} - \boldsymbol{a}$$

and

$$\overrightarrow{PQ} = \overrightarrow{OQ} - \overrightarrow{OP} = \tfrac{1}{2}(\boldsymbol{a} + \boldsymbol{b}) - \tfrac{1}{2}\boldsymbol{a} - \frac{\tfrac{1}{2}\boldsymbol{b} \cdot (\boldsymbol{b} - \boldsymbol{a})}{\boldsymbol{b} \cdot (\hat{\boldsymbol{k}} \times \boldsymbol{a})}\hat{\boldsymbol{k}} \times \boldsymbol{a}$$

Now take the dot product of these two vectors

$$\left[\tfrac{1}{2}\boldsymbol{b} - \frac{\tfrac{1}{2}\boldsymbol{b}\cdot(\boldsymbol{b}-\boldsymbol{a})}{\boldsymbol{b}\cdot(\hat{\boldsymbol{k}}\times\boldsymbol{a})}\hat{\boldsymbol{k}}\times\boldsymbol{a}\right]\cdot(\boldsymbol{b}-\boldsymbol{a}) = \tfrac{1}{2}\boldsymbol{b}\cdot(\boldsymbol{b}-\boldsymbol{a}) - \frac{\tfrac{1}{2}\boldsymbol{b}\cdot(\boldsymbol{b}-\boldsymbol{a})}{\boldsymbol{b}\cdot(\hat{\boldsymbol{k}}\times\boldsymbol{a})}\boldsymbol{b}\cdot(\hat{\boldsymbol{k}}\times\boldsymbol{a}) = 0$$

Since neither $\overrightarrow{PQ}$ nor $\overrightarrow{AB}$ is zero, the two vectors must therefore be perpendicular. Hence the three perpendicular bisectors of the sides of a triangle meet at a point.

**Example 4.33** Three non-zero, non-parallel and non-coplanar vectors $\boldsymbol{a}$, $\boldsymbol{b}$ and $\boldsymbol{c}$ are given. Three further vectors are written in terms of $\boldsymbol{a}$, $\boldsymbol{b}$ and $\boldsymbol{c}$ as

$$\boldsymbol{A} = \alpha\boldsymbol{a} + \beta\boldsymbol{b} + \gamma\boldsymbol{c}$$
$$\boldsymbol{B} = \alpha'\boldsymbol{a} + \beta'\boldsymbol{b} + \gamma'\boldsymbol{c}$$
$$\boldsymbol{C} = \alpha''\boldsymbol{a} + \beta''\boldsymbol{b} + \gamma''\boldsymbol{c}$$

Find how the triple scalar product $\boldsymbol{A}\cdot(\boldsymbol{B}\times\boldsymbol{C})$ is related to $\mathbf{a}\cdot(\mathbf{b}\times\mathbf{c})$.

**Solution** To find the result we use the facts that (i) the vector product of identical vectors is zero and (ii) the triple scalar product is zero if two of the vectors in the product are the same. Now

$$\begin{aligned}
\boldsymbol{A}\cdot(\boldsymbol{B}\times\boldsymbol{C}) &= (\alpha\mathbf{a}+\beta\mathbf{b}+\gamma\mathbf{c})\cdot[(\alpha'\mathbf{a}+\beta'\mathbf{b}+\gamma'\mathbf{c})\times(\alpha''\mathbf{a}+\beta''\mathbf{b}+\gamma''\mathbf{c})]\\
&= (\alpha\mathbf{a}+\beta\mathbf{b}+\gamma\mathbf{c})\cdot[\alpha'\beta''\mathbf{a}\times\mathbf{b}+\alpha'\gamma''\mathbf{a}\times\mathbf{c}+\beta'\alpha''\mathbf{b}\times\mathbf{a}\\
&\qquad +\beta'\gamma''\mathbf{b}\times\mathbf{c}+\gamma'\alpha''\mathbf{c}\times\mathbf{a}+\gamma'\beta''\mathbf{c}\times\mathbf{b}]\\
&= (\alpha\mathbf{a}+\beta\mathbf{b}+\gamma\mathbf{c})\cdot[(\alpha'\beta''-\beta'\alpha'')\mathbf{a}\times\mathbf{b}+(\beta'\gamma''-\gamma'\beta'')\mathbf{b}\times\mathbf{c}\\
&\qquad +(\gamma'\alpha''-\alpha'\gamma'')\mathbf{c}\times\mathbf{a}]\\
&= \gamma(\alpha'\beta''-\beta'\alpha'')\mathbf{c}\cdot\mathbf{a}\times\mathbf{b}+\alpha(\beta'\gamma''-\gamma'\beta'')\mathbf{a}\cdot\mathbf{b}\times\mathbf{c}\\
&\quad +\beta(\gamma'\alpha''-\alpha'\gamma'')\mathbf{b}\cdot\mathbf{c}\times\mathbf{a}\\
&= (\mathbf{a}\cdot\mathbf{b}\times\mathbf{c})[\alpha(\beta'\gamma''-\gamma'\beta'')+\beta(\gamma'\alpha''-\alpha'\gamma'')+\gamma(\alpha'\beta''-\beta'\alpha'')]
\end{aligned}$$

The result can be written most conveniently in determinant form (see Section 5.3 of the next chapter) as

$$\boldsymbol{A}\cdot(\boldsymbol{B}\times\boldsymbol{C}) = \begin{vmatrix}\alpha & \beta & \gamma\\ \alpha' & \beta' & \gamma'\\ \alpha'' & \beta'' & \gamma''\end{vmatrix}(\mathbf{a}\cdot\mathbf{b}\times\mathbf{c})$$

---

### Triple vector product

For the triple vector product we shall show in general that

$$(\mathbf{a}\times\mathbf{b})\times\mathbf{c} = (\mathbf{a}\cdot\mathbf{c})\mathbf{b} - (\mathbf{b}\cdot\mathbf{c})\mathbf{a} \tag{4.13}$$

as suggested in Example 4.24. We have from (4.9)

$$\boldsymbol{a} \times \boldsymbol{b} = (a_2b_3 - a_3b_2, a_3b_1 - a_1b_3, a_1b_2 - a_2b_1)$$

and hence

$$\begin{aligned}(\boldsymbol{a} \times \boldsymbol{b}) \times \boldsymbol{c} = ((a_3b_1 - a_1b_3)c_3 - (a_1b_2 - a_2b_1)c_2,\\ (a_1b_2 - a_2b_1)c_1 - (a_2b_3 - a_3b_2)c_3,\\ (a_2b_3 - a_3b_2)c_2 - (a_3b_1 - a_1b_3)c_1)\end{aligned}$$

The first component of this vector is

$$\begin{aligned}a_3c_3b_1 - b_3c_3a_1 - b_2c_2a_1 + a_2c_2b_1 &= (a_1c_1 + a_2c_2 + a_3c_3)b_1 - (b_1c_1 + b_2c_2 + b_3c_3)a_1\\ &= (\boldsymbol{a}\cdot\boldsymbol{c})b_1 - (\boldsymbol{b}\cdot\boldsymbol{c})a_1\end{aligned}$$

Treating the second and third components similarly, we find

$$\begin{aligned}(\boldsymbol{a} \times \boldsymbol{b}) \times \boldsymbol{c} &= ((\boldsymbol{a}\cdot\boldsymbol{c})b_1 - (\boldsymbol{b}\cdot\boldsymbol{c})a_1, (\boldsymbol{a}\cdot\boldsymbol{c})b_2 - (\boldsymbol{b}\cdot\boldsymbol{c})a_2, (\boldsymbol{a}\cdot\boldsymbol{c})b_3 - (\boldsymbol{b}\cdot\boldsymbol{c})a_3)\\ &= (\boldsymbol{a}\cdot\boldsymbol{c})\boldsymbol{b} - (\boldsymbol{b}\cdot\boldsymbol{c})\boldsymbol{a}\end{aligned}$$

In a similar way we can show that

$$\boldsymbol{a} \times (\boldsymbol{b} \times \boldsymbol{c}) = (\boldsymbol{a}\cdot\boldsymbol{c})\boldsymbol{b} - (\boldsymbol{a}\cdot\boldsymbol{b})\boldsymbol{c} \tag{4.14}$$

We can now see why the associativity of the vector product does not hold in general. The vector in (4.13) is in the plane of ***b*** and ***a***, while the vector in (4.14) is in the plane of ***b*** and ***c***; hence they are not in the same planes in general, as we inferred geometrically in Section 4.2.9. Consequently, in general

$$\boldsymbol{a} \times (\boldsymbol{b} \times \boldsymbol{c}) \neq (\boldsymbol{a} \times \boldsymbol{b}) \times \boldsymbol{c}$$

so use of brackets is essential.

**Example 4.34**

If $\boldsymbol{a} = (3, -2, 1)$, $\boldsymbol{b} = (-1, 3, 4)$ and $\boldsymbol{c} = (2, 1, -3)$, confirm that

$$\boldsymbol{a} \times (\boldsymbol{b} \times \boldsymbol{c}) = (\boldsymbol{a}\cdot\boldsymbol{c})\boldsymbol{b} - (\boldsymbol{a}\cdot\boldsymbol{b})\boldsymbol{c}$$

**Solution**

$$\boldsymbol{b} \times \boldsymbol{c} = \begin{vmatrix} \boldsymbol{i} & \boldsymbol{j} & \boldsymbol{k} \\ -1 & 3 & 4 \\ 2 & 1 & -3 \end{vmatrix} = (-13, 5, -7)$$

$$\boldsymbol{a} \times (\boldsymbol{b} \times \boldsymbol{c}) = \begin{vmatrix} \boldsymbol{i} & \boldsymbol{j} & \boldsymbol{k} \\ 3 & -2 & 1 \\ -13 & 5 & -7 \end{vmatrix} = (9, 8, -11)$$

$$\begin{aligned}(\boldsymbol{a}\cdot\boldsymbol{c})\boldsymbol{b} - (\boldsymbol{a}\cdot\boldsymbol{b})\boldsymbol{c} &= [(3)(2) + (-2)(1) + (1)(-3)](-1, 3, 4) \\ &\quad - [(3)(-1) + (-2)(3) + (1)(4)](2, 1, -3) \\ &= (-1, 3, 4) + 5(2, 1, -3) \\ &= (9, 8, -11)\end{aligned}$$

thus confirming the result

$$\boldsymbol{a}\times(\boldsymbol{b}\times\boldsymbol{c}) = (\boldsymbol{a}\cdot\boldsymbol{c})\boldsymbol{b} - (\boldsymbol{a}\cdot\boldsymbol{b})\boldsymbol{c}$$

**Example 4.35**

Verify that $\boldsymbol{a}\times(\boldsymbol{b}\times\boldsymbol{c}) \neq (\boldsymbol{a}\times\boldsymbol{b})\times\boldsymbol{c}$ for the three vectors $\boldsymbol{a} = (1, 0, 0)$, $\boldsymbol{b} = (-1, 2, 0)$ and $\boldsymbol{c} = (1, 1, 1)$.

**Solution** Evaluate the cross products in turn:

$$\boldsymbol{b}\times\boldsymbol{c} = (-1, 2, 0)\times(1, 1, 1) = (2, 1, -3)$$

and therefore

$$\boldsymbol{a}\times(\boldsymbol{b}\times\boldsymbol{c}) = (1, 0, 0)\times(2, 1, -3) = (0, 3, 1)$$

Similarly for the right-hand side

$$\boldsymbol{a}\times\boldsymbol{b} = (1, 0, 0)\times(-1, 2, 0) = (0, 0, 2)$$

and hence

$$(\boldsymbol{a}\times\boldsymbol{b})\times\boldsymbol{c} = (0, 0, 2)\times(1, 1, 1) = (-2, 2, 0)$$

Clearly for these three vectors $\boldsymbol{a}\times(\boldsymbol{b}\times\boldsymbol{c}) \neq (\boldsymbol{a}\times\boldsymbol{b})\times\boldsymbol{c}$.

**Example 4.36**

The vectors $\boldsymbol{a}$, $\boldsymbol{b}$ and $\boldsymbol{c}$ and the scalar $p$ satisfy the equations

$$\boldsymbol{a}\cdot\boldsymbol{b} = p \quad \text{and} \quad \boldsymbol{a}\times\boldsymbol{b} = \boldsymbol{c}$$

and $\boldsymbol{a}$ is not parallel to $\boldsymbol{b}$. Solve for $\boldsymbol{a}$ in terms of the other quantities and give a geometrical interpretation of the result.

**Solution** First evaluate the cross product of the second equation with $\boldsymbol{b}$

$$\boldsymbol{b}\times(\boldsymbol{a}\times\boldsymbol{b}) = \boldsymbol{b}\times\boldsymbol{c}$$

gives

$$(\boldsymbol{b}\cdot\boldsymbol{b})\boldsymbol{a} - (\boldsymbol{b}\cdot\boldsymbol{a})\boldsymbol{b} = \boldsymbol{b}\times\boldsymbol{c}$$

and hence, using $\boldsymbol{a}\cdot\boldsymbol{b} = p$, and collecting the terms

$$\boldsymbol{a} = \frac{p\boldsymbol{b} + \boldsymbol{b}\times\boldsymbol{c}}{|\boldsymbol{b}|^2}$$

Since $\boldsymbol{b}\times\boldsymbol{c}$ is in the plane of $\boldsymbol{a}$ and $\boldsymbol{b}$, any vector in the plane can be written as a linear combination of $\boldsymbol{b}$ and $\boldsymbol{b}\times\boldsymbol{c}$. The expression for $\boldsymbol{a}$ gives the values of the coefficients in the linear combination.

## 4.2.12 Exercises

Check your answers using MATLAB or MAPLE whenever possible.

**43** Find the volume of the parallelepiped whose edges are represented by the vectors (2, −3, 4), (1, 3, −1), (3, −1, 2).

**44** Prove that the vectors (3, 2, −1), (5, −7, 3) and (11, −3, 1) are coplanar.

**45** Find the constant $\lambda$ such that the three vectors (3, 2, −1), (1, −1, 3) and (2, −3, $\lambda$) are coplanar.

**46** Prove that the four points having position vectors (2, 1, 0), (2, −2, −2), (7, −3, −1) and (13, 3, 5) are coplanar.

**47** Given $\boldsymbol{p} = (1, 4, 1)$, $\boldsymbol{q} = (2, 1, -1)$ and $\boldsymbol{r} = (1, -3, 2)$, find

(a) a unit vector perpendicular to the plane containing $\boldsymbol{p}$ and $\boldsymbol{q}$,

(b) a unit vector in the plane containing $\boldsymbol{p} \times \boldsymbol{q}$ and $\boldsymbol{p} \times \boldsymbol{r}$ that has zero $x$ component.

**48** Show that if $\boldsymbol{a}$ is any vector and $\hat{\boldsymbol{u}}$ any unit vector then

$$\boldsymbol{a} = (\boldsymbol{a} \cdot \hat{\boldsymbol{u}})\hat{\boldsymbol{u}} + \hat{\boldsymbol{u}} \times (\boldsymbol{a} \times \hat{\boldsymbol{u}})$$

and draw a diagram to illustrate this relation geometrically.

The vector (3, −2, 6) is resolved into two vectors along and perpendicular to the line whose direction cosines are proportional to (1, 1, 1). Find these vectors.

**49** Three vectors $\boldsymbol{u}$, $\boldsymbol{v}$, $\boldsymbol{w}$ are expressed in terms of the three vectors $\boldsymbol{l}$, $\boldsymbol{m}$, $\boldsymbol{n}$ in the form

$$\boldsymbol{u} = u_1\boldsymbol{l} + u_2\boldsymbol{m} + u_3\boldsymbol{n}$$

$$\boldsymbol{v} = v_1\boldsymbol{l} + v_2\boldsymbol{m} + v_3\boldsymbol{n}$$

$$\boldsymbol{w} = w_1\boldsymbol{l} + w_2\boldsymbol{m} + w_3\boldsymbol{n}$$

Show that

$$\boldsymbol{u} \cdot (\boldsymbol{v} \times \boldsymbol{w}) = \lambda \boldsymbol{l} \cdot (\boldsymbol{m} \times \boldsymbol{n})$$

and evaluate $\lambda$.

**50** Forces $\boldsymbol{F}_1, \boldsymbol{F}_2, \ldots, \boldsymbol{F}_n$ act at the points $\boldsymbol{r}_1, \boldsymbol{r}_2, \ldots, \boldsymbol{r}_n$ respectively. The total force and the total moment about the origin O are

$$\boldsymbol{F} = \sum \boldsymbol{F}_i \quad \text{and} \quad \boldsymbol{G} = \sum \boldsymbol{r}_i \times \boldsymbol{F}_i$$

Show that for any other origin O′ the moment is given by

$$\boldsymbol{G}' = \boldsymbol{G} + \overrightarrow{\mathrm{O'O}} \times \boldsymbol{F}$$

If O′ lies on the line

$$\overrightarrow{\mathrm{OO'}} = \boldsymbol{r} = \alpha(\boldsymbol{F} \times \boldsymbol{G}) + t\boldsymbol{F}$$

find the constant $\alpha$ that ensures that $\boldsymbol{G}'$ is parallel to $\boldsymbol{F}$. This line is called the central axis of the system of forces.

**51** Extended exercise on products of four vectors.

(a) Use (4.11) to show

$$(\boldsymbol{a} \times \boldsymbol{b}) \cdot (\boldsymbol{c} \times \boldsymbol{d}) = [(\boldsymbol{a} \times \boldsymbol{b}) \times \boldsymbol{c}] \cdot \boldsymbol{d}$$

and use (4.13) to simplify the expression on the right-hand side.

(b) Use (4.13) to show that

$$(\boldsymbol{a} \times \boldsymbol{b}) \times (\boldsymbol{a} \times \boldsymbol{c}) = [\boldsymbol{a} \cdot (\boldsymbol{a} \times \boldsymbol{c})]\boldsymbol{b} - [\boldsymbol{b} \cdot (\boldsymbol{a} \times \boldsymbol{c})]\boldsymbol{a}$$

and show that the right-hand side can be simplified to

$$[(\boldsymbol{a} \times \boldsymbol{b}) \cdot \boldsymbol{c}]\boldsymbol{a}$$

(c) Use (4.14) to show that

$$\boldsymbol{a} \times [\boldsymbol{b} \times (\boldsymbol{a} \times \boldsymbol{c})] = \boldsymbol{a} \times [(\boldsymbol{b} \cdot \boldsymbol{c})\boldsymbol{a} - (\boldsymbol{b} \cdot \boldsymbol{a})\boldsymbol{c}]$$

and simplify the right-hand side further. Note that the product is different from the result in (b), verifying that the position of the brackets matters in cross products.

(d) Use the result in (a) to show that

$$(\boldsymbol{l} \times \boldsymbol{m}) \cdot (\boldsymbol{l} \times \boldsymbol{n}) = l^2(\boldsymbol{m} \cdot \boldsymbol{n}) - (\boldsymbol{l} \cdot \boldsymbol{m})(\boldsymbol{l} \cdot \boldsymbol{n})$$

Take $\boldsymbol{l}$, $\boldsymbol{m}$ and $\boldsymbol{n}$ to be unit vectors along the sides of a regular tetrahedron. Deduce that the angle between two faces of the tetrahedron is $\cos^{-1}\frac{1}{3}$.

## 4.3 The vector treatment of the geometry of lines and planes

### 4.3.1 Vector equation of a line

Take an arbitrary origin O and let $\overrightarrow{OA} = \boldsymbol{a}$, $\overrightarrow{OB} = \boldsymbol{b}$ and $\overrightarrow{OP} = \boldsymbol{r}$, as in Figure 4.48. If P is any point on the line then

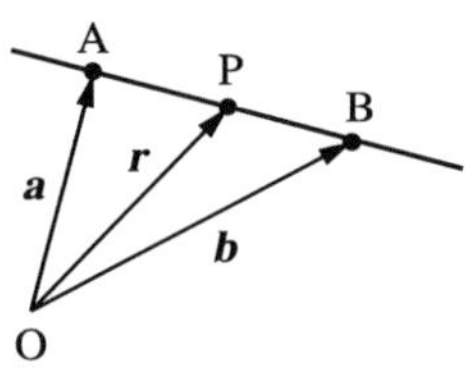


**Figure 4.48**
Line AB in terms of $\boldsymbol{r} = \overrightarrow{OP}$.

$$\overrightarrow{OP} = \overrightarrow{OA} + \overrightarrow{AP}, \quad \text{by the triangle law}$$

giving

$$\boldsymbol{r} = \boldsymbol{a} + t\overrightarrow{AB} \qquad (\text{since } \overrightarrow{AP} \text{ is a multiple of } \overrightarrow{AB})$$
$$= \boldsymbol{a} + t(\boldsymbol{b} - \boldsymbol{a}) \qquad (\text{since } \boldsymbol{a} + \overrightarrow{AB} = \boldsymbol{b})$$

Thus the equation of the line is

$$\boldsymbol{r} = (1 - t)\boldsymbol{a} + t\boldsymbol{b} \tag{4.15}$$

As $t$ varies from $-\infty$ to $+\infty$, the point P sweeps along the line, with $t = 0$ corresponding to point A and $t = 1$ to point B.

Since $\overrightarrow{OP} = \overrightarrow{OA} + \overrightarrow{AP} = \overrightarrow{OA} + t\overrightarrow{AB}$, we have $\boldsymbol{r} = \boldsymbol{a} + t(\boldsymbol{b} - \boldsymbol{a})$. If we write $\boldsymbol{c} = \boldsymbol{b} - \boldsymbol{a}$ then we have an alternative intepretation of a line through A in the direction $\boldsymbol{c}$:

$$\boldsymbol{r} = \boldsymbol{a} + t\boldsymbol{c} \tag{4.16}$$

The cartesian or component form of this equation is

$$\frac{x - a_1}{c_1} = \frac{y - a_2}{c_2} = \frac{z - a_3}{c_3} (= t) \tag{4.17}$$

where $\boldsymbol{a} = (a_1, a_2, a_3)$ and $\boldsymbol{c} = (c_1, c_2, c_3)$. Alternatively the cartesian equation of (4.15) may be written in the form

$$\frac{x - a_1}{b_1 - a_1} = \frac{y - a_2}{b_2 - a_2} = \frac{z - a_3}{b_3 - a_3} (= t)$$

where $\boldsymbol{a} = (a_1, a_2, a_3)$ and $\boldsymbol{b} = (b_1, b_2, b_3)$ are two points on the line. If any of the denominators is zero, then both forms of the equation of a line are interpreted as the corresponding numerator is zero.

**Example 4.37** Find the equation of the lines $L_1$ through the points (0, 1, 0) and (1, 3, −1) and $L_2$ through (1, 1, 1) and (−1, −1, 1). Do the two lines intersect and, if so, at what point?

**Solution** From (4.15) $L_1$ has the equation

$$\boldsymbol{r} = (0, 1 - t, 0) + (t, 3t, -t) = (t, 1 + 2t, -t)$$

and $L_2$ has the equation

$$\boldsymbol{r} = (1 - s, 1 - s, 1 - s) + (-s, -s, s) = (1 - 2s, 1 - 2s, 1)$$

Note that the cartesian equation of $L_2$ reduces to $x = y$; $z = 1$. The two lines intersect if it is possible to find $s$ and $t$ such that

$$t = 1 - 2s, \quad 1 + 2t = 1 - 2s, \quad -t = 1$$

Solving two of these equations will give the values of $s$ and $t$. If these values satisfy the remaining equation then the lines intersect; however, if they do not satisfy the remaining equation then the lines do not intersect. In this particular case, the third equation gives $t = -1$ and the first equation $s = 1$. Putting these values into the second equation the left-hand side equals $-1$ and the right-hand side equals $-1$ so the equations are all satisfied and therefore the lines intersect. Substituting back into either equation, the point of intersection is $(-1, -1, 1)$.

**Example 4.38** The position vectors of the points A and B are

$$(1, 4, 6) \quad \text{and} \quad (3, 5, 7)$$

Find the vector equation of the line AB and find the points where the line intersects the coordinate planes.

**Solution** The line has equation

$$\boldsymbol{r} = (1, 4, 6) + t(2, 1, 1)$$

or in components

$$x = 1 + 2t$$

$$y = 4 + t$$

$$z = 6 + t$$

Thus the line meets the $y$–$z$ plane when $x = 0$ and hence $t = -\frac{1}{2}$ and the point of intersection with the plane is $(0, \frac{7}{2}, \frac{11}{2})$.

The line meets the $z$–$x$ plane when $y = 0$ and hence $t = -4$ and the point of intersection with the plane is $(-7, 0, 2)$.

The line meets the $x$–$y$ plane when $z = 0$ and hence $t = -6$ and the point of intersection with the plane is $(-11, -2, 0)$.

**Example 4.39** The line $L_1$ passes through the points with position vectors

$$(5, 1, 7) \quad \text{and} \quad (6, 0, 8)$$

and the line $L_2$ passes through the points with position vectors

$$(3, 1, 3) \quad \text{and} \quad (-1, 3, \alpha)$$

Find the value of $\alpha$ for which the two lines $L_1$ and $L_2$ intersect.

**Solution** Using the vector form:
From (4.15) the equations of the two lines can be written in vector form as

$$L_1: \quad \boldsymbol{r} = (5, 1, 7) + t(1, -1, 1)$$

$$L_2: \quad \boldsymbol{r} = (3, 1, 3) + s(-4, 2, \alpha - 3)$$

These two lines intersect if $t$, $s$ and $\alpha$ can be chosen so that the two vectors are equal, that is they have the same components. Thus

$$5 + t = 3 - 4s$$

$$1 - t = 1 + 2s$$

$$7 + t = 3 + s(\alpha - 3)$$

The first two of these equations are simultaneous equations for $t$ and $s$. Solving gives $t = 2$ and $s = -1$. Putting these values into the third equation

$$9 = 3 - (\alpha - 3) \Rightarrow \alpha = -3$$

and it can be checked that the point of intersection is $(7, -1, 9)$.

Using the cartesian form:
Equation (4.17) gives the equations of the lines as

$$L_1: \quad \frac{x-5}{6-5} = \frac{y-1}{0-1} = \frac{z-7}{8-7}$$

$$L_2: \quad \frac{x-3}{-1-3} = \frac{y-1}{3-1} = \frac{z-3}{\alpha-3}$$

The two equations for $x$ and $y$ are

$$x - 5 = 1 - y$$

$$\tfrac{1}{4}(3 - x) = \tfrac{1}{2}(y - 1)$$

and are solved to give $x = 7$ and $y = -1$. Putting in these values, the equations for $z$ and $\alpha$ become

$$z - 7 = 2$$

$$\frac{z-3}{\alpha-3} = -1$$

which give $z = 9$ and $\alpha = -3$.

**Example 4.40** A tracking station observes an aeroplane at two successive times to be

$$(-500, 0, 1000) \quad \text{and} \quad (400, 400, 1050)$$

relative to axes $x$ in an easterly direction, $y$ in a northerly direction and $z$ vertically upwards, with distances in metres. Find the equation of the path of the aeroplane. Control advises the aeroplane to change course from its present position to level flight at the current height and turn easterly through an angle of 90°; what is the equation of the new path?

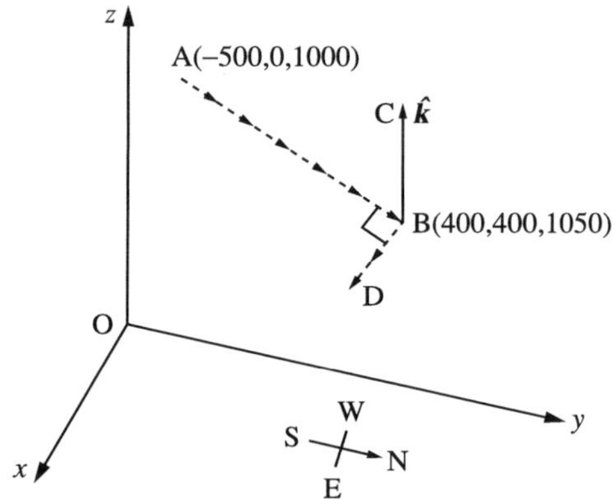


**Figure 4.49**
Path of aeroplane in Example 4.40.

**Solution** The situation is illustrated in Figure 4.49. The equation of the path of the aeroplane is

$$\boldsymbol{r} = (-500, 0, 1000) + t(900, 400, 50)$$

The new path starts at the point (400, 400, 1050). The vector $\overrightarrow{AB} \times \hat{\boldsymbol{k}}$ is a vector in the direction $\overrightarrow{BD}$ which is perpendicular to $\hat{\boldsymbol{k}}$, and is therefore horizontal, and at 90° to AB in the easterly direction. Thus we have 90° turn to horizontal flight. Since

$$(900, 400, 0) \times \boldsymbol{k} = (400, -900, 0)$$

the new path is

$$\boldsymbol{r} = (400, 400, 1050) + s(400, -900, 0)$$

Equating the components

$$x = 400 + 400s$$
$$y = 400 - 900s$$
$$z = 1050$$

In cartesian coordinates the equations are

$$9x + 4y = 5200$$
$$z = 1050$$

**Example 4.41** It is necessary to drill to an underground pipeline in order to undertake repairs, so it is decided to aim for the nearest point from the measuring point. Relative to axes $x$, $y$ in the horizontal ground and with $z$ vertically downwards, remote measuring instruments locate two points on the pipeline at

$$(20, 20, 30) \quad \text{and} \quad (0, 15, 32)$$

with distances in metres. Find the nearest point on the pipeline from the origin O.

**Solution** The situation is illustrated in Figure 4.50. The direction of the pipeline is

$$\boldsymbol{d} = (0, 15, 32) - (20, 20, 30) = (-20, -5, 2).$$

Thus any point on the pipeline will have position vector

$$\boldsymbol{r} = (20, 20, 30) + t(-20, -5, 2)$$

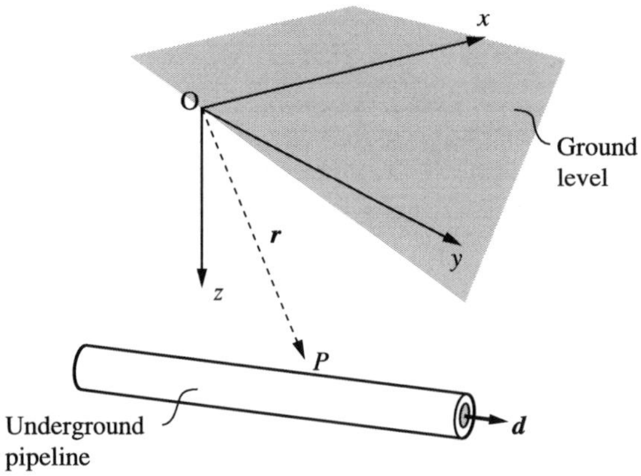


**Figure 4.50** Pipeline of Example 4.41

for some $t$. Note that this is just the equation of the line given in (4.15). At the shortest distance from O to the pipeline the vector $\boldsymbol{r} = \overrightarrow{OP}$ is perpendicular to $\boldsymbol{d}$, so $\boldsymbol{r} \cdot \boldsymbol{d} = 0$ gives the required condition to evaluate $t$. Thus

$$(-20, -5, 2) \cdot [(20, 20, 30) + t(-20, -5, 2)] = 0$$

and hence $-440 + 429t = 0$. Putting this value back into $\boldsymbol{r}$ gives

$$\boldsymbol{r} = (-0.51, 14.87, 32.05)$$

Note that the value of $t$ is close to 1 so the optimum point is not far from the second of the points located.

**Example 4.42** Find the shortest distance between the two skew lines

$$\frac{x}{3} = \frac{y-9}{-1} = \frac{z-2}{1} \quad \text{and} \quad \frac{x+6}{-3} = \frac{y+5}{2} = \frac{z-10}{4}$$

Also determine the equation of the common perpendicular. (Note that two lines are said to be skew if they do not intersect and are not parallel.)

**Solution** In vector form the equations of the lines are

$$\boldsymbol{r} = (0, 9, 2) + t(3, -1, 1)$$

and

$$\boldsymbol{r} = (-6, -5, 10) + s(-3, 2, 4)$$

The shortest distance between the two lines will be their common perpendicular, see Figure 4.51. Let $P_1$ and $P_2$ be the end points of the common perpendicular, having position vectors $\boldsymbol{r}_1$ and $\boldsymbol{r}_2$ respectively, where

$$\boldsymbol{r}_1 = (0, 9, 2) + t_1(3, -1, 1)$$

and

$$\boldsymbol{r}_2 = (-6, -5, 10) + t_2(-3, 2, 4)$$

**Figure 4.51**
Skew lines in Example 4.42.

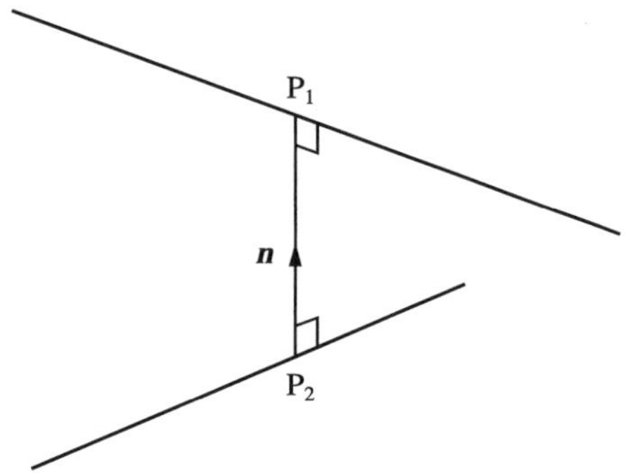


Then the vector $\overrightarrow{P_2P_1}$ is given by

$$\overrightarrow{P_2P_1} = \boldsymbol{r}_1 - \boldsymbol{r}_2 = (6, 14, -8) + t_1(3, -1, 1) - t_2(-3, 2, 4) \quad \textbf{(4.18)}$$

Since (3, –1, 1) and (–3, 2, 4) are vectors in the direction of each of the lines, it follows that a vector $\boldsymbol{n}$ perpendicular to both lines is

$$\boldsymbol{n} = (-3, 2, 4) \times (3, -1, 1) = (6, 15, -3)$$

So a unit vector perpendicular to both lines is

$$\hat{\boldsymbol{n}} = (6, 15, -3)/\sqrt{270} = (2, 5, -1)/\sqrt{30}$$

Thus we can also express $\overrightarrow{P_2P_1}$ as

$$\overrightarrow{P_2P_1} = d\hat{\boldsymbol{n}}$$

where $d$ is the shortest distance between the two lines.

Equating the two expressions for $\overrightarrow{P_2P_1}$ gives

$$(6, 14, -8) + t_1(3, -1, 1) - t_2(-3, 2, 4) = (2, 5, -1)d/\sqrt{30}$$

Taking the scalar product throughout with the vector (2, 5, –1) gives

$$(6, 14, -8)\cdot(2, 5, -1) + t_1(3, -1, 1)\cdot(2, 5, -1) - t_2(-3, 2, 4)\cdot(2, 5, -1)$$
$$= (2, 5, -1)\cdot(2, 5, -1)d/\sqrt{30}$$

which reduces to

$$90 + 0t_1 + 0t_2 = 30d/\sqrt{30}$$

giving the shortest distance between the two lines as

$$d = 3\sqrt{30}$$

To obtain the equation of the common perpendicular, we need to find the coordinates of either $P_1$ or $P_2$ – and to achieve this we need to find the value of either $t_1$ or $t_2$. We therefore take the scalar product of (4.18) with (3, –1, 1) and (–3, 2, 4) in turn, giving respectively

$$11t_1 + 7t_2 = 4$$

and

$$-7t_1 - 29t_2 = 22$$

which on solving simultaneously give $t_1 = 1$ and $t_2 = -1$. Hence the coordinates of the end points $P_1$ and $P_2$ of the common perpendicular are

$$\boldsymbol{r}_1 = (0, 9, 2) + 1(3, -1, 1) = (3, 8, 3)$$

and

$$\boldsymbol{r}_2 = (-6, -5, 10) - 1(-3, 2, 4) = (-3, -7, 6)$$

From (4.16) the equation of the common perpendicular is

$$\boldsymbol{r} = (3, 8, 3) + s(2, 5, -1)$$

or in cartesian form

$$\frac{x-3}{2} = \frac{y-8}{5} = \frac{z-3}{-1} = s$$

MAPLE contains a geometry package which takes a bit of time to master but which can solve many coordinate geometry problems. For the current problem the code is given: note that printing has been largely suppressed, but replace ':' by ';' at the end of statements for more information.

```
with (geom3d):
point (A, [0, 9, 2]): v:= [3, -1, 1]: line
(L1, [A, v]): detail (L1);
point (B, [-6, -5, 10]): w:= [-3, 2, 4]: line
(L2, [B, w]): detail (L2);
distance (L1, L2);                    (gives result 3√30 in the text)
z:= Equation (L1, t): y:= Equation (L2, s):
with (linalg):
m:= innerprod (z - y, v): n:= innerprod (z - y, w):
solve ({m, n}, {s, t});               (gives solution t = 1 and s = −1)
point (P, eval (z, t = 1)): point (Q, eval (y, s = -1)):
line (L3, [P, Q]): detail (L3);       (gives the required equation of
                                       the common perpendicular)
```

**Example 4.43** A box with an open top and unit side length is observed from the direction $(a, b, c)$ as in Figure 4.52. Determine the part of OC that is visible.

**Solution** The line or ray through $Q(0, 0, \alpha)$ parallel to the line of sight has the equation

$$\boldsymbol{r} = (0, 0, \alpha) + t(a, b, c)$$

where $0 \leqslant \alpha \leqslant 1$ to ensure that Q lies between O and C. The line RS passes through $R(1, 0, 1)$ and is in the direction $(0, 1, 0)$ so from (4.16) it has the equation

$$\boldsymbol{r} = (1, 0, 1) + s(0, 1, 0)$$

The ray that intersects RS must therefore satisfy

$$ta = 1, \quad tb = s, \quad \alpha = 1 - \frac{c}{a}$$

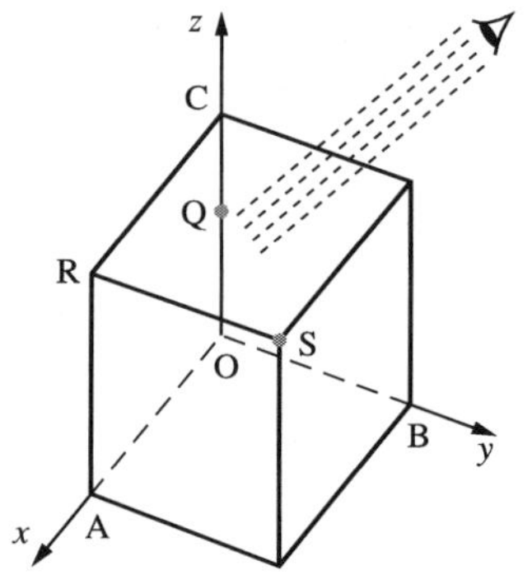


**Figure 4.52**
Looking for hidden lines in Example 4.43.

Note that if $c = 0$ then we are looking parallel to the open top and can only see the point C. If $c < 0$ then we are looking up at the box; since $\alpha > 1$, we cannot see any of side OC, so the line is hidden. If, however, $c > a$ then the solution gives $\alpha$ to be negative, so that all of the side OC is visible. For $0 < c < a$ the parameter $\alpha$ lies between 0 and 1, and only part of the line is visible. A similar analysis needs to be performed for the other sides of the open top. Other edges of the box also need to be analysed to check whether or not they are visible to the ray.

## 4.3.2 Vector equation of a plane

To obtain the equation of a plane, we use the result that the line joining any two points in the plane is perpendicular to the normal to the plane as illustrated in Figure 4.53. The vector $\boldsymbol{n}$ is perpendicular to the plane, $\boldsymbol{a}$ is the position vector of a given point A in the plane and $\boldsymbol{r}$ is the position vector of any point P on the plane. The vector $\overrightarrow{AP} = \boldsymbol{r} - \boldsymbol{a}$ is perpendicular to $\boldsymbol{n}$, and hence

$$(\boldsymbol{r} - \boldsymbol{a}) \cdot \boldsymbol{n} = 0$$

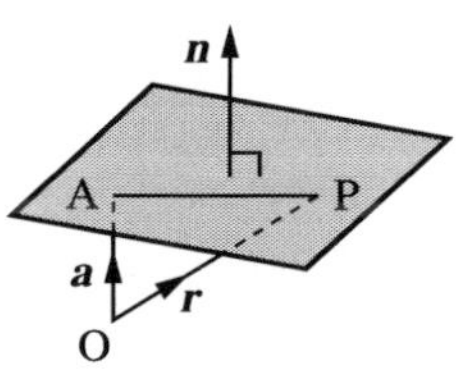


**Figure 4.53**
Equation of a plane; $\boldsymbol{n}$ is perpendicular to the plane.

so that

$$\boldsymbol{r} \cdot \boldsymbol{n} = \boldsymbol{a} \cdot \boldsymbol{n} \quad \text{or} \quad \boldsymbol{r} \cdot \boldsymbol{n} = p \tag{4.19}$$

is the general form for the **equation of a plane** with normal $\boldsymbol{n}$. In the particular case when $\boldsymbol{n}$ is a unit vector, $p$ in (4.19) represents the perpendicular distance from the origin to the plane. In cartesian form we take $\boldsymbol{n} = (\alpha, \beta, \gamma)$, and the equation becomes

$$\alpha x + \beta y + \gamma z = p \tag{4.20}$$

which is just a linear relation between the variables $x$, $y$ and $z$.

**Example 4.44**

Find the equation of the plane through the three points

$$\boldsymbol{a} = (1, 1, 1), \quad \boldsymbol{b} = (0, 1, 2) \quad \text{and} \quad \boldsymbol{c} = (-1, 1, -1)$$

**Solution**

The vectors $\boldsymbol{a} - \boldsymbol{b} = (1, 0, -1)$ and $\boldsymbol{a} - \boldsymbol{c} = (2, 0, 2)$ will lie in the plane. The normal $\boldsymbol{n}$ to the plane can thus be constructed as $(\boldsymbol{a} - \boldsymbol{b}) \times (\boldsymbol{a} - \boldsymbol{c})$, giving

$$\boldsymbol{n} = (1, 0, -1) \times (2, 0, 2) = (0, -4, 0)$$

Thus from (4.19) the equation of the plane is given by

$$\boldsymbol{r} \cdot \boldsymbol{n} = \boldsymbol{a} \cdot \boldsymbol{n}$$

or

$$\boldsymbol{r} \cdot (0, -4, 0) = (1, 1, 1) \cdot (0, -4, 0)$$

giving

$$\boldsymbol{r} \cdot (0, -4, 0) = -4$$

In cartesian form

$$(x, y, z) \cdot (0, -4, 0) = -4$$

or simply $y = 1$.

**Example 4.45** A metal has a simple cubic lattice structure so that the atoms lie on the lattice points given by

$$\boldsymbol{r} = a(l, m, n)$$

where $a$ is the lattice spacing and $l$, $m$, $n$ are integers. The metallurgist requires to identify the points that lie on two lattice planes

$LP_1$ through $a(0, 0, 0)$, $a(1, 1, 0)$ and $a(0, 1, 2)$

$LP_2$ through $a(0, 0, 2)$, $a(1, 1, 0)$ and $a(0, 1, 0)$

**Solution** The direction perpendicular to $LP_1$ is $(1, 1, 0) \times (0, 1, 2) = (2, -2, 1)$ and hence the equation of $LP_1$ is

$$\boldsymbol{r} \cdot (2, -2, 1) = 0 \quad \text{or in cartesian form} \quad 2x - 2y + z = 0 \tag{4.21}$$

The direction perpendicular to $LP_2$ is $(1, 1, -2) \times (0, 1, -2) = (0, 2, 1)$ and hence the equation of $LP_2$ is

$$\boldsymbol{r} \cdot (0, 2, 1) = 2 \quad \text{or in cartesian form} \quad 2y + z = 2 \tag{4.22}$$

Points that lie on both lattice planes must satisfy both (4.21) and (4.22). It is easiest to solve these equations in their cartesian form. The coordinates must be integers so take $y = m$, then $z$ can easily be calculated from (4.22) as

$$z = 2 - 2m$$

and then $x$ is computed from (4.21) to be $x = 2m - 1$.

Hence the required points all lie on a line and take the form

$$\boldsymbol{r} = a(2m - 1, m, 2 - 2m)$$

where $m$ is an integer.

**Example 4.46** Find the point where the plane

$$\boldsymbol{r} \cdot (1, 1, 2) = 3$$

meets the line

$$\boldsymbol{r} = (2, 1, 1) + \lambda(0, 1, 2)$$

**Solution** At the point of intersection $\boldsymbol{r}$ must satisfy both equations, so

$$[(2, 1, 1) + \lambda(0, 1, 2)] \cdot (1, 1, 2) = 3$$

or

$$5 + 5\lambda = 3$$

so

$$\lambda = -\tfrac{2}{5}$$

Substituting back into the equation of the line gives the point of intersection as

$$\boldsymbol{r} = (2, \tfrac{3}{5}, \tfrac{1}{5})$$

**Example 4.47** Find the equation of the line of intersection of the two planes $x + y + z = 5$ and $4x + y + 2z = 15$.

**Solution** In vector form the equations of the two planes are

$$\boldsymbol{r} \cdot (1, 1, 1) = 5$$

and

$$\boldsymbol{r} \cdot (4, 1, 2) = 15$$

The required line lies in both planes, and is therefore perpendicular to the vectors (1, 1, 1) and (4, 1, 2), which are normal to the individual planes. Hence a vector $\mathbf{c}$ in the direction of the line is

$$\mathbf{c} = (1, 1, 1) \times (4, 1, 2) = (1, 2, -3)$$

To find the equation of the line, it remains only to find the coordinates of any point on the line. To do this, we are required to find the coordinates of a point satisfying the equation of the two planes. Taking $x = 0$, the corresponding values of $y$ and $z$ are given by

$$y + z = 5 \quad \text{and} \quad y + 2z = 15$$

that is, $y = -5$ and $z = 10$. Hence it can be checked that the point (0, –5, 10) lies in both planes and is therefore a point on the line. From (4.16) the equation of the line is

$$\boldsymbol{r} = (0, -5, 10) + t(1, 2, -3)$$

or in cartesian form

$$\frac{x}{1} = \frac{y + 5}{2} = \frac{z - 10}{-3} = t$$

The MAPLE instructions to solve this example are

```
with (geom3d):
plane (P1, x + y + z = 5, [x, y, z]): plane (P2, 4*x
+ y + 2*z = 15, [x, y, z]): intersection (L, P1, P2):
detail (L);
```

**Example 4.48** Find the perpendicular distance from the point P(2, −3, 4) to the plane $x + 2y + 2z = 13$.

**Solution** In vector form the equation of the plane is

$$\boldsymbol{r}\cdot(1, 2, 2) = 13$$

and a vector perpendicular to the plane is

$$\boldsymbol{n} = (1, 2, 2)$$

Thus from (4.16) the equation of a line perpendicular to the plane and passing through P(2, −3, 4) is

$$\boldsymbol{r} = (2, -3, 4) + t(1, 2, 2)$$

This will meet the plane when

$$\boldsymbol{r}\cdot(1, 2, 2) = (2, -3, 4)\cdot(1, 2, 2) + t(1, 2, 2)\cdot(1, 2, 2) = 13$$

giving

$$4 + 9t = 13$$

so that

$$t = 1$$

Thus the line meets the plane at N having position vector

$$\boldsymbol{r} = (2, -3, 4) + 1(1, 2, 2) = (3, -1, 6)$$

Hence the perpendicular distance is

$$PN = \sqrt{[(3-2)^2 + (-1+3)^2 + (6-4)^2]} = 3$$

## 4.3.3 Exercises

Many of the exercises can be checked using the geom3d package in MAPLE.

52 If A and B have position vectors (1, 2, 3) and (4, 5, 6) respectively, find

(a) the direction vector of the line through A and B,

(b) the vector equation of the line through A and B,

(c) the cartesian equation of the line.

53 Find the vector equation of the plane that passes through the points (1, 2, 3), (2, 4, 5) and (4, 5, 6). What is its cartesian equation?

54 Show that the line joining (2, 3, 4) to (1, 2, 3) is perpendicular to the line joining (1, 0, 2) to (2, 3, −2).

55 Prove that the lines $\boldsymbol{r} = (1, 2, -1) + t(2, 2, 1)$ and $\boldsymbol{r} = (-1, -2, 3) + s(4, 6, -3)$ intersect, and find the coordinates of their point of intersection. Also find the acute angle between the lines.

56 Find the vector equation of the plane that contains the line $\boldsymbol{r} = \boldsymbol{a} + \lambda\boldsymbol{b}$ and passes through the point with position vector $\boldsymbol{c}$.

57 P is a point on a straight line with position vector $\boldsymbol{r} = \boldsymbol{a} + t\boldsymbol{b}$. Show that

$$r^2 = a^2 + 2\boldsymbol{a}\cdot\boldsymbol{b}t + b^2t^2$$

By completing the square, show that $r^2$ is a minimum for the point P for which $t = -\boldsymbol{a}\cdot\boldsymbol{b}/b^2$

Show that at this point $\overrightarrow{OP}$ is perpendicular to the line $\boldsymbol{r} = \boldsymbol{a} + t\boldsymbol{b}$. (This proves the well-known result that the shortest distance from a point to a line is the length of the perpendicular from that point to the line.)

58 The line of intersection of two planes $\boldsymbol{r} \cdot \boldsymbol{n}_1 = p_1$ and $\boldsymbol{r} \cdot \boldsymbol{n}_2 = p_2$ lies in both planes. It is therefore perpendicular to both $\boldsymbol{n}_1$ and $\boldsymbol{n}_2$. Give an expression for this direction, and so show that the equation of the line of intersection may be written as $\boldsymbol{r} = \boldsymbol{r}_0 + t(\boldsymbol{n}_1 \times \boldsymbol{n}_2)$, where $\boldsymbol{r}_0$ is any vector satisfying $\boldsymbol{r}_0 \cdot \boldsymbol{n}_1 = p_1$ and $\boldsymbol{r}_0 \cdot \boldsymbol{n}_2 = p_2$. Hence find the line of intersection of the planes $\boldsymbol{r} \cdot (1, 1, 1) = 5$ and $\boldsymbol{r} \cdot (4, 1, 2) = 15$.

59 Find the equation of the line through the point (1, 2, 4) and in the direction of the vector (1, 1, 2). Find where this line meets the plane $x + 3y - 4z = 5$.

60 Find the acute angle between the planes $2x + y - 2z = 5$ and $3x - 6y - 2z = 7$.

61 Given that $\boldsymbol{a} = (3, 1, 2)$ and $\boldsymbol{b} = (1, -2, -4)$ are the position vectors of the points P and Q respectively, find

(a) the equation of the plane passing through Q and perpendicular to PQ,

(b) the distance from the point (−1, 1, 1) to the plane obtained in (a).

62 Find the equation of the line joining (1, −1, 3) to (3, 3, −1). Show that it is perpendicular to the plane $2x + 4y - 4z = 5$, and find the angle that the line makes with the plane $12x - 15y + 16z = 10$.

63 Find the vector equation of the line through the points with position vectors $\boldsymbol{a} = (2, 0, -1)$ and $\boldsymbol{b} = (1, 2, 3)$. Write down the equivalent cartesian coordinate form. Does this line intersect the line through the points $\boldsymbol{c} = (0, 0, 1)$ and $\boldsymbol{d} = (1, 0, 1)$?

64 Find the shortest distance between the two lines

$$\boldsymbol{r} = (4, -2, 3) + t(2, 1, -1)$$

and

$$\boldsymbol{r} = (-7, -2, 1) + s(3, 2, 1)$$

65 Find the equation of the plane through the line

$$\boldsymbol{r} = (1, -3, 4) + t(2, 1, 1)$$

and parallel to the line

$$\boldsymbol{r} = s(1, 2, 3)$$

66 Find the equation of the line through $P(-1, 0, 1)$ that cuts the line $\boldsymbol{r} = (3, 2, 1) + t(1, 2, 2)$ at right-angles at $Q$. Also find the length $PQ$ and the equation of the plane containing the two lines.

67 Show that the equation of the plane through the points $P_1$, $P_2$ and $P_3$ with position vectors $\boldsymbol{r}_1$, $\boldsymbol{r}_2$ and $\boldsymbol{r}_3$ respectively takes the form

$$\boldsymbol{r} \cdot [(\boldsymbol{r}_1 \times \boldsymbol{r}_2) + (\boldsymbol{r}_2 \times \boldsymbol{r}_3) + (\boldsymbol{r}_3 \times \boldsymbol{r}_1)] = \boldsymbol{r}_1 \cdot (\boldsymbol{r}_2 \times \boldsymbol{r}_3)$$

## 4.4 Engineering application: spin-dryer suspension

Vectors are at their most powerful when dealing with complicated three-dimensional situations. Geometrical and physical intuition are often difficult to use, and it becomes necessary to work quite formally to analyse such situations. For example, the front suspension of a motor car has two struts supported by a spring-and-damper system and subject to a variety of forces and torques from both the car and the wheels. To analyse the stresses and the vibrations in the various components of the structure is non-trivial, even in a two-dimensional version; the true three-dimensional problem provides a testing exercise for even the most experienced automobile engineer. In the present text a much simpler situation is analysed to illustrate the use of vectors.

### 4.4.1 Point-particle model

As with the car suspension, many machines are mounted on springs to isolate vibrations. A typical example is a spin-dryer, which consists of a drum connected to the

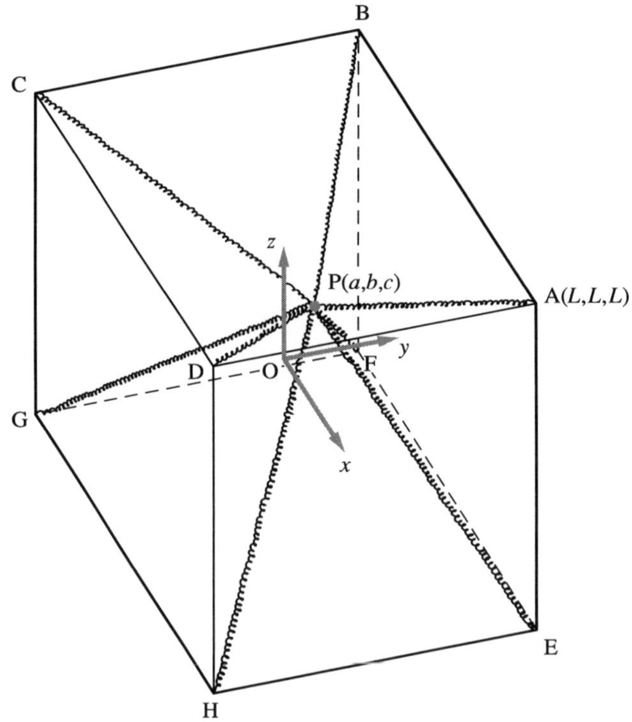


**Figure 4.54**
The particle P is attached by equal springs to the eight corners of the cube.

casing by heavy springs. Oscillations can be very severe when spinning at high speed, and it is essential to know what forces are transmitted to the casing and hence to the mounts. Before the dynamical situation can be analysed, it is necessary to compute the restoring forces on the drum when it is displaced from its equilibrium position. This is a static problem that is best studied using vectors.

We model the spin-dryer as a heavy point particle connected to the eight corners of the casing by springs (Figure 4.54). The drum has weight $W$ and the casing is taken to be a cube of side $2L$. The springs are all equal, having spring constant $k$ and natural length $L\sqrt{3}$. Thus when the drum is at the midpoint of the cube the springs are neither compressed nor extended.

The particle is displaced from its central position by a small amount $(a, b, c)$, where the natural coordinates illustrated in Figure 4.54 are used; the origin is at the centre of the cube and the axes are parallel to the sides. What is required is the total force acting on the particle arising from the weight and the springs. Clearly, this information is needed before any dynamical calculations can be performed. It will be assumed that the displacements are sufficiently small that squares $(a/L)^2$, $(b/L)^2$, $(c/L)^2$ and higher powers are neglected.

Consider a typical spring PA. The tension in the spring is assumed to obey Hooke's law that the force is along PA and has magnitude proportional to extension. $\overrightarrow{PA}/|\overrightarrow{PA}|$ is the unit vector in the direction along PA, and $|\overrightarrow{PA}| - L\sqrt{3}$ is the extension of the spring over its natural length $L\sqrt{3}$ so in vector form the tension can be written as

$$\boldsymbol{T}_A = k\frac{\overrightarrow{PA}}{|\overrightarrow{PA}|}(|\overrightarrow{PA}| - L\sqrt{3}) \tag{4.23}$$

where $k$ is the proportionality constant.

Now

$$\overrightarrow{PA} = \overrightarrow{OA} - \overrightarrow{OP} = (L - a, L - b, L - c)$$

so calculating the modulus squared gives

$$|\overrightarrow{PA}|^2 = (L - a)^2 + (L - b)^2 + (L - c)^2$$

$$= 3L^2 - 2L(a + b + c) + \text{quadratic terms}$$

Thus

$$|\overrightarrow{PA}| = \left[1 - \frac{2}{3L}(a + b + c)\right]^{1/2} L\sqrt{3}$$

and, on using the binomial expansion (see equation (7.16)) and neglecting quadratic and higher terms, we obtain

$$|\overrightarrow{PA}| = \left[1 - \frac{1}{3L}(a + b + c)\right] L\sqrt{3}$$

Putting the information acquired back into (4.23) gives

$$\boldsymbol{T}_{\mathrm{A}} = kL\frac{(1 - a/L, 1 - b/L, 1 - c/L)}{[1 - (a + b + c)/3L]L\sqrt{3}}\frac{(-1)(a + b + c)L\sqrt{3}}{3L}$$

and by expanding again, using the binomial expansion to first order in $a/L$ and so on, we obtain

$$\boldsymbol{T}_{\mathrm{A}} = -\tfrac{1}{3}k(a + b + c)(1, 1, 1)$$

Similar calculations give

$$\boldsymbol{T}_{\mathrm{B}} = -\tfrac{1}{3}k(-a + b + c)(-1, 1, 1)$$

$$\boldsymbol{T}_{\mathrm{C}} = -\tfrac{1}{3}k(-a - b + c)(-1, -1, 1)$$

$$\boldsymbol{T}_{\mathrm{D}} = -\tfrac{1}{3}k(a - b + c)(1, -1, 1)$$

$$\boldsymbol{T}_{\mathrm{E}} = -\tfrac{1}{3}k(a + b - c)(1, 1, -1)$$

$$\boldsymbol{T}_{\mathrm{F}} = -\tfrac{1}{3}k(-a + b - c)(-1, 1, -1)$$

$$\boldsymbol{T}_{\mathrm{G}} = -\tfrac{1}{3}k(-a - b - c)(-1, -1, -1)$$

$$\boldsymbol{T}_{\mathrm{H}} = -\tfrac{1}{3}k(a - b - c)(1, -1, -1)$$

The total spring force is therefore obtained by adding these eight tensions together:

$$\boldsymbol{T} = -\tfrac{8}{3}k(a, b, c)$$

The restoring force is therefore towards the centre of the cube, as expected, in the direction PO and with magnitude $\tfrac{8}{3}k$ times the length of PO.

When the weight is included, the total force is

$$\boldsymbol{F} = (-\tfrac{8}{3}ka, -\tfrac{8}{3}kb, -\tfrac{8}{3}kc - W)$$

If the drum just hangs in equilibrium then $\boldsymbol{F} = 0$, and hence

$$a = b = 0 \quad \text{and} \quad c = -\frac{3W}{8k}$$

Typical values are $W = 400\,\text{N}$ and $k = 10\,000\,\text{N}\,\text{m}^{-1}$, and hence

$$c = -3 \times 400/8 \times 10\,000 = -0.015\,\text{m}$$

so that the centre of the drum hangs 1.5 cm below the midpoint of the centre of the casing.

It is clear that the model used in this section is an idealized one, but it is helpful in describing how to calculate spring forces in complicated three-dimensional static situations. It also gives an idea of the size of the forces involved and the deflections. The next major step is to put these forces into the equations of motion of the drum; this, however, requires a good knowledge of calculus – and, in particular, of differential equations – so it is not appropriate at this point. You may wish to consider this problem after studying the relevant chapters later in this book. A more advanced model must include the fact that the drum is of finite size.

## 4.5 Engineering application: cable stayed bridge

One of the standard methods of supporting bridges is with cables. Readers will no doubt be familiar with suspension bridges such as the Golden Gate in the USA, the Humber bridge in the UK and the Tsing Ma bridge in Hong Kong with their spectacular form. Cable stayed bridges are similar in that they have towers and cables that support a roadway but they are not usually on such a grand scale as suspension bridges. They are often used when the foundations can only support a single tower at one end of the roadway. They are commonly seen on bridges over motorways and footbridges over steep narrow valleys.

In any of the situations described it is essential that information is available on the tension in the wire supports and the forces on the towers. The geometry is fully three-dimensional and quite complicated. Vectors provide a logical and efficient way of dealing with the situation.

### 4.5.1 A simple stayed bridge

There are many configurations that stayed bridges can take; they can have one or more towers and a variety of arrangements of stays. In Figure 4.55 a simple example of a cable stayed footbridge is illustrated. It is constructed with a central vertical pillar with four ties attached by wires to the sides of the pathway.

Relative to the axes, with the $z$ axis vertical, the various points are given, in metres, as A(5, −2, 0.5), B(10, 2, 1), C(15, −2, 1.5), D(20, 2, 1) and S(0, 0, 10). Assuming the weight is evenly distributed, there is an equivalent weight of 2 tonnes at each of the four points A, B, C and D. An estimate is required of the tensions in the wires and force at the tie point S.

The vectors along the ties can easily be evaluated

$$\overrightarrow{AS} = (-5, 2, 9.5), \quad \overrightarrow{BS} = (-10, -2, 9)$$

$$\overrightarrow{CS} = (-15, 2, 8.5), \quad \overrightarrow{DS} = (-20, -2, 9)$$

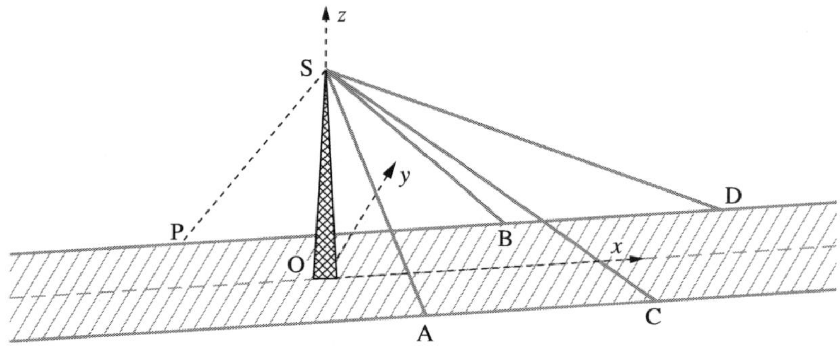


**Figure 4.55** Model of a stayed bridge.

The tension at S in the tie AS can be written $\boldsymbol{T}_A = t_A\overrightarrow{SA}$. Assuming the whole system is in equilibrium, the vertical components at A must be equal

$$\boldsymbol{T}_A \cdot \boldsymbol{k} = 2 \quad \text{and hence} \quad t_A = \frac{2}{9.5}$$

and the four tensions can be computed similarly.

$$\boldsymbol{T}_A = \tfrac{2}{9.5}(5, -2, -9.5) = (1.052, -0.421, -2) \quad \text{and} \quad |\boldsymbol{T}_A| = 2.299 \text{ tonnes}$$

$$\boldsymbol{T}_B = \tfrac{2}{9}(10, 2, -9) = (2.222, 0.444, -2) \quad \text{and} \quad |\boldsymbol{T}_B| = 3.022 \text{ tonnes}$$

$$\boldsymbol{T}_C = \tfrac{2}{8.5}(15, -2, -8.5) = (3.529, -0.471, -2) \quad \text{and} \quad |\boldsymbol{T}_C| = 4.084 \text{ tonnes}$$

$$\boldsymbol{T}_D = \tfrac{2}{9}(20, 2, -9) = (4.444, 0.444, -2) \quad \text{and} \quad |\boldsymbol{T}_D| = 4.894 \text{ tonnes}$$

The total force acting at the tie point S is

$$\boldsymbol{T} = \boldsymbol{T}_A + \boldsymbol{T}_B + \boldsymbol{T}_C + \boldsymbol{T}_D = (11.25, -0.004, -8)$$

Thus with straightforward addition of vectors we have been able to compute the tensions and the total force on the tower.

The question now is how to compensate for the total force on the tower and to try to ensure that it is subject to zero force or a force as small as possible. Suppose that it is decided to have just a single compensating tie wire attached to S and to one side on the pathway at P. It is assumed that on this side of the footbridge the pathway is flat and lies in the $x$–$y$ plane. Where should we position the attachment of the compensating wire so that it produces zero horizontal force at S?

Let the attachment point P on the side of the footbridge be $(-a, 2, 0)$ so that the tension in the compensating cable is

$$\boldsymbol{T}_P = t_P\overrightarrow{SP} = t_P(-a, 2, -10)$$

We require the $y$ component of $(\boldsymbol{T} + \boldsymbol{T}_P)$ to be zero so that

$$2t_P - 0.004 = 0 \quad \text{and hence} \quad t_P = 0.002$$

which in turn gives for the $x$ component

$$at_P = 11.248 \quad \text{and hence} \quad a = 5624 \text{ metres!}$$

Clearly the answer is ridiculous and either more than one compensating cable must be used or the $y$ component can be neglected completely since the force in this direction is only 4 kg.

As a second attempt we specify the attachment wire at P(–5, 2, 0). Requiring the $x$ component of $\boldsymbol{T} + \boldsymbol{T}_P$ to be zero we see that

$$\boldsymbol{T} + \boldsymbol{T}_P = \boldsymbol{T} + t_P\overrightarrow{SP} = (11.25, -0.004, -8) + t_P(-5, 2, -10)$$

gives $t_P = 2.25$. Hence the total force at S is (0, 4.5, –30.5). Although the force in the $x$ direction has been reduced to zero, an unacceptable side force on the tower in the $y$ direction has been introduced.

In a further effort, we introduce two equal compensating wires connected to the points P(–5, –2, 0) and P′(–5, 2, 0). The total force at S is now

$$\boldsymbol{T} + \boldsymbol{T}_P + \boldsymbol{T}_{P'} = \boldsymbol{T} + t_P\overrightarrow{SP} + t_P\overrightarrow{SP'}$$
$$= (11.25, -0.004, -8) + t_P(-5, 2, -10) + t_P(-5, -2, -10)$$

Now choosing $t_P = 1.125$ gives a total force (0, –0.004, –30.5). We now have a satisfactory resolution of the problem with the only significant force being in the downwards direction.

The different forms of stayed bridge construction will require a similar analysis to obtain an estimate of the forces involved. The example given should be viewed as illustrative.

## 4.6 Review exercises (1–24)

Check your answers using MATLAB or MAPLE whenever possible.

1 Given that $\boldsymbol{a} = 3\boldsymbol{i} - \boldsymbol{j} - 4\boldsymbol{k}$, $\boldsymbol{b} = -2\boldsymbol{i} + 4\boldsymbol{j} - 3\boldsymbol{k}$ and $\boldsymbol{c} = \boldsymbol{i} + 2\boldsymbol{j} - \boldsymbol{k}$, find

(a) the magnitude of the vector $\boldsymbol{a} + \boldsymbol{b} + \boldsymbol{c}$,

(b) a unit vector parallel to $3\boldsymbol{a} - 2\boldsymbol{b} + 4\boldsymbol{c}$,

(c) the angles between the vectors $\boldsymbol{a}$ and $\boldsymbol{b}$ and between $\boldsymbol{b}$ and $\boldsymbol{c}$,

(d) the position vector of the centre of mass of particles of masses 1, 2 and 3 placed at points A, B and C with position vectors $\boldsymbol{a}$, $\boldsymbol{b}$ and $\boldsymbol{c}$ respectively.

2 If the vertices X, Y and Z of a triangle have position vectors

$$\boldsymbol{x} = (2, 2, 6), \quad \boldsymbol{y} = (4, 6, 4) \quad \text{and} \quad \boldsymbol{z} = (4, 1, 7)$$

relative to the origin O, find

(a) the midpoint of the side XY of the triangle,

(b) the area of the triangle,

(c) the volume of the tetrahedron OXYZ.

3 The vertices of a tetrahedron are the points

W(2, 1, 3), X(3, 3, 3), Y(4, 2, 4) and Z(3, 3, 5)

Determine

(a) the vectors $\overrightarrow{WX}$ and $\overrightarrow{WY}$,

(b) the area of the face WXZ,

(c) the volume of the tetrahedron WXZY,

(d) the angles between the faces WXY and WYZ.

4 Given $\boldsymbol{a} = (-1, -3, -1)$, $\boldsymbol{b} = (q, 1, 1)$ and $\boldsymbol{c} = (1, 1, q)$ determine the values of $q$ for which

(a) $\boldsymbol{a}$ is perpendicular to $\boldsymbol{b}$

(b) $\boldsymbol{a} \times (\boldsymbol{b} \times \boldsymbol{c}) = 0$

5 Given the vectors $\boldsymbol{a} = (2, 1, 2)$ and $\boldsymbol{b} = (-3, 0, 4)$, evaluate the unit vectors $\hat{\boldsymbol{a}}$ and $\hat{\boldsymbol{b}}$. Use these unit vectors to find a vector that bisects the angle between $\boldsymbol{a}$ and $\boldsymbol{b}$.

6 A triangle, ABC, is inscribed in a circle, centre O, with AOC as a diameter of the circle. Take $\overrightarrow{OA} = \boldsymbol{a}$ and $\overrightarrow{OB} = \boldsymbol{b}$. By evaluating $\overrightarrow{AB} \cdot \overrightarrow{CB}$ show that angle ABC is a right angle.

7 According to the inverse square law, the force on a particle of mass $m_1$ at the point $P_1$ due to a particle of mass $m_2$ at the point $P_2$ is given by

$$\gamma\frac{m_1 m_2}{r^2}\hat{\boldsymbol{r}} \quad \text{where } \boldsymbol{r} = \overrightarrow{P_1P_2}$$

Particles of mass $3m$, $3m$, $m$ are fixed at the points A(1, 0, 1), B(0, 1, 2) and C(2, 1, 2) respectively. Show that the force on the particle at A due to the presence of B and C is

$$\frac{2\gamma m^2}{\sqrt{3}}(-1, 2, 2)$$

8 Show that the vector $\boldsymbol{a}$ which satisfies the vector equation

$$\boldsymbol{a} \times (\boldsymbol{i} + 2\boldsymbol{j}) = -2\boldsymbol{i} + \boldsymbol{j} + \boldsymbol{k}$$

must take the form $\boldsymbol{a} = (\alpha, 2\alpha - 1, 1)$. If in addition the vector $\boldsymbol{a}$ makes an angle $\cos^{-1}(\frac{1}{3})$ with the vector $(\boldsymbol{i} - \boldsymbol{j} + \boldsymbol{k})$ show that there are now two such vectors that satisfy both conditions.

9 The electric field at a point having position vector $\boldsymbol{r}$, due to a charge $e$ at $\boldsymbol{R}$, is $e(\boldsymbol{r} - \boldsymbol{R})/|\boldsymbol{r} - \boldsymbol{R}|^3$. Find the electric field $\boldsymbol{E}$ at the point P(2, 1, 1) given that there is a charge $e$ at each of the points (1, 0, 0), (0, 1, 0) and (0, 0, 1).

10 Given that $\overrightarrow{OP} = (3, 1, 2)$ and $\overrightarrow{OQ} = (1, -2, -4)$ are the position vectors of the points P and Q respectively find

(a) the equation of the plane passing through Q and perpendicular to PQ,

(b) the perpendicular distance from the point (−1, 1, 1) to the plane.

11 (a) Determine the equation of the plane that passes through the points (1, 2, −2), (−1, 1, −9) and (2, −2, −12). Find the perpendicular distance from the origin to this plane.

(b) Calculate the area of the triangle whose vertices are at the points (1, 1, 0), (1, 0, 1) and (0, 1, 1).

12 Find the point P on the line L through the points

A(5, 1, 7) and B(6, 0, 8)

and the point Q on the line M through the points

C(3, 1, 3) and D(−1, 3, 3)

such that the line through P and Q is perpendicular to both lines L and M. Verify that P and Q are at a distance $\sqrt{6}$ apart, and find the point where the line through P and Q intersects the coordinate plane O$xy$.

13 The angular momentum vector $\boldsymbol{H}$ of a particle of mass $m$ is defined by

$$\boldsymbol{H} = \boldsymbol{r} \times (m\boldsymbol{v})$$

where $\boldsymbol{v} = \boldsymbol{\omega} \times \boldsymbol{r}$.

Using the result

$$\boldsymbol{a} \times (\boldsymbol{b} \times \boldsymbol{c}) = (\boldsymbol{a} \cdot \boldsymbol{c})\boldsymbol{b} - (\boldsymbol{a} \cdot \boldsymbol{b})\boldsymbol{c}$$

show that if $\boldsymbol{r}$ is perpendicular to $\boldsymbol{\omega}$ then $\boldsymbol{H} = mr^2\boldsymbol{\omega}$.

Given that $m = 100$, $\boldsymbol{r} = 0.1(\boldsymbol{i} + \boldsymbol{j} + \boldsymbol{k})$ and $\boldsymbol{\omega} = 5\boldsymbol{i} + 5\boldsymbol{j} - 10\boldsymbol{k}$ calculate

(a) $(\boldsymbol{r} \cdot \boldsymbol{\omega})$ (b) $\boldsymbol{H}$

14 A particle of mass $m$, charge $e$ and moving with velocity $\boldsymbol{v}$ in a magnetic field of strength $\boldsymbol{H}$ is known to have acceleration

$$\frac{e}{mc}(\boldsymbol{v} \times \boldsymbol{H})$$

where $c$ is the speed of light. Show that the component of acceleration parallel to $\boldsymbol{H}$ is zero.

15 A force $\boldsymbol{F}$ is of magnitude 14 N and acts at the point A(3, 2, 4) in the direction of the vector $-2\boldsymbol{i} + 6\boldsymbol{j} + 3\boldsymbol{k}$. Find the moment of the force about the point B(1, 5, −2). Find also the angle between $\boldsymbol{F}$ and $\overrightarrow{AB}$.

16 Points A, B, C have coordinates (1, 2, 1), (−1, 1, 3) and (−2, −2, −2) respectively.

Calculate the vector product $\overrightarrow{AB} \times \overrightarrow{AC}$, the angle BAC and a unit vector perpendicular to the plane containing A, B and C. Hence obtain

(a) the equation of the plane ABC,

(b) the equation of a second plane, parallel to ABC, and containing the point D(1, 1, 1),

(c) the shortest distance between the point D and the plane containing A, B and C.

17 A plane Π passes through the three non-collinear points A, B and C having position vectors $\boldsymbol{a}$, $\boldsymbol{b}$ and $\boldsymbol{c}$ respectively. Show that the parametric vector equation of the plane Π is

$$\boldsymbol{r} = \boldsymbol{a} + \lambda(\boldsymbol{b} - \boldsymbol{a}) + \mu(\boldsymbol{c} - \boldsymbol{a})$$

The plane Π passes through the points (−3, 0, 1), (5, −8, −7) and (2, 1, −2) and the plane Θ passes through the points (3, −1, 1), (1, −2, 1) and (2, −1, 2). Find the parametric vector equation of Π and the normal vector equation of Θ, and hence show that their line of intersection is

$$\boldsymbol{r} = (1, -4, -3) + t(5, 1, -3)$$

where $t$ is a scalar variable.

18 Two skew lines $L_1$, $L_2$ have respective equations

$$\frac{x+3}{4} = \frac{y-3}{-1} = \frac{z-2}{1} \quad \text{and}$$

$$\frac{x-1}{2} = \frac{y-5}{1} = \frac{z+3}{2}$$

Obtain the equation of a plane through $L_1$ parallel to $L_2$ and show that the shortest distance between the lines is 6.

19 A particle P of constant mass $m$ moves in a viscous medium under the influence of a uniform gravitational force $-mg\boldsymbol{j}$, where $g$ is a scalar constant and $\boldsymbol{j}$ is a constant unit vector. The medium offers a resistance to the motion of the particle proportional to its momentum (with proportionality constant $K$). The solution of the equation of motion of P gives the velocity as

$$\boldsymbol{v} = \boldsymbol{V}e^{-Kt} - \frac{g}{K}(1 - e^{-Kt})\boldsymbol{j}$$

where $\boldsymbol{V}$ is the velocity at time $t = 0$, and the position vector as

$$\boldsymbol{r} = \boldsymbol{A} - \frac{\boldsymbol{V}e^{-Kt}}{K} - \frac{gt}{K}\boldsymbol{j} - \frac{ge^{-Kt}}{K^2}\boldsymbol{j}$$

where $\boldsymbol{A}$ is some constant vector.

At time $t = 0$, a projectile is introduced into the atmosphere at a height $H$ above the ground with a speed $U$ parallel to the ground. Assuming that the atmosphere behaves as a viscous medium as described above, show that at time $t$ the path of the projectile will be inclined at an angle $\alpha$ to the horizontal, where

$$\alpha = \tan^{-1}\left[\frac{g(e^{Kt} - 1)}{KU}\right]$$

Show also that the time of flight $T$ to hitting the ground is a solution of the equation

$$T + \frac{1}{K}(e^{-KT} - 1) = \frac{HK}{g}$$

and find the horizontal distance travelled in terms of $T$.

20 The three vectors $\mathbf{a} = (1, 0, 0)$, $\mathbf{b} = (1, 1, 0)$ and $\mathbf{c} = (1, 1, 1)$ are given. Evaluate

(a) $\mathbf{a} \times \mathbf{b}$, $\mathbf{b} \times \mathbf{c}$, $\mathbf{c} \times \mathbf{a}$

(b) $\mathbf{a} \cdot (\mathbf{b} \times \mathbf{c})$

For the vector $\boldsymbol{d} = (2, -1, 2)$ calculate

(c) the parameters $\alpha$, $\beta$, $\gamma$ in the expression

$$\boldsymbol{d} = \alpha\boldsymbol{a} + \beta\boldsymbol{b} + \gamma\boldsymbol{c}$$

(d) the parameters $p$, $q$, $r$ in the expression

$$\boldsymbol{d} = p\boldsymbol{a} \times \boldsymbol{b} + q\boldsymbol{b} \times \boldsymbol{c} + r\boldsymbol{c} \times \boldsymbol{a}$$

and show that

$$p = \frac{\mathbf{c} \cdot \mathbf{d}}{\mathbf{a} \cdot (\mathbf{b} \times \mathbf{c})}, \quad q = \frac{\mathbf{a} \cdot \mathbf{d}}{\mathbf{a} \cdot (\mathbf{b} \times \mathbf{c})} \quad \text{and}$$

$$r = \frac{\mathbf{b} \cdot \mathbf{d}}{\mathbf{a} \cdot (\mathbf{b} \times \mathbf{c})}$$

21 Given the line with parametric equation

$$\boldsymbol{r} = \boldsymbol{a} + \lambda\boldsymbol{d}$$

show that the perpendicular distance $p$ from the origin to this line can take either of the forms

$$\text{(i) } p = \frac{|\mathbf{a} \times \mathbf{d}|}{|\mathbf{d}|} \qquad \text{(ii) } p = \left|\mathbf{a} - \frac{\mathbf{a} \cdot \mathbf{d}}{\mathbf{d} \cdot \mathbf{d}}\mathbf{d}\right|$$

Find the parametric equation of the straight line through the points

A(1, 0, 2) and B(2, 3, 0)

and determine

(a) the length of the perpendicular from the origin to the line,

(b) the point at which the line intersects the $y$–$z$ plane,

(c) the coordinates of the foot of the perpendicular to the line from the point (1, 1, 1).

22 Given the three non-coplanar vectors $\mathbf{a}$, $\mathbf{b}$, $\mathbf{c}$, and defining $v = \mathbf{a} \cdot \mathbf{b} \times \mathbf{c}$, three further vectors are defined as

$$\mathbf{a}' = \mathbf{b} \times \mathbf{c}/v \quad \mathbf{b}' = \mathbf{c} \times \mathbf{a}/v \quad \mathbf{c}' = \mathbf{a} \times \mathbf{b}/v$$

Show that

$$\mathbf{a} = \mathbf{b}' \times \mathbf{c}'/v' \quad \mathbf{b} = \mathbf{c}' \times \mathbf{a}'/v' \quad \mathbf{c} = \mathbf{a}' \times \mathbf{b}'/v'$$

where

$$v' = \mathbf{a}' \cdot \mathbf{b}' \times \mathbf{c}'$$

Deduce that

$$\mathbf{a} \cdot \mathbf{a}' = \mathbf{b} \cdot \mathbf{b}' = \mathbf{c} \cdot \mathbf{c}' = 1$$

$$\mathbf{a} \cdot \mathbf{b}' = \mathbf{a} \cdot \mathbf{c}' = \mathbf{b} \cdot \mathbf{a}' = \mathbf{b} \cdot \mathbf{c}' = \mathbf{c} \cdot \mathbf{a}'$$

$$= \mathbf{c} \cdot \mathbf{b}' = 0$$

If a vector is written in terms of $\boldsymbol{a}$, $\boldsymbol{b}$, $\boldsymbol{c}$ as

$$\boldsymbol{r} = \alpha\boldsymbol{a} + \beta\boldsymbol{b} + \gamma\boldsymbol{c}$$

evaluate $\alpha$, $\beta$, $\gamma$ in terms of $\boldsymbol{a}'$, $\boldsymbol{b}'$ and $\boldsymbol{c}'$.

(*Note*: these sets of vectors are called **reciprocal sets** and are widely used in crystallography and materials science.)

23 An unbalanced machine can be approximated by two masses, 2 kg and 1.5 kg, placed at the ends $A$ and $B$ respectively of light rods $OA$ and $OB$ of lengths 0.7 m and 1.1 m. The point $O$ lies on the axis of rotation and $OAB$ forms a plane perpendicular to this axis; $OA$ and $OB$ are at right-angles. The machine rotates about the axis with an angular velocity $\omega$, which gives a centrifugal force $mr\omega^2$ for a mass $m$ and rod length $r$. Find the unbalanced force at the axis. To balance the machine a mass of 1 kg is placed at the end of a light rod $OC$ so that $C$ is coplanar with $OAB$. Determine the position of $C$.

24 In an automated drilling process three holes are drilled simultaneously into the centre of the faces of a block of side 0.2 m, as shown in Figure 4.56. The force exerted by each drill is 25 N, and the couples applied during the drilling are 0.2 N m in the directions indicated. Find the resultant force on the system and the moment of the forces and couples about the corner A. (Take $x$, $y$, $z$ axes along the sides of the block, with origin at A.)

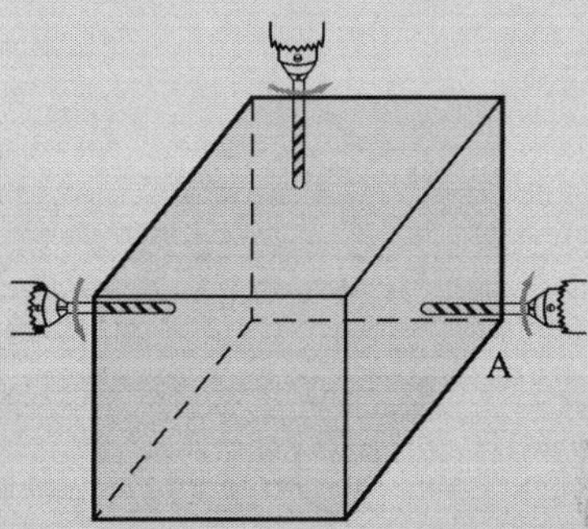


**Figure 4.56** Drilling into a block, Question 24.

## CHAPTER 4
### Exercises

**1** (a) (3, 3, 1) (b) $(2, 4, \frac{5}{2})$ (c) (0, 0, 1)
(d) $\sqrt{2}$ (e) 3 (f) $\sqrt{3}$
(g) $(\sqrt{\frac{1}{2}}, \sqrt{\frac{1}{2}}, 0)$ (h) $(\frac{2}{3}, \frac{2}{3}, \frac{1}{3})$

**2** $\overrightarrow{PQ} = (4, -5, 11)$, $|\overrightarrow{PQ}| = 9\sqrt{2}$
direction cosines $4/(9\sqrt{2})$, $-5/(9\sqrt{2})$, $11/(9\sqrt{2})$

**3** $\sqrt{134}$ N, $(7, 2, 9)/\sqrt{134}$

**4** $\alpha = 4$ $\beta = 1$ $\gamma = 2$

**5** $\sqrt{21}$ $\sqrt{17}$ $\sqrt{38}$

**6** 60° or −60° to the positive $z$ axis

**7** $\overrightarrow{PQ} = \overrightarrow{QR} = (1, 5, -3)$ and PQ : QR = 1 : 1

**8** $8\sqrt{2}$ kilometres per hour from the NW

**9** distance = 13/5, $t = 1/5$

**11** 1 − j2 length = $\sqrt{20}$

**12** $\frac{1}{2} - \text{j}\frac{1}{2}$

**14** $\theta = \sin^{-1}\left(\dfrac{W_1^2 + W_2^2 - W_3^2}{2W_1W_2}\right)$

$\phi = \sin^{-1}\left(\dfrac{W_2^2 + W_3^2 - W_1^2}{2W_2W_3}\right)$

**15** $\boldsymbol{F} = (-940, 124, -31)$ N
(7.93 m, −1.04 m, 0 m), $T = 1342$ N

**16** $T = 539$ N $S = 389$ N

**17** (a) 14 (b) 6 (c) $(2, 1, 6)/\sqrt{41}$
(d) $(12, 0, -6)/\sqrt{5}$ (e) −24 (f) (12, 4, 8)

**18** (a) 98.0° = 1.711 rad (b) 64.8° = 1.130 rad
(c) $\frac{14}{5}$ (d) 3 or −4

**19** 4 units

**20** $\frac{5}{14}$

**21** $\sqrt{5}/2$

**26** (a) 50 N m (b) $\frac{1}{2}Whpn(n + 1)$

**27** $r^2 - (\boldsymbol{r}\cdot\hat{\boldsymbol{a}})^2 = R^2$

**28** $\sqrt{3}$, 70.5° or 1.23 rad

**29** $|X| \leqslant 2.98$ m

**30** $|\theta| \leqslant 36.9°$ or 0.644 rad

**31** (a) (3, −2, −1) (b) (−1, 1, 0) (c) (5, −4, −2)
(d) −1 (e) 1 (f) (2, 2, 1)

**34** (a) (8, 1, 6), (4, 1, 3) (b) $(-\frac{3}{5}, 0, \frac{4}{5})$ (c) $\frac{5}{2}$

**37** $(48, 72, 0)/\sqrt{14}$

**38** $(-8, -32, -4)/\sqrt{21}$

**39** (a) (0, 1, −1) (−2, 1, −1) (−2, 1, 0)
(b) (0, 0, 0) (0, 0, −2) (−3, 3, −1)
(c) (−3, 3, −3)

**40** $\pm(-3, 5, 11)/\sqrt{155}$ 0.9968

**41** Distance = 1.92

**42** $m\omega = eB$

**43** 15

**45** 8

**47** (a) $(-5, 3, -7)/\sqrt{83}$ (b) $(0, 1, -4)/\sqrt{17}$

**48** $\frac{7}{3}(1, 1, 1)$ $\frac{1}{3}(2, -13, 11)$

**49** $\begin{vmatrix} u_1 & u_2 & u_3 \\ v_1 & v_2 & v_3 \\ w_1 & w_2 & w_3 \end{vmatrix}$

**50** $\alpha = -1/\boldsymbol{F}^2$

**51** (a) $(\boldsymbol{c}\cdot\boldsymbol{a})(\boldsymbol{b}\cdot\boldsymbol{d}) - (\boldsymbol{c}\cdot\boldsymbol{b})(\boldsymbol{d}\cdot\boldsymbol{a})$
(c) $-(\boldsymbol{a}\cdot\boldsymbol{b})(\boldsymbol{a}\times\boldsymbol{c})$

**52** (a) (3, 3, 3) (b) $(1 + s, 2 + s, 3 + s)$
(c) $x - 1 = y - 2 = z - 3$

**53** $\boldsymbol{r}\cdot(0, -1, 1) = 1$ $-y + z = 1$

**55** (3, 4, 0), 43.5° = 0.759 rad

**56** $\boldsymbol{r}\cdot[\boldsymbol{b}\times(\boldsymbol{c} - \boldsymbol{a})] = \boldsymbol{a}\cdot(\boldsymbol{b}\times\boldsymbol{c})$

**58** $\boldsymbol{r} = (0, -5, 10) + \lambda(1, 2, -3)$

**59** $\boldsymbol{r} = (1, 2, 4) + t(1, 1, 2)$ $(-\frac{5}{2}, -\frac{3}{2}, -3)$

**60** 79.0° = 1.38 rad

**61** (a) $\boldsymbol{r}\cdot(2, 3, 6) = -28$ (b) 5

**62** $\boldsymbol{r} = (1 + 2t, -1 + 4t, 3 - 4t)$, 41.8° = 0.729 rad

**63** $\boldsymbol{r} = (2 - t, 2t, -1 + 4t)$
$2 - x = \frac{1}{2}y = \frac{1}{4}(1 + z)$, no intersection

**64** $\sqrt{35}$

**65** $\boldsymbol{r}\cdot(1, -5, 3) = 28$

**66** $\boldsymbol{r} = (-1 + 14t, t, 1 - 8t)$
$\frac{2}{3}\sqrt{29}$, $\boldsymbol{r}\cdot(-18, 36, -27) = -9$

### 4.5 Review exercises

**1** (a) $\sqrt{93}$ (b) $(17, -3, -10)/\sqrt{398}$
(c) 85.8° = 1.50 rad, 47.0° = 0.820 rad
(d) (2, 13, −13)/6

**2** (a) (3, 4, 5) (b) $\sqrt{35}$ (c) 34/3

**3** (a) (1, 2, 0), (2, 1, 1) (b) $\sqrt{5}$
(c) 1 (d) 112.2° = 1.96 rad

**4** (a) −4 (b) 1 or −4

**5** $(\frac{2}{3}, \frac{1}{3}, \frac{2}{3})$, $(-\frac{3}{5}, 0, \frac{4}{5})$; (1, 5, 22)

**8** (1, 1, 1), (−5, −11, 1)

**9** $\boldsymbol{E} = e(0.550, 0.282, 0.282)$

**10** (a) $2x + 3y + 6z + 28 = 0$ (b) 5

**11** (a) $2x + 3y - z = 10$; $10/\sqrt{14}$
(b) $\sqrt{3/2}$

**12** P(2, 4, 4), Q(1, 2, 3)
(−2, −4, 0)

**13** (a) 0 (b) 15(1, 1, −2)

**15** (−90, −36, 12), 85.3° or 1.49 rad

**16** (11, −12, 5); 76.8°; $(-11, 12, -5)/\sqrt{290}$
(a) $-11x + 12y - 5z = 8$
(b) $-11x + 12y - 5z = -4$ (c) $12/\sqrt{290}$

**17** $\boldsymbol{r} = (-3, 0, 1) + \lambda(8, -8, -8) + \mu(5, 1, -3)$
$\boldsymbol{r}\cdot(-1, 2, -1) = -6$

**18** $x + 2y - 2z = -1$

**19** $x = \dfrac{U}{K}(1 - e^{-KT})$

**20** (a) (0, 0, 1), (1, −1, 0), (0, 1, −1)
(b) 1 (c) 3, −3, 2 (d) 3, 2, 1

**21** $\boldsymbol{r} = (2 - t, 3 - 3t, 2t)$
(a) $\sqrt{(61/14)}$ (b) (0, −3, 4) (c) (19, 15, 18)/14

**22** $\alpha = \boldsymbol{r}\cdot\boldsymbol{a}'$ $\beta = \boldsymbol{r}\cdot\boldsymbol{b}'$ $\gamma = \boldsymbol{r}\cdot\boldsymbol{c}'$

**23** Taking $\boldsymbol{i}$ along $OA$ and $\boldsymbol{j}$ along $OB$ then
$\boldsymbol{F} = \omega^2(1.4, 1.65)$ and $OC = (-1.4, -1.65)$ m.

**24** (0, 0, −25) N (−2.5, 2.5, −0.2) N m

# Chapter 6
# Vectors in Physics

Vectors are introduced in physics to represent certain physical quantities and to determine the direction of a change. The physical laws can be expressed in simple forms in vector notation. The different concepts of vector algebra are described.

## Introduction to Vectors

### 6.1 Scalars and Vectors

Physical quantities are generally of two types:

- Scalar
- Vector

A quantity, such as the volume of a container, temperature of air, time interval between two events, distance of travel, and speed of a moving object, that can be expressed by a number and its unit is called a *scalar*. However, in some cases, a direction is also needed for the complete specification of a quantity. Examples include the displacement, velocity, and acceleration of an object. These are explained in physics texts and briefly described here.

**Distance and Speed as Examples of Scalars**

The distance of an object from a chosen point of reference at any time is the total length of travel, and it is always positive. For a moving object, its distance changes with time. The time rate at which the distance of a moving object changes is called its *speed.* The *average speed* of a moving object is defined as

$$\text{average speed} = \frac{\text{distance traveled}}{\text{total time to travel the distance}} = \frac{d}{\Delta t} = \frac{d}{t_1 - t_2}$$

where $d$ is the distance traveled and $\Delta t$ $(= t_2 - t_1)$ is the total time elapsed in traveling that distance. The SI unit for the speed is meters per second (m/s). Since *distance* is a *scalar* quantity, *speed* is also a *scalar*.

**Displacement, Velocity, Acceleration, and Force as Examples of Vectors**

If you walk 3 miles due north and 4 miles due east, you have traveled 7 miles but you are only 5 miles from your starting point (Figure 6.1a). That is, the magnitude of your displacement is 5 miles. The reason you cannot add in the ordinary way is that the displacement has *direction* and *magnitude*. The *displacement* of a moving object is the straight-line distance between its final position and its initial position, along with the *direction* from the starting position to the final position.

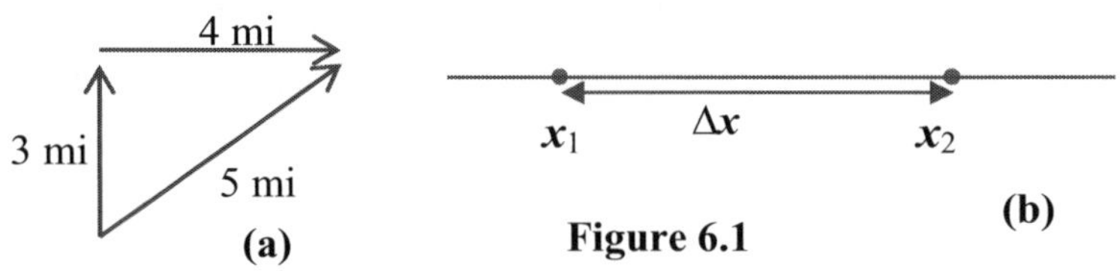


**Figure 6.1**

If the initial and final positions of an object are $x_1$ and $x_2$ at time $t_1$ and $t_2$, respectively, the displacement is (Figure 6.1b)

$$\Delta x = x_2 - x_1$$

In one dimension, there are only two possible directions of motion (left or right or up and down). The $x$-axis is commonly used for horizontal motions and a plus (+) sign is used to indicate the direction to the right and a minus (–) sign is used to indicate the direction to the left. Displacement is expressed in meters and it can be positive or negative. Because of its direction, displacement is a *vector* quantity.

The *velocity* of a moving object tells how fast the object is moving *and* in what direction. The average velocity is the displacement divided by the total travel time:

$$\text{average velocity} = \frac{\text{displacement}}{\text{total travel time}} = \frac{\Delta x}{\Delta t} = \frac{x_2 - x_1}{t_2 - t_1}$$

The SI unit of velocity is meters per second (m/s). Since velocity has a direction, it is a vector quantity.

The *velocity* of a moving object changes when the object speeds up (such as when you press the accelerator of your car) or slows down (such as when you step on the brake) or when the direction of motion of the car changes (such as when you make a turn). The time rate of change of velocity of an object is called its *acceleration*. The *average acceleration* is defined as the change in velocity divided by the time taken to make the change:

$$\text{average acceleration} = \frac{\text{change in velocity}}{\text{time to make the change}} = \frac{\Delta v}{\Delta t} = \frac{v_2 - v_1}{t_2 - t_1}$$

The SI unit of velocity is meters per second per second ($m/s^2$). Since velocity is a vector quantity, *acceleration* is also a *vector* quantity.

*Force* is simply a push or pull. It causes changes in motion or, in other words, causes an acceleration of an object. Force (**F**) is related to acceleration (**a**) by Newton's second law of motion as $\mathbf{F} = m\mathbf{a}$, where $m$ is the mass of an object. Since acceleration is a vector quantity, force is also a *vector* quantity.

> Note: There are other vector quantities in physics. Examples include linear momentum, angular velocity, angular momentum, torque, electric field, and magnetic field.

A *vector* is a physical quantity that has both a magnitude and a direction. Since vectors and scalars are different types of physical quantities, they *cannot be* equal to each other. To distinguish them, different notations are used. Scalars are represented by a single symbol in *italics*. **Boldface** is used to indicate a vector with a written symbol, and *italic* is used for its magnitude. An arrow is drawn to indicate a vector on a graph. The length of the arrow is proportional to the magnitude of the vector, and the direction of the arrowhead specifies the direction of the vector. When writing vectors by hand, draw an arrow over the symbol, such as $\vec{A}$.

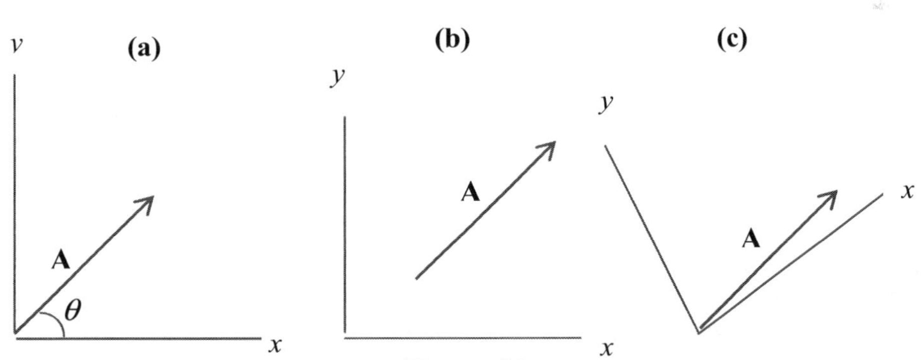


**Figure 6.2**

Figure 6.2 a shows a two-dimensional vector **A** whose magnitude is $A$ and whose direction (as shown by the direction of the arrowhead) is specified by the angle $\theta$ made with the positive $x$-axis. The magnitude of a vector is always a positive number, but the vector can be pointed any direction, depending on the direction or the angle $\theta$. Note that although a vector can be visualized on coordinate axes, it is independent of the coordinate system. In other words, the magnitude or direction of a vector does not change if you change the coordinate system or move the vector from one place to the other in the same coordinate system (Figure 6.2b, c). Thus, you can move a vector anywhere keeping its magnitude and direction the same.

Since a vector is characterized by both its magnitude and direction, *two vectors* are said to be *equal* when both their magnitudes *and* directions are equal.

## 6.2 Components of a Vector

**Rectangular Vector Components**

By rectangular components of a vector we mean those at right angles to each other. Suppose that the two vectors **A** and **B** are at right angles. Then the magnitude of the resultant vector **C** (Figure 6.3 a) is given by the Pythagorean theorem:

$$C = \sqrt{A^2 + B^2}$$

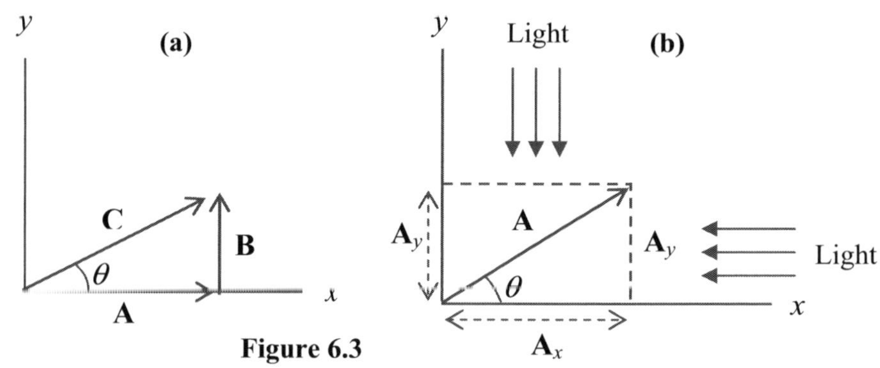


**Figure 6.3**

The orientation of **C** with respect to the $x$-axis is given by the inverse tangent relationship

$$\theta = \tan^{-1}\frac{B}{A}$$

In this case, **C** is the resultant vector and **A** and **B** are called the component vectors.

**Resolving a Vector into Rectangular Components**

Resolving a vector into rectangular components is the reverse of adding the components. To find the components of a vector, you need to set up a coordinate system, say, a Cartesian system. If a vector **A** makes an angle $\theta$ relative to the positive $x$-axis of the coordinate system (Figure 6.3b), the $x$- and $y$-components of the vector are the projections of the vectors on the $x$- and $y$-axes, respectively. To **visualize** the vector components, imagine that a light beam is shining on the vector **A** from above the $x$-axis. Then the length of the shadow of the vector on the $x$-axis is the $x$-component $A_x$

of the vector. Similarly, if you imagine that a light beam is shining on the vector **A** from the right of the *y*-axis, the shadow of **A** on the *y*-axis is the *y* component $A_y$ of the vector.

If $A_x$ and $A_y$ are the *x* and *y* components, respectively, of **A,** then

$$A_x = A \cos \theta$$

and

$$A_y = A \sin \theta.$$

$A_x$ and $A_y$ can be positive, negative, or zero depending on $\theta$. The sign of $A_x$ and $A_y$ in different coordinates are shown in Table 6.1.

**Table 6.1**

| | Quadrant I | Quadrant II | Quadrant III | Quadrant IV |
|---|---|---|---|---|
| $A_x$ | *positive* | *negative* | *negative* | *positive* |
| $A_y$ | *positive* | *positive* | *negative* | *negative* |

The Pythagorean theorem gives the precise value of the magnitude of the vector in terms of its components:

$$A = \sqrt{A_x^2 + A_y^2}$$

The direction of the vector can be obtained from the magnitude of the components and is given by

$$\theta = \tan^{-1} \frac{A_y}{A_x}$$

Note: In determining an angle by means of the inverse tangent function, a calculator always displays the smallest angle. The displayed angle may or may not be the correct angle for a problem. Always utilize the quadrant grid to check your answer when you use the inverse tangent function. If you think the larger angle is the correct angle for the problem, add 180° to the smaller angle for the answer.

**Example 6.2.1**
Find the components of a vector of magnitude 16 m that is applied in a direction of 30º with the positive *x*-axis.

In this case, the vector **A** = 16 m and $\theta$ = 30º. The sketch of the problem follows. Use the relationships $A_x = A \cos \theta$ and $A_y = A \sin \theta$ to determine the components $A_x$ and $A_y$ of **A**:

$$A_x = A \cos \theta = (16\text{ m}).\cos 30^\circ$$
$$= 16 \times 0.866 \text{ m} = 14 \text{ m}$$

$$A_y = A \sin \theta = (16\text{ m}) \sin 30^\circ$$
$$= 16 \times 0.5 \text{ m} = 8 \text{ m}$$

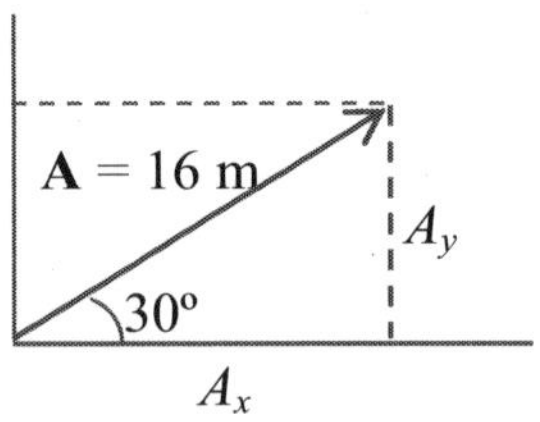


**Example 6.2.2**
A force (**F**) is a push or pull. It is a vector and is measured in the unit of newtons (N). The *x*- and *y*-components of a force are $F_x$ = –4.0 N and $F_y$ = 6.0 N. Find the magnitude and direction of the force.

We have

$$F_x = -4.0 \text{ N}$$
$$F_y = 6.0 \text{ N}$$

In this problem, since the *x* component is negative and the *y* component is positive, the force vector lies in the second quadrant. Hence, the angle $\theta$ is more than 90º.

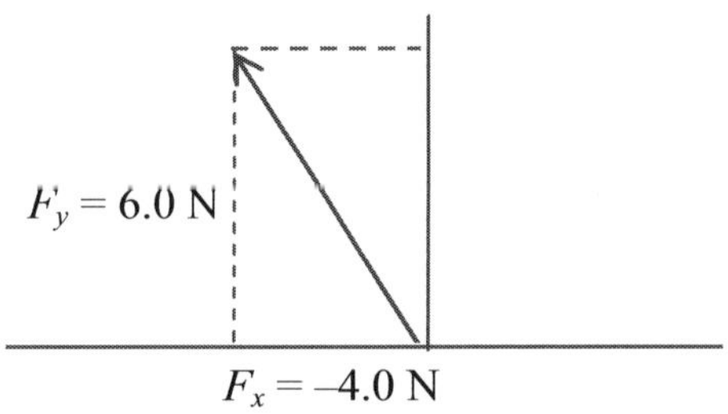


Use the Pythogorean relation and the inverse tangent relation as mentioned in Section 6.2 to solve for the vector magnitude *F* and the angle $\theta$, respectively:

$$F = \sqrt{F_x^2 + F_y^2}$$

Substitute the values of $F_x$ and $F_y$.

$$= \sqrt{(-4.0\text{N})^2 + (6.0\text{N})^2} = 7.2 \text{ N}$$

$$\theta = \tan^{-1} \frac{F_y}{F_x}$$

$$= \tan^{-1}\left(\frac{6.0 \text{ N}}{-4.0 \text{ N}}\right)$$

$= -56.3°$ (using a calculator).

The calculator has given the smallest angle, which is in the fourth quadrant. Since the vector lies in the second quadrant, the correct angle is $180° + (-56.3°) = 123.7°$.

**Exercises**

1. The velocity of a moving object is the rate of change of its displacement with time, and it is a vector. A projectile is shot from the top of a tower with a velocity of 60.0 m/s at an angle of 32° with the horizontal direction. Determine the horizontal and vertical components of the velocity vector of the projectile.

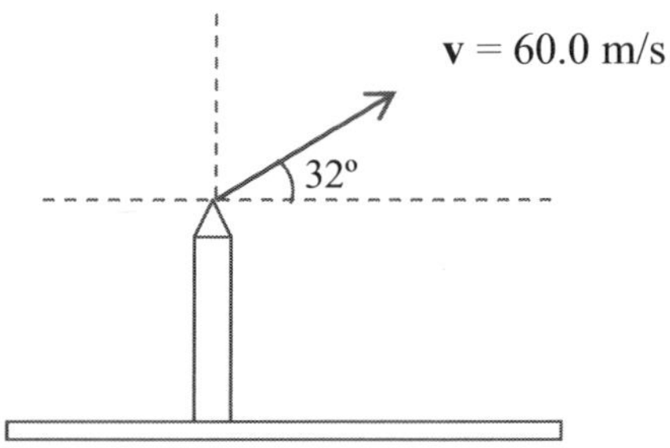


2. An airplane is traveling at a velocity **v** = 701 km/h in a direction 36° west of north. Determine the compentns of its velocity in the northernly and westerly directions.

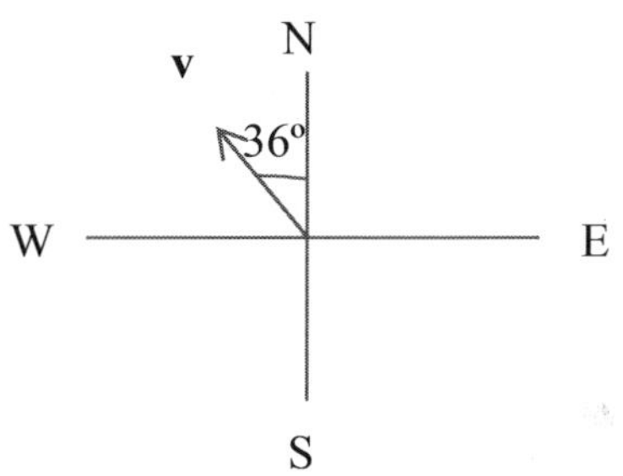


3. The $x$- and $y$-components of a force vector are $F_x = -2.0$ N and $F_y = -4.0$ N, respectively. Determine the force vector and its direction with the positive $x$-axis.

4. If $v_x = 2.21$ units and $v_y = -6.24$ units, deterime the magnitude and direction of the velocity vector **v**.

## 6.3 Unit Vectors

Unit vectors are introduced in mathematics and physics to express vectors in a convenient form. A unit vector is a dimensionless vector whose magnitude is unity and whose direction is usually one of the coordinate axes. There are *several kinds* of unit vectors in physics. Cartesian unit vectors and normal unit vectors are used in introductory physics and are described here.

### Cartesian Unit Vectors

In most situations in introductory physics, you will use *Cartesian unit vectors*. Cartesian unit vectors are written as $\hat{\mathbf{i}}$, $\hat{\mathbf{j}}$, and $\hat{\mathbf{k}}$ or simply **i**, **j**, and **k**, pointing in the positive *x*-, *y*-, and *z*-axes, respectively. The unit vectors **i**, **j**, and **k** are mutually perpendicular and they meet at the origin as shown in Figure 6.4.

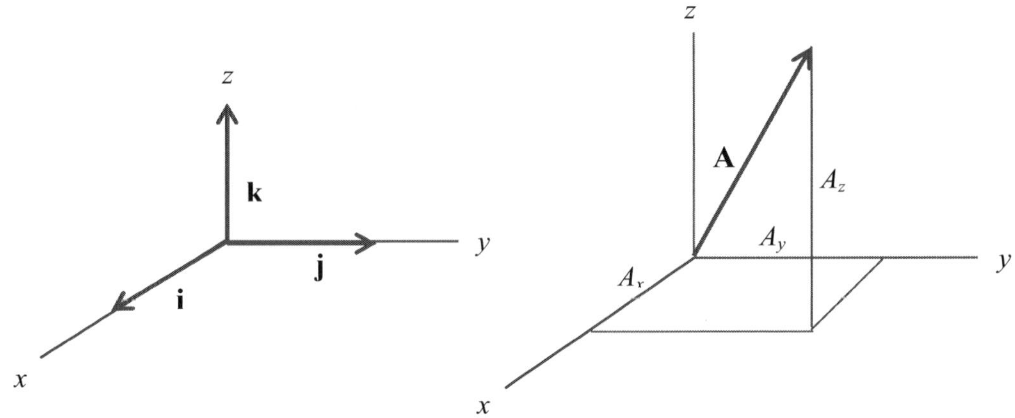


**Figure 6.4** Cartesian unit vectors and Cartesian components of a vector.

An arbitrary vector **A** in space can be written as the sum of its vector components using Cartesian unit vectors as follows:

$$\mathbf{A} = A_x\mathbf{i} + A_y\mathbf{j} + A_z\mathbf{k}; \text{ in two dimensions it reduces to } \mathbf{A} = A_x\mathbf{i} + A_y\mathbf{j}.$$

### Normal Unit Vector

The normal unit vector is usually labeled as $\hat{\mathbf{n}}$ and it is pointed outward in a direction perpendicular to the surface at the point of interest (Figure 6.5). If the surface is a plane, the normal unit vector is directed perpendicularly to the surface area. Use of the normal unit vector is common in electricity to calculate electric flux passing through an area. A small element of area *ds* has some particular orientation with respect to the coordinate axes.

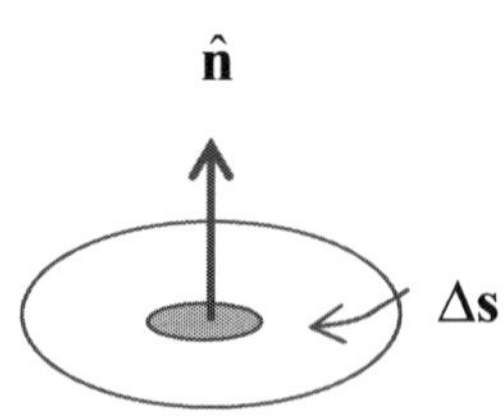


**Figure 6.5**

A direction has been associated with such an area along the unit vector $\hat{\mathbf{n}}$ normal to the surface, and the area is considered to be a vector ($\mathbf{ds} = ds\ \hat{\mathbf{n}}$).

**Polar Unit Vectors**

Polar unit vectors are labeled as $\hat{\mathbf{r}}$ and $\hat{\theta}$ The unit vector $\hat{\mathbf{r}}$ points radially outward and the unit vector $\hat{\theta}$ points perpendicularly counter-clockwise from $\hat{\mathbf{r}}$ (Figure 6.6). Unlike Cartesian unit vectors, the direction of polar unit vectors change depending on the point of interest.

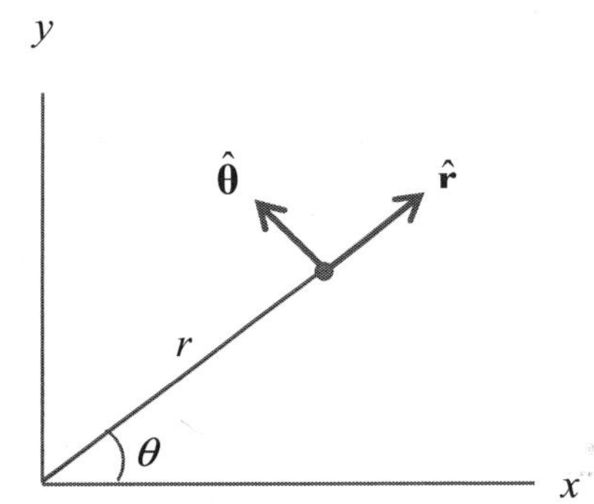


**Figure 6.6**

***Spherical Unit Vectors**

Spherical unit vectors are labeled as $\hat{\mathbf{r}}$, $\hat{\theta}$, and $\hat{\phi}$ and they are mutually perpendicular at the point of interest. Their directions vary with the position. At any point of interest, $\hat{\mathbf{r}}$ points radially outward, $\hat{\theta}$ points perpendicularly downward from along a line tangent to the circle of radius $r$ and $\hat{\phi}$ points perpendicularly counterclockwise from $\hat{\mathbf{r}}$ parallel to the $xy$-plane (Figure 6.7).

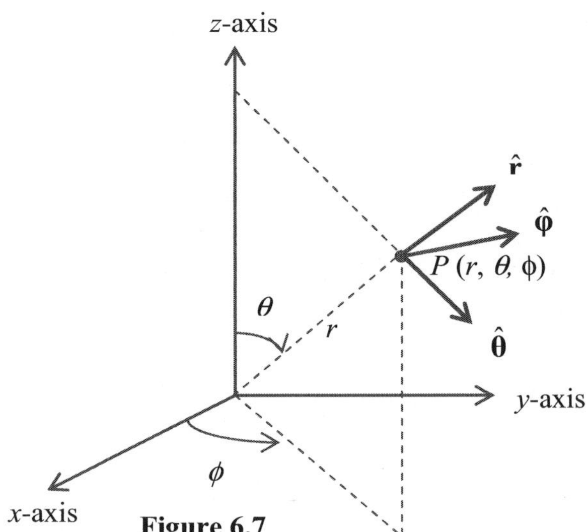


**Figure 6.7**

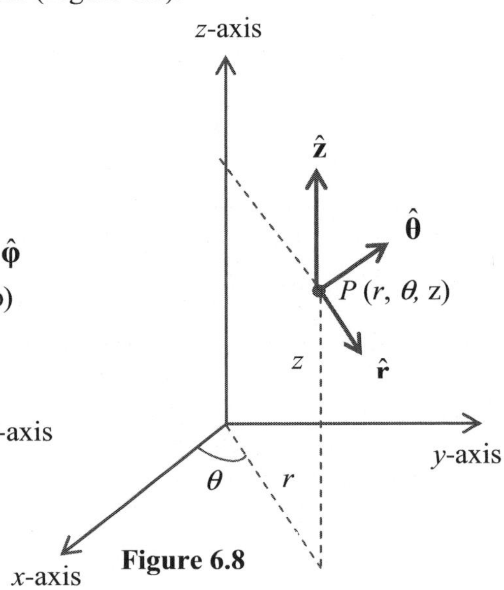


**Figure 6.8**

***Cylindrical Unit Vectors**

Cylindrical unit vectors are labeled as $\hat{\mathbf{r}}$, $\hat{\theta}$, and $\hat{\mathrm{k}}$ and they are mutually perpendicular at the point of interest. Here $\hat{\mathbf{r}}$ and $\hat{\theta}$ are the two polar unit vectors as defined above and $\hat{\mathrm{k}}$ is the Cartesian unit vector $\hat{\mathrm{k}}$ (Figure 6.8). These unit vectors like polar and spherical polar unit vectors vary with position.

Table 6.2 lists how an arbitrary vector **A** is expressed using its components in different systems with different kinds of unit vectors.

The components of a vector in other coordinate systems are related to the Cartesian components of the vector. The relations are given in Appendix F. Also, the Cartesian unit vectors can be expressed in terms of unit vectors in other coordinate systems and vice versa. The relations between the unit vectors are given in Appendix G.

**Table 6.2**

| Unit vector | Vector |
|---|---|
| Cartesian | $\mathbf{A} = A_x\mathbf{i} + A_y\mathbf{j} + A_z\mathbf{k}$ |
| | $\mathbf{A} = A_x\mathbf{i} + A_y\mathbf{j}$ (in two dimensions) |
| Normal | $\mathbf{A} = A\hat{\mathbf{n}}$ |
| Polar | $\mathbf{A} = A_r\hat{\mathbf{r}} + A_\theta\hat{\theta}$ |
| Spherical | $\mathbf{A} = A_r\hat{\mathbf{r}} + A_\theta\hat{\theta} + A_\phi\hat{\Phi}$ |
| Cylindrical | $\mathbf{A} = A_r\hat{\mathbf{r}} + A_\theta\hat{\theta} + A_z\mathbf{k}$ |

# Vector Addition and Subtraction

## 6.4 Vector Addition

Vector quantities (such as displacement, velocity, and acceleration) can be added (*vector addition*) to obtain the *resultant vector*. Either the geometric method or the analytic component method can be used to add two or more vectors.

**Vector Addition: Geometric Method**

Either the triangle method or the parallelogram method can be used to add two vectors geometrically.

**The Triangle Method or the Tip-to-Tail Method**

To add two vectors **A** and **B** by the *triangle method*, first choose a suitable scale to represent the two vectors by two arrows on graph paper, so that the magnitudes of the vectors are proportional to the lengths of the arrows and the directions of the arrowheads show the directions of the vectors. Then, place the tail of vector **B** at the tip of vector **A**. The resultant vector (the vector sum) **R** is the vector joining the tail of **A** to the head of **B**, or **R** = **A** + **B** (Figure 6.9). This method is also called the *tip-to-tail method*, since the tip of one vector is placed at the tail of the second vector.

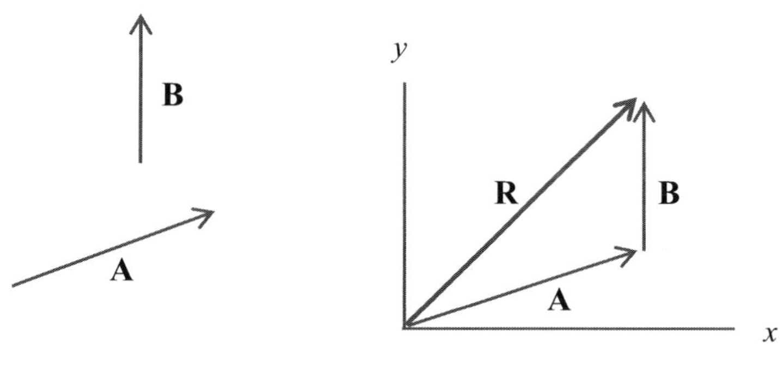


**Figure 6.9**

Measure the length of the resultant vector **R** (with a ruler) and the angle of the vector with the positive $x$-axis (using a protractor) for the direction. Change the length of the arrow to the magnitude of the vector by dividing by the chosen scale factor to get the magnitude of the resultant vector.

**Parallelogram Method**

Another graphical method, similar to the triangular method, is the *parallelogram method.* Draw the vectors **A** and **B** tail to tail, and form a parallelogram, as shown in

Figure 6.10. The diagonal represents the resultant vector **R** whose magnitude and direction can be measured from the diagram in a way similar to the triangular method.

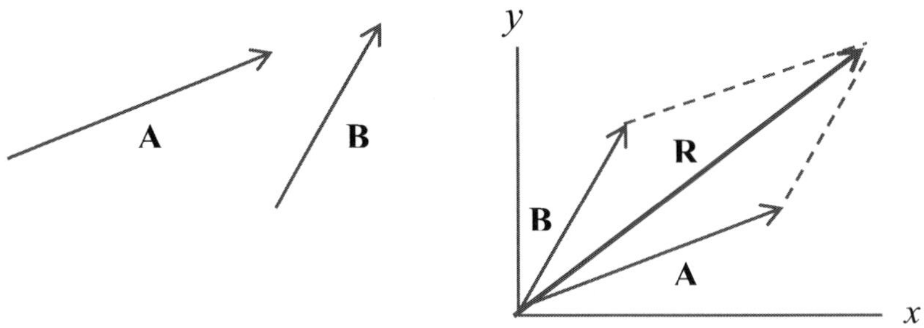


**Figure 6.10**

**Polygon Method**

The triangle method can be extended to add more than two vectors. Place all the vectors head to tail one by one, as shown in Figure 6.11, for the five vectors **A**, **B**, **C**, **D**, and **E**. The line joining the tail of the first vector **A** to the head of the last vector **E** represents the resultant vector. The method is called the polygon method, because the resulting figure is a polygon. In this case, **R** = **A** + **B** + **C** + **D** + **E**. The technique can be used to add any finite number of vectors.

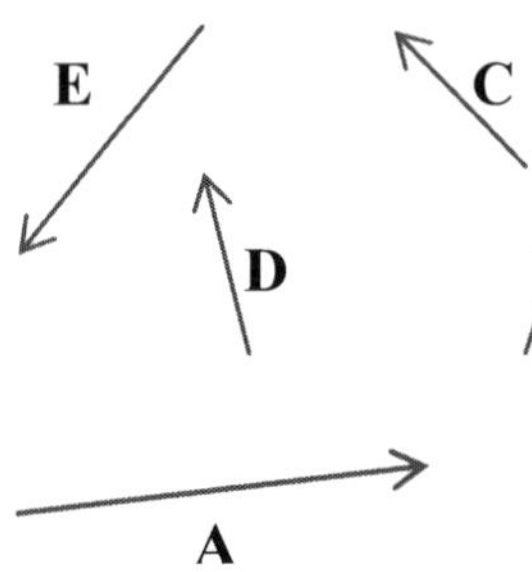


**Figure 6.11**

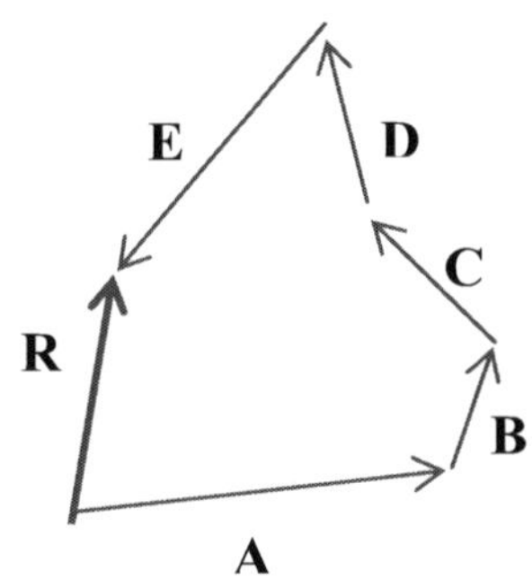


**Vector Subtraction**

An arrow having the same length as the original vector, but pointing in the opposite direction, represents the negative of a vector.

To subtract two vectors, **A** and **B**, add **A** to –**B**. The resultant vector **R** = **A** – **B** = **A** + (–**B**) (Figure 6.12).

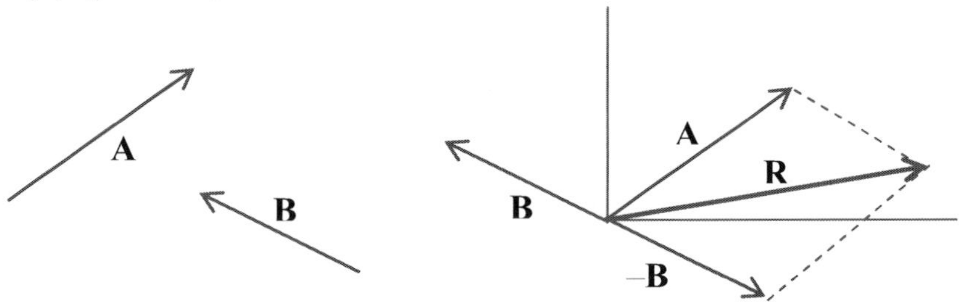


**Figure 6.12**

Even though the graphical methods of adding two or more vectors are useful and easy to understand, they are usually not very accurate.

**Vector Addition Using Components**

The *analytical component method* of vector addition involves resolving the vectors into components and then adding the components for each axis separately. If **A** and **B** are the two plane vectors to be added, and the resultant vector is **R** (= **A** + **B**), then (Figure 6.13)

$$R_x = A_x + B_x \text{ and}$$

$$R_y = A_y + B_y$$

From the Pythagorean theorem,

$$R = \sqrt{R_x^2 + R_y^2},$$

and the angle is given by the inverse tangent relationship,

$$\theta = \tan^{-1}\left(\frac{R_y}{R_x}\right)$$

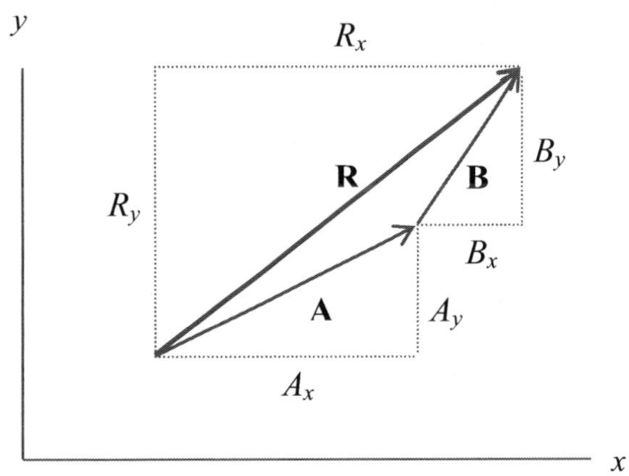


**Figure 6.13**

In the notation of a unit vector,

$$\mathbf{R} = \mathbf{A} + \mathbf{B} = (A_x\mathbf{i} + A_y\mathbf{j}) + (B_x\mathbf{i} + B_y\mathbf{j})$$

$$= (A_x + B_x)\mathbf{i} + (A_y + B_y)\mathbf{j}.$$

If both **A** and **B** have three components,

$$\mathbf{R} = \mathbf{A} + \mathbf{B} = (A_x\mathbf{i} + A_y\mathbf{j} + A_z\mathbf{k}) + (B_x\mathbf{i} + B_y\mathbf{j} + B_z\mathbf{k})$$

$$= (A_x + B_x)\mathbf{i} + (A_y + B_y)\mathbf{j} + (A_z + B_z)\mathbf{k}.$$

Similarly, $\mathbf{A} - \mathbf{B} = (A_x - B_x)\mathbf{I} + (A_y - B_y)\mathbf{j} + (A_z - B_z)\mathbf{k}$.

Vector addition is *commutative*: that is, $\mathbf{A} + \mathbf{B} = \mathbf{B} + \mathbf{A}$.
Vector addition is *associative*: that is, $(\mathbf{A} + \mathbf{B}) + \mathbf{C} = \mathbf{A} + (\mathbf{B} + \mathbf{C})$.

### Example 6.4.1

Two vectors are given by $\mathbf{A} = 2\mathbf{i} + 3\mathbf{j} - 4\mathbf{k}$ and $\mathbf{B} = \mathbf{i} + 2\mathbf{j} + 3\mathbf{k}$. Determine the resultant vector $\mathbf{R} = \mathbf{A} + \mathbf{B}$.

We are given

$$\mathbf{A} = 2\mathbf{i} + 3\mathbf{j} - 4\mathbf{k}$$
$$\mathbf{B} = \mathbf{i} + 2\mathbf{j} + 3\mathbf{k}$$

$$\mathbf{R} = \mathbf{A} + \mathbf{B}$$

Substitute the values of **A** and **B**. $= (2\mathbf{i} + 3\mathbf{j} - 4\mathbf{k}) + (\mathbf{i} + 2\mathbf{j} + 3\mathbf{k})$

Rearrange the terms. $= (2 + 1)\mathbf{i} + (3 + 2)\mathbf{j} + (-4 + 3)\mathbf{k}$

$= 3\mathbf{i} + 5\mathbf{j} - \mathbf{k}$.

### Example 6.4.2

A mail carrier leaves the post office and drives 20.0 mi due north to the next town. He then drives in a direction 30° north of east for 40.0 mi. Determine the displacement (**R**) of the mail carrier.

Let us choose the positive $x$-axis to be east and the positive $y$-axis north. Call the first displacement vector **A** and the second displacement vector **B**.

Since the first displacement **A** is in the $y$-direction (north), it follows that

$A_x = 0$
$A_y = 20.0$ mi.

Since the displacement **B** is 30° with the positive $x$-axis (east), we have

$B_x = (40.0 \text{ mi}) \cos 30° = (40.0 \text{ mi})(0.866) = 34.6$ mi.

$B_y = (40.0 \text{ mi}) \sin 30° = (40.0 \text{ mi})(0.5) = 20.0$ mi.

The resultant displacement is **R**, as shown at the right.

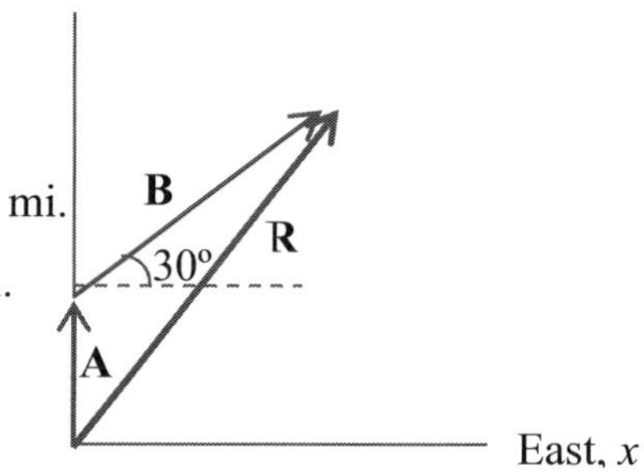


Add the $x$ components to get $R_x$. $R_x = A_x + B_x = 0 + 34.6 \text{ mi} = 34.6$ mi

Add the $y$ components to get $R_y$. $R_y = A_y + B_y = 20.0 \text{ mi} + 20.0 \text{ mi} = 40.0$ mi

Magnitude of $R$

$$R = \sqrt{R_x^2 + R_y^2} = \sqrt{(34.6 \text{ mi})^2 + (40.0 \text{ mi})^2} = 52.9 \text{ mi}$$

Angle $\theta$

$$\theta = \tan^{-1}\left(\frac{R_y}{R_x}\right) = \tan^{-1}\left(\frac{40.0 \text{ mi}}{34.6 \text{ mi}}\right) = 49°$$

You can also solve the problem using unit vector notation.

In unit vector notation, $\mathbf{A} = 0\mathbf{i} + 20.0 \text{ mi } \mathbf{j}$ $\mathbf{B} = 34.6 \text{ mi } \mathbf{i} + 20.0 \text{ mi } \mathbf{j}$, and

$$\mathbf{R} = \mathbf{A} + \mathbf{B}.$$

Substitute the vectors **A** and **B**.

$$= (0 + 34.6 \text{ mi})\,\mathbf{i} + (20.0 \text{ mi} + 20.0 \text{ mi})\,\mathbf{j}$$
$$= (34.6 \text{ mi})\,\mathbf{i} + (40.0 \text{ mi})\,\mathbf{j}$$

**Example 6.4.3**

**Relative Velocity:** Raindrops are falling vertically with a velocity of 4.0 m/s. A bicyclist races through the rain with a horizontal velocity of 6.0 m/s relative to the ground. Determine the magnitude and direction of the velocity of the raindrops with respect to the bicyclist.

Since velocity is a vector quantity, the velocity of the raindrops with respect to the bicyclist is

$\mathbf{v}_{RC} = \mathbf{v}_{RG} - \mathbf{v}_{CG}$,

where $\mathbf{v}_{RG}$ = velocity of the raindrop relative to the ground
and $\mathbf{v}_{CG}$ = velocity of the cyclist relative to the ground.

From the figure at the right, in unit vector notation,

$\mathbf{v}_{RC} = (-6.0 \text{ m/s})\,\mathbf{i} + (-4.0 \text{ m/s})\,\mathbf{j}$.

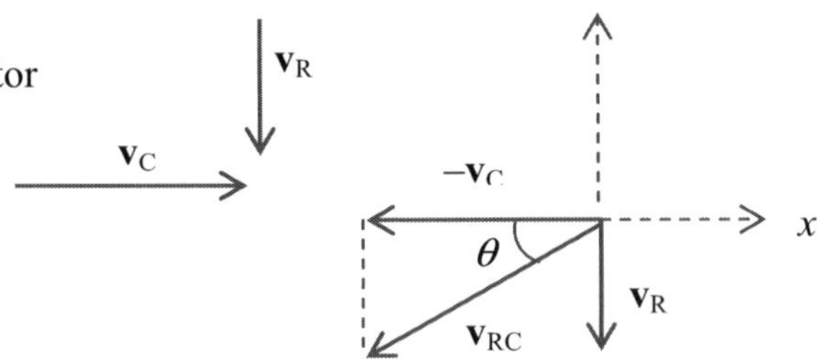


The magnitude $v_{RC} = \sqrt{(-6.0 \text{ m/s})^2 + (-4.0 \text{ m/s})^2} = 7.2 \text{ m/s}$

The angle $\theta = \tan^{-1}\left(\dfrac{-4.0 \text{ m/s}}{-6.0 \text{ m/s}}\right) = 53^\circ$

## Exercises

5. Let $\mathbf{A} = \mathbf{i} - 2\mathbf{j}$ and $\mathbf{B} = 2\mathbf{i} - 3\mathbf{j}$. Express $\mathbf{A} + \mathbf{B}$ and $\mathbf{A} - \mathbf{B}$ in unit vector notation. Determine the magnitude and direction of $\mathbf{A} + \mathbf{B}$ and $\mathbf{A} - \mathbf{B}$.

6. Three vectors are given by $\mathbf{A} = \mathbf{i} - 3\mathbf{j} + 4\mathbf{k}$, $\mathbf{B} = 2\mathbf{i} + 4\mathbf{j} - \mathbf{k}$ and $\mathbf{C} = 3\mathbf{i} - \mathbf{j} + \mathbf{k}$. Determine $\mathbf{A} + \mathbf{B}$, $\mathbf{A} - \mathbf{B}$, $\mathbf{B} - \mathbf{A}$, $\mathbf{A} + \mathbf{B} + \mathbf{C}$, and $\mathbf{A} - \mathbf{B} + \mathbf{C}$.

7. A jogger runs 100.0 m in a direction 30° east of north (call it displacement vector **A**) and then 50.0 m in a direction 60° south of east (call it displacement vector **B**). Determine the resultant displacement **R** of the jogger. Express **A**, **B**, and **R** in unit vector notation.

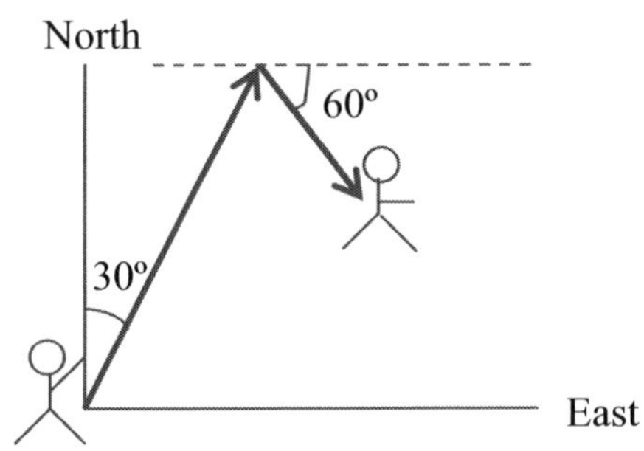

# Vector Products

## 6.5 Products of Vectors

**Multiplying a Vector by a Scalar**
Multiplication of a vector by a positive scalar, *s*, multiplies the magnitude of the vector, but the direction of the vector does not change. If *s* is *negative*, the direction is *reversed* (Figure 6.14).

**Figure 6.14**

Scalar multiplication is distributive. That is, $s(\mathbf{A} + \mathbf{B}) = s\mathbf{A} + s\mathbf{B}$. This is explained in Figure 6.15 for $s = 2$.

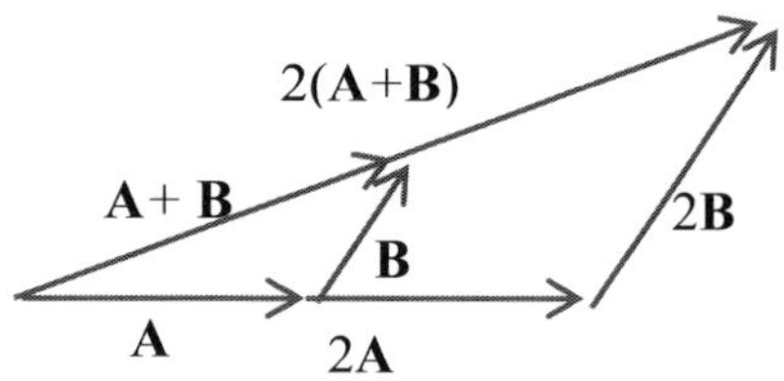

**Figure 6. 15**

> **Note:** When multiplying vectors in component form by a scalar, multiply each component of the vector by the scalar.

**Scalar Product or Dot Product**

The *scalar product* of two vectors is defined as the *scalar* equal to the product of the magnitudes of the vectors and the cosine of the angle between them. That is, (Figure 6.16)

$$\mathbf{A} \cdot \mathbf{B} = A\,B \cos\theta.$$

Because of the notation, the scalar product is also called the *dot product*.

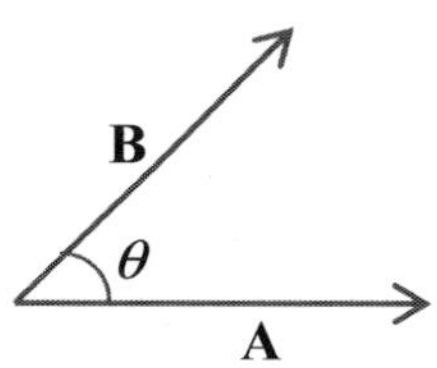

**Figure 6.16**

It is clear from the preceding equation that $\mathbf{A} \cdot \mathbf{B}$ can be positive, negative, or zero (zero when **A** and **B** are perpendicular, since $\cos 90° = 0$) depending on $\theta$. Also, $\mathbf{A}^2 = \mathbf{A} \cdot \mathbf{A} = A\,A \cos 0° = A^2$. In unit vector notation,

$$\mathbf{A} = A_x\,\mathbf{i} + A_y\,\mathbf{j} + A_z\,\mathbf{k}, \quad \mathbf{B} = B_x\,\mathbf{i} + B_y\,\mathbf{j} + B_z\,\mathbf{k}, \text{ and}$$

$$\mathbf{A} \cdot \mathbf{B} = (A_x\mathbf{i} + A_y\mathbf{j} + A_z\mathbf{k}) \cdot (B_x\mathbf{i} + B_y\mathbf{j} + B_z\mathbf{k}).$$

| |
|---|
| $\mathbf{i} \cdot \mathbf{j} = \mathbf{j} \cdot \mathbf{k} = \mathbf{k} \cdot \mathbf{i} = 0$ (since the angle between each pairs is 90º) |
| $\mathbf{i} \cdot \mathbf{i} = \mathbf{j} \cdot \mathbf{j} = \mathbf{k} \cdot \mathbf{k} = 1$ (since the magnitudes of **i**, **j**, and **k** are unity) |

By direct multiplication of **A** and **B**, $\mathbf{A} \cdot \mathbf{B} = A_xB_x + A_yB_y + A_zB_z$.

| |
|---|
| Note: To determine the dot product, multiply like components and then add. |

The dot product is *commutative*, that is, $\mathbf{A} \cdot \mathbf{B} = \mathbf{B} \cdot \mathbf{A}$.
The dot product is *distributive*, that is, $\mathbf{A} \cdot (\mathbf{B} + \mathbf{C}) = \mathbf{A} \cdot \mathbf{B} + \mathbf{A} \cdot \mathbf{C}$.

## Examples of Dot Products in Physics

### Work as a Dot Product

A force can cause an object to move from one place to another. Consider the displacement of a particle of mass, $m$, under the influence of a force as shown in Figure 6.17. In this case, a component of the force acts along the direction of the displacement, and we say that *work* is done.

Quantitatively, we define work $W$ by the force **F** in displacing an object by **r**, as the component of the force causing the displacement multiplied by the displacement. That is,

$$W = Fr\cos\theta = \mathbf{F} \cdot \mathbf{r}.$$

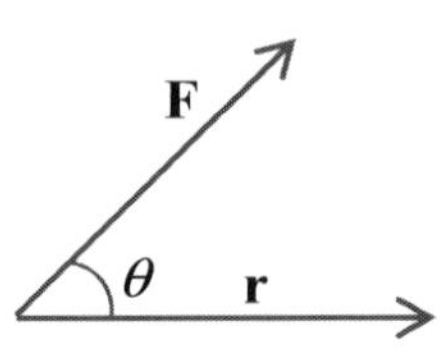

Figure 6.17

In many situations, the force varies in magnitude or direction during the displacement. For example, the force exerted by a spring increases with the amount of stretch. In general, if **F** is the force during an infinitesimal displacement **dr**, the work done for this infinitesimal displacement is $\mathbf{F} \cdot \mathbf{dr}$ (Figure 6.18).

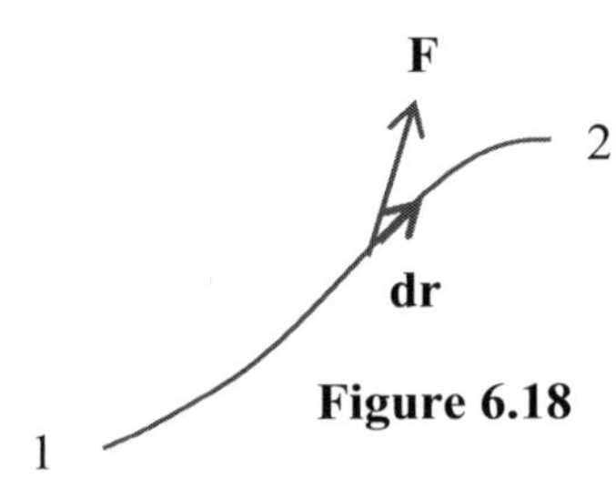

Figure 6.18

The total work in moving from point 1 and 2 is then obtained by summing all these work; that is, total work is obtained from the integration $W = \int_1^2 \mathbf{F} \cdot \mathbf{dr}$. This kind of integration is discussed in Section 9.2 of Chapter 9. A worked-out example is also given in the Section 9.2 and shows how work is calculated for a variable force.

There are other examples of dot products in introductory physics. In electrostatics, you will find that the potential energy $U$ of an electric dipole (two equal and opposite electric charges separated by a small distance) in an electric field **E** is given by $U = -\mathbf{p} \cdot \mathbf{E}$ (where **p** is called the electric dipole moment and **E** is the electric field), and, for a magnetic dipole, the potential energy in a magnetic field **B** is $U = -\boldsymbol{\mu} \cdot \mathbf{B}$ (μ is the magnetic dipole moment) In electricity and magnetism, the magnetic flux $d\phi$ passing through an elementary area $dA$ is given by the dot product $d\phi = \mathbf{B} \cdot dA\,\hat{\mathbf{n}}$.

### Example 6.5.1

Determine the scalar product between vector $\mathbf{A} = 2\mathbf{i} + 4\mathbf{j} + 3\mathbf{k}$ and $\mathbf{B} = 4\mathbf{i} - 2\mathbf{j} + \mathbf{k}$. Find the angle between the two vectors.

$\mathbf{A} = 2\mathbf{i} + 4\mathbf{j} + 3\mathbf{k}$ The components of **A** are $A_x = 2$, $A_y = 4$, and $A_z = 3$.

$\mathbf{B} = 4\mathbf{i} - 2\mathbf{j} + \mathbf{k}$ The components of **B** are $B_x = 4$, $B_y = -2$, and $B_z = 1$.

To determine the angle $\theta$ between the vectors, use the definition $\mathbf{A} \cdot \mathbf{B} = A\,B \cos\theta$. Knowing $\mathbf{A} \cdot \mathbf{B}$, $A$, and $B$, we can determine the angle $\theta$.

$$\mathbf{A} \cdot \mathbf{B} = A_x B_x + A_y B_y + A_z B_z$$

Substitute the values of $A_x$, $A_y$, and $A_z$.
$$= (2)(4) + (4)(-2) + (3)(1) = 3$$

$$A = \sqrt{A_x^2 + A_y^2 + A_z^2}$$

Substitute the values of $A_x$, $A_y$, and $A_z$.
$$= \sqrt{(2)^2 + (4)^2 + (3)^2} = 5.4$$

$$B = \sqrt{B_x^2 + B_y^2 + B_z^2}$$

Substitute the values of $B_x$, $B_y$, and $B_z$.
$$= \sqrt{(4)^2 + (-2)^2 + (1)^2} = 4.6$$

$$\mathbf{A} \cdot \mathbf{B} = A\,B \cos\theta$$

Substitute the values of $\mathbf{A} \cdot \mathbf{B}$, $A$, and $B$.
$$3 = (5.4)(4.6) \cos\theta$$

or $\cos\theta = 0.12$

$\theta = \cos^{-1}(0.12) = 83°$

**Example 6.5.2**

Find the work done by $\mathbf{F} = 4\mathbf{i} - 2\mathbf{j} + 2\mathbf{k}$ in moving an object from a point $P$ (3, 1, 2) to a point $Q$ (2, –1, 6).

Work done $W = \mathbf{F} \cdot \mathbf{r}$

In this case, $\mathbf{r} = (2-3)\mathbf{i} + (-1-1)\mathbf{j} + (6-2)\mathbf{k}$

$= -1\mathbf{i} - 2\mathbf{j} + 45\mathbf{k}.$

$\mathbf{F} = 4\mathbf{i} - 2\mathbf{j} + 2\mathbf{k}$

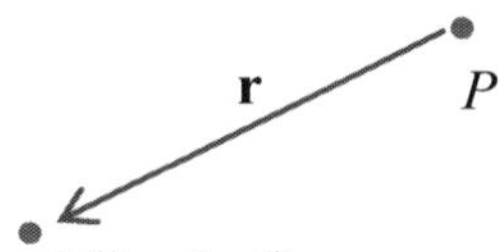


Thus, work done, $W = \mathbf{F} \cdot \mathbf{r}$

$= (4\mathbf{i} - 2\mathbf{j} + 2\mathbf{k}) \cdot (-1\mathbf{i} - 2\mathbf{j} + 4\mathbf{k})$

Use the formula $\mathbf{A} \cdot \mathbf{B} = A_xB_x + A_yB_y + A_zB_z$. $=(4)(-1) + (-2)(-2) + (2)(4)$

$= -4 + 4 + 8 = 8$ units.

**Exercises**

8. $\mathbf{A} = 2\mathbf{i} + 3\mathbf{j} - \mathbf{k}$, $\mathbf{B} = 4\mathbf{i} - 2\mathbf{j} + \mathbf{k}$, and $\mathbf{C} = \mathbf{i} + 3\mathbf{j} - 4\mathbf{k}$. Determine (a) the dot product $\mathbf{A} \cdot \mathbf{B}$, (b) the angle between **A** and **B**, and (c) $\mathbf{A} \cdot (\mathbf{B} + \mathbf{C})$. Also, show that $\mathbf{A} \cdot (\mathbf{B} + \mathbf{C}) = \mathbf{A} \cdot \mathbf{B} + \mathbf{A} \cdot \mathbf{C}$.

9. Starting from the expression $\mathbf{c} = \mathbf{a} - \mathbf{b}$, prove the law of cosines $c^2 = a^2 + b^2 - 2ab\cos\theta$, where $\theta$ is tha angle between the **a** and **b**. (*Hint*: Find $\mathbf{c} \cdot \mathbf{c}$.)

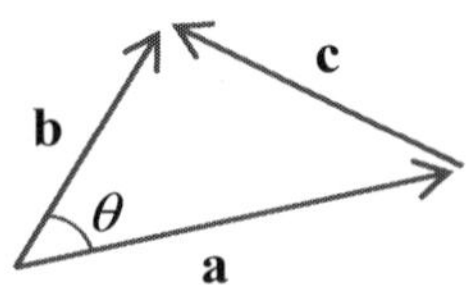


10. Work $W$ is defined as the dot product of the force **F** and the displacement **r**. That is, $W = Fr\cos\theta$. Find the work done in pulling a shopping cart by a force of 20.0 N at an angle of 30° by a distance of 2.0 m.

11. A rocket experiences a constant total thrusting force $\mathbf{F} = (200\text{ N})\mathbf{i} + (20\text{ N})\mathbf{j} + (120\text{ N})\mathbf{k}$. It moves along a straight launch track and its displacement from the origin is $\mathbf{r} = (100\text{ m})\mathbf{i} + (30\text{ m})\mathbf{k}$. Determine the work done by the thursting force.

12. Two forces $\mathbf{F}_1 = (1.2\mathbf{i} - 0.5\mathbf{j} + 0.5\mathbf{k})$ N and $\mathbf{F}_2 = (0.9\mathbf{i} - 1.2\mathbf{j})$ N are applied to a moving object of mass 0.1 kg. The displacement produced by the forces is $\mathbf{r} = (4.0\mathbf{i} + 2.0\mathbf{j} + 2.0\mathbf{k})$ m. Determine the work done by the two forces. [*Hint*: Total work, $W = W_1 + W_2 = \mathbf{F}_1 \cdot \mathbf{r} + \mathbf{F}_2 \cdot \mathbf{r} = (\mathbf{F}_1 + \mathbf{F}_2) \cdot \mathbf{r}$.]

**Vector Product or Cross Product**

The vector product of two vectors **A** and **B** is written as **A X B** (Figure 6.19) and is also called a cross product. It is a vector perpendicular to both **A** and **B**, and its magnitude is defined as

$$|\mathbf{A} \times \mathbf{B}| = A\,B \sin\theta.$$

Geometrically, $|\mathbf{A} \times \mathbf{B}|$ is the area of the parallelogram generated by **A** and **B**.

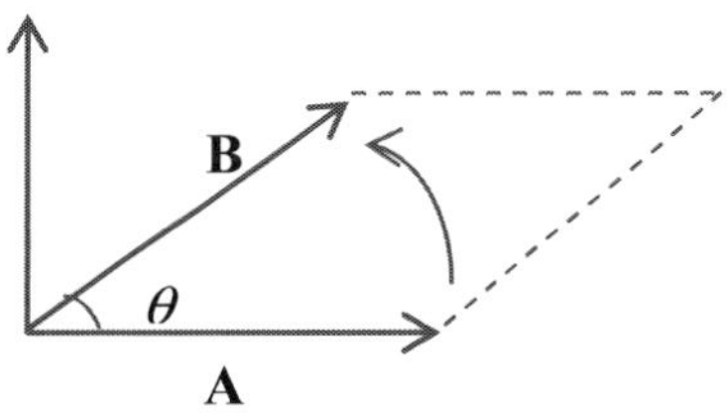


**Figure 6.19**

The direction of **A X B** (as shown in Figure 6.20) is given by the right-hand rule, which states that if the fingers of the right hand are curled in a way that will rotate **A** through the smaller angle into coincidence with **B**, then the thumb will point in the direction of **A X B**.

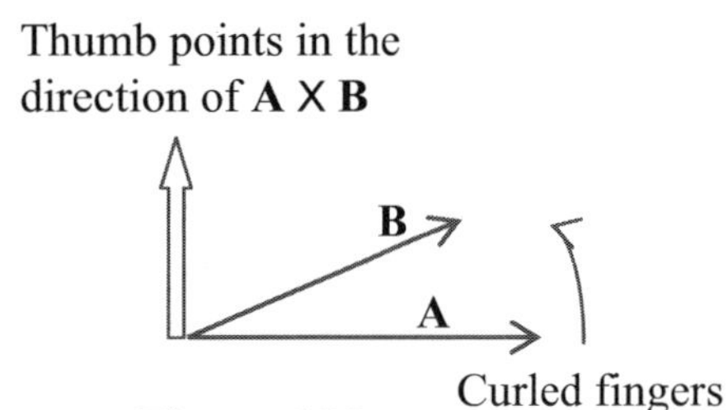


**Figure 6.20**

From the definition, **A X A** = 0 and **A X B** = 0, if **A** and **B** are parallel.

Since the unit vectors **i**, **j**, and **k** are mutually perpendicular, and the cross product is perpendicular to both vectors, it follows that

$$\mathbf{i} \times \mathbf{i} = \mathbf{j} \times \mathbf{j} = \mathbf{k} \times \mathbf{k} = 0 \quad (\text{since } \sin 0^\circ = 0).$$

$\mathbf{i} \times \mathbf{j} = \mathbf{k},\ \mathbf{j} \times \mathbf{k} = \mathbf{i},\ \mathbf{k} \times \mathbf{i} = \mathbf{j}$

$\mathbf{j} \times \mathbf{i} = -\mathbf{k},\ \mathbf{k} \times \mathbf{j} = -\mathbf{i},\ \mathbf{i} \times \mathbf{k} = -\mathbf{j}$

Follow the direction of the arrow in Figure 6.21 to determine the sign of the products.

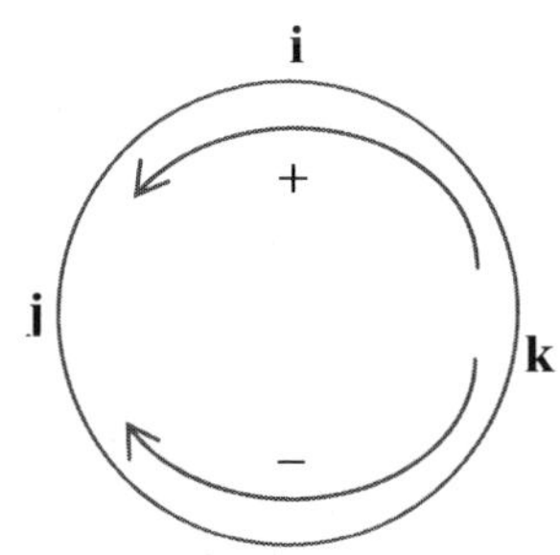


**Figure 6.21**

$$\mathbf{A} \times \mathbf{B} = (A_x\mathbf{i} + A_y\mathbf{j} + A_z\mathbf{k}) \times (B_x\mathbf{i} + B_y\mathbf{j} + B_z\mathbf{k})$$

$$= (A_yB_z - A_zB_y)\mathbf{i} + (A_zB_x - A_xB_z)\mathbf{j} + (A_xB_y - A_yB_x)\mathbf{k}$$

This can be written as an easily remembered determinant:

$$\mathbf{A} \times \mathbf{B} = \begin{vmatrix} \mathbf{i} & \mathbf{j} & \mathbf{k} \\ A_x & A_y & A_z \\ B_x & B_y & B_z \end{vmatrix}$$

> **Note**: To determine the cross product, form the determinant whose first row is **i**, **j**, **k**, whose second row is the components of **A**, and whose third row is the components of **B**.

To get the first term, draw a horizontal line through the first row and a vertical line through the first column. Cross multiply the remaining four terms, obtaining $A_yB_z - A_zB_y$, and then multiply by **i.**

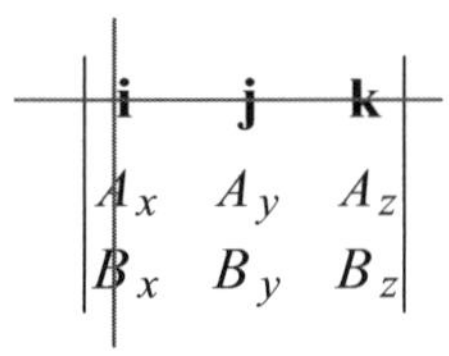

To get the second term, draw a horizontal line through the first row and a vertical line through the second column. Cross multiply the remaining four terms, obtaining $A_xB_z - A_zB_x$, and then multiply by –**j**.

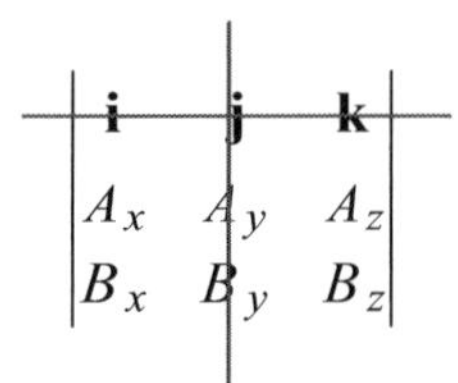

To get the third term, draw a horizontal line through the first row and a vertical line through the third column. Cross multiply the remaining four terms, obtaining $A_xB_y - A_yB_x$, and then multiply by **k.**

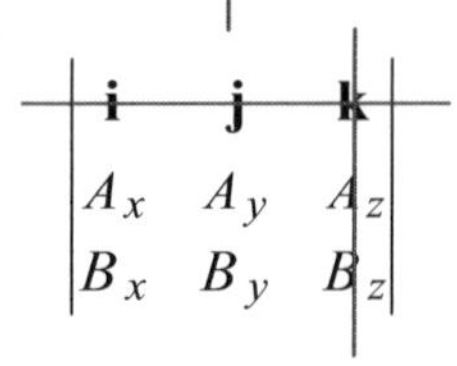

The order of multiplication is important: **A** X **B** = –**B** X **A** (anticommutative law of vector multiplication).

The cross product is distributive: **A** X (**B** + **C**) = (**A** X **B**) + (**A** X **C**).

**Examples of Cross Products in Physics**

There are several examples in physics where a physical quantity is defined as the cross product of two vectors.

Just as a force is needed to cause changes in linear motion, a *torque* is needed to cause changes in rotational motion. Torque is an example of a physical quantity that can be expressed as a cross product. *Torque* is defined as a vector given by $\boldsymbol{\tau} = \mathbf{r} \times \mathbf{F}$, where $\mathbf{r}$ is the position vector of a point on an object and $\mathbf{F}$ is the force acting on the object at the point tending to rotate the object (Figure 6.22). Since the position vector is defined with respect to a suitable point chosen as the origin, torque is defined about a point.

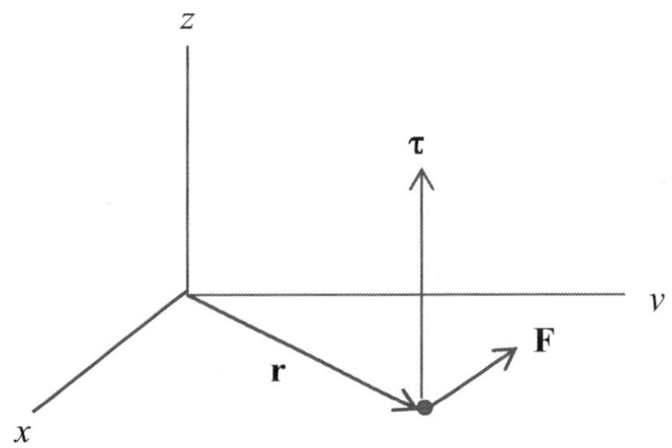

**Figure 6.22**

*Angular momentum* is another example of the cross product of two vectors. Just as an object in linear motion has a linear momentum $\mathbf{p} = m\mathbf{v}$ (where $m$ is the mass and $\mathbf{v}$ is the velocity of the object), an object in rotational motion has a rotational momentum, called angular momentum. Angular momentum is defined as $\mathbf{L} = \mathbf{r} \times \mathbf{p}$.

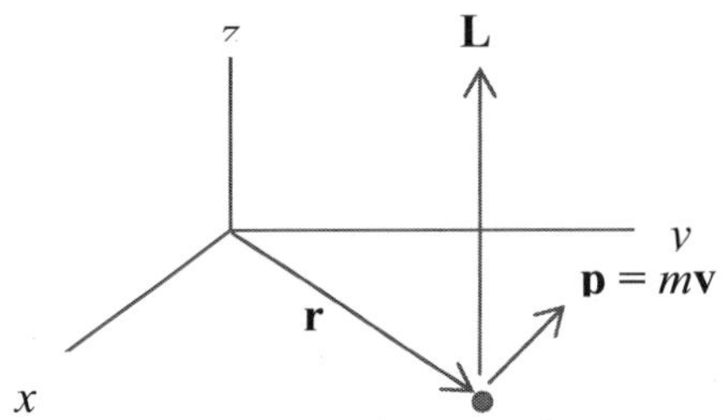


If the angular velocity of a rotating object is $\boldsymbol{\omega}$ about an axis of rotation and if the position vector of a point on the object is $\mathbf{r}$ with respect to a point on the axis of rotation, then the linear velocity $\mathbf{v}$ of the point in the object is given by the cross product $\mathbf{v} = \boldsymbol{\omega} \times \mathbf{r}$.

Particles such as electrons and protons have electric charges. When an electric charge $q$ moves with a velocity $\mathbf{v}$ in a magnetic field $\mathbf{B}$, it is found experimentally that there is a force on the moving charge. This is called magnetic force and its magnitude is found to be $F = qvB \sin\theta$. The direction of the force, as observed experimentally, is perpendicular to the plane defined by $\mathbf{v}$ and $\mathbf{B}$ (Figure 6.23). Thus, the magnitude and direction of the force on a charged particle can be expressed as the cross product

$$\mathbf{F} = q\mathbf{v} \times \mathbf{B}.$$

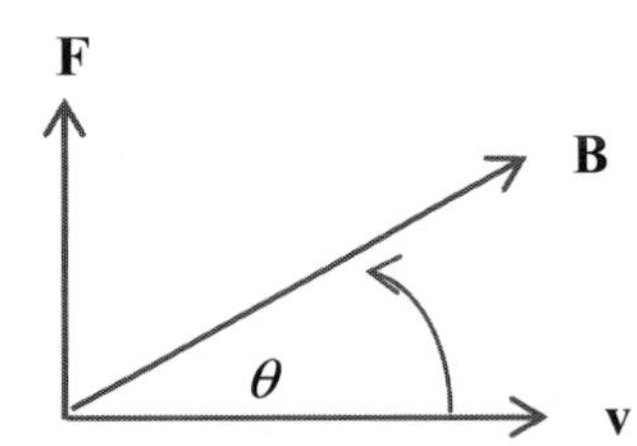

**Figure 6.23**

A current-carrying wire produces a magnetic field, which is a vector. The Biot-Savart law expresses the magnetic field **dB** at a point *P* distant *r* (Figure 6.24) from the small element **dl** of the wire along which the current *I* is flowing by means of the equation

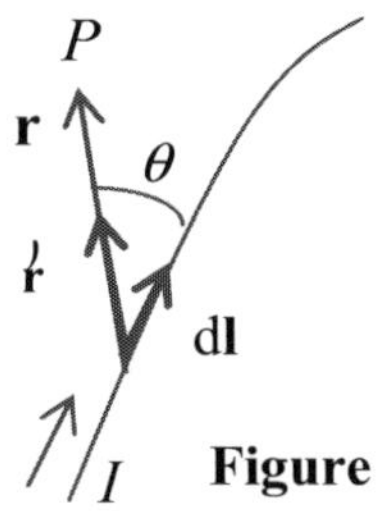

**Figure 6.24**

$$\mathbf{dB} = \frac{\mu_0 I}{4\pi} \frac{\mathbf{dl} \times \hat{\mathbf{r}}}{r^2},$$

where **r** is the displacement vector from the element **dl** of the wire to the point *P*, $\hat{\mathbf{r}}$ is the unit vector along **r**, and $\mu_0$ is a constant. The magnitude of the field is $\frac{\mu_0 I\, dl\, \sin\theta}{4\pi r^2}$, where $\theta$ is the angle between **dl** and **r** and the direction of the field is given by the right-hand rule of the cross product. The total magnetic field at the point *P* due to the wire can be obtained by integrating over all current elements.

There are other examples of cross products in electricity and magnetism in introductory physics. A magnetic field exerts a force on an electric current. If the magnetic field is uniform over a straight wire of length **l**, the force is $\mathbf{F} = I\,\mathbf{l} \times \mathbf{B}$, where *I* is the electric current. Also, a magnetic field tries to rotate a current loop. The torque $\boldsymbol{\tau}$ on a current loop in a magnetic field **B** is given by $\boldsymbol{\tau} = \boldsymbol{\mu} \times \mathbf{B}$, where $\boldsymbol{\mu}$ is called the magnetic dipole moment of the current loop, which is related to the number of turns, the current, and the area of the loop.

### Example 6.5.1

Suppose the position vector is in the *xy*-plane and is given by $\mathbf{r} = 1.8\text{ m } \mathbf{i} + 1.1\text{ m } \mathbf{j}$. If the force vector is $\mathbf{F} = 110\text{ N } \mathbf{j}$, determine the torque vector.

We have

$\mathbf{r} = 1.8\text{ m } \mathbf{i} + 1.1\,\mathbf{j}$ $\quad x = 1.8\text{ m}, y = 1.1\text{ m}, z = 0\text{ m}$

$\mathbf{F} = 110\text{ N } \mathbf{j}$ $\quad F_x = 0\text{ N}, F_y = 110\text{ N}, F_z = 0\text{ N}.$

In determinant form,

$$\boldsymbol{\tau} = \mathbf{r} \times \mathbf{F} = \begin{vmatrix} \mathbf{i} & \mathbf{j} & \mathbf{k} \\ A_x & A_y & A_z \\ B_x & B_y & B_z \end{vmatrix}$$

$$= \begin{vmatrix} \mathbf{i} & \mathbf{j} & \mathbf{k} \\ x & y & z \\ F_x & F_y & F_z \end{vmatrix}$$

Substitute the values.

$$= \begin{vmatrix} \mathbf{i} & \mathbf{j} & \mathbf{k} \\ 1.8\text{ m} & 1.1\text{ m} & 0 \\ 0 & 110\text{ N} & 0 \end{vmatrix}$$

Expand the determinant. $= 0\mathbf{i} + 0\mathbf{j} + (198\text{ m}\cdot\text{N})\mathbf{k} = (198\text{ m}\cdot\text{N})\mathbf{k}$

**Example 6.5.2**

The angular velocity of a rotating object about an axis of rotation is given by **ω** = (4**i** + **j** –2**k**) rad/s. Determine the linear velocity of a point of the object having position vector with respect to a point on the axis of rotations given as **r** = (**i** + 2**j** – **k**) m.

We have **v** = **ω** X **r**:

**ω** = (4**i** + **j** –2**k**) rad/s
**r** = (**i** + 2**j** – **k**) m.

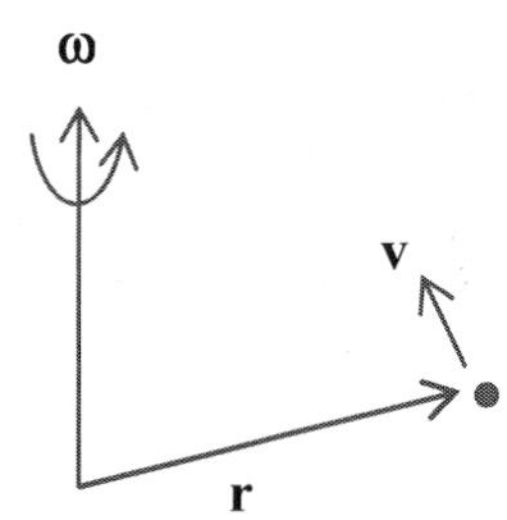


In determinant form,

$$\mathbf{v} = \boldsymbol{\omega} \times \mathbf{r}$$

$$= \begin{vmatrix} \mathbf{i} & \mathbf{j} & \mathbf{k} \\ \omega_x & \omega_y & \omega_z \\ x & y & z \end{vmatrix}$$

Substitute the values.

$$= \begin{vmatrix} \mathbf{i} & \mathbf{j} & \mathbf{k} \\ 4\text{ rad/s} & 1\text{ rad/s} & -2\text{ rad/s} \\ 1\text{ m} & 2\text{ m} & -1\text{ m} \end{vmatrix}$$

Expand the determinant. $= [(1)(-1) - (2)(-2)]\mathbf{i} + [(-2)(1) - (4)(-1]\mathbf{j} + [(4)(2) - (1)(1)]\mathbf{k}$

$= (3\mathbf{i} + 2\mathbf{j} + 7\mathbf{k})$ m/s

**Example 6.5.3**

A circular loop of wire of radius *R* carries a current *I* as shown. Use the Biot-Savart law to determine the magnetic field at the center of the wire.

Use the expression $d\mathbf{B} = \frac{\mu_0 I}{4\pi}\frac{d\mathbf{l} \times \hat{\mathbf{r}}}{r^2}$ to calculate magnetic field due to a small current element. Recall that a tangent line drawn to a circle at any point to a circle is perpendicular to radius of the circle drawn at the point.

Thus, each element **dl** of the circular loop is perpendicular to the radius vector **R**, so that $d\mathbf{l} \times \hat{\mathbf{r}} = dl \sin 90^\circ = dl$.

Thus the magnetic field due to the current element *I* **dl**:

$dB = \frac{\mu_0 I}{4\pi}\frac{d\mathbf{l} \times \hat{\mathbf{r}}}{r^2} = \frac{\mu_0}{4\pi}\frac{I\, dl}{R^2}$. According to the right-hand rule, the direction of the magnetic field due to each elment **dl** of the loop is into the paper at the center.

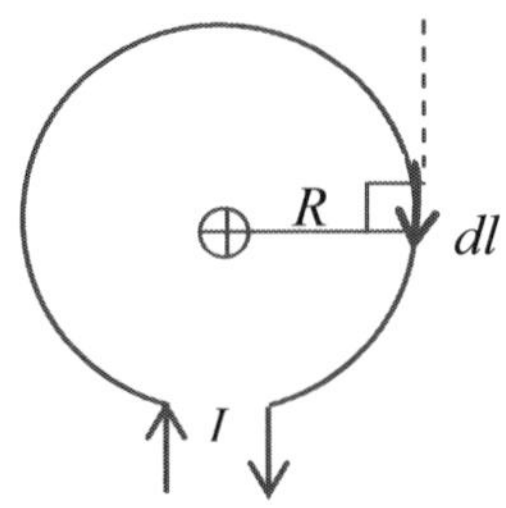


The total magnetic field is obtained by integrating (summing) the field due to each elemtent.

$$B = \frac{\mu_0 I}{4\pi R^2}\int dl = \frac{\mu_0 I}{4\pi R^2}(2\pi R) = \frac{\mu_0 I}{2R}$$

***Triple Product of Vectors**

The cross product of two vectors **A** and **B** is a vector, and the product can be dotted or crossed with a third vector **C** to form of triple product.

**Scalar Triple Product: A · (B X C)**

The scalar triple product is a scalar. Geometrically, it is the volume of the parallelepiped generated by the vectors **A**, **B**, and **C** because $|\mathbf{B} \times \mathbf{C}|$ is the area of the base and $|\mathbf{A} \cos \theta|$ is the altitude of the parallelopiped (Figure 6.25).

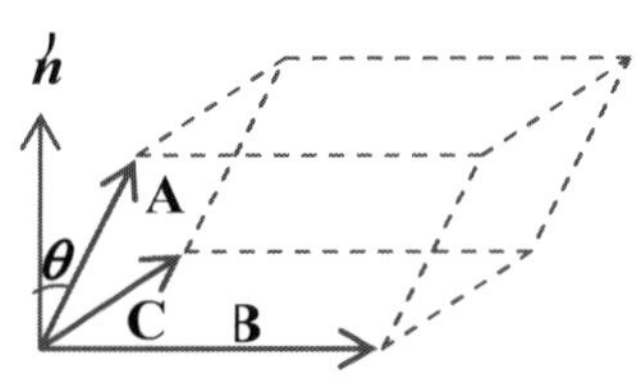


**Figure 6.25**

**A · (B X C) = B · (C X A) = C · (A X B)** since they all represent the same volume of the parallopiped.

**Vector Triple Product**: **A** X (**B** X **C**)

The vector triple product is a vector and we can show that it can be written by the so called BAC-CAB rule as **A** X (**B** X **C**) = **B**(**A** · **C**) – **C**(**A** · **B**).

***Vector Identities**

Vector identities are useful in solving vector problems. Important vector identities, some of which already mentioned, are listed in Table 6.3.

**Table 6.3**

| | |
|---|---|
| $s$ (**A** + **B**) = $s$**A** + $s$**B** | **A** · (**B** + **C**) = **A** · **B** + **A** · **C** |
| ($r + s$)**A** = $r$**A** + $s$**A** | **A** · (**B** X **C**) = **B** · (**C** X **A**) = **C** · (**A** X **B**) |
| $s$(**A** · **B**) = ($s$**A**) · **B** = **A** · ($s$**B**) | **A** X (**B** + **C**) = (**A** X **B**) + (**A** X **C**) |
| $s$(**A** X **B**) = ($s$**A**) X **B** = **A** X ($s$**B**) | **A** X (**B** X **C**) = **B**(**A** · **C**) – **C**(**A** · **B**) |

**Exercises**

13. **A** = 2**i** + 3**j** – **k** and **B** = **i** –2**j** + 3**k**, determine **A** X **B** and **B** X **A**. Find the angle between **A** and **B**.

14. **A** = 2**i** + **j** – 2**k**, **B** = 2**i** –**j** + 3**k** and **C** = **i** + 3**j** –2 **k**. Verify by direct calculation of right- and left-hand sides that (i) **A** X (**B** + **C**) = (**A** X **B**) + (**A** X **C**), and (ii) **A** X (**B** X **C**) = **B**(**A** · **C**) – **C**(**A** · **B**).

15. Use vector cross product to express the area of a triangle in three different ways. Hence, prove the law of sines:

$$\frac{a}{\sin A} = \frac{b}{\sin B} = \frac{c}{\sin C}$$

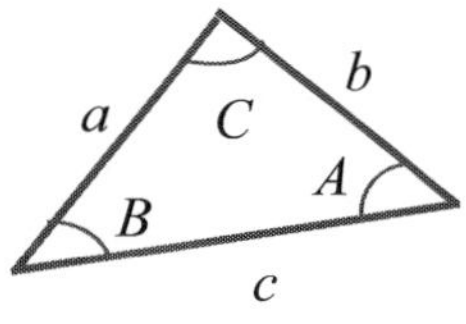


16. A particle is located at **r** = (2.0 m)**i** + (1.0 m)**j** + (3.0 m)**k**. A force **F** = (2.0 N)**j** – (1.0 N)**k** acts on the particle. Determine the torque about the origin.

17. A particle has a momentum **p** = (4**i** + 6**j**) kg · m/s. Find its angular momentum relative to the origin when it is at **r** = (2 **j** + 5**k**) m.

18. A proton in an accelerator is propelled at $2.0 \times 10^6$ m/s perpendicular to a uniform magnetic field of 1.2 T (1 T = 1 N/(m/s)/C). Determine the force experienced by the proton. The charge for the proton, $q = 1.6 \times 10^{-19}$ C. (*Hint*: $\mathbf{F} = q\,\mathbf{v} \times \mathbf{B}$.)

19. Show that $\mathbf{A} \cdot (\mathbf{B} \times \mathbf{C}) = \begin{vmatrix} A_x & A_y & A_z \\ B_x & B_y & B_z \\ C_x & C_y & C_z \end{vmatrix}$

20. Show that $[\mathbf{A} \times (\mathbf{B} \times \mathbf{C})] + [\mathbf{B} \times (\mathbf{C} \times \mathbf{A})] + [\mathbf{C} \times (\mathbf{A} \times \mathbf{B})] = 0$.

## Answers to Exercises in Chapter 6

1. $x$-component = 50.9 m/s, $y$-component = 31.8 m/s
2. 567 km/h in the northernly direction, 412 km/h in the westernly direction
3. $F = 4.5$ N, $\theta = 243°$
4 6.6 units, $\theta = 70.5°$ below the positive $x$-axis.
5. $\mathbf{A} + \mathbf{B} = 3\mathbf{i} - 5\mathbf{j}$, $\mathbf{A} - \mathbf{B} = -\mathbf{i} + \mathbf{j}$
6. $\mathbf{A} + \mathbf{B} = 3\mathbf{i} + \mathbf{j} + 3\mathbf{k}$, $\mathbf{A} - \mathbf{B} = -\mathbf{i} - 7\mathbf{j} + 5\mathbf{k}$, $\mathbf{B} - \mathbf{A} = \mathbf{i} + 7\mathbf{j} - 5\mathbf{k}$,

   $\mathbf{A} + \mathbf{B} + \mathbf{C} = 6\,\mathbf{i} \;\; + 4\mathbf{k}$, $\mathbf{A} - \mathbf{B} + \mathbf{C} = 2\,\mathbf{i} - 8\mathbf{j} + 6\mathbf{k}$
7. $R = 86.6$ m, $\theta = 30°$ north of east, $\mathbf{R} = 75.0\,\mathbf{i} + 43.3\,\mathbf{j}$
8 (a) $\mathbf{A} \cdot \mathbf{B} = 1$ (b) $\theta = 87°$ (c) $\mathbf{A} \cdot (\mathbf{B} + \mathbf{C}) = 16$
10. 34.6 N · m
11. 2.4 X $10^4$ N
12. 6.0 N · m
13. $\mathbf{A} \times \mathbf{B} = 7\mathbf{i} - 7\mathbf{j} - 7\mathbf{k}$, $\mathbf{B} \times \mathbf{A} = -7\mathbf{i} + 7\mathbf{j} + 7\mathbf{k}$, angle $\theta = 60°$
16. $(-7.0\mathbf{i} + 2.0\mathbf{j} + 4.0\,\mathbf{k})$ N · m
17. $(-30\mathbf{i} + 20\mathbf{j} - 8\mathbf{k})$ kg · m$^2$/s
18. 3.8 X $10^{-13}$ N

# Complex Numbers

# 9 Complex numbers

| Chapter 9 | Contents |
|---|---|

## 9.1 Introduction

Complex numbers often seem strange when first encountered but it is worth persevering with them because they provide a powerful mathematical tool for solving several engineering problems. One of the main applications is to the analysis of alternating current (a.c.) circuits. Engineers are very interested in these because the mains supply is itself a.c., and electricity generation and transportation are dominated by a.c. voltages and currents.

A great deal of signal analysis and processing uses mathematical models based on complex numbers because they allow the manipulation of sinusoidal quantities to be undertaken more easily. Furthermore, the design of filters to be used in communications equipment relies heavily on their use.

One area of particular relevance is control engineering – so much so that control engineers often prefer to think of a control system in terms of a 'complex plane' representation rather than a 'time domain' representation. We will develop these concepts in this and subsequent chapters.

## 9.2 Complex numbers

We have already examined quadratic equations such as

$$x^2 - x - 6 = 0 \tag{9.1}$$

and have met techniques for finding the roots of such equations. The formula for obtaining the roots of a quadratic equation $ax^2 + bx + c = 0$ is

$$x = \frac{-b \pm \sqrt{b^2 - 4ac}}{2a} \tag{9.2}$$

Applying this formula to Equation (9.1), we find

$$\begin{aligned} x &= \frac{+1 \pm \sqrt{(-1)^2 - 4(1)(-6)}}{2} \\ &= \frac{1 \pm \sqrt{25}}{2} \\ &= \frac{1 \pm 5}{2} \end{aligned}$$

so that $x = 3$ and $x = -2$ are the two roots. However, if we try to apply the formula to the equation

$$2x^2 + 2x + 5 = 0$$

we find

$$x = \frac{-2 \pm \sqrt{-36}}{4}$$

A problem now arises in that we need to find the square root of a negative number. We know from experience that squaring both positive and negative numbers yields a positive result; thus,

$$6^2 = 36 \qquad \text{and} \qquad (-6)^2 = 36$$

so that there is no real number whose square is $-36$. In the general case, if $ax^2+bx+c = 0$, we see by examining the square root in Equation (9.2) that this problem will always arise whenever $b^2 - 4ac < 0$. Nevertheless, it turns out to be very useful to invent a technique for dealing with such situations, leading to the theory of complex numbers.

To make progress we introduce a number, denoted j, with the property that

$$j^2 = -1$$

We have already seen that using the real number system we cannot obtain a negative number by squaring a real number so the number j is not real – we say it is **imaginary**. This imaginary number has a very useful role to play in engineering mathematics. Using it we can now formally write down an expression for the square root of any negative number. Thus,

$$\begin{aligned}\sqrt{-36} &= \sqrt{36 \times (-1)} \\ &= \sqrt{36 \times j^2} \\ &= 6j\end{aligned}$$

Returning to the solution of the quadratic equation $2x^2 + 2x + 5 = 0$, we find

$$\begin{aligned}x &= \frac{-2 \pm \sqrt{-36}}{4} \\ &= \frac{-2 \pm 6j}{4} \\ &= \frac{-1 \pm 3j}{2}\end{aligned}$$

We have found two roots, namely $x = -\frac{1}{2} + \frac{3}{2}j$ and $x = -\frac{1}{2} - \frac{3}{2}j$. These numbers are called **complex numbers** and we see that they are made up of two parts – a **real part** and an **imaginary part**. For the first complex number the real part is $-\frac{1}{2}$ and the imaginary part is $\frac{3}{2}$. For the second complex number the real part is $-\frac{1}{2}$ and the imaginary part is $-\frac{3}{2}$. In a more general case we usually use the letter $z$ to denote a complex number with real part $a$ and imaginary part $b$, so $z = a + bj$. We write $a = \text{Re}(z)$ and $b = \text{Im}(z)$, and denote the set of all complex numbers by $\mathbb{C}$. Note that $a, b \in \mathbb{R}$ whereas $z \in \mathbb{C}$.

$z = a + bj$, $z$ is a member of the set of complex numbers, that is $z \in \mathbb{C}$
$a = \text{Re}(z) \qquad b = \text{Im}(z)$

Complex numbers which have a zero imaginary part are purely real and hence all real numbers are also complex numbers, that is $\mathbb{R} \subset \mathbb{C}$.

**Example 9.1** Solve the quadratic equation $2s^2 - 3s + 7 = 0$.

**Solution** Using the formula for solving a quadratic equation we find

$$\begin{aligned} s &= \frac{-(-3) \pm \sqrt{(-3)^2 - 4(2)(7)}}{2(2)} \\ &= \frac{3 \pm \sqrt{-47}}{4} \\ &= \frac{3 \pm \sqrt{47}\mathrm{j}}{4} \\ &= 0.75 \pm 1.71\mathrm{j} \end{aligned}$$

---

Using the fact that $\mathrm{j}^2 = -1$ we can develop other quantities.

**Example 9.2** Simplify the expression $\mathrm{j}^3$.

**Solution** We have

$$\begin{aligned} \mathrm{j}^3 &= \mathrm{j}^2 \times \mathrm{j} \\ &= (-1) \times \mathrm{j} \\ &= -\mathrm{j} \end{aligned}$$

---

### 9.2.1 The complex conjugate

If $z = a + b\mathrm{j}$, we define its **complex conjugate** to be the number $\bar{z} = a - b\mathrm{j}$; that is, we change the sign of the imaginary part.

**Example 9.3** Write down the complex conjugates of

(a) $-7 + \mathrm{j}$ (b) $6 - 5\mathrm{j}$ (c) $6$ (d) $\mathrm{j}$

**Solution** To find the complex conjugates of the given numbers we change the sign of the imaginary parts. A purely real number has an imaginary part 0. We find
(a) $-7 - \mathrm{j}$ (b) $6 + 5\mathrm{j}$ (c) 6, there is no imaginary part to alter (d) $-\mathrm{j}$

---

We recall that the solution of the quadratic equation $2x^2 + 2x + 5 = 0$ yielded the two complex numbers $-\frac{1}{2} + \frac{3}{2}\mathrm{j}$ and $-\frac{1}{2} - \frac{3}{2}\mathrm{j}$, and note that these form a complex conjugate pair. This illustrates a more general result:

When the polynomial equation $P(x) = 0$ has real coefficients, any complex roots will always occur in **complex conjugate pairs**.

Consider the following example.

**Example 9.4** Show that the equation $x^3 - 7x^2 + 19x - 13 = 0$ has a root at $x = 1$ and find the other roots.

**Solution** If we let $P(x) = x^3 - 7x^2 + 19x - 13$, then $P(1) = 1 - 7 + 19 - 13 = 0$ so that $x = 1$ is a root. This means that $x - 1$ must be a factor of $P(x)$ and so we can express $P(x)$ in the form

$$\begin{aligned} P(x) = x^3 - 7x^2 + 19x - 13 &= (x - 1)(\alpha x^2 + \beta x + \gamma) \\ &= \alpha x^3 + (\beta - \alpha)x^2 + (\gamma - \beta)x - \gamma \end{aligned}$$

where $\alpha$, $\beta$ and $\gamma$ are coefficients to be determined. Comparing the coefficients of $x^3$ we find $\alpha = 1$. Comparing the constant coefficients we find $\gamma = 13$. Finally, comparing coefficients of $x$ we find $\beta = -6$, and hence

$$P(x) = x^3 - 7x^2 + 19x - 13 = (x - 1)(x^2 - 6x + 13)$$

The other two roots of $P(x) = 0$ are found by solving the quadratic equation $x^2 - 6x + 13 = 0$, that is

$$x = \frac{6 \pm \sqrt{36 - 52}}{2} = \frac{6 \pm \sqrt{-16}}{2} = 3 \pm 2\mathrm{j}$$

and again we note that the complex roots occur as a complex conjugate pair. This illustrates the general result given in Section 1.3 that an $n$th-degree polynomial has $n$ roots.

---

## Exercises 9.2

1. Solve the following equations:

   (a) $x^2 + 1 = 0$

   (b) $x^2 + 4 = 0$

   (c) $3x^2 + 7 = 0$

   (d) $x^2 + x + 1 = 0$

   (e) $\frac{x^2}{2} - x + 2 = 0$

   (f) $-x^2 - 3x - 4 = 0$

   (g) $2x^2 + 3x + 3 = 0$

   (h) $x^2 + 3x + 4 = 0$

2. Solve the cubic equation

   $$3x^3 - 11x^2 + 16x - 12 = 0,$$

   given that one of the roots is $x = 2$.

3. Write down the complex conjugates of the following complex numbers.

   (a) $-11 - 8\mathrm{j}$ (b) $5 + 3\mathrm{j}$

   (c) $\frac{1}{2}\mathrm{j}$ (d) $-17$

   (e) $\cos \omega t + \mathrm{j} \sin \omega t$ (f) $\cos \omega t - \mathrm{j} \sin \omega t$

   (g) $-0.333\mathrm{j} + 1$

4. Recall from Chapter 2 that the poles of a rational function $R(x) = P(x)/Q(x)$ are those values of $x$ for which $Q(x) = 0$. Find any poles of

   (a) $\frac{x}{x - 3}$

   (b) $\frac{3x}{x^2 + 1}$

   (c) $\frac{3}{x^2 + x + 1}$

5 Solve the equation $s^2 + 2s + 5 = 0$.

6 Express as a complex number
(a) $j^4$ (b) $j^5$ (c) $j^6$

7 State Re($z$) and Im($z$) where

(a) $z = 7 + 11j$
(b) $z = -6 + j$
(c) $z = 0$
(d) $z = \dfrac{1+j}{2}$
(e) $z = j$
(f) $z = j^2$

## Solutions

1 (a) $\pm j$ (b) $\pm 2j$
(c) $\pm\sqrt{7/3}j$ (d) $-1/2 \pm (\sqrt{3}/2)j$
(e) $1 \pm \sqrt{3}j$ (f) $-3/2 \pm (\sqrt{7}/2)j$
(g) $-3/4 \pm (\sqrt{15}/4)j$ (h) $-3/2 \pm (\sqrt{7}/2)j$

2 $2, 5/6 \pm (\sqrt{47}/6)j$

3 (a) $-11 + 8j$ (b) $5 - 3j$
(c) $-\frac{1}{2}j$ (d) $-17$
(e) $\cos \omega t - j \sin \omega t$ (f) $\cos \omega t + j \sin \omega t$
(g) $0.333j + 1$

4 (a) $x = 3$
(b) $x = \pm j$
(c) $x = -1/2 \pm (\sqrt{3}/2)j$

5 $s = -1 \pm 2j$

6 (a) 1 (b) $j$ (c) $-1$

7 (a) 7, 11 (b) $-6$, 1
(c) 0, 0 (d) $\frac{1}{2}, \frac{1}{2}$
(e) 0, 1 (f) $-1$, 0

## 9.3 Operations with complex numbers

Two complex numbers are equal if and only if their real parts are equal and their imaginary parts are equal.

**Example 9.5** Find $x$ and $y$ so that $x + 6j$ and $3 - yj$ represent the same complex number.

**Solution** If both quantities represent the same complex number we have

$$x + 6j = 3 - yj$$

Since the real parts must be equal we can equate them, that is

$$x = 3$$

Similarly, we find, by equating imaginary parts

$$6 = -y$$

so that $y = -6$.

The operations of addition, subtraction, multiplication and division can all be performed on complex numbers.

### 9.3.1 Addition and subtraction

To add two complex numbers we simply add the real parts and add the imaginary parts; to subtract a complex number from another we subtract the corresponding real parts and subtract the corresponding imaginary parts as shown in Example 9.6.

**Example 9.6** If $z_1 = 3 - 4j$ and $z_2 = 4 + 2j$ find $z_1 + z_2$ and $z_1 - z_2$.

**Solution**

$$\begin{aligned} z_1 + z_2 &= (3 - 4j) + (4 + 2j) \\ &= (3 + 4) + (-4 + 2)j \\ &= 7 - 2j \\ z_1 - z_2 &= (3 - 4j) - (4 + 2j) \\ &= (3 - 4) + (-4 - 2)j \\ &= -1 - 6j \end{aligned}$$

---

### 9.3.2 Multiplication

We can multiply a complex number by a real number. Both the real and imaginary parts of the complex number are multiplied by the real number. Thus $3(4 - 6j) = 12 - 18j$.

To multiply two complex numbers we use the fact that $j^2 = -1$.

**Example 9.7** If $z_1 = 2 - 2j$ and $z_2 = 3 + 4j$, find $z_1 z_2$.

**Solution**

$$z_1 z_2 = (2 - 2j)(3 + 4j)$$

Removing brackets we find

$$\begin{aligned} z_1 z_2 &= 6 - 6j + 8j - 8j^2 \\ &= 6 - 6j + 8j + 8 \qquad \text{using } j^2 = -1 \\ &= 14 + 2j \end{aligned}$$

**Example 9.8** If $z = 3 - 2j$ find $z\bar{z}$.

**Solution** If $z = 3 - 2j$ then its conjugate is $\bar{z} = 3 + 2j$. Therefore,

$$\begin{aligned} z\bar{z} &= (3 - 2j)(3 + 2j) \\ &= 9 - 6j + 6j - 4j^2 \\ &= 9 - 4j^2 \\ &= 13 \end{aligned}$$

We see that the answer is a real number.

---

Whenever we multiply a complex number by its conjugate the answer is a real number. Thus if $z = a + b\mathrm{j}$

$$\begin{aligned} z\bar{z} &= (a + b\mathrm{j})(a - b\mathrm{j}) \\ &= a^2 + ba\mathrm{j} - ab\mathrm{j} - b^2\mathrm{j}^2 \\ &= a^2 + b^2 \end{aligned}$$

If $z = a + b\mathrm{j}$ then $z\bar{z} = a^2 + b^2$

### 9.3.3 Division

To divide two complex numbers it is necessary to make use of the complex conjugate. We multiply both the numerator and denominator by the conjugate of the denominator and then simplify the result.

**Example 9.9** If $z_1 = 2 + 9\mathrm{j}$ and $z_2 = 5 - 2\mathrm{j}$ find $\dfrac{z_1}{z_2}$.

**Solution** We seek $\dfrac{2 + 9\mathrm{j}}{5 - 2\mathrm{j}}$. The complex conjugate of the denominator is $5 + 2\mathrm{j}$, so we multiply both numerator and denominator by this quantity. The effect of this is to leave the value of $\dfrac{z_1}{z_2}$ unaltered since we have only multiplied by 1. Therefore,

$$\begin{aligned} \frac{z_1}{z_2} = \frac{2 + 9\mathrm{j}}{5 - 2\mathrm{j}} = \frac{(2 + 9\mathrm{j})\,(5 + 2\mathrm{j})}{(5 - 2\mathrm{j})\,(5 + 2\mathrm{j})} &= \frac{10 + 45\mathrm{j} + 4\mathrm{j} + 18\mathrm{j}^2}{25 + 4} = \frac{-8 + 49\mathrm{j}}{29} \\ &= -\frac{8}{29} + \frac{49}{29}\mathrm{j} \end{aligned}$$

The multiplication of two conjugates in the denominator allows a useful simplification. We see that the effect of multiplying by the conjugate of the denominator is to make the denominator of the solution purely real.

---

If $z_1 = x_1 + \mathrm{j}y_1$ and $z_2 = x_2 + \mathrm{j}y_2$ then the quotient $\dfrac{z_1}{z_2}$ is found by multiplying both numerator and denominator by the conjugate of the denominator, that is

$$\begin{aligned} \frac{z_1}{z_2} &= \frac{x_1 + \mathrm{j}y_1}{x_2 + \mathrm{j}y_2} \\ &= \frac{x_1 + \mathrm{j}y_1}{x_2 + \mathrm{j}y_2} \times \frac{x_2 - \mathrm{j}y_2}{x_2 - \mathrm{j}y_2} \\ &= \frac{x_1x_2 + y_1y_2 + \mathrm{j}(x_2y_1 - x_1y_2)}{x_2^2 + y_2^2} \end{aligned}$$

## Exercises 9.3

1 If $z_1 = 3 + 2j$ and $z_2 = 4 - 8j$ find
(a) $z_1 + z_2$ (b) $z_1 - z_2$ (c) $z_2 - z_1$

2 Express the following in the form $a + bj$:

(a) $\dfrac{1}{1+j}$

(b) $\dfrac{-2}{j}$

(c) $\dfrac{1}{j} + \dfrac{1}{2-j}$

(d) $\dfrac{j}{1+j}$

(e) $\dfrac{3}{3+2j} + \dfrac{1}{5-j}$

3 Express the following in the form $a + bj$:

(a) $\dfrac{2}{1-j}$

(b) $\dfrac{-2+3j}{j}$

(c) $3j(4-2j)$

(d) $(7-2j)(5+6j)$

(e) $\dfrac{5+3j}{2+2j}$

4 Find a quadratic equation whose roots are $1 - 3j$ and $1 + 3j$.

5 If $(x + jy)^2 = 3 + 4j$, find $x$ and $y$, where $x, y \in \mathbb{R}$.

6 Find the real and imaginary parts of

(a) $\dfrac{2}{4+j} - \dfrac{3}{2-j}$

(b) $j^4 - j^5$

(c) $\dfrac{1}{j} + j$

(d) $\dfrac{1}{j^3 - 3j}$

## Solutions

1 (a) $7 - 6j$
(b) $-1 + 10j$
(c) $1 - 10j$

2 (a) $\frac{1}{2} - \frac{1}{2}j$
(b) $2j$
(c) $\frac{2}{5} - \frac{4}{5}j$
(d) $\frac{1}{2} + \frac{1}{2}j$
(e) $\dfrac{23-11j}{26}$

3 (a) $1 + j$
(b) $3 + 2j$
(c) $6 + 12j$
(d) $47 + 32j$
(e) $2 - \frac{1}{2}j$

4 $x^2 - 2x + 10 = 0$

5 $x = 2, y = 1; x = -2, y = -1$

6 (a) $-\frac{62}{85}, -\frac{61}{85}$
(b) $1, -1$
(c) $0, 0$
(d) $0, \frac{1}{4}$

## Computer and calculator exercises 9.3

Computer algebra packages allow the user to input and manipulate complex numbers. Investigate how the complex number $a + bj$ is input to the package to which you have access.

1 Use a package to simplify the following complex numbers:

(a) $(1+j)^5$

(b) $\dfrac{3j}{(1-2j)^7}$

(c) $\dfrac{4}{(3+j)^3} - \dfrac{7}{(2-3j)^2}$

2 Solve the polynomial equations

(a) $x^3 + 7x^2 + 9x + 63 = 0$

(b) $x^4 + 15x^2 - 16 = 0$

3 Use a package to find the real and imaginary parts of $\dfrac{15 + \text{j}}{7 - 5\text{j}}$.

4 A common requirement in control theory is to find the poles of a rational function. Use a package to find the poles of the function

$$G(s) = \frac{0.5}{s^3 + 2s^2 + 0.2s + 0.0556}.$$

## 9.4 Graphical representation of complex numbers

Given a complex number $z = a + b\text{j}$ we can obtain a useful graphical interpretation of it by plotting the real part on the horizontal axis and the imaginary part on the vertical axis and obtain a unique point in the $x$–$y$ plane (Figure 9.1). We call the $x$ axis the **real axis** and the $y$ axis the **imaginary axis**, and the whole picture an **Argand diagram**. In this context, the $x$–$y$ plane is often referred to as the **complex plane**.

**Example 9.10** Plot the complex numbers $z_1 = 7 + 2\text{j}$, $z_2 = -3 + 5\text{j}$, $z_3 = -1 - 2\text{j}$ and $z_4 = -4\text{j}$ on an Argand diagram.

**Solution** The Argand diagram is shown in Figure 9.2.

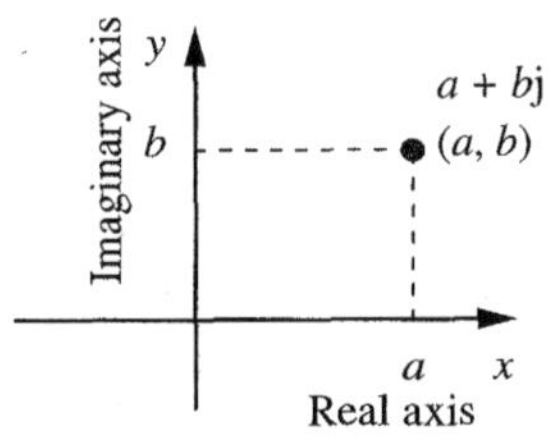


**Figure 9.1** Argand diagram.

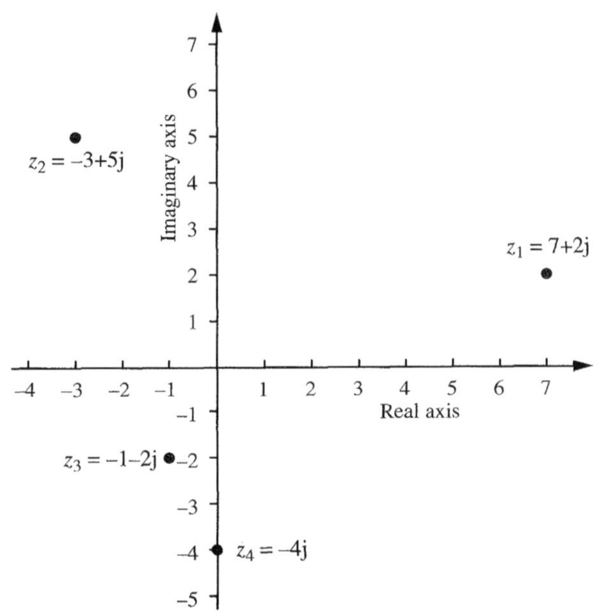


**Figure 9.2** Argand diagram for Example 9.10.

## Exercises 9.4

1 Plot the following complex numbers on an Argand diagram:
(a) $z_1 = -3 - 3j$ (b) $z_2 = 7 + 2j$
(c) $z_3 = 3$ (d) $z_4 = -0.5j$
(e) $z_5 = -2$

2 (a) Plot the complex number $z = 1 + j$ on an Argand diagram.
(b) Simplify the complex number $j(1 + j)$ and plot the result on your Argand diagram. Observe that the effect of multiplying the complex number by j is to rotate the complex number through an angle of $\pi/2$ radians anticlockwise about the origin.

## Solutions

1 See Figure S.12.

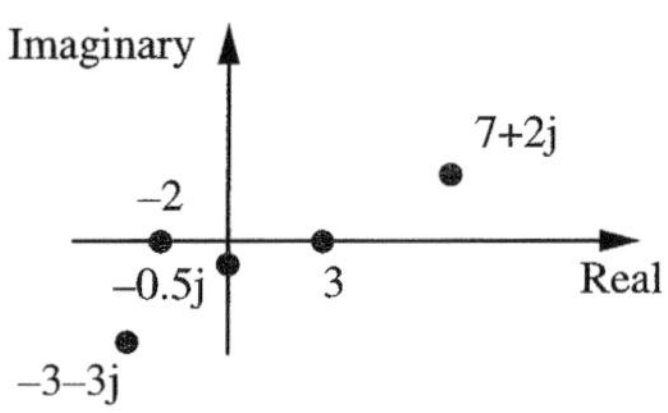


**Figure S.12**

2 (a) See Figure S.13. (b) $j(1 + j) = -1 + j$

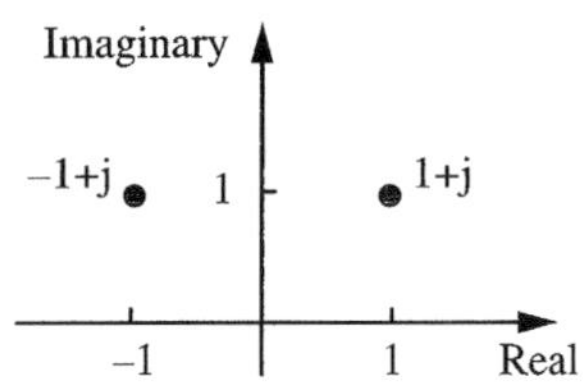


**Figure S.13**

# 9.5 Polar form of a complex number

It is often useful to exchange **Cartesian coordinates** $(a, b)$ for **polar coordinates** $r$ and $\theta$ as depicted in Figure 9.3.

From Figure 9.3 we note that

$$\cos\theta = \frac{a}{r} \qquad \sin\theta = \frac{b}{r}$$

and so,

$$a = r\cos\theta \qquad b = r\sin\theta$$

Furthermore,

$$\tan\theta = \frac{b}{a}$$

Using Pythagoras's theorem we obtain $r = \sqrt{a^2 + b^2}$. By finding $r$ and $\theta$ we can express the complex number $z = a + bj$ in **polar form** as

$$z = r\cos\theta + jr\sin\theta = r(\cos\theta + j\sin\theta)$$

which we often abbreviate to $z = r\angle\theta$. Clearly, $r$ is the 'distance' of the point $(a, b)$ from the origin and is called the **modulus** of the complex number $z$. The modulus is always a non-negative number and is denoted $|z|$. The angle is conventionally measured

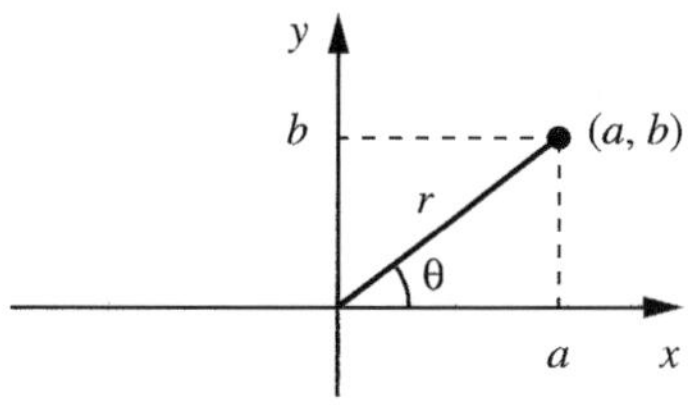


**Figure 9.3** Polar and Cartesian forms of a complex number.

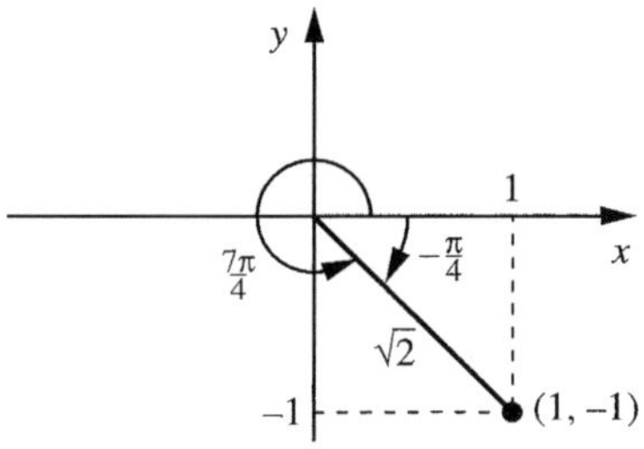


**Figure 9.4** Argand diagram depicting $z = 1 - \mathrm{j}$ in Example 9.11.

from the positive $x$ axis. Angles measured in an anticlockwise sense are regarded as positive while those measured in a clockwise sense are regarded as negative. The angle $\theta$ is called the **argument** of $z$, denoted $\arg(z)$. Since adding or subtracting multiples of $2\pi$ from $\theta$ will result in the 'arm' in Figure 9.3 being in the same position, the argument can have many values. Usually we shall choose $\theta$ to satisfy $-\pi < \theta \leqslant \pi$.

Cartesian form: $z = a + b\mathrm{j}$

Polar form: $z = r(\cos\theta + \mathrm{j}\sin\theta) = r\angle\theta$

$$|z| = r = \sqrt{a^2 + b^2}$$

$$a = r\cos\theta \qquad b = r\sin\theta \qquad \tan\theta = \frac{b}{a}$$

Note that

$$\begin{aligned} r\angle(-\theta) &= r(\cos(-\theta) + \mathrm{j}\sin(-\theta)) \\ &= r(\cos\theta - \mathrm{j}\sin\theta) \\ &= \bar{z} \end{aligned}$$

If $z = a + b\mathrm{j}$ then $\bar{z} = a - b\mathrm{j}$ and $\bar{z} = r\angle(-\theta)$.

**Example 9.11** Depict the complex number $z = 1 - \mathrm{j}$ on an Argand diagram and convert it into polar form.

**Solution** The real part of $z$ is 1 and the imaginary part is $-1$. We therefore plot a point in the $x$–$y$ plane with $x = 1$ and $y = -1$ as shown in Figure 9.4.

From Figure 9.4 we see that $r = \sqrt{1^2 + (-1)^2} = \sqrt{2}$ and $\theta = -45°$ or $-\pi/4$ radians. Therefore $z = 1 - \mathrm{j} = \sqrt{2}\angle(-\pi/4)$.

---

To express a complex number in polar form it is essential to draw an Argand diagram and not simply quote formulae, as the following example will show.

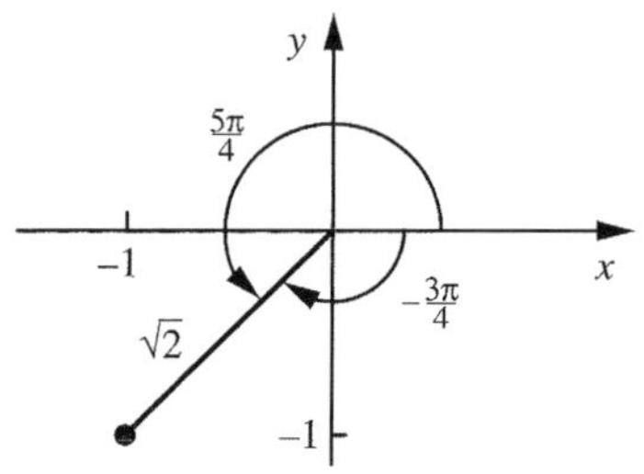


**Figure 9.5** Argand diagram depicting $z = -1 - \mathrm{j}$ in Example 9.12.

**Example 9.12** Express $z = -1 - \mathrm{j}$ in polar form.

**Solution** If we use the formula $|z| = r = \sqrt{a^2 + b^2}$, we find that $r = \sqrt{2}$. Using $\tan\theta = b/a$, we find that $\tan\theta = -1/-1 = 1$ so that you may be tempted to take $\theta = \pi/4$. Figure 9.5 shows the Argand diagram and it is clear that $\theta = -3\pi/4$. Therefore, $z = -1 - \mathrm{j} = \sqrt{2}\angle -3\pi/4$, and we see the importance of drawing an Argand diagram.

---

### 9.5.1 Multiplication and division in polar form

The polar form may seem more complicated than the Cartesian form but it is often more useful. For example, suppose we want to multiply the complex numbers

$$z_1 = r_1(\cos\theta_1 + \mathrm{j}\sin\theta_1) \qquad \text{and} \qquad z_2 = r_2(\cos\theta_2 + \mathrm{j}\sin\theta_2)$$

We find

$$\begin{aligned} z_1 z_2 &= r_1(\cos\theta_1 + \mathrm{j}\sin\theta_1)r_2(\cos\theta_2 + \mathrm{j}\sin\theta_2) \\ &= r_1 r_2\{(\cos\theta_1\cos\theta_2 - \sin\theta_1\sin\theta_2) + \mathrm{j}(\sin\theta_1\cos\theta_2 + \sin\theta_2\cos\theta_1)\} \end{aligned}$$

which can be written as

$$r_1 r_2\{\cos(\theta_1 + \theta_2) + \mathrm{j}\sin(\theta_1 + \theta_2)\}$$

using the trigonometric identities of Section 3.5. This is a new complex number which, if we compare with the general form $r(\cos\theta + \mathrm{j}\sin\theta)$, we see has a modulus of $r_1 r_2$ and an argument of $\theta_1 + \theta_2$. To summarize: to multiply two complex numbers we multiply their moduli and add their arguments, that is

$$z_1 z_2 = r_1 r_2\angle(\theta_1 + \theta_2)$$

**Example 9.13** If $z_1 = 3\angle\pi/3$ and $z_2 = 4\angle\pi/6$ find $z_1 z_2$.

**Solution** Multiplying the moduli we find $r_1 r_2 = 12$, and adding the arguments we find $\theta_1 + \theta_2 = \pi/2$. Therefore $z_1 z_2 = 12\angle\pi/2$.

---

A similar development shows that to divide two complex numbers we divide their moduli and subtract their arguments, that is

$$\frac{z_1}{z_2} = \frac{r_1}{r_2}\angle(\theta_1 - \theta_2)$$

**Example 9.14** If $z_1 = 3\angle\pi/3$ and $z_2 = 4\angle\pi/6$ find $z_1/z_2$.

**Solution** Dividing the respective moduli, we find $r_1/r_2 = 3/4$ and subtracting the arguments, $\pi/3 - \pi/6 = \pi/6$. Hence $z_1/z_2 = 0.75\angle\pi/6$.

## Exercises 9.5

1. Mark on an Argand diagram points representing $z_1 = 3 - 2\text{j}$, $z_2 = -\text{j}$, $z_3 = \text{j}^2$, $z_4 = -2 - 4\text{j}$ and $z_5 = 3$. Find the modulus and argument of each complex number.

2. Express the following complex numbers in polar form:

   (a) $3 - \text{j}$

   (b) $2$

   (c) $-\text{j}$

   (d) $-5 + 12\text{j}$

3. Find the modulus and argument of (a) $z_1 = -\sqrt{3} + \text{j}$ and (b) $z_2 = 4 + 4\text{j}$. Hence express $z_1 z_2$ and $z_1/z_2$ in polar form.

4. Express $\sqrt{2}\angle\pi/4$, $2\angle\pi/6$ and $2\angle - \pi/6$ in Cartesian form $a + b\text{j}$.

5. Prove the result $\dfrac{z_1}{z_2} = \dfrac{r_1}{r_2}\angle\theta_1 - \theta_2$.

6. Express $z = \dfrac{1}{\text{j}\omega C}$, where $\omega$ and $C$ are real constants, in the form $a + b\text{j}$. Plot $z$ on an Argand diagram.

7. If $z_1 = 4(\cos 40° + \text{j}\sin 40°)$ and $z_2 = 3(\cos 70° + \text{j}\sin 70°)$, express $z_1 z_2$ and $z_1/z_2$ in polar form.

8. Simplify

$$\frac{(\sqrt{2}\angle(5\pi/4))^2(2\angle(-\pi/3))^2}{2\angle(-\pi/6)}$$

### Solutions

1. $|z_1| = \sqrt{13}$, $\arg(z_1) = -0.5880$
   $|z_2| = 1$, $\arg(z_2) = -\pi/2$
   $|z_3| = 1$, $\arg(z_3) = \pi$
   $|z_4| = \sqrt{20}$, $\arg(z_4) = -2.0344$
   $|z_5| = 3$, $\arg(z_5) = 0$

2. (a) $\sqrt{10}\angle - 0.3218$

   (b) $2\angle 0$

   (c) $1\angle - \pi/2$

   (d) $13\angle 1.9656$

3. (a) $2, 5\pi/6$

   (b) $4\sqrt{2}, \pi/4$

   $z_1 z_2 = 8\sqrt{2}\angle 13\pi/12$

   $z_1/z_2 = \dfrac{\sqrt{2}}{4}\angle 7\pi/12$

4. $1 + \text{j}$, $\sqrt{3} + \text{j}$, $\sqrt{3} - \text{j}$

6. $-\dfrac{\text{j}}{\omega C}$

7. $z_1 z_2 = 12(\cos 110° + \text{j}\sin 110°)$

   $z_1/z_2 = \frac{4}{3}(\cos 30° - \text{j}\sin 30°)$

8. 4

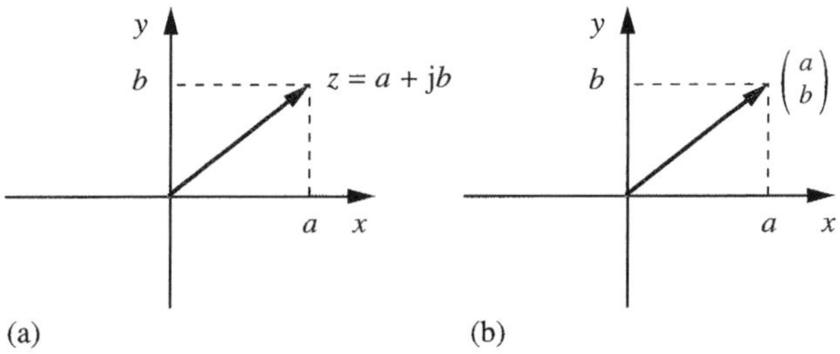


**Figure 9.6** The complex number $z = a + jb$ and its equivalent vector.

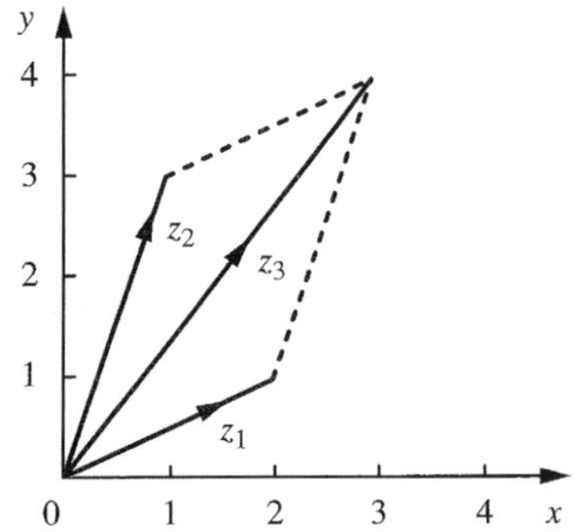


**Figure 9.7** Vector addition in the complex plane.

## 9.6 Vectors and complex numbers

It is often convenient to represent complex numbers by vectors in the $x$–$y$ plane. Figure 9.6(a) shows the complex number $z = a + jb$. Figure 9.6(b) shows the equivalent vector. Figure 9.7 shows the complex numbers $z_1 = 2 + \mathrm{j}$ and $z_2 = 1 + 3\mathrm{j}$.

If we now evaluate $z_3 = z_1 + z_2$ we find $z_3 = 3 + 4\mathrm{j}$ which is also shown. If we form a parallelogram, two sides of which are the representations of $z_1$ and $z_2$, we find that $z_3$ is the diagonal of the parallelogram. If we regard $z_1$ and $z_2$ as vectors in the plane we see that there is a direct analogy between the triangle law of vector addition (see Section 7.2.3) and the addition of complex numbers.

More generally, if $z_1$ and $z_2$ are any complex numbers represented on an Argand diagram by the vectors $\vec{\boldsymbol{OA}}$ and $\vec{\boldsymbol{OB}}$ (Figure 9.8) then upon completing the parallelogram OBCA, the sum $z_1 + z_2$ is represented by the vector $\vec{\boldsymbol{OC}}$. We can also obtain a representation of the difference of two complex numbers in the following way. If we write

$$
\begin{aligned}
z_3 &= z_1 - z_2 \\
&= z_1 + (-z_2)
\end{aligned}
$$

and note that if $z_2$ is represented by the vector $\vec{\boldsymbol{OB}}$, then $-z_2$ is represented by the vector $-\vec{\boldsymbol{OB}} = \vec{\boldsymbol{BO}} = \vec{\boldsymbol{CA}}$. The complex number $z_1$ is represented by $\vec{\boldsymbol{OA}} = \vec{\boldsymbol{BC}}$, so that $z_1 + (-z_2) = \vec{\boldsymbol{BC}} + \vec{\boldsymbol{CA}} = \vec{\boldsymbol{BA}}$. Thus the difference $z_1 - z_2$ is represented by the diagonal BA. To summarize, the sum and difference of $z_1$ and $z_2$ are represented by the two diagonals of the parallelogram OBCA.

**Example 9.15** Represent $z_1 = 6 + \mathrm{j}$ and $z_2 = 3 + 4\mathrm{j}$, and their sum and difference, on an Argand diagram.

**Solution** We draw vectors $\vec{\boldsymbol{OA}}$ and $\vec{\boldsymbol{OB}}$ representing $z_1$ and $z_2$, respectively (Figure 9.9). Then we complete the parallelogram OACB as shown. The sum $z_1 + z_2$ is then represented by

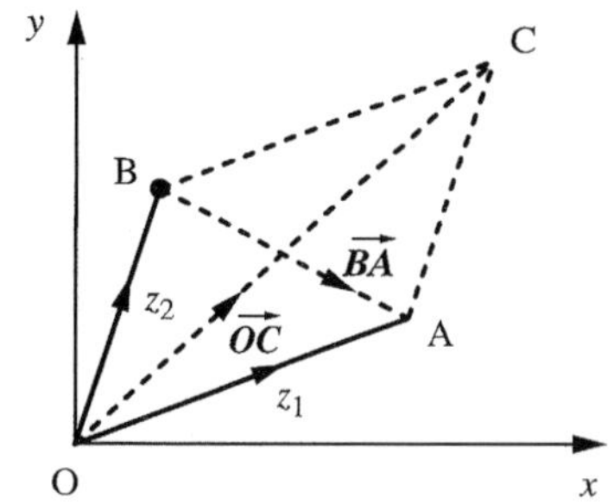


**Figure 9.8** Vector addition and subtraction.

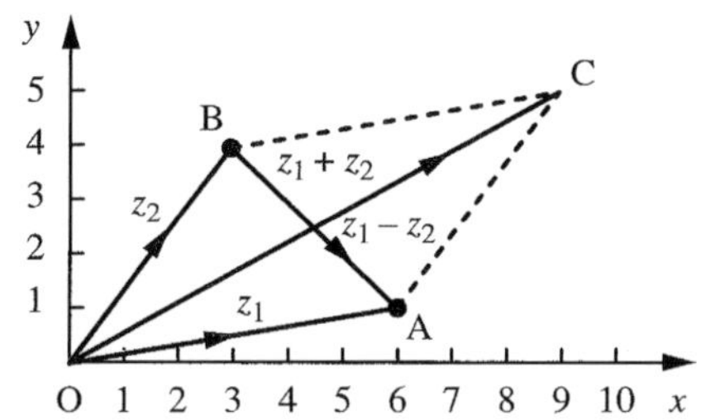


**Figure 9.9** Diagram for Example 9.15.

$\vec{OC}$ and the difference $z_1 - z_2$ by $\vec{BA}$. It is easy to see that the vector $\vec{BA} = \begin{pmatrix} 3 \\ -3 \end{pmatrix}$, that is it represents the complex number $3 - 3\mathrm{j}$, while $\vec{OC} = \begin{pmatrix} 9 \\ 5 \end{pmatrix}$, that is it represents $9 + 5\mathrm{j}$, so that $z_1 + z_2 = 9 + 5\mathrm{j}$ and $z_1 - z_2 = 3 - 3\mathrm{j}$.

---

## 9.7 The exponential form of a complex number

You will recall from Chapter 6 that many functions possess a power series expansion, that is the function can be expressed as the sum of a sequence of terms involving integer powers of $x$. For example,

$$\mathrm{e}^x = 1 + x + \frac{x^2}{2!} + \frac{x^3}{3!} + \cdots$$

and this representation is valid for any real value of $x$. The expression on the r.h.s. is, of course, an infinite sum but its terms get smaller and smaller, and as more are included, the sum we obtain approaches $\mathrm{e}^x$. Other examples of power series include

$$\sin x = x - \frac{x^3}{3!} + \frac{x^5}{5!} - \cdots \qquad (9.3)$$

and

$$\cos x = 1 - \frac{x^2}{2!} + \frac{x^4}{4!} - \cdots \qquad (9.4)$$

which are also valid for any real value of $x$. It is useful to extend the range of applicability of these power series by allowing $x$ to be a complex number. That is, we define the function $\mathrm{e}^z$ to be

$$\mathrm{e}^z = 1 + z + \frac{z^2}{2!} + \frac{z^3}{3!} + \cdots$$

and theory beyond the scope of this book can be used to show that this representation is valid for all complex numbers $z$.

We have already seen that we can express a complex number in polar form:

$$z = r(\cos\theta + \mathrm{j}\sin\theta)$$

Using Equations (9.3) and (9.4) we can write

$$\begin{aligned} z &= r\left\{\left(1 - \frac{\theta^2}{2!} + \frac{\theta^4}{4!} - \cdots\right) + \mathrm{j}\left(\theta - \frac{\theta^3}{3!} + \frac{\theta^5}{5!} - \cdots\right)\right\} \\ &= r\left(1 + \mathrm{j}\theta - \frac{\theta^2}{2!} - \mathrm{j}\frac{\theta^3}{3!} + \frac{\theta^4}{4!} + \mathrm{j}\frac{\theta^5}{5!} \cdots\right) \end{aligned}$$

Furthermore, we note that $\mathrm{e}^{\mathrm{j}\theta}$ can be written as

$$\begin{aligned} \mathrm{e}^{\mathrm{j}\theta} &= 1 + \mathrm{j}\theta + \frac{\mathrm{j}^2\theta^2}{2!} + \frac{\mathrm{j}^3\theta^3}{3!} + \cdots \\ &= 1 + \mathrm{j}\theta - \frac{\theta^2}{2!} - \mathrm{j}\frac{\theta^3}{3!} + \cdots \end{aligned}$$

so that

$$z = r(\cos\theta + \mathrm{j}\sin\theta) = r\mathrm{e}^{\mathrm{j}\theta}$$

This is yet another form of the same complex number which we call the **exponential form**. We see that

$$\mathrm{e}^{\mathrm{j}\theta} = \cos\theta + \mathrm{j}\sin\theta \tag{9.5}$$

It is straightforward to show that

$$\mathrm{e}^{-\mathrm{j}\theta} = \cos\theta - \mathrm{j}\sin\theta$$

Therefore, if $\bar{z} = r(\cos\theta - \mathrm{j}\sin\theta)$ we can equivalently write $\bar{z} = r\mathrm{e}^{-\mathrm{j}\theta}$. The two expressions for $\mathrm{e}^{\mathrm{j}\theta}$ and $\mathrm{e}^{-\mathrm{j}\theta}$ are known as Euler's relations. From these it is easy to obtain the following useful results:

$$\cos\theta = \frac{\mathrm{e}^{\mathrm{j}\theta} + \mathrm{e}^{-\mathrm{j}\theta}}{2} \qquad \sin\theta = \frac{\mathrm{e}^{\mathrm{j}\theta} - \mathrm{e}^{-\mathrm{j}\theta}}{2\mathrm{j}}$$

**Example 9.16**

We saw in Section 3.6 that a waveform can be written in the form $f(t) = A\cos(\omega t + \phi)$. Consider the complex number $\mathrm{e}^{\mathrm{j}(\omega t+\phi)}$. We can use Euler's relations to write

$$\mathrm{e}^{\mathrm{j}(\omega t+\phi)} = \cos(\omega t + \phi) + \mathrm{j}\sin(\omega t + \phi)$$

and hence,

$$f(t) = A\,\mathrm{Re}(\mathrm{e}^{\mathrm{j}(\omega t+\phi)})$$

## Exercises 9.7

1 Find the modulus and argument of
(a) $3e^{j\pi/4}$ (b) $2e^{-j\pi/6}$ (c) $7e^{j\pi/3}$

2 Find the real and imaginary parts of
(a) $5e^{j\pi/3}$ (b) $e^{j2\pi/3}$
(c) $11e^{j\pi}$ (d) $2e^{-j\pi}$

3 Express $z = 6(\cos 30^\circ + j \sin 30^\circ)$ in exponential form. Plot $z$ on an Argand diagram and find its real and imaginary parts.

4 If $\sigma, \omega, T \in \mathbb{R}$, find the real and imaginary parts of $e^{(\sigma + j\omega)T}$.

5 Express $z = e^{1+j\pi/2}$ in the form $a + bj$.

6 Express $-1 - j$ in the form $re^{j\theta}$.

7 Express
(a) $7 + 5j$ and
(b) $\frac{1}{2} - \frac{1}{3}j$ in exponential form.

8 Express $z_1 = 1 - j$ and

$$z_2 = \frac{1+j}{\sqrt{3} - j}$$ in the form $re^{j\theta}$.

### Solutions

1 (a) $3, \pi/4$ (b) $2, -\pi/6$ (c) $7, \pi/3$

2 (a) $2.5, 4.3301$ (b) $-0.5, 0.8660$
(c) $-11, 0$ (d) $-2, 0$

3 $6e^{(\pi/6)j}$, $\text{Re}(z) = 5.1962$, $\text{Im}(z) = 3$

4 Real part: $e^{\sigma T} \cos \omega T$, imaginary part: $e^{\sigma T} \sin \omega T$

5 $ej$

6 $\sqrt{2}e^{(-3\pi/4)j}$

7 (a) $\sqrt{74}e^{0.62j}$ (b) $0.60\, e^{-0.59j}$

8 $\sqrt{2}e^{(-\pi/4)j}$, $\frac{1}{\sqrt{2}}e^{(5\pi/12)j}$

## 9.8 Phasors

Electrical engineers are often interested in analysing circuits in which there is an a.c. power supply. Almost invariably the supply waveform is sinusoidal and the resulting currents and voltages within the circuit are also sinusoidal. For example, a typical voltage is of the form

$$v(t) = V \cos(\omega t + \phi) = V \cos(2\pi f t + \phi) \tag{9.6}$$

where $V$ is the maximum or peak value, $\omega$ is the angular frequency, $f$ is the frequency, and $\phi$ is the phase relative to some reference waveform. This is known as the **time domain representation**. Each of the voltages and currents in the circuit has the same frequency as the supply but differs in magnitude and phase.

In order to analyse such circuits it is necessary to add, subtract, multiply and divide these waveforms. If the time domain representation is used then the mathematics becomes extremely tedious. An alternative approach is to introduce a waveform representation known as a **phasor**. A phasor is an entity consisting of two distinct parts: a magnitude and an angle. It is possible to represent a phasor by a complex number in polar form. The fixed magnitude of this complex number corresponds to the magnitude of the phasor and hence the amplitude of the waveform. The argument of this complex number, $\phi$, corresponds to the angle of the phasor and hence the phase angle of the waveform. Figure 9.10 shows a phasor for the sinusoidal waveform of Equation (9.6).

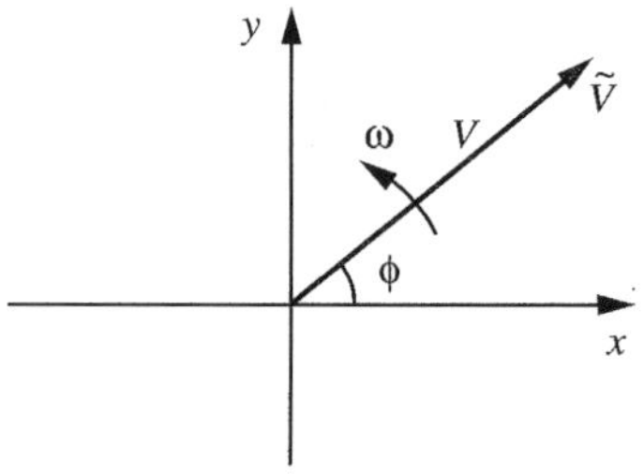


**Figure 9.10**
Illustration of the phasor $\tilde{V} = V\angle\phi$ where $\omega$ = angular frequency with which the phasor rotates.

The time dependency of the waveform is catered for by rotating the phasor anti-clockwise at an angular frequency, $\omega$. The projection of the phasor onto the real axis gives the instantaneous value of the waveform. However, the main interest of an engineer is in the phase relationships between the various sinusoids. Therefore the phasors are 'frozen' at a certain point in time. This may be chosen so that $t = 0$ or it may be chosen so that a convenient phasor, known as the **reference phasor**, aligns with the positive real axis. This approach is valid because the phase and magnitude relationships between the various phasors remain the same at all points in time once a circuit has recovered from any initial transients caused by switching.

Some textbooks refer to phasors as vectors. This can lead to confusion as it is possible to divide phasors whereas division of vectors by other vectors is not defined. In practice this is not a problem as phasors, although thought of as vectors, are manipulated as complex numbers, which can be divided. We will avoid these conceptual difficulties by introducing a different notation. We will denote a phasor by $\tilde{V}$, which corresponds to $V\angle\phi$ in complex number notation (see Figure 9.10). Thus, for example, a current $i(t) = I\cos(\omega t + \phi)$ would be written $\tilde{I}$ in phasor notation and $I\angle\phi$ in complex number notation.

Many engineers use the **root mean square** (r.m.s.) value of a sinusoid as the magnitude of a phasor. The justification for this is that it represents the value of a d.c. signal that would dissipate the same amount of power in a resistor as the sinusoid. For example, in the case of a current signal, $I_{\text{rms}}^2 R$ is the average power dissipated by the sinusoid $I\cos(\omega t + \phi)$ in a resistor $R$. For the case of a sinusoidal signal the r.m.s. value of the signal is $1/\sqrt{2}$ times the peak value of the signal (see Section 15.3, Example 15.6, for a proof of this). We will not adopt this approach but it is a common one.

We start by examining the phasor representation of individual circuit elements. In order to do this we need a phasor form of Ohm's law. This is

$$\tilde{V} = \tilde{I}Z \qquad (9.7)$$

where $\tilde{V}$ is the voltage phasor, $\tilde{I}$ is the current phasor and $Z$ is the impedance of an element or group of elements and may be a complex quantity. Note that phasors and complex numbers are mixed together in the same equation. This is a common practice because phasors are usually manipulated as complex numbers.

## 9.8.1 Resistor

Experimentally it can be shown that if an a.c. voltage is applied to a resistor then the current is in phase with the voltage. The ratio of the magnitude of the two waveforms is equal to the resistance, $R$. So, given $\tilde{I} = I\angle 0$, $Z = R\angle 0$, using Equation (9.7) we have $\tilde{V} = IR\angle 0$. This is illustrated in Figure 9.11.

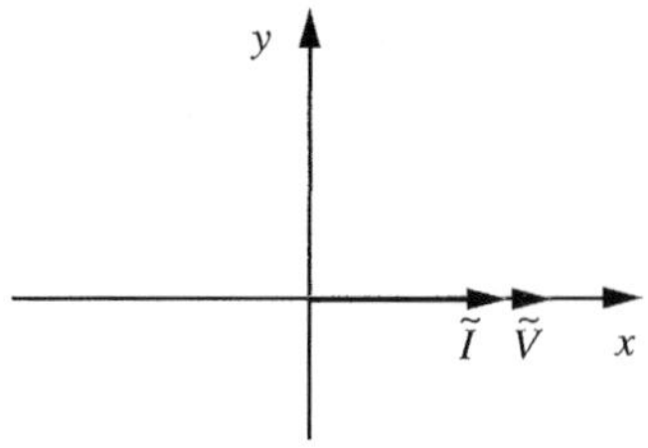


**Figure 9.11** Phasor diagram for a resistor.

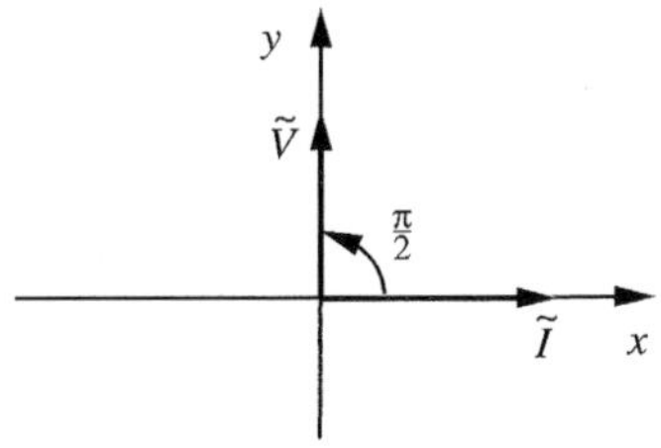


**Figure 9.12** Phasor diagram for an inductor.

### 9.8.2 Inductor

For an inductor we know from experiment that the voltage leads the current by a phase of $\pi/2$, and so the phase angle of the impedance is $\pi/2$. We also know that the magnitude of the impedance is given by $\omega L$. So, given $\tilde{I} = I\angle 0$, $Z = \omega L\angle\pi/2$, using Equation (9.7) we have $\tilde{V} = I\omega L\angle\pi/2$. An alternative way of representing $Z$ for an inductor is to use the Cartesian form, that is

$$\begin{aligned} Z = \omega L e^{j\pi/2} &= \omega L\left(\cos\frac{\pi}{2} + j\sin\frac{\pi}{2}\right) \\ &= j\omega L \end{aligned}$$

This is useful when phasors need to be added and subtracted. The phasor diagram for an inductor is illustrated in Figure 9.12.

### 9.8.3 Capacitor

For a capacitor it is known that the voltage lags the current by a phase of $\pi/2$ and the magnitude of the impedance is given by $\dfrac{1}{\omega C}$. So given $\tilde{I} = I\angle 0$, $Z = \dfrac{1}{\omega C}\angle -\pi/2$, we have, using Equation (9.7), $\tilde{V} = \dfrac{I}{\omega C}\angle -\pi/2$. Alternatively,

$$\begin{aligned} Z = \frac{e^{-j\pi/2}}{\omega C} &= \frac{1}{\omega C}\left(\cos\frac{\pi}{2} - j\sin\frac{\pi}{2}\right) \\ &= -\frac{j}{\omega C} \end{aligned}$$

Engineers often prefer to rewrite this last expression as

$$\frac{1}{j\omega C}$$

The phasor diagram for the capacitor is illustrated in Figure 9.13.

We have shown how phasors can be multiplied by a complex number; division is very similar. Addition of phasors will now be illustrated; subtraction is similar. Consider the circuit shown in Figure 9.14 in which a resistor, capacitor and inductor are connected in series and fed by an a.c. source. As this is a series circuit, the current through each element, $\tilde{I}$, is the same by Kirchhoff's current law. By Kirchhoff's voltage law the voltage rise produced by the supply, $\tilde{V}_S$, must equal the sum of the voltage drops across the elements. Therefore,

$$\tilde{V}_S = \tilde{V}_R + \tilde{V}_C + \tilde{V}_L$$

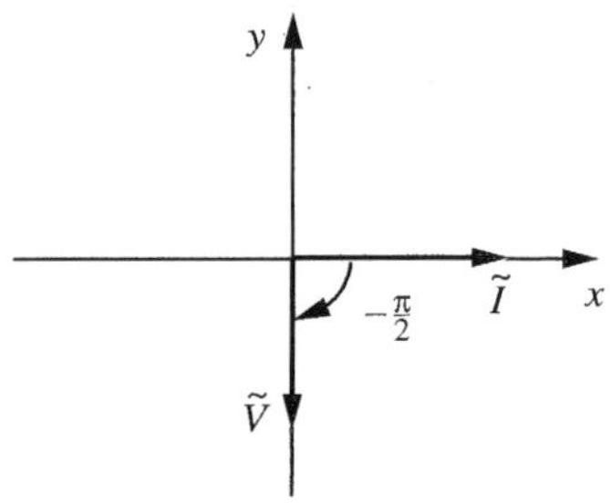


**Figure 9.13** Phasor diagram for a capacitor.

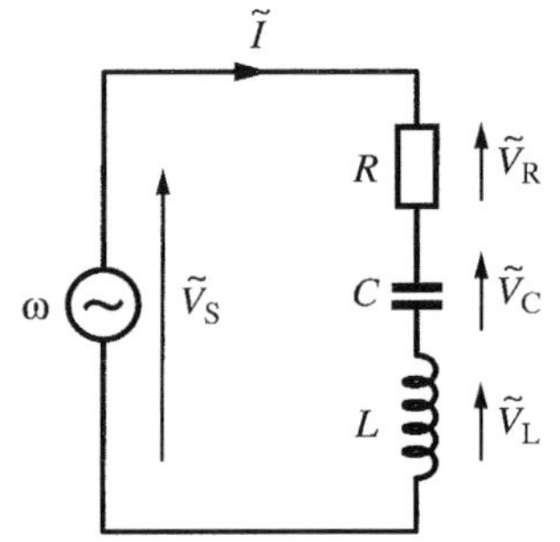


**Figure 9.14** *RLC* circuit.

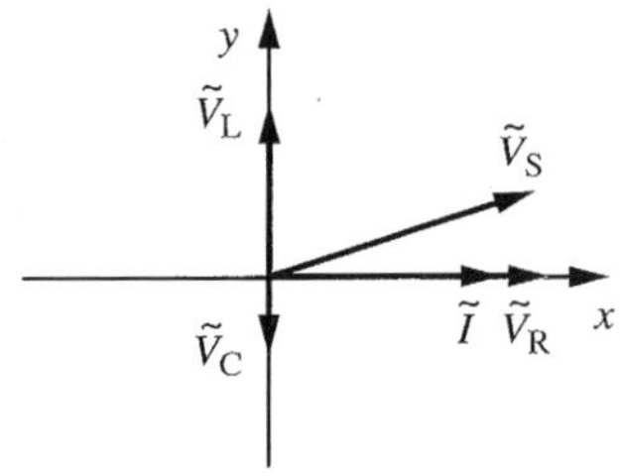


**Figure 9.15** Phasor diagram for the circuit in Figure 9.14.

Note that this is an addition of phasors so that the voltage drops across the elements do not necessarily have the same phase. The phasor diagram for the circuit is shown in Figure 9.15, in this case with $|\tilde{V}_L| > |\tilde{V}_C|$; $\tilde{I}$ is the reference phasor.

Note that the phasor addition of the element voltages gives the overall supply voltage for a particular supply current. If the magnitude of these element voltage phasors is known then it is possible to calculate the supply voltage graphically. In practice it is easier to convert the polar form of the phasors into Cartesian form and use algebra to analyse the circuit.

Now,

$$\tilde{V}_R = \tilde{I}R\angle 0 = \tilde{I}R$$
$$\tilde{V}_L = \tilde{I}\omega L\angle \pi/2 = \tilde{I}\mathrm{j}\omega L$$
$$\tilde{V}_C = \frac{\tilde{I}}{\omega C}\angle -\pi/2 = \frac{\tilde{I}}{\mathrm{j}\omega C}$$

Therefore,

$$\begin{aligned}\tilde{V}_S &= \tilde{V}_R + \tilde{V}_C + \tilde{V}_L \\ &= \tilde{I}R + \tilde{I}\mathrm{j}\omega L + \frac{\tilde{I}}{\mathrm{j}\omega C} \\ &= \tilde{I}\left(R + \mathrm{j}\omega L + \frac{1}{\mathrm{j}\omega C}\right)\end{aligned}$$

Therefore the impedance of the circuit is $Z = R + \mathrm{j}\omega L + \dfrac{1}{\mathrm{j}\omega C}$. We can calculate the frequency for which the impedance of the circuit has minimum magnitude:

$$\begin{aligned}Z &= R + \mathrm{j}\omega L + \frac{1}{\mathrm{j}\omega C} \\ &= R + \mathrm{j}\omega L - \frac{\mathrm{j}}{\omega C} \\ &= R + \mathrm{j}\left(\omega L - \frac{1}{\omega C}\right)\end{aligned}$$

Now

$$|Z| = \sqrt{R^2 + \left(\omega L - \frac{1}{\omega C}\right)^2}$$

and so, as $\omega$ varies $|Z|$ is a minimum when

$$\omega L - \frac{1}{\omega C} = 0$$
$$\omega^2 = \frac{1}{LC}$$
$$\omega = \sqrt{\frac{1}{LC}}$$

This minimum value is $|Z| = R$. Examining Figure 9.15 it is clear that the minimum impedance occurs when $\tilde{V}_\mathrm{L}$ and $\tilde{V}_\mathrm{C}$ have the same magnitude, in which case $\tilde{V}_\mathrm{S}$ has no imaginary component. The frequency at which this occurs is known as the **resonant frequency** of the circuit.

## 9.9 De Moivre's theorem

A very important result in complex number theory is De Moivre's theorem which states that if $n \in \mathbb{N}$,

$$(\cos\theta + \mathrm{j}\sin\theta)^n = \cos n\theta + \mathrm{j}\sin n\theta \qquad (9.8)$$

**Example 9.17** Verify De Moivre's theorem when $n = 1$ and $n = 2$.

**Solution** When $n = 1$, the theorem states:

$$(\cos\theta + \mathrm{j}\sin\theta)^1 = \cos 1\theta + \mathrm{j}\sin 1\theta$$

which is clearly true, and the theorem holds. When $n = 2$, we find

$$\begin{aligned}(\cos\theta + \mathrm{j}\sin\theta)^2 &= (\cos\theta + \mathrm{j}\sin\theta)(\cos\theta + \mathrm{j}\sin\theta)\\ &= \cos^2\theta + \mathrm{j}\sin\theta\cos\theta + \mathrm{j}\cos\theta\sin\theta + \mathrm{j}^2\sin^2\theta\\ &= \cos^2\theta - \sin^2\theta + \mathrm{j}(2\sin\theta\cos\theta)\end{aligned}$$

Recalling the trigonometric identities $\cos 2\theta = \cos^2\theta - \sin^2\theta$ and $\sin 2\theta = 2\sin\theta\cos\theta$, we can write the previous expression as

$$\cos 2\theta + \mathrm{j}\sin 2\theta$$

Therefore,

$$(\cos\theta + \mathrm{j}\sin\theta)^2 = \cos 2\theta + \mathrm{j}\sin 2\theta$$

and De Moivre's theorem has been verified when $n = 2$.

The theorem also holds when $n$ is a rational number, that is $n = p/q$ where $p$ and $q$ are integers. Thus we have

$$(\cos\theta + \mathrm{j}\sin\theta)^{p/q} = \cos\frac{p}{q}\theta + \mathrm{j}\sin\frac{p}{q}\theta$$

In this form it can be used to obtain roots of complex numbers. For example,

$$\sqrt[3]{\cos\theta + \mathrm{j}\sin\theta} = (\cos\theta + \mathrm{j}\sin\theta)^{1/3} = \cos\frac{1}{3}\theta + \mathrm{j}\sin\frac{1}{3}\theta$$

In such a case the expression obtained is only one of the possible roots. Additional roots can be found as illustrated in Example 9.18.

De Moivre's theorem is particularly important for the solution of certain types of equation.

**Example 9.18** Find all complex numbers $z$ which satisfy

$$z^3 = 1 \tag{9.9}$$

**Solution** The solution of this equation is equivalent to finding the solutions of $z = 1^{1/3}$; that is, finding the cube roots of 1. Since we are allowing $z$ to be complex, that is $z \in \mathbb{C}$, we can write

$$z = r(\cos\theta + \mathrm{j}\sin\theta)$$

Then, using De Moivre's theorem,

$$\begin{aligned} z^3 &= r^3(\cos\theta + \mathrm{j}\sin\theta)^3 \\ &= r^3(\cos 3\theta + \mathrm{j}\sin 3\theta) \end{aligned}$$

We next convert the expression on the r.h.s. of Equation (9.9) into polar form. Figure 9.16 shows the number $1 = 1 + 0\mathrm{j}$ on an Argand diagram.

From the Argand diagram we see that its modulus is 1 and its argument is 0, or possibly $\pm 2\pi, \pm 4\pi, \ldots$, that is $2n\pi$ where $n \in \mathbb{Z}$. Consequently, we can write

$$1 = 1(\cos 2n\pi + \mathrm{j}\sin 2n\pi) \qquad n \in \mathbb{Z}$$

Using the polar form, Equation (9.9) becomes

$$r^3(\cos 3\theta + \mathrm{j}\sin 3\theta) = 1(\cos 2n\pi + \mathrm{j}\sin 2n\pi)$$

Comparing both sides of this equation we see that

$$r^3 = 1 \qquad \text{that is} \qquad r = 1 \text{ since } r \in \mathbb{R}$$

and

$$3\theta = 2n\pi \qquad \text{that is} \qquad \theta = 2n\pi/3 \qquad n \in \mathbb{Z}$$

Apparently $\theta$ can take infinitely many values, but, as we shall see, the corresponding complex numbers are simply repetitions. When $n = 0$, we find $\theta = 0$, so that

$$z = z_1 = 1(\cos 0 + \mathrm{j}\sin 0) = 1$$

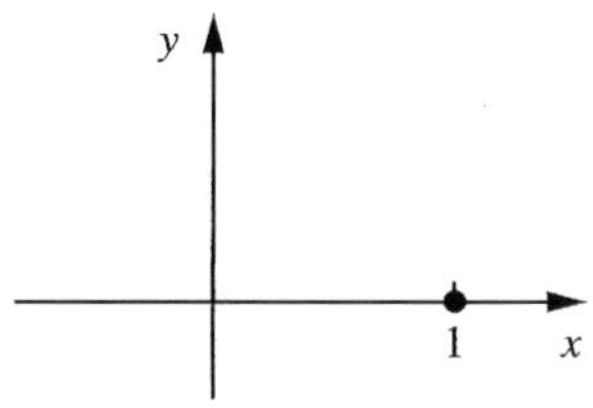


**Figure 9.16** The complex number $z = 1 + 0\mathrm{j}$.

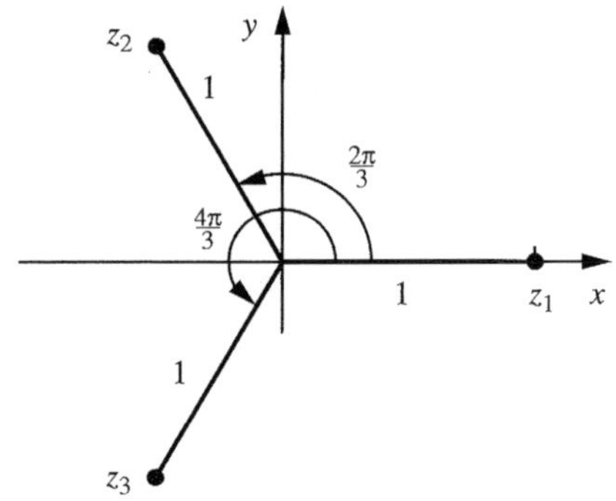


**Figure 9.17** Solutions of $z^3 = 1$.

is the first solution. When $n = 1$ we find $\theta = 2\pi/3$, so that

$$z = z_2 = 1\left(\cos\frac{2\pi}{3} + \mathrm{j}\sin\frac{2\pi}{3}\right) = -\frac{1}{2} + \mathrm{j}\frac{\sqrt{3}}{2}$$

is the second solution. When $n = 2$ we find $\theta = 4\pi/3$, so that

$$z = z_3 = 1\left(\cos\frac{4\pi}{3} + \mathrm{j}\sin\frac{4\pi}{3}\right) = -\frac{1}{2} - \mathrm{j}\frac{\sqrt{3}}{2}$$

is the third solution. If we continue searching for solutions using larger values of $n$ we find that we only repeat solutions already obtained. It is often useful to plot solutions on an Argand diagram and this is easily done directly from the polar form, as shown in Figure 9.17. We note that the solutions are equally spaced at angles of $2\pi/3$.

**Example 9.19** Find the complex numbers $z$ which satisfy $z^2 = 4\mathrm{j}$.

**Solution** Since $z \in \mathbb{C}$ we write $z = r(\cos\theta + \mathrm{j}\sin\theta)$. Therefore,

$$\begin{aligned} z^2 &= r^2(\cos\theta + \mathrm{j}\sin\theta)^2 \\ &= r^2(\cos 2\theta + \mathrm{j}\sin 2\theta) \end{aligned}$$

by De Moivre's theorem. Furthermore, 4j has modulus 4 and argument $\pi/2 + 2n\pi$, $n \in \mathbb{Z}$, that is

$$4\mathrm{j} = 4\{\cos(\pi/2 + 2n\pi) + \mathrm{j}\sin(\pi/2 + 2n\pi)\} \qquad n \in \mathbb{Z}$$

Therefore,

$$r^2(\cos 2\theta + \mathrm{j}\sin 2\theta) = 4\{\cos(\pi/2 + 2n\pi) + \mathrm{j}\sin(\pi/2 + 2n\pi)\}$$

Comparing both sides of this equation, we see that

$$r^2 = 4 \qquad \text{and so} \qquad r = 2$$

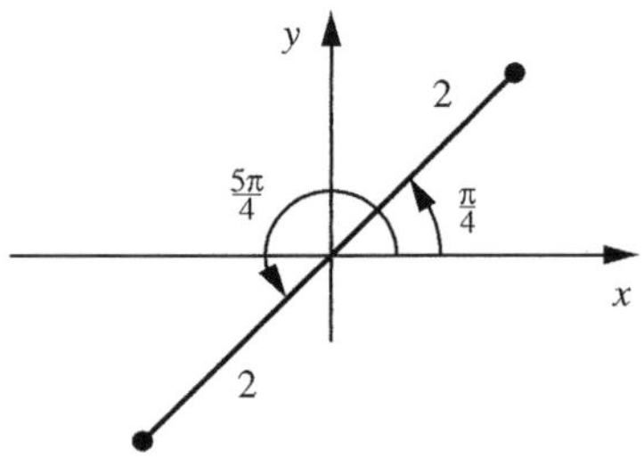


**Figure 9.18**
Solution of $z^2 = 4\text{j}$.

and

$$2\theta = \pi/2 + 2n\pi \qquad \text{and so} \qquad \theta = \pi/4 + n\pi$$

When $n = 0$ we find $\theta = \pi/4$, and when $n = 1$ we find $\theta = 5\pi/4$. Using larger values of $n$ simply repeats solutions already obtained. These solutions are shown in Figure 9.18. We note that in this example the solutions are equally spaced at intervals of $2\pi/2 = \pi$. In Cartesian form,

$$z_1 = \frac{2}{\sqrt{2}} + \text{j}\frac{2}{\sqrt{2}} = \sqrt{2}(1 + \text{j}) \qquad \text{and} \qquad z_2 = -\frac{2}{\sqrt{2}} - \text{j}\frac{2}{\sqrt{2}} = -\sqrt{2}(1 + \text{j})$$

---

In general, the $n$ roots of $z^n = a + \text{j}b$ are equally spaced at angles $2\pi/n$.

Once the technique for solving equations like those in Examples 9.18 and 9.19 has been mastered, engineers find it simpler to work with the abbreviated form $r\angle\theta$. Example 9.19 reworked in this fashion becomes

$$\text{Let } z = r\angle\theta, \qquad \text{then} \qquad z^2 = r^2\angle 2\theta$$

Furthermore, $4\text{j} = 4\angle\pi/2 + 2n\pi$, and hence if $z^2 = 4\text{j}$, we have

$$r^2\angle 2\theta = 4\angle\left(\frac{\pi}{2} + 2n\pi\right)$$

from which

$$r^2 = 4 \qquad \text{and} \qquad 2\theta = \frac{\pi}{2} + 2n\pi$$

as before. Rework Example 9.18 for yourself using this approach.

Another application of De Moivre's theorem is the derivation of trigonometric identities.

**Example 9.20**

Use De Moivre's theorem to show that

$$\cos 3\theta = 4\cos^3\theta - 3\cos\theta$$

and

$$\sin 3\theta = 3\sin\theta - 4\sin^3\theta$$

**Solution** We know that

$$(\cos\theta + \mathrm{j}\sin\theta)^3 = \cos 3\theta + \mathrm{j}\sin 3\theta$$

Expanding the l.h.s. we find

$$\cos^3\theta + 3\mathrm{j}\cos^2\theta\sin\theta - 3\cos\theta\sin^2\theta - \mathrm{j}\sin^3\theta = \cos 3\theta + \mathrm{j}\sin 3\theta$$

Equating the real parts gives

$$\cos^3\theta - 3\cos\theta\sin^2\theta = \cos 3\theta \qquad (9.10)$$

and equating the imaginary parts gives

$$3\cos^2\theta\sin\theta - \sin^3\theta = \sin 3\theta \qquad (9.11)$$

Now, writing $\sin^2\theta = 1 - \cos^2\theta$ in Equation (9.10) and $\cos^2\theta = 1 - \sin^2\theta$ in Equation (9.11), we find

$$\begin{aligned}\cos 3\theta &= \cos^3\theta - 3\cos\theta(1 - \cos^2\theta)\\ &= \cos^3\theta + 3\cos^3\theta - 3\cos\theta\\ &= 4\cos^3\theta - 3\cos\theta\\ \sin 3\theta &= 3(1 - \sin^2\theta)\sin\theta - \sin^3\theta\\ &= 3\sin\theta - 4\sin^3\theta\end{aligned}$$

as required.

---

This technique allows trigonometric functions of multiples of angles to be expressed in terms of powers. Sometimes we want to carry out the reverse process and express a power in terms of multiple angles. Consider Example 9.21.

**Example 9.21** If $z = \cos\theta + \mathrm{j}\sin\theta$ show that

$$z + \frac{1}{z} = 2\cos\theta \qquad z - \frac{1}{z} = 2\mathrm{j}\sin\theta$$

and find similar expressions for $z^n + \dfrac{1}{z^n}$ and $z^n - \dfrac{1}{z^n}$.

**Solution** Consider the complex number

$$z = \cos\theta + \mathrm{j}\sin\theta$$

Using De Moivre's theorem,

$$\frac{1}{z} = z^{-1} = (\cos\theta + \mathrm{j}\sin\theta)^{-1} = \cos(-\theta) + \mathrm{j}\sin(-\theta)$$

But $\cos(-\theta) = \cos\theta$ and $\sin(-\theta) = -\sin\theta$, so that if $z = \cos\theta + \mathrm{j}\sin\theta$

$$\frac{1}{z} = \cos\theta - \mathrm{j}\sin\theta$$

Consequently,

$$z + \frac{1}{z} = 2\cos\theta \qquad \text{and} \qquad z - \frac{1}{z} = 2\mathrm{j}\sin\theta$$

Moreover,

$$z^n = \cos n\theta + \mathrm{j}\sin n\theta \qquad \text{and} \qquad z^{-n} = \cos n\theta - \mathrm{j}\sin n\theta$$

so that

$$z^n + \frac{1}{z^n} = 2\cos n\theta \qquad \text{and} \qquad z^n - \frac{1}{z^n} = 2\mathrm{j}\sin n\theta$$

---

$$z^n + \frac{1}{z^n} = 2\cos n\theta \qquad \text{and} \qquad z^n - \frac{1}{z^n} = 2\mathrm{j}\sin n\theta$$

**Example 9.22** Show that $\cos^2\theta = \frac{1}{2}(\cos 2\theta + 1)$.

**Solution** The formulae obtained in Example 9.21 allow us to obtain expressions for powers of $\cos\theta$ and $\sin\theta$. Since $2\cos\theta = z + \frac{1}{z}$, squaring both sides we have

$$\begin{aligned} 2^2\cos^2\theta &= \left(z + \frac{1}{z}\right)^2 = z^2 + 2 + \frac{1}{z^2} \\ &= \left(z^2 + \frac{1}{z^2}\right) + 2 \end{aligned}$$

But $z^2 + \frac{1}{z^2} = 2\cos 2\theta$, so

$$2^2\cos^2\theta = 2\cos 2\theta + 2$$

and therefore,

$$\begin{aligned} \cos^2\theta &= \tfrac{1}{2}\cos 2\theta + \tfrac{1}{2} \\ &= \tfrac{1}{2}(\cos 2\theta + 1) \end{aligned}$$

as required.

---

## Exercises 9.9

1 Express $(\cos\theta + \mathrm{j}\sin\theta)^9$ and $(\cos\theta + \mathrm{j}\sin\theta)^{1/2}$ in the form $\cos n\theta + \mathrm{j}\sin n\theta$.

2 Use De Moivre's theorem to simplify

(a) $(\cos 3\theta + \mathrm{j}\sin 3\theta)(\cos 4\theta + \mathrm{j}\sin 4\theta)$

(b) $\dfrac{\cos 8\theta + \mathrm{j}\sin 8\theta}{\cos 2\theta - \mathrm{j}\sin 2\theta}$

3 Solve the equations

(a) $z^3 + 1 = 0$

(b) $z^4 = 1 + \mathrm{j}$

4 Find $\sqrt[3]{2 + 2\mathrm{j}}$ and display your solutions on an Argand diagram.

5 Prove the following trigonometric identities:

(a) $\cos 4\theta = 8\cos^4\theta - 8\cos^2\theta + 1$

(b) $32\sin^6\theta = 10 - 15\cos 2\theta + 6\cos 4\theta - \cos 6\theta$

6 Solve the equation $z^4 + 25 = 0$.

7 Find the fifth roots of j and depict your solutions on an Argand diagram.

8 Show that $\cos^3\theta = \frac{1}{4}(\cos 3\theta + 3\cos\theta)$.

9 Show that $\sin^4\theta = \frac{1}{8}(\cos 4\theta - 4\cos 2\theta + 3)$.

10 Express $\cos 5\theta$ in terms of powers of $\cos\theta$.

11 Express $\sin 5\theta$ in terms of powers of $\sin\theta$.

12 Given $e^{\mathrm{j}\theta} = \cos\theta + \mathrm{j}\sin\theta$, prove De Moivre's theorem in the form

$$(e^{\mathrm{j}\theta})^n = \cos n\theta + \mathrm{j}\sin n\theta$$

## Solutions

1 $\cos 9\theta + \mathrm{j}\sin 9\theta$, $\cos(\theta/2) + \mathrm{j}\sin(\theta/2)$

2 (a) $\cos 7\theta + \mathrm{j}\sin 7\theta$

(b) $\cos 10\theta + \mathrm{j}\sin 10\theta$

3 (a) $1\angle\pi/3 + 2n\pi/3 \quad n = 0, 1, 2$

(b) $2^{1/8}\angle\pi/16 + n\pi/2 \quad n = 0, 1, 2, 3$

4 $8^{1/6}\angle\pi/12 + 2n\pi/3 \quad n = 0, 1, 2$

6 $\sqrt{5}\angle\pi/4 + n\pi/2 \quad n = 0, 1, 2, 3$

7 $1\angle\pi/10 + 2n\pi/5 \quad n = 0, 1, 2, 3, 4$

10 $16\cos^5\theta - 20\cos^3\theta + 5\cos\theta$

11 $16\sin^5\theta - 20\sin^3\theta + 5\sin\theta$

## 9.10 Loci and regions of the complex plane

Regions of the complex plane can often be conveniently described by means of complex numbers. For example, the points that lie on a circle of radius 2 centred at the origin (Figure 9.19) represent complex numbers all of which have a modulus of 2. The arguments are any value of $\theta$, $-\pi < \theta \leqslant \pi$. We can describe all the points on this circle by the simple expression

$$|z| = 2$$

that is, all complex numbers with modulus 2. We say that the locus (or path) of the point $z$ is a circle, radius 2, centred at the origin. The interior of the circle is described by $|z| < 2$ while its exterior is described by $|z| > 2$.

Similarly all points lying in the first quadrant (shaded in Figure 9.20) have arguments between 0 and $\pi/2$. This quadrant is therefore described by the expression:

$$0 < \arg(z) < \pi/2$$

**Example 9.23** Sketch the locus of the point satisfying $\arg(z) = \pi/4$.

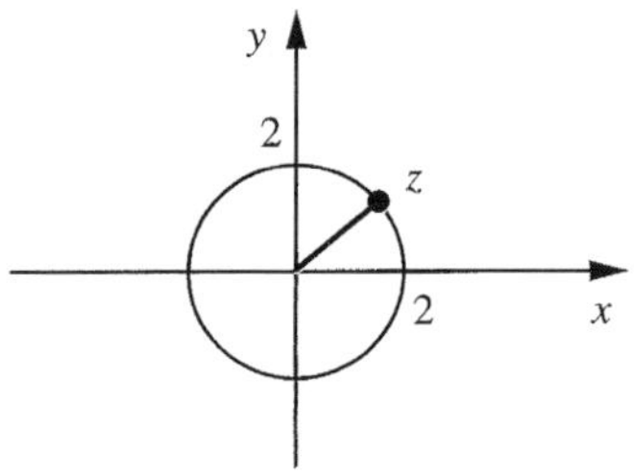


**Figure 9.19** A circle, radius 2, centred at the origin.

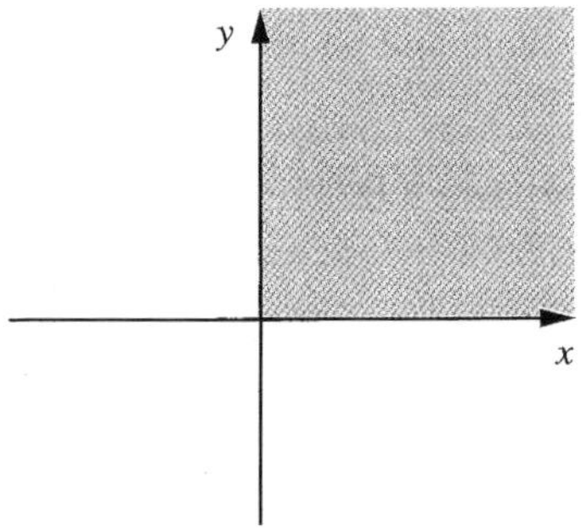


**Figure 9.20** First quadrant of the $x$–$y$ plane.

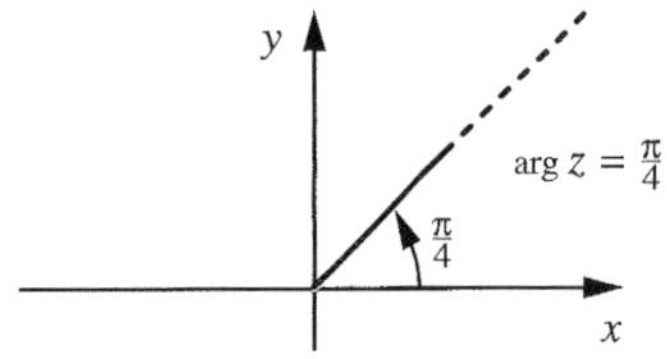


**Figure 9.21** Locus of points satisfying $\arg(z) = \pi/4$.

**Solution** The set of points with $\arg(z) = \pi/4$ comprises complex numbers whose argument is $\pi/4$. All these complex numbers lie on the line shown in Figure 9.21.

**Example 9.24** Sketch the locus of the point satisfying $|z - 2| = 3$.

**Solution** First mark the fixed point 2 on the Argand diagram labelling it 'A' (Figure 9.22). Consider the complex number $z$ represented by the point P. From the vector triangle law of addition

$$\vec{OA} + \vec{AP} = \vec{OP}$$

$$\vec{AP} = \vec{OP} - \vec{OA}$$

Recall from Section 9.6 that the graphical representation of the sum and difference of vectors in the plane, and the sum and difference of complex numbers, are equivalent. Since vector $\vec{OP}$ represents the complex number $z$, and vector $\vec{OA}$ represents the complex number 2, $\vec{AP} = \vec{OP} - \vec{OA}$ will represent $z - 2$. Therefore $|z - 2|$ represents the distance between A and P. We are given that $|z - 2| = 3$, which therefore means that P can be any point such that its distance from A is 3. This means that P can be any point on a circle of radius 3 centred at A(2, 0). The locus is shown in Figure 9.23. $|z - 2| < 3$ represents the interior of the circle while $|z - 2| > 3$ represents the exterior.

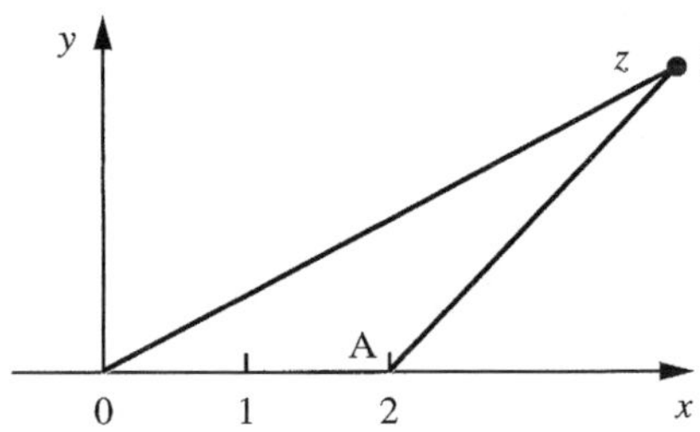


**Figure 9.22** Points $z$ and $2 + 0j$.

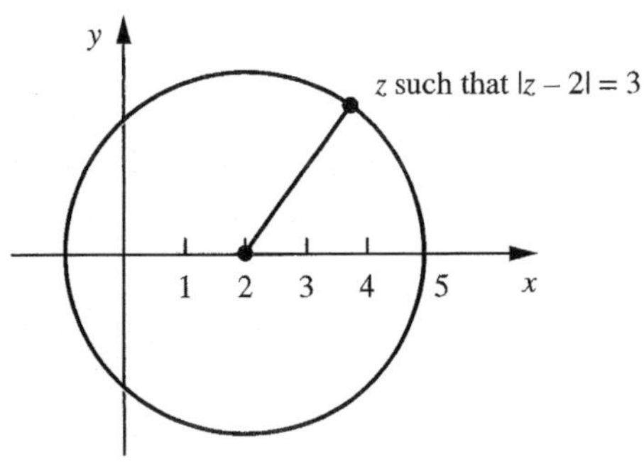


**Figure 9.23** Locus of points satisfying $|z - 2| = 3$.

Alternatively we can obtain the same result algebraically: given $|z-2|=3$ and also that $z=x+\mathrm{j}y$, we can write

$$|z-2| = |(x-2)+\mathrm{j}y| = 3$$

that is

$$\sqrt{(x-2)^2+y^2} = 3$$

or

$$(x-2)^2+y^2 = 9$$

Generally, the equation $(x-a)^2+(y-b)^2=r^2$ represents a circle of radius $r$ centred at $(a, b)$, so we see that $(x-2)^2+y^2=9$ represents a circle of radius 3 centred at $(2, 0)$, as before.

**Example 9.25** Use the algebraic approach to find the locus of the point $z$ which satisfies

$$|z-1| = \tfrac{1}{2}|z-\mathrm{j}|$$

**Solution** If $z=x+\mathrm{j}y$, then we have

$$|(x-1)+\mathrm{j}y| = \tfrac{1}{2}|x+\mathrm{j}(y-1)|$$

Therefore,

$$(x-1)^2+y^2 = \tfrac{1}{4}\{x^2+(y-1)^2\}$$

and so

$$4(x-1)^2+4y^2 = x^2+(y-1)^2$$

that is

$$3x^2-8x+3y^2+2y+3=0$$

By completing the square this may be written in the form

$$3\left(x-\tfrac{4}{3}\right)^2+3\left(y+\tfrac{1}{3}\right)^2=\tfrac{8}{3}$$

that is

$$\left(x-\tfrac{4}{3}\right)^2+\left(y+\tfrac{1}{3}\right)^2=\tfrac{8}{9}$$

which represents a circle of radius $\sqrt{8}/3$ centred at $\left(\tfrac{4}{3}, -\tfrac{1}{3}\right)$.

## Exercises 9.10

1 Sketch the loci defined by

(a) $\arg(z)=0$

(b) $\arg(z)=\pi/2$

(c) $\arg(z-4)=\pi/4$

(d) $|2z|=|z-1|$

**2** Sketch the regions defined by

(a) $\text{Re}(z) \geqslant 0$

(b) $\text{Im}(z) < 3$

(c) $|z| > 3$

(d) $0 \leqslant \arg(z) \leqslant \pi/2$

(e) $|z+2| \leqslant 3$

(f) $|z+\text{j}| > 3$

(g) $|z-1| < |z-2|$

**3** If $s = \sigma + \text{j}\omega$ sketch the regions defined by

(a) $\sigma \leqslant 0$

(b) $\sigma \geqslant 0$

(c) $-2 \leqslant \omega \leqslant 2$

## Solutions

**1** See Figure S.14.

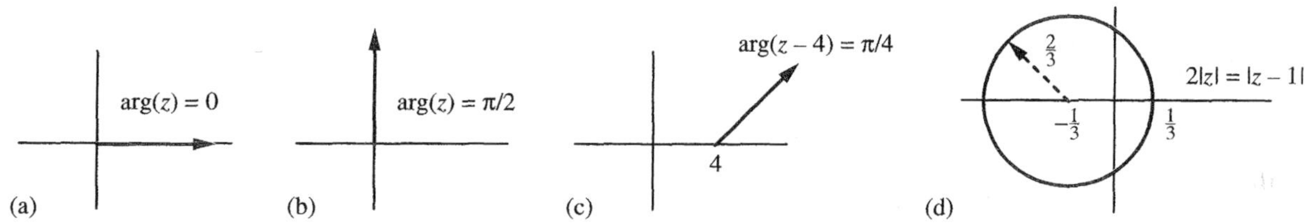


**Figure S.14**

**2** See Figure S.15.

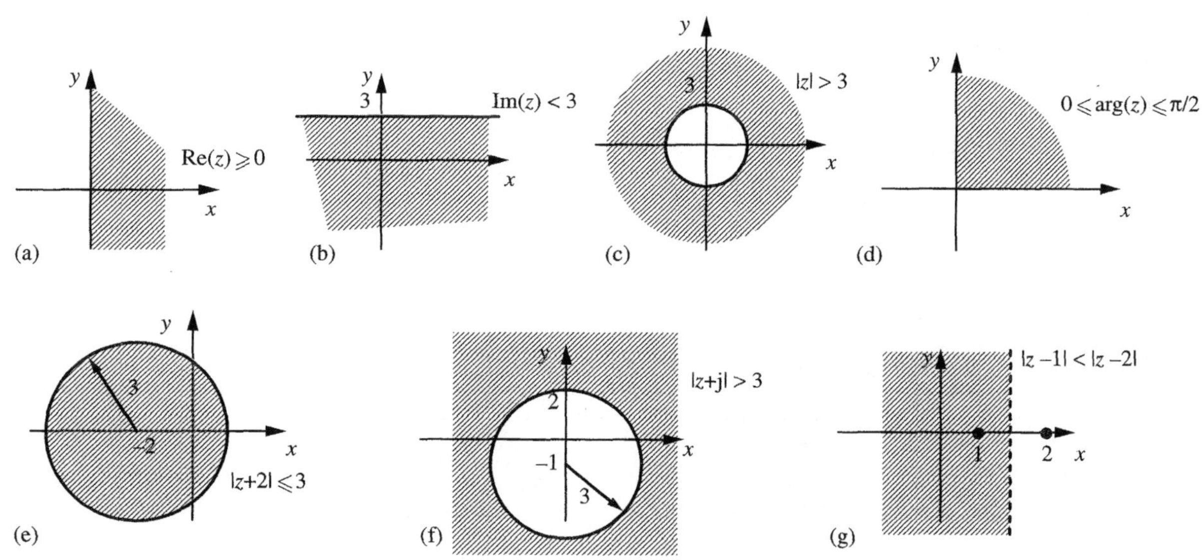


**Figure S.15**

3 See Figure S.16.

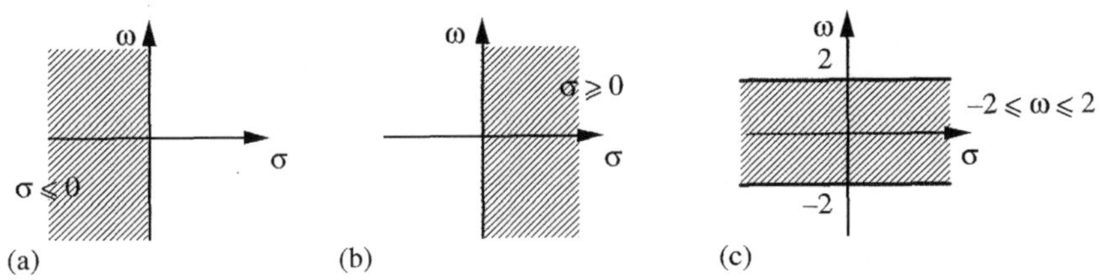


**Figure S.16**

## Review exercises 9

1 Show that $\dfrac{1}{\cos\theta - \mathrm{j}\sin\theta} = \cos\theta + \mathrm{j}\sin\theta$.

2 Express in Cartesian form

(a) $\dfrac{5+4\mathrm{j}}{5-4\mathrm{j}}$

(b) $\dfrac{1}{2+3\mathrm{j}}$

(c) $\dfrac{1}{2+3\mathrm{j}} + \dfrac{1}{2-3\mathrm{j}}$

(d) $\dfrac{1}{x-\mathrm{j}y}$

3 Find the modulus and argument of $-\mathrm{j}$, $-3$, $1+\mathrm{j}$, $\cos\theta + \mathrm{j}\sin\theta$.

4 Mark on an Argand diagram vectors corresponding to the following complex numbers: $-3+2\mathrm{j}$, $-3-2\mathrm{j}$, $\cos\pi + \mathrm{j}\sin\pi$.

5 Express in the form $a + b\mathrm{j}$:

(a) $(\cos\theta + \mathrm{j}\sin\theta)^6$

(b) $\dfrac{1}{(\cos\theta + \mathrm{j}\sin\theta)^3}$

(c) $\dfrac{\cos\theta + \mathrm{j}\sin\theta}{\cos\phi + \mathrm{j}\sin\phi}$

6 If $z \in \mathbb{C}$, show that

(a) $z + \bar{z} = 2\mathrm{Re}(z)$

(b) $z - \bar{z} = 2\mathrm{j}\,\mathrm{Im}(z)$

(c) $z\bar{z} = |z|^2$

7 Show that $e^{\mathrm{j}\omega t} + e^{-\mathrm{j}\omega t} = 2\cos\omega t$ and find an expression for $e^{\mathrm{j}\omega t} - e^{-\mathrm{j}\omega t}$.

8 Express $1 + e^{2\mathrm{j}\omega t}$ in the form $a + b\mathrm{j}$.

9 Sketch the region in the complex plane described by $|z + 2\mathrm{j}| < 1$.

10 Express $e^{(1/2-6\mathrm{j})}$ in the form $a + b\mathrm{j}$.

11 Solve the equation $z^4 + 1 = \mathrm{j}\sqrt{3}$.

12 Express $s^2 + 6s + 13$ in the form $(s-a)(s-b)$ where $a, b \in \mathbb{C}$.

13 Express $2s^2 + 8s + 11$ in the form $2(s-a)(s-b)$ where $a, b \in \mathbb{C}$.

### Solutions

2 (a) $\frac{9}{41} + \frac{40}{41}\mathrm{j}$ (b) $\frac{2}{13} - \frac{3}{13}\mathrm{j}$ (c) $\frac{4}{13}$

(d) $\dfrac{x}{x^2+y^2} + \dfrac{y}{x^2+y^2}\mathrm{j}$

3 $|-\mathrm{j}| = 1$, $\arg(-\mathrm{j}) = -\pi/2$; $|-3| = 3$, $\arg(-3) = \pi$; $|1+\mathrm{j}| = \sqrt{2}$, $\arg(1+\mathrm{j}) = \pi/4$, $|\cos\theta + \mathrm{j}\sin\theta| = 1$, $\arg(\cos\theta + \mathrm{j}\sin\theta) = \theta$

5 (a) $\cos 6\theta + \mathrm{j}\sin 6\theta$ (b) $\cos 3\theta - \mathrm{j}\sin 3\theta$

(c) $\cos(\theta - \phi) + \mathrm{j}\sin(\theta - \phi)$

7 $e^{\mathrm{j}\omega t} - e^{-\mathrm{j}\omega t} = 2\mathrm{j}\sin\omega t$

8 $1 + \cos 2\omega t + \mathrm{j}\sin 2\omega t$

10 $1.5831 + 0.4607\,\mathrm{j}$

11 $2^{1/4}\angle \pi/6 + n\pi/2 \qquad n = 0, 1, 2, 3$

12 $[s - (-3+2\mathrm{j})][s - (-3-2\mathrm{j})]$

13 $2\left[s - \left(-2 + \frac{\sqrt{6}}{2}\mathrm{j}\right)\right]\left[s - \left(-2 - \frac{\sqrt{6}}{2}\mathrm{j}\right)\right]$

# Functions and Curves

# 10 Differentiation

| Chapter 10 | Contents |
|---|---|

## 10.1 Introduction

Differentiation is a mathematical technique for analysing the way in which functions change. In particular, it determines how rapidly a function is changing at any specific point. As the function in question may represent the magnetic field of a motor, the voltage across a capacitor, the temperature of a chemical mix, etc., it is often important to know how quickly these quantities change. For example, if the voltage on an electrical supply network is falling rapidly because of a short circuit, then it is necessary to detect this in order to switch out that part of the network where the fault has occurred. However, the system should not take action for normal voltage fluctuations and so it is important to distinguish different types and rates of change. Another example would be detecting a sudden rise in the pressure of a fermentation vessel and taking appropriate action to stabilize the pressure.

Differentiation will be introduced in this chapter. We shall derive a formula which can be used to find the rate of change of a function. To avoid always having to resort to the formula engineers often use a **table of derivatives**; such a table is given in Section 10.7. The chapter closes with a discussion of an important property of differentiation – that of linearity.

## 10.2 Graphical approach to differentiation

Differentiation is concerned with the rate at which a function is changing, rather than the actual change itself. We can explore the rate of change of a function by examining Figure 10.1. There are several regions to this curve corresponding to different intervals of $t$. In the interval $[0, 5]$ the function does not change at all. The rate of change of $y$ is zero. From $t = 5$ to $t = 7$ the function increases slightly. Thus the rate of change of $y$ as $t$ increases is small. Since $y$ is increasing, the rate of change of $y$ is positive. From $t = 7$ to $t = 8$ there is a rapid rise in the value of the function. The rate of change of $y$ is large and positive. From $t = 8$ to $t = 9$ the value of $y$ decreases very rapidly. The rate of change of $y$ is large and negative. Finally from $t = 9$ to $t = 12$ the function decreases slightly. Thus the rate of change of $y$ is small and negative.

The aim of **differential calculus** is to specify the rate of change of a function precisely. It is not sufficient to say 'the rate of change of a function is large'. We require an exact value or expression for the rate of change. Before being able to do this we need to introduce two concepts concerning the rate of change of a function.

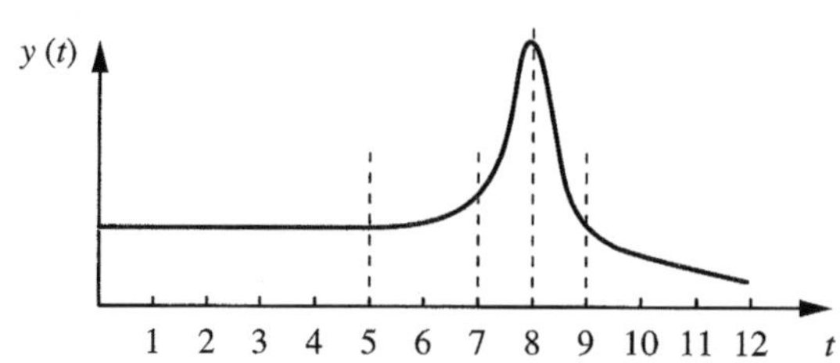


**Figure 10.1** The function $y(t)$ has different rates of change over different regions of $t$.

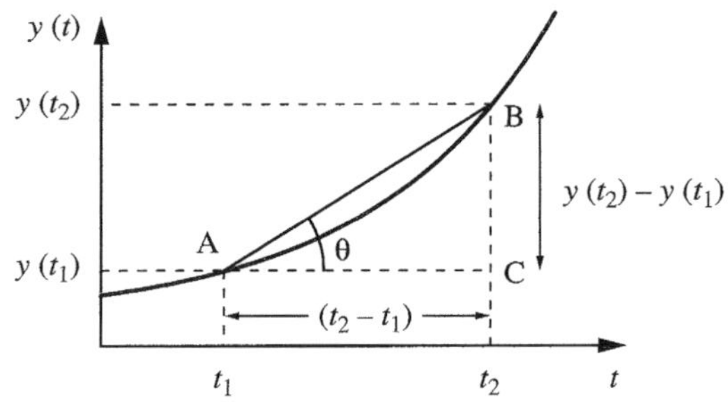


**Figure 10.2** Average rate of change across an interval.

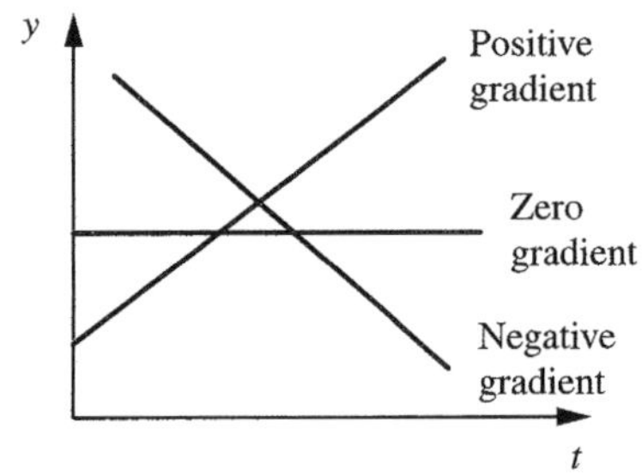


**Figure 10.3** Lines can have different gradients.

## 10.2.1 Average rate of change of a function across an interval

Consider Figure 10.2. When $t = t_1$, the function has a value $y(t_1)$. This is denoted by A on the curve. When $t = t_2$, the function has a value of $y(t_2)$. This point is denoted by B on the curve. The function changes by an amount $y(t_2) - y(t_1)$ over the interval $[t_1, t_2]$. Thus the average rate of change of the function over the interval is

$$\frac{\text{change in } y}{\text{change in } t} = \frac{y(t_2) - y(t_1)}{t_2 - t_1}$$

The straight line joining A and B is known as a **chord**. Graphically, $y(t_2) - y(t_1)$ is the vertical distance and $t_2 - t_1$ the horizontal distance between A and B, so that the **gradient** of the chord AB is given by

$$\frac{\text{BC}}{\text{AC}} = \frac{y(t_2) - y(t_1)}{t_2 - t_1}$$

The gradient or **slope** of a line is a measure of its steepness and lines may have positive, negative or zero gradients as shown in Figure 10.3.

Thus the gradient of the chord AB corresponds to the average rate of change of the function between A and B. To summarize:

The average rate of change of a function between two points A and B is the gradient of the chord AB.

## 10.2.2 Rate of change of a function at a point

Consider again Figure 10.2. Suppose we require the rate of change of the function at point A. We can use the gradient of the chord AB as an approximation to this value. If B is close to A then the approximation is better than if B is not so close to A. Therefore by moving B nearer to A it is possible to improve the accuracy of this approximation (see Figure 10.4).

Suppose the chord AB is extended as a straight line on both sides of AB, and B is moved closer and closer to A until both points eventually coincide. The straight line becomes a **tangent** to the curve at A. This is the straight line that just touches the curve at A. However, the rate of change of this tangent, that is its gradient, still corresponds to the rate of change of the function, but now it is the rate of change of the function at the point A. To summarize:

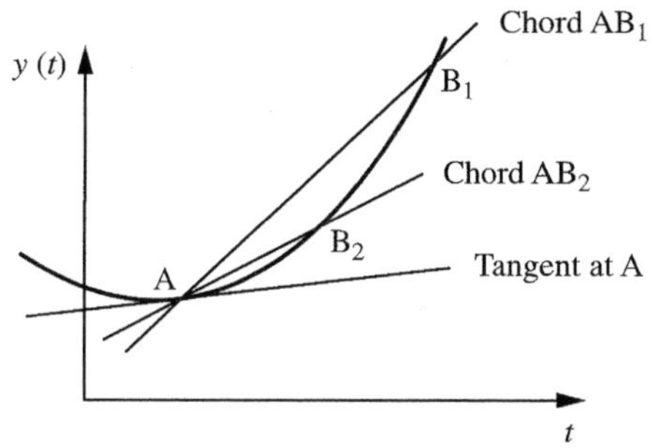


**Figure 10.4**
Point B is moved nearer to A to improve accuracy.

The rate of change of a function at a point A on the curve is the gradient of the tangent to the curve at point A.

We have still to address the question of how the gradients of chords and tangents are found. This requires a knowledge of limits which is the topic of the next section.

## 10.3 Limits and continuity

The concept of a limit is crucial to the development of differentiation. We write $t \to c$ to denote that $t$ approaches, or tends to, the value of $c$. Note carefully that this is distinct from stating $t = c$. As $t$ tends to $c$ we consider the value to which the function approaches and call this value the **limit** of the function as $t \to c$.

**Example 10.1** If $t \to 2$, what value does

$$f(t) = t^2 + 2t - 3$$

approach?

**Solution** Figure 10.5 shows a graph of $f(t)$. Clearly, whether $t = 2$ is approached from the l.h.s. or the r.h.s. the function tends to 5. That is, if $t \to 2$, then $f(t) \to 5$. We note that this is the value of $f(2)$. Informally we are saying that as $t$ gets nearer and nearer to the value 2, so $f(t)$ gets nearer and nearer to 5. This is usually written as

$$\lim_{t\to 2}(t^2 + 2t - 3) = 5$$

where 'lim' is an abbreviation of limit. In this example, the limit of $f(t)$ as $t \to 2$ is simply $f(2)$, but this is not true for all functions.

**Example 10.2** Figure 10.6 illustrates $y(x)$ defined by

$$y(x) = \begin{cases} 1 - x & x < 0 \\ 3 & x = 0 \\ x + 1 & x > 0 \end{cases}$$

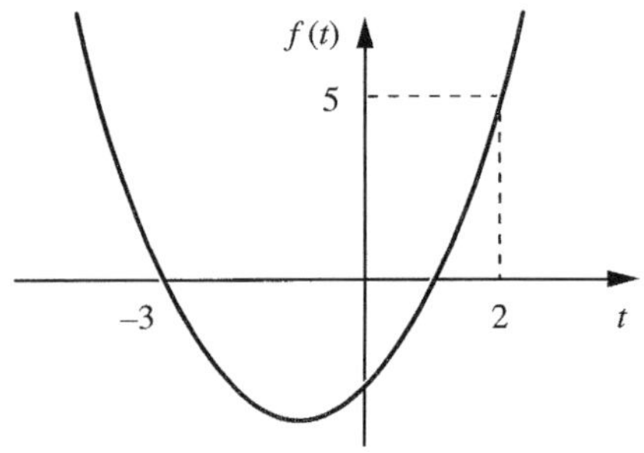


**Figure 10.5** The curve $f(t) = t^2 + 2t - 3$.

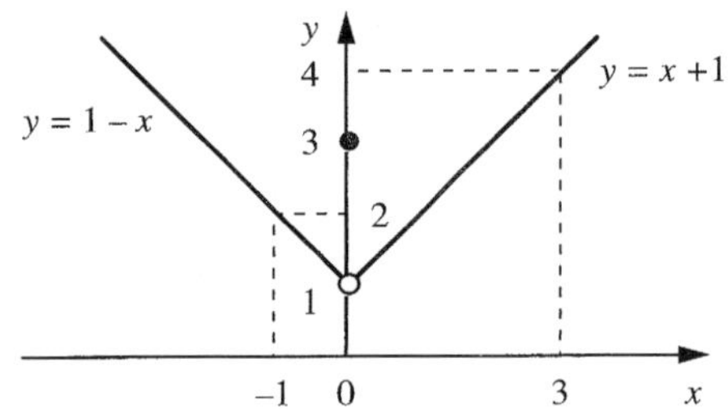


**Figure 10.6** As $x \to 0$, $y \to 1$, even though $y(0) = 3$.

Evaluate:
(a) $\lim_{x\to3} y$ (b) $\lim_{x\to-1} y$ (c) $\lim_{x\to0} y$

**Solution** We note that this function is piecewise continuous. It has a discontinuity at $x = 0$.

(a) We seek the limit of $y$ as $x$ approaches 3. As $x$ approaches 3, we will be on that part of the function defined by $x > 0$, that is $y(x) = x + 1$. As $x \to 3$, then $y \to 3 + 1$, that is $y \to 4$. So

$$\lim_{x\to3} y = 4$$

(b) When $x$ approaches $-1$, we will be on that part of the function defined by $x < 0$, that is $y(x) = 1 - x$. So as $x \to -1$, then $y \to 1 - (-1)$, that is $y \to 2$. Hence

$$\lim_{x\to-1} y = 2$$

(c) As $x$ approaches 0 what value does $y$ approach? Note that we are not evaluating $y(0)$ which actually has a value of 3. We simply ask the question 'What value is $y$ near when $x$ is near, but distinct from, 0?' From Figure 10.6 we see $y$ is near to 1, that is

$$\lim_{x\to0} y = 1$$

**Example 10.3** The function $y(x)$ is defined by

$$y(x) = \begin{cases} 0 & x \leqslant 0 \\ x & 0 < x \leqslant 2 \\ x - 2 & x > 2 \end{cases}$$

(a) Sketch the function.

(b) State the limit of $y$ as $x$ approaches (i) 3, (ii) 2, (iii) 0.

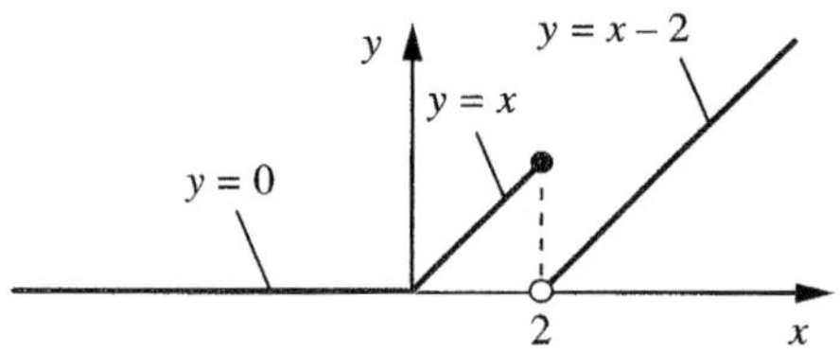


**Figure 10.7** The function $y$ has different limits as $x \to 2$ from the left and the right.

**Solution** (a) The function is shown in Figure 10.7. Note that the figure has three parts; each part corresponds to a part in the algebraic definition.

(b) (i) As $x \to 3$, the relevant part of the function is $y(x) = x - 2$. Hence

$$\lim_{x\to 3} y = 1$$

(ii) Suppose $x < 2$ and gradually increases, approaching the value 2. Then, from the graph, we see that $y$ approaches 2. Now, suppose $x > 2$ and gradually decreases, tending to 2. In this case $y$ approaches 0. Hence, we cannot find the limit of $y$ as $x$ tends to 2. The $\lim_{x\to 2} y$ does not exist.

(iii) As $x$ tends to 0, $y$ tends to 0. This is true whether $x$ approaches 0 from below, that is from the left, or from above, that is from the right. So,

$$\lim_{x\to 0} y = 0$$

---

It is appropriate at this stage to introduce the concept of **left-hand** and **right-hand** limits. Referring to Example 10.3, we see that as $x$ approaches 2 from the left, that is from below, then $y$ approaches 2. We say that the left-hand limit of $y$ as $x$ tends to 2 is 2. This is written as

$$\lim_{x\to 2^-} y = 2$$

Similarly, the right-hand limit of $y$ is obtained by letting $x$ tend to 2 from above. In this case, $y$ approaches 0. This is written as

$$\lim_{x\to 2^+} y = 0$$

Consider a point at which the left-hand and right-hand limits are equal. At such a point we say 'the limit exists at that point'.

The **limit** of a function, at a point $x = a$, exists only if the left-hand and right-hand limits are equal there.

### 10.3.1 Continuous and discontinuous functions

A function $f$ is **continuous** at the point where $x = a$, if

$$\lim_{x\to a} f = f(a)$$

that is, the limit value matches the function value at a point of continuity. A function which is not continuous is **discontinuous**. In Example 10.3, the function is continuous at $x = 0$ because

$$\lim_{x \to 0} y = 0 = f(0)$$

but discontinuous at $x = 2$ because $\lim_{x \to 2} y$ does not exist. In Example 10.2, the function is discontinuous at $x = 0$ because $\lim_{x \to 0} y = 1$ but $y(0) = 3$. The concept of continuity corresponds to our natural understanding of a break in the graph of the function, as discussed in Chapter 2.

> A function $f$ is continuous at a point $x = a$ if and only if
> $\lim_{x \to a} f = f(a)$
> that is, the limit of $f$ exists at $x = a$ and is equal to $f(a)$.

## Exercises 10.3

1 The function, $f(t)$, is defined by

$$f(t) = \begin{cases} 1 & 0 \leqslant t \leqslant 2 \\ 2 & 2 < t \leqslant 3 \\ 3 & t > 3 \end{cases}$$

Sketch a graph of $f(t)$ and state the following limits if they exist.

(a) $\lim_{t \to 1.5} f$

(b) $\lim_{t \to 2^+} f$

(c) $\lim_{t \to 3} f$

(d) $\lim_{t \to 0^+} f$

(e) $\lim_{t \to 3^-} f$

2 The function $g(t)$ is defined by

$$g(t) = \begin{cases} 0 & t < 0 \\ t^2 & 0 \leqslant t \leqslant 3 \\ 2t + 3 & 3 < t \leqslant 4 \\ 12 & t > 4 \end{cases}$$

(a) Sketch $g$.

(b) State any points of discontinuity.

(c) Find, if they exist,

(i) $\lim_{t \to 3} g$

(ii) $\lim_{t \to 4} g$

(iii) $\lim_{t \to 4^-} g$

## Solutions

1 (a) 1 (b) 2 (c) not defined
(d) 1 (e) 2

2 (b) $t = 4$
(c) (i) 9 (ii) not defined (iii) 11

# 10.4 Rate of change at a specific point

We saw in Section 10.2 that the rate of change of a function at a point is the gradient of the tangent to the curve at that point. Also, we can think of a tangent at A as the limit of an extended chord AB as B $\to$ A. We now put these two ideas together to find the rate of change of a function at a point.

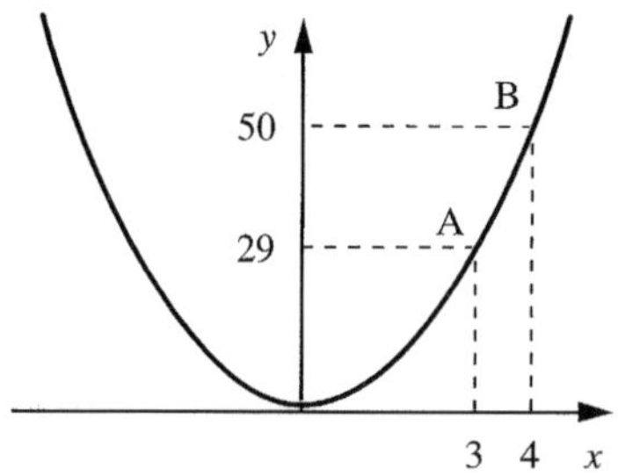


**Figure 10.8**
The function:
$y = 3x^2 + 2$.

**Example 10.4** Given $y = f(x) = 3x^2 + 2$, obtain estimates of the rate of change of $y$ at $x = 3$ by considering the intervals

(a) $[3, 4]$ (b) $[3, 3.1]$ (c) $[3, 3.01]$

**Solution** (a) Consider Figure 10.8.

$$y(3) = 3(3)^2 + 2 = 29$$
$$y(4) = 3(4)^2 + 2 = 50$$

Let A be the point (3, 29) on the curve. Let B be the point (4, 50). Then

$$\text{average rate of change over the interval } [3, 4] = \frac{\text{change in } y}{\text{change in } x} = \frac{y(4) - y(3)}{4 - 3} = \frac{50 - 29}{4 - 3} = 21$$

This is the gradient of the chord AB and is an estimate of the gradient of the tangent at A. That is, the rate of change at A is approximately 21.

(b) $y(3.1) = 30.83$ and so,

$$\text{average rate of change over the interval } [3, 3.1] = \frac{30.83 - 29}{3.1 - 3} = 18.3$$

This is a more accurate estimate of the rate of change at A.

(c) $y(3.01) = 29.1803$ and so,

$$\text{average rate of change over the interval } [3, 3.01] = \frac{29.1803 - 29}{3.01 - 3} = 18.03$$

This is an even better estimate of the rate of change at A. Hence at A, if $x$ increases by 1 unit then $y$ increases by approximately 18 units. This corresponds to a steep upward slope at A.

Example 10.4 illustrates the approach of estimating the rate of change at a point by using the 'shrinking interval' method. By taking smaller and smaller intervals, better and better estimates of the rate of change of the function at $x = 3$ can be obtained. However, we eventually want the interval to 'shrink' to the point $x = 3$. We introduce a small change or **increment** of $x$ denoted by $\delta x$ and consider the interval $[3, 3+\delta x]$. By letting $\delta x$ tend to zero, the interval $[3, 3+\delta x]$ effectively shrinks to the point $x = 3$.

**Example 10.5** Find the rate of change of $y = 3x^2 + 2$ at $x = 3$ by considering the interval $[3, 3+\delta x]$ and letting $\delta x$ tend to 0.

**Solution** When $x = 3$, $y(3) = 29$. When $x = 3 + \delta x$ then

$$\begin{aligned} y(3+\delta x) &= 3(3+\delta x)^2 + 2 \\ &= 3(9 + 6\delta x + (\delta x)^2) + 2 \\ &= 3(\delta x)^2 + 18\delta x + 29 \end{aligned}$$

So,

$$\begin{aligned} \text{average rate of change of } y \text{ across } [3, 3+\delta x] &= \frac{\text{change in } y}{\text{change in } x} \\ &= \frac{(3(\delta x)^2 + 18\delta x + 29) - 29}{\delta x} \\ &= \frac{3(\delta x)^2 + 18\delta x}{\delta x} \\ &= \frac{\delta x(3\delta x + 18)}{\delta x} \\ &= 3\delta x + 18 \end{aligned}$$

We now let $\delta x$ tend to 0, so that the interval shrinks to a point:

$$\text{rate of change of } y \text{ when } x \text{ is } 3 = \lim_{\delta x \to 0} (3\delta x + 18) = 18$$

We have found the rate of change of $y$ at a particular value of $x$, rather than across an interval. We usually write

$$\begin{aligned} \text{rate of change of } y \text{ when } x \text{ is } 3 &= \lim_{\delta x \to 0} \left( \frac{y(3+\delta x) - y(3)}{\delta x} \right) \\ &= \lim_{\delta x \to 0} \left( \frac{3(\delta x)^2 + 18\delta x}{\delta x} \right) = \lim_{\delta x \to 0} (3\delta x + 18) \\ &= 18 \end{aligned}$$

## Exercises 10.4

1 Find the rate of change of $y = 3x^2 + 2$ at

(a) $x = 4$ by considering the interval $[4, 4 + \delta x]$

(b) $x = -2$ by considering the interval $[-2, -2 + \delta x]$

(c) $x = 1$ by considering the interval $[1 - \delta x, 1 + \delta x]$

2 Find the rate of change of $y = 1/x$ at $x = 2$.

3 To determine the rate of change of $y = x^2 - x$ at $x = 1$ the interval $[1, 1 + \delta x]$ could be used. Equally the intervals $[1 - \delta x, 1]$ or $[1 - \delta x, 1 + \delta x]$ could be used. Show that the same answer results regardless of which interval is used.

4 Find the rate of change of $y(x) = 2 - x^2$ at

(a) $x = 3$, by considering the interval $[3, 3 + \delta x]$

(b) $x = -5$, by considering the interval $[-5, -5 + \delta x]$

(c) $x = 1$, by considering the interval $[1 - \delta x, 1 + \delta x]$.

5 Find the rate of change of $y(x) = \dfrac{x}{x+3}$ at $x = 3$ by considering the interval $[3, 3 + \delta x]$.

### Solutions

1 (a) 24 (b) −12 (c) 6

2 −0.25

3 1

4 (a) −6 (b) 10 (c) −2

5 $\frac{1}{12}$

## 10.5 Rate of change at a general point

Example 10.5 shows that the rate of change of a function at a particular point can be found. We will now develop a general terminology for the method. Suppose we have a function of $x$, $y(x)$. We wish to find the rate of change of $y$ at a general value of $x$. We begin by finding the average rate of change of $y(x)$ across an interval and then allow the interval to shrink to a single point. Consider the interval $[x, x + \delta x]$. At the beginning of the interval $y$ has a value of $y(x)$. At the end of the interval $y$ has a value of $y(x + \delta x)$ so that the change in $y$ is $y(x + \delta x) - y(x)$, which we denote by $\delta y$ (see Figure 10.9). So,

$$\text{average rate of change of } y = \frac{\text{change in } y}{\text{change in } x} = \frac{y(x + \delta x) - y(x)}{\delta x} = \frac{\delta y}{\delta x}$$

Now let $\delta x$ tend to 0, so that the interval shrinks to a point. Then

$$\text{rate of change of } y = \lim_{\delta x \to 0} \left( \frac{y(x + \delta x) - y(x)}{\delta x} \right) = \lim_{\delta x \to 0} \left( \frac{\delta y}{\delta x} \right)$$

To see how we proceed to evaluate this limit consider Example 10.6.

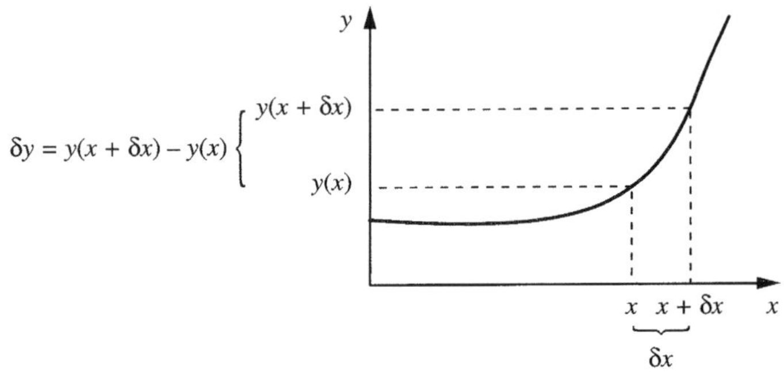


**Figure 10.9**
The rate of change of $y$ at a point is found by letting $\delta x \to 0$.

**Example 10.6** Find the rate of change of $y(x) = 2x^2 + 3x$. Calculate the rate of change of $y$ when $x = 2$ and when $x = -3$.

**Solution** Given $y(x) = 2x^2 + 3x$
then

$$\begin{aligned} y(x + \delta x) &= 2(x + \delta x)^2 + 3(x + \delta x) \\ &= 2x^2 + 4x\delta x + 2(\delta x)^2 + 3x + 3\delta x \end{aligned}$$

Hence

$$y(x + \delta x) - y(x) = 2(\delta x)^2 + 4x\delta x + 3\delta x$$

So,

$$\begin{aligned} \text{rate of change of } y &= \lim_{\delta x \to 0} \left( \frac{y(x + \delta x) - y(x)}{\delta x} \right) \\ &= \lim_{\delta x \to 0} \left( \frac{2(\delta x)^2 + 4x\delta x + 3\delta x}{\delta x} \right) \\ &= \lim_{\delta x \to 0} (2\delta x + 4x + 3) = 4x + 3 \end{aligned}$$

When $x = 2$, the rate of change of $y$ is $4(2) + 3 = 11$. When $x = -3$, the rate of change of $y$ is $4(-3) + 3 = -9$. A positive rate of change shows that the function is increasing at that particular point. A negative rate of change shows that the function is decreasing at that particular point.

---

The rate of change of $y$ is called the **derivative** of $y$. We denote $\lim_{\delta x \to 0} \left( \frac{\delta y}{\delta x} \right)$ by $\frac{dy}{dx}$. This is pronounced 'dee $y$ by dee $x$'.

$$\text{rate of change of } y(x) = \frac{dy}{dx} = \lim_{\delta x \to 0} \left( \frac{y(x + \delta x) - y(x)}{\delta x} \right)$$

Note that the notation $\frac{dy}{dx}$ means $\lim_{\delta x \to 0} \frac{\delta y}{\delta x}$.

Using the previous example, if

$$y(x) = 2x^2 + 3x$$

then

$$\frac{\mathrm{d}y}{\mathrm{d}x} = 4x + 3$$

$\frac{\mathrm{d}y}{\mathrm{d}x}$ is often abbreviated to $y'$

$y'$ is pronounced '$y$ dash' or '$y$ prime'. To stress that $y$ is the dependent variable and $x$ the independent variable we often talk of 'the rate of change of $y$ with respect to $x$', or more compactly, 'the rate of change of $y$ w.r.t. $x$'. The process of finding $y'$ from $y$ is called **differentiation**. This shrinking interval method of finding the derivative is called **differentiation from first principles**. We know that the derivative $\frac{\mathrm{d}y}{\mathrm{d}x}$ is the gradient of the tangent to the function at a point. It is also the rate of change of the function. In many examples, the independent variable is $t$ and we need to find the rate of change of $y$ with respect to $t$; that is, find $\frac{\mathrm{d}y}{\mathrm{d}t}$. This is also often written as $y'$ although $\dot{y}$, pronounced '$y$ dot', is also common. The reader should be aware of both notations. Finally, $y'$ is used to denote the derivative of $y$ whatever the independent variable may be. So $\frac{\mathrm{d}y}{\mathrm{d}z}$, $\frac{\mathrm{d}y}{\mathrm{d}r}$ and $\frac{\mathrm{d}y}{\mathrm{d}w}$ could all be represented by $y'$.

**Example 10.7** Find the gradient of the tangent to $y = x^2$ at $A(1, 1)$, $B(-1, 1)$ and $C(2, 4)$.

**Solution** We have $y = x^2$ and so

$$\begin{aligned} y(x + \delta x) &= (x + \delta x)^2 \\ &= x^2 + 2x\delta x + (\delta x)^2 \end{aligned}$$

and hence

$$\begin{aligned} y(x + \delta x) - y(x) &= x^2 + 2x\delta x + (\delta x)^2 - x^2 \\ &= 2x\delta x + (\delta x)^2 \end{aligned}$$

Then

$$\begin{aligned} \frac{\mathrm{d}y}{\mathrm{d}x} &= \text{gradient of a tangent to curve} \\ &= \lim_{\delta x \to 0}\left(\frac{y(x + \delta x) - y(x)}{\delta x}\right) \\ &= \lim_{\delta x \to 0}\left(\frac{(x + \delta x)^2 - x^2}{\delta x}\right) = \lim_{\delta x \to 0}\left(\frac{2x\delta x + (\delta x)^2}{\delta x}\right) \\ &= \lim_{\delta x \to 0}(2x + \delta x) = 2x \end{aligned}$$

At (1, 1), $\frac{dy}{dx} = 2 =$ gradient of tangent at A. At (−1, 1), $\frac{dy}{dx} = -2 =$ gradient of tangent at B. At (2, 4), $\frac{dy}{dx} = 4 =$ gradient of tangent at C.

---

Suppose we wish to evaluate the derivative, $\frac{dy}{dx}$, at a specific value of $x$, say $x_0$. This is denoted by

$$\frac{dy}{dx}(x = x_0) \qquad \text{or more compactly by } \frac{dy}{dx}(x_0) \qquad \text{or } y'(x_0)$$

An alternative notation is

$$\left.\frac{dy}{dx}\right|_{x=x_0} \qquad \text{or} \qquad \left.\frac{dy}{dx}\right|_{x_0}$$

So, for Example 10.7 we could have written

$$\frac{dy}{dx}(1) = 2 \qquad \frac{dy}{dx}(x = -1) = -2 \qquad \left.\frac{dy}{dx}\right|_{x=2} = 4 \qquad y'(2) = 4$$

**Example 10.8** Refer to Figure 10.10. By considering the gradient of the tangent at the points A, B, C, D and E state whether $\frac{dy}{dx}$ is positive, negative or zero at these points.

**Solution** At A and C the tangent is parallel to the $x$ axis and so $\frac{dy}{dx}$ is zero. At B and E the tangent has a positive gradient and so $\frac{dy}{dx}$ is positive. At D the tangent has a negative gradient and thus $\frac{dy}{dx}$ is negative.

---

As we saw in Chapter 3, functions are used to represent physically important quantities such as voltage and current. When the current through certain devices changes, this can give rise to voltages, the magnitudes of which are proportional to the rate of change of the current. Consequently differentiation is needed to model these effects as illustrated in Examples 10.9 and 10.10.

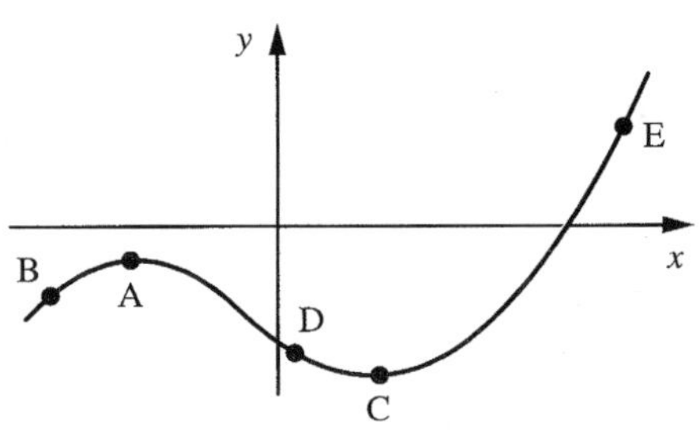


**Figure 10.10** Graph for Example 10.8.

**Example 10.9** **Voltage across an inductor**

The voltage, $v$, across an inductor with inductance, $L$, is related to the current, $i$, through the inductor by

$$v = L\frac{di}{dt}$$

This relationship is a quantification of Faraday's law which states that the voltage induced in a coil is proportional to the rate of change of magnetic flux through it. If the current in a coil is changing then this corresponds to a change in the magnetic flux through the coil. Note that if $\frac{di}{dt}$ is large then $v$ is large.

**Example 10.10** **Current through a capacitor**

The current, $i$, through a capacitor with capacitance, $C$, is related to the voltage, $v$, across the capacitor by

$$i = C\frac{dv}{dt}$$

It may appear confusing to talk of a current flow through a capacitor as no actual charge flows through the capacitor apart from that caused by any leakage current. Instead there is a build-up of charge on the plates of the capacitor. This in turn gives rise to a voltage across the capacitor. If the current flow is large then the rate of change of this voltage will be large. The current flow through the capacitor wires is termed a **conduction current** while that between the capacitor plates is called a **displacement current**.

---

We can relate the small changes $\delta x$ and $\delta y$ to the derivative $\frac{dy}{dx}$.

If $\delta x$ is very small yet still finite we can state that

$$\frac{dy}{dx} \approx \frac{\delta y}{\delta x} \tag{10.1}$$

This result allows an important approximation to be made. From Equation (10.1) we see that if a small change, $\delta x$, is made to the independent variable, the corresponding change in the dependent variable is given by the following formula:

$$\delta y \approx \frac{dy}{dx}\delta x$$

**Example 10.11** If $y = x^2$ estimate the change in $y$ caused by changing $x$ from 3 to 3.1.

**Solution** If $y = x^2$ then $\frac{dy}{dx} = 2x$. The approximate change in the dependent variable is given by

$$\delta y \approx \frac{dy}{dx}\delta x = 2x\delta x$$

Taking $x = 3$ and $\delta x = 0.1$ we have

$$\delta y \approx (2)(3)(0.1) = 0.6$$

We conclude that at the point where $x = 3$ a change in $x$ to 3.1 causes an approximate change of 0.6 in the value of $y$.

## Exercises 10.5

1 Calculate the gradient of the functions at the specified points.

(a) $y = 2x^2$ at (1, 2)

(b) $y = 2x - x^2$ at (0, 0)

(c) $y = 1 + x + x^2$ at (2, 7)

(d) $y = 2x^2 + 1$ at (2, 9)

2 A function, $y$, is such that $\dfrac{dy}{dx}$ is constant. What can you say about the function, $y$?

3 For which graphs in Figure 10.11 is the derivative always (a) positive or (b) negative?

4 Find the derivative of $y(x)$ where $y$ is

(a) $x^2$

(b) $-x^2 + 2x$

5 Differentiate $y = 2x^2 + 9$; that is, find $\dfrac{dy}{dx}$. What is the rate of change of $y$ when $x = 3, -2, 1, 0$?

6 Find the rate of change of $y = 4t - t^2$. What is the value of $\dfrac{dy}{dt}$ when $t = 2$?

7 If $y = x^3 - 3x^2 + x$ then

$$\frac{dy}{dx} = 3x^2 - 6x + 1$$

Estimate the change in $y$ as $x$ changes from

(a) 2 to 2.05

(b) 0 to 0.025

(c) $-1$ to $-1.05$

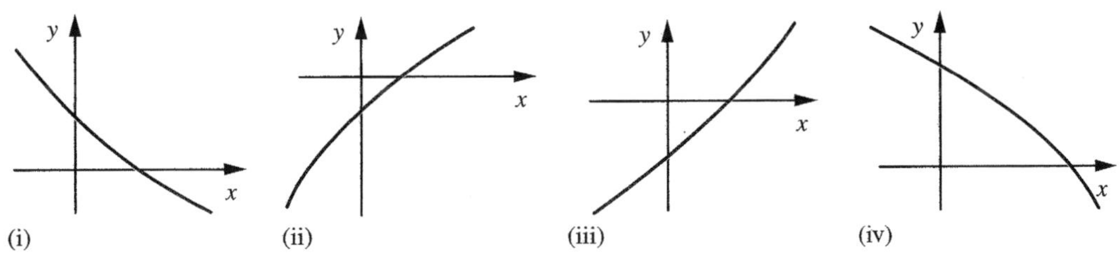


**Figure 10.11**

## Solutions

1 (a) 4 (b) 2 (c) 5 (d) 8

2 $y$ is linear in $x$, that is $y = ax + b$

3 (i) always negative (ii) always positive (iii) always positive (iv) always negative

4 (a) $2x$ (b) $-2x + 2$

5 $4x, 12, -8, 4, 0$

6 $4 - 2t, 0$

7 (a) 0.05 (b) 0.025 (c) $-0.5$

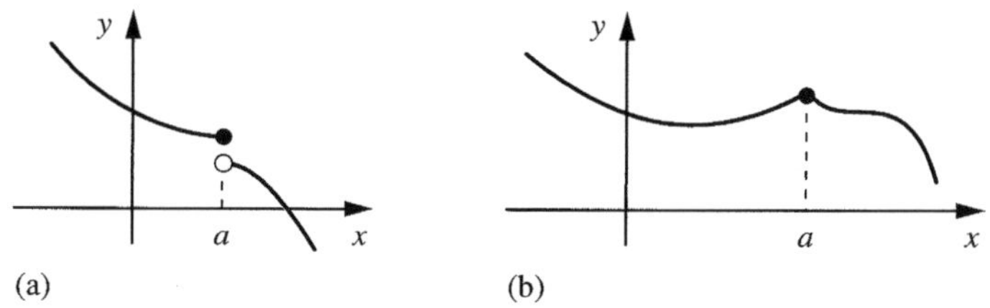


**Figure 10.12**
(a) The graph has a discontinuity at $x = a$.
(b) The graph has a cusp at $x = a$.

## 10.6 Existence of derivatives

So far we have seen that the derivative, $\frac{dy}{dx}$, of a function, $y(x)$, may be viewed either algebraically or geometrically.

$$\frac{dy}{dx} = \lim_{\delta x \to 0} \left( \frac{y(x + \delta x) - y(x)}{\delta x} \right)$$

$$\frac{dy}{dx} = \text{rate of change of } y$$

$$= \text{gradient of the graph of } y$$

We now discuss briefly the existence of $\frac{dy}{dx}$. For some functions the derivative does not exist at certain points and we need to be able to recognize such points. Consider the graphs shown in Figure 10.12. Figure 10.12(a) shows a function with a discontinuity at $x = a$. The function shown in Figure 10.12(b) is continuous but has a **cusp** or **corner** at $x = a$. In both cases it is impossible to draw a tangent at $x = a$, and so $\frac{dy}{dx}$ does not exist at $x = a$. It is impossible to draw a tangent to a curve at a point where the curve is not smooth. Note from Figure 10.12(b) that continuity is not sufficient to guarantee the existence of a derivative.

**Example 10.12** Sketch the following functions. State the values of $t$ for which the derivative does not exist.

(a) $y = |t|$ (b) $y = \tan t$ (c) $y = 1/t$

**Solution**

(a) The graph of $y = |t|$ is shown in Figure 10.13(a). A corner exists at $t = 0$ and so the derivative does not exist here.

(b) A graph of $y = \tan t$ is shown in Figure 10.13(b). There is a discontinuity in $\tan t$ when $t = \ldots - 3\pi/2, -\pi/2, \pi/2, 3\pi/2, \ldots$. No derivative exists at these points.

(c) Figure 10.13(c) shows a graph of $y = 1/t$. The function has one discontinuity at $t = 0$, and so the derivative does not exist here.

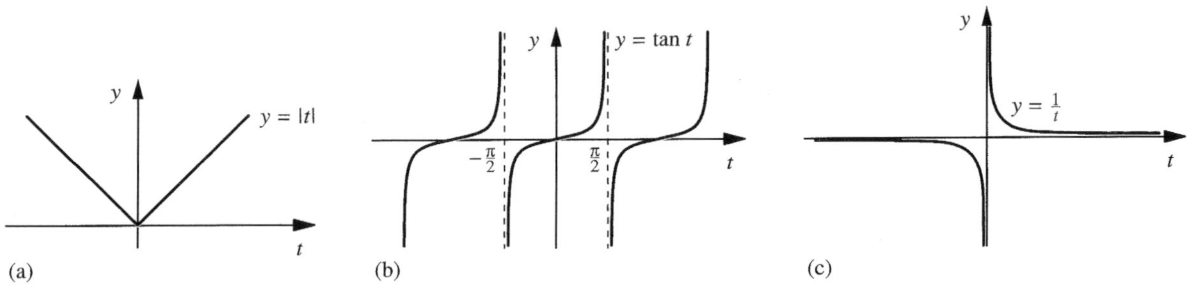


**Figure 10.13** (a) There is a corner at $t = 0$; (b) $\tan t$ has discontinuities; (c) $y = 1/t$ has a discontinuity at $t = 0$.

## Exercises 10.6

**1** Sketch the functions and determine any points where a derivative does not exist.

(a) $y = \dfrac{1}{t-1}$

(b) $y = |\sin t|$

(c) $y = e^t$

(d) $y = |1/t|$

(e) The unit step function $u(t) = \begin{cases} 1 & t \geqslant 0 \\ 0 & t < 0 \end{cases}$

(f) The ramp function $f(t) = \begin{cases} ct & t \geqslant 0 \\ 0 & t < 0 \end{cases}$

## Solutions

**1** See Figure S.17.

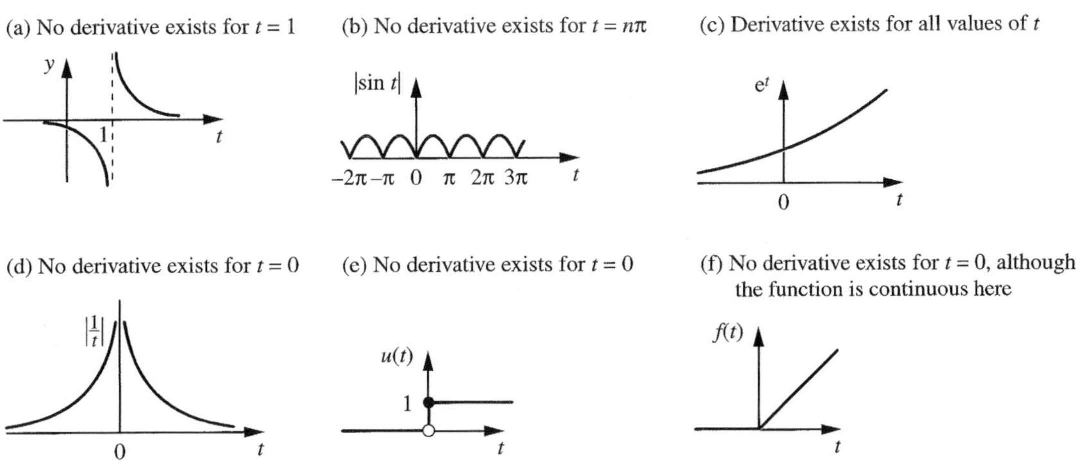


**Figure S.17**

**Table 10.1** Derivatives of commonly used functions.

| Function, $y(x)$ | Derivative, $y'$ | Function, $y(x)$ | Derivative, $y'$ |
|---|---|---|---|
| constant | $0$ | $\cos^{-1}(ax+b)$ | $\dfrac{-a}{\sqrt{1-(ax+b)^2}}$ |
| $x^n$ | $nx^{n-1}$ | | |
| $e^x$ | $e^x$ | $\tan^{-1}(ax+b)$ | $\dfrac{a}{1+(ax+b)^2}$ |
| $e^{-x}$ | $-e^{-x}$ | | |
| $e^{ax}$ | $ae^{ax}$ | $\sinh(ax+b)$ | $a\cosh(ax+b)$ |
| | | $\cosh(ax+b)$ | $a\sinh(ax+b)$ |
| $\ln x$ | $\dfrac{1}{x}$ | $\tanh(ax+b)$ | $a\,\text{sech}^2(ax+b)$ |
| $\sin x$ | $\cos x$ | $\text{cosech}(ax+b)$ | $-a\,\text{cosech}(ax+b)\times \coth(ax+b)$ |
| $\cos x$ | $-\sin x$ | | |
| $\sin(ax+b)$ | $a\cos(ax+b)$ | $\text{sech}(ax+b)$ | $-a\,\text{sech}(ax+b)\times \tanh(ax+b)$ |
| $\cos(ax+b)$ | $-a\sin(ax+b)$ | | |
| $\tan(ax+b)$ | $a\sec^2(ax+b)$ | $\coth(ax+b)$ | $-a\,\text{cosech}^2(ax+b)$ |
| $\text{cosec}(ax+b)$ | $-a\,\text{cosec}(ax+b)\cot(ax+b)$ | $\sinh^{-1}(ax+b)$ | $\dfrac{a}{\sqrt{(ax+b)^2+1}}$ |
| $\sec(ax+b)$ | $a\sec(ax+b)\tan(ax+b)$ | | |
| $\cot(ax+b)$ | $-a\,\text{cosec}^2(ax+b)$ | $\cosh^{-1}(ax+b)$ | $\dfrac{a}{\sqrt{(ax+b)^2-1}}$ |
| $\sin^{-1}(ax+b)$ | $\dfrac{a}{\sqrt{1-(ax+b)^2}}$ | $\tanh^{-1}(ax+b)$ | $\dfrac{a}{1-(ax+b)^2}$ |

## 10.7 Common derivatives

It is time consuming to find the derivative of $y(x)$ using the 'shrinking interval' method (often referred to as **differentiation from first principles**). Consequently the derivatives of commonly used functions are listed for reference in Table 10.1. It will be helpful to memorize the most common derivatives. Note that $a$, $b$ and $n$ are constants. In the trigonometric functions, the quantity $ax + b$, being an angle, must be measured in radians.

A shorter table of the more common derivatives is given on the inside back cover of this book for easy reference.

**Example 10.13** Use Table 10.1 to find $y'$ when

(a) $y = e^{-7x}$

(b) $y = x^5$

(c) $y = \tan(3x - 2)$

(d) $y = \sin(\omega x + \phi)$

(e) $y = \dfrac{1}{\sqrt{x}}$

(f) $y = \dfrac{1}{x^5}$

(g) $y = \cosh^{-1} 5x$

**Solution** (a) From Table 10.1, we find that if

$$y = e^{ax} \qquad \text{then} \qquad y' = a\,e^{ax}$$

In this case, $a = -7$ and so if

$$y = e^{-7x} \qquad \text{then} \qquad y' = -7\,e^{-7x}$$

(b) From Table 10.1, we find that if

$$y = x^n \qquad \text{then} \qquad y' = nx^{n-1}$$

In this case, $n = 5$ and so if

$$y = x^5 \qquad \text{then} \qquad y' = 5x^4$$

(c) If $y = \tan(ax + b)$ then $y' = a\sec^2(ax + b)$. In this case, $a = 3$ and $b = -2$. Hence if

$$y = \tan(3x - 2) \qquad \text{then} \qquad y' = 3\sec^2(3x - 2)$$

(d) If $y = \sin(ax + b)$ then $y' = a\cos(ax + b)$. Here $a = \omega$ and $b = \phi$, and so if

$$y = \sin(\omega x + \phi) \qquad \text{then} \qquad y' = \omega\cos(\omega x + \phi)$$

(e) Note that $\dfrac{1}{\sqrt{x}} = x^{-1/2}$. From Table 10.1 we find that if $y = x^n$ then $y' = nx^{n-1}$. In this case, $n = -1/2$ and so if

$$y = \frac{1}{\sqrt{x}} \qquad \text{then} \qquad y' = -\frac{1}{2}x^{-3/2}$$

(f) Note that $\dfrac{1}{x^5} = x^{-5}$. Using Table 10.1, we find that if $y = x^{-5}$ then $y' = -5x^{-6}$.

(g) From Table 10.1, if $y = \cosh^{-1}(ax + b)$ then

$$y' = \frac{a}{\sqrt{(ax + b)^2 - 1}}$$

In this case, $a = 5$ and $b = 0$. Hence, if

$$y = \cosh^{-1} 5x \qquad \text{then} \qquad y' = \frac{5}{\sqrt{25x^2 - 1}}$$

**Example 10.14** Differentiate $y(t) = e^t$.

**Solution** We note that the independent variable is $t$. However, Table 10.1 can still be used. From Table 10.1, we find

$$\frac{dy}{dt} = e^t = y$$

We note that the derivative of $e^t$ is again $e^t$. This is the only function which reproduces itself upon differentiation.

## Exercises 10.7

1 Use Table 10.1 to find $y'$ given:

(a) $y = t^2$
(b) $y = t^9$
(c) $y = t^{-3}$
(d) $y = t$
(e) $y = \frac{1}{t}$
(f) $y = \frac{1}{t^2}$
(g) $y = e^{3t}$
(h) $y = e^{-3t}$
(i) $y = \frac{1}{e^{5t}}$
(j) $y = t^{1/2}$
(k) $y = \sin(2t + 3)$
(l) $y = \cos(4 - t)$
(m) $y = \tan\left(\frac{t}{2} + 1\right)$
(n) $y = \text{cosec}(3t + 7)$
(o) $y = \cot(1 - t)$
(p) $y = \sec(2t - \pi)$
(q) $y = \sin^{-1}(t + \pi)$
(r) $y = \pi$
(s) $y = \tan^{-1}(-2t - 1)$
(t) $y = \cos^{-1}(4t - 3)$
(u) $y = \tanh(6t)$
(v) $y = \cosh(2t + 5)$
(w) $y = \sinh\left(\frac{t + 3}{2}\right)$
(x) $y = \text{sech}(-t)$
(y) $y = \coth\left(\frac{2t}{3} - \frac{1}{2}\right)$
(z) $y = \cosh^{-1}(t + 3)$

2 Find $\frac{dy}{dx}$ when

(a) $y = \frac{1}{\sqrt{x}}$
(b) $y = e^{2x/3}$
(c) $y = e^{-x/2}$
(d) $y = \ln x$
(e) $y = \text{cosec}\left(\frac{2x - 1}{3}\right)$
(f) $y = \tan^{-1}(\pi x + 3)$
(g) $y = \tanh(2x + 1)$
(h) $y = \sinh^{-1}(-3x)$
(i) $y = \cot(\omega x + \pi)$ $\quad\omega$ constant
(j) $y = \frac{1}{\sin(5x + 3)}$
(k) $y = \cos 3x$
(l) $y = \frac{1}{\cos 3x}$
(m) $y = \tan(2x + \pi)$
(n) $y = \text{cosech}\left(\frac{x - 1}{2}\right)$
(o) $y = \tanh^{-1}\left(\frac{2x + 3}{7}\right)$

## Solutions

**1**

(a) $2t$

(b) $9t^8$

(c) $-3t^{-4}$

(d) $1$

(e) $-t^{-2}$

(f) $-2t^{-3}$

(g) $3\,\mathrm{e}^{3t}$

(h) $-3\,\mathrm{e}^{-3t}$

(i) $-5\,\mathrm{e}^{-5t}$

(j) $0.5t^{-1/2}$

(k) $2\cos(2t+3)$

(l) $\sin(4-t)$

(m) $0.5\sec^2(t/2+1)$

(n) $-3\,\mathrm{cosec}(3t+7)\cot(3t+7)$

(o) $\mathrm{cosec}^2(1-t)$

(p) $2\sec(2t-\pi)\tan(2t-\pi)$

(q) $\dfrac{1}{\sqrt{1-(t+\pi)^2}}$

(r) $0$

(s) $-\dfrac{2}{1+(-2t-1)^2}$

(t) $-\dfrac{4}{\sqrt{1-(4t-3)^2}}$

(u) $6\,\mathrm{sech}^2\,6t$

(v) $2\sinh(2t+5)$

(w) $0.5\cosh\left(\dfrac{t+3}{2}\right)$

(x) $\mathrm{sech}(-t)\tanh(-t)$

(y) $-\dfrac{2}{3}\,\mathrm{cosech}^2\left(\dfrac{2t}{3}-\dfrac{1}{2}\right)$

(z) $\dfrac{1}{\sqrt{(t+3)^2-1}}$

**2**

(a) $-0.5x^{-3/2}$

(b) $\frac{2}{3}\,\mathrm{e}^{2x/3}$

(c) $-0.5\,\mathrm{e}^{-x/2}$

(d) $1/x$

(e) $-\dfrac{2}{3}\,\mathrm{cosec}\left(\dfrac{2x-1}{3}\right)\cot\left(\dfrac{2x-1}{3}\right)$

(f) $\dfrac{\pi}{1+(\pi x+3)^2}$

(g) $2\,\mathrm{sech}^2(2x+1)$

(h) $-\dfrac{3}{\sqrt{9x^2+1}}$

(i) $-\omega\,\mathrm{cosec}^2(\omega x+\pi)$

(j) $-5\,\mathrm{cosec}(5x+3)\cot(5x+3)$

(k) $-3\sin 3x$

(l) $3\sec 3x\tan 3x$

(m) $2\sec^2(2x+\pi)$

(n) $-0.5\,\mathrm{cosech}\left(\dfrac{x-1}{2}\right)\coth\left(\dfrac{x-1}{2}\right)$

(o) $\dfrac{2}{7\left[1-\left(\dfrac{2x+3}{7}\right)^2\right]}$

## 10.8 Differentiation as a linear operator

In mathematical language differentiation is a **linear operator**. This means that if we wish to differentiate the sum of two functions we can differentiate each function separately and then simply add the two derivatives, that is

derivative of $(f+g)$ = derivative of $f$ + derivative of $g$

This is expressed mathematically as

$$\frac{\mathrm{d}}{\mathrm{d}x}(f+g)=\frac{\mathrm{d}f}{\mathrm{d}x}+\frac{\mathrm{d}g}{\mathrm{d}x}$$

We can regard $\frac{d}{dx}$ as the operation of differentiation being applied to the expression which follows it. The properties of a linear operator also make the handling of constant factors easy. To differentiate $kf$, where $k$ is a constant, we take $k$ times the derivative of $f$, that is

$$\text{derivative of } (kf) = k \times \text{derivative of } f$$

Mathematically, we would state:

$$\frac{d}{dx}(kf) = k\frac{df}{dx}$$

Table 10.1 together with these two linearity properties allows us to differentiate some quite complicated functions.

**Example 10.15** Differentiate

(a) $3x^2$ (b) $9x$ (c) $7$ (d) $3x^2 + 9x + 7$

**Solution** (a) Let $y = 3x^2$, then

$$\begin{aligned}\frac{dy}{dx} &= \frac{d}{dx}(3x^2)\\ &= 3\frac{d}{dx}(x^2) \text{ using linearity}\\ &= 3(2x) \text{ from the table}\\ &= 6x\end{aligned}$$

(b) Let $y = 9x$, then

$$\begin{aligned}\frac{dy}{dx} &= \frac{d}{dx}(9x)\\ &= 9\frac{d}{dx}(x) \text{ using linearity}\\ &= 9\end{aligned}$$

(c) Let $y = 7$, then $y' = 0$.

(d) Let $y = 3x^2 + 9x + 7$

$$\begin{aligned}\frac{dy}{dx} &= \frac{d}{dx}(3x^2 + 9x + 7)\\ \frac{dy}{dx} &= 3\frac{d}{dx}(x^2) + 9\frac{d}{dx}(x) + \frac{d}{dx}(7) \text{ using linearity}\\ &= 6x + 9\end{aligned}$$

**Example 10.16** **Fluid flow into a tank**

If fluid is being poured into a tank at a rate of $q$ m$^3$ s$^{-1}$, then this will result in an increase in volume, $V$, of fluid in the tank. The rate of increase in volume, $\frac{dV}{dt}$ m$^3$ s$^{-1}$, is given by

$$\frac{dV}{dt} = q$$

This relationship follows from the principle of conservation of mass. If $q$ is large, then $\frac{dV}{dt}$ is large, which corresponds to the fluid volume in the tank increasing at a fast rate. Consequently, the height of the fluid, $h$, also increases at a fast rate. If the cross-sectional area of the tank, $A$, is constant, then $V = Ah$. Therefore,

$$\frac{dV}{dt} = \frac{d}{dt}(Ah) = A\frac{dh}{dt}$$

because differentiation is a linear operator. So,

$$A\frac{dh}{dt} = q$$

**Example 10.17** Use Table 10.1 and the linearity properties of differentiation to find $y'$ where

(a) $y = 3\,e^{2x}$

(b) $y = 1/x$

(c) $y = 3\sin 4x$

(d) $y = \sin 2x - \cos 5x$

(e) $y = 3\ln x$

(f) $y = \ln 2x$

(g) $y = 3x^2 + 7x - 5$

**Solution** (a) If $y = 3\,e^{2x}$, then

$$\frac{dy}{dx} = \frac{d}{dx}(3e^{2x}) = 3\frac{d}{dx}(e^{2x}) \qquad \text{using linearity}$$

$$= 3(2e^{2x}) \qquad \text{using Table 10.1}$$

$$= 6\,e^{2x}$$

(b) If $y = x^{-1}$, then

$$y' = -1x^{-2} \qquad \text{from Table 10.1}$$

$$= -\frac{1}{x^2}$$

(c) If $y = 3\sin 4x$, then

$$\frac{dy}{dx} = \frac{d}{dx}(3\sin 4x) = 3\frac{d}{dx}(\sin 4x) \qquad \text{using linearity}$$
$$= 3(4\cos 4x) \qquad \text{using Table 10.1}$$
$$= 12\cos 4x$$

(d) The linearity properties allow us to differentiate each term individually. If,

$$y = \sin 2x - \cos 5x \qquad \text{then} \qquad \frac{dy}{dx} = \frac{d}{dx}(\sin 2x) - \frac{d}{dx}(\cos 5x)$$
$$= 2\cos 2x + 5\sin 5x$$

(e) If $y = 3\ln x$, then

$$\frac{dy}{dx} = \frac{d}{dx}(3\ln x) = 3\frac{d}{dx}(\ln x) \qquad \text{using linearity}$$
$$= \frac{3}{x} \qquad \text{using Table 10.1}$$

(f) If $y = \ln 2x$, then

$$y = \ln 2 + \ln x \qquad \text{using laws of logarithms}$$

and so

$$\frac{dy}{dx} = 0 + \frac{1}{x} = \frac{1}{x} \qquad \text{since } \ln 2 \text{ is constant}$$

(g) Each term is differentiated:

$$y' = 6x + 7 - 0 = 6x + 7$$

**Example 10.18** **Small-signal resistance**

In Chapter 2, Example 2.18, we examined the mathematical model of a semiconductor diode. At room temperature this was

$$I = I_s(e^{40V} - 1)$$

where $I$ is the diode current, $V$ is the applied voltage and $I_s$ is the constant reverse saturation current. Sometimes when a diode is used in a circuit it may be **biased** to operate in a certain region of its $I$–$V$ characteristic. This means that its use is restricted to a certain voltage range. The point around which it operates is known as its **operating point**. This is illustrated in Figure 10.14.

Deviations from this operating point may be small in certain cases. If so, they are known as **small-signal** variations and are caused by small a.c. voltages being superimposed on the main d.c. bias voltage. In calculating how the diode will react to such small-signal voltages, the slope of the diode characteristic around the operating point is

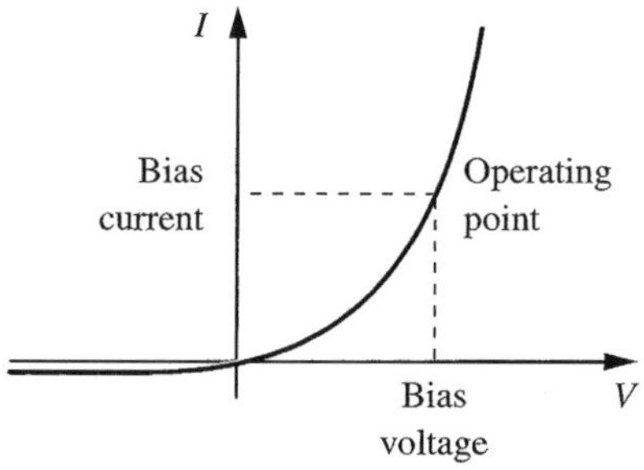


**Figure 10.14** Diode characteristic showing operating point.

more relevant than the overall ratio of current to voltage. Provided the deviations from the operating point are not large, the tangent to the $I$–$V$ curve at the operating point provides an adequate model for how the diode will behave. The slope of the curve can be obtained by differentiating the diode equation. If

$$I = I_s(e^{40V} - 1) = I_s e^{40V} - I_s$$

then

$$\frac{dI}{dV} = 40 I_s e^{40V}$$

since $I_s$ is constant.

It is usual to write small changes in current and voltage as $\delta I$ and $\delta V$. Therefore, since

$$\frac{\delta I}{\delta V} \approx \frac{dI}{dV}$$
$$\delta I \approx 40 I_s e^{40V} \delta V$$

This expression allows the change in diode current, $\delta I$, to be estimated given a change in diode voltage, $\delta V$, provided the operating point is known and the changes are small.

**Example 10.19** Find the derivative of $y = e^{-t} + t^2$, when

(a) $t = 1$

(b) $t = 0$

**Solution**

$$y = e^{-t} + t^2$$
$$y' = -e^{-t} + 2t$$

(a) When $t = 1$, $y' = -e^{-1} + 2 = 1.632$, that is $y'(1) = 1.632$.

(b) When $t = 0$, $y' = -1$, that is $y'(0) = -1$.

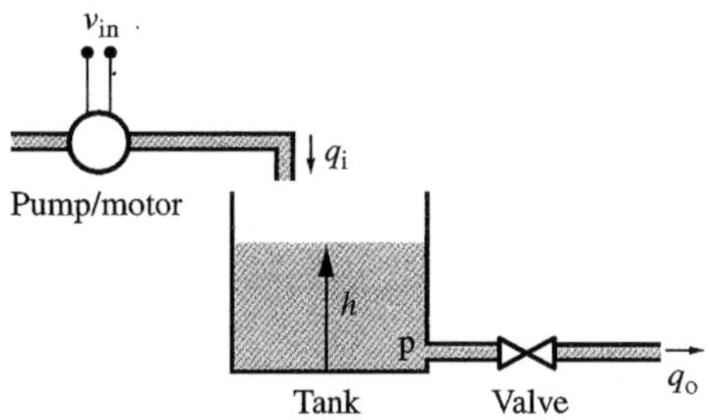


**Figure 10.15**
A fluid system comprising pump, tank and valve.

**Example 10.20** **Obtaining a linear model for a simple fluid system**

Consider the fluid system illustrated in Figure 10.15. The pump is driven by a d.c. motor. The pump/motor can be modelled by a linear relationship in which the fluid flow rate, $q_i$, is proportional to the control voltage, $v_{in}$, that is

$$q_i = k_p v_{in}$$

where $k_p$ = pump/motor constant, $v_{in}$ = control voltage (V), $q_i$ = flow rate into the tank ($m^3\ s^{-1}$). The valve has a non-linear characteristic given by the quadratic polynomial

$$p = 20\,000\, q_o^2$$

where $p$ = pressure at the base of the tank ($N\ m^{-2}$), $q_o$ = flow out of the tank ($m^3\ s^{-1}$). The fluid being used is water which has a density $\rho = 998\ kg\ m^{-3}$. Assume $g = 9.81\ m\ s^{-2}$ and that $k_p = 0.03\ m^3\ s^{-1} V^{-1}$. Carry out the following:

(a) Calculate the flow rate out of the tank, $q_o$, and the control voltage, $v_{in}$, when the system is in equilibrium and the height of the water in the tank, $h$, is 0.25 m.

(b) Obtain a linear model for the system, valid for small changes about a water height of 0.25 m. Use this model to calculate the new water height and flow rate out of the tank when the control voltage is increased by 0.4 V.

**Solution** (a) The pressure at the bottom of the tank is given by

$$p = \rho g h = 998 \times 9.81 \times 0.25 = 2448$$

The flow rate through the valve is given by

$$q_o^2 = \frac{p}{20\,000}$$

$$q_o = \sqrt{\frac{p}{20\,000}} = \sqrt{\frac{2448}{20\,000}} = 0.350\ m^3\ s^{-1}$$

Now if the system is in equilibrium, then the height of the water in the tank must have stabilized to a constant value. Therefore,

$$q_i = q_o = 0.350$$

and so

$$v_{in} = \frac{q_i}{k_p} = \frac{0.350}{0.03} = 11.7\ V$$

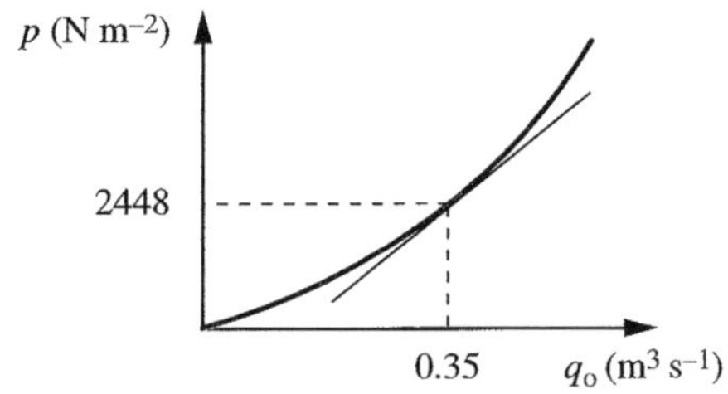


**Figure 10.16** Relationship between pressure across valve ($p$) and flow through valve ($q_o$).

(b) Before answering this part it is worth examining what is meant by a **linear model**. Figure 10.16 shows the valve characteristic together with a linear approximation around an output flow rate of $q_o = 0.350$ m$^3$ s$^{-1}$. This corresponds to a water height of 0.25 m.

A linear model for the valve is one in which the relationship between $p$ and $q_o$ is approximated by the straight line which forms a tangent to the curve at the operating point. The operating point is the point around which the model is valid. It is clear that if the straight line approximation is used for points that are a large distance from the operating point, then the linear model will not be very accurate. However, for small changes around the operating point the approximation is reasonably accurate. Clearly a different operating point will require a different linear approximation. In order to obtain the gradient of this line it is necessary to differentiate the function relating valve pressure to valve flow. So,

$$p = 20\,000q_o^2$$

$$\frac{dp}{dq_o} = 40\,000q_o$$

At the operating point $q_o = 0.350$. Therefore,

$$\left.\frac{dp}{dq_o}\right|_{q_o=0.350} = 40\,000 \times 0.350 = 14\,000$$

This value is the gradient of the tangent to the curve at the operating point. Small changes around an operating point are usually indicated by the notation $\delta$. Therefore,

$$\frac{\delta p}{\delta q_o} \approx \left.\frac{dp}{dq_o}\right|_{q_o=0.350} = 14\,000$$

$$\delta p = 14\,000\delta q_o \qquad (10.2)$$

Note that equality has been assumed for the purposes of the linear model. It is easy to relate a change in pump flow to a change in control voltage because the relationship is linear and so a linear approximation is not required. So,

$$q_i = k_p v_{in}$$

Differentiating this equation w.r.t. $v_{in}$ yields

$$\frac{dq_i}{dv_{in}} = k_p$$

In this case

$$\frac{\delta q_{\mathrm{i}}}{\delta v_{\mathrm{in}}} = \frac{\mathrm{d}q_{\mathrm{i}}}{\mathrm{d}v_{\mathrm{in}}} = k_{\mathrm{p}}$$

and has a constant value independent of the operating point:

$$\delta q_{\mathrm{i}} = k_{\mathrm{p}}\,\delta v_{\mathrm{in}} \qquad (10.3)$$

The relationship between pressure at the bottom of the tank and the water height is also linear.

Since $p = \rho g h$ we have $\frac{\mathrm{d}p}{dh} = \rho g$. Because $\frac{\mathrm{d}p}{dh}$ is a constant we can write

$$\frac{\delta p}{\delta h} = \frac{\mathrm{d}p}{dh} = \rho g$$

$$\delta p = \rho g\,\delta h \qquad (10.4)$$

The change in control voltage, $\delta v_{\mathrm{in}}$, is given as 0.4. We also know that $k_{\mathrm{p}} = 0.03$. Therefore, using Equation (10.3), we have

$$\delta q_{\mathrm{i}} = 0.03 \times 0.4 = 0.012$$

Now if time is allowed for the system to reach equilibrium with this increased input flow, then $\delta q_{\mathrm{o}} = \delta q_{\mathrm{i}}$. In other words, the output flow increases by the same amount as the input flow and the water height once again stabilizes to a fixed value. Therefore,

$$\delta q_{\mathrm{o}} = \delta q_{\mathrm{i}} = 0.012$$

Using Equation (10.2), we find

$$\delta p = 14\,000\,\delta q_{\mathrm{o}} = 14\,000 \times 0.012 = 168$$

Using Equation (10.4), we get

$$\delta h = \frac{\delta p}{\rho g} = \frac{168}{998 \times 9.81} = 0.0172$$

Therefore the new water height is $0.25 + 0.0172 = 0.267$ m to three significant figures. The new water flow rate is $0.35 + 0.012 = 0.362\ \mathrm{m}^3\ \mathrm{s}^{-1}$.

To recap, all the elements of the fluid system were linear apart from the valve. By obtaining a linear model for the valve, valid for values close to the operating point, it was possible to calculate the effect of changing the control voltage to the motor. It is important to stress that the linear model for the valve is only good for small changes around the operating point. In this case the increase in control voltage was approximately 3%. The model would not have been very good for predicting the effect of a 50% increase in control voltage. Linear models of non-linear systems are particularly useful when several components are non-linear, as they are much easier to analyse. We examine these concepts in more detail in Chapter 18.

## Exercises 10.8

1 Differentiate the following functions.

(a) $y = 4x^3 - 5x^2$

(b) $y = 3\sin(5t) + 2\,e^{4t}$

(c) $y = \sin(4t) + 3\cos(2t) - t$

(d) $y = \tan(3z)$

(e) $y = 2\,e^{3t} + 17 - 4\sin(2t)$

(f) $y = \dfrac{1}{t^3} + \dfrac{\cos 5t}{2}$

(g) $y = \dfrac{2w^3}{3} + \dfrac{e^{4w}}{2}$

(h) $y = \sqrt{x} + \ln(\sqrt{x})$. [*Hint*: $\sqrt{x} = x^{1/2}$, and use the laws of logarithms.]

2 Evaluate the derivatives of the functions at the given value.

(a) $y = 2t + 9 + e^{t/2}$ $\quad t = 1$

(b) $y = \dfrac{t^2 - 4t + 6}{3}$ $\quad t = 2$

(c) $y = \sin t + \cos t$ $\quad t = 1$

(d) $y = 3\,e^{2t} - 2\sin\left(\dfrac{t}{2}\right)$ $\quad t = 0$

(e) $y = 5\tan(2x) + \dfrac{1}{e^{2x}}$ $\quad x = 0.5$

(f) $y = 3\ln t + \sin(3t)$ $\quad t = 0.25$

3 Find $\dfrac{dx}{dt}$, if

(a) $x = e^{\omega t}$

(b) $x = e^{-\omega t}$

where $\omega$ is a constant.

4 Find the derivative of

(a) $y = 3\sin^{-1}(2t) - 5\cos^{-1}(3t)$

(b) $y = \frac{1}{2}\tan^{-1}(t + 2) + 4\cos^{-1}(2t - 1)$

(c) $y = 2\sinh(3t - 1) - 4\cosh\left(\dfrac{t - 3}{2}\right)$

(d) $y = \dfrac{\operatorname{cosech}(4t) + 3\operatorname{sech}(6t)}{2}$

(e) $y = 2\sinh^{-1}\left(\dfrac{t + 1}{2}\right) - 3\cosh^{-1}\left(\dfrac{1 - t}{2}\right)$

(f) $y = 3\tanh^{-1}(2t + 3) - 2\tanh^{-1}(3t + 2)$

5 A function, $y(t)$, is given by

$$y(t) = \frac{t^3}{3} - \frac{5t^2}{2} + 4t + 1$$

(a) Find $\dfrac{dy}{dt}$.

(b) For which values of $t$ is the derivative zero?

6 Find the equation of the tangent to the curve

$$y(x) = x^3 + 7x^2 - 9$$

at the point (2, 27).

7 Find values of $t$ in the interval $[0, \pi]$ for which the tangent to $x(t) = \sin 2t$ has zero gradient.

8 Find the rate of change of

$$z(t) = 2\,e^{t/2} - t^2$$

when

(a) $t = 0$

(b) $t = 3$

## Solutions

1 (a) $12x^2 - 10x$

(b) $15\cos 5t + 8\,e^{4t}$

(c) $4\cos 4t - 6\sin 2t - 1$

(d) $3\sec^2 3z$

(e) $6\,e^{3t} - 8\cos 2t$

(f) $-\dfrac{3}{t^4} - 2.5\sin 5t$

(g) $2w^2 + 2\,e^{4w}$

(h) $0.5x^{-1/2} + \dfrac{1}{2x}$

2 (a) 2.8244 (b) 0
(c) −0.3012 (d) 5
(e) 33.5194 (f) 14.195

3 (a) $\omega\,e^{\omega t}$ (b) $-\omega\,e^{-\omega t}$

4 (a) $\dfrac{6}{\sqrt{1-4t^2}}+\dfrac{15}{\sqrt{1-9t^2}}$

(b) $\dfrac{1}{2[1+(t+2)^2]}-\dfrac{4}{\sqrt{t(1-t)}}$

(c) $6\cosh(3t-1)-2\sinh\dfrac{t-3}{2}$

(d) $-2\,\mathrm{cosech}\,4t\coth 4t-9\,\mathrm{sech}\,6t\tanh 6t$

(e) $\dfrac{1}{\sqrt{\left(\frac{1}{2}(t+1)\right)^2+1}}+\dfrac{3}{2\sqrt{\left(\frac{1}{2}(1-t)\right)^2-1}}$

(f) $\dfrac{6}{1-(2t+3)^2}-\dfrac{6}{1-(3t+2)^2}$

5 (a) $t^2-5t+4$ (b) $1, 4$

6 $y=40x-53$

7 $\pi/4, 3\pi/4$

8 (a) 1 (b) $-1.5183$

## Review exercises 10

1 Find the rate of change of $f(x)=5+3x^2$ at $x=2$ by considering each of the intervals $[2-\delta x, 2]$, $[2, 2+\delta x]$, $[2-\delta x, 2+\delta x]$. Show that the same result is obtained in each case.

2 Use a table of derivatives and the linearity rules to differentiate

(a) $y=4x^2+6x-11$

(b) $y=-x^2+2x-10$

(c) $y=x^{1/3}-x^{1/4}$

(d) $y=5\cos 4x-3\cos 2x$

(e) $y=\sin^{-1}(4x+3)$

(f) $y=\sqrt{2x^4}-\dfrac{5}{3x^2}$

(g) $y=t^{3/2}+\cos t$

(h) $y=t^2-14t+8$

(i) $y=5\ln t+\sin 4t$

(j) $y=\dfrac{1}{2}x-\dfrac{1}{3}x^2$

(k) $y=\dfrac{2t^2}{3}+e^{2t}$

3 Find the equation of the tangent to $y=x^2+7x-4$ at the point on the graph where $x=2$.

4 Find the rate of change of $f(t)=2\cos t+3\sin t$ at $t=1$.

5 At any time $t$, the voltage, $v$, across an inductor of inductance $L$ is related to the current, $i$, through the inductor by $v=L\dfrac{di}{dt}$.

(a) Find an expression for the voltage when $i=5\cos\omega t$ where $\omega$ is the constant angular frequency.

(b) Find an expression for the voltage when the current takes the form of a sine wave with amplitude 10 and period 0.01 seconds.

6 Use the shrinking interval method to find the rate of change of $f(t)=\sin t$ at $t=0$ by considering the interval $[0, \delta t]$. [*Hint*: use the trigonometric identities in Section 3.5 and the small-angle approximation in Section 6.5.] Use the shrinking interval method to find the rate of change of $f(t)=\sin t$ at a general point.

7 Given $y(t)=3+\sin 2t$, find the average rate of change of $y$ as $t$ varies from 0 to 2.

8 Explain the essential difference between $\dfrac{\delta y}{\delta x}$ and $\dfrac{dy}{dx}$.

9 Find $y'$ for the following functions:

(a) $y=2e^{-t}+6\cos(t/2)$

(b) $y=(-t+2)^2$

10 Using derivatives, estimate the change in $y$ as $x$ changes from 1.5 to 1.55 where $y=2e^{2x}+x^3$.

## Solutions

1 12

2 (a) $8x + 6$

(b) $-2x + 2$

(c) $\frac{1}{3}x^{-2/3} - \frac{1}{4}x^{-3/4}$

(d) $-20 \sin 4x + 6 \sin 2x$

(e) $\dfrac{4}{\sqrt{1 - (4x + 3)^2}}$

(f) $2\sqrt{2x} + \dfrac{10}{3x^3}$

(g) $\frac{3}{2}t^{1/2} - \sin t$

(h) $2t - 14$

(i) $\dfrac{5}{t} + 4 \cos 4t$

(j) $\frac{1}{2} - \frac{2}{3}x$

(k) $\frac{4}{3}t + 2\,e^{2t}$

3 $y = 11x - 8$

4 $-0.062$

5 (a) $-5\omega L \sin \omega t$ (b) $2000\pi L \cos 200\pi t$

7 $-0.3784$

9 (a) $-2\,e^{-t} - 3 \sin\left(\dfrac{t}{2}\right)$ (b) $2t - 4$

10 4.355

# 11 Techniques of differentiation

**Chapter 11 Contents**

## 11.1 Introduction

In this chapter we develop the techniques of differentiation introduced in Chapter 10 so that rates of change of more complicated functions can be found. We introduce rules for differentiating products and quotients of functions. The chain rule is used for differentiating functions of functions. We explain what is meant by defining functions implicitly and parametrically and show how these can be differentiated. The technique of logarithmic differentiation allows complicated products of functions to be simplified and then differentiated. Finally derivatives of functions can themselves be differentiated. This involves the use of higher derivatives which are explained towards the end of the chapter.

## 11.2 Rules of differentiation

There are three rules which enable us to differentiate more complicated functions. They are (a) the product rule, (b) the quotient rule, (c) the chain rule. Traditionally they are written with $x$ as the independent variable but apply in an analogous way for other independent variables.

### 11.2.1 The product rule

As the name suggests, this rule allows us to differentiate a product of functions, such as $x \sin x$, $t^2 \cos 2t$ and $e^z \ln z$.

The product rule states: if

$$y(x) = u(x)\, v(x)$$

then

$$\frac{dy}{dx} = \frac{du}{dx}v + u\frac{dv}{dx} = u'v + uv'$$

To apply this rule one of the functions in the product must be chosen to be $u$, and the other, $v$. Before we can apply the rule we need to calculate $u'$ and $v'$.

**Example 11.1** Find $y'$ given

(a) $y = x \sin x$

(b) $y = t^2 e^t$

(c) $y = e^{-2t} \cos 3t$

**Solution** (a) $y = x \sin x = uv$. Choose $u = x$ and $v = \sin x$. Then $u' = 1$, $v' = \cos x$. Applying the product rule to $y$ yields

$$y' = \sin x + x \cos x$$

(b) $y = t^2 e^t = uv$. Choose $u = t^2$ and $v = e^t$. Then $u' = 2t$ and $v' = e^t$. Applying the product rule to $y$ yields

$$y' = 2te^t + t^2 e^t$$

(c) $y = e^{-2t} \cos 3t = uv$. Choose $u = e^{-2t}$ and $v = \cos 3t$. Then $u' = -2e^{-2t}$ and $v' = -3 \sin 3t$. Applying the product rule yields

$$y' = -2e^{-2t} \cos 3t + e^{-2t}(-3 \sin 3t) = -e^{-2t}(2 \cos 3t + 3 \sin 3t)$$

---

### 11.2.2 The quotient rule

This rule allows us to differentiate a quotient of functions, such as $\dfrac{x}{\sin x}$, $\dfrac{t^2 - t + 3}{t + 2}$ and $\dfrac{e^{-3z}}{z^2 - 1}$.

> The quotient rule states: when
>
> $$y(x) = \frac{u(x)}{v(x)}$$
>
> then
>
> $$y' = \frac{v\left(\dfrac{du}{dx}\right) - u\left(\dfrac{dv}{dx}\right)}{v^2} = \frac{vu' - uv'}{v^2}$$

**Example 11.2** Find $y'$ given

(a) $y = \dfrac{\sin x}{x}$ (b) $y = \dfrac{t^2}{2t + 1}$ (c) $y = \dfrac{e^{2t}}{t^2 + 1}$

**Solution** (a) $y = \dfrac{\sin x}{x} = \dfrac{u}{v}$. So $u = \sin x$, $v = x$ and $u' = \cos x$, $v' = 1$. Using the quotient rule the derivative of $y$ is found:

$$y' = \frac{x \cos x - \sin x}{x^2}$$

(b) $y = \dfrac{t^2}{2t + 1} = \dfrac{u}{v}$. So $u = t^2$, $v = 2t + 1$ and $u' = 2t$, $v' = 2$. Hence,

$$y' = \frac{(2t + 1)2t - (t^2)(2)}{(2t + 1)^2} = \frac{2t(t + 1)}{(2t + 1)^2}$$

(c) $y = \dfrac{e^{2t}}{t^2+1}$. So $u = e^{2t}$, $v = t^2+1$ and $u' = 2e^{2t}$, $v' = 2t$. Application of the quotient rule yields

$$y' = \frac{(t^2+1)2e^{2t} - e^{2t}2t}{(t^2+1)^2} = \frac{2e^{2t}(t^2-t+1)}{(t^2+1)^2}$$

### 11.2.3 The chain rule

This rule helps us to differentiate complicated functions, where a substitution can be used to simplify the function. Suppose $y = y(z)$ and $z = z(x)$. Then $y$ may be considered as a function of $x$. For example, if $y = z^3 - z$ and $z = \sin 3x$, then $y = (\sin 3x)^3 - \sin(3x)$. Suppose we seek the derivative, $\dfrac{dy}{dx}$. Note that the derivative w.r.t. $x$ is sought.

The chain rule states:

$$\frac{dy}{dx} = \frac{dy}{dz} \times \frac{dz}{dx}$$

**Example 11.3** Given $y = z^6$ where $z = x^2 + 1$ find $\dfrac{dy}{dx}$.

**Solution** If $y = z^6$ and $z = x^2 + 1$, then $y = (x^2+1)^6$. We recognize this as the composition $y(z(x))$ (see Section 2.3.6). Now $y = z^6$ and so $\dfrac{dy}{dz} = 6z^5$. Also $z = x^2 + 1$ and so $\dfrac{dz}{dx} = 2x$. Using the chain rule,

$$\frac{dy}{dx} = \frac{dy}{dz} \times \frac{dz}{dx} = 6z^5 2x = 12x(x^2+1)^5$$

**Example 11.4** If $y = \ln(3x^2 + 5x + 7)$, find $\dfrac{dy}{dx}$.

**Solution** We use a substitution to simplify the given function: let $z = 3x^2 + 5x + 7$ so that $y = \ln z$. Since

$$y = \ln z \quad \text{then} \quad \frac{dy}{dz} = \frac{1}{z}$$

Also

$$z = 3x^2 + 5x + 7 \quad \text{and so} \quad \frac{dz}{dx} = 6x + 5$$

Using the chain rule we find

$$\frac{dy}{dx} = \frac{dy}{dz} \times \frac{dz}{dx}$$

$$= \frac{1}{z} \times (6x + 5)$$

$$= \frac{6x + 5}{3x^2 + 5x + 7}$$

---

Note that in the previous answer the numerator is the derivative of the denominator. This result is true more generally and can be applied when differentiating the natural logarithm of any function:

When $y = \ln f(x)$ then $\dfrac{dy}{dx} = \dfrac{f'(x)}{f(x)}$

**Example 11.5** Find $y'$ when

(a) $y = \ln(x^5 + 8)$ (b) $y = \ln(1 - t)$ (c) $y = 8\ln(2 - 3t)$

(d) $y = \ln(1 + x)$ (e) $y = \ln(1 + \cos x)$

**Solution** In each case we apply the previous rule.

(a) If $y = \ln(x^5 + 8)$, then $y' = \dfrac{5x^4}{x^5 + 8}$.

(b) If $y = \ln(1 - t)$, then $y' = \dfrac{-1}{1 - t} = -\dfrac{1}{1 - t} = \dfrac{1}{t - 1}$.

(c) If $y = 8\ln(2 - 3t)$, then $y' = 8\dfrac{-3}{2 - 3t} = -\dfrac{24}{2 - 3t} = \dfrac{24}{3t - 2}$.

(d) If $y = \ln(1 + x)$ then $y' = \dfrac{1}{1 + x}$.

(e) If $y = \ln(1 + \cos x)$ then $y' = \dfrac{-\sin x}{1 + \cos x} = -\dfrac{\sin x}{1 + \cos x}$.

**Example 11.6** Differentiate

(a) $y = 3e^{\sin x}$

(b) $y = (3t^2 + 2t - 9)^{10}$

(c) $y = \sqrt{1 + t^2}$

**Solution** In these examples we must formulate the function $z$ ourselves.

(a) Let $z(x) = \sin x$. Then $y(z) = 3e^z$ so $\frac{dy}{dz} = 3e^z$; $z(x) = \sin x$ and so $\frac{dz}{dx} = \cos x$. The chain rule is used to find $\frac{dy}{dx}$.

$$\frac{dy}{dx} = \frac{dy}{dz} \times \frac{dz}{dx} = 3e^z \cos x = 3e^{\sin x} \cos x$$

(b) Let $z(t) = 3t^2 + 2t - 9$. Then $y(z) = z^{10}$, $\frac{dy}{dz} = 10z^9$, $\frac{dz}{dt} = 6t + 2$. Using the chain rule $\frac{dy}{dt}$ is found:

$$\frac{dy}{dt} = \frac{dy}{dz} \times \frac{dz}{dt} = 10z^9(6t + 2) = 20(3t + 1)(3t^2 + 2t - 9)^9$$

(c) Let $z(t) = 1 + t^2$. Then $y = \sqrt{z} = z^{1/2}$, $\frac{dy}{dz} = \frac{1}{2}z^{-1/2}$ and $\frac{dz}{dt} = 2t$. Using the chain rule, we obtain

$$\frac{dy}{dt} = \frac{dy}{dz} \times \frac{dz}{dt} = \frac{1}{2}z^{-1/2}2t = \frac{t}{\sqrt{z}} = \frac{t}{\sqrt{1+t^2}}$$

## Exercises 11.2

1 Use the product rule to differentiate the following functions.

(a) $y = \sin x \cos x$

(b) $y = \ln t \tan t$

(c) $y = (t^3 + 1)e^{2t}$

(d) $y = \sqrt{x}e^x$

(e) $y = e^t \sin t \cos t$

(f) $y = 3 \sinh 2t \cosh 3t$

(g) $y = (1 + \sin t) \tan t$

(h) $y = 4 \sinh(t + 1) \cosh(1 - t)$

2 Use the quotient rule to find the derivatives of the following:

(a) $\frac{\cos x}{\sin x}$

(b) $\frac{\tan t}{\ln t}$

(c) $\frac{e^{2t}}{t^3 + 1}$

(d) $\frac{3x^2 + 2x - 9}{x^3 + 1}$

(e) $\frac{x^2 + x + 1}{1 + e^x}$

(f) $\frac{\sinh 2t}{\cosh 3t}$

(g) $\frac{1 + e^t}{1 + e^{2t}}$

3 Use the chain rule to differentiate the following.

(a) $(t^3 + 1)^{100}$

(b) $\sin^3(3t + 2)$

(c) $\ln(x^2 + 1)$

(d) $(2t + 1)^{1/2}$

(e) $3\sqrt{\cos(2x - 1)}$

(f) $\frac{1}{t + 1}$

(g) $(at + b)^n$, $a$ and $b$ constants

**4** Differentiate each of the following functions:

(a) $y = 5\sin x$

(b) $y = 5e^x \sin x$

(c) $y = 5e^{\sin x}$

(d) $y = \dfrac{5\sin x}{e^{-x}}$

(e) $y = (t^3 + 4t)^{15}$

(f) $y = 7e^{-3t^2}$

(g) $y = \dfrac{\sin x}{4\cos x + 1}$

**5** For which values of $t$ is the derivative of $y(t) = e^{-t}t^2$ zero?

**6** Find the rate of change of $y$ at the specified values of $t$.

(a) $y = \sin \dfrac{1}{t}$ $\quad t = 1$

(b) $y = (t^2 - 1)^{17}$ $\quad t = 1$

(c) $y = \sinh(t^2)$ $\quad t = 2$

(d) $y = \dfrac{1 + t + t^2}{1 - t}$ $\quad t = 2$

(e) $y = \dfrac{e^t}{t\sin t}$ $\quad t = 1$

**7** Find the equation of the tangent to

$$y(x) = e^{3x}(1 - x) \quad \text{at the point } (0, 1)$$

**8** Differentiate

(a) $y = \ln x$

(b) $y = \ln 2x$

(c) $y = \ln kx$, $k$ constant

(d) $y = \ln(1 + t)$

(e) $y = \ln(3 + 4t)$

(f) $y = \ln(5 + 7\sin x)$

## Solutions

**1** (a) $\cos^2 x - \sin^2 x$

(b) $\dfrac{1}{t}\tan t + \ln t \sec^2 t$

(c) $e^{2t}(2t^3 + 3t^2 + 2)$

(d) $e^x\left(\sqrt{x} + \dfrac{1}{2\sqrt{x}}\right)$

(e) $e^t(2\cos^2 t + \sin t\cos t - 1)$

(f) $3[2\cosh 2t \cosh 3t + 3\sinh 2t \sinh 3t]$

(g) $(1 + \sin t)\sec^2 t + \sin t$

(h) $4[\cosh(t + 1)\cosh(1 - t) - \sinh(t + 1)\sinh(1 - t)]$

**2** (a) $-\operatorname{cosec}^2 x$

(b) $\dfrac{\ln t \sec^2 t - (\tan t)/t}{(\ln t)^2}$

(c) $\dfrac{e^{2t}(2t^3 - 3t^2 + 2)}{(t^3 + 1)^2}$

(d) $\dfrac{-3x^4 - 4x^3 + 27x^2 + 6x + 2}{(x^3 + 1)^2}$

(e) $\dfrac{e^x(-x^2 + x) + 2x + 1}{(e^x + 1)^2}$

(f) $\dfrac{2\cosh 2t \cosh 3t - 3\sinh 2t \sinh 3t}{(\cosh 3t)^2}$

(g) $\dfrac{-e^{3t} - 2e^{2t} + e^t}{(e^{2t} + 1)^2}$

**3** (a) $300t^2(t^3 + 1)^{99}$

(b) $9\sin^2(3t + 2)\cos(3t + 2)$

(c) $\dfrac{2x}{x^2 + 1}$

(d) $(2t + 1)^{-1/2}$

(e) $\dfrac{-3\sin(2x - 1)}{\sqrt{\cos(2x - 1)}}$

(f) $-(t + 1)^{-2}$

(g) $an(at + b)^{n-1}$

**4** (a) $5\cos x$

(b) $5e^x(\cos x + \sin x)$

(c) $5e^{\sin x}\cos x$

(d) $5e^x(\cos x + \sin x)$

(e) $15(t^3 + 4t)^{14}(3t^2 + 4)$

(f) $-42te^{-3t^2}$

(g) $\dfrac{4 + \cos x}{(4\cos x + 1)^2}$

5 0, 2

6 (a) −0.5403 (b) 0 (c) 109.2
(d) 2 (e) −2.0742

7 $y = 2x + 1$

8 (a) $\frac{1}{x}$ (b) $\frac{1}{x}$ (c) $\frac{1}{x}$
(d) $\frac{1}{1+t}$ (e) $\frac{4}{3+4t}$ (f) $\frac{7\cos x}{5+7\sin x}$

# 11.3 Parametric, implicit and logarithmic differentiation

## 11.3.1 Parametric differentiation

In some circumstances both $y$ and $x$ depend upon a third variable, $t$. This third variable is often called a **parameter**. By eliminating $t$, $y$ can be found as a function of $x$. For example, if $y = (1+t)^2$ and $x = 2t$ then, eliminating $t$, we can write $y = (1 + x/2)^2$. Hence, $y$ may be considered as a function of $x$, and so the derivative $\frac{dy}{dx}$ can be found. However, sometimes the elimination of $t$ is difficult or even impossible. Consider the example $y = \sin t + t$, $x = t^2 + e^t$. In this case, it is impossible to obtain $y$ in terms of $x$. The derivative $\frac{dy}{dx}$ can still be found using the chain rule.

$$\frac{dy}{dx} = \frac{dy}{dt} \times \frac{dt}{dx} = \frac{dy}{dt} \Big/ \frac{dx}{dt}$$

Finding $\frac{dy}{dx}$ by this method is known as **parametric differentiation**.

**Example 11.7** Given $y = (1+t)^2$, $x = 2t$ find $\frac{dy}{dx}$.

**Solution** By eliminating $t$, we see

$$y = \left(1 + \frac{x}{2}\right)^2 = 1 + x + \frac{x^2}{4}$$

and so

$$\frac{dy}{dx} = 1 + \frac{x}{2}$$

Parametric differentiation is an alternative method of finding $\frac{dy}{dx}$ which does not require the elimination of $t$.

$$\frac{dy}{dt} = 2(1+t) \qquad \frac{dx}{dt} = 2$$

Using the chain rule, we obtain

$$\frac{dy}{dx} = \frac{dy}{dt} \Big/ \frac{dx}{dt} = \frac{2(1+t)}{2} = 1 + t = 1 + \frac{x}{2}$$

**Example 11.8** Given $y = e^t + t$, $x = t^2 + 1$, find $\frac{dy}{dx}$ using parametric differentiation.

**Solution**

$$\frac{dy}{dt} = e^t + 1 \qquad \frac{dx}{dt} = 2t$$

Hence,

$$\frac{dy}{dx} = \frac{dy}{dt} \bigg/ \frac{dx}{dt} = \frac{e^t + 1}{2t}$$

In this example, the derivative is expressed in terms of $t$. This will always be the case when $t$ has not been eliminated between $x$ and $y$.

**Example 11.9** If $x = \sin t + \cos t$ and $y = t^2 - t + 1$ find $\frac{dy}{dx}(t = 0)$.

**Solution**

$$\frac{dy}{dt} = 2t - 1 \qquad \frac{dx}{dt} = \cos t - \sin t$$

Hence,

$$\frac{dy}{dx} = \frac{2t - 1}{\cos t - \sin t}$$

When $t = 0$, $\frac{dy}{dx} = \frac{-1}{1} = -1$.

### 11.3.2 Implicit differentiation

Suppose we are told that

$$y^3 + x^3 = 5 \sin x + 10 \cos y$$

Although $y$ depends upon $x$, it is impossible to write the equation in the form $y = f(x)$. We say $y$ is expressed **implicitly** in terms of $x$. The form $y = f(x)$ is an **explicit** expression for $y$ in terms of $x$. However, given an implicit expression for $y$ it is still possible to find $\frac{dy}{dx}$. Usually $\frac{dy}{dx}$ will be expressed in terms of both $x$ and $y$. Essentially, the chain rule is used when differentiating implicit expressions.

When calculating $\frac{dy}{dx}$ we need to differentiate a function of $y$, as opposed to a function of $x$. For example, we may need to find $\frac{d}{dx}(y^4)$.

**Example 11.10** Find

(a) $\frac{d}{dx}(y^4)$ (b) $\frac{d}{dx}(y^{-3})$

**Solution** (a) We make a substitution and let $z = y^4$ so that the problem becomes that of finding $\frac{dz}{dx}$. Now, using the chain rule,

$$\frac{dz}{dx} = \frac{dz}{dy} \times \frac{dy}{dx}$$

If $z = y^4$ then $\dfrac{dz}{dy} = 4y^3$ and so

$$\frac{dz}{dx} = 4y^3\frac{dy}{dx}$$

We conclude that

$$\frac{d}{dx}(y^4) = 4y^3\frac{dy}{dx}$$

(b) We make a substitution and let $z = y^{-3}$ so that the problem becomes that of finding $\dfrac{dz}{dx}$.

If $z = y^{-3}$ then $\dfrac{dz}{dy} = -3y^{-4}$ and so

$$\frac{d}{dx}(y^{-3}) = \frac{dz}{dx} = \frac{dz}{dy} \times \frac{dy}{dx} = -3y^{-4}\frac{dy}{dx}$$

**Example 11.11** Find $\dfrac{d}{dt}(\ln y)$.

**Solution** We let $z = \ln y$ so that the problem becomes that of finding $\dfrac{dz}{dt}$. If $z = \ln y$ then $\dfrac{dz}{dy} = \dfrac{1}{y}$ and so using the chain rule

$$\frac{dz}{dt} = \frac{dz}{dy} \times \frac{dy}{dt} = \frac{1}{y}\frac{dy}{dt}$$

we conclude that

$$\frac{d}{dt}(\ln y) = \frac{1}{y}\frac{dy}{dt}$$

---

Examples 11.10 and 11.11 illustrate the general formula:

$$\frac{d}{dx}(f(y)) = \frac{df}{dy} \times \frac{dy}{dx}.$$

This is simply the chain rule expressed in a slightly different form.

**Example 11.12** Find $\dfrac{d}{dx}(y)$.

**Solution** We have

$$\frac{d}{dx}(y) = \frac{dy}{dy} \times \frac{dy}{dx} = \frac{dy}{dx}$$

**Example 11.13** Given

$$x^3 + y = 1 + y^3$$

find $\dfrac{dy}{dx}$.

**Solution** Consider differentiation of the l.h.s. w.r.t. $x$.

$$\frac{d}{dx}(x^3 + y) = \frac{d}{dx}(x^3) + \frac{dy}{dx} = 3x^2 + \frac{dy}{dx}$$

Now consider differentiation of the r.h.s. w.r.t. $x$.

$$\frac{d}{dx}(1 + y^3) = \frac{d}{dx}(1) + \frac{d}{dx}(y^3) = \frac{d}{dx}(y^3)$$

We note from the formula following Example 11.11 that $\dfrac{d}{dx}(y^3) = 3y^2\dfrac{dy}{dx}$. So finally,

$$3x^2 + \frac{dy}{dx} = 3y^2\frac{dy}{dx}$$

from which

$$\frac{dy}{dx} = \frac{3x^2}{3y^2 - 1}$$

Note that $\dfrac{dy}{dx}$ is expressed in terms of $x$ and $y$.

**Example 11.14** Find $\dfrac{dy}{dx}$ given

(a) $\ln y = y - x^2$

(b) $x^2y^3 - e^y = e^{2x}$

**Solution** (a) Differentiating the given equation w.r.t. $x$ yields

$$\frac{1}{y}\frac{dy}{dx} = \frac{dy}{dx} - 2x$$

from which

$$\frac{dy}{dx} = \frac{2xy}{y - 1}$$

(b) Consider $\dfrac{d}{dx}(x^2y^3)$. Using the product rule we find

$$\frac{d}{dx}(x^2y^3) = \frac{d}{dx}(x^2)y^3 + x^2\frac{d}{dx}(y^3) = 2xy^3 + x^2 3y^2\frac{dy}{dx}$$

Consider $\frac{d}{dx}(e^y)$. Let $z = e^y$ so $\frac{dz}{dy} = e^y$. Hence,

$$\frac{d}{dx}(e^y) = \frac{dz}{dx} = \frac{dz}{dy}\frac{dy}{dx} = e^y\frac{dy}{dx}$$

So, upon differentiating, the equation becomes

$$2xy^3 + x^2 3y^2\frac{dy}{dx} - e^y\frac{dy}{dx} = 2e^{2x}$$

So,

$$\frac{dy}{dx}(3x^2y^2 - e^y) = 2e^{2x} - 2xy^3$$

from which

$$\frac{dy}{dx} = \frac{2e^{2x} - 2xy^3}{3x^2y^2 - e^y}$$

### 11.3.3 Logarithmic differentiation

The technique of **logarithmic differentiation** is useful when we need to differentiate a cumbersome product. The method involves taking the natural logarithm of the function to be differentiated. This is illustrated in the following examples.

**Example 11.15** Given that $y = t^2(1-t)^8$ find $\frac{dy}{dt}$.

**Solution** The product rule could be used but we will demonstrate an alternative technique. Taking the natural logarithm of both sides of the given equation yields

$$\ln y = \ln(t^2(1-t)^8)$$

Using the laws of logarithms we can write this as

$$\begin{aligned}\ln y &= \ln t^2 + \ln(1-t)^8 \\ &= 2\ln t + 8\ln(1-t)\end{aligned}$$

Both sides of this equation are now differentiated w.r.t. $t$ to give

$$\frac{d}{dt}(\ln y) = \frac{d}{dt}(2\ln t) + \frac{d}{dt}(8\ln(1-t))$$

The evaluation of $\frac{d}{dt}(\ln y)$ has already been found in Example 11.11, and so

$$\frac{1}{y}\frac{dy}{dt} = \frac{2}{t} - \frac{8}{1-t}$$

Hence

$$\frac{dy}{dt} = y\left(\frac{2}{t} - \frac{8}{1-t}\right)$$

Finally, replacing $y$ by $t^2(1-t)^8$ we have

$$\frac{dy}{dt} = t^2(1-t)^8\left(\frac{2}{t} - \frac{8}{1-t}\right)$$

**Example 11.16** Given

$$y = x^3(1+x)^9e^{6x}$$

find $\dfrac{dy}{dx}$.

**Solution** The product rule could be used. However, we will use logarithmic differentiation. Taking the natural logarithm of the equation and applying the laws of logarithms produces

$$\ln y = \ln(x^3(1+x)^9e^{6x}) = \ln x^3 + \ln(1+x)^9 + \ln e^{6x}$$
$$\ln y = 3\ln x + 9\ln(1+x) + 6x$$

This equation is now differentiated.

$$\frac{1}{y}\frac{dy}{dx} = \frac{3}{x} + \frac{9}{1+x} + 6$$

and so

$$\frac{dy}{dx} = y\left(\frac{3}{x} + \frac{9}{1+x} + 6\right)$$
$$= 3x^2(1+x)^9e^{6x} + 9x^3(1+x)^8e^{6x} + 6x^3(1+x)^9e^{6x}$$

**Example 11.17** If $y = \sqrt{1+t^2}\sin^2 t$ find $y'$.

**Solution** Taking logarithms we find

$$\ln y = \ln(\sqrt{1+t^2}\sin^2 t)$$
$$= \ln\sqrt{1+t^2} + \ln(\sin^2 t)$$
$$= \frac{1}{2}\ln(1+t^2) + 2\ln(\sin t)$$

Differentiation yields

$$\frac{1}{y}y' = \frac{1}{2}\frac{2t}{1+t^2} + 2\frac{\cos t}{\sin t}$$

$$y' = y\left(\frac{t}{1+t^2} + 2\cot t\right) = \sqrt{1+t^2}\sin^2 t\left(\frac{t}{1+t^2} + 2\cot t\right)$$

---

## Exercises 11.3

**1** Find each of the following:

(a) $\frac{d}{dx}(x^5)$

(b) $\frac{d}{dx}(y^5)$

(c) $\frac{d}{dt}(y^5)$

(d) $\frac{d}{dx}(y^2)$

(e) $\frac{d}{dx}(5y)$

(f) $\frac{d}{dx}(y)$

(g) $\frac{d}{dx}(y^2 + y^3)$

**2** Find each of the following:

(a) $\frac{d}{dx}(e^y)$

(b) $\frac{d}{dx}(\sin y)$

(c) $\frac{d}{dx}(\cos 2y)$

(d) $\frac{d}{dx}(e^{-3y})$

(e) $\frac{d}{dx}(\sqrt{y})$

(f) $\frac{d}{dx}(x + y)$

(g) $\frac{d}{dx}(\cos(x + y))$

(h) $\frac{d}{dx}(\ln y)$

(i) $\frac{d}{dx}(\ln 7y)$

**3** Find $\frac{dy}{dx}$ given

(a) $2y^2 - 3x^3 = x + y$

(b) $\sqrt{y} + \sqrt{x} = x^2 + y^3$

(c) $\sqrt{2x + 3y} = 1 + e^x$

(d) $y = \frac{e^x\sqrt{1+x}}{x^2}$

(e) $2xy^4 = x^3 + 3xy^2$

(f) $\sin(x + y) = 1 + y$

(g) $\ln(x^2 + y^2) = 2x - 3y$

(h) $ye^{2y} = x^2e^{x/2}$

**4** Find $\frac{dy}{dx}$, given

(a) $x = t^2 \quad y = 1 + t^3$

(b) $x = \sin t \quad y = e^t$

(c) $x = (1 + t)^3 \quad y = 1 + t^3$

(d) $x = \cos 2t \quad y = 3t$

(e) $x = \frac{3}{t} \quad y = e^{2t}$

(f) $x = e^t - e^{-t} \quad y = e^t + e^{-t}$

**5** Use logarithmic differentiation to find the derivatives of the following functions:

(a) $y = x^4e^x$

(b) $y = \frac{1}{x}e^{-x}$

(c) $z = t^3(1 + t)^9$

(d) $y = e^x \sin x$

(e) $y = x^7 \sin^4 x$

**6** Use logarithmic differentiation to find the derivatives of the following functions:

(a) $z = t^4(1-t)^6(2+t)^4$

(b) $y = \dfrac{(1+x^2)^3 e^{7x}}{(2+x)^6}$

(c) $x = (1+t)^3(2+t)^4(3+t)^5$

(d) $y = \dfrac{(\sin^4 t)(2-t^2)^4}{(1+e^t)^6}$

(e) $y = x^3 e^x \sin x$

**7** If $x = t + t^2 + t^3$ and $y = \sin 2t$, find $\dfrac{dy}{dx}$ when $t = 1$.

**8** Given $x = 1 + t^6$ and $y = 1 - t^2$, find:

(a) the rate of change of $x$ w.r.t. $t$ when $t = 2$

(b) the rate of change of $y$ w.r.t. $t$ when $t = 1$

(c) the rate of change of $y$ w.r.t. $x$ when $t = 1$

(d) the rate of change of $x$ w.r.t. $y$ when $t = 2$

**9** Find the equations of the tangents to

$$y^2 = x^2 + 6y$$

when $x = 4$.

**10** Given the implicit function $3x^2 + y^3 = y$ find an expression for $\dfrac{dy}{dx}$.

## Solutions

**1** (a) $5x^4$

(b) $5y^4\dfrac{dy}{dx}$

(c) $5y^4\dfrac{dy}{dt}$

(d) $2y\dfrac{dy}{dx}$

(e) $5\dfrac{dy}{dx}$

(f) $\dfrac{dy}{dx}$

(g) $(2y+3y^2)\dfrac{dy}{dx}$

**2** (a) $e^y\dfrac{dy}{dx}$

(b) $\cos y\dfrac{dy}{dx}$

(c) $-2\sin 2y\dfrac{dy}{dx}$

(d) $-3e^{-3y}\dfrac{dy}{dx}$

(e) $\frac{1}{2}y^{-1/2}\dfrac{dy}{dx}$

(f) $1 + \dfrac{dy}{dx}$

(g) $-\sin(x+y)\left(1 + \dfrac{dy}{dx}\right)$

(h) $\dfrac{1}{y}\dfrac{dy}{dx}$

(i) $\dfrac{1}{y}\dfrac{dy}{dx}$

**3** (a) $\dfrac{1+9x^2}{4y-1}$

(b) $\dfrac{(4x\sqrt{x}-1)\sqrt{y}}{(1-6y^2\sqrt{y})\sqrt{x}}$

(c) $\frac{2}{3}(e^x\sqrt{2x+3y}-1)$

(d) $y\left(\frac{1}{2(1+x)} + 1 - \frac{2}{x}\right)$

(e) $\dfrac{3x^2+3y^2-2y^4}{2xy(4y^2-3)}$

(f) $\dfrac{\cos(x+y)}{1-\cos(x+y)}$

(g) $\dfrac{2(x^2+y^2-x)}{3x^2+3y^2+2y}$

(h) $\dfrac{e^{(x/2-2y)}x(x+4)}{2(1+2y)}$

**4** (a) $3t/2$ (b) $\dfrac{e^t}{\cos t}$

(c) $\left(\dfrac{t}{1+t}\right)^2$ (d) $\dfrac{-3}{2\sin 2t}$

(e) $-2e^{2t}t^2/3$ (f) $\dfrac{e^t - e^{-t}}{e^t + e^{-t}}$

**5** (a) $(4x^3 + x^4)e^x$

(b) $-e^{-x}\left(\dfrac{1}{x^2} + \dfrac{1}{x}\right)$

(c) $t^3(1+t)^9\left(\dfrac{3}{t} + \dfrac{9}{1+t}\right)$

(d) $e^x \sin x(1 + \cot x)$

(e) $x^7 \sin^4 x\left(\frac{7}{x} + 4\cot x\right)$

6 (a) $z\left(\frac{4}{t} - \frac{6}{1-t} + \frac{4}{2+t}\right)$

(b) $y\left(\frac{6x}{1+x^2} + 7 - \frac{6}{2+x}\right)$

(c) $x\left(\frac{3}{1+t} + \frac{4}{2+t} + \frac{5}{3+t}\right)$

(d) $y\left(4\cot t - \frac{8t}{2-t^2} - \frac{6e^t}{1+e^t}\right)$

(e) $x^3 e^x \sin x\left(\frac{3}{x} + 1 + \cot x\right)$

7 $-0.1387$

8 (a) 192

(b) $-2$

(c) $-\frac{1}{3}$

(d) $\frac{dx}{dy} = -3t^4$; when $t = 2$, $\frac{dx}{dy} = -48$

9 $y = \frac{-4x+6}{5}$, $y = \frac{4x+24}{5}$

10 $y' = \frac{6x}{1-3y^2}$

## 11.4 Higher derivatives

The derivative, $y'$, of a function $y(x)$ is more correctly called the **first derivative** of $y$ w.r.t. $x$. Since $y'$ itself is a function of $x$, then it is often possible to differentiate this too. The derivative of $y'$ is called the **second derivative** of $y$.

$$\text{second derivative of } y = \frac{d}{dx}\left(\frac{dy}{dx}\right)$$

which is written as $\frac{d^2y}{dx^2}$ or more compactly as $y''$.

**Example 11.18** If $y(x) = 3x^2 + 8x + 9$, find $y'$ and $y''$.

**Solution**

$$y' = 6x + 8 \qquad y'' = \frac{d}{dx}(6x + 8) = 6$$

**Example 11.19** If $y(t) = 2\sin 3t$, find $y'$ and $y''$.

**Solution**

$$y' = 6\cos 3t \qquad y'' = -18\sin 3t$$

The first and second derivatives w.r.t. time, $t$, are also denoted by $\dot{y}$ and $\ddot{y}$.

**Example 11.20** Find $y''$ given

$$1 + xy = x^2 + y^2$$

**Solution** The equation is differentiated implicitly to obtain $\frac{dy}{dx}$.

$$0 + y + xy' = 2x + 2yy'$$

$$y' = \frac{2x - y}{x - 2y}$$

The quotient rule is now used with $u = 2x - y$ and $v = x - 2y$. The derivatives of $u$ and $v$ are

$$\frac{du}{dx} = u' = 2 - y' \qquad \frac{dv}{dx} = v' = 1 - 2y'$$

Then,

$$y'' = \frac{(x - 2y)(2 - y') - (2x - y)(1 - 2y')}{(x - 2y)^2}$$

This is simplified to

$$y'' = \frac{3xy' - 3y}{(x - 2y)^2}$$

Replacing $y'$ by $\dfrac{2x - y}{x - 2y}$ and simplifying yields

$$y'' = \frac{6(x^2 - xy + y^2)}{(x - 2y)^3}$$

Note that it is possible to simplify this further by observing that $x^2 + y^2 = 1 + xy$ as given. Therefore,

$$y'' = \frac{6(1 + xy - xy)}{(x - 2y)^3} = \frac{6}{(x - 2y)^3}$$

---

Just as the first derivative may be differentiated to obtain the second derivative, so the second derivative may be differentiated to find the third derivative and so on. A similar notation is used. The third derivative is written $\dfrac{d^3y}{dx^3}$ or $y'''$ or $y^{(3)}$. The fourth derivative is written $\dfrac{d^4y}{dx^4}$ or $y^{\text{iv}}$ or $y^{(4)}$. The fifth derivative is written $\dfrac{d^5y}{dx^5}$ or $y^{\text{v}}$ or $y^{(5)}$.

**Example 11.21** Find the first five derivatives of $z(t) = 2t^3 + \sin t$.

**Solution**

$$z' = 6t^2 + \cos t \qquad z^{\text{iv}} = \sin t$$
$$z'' = 12t - \sin t \qquad z^{\text{v}} = \cos t$$
$$z''' = 12 - \cos t$$

**Example 11.22** Calculate the values of $x$ for which $y'' = 0$, given $y = x^4 - x^3$.

**Solution**

$$y = x^4 - x^3 \qquad y' = 4x^3 - 3x^2 \qquad y'' = 12x^2 - 6x$$

Putting $y'' = 0$ gives

$$12x^2 - 6x = 0 \qquad \text{and so} \qquad 6x(2x - 1) = 0$$

Hence

$$x = 0, \tfrac{1}{2}$$

---

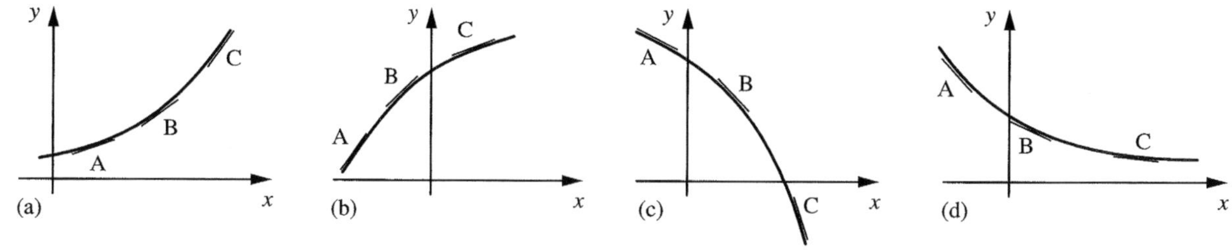


**Figure 11.1** (a) $y$ is concave up ($y' > 0$, $y'' > 0$); (b) $y$ is concave down ($y' > 0$, $y'' < 0$); (c) $y$ is concave down ($y' < 0$, $y'' < 0$); (d) $y$ is concave up ($y' < 0$, $y'' > 0$).

The first and second derivatives can be used to describe the nature of increasing and decreasing functions. In Figure 11.1(a, b) the tangents to the curves have positive gradients, that is $y' > 0$. As can be seen, as $x$ increases the value of the function increases. Conversely, in Figure 11.1(c, d) the tangents have negative gradients ($y' < 0$) and as $x$ increases the value of the function decreases. The sign of the first derivative tells us whether $y$ is increasing or decreasing. However, the curves in (a) and (b) both show $y$ increasing but, clearly, there is a difference in the way $y$ changes.

Consider again Figure 11.1(a). The tangents at A, B and C are shown. As $x$ increases the gradient of the tangent increases, that is $y'$ increases as $x$ increases. Since $y'$ increases as $x$ increases then the derivative of $y'$ is positive, that is $y'' > 0$. (Compare with: $y$ increases when its derivative is positive.) So for the curve shown in Figure 11.1(a), $y' > 0$ and $y'' > 0$.

For that shown in Figure 11.1(b) the situation is different. The value of $y'$ decreases as $x$ increases, as can be seen by considering the gradients of the tangents at A, B and C, that is the derivative of $y'$ must be negative. For this curve $y' > 0$ and $y'' < 0$.

A function is **concave down** when $y'$ decreases and **concave up** when $y'$ increases. Hence Figure 11.1(a) illustrates a concave up function; Figure 11.1(b) illustrates a concave down function. The sign of the second derivative can be used to distinguish between concave up and concave down functions.

Consider now the functions shown in Figure 11.1(c) and Figure 11.1(d). In both (c) and (d), $y$ is decreasing and so $y' < 0$. In (c) the gradient of the tangent becomes increasingly negative; that is, it is decreasing. Hence, for the function in (c) $y'' < 0$. Conversely, for the function in (d) the gradient of the tangent is increasing as $x$ increases, although it is always negative, that is $y'' > 0$. So for the function in (c) $y' < 0$ and $y'' < 0$; that is, the function is concave down. For the function in (d) $y' < 0$ and $y'' > 0$; that is, the function is concave up. In summary, we can state:

When $y' > 0$, $y$ is increasing. When $y' < 0$, $y$ is decreasing.
When $y'$ is increasing the function is concave up. In this case $y'' > 0$.
When $y'$ is decreasing the function is concave down. In this case $y'' < 0$.

An easy way of determining the concavity of a curve is to note that as the curve is traced from left to right, an anticlockwise motion reveals that the curve is concave up. A clockwise motion means that the curve is concave down.

As will be seen in the next chapter, higher derivatives are used to determine the location and nature of important points called maximum points, minimum points and points of inflexion.

## Exercises 11.4

**1** Calculate $\frac{dy}{dt}$ and $\frac{d^2y}{dt^2}$ given

(a) $y = t^2 + t$

(b) $y = 2t^3 - t^2 + 1$

(c) $y = \sin 2t$

(d) $y = \sin kt \quad k$ constant

(e) $y = 2e^{3t} - t^2 + 1$

(f) $y = \frac{t}{t+1}$

(g) $y = 4\cos\frac{t}{2}$

(h) $y = e^t t$

(i) $y = \sinh 4t$

(j) $y = \sin^2 t$

**2** If

$$y = 2x^3 + 3x^2 - 12x + 1$$

find values of $x$ for which $y'' = 0$.

**3** If $\frac{dy}{dt} = 3t^2 + t$, find

(a) $\frac{d^2y}{dt^2}$ (b) $\frac{d^3y}{dt^3}$

**4** Find values of $t$ at which $y'' = 0$, where

$$y = \frac{t^3}{3} - \frac{7t^2}{2} + 12t - 1$$

**5** Determine whether the following functions are concave up or concave down.

(a) $y = e^t$

(b) $y = t^2$

(c) $y = 1 + t - t^2$

**6** Determine the interval on which $y = t^3$ is

(a) concave up,

(b) concave down.

**7** Evaluate $y''$ at the specified value of $t$.

(a) $y = 2\cos t - t^2 \quad t = 1$

(b) $y = \frac{\sin t + \cos t}{2} \quad t = \pi/2$

(c) $y = (1+t)e^t \quad t = 0$

**8** Find $\frac{d^2y}{dx^2}$ given $xy + x^2 = y^2$.

**9** Find $\frac{dx}{dt}$ when $x^3 + \frac{x}{t} = t^2 + x^2 t$.

## Solutions

**1** (a) $2t + 1, 2$

(b) $6t^2 - 2t, 12t - 2$

(c) $2\cos 2t, -4\sin 2t$

(d) $k\cos kt, -k^2 \sin kt$

(e) $6e^{3t} - 2t, 18e^{3t} - 2$

(f) $\frac{1}{(t+1)^2}, -\frac{2}{(t+1)^3}$

(g) $-2\sin(t/2), -\cos(t/2)$

(h) $e^t(t+1), e^t(t+2)$

(i) $4\cosh 4t, 16\sinh 4t$

(j) $2\sin t\cos t, 2\cos 2t$

**2** $-\frac{1}{2}$

**3** (a) $6t + 1$ (b) 6

**4** $\frac{7}{2}$

**5** (a) concave up

(b) concave up

(c) concave down

**6** (a) concave up on $(0, \infty)$

(b) concave down on $(-\infty, 0)$

**7** (a) $-3.08$ (b) $-\frac{1}{2}$ (c) 3

**8** $\frac{10y^2 - 10x^2 - 10yx}{(2y-x)^3}$

**9** $\frac{x + 2t^3 + x^2t^2}{3x^2t^2 + t - 2xt^3}$

## Review exercises 11

1 Differentiate each of the following functions:

(a) $y = \sin(5+x)^2$
(b) $y = e^{2\sin x}$
(c) $y = (4x+7)^5$
(d) $y = x^4 \sin 3x$
(e) $y = \dfrac{e^{4x}}{x^3+11}$
(f) $y = x^2 \tan x$
(g) $y = \dfrac{\cos 3x}{x^2}$
(h) $y = e^{-x}\cos 5x$
(i) $y = \ln \cos 4x$
(j) $y = \sin 2t \cos 2t$
(k) $y = \dfrac{1}{x^2+1}$

2 Find $\dfrac{dy}{dx}$ in each of the following cases:

(a) $y = \dfrac{x^3 \sin 2x}{\cos x}$
(b) $y = x^3 e^{-x}\tan x$
(c) $y = \dfrac{xe^{5x}}{\sin x}$
(d) $x^2 + 3xy + y^2 = 5$
(e) $9 = 3x^3 + 2xy^2 - y$

3 If $x = \dfrac{5+3t}{1-t}$ and $y = \dfrac{2-t}{1-t}$ find $\dfrac{dy}{dx}$ and $\dfrac{d^2y}{dx^2}$.

4 If $x = 4(1+\cos\theta)$ and $y = 3(\theta - \sin\theta)$ find $\dfrac{dy}{dx}$.

5 If $x = 3\cos^2\theta$ and $y = 2\sin^2\theta$ find $\dfrac{dy}{dx}$ and $\dfrac{d^2y}{dx^2}$.

6 Show that $y = e^{-4x}\sin 8x$ satisfies the equation $y'' + 8y' + 80y = 0$.

7 Differentiate $y = x^x$.

8 Given $y = x^3 e^{2x}$ find

(a) $\dfrac{dy}{dx}$ (b) $\dfrac{d^2y}{dx^2}$ (c) $\dfrac{d^3y}{dx^3}$

9 Use logarithmic differentiation to find $\dfrac{dx}{dt}$ given

(a) $x = te^t \sin t$
(b) $x = t^2 e^{-t}\cos 3t$
(c) $x = t^2 e^{3t}\sin 4t \cos 3t$

10 Show that if $y(t) = A\sin\omega t + B\cos\omega t$, where $\omega$ is a constant, then

$$y'' + \omega^2 y = 0$$

## Solutions

1 (a) $2(5+x)\cos(5+x)^2$
(b) $2\cos x e^{2\sin x}$
(c) $20(4x+7)^4$
(d) $3x^4\cos 3x + 4x^3 \sin 3x$
(e) $\dfrac{e^{4x}(4x^3 - 3x^2 + 44)}{(x^3+11)^2}$
(f) $x^2\sec^2 x + 2x\tan x$
(g) $\dfrac{-3x\sin 3x - 2\cos 3x}{x^3}$
(h) $-e^{-x}(5\sin 5x + \cos 5x)$
(i) $-4\tan 4x$
(j) $2\cos 4t$
(k) $\dfrac{-2x}{(x^2+1)^2}$

2 (a) $\dfrac{\cos x(2x^3\cos 2x + 3x^2\sin 2x) + x^3 \sin 2x \sin x}{\cos^2 x}$
which simplifies to $2x^3\cos x + 6x^2 \sin x$
(b) $e^{-x}(x^3\sec^2 x - x^3\tan x + 3x^2\tan x)$
(c) $\dfrac{e^{5x}(5x\sin x + \sin x - x\cos x)}{\sin^2 x}$
(d) $-\dfrac{2x+3y}{3x+2y}$
(e) $\dfrac{9x^2+2y^2}{1-4xy}$

3 $\frac{1}{8}, 0$

4 $-\dfrac{3(1-\cos\theta)}{4\sin\theta}$

5 $-\frac{2}{3}, 0$

7 $x^x(\ln x+1)$

8 (a) $e^{2x}(2x^3+3x^2)$

(b) $2xe^{2x}(2x^2+6x+3)$

(c) $2e^{2x}(4x^3+18x^2+18x+3)$

9 (a) $e^t(t\cos t+(t+1)\sin t)$

(b) $-e^{-t}((t^2-2t)\cos 3t+3t^2\sin 3t)$

(c) $t^2e^{3t}\sin 4t\cos 3t\left(\dfrac{2}{t}+3+\dfrac{4\cos 4t}{\sin 4t}-\dfrac{3\sin 3t}{\cos 3t}\right)$

# Chapter 7
# Differential Calculus

## 7.1 Introduction to Calculus: A Way of Probing the Changing World

Calculus is the branch of mathematics that studies changes. Many physical quantities, which you will study in physics, change. Examples include the following: For a moving object, its position changes with time; for a rotating object, its angular displacement changes with time; for a radioactive substance, its number of radioactive nuclei changes with time; for an ideal gas kept in a closed container, its pressure changes with temperature and so on. Calculus not only is the most important tool that you will need to study such changes, many fundamental principles of physics can be conveniently expressed in simple equations using the notations of calculus.

Calculus is subdivided into two different parts: *differential* calculus and *integral* calculus. Just as the operations addition and subtraction are inverse and complementary, the two operations called differentiation in differential calculus and integration in integral calculus are inverse and complementary. Differential calculus is the study of rates of changes. More definitely, it is the study of the rate of change of one variable quantity with respect to a second variable quantity.

Although calculus can be challenging for some students, the fact is that physics would have been more difficult without the use of calculus. It is therefore important to understand the basic operations and principles of calculus before taking a calculus-based physics course. The calculus is based on two concepts of outstanding importance, namely the concept of *function* and the concept of *limit*.

## 7.2 Functions: Charting the Changes

Many problems in physics lead to the study of two related variables. For example, the period of a pendulum depends on the length of the pendulum, the kinetic energy of a gas depends on its velocity, and so on. When such dependence exists between two variables, either one of them is said to be a *function* of the other. Mathematically, a variable $y$ is said to be a function of a variable $x$, if, for a definite value of $x$, a definite value of $y$ is determined. A function of $x$ is usually denoted by the form, $f(x)$, which is read as "the $f$-function of $x$."

For example, if $y = f(x) = x^2$, the $f$-function of any variable or a constant is obtained by substituting the variable or the constant for $x$. In this example, $x$ is called the *independent* variable and $y$ is called the *dependent* variable.

Thus, $f(2) = 2^2 = 4$,

$f(z) = z^2$,

$f(x + b) = (x + b)^2 = x^2 + 2bx + b^2$, etc.

**Single-Valued and Multiple-Valued Functions**

A function is said to be *single valued* if it has only one value for each value of the independent variable. For example, all polynomial functions of the form $f(x) = x^n + \cdots + ax^2 + bx + c$ that contain only integral exponents are single valued. A function is said to be *multiple valued* if it has more than one value for each value of the independent variable. For example, $f(x) = \pm\sqrt{x}$ is a multiple valued function because it has two values corresponding to each value of $x$.

**Constant Function**

A function that has the same value $f(x) = a$ for all values of $x$ in an interval is called a *constant* function. A constant function is graphically represented by a straight line parallel to $x$-axis as shown in Figure 7.1.

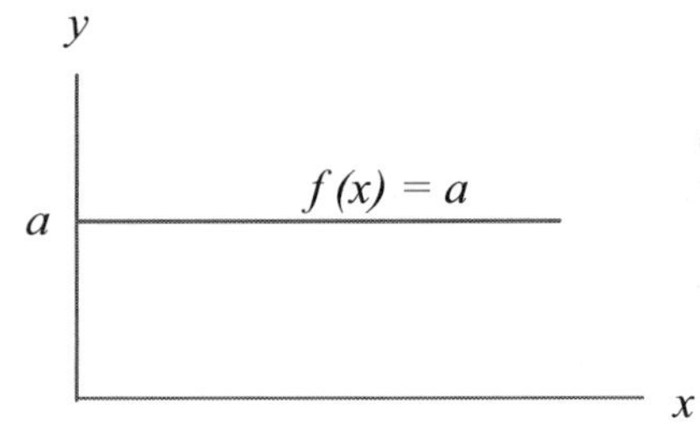


**Figure 7.1**

**Monotonic Increasing and Monotonic Decreasing Functions**

A function $f(x)$ for which an increase in the value of $x$ throughout the interval causes an increase in the value of $f(x)$, is called a *monotonic increasing* function (Figure 7.2). On the other hand, a function $f(x)$ for which an increase in the value of $x$ always causes a decrease in the value of $f(x)$ is called a *monotonic decreasing* function (Figure 7.3).

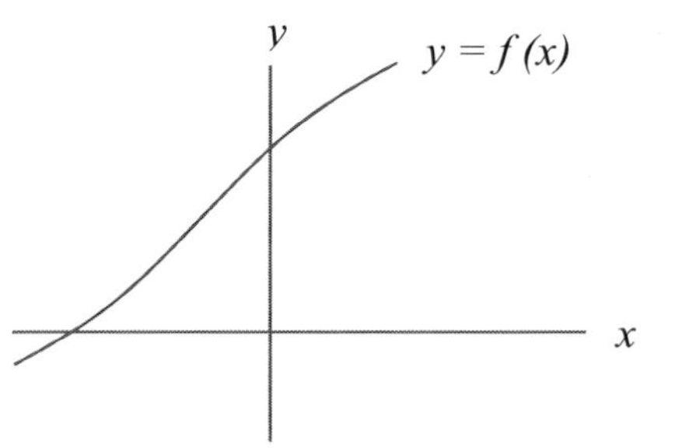


**Figure 7.2**

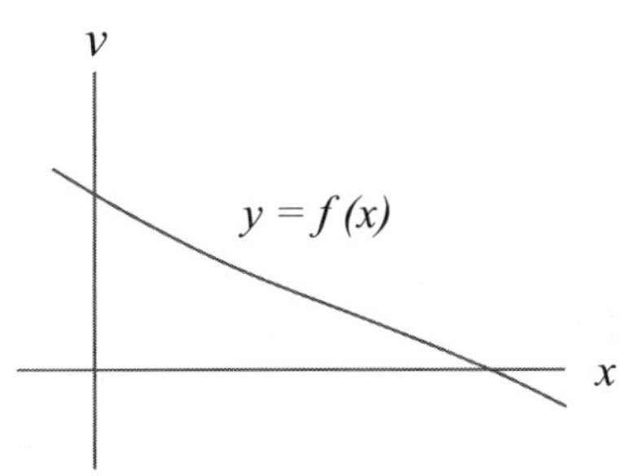


**Figure 7.3**

**Even and Odd Functions**

A function $f(x)$ is said to be *even* if $f(-x) = f(x)$. The curve represented by an even function $y = f(x)$ is symmetrical with respect to the $y$-axis. From the plot of $y = \cos x$

(Figure 7.4a.) it is seen that cos $x$ is an even function of $x$. The function $y = f(x) = x^2$ is also an even function of $x$, as shown in Figure 7.4b.

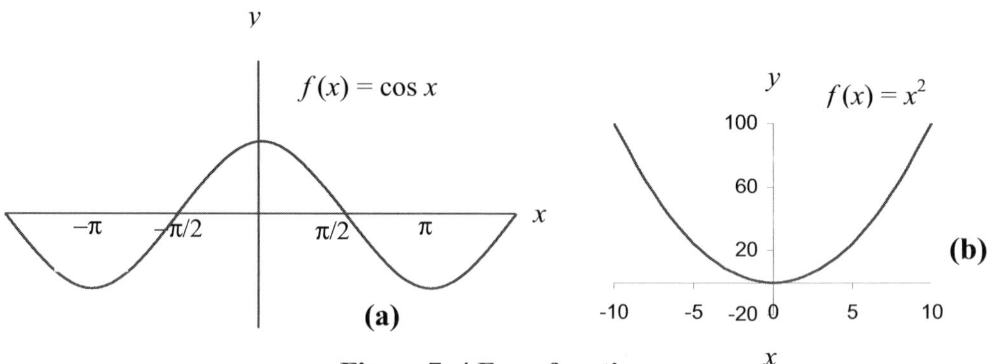


**Figure 7. 4 Even functions.**

A function $f(x)$ is said to be *odd* if $f(-x) = -f(x)$. The curve represented by an odd function is symmetrical with respect to the origin. From the plot of $y = \sin x$ (Figure 7.5a) it is seen that sin $x$ is an odd function of $x$. The functions $y = x$ and $y = x^3$ (Figure 7.5b) are also odd. The concept of even and odd functions is important in introductory quantum physics.

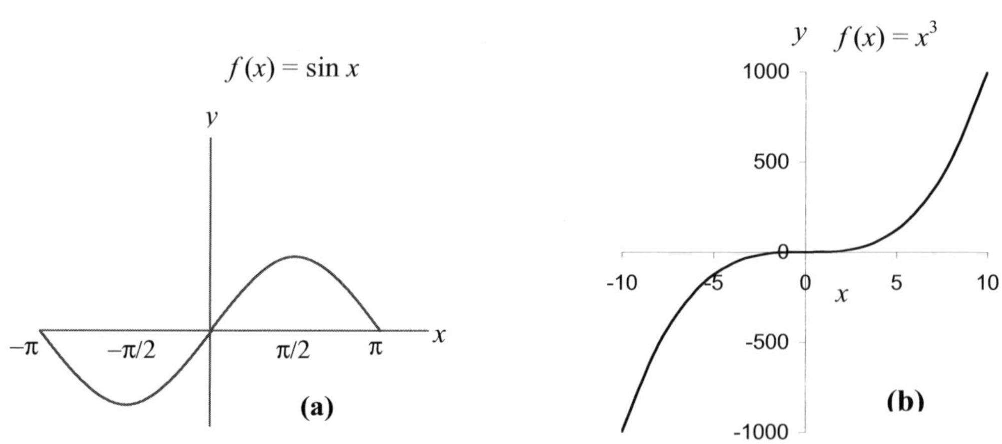


**Figure 7. 5 Odd functions.**

## 7.3 Limit and Continuity

### Limit

The whole structure of calculus is based on a concept called the *limit*. By the statement "the variable $x$ approaches the limit $a$," or "$x$ tends to $a$" in calculus, we mean that $x$ assumes successive values whose numerical differences from $a$ become gradually less and less and finally becomes less than any small quantity that we can imagine. This is denoted by the symbol $x \to a$. The successive values of $x$ can be greater than or less than $a$.

As $x$ approaches the number $a$ (*but is not equal to* $a$), if there exists a finite number $L$ toward which the function $f(x)$ approaches such that the numerical difference between $f(x)$ and $L$ becomes as small as we can imagine by approaching $x$ very close to $a$, then $L$ is called the limit of the function $f(x)$ as $x$ tends to $a$. This is mathematically written as $\lim_{x \to a} f(x) = L$.

> **Important Note**: Consider the function $f(x) = \dfrac{x^2-4}{x-2}$. The function $f(x)$ is undefined at $x = 2$; that is, $f(2)$ does not exist since the denominator becomes zero for $x = 2$. But $\lim_{x \to 2} f(x) = \lim_{x \to 2} \dfrac{x^2-4}{x-2} = \lim_{x \to 2} \dfrac{(x+2)(x-2)}{x-2}$ $= \lim_{x \to 2} (x+2) = 2 + 2 = 4$. Note that in this case we could cancel $x-2$ from both the numerator and the denominator since $x-2$ is not zero because $x \neq 2$.

### Continuity and Discontinuity of Functions

A function $f(x)$ is said to be *continuous* if the plot of $f(x)$ is a continuous curve. But if there is a break or discontinuity at a point on the curve of $f(x)$, the function $f(x)$ is discontinuous for the corresponding value of $x$. For example, consider two functions of $x$: $f(x) = x$ and $g(x) = x^2/x$. Their plots are shown in Figures 7.6 and 7.7, respectively. Note that $f(x)$ is a continuous function of $x$ passing through $x = 0$. But the function $g(x)$ is discontinuous at $x = 0$ because for $x = 0$, $g(x) = x^2/x$ is undefined, as its denominator is zero for $x = 0$.

> Mathematically, a function $f(x)$ is said to be continuous at a point $x = a$ if $\lim_{x \to a} f(x)$ exists, is finite, and is equal to the value $f(a)$.

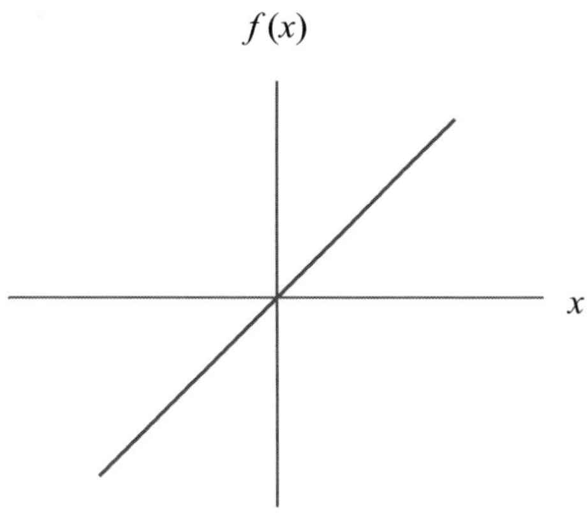


**Figure 7.6**

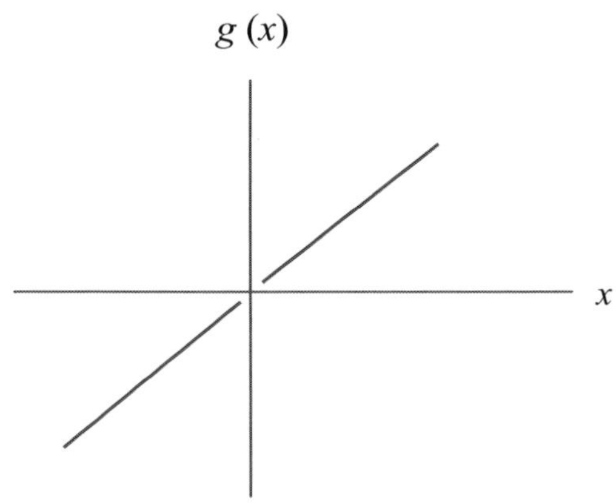


**Figure 7.7**

## 7.4 Derivative as the Rate of a Change

Let $y$ be a function of the variable $x$, that is, $y = f(x)$. Let $\Delta y$ be the change in $y$ corresponding to a change $\Delta x$ of $x$. This can be written as $y + \Delta y = f(x + \Delta x)$. Then the derivative of $y$ or $f(x)$ with respect to $x$ is mathematically defined as the limit

$$\frac{dy}{dx} = \lim_{\Delta x \to 0} \frac{\Delta y}{\Delta x} = \lim_{\Delta x \to 0} \frac{f(x+\Delta x) - f(x)}{\Delta x}.$$

For example, consider the function $y = f(x) = x^2$. From the definition,

$$\frac{dy}{dx} = \lim_{\Delta x \to 0} \frac{(x+\Delta x)^2 - x^2}{\Delta x} = \lim_{\Delta x \to 0} \frac{x^2 + 2x\,\Delta x + (\Delta x)^2 - x^2}{\Delta x}$$

$$= \lim_{\Delta x \to 0} \frac{\Delta x(2x+\Delta x)}{\Delta x} = \lim_{\Delta x \to 0} (2x + \Delta x) = 2x.$$

The derivative of the function $y = f(x)$ is also written as $y'$, $df/dx$, or $f'(x)$. The process of finding a derivative is called *differentiation.* An important aspect of derivative that follows from the preceding definition is that the *derivative is the rate of change of one variable with respect to the other; that is, dy/dx is the rate of change of y with respect to x*. This will be clear from the following examples of physics.

**Speed, Velocity, and Acceleration as Derivatives (Time Rate of Change)**

For an object moving along the $x$-axis, its position $x$ changes with time $t$. That is, the position $x$ is a function of time $t$. If $x$ and $x + \Delta x$ represent the position of the object at time $t$ and $t + \Delta t$, respectively, then $\Delta x$ denotes the distance covered by the object in time $\Delta t$ (Figure 7.8).

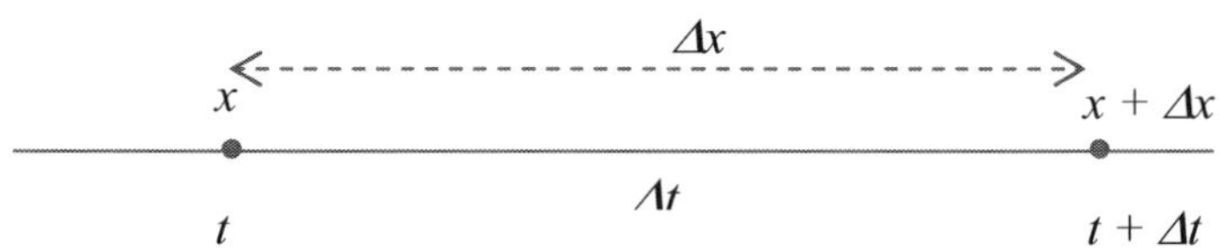


**Figure 7.8**

The ratio $\Delta x/\Delta t$ in the limit $\Delta t$ tends to zero represents the instantaneous rate at which the object is describing its path in unit time. On the other hand, by definition, $dx/dt$ is the derivative of $x$ with respect to $t$. Thus, the derivative $dx/dt$ represents the instantaneous rate of change of $x$ with respect to $t$, or the *instantaneous speed*, $v$, of the object. That is,

$$v = \lim_{\Delta t \to 0} \frac{\Delta x}{\Delta t} = \frac{dx}{dt}.$$

Instantaneous velocity of an object is its instantaneous speed with direction.

Also, if $v$ represents the velocity of a moving object at time $t$, $dv/dt$ represents the instantaneous time-rate of change of velocity, that is, its *instantaneous acceleration*, $a$, or,

$$a = \lim_{\Delta x \to 0} \frac{\Delta v}{\Delta t} = \frac{dv}{dt}.$$

Similarly, if the pressure of a gas is $p$ and its temperature is $T$, then for the gas kept in a closed container (that is, volume constant), the derivative $dp/dT$ represents the rate of change of pressure with temperature and so on.

> **Note**: In general, *if y is a function of x, the derivative dy/dx represents the rate of change of y with respect to x.*

- Note that for the function $y = f(x)$, if *$y$ increases when $x$ is increased* and *decreases when $x$ is decreased*, the corresponding changes $\Delta y$ and $\Delta x$ are of the same sign and, hence, the ratio $\Delta y/\Delta x$ and the derivative $dy/dx$ is *positive*.
- But if *$y$ decreases when $x$ is increased, or increases when $x$ is decreased*, $dy/dx$ is *negative*.

- If $y$ remains constant as $x$ increases or decreases, $dy/dx$ is zero.

**Geometrical Significance of Derivatives**

The geometrical significance of derivatives is represented graphically as shown in Figure 7.9. Let $A$ be a point $(x, y)$ on the curve and $B$ a neighboring point $(x + \Delta x, y + \Delta y)$ that may be on either side of $A$ so that $\Delta x$ can be positive or negative. If $\phi$ be the inclination of the line $AB$ with $x$-axis, the slope of the line $AB$ is given by

$$\tan\phi = \frac{(y+\Delta y)-y}{(x+\Delta x)-x} = \frac{\Delta y}{\Delta x}.$$

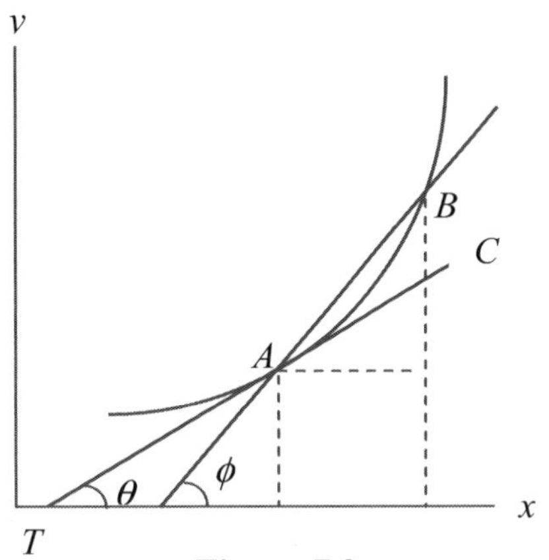


**Figure 7.9**

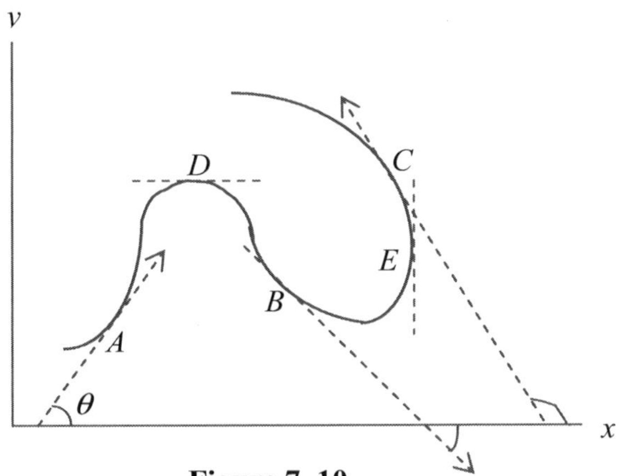


**Figure 7. 10**

Now let $B$ approach $A$ along the curve indefinitely closely so that $\Delta x \to 0$. As $B$ approaches $A$, the line $AB$ tends to a definite limiting position $TAC$, which is the tangent to the curve drawn at the point $A$. In this case, if $\theta$ is the inclination of the straight line $TAC$ to the $x$-axis, then as $AB$ tends to TAC, $\phi \to \theta$. Also, as $\Delta x \to 0$, $\frac{dy}{dx} = \lim_{\Delta x \to 0} \frac{\Delta y}{\Delta x}$ from the definition of the derivative. Thus,

$$\tan\theta = \frac{dy}{dx} = \text{slope of the tangent to the curve drawn at } A.$$

> Therefore, *the derivative dy/dx for any value of x (when it exists) is the trigonometrical tangent of the inclination of the tangent line of the curve with positive x-axis at the point x,* or *the slope of the curve at the point x.*

- If $dy/dx$ is positive (such as point $A$ of Figure 7.10), tan $\theta$ is positive, the angle $\theta$ is acute, and at that point $y$ increases with $x$.
- If $dy/dx$ is negative (such as point $B$ of Figure 7.10), tan $\theta$ is negative, the angle $\theta$ is negative or the angle $\theta$ is obtuse (such as point $C$ Figure 7.10), and $y$ decreases when $x$ increases or vice versa.
- If $dy/dx = 0$ (such as point $D$ of Figure 7.10), the tangent line is parallel to the $x$-axis.
- If $dy/dx \rightarrow \infty$, that is, $dx/dy = 0$, (such as point $E$, Figure 7.10), the tangent line is parallel to the $y$-axis.

## 7.5 Derivatives of Common Functions

To determine the derivatives of single-term common mathematical functions with respect to the variables that are in the functions, you do not need to determine the slopes or the tangent lines. These can be done from the mathematical definition of the derivative, that is, by evaluating the limit that occurs in the definition. These are done in any standard text on differential calculus. The results of these derivatives are useful in physics. Derivatives of most common single-term functions are listed below. Here $c$ and $n$ are constants.

$$\frac{d}{dx}(c) = 0 \qquad \frac{d}{dx}[c\,f(x)] = c\,\frac{d}{dx}[f(x)]$$

$$\frac{d}{dx}(x^n) = nx^{n-1} \qquad \frac{d}{dx}(e^{cx}) = ce^{cx}$$

$$\frac{d}{dx}(ln\ cx) = \frac{1}{x} \qquad \frac{d}{dx}(\sin cx) = c \cos cx$$

$$\frac{d}{dx}(\cos cx) = -c \sin cx \qquad \frac{d}{dx}(\tan cx) = c \sec^2 cx$$

$$\frac{d}{dx}(\cot cx) = -c \csc^2 cx \qquad \frac{d}{dx}(\csc cx) = -c \csc cx \cot cx$$

$$\frac{d}{dx}(\sec cx) = c \sec cx \tan cx \qquad \frac{d}{dx}(\sin^{-1} cx) = c\,\frac{1}{\sqrt{1-(cx)^2}}$$

$$\frac{d}{dx}(\cos^{-1} cx) = c\,\frac{-1}{\sqrt{1-(cx)^2}} \qquad \frac{d}{dx}(\tan^{-1} cx) = c\,\frac{1}{1+(cx)^2}$$

$$\frac{d}{dx}(\cot^{-1} cx) = c\,\frac{-1}{1+(cx)^2} \qquad \frac{d}{dx}(\sinh cx) = c\cosh cx$$

$$\frac{d}{dx}(\cosh cx) = c\sinh cx \qquad \frac{d}{dx}(\tanh cx) = c\,\mathrm{sech}^2\, cx$$

$$\frac{d}{dx}(\coth cx) = -c\,\mathrm{csch}^2\, cx \qquad \frac{d}{dx}(\sinh^{-1} cx) = c\,\frac{1}{\sqrt{(cx)^2+1}}$$

$$\frac{d}{dx}(\tanh^{-1} cx) = c\,\frac{1}{1-(cx)^2} \qquad \frac{d}{dx}(\cosh^{-1} cx) = c\,\frac{\pm 1}{\sqrt{(cx)^2-1}}$$

[+ if $\cosh^{-1} cx > 0$, – if $\cosh^{-1} cx < 0$]

In case it is not possible to remember all of the preceding derivatives, *remember* the following simple results that are often useful in physics:

The derivative of a constant = 0.

The derivative of the product of a constant and a function = product of the constant and the derivative of the function.

The derivative of $x^n = nx^{n-1}$.

The derivative of $e^x = e^x$.

The derivative of $\ln x = 1/x$.

The derivative of $\sin x = \cos x$.

The derivative of $\cos x = -\sin x$.

The derivative of $\tan x = \sec^2 x$.

## 7.6 Rules of Derivatives

In many situations in physics you will find derivatives of functions, which are more complicated than the functions listed in the preceding section. The following rules will be useful in those situations. Here $u$ and $v$ are functions of $x$.

1. **The Addition-Subtraction Rule**: *The derivative of the sum or difference of two functions is equal to the sum or difference of their derivatives*:

$$\frac{d}{dx}[u \pm v \pm \cdots] = \frac{du}{dx} \pm \frac{dv}{dx} \pm \cdots$$

2. **The Product Rule**: *The derivative of the product of two functions = first function* X *derivative of the second + second function* X *derivative of the first*:

$$\frac{d}{dx}[u \cdot v] = u\,\frac{dv}{dx} + v\,\frac{du}{dx}$$

3. **The Quotient Rule**: *The derivative of the quotient of two functions* =

$$\frac{\textit{derivative of the num.} \times \textit{denom.} - \textit{derivative of denom.} \times \textit{num}}{\textit{square of denom.}}$$

$$\frac{d}{dx}\left(\frac{u}{v}\right) = \frac{v(du/dx) - u(dv/dx)}{v^2}$$

4. **Generalized Product Rule**: *The derivative of $u^n$ with respect to x is given by the derivative of the function times the derivative of u with respect to x*:

$$\frac{d}{dx}(u^n) = n\,u^{n-1}\,\frac{du}{dx}$$

5. **The Chain Rule**: If $y$ is a function of the variable $t$, $y = f(t)$, and $t$ is a function of $x$, $t = f(x)$, then the derivative of $y$ with respect to $x$ is given by the chain rule:

$$\frac{dy}{dx} = \frac{dy}{dt} \cdot \frac{dt}{dx}$$

Also, note that $\frac{dt}{dx} = \frac{1}{dx/dt}$ (provided neither derivative is zero).

Thus,
$$\frac{dy}{dx} = \frac{dy/dt}{dx/dt}$$

The preceding expression for $dy/dx$ is useful to calculate derivative of parametric equations where both $x$ and $y$ can be expressed separately in terms of the parameter $t$.

**Example 7.6.1**

Find the derivative of the function $f(x) = 2x^5 - 4x^3 + 2x^2 + 6$ with respect to $x$.

$$f'(x) = \frac{d}{dx}(2x^5 - 4x^3 + 2x^2 + 6)$$

Use the addition-subtraction rule.
$$= \frac{d}{dx}(2x^5) - \frac{d}{dx}(4x^3) + \frac{d}{dx}(2x^2) + \frac{d}{dx}(6)$$

Take the constants out.
$$= 2\frac{d}{dx}(x^5) - 4\frac{d}{dx}(x^3) + 2\frac{d}{dx}(x^2) + \frac{d}{dx}(6)$$

Use the rules for derivative, $\frac{d}{dx}(c) = 0$ and $\frac{d}{dx}(x^n) = nx^{n-1}$

Thus,
$$f'(x) = 2(5x^{5-1}) - 4(3x^{3-1}) + 2(2x^{2-1}) + 0$$
$$= 10x^4 - 12x^2 + 4x$$

Factor out $2x$.
$$= 2x(5x^3 - 6x + 2).$$

**Example 7.6.2**

A prticle moves along the $x$-axis and is postion $x$ changes with time $t$ according to the equation $x = (4.0\text{ m})\,t + (2.4\text{ m/s}^2)\,t^2$. Determine the velocity $v = dx/dt$ and acceleration $a = dv/dt$ of the particle as a function of time.

$$x = (4.0\text{ m/s})\,t + (2.4\text{ m/s}^2)t^2$$

Take the derivative with respect to $t$.
$$v = \frac{dx}{dt} = \frac{d}{dt}[(4.0\text{ m/s})t + (2.4\text{ m/s}^2)t^2]$$

Use the addition-subtraction rule.
$$= \frac{d}{dt}[(4.0\text{ m/s})t] + \frac{d}{dt}[(2.4\text{ m/s}^2)t^2]$$

Take the constants out and use the formula $\frac{d}{dx}(x^n) = nx^{n-1}$

Thus, $v = (4.0 \text{ m/s})\,(1) + (2.4 \text{ m/s}^2)\,(2t^{2-1}) = 4.0 \text{ m/s} + (4.8 \text{ m/s}^2)t$.

Take the derivative with respect to $t$.

$$a = \frac{dv}{dt} = \frac{d}{dt}[(4.0 \text{ m/s})t + (4.8 \text{ m/s}^2)t]$$

$$= \frac{d}{dt}(4.0 \text{ m/s}) + \frac{d}{dt}[(4.8 \text{ m/s}^2)t]$$

$$= 0 + (4.8 \text{ m/s}^2)\,(1) = 4.8 \text{ m/s}^2.$$

**Example 7.6.3**

Find the derivative of the function $f(x) = e^x \cos x$ with respect to $x$.

$$f'(x) = \frac{d}{dx}(e^x \cos x)$$

Use the product rule.

$$= e^x \frac{d}{dx}(\cos x) + \cos x \frac{d}{dx}(e^x)$$

Use the results for derivatives of $\sin x$ and $\cos x$.

$$= e^x(-\sin x) + \cos x\,(e^x)$$

Factor out $e^x$.

$$= e^x(\cos x - \sin x)$$

**Example 7.6.4**

Find the derivative of the function $y = \dfrac{\sin x}{x^3}$ with respect to $x$.

$$\frac{dy}{dx} = \frac{d}{dx}\left(\frac{\sin x}{x^3}\right)$$

Use the quotient rule.

$$= \frac{x^3 \frac{d}{dx}(\sin x) - \sin x \frac{d}{dx}(x^3)}{(x^3)^2}$$

Use the results for derivatives.

$$= \frac{x^3(\cos x) - \sin x(3x^{3-1})}{x^6}$$

$$= \frac{x^3 \cos x - 3x^2 \sin x}{x^6}$$

Factor out $x^2$

$$= \frac{x^2(x\cos x - 3\sin x)}{x^6}$$

$$= \frac{(x\cos x - 3\sin x)}{x^4}$$

**Example 7.6.5**

Find $\frac{dy}{dx}$ if $x = a\,(t - \sin t)$, $y = a\,(1 + \cos t)$.

In this case, $x$ and $y$ have been expressed in terms of a third parameter $t$. Thus,

$$\frac{dy}{dx} = \frac{dy/dt}{dx/dt}$$

$$\frac{dx}{dt} = \frac{d}{dt}[a\,(t - \sin t)] = a\frac{d}{dt}\,(t - \sin t) = a\,(1 - \cos t)$$

$$\frac{dy}{dt} = \frac{d}{dt}[a\,(1 + \cos t)] = a\frac{d}{dt}\,(1 + \cos t) = a\,(0 - \sin t) = -\,a \sin t.$$

Therefore,

$$\frac{dy}{dx} = \frac{dy/dt}{dx/dt} = \frac{-\cancel{a}\sin t}{\cancel{a}(1 - \cos t)} = -\frac{2\sin\frac{t}{2}\cos\frac{t}{2}}{2\sin^2\frac{t}{2}} = -\cot\frac{t}{2}.$$

## 7.7 Derivatives of Implicit Functions

In many situations in physics, it may be inconvenient or even impossible to solve an equation of the form, say, $f(x, y) = 0$ for $y$ in terms of $x$. In such cases, $y$ is said to be an *implicit function* of $x$. To find derivative of such implicit functions, *take the derivative of each term* of the equation with respect to $x$ regarding $y$ as an unknown function of $x$ having a derivative $dy/dx$. Then use algebra to solve the resulting equation for $dy/dx$.

**Example 7.7.1**

Find $\frac{dy}{dx}$, if $x^3 - xy^3 - 2y + 6 = 0$.

This equation cannot be solved easily for $y$ in terms of $x$. Therefore, we must use implicit derivation to find the derivative. Differentiating each term of the equation with respect to $x$,

$$3x^2 - (x \cdot 3y^2 \frac{dy}{dx} + y^3 \cdot 1) - 2\frac{dy}{dx} + 0 = 0$$

Collect terms involving $\frac{dy}{dx}$ $\quad (3xy^2 + 2)\frac{dy}{dx} = 3x^2 - y^3$

Divide by $(3xy^2 + 2)$. $\quad \frac{dy}{dx} = \frac{3x^2 - y^3}{3xy^2 + 2}$

Note that the final answer contains $y$.

**Example 7.7.2 (thermal physics)**
In an isothermal process of an ideal gas $PV$ = constant, while for an adiabatic process for an ideal gas $PV^{\gamma}$ = constant, where $\gamma$ is a constant (greater than one) of the gas and $P$ and $V$ represent the pressure and the volume of the gas, respectively. If $V$ is plotted along the $x$-axis and $P$ is plotted along the $y$-axis, compare the slope the isothermal and the adabatic curves.

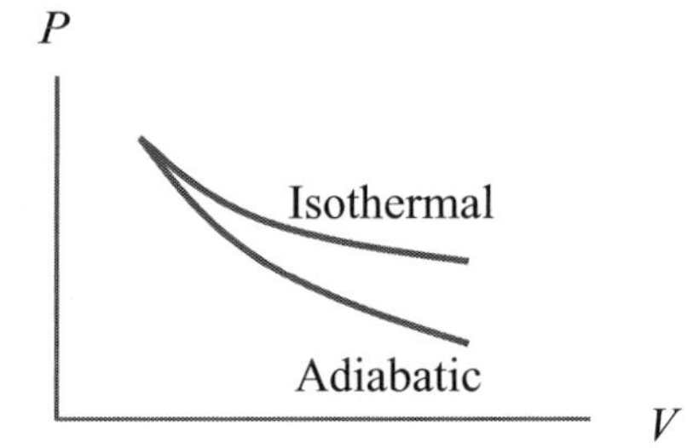


For an isothermal process $PV$ = constant.
Differentiate both sides with respect to $V$.

Use the product rule. $\quad P \cdot 1 + V\frac{dP}{dV} = 0$

Solve for $\frac{dP}{dV}$ $\quad \frac{dP}{dV} = -\frac{P}{V}$

= slope of the isothermal curve.

For an adiabatic process $PV^{\gamma}$ = constant.

Differentiate both sides with respect to $V$.

Use the product rule. $\quad P \cdot (\gamma V^{\gamma - 1}) + V^{\gamma}\frac{dP}{dV} = 0$

Solve for $\frac{dP}{dV}$. $\quad \frac{dP}{dV} = -\frac{\gamma P V^{\gamma - 1}}{V^{\gamma}} = -\frac{\gamma P}{V}$

= Slope of the adiabatic curve.

Thus, the ratio of the two slopes = $-\frac{\gamma P}{V} \Big/ -\frac{P}{V} = \gamma\,(>1)$.

**Exercises**

Find the derivative of the following functions of $x$.

1. $3x^7 + 4x^4 - 2x^2 - x + 6$ 2. $x^2 \log x$ 3. $(x^2 + 1) \sin x$

4. $\dfrac{\sin x}{x}$ 5. $\dfrac{1+\sin x}{1-\sin x}$

Find $\dfrac{dy}{dx}$ for the following cases:

6. $x = a \cos t$, $y = b \sin t$ 7. $x = a(2\cos t + \cos 2t)$, $y = a\,(2\sin t - \sin 2t)$

8. $3x^4 - x^2y + 2y^3 = 0$ 9. $x^{2/3} + y^{2/3} = a^{2/3}$

10. Determine the velocity ($v$) and acceleration ($a$) of a particle whose position ($x$) changes with time according to the equation $x$ = (1.2 m) + (2.8 m/s) $t$ + (4.2 m/s$^2$)$t^2$.

11. The force of gravity on a person of mass $m$ at a distance $r$ from the center of the earth is given by $F = GM_Em/r^2$, where $G$ is a constant (called gravitational constant) and $M_E$ is the constant mass of the earth. The force of gravity acting on a person is called his weight. If the person travels at a constant velocity $v$ directly away from the earth, show that the time ($t$) rate of change of the weight of the person is $-(2GM_Em/r^3)v$. (*Hint*: $v = dr/dt$.)

## 7.8 Differentials

Let $f'(x)$ be the derivative of the function $y = f(x)$ and $\Delta x$ be the increment or the change of $x$. Then the differential of $y$ or $f(x)$, which is denoted by the symbol $dy$ or $df(x)$, is given by

$$dy = df(x) = f'(x)\,\Delta x.$$

If $f(x) = x$, or, $f'(x) = 1$, then from the preceding equation, $dx = 1 \cdot \Delta x = \Delta x$. Therefore, if $x$ is the independent variable, the differential of $x$, written as $dx$, is identical with $\Delta x$.

Thus, $dy = df(x) = f'(x)\,dx$.

That is, the *differential of a function is equal to the derivative of the function multiplied by the differential of the independent variable.*

Thus, if $y = x^n$, $dy = nx^{n-1}\,dx$. If $y = \tan x$, $dy = \sec^2 x\,dx$.

**Rules for Differentials**

The rules for differentials are exactly analogous to those for derivatives:

$$d(c) = 0$$

$$d(u \pm v \pm w \pm \cdots) = du \pm dv \pm dw \pm \cdots$$

$$d(uv) = u\,dv + v\,du$$

$$d\left(\frac{u}{v}\right) = \frac{v\,du - u\,dv}{v^2}$$

$$d(\sin x) = \cos x\,dx$$

$$d(\cos x) = -\sin x\,dx.$$

## 7.9 Higher Derivatives of a Function

It is possible to take the derivative of derivatives of a function. The second derivative of the function $y = f(x)$ is the derivative of its first derivative. It is written as follows:

$$\text{Second derivative of } y \text{ or } f(x) = \frac{d}{dx}\left(\frac{dy}{dx}\right) = f''(x) = y''.$$

For example, the velocity $v = \frac{dx}{dt}$ and the acceleration $a = \frac{dv}{dt}$. Thus, the acceleration $a$ can be written as the second derivative of the position $x$ with respect to time $t$ as follows:

$$a = \frac{dv}{dt} = \frac{d}{dt}\left(\frac{dx}{dt}\right) = \frac{d^2x}{d_t{}^2}$$

Recall, from Section 7.4, that first derivative of a function at a point is the value of the slope of the curve representing the function at the point. Since the second derivative of a function is the derivative of its first derivative, it represents the rate at which the slope (or first derivative) changes with respect to $x$, or, in other words, it is a measure of how much curvature or concavity a function has. For a function that is *concaving up*, the second derivative is *positive* (Figure 7.11), while for a function that is *concaving down* (Figure 7.12), the second derivative is *negative*.

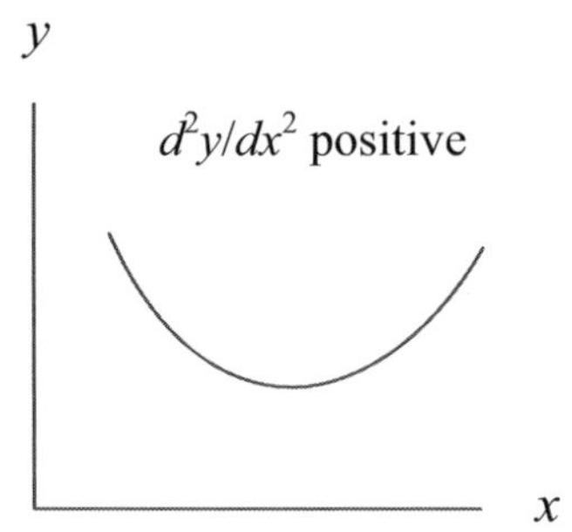


**Figure 7.11**

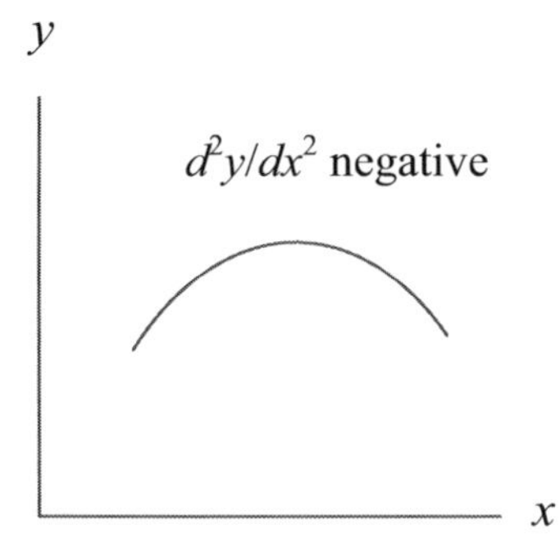


**Figure 7.12**

Higher derivatives beyond second derivatives can also be found by continuing taking derivatives of derivatives.

$$\text{Third derivative of } y = f(x) \text{ with respect to } x = \frac{d}{dx}\left(\frac{d^2y}{dx^2}\right)$$

$$= \frac{d^3y}{dx^3} = f'''(x) = y'''$$

In general,

$$n\text{th derivative of } y \text{ with respect to } x = \frac{d}{dx}\left(\frac{d^{n-1}y}{dx^{n-1}}\right) = \frac{d^n y}{dx^n} = f^{(n)}(x) = y^{(n)}$$

Higher derivatives beyond the second derivative are rarely used in introductory or intermediate physics.

## 7.10 Maxima and Minima of a Function

The concept of derivative is directly used in physics to determine the maxima and minima of a function representing a physical quantity.

By the maximum value of a function $y = f(x)$ in calculus, we do not necessarily mean the absolutely greatest value attainable by the function. A function may have several maxima and minima. A function $y = f(x)$ is said to be a minimum at a point $x = a$ if $f(a)$ is less than every other value assumed by $f(x)$ in the immediate neighborhood of $x = a$. Similarly, a function $y = f(x)$ is said to be a *maximum* at a point $x = b$ if $f(b)$ is greater than every other value assumed by $f(x)$ in the *immediate neighborhood* of $x = b$. These maxima and minima points on the curve are called *critical points*.

For all critical points on the curve, the tangent line is horizontal, that is, the first derivative $dy/dx$ or $f'(x)$ is zero. In Figure 7.13 the function $f(x)$ has a minimum at $x = a$ and $x = c$ and a maximum at $x = b$. Thus, $f'(a) = f'(b) = f'(c) = 0$. This is a *necessary condition* for maximum and minimum. You can use this condition to determine the locations of maxima and minima of a function. This technique is useful in different areas of physics especially for potential energy analyses. The maxima and minima are collectively called *extrema* on the function.

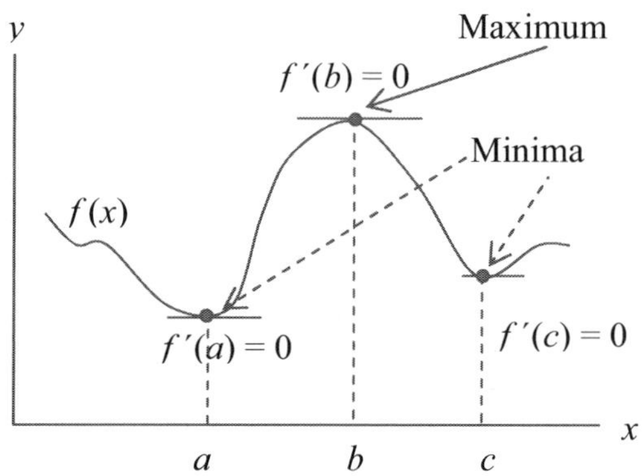


**Figure 7.13**

Follow these steps to determine the extrema of a function $y = f(x)$:

- Determine the first derivative $dy/dx$, that is, $f'(x)$.
- Set $f'(x) = 0$, and solve the resulting equation for $x$. The values of $x$ are the critical points.
- Determine the second derivative $f''(x)$ and find the value of the second derivative for each critical point.
- If the result is negative, then $f(x)$ has a maximum at the corresponding critical point. Plug the value of $x$ for which $f(x)$ has a maximum to the original function to determine the maximum value of the function $f(x)$.
- If the result is positive, then $f(x)$ has a minimum at the corresponding critical point. Plug the value of $x$ for which $f(x)$ has a maximum to the original function to determine the maximum value of the function $f(x)$.
- If the result is zero, pick a number greater than and a number less than the critical point. The number must be close to the test point so that the value of another critical point is not inadvertently tested. Substitute these two numbers into the second derivative.

  If both numbers are negative, $f(x)$ has a maximum at the corresponding critical point.

If both numbers are positive, $f(x)$ has a minimum at the corresponding critical point.

If one number is positive and the other negative, $f(x)$ has an inflection point. At inflection points the curve change concavity. Ignore any inflection point. If an extrema is found, plug the value of $x$ to the original function to determine the maximum or minimum value of the function $f(x)$.

> Note: A point at which the slope of a curve has a maximum or minimum value is called a point of inflection. A curve bends upward if second derivative is *positive*, and bends downward if second derivative is *negative*.

**Example 7.10.1**

Investigate for what values of $x$ the function $f(x) = 2x^3 - 21x^2 + 36x - 21$ is a minimum or maximum. Find also the minimum and maximum values of $f(x)$.

$$f(x) = 2x^3 - 21x^2 + 36x - 21$$

A necessary condition for maximum and minimum is that the first derivative $f'(x) = 0$. Find the first derivative $f'(x)$.

$$f'(x) = 2(3x^2) - 21(2x) + 36 + 0 = 6x^2 - 42x + 36$$

Set $f'(x) = 0$, to determine maximum or minimum. Thus,

$$6x^2 - 42x + 36 = 0$$

Factor out 6. $\quad 6(x^2 - 7x + 6) = 0$

Divide by 6. $\quad x^2 - 7x + 6 = 0$

Factor the left-hand side. $\quad (x - 1)(x - 6) = 0$

or $\quad x = 1$ or $6$.

Determine the second derivative $f''(x)$.

$$f''(x) = 6(2x) - 42 = 12x - 42 = 6(2x - 7)$$

For $x = 1$, $\quad f''(x) = 6(2 \cdot 1 - 7) = -30$, which is *negative*.

Thus, $f(x)$ is the *maximum* for $x = 1$.

For $x = 6$, $\quad f''(x) = 6(2 \cdot 6 - 7) = 30$, which is *positive*.

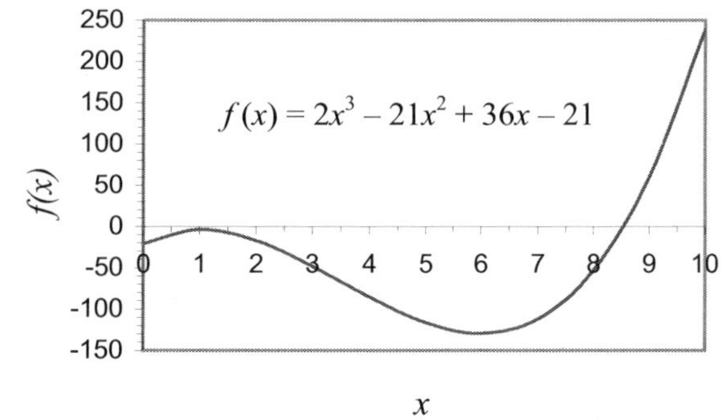


Thus, $f(x)$ is minimum for $x = 6$.

To determine the maximum and minimum values of the function, substitute the values of $x = 1$ and $x = 6$, respectively.

The maximum value of $f(x) = f(1) = 2(1^3) - 21(1^2) + 36(1) - 21 = -4$.

The minimum value of $f(x) = f(6) = 2(6^3) - 21(6^2) + 36(6) - 21 = -129$.

The plot of the function $f(x) = 2x^3 - 21x^2 + 36x - 21$ is shown showing that it has a maximum at $x = 1$ and minimum at $x = 6$.

### Example 7.10.2

Investigate whether the function $f(x) = x^3 - 6x^2 + 18x + 10$ has a minimum or maximum.

$f(x) = x^3 - 6x^2 + 184x + 10$. The plot of $f(x)$ is shown below for $x = -10$ to 10.

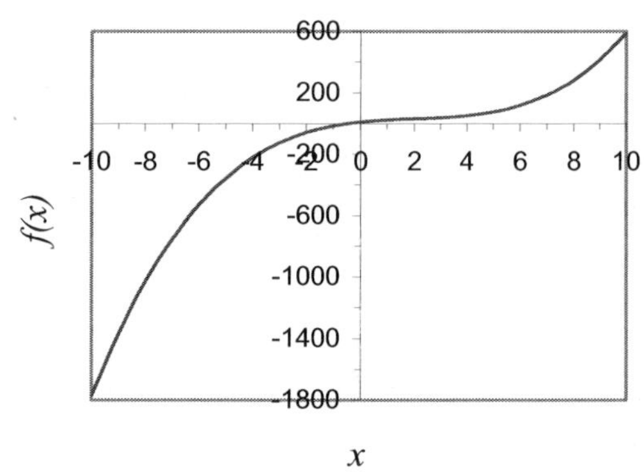

Take the derivative with respect to $x$. $f'(x) = 3x^2 - 6(2x) + 18$

$= 3x^2 - 12x + 18$

Factor out 3. $= 3(x^2 - 4x + 6)$

Write as a perfect square plus a number. $= 3[(x^2 - 4x + 4) + 2]$

$= 3[(x - 2)^2 + 2]$

Since $(x - 2)^2$ is always positive, $f'(x)$ is always positive and can never be zero. Therefore, $f(x)$ does not have a maximum nor a minimum.

### Example 7.10.3 (from modern physics)

**Most probable radius for an electron in a hydrogen atom**: The electron in a normal hydrogen atom is at the ground state and has a radial probability distribution function (which gives the probability of finding an electron at a distance $r$ from the nucleus of the atom) given by $P_r = 4\frac{r^2}{r_0^3}e^{-2r/r_0}$, where $r_0$ has the dimension of length and is called the *Bohr radius*. Determine the most probable distance $r$ at which to find the electron in the ground state for a hydrogen atom.

The plot of the radial probability distribution function $P_r$ is shown at right. The peak of the curve corresponds to the most probable distance, $r$. At the peak, the curve has a zero slope (that is, first derivative is zero). Therefore, take the first derivative of $P_r$ and set it equal to zero.

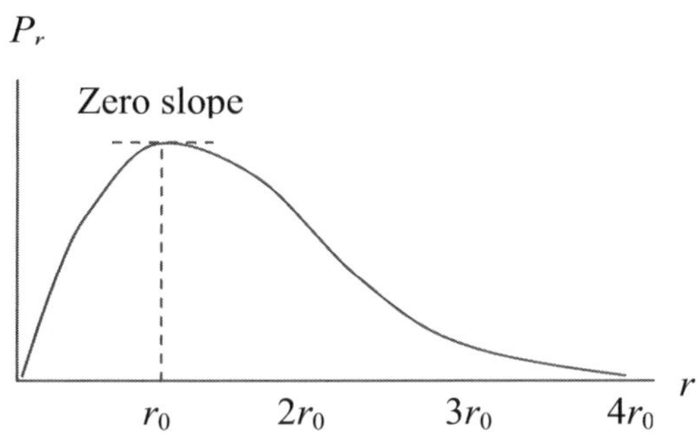


$$\frac{\mathrm{d}}{\mathrm{dr}}\left(4\frac{r^2}{r_0^3}e^{-2r/r_0}\right) = 0$$

Use the rule of derivative for the product of two functions.

Thus, $$\left(8\frac{\mathrm{r}}{\mathrm{r}_0^3} - 8\frac{\mathrm{r}^2}{\mathrm{r}_0^4}\right)e^{-2r/r_0} = 0.$$

Divide by $e^{-2r/r_0}$, since it is not equal to zero except when $r = \infty$.

Thus, $$8\frac{r}{r_0^3} - 8\frac{r^2}{r_0^4} = 0$$

Divide by 8. $$\frac{r}{r_0^3} = \frac{r^2}{r_0^4}$$

Cancel the same quantities on both sides. $r = r_0$

Thus, the most probable distance for the electron is equal to the Bohr radius $r_0$ in a normal hydrogen atom.

**Example 7.10.4 (from thermal physics)**

**Most probable speed**: The velocity ($v$) distribution of a system of $N$ molecules each of mass $m$ at any temperature $T$ (in kelvin) is given by Maxwell velocity distribution, which is expressed as

$$f(v) = 4\pi N \left(m/2\pi kT\right)^{3/2} v^2 e^{-mv^2/2kT}$$

where $k$ is a constant called the Boltzmann constnat. *Most probable speed*, $v_p$, is the speed at which the number of molecules is a maximum. Determine the most probable speed.

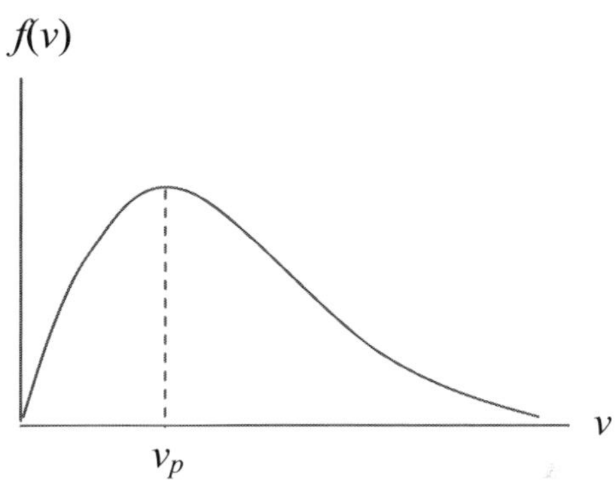


The plot of $f(v)$ is shown. For the most probable speed, $f(v)$ is a maximum,. That is, $df(v)/dv = 0$.

Thus, $$\frac{df(v)}{dv} = \frac{d}{dv}\left(4\pi N\left(\frac{m}{2\pi kT}\right)^{3/2} v^2 e^{-mv^2/2kT}\right) = 0$$

Use the rule of products. $$4\pi N\left(\frac{m}{2\pi kT}\right)^{3/2}\left(2ve^{-mv^2/2kT} - \frac{2mv^3}{2kT}e^{-mv^2/2kT}\right) = 0$$

Factor out $2v\,e^{-mv^2/2kT}$ $$4\pi N 2v\,e^{-mv^2/2kT}\left(\frac{m}{2\pi kT}\right)^{3/2}\left(1 - \frac{mv^2}{2kT}\right) = 0$$

Divide by the common factor. $\left(1 - \dfrac{mv^2}{2kT}\right) = 0$

The solution for $v$ is the most probable speed, $v_p$. Therefore, $v_p = \sqrt{\dfrac{2kT}{m}}$

### Example 7.10.5 (from optics)

***Principle of least time**: According to *Fermat's principle* in optics, a ray of light in passing from a point $P$ in one medium to a point $Q$ in another medium follows the path for which the time is a minimum. Prove the law of refraction from Fermat's principle.

Let a ray of light meet the surface of separation between the two media and $POQ$ be a possible path of the ray. $PM$ (= $a$) and $QN$ (= $b$) are two perpendiculars drawn from $P$ and $Q$ to the surface. The line $AOB$ is normal to the surface passing through the point of incidence, $O$. From the following figure, if $v$ and $v'$ are the velocities of light in the two media, the total time $t$ taken by the ray of light is

$$t = \frac{PO}{v} + \frac{OQ}{v'} = \frac{a\sec\theta}{v} + \frac{a\sec\phi}{v'}$$

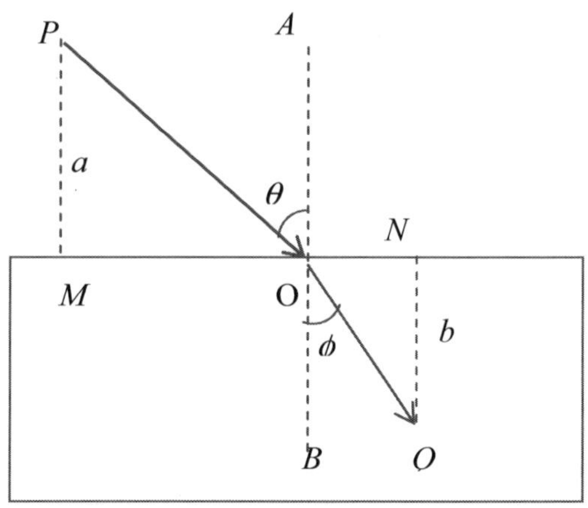


For the time $t$ to be a minimum, set $\dfrac{dt}{d\theta} = 0$. Thus from the preceding equation for $t$,

$$\frac{a}{v}\sec\theta\tan\theta + \frac{b}{v'}\sec\phi\tan\phi\frac{d\phi}{d\theta} = 0. \qquad (7.1)$$

Since the points $P$ and $Q$ are fixed, distance $MN = MO + ON = a \tan\theta + b \tan\phi =$ constant. Take derivative with respect to $\theta$.

$$a \sec^2\theta + b \sec^2\phi \frac{d\phi}{d\theta} = 0 \tag{7.2}$$

Eliminate $\frac{d\phi}{d\theta}$ from Equations (7.1) and (7.2). You will get after simplification (to show this determine $\frac{d\phi}{d\theta}$ from Equation 2 and substitute in Equation 1),

$$\frac{\sin\theta}{v} = \frac{\sin\phi}{v'}$$

$$\frac{\sin\theta}{\sin\phi} = \frac{v}{v'}$$

This is the law of refraction.

## Exercises

Find the values of $x$ for which the following functions (Exercises 12 and 13) are maximum or minimum. Also find the maximum and minimum values of the function.

12. $f(x) = 2x^3 - 15x^2 + 36x + 9$

13. $f(x) = 2x^3 + 3x^2 - 12x + 10$

14. The force $F$ exerted by a circular electric current of radius a on a magnet whose axis coincides with the axis of the coil is $F = kx\,(a^2 + x^2)^{-5/2}$, where $k$ is a constant and $x$ is the distance of the magnet from the center of the coil. Show that the force $F$ is greatest for $x = a/2$. (*Hint*: To determine $dF/dx$, use the product rule or the quotient rule.)

15. The potential energy of two atoms in a diatomic molecule can be expressed by $U(r) = -a/r^6 + b/r^{12}$, where $a$ and $b$ are positive constants and $r$ is the separation between the atoms. Show that $U(r)$ is minimum for $r = (2b/a)^{1/6}$. Find the value of $U(r)$ as $r$ tends to 0 and $\infty$. Also, find $r$ for which $U(r) = 0$. From these information, plot $U(r)$ as a function of $r$.

*16 According to Fermat's principle in optics, a ray of light in passing from a point $P$ in one medium to a point $Q$ in the same medium after reflection from a surface follows the path for which the time is a minimum. Prove the law of reflection (angle of incidence = angle of reflection) from Fermat's principle.

*17. The Planck's law for the radiation intensity $I$ for a blackbody can be written as $I(x) = (2\pi kT^5/h^4c^3)\, x^5\, [\exp(x) - 1]^{-1}$, where $x = hc/\lambda kT$ ($h$, $c$, $k$ are constants, $\lambda$ is wavelength, and $T$ is the temperature of the blackbody). For the wavelength for which the radiated intensity is a maximum, the derivative of $I(x)$ with respect to $x$ is zero. Show that this leads to a transcendental equation $5e^{-x} + x - 5 = 0$.

## 7.11 Partial Derivatives

If there is a function of more than one independent variable, then the differentiation of the function with respect to any one of the variables is termed as *partial differentiation*. Partial differentials are common in different areas of physics especially in thermodynamics. For example, a thermodynamic system is characterized by thermodynamic variables such as pressure, volume, and temperature. All these variables cannot be changed independently; when certain ones are changed, the remaining ones are automatically fixed in value. This situation is mathematically represented by partial differentiation.

If $z = f(x, y)$, the partial derivative of $f(x, y)$ with respect to $x$, keeping $y$ constant, is mathematically defined as

$$\frac{\partial f}{\partial x} = \lim_{\Delta x \to 0} \frac{f(x + \Delta x, y) - f(x, y)}{\Delta x}$$

Similarly, the partial derivative of $f(x, y)$ with respect to $y$, keeping $x$ constant, is defined as

$$\frac{\partial f}{\partial y} = \lim_{\Delta y \to 0} \frac{f(x, y + \Delta y) - f(x, y)}{\Delta y}$$

To take the partial derivative of a function $z = f(x, y, \ldots)$ with respect to $x$, first pretend all variables, except the first variable $x$, are constant and take the derivative of the function with respect to $x$. This is $\frac{\partial f}{\partial x}$. Next, pretend all variables except the second variable $y$ are constant and take the derivative with respect to $y$. This is $\frac{\partial f}{\partial y}$.

Repeat this process for any other variables in the function.

Note: The curly $\partial$ is commonly used to denote the symbol of partial derivative, to distinguish it from the symbol $d$ of ordinary derivative.

**Example 7.11.1**

Determine $\dfrac{\partial f}{\partial x}$ or $\dfrac{\partial z}{\partial x}$ and $\dfrac{\partial f}{\partial y}$ or $\dfrac{\partial z}{\partial y}$ for the function $z = f(x, y) = x^2 + 2xy + y^3$.

The partial derivative of the function with respect to $x$,

$$\frac{\partial f}{\partial x} \text{ or } \frac{\partial z}{\partial x} = \frac{\partial}{\partial x}(x^2 + 2xy + y^3)$$

Take the derivative, assuming $y$ is constant.

$$= 2x + 2y \cdot 1 + 0$$
$$= 2(x + y).$$

The partial derivative of $f(x, y)$ with respect to $y$,

$$\frac{\partial f}{\partial y} \text{ or } \frac{\partial z}{\partial y} = \frac{\partial}{\partial y}(x^2 + 2xy + y^3)$$

Take the derivative, assuming $x$ constant.

$$= 0 + 2x \cdot 1 + 3y^2$$
$$= 2x + 3y^2$$

The partial derivatives of second order are defined as follows:

$$\frac{\partial^2 f}{\partial x^2} = \frac{\partial}{\partial x}\left(\frac{\partial f}{\partial x}\right) \qquad \frac{\partial^2 f}{\partial y^2} = \frac{\partial}{\partial y}\left(\frac{\partial f}{\partial y}\right)$$

$$\frac{\partial^2 f}{\partial x\, \partial y} = \frac{\partial}{\partial x}\left(\frac{\partial f}{\partial y}\right) \qquad \frac{\partial^2 f}{\partial y\, \partial x} = \frac{\partial}{\partial y}\left(\frac{\partial f}{\partial x}\right)$$

The results of differentiation from the bottom two expressions will be the same if the function and its partial derivative are continuous. In this case, the order of differentiation is not important. Similarly, other higher-order partial derivates are defined.

**Example 7.11.2**

A wave propagating to the left can be expreseed by the function $y(x, t) = A \sin(kx + \omega t)$ where $A$, $k$ and $\omega$ are constants, called the amplitude, wave number, and the angular frequency of the wave, respectively. Show that the wave satisfies the equation $\partial^2 y/\partial t^2 = v^2\, \partial^2 y/\partial x^2$, where $v = \omega/k$.

$y(x, t) = A \sin(kx + \omega t)$. Here the variables are $x$ and $t$.
First, take the partial derivative of the equation twice with respect to $t$: Use the results for the derivatives of sin and cos functions from Section 7.5.

$$\frac{\partial y}{\partial t} = \frac{\partial}{\partial t}[A \sin(kx + \omega t)] = A\,\omega \cos(kx + \omega t)$$

$$\frac{\partial^2 y}{\partial t^2} = \frac{\partial}{\partial t}[A\,\omega \cos(kx + \omega t)] = A\omega[-\omega \sin(kx + \omega t)] = -A\omega^2 \sin(kx + \omega t)$$

Next, take the partial derivative of the equation twice with respect to $x$.

$$\frac{\partial y}{\partial x} = \frac{\partial}{\partial x}[A \sin(kx + \omega t)] = A\,k \cos(kx + \omega t)$$

$$\frac{\partial^2 y}{\partial x^2} = \frac{\partial}{\partial x}[A\,k \cos(kx + \omega t)] = Ak\,[-k \sin(kx + \omega t)] = -Ak^2 \sin(kx + \omega t)$$

Thus, dividing the two second derivatives, we get

$$\frac{\partial^2 y}{\partial t^2} \bigg/ \frac{\partial^2 y}{\partial x^2} = \frac{-A\omega^2 \sin(kx - \omega t)}{-Ak^2 \sin(kx - \omega t)} = \frac{\omega^2}{k^2} = v^2 \text{ (since } v = \omega/k)$$

or $$\frac{\partial^2 y}{\partial t^2} = v^2 \frac{\partial^2 y}{\partial x^2}$$

This equation is called the wave equation in physics.

**Exercises**

18. Show that $\dfrac{\partial^2 z}{\partial x^2} + \dfrac{\partial^2 z}{\partial y^2} = 0$, if $z = \log(x^2 + y^2)$.

19. If $f(x, y) = x^3 + x^2y^2 + y^3$, show that $\dfrac{\partial^2 f}{\partial x\,\partial y} = \dfrac{\partial^2 f}{\partial y\,\partial x}$

20 . If $y = f(x + vt) + \phi(x - vt)$, show that $\dfrac{\partial^2 y}{\partial t^2} = v^2 \dfrac{\partial^2 y}{\partial x^2}$

21. The relation between pressure $P$, volume $V$ and temperature $T$ of $n$ mols of a perfect gas is $PV = nRT$ where $R$ is a constant. Show that $(dP/dV)_T = -nRT/V^2$ and $(dP/dT)_V = nR/V$, where $(dP/dV)_T$ means the partial derivative of $P$ with respect to $V$ at constant $T$, etc.

## *7.12 Exact or Perfect Differential

The *differential* $dz$ of the function $z = f(x, y)$ is defined as

$$dz = \left(\frac{\partial z}{\partial x}\right)_y dx + \left(\frac{\partial z}{\partial y}\right)_x dy.$$

Here, the subscript $x$ (or $y$) means that the derivative was taken when $x$ (or $y$) was constant.

The expression $dz = M(x, y)\ dx + N(x, y)\ dy$ is said to an *exact or perfect differential* if a function $z$ of $x$, $y$ exists such that $\left(\frac{\partial M}{\partial y}\right)_x = \left(\frac{\partial N}{\partial x}\right)_y$

Taking derivatives of the preceding expressions with respect to $y$ and $x$, respectively,

$$\frac{\partial^2 z}{\partial y\,\partial x} = \left(\frac{\partial M}{\partial y}\right)_x \quad \text{and} \quad \frac{\partial^2 z}{\partial x\,\partial y} = \left(\frac{\partial N}{\partial x}\right)_y$$

Thus, the condition for perfect differential is

$$\left(\frac{\partial M}{\partial y}\right)_x = \left(\frac{\partial N}{\partial x}\right)_y \quad \text{or} \quad \frac{\partial^2 z}{\partial y\,\partial x} = \frac{\partial^2 z}{\partial x\,\partial y}$$

### *Example 7.12.1 (from thermodynamics)

The four thermodynamic functions called internal energy ($U$), enthalpy ($H$), free energy ($F$), and Gibbs's potential ($G$) are perfect differentials. The differentials of these functions are expressed as, respectively,

$$dU = T\,dS - P\,dV,$$

$$dH = T\,dS + V\,dP,$$

$$dF = -S\,dT - P\,dV,$$

$$dG = -S\,dT + V\,dP.$$

Here, $P$, $V$, $T$, and $S$ are other thermodynamic variables called pressure, volume, temperature, and entropy, respectively. Express the condition for each of these perfect differentials.

To solve this problem, compare the differentials with the expression $M\,dx + N\,dy$ and write down condition as $\left(\frac{\partial M}{\partial y}\right)_x = \left(\frac{\partial N}{\partial x}\right)_y$

Thus, from the expression for $dU$, $\left(\frac{\partial T}{\partial V}\right)_S = -\left(\frac{\partial P}{\partial S}\right)_V$

From the expression for $dH$, $\left(\frac{\partial T}{\partial P}\right)_S = \left(\frac{\partial V}{\partial S}\right)_P$

From the expression for $dF$, $\left(\frac{\partial S}{\partial V}\right)_T = \left(\frac{\partial P}{\partial T}\right)_V$

From the expression for $dG$, $\left(\frac{\partial S}{\partial P}\right)_T = -\left(\frac{\partial V}{\partial T}\right)_P$

These four relations are called *Maxwell's four thermodynamic relations.*

***Example 7.12.2 (from thermodynamics)**

The relationship between pressure $P$ volume $V$ and temperature $T$ of a thermodynamic system can be expressed by the function $f(P, V, T) = 0$. The equation can be written as $T = T(P, V)$ (that is, $T$ is a function of $P$ and $V$) and also as $P = P(T, V)$. Show that (i)

(i) $\left(\frac{\partial P}{\partial T}\right)_V = 1\Big/\left(\frac{\partial T}{\partial P}\right)_V$ and (ii) $\left(\frac{\partial P}{\partial T}\right)_V \left(\frac{\partial T}{\partial V}\right)_P \left(\frac{\partial V}{\partial P}\right)_T = -1.$

From the function $T = T(P, V)$, $dT = \left(\frac{\partial T}{\partial P}\right)_V dP + \left(\frac{\partial T}{\partial V}\right)_P dV$

From the function $P = P(T, V)$, $dP = \left(\frac{\partial P}{\partial T}\right)_V dT + \left(\frac{\partial P}{\partial V}\right)_T dV$

Substituting the value of $dT$,

$$dP = \left(\frac{\partial P}{\partial T}\right)_V \left[\left(\frac{\partial T}{\partial P}\right)_V dP + \left(\frac{\partial T}{\partial V}\right)_P dV\right] + \left(\frac{\partial P}{\partial V}\right)_T dV$$

$$= \left(\frac{\partial P}{\partial T}\right)_V \left(\frac{\partial T}{\partial P}\right)_V dP + \left[\left(\frac{\partial P}{\partial T}\right)_V \left(\frac{\partial T}{\partial V}\right)_P + \left(\frac{\partial P}{\partial V}\right)_T\right] dV$$

Transferring all terms to the left-hand side,

$$\left[1-\left(\frac{\partial P}{\partial T}\right)_V\left(\frac{\partial T}{\partial P}\right)_V\right]dP-\left[\left(\frac{\partial P}{\partial T}\right)_V\left(\frac{\partial T}{\partial V}\right)_P+\left(\frac{\partial P}{\partial V}\right)_T\right]dV=0$$

Since $P$ and $V$ can be independent variables, the left-hand side can be zero only if the coefficients of $dP$ and $dV$ are zero; that is,

(i) $1-\left(\frac{\partial P}{\partial T}\right)_V\left(\frac{\partial T}{\partial P}\right)_V=0.$

That is, $\left(\frac{\partial P}{\partial T}\right)_V\left(\frac{\partial T}{\partial P}\right)_V=1$ or $\left(\frac{\partial P}{\partial T}\right)_V=1\Big/\left(\frac{\partial T}{\partial P}\right)_V$

(ii) $\left(\frac{\partial P}{\partial T}\right)_V\left(\frac{\partial T}{\partial V}\right)_P+\left(\frac{\partial P}{\partial V}\right)_T=0$

$$\left(\frac{\partial P}{\partial T}\right)_V\left(\frac{\partial T}{\partial V}\right)_P=-\left(\frac{\partial P}{\partial V}\right)_T=-1\Big/\left(\frac{\partial V}{\partial P}\right)_T \quad \text{or} \quad \left(\frac{\partial P}{\partial T}\right)_V\left(\frac{\partial T}{\partial V}\right)_P\left(\frac{\partial V}{\partial P}\right)_T=-1$$

Extension of partial differentiation and differential to functions of more than two variables are exactly analogous.

**Exercise**

22. Show that

(a) $\left(\frac{\partial V}{\partial T}\right)_P=-\left(\frac{\partial P}{\partial T}\right)_V\Big/\left(\frac{\partial P}{\partial V}\right)_T$ (b) $\left(\frac{\partial P}{\partial T}\right)_V=-\left(\frac{\partial V}{\partial T}\right)_P\Big/\left(\frac{\partial V}{\partial P}\right)_T$

## *7.13 Partial Derivatives of a Function of Two Functions

Let $z=f(x_1, x_2)$, where $x_1=f_1(x, y)$ and $x_2=f_2(x, y)$ and $x$, $y$ are independent variables. Then

$$\frac{\partial z}{\partial x}=\frac{\partial z}{\partial x_1}\frac{\partial x_1}{\partial x}+\frac{\partial z}{\partial x_2}\frac{\partial x_2}{\partial x}$$

$$\frac{\partial z}{\partial y}=\frac{\partial z}{\partial x_1}\frac{\partial x_1}{\partial y}+\frac{\partial z}{\partial x_2}\frac{\partial x_2}{\partial y}$$

The result can be generalized to the cases of more than two variables.

# Answers to Exercises in Chapter 7

1. $21x^6 + 16x^3 - 4x - 1$
2. $x + 2x \log x$
3. $(x^2 + 1) \cos x + 2x \sin x$
4. $(x \cos x - \sin x)/x^2$
5. $\dfrac{2\cos x}{(1 - \sin x)^2}$
6. $-(b/a)\cot t$
7. $-\tan \dfrac{1}{2} t$
8. $\dfrac{2x(6x^2 - y)}{x^2 - 6y^2}$
9. $-\left(\dfrac{y}{x}\right)^{\frac{1}{3}}$

10. $v = (2.8 + 8.4\, t)$ m/s, $a = 8.4$ m/s$^2$

12. $f(x)$ is maximum for $x = 2$ and minimum for $x = 3$; $f_{max} = f(2) = 37$ and $f_{min} = f(3) = 36$.

13. $f(x)$ is maximum for $x = -2$ and minimum for $x = 1$; $f_{max} = f(-2) = 30$ and $f_{min} = f(1) = 3$.

15. At $r \to 0$, $U(r) \to \infty$; as $r \to \infty$, $U(r) \to 0$, $U(r) = 0$ for $r = (b/a)^{1/6}$.

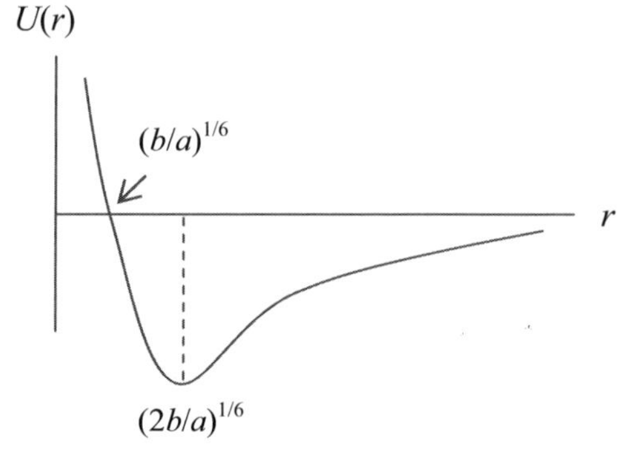

# Sequences and Convergence

CHAPTER 9

# Sequences, Series, and Power Series

> 'Then you should say what you mean,' the March Hare went on.
> 'I do,' Alice hastily replied; 'at least — at least I mean what I say — that's the same thing, you know.'
> 'Not the same thing a bit!' said the Hatter. 'Why, you might just as well say that "I see what I eat" is the same thing as "I eat what I see!"'

**Lewis Carroll (Charles Lutwidge Dodgson) 1832–1898**
**from *Alice's Adventures in Wonderland***

## Introduction

An infinite series is a sum that involves infinitely many terms. Since addition is carried out on two numbers at a time, the evaluation of the sum of an infinite series necessarily involves finding a limit. Complicated functions $f(x)$ can frequently be expressed as series of simpler functions. For example, many of the transcendental functions we have encountered can be expressed as series of powers of $x$ so that they resemble polynomials of infinite degree. Such series can be differentiated and integrated term by term, and they play a very important role in the study of calculus.

## 9.1 Sequences and Convergence

By a **sequence** (or an **infinite sequence**) we mean an ordered list having a first element but no last element. For our purposes, the elements (called **terms**) of a sequence will always be real numbers, although much of our discussion could be applied to complex numbers as well. Examples of sequences are:

$\{1, 2, 3, 4, 5, \ldots\}$ the sequence of positive integers,

$\left\{-\frac{1}{2}, \frac{1}{4}, -\frac{1}{8}, \frac{1}{16}, \ldots\right\}$ the sequence of positive integer powers of $-\frac{1}{2}$.

The terms of a sequence are usually listed in braces as shown. The ellipsis points $(\ldots)$ should be read "and so on."

An infinite sequence is a special kind of function, one whose domain is a set of integers extending from some starting integer to infinity. The starting integer is usually 1, so the domain is the set of positive integers. The sequence $\{a_1, a_2, a_3, a_4, \ldots\}$ is the function $f$ that takes the value $f(n) = a_n$ at each positive integer $n$. A sequence can be specified in three ways:

(i) We can list the first few terms followed by ... *if the pattern is obvious.*

(ii) We can provide a formula for the **general term** $a_n$ as a function of $n$.

(iii) We can provide a formula for calculating the term $a_n$ as a function of earlier terms $a_1, a_2, \ldots, a_{n-1}$ and specify enough of the beginning terms so the process of computing higher terms can begin.

In each case it must be possible to determine any term of the sequence, although it may be necessary to calculate all the preceding terms first.

**EXAMPLE 1** **(Some examples of sequences)**

(a) $\{n\} = \{1, 2, 3, 4, 5, \ldots\}$

(b) $\left\{\left(-\frac{1}{2}\right)^n\right\} = \left\{-\frac{1}{2}, \frac{1}{4}, -\frac{1}{8}, \frac{1}{16}, \ldots\right\}$

(c) $\left\{\frac{n-1}{n}\right\} = \left\{0, \frac{1}{2}, \frac{2}{3}, \frac{3}{4}, \frac{4}{5}, \ldots\right\}$

(d) $\{(-1)^{n-1}\} = \{\cos((n-1)\pi)\} = \{1, -1, 1, -1, 1, \ldots\}$

(e) $\left\{\frac{n^2}{2^n}\right\} = \left\{\frac{1}{2}, 1, \frac{9}{8}, 1, \frac{25}{32}, \frac{36}{64}, \frac{49}{128}, \ldots\right\}$

(f) $\left\{\left(1+\frac{1}{n}\right)^n\right\} = \left\{2, \left(\frac{3}{2}\right)^2, \left(\frac{4}{3}\right)^3, \left(\frac{5}{4}\right)^4, \ldots\right\}$

(g) $\left\{\frac{\cos(n\pi/2)}{n}\right\} = \left\{0, -\frac{1}{2}, 0, \frac{1}{4}, 0, -\frac{1}{6}, 0, \frac{1}{8}, 0, \ldots\right\}$

(h) $a_1 = 1, \quad a_{n+1} = \sqrt{6 + a_n}, \quad (n = 1, 2, 3, \ldots)$
In this case $\{a_n\} = \{1, \sqrt{7}, \sqrt{6+\sqrt{7}}, \ldots\}$. Note that there is no *obvious* formula for $a_n$ as an explicit function of $n$ here, but we can still calculate $a_n$ for any desired value of $n$ provided we first calculate all the earlier values $a_2, a_3, \ldots, a_{n-1}$.

(i) $a_1 = 1, a_2 = 1, a_{n+2} = a_n + a_{n+1}, \quad (n = 1, 2, 3, \ldots)$
Here $\{a_n\} = \{1, 1, 2, 3, 5, 8, 13, 21, \ldots\}$. This is called the **Fibonacci sequence**. Each term after the second is the sum of the previous two terms.

In parts (a)–(g) of Example 1, the formulas on the left sides define the general term of each sequence $\{a_n\}$ as an explicit function of $n$. In parts (h) and (i) we say the sequence $\{a_n\}$ is defined **recursively** or **inductively**; each term must be calculated from previous ones rather than directly as a function of $n$. We now introduce terminology used to describe various properties of sequences.

**DEFINITION 1**

**Terms for describing sequences**

(a) The sequence $\{a_n\}$ is **bounded below** by $L$, and $L$ is a **lower bound** for $\{a_n\}$, if $a_n \geq L$ for every $n = 1, 2, 3, \ldots$. The sequence is **bounded above** by $M$, and $M$ is an **upper bound**, if $a_n \leq M$ for every such $n$.

The sequence $\{a_n\}$ is **bounded** if it is both bounded above and bounded below. In this case there is a constant $K$ such that $|a_n| \leq K$ for every $n = 1, 2, 3, \ldots$. (We can take $K$ to be the larger of $|L|$ and $|M|$.)

(b) The sequence $\{a_n\}$ is **positive** if it is bounded below by zero, that is, if $a_n \geq 0$ for every $n = 1, 2, 3, \ldots$; it is **negative** if $a_n \leq 0$ for every $n$.

(c) The sequence $\{a_n\}$ is **increasing** if $a_{n+1} \geq a_n$ for every $n = 1, 2, 3, \ldots$; it is **decreasing** if $a_{n+1} \leq a_n$ for every such $n$. The sequence is said to be **monotonic** if it is either increasing or decreasing. (The terminology here is looser than that used for functions, where we would have used *nondecreasing* and *nonincreasing* to describe this behaviour. The distinction between $a_{n+1} > a_n$ and $a_{n+1} \geq a_n$ is not as important for sequences as it is for functions defined on intervals.)

(d) The sequence $\{a_n\}$ is **alternating** if $a_n a_{n+1} < 0$ for every $n = 1, 2, \ldots$, that is, if any two consecutive terms have opposite sign. Note that this definition requires $a_n \neq 0$ for each $n$.

**EXAMPLE 2** **(Describing some sequences)**

(a) The sequence $\{n\} = \{1, 2, 3, \ldots\}$ is positive, increasing, and bounded below. A lower bound for the sequence is 1 or any smaller number. The sequence is not bounded above.

(b) $\left\{\frac{n-1}{n}\right\} = \left\{0, \frac{1}{2}, \frac{2}{3}, \frac{3}{4}, \ldots\right\}$ is positive, bounded, and increasing. Here, 0 is a lower bound and 1 is an upper bound.

(c) $\left\{\left(-\frac{1}{2}\right)^n\right\} = \left\{-\frac{1}{2}, \frac{1}{4}, -\frac{1}{8}, \frac{1}{16}, \ldots\right\}$ is bounded and alternating. Here, $-1/2$ is a lower bound and $1/4$ is an upper bound.

(d) $\{(-1)^n n\} = \{-1, 2, -3, 4, -5, \ldots\}$ is alternating but not bounded either above or below.

When you want to show that a sequence is increasing, you can try to show that the inequality $a_{n+1} - a_n \geq 0$ holds for $n \geq 1$. Alternatively, if $a_n = f(n)$ for a differentiable function $f(x)$, you can show that $f$ is a nondecreasing function on $[1, \infty)$ by showing that $f'(x) \geq 0$ there. Similar approaches are useful for showing that a sequence is decreasing.

**EXAMPLE 3** If $a_n = \dfrac{n}{n^2+1}$, show that the sequence $\{a_n\}$ is decreasing.

***Solution*** Since $a_n = f(n)$, where $f(x) = \dfrac{x}{x^2+1}$ and

$$f'(x) = \frac{(x^2+1)(1) - x(2x)}{(x^2+1)^2} = \frac{1-x^2}{(x^2+1)^2} \leq 0 \quad \text{for } x \geq 1,$$

the function $f(x)$ is decreasing on $[1, \infty)$; therefore, $\{a_n\}$ is a decreasing sequence.

The sequence $\left\{\frac{n^2}{2^n}\right\} = \left\{\frac{1}{2}, 1, \frac{9}{8}, 1, \frac{25}{32}, \frac{36}{64}, \frac{49}{128}, \ldots\right\}$ is positive and therefore bounded below. It seems clear that from the fourth term on, all the terms are getting smaller. However, $a_2 > a_1$ and $a_3 > a_2$. Since $a_{n+1} \leq a_n$ only if $n \geq 3$, we say that this sequence is **ultimately decreasing**. The adverb *ultimately* is used to describe any termwise property of a sequence that the terms have from some point on, but not necessarily at the beginning of the sequence. Thus, the sequence

$$\{n - 100\} = \{-99, -98, \ldots, -2, -1, 0, 1, 2, 3, \ldots\}$$

is *ultimately positive* even though the first 99 terms are negative, and the sequence

$$\left\{(-1)^n + \frac{4}{n}\right\} = \left\{3, 3, \frac{1}{3}, 2, -\frac{1}{5}, \frac{5}{3}, -\frac{3}{7}, \frac{3}{2}, \ldots\right\}$$

is *ultimately alternating* even though the first few terms do not alternate.

## Convergence of Sequences

Central to the study of sequences is the notion of convergence. The concept of the limit of a sequence is a special case of the concept of the limit of a function $f(x)$ as $x \to \infty$. We say that the sequence $\{a_n\}$ **converges to the limit** $L$, and we write $\lim_{n\to\infty} a_n = L$, provided the distance from $a_n$ to $L$ on the real line approaches 0 as $n$ increases toward $\infty$. We state this definition more formally as follows:

**DEFINITION 2**

**Limit of a sequence**

We say that sequence $\{a_n\}$ converges to the limit $L$, and we write $\lim_{n\to\infty} a_n = L$, if for every positive real number $\epsilon$ there exists an integer $N$ (which may depend on $\epsilon$) such that if $n \geq N$, then $|a_n - L| < \epsilon$.

This definition is illustrated in Figure 9.1.

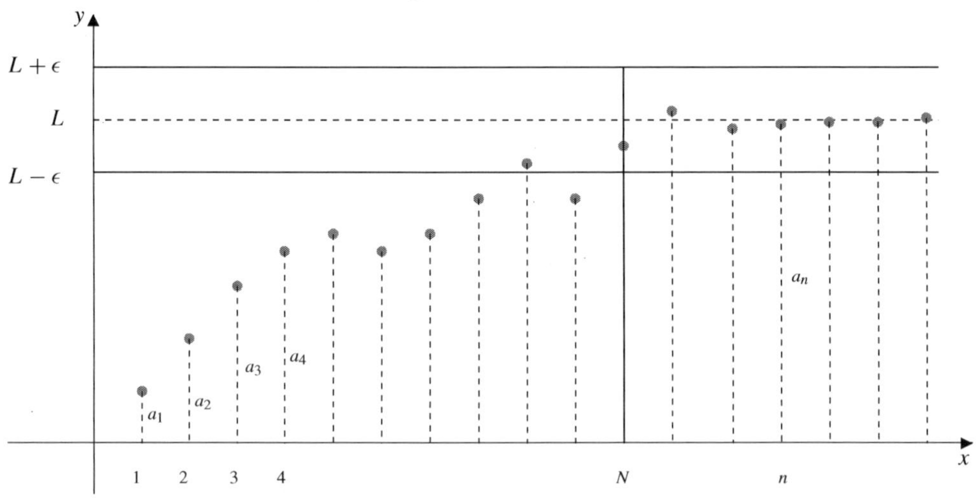


Figure 9.1 A convergent sequence

**EXAMPLE 4** Show that $\lim_{n\to\infty} \dfrac{c}{n^p} = 0$ for any real number $c$ and any $p > 0$.

***Solution*** Let $\epsilon > 0$ be given. Then

$$\left|\frac{c}{n^p}\right| < \epsilon \quad \text{if} \quad n^p > \frac{|c|}{\epsilon},$$

that is, if $n \geq N$, the least integer greater than $(|c|/\epsilon)^{1/p}$. Therefore, by Definition 2, $\lim_{n\to\infty} \dfrac{c}{n^p} = 0$.

Every sequence $\{a_n\}$ must either **converge** to a finite limit $L$ or **diverge**. That is, either $\lim_{n\to\infty} a_n = L$ exists (is a real number) or $\lim_{n\to\infty} a_n$ does not exist. If $\lim_{n\to\infty} a_n = \infty$, we can say that the sequence diverges to $\infty$; if $\lim_{n\to\infty} a_n = -\infty$, we can say that it diverges to $-\infty$. If $\lim_{n\to\infty} a_n$ simply does not exist (but is not $\infty$ or $-\infty$), we can only say that the sequence diverges.

**EXAMPLE 5** **(Examples of convergent and divergent sequences)**

(a) $\{(n-1)/n\}$ converges to 1; $\lim_{n\to\infty}(n-1)/n = \lim_{n\to\infty}\big(1-(1/n)\big) = 1$.

(b) $\{n\} = \{1, 2, 3, 4, \ldots\}$ diverges to $\infty$.

(c) $\{-n\} = \{-1, -2, -3, -4, \ldots\}$ diverges to $-\infty$.

(d) $\{(-1)^n\} = \{-1, 1, -1, 1, -1, \ldots\}$ simply diverges.

(e) $\{(-1)^n n\} = \{-1, 2, -3, 4, -5, \ldots\}$ diverges (but not to $\infty$ or $-\infty$ even though $\lim_{n\to\infty} |a_n| = \infty$).

The limit of a sequence is equivalent to the limit of a function as its argument approaches infinity:

If $\lim\limits_{x\to\infty} f(x) = L$ and $a_n = f(n)$, then $\lim\limits_{n\to\infty} a_n = L$.

Because of this, the standard rules for limits of functions (Theorems 2 and 4 of Section 1.2) also hold for limits of sequences, with the appropriate changes of notation. Thus, if $\{a_n\}$ and $\{b_n\}$ converge, then

$$\lim_{n\to\infty}(a_n \pm b_n) = \lim_{n\to\infty} a_n \pm \lim_{n\to\infty} b_n,$$

$$\lim_{n\to\infty} ca_n = c \lim_{n\to\infty} a_n,$$

$$\lim_{n\to\infty} a_n b_n = \left(\lim_{n\to\infty} a_n\right)\left(\lim_{n\to\infty} b_n\right),$$

$$\lim_{n\to\infty} \frac{a_n}{b_n} = \frac{\lim_{n\to\infty} a_n}{\lim_{n\to\infty} b_n} \quad \text{assuming } \lim_{n\to\infty} b_n \neq 0.$$

If $a_n \le b_n$ ultimately, then $\lim_{n\to\infty} a_n \le \lim_{n\to\infty} b_n$.

If $a_n \le b_n \le c_n$ ultimately, and $\lim_{n\to\infty} a_n = L = \lim_{n\to\infty} c_n$, then $\lim_{n\to\infty} b_n = L$.

The limits of many explicitly defined sequences can be evaluated using these properties in a manner similar to the methods used for limits of the form $\lim_{x\to\infty} f(x)$ in Section 1.3.

**EXAMPLE 6** Calculate the limits of the sequences

$$\text{(a) } \left\{\frac{2n^2 - n - 1}{5n^2 + n - 3}\right\}, \quad \text{(b) } \left\{\frac{\cos n}{n}\right\}, \quad \text{and} \quad \text{(c) } \{\sqrt{n^2 + 2n} - n\}.$$

### *Solution*

(a) We divide the numerator and denominator of the expression for $a_n$ by the highest power of $n$ in the denominator, that is, by $n^2$:

$$\lim_{n\to\infty} \frac{2n^2 - n - 1}{5n^2 + n - 3} = \lim_{n\to\infty} \frac{2 - (1/n) - (1/n^2)}{5 + (1/n) - (3/n^2)} = \frac{2 - 0 - 0}{5 + 0 - 0} = \frac{2}{5},$$

since $\lim_{n\to\infty} 1/n = 0$ and $\lim_{n\to\infty} 1/n^2 = 0$. The sequence converges and its limit is 2/5.

(b) Since $|\cos n| \le 1$ for every $n$, we have

$$-\frac{1}{n} \le \frac{\cos n}{n} \le \frac{1}{n} \quad \text{for} \quad n \ge 1.$$

Now, $\lim_{n\to\infty} -1/n = 0$ and $\lim_{n\to\infty} 1/n = 0$. Therefore, by the sequence version of the Squeeze Theorem, $\lim_{n\to\infty}(\cos n)/n = 0$. The given sequence converges to 0.

(c) For this sequence we multiply the numerator and the denominator (which is 1) by the conjugate of the expression in the numerator:

$$\begin{aligned}\lim_{n\to\infty}(\sqrt{n^2+2n} - n) &= \lim_{n\to\infty} \frac{(\sqrt{n^2+2n} - n)(\sqrt{n^2+2n} + n)}{\sqrt{n^2+2n} + n} \\ &= \lim_{n\to\infty} \frac{2n}{\sqrt{n^2+2n} + n} = \lim_{n\to\infty} \frac{2}{\sqrt{1 + (2/n)} + 1} = 1.\end{aligned}$$

The sequence converges to 1.

**EXAMPLE 7** Evaluate $\lim_{n\to\infty} n \tan^{-1}\left(\frac{1}{n}\right)$.

***Solution*** For this example it is best to replace the $n$th term of the sequence by the corresponding function of a real variable $x$ and take the limit as $x \to \infty$. We use l'Hôpital's Rule:

$$\begin{aligned}
\lim_{n\to\infty} n \tan^{-1}\left(\frac{1}{n}\right) &= \lim_{x\to\infty} x \tan^{-1}\left(\frac{1}{x}\right) \\
&= \lim_{x\to\infty} \frac{\tan^{-1}\left(\frac{1}{x}\right)}{\frac{1}{x}} \qquad \left[\frac{0}{0}\right] \\
&= \lim_{x\to\infty} \frac{\frac{1}{1+(1/x^2)}\left(-\frac{1}{x^2}\right)}{-\left(\frac{1}{x^2}\right)} = \lim_{x\to\infty} \frac{1}{1+\frac{1}{x^2}} = 1.
\end{aligned}$$

**THEOREM 1** If $\{a_n\}$ converges, then $\{a_n\}$ is bounded.

***PROOF*** Suppose $\lim_{n\to\infty} a_n = L$. According to Definition 2, for $\epsilon = 1$ there exists a number $N$ such that if $n > N$, then $|a_n - L| < 1$; therefore $|a_n| < 1 + |L|$ for such $n$. (Why is this true?) If $K$ denotes the largest of the numbers $|a_1|, |a_2|, \ldots, |a_N|$, and $1 + |L|$, then $|a_n| \le K$ for every $n = 1, 2, 3, \ldots$. Hence $\{a_n\}$ is bounded.

The converse of Theorem 1 is false; the sequence $\{(-1)^n\}$ is bounded but does not converge.

The *completeness property* of the real number system (see Section P.1) can be reformulated in terms of sequences to read as follows:

**Bounded monotonic sequences converge**

If the sequence $\{a_n\}$ is bounded above and is (ultimately) increasing, then it converges. The same conclusion holds if $\{a_n\}$ is bounded below and is (ultimately) decreasing.

Thus, a bounded, ultimately monotonic sequence is convergent. (See Figure 9.2.)

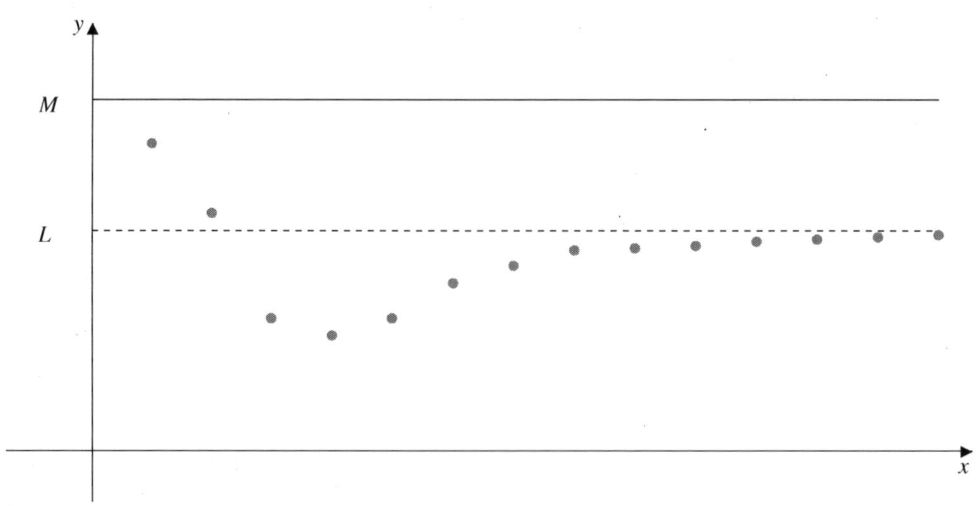


Figure 9.2 An ultimately increasing sequence that is bounded above

> There is a subtle point to note in this solution. Showing that $\{a_n\}$ is increasing is pretty obvious, but how did we know to try and show that 3 (rather than some other number) was an upper bound? The answer is that we actually did the last part first and showed that *if* $\lim a_n = a$ exists, *then* $a = 3$. It then makes sense to try and show that $a_n < 3$ for all $n$.
>
> Of course we can easily show that any number greater than 3 is an upper bound.

**EXAMPLE 8** Let $a_n$ be defined recursively by

$$a_1 = 1, \qquad a_{n+1} = \sqrt{6 + a_n} \qquad (n = 1, 2, 3, \ldots).$$

Show that $\lim_{n\to\infty} a_n$ exists and find its value.

***Solution*** Observe that $a_2 = \sqrt{6+1} = \sqrt{7} > a_1$. If $a_{k+1} > a_k$, then $a_{k+2} = \sqrt{6 + a_{k+1}} > \sqrt{6 + a_k} = a_{k+1}$, so $\{a_n\}$ is increasing, by induction. Now observe that $a_1 = 1 < 3$. If $a_k < 3$, then $a_{k+1} = \sqrt{6 + a_k} < \sqrt{6+3} = 3$, so $a_n < 3$ for every $n$ by induction. Since $\{a_n\}$ is increasing and bounded above, $\lim_{n\to\infty} a_n = a$ exists, by completeness. Since $\sqrt{6+x}$ is a continuous function of $x$, we have

$$a = \lim_{n\to\infty} a_{n+1} = \lim_{n\to\infty} \sqrt{6 + a_n} = \sqrt{6 + \lim_{n\to\infty} a_n} = \sqrt{6 + a}.$$

Thus, $a^2 = 6 + a$, or $a^2 - a - 6 = 0$, or $(a-3)(a+2) = 0$. This quadratic has roots $a = 3$ and $a = -2$. Since $a_n \ge 1$ for every $n$, we must have $a \ge 1$. Therefore, $a = 3$ and $\lim_{n\to\infty} a_n = 3$.

**EXAMPLE 9** Does $\left\{\left(1 + \frac{1}{n}\right)^n\right\}$ converge or diverge?

***Solution*** We could make an effort to show that the given sequence is, in fact, increasing and bounded above. (See Exercise 32 at the end of this section.) However, we already know the answer. The sequence converges by Theorem 6 of Section 3.4:

$$\lim_{n\to\infty} \left(1 + \frac{1}{n}\right)^n = e^1 = e.$$

**THEOREM 2**

If $\{a_n\}$ is (ultimately) increasing, then either it is bounded above, and therefore convergent, or it is not bounded above and diverges to infinity.

The proof of this theorem is left as an exercise. A corresponding result holds for (ultimately) decreasing sequences.

The following theorem evaluates two important limits that find frequent application in the study of series.

**THEOREM 3**

(a) If $|x| < 1$, then $\lim_{n\to\infty} x^n = 0$.

(b) If $x$ is any real number, then $\lim_{n\to\infty} \dfrac{x^n}{n!} = 0$.

***PROOF*** For part (a) observe that

$$\lim_{n\to\infty} \ln|x|^n = \lim_{n\to\infty} n \ln|x| = -\infty,$$

since $\ln|x| < 0$ when $|x| < 1$. Accordingly, since $e^x$ is continuous,

$$\lim_{n\to\infty} |x|^n = \lim_{n\to\infty} e^{\ln|x|^n} = e^{\lim_{n\to\infty} \ln|x|^n} = 0.$$

Since $-|x|^n \le x^n \le |x|^n$, we have $\lim_{n\to\infty} x^n = 0$ by the Squeeze Theorem.

For part (b), pick any $x$ and let $N$ be an integer such that $N > |x|$. If $n > N$ we have

$$\begin{aligned}\left|\frac{x^n}{n!}\right| &= \frac{|x|}{1}\frac{|x|}{2}\frac{|x|}{3}\cdots\frac{|x|}{N-1}\frac{|x|}{N}\frac{|x|}{N+1}\cdots\frac{|x|}{n}\\ &< \frac{|x|^{N-1}}{(N-1)!}\frac{|x|}{N}\frac{|x|}{N}\frac{|x|}{N}\cdots\frac{|x|}{N}\\ &= \frac{|x|^{N-1}}{(N-1)!}\left(\frac{|x|}{N}\right)^{n-N+1} = K\left(\frac{|x|}{N}\right)^n,\end{aligned}$$

where $K = \dfrac{|x|^{N-1}}{(N-1)!}\left(\dfrac{|x|}{N}\right)^{1-N}$ is a constant that is independent of $n$. Since $|x|/N < 1$, we have $\lim_{n\to\infty}(|x|/N)^n = 0$ by part (a). Thus $\lim_{n\to\infty}|x^n/n!| = 0$, so $\lim_{n\to\infty} x^n/n! = 0$.

**EXAMPLE 10** Find $\lim_{n\to\infty} \dfrac{3^n + 4^n + 5^n}{5^n}$.

***Solution*** $\lim\limits_{n\to\infty} \dfrac{3^n + 4^n + 5^n}{5^n} = \lim\limits_{n\to\infty}\left[\left(\dfrac{3}{5}\right)^n + \left(\dfrac{4}{5}\right)^n + 1\right] = 0 + 0 + 1 = 1$, by Theorem 3(a).

## EXERCISES 9.1

In Exercises 1–13, determine whether the given sequence is (a) bounded (above or below), (b) positive or negative (ultimately), (c) increasing, decreasing, or alternating, and (d) convergent, divergent, divergent to $\infty$ or $-\infty$.

**1.** $\left\{\dfrac{2n^2}{n^2+1}\right\}$

**2.** $\left\{\dfrac{2n}{n^2+1}\right\}$

**3.** $\left\{4 - \dfrac{(-1)^n}{n}\right\}$

**4.** $\left\{\sin\dfrac{1}{n}\right\}$

**5.** $\left\{\dfrac{n^2-1}{n}\right\}$

**6.** $\left\{\dfrac{e^n}{\pi^n}\right\}$

**7.** $\left\{\dfrac{e^n}{\pi^{n/2}}\right\}$

**8.** $\left\{\dfrac{(-1)^n n}{e^n}\right\}$

**9.** $\left\{\dfrac{2^n}{n^n}\right\}$

**10.** $\left\{\dfrac{(n!)^2}{(2n)!}\right\}$

**11.** $\left\{n\cos\left(\dfrac{n\pi}{2}\right)\right\}$

**12.** $\left\{\dfrac{\sin n}{n}\right\}$

**13.** $\{1, 1, -2, 3, 3, -4, 5, 5, -6, \ldots\}$

In Exercises 14–29, evaluate, wherever possible, the limit of the sequence $\{a_n\}$.

**14.** $a_n = \dfrac{5-2n}{3n-7}$

**15.** $a_n = \dfrac{n^2-4}{n+5}$

**16.** $a_n = \dfrac{n^2}{n^3+1}$

**17.** $a_n = (-1)^n\dfrac{n}{n^3+1}$

**18.** $a_n = \dfrac{n^2 - 2\sqrt{n}+1}{1-n-3n^2}$

**19.** $a_n = \dfrac{e^n - e^{-n}}{e^n + e^{-n}}$

**20.** $a_n = n\sin\dfrac{1}{n}$

**21.** $a_n = \left(\dfrac{n-3}{n}\right)^n$

**22.** $a_n = \dfrac{n}{\ln(n+1)}$

**23.** $a_n = \sqrt{n+1} - \sqrt{n}$

**24.** $a_n = n - \sqrt{n^2-4n}$

**25.** $a_n = \sqrt{n^2+n} - \sqrt{n^2-1}$

**26.** $a_n = \left(\dfrac{n-1}{n+1}\right)^n$

**27.** $a_n = \dfrac{(n!)^2}{(2n)!}$

**28.** $a_n = \dfrac{n^2 2^n}{n!}$

**29.** $a_n = \dfrac{\pi^n}{1+2^{2n}}$

**30.** Let $a_1 = 1$ and $a_{n+1} = \sqrt{1+2a_n}$ $(n = 1, 2, 3, \ldots)$. Show that $\{a_n\}$ is increasing and bounded above. (*Hint:* Show that 3 is an upper bound.) Hence, conclude that the sequence converges, and find its limit.

**31.** Repeat Exercise 30 for the sequence defined by $a_1 = 3$, $a_{n+1} = \sqrt{15+2a_n}$, $n = 1, 2, 3, \ldots$. This time you will have to guess an upper bound.

**32.** Let $a_n = \left(1+\dfrac{1}{n}\right)^n$ so that $\ln a_n = n\ln\left(1+\dfrac{1}{n}\right)$. Use properties of the logarithm function to show that (a) $\{a_n\}$ is increasing and (b) $e$ is an upper bound for $\{a_n\}$.

**33.** Prove Theorem 2. Also, state an analogous theorem pertaining to ultimately decreasing sequences.

**34.** If $\{|a_n|\}$ is bounded, prove that $\{a_n\}$ is bounded.

**35.** If $\lim_{n\to\infty}|a_n| = 0$, prove that $\lim_{n\to\infty} a_n = 0$.

**36.** Which of the following statements are TRUE and which are FALSE? Justify your answers.

(a) If $\lim_{n\to\infty} a_n = \infty$ and $\lim_{n\to\infty} b_n = L > 0$, then $\lim_{n\to\infty} a_n b_n = \infty$.

(b) If $\lim_{n\to\infty} a_n = \infty$ and $\lim_{n\to\infty} b_n = -\infty$, then $\lim_{n\to\infty}(a_n + b_n) = 0$.

(c) If $\lim_{n\to\infty} a_n = \infty$ and $\lim_{n\to\infty} b_n = -\infty$, then $\lim_{n\to\infty} a_n b_n = -\infty$.

(d) If neither $\{a_n\}$ nor $\{b_n\}$ converges, then $\{a_n b_n\}$ does not converge.

(e) If $\{|a_n|\}$ converges, then $\{a_n\}$ converges.

# 9.2 Infinite Series

An **infinite series**, usually just called a **series**, is a formal sum of infinitely many terms; for instance, $a_1 + a_2 + a_3 + a_4 + \cdots$ is a series formed by adding the terms of the sequence $\{a_n\}$. This series is also denoted $\sum_{n=1}^{\infty} a_n$:

$$\sum_{n=1}^{\infty} a_n = a_1 + a_2 + a_3 + a_4 + \cdots.$$

For example,

$$\sum_{n=1}^{\infty} \frac{1}{n} = 1 + \frac{1}{2} + \frac{1}{3} + \frac{1}{4} + \cdots$$

$$\sum_{n=1}^{\infty} \frac{(-1)^{n-1}}{2^{n-1}} = 1 - \frac{1}{2} + \frac{1}{4} - \frac{1}{8} + \frac{1}{16} - \cdots.$$

It is sometimes necessary or useful to start the sum from some index other than 1:

$$\sum_{n=0}^{\infty} a^n = 1 + a + a^2 + a^3 + \cdots$$

$$\sum_{n=2}^{\infty} \frac{1}{\ln n} = \frac{1}{\ln 2} + \frac{1}{\ln 3} + \frac{1}{\ln 4} + \cdots.$$

Note that the latter series would make no sense if we had started the sum from $n = 1$; the first term would have been undefined.

When necessary, we can change the index of summation to start at a different value. This is accomplished by a substitution as illustrated in Example 3 of Section 5.1. For instance, using the substitution $n = m - 2$, we can rewrite $\sum_{n=1}^{\infty} a_n$ in the form $\sum_{m=3}^{\infty} a_{m-2}$. Both sums give rise to the same expansion

$$\sum_{n=1}^{\infty} a_n = a_1 + a_2 + a_3 + \cdots = \sum_{m=3}^{\infty} a_{m-2}.$$

Addition is an operation that is carried out on two numbers at a time. If we want to calculate the finite sum $a_1 + a_2 + a_3$, we could proceed by adding $a_1 + a_2$ and then adding $a_3$ to this sum, or else we might first add $a_2 + a_3$ and then add $a_1$ to the sum. Of course, the associative law for addition assures us we will get the same answer both ways. This is the reason the symbol $a_1 + a_2 + a_3$ makes sense; we would otherwise have to write $(a_1 + a_2) + a_3$ or $a_1 + (a_2 + a_3)$. This reasoning extends to any sum $a_1 + a_2 + \cdots + a_n$ of finitely many terms, but it is not obvious what should be meant by a sum with infinitely many terms:

$$a_1 + a_2 + a_3 + a_4 + \cdots.$$

We no longer have any assurance that the terms can be added up in any order to yield the same sum. In fact, we will see in Section 9.4 that in certain circumstances, changing the order of terms in a series can actually change the sum of the series. The interpretation we place on the infinite sum is that of adding from left to right, as suggested by the grouping

$$\cdots((((a_1 + a_2) + a_3) + a_4) + a_5) + \cdots.$$

We accomplish this by defining a new sequence $\{s_n\}$, called the **sequence of partial sums** of the series $\sum_{n=1}^{\infty} a_n$, so that $s_n$ is the sum of the first $n$ terms of the series:

$$\begin{aligned}
s_1 &= a_1\\
s_2 &= s_1 + a_2 = a_1 + a_2\\
s_3 &= s_2 + a_3 = a_1 + a_2 + a_3\\
&\vdots\\
s_n &= s_{n-1} + a_n = a_1 + a_2 + a_3 + \cdots + a_n = \sum_{j=1}^{n} a_j\\
&\vdots
\end{aligned}$$

We then define the sum of the infinite series to be the limit of this sequence of partial sums.

DEFINITION 3

**Convergence of a series**

We say that the series $\sum_{n=1}^{\infty} a_n$ **converges to the sum** $s$, and we write

$$\sum_{n=1}^{\infty} a_n = s,$$

if $\lim_{n\to\infty} s_n = s$, where $s_n$ is the $n$th partial sum of $\sum_{n=1}^{\infty} a_n$:

$$s_n = a_1 + a_2 + a_3 + \cdots + a_n = \sum_{j=1}^{n} a_j.$$

Thus, a *series* converges if and only if the *sequence* of its partial sums converges.

Similarly, a series is said to diverge to infinity, diverge to negative infinity, or simply diverge if its sequence of partial sums does so. It must be stressed that the convergence of the series $\sum_{n=1}^{\infty} a_n$ depends on the convergence of the sequence $\{s_n\} = \{\sum_{j=1}^{n} a_j\}$, *not* the sequence $\{a_n\}$.

## Geometric Series

DEFINITION 4

**Geometric series**

A series of the form $\sum_{n=1}^{\infty} a\, r^{n-1} = a + ar + ar^2 + ar^3 + \cdots$, whose $n$th term is $a_n = a\, r^{n-1}$, is called a **geometric series**. The number $a$ is the first term. The number $r$ is called the **common ratio** of the series, since it is the value of the ratio of the $(n+1)$st term to the $n$th term for any $n \geq 1$:

$$\frac{a_{n+1}}{a_n} = \frac{ar^n}{ar^{n-1}} = r, \qquad n = 1, 2, 3, \ldots.$$

The $n$th partial sum $s_n$ of a geometric series is calculated as follows:

$$\begin{aligned}
s_n &= a + ar + ar^2 + ar^3 + \cdots + ar^{n-1}\\
rs_n &= \phantom{a + {}} ar + ar^2 + ar^3 + \cdots + ar^{n-1} + ar^n.
\end{aligned}$$

The second equation is obtained by multiplying the first by $r$. Subtracting these two equations (note the cancellations), we get $(1-r)s_n = a - ar^n$. If $r \neq 1$, we can divide by $1 - r$ and get a formula for $s_n$.

**Partial sums of geometric series**

If $r = 1$, then the $n$th partial sum of a geometric series $\sum_{n=1}^{\infty} ar^{n-1}$ is $s_n = a + a + \cdots + a = na$. If $r \neq 1$, then

$$s_n = a + ar + ar^2 + \cdots + ar^{n-1} = \frac{a(1-r^n)}{1-r}.$$

If $a = 0$, then $s_n = 0$ for every $n$, and $\lim_{n\to\infty} s_n = 0$. Now suppose $a \neq 0$. If $|r| < 1$, then $\lim_{n\to\infty} r^n = 0$, so $\lim_{n\to\infty} s_n = a/(1-r)$. If $r > 1$, then $\lim_{n\to\infty} r^n = \infty$, and $\lim_{n\to\infty} s_n = \infty$ if $a > 0$, or $\lim_{n\to\infty} s_n = -\infty$ if $a < 0$. The same conclusion holds if $r = 1$, since $s_n = na$ in this case. If $r \leq -1$, $\lim_{n\to\infty} r^n$ does not exist and neither does $\lim_{n\to\infty} s_n$. Hence we conclude that

$$\sum_{n=1}^{\infty} ar^{n-1} \begin{cases} \text{converges to } 0 & \text{if } a = 0 \\ \text{converges to } \dfrac{a}{1-r} & \text{if } |r| < 1 \\ \text{diverges to } \infty & \text{if } r \geq 1 \text{ and } a > 0 \\ \text{diverges to } -\infty & \text{if } r \geq 1 \text{ and } a < 0 \\ \text{diverges} & \text{if } r \leq -1 \text{ and } a \neq 0. \end{cases}$$

The representation of the function $1/(1-x)$ as the sum of a geometric series,

$$\frac{1}{1-x} = \sum_{n=0}^{\infty} x^n = 1 + x + x^2 + x^3 + \cdots \quad \text{for } -1 < x < 1,$$

will be important in our discussion of power series later in this chapter.

**EXAMPLE 1** **(Examples of geometric series and their sums)**

(a) $1 + \dfrac{1}{2} + \dfrac{1}{4} + \dfrac{1}{8} + \cdots = \displaystyle\sum_{n=1}^{\infty} \left(\frac{1}{2}\right)^{n-1} = \frac{1}{1-\frac{1}{2}} = 2$. Here $a = 1$ and $r = \dfrac{1}{2}$.

Since $|r| < 1$, the series converges.

(b) $\pi - e + \dfrac{e^2}{\pi} - \dfrac{e^3}{\pi^2} + \cdots = \displaystyle\sum_{n=1}^{\infty} \pi\left(-\frac{e}{\pi}\right)^{n-1}$ Here $a = \pi$ and $r = -\dfrac{e}{\pi}$.

$$= \frac{\pi}{1-\left(-\frac{e}{\pi}\right)} = \frac{\pi^2}{\pi + e}.$$

The series converges since $\left|-\dfrac{e}{\pi}\right| < 1$.

(c) $1 + 2^{1/2} + 2 + 2^{3/2} + \cdots = \displaystyle\sum_{n=1}^{\infty} (\sqrt{2})^{n-1}$. This series diverges to $\infty$ since $a = 1 > 0$ and $r = \sqrt{2} > 1$.

(d) $1 - 1 + 1 - 1 + 1 - \cdots = \displaystyle\sum_{n=1}^{\infty} (-1)^{n-1}$. This series diverges since $r = -1$.

(e) Let $x = 0.32\,32\,32\cdots = 0.\overline{32}$; then

$$x = \frac{32}{100} + \frac{32}{100^2} + \frac{32}{100^3} + \cdots = \sum_{n=1}^{\infty} \frac{32}{100}\left(\frac{1}{100}\right)^{n-1} = \frac{32}{100}\,\frac{1}{1-\frac{1}{100}} = \frac{32}{99}.$$

This is an alternative to the method of Example 1 of Section P.1 for representing repeating decimals as quotients of integers.

**EXAMPLE 2** If money earns interest at a constant effective rate of 5% per year, how much should you pay today for an annuity that will pay you (a) \$1,000 at the end of each of the next 10 years and (b) \$1,000 at the end of every year forever?

**Solution** A payment of \$1,000 that is due to be received $n$ years from now has present value $\$1{,}000 \times \left(\frac{1}{1.05}\right)^n$ (since $\$A$ would grow to $\$A(1.05)^n$ in $n$ years). Thus, \$1,000 payments at the end of each of the next $n$ years are worth $\$s_n$ at the present time, where

$$\begin{aligned} s_n &= 1{,}000\left[\frac{1}{1.05} + \left(\frac{1}{1.05}\right)^2 + \cdots + \left(\frac{1}{1.05}\right)^n\right] \\ &= \frac{1{,}000}{1.05}\left[1 + \frac{1}{1.05} + \left(\frac{1}{1.05}\right)^2 + \cdots + \left(\frac{1}{1.05}\right)^{n-1}\right]. \\ &= \frac{1{,}000}{1.05}\,\frac{1 - \left(\frac{1}{1.05}\right)^n}{1 - \frac{1}{1.05}} = \frac{1{,}000}{0.05}\left[1 - \left(\frac{1}{1.05}\right)^n\right] \end{aligned}$$

(a) The present value of 10 future payments is $\$s_{10} = \$7{,}721.73$.

(b) The present value of future payments continuing forever is

$$\$\lim_{n\to\infty} s_n = \frac{\$1{,}000}{0.05} = \$20{,}000.$$

## Telescoping Series and Harmonic Series

**EXAMPLE 3** Show that the series

$$\sum_{n=1}^{\infty} \frac{1}{n(n+1)} = \frac{1}{1\times 2} + \frac{1}{2\times 3} + \frac{1}{3\times 4} + \frac{1}{4\times 5} + \cdots$$

converges and find its sum.

**Solution** Since $\frac{1}{n(n+1)} = \frac{1}{n} - \frac{1}{n+1}$, we can write the partial sum $s_n$ in the form

$$\begin{aligned} s_n &= \frac{1}{1\times 2} + \frac{1}{2\times 3} + \frac{1}{3\times 4} + \cdots + \frac{1}{(n-1)n} + \frac{1}{n(n+1)} \\ &= \left(1 - \frac{1}{2}\right) + \left(\frac{1}{2} - \frac{1}{3}\right) + \left(\frac{1}{3} - \frac{1}{4}\right) \\ &\quad + \cdots + \left(\frac{1}{n-1} - \frac{1}{n}\right) + \left(\frac{1}{n} - \frac{1}{n+1}\right) \\ &= 1 - \frac{1}{2} + \frac{1}{2} - \frac{1}{3} + \frac{1}{3} - \cdots - \frac{1}{n} + \frac{1}{n} - \frac{1}{n+1} \\ &= 1 - \frac{1}{n+1}. \end{aligned}$$

Therefore, $\lim_{n\to\infty} s_n = 1$ and the series converges to 1:

$$\sum_{n=1}^{\infty} \frac{1}{n(n+1)} = 1.$$

This is an example of a **telescoping series**, so called because the partial sums *fold up* into a simple form when the terms are expanded in partial fractions. Other examples can be found in the exercises at the end of this section. As these examples show, the method of partial fractions can be a useful tool for series as well as for integrals.

**EXAMPLE 4** Show that the **harmonic series**

$$\sum_{n=1}^{\infty} \frac{1}{n} = 1 + \frac{1}{2} + \frac{1}{3} + \frac{1}{4} + \cdots$$

diverges to infinity.

***Solution*** If $s_n$ is the $n$th partial sum of the harmonic series, then

$$\begin{aligned} s_n &= 1 + \frac{1}{2} + \frac{1}{3} + \cdots + \frac{1}{n} \\ &= \text{sum of areas of rectangles shaded in Figure 9.3} \\ &> \text{area under } y = \frac{1}{x} \text{ from } x = 1 \text{ to } x = n+1 \\ &= \int_1^{n+1} \frac{dx}{x} = \ln(n+1). \end{aligned}$$

Now $\lim_{n\to\infty} \ln(n+1) = \infty$. Therefore, $\lim_{n\to\infty} s_n = \infty$ and

$$\sum_{n=1}^{\infty} \frac{1}{n} = 1 + \frac{1}{2} + \frac{1}{3} + \cdots \qquad \text{diverges to infinity.}$$

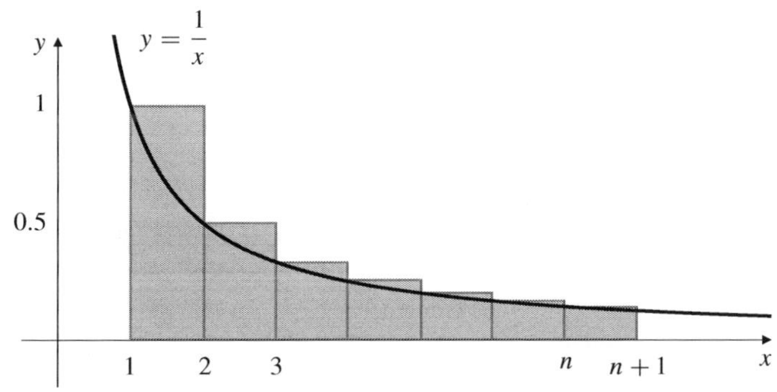


**Figure 9.3** A partial sum of the harmonic series

Like geometric series, the harmonic series will often be encountered in subsequent sections.

## Some Theorems About Series

**THEOREM 4**

If $\sum_{n=1}^{\infty} a_n$ converges, then $\lim_{n\to\infty} a_n = 0$. Therefore, if $\lim_{n\to\infty} a_n$ does not exist, or exists but is not zero, then the series $\sum_{n=1}^{\infty} a_n$ is divergent. (This amounts to an ***n*th term test for divergence of a series.**)

***PROOF*** If $s_n = a_1 + a_2 + \cdots + a_n$, then $s_n - s_{n-1} = a_n$. If $\sum_{n=1}^{\infty} a_n$ converges, then $\lim_{n\to\infty} s_n = s$ exists, and $\lim_{n\to\infty} s_{n-1} = s$. Hence $\lim_{n\to\infty} a_n = s - s = 0$.

**Remark** Theorem 4 is *very important* for the understanding of infinite series. Students often err either in forgetting that *a series cannot converge if its terms do not approach zero* or in confusing this result with its *converse*, which is false. The converse would say that if $\lim_{n\to\infty} a_n = 0$, then $\sum_{n=1}^{\infty} a_n$ must converge. The harmonic series is a counterexample showing the falsehood of this assertion:

$$\lim_{n\to\infty} \frac{1}{n} = 0 \qquad \text{but} \qquad \sum_{n=1}^{\infty} \frac{1}{n} \text{ diverges to infinity.}$$

When considering whether a given series converges, the first question you should ask yourself is: "Does the $n$th term approach 0 as $n$ approaches $\infty$?" If the answer is *no*, then the series does *not* converge. If the answer is *yes*, then the series *may or may not* converge. If the sequence of terms $\{a_n\}$ tends to a nonzero limit $L$, then $\sum_{n=1}^{\infty} a_n$ diverges to infinity if $L > 0$ and diverges to negative infinity if $L < 0$.

**EXAMPLE 5**

(a) $\displaystyle\sum_{n=1}^{\infty} \frac{n}{2n-1}$ diverges to infinity since $\lim_{n\to\infty} \dfrac{n}{2n-1} = 1/2 > 0$.

(b) $\sum_{n=1}^{\infty} (-1)^n n \sin(1/n)$ diverges since

$$\lim_{n\to\infty} \left|(-1)^n n \sin\frac{1}{n}\right| = \lim_{n\to\infty} \frac{\sin(1/n)}{1/n} = \lim_{x\to 0+} \frac{\sin x}{x} = 1 \neq 0.$$

The following theorem asserts that it is only the *ultimate* behaviour of $\{a_n\}$ that determines whether $\sum_{n=1}^{\infty} a_n$ converges. Any finite number of terms can be dropped from the beginning of a series without affecting the convergence; the convergence depends only on the *tail* of the series. Of course, the actual sum of the series depends on *all* the terms.

**THEOREM 5**

$\sum_{n=1}^{\infty} a_n$ converges if and only if $\sum_{n=N}^{\infty} a_n$ converges for any integer $N \geq 1$.

**THEOREM 6**

If $\{a_n\}$ is ultimately positive, then the series $\sum_{n=1}^{\infty} a_n$ must either converge (if its partial sums are bounded above) or diverge to infinity (if its partial sums are not bounded above).

The proofs of these two theorems are posed as exercises at the end of this section. The following theorem is just a reformulation of standard laws of limits.

**THEOREM 7**

If $\sum_{n=1}^{\infty} a_n$ and $\sum_{n=1}^{\infty} b_n$ converge to $A$ and $B$, respectively, then

(a) $\sum_{n=1}^{\infty} ca_n$ converges to $cA$ (where $c$ is any constant);

(b) $\sum_{n=1}^{\infty} (a_n \pm b_n)$ converges to $A \pm B$;

(c) if $a_n \leq b_n$ for all $n = 1, 2, 3, \ldots$, then $A \leq B$.

**EXAMPLE 6** Find the sum of the series $\displaystyle\sum_{n=1}^{\infty} \frac{1+2^{n+1}}{3^n}$.

**Solution** The given series is the sum of two geometric series,

$$\sum_{n=1}^{\infty} \frac{1}{3^n} = \sum_{n=1}^{\infty} \frac{1}{3}\left(\frac{1}{3}\right)^{n-1} = \frac{1/3}{1-(1/3)} = \frac{1}{2} \quad \text{and}$$

$$\sum_{n=1}^{\infty} \frac{2^{n+1}}{3^n} = \sum_{n=1}^{\infty} \frac{4}{3}\left(\frac{2}{3}\right)^{n-1} = \frac{4/3}{1-(2/3)} = 4.$$

Thus, its sum is $\frac{1}{2} + 4 = \frac{9}{2}$ by Theorem 7(b).

## EXERCISES 9.2

In Exercises 1–18, find the sum of the given series, or show that the series diverges (possibly to infinity or negative infinity). Exercises 11–14 are telescoping series and should be done by partial fractions as suggested in Example 3 in this section.

**1.** $\frac{1}{3} + \frac{1}{9} + \frac{1}{27} + \cdots = \sum_{n=1}^{\infty} \frac{1}{3^n}$

**2.** $3 - \frac{3}{4} + \frac{3}{16} - \frac{3}{64} + \cdots = \sum_{n=1}^{\infty} 3\left(-\frac{1}{4}\right)^{n-1}$

**3.** $\sum_{n=5}^{\infty} \frac{1}{(2+\pi)^{2n}}$

**4.** $\sum_{n=0}^{\infty} \frac{5}{10^{3n}}$

**5.** $\sum_{n=2}^{\infty} \frac{(-5)^n}{8^{2n}}$

**6.** $\sum_{n=0}^{\infty} \frac{1}{e^n}$

**7.** $\sum_{k=0}^{\infty} \frac{2^{k+3}}{e^{k-3}}$

**8.** $\sum_{j=1}^{\infty} \pi^{j/2} \cos(j\pi)$

**9.** $\sum_{n=1}^{\infty} \frac{3+2^n}{2^{n+2}}$

**10.** $\sum_{n=0}^{\infty} \frac{3+2^n}{3^{n+2}}$

**11.** $\sum_{n=1}^{\infty} \frac{1}{n(n+2)} = \frac{1}{1\times 3} + \frac{1}{2\times 4} + \frac{1}{3\times 5} + \cdots$

**12.** $\sum_{n=1}^{\infty} \frac{1}{(2n-1)(2n+1)} = \frac{1}{1\times 3} + \frac{1}{3\times 5} + \frac{1}{5\times 7} + \cdots$

**13.** $\sum_{n=1}^{\infty} \frac{1}{(3n-2)(3n+1)} = \frac{1}{1\times 4} + \frac{1}{4\times 7} + \frac{1}{7\times 10} + \cdots$

**14.** $\sum_{n=1}^{\infty} \frac{1}{n(n+1)(n+2)}$
$= \frac{1}{1\times 2\times 3} + \frac{1}{2\times 3\times 4} + \frac{1}{3\times 4\times 5} + \cdots$

**15.** $\sum_{n=1}^{\infty} \frac{1}{2n-1}$

**16.** $\sum_{n=1}^{\infty} \frac{n}{n+2}$

**17.** $\sum_{n=1}^{\infty} n^{-1/2}$

**18.** $\sum_{n=1}^{\infty} \frac{2}{n+1}$

**19.** Obtain a simple expression for the partial sum $s_n$ of the series $\sum_{n=1}^{\infty}(-1)^n$, and use it to show that the series diverges.

**20.** Find the sum of the series

$$\frac{1}{1} + \frac{1}{1+2} + \frac{1}{1+2+3} + \frac{1}{1+2+3+4} + \cdots.$$

**21.** When dropped, an elastic ball bounces back up to a height three-quarters of that from which it fell. If the ball is dropped from a height of 2 m and allowed to bounce up and down indefinitely, what is the total distance it travels before coming to rest?

**22.** If a bank account pays 10% simple interest into an account once a year, what is the balance in the account at the end of 8 years if \$1,000 is deposited into the account at the beginning of each of the 8 years? (Assume there was no balance in the account initially.)

**23.** Prove Theorem 5.

**24.** Prove Theorem 6.

**25.** State a theorem analogous to Theorem 6 but for a negative sequence.

In Exercises 26–31, decide whether the given statement is TRUE or FALSE. If it is true, prove it. If it is false, give a counterexample showing the falsehood.

**26.** If $a_n = 0$ for every $n$, then $\sum a_n$ converges.

**27.** If $\sum a_n$ converges, then $\sum(1/a_n)$ diverges to infinity.

**28.** If $\sum a_n$ and $\sum b_n$ both diverge, then so does $\sum(a_n + b_n)$.

**29.** If $a_n \ge c > 0$ for every $n$, then $\sum a_n$ diverges to infinity.

**30.** If $\sum a_n$ diverges and $\{b_n\}$ is bounded, then $\sum a_n b_n$ diverges.

**31.** If $a_n > 0$ and $\sum a_n$ converges, then $\sum(a_n)^2$ converges.

## 9.3 Convergence Tests for Positive Series

In the previous section we saw a few examples of convergent series (geometric and telescoping series) whose sums could be determined exactly because the partial sums $s_n$ could be expressed in closed form as explicit functions of $n$ whose limits as $n \to \infty$ could be evaluated. It is not usually possible to do this with a given series, and therefore it is not usually possible to determine the sum of the series exactly. However, there are many techniques for determining whether a given series converges and, if it does, for approximating the sum to any desired degree of accuracy.

In this section we deal exclusively with *positive series*, that is, series of the form

$$\sum_{n=1}^{\infty} a_n = a_1 + a_2 + a_3 + \cdots,$$

where $a_n \ge 0$ for all $n \ge 1$. As noted in Theorem 6, such a series will converge if its partial sums are bounded above and will diverge to infinity otherwise. All our results apply equally well to *ultimately* positive series since convergence or divergence depends only on the *tail* of a series.

### The Integral Test

The integral test provides a means for determining whether an ultimately positive series converges or diverges by comparing it with an improper integral that behaves similarly. Example 4 in Section 9.2 is an example of the use of this technique. We formalize the method in the following theorem.

**THEOREM 8**

**The integral test**

Suppose that $a_n = f(n)$, where $f$ is positive, continuous, and nonincreasing on an interval $[N, \infty)$ for some positive integer $N$. Then

$$\sum_{n=1}^{\infty} a_n \qquad \text{and} \qquad \int_N^{\infty} f(t)\, dt$$

either both converge or both diverge to infinity.

***PROOF*** Let $s_n = a_1 + a_2 + \cdots + a_n$. If $n > N$, we have

$$\begin{aligned} s_n &= s_N + a_{N+1} + a_{N+2} + \cdots + a_n \\ &= s_N + f(N+1) + f(N+2) + \cdots + f(n) \\ &= s_N + \text{ sum of areas of rectangles shaded in Figure 9.4(a)} \\ &\le s_N + \int_N^{\infty} f(t)\, dt. \end{aligned}$$

If the improper integral $\int_N^{\infty} f(t)\, dt$ converges, then the sequence $\{s_n\}$ is bounded above and $\sum_{n=1}^{\infty} a_n$ converges.

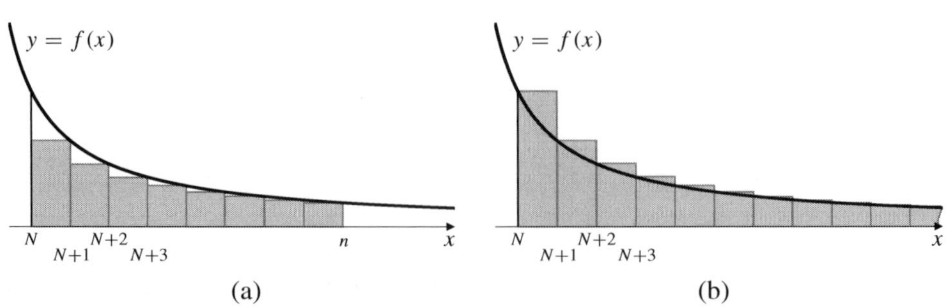


Figure 9.4 Comparing integrals and series

Conversely, suppose that $\sum_{n=1}^{\infty} a_n$ converges to the sum $s$. Then

$$\begin{aligned}\int_N^{\infty} f(t)\,dt &= \text{area under } y = f(t) \text{ above } y = 0 \text{ from } t = N \text{ to } t = \infty \\ &\le \text{sum of areas of shaded rectangles in Figure 9.4(b)} \\ &= a_N + a_{N+1} + a_{N+2} + \cdots \\ &= s - s_{N-1} < \infty,\end{aligned}$$

so the improper integral represents a finite area and is thus convergent. (We omit the remaining details showing that $\lim_{R\to\infty} \int_N^R f(t)\,dt$ exists; like the series case, the argument depends on the completeness of the real numbers.)

---

***Remark*** If $a_n = f(n)$, where $f$ is positive, continuous, and nonincreasing on $[1, \infty)$, then Theorem 8 assures us that $\sum_{n=1}^{\infty} a_n$ and $\int_1^{\infty} f(x)\,dx$ both converge or both diverge to infinity. It does *not* tell us that the sum of the series is equal to the value of the integral. The two are not likely to be equal in the case of convergence. However, as we see below, integrals can help us approximate the sum of a series.

The principal use of the integral test is to establish the result of the following example concerning the series $\sum_{n=1}^{\infty} n^{-p}$, which is called a ***p*-series**. This result should be memorized; we will frequently compare the behaviour of other series with $p$-series later in this and subsequent sections.

**EXAMPLE 1** **($p$-series)** Show that

$$\sum_{n=1}^{\infty} n^{-p} = \sum_{n=1}^{\infty} \frac{1}{n^p} \begin{cases} \text{converges if } p > 1 \\ \text{diverges to infinity if } p \le 1. \end{cases}$$

***Solution*** Observe that if $p > 0$, then $f(x) = x^{-p}$ is positive, continuous, and decreasing on $[1, \infty)$. By the integral test, the $p$-series converges for $p > 1$ and diverges for $0 < p \le 1$ by comparison with $\int_1^{\infty} x^{-p}\,dx$. (See Theorem 2(a) of Section 6.5.) If $p \le 0$, then $\lim_{n\to\infty}(1/n^p) \ne 0$, so the series cannot converge in this case. Being a positive series, it must diverge to infinity.

---

***Remark*** The harmonic series $\sum_{n=1}^{\infty} n^{-1}$ (the case $p = 1$ of the $p$-series) is on the borderline between convergence and divergence, although it diverges. While its terms decrease toward 0 as $n$ increases, they do not decrease *fast enough* to allow the sum of the series to be finite. If $p > 1$, the terms of $\sum_{n=1}^{\infty} n^{-p}$ decrease toward zero fast enough that their sum is finite. We can refine the distinction between convergence and divergence at $p = 1$ by using terms that decrease faster than $1/n$, but not as fast as $1/n^q$ for any $q > 1$. If $p > 0$, the terms $1/\big(n(\ln n)^p\big)$ have this property since $\ln n$ grows more slowly than any positive power of $n$ as $n$ increases. The question now arises whether $\sum_{n=2}^{\infty} 1/(n(\ln n)^p)$ converges. It does, provided again that $p > 1$; you can use the substitution $u = \ln x$ to check that

$$\int_2^{\infty} \frac{dx}{x(\ln x)^p} = \int_{\ln 2}^{\infty} \frac{du}{u^p},$$

which converges if $p > 1$ and diverges if $0 < p \le 1$. This process of fine-tuning Example 1 can be extended even further. (See Exercise 36 below.)

## Using Integral Bounds to Estimate the Sum of a Series

Suppose that $a_k = f(k)$ for $k = n+1, n+2, n+3, \ldots$, where $f$ is a positive, continuous function, decreasing at least on the interval $[n, \infty)$. We have:

$$\begin{aligned} s - s_n &= \sum_{k=n+1}^{\infty} f(k) \\ &= \text{sum of areas of rectangles shaded in Figure 9.5(a)} \\ &\leq \int_n^{\infty} f(x)\,dx. \end{aligned}$$

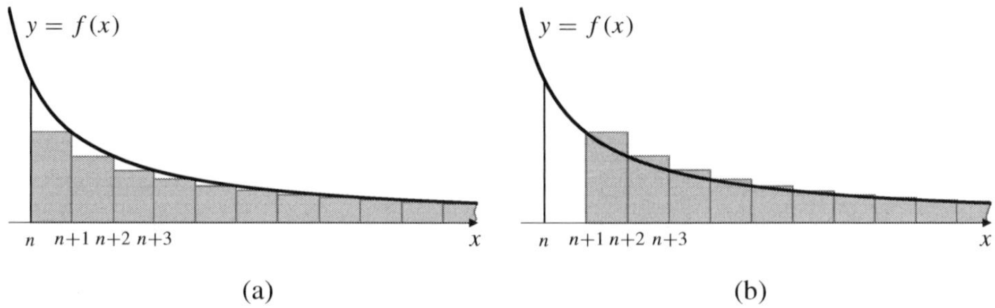


Figure 9.5 Using integrals to estimate the tail of a series

Similarly,

$$\begin{aligned} s - s_n &= \text{sum of areas of rectangles in Figure 9.5(b)} \\ &\geq \int_{n+1}^{\infty} f(x)\,dx. \end{aligned}$$

If we define

$$A_n = \int_n^{\infty} f(x)\,dx,$$

then we can combine the above inequalities to obtain

$$A_{n+1} \leq s - s_n \leq A_n,$$

or, equivalently:

$$s_n + A_{n+1} \leq s \leq s_n + A_n.$$

The error in the approximation $s \approx s_n$ satisfies $0 \leq s - s_n \leq A_n$. However, since $s$ must lie in the interval $[s_n + A_{n+1}, s_n + A_n]$, we can do better by using the midpoint $s_n^*$ of this interval as an approximation for $s$. The error is then less than half the length $A_n - A_{n+1}$ of the interval:

**A better integral approximation**

The error $|s - s_n^*|$ in the approximation

$$s \approx s_n^* = s_n + \frac{A_{n+1} + A_n}{2}, \qquad \text{where} \quad A_n = \int_n^{\infty} f(x)\,dx,$$

satisfies $\quad |s - s_n^*| \leq \dfrac{A_n - A_{n+1}}{2}.$

(Whenever a quantity is known to lie in a certain interval, the midpoint of that interval can be used to approximate the quantity, and the absolute value of the error in that approximation does not exceed half the length of the interval.)

**EXAMPLE 2** Find the best approximation $s_n^*$ to the sum $s$ of the series $\sum_{n=1}^{\infty} 1/n^2$, making use of the partial sum $s_n$ of the first $n$ terms. How large would $n$ have to be to ensure that the approximation $s \approx s_n^*$ has error less than 0.001 in absolute value? How large would $n$ have to be to ensure that the approximation $s \approx s_n$ has error less than 0.001 in absolute value?

**Solution** Since $f(x) = 1/x^2$ is positive, continuous, and decreasing on $[1, \infty)$ for any $n = 1, 2, 3, \ldots$, we have

$$s_n + A_{n+1} \le s \le s_n + A_n,$$

where

$$A_n = \int_n^{\infty} \frac{dx}{x^2} = \lim_{R\to\infty} \left(-\frac{1}{x}\right)\bigg|_n^R = \frac{1}{n}.$$

The best approximation to $s$ using $s_n$ is

$$\begin{aligned} s_n^* &= s_n + \frac{1}{2}\left(\frac{1}{n+1} + \frac{1}{n}\right) = s_n + \frac{2n+1}{2n(n+1)} \\ &= 1 + \frac{1}{4} + \frac{1}{9} + \cdots + \frac{1}{n^2} + \frac{2n+1}{2n(n+1)}. \end{aligned}$$

The error in this approximation satisfies

$$|s - s_n^*| \le \frac{1}{2}\left(\frac{1}{n} - \frac{1}{n+1}\right) = \frac{1}{2n(n+1)} \le 0.001,$$

provided $2n(n+1) \ge 1/0.001 = 1{,}000$. It is easily checked that this condition is satisfied if $n \ge 22$; the approximation

$$s \approx s_{22}^* = 1 + \frac{1}{4} + \frac{1}{9} + \cdots + \frac{1}{22^2} + \frac{45}{44 \times 23}$$

will have error with absolute value not exceeding 0.001. Had we used the approximation $s \approx s_n$ we could only have concluded that

$$0 \le s - s_n \le A_n = \frac{1}{n} < 0.001,$$

provided $n > 1{,}000$; we would need 1,000 terms of the series to get the desired accuracy.

## Comparison Tests

The next test we consider for positive series is analogous to the comparison theorem for improper integrals. (See Theorem 3 of Section 6.5.) It enables us to determine the convergence or divergence of one series by comparing it with another series that is known to converge or diverge.

**THEOREM 9**

**A comparison test**

Let $\{a_n\}$ and $\{b_n\}$ be sequences for which there exists a positive constant $K$ such that, ultimately, $0 \le a_n \le K b_n$.

(a) If the series $\sum_{n=1}^{\infty} b_n$ converges, then so does the series $\sum_{n=1}^{\infty} a_n$.

(b) If the series $\sum_{n=1}^{\infty} a_n$ diverges to infinity, then so does the series $\sum_{n=1}^{\infty} b_n$.

BEWARE! Theorem 9 does *not* say that if $\sum a_n$ converges, then $\sum b_n$ converges. It is possible that the *smaller* sum may be finite while the *larger* one is infinite. (Do not confuse a theorem with its converse.)

***PROOF*** Since a series converges if and only if its tail converges (Theorem 5), we can assume, without loss of generality, that the condition $0 \le a_n \le K b_n$ holds for all $n \ge 1$. Let $s_n = a_1 + a_2 + \cdots + a_n$ and $S_n = b_1 + b_2 + \cdots + b_n$. Then $s_n \le K S_n$. If $\sum b_n$ converges, then $\{S_n\}$ is convergent and hence is bounded by Theorem 1. Hence $\{s_n\}$ is bounded above. By Theorem 6, $\sum a_n$ converges. Since the convergence of $\sum b_n$ guarantees that of $\sum a_n$, if the latter series diverges to infinity, then the former cannot converge either, so it must diverge to infinity too.

**EXAMPLE 3** Which of the following series converge? Give reasons for your answers.

(a) $\displaystyle\sum_{n=1}^{\infty} \frac{1}{2^n + 1}$, (b) $\displaystyle\sum_{n=1}^{\infty} \frac{3n+1}{n^3+1}$, (c) $\displaystyle\sum_{n=2}^{\infty} \frac{1}{\ln n}$.

***Solution*** In each case we must find a suitable comparison series that we already know converges or diverges.

(a) Since $0 < \dfrac{1}{2^n+1} < \dfrac{1}{2^n}$ for $n = 1, 2, 3, \ldots$, and since $\sum_{n=1}^{\infty} \dfrac{1}{2^n}$ is a convergent geometric series, the series $\sum_{n=1}^{\infty} \dfrac{1}{2^n+1}$ also converges by comparison.

(b) Observe that $\dfrac{3n+1}{n^3+1}$ behaves like $\dfrac{3}{n^2}$ for large $n$, so we would expect to compare the series with the convergent $p$-series $\sum_{n=1}^{\infty} n^{-2}$. We have, for $n \ge 1$,

$$\frac{3n+1}{n^3+1} = \frac{3n}{n^3+1} + \frac{1}{n^3+1} < \frac{3n}{n^3} + \frac{1}{n^3} < \frac{3}{n^2} + \frac{1}{n^2} = \frac{4}{n^2}.$$

Thus, the given series converges by Theorem 9.

(c) For $n = 2, 3, 4, \ldots$, we have $0 < \ln n < n$. Thus $\dfrac{1}{\ln n} > \dfrac{1}{n}$. Since $\sum_{n=2}^{\infty} \dfrac{1}{n}$ diverges to infinity (it is a harmonic series), so does $\sum_{n=2}^{\infty} \dfrac{1}{\ln n}$ by comparison.

The following theorem provides a version of the comparison test that is not quite as general as Theorem 9 but is often easier to apply in specific cases.

**THEOREM 10**

**A limit comparison test**

Suppose that $\{a_n\}$ and $\{b_n\}$ are positive sequences and that

$$\lim_{n\to\infty} \frac{a_n}{b_n} = L,$$

where $L$ is either a nonnegative finite number or $+\infty$.

(a) If $L < \infty$ and $\sum_{n=1}^{\infty} b_n$ converges, then $\sum_{n=1}^{\infty} a_n$ also converges.

(b) If $L > 0$ and $\sum_{n=1}^{\infty} b_n$ diverges to infinity, then so does $\sum_{n=1}^{\infty} a_n$.

***PROOF*** If $L < \infty$, then for $n$ sufficiently large, we have $b_n > 0$ and

$$0 \le \frac{a_n}{b_n} \le L + 1,$$

so $0 \le a_n \le (L+1)b_n$. Hence $\sum_{n=1}^{\infty} a_n$ converges if $\sum_{n=1}^{\infty} b_n$ converges, by Theorem 9(a).

If $L > 0$, then for $n$ sufficiently large

$$\frac{a_n}{b_n} \ge \frac{L}{2}.$$

Therefore, $0 < b_n \le (2/L)a_n$, and $\sum_{n=1}^{\infty} a_n$ diverges to infinity if $\sum_{n=1}^{\infty} b_n$ does, by Theorem 9(b).

**EXAMPLE 4** Which of the following series converge? Give reasons for your answers.

(a) $\displaystyle\sum_{n=1}^{\infty} \frac{1}{1+\sqrt{n}}$, (b) $\displaystyle\sum_{n=1}^{\infty} \frac{n+5}{n^3-2n+3}$.

***Solution*** Again we must make appropriate choices for comparison series.

(a) The terms of this series decrease like $1/\sqrt{n}$. Observe that

$$L = \lim_{n\to\infty} \frac{\dfrac{1}{1+\sqrt{n}}}{\dfrac{1}{\sqrt{n}}} = \lim_{n\to\infty} \frac{\sqrt{n}}{1+\sqrt{n}} = \lim_{n\to\infty} \frac{1}{(1/\sqrt{n})+1} = 1.$$

Since the $p$-series $\sum_{n=1}^{\infty} \dfrac{1}{\sqrt{n}}$ diverges to infinity ($p = 1/2$), so does the series $\sum_{n=1}^{\infty} \dfrac{1}{1+\sqrt{n}}$, by the limit comparison test.

(b) For large $n$, the terms behave like $n/n^3$, so let us compare the series with the $p$-series $\sum_{n=1}^{\infty} 1/n^2$, which we know converges.

$$L = \lim_{n\to\infty} \frac{\dfrac{n+5}{n^3-2n+3}}{\dfrac{1}{n^2}} = \lim_{n\to\infty} \frac{n^3+5n^2}{n^3-2n+3} = 1.$$

Since $L < \infty$, the series $\displaystyle\sum_{n=1}^{\infty} \frac{n+5}{n^3-2n+3}$ also converges by the limit comparison test.

---

In order to apply the original version of the comparison test (Theorem 9) successfully, it is important to have an intuitive feeling for whether the given series converges or diverges. The form of the comparison will depend on whether you are trying to prove convergence or divergence. For instance, if you did not know intuitively that

$$\sum_{n=1}^{\infty} \frac{1}{100n + 20{,}000}$$

would have to diverge to infinity, you might try to argue that

$$\frac{1}{100n+20{,}000} < \frac{1}{n} \qquad \text{for } n = 1, 2, 3, \ldots.$$

While true, this doesn't help at all. $\sum_{n=1}^{\infty} 1/n$ diverges to infinity; therefore Theorem 9 yields no information from this comparison. We could, of course, argue instead that

$$\frac{1}{100n+20{,}000} \ge \frac{1}{20{,}100n} \qquad \text{if } n \ge 1,$$

and conclude by Theorem 9 that $\sum_{n=1}^{\infty}(1/(100n + 20{,}000))$ diverges to infinity by comparison with the divergent series $\sum_{n=1}^{\infty} 1/n$. An easier way is to use Theorem 10 and the fact that

$$L = \lim_{n\to\infty} \frac{\dfrac{1}{100n+20{,}000}}{\dfrac{1}{n}} = \lim_{n\to\infty} \frac{n}{100n+20{,}000} = \frac{1}{100} > 0.$$

However, the limit comparison test Theorem 10 has a disadvantage when compared to the ordinary comparison test Theorem 9. It can fail in certain cases because the limit $L$ does not exist. In such cases it is possible that the ordinary comparison test may still work.

**EXAMPLE 5** Test the series $\displaystyle\sum_{n=1}^{\infty} \frac{1+\sin n}{n^2}$ for convergence.

***Solution*** Since

$$\lim_{n\to\infty} \frac{\dfrac{1+\sin n}{n^2}}{\dfrac{1}{n^2}} = \lim_{n\to\infty} (1+\sin n)$$

does not exist, the limit comparison test gives us no information. However, since $\sin n \le 1$, we have

$$0 \le \frac{1+\sin n}{n^2} \le \frac{2}{n^2} \qquad \text{for } n = 1, 2, 3, \ldots.$$

The given series does, in fact, converge by comparison with $\sum_{n=1}^{\infty} 1/n^2$, using the ordinary comparison test.

## The Ratio and Root Tests

**THEOREM 11**

**The ratio test**

Suppose that $a_n > 0$ (ultimately) and that $\rho = \displaystyle\lim_{n\to\infty} \frac{a_{n+1}}{a_n}$ exists or is $+\infty$.

(a) If $0 \le \rho < 1$, then $\sum_{n=1}^{\infty} a_n$ converges.

(b) If $1 < \rho \le \infty$, then $\lim_{n\to\infty} a_n = \infty$ and $\sum_{n=1}^{\infty} a_n$ diverges to infinity.

(c) If $\rho = 1$, this test gives no information; the series may either converge or diverge to infinity.

***PROOF*** Here $\rho$ is the lowercase Greek letter "rho" (pronounced "roh").

(a) Suppose $\rho < 1$. Pick a number $r$ such that $\rho < r < 1$. Since we are given that $\lim_{n\to\infty} a_{n+1}/a_n = \rho$, we have $a_{n+1}/a_n \le r$ for $n$ sufficiently large; that is, $a_{n+1} \le r a_n$ for $n \ge N$, say. In particular,

$$\begin{aligned}
a_{N+1} &\le r a_N \\
a_{N+2} &\le r a_{N+1} \le r^2 a_N \\
a_{N+3} &\le r a_{N+2} \le r^3 a_N \\
&\ \vdots \\
a_{N+k} &\le r^k a_N \qquad (k = 0, 1, 2, 3, \ldots).
\end{aligned}$$

Hence, $\sum_{n=N}^{\infty} a_n$ converges by comparison with the convergent geometric series $\sum_{k=0}^{\infty} r^k$. It follows that $\sum_{n=1}^{\infty} a_n = \sum_{n=1}^{N-1} a_n + \sum_{n=N}^{\infty} a_n$ must also converge.

(b) Now suppose that $\rho > 1$. Pick a number $r$ such that $1 < r < \rho$. Since $\lim_{n\to\infty} a_{n+1}/a_n = \rho$, we have $a_{n+1}/a_n \ge r$ for $n$ sufficiently large, say for $n \ge N$. We assume $N$ is chosen large enough that $a_N > 0$. It follows by an argument similar to that used in part (a) that $a_{N+k} \ge r^k a_N$ for $k = 0, 1, 2, \ldots,$ and since $r > 1$, $\lim_{n\to\infty} a_n = \infty$. Therefore $\sum_{n=1}^{\infty} a_n$ diverges to infinity.

(c) If $\rho$ is computed for the series $\sum_{n=1}^{\infty} 1/n$ and $\sum_{n=1}^{\infty} 1/n^2$, we get $\rho = 1$ in each case. Since the first series diverges to infinity and the second converges, the ratio test cannot distinguish between convergence and divergence if $\rho = 1$.

All $p$-series fall into the indecisive category where $\rho = 1$, as does $\sum_{n=1}^{\infty} a_n$, where $a_n$ is any rational function of $n$. The ratio test is most useful for series whose terms decrease at least exponentially fast. The presence of factorials in a term also suggests that the ratio test might be useful.

**EXAMPLE 6** Test the following series for convergence:

(a) $\displaystyle\sum_{n=1}^{\infty} \frac{99^n}{n!}$, (b) $\displaystyle\sum_{n=1}^{\infty} \frac{n^5}{2^n}$, (c) $\displaystyle\sum_{n=1}^{\infty} \frac{n!}{n^n}$, (d) $\displaystyle\sum_{n=1}^{\infty} \frac{(2n)!}{(n!)^2}$.

***Solution*** We use the ratio test for each of these series.

(a) $$\rho = \lim_{n\to\infty} \frac{99^{n+1}}{(n+1)!} \bigg/ \frac{99^n}{n!} = \lim_{n\to\infty} \frac{99}{n+1} = 0 < 1.$$

Thus $\sum_{n=1}^{\infty}(99^n/n!)$ converges.

(b) $$\rho = \lim_{n\to\infty} \frac{(n+1)^5}{2^{n+1}} \bigg/ \frac{n^5}{2^n} = \lim_{n\to\infty} \frac{1}{2}\left(\frac{n+1}{n}\right)^5 = \frac{1}{2} < 1.$$

Hence $\sum_{n=1}^{\infty}(n^5/2^n)$ converges.

(c) $$\rho = \lim_{n\to\infty} \frac{(n+1)!}{(n+1)^{n+1}} \bigg/ \frac{n!}{n^n} = \lim_{n\to\infty} \frac{(n+1)!\,n^n}{(n+1)^{n+1}n!} = \lim_{n\to\infty}\left(\frac{n}{n+1}\right)^n$$
$$= \lim_{n\to\infty} \frac{1}{\left(1+\dfrac{1}{n}\right)^n} = \frac{1}{e} < 1.$$

Thus $\sum_{n=1}^{\infty}(n!/n^n)$ converges.

(d) $$\rho = \lim_{n\to\infty} \frac{(2(n+1))!}{((n+1)!)^2} \bigg/ \frac{(2n)!}{(n!)^2} = \lim_{n\to\infty} \frac{(2n+2)(2n+1)}{(n+1)^2} = 4 > 1.$$

Thus $\sum_{n=1}^{\infty}(2n)!/(n!)^2$ diverges to infinity.

The following theorem is very similar to the ratio test but is less frequently used. Its proof is left as an exercise. (See Exercise 37.) For examples of series to which it can be applied, see Exercises 38 and 39.

**THEOREM 12**

**The root test**

Suppose that $a_n > 0$ (ultimately) and that $\sigma = \lim_{n\to\infty}(a_n)^{1/n}$ exists or is $+\infty$.

(a) If $0 \le \sigma < 1$, then $\sum_{n=1}^{\infty} a_n$ converges.

(b) If $1 < \sigma \le \infty$, then $\lim_{n\to\infty} a_n = \infty$ and $\sum_{n=1}^{\infty} a_n$ diverges to infinity.

(c) If $\sigma = 1$, this test gives no information; the series may either converge or diverge to infinity.

## Using Geometric Bounds to Estimate the Sum of a Series

Suppose that an inequality of the form

$$0 \le a_k \le K r^k$$

holds for $k = n+1, n+2, n+3, \ldots$, where $K$ and $r$ are constants and $r < 1$. We can then use a geometric series to bound the tail of $\sum_{n=1}^{\infty} a_n$.

$$\begin{aligned} 0 \le s - s_n &= \sum_{k=n+1}^{\infty} a_k \le \sum_{k=n+1}^{\infty} K r^k \\ &= K r^{n+1}(1 + r + r^2 + \cdots) \\ &= \frac{K r^{n+1}}{1-r}. \end{aligned}$$

Since $r < 1$, the series converges and the error approaches 0 at an exponential rate as $n$ increases.

**EXAMPLE 7** In Section 9.6 we will show that

$$e = \frac{1}{0!} + \frac{1}{1!} + \frac{1}{2!} + \frac{1}{3!} + \cdots = \sum_{n=0}^{\infty} \frac{1}{n!}.$$

(Recall that $0! = 1$.) Estimate the error if the sum $s_n$ of the first $n$ terms of the series is used to approximate $e$. Find $e$ to 3-decimal-place accuracy using the series.

**Solution** We have

$$\begin{aligned} s_n &= \frac{1}{0!} + \frac{1}{1!} + \frac{1}{2!} + \frac{1}{3!} + \cdots + \frac{1}{(n-1)!} \\ &= 1 + 1 + \frac{1}{2} + \frac{1}{6} + \frac{1}{24} + \cdots + \frac{1}{(n-1)!}. \end{aligned}$$

(Since the series starts with the term for $n = 0$, the $n$th term is $1/(n-1)!$.) We can estimate the error in the approximation $s \approx s_n$ as follows:

$$\begin{aligned} 0 < s - s_n &= \frac{1}{n!} + \frac{1}{(n+1)!} + \frac{1}{(n+2)!} + \frac{1}{(n+3)!} + \cdots \\ &= \frac{1}{n!}\left(1 + \frac{1}{n+1} + \frac{1}{(n+1)(n+2)} + \frac{1}{(n+1)(n+2)(n+3)} + \cdots\right) \\ &< \frac{1}{n!}\left(1 + \frac{1}{n+1} + \frac{1}{(n+1)^2} + \frac{1}{(n+1)^3} + \cdots\right) \end{aligned}$$

since $n + 2 > n + 1$, $n + 3 > n + 1$, and so on. The latter series is geometric, so

$$0 < s - s_n < \frac{1}{n!} \frac{1}{1 - \dfrac{1}{n+1}} = \frac{n+1}{n!n}.$$

If we want to evaluate $e$ accurately to 3 decimal places, then we must ensure that the error is less than 5 in the fourth decimal place, that is, that the error is less than 0.0005. Hence we want

$$\frac{n+1}{n} \frac{1}{n!} < 0.0005 = \frac{1}{2{,}000}.$$

Since $7! = 5{,}040$ but $6! = 720$, we can use $n = 7$ but no smaller. We have

$$\begin{aligned} e \approx s_7 &= 1 + 1 + \frac{1}{2!} + \frac{1}{3!} + \frac{1}{4!} + \frac{1}{5!} + \frac{1}{6!} \\ &= 2 + \frac{1}{2} + \frac{1}{6} + \frac{1}{24} + \frac{1}{120} + \frac{1}{720} \approx 2.718 \quad \text{to 3 decimal places.} \end{aligned}$$

It is appropriate to use geometric series to bound the tails of positive series whose convergence would be demonstrated by the ratio test. Such series converge ultimately faster than any $p$-series $\sum_{n=1}^{\infty} n^{-p}$, for which the limit ratio is $\rho = 1$.

## EXERCISES 9.3

In Exercises 1–26, determine whether the given series converges or diverges by using any appropriate test. The $p$-series can be used for comparison, as can geometric series. Be alert for series whose terms do not approach 0.

**1.** $\displaystyle\sum_{n=1}^{\infty} \frac{1}{n^2+1}$

**2.** $\displaystyle\sum_{n=1}^{\infty} \frac{n}{n^4-2}$

**3.** $\displaystyle\sum_{n=1}^{\infty} \frac{n^2+1}{n^3+1}$

**4.** $\displaystyle\sum_{n=1}^{\infty} \frac{\sqrt{n}}{n^2+n+1}$

**5.** $\displaystyle\sum_{n=1}^{\infty} \left|\sin\frac{1}{n^2}\right|$

**6.** $\displaystyle\sum_{n=8}^{\infty} \frac{1}{\pi^n+5}$

**7.** $\displaystyle\sum_{n=2}^{\infty} \frac{1}{(\ln n)^3}$

**8.** $\displaystyle\sum_{n=1}^{\infty} \frac{1}{\ln(3n)}$

**9.** $\displaystyle\sum_{n=1}^{\infty} \frac{1}{\pi^n-n^\pi}$

**10.** $\displaystyle\sum_{n=0}^{\infty} \frac{1+n}{2+n}$

**11.** $\displaystyle\sum_{n=1}^{\infty} \frac{1+n^{4/3}}{2+n^{5/3}}$

**12.** $\displaystyle\sum_{n=1}^{\infty} \frac{n^2}{1+n\sqrt{n}}$

**13.** $\displaystyle\sum_{n=3}^{\infty} \frac{1}{n\ln n\sqrt{\ln\ln n}}$

**14.** $\displaystyle\sum_{n=2}^{\infty} \frac{1}{n\ln n(\ln\ln n)^2}$

**15.** $\displaystyle\sum_{n=1}^{\infty} \frac{1-(-1)^n}{n^4}$

**16.** $\displaystyle\sum_{n=1}^{\infty} \frac{1+(-1)^n}{\sqrt{n}}$

**17.** $\displaystyle\sum_{n=1}^{\infty} \frac{1}{2^n(n+1)}$

**18.** $\displaystyle\sum_{n=1}^{\infty} \frac{n^4}{n!}$

**19.** $\displaystyle\sum_{n=1}^{\infty} \frac{n!}{n^2e^n}$

**20.** $\displaystyle\sum_{n=1}^{\infty} \frac{(2n)!6^n}{(3n)!}$

**21.** $\displaystyle\sum_{n=2}^{\infty} \frac{\sqrt{n}}{3^n\ln n}$

**22.** $\displaystyle\sum_{n=0}^{\infty} \frac{n^{100}2^n}{\sqrt{n!}}$

**23.** $\displaystyle\sum_{n=1}^{\infty} \frac{(2n)!}{(n!)^3}$

**24.** $\displaystyle\sum_{n=1}^{\infty} \frac{1+n!}{(1+n)!}$

**25.** $\displaystyle\sum_{n=4}^{\infty} \frac{2^n}{3^n-n^3}$

**26.** $\displaystyle\sum_{n=1}^{\infty} \frac{n^n}{\pi^n n!}$

In Exercises 27–30, use $s_n$ and integral bounds to find the smallest interval that you can be sure contains the sum $s$ of the series. If the midpoint $s_n^*$ of this interval is used to approximate $s$, how large should $n$ be chosen to ensure that the error is less than 0.001?

**27.** $\displaystyle\sum_{k=1}^{\infty} \frac{1}{k^4}$

**28.** $\displaystyle\sum_{k=1}^{\infty} \frac{1}{k^3}$

**29.** $\displaystyle\sum_{k=1}^{\infty} \frac{1}{k^{3/2}}$

**30.** $\displaystyle\sum_{k=1}^{\infty} \frac{1}{k^2+4}$

For each positive series in Exercises 31–34, find the best upper bound you can for the error $s-s_n$ encountered if the partial sum $s_n$ is used to approximate the sum $s$ of the series. How many terms of each series do you need to be sure that the approximation has error less than 0.001?

**31.** $\displaystyle\sum_{k=1}^{\infty} \frac{1}{2^k k!}$

**32.** $\displaystyle\sum_{n=1}^{\infty} \frac{1}{(2n-1)!}$

**33.** $\displaystyle\sum_{n=0}^{\infty} \frac{2^n}{(2n)!}$

**34.** $\displaystyle\sum_{n=1}^{\infty} \frac{1}{n^n}$

**35.** Use the integral test to show that $\displaystyle\sum_{n=1}^{\infty} \frac{1}{1+n^2}$ converges. Show that the sum $s$ of the series is less than $\pi/2$.

**36.** Show that $\sum_{n=3}^{\infty}(1/(n\ln n(\ln\ln n)^p))$ converges if and only if $p>1$. Generalize this result to series of the form

$$\sum_{n=N}^{\infty} \frac{1}{n(\ln n)(\ln\ln n)\cdots(\ln_j n)(\ln_{j+1} n)^p},$$

where $\ln_j n = \underbrace{\ln\ln\ln\ln\cdots\ln}_{j \text{ ln's}} n.$

**37.** Prove the root test. *Hint:* Mimic the proof of the ratio test.

**38.** Use the root test to show that $\displaystyle\sum_{n=1}^{\infty} \frac{2^{n+1}}{n^n}$ converges.

**39.** Use the root test to test the following series for convergence:

$$\sum_{n=1}^{\infty} \left(\frac{n}{n+1}\right)^{n^2}.$$

**40.** Repeat Exercise 38, but use the ratio test instead of the root test.

**41.** Try to use the ratio test to determine whether $\displaystyle\sum_{n=1}^{\infty} \frac{2^{2n}(n!)^2}{(2n)!}$ converges. What happens? Now observe that

$$\begin{aligned}\frac{2^{2n}(n!)^2}{(2n)!} &= \frac{[2n(2n-2)(2n-4)\cdots 6\times 4\times 2]^2}{2n(2n-1)(2n-2)\cdots 4\times 3\times 2\times 1}\\ &= \frac{2n}{2n-1}\times\frac{2n-2}{2n-3}\times\cdots\times\frac{4}{3}\times\frac{2}{1}.\end{aligned}$$

Does the given series converge? Why or why not?

**42.** Determine whether the series $\displaystyle\sum_{n=1}^{\infty} \frac{(2n)!}{2^{2n}(n!)^2}$ converges. *Hint:* Proceed as in Exercise 41. Show that $a_n \ge 1/(2n)$.

**43.** (a) Show that if $k>0$ and $n$ is a positive integer, then $n < \dfrac{1}{k}(1+k)^n$.

(b) Use the estimate in (a) with $0<k<1$ to obtain an upper bound for the sum of the series $\sum_{n=0}^{\infty} n/2^n$. For what value of $k$ is this bound least?

(c) If we use the sum $s_n$ of the first $n$ terms to approximate the sum $s$ of the series in (b), obtain an upper bound for the error $s-s_n$ using the inequality from (a). For given $n$, find $k$ to minimize this upper bound.

**44. (Improving the convergence of a series)** We know that $\sum_{n=1}^{\infty} 1/\big(n(n+1)\big) = 1$. (See Example 3 of Section 9.2.)

Since

$$\frac{1}{n^2} = \frac{1}{n(n+1)} + c_n, \quad \text{where} \quad c_n = \frac{1}{n^2(n+1)},$$

we have $\displaystyle\sum_{n=1}^{\infty} \frac{1}{n^2} = 1 + \sum_{n=1}^{\infty} c_n$.

The series $\sum_{n=1}^{\infty} c_n$ converges more rapidly than does $\sum_{n=1}^{\infty} 1/n^2$ because its terms decrease like $1/n^3$. Hence, fewer terms of that series will be needed to compute $\sum_{n=1}^{\infty} 1/n^2$ to any desired degree of accuracy than would be needed if we calculated with $\sum_{n=1}^{\infty} 1/n^2$ directly. Using integral upper and lower bounds, determine a value of $n$ for which the modified partial sum $s_n^*$ for the series $\sum_{n=1}^{\infty} c_n$ approximates the sum of that series with error less than 0.001 in absolute value. Hence, determine $\sum_{n=1}^{\infty} 1/n^2$ to within 0.001 of its true value. (The technique exibited in this exercise is known as **improving the convergence** of a series. It can be applied to estimating the sum $\sum a_n$ if we know the sum $\sum b_n$ and if $a_n - b_n = c_n$, where $|c_n|$ decreases faster than $|a_n|$ as $n$ tends to infinity.)

**45.** Consider the series $s = \sum_{n=1}^{\infty} 1/(2^n + 1)$, and the partial sum $s_n$ of its first $n$ terms.

(a) How large need $n$ be taken to ensure that the error in the approximation $s \approx s_n$ is less than 0.001 in absolute value?

(b) The geometric series $\sum_{n=1}^{\infty} 1/2^n$ converges to 1. If

$$b_n = \frac{1}{2^n} - \frac{1}{2^n + 1}$$

for $n = 1, 2, 3, \ldots$, how many terms of the series $\sum_{n=1}^{\infty} b_n$ are needed to calculate its sum to within 0.001?

(c) Use the result of part (b) to calculate the $\sum_{n=1}^{\infty} 1/(2^n + 1)$ to within 0.001.

## 9.4 Absolute and Conditional Convergence

All of the series $\sum_{n=1}^{\infty} a_n$ considered in the previous section were ultimately positive; that is, $a_n \geq 0$ for $n$ sufficiently large. We now drop this restriction and allow arbitrary real terms $a_n$. We can, however, always obtain a positive series from any given series by replacing all the terms with their absolute values.

**DEFINITION 5**

**Absolute convergence**

The series $\sum_{n=1}^{\infty} a_n$ is said to be **absolutely convergent** if $\sum_{n=1}^{\infty} |a_n|$ converges.

The series

$$s = \sum_{n=1}^{\infty} \frac{(-1)^n}{n^2} = -1 + \frac{1}{4} - \frac{1}{9} + \frac{1}{16} - \cdots$$

converges absolutely since

$$S = \sum_{n=1}^{\infty} \left| \frac{(-1)^n}{n^2} \right| = \sum_{n=1}^{\infty} \frac{1}{n^2} = 1 + \frac{1}{4} + \frac{1}{9} + \frac{1}{16} + \cdots$$

converges. It seems reasonable that the first series must converge, and its sum $s$ should satisfy $-S \leq s \leq S$. In general, the cancellation that occurs because some terms are negative and others positive makes it *easier* for a series to converge than if all the terms are of one sign. We verify this insight in the following theorem.

**THEOREM 13**

If a series converges absolutely, then it converges.

***PROOF*** Let $\sum_{n=1}^{\infty} a_n$ be absolutely convergent, and let $b_n = a_n + |a_n|$ for each $n$. Since $-|a_n| \leq a_n \leq |a_n|$, we have $0 \leq b_n \leq 2|a_n|$ for each $n$. Thus $\sum_{n=1}^{\infty} b_n$ converges by the comparison test. Therefore, $\sum_{n=1}^{\infty} a_n = \sum_{n=1}^{\infty} b_n - \sum_{n=1}^{\infty} |a_n|$ also converges. ∎

Again you are cautioned not to confuse the statement of Theorem 13 with the converse statement, which is false. We will show later in this section that the **alternating harmonic series**

$$\sum_{n=1}^{\infty} \frac{(-1)^{n-1}}{n} = 1 - \frac{1}{2} + \frac{1}{3} - \frac{1}{4} + \frac{1}{5} - \cdots$$

converges, although it does not converge absolutely. If we replace all the terms by their absolute values, we get the divergent harmonic series

$$\sum_{n=1}^{\infty} \frac{1}{n} = 1 + \frac{1}{2} + \frac{1}{3} + \frac{1}{4} + \cdots = \infty.$$

BEWARE! Although absolute convergence implies convergence, convergence does *not* imply absolute convergence.

**DEFINITION 6**

**Conditional convergence**

If $\sum_{n=1}^{\infty} a_n$ is convergent, but not absolutely convergent, then we say that it is **conditionally convergent** or that it **converges conditionally**.

The alternating harmonic series is an example of a conditionally convergent series.

The comparison tests, the integral test, and the ratio test can each be used to test for absolute convergence. They should be applied to the series $\sum_{n=1}^{\infty} |a_n|$. For the ratio test we calculate $\rho = \lim_{n\to\infty} |a_{n+1}/a_n|$. If $\rho < 1$, then $\sum_{n=1}^{\infty} a_n$ converges absolutely. If $\rho > 1$, then $\lim_{n\to\infty} |a_n| = \infty$, so both $\sum_{n=1}^{\infty} |a_n|$ and $\sum_{n=1}^{\infty} a_n$ must diverge. If $\rho = 1$, we get no information; the series $\sum_{n=1}^{\infty} a_n$ may converge absolutely, it may converge conditionally, or it may diverge.

**EXAMPLE 1** Test the following series for absolute convergence:

(a) $\displaystyle\sum_{n=1}^{\infty} \frac{(-1)^{n-1}}{2n-1}$, (b) $\displaystyle\sum_{n=1}^{\infty} \frac{n\cos(n\pi)}{2^n}$.

***Solution***

(a) $\displaystyle\lim_{n\to\infty} \left|\frac{(-1)^{n-1}}{2n-1}\right| \bigg/ \frac{1}{n} = \lim_{n\to\infty} \frac{n}{2n-1} = \frac{1}{2} > 0.$

Since the harmonic series $\sum_{n=1}^{\infty}(1/n)$ diverges to infinity, the comparison test assures us that $\sum_{n=1}^{\infty}((-1)^{n-1}/(2n-1))$ does not converge absolutely.

(b) $\displaystyle\rho = \lim_{n\to\infty} \left| \frac{(n+1)\cos((n+1)\pi)}{2^{n+1}} \bigg/ \frac{n\cos(n\pi)}{2^n} \right| = \lim_{n\to\infty} \frac{n+1}{2n} = \frac{1}{2} < 1.$

(Note that $\cos(n\pi)$ is just a fancy way of writing $(-1)^n$.) Therefore (ratio test) $\sum_{n=1}^{\infty}((n\cos(n\pi))/2^n)$ converges absolutely.

## The Alternating Series Test

We cannot use any of the previously developed tests to show that the alternating harmonic series converges; all of those tests apply only to (ultimately) positive series, so they can test only for absolute convergence. Demonstrating convergence that is not absolute is generally more difficult to do. We present only one test that can establish such convergence; this test can only be used on a very special kind of series.

**THEOREM 14**

**The alternating series test**

Suppose $\{a_n\}$ is a sequence whose terms satisfy, for some positive integer $N$,

(i) $a_n a_{n+1} < 0$ for $n \ge N$,

(ii) $|a_{n+1}| \le |a_n|$ for $n \ge N$, and

(iii) $\lim_{n\to\infty} a_n = 0$,

that is, the terms are ultimately alternating in sign and decreasing in size, and the sequence has limit zero. Then the series $\sum_{n=1}^{\infty} a_n$ converges.

***PROOF*** Without loss of generality we can assume $N = 1$ because convergence only depends on the tail of a series. We also assume $a_1 > 0$; the proof if $a_1 < 0$ is similar. If $s_n = a_1 + a_2 + \cdots + a_n$ is the $n$th partial sum of the series, it follows from the alternation of $\{a_n\}$ that $a_{2n+1} > 0$ and $a_{2n} < 0$ for each $n$. Since the terms decrease in size, $a_{2n+1} \geq -a_{2n+2}$. Therefore $s_{2n+2} = s_{2n} + a_{2n+1} + a_{2n+2} \geq s_{2n}$ for $n = 1, 2, 3, \ldots$; the even partial sums $\{s_{2n}\}$ form an increasing sequence. Similarly $s_{2n+1} = s_{2n-1} + a_{2n} + a_{2n+1} \leq s_{2n-1}$, so the odd partial sums $\{s_{2n-1}\}$ form a decreasing sequence. Since $s_{2n} = s_{2n-1} + a_{2n} \leq s_{2n-1}$, we can say, for any $n$, that

BEWARE! Read this proof slowly and think about why each statement is true.

$$s_2 \leq s_4 \leq s_6 \leq \cdots \leq s_{2n} \leq s_{2n-1} \leq s_{2n-3} \leq \cdots \leq s_5 \leq s_3 \leq s_1.$$

Hence, $s_2$ is a lower bound for the decreasing sequence $\{s_{2n-1}\}$, and $s_1$ is an upper bound for the increasing sequence $\{s_{2n}\}$. Both of these sequences therefore converge by the completeness of the real numbers:

$$\lim_{n\to\infty} s_{2n-1} = s_{\text{odd}}, \qquad \lim_{n\to\infty} s_{2n} = s_{\text{even}}.$$

Now $a_{2n} = s_{2n} - s_{2n-1}$, so $0 = \lim_{n\to\infty} a_{2n} = \lim_{n\to\infty}(s_{2n} - s_{2n-1}) = s_{\text{even}} - s_{\text{odd}}$. Therefore $s_{\text{odd}} = s_{\text{even}} = s$, say. Every partial sum $s_n$ is either of the form $s_{2n-1}$ or of the form $s_{2n}$. Thus, $\lim_{n\to\infty} s_n = s$ exists and the series $\sum(-1)^{n-1}a_n$ converges to this sum $s$.

***Remark*** The proof of Theorem 14 shows that the sum $s$ of the series always lies between any two consecutive partial sums of the series:

$$\text{either} \quad s_n < s < s_{n+1} \quad \text{or} \quad s_{n+1} < s < s_n.$$

This proves the following theorem.

**THEOREM 15**

**Error estimate for alternating series**

If the sequence $\{a_n\}$ satisfies the conditions of the alternating series test (Theorem 14), so that the series $\sum_{n=1}^{\infty} a_n$ converges to the sum $s$, then the error in the approximation $s \approx s_n$ (where $n \geq N$) has the same sign as the first omitted term $a_{n+1} = s_{n+1} - s_n$, and it size is no greater than the size of that term:

$$|s - s_n| \leq |s_{n+1} - s_n| = |a_{n+1}|.$$

**EXAMPLE 2** How many terms of the series $\displaystyle\sum_{n=1}^{\infty} \frac{(-1)^n}{1+2^n}$ are needed to compute the sum of the series with error less than 0.001?

***Solution*** This series satisfies the hypotheses for Theorem 15. If we use the partial sum of the first $n$ terms of the series to approximate the sum of the series, the error will satisfy

$$|\text{error}| \leq |\text{first omitted term}| = \frac{1}{1+2^{n+1}}.$$

This error is less than 0.001 if $1 + 2^{n+1} > 1{,}000$. Since $2^{10} = 1{,}024$, $n + 1 = 10$ will do; we need 9 terms of the series to compute the sum to within 0.001 of its actual value.

When determining the convergence of a given series, it is best to consider first whether the series converges absolutely. If it does not, then there remains the possibility of conditional convergence.

**EXAMPLE 3** Test the following series for absolute and conditional convergence:

$$\text{(a)}\ \sum_{n=1}^{\infty} \frac{(-1)^{n-1}}{n}, \qquad \text{(b)}\ \sum_{n=2}^{\infty} \frac{\cos(n\pi)}{\ln n}, \qquad \text{(c)}\ \sum_{n=1}^{\infty} \frac{(-1)^{n-1}}{n^4}.$$

**Solution** The absolute values of the terms in series (a) and (b) are $1/n$ and $1/(\ln n)$, respectively. Since $1/(\ln n) > 1/n$, and $\sum_{n=1}^{\infty} 1/n$ diverges to infinity, neither series (a) nor (b) converges absolutely. However, both series satisfy the requirements of Theorem 14 and so both converge. Each of these series is conditionally convergent.

Series (c) is absolutely convergent because $|(-1)^{n-1}/n^4| = 1/n^4$, and $\sum_{n=1}^{\infty} 1/n^4$ is a convergent $p$-series ($p = 4 > 1$). We could establish its convergence using Theorem 14, but there is no need to do that since every absolutely convergent series is convergent (Theorem 13).

**EXAMPLE 4** For what values of $x$ does the series $\displaystyle\sum_{n=1}^{\infty} \frac{(x-5)^n}{n\,2^n}$ converge absolutely? converge conditionally? diverge?

**Solution** For such series whose terms involve functions of a variable $x$, it is usually wisest to begin testing for absolute convergence with the ratio test. We have

$$\rho = \lim_{n\to\infty} \left| \frac{(x-5)^{n+1}}{(n+1)2^{n+1}} \bigg/ \frac{(x-5)^n}{n\,2^n} \right| = \lim_{n\to\infty} \frac{n}{n+1} \left| \frac{x-5}{2} \right| = \left| \frac{x-5}{2} \right|.$$

The series converges absolutely if $|(x-5)/2| < 1$. This inequality is equivalent to $|x-5| < 2$ (the distance from $x$ to 5 is less than 2), that is, $3 < x < 7$. If $x < 3$ or $x > 7$, then $|(x-5)/2| > 1$. The series diverges; its terms do not approach zero.

If $x = 3$, the series is $\sum_{n=1}^{\infty}((-1)^n/n)$, which converges conditionally (it is an alternating harmonic series); if $x = 7$, the series is the harmonic series $\sum_{n=1}^{\infty} 1/n$, which diverges to infinity. Hence, the given series converges absolutely on the open interval (3, 7), converges conditionally at $x = 3$, and diverges everywhere else.

**EXAMPLE 5** For what values of $x$ does the series $\displaystyle\sum_{n=0}^{\infty} (n+1)^2 \left(\frac{x}{x+2}\right)^n$ converge absolutely? converge conditionally? diverge?

**Solution** Again we begin with the ratio test.

$$\begin{aligned} \rho &= \lim_{n\to\infty} \left| (n+2)^2 \left(\frac{x}{x+2}\right)^{n+1} \bigg/ (n+1)^2 \left(\frac{x}{x+2}\right)^n \right| \\ &= \lim_{n\to\infty} \left(\frac{n+2}{n+1}\right)^2 \left|\frac{x}{x+2}\right| = \left|\frac{x}{x+2}\right| = \frac{|x|}{|x+2|} \end{aligned}$$

The series converges absolutely if $|x|/|x+2| < 1$. This condition says that the distance from $x$ to 0 is less than the distance from $x$ to $-2$. Hence $x > -1$. The series diverges if $|x|/|x+2| > 1$, that is, if $x < -1$. If $x = -1$, the series is $\sum_{n=0}^{\infty}(-1)^n(n+1)^2$, which diverges. We conclude that the series converges absolutely for $x > -1$, converges conditionally nowhere, and diverges for $x \le -1$.

When using the alternating series test, it is important to verify (at least mentally) that *all three conditions* (i)–(iii) are satisfied.

**EXAMPLE 6** Test the following series for convergence:

(a) $\sum_{n=1}^{\infty}(-1)^{n-1}\frac{n+1}{n}$,

(b) $1 - \frac{1}{4} + \frac{1}{3} - \frac{1}{16} + \frac{1}{5} - \cdots = \sum_{n=1}^{\infty} a_n$, where

$$a_n = \begin{cases} 1/n & \text{if } n \text{ is odd,} \\ -1/n^2 & \text{if } n \text{ is even.} \end{cases}$$

***Solution***

(a) Here, the terms $a_n$ alternate and decrease in size as $n$ increases. However, $\lim_{n\to\infty} |a_n| = 1 \neq 0$. The alternating series test does not apply. In fact, the given series diverges because its terms do not approach 0.

(b) This series alternates and its terms have limit zero, However, the terms are not decreasing in size (even ultimately). Once again, the alternating series test cannot be applied. In fact, since

$$-\frac{1}{4} - \frac{1}{16} - \cdots - \frac{1}{(2n)^2} - \cdots \qquad \text{converges, and}$$

$$1 + \frac{1}{3} + \frac{1}{5} + \cdots + \frac{1}{2n-1} + \cdots \qquad \text{diverges to infinity,}$$

it is readily seen that the given series diverges to infinity.

## Rearranging the Terms in a Series

The basic difference between absolute and conditional convergence is that when a series $\sum_{n=1}^{\infty} a_n$ converges absolutely, it does so because its terms $\{a_n\}$ decrease in size fast enough that their sum can be finite even if no cancellation occurs due to terms of opposite sign. If cancellation is required to make the series converge (because the terms decrease slowly), then the series can only converge conditionally.

Consider the alternating harmonic series

$$1 - \frac{1}{2} + \frac{1}{3} - \frac{1}{4} + \frac{1}{5} - \frac{1}{6} + \cdots.$$

This series converges, but only conditionally. If we take the subseries containing only the positive terms, we get the series

$$1 + \frac{1}{3} + \frac{1}{5} + \frac{1}{7} + \cdots,$$

which diverges to infinity. Similarly, the subseries of negative terms

$$-\frac{1}{2} - \frac{1}{4} - \frac{1}{6} - \frac{1}{8} - \cdots$$

diverges to negative infinity.

If a series converges absolutely, the subseries consisting of positive terms and the subseries consisting of negative terms must each converge to a finite sum. If a series converges conditionally, the positive and negative subseries will both diverge, to $\infty$ and $-\infty$, respectively.

Using these facts we can answer a question raised at the beginning of Section 9.2. If we rearrange the terms of a convergent series so that they are added in a different order, must the rearranged series converge, and if it does will it converge to the same sum as the original series? The answer depends on whether the original series was absolutely convergent or merely conditionally convergent.

**THEOREM 16** **Convergence of rearrangements of a series**

(a) If the terms of an absolutely convergent series are rearranged so that addition occurs in a different order, the rearranged series still converges to the same sum as the original series.

(b) If a series is conditionally convergent, and $L$ is any real number, then the terms of the series can be rearranged so as to make the series converge (conditionally) to the sum $L$. It can also be rearranged so as to diverge to $\infty$ or to $-\infty$, or just to diverge.

Part (b) shows that conditional convergence is a rather suspect kind of convergence, being dependent on the order in which the terms are added. We will not present a formal proof of the theorem but will give an example suggesting what is involved. (See also Exercise 30 below.)

**EXAMPLE 7** In Section 9.5 we will show that the alternating harmonic series

$$\sum_{n=1}^{\infty} \frac{(-1)^{n-1}}{n} = 1 - \frac{1}{2} + \frac{1}{3} - \frac{1}{4} + \frac{1}{5} - \frac{1}{6} + \frac{1}{7} - \cdots$$

converges (conditionally) to the sum $\ln 2$. Describe how to rearrange its terms so that it converges to 8 instead.

***Solution*** Start adding terms of the positive subseries

$$1 + \frac{1}{3} + \frac{1}{5} + \cdots,$$

and keep going until the partial sum exceeds 8. (It will, eventually, because the positive subseries diverges to infinity.) Then add the first term $-1/2$ of the negative subseries

$$-\frac{1}{2} - \frac{1}{4} - \frac{1}{6} - \cdots.$$

This will reduce the partial sum below 8 again. Now resume adding terms of the positive subseries until the partial sum climbs above 8 once more. Then add the second term of the negative subseries and the partial sum will drop below 8. Keep repeating this procedure, alternately adding terms of the positive subseries to force the sum above 8 and then terms of the negative subseries to force it below 8. Since both subseries have infinitely many terms and diverge to $\infty$ and $-\infty$, respectively, eventually every term of the original series will be included, and the partial sums of the new series will oscillate back and forth around 8, converging to that number. Of course, any number other than 8 could also be used in place of 8.

## EXERCISES 9.4

Determine whether the series in Exercises 1–12 converge absolutely, converge conditionally, or diverge.

1. $\displaystyle\sum_{n=1}^{\infty} \frac{(-1)^{n-1}}{\sqrt{n}}$

2. $\displaystyle\sum_{n=1}^{\infty} \frac{(-1)^{n}}{n^2 + \ln n}$

3. $\displaystyle\sum_{n=1}^{\infty} \frac{\cos(n\pi)}{(n+1)\ln(n+1)}$

4. $\displaystyle\sum_{n=1}^{\infty} \frac{(-1)^{2n}}{2^n}$

5. $\displaystyle\sum_{n=0}^{\infty} \frac{(-1)^{n}(n^2-1)}{n^2+1}$

6. $\displaystyle\sum_{n=1}^{\infty} \frac{(-2)^{n}}{n!}$

7. $\displaystyle\sum_{n=1}^{\infty} \frac{(-1)^{n}}{n\pi^n}$

8. $\displaystyle\sum_{n=0}^{\infty} \frac{-n}{n^2+1}$

9. $\displaystyle\sum_{n=1}^{\infty} (-1)^n \frac{20n^2 - n - 1}{n^3 + n^2 + 33}$

10. $\displaystyle\sum_{n=1}^{\infty} \frac{100\cos(n\pi)}{2n+3}$

**11.** $\sum_{n=1}^{\infty} \frac{n!}{(-100)^n}$ **12.** $\sum_{n=10}^{\infty} \frac{\sin(n+1/2)\pi}{\ln\ln n}$

For the series in Exercises 13–16, find the smallest integer $n$ that ensures that the partial sum $s_n$ approximates the sum $s$ of the series with error less than 0.001 in absolute value.

**13.** $\sum_{n=1}^{\infty}(-1)^{n-1}\frac{n}{n^2+1}$ **14.** $\sum_{n=0}^{\infty}\frac{(-1)^n}{(2n)!}$

**15.** $\sum_{n=1}^{\infty}(-1)^{n-1}\frac{n}{2^n}$ **16.** $\sum_{n=0}^{\infty}(-1)^n\frac{3^n}{n!}$

Determine the values of $x$ for which the series in Exercises 17–24 converge absolutely, converge conditionally, or diverge.

**17.** $\sum_{n=0}^{\infty}\frac{x^n}{\sqrt{n+1}}$ **18.** $\sum_{n=1}^{\infty}\frac{(x-2)^n}{n^2 2^{2n}}$

**19.** $\sum_{n=0}^{\infty}(-1)^n\frac{(x-1)^n}{2n+3}$ **20.** $\sum_{n=1}^{\infty}\frac{1}{2n-1}\left(\frac{3x+2}{-5}\right)^n$

**21.** $\sum_{n=2}^{\infty}\frac{x^n}{2^n \ln n}$ **22.** $\sum_{n=1}^{\infty}\frac{(4x+1)^n}{n^3}$

**23.** $\sum_{n=1}^{\infty}\frac{(2x+3)^n}{n^{1/3}4^n}$ **24.** $\sum_{n=1}^{\infty}\frac{1}{n}\left(1+\frac{1}{x}\right)^n$

**25.** Does the alternating series test apply directly to the series $\sum_{n=1}^{\infty}(1/n)\sin(n\pi/2)$? Determine whether the series converges.

**26.** Show that the series $\sum_{n=1}^{\infty} a_n$ converges absolutely if $a_n = 10/n^2$ for even $n$ and $a_n = -1/10n^3$ for odd $n$.

**27.** Which of the following statements are TRUE and which are FALSE? Justify your assertion of truth, or give a counterexample to show falsehood.

(a) If $\sum_{n=1}^{\infty} a_n$ converges, then $\sum_{n=1}^{\infty}(-1)^n a_n$ converges.

(b) If $\sum_{n=1}^{\infty} a_n$ converges and $\sum_{n=1}^{\infty}(-1)^n a_n$ converges, then $\sum_{n=1}^{\infty} a_n$ converges absolutely.

(c) If $\sum_{n=1}^{\infty} a_n$ converges absolutely, then $\sum_{n=1}^{\infty}(-1)^n a_n$ converges absolutely.

**28.** (a) Use a Riemann sum argument to show that

$$\ln n! \ge \int_1^n \ln t\, dt = n\ln n - n + 1.$$

(b) For what values of $x$ does the series $\sum_{n=1}^{\infty}\frac{n!x^n}{n^n}$ converge absolutely? converge conditionally? diverge? (*Hint:* First use the ratio test. To test the cases where $\rho = 1$, you may find the inequality in part (a) useful.)

**29.** For what values of $x$ does the series $\sum_{n=1}^{\infty}\frac{(2n)!x^n}{2^{2n}(n!)^2}$ converge absolutely? converge conditionally? diverge? *Hint:* See Exercise 42 of Section 9.3.

**30.** Devise procedures for rearranging the terms of the alternating harmonic series so that the rearranged series (a) diverges to $\infty$, (b) converges to $-2$.

## 9.5 Power Series

This section is concerned with a special kind of infinite series called a *power series*, which may be thought of as a polynomial of infinite degree.

**DEFINITION 7**

**Power series**

A series of the form

$$\sum_{n=0}^{\infty} a_n(x-c)^n = a_0 + a_1(x-c) + a_2(x-c)^2 + a_3(x-c)^3 + \cdots$$

is called a **power series in powers of $x - c$** or a **power series about $c$**. The constants $a_0, a_1, a_2, \ldots$ are called the **coefficients** of the power series.

Since the terms of a power series are functions of a variable $x$, the series may or may not converge for each value of $x$. For those values of $x$ for which the series does converge, the sum defines a function of $x$. For example, if $-1 < x < 1$, then

$$1 + x + x^2 + x^3 + \cdots = \frac{1}{1-x}.$$

The geometric series on the left side is a power series *representation* of the function $1/(1-x)$ in powers of $x$ (or about 0). Note that the representation is valid only in the open interval $(-1, 1)$ even though $1/(1-x)$ is defined for all real $x$ except $x = 1$. For

$x = -1$ and for $|x| > 1$ the series does not converge, so it cannot represent $1/(1-x)$ at these points.

The point $c$ is the **centre of convergence** of the power series $\sum_{n=0}^{\infty} a_n(x-c)^n$. The series certainly converges (to $a_0$) at $x = c$. (All the terms except possibly the first are 0.) Theorem 17 below shows that if the series converges anywhere else, then it converges on an interval (possibly infinite) centred at $x = c$, and it converges absolutely everywhere on that interval except possibly at one or both of the endpoints if the interval is finite. The geometric series

$$1 + x + x^2 + x^3 + \cdots$$

is an example of this behaviour. It has centre of convergence $c = 0$, and converges only on the interval $(-1, 1)$, centred at 0. The convergence is absolute at every point of the interval. Another example is the series

$$\sum_{n=1}^{\infty} \frac{1}{n\,2^n}(x-5)^n = \frac{x-5}{2} + \frac{(x-5)^2}{2 \times 2^2} + \frac{(x-5)^3}{3 \times 2^3} + \cdots,$$

which we discussed in Example 4 of Section 9.4. We showed that this series converges on the interval $[3, 7)$, an interval with centre $x = 5$, and that the convergence is absolute on the open interval $(3, 7)$ but is only conditional at the endpoint $x = 3$.

**THEOREM 17**

For any power series $\sum_{n=0}^{\infty} a_n\,(x-c)^n$ one of the following alternatives must hold:

(i) the series may converge only at $x = c$,

(ii) the series may converge at every real number $x$, or

(iii) there may exist a positive real number $R$ such that the series converges at every $x$ satisfying $|x-c| < R$ and diverges at every $x$ satisfying $|x-c| > R$. In this case the series may or may not converge at either of the two *endpoints* $x = c - R$ and $x = c + R$.

In each of these cases the convergence is absolute except possibly at the endpoints $x = c - R$ and $x = c + R$ in case (iii).

***PROOF*** We observed above that every power series converges at its centre of convergence; only the first term can be nonzero so the convergence is absolute. To prove the rest of this theorem, it suffices to show that if the series converges at any number $x_0 \neq c$, then it converges absolutely at every number $x$ closer to $c$ than $x_0$ is, that is, at every $x$ satisfying $|x-c| < |x_0 - c|$. This means that convergence at any $x_0 \neq c$ implies absolute convergence on $(c - x_0, c + x_0)$, so the set of points $x$ where the series converges must be an interval centred at $c$.

Suppose, therefore, that $\sum_{n=0}^{\infty} a_n(x_0-c)^n$ converges. Then $\lim a_n(x_0-c)^n = 0$, so $|a_n(x_0-c)^n| \le K$ for all $n$, where $K$ is some constant (Theorem 1 of Section 9.1). If $r = |x-c|/|x_0-c| < 1$, then

$$\sum_{n=0}^{\infty} |a_n(x-c)^n| = \sum_{n=0}^{\infty} |a_n(x_0-c)^n| \left|\frac{x-c}{x_0-c}\right|^n \le K \sum_{n=0}^{\infty} r^n = \frac{K}{1-r} < \infty.$$

Thus, $\sum_{n=0}^{\infty} a_n(x-c)^n$ converges absolutely. ■

By Theorem 17, the set of values $x$ for which the power series $\sum_{n=0}^{\infty} a_n(x-c)^n$ converges is an interval centred at $x = c$. We call this interval the **interval of convergence** of the power series. It must be of one of the following forms:

(i) the isolated point $x = c$ (a degenerate closed interval $[c, c]$),

(ii) the entire line $(-\infty, \infty)$,

(iii) a finite interval centred at $c$:
$[c-R, c+R]$, or $[c-R, c+R)$, or $(c-R, c+R]$, or $(c-R, c+R)$.

The number $R$ in (iii) is called the **radius of convergence** of the power series. In case (i) we say the radius of convergence is $R = 0$; in case (ii) it is $R = \infty$.

The radius of convergence, $R$, can often be found by using the ratio test on the power series: if

$$\rho = \lim_{n\to\infty} \left| \frac{a_{n+1}(x-c)^{n+1}}{a_n(x-c)^n} \right| = \left( \lim_{n\to\infty} \left| \frac{a_{n+1}}{a_n} \right| \right) |x-c|$$

exists, then the series $\sum_{n=0}^{\infty} a_n(x-c)^n$ converges absolutely where $\rho < 1$, that is, where

$$|x-c| < R = 1 \Bigg/ \lim_{n\to\infty} \left| \frac{a_{n+1}}{a_n} \right|.$$

The series diverges if $|x-c| > R$.

**Radius of convergence**

Suppose that $L = \lim_{n\to\infty} \left| \frac{a_{n+1}}{a_n} \right|$ exists or is $\infty$. Then the power series $\sum_{n=0}^{\infty} a_n(x-c)^n$ has radius of convergence $R = 1/L$. (If $L = 0$, then $R = \infty$; if $L = \infty$, then $R = 0$.)

**EXAMPLE 1** Determine the centre, radius, and interval of convergence of

$$\sum_{n=0}^{\infty} \frac{(2x+5)^n}{(n^2+1)3^n}.$$

***Solution*** The series can be rewritten

$$\sum_{n=0}^{\infty} \left(\frac{2}{3}\right)^n \frac{1}{n^2+1} \left(x + \frac{5}{2}\right)^n.$$

The centre of convergence is $x = -5/2$. The radius of convergence, $R$, is given by

$$\frac{1}{R} = L = \lim \left| \frac{\left(\frac{2}{3}\right)^{n+1} \frac{1}{(n+1)^2+1}}{\left(\frac{2}{3}\right)^n \frac{1}{n^2+1}} \right| = \lim \frac{2}{3} \frac{n^2+1}{(n+1)^2+1} = \frac{2}{3}.$$

Thus $R = 3/2$. The series converges absolutely on $(-5/2 - 3/2, -5/2 + 3/2) = (-4, -1)$, and it diverges on $(-\infty, -4)$ and on $(-1, \infty)$. At $x = -1$ the series is $\sum_{n=0}^{\infty} 1/(n^2+1)$; at $x = -4$ it is $\sum_{n=0}^{\infty} (-1)^n/(n^2+1)$. Both series converge (absolutely). The interval of convergence of the given power series is therefore $[-4, -1]$.

**EXAMPLE 2** Determine the radii of convergence of the series

$$\text{(a)} \quad \sum_{n=0}^{\infty} \frac{x^n}{n!} \qquad \text{and} \qquad \text{(b)} \quad \sum_{n=0}^{\infty} n!\,x^n.$$

***Solution***

(a) $L = \left| \lim \frac{1}{(n+1)!} \Big/ \frac{1}{n!} \right| = \lim \frac{n!}{(n+1)!} = \lim \frac{1}{n+1} = 0$. Thus $R = \infty$.
This series converges (absolutely) for all $x$. The sum is $e^x$, as will be shown in Example 1 in the next section.

(b) $L = \left| \lim \frac{(n+1)!}{n!} \right| = \lim(n+1) = \infty$. Thus $R = 0$.
This series converges only at its centre of convergence, $x = 0$.

## Algebraic Operations on Power Series

To simplify the following discussion, we will consider only power series with centre of convergence 0, that is, series of the form

$$\sum_{n=0}^{\infty} a_n x^n = a_0 + a_1 x + a_2 x^2 + a_3 x^3 + \cdots.$$

Any properties we demonstrate for such series extend automatically to power series of the form $\sum_{n=0}^{\infty} a_n (y-c)^n$ via the change of variable $x = y - c$.

First, we observe that series having the same centre of convergence can be added or subtracted on whatever interval is common to their intervals of convergence. The following theorem is a simple consequence of Theorem 7 of Section 9.2 and does not require a proof.

**THEOREM 18**

Let $\sum_{n=0}^{\infty} a_n\, x^n$ and $\sum_{n=0}^{\infty} b_n\, x^n$ be two power series with radii of convergence $R_a$ and $R_b$, respectively, and let $c$ be a constant. Then

(i) $\sum_{n=0}^{\infty} (ca_n)\, x^n$ has radius of convergence $R_a$, and

$$\sum_{n=0}^{\infty} (ca_n)\, x^n = c \sum_{n=0}^{\infty} a_n\, x^n$$

wherever the series on the right converges.

(ii) $\sum_{n=0}^{\infty} (a_n + b_n)\, x^n$ has radius of convergence $R$ at least as large as the smaller of $R_a$ and $R_b$ ($R \ge \min\{R_a, R_b\}$), and

$$\sum_{n=0}^{\infty} (a_n + b_n)\, x^n = \sum_{n=0}^{\infty} a_n\, x^n + \sum_{n=0}^{\infty} b_n\, x^n$$

wherever both series on the right converge.

The situation regarding multiplication and division of power series is more complicated. We will mention only the results and will not attempt any proofs of our assertions. A textbook in mathematical analysis will provide more details.

Long multiplication of the form

$$\begin{aligned}(a_0 + a_1 x + a_2 x^2 + \cdots)&(b_0 + b_1 x + b_2 x^2 + \cdots)\\ &= a_0 b_0 + (a_0 b_1 + a_1 b_0)x + (a_0 b_2 + a_1 b_1 + a_2 b_0)x^2 + \cdots\end{aligned}$$

leads us to conjecture the formula

$$\left(\sum_{n=0}^{\infty} a_n x^n\right)\left(\sum_{n=0}^{\infty} b_n x^n\right) = \sum_{n=0}^{\infty} c_n x^n,$$

where

$$c_n = a_0 b_n + a_1 b_{n-1} + \cdots + a_n b_0 = \sum_{j=0}^{n} a_j b_{n-j}.$$

The series $\sum_{n=0}^{\infty} c_n x^n$ is called the **Cauchy product** of the series $\sum_{n=0}^{\infty} a_n x^n$ and $\sum_{n=0}^{\infty} b_n x^n$. Like the sum, the Cauchy product also has radius of convergence at least equal to the lesser of those of the factor series.

**EXAMPLE 3** Since

$$\frac{1}{1-x} = 1 + x + x^2 + x^3 + \cdots = \sum_{n=0}^{\infty} x^n$$

holds for $-1 < x < 1$, we can determine a power series representation for $1/(1-x)^2$ by taking the Cauchy product of this series with itself. Since $a_n = b_n = 1$ for $n = 0, 1, 2, \ldots$, we have

$$c_n = \sum_{j=0}^{n} 1 = n + 1 \qquad \text{and}$$

$$\frac{1}{(1-x)^2} = 1 + 2x + 3x^2 + 4x^3 + \cdots = \sum_{n=0}^{\infty} (n+1)x^n,$$

which must also hold for $-1 < x < 1$. The same series can be obtained by direct long multiplication of the series:

$$\begin{array}{rccccccccc}
 & 1 & + & x & + & x^2 & + & x^3 & + & \cdots \\
\times & 1 & + & x & + & x^2 & + & x^3 & + & \cdots \\
\hline
 & 1 & + & x & + & x^2 & + & x^3 & + & \cdots \\
 & & & x & + & x^2 & + & x^3 & + & \cdots \\
 & & & & & x^2 & + & x^3 & + & \cdots \\
 & & & & & & & x^3 & + & \cdots \\
 & & & & & & & & & \cdots \\
\hline
 & 1 & + & 2x & + & 3x^2 & + & 4x^3 & + & \cdots
\end{array}$$

Long division can also be performed on power series, but there is no simple rule for determining the coefficients of the quotient series. The radius of convergence of the quotient series is not less than the least of the three numbers $R_1$, $R_2$, and $R_3$, where $R_1$ and $R_2$ are the radii of convergence of the numerator and denominator series and $R_3$ is the distance from the centre of convergence to the nearest *complex number* where the denominator series has sum equal to 0. To illustrate this point, observe that 1 and $1 - x$ are both power series with infinite radii of convergence:

$$\begin{aligned}
1 &= 1 + 0x + 0x^2 + 0x^3 + \cdots && \text{for all } x, \\
1 - x &= 1 - \phantom{0}x + 0x^2 + 0x^3 + \cdots && \text{for all } x.
\end{aligned}$$

Their quotient, $1/(1-x)$, however, only has radius of convergence 1, the distance from the centre of convergence $x = 0$ to the point $x = 1$ where the denominator vanishes:

$$\frac{1}{1-x} = 1 + x + x^2 + x^3 + \cdots \qquad \text{for} \quad |x| < 1.$$

## Differentiation and Integration of Power Series

If a power series has a positive radius of convergence, it can be differentiated or integrated term by term. The resulting series will converge to the appropriate derivative or integral of the sum of the original series everywhere except possibly at the endpoints of the interval of convergence of the original series. This very important fact ensures that, for purposes of calculation, power series behave just like polynomials, the easiest functions to differentiate and integrate. We formalize the differentiation and integration properties of power series in the following theorem.

**THEOREM 19**

**Term-by-term differentiation and integration of power series**

If the series $\sum_{n=0}^{\infty} a_n x^n$ converges to the sum $f(x)$ on an interval $(-R, R)$, where $R > 0$, that is,

$$f(x) = \sum_{n=0}^{\infty} a_n x^n = a_0 + a_1 x + a_2 x^2 + a_3 x^3 + \cdots, \qquad (-R < x < R),$$

then $f$ is differentiable on $(-R, R)$ and

$$f'(x) = \sum_{n=1}^{\infty} n a_n x^{n-1} = a_1 + 2a_2 x + 3a_3 x^2 + \cdots, \qquad (-R < x < R).$$

Also, $f$ is integrable over any closed subinterval of $(-R, R)$, and if $|x| < R$, then

$$\int_0^x f(t)\,dt = \sum_{n=0}^{\infty} \frac{a_n}{n+1} x^{n+1} = a_0 x + \frac{a_1}{2} x^2 + \frac{a_2}{3} x^3 + \cdots.$$

While understanding the statement of this theorem is very important for what follows, understanding the proof is not. Feel free to skip the proof and go on to the applications.

***PROOF*** Let $x$ satisfy $-R < x < R$ and choose $H > 0$ such that $|x| + H < R$. By Theorem 17 we then have[1]

$$\sum_{n=1}^{\infty} |a_n|(|x| + H)^n = K < \infty.$$

The Binomial Theorem (see Section 9.9) shows that if $n \ge 1$, then

$$(x+h)^n = x^n + nx^{n-1}h + \sum_{k=2}^{n} \binom{n}{k} x^{n-k} h^k.$$

Therefore, if $|h| \le H$ we have

$$\begin{aligned}
|(x+h)^n - x^n - nx^{n-1}h| &= \left| \sum_{k=2}^{n} \binom{n}{k} x^{n-k} h^k \right| \\
&\le \sum_{k=2}^{n} \binom{n}{k} |x|^{n-k} \frac{|h|^k}{H^k} H^k \\
&\le \frac{|h|^2}{H^2} \sum_{k=0}^{n} \binom{n}{k} |x|^{n-k} H^k \\
&= \frac{|h|^2}{H^2} (|x| + H)^n.
\end{aligned}$$

Also,

$$|nx^{n-1}| = \frac{n|x|^{n-1}H}{H} \le \frac{1}{H}(|x| + H)^n.$$

Thus,

$$\sum_{n=1}^{\infty} |na_n x^{n-1}| \le \frac{1}{H} \sum_{n=1}^{\infty} |a_n|(|x| + H)^n = \frac{K}{H} < \infty,$$

[1] This proof is due to R. Výborný, *American Mathematical Monthly*, April 1987.

so the series $\sum_{n=1}^{\infty} na_n x^{n-1}$ converges (absolutely) to $g(x)$, say. Now

$$\begin{aligned}\left|\frac{f(x+h)-f(x)}{h} - g(x)\right| &= \left|\sum_{n=1}^{\infty} \frac{a_n(x+h)^n - a_n x^n - na_n x^{n-1}h}{h}\right| \\ &\le \frac{1}{|h|}\sum_{n=1}^{\infty} |a_n||(x+h)^n - x^n - nx^{n-1}h| \\ &\le \frac{|h|}{H^2}\sum_{n=1}^{\infty} |a_n|\big(|x|+H\big)^n \le \frac{K|h|}{H^2}.\end{aligned}$$

Letting $h$ approach zero, we obtain $|f'(x) - g(x)| \le 0$, so $f'(x) = g(x)$, as required.

Now observe that since $|a_n/(n+1)| \le |a_n|$, the series

$$h(x) = \sum_{n=0}^{\infty} \frac{a_n}{n+1} x^{n+1}$$

converges (absolutely) at least on the interval $(-R, R)$. Using the differentiation result proved above, we obtain

$$h'(x) = \sum_{n=0}^{\infty} a_n x^n = f(x).$$

Since $h(0) = 0$, we have

$$\int_0^x f(t)\, dt = \int_0^x h'(t)\, dt = h(t)\Big|_0^x = h(x),$$

as required.

---

Together, these results imply that the termwise differentiated or integrated series have the same radius of convergence as the given series. In fact, as the following examples illustrate, the interval of convergence of the differentiated series is the same as that of the original series except for the *possible* loss of one or both endpoints if the original series converges at endpoints of its interval of convergence. Similarly, the integrated series will converge everywhere on the interval of convergence of the original series and possibly at one or both endpoints of that interval, even if the original series does not converge at the endpoints.

Being differentiable on $(-R, R)$, where $R$ is the radius of convergence, the sum $f(x)$ of a power series is necessarily continuous on that open interval. If the series happens to converge at either or both of the endpoints $-R$ and $R$, then $f$ is also continuous (on one side) up to these endpoints. This result is stated formally in the following theorem. We will not prove it here; the interested reader is referred to textbooks on mathematical analysis for a proof.

**THEOREM 20** **Abel's Theorem**

The sum of a power series is a continuous function everywhere on the interval of convergence of the series. In particular, if $\sum_{n=0}^{\infty} a_n R^n$ converges for some $R > 0$, then

$$\lim_{x\to R-} \sum_{n=0}^{\infty} a_n x^n = \sum_{n=0}^{\infty} a_n R^n,$$

and if $\sum_{n=0}^{\infty} a_n(-R)^n$ converges, then

$$\lim_{x\to -R+} \sum_{n=0}^{\infty} a_n x^n = \sum_{n=0}^{\infty} a_n(-R)^n.$$

---

The following examples show how the above theorems are applied to obtain power series representations for functions.

**EXAMPLE 4** Find power series representations for the functions

$$\text{(a)}\quad \frac{1}{(1-x)^2}, \qquad \text{(b)}\quad \frac{1}{(1-x)^3}, \qquad \text{and} \qquad \text{(c)}\quad \ln(1+x)$$

by starting with the geometric series

$$\frac{1}{1-x} = \sum_{n=0}^{\infty} x^n = 1 + x + x^2 + x^3 + \cdots \qquad (-1 < x < 1)$$

and using differentiation, integration, and substitution. Where is each series valid?

### *Solution*

(a) Differentiate the geometric series term by term to obtain

$$\frac{1}{(1-x)^2} = \sum_{n=1}^{\infty} n x^{n-1} = 1 + 2x + 3x^2 + 4x^3 + \cdots \qquad (-1 < x < 1).$$

This is the same result obtained by multiplication of series in Example 3 above.

(b) Differentiate again to get, for $-1 < x < 1$,

$$\frac{2}{(1-x)^3} = \sum_{n=2}^{\infty} n(n-1)\, x^{n-2} = (1 \times 2) + (2 \times 3)x + (3 \times 4)x^2 + \cdots.$$

Now divide by 2:

$$\frac{1}{(1-x)^3} = \sum_{n=2}^{\infty} \frac{n(n-1)}{2} x^{n-2} = 1 + 3x + 6x^2 + 10x^3 + \cdots \qquad (-1 < x < 1).$$

(c) Substitute $-t$ in place of $x$ in the original geometric series:

$$\frac{1}{1+t} = \sum_{n=0}^{\infty} (-1)^n t^n = 1 - t + t^2 - t^3 + t^4 - \cdots \qquad (-1 < t < 1).$$

Integrate from 0 to $x$, where $|x| < 1$, to get

$$\begin{aligned}\ln(1+x) &= \int_0^x \frac{dt}{1+t} = \sum_{n=0}^{\infty} (-1)^n \int_0^x t^n\, dt \\ &= \sum_{n=0}^{\infty} (-1)^n \frac{x^{n+1}}{n+1} = x - \frac{x^2}{2} + \frac{x^3}{3} - \frac{x^4}{4} + \cdots \qquad (-1 < x \le 1).\end{aligned}$$

Note that the latter series converges (conditionally) at the endpoint $x = 1$ as well as on the interval $-1 < x < 1$. Since $\ln(1+x)$ is continuous at $x = 1$, Theorem 20 assures us that the series must converge to that function at $x = 1$ also. In particular, therefore, the alternating harmonic series converges to $\ln 2$:

$$\ln 2 = 1 - \frac{1}{2} + \frac{1}{3} - \frac{1}{4} + \frac{1}{5} - \cdots = \sum_{n=0}^{\infty} \frac{(-1)^n}{n+1}.$$

This would not, however, be a very useful formula for calculating the value of $\ln 2$. (Why not?)

**EXAMPLE 5** Use the geometric series of the previous example to find a power series representation for $\tan^{-1} x$.

***Solution*** Substitute $-t^2$ for $x$ in the geometric series. Since $0 \le t^2 < 1$ whenever $-1 < t < 1$, we obtain

$$\frac{1}{1+t^2} = 1 - t^2 + t^4 - t^6 + t^8 - \cdots \qquad (-1 < t < 1).$$

Now integrate from 0 to $x$, where $|x| < 1$:

$$\begin{aligned}\tan^{-1} x &= \int_0^x \frac{dt}{1+t^2} = \int_0^x (1 - t^2 + t^4 - t^6 + t^8 - \cdots)\,dt \\ &= x - \frac{x^3}{3} + \frac{x^5}{5} - \frac{x^7}{7} + \frac{x^9}{9} - \cdots \\ &= \sum_{n=0}^{\infty} (-1)^n \frac{x^{2n+1}}{2n+1} \qquad (-1 < x < 1).\end{aligned}$$

However, note that the series also converges (conditionally) at $x = -1$ and 1. Since $\tan^{-1}$ is continuous at $\pm 1$, the above series representation for $\tan^{-1} x$ also holds for these values, by Theorem 20. Letting $x = 1$ we get another interesting result:

$$\frac{\pi}{4} = 1 - \frac{1}{3} + \frac{1}{5} - \frac{1}{7} + \frac{1}{9} - \cdots.$$

Again, however, this would not be a good formula with which to calculate a numerical value of $\pi$. (Why not?)

**EXAMPLE 6** Find the sum of the series $\sum_{n=1}^{\infty} \frac{n^2}{2^n}$ by first finding the sum of the power series

$$\sum_{n=1}^{\infty} n^2 x^n = x + 4x^2 + 9x^3 + 16x^4 + \cdots.$$

***Solution*** Observe in Example 4(a) how the process of differentiating the geometric series produces a series with coefficients 1, 2, 3, .... Start with the series obtained for $1/(1-x)^2$ and multiply it by $x$ to obtain

$$\sum_{n=1}^{\infty} n x^n = x + 2x^2 + 3x^3 + 4x^4 + \cdots = \frac{x}{(1-x)^2}.$$

Now differentiate again to get a series with coefficients $1^2$, $2^2$, $3^2$, ...:

$$\sum_{n=1}^{\infty} n^2 x^{n-1} = 1 + 4x + 9x^2 + 16x^3 + \cdots = \frac{d}{dx}\frac{x}{(x-1)^2} = \frac{1+x}{(1-x)^3}.$$

Multiplication by $x$ again gives the desired power series:

$$\sum_{n=1}^{\infty} n^2 x^n = x + 4x^2 + 9x^3 + 16x^4 + \cdots = \frac{x(1+x)}{(1-x)^3}.$$

Differentiation and multiplication by $x$ do not change the radius of convergence, so this series converges to the indicated function for $-1 < x < 1$. Putting $x = 1/2$, we get

$$\sum_{n=1}^{\infty} \frac{n^2}{2^n} = \frac{\frac{1}{2} \times \frac{3}{2}}{\frac{1}{8}} = 6.$$

The following example illustrates how substitution can be used to obtain power series representations of functions with centres of convergence different from 0.

**EXAMPLE 7** Find a series representation of $f(x) = 1/(2+x)$ in powers of $x-1$. What is the interval of convergence of this series?

***Solution*** Let $t = x - 1$ so that $x = t + 1$. We have

$$\begin{aligned}
\frac{1}{2+x} &= \frac{1}{3+t} = \frac{1}{3}\,\frac{1}{1+\dfrac{t}{3}} \\
&= \frac{1}{3}\left(1 - \frac{t}{3} + \frac{t^2}{3^2} - \frac{t^3}{3^3} + \cdots\right) && (-1 < t/3 < 1) \\
&= \sum_{n=0}^{\infty} (-1)^n \frac{t^n}{3^{n+1}} && (-3 < t < 3) \\
&= \sum_{n=0}^{\infty} (-1)^n \frac{(x-1)^n}{3^{n+1}} && (-2 < x < 4).
\end{aligned}$$

Note that the radius of convergence of this series is 3, the distance from the centre of convergence, 1, to the point $-2$ where the denominator is 0. We could have predicted this in advance.

## Maple Calculations

Maple can find the sums of many kinds of series, including absolutely and conditionally convergent numerical series and many power series. Even when Maple can't find the formal sum of a (convergent) series, it can provide a decimal approximation to the precision indicated by the current value of its variable `Digits`, which defaults to 10. Here are some examples.

```
> sum(n^4/2^n, n=1..infinity);
```

$$150$$

```
> sum(1/n^2, n=1..infinity);
```

$$\frac{1}{6}\pi^2$$

```
> sum(exp(-n^2), n=0..infinity);
```

$$\sum_{n=0}^{\infty} e^{(-n^2)}$$

```
> evalf(%);
```

$$1.386\,318\,602$$

```
> f := x -> sum(x^(n-1)/n, n=1..infinity);
```

$$f := x \to \sum_{n=1}^{\infty}\left(\frac{x^{(n-1)}}{n}\right)$$

```
> f(1); f(-1); f(1/2);
```

$$\infty$$

$$\ln(2)$$

$$2\ln(2)$$

## EXERCISES 9.5

Determine the centre, radius, and interval of convergence of each of the power series in Exercises 1–8.

**1.** $\sum_{n=0}^{\infty} \frac{x^{2n}}{\sqrt{n+1}}$

**2.** $\sum_{n=0}^{\infty} 3n\,(x+1)^n$

**3.** $\sum_{n=1}^{\infty} \frac{1}{n}\left(\frac{x+2}{2}\right)^n$

**4.** $\sum_{n=1}^{\infty} \frac{(-1)^n}{n^4 2^{2n}} x^n$

**5.** $\sum_{n=0}^{\infty} n^3 (2x-3)^n$

**6.** $\sum_{n=1}^{\infty} \frac{e^n}{n^3}(4-x)^n$

**7.** $\sum_{n=0}^{\infty} \frac{(1+5^n)}{n!} x^n$

**8.** $\sum_{n=1}^{\infty} \frac{(4x-1)^n}{n^n}$

**9.** Use multiplication of series to find a power series representation of $1/(1-x)^3$ valid in the interval $(-1, 1)$.

**10.** Determine the Cauchy product of the series $1 + x + x^2 + x^3 + \cdots$ and $1 - x + x^2 - x^3 + \cdots$. On what interval and to what function does the product series converge?

**11.** Determine the power series expansion of $1/(1-x)^2$ by formally dividing $1 - 2x + x^2$ into 1.

Starting with the power series representation

$$\frac{1}{1-x} = 1 + x + x^2 + x^3 + \cdots, \qquad (-1 < x < 1),$$

determine power series representations for the functions indicated in Exercises 12–20. On what interval is each representation valid?

**12.** $\frac{1}{2-x}$ in powers of $x$

**13.** $\frac{1}{(2-x)^2}$ in powers of $x$

**14.** $\frac{1}{1+2x}$ in powers of $x$

**15.** $\ln(2-x)$ in powers of $x$

**16.** $\frac{1}{x}$ in powers of $x-1$

**17.** $\frac{1}{x^2}$ in powers of $x+2$

**18.** $\frac{1-x}{1+x}$ in powers of $x$

**19.** $\frac{x^3}{1-2x^2}$ in powers of $x$

**20.** $\ln x$ in powers of $x-4$

Determine the interval of convergence and the sum of each of the series in Exercises 21–26.

**21.** $1 - 4x + 16x^2 - 64x^3 + \cdots = \sum_{n=0}^{\infty} (-1)^n (4x)^n$

**22.** $3 + 4x + 5x^2 + 6x^3 + \cdots = \sum_{n=0}^{\infty} (n+3)x^n$

**23.** $\frac{1}{3} + \frac{x}{4} + \frac{x^2}{5} + \frac{x^3}{6} + \cdots = \sum_{n=0}^{\infty} \frac{x^n}{n+3}$

**24.** $1 \times 3 - 2 \times 4x + 3 \times 5x^2 - 4 \times 6x^3 + \cdots$
$= \sum_{n=0}^{\infty} (-1)^n (n+1)(n+3)\, x^n$

**25.** $2 + 4x^2 + 6x^4 + 8x^6 + 10x^8 + \cdots = \sum_{n=0}^{\infty} 2(n+1)\, x^{2n}$

**26.** $1 - \frac{x^2}{2} + \frac{x^4}{3} - \frac{x^6}{4} + \frac{x^8}{5} - \cdots = \sum_{n=0}^{\infty} \frac{(-1)^n x^{2n}}{n+1}$

Use the technique (or the result) of Example 6 to find the sums of the numerical series in Exercises 27–32.

**27.** $\sum_{n=1}^{\infty} \frac{n}{3^n}$

**28.** $\sum_{n=0}^{\infty} \frac{n+1}{2^n}$

**29.** $\sum_{n=0}^{\infty} \frac{(n+1)^2}{\pi^n}$

**30.** $\sum_{n=1}^{\infty} \frac{(-1)^n n(n+1)}{2^n}$

**31.** $\sum_{n=1}^{\infty} \frac{(-1)^{n-1}}{n 2^n}$

**32.** $\sum_{n=3}^{\infty} \frac{1}{n 2^n}$

## 9.6 Taylor and Maclaurin Series

If a power series $\sum_{n=0}^{\infty} a_n (x-c)^n$ has a positive radius of convergence $R$, then the sum of the series defines a function $f(x)$ on the interval $(c-R, c+R)$. We say that the power series is a **representation** of $f(x)$ on that interval. What relationship exists between the function $f(x)$ and the coefficients $a_0, a_1, a_2, \ldots$ of the power series? The following theorem answers this question.

**THEOREM 21**

Suppose the series

$$f(x) = \sum_{n=0}^{\infty} a_n (x-c)^n = a_0 + a_1(x-c) + a_2(x-c)^2 + a_3(x-c)^3 + \cdots$$

converges to $f(x)$ for $c - R < x < c + R$, where $R > 0$. Then

$$a_k = \frac{f^{(k)}(c)}{k!} \qquad \text{for } k = 0, 1, 2, 3, \ldots.$$

***PROOF*** This proof requires that we differentiate the series for $f(x)$ term by term several times, a process justified by Theorem 19 (suitably reformulated for powers of $x - c$):

$$f'(x) = \sum_{n=1}^{\infty} n a_n (x-c)^{n-1} = a_1 + 2a_2(x-c) + 3a_3(x-c)^2 + \cdots$$

$$f''(x) = \sum_{n=2}^{\infty} n(n-1) a_n (x-c)^{n-2} = 2a_2 + 6a_3(x-c) + 12a_4(x-c)^2 + \cdots$$

$$\vdots$$

$$\begin{aligned} f^{(k)}(x) &= \sum_{n=k}^{\infty} n(n-1)(n-2)\cdots(n-k+1) a_n (x-c)^{n-k} \\ &= k!a_k + \frac{(k+1)!}{1!}a_{k+1}(x-c) + \frac{(k+2)!}{2!}a_{k+2}(x-c)^2 + \cdots. \end{aligned}$$

Each series converges for $c - R < x < c + R$. Setting $x = c$, we obtain $f^{(k)}(c) = k!a_k$, which proves the theorem. ■

Theorem 21 shows that a function $f(x)$ that has a power series representation with centre at $c$ and positive radius of convergence must have derivatives of all orders in an interval around $x = c$, and it can have only one representation as a power series in powers of $x - c$, namely

$$f(x) = \sum_{n=0}^{\infty} \frac{f^{(n)}(c)}{n!}(x-c)^n = f(c) + f'(c)(x-c) + \frac{f''(c)}{2!}(x-c)^2 + \cdots.$$

Such a series is called a Taylor series or, if $c = 0$, a Maclaurin series.

**DEFINITION 8**

**Taylor and Maclaurin series**

If $f(x)$ has derivatives of all orders at $x = c$ (i.e., if $f^{(k)}(c)$ exists for $k = 0, 1, 2, 3, \ldots$), then the series

$$\begin{aligned} &\sum_{k=0}^{\infty} \frac{f^{(k)}(c)}{k!}(x-c)^k \\ &= f(c) + f'(c)(x-c) + \frac{f''(c)}{2!}(x-c)^2 + \frac{f^{(3)}(c)}{3!}(x-c)^3 + \cdots \end{aligned}$$

is called the **Taylor series of $f$ about $c$** (or the **Taylor series of $f$ in powers of $x - c$**). If $c = 0$, the term **Maclaurin series** is usually used in place of Taylor series.

Note that the partial sums of such Taylor (or Maclaurin) series are just the Taylor (or Maclaurin) polynomials studied in Section 4.10.

The Taylor series is a power series as defined in the previous section. Theorem 17 implies that $c$ must be the centre of any interval on which such a series converges, but the definition of Taylor series makes no requirement that the series should converge anywhere except at the point $x = c$ where the series is just $f(c) + 0 + 0 + \cdots$. The series exists provided all the derivatives of $f$ exist at $x = c$; in practice this means that each derivative must exist in an open interval containing $x = c$. (Why?) However, the series may converge nowhere except at $x = c$, and if it does converge elsewhere, it may converge to something other than $f(x)$. (See Exercise 40 at the end of this section for an example where this happens.) If the Taylor series does converge to $f(x)$ in an open interval containing $c$, then we will say that $f$ is analytic at $c$.

DEFINITION 9

**Analytic functions**

A function $f$ is **analytic at $c$** if $f$ has a Taylor series at $c$ and that series converges to $f(x)$ in an open interval containing $c$. If $f$ is analytic at each point of an open interval, then we say it is analytic on that interval.

Most, but not all, of the elementary functions encountered in calculus are analytic wherever they have derivatives of all orders. On the other hand, whenever a power series in powers of $x - c$ converges for all $x$ in an open interval containing $c$, then its sum $f(x)$ is analytic at $c$, and the given series is the Taylor series of $f$ about $c$.

## Maclaurin Series for Some Elementary Functions

Calculating Taylor and Maclaurin series for a function $f$ directly from Definition 8 is practical only when we can find a formula for the $n$th derivative of $f$. Examples of such functions include $(ax+b)^r$, $e^{ax+b}$, $\ln(ax+b)$, $\sin(ax+b)$, $\cos(ax+b)$, and sums of such functions.

**EXAMPLE 1** Find the Taylor series for $e^x$ about $x = c$. Where does the series converge to $e^x$? Where is $e^x$ analytic? What is the Maclaurin series for $e^x$?

*Solution* Since all the derivatives of $f(x) = e^x$ are $e^x$, we have $f^{(n)}(c) = e^c$ for every integer $n \geq 0$. Thus, the Taylor series for $e^x$ about $x = c$ is

$$\sum_{n=0}^{\infty} \frac{e^c}{n!}(x-c)^n = e^c + e^c(x-c) + \frac{e^c}{2!}(x-c)^2 + \frac{e^c}{3!}(x-c)^3 + \cdots.$$

The radius of convergence $R$ of this series is given by

$$\frac{1}{R} = \lim_{n\to\infty}\left|\frac{e^c/(n+1)!}{e^c/n!}\right| = \lim_{n\to\infty}\frac{n!}{(n+1)!} = \lim_{n\to\infty}\frac{1}{n+1} = 0.$$

Thus, the radius of convergence is $R = \infty$ and the series converges for all $x$.

Suppose the sum is $g(x)$:

$$g(x) = e^c + e^c(x-c) + \frac{e^c}{2!}(x-c)^2 + \frac{e^c}{3!}(x-c)^3 + \cdots.$$

By Theorem 19, we have

$$\begin{aligned} g'(x) &= 0 + e^c + \frac{e^c}{2!}2(x-c) + \frac{e^c}{3!}3(x-c)^2 + \cdots \\ &= e^c + e^c(x-c) + \frac{e^c}{2!}(x-c)^2 + \cdots = g(x). \end{aligned}$$

Also, $g(c) = e^c + 0 + 0 + \cdots = e^c$. Since $g(x)$ satisfies the differential equation $g'(x) = g(x)$ of exponential growth, we have $g(x) = Ce^x$. Substituting $x = c$ gives $e^c = g(c) = Ce^c$, so $C = 1$. Thus, the Taylor series for $e^x$ in powers of $x - c$ converges to $e^x$ for every real number $x$:

$$\begin{aligned} e^x &= \sum_{n=0}^{\infty}\frac{e^c}{n!}(x-c)^n \\ &= e^c + e^c(x-c) + \frac{e^c}{2!}(x-c)^2 + \frac{e^c}{3!}(x-c)^3 + \cdots \qquad \text{(for all } x). \end{aligned}$$

In particular, $e^x$ is analytic on the whole real line $\mathbb{R}$. Setting $c = 0$ we obtain the Maclaurin series for $e^x$:

$$e^x = \sum_{n=0}^{\infty} \frac{x^n}{n!} = 1 + x + \frac{x^2}{2!} + \frac{x^3}{3!} + \cdots \qquad \text{(for all } x\text{)}.$$

**EXAMPLE 2** Find the Maclaurin series for (a) $\sin x$ and (b) $\cos x$. Where does each series converge?

***Solution*** Let $f(x) = \sin x$. Then we have $f(0) = 0$ and

$$\begin{aligned}
f'(x) &= \cos x & f'(0) &= 1\\
f''(x) &= -\sin x & f''(0) &= 0\\
f^{(3)}(x) &= -\cos x & f^{(3)}(0) &= -1\\
f^{(4)}(x) &= \sin x & f^{(4)}(0) &= 0\\
f^{(5)}(x) &= \cos x & f^{(5)}(0) &= 1\\
&\vdots & &\vdots
\end{aligned}$$

Thus, the Maclaurin series for $\sin x$ is

$$\begin{aligned}
g(x) &= 0 + x + 0 - \frac{x^3}{3!} + 0 + \frac{x^5}{5!} + 0 - \cdots\\
&= x - \frac{x^3}{3!} + \frac{x^5}{5!} - \frac{x^7}{7!} + \cdots = \sum_{n=0}^{\infty} \frac{(-1)^n}{(2n+1)!} x^{2n+1}.
\end{aligned}$$

We have denoted the sum by $g(x)$ since we don't yet know whether the series converges to $\sin x$. The series does converge for all $x$ by the ratio test:

$$\begin{aligned}
\lim_{n\to\infty} \left| \frac{\dfrac{(-1)^{n+1}}{(2(n+1)+1)!} x^{2(n+1)+1}}{\dfrac{(-1)^n}{(2n+1)!} x^{2n+1}} \right| &= \lim_{n\to\infty} \frac{(2n+1)!}{(2n+3)!} |x|^2\\
&= \lim_{n\to\infty} \frac{|x|^2}{(2n+3)(2n+2)} = 0.
\end{aligned}$$

Now we can differentiate the function $g(x)$ twice to get

$$\begin{aligned}
g'(x) &= 1 - \frac{x^2}{2!} + \frac{x^4}{4!} - \frac{x^6}{6!} + \cdots\\
g''(x) &= -x + \frac{x^3}{3!} - \frac{x^5}{5!} + \frac{x^7}{7!} - \cdots = -g(x).
\end{aligned}$$

Thus, $g(x)$ satisfies the differential equation $g''(x) + g(x) = 0$ of simple harmonic motion. The general solution of this equation, as observed in Section 3.7, is

$$g(x) = A\cos x + B\sin x.$$

Observe, from the series, that $g(0) = 0$ and $g'(0) = 1$. These values determine that $A = 0$ and $B = 1$. Thus, $g(x) = \sin x$ and $g'(x) = \cos x$ for all $x$.

We have therefore demonstrated that

$$\sin x = \sum_{n=0}^{\infty} \frac{(-1)^n}{(2n+1)!} x^{2n+1} = x - \frac{x^3}{3!} + \frac{x^5}{5!} - \frac{x^7}{7!} + \cdots \quad \text{(for all } x\text{)},$$

$$\cos x = \sum_{n=0}^{\infty} \frac{(-1)^n}{(2n)!} x^{2n} = 1 - \frac{x^2}{2!} + \frac{x^4}{4!} - \frac{x^6}{6!} + \cdots \quad \text{(for all } x\text{)}.$$

Theorem 21 shows that we can use any available means to find a power series converging to a given function on an interval, and the series obtained will turn out to be the Taylor series. In Section 9.5 several series were constructed by manipulating a geometric series. These include:

**Some Maclaurin series**

$$\frac{1}{1-x} = \sum_{n=0}^{\infty} x^n = 1 + x + x^2 + x^3 + \cdots \quad (-1 < x < 1)$$

$$\frac{1}{(1-x)^2} = \sum_{n=1}^{\infty} nx^{n-1} = 1 + 2x + 3x^2 + 4x^3 + \cdots \quad (-1 < x < 1)$$

$$\ln(1+x) = \sum_{n=1}^{\infty} \frac{(-1)^{n-1}}{n} x^n = x - \frac{x^2}{2} + \frac{x^3}{3} - \frac{x^4}{4} + \cdots \quad (-1 < x \le 1)$$

$$\tan^{-1} x = \sum_{n=0}^{\infty} \frac{(-1)^n}{2n+1} x^{2n+1} = x - \frac{x^3}{3} + \frac{x^5}{5} - \frac{x^7}{7} + \cdots \quad (-1 \le x \le 1)$$

These series, together with the intervals on which they converge, are frequently used hereafter and should be memorized.

## Other Maclaurin and Taylor Series

Series can be combined in various ways to generate new series. For example, we can find the Maclaurin series for $e^{-x}$ by replacing $x$ with $-x$ in the series for $e^x$:

$$e^{-x} = \sum_{n=0}^{\infty} \frac{(-1)^n}{n!} x^n = 1 - x + \frac{x^2}{2!} - \frac{x^3}{3!} + \cdots \quad \text{(for all } x\text{)}.$$

The series for $e^x$ and $e^{-x}$ can then be subtracted or added and the results divided by 2 to obtain Maclaurin series for the hyperbolic functions $\sinh x$ and $\cosh x$:

$$\sinh x = \frac{e^x - e^{-x}}{2} = \sum_{n=0}^{\infty} \frac{x^{2n+1}}{(2n+1)!} = x + \frac{x^3}{3!} + \frac{x^5}{5!} + \cdots \quad \text{(for all } x\text{)}$$

$$\cosh x = \frac{e^x + e^{-x}}{2} = \sum_{n=0}^{\infty} \frac{x^{2n}}{(2n)!} = 1 + \frac{x^2}{2!} + \frac{x^4}{4!} + \cdots \quad \text{(for all } x\text{)}.$$

***Remark*** Observe the similarity between the series for $\sin x$ and $\sinh x$ and between those for $\cos x$ and $\cosh x$. If we were to allow complex numbers (numbers of the form $z = x + iy$, where $i^2 = -1$ and $x$ and $y$ are real; see Appendix I) as arguments for our functions, and if we were to demonstrate that our operations on series could be extended to series of complex numbers, we would see that $\cos x = \cosh(ix)$ and $\sin x = -i \sinh(ix)$. In fact, $e^{ix} = \cos x + i \sin x$ and $e^{-ix} = \cos x - i \sin x$, so

$$\cos x = \frac{e^{ix} + e^{-ix}}{2}, \quad \text{and} \quad \sin x = \frac{e^{ix} - e^{-ix}}{2i}.$$

Such formulas are encountered in the study of functions of a complex variable (see Appendix II); from the complex point of view the trigonometric and exponential functions are just different manifestations of the same basic function, a complex exponential $e^z = e^{x+iy}$. We content ourselves here with having mentioned the interesting relationships above and invite the reader to verify them formally by calculating with series. (Such formal calculations do not, of course, constitute a proof, since we have not established the various rules covering series of complex numbers.)

**EXAMPLE 3** Obtain Maclaurin series for the following functions:

(a) $e^{-x^2/3}$, (b) $\dfrac{\sin(x^2)}{x}$, (c) $\sin^2 x$.

***Solution***

(a) We substitute $-x^2/3$ for $x$ in the Maclaurin series for $e^x$:

$$\begin{aligned} e^{-x^2/3} &= 1 - \frac{x^2}{3} + \frac{1}{2!}\left(\frac{x^2}{3}\right)^2 - \frac{1}{3!}\left(\frac{x^2}{3}\right)^3 + \cdots \\ &= \sum_{n=0}^{\infty} (-1)^n \frac{1}{3^n n!} x^{2n} \qquad \text{(for all real } x\text{).} \end{aligned}$$

(b) For all $x \neq 0$ we have

$$\begin{aligned} \frac{\sin(x^2)}{x} &= \frac{1}{x}\left(x^2 - \frac{(x^2)^3}{3!} + \frac{(x^2)^5}{5!} - \cdots\right) \\ &= x - \frac{x^5}{3!} + \frac{x^9}{5!} - \cdots = \sum_{n=0}^{\infty} (-1)^n \frac{x^{4n+1}}{(2n+1)!}. \end{aligned}$$

Note that $f(x) = (\sin(x^2))/x$ is not defined at $x = 0$ but does have a limit (namely 0) as $x$ approaches 0. If we define $f(0) = 0$ (the continuous extension of $f(x)$ to $x = 0$), then the series converges to $f(x)$ for all $x$.

(c) We use a trigonometric identity to express $\sin^2 x$ in terms of $\cos 2x$ and then use the Maclaurin series for $\cos x$ with $x$ replaced by $2x$.

$$\begin{aligned} \sin^2 x &= \frac{1 - \cos 2x}{2} = \frac{1}{2} - \frac{1}{2}\left(1 - \frac{(2x)^2}{2!} + \frac{(2x)^4}{4!} - \cdots\right) \\ &= \frac{1}{2}\left(\frac{(2x)^2}{2!} - \frac{(2x)^4}{4!} + \frac{(2x)^6}{6!} - \cdots\right) \\ &= \sum_{n=0}^{\infty} (-1)^n \frac{2^{2n+1}}{(2n+2)!} x^{2n+2} \qquad \text{(for all real } x\text{).} \end{aligned}$$

Taylor series about points other than 0 can often be obtained from known Maclaurin series by a change of variable.

**EXAMPLE 4** Find the Taylor series for $\ln x$ in powers of $x - 2$. Where does the series converge to $\ln x$?

**Solution** Note that if $t = (x-2)/2$, then

$$\ln x = \ln\bigl(2 + (x-2)\bigr) = \ln\left[2\left(1 + \frac{x-2}{2}\right)\right] = \ln 2 + \ln(1+t).$$

We use the known Maclaurin series for $\ln(1+t)$:

$$\begin{aligned}\ln x &= \ln 2 + \ln(1+t)\\ &= \ln 2 + t - \frac{t^2}{2} + \frac{t^3}{3} - \frac{t^4}{4} - \cdots\\ &= \ln 2 + \frac{x-2}{2} - \frac{(x-2)^2}{2\times 2^2} + \frac{(x-2)^3}{3\times 2^3} - \frac{(x-2)^4}{4\times 2^4} + \cdots\\ &= \ln 2 + \sum_{n=1}^{\infty} \frac{(-1)^{n-1}}{n\,2^n}(x-2)^n.\end{aligned}$$

Since the series for $\ln(1+t)$ is valid for $-1 < t \le 1$, this series for $\ln x$ is valid for $-1 < (x-2)/2 \le 1$, that is, for $0 < x \le 4$.

**EXAMPLE 5** Find the Taylor series for $\cos x$ about $\pi/3$. Where is the series valid?

**Solution** We use the addition formula for cosine:

$$\begin{aligned}\cos x &= \cos\left(x - \frac{\pi}{3} + \frac{\pi}{3}\right) = \cos\left(x - \frac{\pi}{3}\right)\cos\frac{\pi}{3} - \sin\left(x - \frac{\pi}{3}\right)\sin\frac{\pi}{3}\\ &= \frac{1}{2}\left[1 - \frac{1}{2!}\left(x - \frac{\pi}{3}\right)^2 + \frac{1}{4!}\left(x - \frac{\pi}{3}\right)^4 - \cdots\right]\\ &\quad - \frac{\sqrt{3}}{2}\left[\left(x - \frac{\pi}{3}\right) - \frac{1}{3!}\left(x - \frac{\pi}{3}\right)^3 + \cdots\right]\\ &= \frac{1}{2} - \frac{\sqrt{3}}{2}\left(x - \frac{\pi}{3}\right) - \frac{1}{2}\frac{1}{2!}\left(x - \frac{\pi}{3}\right)^2 + \frac{\sqrt{3}}{2}\frac{1}{3!}\left(x - \frac{\pi}{3}\right)^3\\ &\quad + \frac{1}{2}\frac{1}{4!}\left(x - \frac{\pi}{3}\right)^4 - \cdots.\end{aligned}$$

This series representation is valid for all $x$. A similar calculation would enable us to expand $\cos x$ or $\sin x$ in powers of $x - c$ for any real $c$; both functions are analytic at every point of the real line.

Sometimes it is quite difficult, if not impossible, to find a formula for the general term of a Maclaurin or Taylor series. In such cases it is usually possible to obtain the first few terms before the calculations get too cumbersome. Had we attempted to solve Example 3(c) by multiplying the series for $\sin x$ by itself we might have found ourselves in this bind. Other examples occur when it is necessary to substitute one series into another or to divide one by another.

**EXAMPLE 6** Obtain the first three nonzero terms of the Maclaurin series for (a) $\tan x$ and (b) $\ln\cos x$.

**Solution**

(a) $\tan x = (\sin x)/(\cos x)$. We can obtain the first three terms of the Maclaurin series for $\tan x$ by long division of the series for $\cos x$ into that for $\sin x$:

$$
\begin{array}{rrrrrrrrr}
 & & & x & + & \frac{x^3}{3} & + & \frac{2}{15}x^5 & + \cdots \\
\cline{4-9}
1 - \frac{x^2}{2} + \frac{x^4}{24} & \Big) & & x & - & \frac{x^3}{6} & + & \frac{x^5}{120} & - \cdots \\
 & & & x & - & \frac{x^3}{2} & + & \frac{x^5}{24} & - \cdots \\
\cline{4-9}
 & & & & & \frac{x^3}{3} & - & \frac{x^5}{30} & + \cdots \\
 & & & & & \frac{x^3}{3} & - & \frac{x^5}{6} & + \cdots \\
\cline{6-9}
 & & & & & & & \frac{2x^5}{15} & - \cdots \\
 & & & & & & & \frac{2x^5}{15} & - \cdots \\
\cline{8-9}
\end{array}
$$

Thus, $\tan x = x + \frac{1}{3}x^3 + \frac{2}{15}x^5 + \cdots$.

We cannot easily find all the terms of the series; only with considerable computational effort can we find many more terms than we have already found. This Maclaurin series for $\tan x$ converges for $|x| < \pi/2$, but we cannot demonstrate this fact by the techniques we have at our disposal now. (It is true because the complex number $z = x + iy$ closest to 0 where the "denominator" of $\tan z$, that is, $\cos z$, is zero, is, in fact, the real value $z = \pi/2$.)

(b)
$$
\begin{aligned}
\ln \cos x &= \ln\left(1 + \left(-\frac{x^2}{2!} + \frac{x^4}{4!} - \frac{x^6}{6!} + \cdots\right)\right) \\
&= \left(-\frac{x^2}{2!} + \frac{x^4}{4!} - \frac{x^6}{6!} + \cdots\right) - \frac{1}{2}\left(-\frac{x^2}{2!} + \frac{x^4}{4!} - \frac{x^6}{6!} + \cdots\right)^2 \\
&\quad + \frac{1}{3}\left(-\frac{x^2}{2!} + \frac{x^4}{4!} - \frac{x^6}{6!} + \cdots\right)^3 - \cdots \\
&= -\frac{x^2}{2} + \frac{x^4}{24} - \frac{x^6}{720} + \cdots - \frac{1}{2}\left(\frac{x^4}{4} - \frac{x^6}{24} + \cdots\right) \\
&\quad + \frac{1}{3}\left(-\frac{x^6}{8} + \cdots\right) - \cdots \\
&= -\frac{x^2}{2} - \frac{x^4}{12} - \frac{x^6}{45} - \cdots.
\end{aligned}
$$

Note that at each stage of the calculation we kept only enough terms to ensure that we could get all the terms with powers up to $x^6$. Being an even function, $\ln \cos x$ has only even powers in its Maclaurin series. Again, we cannot find the general term of this series. We could try to calculate terms by using the formula $a_k = f^{(k)}(0)/k!$ but even this becomes difficult after the first few values of $k$.

Observe that the series for $\tan x$ can also have been derived from that of $\ln \cos x$ because we have $\tan x = -\frac{d}{dx} \ln \cos x$.

## Taylor's Formula Revisited

In the examples above we have used a variety of techniques to obtain Taylor series for functions and verify that functions are analytic. As shown in Section 4.10, Taylor's Theorem provides a means for estimating the size of the error $E_n(x) = f(x) - P_n(x)$

involved when the Taylor polynomial

$$P_n(x) = \sum_{k=0}^{n} \frac{f^{(k)}(c)}{k!}(x-c)^k$$

is used to approximate the value of $f(x)$ for $x \neq c$. Since the Taylor polynomials are partial sums of the Taylor series for $f$ at $c$ (if the latter exists), another technique for verifying the convergence of a Taylor series is to use the formula for $E_n(x)$ provided by Taylor's Theorem to show, at least for an interval of values of $x$ containing $c$, that $\lim_{n\to\infty} E_n(x) = 0$. This implies that $\lim_{n\to\infty} P_n(x) = f(x)$ so that $f$ is indeed the sum of its Taylor series about $c$ on that inverval, and $f$ is analytic at $c$. Here is a somewhat more general version of Taylor's theroem.

**THEOREM 22**

**Taylor's Theorem**

If the $(n+1)$st derivative of $f$ exists on an interval containing $c$ and $x$, and if $P_n(x)$ is the Taylor polynomial of degree $n$ for $f$ about the point $x = c$, then

$$f(x) = P_n(x) + E_n(x) \qquad \textbf{Taylor's Formula}$$

holds, where the error term $E_n(x)$ is given by *either* of the following formulas:

**Lagrange remainder** $\quad E_n(x) = \dfrac{f^{(n+1)}(s)}{(n+1)!}(x-c)^{n+1},$

for some $s$ between $c$ and $x$

**Integral remainder** $\quad E_n(x) = \dfrac{1}{n!}\displaystyle\int_c^x (x-t)^n f^{(n+1)}(t)\,dt.$

Taylor's Theorem with Lagrange remainder was proved in Section 4.10 (Theorem 12) by using the Mean-Value Theorem and induction on $n$. The Integral remainder version is also proved by induction on $n$. See Exercise 42 for hints on how to carry out the proof. We will not make any use of the Integral form of the remainder here.

Our final example in this section reestablishes the Maclaurin series for $e^x$ by finding the limit of the Lagrange remainder as suggested above.

**EXAMPLE 7** Use Taylor's Theorem to find the Maclaurin series for $f(x) = e^x$. Where does the series converge to $f(x)$?

***Solution*** Since $e^x$ is positive and increasing, $e^s \leq e^{|x|}$ for any $s \leq |x|$. Since $f^{(k)}(x) = e^x$ for any $k$ we have, taking $c = 0$ in the Lagrange remainder in Taylor's Formula,

$$\begin{aligned} |E_n(x)| &= \left| \frac{f^{(n+1)}(s)}{(n+1)!} x^{n+1} \right| \qquad \text{for some } s \text{ between 0 and } x \\ &= \frac{e^s}{(n+1)!}|x|^{n+1} \leq e^{|x|} \frac{|x|^{n+1}}{(n+1)!} \to 0 \text{ as } n \to \infty \end{aligned}$$

for any real $x$, as shown in Theorem 3(b) of Section 9.1. Thus, $\lim_{n\to\infty} E_n(x) = 0$. Since the $n$th-order Maclaurin polynomial for $e^x$ is $\sum_{k=0}^{n}(x^k/k!)$,

$$e^x = \lim_{n\to\infty} \left( \sum_{k=0}^{n} \frac{x^k}{k!} + E_n(x) \right) = \sum_{k=0}^{\infty} \frac{x^k}{k!} = 1 + x + \frac{x^2}{2!} + \frac{x^3}{3!} + \cdots,$$

and the series converges to $e^x$ for all real numbers $x$.

## EXERCISES 9.6

Find Maclaurin series representations for the functions in Exercises 1–14. For what values of $x$ is each representation valid?

**1.** $e^{3x+1}$

**2.** $\cos(2x^3)$

**3.** $\sin(x - \pi/4)$

**4.** $\cos(2x - \pi)$

**5.** $x^2 \sin(x/3)$

**6.** $\cos^2(x/2)$

**7.** $\sin x \cos x$

**8.** $\tan^{-1}(5x^2)$

**9.** $\dfrac{1+x^3}{1+x^2}$

**10.** $\ln(2 + x^2)$

**11.** $\ln \dfrac{1+x}{1-x}$

**12.** $(e^{2x^2} - 1)/x^2$

**13.** $\cosh x - \cos x$

**14.** $\sinh x - \sin x$

Find the required Taylor series representations of the functions in Exercises 15–26. Where is each series representation valid?

**15.** $f(x) = e^{-2x}$ about $-1$

**16.** $f(x) = \sin x$ about $\pi/2$

**17.** $f(x) = \cos x$ in powers of $x - \pi$

**18.** $f(x) = \ln x$ in powers of $x - 3$

**19.** $f(x) = \ln(2 + x)$ in powers of $x - 2$

**20.** $f(x) = e^{2x+3}$ in powers of $x + 1$

**21.** $f(x) = \sin x - \cos x$ about $\dfrac{\pi}{4}$

**22.** $f(x) = \cos^2 x$ about $\dfrac{\pi}{8}$

**23.** $f(x) = 1/x^2$ in powers of $x + 2$

**24.** $f(x) = \dfrac{x}{1+x}$ in powers of $x - 1$

**25.** $f(x) = x \ln x$ in powers of $x - 1$

**26.** $f(x) = xe^x$ in powers of $x + 2$

Find the first three nonzero terms in the Maclaurin series for the functions in Exercises 27–30.

**27.** $\sec x$

**28.** $\sec x \tan x$

**29.** $\tan^{-1}(e^x - 1)$

**30.** $e^{\tan^{-1} x} - 1$

**31.** Use the fact that $(\sqrt{1+x})^2 = 1 + x$ to find the first three nonzero terms of the Maclaurin series for $\sqrt{1+x}$.

**32.** Does $\csc x$ have a Maclaurin series? Why? Find the first three nonzero terms of the Taylor series for $\csc x$ about the point $x = \pi/2$.

Find the sums of the series in Exercises 33–36.

**33.** $1 + x^2 + \dfrac{x^4}{2!} + \dfrac{x^6}{3!} + \dfrac{x^8}{4!} + \cdots$

**34.** $x^3 - \dfrac{x^9}{3! \times 4} + \dfrac{x^{15}}{5! \times 16} - \dfrac{x^{21}}{7! \times 64} + \dfrac{x^{27}}{9! \times 256} - \cdots$

**35.** $1 + \dfrac{x^2}{3!} + \dfrac{x^4}{5!} + \dfrac{x^6}{7!} + \dfrac{x^8}{9!} + \cdots$

**36.** $1 + \dfrac{1}{2 \times 2!} + \dfrac{1}{4 \times 3!} + \dfrac{1}{8 \times 4!} + \cdots$

**37.** Let $P(x) = 1 + x + x^2$. Find (a) the Maclaurin series for $P(x)$ and (b) the Taylor series for $P(x)$ about 1.

**38.** Verify by direct calculation that $f(x) = 1/x$ is analytic at $a$ for every $a \neq 0$.

**39.** Verify by direct calculation that $\ln x$ is analytic at $a$ for every $a > 0$.

**40.** Review Exercise 41 of Section 4.5. It shows that the function

$$f(x) = \begin{cases} e^{-1/x^2} & \text{if } x \neq 0 \\ 0 & \text{if } x = 0 \end{cases}$$

has derivatives of all orders at every point of the real line, and $f^{(k)}(0) = 0$ for every positive integer $k$. What is the Maclaurin series for $f(x)$? What is the interval of convergence of this Maclaurin series? On what interval does the series converge to $f(x)$? Is $f$ analytic at 0?

**41.** By direct multiplication of the Maclaurin series for $e^x$ and $e^y$ show that $e^x e^y = e^{x+y}$.

**42.** **(Taylor's Formula with integral remainder)** Verify that if $f^{(n+1)}$ exists on an interval containing $c$ and $x$, and if $P_n(x)$ is the $n$th-order Taylor polynomial for $f$ about $c$, then $f(x) = P_n(x) + E_n(x)$, where

$$E_n(x) = \frac{1}{n!} \int_c^x (x - t)^n f^{(n+1)}(t)\, dt.$$

Proceed as follows:

(a) First observe that the case $n = 0$ is just the Fundamental Theorem of Calculus:

$$f(x) = f(c) + \int_c^x f'(t)\, dt.$$

Now integrate by parts in this formula, taking $U = f'(t)$ and $dV = dt$. Contrary to our usual policy of not including a constant of integration in $V$, here write $V = -(x - t)$ rather than just $V = t$. Observe that the result of the integration by parts is the case $n = 1$ of the formula.

(b) Use induction argument (and integration by parts again) to show that if the formula is valid for $n = k$, then it is also valid for $n = k + 1$.

**43.** Use Taylor's formula with integral remainder to reprove that the Maclaurin series for $\ln(1 + x)$ converges to $\ln(1 + x)$ for $-1 < x \leq 1$.

**44.** **(Stirling's Formula)** The limit

$$\lim_{n\to\infty} \frac{n!}{\sqrt{2\pi}\, n^{n+1/2} e^{-n}} = 1$$

says that the *relative error* in the approximation

$$n! \approx \sqrt{2\pi}\, n^{n+1/2} e^{-n}$$

approaches zero as $n$ increases. That is, $n!$ grows at a rate comparable to $\sqrt{2\pi}\, n^{n+1/2} e^{-n}$. This result, known as Stirling's Formula, is often very useful in applied mathematics and statistics. Prove it by carrying out the following steps.

(a) Use the identity $\ln(n!) = \sum_{j=1}^{n} \ln j$ and the increasing nature of ln to show that if $n \geq 1$,

$$\int_0^n \ln x\, dx < \ln(n!) < \int_1^{n+1} \ln x\, dx$$

and hence that

$$n \ln n - n < \ln(n!) < (n+1)\ln(n+1) - n.$$

(b) If $c_n = \ln(n!) - \left(n + \frac{1}{2}\right)\ln n + n$, show that

$$\begin{aligned} c_n - c_{n+1} &= \left(n + \frac{1}{2}\right) \ln \frac{n+1}{n} - 1 \\ &= \left(n + \frac{1}{2}\right) \ln \frac{1 + 1/(2n+1)}{1 - 1/(2n+1)} - 1. \end{aligned}$$

(c) Use the Maclaurin series for $\ln \dfrac{1+t}{1-t}$ (see Exercise 11) to show that

$$\begin{aligned} 0 < c_n - c_{n+1} &< \frac{1}{3}\left(\frac{1}{(2n+1)^2} + \frac{1}{(2n+1)^4} + \cdots\right) \\ &= \frac{1}{12}\left(\frac{1}{n} - \frac{1}{n+1}\right), \end{aligned}$$

and therefore that $\{c_n\}$ is decreasing and $\left\{c_n - \frac{1}{12n}\right\}$ is increasing. Hence conclude that $\lim_{n\to\infty} c_n = c$ exists, and that

$$\lim_{n\to\infty} \frac{n!}{n^{n+1/2}e^{-n}} = \lim_{n\to\infty} e^{c_n} = e^c.$$

(d) Now use the Wallis Product from Exercise 38 of Section 6.1 to show that

$$\lim_{n\to\infty} \frac{(2^n n!)^2}{(2n)!\sqrt{2n}} = \sqrt{\frac{\pi}{2}},$$

and hence deduce that $e^c = \sqrt{2\pi}$, which completes the proof.

## 9.7 Applications of Taylor and Maclaurin Series

### Approximating the Values of Functions

We saw in Section 4.10 how Taylor and Maclaurin polynomials (the partial sums of Taylor and Maclaurin series) can be used as polynomial approximations to more complicated functions. In Example 5 of that section we used the Lagrange remainder in Taylor's Formula to determine how many terms of the Maclaurin series for $e^x$ are needed to calculate $e^1 = e$ correct to 3 decimal places. For comparison, we obtained the same result in Example 7 in Section 9.3 by using a geometric series to bound the tail of the series for $e$.

The following example shows how the error bound associated with the alternating series test (see Theorem 15 in Section 9.4) can also be used for such approximations. When the terms $a_n$ of a series (i) alternate in sign, (ii) decrease steadily in size, and (iii) approach zero as $n \to \infty$, then the error involved in using a partial sum of the series as an approximation to the sum of the series has the same sign as, and is no greater in absolute value than, the first omitted term.

**EXAMPLE 1** Find $\cos 43°$ with error less than 1/10,000.

***Solution*** We give two alternative solutions:

**METHOD I.** We can use the Maclaurin series for cosine:

$$\cos 43° = \cos \frac{43\pi}{180} = 1 - \frac{1}{2!}\left(\frac{43\pi}{180}\right)^2 + \frac{1}{4!}\left(\frac{43\pi}{180}\right)^4 - \cdots.$$

Now $43\pi/180 \approx 0.750\,49\cdots < 1$, so the series above must satisfy the conditions (i)–(iii) mentioned above. If we truncate the series after the $n$th term

$$(-1)^{n-1}\frac{1}{(2n-2)!}\left(\frac{43\pi}{180}\right)^{2n-2},$$

then the error $E$ will be bounded by the size of the first omitted term:

$$|E| \le \frac{1}{(2n)!}\left(\frac{43\pi}{180}\right)^{2n} < \frac{1}{(2n)!}.$$

The error will not exceed $1/10{,}000$ if $(2n)! > 10{,}000$, so $n = 4$ will do $(8! = 40{,}320)$.

$$\cos 43^\circ \approx 1 - \frac{1}{2!}\left(\frac{43\pi}{180}\right)^2 + \frac{1}{4!}\left(\frac{43\pi}{180}\right)^4 - \frac{1}{6!}\left(\frac{43\pi}{180}\right)^6 \approx 0.731\,35\cdots$$

**METHOD II.** Since $43^\circ$ is close to $45^\circ = \pi/4$ rad, we can do a bit better by using the Taylor series about $\pi/4$ instead of the Maclaurin series:

$$\begin{aligned}
\cos 43^\circ &= \cos\left(\frac{\pi}{4} - \frac{\pi}{90}\right) \\
&= \cos\frac{\pi}{4}\cos\frac{\pi}{90} + \sin\frac{\pi}{4}\sin\frac{\pi}{90} \\
&= \frac{1}{\sqrt{2}}\left[\left(1 - \frac{1}{2!}\left(\frac{\pi}{90}\right)^2 + \frac{1}{4!}\left(\frac{\pi}{90}\right)^4 - \cdots\right)\right. \\
&\qquad \left. + \left(\frac{\pi}{90} - \frac{1}{3!}\left(\frac{\pi}{90}\right)^3 + \cdots\right)\right].
\end{aligned}$$

Since

$$\frac{1}{4!}\left(\frac{\pi}{90}\right)^4 < \frac{1}{3!}\left(\frac{\pi}{90}\right)^3 < \frac{1}{20{,}000},$$

we need only the first two terms of the first series and the first term of the second series:

$$\cos 43^\circ \approx \frac{1}{\sqrt{2}}\left(1 + \frac{\pi}{90} - \frac{1}{2}\left(\frac{\pi}{90}\right)^2\right) \approx 0.731\,358\cdots.$$

(In fact, $\cos 43^\circ = 0.731\,353\,7\cdots$.)

When finding approximate values of functions, it is best, whenever possible, to use a power series about a point as close as possible to the point where the approximation is desired.

## Functions Defined by Integrals

Many functions that can be expressed as simple combinations of elementary functions cannot be antidifferentiated by elementary techniques; their antiderivatives are not simple combinations of elementary functions. We can, however, often find the Taylor series for the antiderivatives of such functions and hence approximate their definite integrals.

**EXAMPLE 2** Find the Maclaurin series for

$$E(x) = \int_0^x e^{-t^2}\,dt,$$

and use it to evaluate $E(1)$ correct to 3 decimal places.

***Solution*** The Maclaurin series for $E(x)$ is given by

$$\begin{aligned}
E(x) &= \int_0^x \left(1 - t^2 + \frac{t^4}{2!} - \frac{t^6}{3!} + \frac{t^8}{4!} - \cdots\right) dt \\
&= \left(t - \frac{t^3}{3} + \frac{t^5}{5 \times 2!} - \frac{t^7}{7 \times 3!} + \frac{t^9}{9 \times 4!} - \cdots\right)\Bigg|_0^x \\
&= x - \frac{x^3}{3} + \frac{x^5}{5 \times 2!} - \frac{x^7}{7 \times 3!} + \frac{x^9}{9 \times 4!} - \cdots = \sum_{n=0}^{\infty}(-1)^n \frac{x^{2n+1}}{(2n+1)n!},
\end{aligned}$$

and is valid for all $x$ because the series for $e^{-t^2}$ is valid for all $t$. Therefore,

$$E(1) = 1 - \frac{1}{3} + \frac{1}{5 \times 2!} - \frac{1}{7 \times 3!} + \cdots$$
$$\approx 1 - \frac{1}{3} + \frac{1}{5 \times 2!} - \frac{1}{7 \times 3!} + \cdots + \frac{(-1)^{n-1}}{(2n-1)(n-1)!}.$$

We stopped with the $n$th term. Again, the alternating series test assures us that the error in this approximation does not exceed the first omitted term, so it will be less than 0.0005, provided $(2n+1)n! > 2{,}000$. Since $13 \times 6! = 9{,}360$, $n = 6$ will do. Thus,

$$E(1) \approx 1 - \frac{1}{3} + \frac{1}{10} - \frac{1}{42} + \frac{1}{216} - \frac{1}{1{,}320} \approx 0.747,$$

rounded to 3 decimal places.

## Indeterminate Forms

Examples 9 and 10 of Section 4.10 showed how Maclaurin polynomials could be used for evaluating the limits of indeterminate forms. Here are two more examples, this time using the series directly and keeping enough terms to allow cancellation of the [0/0] factors.

**EXAMPLE 3** Evaluate (a) $\lim_{x\to 0} \dfrac{x - \sin x}{x^3}$ and (b) $\lim_{x\to 0} \dfrac{(e^{2x}-1)\ln(1+x^3)}{(1-\cos 3x)^2}$.

***Solution***

(a) $$\lim_{x\to 0} \frac{x - \sin x}{x^3} \qquad \left[\frac{0}{0}\right]$$

$$= \lim_{x\to 0} \frac{x - \left(x - \dfrac{x^3}{3!} + \dfrac{x^5}{5!} - \cdots\right)}{x^3}$$

$$= \lim_{x\to 0} \frac{\dfrac{x^3}{3!} - \dfrac{x^5}{5!} + \cdots}{x^3}$$

$$= \lim_{x\to 0} \left(\frac{1}{3!} - \frac{x^2}{5!} + \cdots\right) = \frac{1}{3!} = \frac{1}{6}.$$

(b) $$\lim_{x\to 0} \frac{(e^{2x}-1)\ln(1+x^3)}{(1-\cos 3x)^2} \qquad \left[\frac{0}{0}\right]$$

$$= \lim_{x\to 0} \frac{\left(1 + (2x) + \dfrac{(2x)^2}{2!} + \dfrac{(2x)^3}{3!} + \cdots - 1\right)\left(x^3 - \dfrac{x^6}{2} + \cdots\right)}{\left(1 - \left(1 - \dfrac{(3x)^2}{2!} + \dfrac{(3x)^4}{4!} - \cdots\right)\right)^2}$$

$$= \lim_{x\to 0} \frac{2x^4 + 2x^5 + \cdots}{\left(\dfrac{9}{2}x^2 - \dfrac{3^4}{4!}x^4 + \cdots\right)^2}$$

$$= \lim_{x\to 0} \frac{2 + 2x + \cdots}{\left(\dfrac{9}{2} - \dfrac{3^4}{4!}x^2 + \cdots\right)^2} = \frac{2}{\left(\dfrac{9}{2}\right)^2} = \frac{8}{81}.$$

You can check that the second of these examples is much more difficult if attempted using l'Hôpital's Rule.

## EXERCISES 9.7

1. Estimate the error if the Maclaurin polynomial of degree 5 for $\sin x$ is used to approximate $\sin(0.2)$.

2. Estimate the error if the Taylor polynomial of degree 4 for $\ln x$ in powers of $x - 2$ is used to approximate $\ln(1.95)$.

Use Maclaurin or Taylor series to calculate the function values indicated in Exercises 3–14, with error less than $5 \times 10^{-5}$ in absolute value.

3. $e^{0.2}$
4. $1/e$
5. $e^{1.2}$
6. $\sin(0.1)$
7. $\cos 5°$
8. $\ln(6/5)$
9. $\ln(0.9)$
10. $\sin 80°$
11. $\cos 65°$
12. $\tan^{-1} 0.2$
13. $\cosh(1)$
14. $\ln(3/2)$

Find Maclaurin series for the functions in Exercises 15–19.

15. $I(x) = \int_0^x \frac{\sin t}{t}\, dt$
16. $J(x) = \int_0^x \frac{e^t - 1}{t}\, dt$
17. $K(x) = \int_1^{1+x} \frac{\ln t}{t-1}\, dt$
18. $L(x) = \int_0^x \cos(t^2)\, dt$
19. $M(x) = \int_0^x \frac{\tan^{-1} t^2}{t^2}\, dt$

20. Find $L(0.5)$ correct to 3 decimal places, with $L$ defined as in Exercise 16.

21. Find $I(1)$ correct to 3 decimal places, with $I$ defined as in Exercise 13.

Evaluate the limits in Exercises 22–27.

22. $\lim_{x\to 0} \frac{\sin(x^2)}{\sinh x}$
23. $\lim_{x\to 0} \frac{1-\cos(x^2)}{(1-\cos x)^2}$
24. $\lim_{x\to 0} \frac{(e^x - 1 - x)^2}{x^2 - \ln(1+x^2)}$
25. $\lim_{x\to 0} \frac{2\sin 3x - 3\sin 2x}{5x - \tan^{-1} 5x}$
26. $\lim_{x\to 0} \frac{\sin(\sin x) - x}{x(\cos(\sin x) - 1)}$
27. $\lim_{x\to 0} \frac{\sinh x - \sin x}{\cosh x - \cos x}$

# 9.8 The Binomial Theorem and Binomial Series

**EXAMPLE 1** Use Taylor's Formula to prove the Binomial Theorem: if $n$ is a positive integer, then

$$(a+x)^n = a^n + n\,a^{n-1}x + \frac{n(n-1)}{2!}a^{n-2}x^2 + \cdots + n\,ax^{n-1} + x^n$$
$$= \sum_{k=0}^{n} \binom{n}{k} a^{n-k}x^k,$$

where $\binom{n}{k} = \frac{n!}{(n-k)!k!}$.

***Solution*** Let $f(x) = (a+x)^n$. Then

$$f'(x) = n(a+x)^{n-1} = \frac{n!}{(n-1)!}(a+x)^{n-1}$$
$$f''(x) = \frac{n!}{(n-1)!}(n-1)(a+x)^{n-2} = \frac{n!}{(n-2)!}(a+x)^{n-2}$$
$$\vdots$$
$$f^{(k)}(x) = \frac{n!}{(n-k)!}(a+x)^{n-k} \qquad (0 \le k \le n).$$

In particular, $f^{(n)}(x) = \frac{n!}{0!}(a+x)^{n-n} = n!$, a constant, and so

$$f^{(k)}(x) = 0 \qquad \text{for all } x, \text{ if } k > n.$$

For $0 \le k \le n$ we have $f^{(k)}(0) = \dfrac{n!}{(n-k)!}\, a^{n-k}$. Thus, by Taylor's Theorem with Lagrange remainder, for some $s$ between $a$ and $x$,

$$\begin{aligned}(a+x)^n = f(x) &= \sum_{k=0}^{n} \frac{f^{(k)}(0)}{k!} x^k + \frac{f^{(n+1)}(s)}{(n+1)!} x^{n+1} \\ &= \sum_{k=0}^{n} \frac{n!}{(n-k)!k!} a^{n-k} x^k + 0 = \sum_{k=0}^{n} \binom{n}{k} a^{n-k} x^k.\end{aligned}$$

This is, in fact, the Maclaurin *series* for $(a+x)^n$, not just the Maclaurin polynomial of degree $n$. Since all higher-degree terms are zero, the series has only finitely many nonzero terms and so converges for all $x$.

---

**Remark** If $f(x) = (a+x)^r$, where $a > 0$ and $r$ is any real number, then calculations similar to those above show that the Maclaurin polynomial of degree $n$ for $f$ is

$$P_n(x) = a^r + \sum_{k=1}^{n} \frac{r(r-1)(r-2)\cdots(r-k+1)}{k!} a^{r-k} x^k.$$

However, if $r$ is not a positive integer, then there will be no positive integer $n$ for which the remainder $E_n(x) = f(x) - P_n(x)$ vanishes identically, and the corresponding Maclaurin series will not be a polynomial.

## The Binomial Series

To simplify the discussion of the function $(a+x)^r$ when $r$ is not a positive integer, we take $a = 1$ and consider the function $(1+x)^r$. Results for the general case follow via the identity

$$(a+x)^r = a^r \left(1 + \frac{x}{a}\right)^r,$$

valid for any $a > 0$.

If $r$ is any real number and $x > -1$, then the $k$th derivative of $(1+x)^r$ is

$$r(r-1)(r-2)\cdots(r-k+1)\,(1+x)^{r-k}, \qquad (k = 1, 2, \ldots).$$

Thus, the Maclaurin series for $(1+x)^r$ is

$$1 + \sum_{k=1}^{\infty} \frac{r(r-1)(r-2)\cdots(r-k+1)}{k!} x^k,$$

which is called the **binomial series**. The following theorem shows that the binomial series does, in fact, converge to $(1+x)^r$ if $|x| < 1$. We could accomplish this by writing Taylor's Formula for $(1+x)^r$ with $c = 0$ and showing that the remainder $E_n(x) \to 0$ as $n \to \infty$. (We would need to use the integral form of the remainder to prove this for all $|x| < 1$.) However, we will use an easier method, similar to the one used for the exponential and trigonometric functions in Section 9.6.

**THEOREM 23** **The binomial series**

If $|x| < 1$, then

$$\begin{aligned}(1+x)^r &= 1 + rx + \frac{r(r-1)}{2!} x^2 + \frac{r(r-1)(r-2)}{3!} x^3 + \cdots \\ &= 1 + \sum_{n=1}^{\infty} \frac{r(r-1)(r-2)\cdots(r-n+1)}{n!} x^n \quad (-1 < x < 1).\end{aligned}$$

***PROOF*** If $|x| < 1$, then the series

$$f(x) = 1 + \sum_{n=1}^{\infty} \frac{r(r-1)(r-2)\cdots(r-n+1)}{n!} x^n$$

converges by the ratio test, since

$$\begin{aligned}
\rho &= \lim_{n\to\infty} \left| \frac{\dfrac{r(r-1)(r-2)\cdots(r-n+1)(r-n)}{(n+1)!} x^{n+1}}{\dfrac{r(r-1)(r-2)\cdots(r-n+1)}{n!} x^n} \right| \\
&= \lim_{n\to\infty} \left| \frac{r-n}{n+1} \right| |x| = |x| < 1.
\end{aligned}$$

Note that $f(0) = 1$. We need to show that $f(x) = (1+x)^r$ for $|x| < 1$.

By Theorem 19, we can differentiate the series for $f(x)$ termwise on $|x| < 1$ to obtain

$$\begin{aligned}
f'(x) &= \sum_{n=1}^{\infty} \frac{r(r-1)(r-2)\cdots(r-n+1)}{(n-1)!} x^{n-1} \\
&= \sum_{n=0}^{\infty} \frac{r(r-1)(r-2)\cdots(r-n)}{n!} x^n.
\end{aligned}$$

We have replaced $n$ with $n+1$ to get the second version of the sum from the first version. Adding the second version to $x$ times the first version, we get

$$\begin{aligned}
(1+x)f'(x) &= \sum_{n=0}^{\infty} \frac{r(r-1)(r-2)\cdots(r-n)}{n!} x^n \\
&\quad + \sum_{n=1}^{\infty} \frac{r(r-1)(r-2)\cdots(r-n+1)}{(n-1)!} x^n \\
&= r + \sum_{n=1}^{\infty} \frac{r(r-1)(r-2)\cdots(r-n+1)}{n!} x^n \big[(r-n)+n\big] \\
&= r\,f(x).
\end{aligned}$$

The differential equation $(1+x)f'(x) = rf(x)$ implies that

$$\frac{d}{dx}\frac{f(x)}{(1+x)^r} = \frac{(1+x)^r f'(x) - r(1+x)^{r-1} f(x)}{(1+x)^{2r}} = 0$$

for all $x$ satisfying $|x| < 1$. Thus, $f(x)/(1+x)^r$ is constant on that interval, and since $f(0) = 1$, the constant must be 1. Thus $f(x) = (1+x)^r$.

***Remark*** For some values of $r$ the binomial series may converge at the endpoints $x = 1$ or $x = -1$. As observed above, if $r$ is a positive integer, the series has only finitely many nonzero terms, and so converges for all $x$.

**EXAMPLE 2** Find the Maclaurin series for $\dfrac{1}{\sqrt{1+x}}$.

***Solution*** Here $r = -(1/2)$:

$$\begin{aligned}\frac{1}{\sqrt{1+x}} &= (1+x)^{-1/2} \\ &= 1 - \frac{1}{2}x + \frac{1}{2!}\left(-\frac{1}{2}\right)\left(-\frac{3}{2}\right)x^2 + \frac{1}{3!}\left(-\frac{1}{2}\right)\left(-\frac{3}{2}\right)\left(-\frac{5}{2}\right)x^3 + \cdots \\ &= 1 - \frac{1}{2}x + \frac{1\times 3}{2^2 2!}x^2 - \frac{1\times 3\times 5}{2^3 3!}x^3 + \cdots \\ &= 1 + \sum_{n=1}^{\infty}(-1)^n \frac{1\times 3\times 5\times\cdots\times(2n-1)}{2^n n!}x^n.\end{aligned}$$

This series converges for $-1 < x \le 1$. (Use the alternating series test to get the endpoint $x = 1$.)

**EXAMPLE 3** Find the Maclaurin series for $\sin^{-1} x$.

***Solution*** Replace $x$ with $-t^2$ in the series obtained in the previous example to get

$$\frac{1}{\sqrt{1-t^2}} = 1 + \sum_{n=1}^{\infty}\frac{1\times 3\times 5\times\cdots\times(2n-1)}{2^n n!}t^{2n} \qquad (-1 < t < 1).$$

Now integrate $t$ from 0 to $x$:

$$\begin{aligned}\sin^{-1} x &= \int_0^x \frac{dt}{\sqrt{1-t^2}} = \int_0^x \left(1 + \sum_{n=1}^{\infty}\frac{1\times 3\times 5\times\cdots\times(2n-1)}{2^n n!}t^{2n}\right)dt \\ &= x + \sum_{n=1}^{\infty}\frac{1\times 3\times 5\times\cdots\times(2n-1)}{2^n n!(2n+1)}x^{2n+1} \\ &= x + \frac{x^3}{6} + \frac{3}{40}x^5 + \cdots \qquad (-1 < x < 1).\end{aligned}$$

## EXERCISES 9.8

Find Maclaurin series representations for the functions in Exercises 1–6. Use the binomial series to calculate the answers.

**1.** $\sqrt{1+x}$

**2.** $x\sqrt{1-x}$

**3.** $\sqrt{4+x}$

**4.** $\dfrac{1}{\sqrt{4+x^2}}$

**5.** $(1-x)^{-2}$

**6.** $(1+x)^{-3}$

**7.** $\cos^{-1} x$

**8.** $\sinh^{-1} x$

**9.** **(Binomial coefficients)** Show that the binomial coefficients $\binom{n}{k} = \dfrac{n!}{k!\,(n-k)!}$ satisfy

(i) $\binom{n}{0} = \binom{n}{n} = 1$ for every $n$, and

(ii) if $0 \le k \le n$, then $\binom{n}{k-1} + \binom{n}{k} = \binom{n+1}{k}$.

It follows that, for fixed $n \ge 1$, the binomial coefficients

$$\binom{n}{0}, \binom{n}{1}, \binom{n}{2}, \ldots, \binom{n}{n}$$

are the elements of the $n$th row of **Pascal's triangle** below, where each element with value greater than 1 is the sum of the two diagonally above it.

$$\begin{array}{ccccccccccc} &&&&& 1 &&&&& \\ &&&& 1 && 1 &&&& \\ &&& 1 && 2 && 1 &&& \\ && 1 && 3 && 3 && 1 && \\ & 1 && 4 && 6 && 4 && 1 & \\ 1 && 5 && 10 && 10 && 5 && 1 \\ . &&&&&&&&&& . \\ . &&&&&&&&&& . \end{array}$$

**10. (An inductive proof of the Binomial Theorem)** Use mathematical induction and the results of Exercise 9 to prove the Binomial Theorem:

$$(a+b)^n = \sum_{k=0}^{n} \binom{n}{k} a^{n-k} b^k$$
$$= a^n + na^{n-1}b + \binom{n}{2} a^{n-2}b^2 + \binom{n}{3} a^{n-3}b^3 + \cdots + b^n.$$

**11. (The Leibniz Rule)** Use mathematical induction, the Product Rule, and Exercise 9 to verify the Leibniz Rule for the $n$th derivative of a product of two functions:

$$(fg)^{(n)} = \sum_{k=0}^{n} \binom{n}{k} f^{(n-k)} g^{(k)}$$
$$= f^{(n)}g + nf^{(n-1)}g' + \binom{n}{2} f^{(n-2)}g''$$
$$+ \binom{n}{3} f^{(n-3)}g^{(3)} + \cdots + fg^{(n)}.$$

## 9.9 Fourier Series

As we have seen, power series representations of functions make it possible to approximate those functions as closely as we want in intervals near a particular point of interest by using partial sums of the series, that is, polynomials. However, in many important applications of mathematics, the functions involved are required to be periodic. For example, much of electrical engineering is concerned with the analysis and manipulation of *waveforms*, which are periodic functions of time. Polynomials are not periodic functions, and for this reason power series are not well suited to representing such functions.

Much more appropriate for the representations of periodic functions over extended intervals are certain infinite series of periodic functions called Fourier series.

### Periodic Functions

Recall that a function $f$ defined on the real line is **periodic** with period $T$ if

$$f(t+T) = f(t) \quad \text{for all real } t. \qquad (*)$$

This implies that $f(t+mT) = f(t)$ for any integer $m$, so that if $T$ is a period of $f$, then so is any multiple $mT$ of $T$. The smallest positive number $T$ for which $(*)$ holds is called the **fundamental period**, or simply **the period** of $f$.

The entire graph of a function with period $T$ can be obtained by shifting the part of the graph in any half-open interval of length $T$ (e.g., the interval $[0, T)$) to the left or right by integer multiples of the period $T$. Figure 9.6 shows the graph of a function of period 2.

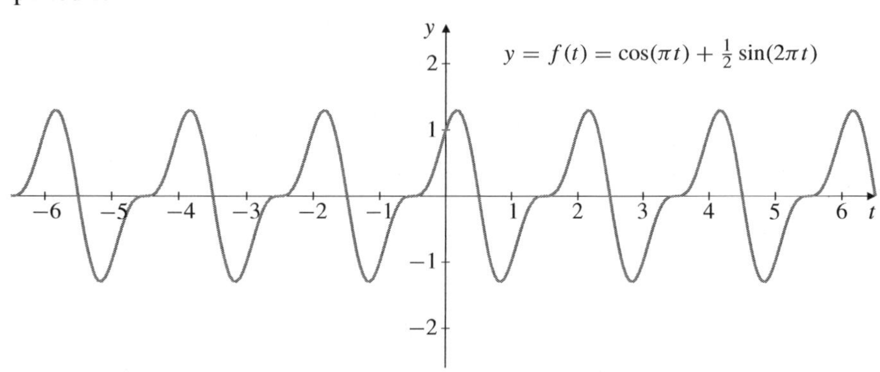


Figure 9.6 This function has period 2. Observe how the graph repeats the part in the interval $[0, 2)$ over and over to the left and right

**EXAMPLE 1** The functions $g(t) = \cos(\pi t)$ and $h(t) = \sin(\pi t)$ are both periodic with period 2:

$$g(t+2) = \cos(\pi t + 2\pi) = \cos(\pi t) = g(t).$$

The function $k(t) = \sin(2\pi t)$ also has period 2, but this is not its fundamental period. The fundamental period is 1:

$$k(t+1) = \sin(2\pi t + 2\pi) = \sin(2\pi t) = k(t).$$

The sum $f(t) = g(t) + \frac{1}{2}k(t) = \cos(\pi t) + \frac{1}{2}\sin(2\pi t)$, graphed in Figure 9.6, has period 2, the least common multiple of the periods of its two terms.

---

**EXAMPLE 2** For any positive integer $n$, the functions

$$f_n(t) = \cos(n\omega t) \qquad \text{and} \qquad g_n(t) = \sin(n\omega t)$$

both have fundamental period $T = 2\pi/(n\omega)$. The collection of all such functions corresponding to all positive integers $n$ have common period $T = 2\pi/\omega$, the fundamental period of $f_1$ and $g_1$. $T$ is an integer multiple of the fundamental periods of all the functions $f_n$ and $g_n$. The subject of Fourier series is concerned with expressing general functions with period $T$ as series whose terms are real multiples of these functions.

---

## Fourier Series

It can be shown (but we won't do it here) that if $f(t)$ is periodic with fundamental period $T$, is continuous, and has a piecewise continuous derivative on the real line, then $f(t)$ is everywhere the sum of a series of the form

$$f(t) = \frac{a_0}{2} + \sum_{n=1}^{\infty}\big(a_n\cos(n\omega t) + b_n\sin(n\omega t)\big), \qquad (**)$$

called the **Fourier series** of $f$, where $\omega = 2\pi/T$ and the sequences $\{a_n\}_{n=0}^{\infty}$ and $\{b_n\}_{n=1}^{\infty}$ are the **Fourier coefficients** of $f$. Determining the values of these coefficients for a given such function $f$ is made possible by the following identities, valid for integers $m$ and $n$, which are easily proved by using the addition formulas for sine and cosine. (See Exercises 49–51 in Section 5.6.)

$$\int_0^T \cos(n\omega t)\,dt = \begin{cases} 0 & \text{if } n \neq 0 \\ T & \text{if } n = 0 \end{cases}$$

$$\int_0^T \sin(n\omega t)\,dt = 0$$

$$\int_0^T \cos(m\omega t)\cos(n\omega t)\,dt = \begin{cases} 0 & \text{if } m \neq n \\ T/2 & \text{if } m = n \end{cases}$$

$$\int_0^T \sin(m\omega t)\sin(n\omega t)\,dt = \begin{cases} 0 & \text{if } m \neq n \\ T/2 & \text{if } m = n \end{cases}$$

$$\int_0^T \cos(m\omega t)\sin(n\omega t)\,dt = 0.$$

If we multiply equation $(**)$ by $\cos(m\omega t)$ (or by $\sin(m\omega t)$) and integrate the resulting equation over $[0, T]$ term by term, all the terms on the right except the one involving $a_m$ (or $b_m$) will be 0. (The term-by-term integration requires justification, but we won't try to do that here either.) The integration results in

$$\int_0^T f(t)\cos(m\omega t)\,dt = \frac{1}{2}Ta_m$$

$$\int_0^T f(t)\sin(m\omega t)\,dt = \frac{1}{2}Tb_m.$$

(Note that the first of these formulas is even valid for $m = 0$ because we chose to call the constant term in the Fourier series $a_0/2$ instead of $a_0$.) Since the integrands are all periodic with period $T$, the integrals can be taken over any interval of length $T$; it is often convenient to use $[-T/2, T/2]$ instead of $[0, T]$. The Fourier coefficients of $f$ are therefore given by

$$a_n = \frac{2}{T}\int_{-T/2}^{T/2} f(t)\cos(n\omega t)\,dt \quad (n = 0,\ 1,\ 2,\ \ldots)$$
$$b_n = \frac{2}{T}\int_{-T/2}^{T/2} f(t)\sin(n\omega t)\,dt \quad (n = 1,\ 2,\ 3,\ \ldots),$$

where $\omega = 2\pi/T$.

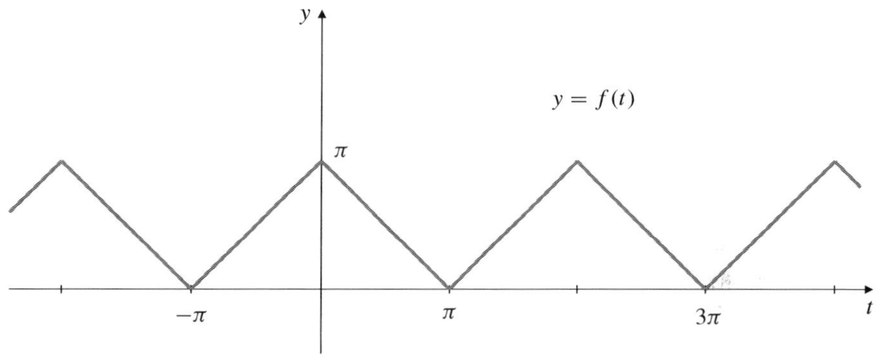


**Figure 9.7** A sawtooth function of period $2\pi$

**EXAMPLE 3** Find the Fourier series of the sawtooth function $f(t)$ of period $2\pi$ whose values in the interval $[-\pi, \pi]$ are given by $f(t) = \pi - |t|$. (See Figure 9.7.)

***Solution*** Here $T = 2\pi$ and $\omega = 2\pi/(2\pi) = 1$. Since $f(t)$ is an even function, $f(t)\sin(nt)$ is odd, so all the Fourier sine coefficients $b_n$ are zero:

$$b_n = \frac{2}{2\pi}\int_{-\pi}^{\pi} f(t)\sin(nt)\,dt = 0.$$

Also, $f(t)\cos(nt)$ is an even function, so

$$\begin{aligned} a_n &= \frac{2}{2\pi}\int_{-\pi}^{\pi} f(t)\cos(nt)\,dt = \frac{4}{2\pi}\int_{0}^{\pi} f(t)\cos(nt)\,dt \\ &= \frac{2}{\pi}\int_0^{\pi}(\pi - t)\cos(nt)\,dt \\ &= \begin{cases} \pi & \text{if } n = 0 \\ 0 & \text{if } n \neq 0 \text{ and } n \text{ is even} \\ 4/(\pi n^2) & \text{if } n \text{ is odd.} \end{cases} \end{aligned}$$

Since odd positive integers $n$ are of the form $n = 2k - 1$, where $k$ is a positive integer, the Fourier series of $f$ is given by

$$f(t) = \frac{\pi}{2} + \sum_{k=1}^{\infty} \frac{4}{\pi(2k-1)^2}\cos\big((2k-1)t\big).$$

## Convergence of Fourier Series

The partial sums of a Fourier series are called Fourier polynomials because they can be expressed as polynomials in $\sin(\omega t)$ and $\cos(\omega t)$, although we will not actually try to write them that way. The Fourier polynomial of order $m$ of the periodic function $f$ having period $T$ is

$$f_m(t) = \frac{a_0}{2} + \sum_{n=1}^{m}\big(a_n\cos(n\omega t) + b_n\sin(n\omega t)\big),$$

where $\omega = 2\pi/T$ and the coefficients $a_n$ $(0 \le n \le m)$ and $b_n$ $(1 \le n \le m)$ are given by the integral formulas developed earlier.

**EXAMPLE 4** The Fourier polynomial of order 3 of the sawtooth function of Example 3 is

$$f_3(t) = \frac{\pi}{2} + \frac{4}{\pi}\cos t + \frac{4}{9\pi}\cos(3t).$$

The graph of this function is shown in Figure 9.8. Observe that it appears to be a reasonable approximation to the graph of $f$ in Figure 9.7, but, being a finite sum of differentiable functions, $f_3(t)$ is itself differentiable everywhere, even at the integer multiples of $\pi$ where $f$ is not differentiable.

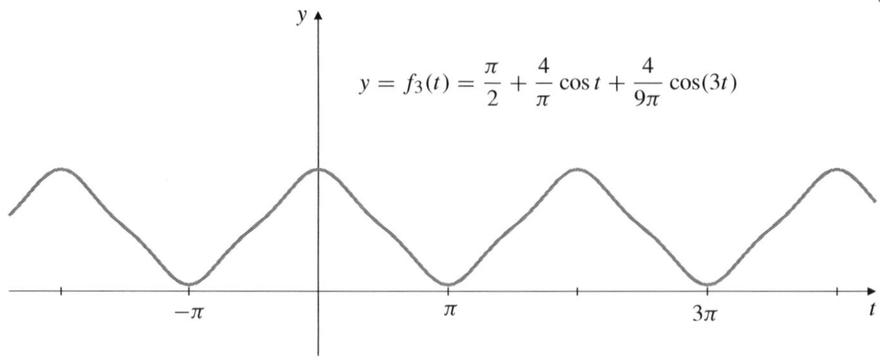


**Figure 9.8** The Fourier polynomial approximation $f_3(t)$ to the sawtooth function of Example 3

As noted earlier, the Fourier series of a function $f(t)$ that is periodic, continuous, and has a piecewise continuous derivative on the real line converges to $f(t)$ at each real number $t$. However, the Fourier coefficients (and hence the Fourier series) can be calculated (by the formulas given above) for periodic functions with piecewise continuous derivative even if the functions are not themselves continuous, but only piecewise continuous.

Recall that $f(t)$ is piecewise continuous on the interval $[a, b]$ if there exists a partition $\{a = x_0 < x_1 < x_2 < \cdots < x_k = b\}$ of $[a, b]$ and functions $F_1, F_2, \ldots, F_k$, such that

(i) $F_i$ is continuous on $[x_{i-1}, x_i]$, and

(ii) $f(t) = F_i(t)$ on $(x_{i-1}, x_i)$.

The integral of such a function $f$ is the sum of integrals of the functions $F_i$:

$$\int_a^b f(t)\,dt = \sum_{i=1}^{k} \int_{x_{i-1}}^{x_i} F_i(t)\,dt.$$

Since $f(t)\cos(n\omega t)$ and $f(t)\sin(n\omega t)$ are piecewise continuous if $f$ is, the Fourier coefficients of a piecewise continuous, periodic function can be calculated by the same formulas given for a continuous periodic function. The question of where and to what the Fourier series converges in this case is answered by the following theorem, proved in textbooks on Fourier analysis.

**THEOREM 24**

The Fourier series of a piecewise continuous, periodic function $f$ with piecewise continuous derivative converges to that function at every point $t$ where $f$ is continuous. Moreover, if $f$ is discontinuous at $t = c$, then $f$ has different, but finite, left and right limits at $c$:

$$\lim_{t\to c-} f(t) = f(c-), \qquad \text{and} \qquad \lim_{t\to c+} f(t) = f(c+).$$

The Fourier series of $f$ converges at $t = c$ to the average of these left and right limits:

$$\frac{a_0}{2} + \sum_{n=1}^{\infty}\big(a_n\cos(n\omega c) + b_n\sin(n\omega c)\big) = \frac{f(c-) + f(c+)}{2},$$

where $\omega = 2\pi/T$.

**EXAMPLE 5** Calculate the Fourier series for the periodic function $f$ with period 2 satisfying

$$f(t) = \begin{cases} -1 & \text{if } -1 < x < 0 \\ 1 & \text{if } 0 < x < 1. \end{cases}$$

Where does $f$ fail to be continuous? To what does the Fourier series of $f$ converge at these points?

***Solution*** Here $T = 2$ and $\omega = 2\pi/2 = \pi$. Since $f$ is an odd function, its cosine coefficients are all zero:

$$a_n = \int_{-1}^{1} f(t)\cos(n\pi t)\,dt = 0. \qquad \text{(The integrand is odd.)}$$

The same symmetry implies that

$$\begin{aligned} b_n &= \int_{-1}^{1} f(t)\sin(n\pi t)\,dt \\ &= 2\int_{0}^{1} \sin(n\pi t)\,dt = -\frac{2\cos(n\pi t)}{n\pi}\bigg|_0^1 \\ &= -\frac{2}{n\pi}\big((-1)^n - 1\big) = \begin{cases} 4/(n\pi) & \text{if } n \text{ is odd} \\ 0 & \text{if } n \text{ is even.} \end{cases} \end{aligned}$$

Odd integers $n$ are of the form $n = 2k - 1$ for $k = 1, 2, 3, \ldots$. Therefore, the Fourier series of $f$ is

$$\begin{aligned} &\frac{4}{\pi}\sum_{k=1}^{\infty} \frac{1}{2k-1}\sin\big((2k-1)\pi t\big) \\ &= \frac{4}{\pi}\left(\sin(\pi t) + \frac{1}{3}\sin(3\pi t) + \frac{1}{5}\sin(5\pi t) + \cdots\right). \end{aligned}$$

Note that $f$ is continuous except at the points where $t$ is an integer. At each of these points $f$ jumps from $-1$ to 1 or from 1 to $-1$, so the average of the left and right limits of $f$ at these points is 0. Observe that the sum of the Fourier series is 0 at integer values of $t$, in accordance with Theorem 24. See Figure 9.9.

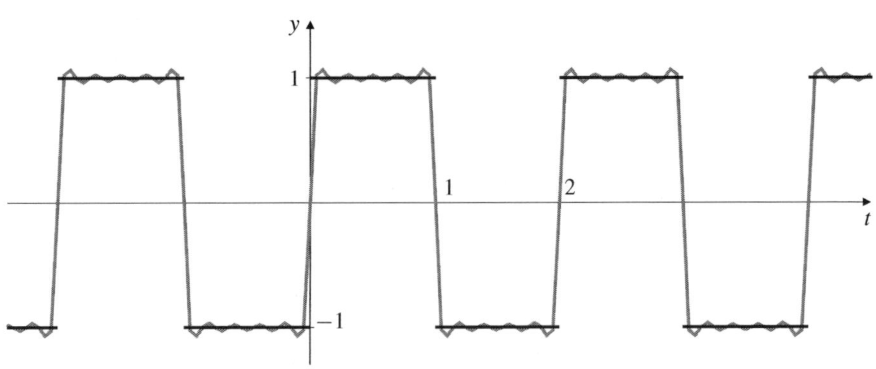


Figure 9.9 The piecewise continuous function $f$ (black) of Example 5 and its Fourier polynomial $f_{15}$ (colour)

$$f_{15}(t) = \sum_{k=1}^{8} \frac{4\sin\big((2k-1)\pi t\big)}{(2k-1)\pi}$$

## Fourier Cosine and Sine Series

As observed in Example 3 and Example 5, even functions have no sine terms in their Fourier series, and odd functions have no cosine terms (including the constant term $a_0/2$). It is often necessary in applications to find a Fourier series representation of a given function defined on a finite interval $[0, a]$ having either no sine terms (a **Fourier cosine series**) or no cosine terms (a **Fourier sine series**). This is accomplished by extending the domain of $f$ to $[-a, 0)$ so as to make $f$ either even or odd on $[-a, a]$,

$$\begin{aligned} f(-t) &= f(t) \text{ if } -a \le t < 0 \text{ for the even extension} \\ f(-t) &= -f(t) \text{ if } -a \le t < 0 \text{ for the odd extension,} \end{aligned}$$

and then calculating its Fourier series considering the extended $f$ to have period $2a$. (If we want the odd extension, we may have to redefine $f(0)$ to be 0.)

**EXAMPLE 6** Find the Fourier cosine series of $g(t) = \pi - t$ defined on $[0, \pi]$.

***Solution*** The even extension of $g(t)$ to $[-\pi, \pi]$ is the function $f$ of Example 3. Thus, the Fourier cosine series of $g$ is

$$\frac{\pi}{2} + \sum_{k=1}^{\infty} \frac{4}{\pi(2k-1)^2} \cos\big((2k-1)t\big).$$

**EXAMPLE 7** Find the Fourier sine series of $h(t) = 1$ defined on $[0, 1]$.

***Solution*** If we redefine $h(0) = 0$, then the odd extension of $h$ to $[-1, 1]$ coincides with the function $f(t)$ of Example 5 except that the latter function is undefined at $t = 0$. The Fourier sine series of $h$ is the series obtained in Example 5, namely,

$$\frac{4}{\pi} \sum_{k=1}^{\infty} \frac{1}{2k-1} \sin\big((2k-1)\pi t\big).$$

***Remark*** Fourier cosine and sine series are treated from a different perspective in Section 13.4.

## EXERCISES 9.9

In Exercises 1–4, what is the fundamental period of the given function?

**1.** $f(t) = \sin(3t)$

**2.** $g(t) = \cos(3 + \pi t)$

**3.** $h(t) = \cos^2 t$

**4.** $k(t) = \sin(2t) + \cos(3t)$

In Exercises 5–8, find the Fourier series of the given function.

**5.** $f(t) = t, -\pi < t \le \pi$, $f$ has period $2\pi$.

**6.** $f(t) = \begin{cases} 0 & \text{if } 0 \le t < 1 \\ 1 & \text{if } 1 \le t < 2, \end{cases}$ $f$ has period 2.

**7.** $f(t) = \begin{cases} 0 & \text{if } -1 \le t < 0 \\ t & \text{if } 0 \le t < 1, \end{cases}$ $f$ has period 2.

**8.** $f(t) = \begin{cases} t & \text{if } 0 \le t < 1 \\ 1 & \text{if } 1 \le t < 2 \\ 3-t & \text{if } 2 \le t < 3, \end{cases}$ $f$ has period 3.

**9.** What is the Fourier cosine series of the function $h(t)$ of Example 7?

**10.** Calculate the Fourier sine series of the function $g(t)$ of Example 6.

**11.** Find the Fourier sine series of $f(t) = t$ on $[0, 1]$.

**12.** Find the Fourier cosine series of $f(t) = t$ on $[0, 1]$.

**13.** Use the result of Example 3 to evaluate

$$\sum_{n=1}^{\infty} \frac{1}{(2n-1)^2} = 1 + \frac{1}{3^2} + \frac{1}{5^2} + \cdots.$$

**14.** Verify that if $f$ is an even function of period $T$, then the Fourier sine coefficients $b_n$ of $f$ are all zero and the Fourier cosine coefficients $a_n$ of $f$ are given by

$$a_n = \frac{4}{T}\int_0^{T/2} f(t)\cos(n\omega t)\,dt, \qquad n = 0, 1, 2, \ldots,$$

where $\omega = 2\pi/T$. State and verify the corresponding result for odd functions $f$.

# CHAPTER REVIEW

## Key Ideas

- **What does it mean to say that the sequence $\{a_n\}$**
  - ◇ is bounded above?
  - ◇ is ultimately positive?
  - ◇ is alternating?
  - ◇ is increasing?
  - ◇ converges?
  - ◇ diverges to infinity?
- **What does it mean to say that the series $\sum_{n=1}^{\infty} a_n$**
  - ◇ converges?
  - ◇ diverges?
  - ◇ is geometric?
  - ◇ is telescoping?
  - ◇ is a $p$-series?
  - ◇ is positive?
  - ◇ converges absolutely?
  - ◇ converges conditionally?
- **State the following convergence tests for series.**
  - ◇ the integral test
  - ◇ the comparison test
  - ◇ the limit comparison test
  - ◇ the ratio test
  - ◇ the alternating series test
- **How can you find bounds for the tail of a series?**
- **What is a bound for the tail of an alternating series?**
- **What do the following terms and phrases mean?**
  - ◇ a power series
  - ◇ interval of convergence
  - ◇ radius of convergence
  - ◇ centre of convergence
  - ◇ a Taylor series
  - ◇ a Maclaurin series
  - ◇ a Taylor polynomial
  - ◇ a binomial series
  - ◇ an analytic function
- **Where is the sum of a power series differentiable?**
- **Where does the integral of a power series converge?**
- **Where is the sum of a power series continuous?**
- **State Taylor's Theorem with Lagrange remainder.**
- **State Taylor's Theorem with integral remainder.**
- **What is the binomial theorem?**
- **What is a Fourier series?**
- **What is a Fourier cosine series? a Fourier sine series?**

## Review Exercises

In Exercises 1–4, determine whether the given sequence converges, and find its limit if it does converge.

**1.** $\left\{\dfrac{(-1)^n e^n}{n!}\right\}$ **2.** $\left\{\dfrac{n^{100} + 2^n\pi}{2^n}\right\}$

**3.** $\left\{\dfrac{\ln n}{\tan^{-1} n}\right\}$ **4.** $\left\{\dfrac{(-1)^n n^2}{\pi n(n-\pi)}\right\}$

**5.** Let $a_1 > \sqrt{2}$, and let

$$a_{n+1} = \frac{a_n}{2} + \frac{1}{a_n} \quad \text{for} \quad n = 1, 2, 3, \ldots$$

Show that $\{a_n\}$ is decreasing and that $a_n > \sqrt{2}$ for $n \ge 1$. Why must $\{a_n\}$ converge? Find $\lim_{n\to\infty} a_n$.

**6.** Find the limit of the sequence $\{\ln\ln(n+1) - \ln\ln n\}$.

Evaluate the sums of the series in Exercises 7–10.

**7.** $\displaystyle\sum_{n=1}^{\infty} 2^{-(n-5)/2}$ **8.** $\displaystyle\sum_{n=0}^{\infty} \frac{4^{n-1}}{(\pi-1)^{2n}}$

**9.** $\displaystyle\sum_{n=1}^{\infty} \frac{1}{n^2 - \frac{1}{4}}$ **10.** $\displaystyle\sum_{n=1}^{\infty} \frac{1}{n^2 - \frac{9}{4}}$

Determine whether the series in Exercises 11–16 converge or diverge. Give reasons for your answers.

**11.** $\displaystyle\sum_{n=1}^{\infty} \frac{n-1}{n^3}$ **12.** $\displaystyle\sum_{n=1}^{\infty} \frac{n+2^n}{1+3^n}$

**13.** $\displaystyle\sum_{n=1}^{\infty} \frac{n}{(1+n)(1+n\sqrt{n})}$ **14.** $\displaystyle\sum_{n=1}^{\infty} \frac{n^2}{(1+2^n)(1+n\sqrt{n})}$

**15.** $\displaystyle\sum_{n=1}^{\infty} \frac{3^{2n+1}}{n!}$ **16.** $\displaystyle\sum_{n=1}^{\infty} \frac{n!}{(n+2)!+1}$

Do the series in Exercises 17–20 converge absolutely, converge conditionally, or diverge?

**17.** $\displaystyle\sum_{n=1}^{\infty} \frac{(-1)^{n-1}}{1+n^3}$ **18.** $\displaystyle\sum_{n=1}^{\infty} \frac{(-1)^n}{2^n - n}$

**19.** $\displaystyle\sum_{n=10}^{\infty} \frac{(-1)^{n-1}}{\ln\ln n}$ **20.** $\displaystyle\sum_{n=1}^{\infty} \frac{n^2\cos(n\pi)}{1+n^3}$

For what values of $x$ do the series in Exercises 21–22 converge absolutely? converge conditionally? diverge?

**21.** $\displaystyle\sum_{n=1}^{\infty} \frac{(x-2)^n}{3^n\sqrt{n}}$ **22.** $\displaystyle\sum_{n=1}^{\infty} \frac{(5-2x)^n}{n}$

Determine the sums of the series in Exercises 23–24 to within 0.001.

**23.** $\displaystyle\sum_{n=1}^{\infty} \frac{1}{n^3}$ **24.** $\displaystyle\sum_{n=1}^{\infty} \frac{1}{4+n^2}$

In Exercises 25–32, find Maclaurin series for the given functions. State where each series converges to the function.

**25.** $\dfrac{1}{3-x}$ **26.** $\dfrac{x}{3-x^2}$

**27.** $\ln(e+x^2)$ **28.** $\dfrac{1-e^{-2x}}{x}$

**29.** $x\cos^2 x$ **30.** $\sin(x+(\pi/3))$

**31.** $(8+x)^{-1/3}$ **32.** $(1+x)^{1/3}$

Find Taylor series for the functions in Exercises 33–34 about the indicated points $x=c$.

**33.** $1/x, \quad c=\pi$ **34.** $\sin x+\cos x, \quad c=\pi/4$

Find the Maclaurin polynomial of the indicated degree for the functions in Exercises 35–38.

**35.** $e^{x^2+2x}$, degree 3 **36.** $\sin(1+x)$, degree 3

**37.** $\cos(\sin x)$, degree 4 **38.** $\sqrt{1+\sin x}$, degree 4

**39.** What function has Maclaurin series

$$1-\frac{x}{2!}+\frac{x^2}{4!}-\cdots=\sum_{n=0}^{\infty}\frac{(-1)^n x^n}{(2n)!}?$$

**40.** A function $f(x)$ has Maclaurin series

$$1+x^2+\frac{x^4}{2^2}+\frac{x^6}{3^2}+\cdots=1+\sum_{n=1}^{\infty}\frac{x^{2n}}{n^2}.$$

Find $f^{(k)}(0)$ for all positive integers $k$.

Find the sums of the series in Exercises 41–44.

**41.** $\displaystyle\sum_{n=0}^{\infty}\frac{n+1}{\pi^n}$ **42.** $\displaystyle\sum_{n=0}^{\infty}\frac{n^2}{\pi^n}$

**43.** $\displaystyle\sum_{n=1}^{\infty}\frac{1}{ne^n}$ **44.** $\displaystyle\sum_{n=2}^{\infty}\frac{(-1)^n\pi^{2n-4}}{(2n-1)!}$

**45.** If $S(x)=\displaystyle\int_0^x\sin(t^2)\,dt$, find $\displaystyle\lim_{x\to 0}\frac{x^3-3S(x)}{x^7}$.

**46.** Use series to evaluate $\displaystyle\lim_{x\to 0}\frac{(x-\tan^{-1}x)(e^{2x}-1)}{2x^2-1+\cos(2x)}$.

**47.** How many nonzero terms in the Maclaurin series for $e^{-x^4}$ are needed to evaluate $\int_0^{1/2}e^{-x^4}\,dx$ correct to 5 decimal places? Evaluate the integral to that accuracy.

**48.** Estimate the size of the error if the Taylor polynomial of degree 4 about $x=\pi/2$ for $f(x)=\ln\sin x$ is used to approximate $\ln\sin(1.5)$.

**49.** Find the Fourier sine series for $f(t)=\pi-t$ on $[0,\pi]$.

**50.** Find the Fourier series for $f(t)=\begin{cases}1 & \text{if } -\pi<t\le 0\\ t & \text{if } 0<t\le\pi.\end{cases}$

## Challenging Problems

**1. (A refinement of the ratio test)** Suppose $a_n>0$ and $a_{n+1}/a_n\ge n/(n+1)$ for all $n$. Show that $\sum_{n=1}^{\infty}a_n$ diverges. *Hint:* $a_n\ge K/n$ for some constant $K$.

**2. (Summation by parts)** Let $\{u_n\}$ and $\{v_n\}$ be two sequences, and let $s_n=\sum_{k=1}^{n}v_k$.

(a) Show that $\sum_{k=1}^{n}u_kv_k=u_{n+1}s_n+\sum_{k=1}^{n}(u_k-u_{k+1})s_n$. (*Hint:* Write $v_n=s_n-s_{n-1}$, with $s_0=0$, and rearrange the sum.)

(b) If $\{u_n\}$ is positive, decreasing, and convergent to 0, and if $\{v_n\}$ has bounded partial sums, $|s_n|\le K$ for all $n$, where $K$ is a constant, show that $\sum_{n=1}^{\infty}u_nv_n$ converges. (*Hint:* Show that the series $\sum_{n=1}^{\infty}(u_n-u_{n+1})s_n$ converges by comparing it to the telescoping series $\sum_{n=1}^{\infty}(u_n-u_{n+1})$.)

**3.** Show that $\sum_{n=1}^{\infty}(1/n)\sin(nx)$ converges for every $x$. *Hint:* If $x$ is an integer multiple of $\pi$, all the terms in the series are 0 so there is nothing to prove. Otherwise, $\sin(x/2)\ne 0$. In this case show that

$$\sum_{n=1}^{N}\sin(nx)=\frac{\cos(x/2)-\cos((N+1/2)x)}{2\sin(x/2)}$$

using the identity

$$\sin a\sin b=\frac{\cos(a-b)-\cos(a+b)}{2}$$

to make the sum telescope. Then apply the result of Problem 2(b) with $u_n=1/n$ and $v_n=\sin(nx)$.

**4.** Let $a_1, a_2, a_3, \ldots$ be those positive integers that do not contain the digit 0 in their decimal representations. Thus $a_1=1$, $a_2=2, \ldots, a_9=9, a_{10}=11, \ldots, a_{18}=19, a_{19}=21, \ldots, a_{90}=99, a_{91}=111$, etc. Show that the series $\sum_{n=1}^{\infty}\frac{1}{a_n}$ converges and that the sum is less than 90. (*Hint:* How many of these integers have $m$ digits? Each term $1/a_n$, where $a_n$ has $m$ digits, is less than $10^{-m+1}$.)

**5. (Using an integral to improve convergence)** Recall the error formula for the Midpoint Rule, according to which

$$\int_{k-1/2}^{k+1/2}f(x)\,dx-f(k)=\frac{f''(c)}{24},$$

where $k-(1/2)\le c\le k+(1/2)$.

(a) If $f''(x)$ is a decreasing function of $x$, show that

$$f'(k+\tfrac{3}{2})-f'(k+\tfrac{1}{2})\le f''(c)\le f'(k-\tfrac{1}{2})-f'(k-\tfrac{3}{2}).$$

(b) If (i) $f''(x)$ is a decreasing function of $x$, (ii) $\int_{N+1/2}^{\infty}f(x)\,dx$ converges, and (iii) $f'(x)\to 0$ as $x\to\infty$, show that

$$\frac{f'(N-\frac{1}{2})}{24}\le\sum_{n=N+1}^{\infty}f(n)-\int_{N+1/2}^{\infty}f(x)\,dx\le\frac{f'(N+\frac{3}{2})}{24}.$$

(c) Use the result of part (b) to approximate $\sum_{n=1}^{\infty}1/n^2$ to within 0.001.

**6. (The number *e* is irrational)** Start with $e=\sum_{n=0}^{\infty}1/n!$.

(a) Use the technique of Example 7 in Section 9.3 to show that for any $n>0$,

$$0<e-\sum_{j=0}^{n}\frac{1}{j!}<\frac{1}{n!n}.$$

(Note that the sum here has $n+1$ terms, not $n$ terms.)

(b) Suppose that $e$ is a rational number, say $e = M/N$ for certain positive integers $M$ and $N$. Show that $N!\left(e - \sum_{j=0}^{N}(1/j!)\right)$ is an integer.

(c) Combine parts (a) and (b) to show that there is an integer between 0 and $1/N$. Why is this not possible? Conclude that $e$ cannot be a rational number.

**7.** Let

$$f(x) = \sum_{k=0}^{\infty} \frac{2^{2k}k!}{(2k+1)!}x^{2k+1}$$
$$= x + \frac{2}{3}x^3 + \frac{4}{3\times 5}x^5 + \frac{8}{3\times 5\times 7}x^7 + \dots.$$

(a) Find the radius of convergence of this power series.

(b) Show that $f'(x) = 1 + 2xf(x)$.

(c) What is $\frac{d}{dx}\left(e^{-x^2}f(x)\right)$?

(d) Express $f(x)$ in terms of an integral.

**8. (The number $\pi$ is irrational)** Problem 6 above shows how to prove that $e$ is irrational by assuming the contrary and deducing a contradiction. In this problem you will show that $\pi$ is also irrational. The proof for $\pi$ is also by contradiction but is rather more complicated, so it will be broken down into several parts.

(a) Let $f(x)$ be a polynomial, and let

$$g(x) = f(x) - f''(x) + f^{(4)}(x) - f^{(6)}(x) + \cdots$$
$$= \sum_{j=0}^{\infty}(-1)^j f^{(2j)}(x).$$

(Since $f$ is a polynomial, all but a finite number of terms in the above sum are identically zero, so there are no convergence problems.) Verify that

$$\frac{d}{dx}\left(g'(x)\sin x - g(x)\cos x\right) = f(x)\sin x,$$

and hence that $\displaystyle\int_0^{\pi} f(x)\sin x\,dx = g(\pi) + g(0)$.

(b) Suppose that $\pi$ is rational, say, $\pi = m/n$, where $m$ and $n$ are positive integers. You will show that this leads to a contradiction and thus cannot be true. Choose a positive integer $k$ such that $(\pi m)^k/k! < 1/2$. (Why is this possible?) Consider the polynomial

$$f(x) = \frac{x^k(m-nx)^k}{k!} = \frac{1}{k!}\sum_{j=0}^{k}\binom{k}{j}m^{k-j}(-n)^j x^{j+k}.$$

Show that $0 < f(x) < 1/2$ for $0 < x < \pi$, and hence that $0 < \displaystyle\int_0^{\pi} f(x)\sin x\,dx < 1$. Thus, $0 < g(\pi) + g(0) < 1$, where $g(x)$ is defined as in part (a).

(c) Show that the $i$th derivative of $f(x)$ is given by

$$f^{(i)}(x) = \frac{1}{k!}\sum_{j=0}^{k}\binom{k}{j}m^{k-j}(-n)^j\frac{(j+k)!}{(j+k-i)!}x^{j+k-i}.$$

(d) Show that $f^{(i)}(0)$ is an integer for $i = 0, 1, 2, \dots$. (*Hint:* Observe for $i < k$ that $f^{(i)}(0) = 0$, and for $i > 2k$ that $f^{(i)}(x) = 0$ for all $x$. For $k \le i \le 2k$, show that only one term in the sum for $f^{(i)}(0)$ is not 0, and that this term is an integer. You will need the fact that the binomial coefficients $\binom{k}{j}$ are integers.)

(e) Show that $f(\pi - x) = f(x)$ for all $x$, and hence that $f^{(i)}(\pi)$ is also an integer for each $i = 0, 1, 2, \dots$. Therefore, if $g(x)$ is defined as in (a), then $g(\pi) + g(0)$ is an integer. This contradicts the conclusion of part (b) and so shows that $\pi$ cannot be rational.

**9. (An asymptotic series)** Integrate by parts to show that

$$\int_0^x e^{-1/t}\,dt = e^{-1/x}\sum_{n=2}^{N}(-1)^n(n-1)!x^n$$
$$+ (-1)^{N+1}N!\int_0^x t^{N-1}e^{-1/t}\,dt.$$

Why can't you just use a Maclaurin series to approximate this integral? Using $N = 5$, find an approximate value for $\int_0^{0.1} e^{-1/t}\,dt$, and estimate the error. Estimate the error for $N = 10$ and $N = 20$.

Note that the series $\sum_{n=2}^{\infty}(-1)^n(n-1)!x^n$ **diverges** for any $x \ne 0$. This is an example of what is called an **asymptotic series**. Even though it diverges, a properly chosen partial sum gives a good approximation to our function when $x$ is small.

# Chapter 9
# Sequences, Series, and Power Series

## Section 9.1

**1.** bounded, positive, increasing, convergent to 2
**3.** bounded, positive, convergent to 4
**5.** bounded below, positive, increasing, divergent to infinity
**7.** bounded below, positive, increasing, divergent to infinity
**9.** bounded, positive, decreasing, convergent to 0
**11.** divergent
**13.** divergent
**15.** $\infty$
**17.** 0
**19.** 1
**21.** $e^{-3}$
**23.** 0
**25.** 1/2
**27.** 0
**29.** 0
**31.** $\lim_{n\to\infty} a_n = 5$
**33.** If $\{a_n\}$ is (ultimately) decreasing, then either it is bounded below, and therefore convergent, or else it is unbounded below and therefore divergent to negative infinity.

## Section 9.2

**1.** $\frac{1}{2}$
**3.** $\frac{1}{(2+\pi)^8\big((2+\pi)^2-1\big)}$
**5.** $\frac{25}{4,416}$
**7.** $\frac{8e^4}{e-2}$
**9.** diverges to $\infty$
**11.** $\frac{3}{4}$
**13.** $\frac{1}{3}$
**15.** div. to $\infty$
**17.** div. to $\infty$
**19.** diverges
**21.** 14 m
**25.** If $\{a_n\}$ is ultimately negative, then the series $\sum a_n$ must either converge (if its partial sums are bounded below), or diverge to $-\infty$ (if its partial sums are not bounded below).
**27.** false, e.g. $\sum \frac{(-1)^n}{2^n}$
**29.** true
**31.** true

## Section 9.3

**1.** converges
**3.** diverges to $\infty$
**5.** converges
**7.** diverges to $\infty$
**9.** converges
**11.** diverges to $\infty$
**13.** diverges to $\infty$
**15.** converges
**17.** converges
**19.** diverges to $\infty$
**21.** converges
**23.** converges
**25.** converges
**27.** $s_n + \frac{1}{3(n+1)^3} \le s \le s_n + \frac{1}{3n^3}$; $n = 6$
**29.** $s_n + \frac{2}{\sqrt{n+1}} \le s \le s_n + \frac{2}{\sqrt{n}}$; $n = 63$
**31.** $0 < s - s_n \le \frac{n+2}{2^n(n+1)!(2n+3)}$; $n = 4$
**33.** $0 < s - s_n \le \frac{2^n(4n^2+6n+2)}{(2n)!(4n^2+6n)}$; $n = 4$
**39.** converges, $a_n^{1/n} \to (1/e) < 1$
**41.** no info from ratio test, but series diverges to infinity since all terms exceed 1.
**43.** (b) $s \le \frac{2}{k(1-k)}$, $k = \frac{1}{2}$,
(c) $0 < s - s_n < \frac{(1+k)^{n+1}}{2^n k(1-k)}$, $k = \frac{n+2-\sqrt{n^2+8}}{2(n-1)}$
for $n \ge 2$
**45.** (a) 10, (b) 5, (c) 0.765

## Section 9.4

**1.** conv. conditionally
**3.** conv. conditionally
**5.** diverges
**7.** conv. absolutely
**9.** conv. conditionally
**11.** diverges
**13.** 999
**15.** 13
**17.** converges absolutely if $-1 < x < 1$, conditionally if $x = -1$, diverges elsewhere
**19.** converges absolutely if $0 < x < 2$, conditionally if $x = 2$, diverges elsewhere
**21.** converges absolutely if $-2 < x < 2$, conditionally if $x = -2$, diverges elsewhere
**23.** converges absolutely if $-\frac{7}{2} < x < \frac{1}{2}$, conditionally if $x = -\frac{7}{2}$, diverges elsewhere
**25.** AST does not apply directly, but does if we remove all the 0 terms; series converges conditionally
**27.** (a) false, e.g. $a_n = \frac{(-1)^n}{n}$,
(b) false, e.g. $a_n = \frac{\sin(n\pi/2)}{n}$, (see Exercise 25),
(c) true
**29.** converges absolutely for $-1 < x < 1$, conditionally if $x = -1$, diverges elsewhere

## Section 9.5

**1.** centre 0, radius 1, interval $(-1, 1)$
**3.** centre $-2$, radius 2, interval $[-4, 0)$
**5.** centre $\frac{3}{2}$, radius $\frac{1}{2}$, interval $(1, 2)$
**7.** centre 0, radius $\infty$, interval $(-\infty, \infty)$
**9.** $\frac{1}{(1-x)^3} = \sum_{n=0}^{\infty} \frac{(n+1)(n+2)}{2} x^n$, $(-1 < x < 1)$
**11.** $\frac{1}{(1-x)^2} = \sum_{n=0}^{\infty} (n+1)x^n$, $(-1 < x < 1)$

**13.** $\frac{1}{(2-x)^2} = \sum_{n=0}^{\infty} \frac{n+1}{2^{n+2}} x^n, \quad (-2 < x < 2)$

**15.** $\ln(2-x) = \ln 2 - \sum_{n=1}^{\infty} \frac{x^n}{2^n n}, \quad (-2 \le x < 2)$

**17.** $\frac{1}{x^2} = \sum_{n=0}^{\infty} \frac{n+1}{2^{n+2}} (x+2)^n, \quad (-4 < x < 0)$

**19.** $\frac{x^3}{1-2x^2} = \sum_{n=0}^{\infty} 2^n x^{2n+3}, \quad \left(-\frac{1}{\sqrt{2}} < x < \frac{1}{\sqrt{2}}\right)$

**21.** $\left(-\frac{1}{4}, \frac{1}{4}\right); \quad \frac{1}{1+4x}$

**23.** $[-1, 1); \quad \frac{1}{3}$ if $x = 0$, $-\frac{1}{x^3}\ln(1-x) - \frac{1}{x^2} - \frac{1}{2x}$ otherwise

**25.** $(-1, 1); \quad \frac{2}{(1-x^2)^2}$

**27.** $3/4$

**29.** $\pi^2(\pi+1)/(\pi-1)^3$

**31.** $\ln(3/2)$

## Section 9.6

**1.** $e^{3x+1} = \sum_{n=0}^{\infty} \frac{3^n e}{n!} x^n$, (all $x$)

**3.** $\sin\left(x - \frac{\pi}{4}\right) = \frac{1}{\sqrt{2}} \sum_{n=0}^{\infty} (-1)^n \left[-\frac{x^{2n}}{(2n)!} + \frac{x^{2n+1}}{(2n+1)!}\right]$, (all $x$)

**5.** $x^2 \sin\left(\frac{x}{3}\right) = \sum_{n=0}^{\infty} \frac{(-1)^n}{3^{2n+1}(2n+1)!} x^{2n+3}$, (all $x$)

**7.** $\sin x \cos x = \sum_{n=0}^{\infty} \frac{(-1)^n 2^{2n}}{(2n+1)!} x^{2n+1}$, (all $x$)

**9.** $\frac{1+x^3}{1+x^2} = 1 - x^2 + \sum_{n=2}^{\infty} (-1)^n (x^{2n-1} + x^{2n})$, $(-1 < x < 1)$

**11.** $\ln \frac{1+x}{1-x} = 2\sum_{n=1}^{\infty} \frac{x^{2n-1}}{2n-1}, \quad (-1 < x < 1)$

**13.** $\cosh x - \cos x = 2\sum_{n=0}^{\infty} \frac{x^{4n+2}}{(4n+2)!}$, (all $x$)

**15.** $e^{-2x} = e^2 \sum_{n=0}^{\infty} \frac{(-1)^n 2^n}{n!} (x+1)^n$, (all $x$)

**17.** $\cos x = \sum_{n=0}^{\infty} \frac{(-1)^{n+1}}{(2n)!} (x-\pi)^{2n}$, (all $x$)

**19.** $\ln 4 + \sum_{n=1}^{\infty} \frac{(-1)^{n-1}}{4^n n} (x-2)^n, \quad (-2 < x \le 6)$

**21.** $\sin x - \cos x = \sqrt{2}\sum_{n=0}^{\infty} \frac{(-1)^n}{(2n+1)!} \left(x - \frac{\pi}{4}\right)^{2n+1}$, (all $x$)

**23.** $\frac{1}{x^2} = \frac{1}{4} \sum_{n=0}^{\infty} \frac{n+1}{2^n} (x+2)^n, \quad (-4 < x < 0)$

**25.** $(x-1) + \sum_{n=2}^{\infty} \frac{(-1)^n}{n(n-1)} (x-1)^n, \quad (0 \le x \le 2)$

**27.** $1 + \frac{x^2}{2} + \frac{5x^4}{24}$

**29.** $x + \frac{x^2}{2} - \frac{x^3}{6}$

**31.** $1 + \frac{x}{2} - \frac{x^2}{8}$

**33.** $e^{x^2}$ (all $x$)

**35.** $\frac{e^x - e^{-x}}{2x} = \frac{\sinh x}{x}$ if $x \ne 0$, $1$ if $x = 0$

**37.** (a) $1 + x + x^2$, (b) $3 + 3(x-1) + (x-1)^2$

## Section 9.7

**1.** $\frac{1}{720}(0.2)^7$

**3.** 1.22140

**5.** 3.32011

**7.** 0.99619

**9.** −0.10533

**11.** 0.42262

**13.** 1.54306

**15.** $I(x) = \sum_{n=0}^{\infty} \frac{(-1)^n}{(2n+1)(2n+1)!} x^{2n+1}$, (all $x$)

**17.** $K(x) = \sum_{n=0}^{\infty} \frac{(-1)^n}{(n+1)^2} x^{n+1}, \quad (-1 \le x \le 1)$

**19.** $M(x) = \sum_{n=0}^{\infty} \frac{(-1)^n}{(2n+1)(4n+1)} x^{4n+1}$, $(-1 \le x \le 1)$

**21.** 0.946

**23.** 2

**25.** −3/25

**27.** 0

## Section 9.8

**1.** $\sqrt{1+x} = 1 + \sum_{n=1}^{\infty} \frac{(-1)^{n-1} 1 \times 3 \times 5 \times \cdots \times (2n-3)}{2^n n!} x^n$, $|x| < 1$

**3.** $\sqrt{4+x} = 2 + \frac{x}{4} + 2\sum_{n=2}^{\infty} (-1)^{n-1} \frac{1 \times 3 \times 5 \times \cdots \times (2n-3)}{2^{3n} n!} x^n$, $(-4 < x \le 4)$

**5.** $\sum_{n=0}^{\infty} (n+1)x^n, \quad |x| < 1$

**7.** $\frac{\pi}{2} - x - \sum_{n=1}^{\infty} \frac{1 \times 3 \times 5 \times \cdots \times (2n-1)}{2^n n!(2n+1)} x^{2n+1}$, $(-1 < x < 1)$

## Section 9.9

**1.** $2\pi/3$

**3.** $\pi$

**5.** $2\sum_{n=1}^{\infty} (-1)^{n-1}(\sin(nt))/n$

**7.** $\frac{1}{4} - \sum_{n=1}^{\infty} \left(\frac{2\cos((2n-1)\pi t)}{(2n-1)^2\pi^2} + \frac{(-1)^n \sin(n\pi t)}{n\pi}\right)$

**9.** 1

**11.** $2\sum_{n=1}^{\infty} \frac{(-1)^n}{n\pi} \sin(n\pi t)$

**13.** $\pi^2/8$

## Review Exercises

**1.** conv. to 0

**3.** div. to $\infty$

**5.** $\lim_{n\to\infty} a_n = \sqrt{2}$

**7.** $4\sqrt{2}/(\sqrt{2}-1)$

**9.** 2

**11.** converges

**13.** converges
**15.** converges
**17.** conv. abs.
**19.** conv. cond.
**21.** conv. abs. for $x$ in $(-1, 5)$, cond. for $x = -1$, div. elsewhere
**23.** 1.202
**25.** $\sum_{n=0}^{\infty} x^n/3^{n+1}, \ |x| < 3$
**27.** $1 + \sum_{n=1}^{\infty}(-1)^{n-1}x^{2n}/(ne^n), \ -\sqrt{e} < x \leq \sqrt{e}$
**29.** $x + \sum_{n=1}^{\infty}(-1)^n 2^{2n-1}x^{2n+1}/(2n)!$, all $x$
**31.** $(1/2) + \sum_{n=1}^{\infty} \dfrac{(-1)^n\, 1 \times 4 \times 7 \times \cdots \times (3n-2)x^n}{2 \times 24^n\, n!}$, $-8 < x \leq 8$
**33.** $\sum_{n=0}^{\infty}(-1)^n(x-\pi)^n/\pi^{n+1}, \ 0 < x < 2\pi$
**35.** $1 + 2x + 3x^2 + \frac{10}{3}x^3$
**37.** $1 - \frac{1}{2}x^2 + \frac{5}{24}x^4$
**39.** $\begin{cases} \cos\sqrt{x} & \text{if } x \geq 0 \\ \cosh\sqrt{|x|} & \text{if } x < 0 \end{cases}$
**41.** $\pi^2/(\pi-1)^2$
**43.** $\ln(e/(e-1))$
**45.** $1/14$
**47.** 3, 0.49386
**49.** $\sum_{n=1}^{\infty} \dfrac{2}{n}\sin(nt)$

## Challenging Problems

**5.** (c) 1.645
**7.** (a) $\infty$, (c) $e^{-x^2}$, (d) $f(x) = e^{x^2}\int_0^x e^{-t^2}\,dt$

# Differential Equations

# 19 Ordinary differential equations I

Chapter 19 Contents

## 19.1 Introduction

The solution of problems concerning the motion of objects, the flow of charged particles, heat transport, etc., often involves discussion of relations of the form

$$\frac{d^2x}{dt^2} + 6\frac{dx}{dt} + 2x = 3t \qquad \text{or} \qquad \frac{dq}{dt} + 8q = \sin t$$

In the first equation, $x$ might represent distance. For this case $\frac{dx}{dt}$ is the rate of change of distance with respect to time $t$, that is speed, and $\frac{d^2x}{dt^2}$ represents acceleration. In the second equation, $q$ might be charge and $\frac{dq}{dt}$ the rate of flow of charge, that is current. These are examples of **differential equations**, so called because they are equations involving the derivatives of various quantities. Such equations arise out of situations in which change is occurring. To solve such a differential equation means to find the function $x(t)$ or $q(t)$ when we are given the differential equation. Solutions to these equations may be **analytical** in that we can write down an answer in terms of common elementary functions such as $e^t$, $\sin t$ and so on. Alternatively, the problem may be so difficult that only **numerical methods** are available, which produce approximate solutions.

In engineering, differential equations are most commonly used to model **dynamic systems**. These are systems which change with time. Examples include an electronic circuit with time-dependent currents and voltages, a chemical production line in which pressures, tank levels, flow rates, etc., vary with time, and a semiconductor device in which hole and electron densities change with time.

## 19.2 Basic definitions

In order to solve a differential equation it is important to identify certain features. Recall from Chapter 2 that in a function such as $y = x^2 + 3x$ we say $x$ is the independent variable and $y$ is the dependent variable since the value of $y$ depends upon the choice we have made for $x$.

In a differential equation such as

$$\frac{dy}{dx} - 2y = 3x^2$$

$x$ is the independent variable, and $y$ is the dependent variable.

Similarly, for the differential equation

$$\frac{dx}{dt} + 7x = e^t$$

$t$ is the independent variable and $x$ is the dependent variable.

We see that the variable being differentiated is the dependent variable.

Before classifying differential equations, we will derive one.

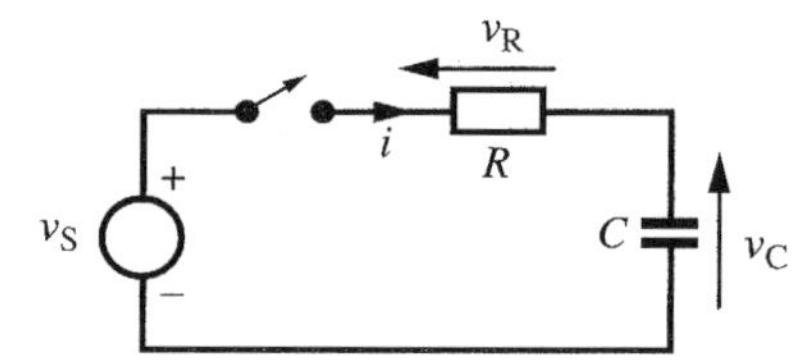


**Figure 19.1**
An $RC$ charging circuit.

**Example 19.1** **An *RC* charging circuit**

Consider the $RC$ circuit of Figure 19.1. Suppose we wish to derive a differential equation which models the circuit so that we can determine the voltage across the capacitor at any time, $t$. Clearly there are two different cases corresponding to the switch being open and the switch being closed. We will concentrate on the latter and for convenience assume that the switch is closed at $t = 0$. From Kirchhoff's voltage law we have

$$v_S = v_R + v_C \qquad \text{that is} \qquad v_R = v_S - v_C$$

where $v_S$ is the voltage of the supply, $v_C$ is the voltage across the capacitor, and $v_R$ is the voltage across the resistor. Using Ohm's law for the resistor then gives

$$i = \frac{v_S - v_C}{R}$$

where $i$ is the current flowing in the circuit after the switch is closed. For the capacitor

$$i = C\frac{dv_C}{dt}$$

Combining these equations gives

$$C\frac{dv_C}{dt} = \frac{v_S - v_C}{R}$$

and hence

$$RC\frac{dv_C}{dt} + v_C = v_S$$

This is the differential equation which models the variation in voltage across the capacitor with time. Here $v_C$ is the dependent variable and $t$ is the independent variable, and when we are required to solve this differential equation we must attempt to find $v_C$ as a function of $t$.

---

Differential equations which have features in common are often grouped together and given certain classifications and it is usually the case that appropriate methods of solution depend upon the classifications. Some important terminology is now given.

### 19.2.1 Order

The **order** of a differential equation is the order of its highest derivative.

**Example 19.2** State the order of

(a) $\dfrac{d^2y}{dx^2} + \dfrac{dy}{dx} = x$ (b) $\dfrac{dx}{dt} = (xt)^5$

**Solution** (a) The highest derivative is $\dfrac{d^2y}{dx^2}$, a second derivative. The order is therefore two.

(b) The only derivative appearing is $\dfrac{dx}{dt}$, a first derivative. The order is therefore one.

### 19.2.2 Linearity

Recall that in a differential equation such as $\dfrac{dy}{dx} + 3y = x^2$, the independent variable is $x$ and the dependent variable is $y$.

A differential equation is said to be **linear** if:

(1) the dependent variable and its derivatives occur to the first power only,

(2) there are no products involving the dependent variable with its derivatives, and

(3) there are no non-linear functions of the dependent variable such as sine, exponential, etc.

If an equation is not linear, then it is said to be **non-linear**. Note from (2) that a product of terms involving the dependent variable such as $y\dfrac{dy}{dx}$ is non-linear. Note from (3) that the existence of terms such as $y^2$, $\sin y$ and $e^y$ causes an equation to be non-linear.

Note also that the conditions for linearity are conditions on the dependent variable. The linearity of a differential equation is not determined or affected by the presence of non-linear terms involving the independent variable.

The distinction between a linear and a non-linear differential equation is important because the methods of solution depend upon whether an equation is linear or non-linear. Furthermore, it is usually the case that a linear differential equation is easier to solve.

**Example 19.3** Decide whether or not the following equations are linear.

(a) $\sin x\dfrac{dy}{dx} + y = x$

(b) $\dfrac{dx}{dt} + x = t^3$

(c) $\dfrac{d^2y}{dx^2} + y^2 = 0$

(d) $\dfrac{dy}{dx} + \sin y = 0$

**Solution** In (a), (c) and (d) the dependent variable is $y$, and the independent variable is $x$. In (b) the dependent variable is $x$ and the independent variable is $t$.

(a) This equation is linear.

(b) This equation is linear. It does not matter that the term in $t$, the independent variable, is raised to the power 3.

(c) This equation is non-linear, the non-linearity arising through the term $y^2$.

(d) This equation is non-linear, the non-linearity arising through the term $\sin y$.

---

### 19.2.3 The solution of a differential equation

The **solution** of a differential equation is a relationship between the dependent and independent variables such that the differential equation is satisfied for all values of the independent variable over a specified domain.

**Example 19.4** Verify that $y = \mathrm{e}^x$ is a solution of the differential equation

$$\frac{\mathrm{d}y}{\mathrm{d}x} = y$$

**Solution** If $y = \mathrm{e}^x$ then $\frac{\mathrm{d}y}{\mathrm{d}x} = \mathrm{e}^x$. For all values of $x$, we see that $\frac{\mathrm{d}y}{\mathrm{d}x} = y$ and so $y = \mathrm{e}^x$ is a solution. Note also that this equation is first order and linear.

---

There are frequently many different functions which satisfy a differential equation; that is, there are many solutions. The **general solution** embraces all of these and all possible solutions can be obtained from it.

**Example 19.5** Verify that $y = C\,\mathrm{e}^x$ is a solution of $\frac{\mathrm{d}y}{\mathrm{d}x} = y$, where $C$ is any constant.

**Solution** If $y = C\,\mathrm{e}^x$, then $\frac{\mathrm{d}y}{\mathrm{d}x} = C\,\mathrm{e}^x$. Therefore, for all values of $x$, $\frac{\mathrm{d}y}{\mathrm{d}x} = y$ and the equation is satisfied for any constant $C$; $C$ is called an **arbitrary constant** and by varying it, all possible solutions can be obtained. For example, by choosing $C$ to be 1, we obtain the solution of the previous example. In fact, $y = C\,\mathrm{e}^x$ is the general solution of $\frac{\mathrm{d}y}{\mathrm{d}x} = y$.

---

More generally, to determine $C$ we require more information given in the form of a **condition**. For example, if we are told that at $x = 0$, $y = 4$ then from $y = C\,e^x$ we have

$$4 = C\,e^0 = C$$

so that $C = 4$. Therefore $y = 4\,e^x$ is the solution of the differential equation which additionally satisfies the condition $y(0) = 4$. This is called a **particular solution**. In general, application of conditions to the general solution yields the particular solution. To obtain a particular solution, the number of given independent conditions must be the same as the number of constants.

Consider the following example.

**Example 19.6** Consider the second-order differential equation

$$\frac{d^2y}{dx^2} + y = 0$$

The general solution of this equation can be shown to be

$$y = A\cos x + B\sin x$$

where $A$ and $B$ are arbitrary constants.

Find the particular solution which satisfies the conditions

(a) when $x = 0$, then $y = 0$, and

(b) when $x = \frac{3\pi}{2}$, then $y = 1$.

**Solution** We note that because the general solution has two arbitrary constants, $A$ and $B$, then two conditions are necessary to obtain a particular solution. Applying the first condition to the general solution gives

$$\begin{aligned} 0 &= A\cos 0 + B\sin 0 \\ &= A \end{aligned}$$

Therefore $A = 0$, and the solution reduces to $y = B\sin x$. Applying the second condition we find

$$1 = B\sin\frac{3\pi}{2}$$

from which

$$\begin{aligned} 1 &= B(-1) \\ B &= -1 \end{aligned}$$

The particular solution becomes $y = -\sin x$.

Sometimes the conditions involve derivatives.

**Example 19.7** For the differential equation of Example 19.6 find the particular solution which satisfies the conditions

(a) when $x = 0$, then $y = 0$, and

(b) when $x = 0$, then $\dfrac{dy}{dx} = 5$.

**Solution** Application of the first condition to the general solution $y = A\cos x + B\sin x$ gives

$$\begin{aligned} 0 &= A\cos 0 + B\sin 0 \\ &= A \end{aligned}$$

Therefore $A = 0$ and the solution becomes $y = B\sin x$. To apply the second condition we must differentiate $y$.

$$\frac{dy}{dx} = B\cos x$$

Then applying the second condition we get

$$\begin{aligned} 5 &= B\cos 0 \\ &= B \end{aligned}$$

so that $B = 5$. Finally the required particular solution is $y = 5\sin x$.

In this example both conditions have been specified at $x = 0$, and are often referred to as **initial conditions**.

---

## Exercises 19.2

1. Verify that $y = 3\sin 2x$ is a solution of
$$\frac{d^2y}{dx^2} + 4y = 0.$$

2. Verify that $3e^x$, $Ax e^x$, $Ax e^x + B e^x$, where $A$, $B$ are constants, all satisfy the differential equation
$$\frac{d^2y}{dx^2} - 2\frac{dy}{dx} + y = 0$$

3. Verify that $x = t^2 + A\ln t + B$ is a solution of
$$t\frac{d^2x}{dt^2} + \frac{dx}{dt} = 4t$$

4. Verify that $y = A\cos x + B\sin x$ satisfies the differential equation
$$\frac{d^2y}{dx^2} + y = 0$$
Verify also that $y = A\cos x$ and $y = B\sin x$ each individually satisfy the equation.

5. If $y = A e^{2x}$ is the general solution of $\dfrac{dy}{dx} = 2y$, find the particular solution satisfying $y(0) = 3$. What is the particular solution satisfying $\dfrac{dy}{dx} = 2$ when $x = 0$?

6. Identify the dependent and independent variables of the following differential equations. Give the order of the equations and state which are linear.

(a) $\dfrac{dy}{dx} + 9y = 0$

(b) $\left(\dfrac{dy}{dx}\right)\left(\dfrac{d^2y}{dx^2}\right) + 3\dfrac{dy}{dx} = 0$

(c) $\dfrac{d^3x}{dt^3} + 5\dfrac{dx}{dt} = \sin x$

7 Show that $x(t) = 7\cos 3t - 2\sin 2t$ is a solution of:

$$\frac{d^2x}{dt^2} + 2x = -49\cos 3t + 4\sin 2t$$

8 The general solution of the equation $\dfrac{d^2x}{dt^2} - 3\dfrac{dx}{dt} + 2x = 0$ is given by

$$x = A\,e^t + B\,e^{2t}$$

Find the particular solution which satisfies $x = 3$ and $\dfrac{dx}{dt} = 5$ when $t = 0$.

9 The general solution of $\dfrac{d^2y}{dx^2} - 2\dfrac{dy}{dx} + y = 0$ is $y = Ax\,e^x + B\,e^x$. Find the particular solution satisfying $y(0) = 0$, $\dfrac{dy}{dx}(0) = 1$.

10 The general solution of $\dfrac{d^2x}{dt^2} = -\omega^2 x$ is $x = A\,e^{j\omega t} + B\,e^{-j\omega t}$, where $j^2 = -1$. Verify that this is indeed a solution. What is the particular solution satisfying $x(0) = 0$, $\dfrac{dx}{dt}(0) = 1$? Express the general solution and the particular solution in terms of trigonometric functions.

## Solutions

5 $y(x) = 3\,e^{2x}$, $y(x) = e^{2x}$

6 (a) $y$ is the dependent variable; $x$ is the independent variable; first order, linear

(b) $y$ is the dependent variable; $x$ is the independent variable; second order, non-linear

(c) $x$ is the dependent variable; $t$ is the independent variable; third order, non-linear.

8 $x = e^t + 2\,e^{2t}$

9 $y = x\,e^x$

10 particular solution: $\sin\omega t/\omega$
general solution:
$(A + B)\cos\omega t + (A - B)j\sin\omega t$

## 19.3 First order equations: simple equations and separation of variables

### 19.3.1 Simple equations

The simplest first-order equations to deal with are those of the form

$$\frac{dy}{dx} = f(x)$$

where the r.h.s. is a function of the independent variable only. No special treatment is necessary and direct integration yields $y$ as a function of $x$, that is

$$y = \int f(x)\,dx$$

**Example 19.8** Find the general solution of $\dfrac{dy}{dx} = 3\cos 2x$.

**Solution** Given that $\frac{dy}{dx} = 3\cos 2x$, then $y = \int 3\cos 2x\,dx = \frac{3}{2}\sin 2x + C$. This is the required general solution.

---

If $\frac{dy}{dx} = f(x)$ then $y = \int f(x)\,dx$.

## 19.3.2 Separation of variables

When the function $f$ on the r.h.s. of the equation depends upon both independent and dependent variables this approach is not possible. However, first-order equations which can be written in the form

$$\frac{dy}{dx} = f(x)g(y) \tag{19.1}$$

form an important class known as **separable equations**. For example,

$$\frac{dy}{dx} = 3x^2 e^{-4y}$$

is a separable equation for which

$$f(x) = 3x^2 \qquad \text{and} \qquad g(y) = e^{-4y}$$

To obtain a solution we first divide both sides of Equation (19.1) by $g(y)$ to give

$$\frac{1}{g(y)}\frac{dy}{dx} = f(x)$$

Integrating both sides with respect to $x$ yields

$$\int \frac{1}{g(y)}\frac{dy}{dx}\,dx = \int \frac{1}{g(y)}\,dy = \int f(x)\,dx$$

The equation is then said to be separated. If the last two integrals can be found, we obtain a relationship between $y$ and $x$, although it is not always possible to write $y$ explicitly in terms of $x$ as the following examples will show.

Separation of variables:
The solution of $\frac{dy}{dx} = f(x)g(y)$ is found from

$$\int \frac{1}{g(y)}\,dy = \int f(x)\,dx$$

**Example 19.9** Solve $\frac{dy}{dx} = \frac{e^{-x}}{y}$.

**Solution** Here $f(x) = e^{-x}$ and $g(y) = \dfrac{1}{y}$. Multiplication through by $y$ yields

$$y\frac{dy}{dx} = e^{-x}$$

Integration of both sides with respect to $x$ gives

$$\int y\,dy = \int e^{-x}\,dx$$

so that

$$\frac{y^2}{2} = -e^{-x} + C$$

Note that the constants arising from the two integrals have been combined to give a single constant, $C$. Finally we can rearrange this expression to give $y$ in terms of $x$:

$$y^2 = -2\,e^{-x} + 2C$$

that is,

$$y = \pm\sqrt{D - 2\,e^{-x}}$$

where $D = 2C$.

---

It is important to stress that the constant of integration must be inserted at the stage at which the integration is actually carried out, and not simply added to the answer at the end.

**Example 19.10** Solve $\dfrac{dy}{dx} = 3x^2\,e^{-y}$ subject to $y(0) = 1$.

**Solution** Here $g(y) = e^{-y}$ and $f(x) = 3x^2$. Separating the variables and integrating we find

$$\int e^y\,dy = \int 3x^2\,dx$$

so that $e^y = x^3 + C$. Imposing the initial condition $y(0) = 1$ we find

$$e^1 = (0)^3 + C$$

so that $C = e$. Therefore,

$$e^y = x^3 + e$$

Note that since the exponential function is always positive, the solution will be valid only for $x^3 + e > 0$. Taking natural logarithms gives the particular solution explicitly:

$$y = \ln(x^3 + e)$$

**Example 19.11** Solve

$$\frac{dx}{dt} = \frac{t^2 + 1}{x^2 + 1}$$

**Solution** Separating the variables and integrating we find

$$\int x^2 + 1 \, dx = \int t^2 + 1 \, dt$$

Therefore,

$$\frac{x^3}{3} + x = \frac{t^3}{3} + t + C$$

which is the general solution. Here we note that $x$ has not been obtained explicitly in terms of $t$, although we have found a relationship between $x$ and $t$ which satisfies the differential equation. To obtain the value of $x$ at any given $t$ it would be necessary to solve the cubic equation.

---

Sometimes, equations which are not immediately separable can be reduced to separable form by an appropriate substitution as the following example shows.

**Example 19.12** By means of the substitution $z = \frac{y}{x}$, solve the equation

$$\frac{dy}{dx} = \frac{y^2}{x^2} + \frac{y}{x} + 1 \qquad (19.2)$$

**Solution** If $z = \frac{y}{x}$ then $y = zx$. Because the solution, $y$, is a function of $x$ the variable $z$ depends upon $x$ also. The product rule gives $\frac{dy}{dx} = z + x\frac{dz}{dx}$, so that Equation (19.2) becomes

$$z + x\frac{dz}{dx} = z^2 + z + 1$$

that is,

$$x\frac{dz}{dx} = z^2 + 1$$

This new equation has independent variable $x$ and dependent variable $z$, and is separable. We find

$$\int \frac{dz}{z^2 + 1} = \int \frac{dx}{x}$$

so that $\tan^{-1} z = \ln|x| + C$. Writing $C = \ln|D|$ we have

$$\tan^{-1} z = \ln|x| + \ln|D| = \ln|Dx|$$

so that $z = \tan(\ln|Dx|)$. Returning to the original variables we see that the general solution is

$$y = zx = x\tan(\ln|Dx|)$$

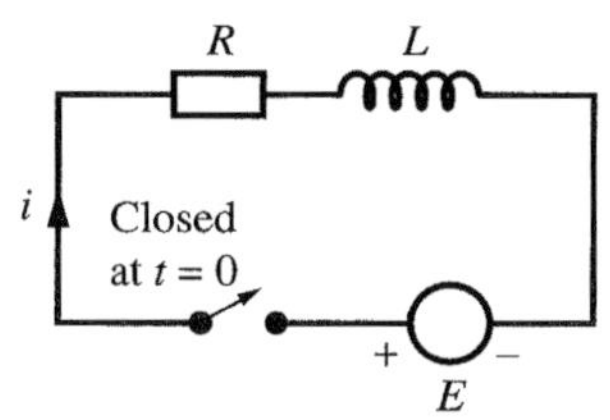


**Figure 19.2** A step voltage is applied to the circuit at $t = 0$.

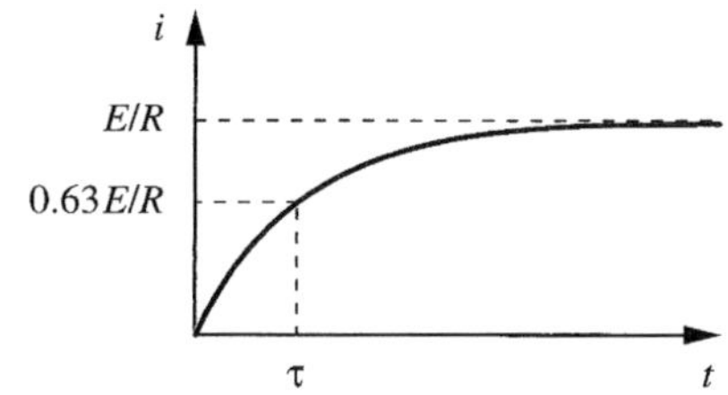


**Figure 19.3** Response of the circuit of Figure 19.2 to a step input.

**Example 19.13** ***RL* circuit with step input**

Write down the differential equation governing the current, $i$, flowing in the $RL$ circuit shown in Figure 19.2 when a step voltage of magnitude $E$ is applied to the circuit at $t = 0$. Solve this differential equation to obtain $i(t)$. Assume that when $t = 0$, $i = 0$.

**Solution** Applying Kirchhoff's voltage law and Ohm's law to the circuit we find

$$iR + L\frac{di}{dt} = E \qquad \text{for} \qquad t \geqslant 0$$

that is,

$$L\frac{di}{dt} = E - iR$$

so that

$$\int \frac{L}{E - iR}\, di = \int dt$$

Note in particular that in this equation $L$, $E$ and $R$ are constants and so the variables $i$ and $t$ have been separated. If the applied voltage, $E$, varied with time this would not have been the case since the l.h.s. would contain terms dependent upon $t$. Integrating, we find

$$\int \frac{L}{E - iR}\, di = \frac{-L}{R}\int \frac{-R}{E - iR}\, di = -\frac{L}{R}\ln(E - iR) = t + C$$

To find the constant of integration, $C$, a condition is required. The physical condition $i = 0$ at $t = 0$ provides this. Applying $i = 0$ when $t = 0$ we find

$$C = -\frac{L}{R}\ln E$$

Substituting this value gives

$$-\frac{L}{R}\ln(E - iR) = t - \frac{L}{R}\ln E$$

Thus,

$$\frac{L}{R}[\ln E - \ln(E - iR)] = t$$

so that

$$\frac{L}{R}\ln\frac{E}{E-iR}=t$$

Then

$$\ln\frac{E}{E-iR}=\frac{Rt}{L}$$

hence

$$\frac{E}{E-iR}=\mathrm{e}^{Rt/L}$$

Rearranging to obtain $E$ gives

$$E=(E-iR)\,\mathrm{e}^{Rt/L}$$

hence

$$E=E\mathrm{e}^{Rt/L}-iR\mathrm{e}^{Rt/L}$$

and so

$$iR\mathrm{e}^{Rt/L}=E(\mathrm{e}^{Rt/L}-1)$$

so

$$iR=E(1-\mathrm{e}^{-Rt/L})$$

Finally we have

$$i=\frac{E}{R}(1-\mathrm{e}^{-Rt/L})$$

The graph of this current against time is shown in Figure 19.3. We note that as $t\to\infty$, $i\to\frac{E}{R}$. The rate at which the current increases towards its final value depends upon the values of the components $R$ and $L$. It is common to define a **time constant**, $\tau$, for the circuit. In this case $\tau=\frac{L}{R}$ and the equation for the current can be written as

$$i=\frac{E}{R}(1-\mathrm{e}^{-t/\tau})$$

The smaller the value of $\tau$, the more rapidly the current reaches its final value. It is possible to estimate a value of $\tau$ from a laboratory test curve by noting that after one time constant, that is $t=\tau$, $i$ has reached $1-\mathrm{e}^{-1}\approx 0.63$ of its final value.

## Exercises 19.3

1 Find the general solution of the following equations:

(a) $\frac{\mathrm{d}y}{\mathrm{d}x}=3$

(b) $\dfrac{dx}{dt} = 5$

(c) $\dfrac{dy}{dx} = 2x$

(d) $\dfrac{dy}{dt} = 6t$

(e) $\dfrac{dy}{dx} = 8x^2$

(f) $\dfrac{dx}{dt} = 3t^3$

(g) $\dfrac{dy}{dx} = \dfrac{x^2}{y}$

(h) $\dfrac{dx}{dt} = \dfrac{t^3}{x^2}$

(i) $\dfrac{dx}{dt} = \dfrac{e^t}{x}$

(j) $\dfrac{dy}{dx} = \dfrac{e^{-2x}}{y^2}$

(k) $\dfrac{dy}{dx} = \dfrac{6 \sin x}{y}$

(l) $\dfrac{dx}{dt} = \dfrac{9 \cos 4t}{x^2}$

(m) $\dfrac{dx}{dt} = \dfrac{3 \cos 2t + 8 \sin 4t}{x^2 + x}$

**2** Find the particular solution of the following equations:

(a) $\dfrac{dx}{dt} = 3t, \quad x(0) = 1$

(b) $\dfrac{dy}{dx} = \dfrac{6x^2}{y}, \quad y(0) = 1$

(c) $\dfrac{dy}{dt} = \dfrac{3 \sin t}{y}, \quad y(0) = 2$

(d) $\dfrac{dy}{dx} = \dfrac{e^{-x}}{y}, \quad y(0) = 3$

(e) $\dfrac{dx}{dt} = \dfrac{4 \sin t + 6 \cos 2t}{x}, \quad x(0) = 2$

**3** Find the general solution of $\dfrac{dx}{dt} = \ln t$. Find the particular solution satisfying $x(1) = 1$.

**4** Find the general solutions of the following equations:

(a) $\dfrac{dy}{dx} = kx, \quad k$ constant

(b) $\dfrac{dy}{dx} = -ky, \quad k$ constant

(c) $\dfrac{dy}{dx} = y^2$

(d) $y\dfrac{dy}{dx} = \sin x$

(e) $y\dfrac{dy}{dx} = x + 2$

(f) $x^2\dfrac{dy}{dx} = 2y^2 + yx$

(g) $\dfrac{dx}{dt} = \dfrac{t^4}{x^5}$

**5** Find the general solutions of the following equations:

(a) $\dfrac{dx}{dt} = xt$

(b) $\dfrac{dy}{dx} = \dfrac{x}{y}$

(c) $t\dfrac{dx}{dt} = \tan x$

(d) $\dfrac{dx}{dt} = \dfrac{x^2 - 1}{t}$

**6** Find the general solution of the equation $\dfrac{dx}{dt} = t(x - 2)$. Find the particular solution which satisfies $x(0) = 5$.

## Solutions

**1** (a) $y = 3x + c$

(b) $x = 5t + c$

(c) $y = x^2 + c$

(d) $y = 3t^2 + c$

(e) $y = \frac{8}{3}x^3 + c$

(f) $x = \frac{3}{4}t^4 + c$

(g) $\dfrac{y^2}{2} = \dfrac{x^3}{3} + c$

(h) $\dfrac{x^3}{3} = \dfrac{t^4}{4} + c$

(i) $\dfrac{x^2}{2} = e^t + c$

(j) $\dfrac{y^3}{3} = c - \dfrac{e^{-2x}}{2}$

(k) $\frac{y^2}{2} = c - 6\cos x$

(l) $\frac{x^3}{3} = \frac{9}{4}\sin 4t + c$

(m) $\frac{x^3}{3} + \frac{x^2}{2} = \frac{3}{2}\sin 2t - 2\cos 4t + c$

**2** (a) $x = \frac{3}{2}t^2 + 1$

(b) $y^2 = 4x^3 + 1$

(c) $\frac{y^2}{2} = 5 - 3\cos t$

(d) $y^2 = 11 - 2\,\mathrm{e}^{-x}$

(e) $\frac{x^2}{2} = 3\sin 2t - 4\cos t + 6$

**3** $t\ln|t| - t + c$, $t\ln|t| - t + 2$

**4** (a) $\frac{kx^2}{2} + c$

(b) $A\,\mathrm{e}^{-kx}$

(c) $-\frac{1}{x + c}$

(d) $y^2 = 2(c - \cos x)$

(e) $y^2 = x^2 + 4x + c$

(f) $\frac{x}{A - 2\ln|x|}$

(g) $\frac{x^6}{6} = \frac{t^5}{5} + c$

**5** (a) $x = A\,\mathrm{e}^{t^2/2}$

(b) $y^2 = x^2 + c$

(c) $x = \sin^{-1}(kt)$

(d) $x = \frac{1 + At^2}{1 - At^2}$

**6** $2 + A\,\mathrm{e}^{t^2/2}$, $2 + 3\,\mathrm{e}^{t^2/2}$

## 19.4 First order linear equations: use of an integrating factor

In this section we develop a method for solving first-order linear differential equations.

### 19.4.1 Exact equations

Consider the differential equation

$$\frac{\mathrm{d}y}{\mathrm{d}x} = 3x^2$$

This can be solved very easily by simply integrating both sides to give

$$\begin{aligned} y &= \int 3x^2 \mathrm{d}x \\ &= x^3 + c \end{aligned}$$

where $c$ is the constant of integration. An equation which can be solved by integrating both sides is said to be an **exact** equation. A more complicated example which, nevertheless, can be solved in the same way is

$$\frac{\mathrm{d}}{\mathrm{d}x}(xy) = 3x^2$$

Integrating both sides we find

$$\begin{aligned} xy &= \int 3x^2 \mathrm{d}x \\ &= x^3 + c \end{aligned}$$

and dividing through by $x$ gives the general solution

$$y = x^2 + \frac{c}{x}$$

The differential equation we have just solved is an exact equation.

**Example 19.14** Solve the equation

$$\frac{d}{dx}(x^2 y) = \cos x$$

**Solution** Integrating both sides we find

$$\begin{aligned} x^2 y &= \int \cos x \, dx \\ &= \sin x + c \end{aligned}$$

so that

$$y = \frac{\sin x}{x^2} + \frac{c}{x^2}$$

---

Consider again the differential equation of the previous example:

$$\frac{d}{dx}(x^2 y) = \cos x$$

Using the product rule for differentiation we can expand the l.h.s. as follows:

$$\frac{d}{dx}(x^2 y) = x^2 \frac{dy}{dx} + 2xy$$

Doing this, the differential equation can be written in the equivalent form

$$x^2 \frac{dy}{dx} + 2xy = \cos x$$

Suppose we had posed the question in this form. A method of solving this equation would be to recognize that the equation is exact and that the l.h.s. could be written as $\frac{d}{dx}(x^2 y)$.

It is easy to recognize an exact equation because it will always take the form

$$\mu \frac{dy}{dx} + \mu' y = f(x)$$

where $\mu$ is some function of $x$. That is, the coefficient of $y$ is the derivative of the coefficient of $\frac{dy}{dx}$. When this is the case the l.h.s. can be written $\frac{d}{dx}(\mu y)$.

**Example 19.15** The following equations are exact. Note in each case that the coefficient of $y$ is the derivative of the coefficient of $\frac{\mathrm{d}y}{\mathrm{d}x}$. Solve them.

(a) $x^3\frac{\mathrm{d}y}{\mathrm{d}x} + 3x^2y = \mathrm{e}^{2x}$

(b) $\cos x\frac{\mathrm{d}y}{\mathrm{d}x} - (\sin x)y = 1$

**Solution** (a) The equation can be written

$$\frac{\mathrm{d}}{\mathrm{d}x}(x^3y) = \mathrm{e}^{2x}$$

and so, upon integrating,

$$x^3y = \int \mathrm{e}^{2x}\,\mathrm{d}x$$
$$= \frac{\mathrm{e}^{2x}}{2} + c$$

so that

$$y = \frac{\mathrm{e}^{2x}}{2x^3} + \frac{c}{x^3}$$

(b) The equation can be written

$$\frac{\mathrm{d}}{\mathrm{d}x}((\cos x)\,y) = 1$$

and so, upon integrating,

$$(\cos x)\,y = x + c$$

so that

$$y = \frac{x}{\cos x} + \frac{c}{\cos x}$$

## Exercises 19.4.1

1 Each of the following equations is exact. Solve them.

(a) $x^2\frac{\mathrm{d}y}{\mathrm{d}x} + 2xy = x^3$

(b) $\frac{1}{x^2}\frac{\mathrm{d}y}{\mathrm{d}x} - \frac{2}{x^3}y = 5x^3$

(c) $\mathrm{e}^x\left(y + \frac{\mathrm{d}y}{\mathrm{d}x}\right) = \cos x$

## Solutions

1 (a) $y = \frac{x^2}{4} + \frac{C}{x^2}$.

(b) $y = \frac{5x^6}{4} + Cx^2$.

(c) $y = \mathrm{e}^{-x}\sin x + C\,\mathrm{e}^{-x}$

### 19.4.2 A preliminary result involving separation of variables

Consider the following differential equation for the dependent variable $\mu$:

$$\frac{\mathrm{d}\mu}{\mathrm{d}x} = \mu P \tag{19.3}$$

where $P$ is some function of $x$ only. Using separation of variables we have

$$\frac{1}{\mu}\frac{\mathrm{d}\mu}{\mathrm{d}x} = P$$

and integrating both sides

$$\int \frac{1}{\mu}\mathrm{d}\mu = \int P\,\mathrm{d}x$$

$$\ln\mu = \int P\,\mathrm{d}x$$

$$\mu = \mathrm{e}^{\int P\,\mathrm{d}x}$$

In this development the constant of integration has been omitted. The reason for this will be apparent in what follows. So the solution of Equation (19.3), for any function $P(x)$, is $\mu = \mathrm{e}^{\int P\mathrm{d}x}$.

For example, if $P(x) = \frac{1}{x}$, then Equation (19.3) is $\frac{\mathrm{d}\mu}{\mathrm{d}x} = \frac{\mu}{x}$ and its solution is $\mu = \mathrm{e}^{\int(1/x)\mathrm{d}x} = \mathrm{e}^{\ln x} = x$.

### 19.4.3 First-order linear equations

First-order linear differential equations can always be written in the 'standard' form

$$\frac{\mathrm{d}y}{\mathrm{d}x} + P(x)y = Q(x) \tag{19.4}$$

where $P$ and $Q$ are both functions of the independent variable, $x$, only. In some cases, either of these may be simply constants.

An example of such an equation is

$$\frac{\mathrm{d}y}{\mathrm{d}x} + 3xy = 7x^2$$

Comparing this with the standard form in Equation (19.4), note that $P(x) = 3x$ and $Q(x) = 7x^2$. As a second example consider

$$\frac{\mathrm{d}y}{\mathrm{d}x} - \frac{2y}{x} = 4\,\mathrm{e}^{-x}$$

Here $P(x) = -\frac{2}{x}$ (note in particular the minus sign) and $Q(x) = 4\,e^{-x}$.

Finally, in the equation

$$\frac{dy}{dx} - 5y = \sin x$$

note that $P(x)$ is simply the constant $-5$.

Variables other than $y$ and $x$ may be used. So, for example,

$$\frac{dx}{dt} + 8t\,x = 3t^2 - 5t$$

is a first-order linear equation in the form of Equation (19.4) but with independent variable $t$ and dependent variable $x$. Here $P(t) = 8t$ and $Q(t) = 3t^2 - 5t$.

In what follows it will be important that you can distinguish between the dependent and independent variables, and also that you are able to identify the functions $P$ and $Q$.

Equations such as these arise naturally when modelling many engineering applications. For example, the equation which determines the current flow in a series *RL* circuit when the applied voltage takes the form of a ramp is given by

$$\frac{di}{dt} + \frac{R}{L}i = \frac{t}{L}$$

This is a first-order linear equation in which $P(t)$ is the constant $\frac{R}{L}$ and $Q(t) = \frac{t}{L}$. You will learn how to solve such equations in the following section.

### 19.4.4 The integrating factor method

All first-order linear equations, even when they are not exact, can be made exact by multiplying them through by a function known as an **integrating factor**. As we have seen, the solution then follows by performing an integration. For example, the linear equation

$$\frac{dy}{dx} + \frac{3}{x}y = \frac{e^{2x}}{x^3}$$

is not exact, but multiplying it through by $x^3$ produces the differential equation in Example 19.15(a) which is exact.

Consider again a first-order linear equation in standard form:

$$\frac{dy}{dx} + Py = Q \qquad (19.5)$$

where $P$ and $Q$ are functions of $x$ only. We are aiming to solve this and express the dependent variable $y$ in terms of the independent variable $x$. The aim is to multiply (19.5) through by a function $\mu$ to make the equation exact. That is, so that the l.h.s. can be written in the form

$$\frac{d}{dx}(\mu y)$$

At this stage the function $\mu$ is not known. Multiplying (19.5) through by $\mu$ yields

$$\mu\frac{dy}{dx} + \mu P y = \mu Q \qquad (19.6)$$

If the l.h.s. is to equal $\frac{\mathrm{d}}{\mathrm{d}x}(\mu y)$ then we must have

$$\frac{\mathrm{d}}{\mathrm{d}x}(\mu y) = \mu\frac{\mathrm{d}y}{\mathrm{d}x} + \mu P y$$

Expanding the l.h.s. using the product rule gives

$$\mu\frac{\mathrm{d}y}{\mathrm{d}x} + y\frac{\mathrm{d}\mu}{\mathrm{d}x} = \mu\frac{\mathrm{d}y}{\mathrm{d}x} + \mu P y$$

which simplifies to

$$y\frac{\mathrm{d}\mu}{\mathrm{d}x} = \mu P y$$

and consequently

$$\frac{\mathrm{d}\mu}{\mathrm{d}x} = \mu P$$

Using the result in Section 19.4.2 we see that this equation has solution

$$\mu = \mathrm{e}^{\int P\,\mathrm{d}x}$$

The function $\mu$ is called an **integrating factor** and is a function of $x$ only. With this choice of $\mu$, the l.h.s. of (19.6) is the same as $\frac{\mathrm{d}}{\mathrm{d}x}(\mu y)$ and hence (19.6) can be written

$$\frac{\mathrm{d}}{\mathrm{d}x}(\mu y) = \mu Q$$

This exact equation can be solved by integration to give

$$\mu\, y = \int \mu Q\,\mathrm{d}x$$

and consequently

$$y = \frac{1}{\mu}\int \mu Q\,\mathrm{d}x$$

In summary:

Given any first-order linear equation in standard form

$$\frac{\mathrm{d}y}{\mathrm{d}x} + Py = Q$$

where $P$ and $Q$ are functions of $x$, the integrating factor $\mu$ is given by

$$\mu = \mathrm{e}^{\int P\,\mathrm{d}x}$$

and the solution of the equation is then obtained from

$$\mu y = \int \mu\, Q\,\mathrm{d}x$$

It is important when working on a particular differential equation to rewrite the standard formulae in the correct form before use. Essentially this means using the correct dependent and independent variables in the equations. For example, if $x$ is the dependent variable and $t$ is the independent variable then the equations are as follows:

The integrating factor for

$$\frac{dx}{dt} + Px = Q$$

where $P$ and $Q$ are functions of $t$, is given by

$$\mu = e^{\int P\,dt}$$

and the solution of the equation is obtained from

$$\mu x = \int \mu Q\,dt$$

These results are illustrated in the examples which follow.

**Example 19.16** Solve the differential equation $\frac{dy}{dx} + \frac{y}{x} = 1$ using the integrating factor method.

**Solution** Referring to the standard first-order linear equation

$$\frac{dy}{dx} + P(x)y = Q(x)$$

we see that $P(x) = \frac{1}{x}$ and $Q(x) = 1$. Using the previous formula for $\mu(x)$, we find

$$\begin{aligned}\mu(x) &= e^{\int (1/x)\,dx} \\ &= e^{\ln x} \\ &= x\end{aligned}$$

Then from the key point on page 540 with $\mu = x$ and $Q = 1$ we have

$$xy = \int x\,dx = \frac{x^2}{2} + C$$

and finally $y = \frac{x}{2} + \frac{C}{x}$ is the required general solution.

**Example 19.17** ***RL* circuit with ramp input**

The differential equation governing current flow, $i(t)$, in a series $RL$ circuit, when a voltage $u(t)t$ is applied, is given by

$$iR + L\frac{di}{dt} = t \qquad \text{for} \qquad t \geqslant 0 \qquad i(0) = 0$$

Show that this equation can be written in the form of Equation (19.4). Hence use the integrating factor method to find $i(t)$.

**Solution** This equation can be written as

$$\frac{\mathrm{d}i}{\mathrm{d}t} + \frac{R}{L}i = \frac{t}{L} \qquad \text{for} \qquad t \geqslant 0$$

which is a first-order linear equation.

Note in this case that the independent variable is $t$ and the dependent variable is $i$. In standard form, we have

$$\frac{\mathrm{d}i}{\mathrm{d}t} + P(t)i = Q(t)$$

where $P(t) = \frac{R}{L}$ and $Q(t) = \frac{t}{L}$. The integrating factor, $\mu$, is given by

$$\begin{aligned}\mu &= \mathrm{e}^{\int P(t)\,\mathrm{d}t} \\ &= \mathrm{e}^{\int (R/L)\,\mathrm{d}t} \\ &= \mathrm{e}^{Rt/L}\end{aligned}$$

Then

$$\begin{aligned}i\mathrm{e}^{Rt/L} &= \frac{1}{L}\int t\mathrm{e}^{Rt/L}\,\mathrm{d}t \\ &= \frac{1}{L}\left(\frac{t\mathrm{e}^{Rt/L}}{R/L} - \int \frac{\mathrm{e}^{Rt/L}}{R/L}\,\mathrm{d}t\right) \\ &= \frac{t\mathrm{e}^{Rt/L}}{R} - \frac{L}{R^2}\mathrm{e}^{Rt/L} + K\end{aligned}$$

where $K$ is the constant of integration. The general solution is

$$i = \frac{t}{R} - \frac{L}{R^2} + K\mathrm{e}^{-Rt/L}$$

When $t = 0$, $i = 0$. This gives the initial condition required to find $K$. Applying $i(0) = 0$ gives $K = L/R^2$ so that the particular solution is

$$i = \frac{t}{R} + \frac{L}{R^2}(\mathrm{e}^{-Rt/L} - 1)$$

---

In many engineering applications the terms transient response, steady-state response, zero-input response, and zero-state response arise through the solution of differential equations. These terms are explained in the following example.

**Example 19.18** ***RC*** **circuit: zero-input response and zero-state response**

The differential equation which is used to model the variation in voltage across a capacitor, $v_C(t)$, in a series $RC$ circuit was derived in Example 19.1:

$$RC\frac{\mathrm{d}v_C}{\mathrm{d}t} + v_C = v_S(t)$$

where $v_S(t)$ is the applied voltage. Suppose that this applied voltage takes the form $v_S(t) = V\cos\omega t$. Suppose also that when the switch is closed at $t = 0$, the initial voltage across the capacitor is $V_0$, that is $v_C(0) = V_0$.

(a) Show that this equation can be written in the form of Equation (19.4); that is, it is a first-order linear equation.

(b) Use the integrating factor method to obtain the particular solution of this equation which satisfies the given initial condition.

(c) Obtain the particular solution of the equation subject instead to the initial condition $v_C(0) = 0$. It corresponds to the response of the system when there is no initial energy in the circuit. This solution is referred to as the **zero-state response**.

(d) Obtain the solution of the equation in the case when the supply voltage is identically zero, $v_S(t) = 0$, subject to the given condition $v_C(0) = V_0$. This solution is often referred to as the **zero-input response**, and represents the response of the system when the input is zero.

(e) Show that the solution in (b) can be written as the sum of the zero-state response and the zero-input response.

(f) Identify the transient and steady-state terms in the solution to part (e).

**Solution** (a) The given differential equation can be rewritten as

$$\frac{\mathrm{d}v_C}{\mathrm{d}t} + \frac{1}{RC}v_C = \frac{1}{RC}v_S(t)$$

Comparing the form of this equation with (19.4) we see that it is a first-order linear equation, with independent variable $t$, and dependent variable $v_C$, in which $P(t) = \frac{1}{RC}$ and $Q(t) = \frac{1}{RC}v_S(t)$.

(b) The integrating factor is given by

$$\mu = \mathrm{e}^{\int (1/RC)\mathrm{d}t} = \mathrm{e}^{t/(RC)}$$

It follows from the key point on page 541 that

$$\mathrm{e}^{t/(RC)}v_C = \frac{V}{RC}\int \mathrm{e}^{t/(RC)} \cos \omega t \, \mathrm{d}t$$

This integral can be evaluated using integration by parts twice following the technique in Example 14.4. You should verify that

$$\int \mathrm{e}^{t/(RC)} \cos \omega t \, \mathrm{d}t = \frac{R^2C^2\,\mathrm{e}^{t/(RC)}}{R^2C^2\omega^2 + 1}\left[\omega \sin \omega t + \frac{\cos \omega t}{RC}\right]$$
$$+ \text{ constant of integration}$$

Then

$$\mathrm{e}^{t/(RC)}v_C = \frac{VRC\mathrm{e}^{t/(RC)}}{R^2C^2\omega^2 + 1}\left[\omega \sin \omega t + \frac{\cos \omega t}{RC}\right] + K$$

from which

$$v_C = \frac{VRC}{R^2C^2\omega^2 + 1}\left[\omega \sin \omega t + \frac{\cos \omega t}{RC}\right] + K\,e^{-t/(RC)}$$

This is the general solution of the differential equation. Applying the initial condition gives us a value for $K$. When $t = 0$, $v_C = V_0$, so

$$V_0 = \frac{VRC}{R^2C^2\omega^2 + 1}\left[\frac{1}{RC}\right] + K$$

from which

$$K = V_0 - \frac{V}{R^2C^2\omega^2 + 1}$$

Finally,

$$v_C = \frac{VRC}{R^2C^2\omega^2 + 1}\left[\omega \sin \omega t + \frac{\cos \omega t}{RC}\right] + \left(V_0 - \frac{V}{R^2C^2\omega^2 + 1}\right) e^{-t/(RC)}$$

This is the particular solution which satisfies the given initial condition. It tells us the voltage across the capacitor as a function of time $t$.

(c) To find the particular solution subject to the condition $v_C(0) = 0$ we need only replace $V_0$ by 0 in the particular solution obtained in part (b). Hence the zero-state response is

$$v_C(t) = \frac{VRC}{R^2C^2\omega^2 + 1}\left[\omega \sin \omega t + \frac{\cos \omega t}{RC}\right] - \frac{V}{R^2C^2\omega^2 + 1}\,e^{-t/(RC)}$$

(d) In the case of zero input we have $v_S(t) = 0$. In part (b) we solved the equation with $v_S(t) = V \cos \omega t$. Hence, putting $V = 0$ in the solution to part (b) will yield the solution when $v_S(t) = 0$. So,

$$v_C(t) = V_0\,e^{-t/(RC)}$$

Alternatively we can note that when $v_S(t) = 0$ the original equation becomes

$$\frac{dv_C}{dt} + \frac{1}{RC}v_C = 0$$

subject to $v_C(0) = V_0$. This can be solved using separation of variables. So

$$\frac{1}{v_C}\frac{dv_C}{dt} = -\frac{1}{RC}$$

Integration yields

$$\int \frac{1}{v_C} dv_C = -\int \frac{1}{RC} dt$$

$$\ln v_C = -\frac{t}{RC} + k \qquad (k \text{ a constant})$$

$$v_C = e^{-t/(RC)+k}$$

$$= e^k e^{-t/(RC)}$$

$$= A e^{-t/(RC)}$$

where $A$ is the constant $e^k$. Applying the initial condition $v_C(0) = V_0$ we find $V_0 = A$ and so finally

$$v_C(t) = V_0 e^{-t/(RC)}$$

as before.

(e) Inspection of part (b) shows that it is the sum of the zero-input response and the zero-state response.

$$v_C(t) = \overbrace{V_0 e^{-t/(RC)}}^{\text{zero-input response}} + \overbrace{\frac{VRC}{R^2C^2\omega^2+1}\left[\omega \sin \omega t + \frac{\cos \omega t}{RC}\right] - \frac{V}{R^2C^2\omega^2+1} e^{-t/(RC)}}^{\text{zero-state response}}$$

(f) In this example, the terms involving $e^{-t/(RC)}$ tend to zero as $t$ increases, and are termed **transients**. Once the system has settled down their contribution will not be important. The remaining terms represent the longer term behaviour of the system or the so-called **steady state**.

Hence the transient terms are

$$V_0 e^{-t/(RC)} - \frac{V}{R^2C^2\omega^2 + 1} e^{-t/(RC)}$$

and the steady-state terms are

$$\frac{VRC}{R^2C^2\omega^2 + 1}\left[\omega \sin \omega t + \frac{\cos \omega t}{RC}\right]$$

## Exercises 19.4.4

1 Find the general solution of the following equations:

(a) $\dfrac{dy}{dx} + y = 1$

(b) $\dfrac{dy}{dx} + 2y = 6$

(c) $\dfrac{dx}{dt} + 6x = 4$

(d) $\dfrac{dy}{dx} - 3y = 2$

(e) $\dfrac{dy}{dx} = 6y + 9$

(f) $\dfrac{dx}{dt} = 3x - 8$

2 Find the particular solution of the following equations:

(a) $\dfrac{dy}{dx} + 4y = 7, \quad y(0) = 1$

(b) $\dfrac{dx}{dt} - x = 4, \quad x(0) = 2$

(c) $\dfrac{dy}{dt} = 3y + 2, \quad y(0) = 2$

(d) $\dfrac{dy}{dx} = 4y - 8, \quad y(1) = 2$

3 Find the general solution of $\dfrac{dx}{dt} = 2x + 4t$. What is the particular solution which satisfies $x(1) = 2$?

4 Find the general solution of $\dfrac{dy}{dx} + y = 2x + 5$.

5 Solve $\dfrac{dx}{dt} = t - tx$, $x(0) = 0$.

6 Use an integrating factor to obtain the general solution of $iR + L\dfrac{di}{dt} = \sin \omega t$ where $R$, $L$ and $\omega$ are constants.

7 Solve $x\dfrac{dy}{dx} + y = x^4$.

8 Use an integrating factor to find the general solution of $t\dfrac{dx}{dt} + x = 3t$.

9 Find the general solution of $\dfrac{dx}{dt} + 2xt = t$. Find the particular solution satisfying the condition $x(0) = -1$.

10 Find the general solution of

$$t\dot{x} + 3x = \frac{e^t}{t^2}.$$

## Solutions

1 (a) $y = 1 + c\,e^{-x}$

(b) $y = 3 + c\,e^{-2x}$

(c) $x = \frac{2}{3} + c\,e^{-6t}$

(d) $y = c\,e^{3x} - \frac{2}{3}$

(e) $y = c\,e^{6x} - \frac{3}{2}$

(f) $x = \frac{8}{3} + c\,e^{3t}$

2 (a) $y = \frac{7}{4} - \frac{3}{4}e^{-4x}$

(b) $x = 6e^t - 4$

(c) $y = \frac{8}{3}e^{3t} - \frac{2}{3}$

(d) $y = 2$

3 $-2t - 1 + c\,e^{2t}$, $-2t - 1 + 5\,e^{2(t-1)}$

4 $2x + 3 + c\,e^{-x}$

5 $1 - e^{-t^2/2}$

6 $\dfrac{L((R/L)\sin \omega t - \omega \cos \omega t)}{R^2 + L^2\omega^2} + c\,e^{-Rt/L}$

7 $\dfrac{x^4}{5} + \dfrac{c}{x}$

8 $\dfrac{3t}{2} + \dfrac{c}{t}$

9 $\frac{1}{2} - \frac{3}{2}e^{-t^2}$

10 $\dfrac{e^t + c}{t^3}$

## 19.5 Second order linear equations

The general form of a second-order linear ordinary differential equation is

$$p(x)\frac{d^2y}{dx^2} + q(x)\frac{dy}{dx} + r(x)y = f(x) \tag{19.7}$$

where $p(x)$, $q(x)$, $r(x)$ and $f(x)$ are functions of $x$ only.

An important relative of this equation is

$$p(x)\frac{d^2y}{dx^2} + q(x)\frac{dy}{dx} + r(x)y = 0 \tag{19.8}$$

which is obtained from Equation (19.7) by ignoring the term which is independent of $y$. Equation (19.8) is said to be a **homogeneous** equation – all its terms contain $y$ or its derivatives. Equation (19.7) is said to be **inhomogeneous**.

For example,

$$x^2\frac{d^2y}{dx^2} + x\frac{dy}{dx} + (x^2 - 1)y = e^{-x}$$

is an inhomogeneous second-order linear equation in which $p(x) = x^2$, $q(x) = x$, $r(x) = x^2 - 1$ and $f(x) = e^{-x}$. The associated homogeneous equation is

$$x\frac{d^2y}{dx^2} + x\frac{dy}{dx} + (x^2 - 1)y = 0$$

The following properties of linear equations are necessary for finding solutions of second-order linear equations.

### 19.5.1 Property 1

If $y_1(x)$ and $y_2(x)$ are any two linearly independent solutions of a second-order homogeneous equation then the general solution, $y_H(x)$, is

$$y_H(x) = Ay_1(x) + By_2(x)$$

where $A$, $B$ are constants.

We see that the second-order linear ordinary differential equation has two arbitrary constants in its general solution. The functions $y_1(x)$ and $y_2(x)$ are **linearly independent** if one is not simply a multiple of the other.

### 19.5.2 Property 2

Let $y_p(x)$ be any solution of an inhomogeneous equation. Let $y_H(x)$ be the general solution of the associated homogeneous equation. The general solution of the inhomogeneous equation is then given by

$$y(x) = y_H(x) + y_P(x)$$

In other words, to find the general solution of an inhomogeneous equation we must first find the general solution of the corresponding homogeneous problem, and then add to it any solution of the inhomogeneous equation.

The function $y_H(x)$ is known as the **complementary function** and $y_P(x)$ is called the **particular integral**. Clearly the complementary function of a homogeneous problem is the same as its general solution; we shall often write $y(x)$ for both. If conditions are given they are applied to the general solution of the inhomogeneous equation to determine any unknown constants. This yields the particular solution satisfying the given conditions.

**Example 19.19** Verify that $y_1(x) = x$ and $y_2(x) = 1$ both satisfy $\frac{d^2y}{dx^2} = 0$. Write down the general solution of this equation and verify that this indeed satisfies the equation.

**Solution** If $y_1(x) = x$ then $\frac{dy_1}{dx} = 1$ and $\frac{d^2y_1}{dx^2} = 0$, so that $y_1$ satisfies $\frac{d^2y}{dx^2} = 0$. If $y_2(x) = 1$, then $\frac{dy_2}{dx} = 0$ and $\frac{d^2y_2}{dx^2} = 0$, so that $y_2$ satisfies $\frac{d^2y}{dx^2} = 0$. From Property 1, the general solution of $\frac{d^2y}{dx^2} = 0$ is

$$\begin{aligned} y_H(x) &= Ax + B(1) \\ &= Ax + B \end{aligned}$$

To verify that this satisfies the equation proceed as follows:

$$\frac{dy_H}{dx} = A$$

$$\frac{d^2y_H}{dx^2} = 0$$

and so $y_H(x)$ satisfies $\frac{d^2y}{dx^2} = 0$.

**Example 19.20** Given

$$\frac{d^2y}{dx^2} + y = x \qquad (19.9)$$

(a) Show that $y_H = A\cos x + B\sin x$ is a solution of the corresponding homogeneous equation.

(b) Verify that $y_P = x$ is a particular integral.

(c) Verify that $y_H + y_P$ does indeed satisfy the inhomogeneous equation.

**Solution** (a) If $y_H = A\cos x + B\sin x$, then

$$y'_H = -A\sin x + B\cos x \qquad y''_H = -A\cos x - B\sin x$$

We see immediately that $y_H + y''_H = 0$ so that $y_H$ is a solution of the homogeneous equation.

(b) If $y_P = x$ then $y'_P = 1$ and $y''_P = 0$. Substitution into the inhomogeneous equation shows that $y_P$ satisfies Equation (19.9), that is $y_P = x$ is a particular integral.

(c) Writing

$$y = A\cos x + B\sin x + x$$

we have

$$y' = -A\sin x + B\cos x + 1 \qquad y'' = -A\cos x - B\sin x$$

Substitution into the l.h.s. of Equation (19.9) gives

$$(-A\cos x - B\sin x) + (A\cos x + B\sin x + x)$$

which equals $x$, and so the complementary function plus the particular integral is indeed a solution of the inhomogeneous equation, as required by Property 2.

---

### 19.5.3 Constant coefficient equations

We now proceed to study in detail those second-order linear equations which have constant coefficients. The general form of such an equation is

$$a\frac{d^2y}{dx^2} + b\frac{dy}{dx} + cy = f(x) \tag{19.10}$$

where $a$, $b$, $c$ are constants. The homogeneous form of Equation (19.10) is

$$a\frac{d^2y}{dx^2} + b\frac{dy}{dx} + cy = 0 \tag{19.11}$$

Equations of this form arise in the analysis of circuits. Consider the following example.

**Example 19.21** **The *LCR* circuit**

Write down the differential equation governing the current flowing in the series *LCR* circuit shown in Figure 19.4.

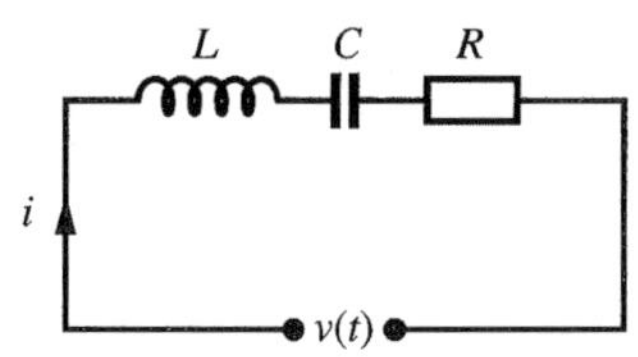


**Figure 19.4**
An $LCR$ circuit.

**Solution** Using Kirchhoff's voltage law and the individual laws for each component we find

$$L\frac{di}{dt} + iR + \frac{1}{C}\int i\,dt = v(t)$$

If this equation is now differentiated w.r.t. $t$ we find

$$L\frac{d^2i}{dt^2} + R\frac{di}{dt} + \frac{1}{C}i = \frac{dv(t)}{dt}$$

This is an inhomogeneous second-order differential equation, with the inhomogeneity arising from the term $\frac{dv}{dt}$. When the circuit components $L$, $R$ and $C$ are constants we have what is termed a **linear time-invariant system**, and the differential equation then has constant coefficients.

---

A linear time-invariant system has components whose properties do not vary with time and as such can be modelled by a linear constant coefficient differential equation.

## 19.5.4 Finding the complementary function

As stated in Property 2, finding the general solution of $ay''+by'+cy = f$ is a two-stage process. The first task is to determine the complementary function. This is the general solution of the corresponding homogeneous equation, that is $ay'' + by' + cy = 0$. We now focus attention on the solution of such equations.

**Example 19.22** Verify that $y_1 = e^{4x}$ and $y_2 = e^{2x}$ both satisfy the constant coefficient homogeneous equation

$$\frac{d^2y}{dx^2} - 6\frac{dy}{dx} + 8y = 0 \tag{19.12}$$

Write down the general solution of this equation.

**Solution** If $y_1 = e^{4x}$, differentiation yields

$$\frac{dy_1}{dx} = 4\,e^{4x}$$

and similarly,

$$\frac{d^2y_1}{dx^2} = 16\,e^{4x}$$

Substitution into Equation (19.12) gives

$$16\,e^{4x} - 6(4\,e^{4x}) + 8\,e^{4x} = 0$$

so that $y_1 = e^{4x}$ is indeed a solution. Similarly if $y_2 = e^{2x}$, then $\frac{dy_2}{dx} = 2\,e^{2x}$ and $\frac{d^2y_2}{dx^2} = 4\,e^{2x}$. Substitution into Equation (19.12) gives

$$4\,e^{2x} - 6(2\,e^{2x}) + 8\,e^{2x} = 0$$

so that $y_2 = e^{2x}$ is also a solution of Equation (19.12). Now $e^{2x}$ and $e^{4x}$ are linearly independent functions. So, from Property 1 we have

$$y_H(x) = A\,e^{4x} + B\,e^{2x}$$

as the general solution of Equation (19.12).

**Example 19.23** Find values of $k$ so that $y = e^{kx}$ is a solution of

$$\frac{d^2y}{dx^2} - \frac{dy}{dx} - 6y = 0$$

Hence state the general solution.

**Solution** As suggested we try a solution of the form $y = e^{kx}$. Differentiating we find $\frac{dy}{dx} = k\,e^{kx}$ and $\frac{d^2y}{dx^2} = k^2\,e^{kx}$. Substitution into the given equation yields

$$k^2\,e^{kx} - k\,e^{kx} - 6\,e^{kx} = 0$$

that is,

$$(k^2 - k - 6)\,e^{kx} = 0$$

The only way this equation can be satisfied for all values of $x$ is if

$$k^2 - k - 6 = 0 \qquad (19.13)$$

that is,

$$(k - 3)(k + 2) = 0$$

so that $k = 3$ or $k = -2$. That is to say, if $y = e^{kx}$ is to be a solution of the differential equation $k$ must be either 3 or $-2$. We therefore have found two solutions

$$y_1(x) = e^{3x} \qquad \text{and} \qquad y_2(x) = e^{-2x}$$

These two functions are linearly independent and we can therefore apply Property 1 to give the general solution:

$$y_H(x) = A\,e^{3x} + B\,e^{-2x}$$

Equation (19.13) for determining $k$ is called the **auxiliary equation**.

**Example 19.24** Find the auxiliary equation of the differential equation

$$a\frac{d^2y}{dx^2} + b\frac{dy}{dx} + cy = 0$$

**Solution** We try a solution of the form $y = e^{kx}$ so that $\frac{dy}{dx} = k\,e^{kx}$ and $\frac{d^2y}{dx^2} = k^2\,e^{kx}$. Substitution into the given differential equation yields

$$ak^2\,e^{kx} + bk\,e^{kx} + c\,e^{kx} = 0$$

that is,

$$(ak^2 + bk + c)\,e^{kx} = 0$$

Since this equation is to be satisfied for all values of $x$, then

$$ak^2 + bk + c = 0$$

is the required auxiliary equation.

---

The auxiliary equation of $a\frac{d^2y}{dx^2} + b\frac{dy}{dx} + cy = 0$ is

$$ak^2 + bk + c = 0$$

Solution of this quadratic equation gives the values of $k$ which we seek. Clearly the nature of the roots will depend upon the values of $a$, $b$ and $c$. If $b^2 > 4ac$ the roots will be real and distinct. The two values of $k$ thus obtained, $k_1$ and $k_2$, will allow us to write down two independent solutions:

$$y_1(x) = e^{k_1x} \qquad y_2(x) = e^{k_2x}$$

and so the general solution of the differential equation will be

$$y(x) = A\,e^{k_1 x} + B\,e^{k_2 x}$$

If the auxiliary equation has real, distinct roots $k_1$ and $k_2$, the complementary function will be

$$y(x) = A\,e^{k_1 x} + B\,e^{k_2 x}$$

On the other hand, if $b^2 = 4ac$ the two roots of the auxiliary equation will be equal and this method will therefore only yield one independent solution. In this case, special treatment is required. If $b^2 < 4ac$ the two roots of the auxiliary equation will be complex, that is $k_1$ and $k_2$ will be complex numbers. The procedure for dealing with such cases will become apparent in the following examples.

**Example 19.25** Find the general solution of

$$\frac{d^2y}{dx^2} + 3\frac{dy}{dx} - 10y = 0$$

Find the particular solution which satisfies the conditions $y(0) = 1$ and $y'(0) = 1$.

**Solution** By letting $y = e^{kx}$, so that $\dfrac{dy}{dx} = k\,e^{kx}$ and $\dfrac{d^2y}{dx^2} = k^2\,e^{kx}$, the auxiliary equation is found to be

$$k^2 + 3k - 10 = 0$$

Therefore,

$$(k - 2)(k + 5) = 0$$

so that $k = 2$ and $k = -5$. Thus there exist two solutions, $y_1 = e^{2x}$ and $y_2 = e^{-5x}$. From Property 1 we can write the general solution as

$$y = A\,e^{2x} + B\,e^{-5x}$$

To find the particular solution we must now impose the given conditions:

$$\begin{aligned} y(0) &= 1 \quad \text{gives} \quad 1 = A + B \\ y'(0) &= 1 \quad \text{gives} \quad 1 = 2A - 5B \end{aligned}$$

from which $A = \frac{6}{7}$ and $B = \frac{1}{7}$. Finally, the required particular solution is $y = \frac{6}{7}\,e^{2x} + \frac{1}{7}\,e^{-5x}$.

**Example 19.26** Find the general solution of

$$\frac{d^2y}{dx^2} + 4y = 0$$

**Solution** As before, let $y = e^{kx}$ so that $\frac{dy}{dx} = k\,e^{kx}$ and $\frac{d^2y}{dx^2} = k^2\,e^{kx}$. The auxiliary equation is easily found to be

$$k^2 + 4 = 0$$

that is

$$k^2 = -4$$

so that

$$k = \pm 2j$$

that is, we have complex roots. The two independent solutions of the equation are thus

$$y_1(x) = e^{2jx} \qquad \text{and} \qquad y_2(x) = e^{-2jx}$$

so that the general solution can be written in the form

$$y(x) = A\,e^{2jx} + B\,e^{-2jx}$$

However, in cases such as this, it is usual to rewrite the solution in the following way. Recall from Chapter 9 that Euler's relations give

$$e^{2jx} = \cos 2x + j \sin 2x$$

and

$$e^{-2jx} = \cos 2x - j \sin 2x$$

so that

$$y(x) = A(\cos 2x + j \sin 2x) + B(\cos 2x - j \sin 2x)$$

If we now relabel the constants such that

$$A + B = C \qquad \text{and} \qquad Aj - Bj = D$$

we can write the general solution in the form

$$y(x) = C \cos 2x + D \sin 2x$$

**Example 19.27** Given $ay'' + by' + cy = 0$, write down the auxiliary equation. If the roots of the auxiliary equation are complex and are denoted by

$$k_1 = \alpha + \beta j \qquad k_2 = \alpha - \beta j$$

show that the general solution is

$$y(x) = e^{\alpha x}(A \cos \beta x + B \sin \beta x)$$

**Solution** Substitution of $y = e^{kx}$ into the differential equation yields

$$(ak^2 + bk + c)\,e^{kx} = 0$$

and so

$$ak^2 + bk + c = 0$$

This is the auxiliary equation. If $k_1 = \alpha + \beta\text{j}$, $k_2 = \alpha - \beta\text{j}$ then the general solution is

$$y = C\,\text{e}^{(\alpha+\beta\text{j})x} + D\,\text{e}^{(\alpha-\beta\text{j})x}$$

where $C$ and $D$ are arbitrary constants. Using the laws of indices this is rewritten as

$$y = C\,\text{e}^{\alpha x}\,\text{e}^{\beta\text{j}x} + D\,\text{e}^{\alpha x}\,\text{e}^{-\beta\text{j}x} = \text{e}^{\alpha x}(C\,\text{e}^{\beta\text{j}x} + D\,\text{e}^{-\beta\text{j}x})$$

Then, using Euler's relations, we obtain

$$\begin{aligned} y &= \text{e}^{\alpha x}(C\cos\beta x + C\text{j}\sin\beta x + D\cos\beta x - D\text{j}\sin\beta x) \\ &= \text{e}^{\alpha x}\{(C + D)\cos\beta x + (C\text{j} - D\text{j})\sin\beta x\} \end{aligned}$$

Writing $A = C + D$ and $B = C\text{j} - D\text{j}$, we find

$$y = \text{e}^{\alpha x}(A\cos\beta x + B\sin\beta x)$$

This is the required solution.

---

If the auxiliary equation has complex roots $\alpha+\beta\text{j}$ and $\alpha-\beta\text{j}$, then the complementary function is

$$y = \text{e}^{\alpha x}(A\cos\beta x + B\sin\beta x)$$

Note that Example 19.26 is a special case of Example 19.27 with $\alpha = 0$ and $\beta = 2$.

**Example 19.28** Find the general solution of $y'' + 2y' + 4y = 0$.

**Solution** The auxiliary equation is $k^2 + 2k + 4 = 0$. This equation has complex roots given by

$$\begin{aligned} k &= \frac{-2 \pm \sqrt{4 - 16}}{2} \\ &= \frac{-2 \pm \sqrt{12}\text{j}}{2} \\ &= -1 \pm \sqrt{3}\text{j} \end{aligned}$$

Using the result of Example 19.27 with $\alpha = -1$ and $\beta = \sqrt{3}$ we find the general solution is

$$y = \text{e}^{-x}(A\cos\sqrt{3}x + B\sin\sqrt{3}x)$$

**Example 19.29** The auxiliary equation of $ay''+by'+cy=0$ is $ak^2+bk+c=0$. Suppose this equation has equal roots $k=k_1$. Verify that $y=x\,\mathrm{e}^{k_1x}$ is a solution of the differential equation.

**Solution** We have

$$y=x\,\mathrm{e}^{k_1x} \qquad y'=\mathrm{e}^{k_1x}(1+k_1x) \qquad y''=\mathrm{e}^{k_1x}(k_1^2x+2k_1)$$

Substitution into the l.h.s. of the differential equation yields

$$\mathrm{e}^{k_1x}\{a(k_1^2x+2k_1)+b(1+k_1x)+cx\}=\mathrm{e}^{k_1x}\{(ak_1^2+bk_1+c)x+2ak_1+b\}$$

But $ak_1^2+bk_1+c=0$ since $k_1$ satisfies the auxiliary equation. Also,

$$k_1=\frac{-b\pm\sqrt{b^2-4ac}}{2a}$$

but since the roots are equal, then $b^2-4ac=0$ and hence $k_1=-\dfrac{b}{2a}$. So $2ak_1+b=0$. We conclude that $y=x\,\mathrm{e}^{k_1x}$ is a solution of $ay''+by'+cy=0$ when the roots of the auxiliary equation are equal.

---

If the auxiliary equation has two equal roots, $k_1$, the complementary function is

$$y=A\,\mathrm{e}^{k_1x}+Bx\,\mathrm{e}^{k_1x}$$

**Example 19.30** Obtain the general solution of the equation

$$\frac{\mathrm{d}^2y}{\mathrm{d}x^2}+8\frac{\mathrm{d}y}{\mathrm{d}x}+16y=0$$

**Solution** As before, a trial solution of the form $y=\mathrm{e}^{kx}$ yields an auxiliary equation:

$$k^2+8k+16=0$$

This equation factorizes so that

$$(k+4)(k+4)=0$$

and we obtain equal roots, that is $k=-4$ (twice). If we proceed as before, writing $y_1(x)=\mathrm{e}^{-4x}$, $y_2(x)=\mathrm{e}^{-4x}$, it is clear that the two solutions are not independent. To apply Property 1 we need to find a second independent solution. Using the result of Example 19.29 we conclude that, because the roots of the auxiliary equation are equal, the second independent solution is $y_2=x\,\mathrm{e}^{-4x}$. The general solution is then

$$y(x)=A\,\mathrm{e}^{-4x}+Bx\,\mathrm{e}^{-4x}$$

---

## Exercises 19.5.4

1 Obtain the general solutions, that is the complementary functions, of the following homogeneous equations:

(a) $\dfrac{d^2y}{dx^2} - 3\dfrac{dy}{dx} + 2y = 0$

(b) $\dfrac{d^2y}{dx^2} + 7\dfrac{dy}{dx} + 6y = 0$

(c) $\dfrac{d^2x}{dt^2} + 5\dfrac{dx}{dt} + 6x = 0$

(d) $\dfrac{d^2y}{dt^2} + 2\dfrac{dy}{dt} + y = 0$

(e) $\dfrac{d^2y}{dx^2} - 4\dfrac{dy}{dx} + 4y = 0$

(f) $\dfrac{d^2y}{dt^2} + \dfrac{dy}{dt} + 8y = 0$

(g) $\dfrac{d^2y}{dx^2} - 2\dfrac{dy}{dx} + y = 0$

(h) $\dfrac{d^2y}{dt^2} + \dfrac{dy}{dt} + 5y = 0$

(i) $\dfrac{d^2y}{dx^2} + \dfrac{dy}{dx} - 2y = 0$

(j) $\dfrac{d^2y}{dx^2} + 9y = 0$

(k) $\dfrac{d^2y}{dx^2} - 2\dfrac{dy}{dx} = 0$

(l) $\dfrac{d^2x}{dt^2} - 16x = 0$

2 Find the auxiliary equation for the differential equation

$$L\frac{d^2i}{dt^2} + R\frac{di}{dt} + \frac{1}{C}i = 0$$

Hence write down the complementary function.

3 Find the complementary function of the equation

$$\frac{d^2y}{dx^2} + \frac{dy}{dx} + y = 0$$

## Solutions

1 (a) $y = A\,e^{x} + B\,e^{2x}$

(b) $y = A\,e^{-x} + B\,e^{-6x}$

(c) $x = A\,e^{-2t} + B\,e^{-3t}$

(d) $y = A\,e^{-t} + Bt\,e^{-t}$

(e) $y = A\,e^{2x} + Bx\,e^{2x}$

(f) $y = e^{-0.5t}(A\cos 2.78t + B\sin 2.78t)$

(g) $y = A\,e^{x} + Bx\,e^{x}$

(h) $y = e^{-0.5t}(A\cos 2.18t + B\sin 2.18t)$

(i) $y = A\,e^{-2x} + B\,e^{x}$

(j) $y = A\cos 3x + B\sin 3x$

(k) $y = A + B\,e^{2x}$

(l) $x = A\,e^{4t} + B\,e^{-4t}$

2 $Lk^2 + Rk + \dfrac{1}{C} = 0 \qquad i(t) = A\,e^{k_1 t} + B\,e^{k_2 t}$

where

$$k_1, k_2 = \frac{-R \pm \sqrt{\dfrac{R^2C - 4L}{C}}}{2L}$$

3 $e^{-x/2}\left(A\cos\dfrac{\sqrt{3}x}{2} + B\sin\dfrac{\sqrt{3}x}{2}\right)$

### 19.5.5 Finding a particular integral

We stated in Property 2 that the general solution of an inhomogeneous equation is the sum of the complementary function and a particular integral. We have seen how to find the complementary function in the case of a constant coefficient equation. We shall now deal with the problem of finding a particular integral. Recall that the particular integral is any solution of the inhomogeneous equation. There are a number of advanced techniques available for finding such solutions but these are beyond the scope of this book. We shall adopt a simpler strategy. Since any solution will do we shall try to find such a solution by a combination of educated guesswork and trial and error.

**Example 19.31** Find the general solution of the equation

$$\frac{d^2y}{dx^2} - \frac{dy}{dx} - 6y = e^{2x} \tag{19.14}$$

**Solution** The complementary function for this equation has already been shown in Example 19.23 to be

$$y_H = A\,e^{3x} + B\,e^{-2x}$$

We shall attempt to find a solution of the inhomogeneous problem by trying a function of the same form as that on the r.h.s. In particular, let us try $y_P(x) = \alpha\,e^{2x}$, where $\alpha$ is a constant that we shall now determine. If $y_P(x) = \alpha\,e^{2x}$ then $\dfrac{dy_P}{dx} = 2\alpha\,e^{2x}$ and $\dfrac{d^2y_P}{dx^2} = 4\alpha\,e^{2x}$. Substitution in Equation (19.14) gives

$$4\alpha\,e^{2x} - 2\alpha\,e^{2x} - 6\alpha\,e^{2x} = e^{2x}$$

that is,

$$-4\alpha\,e^{2x} = e^{2x}$$

so that $y_P$ will be a solution if $\alpha$ is chosen so that $-4\alpha = 1$, that is $\alpha = -\frac{1}{4}$. Therefore the particular integral is $y_P(x) = -\dfrac{e^{2x}}{4}$. From Property 2 the general solution of the inhomogeneous equation is found by summing this particular integral and the complementary function

$$y(x) = A\,e^{3x} + B\,e^{-2x} - \tfrac{1}{4}\,e^{2x}$$

**Example 19.32** Obtain a particular integral of the equation

$$\frac{d^2y}{dx^2} - 6\frac{dy}{dx} + 8y = x$$

**Solution** In the last example, we found that a fruitful approach was to assume a solution in the same form as that on the r.h.s. Suppose we assume a solution $y_p(x) = \alpha x$ and proceed to determine $\alpha$. This approach will actually fail, but let us see why. If $y_P(x) = \alpha x$ then $\dfrac{dy_P}{dx} = \alpha$ and $\dfrac{d^2y_P}{dx^2} = 0$. Substitution into the differential equation yields

$$0 - 6\alpha + 8\alpha x = x$$

and $\alpha$ ought now to be chosen so that this expression is true for all $x$. If we equate the coefficients of $x$ we find $8\alpha = 1$ so that $\alpha = \frac{1}{8}$, but with this value of $\alpha$ the constant terms are inconsistent. Clearly a particular integral of the form $\alpha x$ is not possible. The problem arises because differentiation of the term $\alpha x$ produces constant terms which are unbalanced on the r.h.s. So, we try a solution of the form

$$y_P(x) = \alpha x + \beta$$

with $\alpha$, $\beta$ constants. Proceeding as before, $\frac{dy_P}{dx} = \alpha$, $\frac{d^2y_P}{dx^2} = 0$. Substitution in the differential equation now gives

$$0 - 6\alpha + 8(\alpha x + \beta) = x$$

Equating coefficients of $x$ we find

$$8\alpha = 1 \tag{19.15}$$

and equating constant terms we find

$$-6\alpha + 8\beta = 0 \tag{19.16}$$

From Equation (19.15), $\alpha = \frac{1}{8}$ and then from Equation (19.16)

$$-6\left(\tfrac{1}{8}\right) + 8\beta = 0$$

so that

$$8\beta = \tfrac{3}{4}$$

that is,

$$\beta = \tfrac{3}{32}$$

The required particular integral is $y_P(x) = \frac{x}{8} + \frac{3}{32}$.

Experience leads to the trial solutions suggested in Table 19.1.

**Table 19.1**
Trial solutions to find the particular integral.

| $f(x)$ | **Trial solution** |
|---|---|
| constant | constant |
| polynomial in $x$ of degree $r$ | polynomial in $x$ of degree $r$ |
| $\cos kx$ | $a\cos kx + b\sin kx$ |
| $\sin kx$ | $a\cos kx + b\sin kx$ |
| $a\,e^{kx}$ | $\alpha\,e^{kx}$ |

**Example 19.33** Find a particular integral for the equation

$$\frac{d^2y}{dx^2} - 6\frac{dy}{dx} + 8y = 3\cos x$$

**Solution** We shall try a solution of the form

$$y_P(x) = \alpha \cos x + \beta \sin x$$

Differentiating, we find

$$\frac{dy_P}{dx} = -\alpha \sin x + \beta \cos x$$

$$\frac{d^2 y_P}{dx^2} = -\alpha \cos x - \beta \sin x$$

Substitution into the differential equation gives

$$(-\alpha \cos x - \beta \sin x) - 6(-\alpha \sin x + \beta \cos x) + 8(\alpha \cos x + \beta \sin x)$$
$$= 3 \cos x$$

Equating coefficients of $\cos x$ we find

$$-\alpha - 6\beta + 8\alpha = 3 \tag{19.17}$$

while those of $\sin x$ give

$$-\beta + 6\alpha + 8\beta = 0 \tag{19.18}$$

Solving Equations (19.17) and (19.18) simultaneously we find $\alpha = \frac{21}{85}$ and $\beta = -\frac{18}{85}$, so that the particular integral is

$$y_P(x) = \frac{21}{85} \cos x - \frac{18}{85} \sin x$$

**Example 19.34** **An *LC* circuit with sinusoidal input**

The differential equation governing the flow of current in a series $LC$ circuit when subject to an applied voltage $v(t) = V_0 \sin \omega t$ is

$$L\frac{d^2 i}{dt^2} + \frac{1}{C}i = \omega V_0 \cos \omega t$$

Derive this equation and then obtain its general solution.

**Solution** Kirchhoff's voltage law and the component laws give

$$L\frac{di}{dt} + \frac{1}{C}\int i \, dt = V_0 \sin \omega t$$

To avoid processes of differentiation and integration in the same equation let us differentiate this equation w.r.t. $t$. This yields

$$L\frac{d^2 i}{dt^2} + \frac{1}{C}i = \omega V_0 \cos \omega t$$

as required.

The homogeneous equation is $L\frac{\mathrm{d}^2 i}{\mathrm{d}t^2} + \frac{i}{C} = 0$. Letting $i = \mathrm{e}^{kt}$ we find the auxiliary equation is $Lk^2 + \frac{1}{C} = 0$ so that $k = \pm\frac{\mathrm{j}}{\sqrt{LC}}$. Therefore, using the result of Example 19.27, with $\alpha = 0$ and $\beta = \frac{1}{\sqrt{LC}}$, the complementary function is

$$i = A\cos\frac{t}{\sqrt{LC}} + B\sin\frac{t}{\sqrt{LC}}$$

To find a particular integral, try $i = E\cos\omega t + F\sin\omega t$, where $E$ and $F$ are constants. We find

$$\frac{\mathrm{d}i}{\mathrm{d}t} = -\omega E\sin\omega t + \omega F\cos\omega t$$

$$\frac{\mathrm{d}^2 i}{\mathrm{d}t^2} = -\omega^2 E\cos\omega t - \omega^2 F\sin\omega t$$

Substitution into the inhomogeneous equation yields

$$L(-\omega^2 E\cos\omega t - \omega^2 F\sin\omega t) + \frac{1}{C}(E\cos\omega t + F\sin\omega t) = V_0\omega\cos\omega t$$

Equating coefficients of $\sin\omega t$ gives

$$-\omega^2 LF + \frac{F}{C} = 0$$

Equating coefficients of $\cos\omega t$ gives

$$-\omega^2 LE + \frac{E}{C} = V_0\omega$$

so that $F = 0$ and $E = \frac{CV_0\omega}{1-\omega^2 LC}$. It follows that the particular integral is $i = \frac{CV_0\omega}{1-\omega^2 LC}\cos\omega t$. Finally, the general solution is

$$i = A\cos\frac{t}{\sqrt{LC}} + B\sin\frac{t}{\sqrt{LC}} + \frac{CV_0\omega\cos\omega t}{1-\omega^2 LC}$$

---

The terms zero-input response and zero-state response were introduced in Section 19.4 in connection with first-order equations. This terminology is identical when we deal with second-order equations as the following example illustrates.

**Example 19.35** **Parallel *RLC* circuit**

Figure 19.5 shows a parallel $RLC$ circuit which has a current source $i_S(t)$. The inductor current, $i$, can be found by solving the second-order differential equation

$$LC\frac{\mathrm{d}^2 i}{\mathrm{d}t^2} + \frac{L}{R}\frac{\mathrm{d}i}{\mathrm{d}t} + i = i_S(t) \qquad \text{for } t \geqslant 0$$

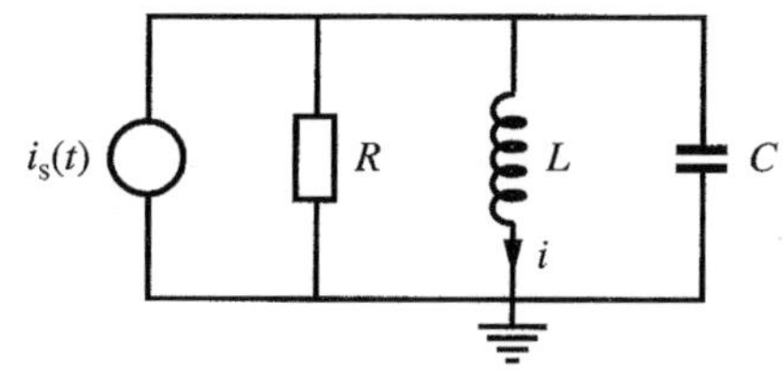


**Figure 19.5**
A parallel *RLC* circuit.

It would be a useful exercise for you to derive this equation. Note that this equation is second order, and inhomogeneous due to the source term $i_S(t)$.

Suppose $L = 10$ H, $R = 10\ \Omega$, $C = 0.1$ F and $i_S(t) = e^{-2t}$ and that the initial conditions are $i = 1$ and $\dfrac{di}{dt} = 2$ when $t = 0$.

(a) Obtain the solution of this equation subject to the given initial conditions and hence state the inductor current $i$.

(b) Obtain the zero-input response. This is the solution when $i_S(t) = 0$.

(c) Obtain the zero-state response. This is the solution of the inhomogeneous equation subject to the conditions $i = 0$ and $\dfrac{di}{dt} = 0$ at $t = 0$. It corresponds to there being no initial energy in the circuit.

(d) Show that the solution in (a) is the sum of the zero-input response and the zero-state response.

**Solution** (a) With the given parameter values the differential equation becomes

$$\frac{d^2 i}{dt^2} + \frac{di}{dt} + i = e^{-2t}$$

It is first necessary to find the complementary function. Letting $i = e^{kt}$, the auxiliary equation is $k^2 + k + 1 = 0$ which has complex solutions

$$k = -\frac{1}{2} \pm \frac{\sqrt{3}}{2} j$$

The complementary function is therefore

$$i = e^{-t/2}\left(A \cos \frac{\sqrt{3}}{2} t + B \sin \frac{\sqrt{3}}{2} t\right)$$

For a particular integral we try a solution of the form $i = \alpha\, e^{-2t}$. Substitution into the differential equation gives

$$4\alpha\, e^{-2t} - 2\alpha\, e^{-2t} + \alpha\, e^{-2t} = e^{-2t}$$

so that

$$3\alpha = 1, \qquad \text{that is} \qquad \alpha = \frac{1}{3}$$

Hence a particular integral is $i = \frac{1}{3}\mathrm{e}^{-2t}$. The general solution is the sum of the complementary function and the particular integral:

$$i = \mathrm{e}^{-t/2}\left(A\cos\frac{\sqrt{3}}{2}t + B\sin\frac{\sqrt{3}}{2}t\right) + \frac{1}{3}\mathrm{e}^{-2t}$$

We now apply the initial conditions to find the constants $A$ and $B$. Given $i = 1$ when $t = 0$ means

$$1 = A + \frac{1}{3} \qquad \text{so that} \qquad A = \frac{2}{3}$$

To apply the second condition we need to find $\frac{\mathrm{d}i}{\mathrm{d}t}$:

$$\frac{\mathrm{d}i}{\mathrm{d}t} = \mathrm{e}^{-t/2}\left(-\frac{\sqrt{3}}{2}A\sin\frac{\sqrt{3}}{2}t + \frac{\sqrt{3}}{2}B\cos\frac{\sqrt{3}}{2}t\right)$$

$$-\frac{1}{2}\mathrm{e}^{-t/2}\left(A\cos\frac{\sqrt{3}}{2}t + B\sin\frac{\sqrt{3}}{2}t\right) - \frac{2}{3}\mathrm{e}^{-2t}$$

Given $\frac{\mathrm{d}i}{\mathrm{d}t} = 2$ when $t = 0$ means

$$\begin{aligned}
2 &= \frac{\sqrt{3}}{2}B - \frac{1}{2}(A) - \frac{2}{3} \\
2 &= \frac{\sqrt{3}}{2}B - \frac{1}{2}\left(\frac{2}{3}\right) - \frac{2}{3} \\
2 &= \frac{\sqrt{3}}{2}B - 1 \\
3 &= \frac{\sqrt{3}}{2}B \\
B &= \frac{6}{\sqrt{3}} \\
&= 2\sqrt{3}
\end{aligned}$$

Finally, the required particular solution which gives the current through the inductor at any time is

$$i = \mathrm{e}^{-t/2}\left(\frac{2}{3}\cos\frac{\sqrt{3}}{2}t + 2\sqrt{3}\sin\frac{\sqrt{3}}{2}t\right) + \frac{1}{3}\mathrm{e}^{-2t}$$

(b) The zero-input response is obtained by ignoring the source term $i_S(t)$. From (a) we see that this is just the complementary function:

$$i = \mathrm{e}^{-t/2}\left(A\cos\frac{\sqrt{3}}{2}t + B\sin\frac{\sqrt{3}}{2}t\right)$$

Applying the given initial conditions to this solution gives $A = 1$ and $B = \dfrac{5}{\sqrt{3}}$ and so the zero-input response is

$$i = e^{-t/2}\left(\cos\frac{\sqrt{3}}{2}t + \frac{5}{\sqrt{3}}\sin\frac{\sqrt{3}}{2}t\right)$$

(c) The zero-state response of the inhomogeneous equation is found by applying the conditions $i = 0$ and $\dfrac{di}{dt} = 0$ at $t = 0$ to the general solution already obtained in (a). It is straightforward to show that $A = -\dfrac{1}{3}$ and $B = \dfrac{1}{\sqrt{3}}$. So the zero-state response is

$$i = e^{-t/2}\left(-\frac{1}{3}\cos\frac{\sqrt{3}}{2}t + \frac{1}{\sqrt{3}}\sin\frac{\sqrt{3}}{2}t\right) + \frac{1}{3}e^{-2t}$$

(d) Inspection of the previous working shows that the particular solution obtained in (a) is the sum of the zero-state response and zero-input response.

**Example 19.36** **Transmission lines**

A transmission line is an arrangement of electrical conductors for transporting electromagnetic waves. Although this definition could be applied to most electrical cables, it is usually restricted to cables used to transport high-frequency electromagnetic waves. There are several different types of transmission lines. The most familiar one is the coaxial cable which is used to carry the signal from a television aerial to a television set (see Figure 19.6). When a high-frequency wave is being carried by a cable several effects become important which can usually be neglected when dealing with a low-frequency wave. These are

(1) the capacitance, $C$, between the two conductors,

(2) the series inductance, $L$, of the two conductors,

(3) the leakage current through the insulation layer that separates the two conductors.

The electrical parameters of a coaxial cable are evenly distributed along its length. This is true for transmission lines in general and so it is usual to specify per unit length values for the parameters. When constructing a mathematical model of a transmission line it is easier to think in terms of lumped components spanning a distance $\delta z$ and then allow $\delta z$ to tend to zero (see Figure 19.7). The leakage between the two conductors is conventionally modelled by a conductance, $G$, as this simplifies the mathematics and avoids confusion with the line resistance, $R$. Note that $C$, $G$, $L$ and $R$ are per unit length values for the transmission line.

For most transmission lines of interest the signal that is being carried varies sinusoidally with time. Therefore the voltage and current depend on both position along the line, $z$, and time, $t$. However, it is common to separate the time dependence from the voltage and current expressions in order to simplify the analysis. It must be remembered that any voltage and current variation with position has superimposed upon it a

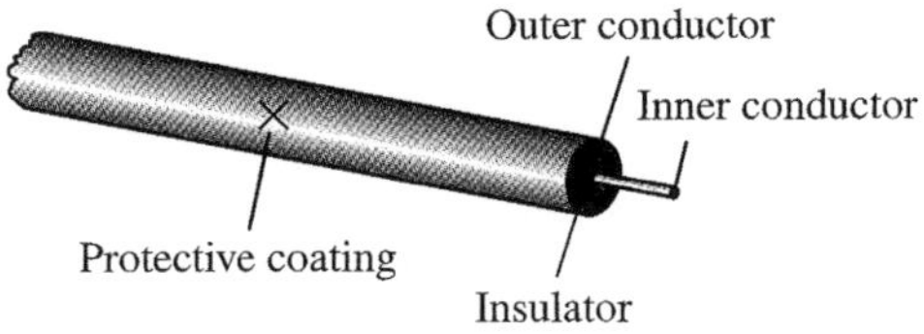


**Figure 19.6** A coaxial cable.

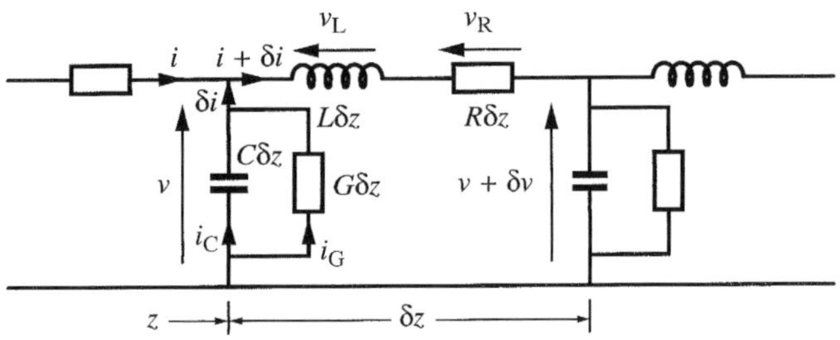


**Figure 19.7** A section of a transmission line.

sinusoidal variation with time. Therefore, ignoring the time-dependent element we write the voltage as $v$ and the current as $i$, knowing that they are functions of $z$.

Consider the circuit of Figure 19.7 which represents a section of the transmission line of length $\delta z$. Applying Kirchhoff's voltage law to the circuit yields

$$v + \delta v - v + v_{\mathrm{L}} + v_{\mathrm{R}} = 0$$
$$\delta v = -v_{\mathrm{L}} - v_{\mathrm{R}}$$

where $v_{\mathrm{L}}$ is the voltage across the inductor and $v_{\mathrm{R}}$ is the voltage across the resistor. Using the individual component laws for the inductor and resistor gives

$$\begin{aligned}\delta v &= -i\mathrm{j}\omega L\delta z - iR\delta z \\ &= -i(R + \mathrm{j}\omega L)\delta z\end{aligned}$$

Note that $\delta i$ has been ignored because it is small compared to $i$. Now consider the parallel combination of the capacitor and resistor (with units of conductance). Applying Kirchhoff's current law to this combination yields

$$\delta i = i_{\mathrm{C}} + i_{\mathrm{G}}$$

where $i_{\mathrm{C}}$ is the current through the capacitor and $i_{\mathrm{G}}$ is the current through the resistor. Using the individual component laws for the capacitor and resistor gives

$$\begin{aligned}\delta i &= -v\mathrm{j}\omega C\delta z - vG\delta z \\ &= -v(G + \mathrm{j}\omega C)\delta z\end{aligned}$$

Dividing these two circuit equations by $\delta z$ yields

$$\frac{\delta v}{\delta z} = -i(R + \mathrm{j}\omega L)$$

$$\frac{\delta i}{\delta z} = -v(G + \mathrm{j}\omega C)$$

In order to model a continuous transmission line with evenly distributed parameters, $\delta z$ is allowed to tend to zero. In the limit the two circuit equations become

$$\frac{\mathrm{d}v}{\mathrm{d}z} = -i(R + \mathrm{j}\omega L) \tag{19.19}$$

$$\frac{\mathrm{d}i}{\mathrm{d}z} = -v(G + \mathrm{j}\omega C) \tag{19.20}$$

Differentiating Equation (19.19) yields

$$\frac{d^2v}{dz^2} = -(R + j\omega L)\frac{di}{dz}$$

Substituting for $\frac{di}{dz}$ from Equation (19.20) yields

$$\frac{d^2v}{dz^2} = (R + j\omega L)(G + j\omega C)v$$

This is usually written as

$$\frac{d^2v}{dz^2} = \gamma^2 v \qquad \text{where} \qquad \gamma^2 = (R + j\omega L)(G + j\omega C) \tag{19.21}$$

This is the differential equation that describes the variation of the voltage, $v$, with position, $z$, along the transmission line. The general solution of this equation is easily shown to be

$$v = v_1\,e^{-\gamma z} + v_2\,e^{\gamma z} \tag{19.22}$$

where $v_1$ and $v_2$ are constants that depend on the initial conditions for the transmission line. It is useful to write $\gamma = \alpha + j\beta$ thus separating the real and imaginary parts of $\gamma$. Equation (19.22) can then be written as

$$v = v_1\,e^{-\alpha z}\,e^{-j\beta z} + v_2\,e^{\alpha z}\,e^{j\beta z} \tag{19.23}$$

The quantity $v_1\,e^{-\alpha z}\,e^{-j\beta z}$ represents the forward wave on the transmission line. It consists of a decaying exponential multiplied by a sinusoidal term. The decaying exponential represents a gradual attenuation of the wave caused by losses as it travels along the transmission line. The quantity $v_2\,e^{\alpha z}\,e^{j\beta z}$ represents the backward wave produced by reflection. Reflection occurs if the transmission line is not matched with its load. As the wave is travelling in the opposite direction to the forward wave, $e^{\alpha z}$ still represents an attenuation but in this case an attenuation as $z$ decreases.

A **loss-less** line is one in which the attenuation is negligible. This case corresponds to $\alpha = 0$, and so $\gamma = j\beta$. If $\gamma = j\beta$ then $\gamma^2 = -\beta^2$ so that, from Equation (19.21), $(R+j\omega L)(G+j\omega C)$ must be real and negative. We see that this is the case when $R = 0$ and $G = 0$. This agrees with what would be expected in practice as it is the resistive and conductive terms that lead to energy dissipation.

---

### 19.5.6 Inhomogeneous term appears in the complementary function

In some examples, terms which form part of the complementary function also appear in the inhomogeneous term. This gives rise to an additional complication. Consider Example 19.37.

**Example 19.37** Consider the equation $y'' - y' - 6y = e^{3x}$. It is straightforward to show that the complementary function is

$$y = A\,e^{3x} + B\,e^{-2x}$$

Find a particular integral and deduce the general solution.

**Solution** Suppose we try to find a particular integral by using a trial solution of the form $y_P = \alpha\,e^{3x}$. Substitution into the l.h.s. of the inhomogeneous equation yields

$$9\alpha\,e^{3x} - 3\alpha\,e^{3x} - 6\alpha\,e^{3x} \text{ which simplifies to } 0$$

so that $\alpha\,e^{3x}$ is clearly not a solution of the inhomogeneous equation. The reason is that $e^{3x}$ is part of the complementary function and so causes the l.h.s. to vanish. To obtain a particular integral in such a case, we carry out the procedure required when the auxiliary equation has equal roots. That is, we try $y_P = \alpha x\,e^{3x}$. We find

$$y' = \alpha\,e^{3x}(3x+1) \qquad y'' = \alpha\,e^{3x}(9x+6)$$

Substitution into the inhomogeneous equation yields

$$\alpha\,e^{3x}(9x+6) - \alpha\,e^{3x}(3x+1) - 6\alpha x\,e^{3x} = e^{3x}$$

Most terms cancel, leaving

$$5\alpha\,e^{3x} = e^{3x}$$

so that $\alpha = \frac{1}{5}$. Finally, the required particular integral is $y_P = \dfrac{x\,e^{3x}}{5}$. The general solution is then $y = A\,e^{3x} + B\,e^{-2x} + \dfrac{x\,e^{3x}}{5}$.

## Exercises 19.5.6

1. Find the general solution of the following equations:

(a) $\dfrac{d^2x}{dt^2} - 2\dfrac{dx}{dt} - 3x = 6$

(b) $\dfrac{d^2y}{dx^2} + 5\dfrac{dy}{dx} + 4y = 8$

(c) $\dfrac{d^2y}{dt^2} + 5\dfrac{dy}{dt} + 6y = 2t$

(d) $\dfrac{d^2x}{dt^2} + 11\dfrac{dx}{dt} + 30x = 8t$

(e) $\dfrac{d^2y}{dx^2} + 2\dfrac{dy}{dx} + 3y = 2\sin 2x$

(f) $\dfrac{d^2y}{dt^2} + \dfrac{dy}{dt} + y = 4\cos 3t$

(g) $\dfrac{d^2y}{dx^2} + 9y = 4\,e^{8x}$

(h) $\dfrac{d^2x}{dt^2} - 16x = 9\,e^{6t}$

2. Find a particular integral for the equation

$$\frac{d^2x}{dt^2} - 3\frac{dx}{dt} + 2x = 5\,e^{3t}$$

3. Find a particular integral for the equation

$$\frac{d^2x}{dt^2} - x = 4\,e^{-2t}$$

4. Obtain the general solution of $y'' - y' - 2y = 6$.

5. Obtain the general solution of the equation

$$\frac{d^2y}{dx^2} + 3\frac{dy}{dx} + 2y = 10\cos 2x$$

Find the particular solution satisfying

$$y(0) = 1, \quad \frac{dy}{dx}(0) = 0.$$

6. Find a particular integral for the equation

$$\frac{d^2y}{dx^2} + \frac{dy}{dx} + y = 1 + x$$

7. Find the general solution of

(a) $\dfrac{d^2x}{dt^2} - 6\dfrac{dx}{dt} + 5x = 3$

(b) $\dfrac{d^2x}{dt^2} - 2\dfrac{dx}{dt} + x = e^t$

**8** For the circuit shown in Figure 19.8 show that

$$RCL\frac{d^2i_2}{dt^2} + L\frac{di_2}{dt} + Ri_2 = E(t)$$

If $L = 1$ mH, $R = 10\ \Omega$, $C = 1\ \mu$F and $E(t) = 2\sin 100\pi t$, find the complementary function.

**9** Find the general solution of

$$\frac{d^2i}{dt^2} + 8\frac{di}{dt} + 25i = 48\cos 3t - 16\sin 3t$$

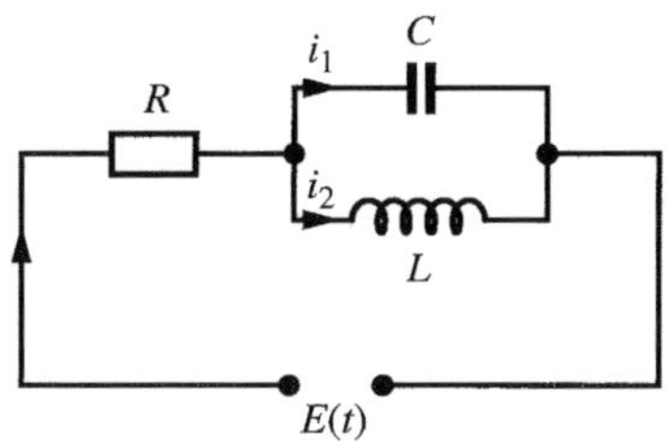


**Figure 19.8**

## Solutions

**1** (a) $x = A\,e^{-t} + B\,e^{3t} - 2$

(b) $y = A\,e^{-x} + B\,e^{-4x} + 2$

(c) $y = A\,e^{-2t} + B\,e^{-3t} + \dfrac{t}{3} - \dfrac{5}{18}$

(d) $x = A\,e^{-6t} + B\,e^{-5t} + 0.267t - 0.0978$

(e) $y = e^{-x}[A\sin\sqrt{2}x + B\cos\sqrt{2}x] - \dfrac{8}{17}\cos 2x - \dfrac{2}{17}\sin 2x$

(f) $y = e^{-0.5t}(A\cos 0.866t + B\sin 0.866t) - 0.438\cos 3t + 0.164\sin 3t$

(g) $y = A\cos 3x + B\sin 3x + 0.0548\,e^{8x}$

(h) $x = A\,e^{4t} + B\,e^{-4t} + \frac{9}{20}e^{6t}$

**2** $x = 2.5\,e^{3t}$

**3** $x = \frac{4}{3}e^{-2t}$

**4** $A\,e^{2x} + B\,e^{-x} - 3$

**5** $A\,e^{-2x} + B\,e^{-x} + \frac{3}{2}\sin 2x - \frac{1}{2}\cos 2x$, $\frac{3}{2}e^{-2x} + \frac{3}{2}\sin 2x - \frac{1}{2}\cos 2x$

**6** $x$

**7** (a) $A\,e^t + B\,e^{5t} + \frac{3}{5}$

(b) $A\,e^t + Bt\,e^t + \frac{1}{2}t^2\,e^t$

**8** $A\,e^{-11270t} + B\,e^{-88730t}$

**9** $e^{-4t}(A\sin 3t + B\cos 3t) + \dfrac{14\sin 3t + 18\cos 3t}{13}$

## Review exercises 19

**1** Find the general solution of the following equations:

(a) $\dfrac{dx}{dt} = 2x$

(b) $(1+t)\dfrac{dx}{dt} = 3$

(c) $\dfrac{dy}{dx} = y^2\cos x$

**2** Solve $\dfrac{dy}{dx} = 2$, subject to $y(0) = 3$.

**3** Find the general solution of $t\dot{x} + x = 2t$.

**4** Solve $\dfrac{dx}{dt} + 2x = e^{2t}\cos t$

(a) by using an integrating factor

(b) by finding its complementary function and a particular integral.

**5** Find the general solution of $y'' + 16y = x^2$.

**6** Find the particular solution of $y'' + 3y' - 4y = e^x$, $y(0) = 2$, $y'(0) = 0$.

**7** A particle moves in a straight line such that its displacement from the origin O is $x$, where $x$ satisfies the differential equation

$$\frac{d^2x}{dt^2} + 16x = 0$$

(a) Find the general solution of this equation.

(b) If $x\left(\frac{\pi}{4}\right) = -12$, and $\dot{x}\left(\frac{\pi}{4}\right) = 20$, find the displacement of the particle when $t = \frac{\pi}{2}$.

8 Use an integrating factor to solve the differential equation

$$\frac{dx}{dt} + x\cot t = \cos 3t$$

## Solutions

1 (a) $x = A\,e^{2t}$

(b) $x = 3\ln|1+t| + c$

(c) $y = \dfrac{1}{A - \sin x}$

2 $y = 2x + 3$

3 $x = t + \dfrac{c}{t}$

4 $x = \dfrac{e^{2t}(4\cos t + \sin t)}{17} + c\,e^{-2t}$

5 $y = A\cos 4x + B\sin 4x + \dfrac{x^2}{16} - \dfrac{1}{128}$

6 $y = \dfrac{39\,e^x + 11\,e^{-4x}}{25} + \dfrac{x\,e^x}{5}$

7 (a) $A\sin 4t + B\cos 4t$ (b) 12

8 $\sin t$; $x(t) = \dfrac{\cos 2t - \frac{1}{2}\cos 4t + c}{4\sin t}$

# Functions of More Than One Variable

# 25 Functions of several variables

| Chapter 25 | Contents |
| --- | --- |

## 25.1 Introduction

In engineering there are many functions which depend upon more than one variable. For example, the voltage on a transmission line depends upon position along the transmission line as well as time. The height of liquid in a tank depends upon the flow rates into and out of the tank. We shall examine some more examples in this chapter.

We have already discussed differentiation of functions of one variable. However, we also need to be able to differentiate functions of two or more variables. This is achieved by allowing one variable to change at a time, holding the others fixed. Differentiation under these conditions is called **partial differentiation**.

## 25.2 Functions of more than one variable

In Chapter 10 we saw how to differentiate a function $y(x)$ with respect to $x$. Many standard derivatives were listed and some techniques explained. Since $y$ is a function of $x$ we call $y$ the dependent variable and $x$ the independent variable. The function $y$ depends upon the one variable $x$. Consider the following example.

The area, $A$, of a circle depends only upon the radius, $r$, and is given by

$$A(r) = \pi r^2$$

The rate of change of area w.r.t. the radius is $\frac{\mathrm{d}A}{\mathrm{d}r} = 2\pi r$. In practice functions often depend upon more than one variable. For example, the volume, $V$, of a cylinder depends upon the radius, $r$, and the height, $h$, and is given by

$$V = \pi r^2 h$$

where $V$ is the dependent variable; $r$ and $h$ are independent variables. $V$ is a function of the two independent variables, $r$ and $h$. We write $V = V(r, h)$.

### Example 25.1 Electrical potential inside a cathode ray tube

Within a cathode ray tube the electrical potential, $V$, will vary with spatial position and time. Given Cartesian coordinates $x$, $y$ and $z$, we can write

$$V = V(x, y, z, t)$$

to show this dependence. Note that $V$ is a function of four independent variables.

### Example 25.2 Power dissipated in a variable resistor

The power, $P$, dissipated in a variable resistor depends upon the instantaneous voltage across the resistor, $v$, and the resistance, $r$. It is given by

$$P = \frac{v^2}{r}$$

Hence we may write $P = P(v, r)$ to show this dependence. The power is a function of two independent variables.

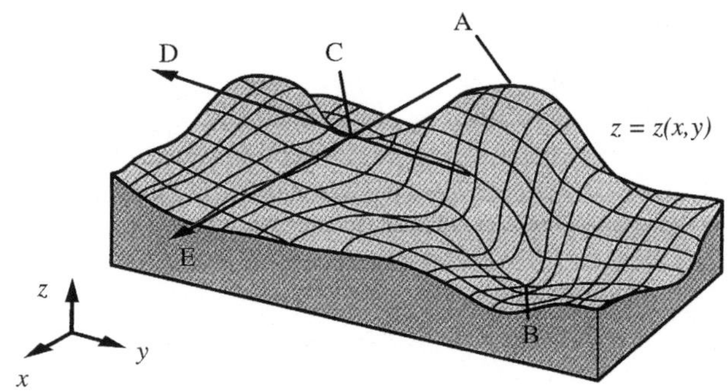


**Figure 25.1**
The height of the surface above the $x$–$y$ plane is $z$.

As another example of a function of more than one variable consider a three-dimensional surface as shown in Figure 25.1. The height, $z$, of the surface above the $x$–$y$ plane depends upon the $x$ and $y$ coordinates, that is $z = z(x, y)$. If we are given values of $x$ and $y$, then $z(x, y)$ can be evaluated. This value of $z$ is the height of the surface above the point $(x, y)$. We write, for example, $z(3, -1)$ for the value of $z$ evaluated when $x = 3$ and $y = -1$. The dependent variable, $z$, is a function of the independent variables $x$ and $y$.

Some important features are shown in Figure 25.1. The value of $z$ at a **maximum point** is greater than the values of $z$ at nearby points. Point A is such a point. As you move away from A the value of $z$ decreases. A **minimum point** is similarly defined. At a minimum point, the value of $z$ is smaller than the $z$ value at nearby points. This is illustrated by point B. Point C illustrates a **saddle point**. At a saddle point, $z$ increases in one direction, axis D on the figure, but decreases in the direction of axis E. These axes are at right angles to each other. The term 'saddle' is descriptive as a horse saddle has a similar shape. Maximum points, minimum points and saddle points are considered in greater depth in Section 25.7.

## 25.3 Partial derivatives

Consider

$$z = z(x, y)$$

that is, $z$ is a function of the independent variables $x$ and $y$. We can differentiate $z$ either w.r.t $x$, or w.r.t. $y$. We need symbols to distinguish between these two cases. When finding the derivative w.r.t. $x$, the other independent variable, $y$, is held constant and only $x$ changes. Similarly when differentiating w.r.t. $y$, the variable $x$ is held constant. We write $\dfrac{\partial z}{\partial x}$ to denote differentiation of $z$ w.r.t. $x$ for a constant $y$. It is called the first partial derivative of $z$ w.r.t. $x$. Similarly, the first partial derivative of $z$ w.r.t. $y$ is denoted $\dfrac{\partial z}{\partial y}$. Referring to the surface $z(x, y)$, $\dfrac{\partial z}{\partial x}$ gives the rate of change of $z$ moving only in the $x$ direction, and hence $y$ is held fixed.

If $z = z(x, y)$, then the **first partial derivatives** of $z$ are

$$\frac{\partial z}{\partial x} \quad \text{and} \quad \frac{\partial z}{\partial y}$$

If we wish to evaluate a partial derivative, say $\frac{\partial z}{\partial x}$, at a particular point $(x_0, y_0)$, we indicate this by

$$\frac{\partial z}{\partial x}(x_0, y_0) \qquad \text{or} \qquad \left.\frac{\partial z}{\partial x}\right|_{(x_0, y_0)}$$

just as we did for functions of one variable.

**Example 25.3** Given $z(x, y) = x^2y + \sin x + x \cos y$ find $\frac{\partial z}{\partial x}$ and $\frac{\partial z}{\partial y}$.

**Solution** To find $\frac{\partial z}{\partial x}$ we differentiate $z$ w.r.t. $x$, treating $y$ as a constant. Note that since $y$ is a constant then so is $\cos y$.

$$\frac{\partial z}{\partial x} = 2xy + \cos x + \cos y$$

In finding $\frac{\partial z}{\partial y}$, $x$ and hence $x^2$ and $\sin x$ are held fixed, thus

$$\frac{\partial z}{\partial y} = x^2 - x \sin y$$

**Example 25.4** Given $z(x, y) = 3\,\mathrm{e}^x - 2\,\mathrm{e}^y + x^2y^3$

(a) find $z(1, 1)$

(b) find $\frac{\partial z}{\partial x}$ and $\frac{\partial z}{\partial y}$ when $x = y = 1$.

**Solution** (a) $z(1, 1) = 3\,\mathrm{e}^1 - 2\,\mathrm{e}^1 + 1 = 3.718$

(b)
$$\frac{\partial z}{\partial x} = 3\,\mathrm{e}^x + 2xy^3$$

$$\frac{\partial z}{\partial y} = -2\,\mathrm{e}^y + 3x^2y^2$$

When $x = y = 1$, then

$$\frac{\partial z}{\partial x} = 3\,\mathrm{e} + 2 = 10.155$$

$$\frac{\partial z}{\partial y} = -2\,\mathrm{e} + 3 = -2.437$$

At the point (1, 1, 3.718) on the surface defined by $z(x, y)$, the height of the surface above the $x$–$y$ plane is increasing in the $x$ direction, and decreasing in the $y$ direction. Note that we could also write

$$\left.\frac{\partial z}{\partial x}\right|_{(1,1)} = 10.155 \quad \text{and} \quad \left.\frac{\partial z}{\partial y}\right|_{(1,1)} = -2.437$$

or

$$\frac{\partial z}{\partial x}(1, 1) = 10.155 \quad \text{and} \quad \frac{\partial z}{\partial y}(1, 1) = -2.437$$

Both notations are in common use.

**Example 25.5** **Eddy current losses**

Eddy currents are circulating currents that arise in iron cores of electrical equipment as a result of an a.c. magnetic field. They lead to energy losses given by

$$P_e = k_e f^2 B_{max}^2$$

where

$P_e$ = eddy current losses (W per unit mass),
$B_{max}$ = maximum value of the magnetic field wave (T),
$f$ = frequency of the magnetic field wave (Hz),
$k_e$ = a constant that depends upon factors such as the lamination thickness of the iron core.

Calculate $\dfrac{\partial P_e}{\partial f}$, and $\dfrac{\partial P_e}{\partial B_{max}}$.

**Solution**

$$\frac{\partial P_e}{\partial f} = 2k_e f B_{max}^2 \quad \text{and} \quad \frac{\partial P_e}{\partial B_{max}} = 2k_e f^2 B_{max}$$

**Example 25.6** If $V(x, y) = \sin(xy)$, find $\dfrac{\partial V}{\partial x}$ and $\dfrac{\partial V}{\partial y}$.

**Solution** To find $\dfrac{\partial V}{\partial x}$ we treat $y$ as a constant. Recalling that $\dfrac{d}{dx}(\sin kx) = k \cos kx$ we find $\dfrac{\partial V}{\partial x} = y\cos(xy)$. To find $\dfrac{\partial V}{\partial y}$ we treat $x$ as a constant. Thus $\dfrac{\partial V}{\partial y} = x\cos(xy)$.

**Example 25.7** Find the first partial derivatives of $z$ where

(a) $z(x, y) = yx\,e^x$

(b) $z(x, y) = x^2 \sin(xy)$

**Solution** (a) To find $\frac{\partial z}{\partial x}$ we must treat $y$ as a constant. However, the differentiation of the factor $x\,e^x$ will require use of the product rule. We find

$$\begin{aligned}\frac{\partial z}{\partial x} &= y\frac{\partial}{\partial x}(x\,e^x)\\ &= y((1)\,e^x + x\,e^x)\\ &= y\,e^x(x+1)\end{aligned}$$

To find $\frac{\partial z}{\partial y}$ the variable $x$ is held constant and so

$$\frac{\partial z}{\partial y} = x\,e^x$$

(b) Observe the product term in the variable $x$ which means we shall need to use the product rule. We find

$$\frac{\partial z}{\partial x} = 2x\sin(xy) + x^2(y\cos(xy)) = 2x\sin(xy) + x^2y\cos(xy)$$

To find $\frac{\partial z}{\partial y}$ we treat $x$ as a constant and find

$$\frac{\partial z}{\partial y} = x^2(x\cos(xy)) = x^3\cos(xy)$$

## Exercises 25.3

1 Find the first partial derivatives of

(a) $z = 2x + 3y$

(b) $z = x - y + x^2$

(c) $z = x^2 + y^2 + 3$

(d) $z = xy - 1$

(e) $z = x^2y + xy^2$

(f) $z = x^3 + 2x^2y - 4xy^2 + 2y^3$

2 Find the first partial derivatives of

(a) $z = \frac{x}{y}$

(b) $z = \sqrt{x}\,y$

(c) $z = \frac{y^2}{x^3} + 2$

(d) $z = \frac{1}{xy}$

(e) $z = \frac{3x^2}{y} - \frac{\sqrt{y}}{x}$

(f) $z = \sqrt{xy} - 3(x + y)$

**3** Find the first partial derivatives of

(a) $z = 2\sin x + 3\cos y$

(b) $z = x\sin y$

(c) $z = x\tan y - y^2\sin x$

(d) $z = xy\sin y$

(e) $z = \sin(x + y)$

(f) $z = 4\cos(4x - 6y)$

(g) $z = \dfrac{\sin y}{x}$

**4** Find the first partial derivatives of $y$. Note that $y$ is a function of $x$ and $t$.

(a) $y = t\,e^x$

(b) $y = x^2\,e^{-t}$

(c) $y = t\,e^t + x$

(d) $y = 3x^2\,e^{2t} + t^3\,e^{-x}$

(e) $y = e^{xt}$

(f) $y = e^{2x+3t}$

**5** Find the first partial derivatives of $z$ where

(a) $z = \sqrt{x^2 + y^2}$

(b) $z = \dfrac{x}{2x + 3y}$

(c) $z = \sin\left(\dfrac{x}{y}\right)$

(d) $z = e^{3xy}$

(e) $z = \ln(2x - 3y)$

(f) $z = \ln(xy)$

(g) $z = x\ln(xy)$

(h) $z = x\ln\left(\dfrac{y}{x}\right)$

**6** Evaluate the first partial derivatives of $f$ at $x = 1$, $y = 2$.

(a) $f = 3x^2y - 2xy$

(b) $f = \dfrac{x + y}{y}$

(c) $f = 2\sin(3x + 2y)$

(d) $f = 2e^{xy}$

(e) $f = y\ln x + \ln(xy)$

(f) $f = \sqrt{3x + y}$

**7** Given

$$f(r, h) = 2r^2h - \sqrt{r}h$$

evaluate the first partial derivatives of $f$ when $r = 2$, $h = 1$.

## Solutions

**1** (a) $\dfrac{\partial z}{\partial x} = 2,\ \dfrac{\partial z}{\partial y} = 3$

(b) $1 + 2x, -1$

(c) $2x, 2y$

(d) $y, x$

(e) $2xy + y^2, x^2 + 2xy$

(f) $3x^2 + 4xy - 4y^2, 2x^2 - 8xy + 6y^2$

**2** (a) $\dfrac{\partial z}{\partial x} = \dfrac{1}{y},\ \dfrac{\partial z}{\partial y} = -\dfrac{x}{y^2}$

(b) $\dfrac{y}{2\sqrt{x}}, \sqrt{x}$

(c) $-\dfrac{3y^2}{x^4}, \dfrac{2y}{x^3}$

(d) $-\dfrac{1}{x^2y}, -\dfrac{1}{xy^2}$

(e) $\dfrac{6x}{y} + \dfrac{\sqrt{y}}{x^2}, -\dfrac{3x^2}{y^2} - \dfrac{1}{2x\sqrt{y}}$

(f) $\dfrac{1}{2}\sqrt{\dfrac{y}{x}} - 3, \dfrac{1}{2}\sqrt{\dfrac{x}{y}} - 3$

**3** (a) $\dfrac{\partial z}{\partial x} = 2\cos x,\ \dfrac{\partial z}{\partial y} = -3\sin y$

(b) $\sin y, x\cos y$

(c) $\tan y - y^2\cos x, x\sec^2 y - 2y\sin x$

(d) $y\sin y, x\sin y + xy\cos y$

(e) $\cos(x + y), \cos(x + y)$

(f) $-16\sin(4x - 6y), 24\sin(4x - 6y)$

(g) $-\dfrac{\sin y}{x^2}, \dfrac{\cos y}{x}$

**4** (a) $\dfrac{\partial y}{\partial x} = t\,e^x,\ \dfrac{\partial y}{\partial t} = e^x$

(b) $2x\,e^{-t}, -x^2\,e^{-t}$

(c) $1, e^t(1+t)$

(d) $6x\,e^{2t} - t^3\,e^{-x}, 6x^2\,e^{2t} + 3t^2\,e^{-x}$

(e) $t\,e^{xt}, x\,e^{xt}$

(f) $2\,e^{2x+3t}, 3\,e^{2x+3t}$

(f) $\frac{1}{x}, \frac{1}{y}$

(g) $1 + \ln(xy), \frac{x}{y}$

(h) $\ln\left(\frac{y}{x}\right) - 1, \frac{x}{y}$

5 (a) $\frac{\partial z}{\partial x} = \frac{x}{\sqrt{x^2+y^2}}, \frac{\partial z}{\partial y} = \frac{y}{\sqrt{x^2+y^2}}$

(b) $\frac{3y}{(2x+3y)^2}, -\frac{3x}{(2x+3y)^2}$

(c) $\frac{1}{y}\cos\left(\frac{x}{y}\right), -\frac{x}{y^2}\cos\left(\frac{x}{y}\right)$

(d) $3y\,e^{3xy}, 3x\,e^{3xy}$

(e) $\frac{2}{2x-3y}, -\frac{3}{2x-3y}$

6 (a) $\frac{\partial f}{\partial x}(1,2) = 8, \frac{\partial f}{\partial y}(1,2) = 1$

(b) 0.5, −0.25

(c) 4.5234, 3.0156

(d) 29.5562, 14.7781

(e) 3, 0.5

(f) 0.6708, 0.2236

7 $\frac{\partial f}{\partial r}(2,1) = 7.6464, \frac{\partial f}{\partial h}(2,1) = 6.5858$

## 25.4 Higher order derivatives

Just as functions of one variable have second and higher derivatives, so do functions of several variables. Consider

$$z = z(x, y)$$

The first partial derivatives of $z$ are $\frac{\partial z}{\partial x}$ and $\frac{\partial z}{\partial y}$. The second partial derivatives are found by differentiating the first derivatives. We can differentiate first partial derivatives either w.r.t. $x$ or w.r.t. $y$ to obtain various second partial derivatives:

differentiating $\frac{\partial z}{\partial x}$ w.r.t. $x$ produces $\frac{\partial}{\partial x}\left(\frac{\partial z}{\partial x}\right) = \frac{\partial^2 z}{\partial x^2}$

differentiating $\frac{\partial z}{\partial x}$ w.r.t. $y$ produces $\frac{\partial}{\partial y}\left(\frac{\partial z}{\partial x}\right) = \frac{\partial^2 z}{\partial y \partial x}$

differentiating $\frac{\partial z}{\partial y}$ w.r.t. $x$ produces $\frac{\partial}{\partial x}\left(\frac{\partial z}{\partial y}\right) = \frac{\partial^2 z}{\partial x \partial y}$

differentiating $\frac{\partial z}{\partial y}$ w.r.t. $y$ produces $\frac{\partial}{\partial y}\left(\frac{\partial z}{\partial y}\right) = \frac{\partial^2 z}{\partial y^2}$

For most common functions, the mixed derivatives $\frac{\partial^2 z}{\partial y \partial x}$ and $\frac{\partial^2 z}{\partial x \partial y}$ are equal.

**Example 25.8** Given

$$z(x, y) = 3xy^3 - 2xy + \sin x$$

find all second partial derivatives of $z$.

**Solution**

$$\frac{\partial z}{\partial x} = 3y^3 - 2y + \cos x \qquad \frac{\partial z}{\partial y} = 9xy^2 - 2x$$

$$\frac{\partial^2 z}{\partial x^2} = \frac{\partial}{\partial x}\left(\frac{\partial z}{\partial x}\right) = -\sin x \qquad \frac{\partial^2 z}{\partial y^2} = \frac{\partial}{\partial y}\left(\frac{\partial z}{\partial y}\right) = 18xy$$

$$\frac{\partial^2 z}{\partial x \partial y} = \frac{\partial}{\partial x}\left(\frac{\partial z}{\partial y}\right) = 9y^2 - 2 \qquad \frac{\partial^2 z}{\partial y \partial x} = \frac{\partial}{\partial y}\left(\frac{\partial z}{\partial x}\right) = 9y^2 - 2$$

Note that $\dfrac{\partial^2 z}{\partial x \partial y} = \dfrac{\partial^2 z}{\partial y \partial x}$.

**Example 25.9** Given

$$H(x, t) = 3x^2 + t^2 + e^{xt}$$

verify that $\dfrac{\partial^2 H}{\partial x \partial t} = \dfrac{\partial^2 H}{\partial t \partial x}$.

**Solution**

$$\frac{\partial H}{\partial x} = 6x + t\,e^{xt} \qquad \frac{\partial H}{\partial t} = 2t + x\,e^{xt}$$

$$\frac{\partial^2 H}{\partial t \partial x} = \frac{\partial}{\partial t}\left(\frac{\partial H}{\partial x}\right) = \frac{\partial}{\partial t}(6x + t\,e^{xt}) = e^{xt} + tx\,e^{xt}$$

$$\frac{\partial^2 H}{\partial x \partial t} = \frac{\partial}{\partial x}\left(\frac{\partial H}{\partial t}\right) = \frac{\partial}{\partial x}(2t + x\,e^{xt}) = e^{xt} + xt\,e^{xt}$$

---

Third, fourth and higher derivatives are found in a similar way to finding second derivatives. The third derivatives are found by differentiating the second derivatives and so on.

**Example 25.10** Find all third derivatives of $f(r, s) = \sin(2r) - 3r^4s^2$.

**Solution**

$$\frac{\partial f}{\partial r} = 2\cos(2r) - 12r^3s^2 \qquad \frac{\partial f}{\partial s} = -6r^4s$$

$$\frac{\partial^2 f}{\partial r^2} = -4\sin(2r) - 36r^2s^2 \qquad \frac{\partial^2 f}{\partial s^2} = -6r^4$$

$$\frac{\partial^2 f}{\partial r \partial s} = -24r^3s$$

The third derivatives are $\dfrac{\partial^3 f}{\partial r^3}$, $\dfrac{\partial^3 f}{\partial r^2 \partial s}$, $\dfrac{\partial^3 f}{\partial r \partial s^2}$ and $\dfrac{\partial^3 f}{\partial s^3}$, and these are found by differentiating the second derivatives.

$$\frac{\partial^3 f}{\partial r^3} = \frac{\partial}{\partial r}\left(\frac{\partial^2 f}{\partial r^2}\right) = -8\cos(2r) - 72rs^2$$

$$\frac{\partial^3 f}{\partial r^2 \partial s} = \frac{\partial}{\partial r}\left(\frac{\partial^2 f}{\partial r \partial s}\right) = -72r^2 s$$

$$\frac{\partial^3 f}{\partial r \partial s^2} = \frac{\partial}{\partial r}\left(\frac{\partial^2 f}{\partial s^2}\right) = -24r^3$$

$$\frac{\partial^3 f}{\partial s^3} = \frac{\partial}{\partial s}\left(\frac{\partial^2 f}{\partial s^2}\right) = 0$$

Note that the mixed derivatives can be calculated in a variety of ways.

$$\frac{\partial^3 f}{\partial r^2 \partial s} = \frac{\partial}{\partial r}\left(\frac{\partial^2 f}{\partial r \partial s}\right) = \frac{\partial}{\partial s}\left(\frac{\partial^2 f}{\partial r^2}\right)$$

$$\frac{\partial^3 f}{\partial r \partial s^2} = \frac{\partial}{\partial r}\left(\frac{\partial^2 f}{\partial s^2}\right) = \frac{\partial}{\partial s}\left(\frac{\partial^2 f}{\partial r \partial s}\right)$$

## Exercises 25.4

**1** Calculate all second derivatives of $v$ where

$$v(h, r) = r^2\sqrt{h}$$

**2** Find the second partial derivatives of $f$ given

(a) $f = x^2 y + y^3$

(b) $f = 2x^4 y^3 - 3x^3 y^5$

(c) $f = 4\sqrt{x}y^2$

(d) $f = \dfrac{x^2 + 1}{y}$

(e) $f = \dfrac{3x^3}{\sqrt{y}}$

(f) $f = 4\sqrt{xy}$

**3** Find all second partial derivatives of

(a) $z = x\,e^{2y}$

(b) $z = 2\sin(xy)$

(c) $z = x\cos(2x + 3y)$

(d) $z = y\sin(4xy)$

(e) $z = e^x \sin y$

(f) $z = e^{3x-y}$

(g) $z = e^{xy}$

**4** Find all second partial derivatives of

(a) $z = (3x - 2y)^{20}$

(b) $z = \sqrt{2x + 5y}$

(c) $z = \sin(x^2 + y^2)$

(d) $z = \ln(2x + 5y)$

(e) $z = \dfrac{1}{3x - 2y}$

**5** Find all third partial derivatives of $z$ where

$$z(x, y) = \frac{x^2}{y + 1}$$

**6** Evaluate all second partial derivatives of $f$ at $x = 2$, $y = 1$.

(a) $f = y\,e^x$

(b) $f = \sin(2x - y)$

(c) $f = \ln\left(\dfrac{y}{x}\right)$

## Solutions

1 $\frac{\partial^2 v}{\partial h^2} = -\frac{r^2}{4h^{3/2}}, \frac{\partial^2 v}{\partial h \partial r} = \frac{r}{\sqrt{h}}, \frac{\partial^2 v}{\partial r^2} = 2\sqrt{h}$

2 (a) $\frac{\partial^2 f}{\partial x^2} = 2y, \frac{\partial^2 f}{\partial x \partial y} = 2x, \frac{\partial^2 f}{\partial y^2} = 6y$

(b) $24x^2y^3 - 18xy^5$,
$24x^3y^2 - 45x^2y^4$,
$12x^4y - 60x^3y^3$

(c) $-x^{-3/2}y^2, 4x^{-1/2}y, 8\sqrt{x}$

(d) $\frac{2}{y}, -\frac{2x}{y^2}, \frac{2(x^2+1)}{y^3}$

(e) $18xy^{-1/2}, -\frac{9}{2}x^2y^{-3/2}, \frac{9}{4}x^3y^{-5/2}$

(f) $-x^{-3/2}y^{1/2}, x^{-1/2}y^{-1/2}, -x^{1/2}y^{-3/2}$

3 (a) $\frac{\partial^2 z}{\partial x^2} = 0, \frac{\partial^2 z}{\partial x \partial y} = 2\,e^{2y}, \frac{\partial^2 z}{\partial y^2} = 4x\,e^{2y}$

(b) $-2y^2 \sin(xy)$,
$2\cos(xy) - 2xy\sin(xy)$,
$-2x^2\sin(xy)$

(c) $-4\sin(2x+3y) - 4x\cos(2x+3y)$,
$-3\sin(2x+3y) - 6x\cos(2x+3y)$,
$-9x\cos(2x+3y)$

(d) $-16y^3\sin(4xy)$,
$8y\cos(4xy) - 16xy^2\sin(4xy)$,
$8x\cos(4xy) - 16x^2y\sin(4xy)$

(e) $e^x \sin y, e^x \cos y, -e^x \sin y$

(f) $9\,e^{3x-y}, -3\,e^{3x-y}, e^{3x-y}$

(g) $y^2 e^{xy}, e^{xy}(1+xy), x^2 e^{xy}$

4 (a) $\frac{\partial^2 z}{\partial x^2} = 3420(3x-2y)^{18}$,

$\frac{\partial^2 z}{\partial x \partial y} = -2280(3x-2y)^{18}$,

$\frac{\partial^2 z}{\partial y^2} = 1520(3x-2y)^{18}$

(b) $-(2x+5y)^{-3/2}$,
$-\frac{5}{2}(2x+5y)^{-3/2}$,
$-\frac{25}{4}(2x+5y)^{-3/2}$

(c) $2\cos(x^2+y^2) - 4x^2\sin(x^2+y^2)$,
$-4xy\sin(x^2+y^2)$,
$2\cos(x^2+y^2) - 4y^2\sin(x^2+y^2)$

(d) $-\frac{4}{(2x+5y)^2}$,

$-\frac{10}{(2x+5y)^2}$,

$-\frac{25}{(2x+5y)^2}$

(e) $\frac{18}{(3x-2y)^3}, -\frac{12}{(3x-2y)^3}, \frac{8}{(3x-2y)^3}$

5 $\frac{\partial^3 z}{\partial x^3} = 0, \frac{\partial^3 z}{\partial x^2 \partial y} = -\frac{2}{(y+1)^2}$,

$\frac{\partial^3 z}{\partial x \partial y^2} = \frac{4x}{(y+1)^3}, \frac{\partial^3 z}{\partial y^3} = -\frac{6x^2}{(y+1)^4}$

6 (a) $\frac{\partial^2 f}{\partial x^2}(2, 1) = 7.3891$,

$\frac{\partial^2 f}{\partial x \partial y}(2, 1) = 7.3891$,

$\frac{\partial^2 f}{\partial y^2}(2, 1) = 0$

(b) $-0.5645, 0.2822, -0.1411$

(c) $0.25, 0, -1$

## 25.5 Partial differential equations

Partial differential equations (p.d.e.s) occur in many areas of engineering. If a variable depends upon two or more independent variables, then it is likely this dependence can be described by a p.d.e. The independent variables are often time, $t$, and space coordinates $x$, $y$, $z$.

One example is the wave equation. The displacement, $u$, of the wave depends upon time and position. Under certain assumptions, the displacement of a wave travelling in one direction satisfies

$$\frac{\partial^2 u}{\partial t^2} = c^2 \frac{\partial^2 u}{\partial x^2}$$

where $c$ is the speed of the wave. This p.d.e. is called the one-dimensional wave equation. Under prescribed conditions the subsequent displacement of the wave can be calculated as a function of position and time.

**Example 25.11** Verify that

$$u(x, t) = \sin(x + 2t)$$

is a solution of the one-dimensional wave equation

$$\frac{\partial^2 u}{\partial t^2} = 4 \frac{\partial^2 u}{\partial x^2}$$

**Solution** The first partial derivatives are calculated.

$$\frac{\partial u}{\partial x} = \cos(x + 2t) \qquad \frac{\partial u}{\partial t} = 2\cos(x + 2t)$$

The second derivatives, $\frac{\partial^2 u}{\partial x^2}$ and $\frac{\partial^2 u}{\partial t^2}$, are now found.

$$\frac{\partial^2 u}{\partial x^2} = -\sin(x + 2t) \qquad \frac{\partial^2 u}{\partial t^2} = -4\sin(x + 2t)$$

Now

$$\frac{\partial^2 u}{\partial t^2} = -4\sin(x + 2t) = 4[-\sin(x + 2t)] = 4\frac{\partial^2 u}{\partial x^2}$$

Hence $u(x, t) = \sin(x + 2t)$ is a solution of the given wave equation.

---

Another equally important p.d.e. is Laplace's equation. This equation is used extensively in electrostatics. Under certain conditions the electrostatic potential in a region is described by a function $\phi(x, y)$ which satisfies Laplace's equation in two dimensions.

$$\frac{\partial^2 \phi}{\partial x^2} + \frac{\partial^2 \phi}{\partial y^2} = 0$$

This equation is so important that a whole area of applied mathematics, called potential theory, is devoted to the study of its solution.

**Example 25.12** Verify that

$$\phi(x, y, z) = \frac{1}{\sqrt{x^2 + y^2 + z^2}}$$

satisfies the three-dimensional Laplace's equation

$$\frac{\partial^2\phi}{\partial x^2} + \frac{\partial^2\phi}{\partial y^2} + \frac{\partial^2\phi}{\partial z^2} = 0$$

**Solution** We begin by calculating the first partial derivative, $\frac{\partial\phi}{\partial x}$. We are given

$$\phi = (x^2 + y^2 + z^2)^{-1/2}$$

and so

$$\frac{\partial\phi}{\partial x} = -\frac{1}{2}(x^2 + y^2 + z^2)^{-3/2}(2x) = -x(x^2 + y^2 + z^2)^{-3/2}$$

We use the product rule to find $\frac{\partial^2\phi}{\partial x^2}$.

$$\begin{aligned}\frac{\partial^2\phi}{\partial x^2} &= -1(x^2 + y^2 + z^2)^{-3/2} - x\left(-\tfrac{3}{2}\right)(x^2 + y^2 + z^2)^{-5/2}2x \\ &= (x^2 + y^2 + z^2)^{-5/2}[-(x^2 + y^2 + z^2) + 3x^2]\end{aligned}$$

By a similar analysis we have

$$\frac{\partial^2\phi}{\partial y^2} = (x^2 + y^2 + z^2)^{-5/2}[-(x^2 + y^2 + z^2) + 3y^2]$$

$$\frac{\partial^2\phi}{\partial z^2} = (x^2 + y^2 + z^2)^{-5/2}[-(x^2 + y^2 + z^2) + 3z^2]$$

So

$$\begin{aligned}\frac{\partial^2\phi}{\partial x^2} + \frac{\partial^2\phi}{\partial y^2} + \frac{\partial^2\phi}{\partial z^2} &= (x^2 + y^2 + z^2)^{-5/2}[-3(x^2 + y^2 + z^2) + 3x^2 + 3y^2 + 3z^2] \\ &= 0\end{aligned}$$

Hence $\phi = \frac{1}{\sqrt{x^2 + y^2 + z^2}}$ is a solution of the three-dimensional Laplace's equation.

---

The transmission equation is another important p.d.e. The potential, $u$, in a transmission cable with leakage satisfies a p.d.e. of the form

$$\frac{\partial^2 u}{\partial x^2} = A\frac{\partial^2 u}{\partial t^2} + B\frac{\partial u}{\partial t} + Cu$$

where $A$, $B$ and $C$ are constants relating to the physical properties of the cable.

The analytical and numerical solution of p.d.e.s is an important topic in engineering. Coverage is beyond the scope of this book.

## Exercises 25.5

1 Verify that

$$u(x, y) = x^2 + xy$$

is a solution of the p.d.e.

$$\frac{\partial u}{\partial x} - 2\frac{\partial u}{\partial y} = y$$

2 Verify that

$$\phi = \sin(xy)$$

satisfies the equation

$$\frac{\partial^2 \phi}{\partial x^2} + \frac{\partial^2 \phi}{\partial y^2} + (x^2 + y^2)\phi = 0$$

3 Verify that

$$u(x, y) = x^3 y + xy^3$$

is a solution of the equation

$$xy\frac{\partial^2 u}{\partial x \partial y} + x\frac{\partial u}{\partial x} + y\frac{\partial u}{\partial y} = 7u$$

4 Verify that

$$u(x, y) = xy + \frac{x}{y}$$

is a solution of

$$y\frac{\partial^2 u}{\partial y^2} + 2x\frac{\partial^2 u}{\partial x \partial y} = 2x$$

5 Verify that

$$\phi(x, y) = x \sin y + e^x \cos y$$

satisfies

$$\frac{\partial^2 \phi}{\partial x^2} + \frac{\partial^2 \phi}{\partial y^2} = -x \sin y$$

6 Given

$$\phi = \sqrt{x^2 + y^2}$$

(a) Show

$$\frac{\partial^2 \phi}{\partial x^2} = y^2(x^2 + y^2)^{-3/2}$$

(b) Verify that $\phi$ is a solution of

$$\frac{\partial^2 \phi}{\partial x^2} + \frac{\partial^2 \phi}{\partial y^2} = (x^2 + y^2)^{-1/2}$$

## 25.6 Taylor polynomials and Taylor series in two variables

In Chapter 18 we introduced Taylor polynomials and Taylor series for functions of a single variable. We now extend this to include functions of two variables. Recall the main idea behind Taylor polynomials and series for a function of one variable. Knowing the values of a function, $f(x)$, and its derivatives at $x = a$ we can write down the Taylor polynomial generated by $f$ about $x = a$. This polynomial approximates to the function $f$. The values of the Taylor polynomial and the function are usually in close agreement for values of $x$ near to $x = a$. To put it another way, knowing the value of $f$ and its derivatives at $x = a$ allows us to estimate the value of $f$ near to $x = a$.

The same idea holds when $f$ is a function of two variables, $x$ and $y$. If we know the value of $f$ and its partial derivatives at a point $x = a$, $y = b$, then the Taylor polynomials allow us to estimate $f$ at points near to $(a, b)$.

### 25.6.1 First-order Taylor polynomial in two variables

Suppose $f$ is a function of two independent variables, $x$ and $y$, and that the values of $f$, $\frac{\partial f}{\partial x}$ and $\frac{\partial f}{\partial y}$ are known at the point $x = a$, $y = b$, that is we know

$$f(a, b) \qquad \frac{\partial f}{\partial x}(a, b) \qquad \frac{\partial f}{\partial y}(a, b)$$

The first-order Taylor polynomial, $p_1(x, y)$, generated by $f$ about $(a, b)$ is given by

$$p_1(x, y) = f(a, b) + (x - a)\frac{\partial f}{\partial x}(a, b) + (y - b)\frac{\partial f}{\partial y}(a, b)$$

We note the following properties of a first-order Taylor polynomial:

(1) The values of the Taylor polynomial and the function are identical at the point $(a, b)$.

(2) The values of the first partial derivatives of the Taylor polynomial and the function are identical at the point $(a, b)$.

(3) The highest derivative needed to calculate the Taylor polynomial is the first derivative.

(4) The first-order Taylor polynomial contains only linear terms; that is, there are no powers of $x$ or $y$ higher than 1.

The first-order Taylor polynomial represents a plane which is tangent to the surface $f(x, y)$ at $(a, b)$.

We can use $p_1(x, y)$ to estimate the value of $f$ near to $(a, b)$.

**Example 25.13** A function, $f$, is such that

$$f(3, 1) = 2 \qquad \frac{\partial f}{\partial x}(3, 1) = -1 \qquad \frac{\partial f}{\partial y}(3, 1) = 4$$

(a) State the first-order Taylor polynomial generated by $f$ about (3, 1).

(b) Estimate the values of $f(3.5, 1.2)$ and $f(3.2, 0.7)$.

(c) Verify that the Taylor polynomial and the function have identical values at (3, 1).

(d) Verify that the first partial derivatives of the Taylor polynomial and the function are identical at (3, 1).

**Solution** (a) In this example $a = 3$ and $b = 1$. Hence

$$\begin{aligned} p_1(x, y) &= f(3, 1) + (x - 3)\frac{\partial f}{\partial x}(3, 1) + (y - 1)\frac{\partial f}{\partial y}(3, 1) \\ &= 2 + (x - 3)(-1) + (y - 1)4 \\ &= 4y - x + 1 \end{aligned}$$

The first-order Taylor polynomial generated by $f$ about (3, 1) is

$$p_1(x, y) = 4y - x + 1$$

(b) We use $p_1(x, y)$ to estimate $f(3.5, 1.2)$ and $f(3.2, 0.7)$.

$$p_1(3.5, 1.2) = 4(1.2) - 3.5 + 1 = 2.3$$
$$p_1(3.2, 0.7) = 4(0.7) - 3.2 + 1 = 0.6$$

Hence 2.3 is an estimate of $f(3.5, 1.2)$ and 0.6 is an estimate of $f(3.2, 0.7)$.

(c) We are given $f(3, 1) = 2$. Also

$$p_1(3, 1) = 4(1) - 3 + 1 = 2$$

and so $f(3, 1) = p_1(3, 1)$.

(d) We are given $\frac{\partial f}{\partial x}(3, 1) = -1$ and $\frac{\partial f}{\partial y}(3, 1) = 4$. Now

$$p_1(x, y) = 4y - x + 1$$

and so

$$\frac{\partial p_1}{\partial x} = -1 \qquad \frac{\partial p_1}{\partial y} = 4$$

Hence

$$\frac{\partial p_1}{\partial x}(3, 1) = \frac{\partial f}{\partial x}(3, 1) = -1 \qquad \frac{\partial p_1}{\partial y}(3, 1) = \frac{\partial f}{\partial y}(3, 1) = 4$$

**Example 25.14** A function, $f(x, y)$, is defined by

$$f(x, y) = x^2 + xy - y^3$$

(a) State the first-order Taylor polynomial generated by $f$ about (1, 2).

(b) Verify that the Taylor polynomial in (a) and the function $f$ have identical values at (1, 2).

(c) Verify that the first partial derivatives of the Taylor polynomial and $f$ have identical values at (1, 2).

(d) Estimate $f(1.1, 1.9)$ using the Taylor polynomial. Compare this with the true value.

**Solution** (a) We are given $f = x^2 + xy - y^3$ and so

$$\frac{\partial f}{\partial x} = 2x + y \qquad \frac{\partial f}{\partial y} = x - 3y^2$$

Evaluating these at the point (1, 2) gives

$$f(1, 2) = -5 \qquad \frac{\partial f}{\partial x}(1, 2) = 4 \qquad \frac{\partial f}{\partial y}(1, 2) = -11$$

Putting $a = 1$ and $b = 2$ in the formula for $p_1(x, y)$ we are able to write down the Taylor polynomial:

$$\begin{aligned} p_1(x, y) &= f(1,2) + (x-1)\frac{\partial f}{\partial x}(1,2) + (y-2)\frac{\partial f}{\partial y}(1,2) \\ &= -5 + (x-1)4 + (y-2)(-11) \\ &= 4x - 11y + 13 \end{aligned}$$

The first-order Taylor polynomial is $p_1(x, y) = 4x - 11y + 13$.

(b) We can evaluate the Taylor polynomial and the function at $(1, 2)$.

$$p_1(1,2) = 4 - 22 + 13 = -5 \qquad f(1,2) = -5$$

Hence $p_1(1, 2) = f(1, 2)$; that is, the Taylor polynomial and the function have identical values at $(1, 2)$.

(c) The first partial derivatives of $p_1(x, y)$ are found.

$$\frac{\partial p_1}{\partial x} = 4 \qquad \frac{\partial p_1}{\partial y} = -11 \qquad \frac{\partial f}{\partial x}(1,2) = 4 \qquad \frac{\partial f}{\partial y}(1,2) = -11$$

Hence the first partial derivatives of $p_1$ and $f$ are identical at $(1, 2)$.

(d) $p_1(1.1, 1.9) = 4(1.1) - 11(1.9) + 13 = -3.5$

$f(1.1, 1.9) = (1.1)^2 + (1.1)(1.9) - (1.9)^3 = -3.559$

The values of the Taylor polynomial and the function are in close agreement near to the point $(1, 2)$.

---

### 25.6.2 Second-order Taylor polynomial in two variables

Given a function, $f$, and its first and second partial derivatives at $(a, b)$ we can write down the second-order Taylor polynomial, $p_2(x, y)$.

$$\begin{aligned} p_2(x, y) &= f(a,b) + (x-a)\frac{\partial f}{\partial x}(a,b) + (y-b)\frac{\partial f}{\partial y}(a,b) \\ &+ \frac{1}{2!}\left((x-a)^2\frac{\partial^2 f}{\partial x^2}(a,b) + 2(x-a)(y-b)\frac{\partial^2 f}{\partial x \partial y}(a,b) + (y-b)^2\frac{\partial^2 f}{\partial y^2}(a,b)\right) \end{aligned}$$

We note the following properties of the second-order Taylor polynomial:

(1) The values of the Taylor polynomial and the function are identical at $(a, b)$.

(2) The values of the first partial derivatives of the Taylor polynomial and the function are identical at $(a, b)$.

(3) The values of the second partial derivatives of the Taylor polynomial and the function are identical at $(a, b)$.

(4) The second-order Taylor polynomial contains quadratic terms, that is terms involving $x^2$, $y^2$ and $xy$.

**Example 25.15** A function, $f$, and its first and second partial derivatives are evaluated at $(2, -1)$. The values are

$$f = 3 \qquad \frac{\partial f}{\partial x} = 4 \qquad \frac{\partial f}{\partial y} = -3 \qquad \frac{\partial^2 f}{\partial x^2} = 1 \qquad \frac{\partial^2 f}{\partial x \partial y} = 2 \qquad \frac{\partial^2 f}{\partial y^2} = -1$$

(a) State the second-order Taylor polynomial generated by $f$ about $(2, -1)$.

(b) Estimate $f(1.8, -0.9)$.

(c) Verify that the Taylor polynomial and $f$ have identical values at $(2, -1)$.

(d) Verify that the first partial derivatives of the Taylor polynomial and $f$ are identical at $(2, -1)$.

(e) Verify that the second partial derivatives of the Taylor polynomial and $f$ are identical at $(2, -1)$.

**Solution** (a) We put $a = 2$ and $b = -1$ in the formula for $p_2(x, y)$.

$$p_2(x, y) = f + (x-2)\frac{\partial f}{\partial x} + (y+1)\frac{\partial f}{\partial y} + \frac{1}{2}\left((x-2)^2\frac{\partial^2 f}{\partial x^2} + 2(x-2)(y+1)\frac{\partial^2 f}{\partial x \partial y} + (y+1)^2\frac{\partial^2 f}{\partial y^2}\right)$$

where $f$ and its derivatives are evaluated at $(2, -1)$. So

$$p_2(x, y) = 3 + (x-2)4 + (y+1)(-3) + \tfrac{1}{2}\{(x-2)^2 + 2(x-2)(y+1)2 + (y+1)^2(-1)\} = \frac{x^2}{2} - \frac{y^2}{2} + 2xy + 4x - 8y - \frac{21}{2}$$

(b) The value of $p_2(1.8, -0.9)$ is an estimate of $f(1.8, -0.9)$.

$$p_2(1.8, -0.9) = \frac{(1.8)^2}{2} - \frac{(-0.9)^2}{2} + 2(1.8)(-0.9) + 4(1.8) - 8(-0.9) - \frac{21}{2}$$
$$= 1.875$$

(c) $$p_2(2, -1) = \frac{2^2}{2} - \frac{(-1)^2}{2} + 2(2)(-1) + 4(2) - 8(-1) - \frac{21}{2} = 3$$

$$f(2, -1) = 3$$

Hence $p_2(2, -1) = f(2, -1)$; that is, the Taylor polynomial and the function have identical values at $(2, -1)$.

(d) The first partial derivatives of $p_2$ are

$$\frac{\partial p_2}{\partial x} = x + 2y + 4 \qquad \frac{\partial p_2}{\partial y} = -y + 2x - 8$$

so

$$\frac{\partial p_2}{\partial x}(2, -1) = 2 + 2(-1) + 4 = 4 \qquad \frac{\partial p_2}{\partial y}(2, -1) = 1 + 4 - 8 = -3$$

Hence

$$\frac{\partial p_2}{\partial x}(2, -1) = \frac{\partial f}{\partial x}(2, -1) \qquad \frac{\partial p_2}{\partial y}(2, -1) = \frac{\partial f}{\partial y}(2, -1)$$

that is, the first partial derivatives of the Taylor polynomial and the function have identical values at $(2, -1)$.

(e) The second partial derivatives of $p_2$ are found.

$$\frac{\partial^2 p_2}{\partial x^2} = 1 \qquad \frac{\partial^2 p_2}{\partial x \partial y} = 2 \qquad \frac{\partial^2 p_2}{\partial y^2} = -1$$

These values are identical to the second partial derivatives of $f$ at $(2, -1)$.

**Example 25.16** A function $f$ is given by

$$f(x, y) = x^3 + x^2y + y^4$$

(a) State the second-order Taylor polynomial generated by $f$ about $(1, 1)$.

(b) Use the polynomial to estimate $f(1.2, 0.9)$. Compare this value with the true value.

(c) Verify that the second partial derivatives of the function and the Taylor polynomial are identical at $(1, 1)$.

**Solution** (a) Here $a = 1$ and $b = 1$. We are given that $f = x^3 + x^2y + y^4$ and so

$$\frac{\partial f}{\partial x} = 3x^2 + 2xy \qquad \frac{\partial f}{\partial y} = x^2 + 4y^3 \qquad \frac{\partial^2 f}{\partial x^2} = 6x + 2y$$

$$\frac{\partial^2 f}{\partial x \partial y} = 2x \qquad \frac{\partial^2 f}{\partial y^2} = 12y^2$$

Evaluation of $f$ and its derivatives at $(1, 1)$ yields

$$f = 3 \qquad \frac{\partial f}{\partial x} = 5 \qquad \frac{\partial f}{\partial y} = 5 \qquad \frac{\partial^2 f}{\partial x^2} = 8 \qquad \frac{\partial^2 f}{\partial x \partial y} = 2 \qquad \frac{\partial^2 f}{\partial y^2} = 12$$

The second-order Taylor polynomial is $p_2(x, y)$:

$$
\begin{aligned}
p_2(x, y) &= f + (x-1)\frac{\partial f}{\partial x} + (y-1)\frac{\partial f}{\partial y} \\
&\quad + \frac{1}{2}\left((x-1)^2\frac{\partial^2 f}{\partial x^2} + 2(x-1)(y-1)\frac{\partial^2 f}{\partial x \partial y} + (y-1)^2\frac{\partial^2 f}{\partial y^2}\right) \\
&= 3+5(x-1)+5(y-1)+\frac{1}{2}(8(x-1)^2+4(x-1)(y-1)+12(y-1)^2) \\
&= 4x^2 + 6y^2 + 2xy - 5x - 9y + 5
\end{aligned}
$$

(b) The value of $p_2(1.2, 0.9)$ is an estimate of $f(1.2, 0.9)$.

$$p_2(1.2, 0.9) = 4(1.2)^2 + 6(0.9)^2 + 2(1.2)(0.9) - 5(1.2) - 9(0.9) + 5 = 3.68$$

The actual value is

$$f(1.2, 0.9) = (1.2)^3 + (1.2)^2(0.9) + (0.9)^4 = 3.6801$$

(c) The partial derivatives of $p_2(x, y)$ are found.

$$\frac{\partial p_2}{\partial x} = 8x + 2y - 5 \qquad \frac{\partial p_2}{\partial y} = 12y + 2x - 9$$

$$\frac{\partial^2 p_2}{\partial x^2} = 8 \qquad \frac{\partial^2 p_2}{\partial x \partial y} = 2 \qquad \frac{\partial^2 p_2}{\partial y^2} = 12$$

The second partial derivatives of $p_2$ are identical to the second partial derivatives of $f$ evaluated at (1, 1).

---

### 25.6.3 Taylor series in two variables

The third-order Taylor polynomial involves all the third-order partial derivatives of $f$, the fourth-order Taylor polynomial involves all the fourth-order partial derivatives of $f$ and so on. Taylor polynomials approximate more and more closely to the generating function as more and more terms are included. As more and more terms are included, we obtain an infinite series known as a Taylor series in two variables. The general form of this series is beyond the scope of this book.

## Exercises 25.6

1 Use a first-order Taylor polynomial to estimate $f(2.1, 3.2)$ given

$$f(2,3) = 4 \qquad \frac{\partial f}{\partial x}(2,3) = -2$$

$$\frac{\partial f}{\partial y}(2,3) = 3$$

2 Use a first-order Taylor polynomial to estimate $g(-1.1, 0.2)$ given

$$g(-1,0) = 6 \qquad \frac{\partial g}{\partial x}(-1,0) = 2$$

$$\frac{\partial g}{\partial y}(-1,0) = -1$$

**3** Use a first-order Taylor polynomial to estimate $h(-1.2, -0.7)$ given

$$h(-1.3, -0.6) = 4$$
$$\frac{\partial h}{\partial x}(-1.3, -0.6) = -1$$
$$\frac{\partial h}{\partial y}(-1.3, -0.6) = 1$$

**4** Use a second-order Taylor polynomial to estimate $f(3.1, 4.2)$ given

$$f(3,4) = 1 \qquad \frac{\partial f}{\partial x}(3,4) = 0$$
$$\frac{\partial f}{\partial y}(3,4) = 2 \qquad \frac{\partial^2 f}{\partial x^2}(3,4) = -1$$
$$\frac{\partial^2 f}{\partial x \partial y}(3,4) = 3 \qquad \frac{\partial^2 f}{\partial y^2}(3,4) = 0.5$$

**5** Use a second-order Taylor polynomial to estimate $g(-2.9, 3.1)$ given

$$g(-3,3) = 1 \qquad \frac{\partial g}{\partial x}(-3,3) = -1$$
$$\frac{\partial g}{\partial y}(-3,3) = 4 \qquad \frac{\partial^2 g}{\partial x^2}(-3,3) = 3$$
$$\frac{\partial^2 g}{\partial x \partial y}(-3,3) = -2 \qquad \frac{\partial^2 g}{\partial y^2}(-3,3) = 2$$

**6** Use a second-order Taylor polynomial to estimate $h(0.1, 0.1)$ given

$$h(0,0) = 4 \qquad \frac{\partial h}{\partial x}(0,0) = -1$$
$$\frac{\partial h}{\partial y}(0,0) = -3 \qquad \frac{\partial^2 h}{\partial x^2}(0,0) = 2$$
$$\frac{\partial^2 h}{\partial x \partial y}(0,0) = 2 \qquad \frac{\partial^2 h}{\partial y^2}(0,0) = -1$$

**7** A function, $f(x, y)$, is defined by

$$f(x, y) = x^3 y + x y^3$$

(a) Calculate the first-order Taylor polynomial generated by $f$ about $(1, 1)$.

(b) Calculate the second-order Taylor polynomial generated by $f$ about $(1, 1)$.

(c) Estimate $f(1.2, 1.2)$ using the first-order Taylor polynomial.

(d) Estimate $f(1.2, 1.2)$ using the second-order Taylor polynomial.

(e) Compare your answers in (c) and (d) with the true value of $f(1.2, 1.2)$.

**8** A function $g(x, y)$ is defined by

$$g(x, y) = x \sin y + \frac{x}{y}$$

(a) Calculate the first-order Taylor polynomial generated by $g$ about $(0, 1)$.

(b) Calculate the second-order Taylor polynomial generated by $g$ about $(0, 1)$.

(c) Estimate $g(0.2, 0.9)$ using the polynomial in (a).

(d) Estimate $g(0.2, 0.9)$ using the polynomial in (b).

(e) Compare your estimates with the exact value of $g(0.2, 0.9)$.

**9** A function $h(x, y)$ is defined by

$$h(x, y) = e^x y + x^2 e^y$$

(a) Calculate the first-order Taylor polynomial generated by $h$ about $(0, 0)$.

(b) Calculate the second-order Taylor polynomial generated by $h$ about $(0, 0)$.

(c) Estimate $h(0.2, 0.15)$ using the polynomial from (a).

(d) Estimate $h(0.2, 0.15)$ using the polynomial from (b).

(e) Compare your answers in (c) and (d) to the exact value of $h(0.2, 0.15)$.

**10** A function, $f(x, y, z)$, is defined by

$$f(x, y, z) = x^2 + xyz + yz^2$$

(a) Write down the first-order Taylor polynomial generated by $f$ about $(0, 1, 2)$.

(b) Use the polynomial from (a) to estimate $f(0.1, 1.2, 1.9)$.

(c) Compare your answer in (b) to the exact value of $f(0.1, 1.2, 1.9)$.

## Solutions

1. 4.4
2. 5.6
3. 3.8
4. 1.465
5. 1.305
6. 3.625
7. (a) $4x + 4y - 6$
   (b) $3x^2 + 3y^2 + 6xy - 8x - 8y + 6$
   (c) 3.6
   (d) 4.08
   (e) 4.1472
8. (a) $1.8415x$
   (b) $2.3012x - 0.4597xy$
   (c) 0.3683
   (d) 0.3775
   (e) 0.3789
9. (a) $y$
   (b) $x^2 + xy + y$
   (c) 0.15
   (d) 0.22
   (e) 0.2297
10. (a) $2x + 4y + 4z - 8$
    (b) 4.6
    (c) 4.57

## 25.7 Maximum and minimum points of a function of two variables

We saw in Chapter 12 that to find the turning points of $y(x)$ we solve

$$\frac{dy}{dx} = 0$$

The sign of the second derivative, $\frac{d^2y}{dx^2}$, is then used to distinguish between a maximum point and a minimum point. The analysis is very similar for a function of two variables.

When considering a function of two variables, $f(x, y)$, we often seek maximum points, minimum points and saddle points. Collectively these are known as **stationary points**. Figure 25.1 illustrates a maximum point at A, a minimum point at B and a saddle point at C. When leaving a maximum point the value of the function decreases, when leaving a minimum point the value of the function increases. When leaving a saddle point, the function increases in one direction, axis D on the figure, and decreases in the other direction, axis E on the figure.

To locate stationary points we equate both first partial derivatives to zero, that is we solve

$$\frac{\partial f}{\partial x} = 0 \qquad \frac{\partial f}{\partial y} = 0$$

Stationary points are located by solving

$$\frac{\partial f}{\partial x} = 0 \qquad \frac{\partial f}{\partial y} = 0$$

**Example 25.17** Locate the stationary points of

(a) $f(x, y) = 2x^2 - xy - 7y + y^2$

(b) $f(x, y) = x^2 - 6x + 4xy + y^2$

**Solution** (a) The first partial derivatives are found.

$$\frac{\partial f}{\partial x} = 4x - y \qquad \frac{\partial f}{\partial y} = -x - 7 + 2y$$

The stationary points are located by solving $\frac{\partial f}{\partial x} = 0$ and $\frac{\partial f}{\partial y} = 0$ simultaneously, that is

$$\begin{aligned} 4x - y &= 0 \\ -x + 2y - 7 &= 0 \end{aligned}$$

Solving these equations yields $x = 1$, $y = 4$. Hence the function $f(x, y)$ has one stationary point and it is located at (1, 4).

(b) The first partial derivatives are found.

$$\frac{\partial f}{\partial x} = 2x - 6 + 4y \qquad \frac{\partial f}{\partial y} = 4x + 2y$$

The first partial derivatives are equated to zero.

$$\begin{aligned} 2x + 4y - 6 &= 0 \\ 4x + 2y &= 0 \end{aligned}$$

Solving the equations simultaneously yields $x = -1$, $y = 2$. Thus the function has one stationary point located at $(-1, 2)$.

**Example 25.18** Locate the stationary points of

$$f(x, y) = \frac{x^3}{3} + 3x^2 + xy + \frac{y^2}{2} + 6y$$

**Solution** The first partial derivatives are found.

$$\frac{\partial f}{\partial x} = x^2 + 6x + y \qquad \frac{\partial f}{\partial y} = x + y + 6$$

These derivatives are equated to zero.

$$x^2 + 6x + y = 0 \qquad (25.1)$$

$$x + y + 6 = 0 \qquad (25.2)$$

Equations (25.1) and (25.2) are solved simultaneously. From (25.2) $y = -x - 6$, and substituting this into Equation (25.1) yields $x^2 + 5x - 6 = 0$. Solving this quadratic equation gives $x = 1, -6$. When $x = 1$, $y = -7$, and when $x = -6$, $y = 0$. The function has stationary values at $(1, -7)$ and $(-6, 0)$.

---

Equating the first partial derivatives to zero locates the stationary points, but does not identify them as maximum points, minimum points or saddle points. To distinguish between these various points a test involving second partial derivatives must be made. Note that this is similar to locating and identifying turning points of a function of one variable.

To identify the stationary points we consider the expression

$$\frac{\partial^2 f}{\partial x^2}\frac{\partial^2 f}{\partial y^2} - \left(\frac{\partial^2 f}{\partial x \partial y}\right)^2$$

If the expression is negative at a stationary point, then that point is a saddle point.

If the expression is positive and in addition $\dfrac{\partial^2 f}{\partial x^2}$ is positive at a stationary point, then that point is a minimum point.

If the expression is positive and in addition $\dfrac{\partial^2 f}{\partial x^2}$ is negative at a stationary point, then that point is a maximum point.

If the expression is zero then further tests are required. These are beyond the scope of the book.

In summary:

| | | | |
|---|---|---|---|
| $\dfrac{\partial^2 f}{\partial x^2}\dfrac{\partial^2 f}{\partial y^2} - \left(\dfrac{\partial^2 f}{\partial x \partial y}\right)^2 < 0$ | | | Saddle point |
| $\dfrac{\partial^2 f}{\partial x^2}\dfrac{\partial^2 f}{\partial y^2} - \left(\dfrac{\partial^2 f}{\partial x \partial y}\right)^2 > 0$ | and | $\dfrac{\partial^2 f}{\partial x^2} > 0$ | Minimum point |
| $\dfrac{\partial^2 f}{\partial x^2}\dfrac{\partial^2 f}{\partial y^2} - \left(\dfrac{\partial^2 f}{\partial x \partial y}\right)^2 > 0$ | and | $\dfrac{\partial^2 f}{\partial x^2} < 0$ | Maximum point |

**Example 25.19** Locate and identify the stationary values of

$$f(x, y) = x^2 + xy + y$$

**Solution** The first partial derivatives are found.

$$\frac{\partial f}{\partial x} = 2x + y \qquad \frac{\partial f}{\partial y} = x + 1$$

The first partial derivatives are equated to zero.

$$2x + y = 0$$
$$x + 1 = 0$$

This yields $x = -1$, $y = 2$. Thus there is one stationary point, positioned at $(-1, 2)$.

The second partial derivatives are found.

$$\frac{\partial^2 f}{\partial x^2} = 2 \qquad \frac{\partial^2 f}{\partial x \partial y} = 1 \qquad \frac{\partial^2 f}{\partial y^2} = 0$$

Now

$$\frac{\partial^2 f}{\partial x^2}\frac{\partial^2 f}{\partial y^2} - \left(\frac{\partial^2 f}{\partial x \partial y}\right)^2 = 2(0) - (1)^2 = -1$$

Since the expression is negative, we conclude that $(-1, 2)$ is a saddle point.

**Example 25.20** Locate and identify the stationary points of

$$f(x, y) = xy - x^2 - y^2$$

**Solution** The first partial derivatives are found.

$$\frac{\partial f}{\partial x} = y - 2x \qquad \frac{\partial f}{\partial y} = x - 2y$$

Solving $\frac{\partial f}{\partial x} = 0$, $\frac{\partial f}{\partial y} = 0$ yields $x = 0$, $y = 0$.

The second partial derivatives are found.

$$\frac{\partial^2 f}{\partial x^2} = -2 \qquad \frac{\partial^2 f}{\partial x \partial y} = 1 \qquad \frac{\partial^2 f}{\partial y^2} = -2$$

The second derivative test to identify the stationary point is used. Now

$$\frac{\partial^2 f}{\partial x^2}\frac{\partial^2 f}{\partial y^2} - \left(\frac{\partial^2 f}{\partial x \partial y}\right)^2 = (-2)(-2) - (1)^2 = 3$$

Since $\frac{\partial^2 f}{\partial x^2} < 0$ and $\frac{\partial^2 f}{\partial x^2}\frac{\partial^2 f}{\partial y^2} - \left(\frac{\partial^2 f}{\partial x \partial y}\right)^2 > 0$ then $(0, 0)$ is a maximum point.

**Example 25.21** Locate and identify the stationary points of

$$f(x, y) = \frac{x^3}{3} - x + \frac{y^2}{2} + 2y$$

**Solution** The first partial derivatives are found.

$$\frac{\partial f}{\partial x} = x^2 - 1 \qquad \frac{\partial f}{\partial y} = y + 2$$

The first partial derivatives are equated to zero.

$$x^2 - 1 = 0$$
$$y + 2 = 0$$

These equations have two solutions: $x = 1$, $y = -2$ and $x = -1$, $y = -2$.

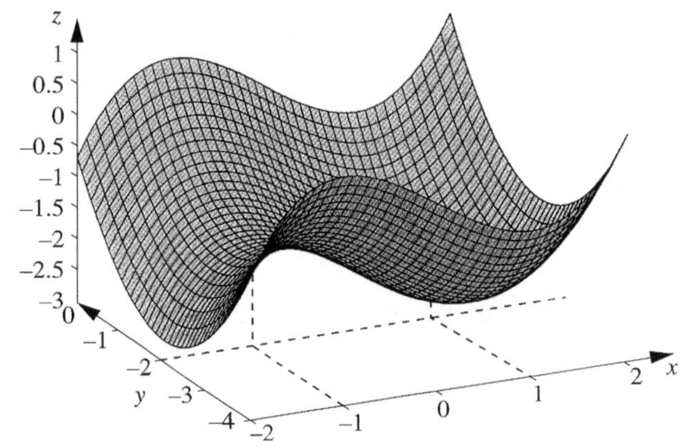


**Figure 25.2** The function $f(x, y) = \frac{x^3}{3} - x + \frac{y^2}{2} + 2y$ has a minimum at $(1, -2)$ and a saddle point at $(-1, -2)$.

In order to identify the nature of each stationary point, the second derivatives are found.

$$\frac{\partial^2 f}{\partial x^2} = 2x \qquad \frac{\partial^2 f}{\partial x \partial y} = 0 \qquad \frac{\partial^2 f}{\partial y^2} = 1$$

Each stationary point is examined in turn.

*At* $(1, -2)$

$$\frac{\partial^2 f}{\partial x^2}\frac{\partial^2 f}{\partial y^2} - \left(\frac{\partial^2 f}{\partial x \partial y}\right)^2 = 2x(1) - 0^2 = 2x = 2 \text{ since } x = 1$$

$$\frac{\partial^2 f}{\partial x^2} = 2x = 2$$

Since both expressions are positive the point $(1, -2)$ is a minimum point.

*At* $(-1, -2)$

Here

$$\frac{\partial^2 f}{\partial x^2}\frac{\partial^2 f}{\partial y^2} - \left(\frac{\partial^2 f}{\partial x \partial y}\right)^2 = 2x = -2 \text{ since } x = -1$$

Since the expression is negative then $(-1, -2)$ is a saddle point.

Figure 25.2 illustrates a plot of the surface defined by $f(x, y)$.

## Exercises 25.7

1 Determine the position and nature of the stationary points of the following functions.

(a) $f(x, y) = x + y + xy$

(b) $f(x, y) = x^2 + y^2 - 2y$

(c) $f(x, y) = x^2 + xy - y$

(d) $f(x, y) = x^2 + y^2 - xy$

(e) $f(x, y) = x^2 + 2y^2 - 3xy + x$

2 Determine the position and nature of the stationary points of the following functions.

(a) $z(x, y) = x^2 + y^2 - 3xy + 2x$

(b) $z(x, y) = x^3 + xy + y^2$

(c) $z(x, y) = \dfrac{y^3}{3} - x^2 - y$

(d) $z(x, y) = \dfrac{1}{x} + \dfrac{1}{y} - \dfrac{1}{xy}$

(e) $z(x, y) = 4x^2y - 6xy$

3 Locate and identify the stationary points of the following:

(a) $f(x, y) = x^2y - x^2 + y^2$

(b) $f(x, y) = \dfrac{x}{y} + x + y$

(c) $f(x, y) = x^4 + 16xy + y^4$

(d) $f(x, y) = y - y^2 - e^x x$

(e) $f(x, y) = \dfrac{e^x}{y^4} - xy$

## Solutions

1 (a) $(-1, -1)$, saddle point

(b) $(0, 1)$, minimum

(c) $(1, -2)$, saddle point

(d) $(0, 0)$, minimum

(e) $(4, 3)$, saddle point

2 (a) $\left(\frac{4}{5}, \frac{6}{5}\right)$, saddle point

(b) $(0, 0)$, saddle point; $\left(\frac{1}{6}, -\frac{1}{12}\right)$, minimum

(c) $(0, 1)$, saddle point; $(0, -1)$, maximum

(d) $(1, 1)$, saddle point

(e) $(0, 0)$, $(1.5, 0)$, saddle points

3 (a) $(0, 0)$, saddle point

(b) $(1, -1)$, saddle point

(c) $(0, 0)$, saddle point; $(2, -2)$, minimum; $(-2, 2)$, minimum

(d) $(-1, 0.5)$, maximum

(e) $(-4, 0.4493)$, saddle point

## Review exercises 25

1 Find all first partial derivatives of the following functions:

(a) $z(x, y) = 9x^2 + 2y^2$

(b) $z(x, y) = 3x^3y^6$

(c) $z(x, y) = 4x^3 - 5y^3$

(d) $z(x, y) = xy + x^2y^2$

(e) $z(x, y) = \sin(2xy)$

(f) $z(x, y) = 2\,e^{3xy}$

2 Evaluate the first partial derivatives of $f$ at $x = -1$, $y = 2$.

(a) $f(x, y) = 3x^3 - y^3 + x^2y^2$

(b) $f(x, y) = \dfrac{4x}{y}$

(c) $f(x, y) = \sin x + 2\cos y$

(d) $f(x, y) = (xy)^3 + x$

(e) $f(x, y) = \dfrac{x + y}{x - y}$

(f) $f(x, y) = 2\,e^x\,e^y$

3 Find all second partial derivatives of $z$ where

(a) $z(x, y) = 3x^4 - 9y^4 + x^3y^3$

(b) $z(x, y) = (x^2 + y^2)^2$

(c) $z(x, y) = 2\,e^{4x-3y}$

(d) $z(x, y) = \dfrac{2}{x + y}$

(e) $z(x, y) = 2\sqrt{x + y}$

(f) $z(x, y) = (\sin x)(\cos y)$

4 Find all first and second partial derivatives of

$$f(x, y) = (ax + by)^n$$

where $a$, $b$ and $n$ are constants.

5 Find the first partial derivatives of

$$f(x, y) = (ax^2 + by^2 + cxy)^n$$

where $a$, $b$, $c$ and $n$ are constants.

**6** Verify that

$$z(x, y) = 3x + 2y + 1$$

is a solution of

$$\frac{\partial z}{\partial x} - \frac{\partial z}{\partial y} = 1$$

**7** Verify that

$$z(x, y) = 2xy - x + y$$

is a solution of

$$\frac{\partial z}{\partial x} + \frac{\partial z}{\partial y} = 2(x + y)$$

**8** Verify that

$$f(x, y) = x^2 + y^2 - 2xy$$

is a solution of

$$\frac{\partial f}{\partial x} + \frac{\partial f}{\partial y} = 0$$

**9** Verify that

$$z(x, y) = \sin x + \cos y$$

is a solution of

$$\frac{\partial^2 z}{\partial x^2} + \frac{\partial^2 z}{\partial y^2} + z = 0$$

**10** Verify that

$$z(x, y) = xy\,e^x$$

is a solution of

$$\frac{\partial^2 z}{\partial x^2} + \frac{\partial^2 z}{\partial y^2} - y\frac{\partial^2 z}{\partial x \partial y} = y\,e^x$$

**11** (a) Write down the second-order Taylor polynomial generated by $f(x, y)$ about $x = 2$, $y = 3$ given

$$f(x, y) = 3x^3y - x^2y^3$$

(b) Estimate $f(2.1, 2.9)$ using your polynomial from (a) and compare this with the exact answer.

**12** Write down the second-order Taylor polynomial generated by $z(x, y)$ about $x = 1$, $y = 1$ given

$$z(x, y) = \frac{x + y}{x}$$

**13** Calculate the second-order Taylor polynomial generated by

$$f(x, y) = \sqrt{x^2 + y^2}$$

about $x = 1$, $y = 0$.

**14** Locate and identify all the stationary points of the following functions:

(a) $f(x, y) = x^2 + y^3 - 3y$

(b) $f(x, y) = 4xy - x^2y$

(c) $f(x, y) = x^3 + 2y^2 - 12x$

(d) $f(x, y) = xy - y^2 - x^3$

**15** Locate and identify the stationary points of

$$f(x, y) = \frac{y}{x} - x^2 + y^2$$

## Solutions

**1** (a) $\frac{\partial z}{\partial x} = 18x$, $\frac{\partial z}{\partial y} = 4y$

(b) $9x^2y^6$, $18x^3y^5$

(c) $12x^2$, $-15y^2$

(d) $y + 2xy^2$, $x + 2x^2y$

(e) $2y\cos(2xy)$, $2x\cos(2xy)$

(f) $6y\,e^{3xy}$, $6x\,e^{3xy}$

**2** (a) $\frac{\partial f}{\partial x}(-1, 2) = 1$, $\frac{\partial f}{\partial y}(-1, 2) = -8$

(b) 2, 1

(c) 0.5403, −1.8186

(d) 25, −12

(e) $-\frac{4}{9}$, $-\frac{2}{9}$

(f) 5.4366, 5.4366

**3** (a) $\frac{\partial^2 z}{\partial x^2} = 36x^2 + 6xy^3$,

$\frac{\partial^2 z}{\partial x \partial y} = 9x^2y^2$,

$\frac{\partial^2 z}{\partial y^2} = -108y^2 + 6x^3y$

(b) $12x^2 + 4y^2$, $8xy$, $4x^2 + 12y^2$

(c) $32\,e^{4x-3y}$, $-24\,e^{4x-3y}$, $18\,e^{4x-3y}$

(d) $\frac{4}{(x + y)^3}$, $\frac{4}{(x + y)^3}$, $\frac{4}{(x + y)^3}$

(e) $-\frac{1}{2}(x+y)^{-3/2}$,

$-\frac{1}{2}(x+y)^{-3/2}$,

$-\frac{1}{2}(x+y)^{-3/2}$

(f) $-(\sin x)(\cos y)$,

$-(\cos x)(\sin y)$,

$-(\sin x)(\cos y)$

4 $\frac{\partial f}{\partial x} = an(ax+by)^{n-1}$,

$\frac{\partial f}{\partial y} = bn(ax+by)^{n-1}$,

$\frac{\partial^2 f}{\partial x^2} = a^2 n(n-1)(ax+by)^{n-2}$,

$\frac{\partial^2 f}{\partial x \partial y} = abn(n-1)(ax+by)^{n-2}$,

$\frac{\partial^2 f}{\partial y^2} = b^2 n(n-1)(ax+by)^{n-2}$

5 $\frac{\partial f}{\partial x} = (2ax+cy)n(ax^2+by^2+cxy)^{n-1}$,

$\frac{\partial f}{\partial y} = (2by+cx)n(ax^2+by^2+cxy)^{n-1}$

11 (a) $27x^2 - 36y^2 - 72xy + 108x + 276y - 432$

(b) $p_2(2.1, 2.9) = -26.97$,

$f(2.1, 2.9) = -26.985$

12 $x^2 - xy - 2x + 2y + 2$

13 $\frac{y^2}{2} + x$

14 (a) (0, 1) minimum; (0, −1) saddle point

(b) (0, 0), (4, 0) saddle points

(c) (2, 0) minimum; (−2, 0) saddle point

(d) (0, 0) saddle point; $\left(\frac{1}{6}, \frac{1}{12}\right)$ maximum

15 $\left(\frac{1}{\sqrt{2}}, -\frac{1}{2\sqrt{2}}\right), \left(-\frac{1}{\sqrt{2}}, \frac{1}{2\sqrt{2}}\right)$; saddle points

# 26 Vector calculus

Chapter 26 Contents

## 26.1 Introduction

This chapter draws together several threads from previous chapters. It builds upon differential and integral calculus, functions of several variables and the study of vectors. These topics together form a branch of engineering mathematics known as **vector calculus**. Vector calculus is used to model a vast range of engineering phenomena including electrostatic charges, electromagnetic fields, air flow around aircraft, cars and other solid objects, fluid flow around ships and heat flow in nuclear reactors. The chapter starts by explaining what is meant by the operators grad, div and curl. These are used to carry out various differentiation operations on the fields.

## 26.2 Partial differentiation of vectors

Consider the vector field $\mathbf{v} = v_x\mathbf{i} + v_y\mathbf{j} + v_z\mathbf{k}$, where each component $v_x$, $v_y$ and $v_z$ is a function of $x$, $y$ and $z$. We can partially differentiate the vector w.r.t. $x$ as follows:

$$\frac{\partial \mathbf{v}}{\partial x} = \frac{\partial v_x}{\partial x}\mathbf{i} + \frac{\partial v_y}{\partial x}\mathbf{j} + \frac{\partial v_z}{\partial x}\mathbf{k}$$

This is a new vector with a magnitude and direction different from those of $\mathbf{v}$.

Partial differentiation w.r.t. $y$ and $z$ is defined in a similar way, as are higher derivatives. For example,

$$\frac{\partial^2 \mathbf{v}}{\partial x^2} = \frac{\partial^2 v_x}{\partial x^2}\mathbf{i} + \frac{\partial^2 v_y}{\partial x^2}\mathbf{j} + \frac{\partial^2 v_z}{\partial x^2}\mathbf{k}$$

**Example 26.1** If $\mathbf{v} = 3x^2y\mathbf{i} + 2xyz\mathbf{j} - 3x^4y^2\mathbf{k}$, find $\frac{\partial \mathbf{v}}{\partial x}, \frac{\partial \mathbf{v}}{\partial y}, \frac{\partial \mathbf{v}}{\partial z}$. Further, find $\frac{\partial^2 \mathbf{v}}{\partial x^2}$ and $\frac{\partial^2 \mathbf{v}}{\partial x \partial z}$.

**Solution** We find

$$\frac{\partial \mathbf{v}}{\partial x} = 6xy\mathbf{i} + 2yz\mathbf{j} - 12x^3y^2\mathbf{k}$$

$$\frac{\partial \mathbf{v}}{\partial y} = 3x^2\mathbf{i} + 2xz\mathbf{j} - 6x^4y\mathbf{k}$$

$$\frac{\partial \mathbf{v}}{\partial z} = 2xy\mathbf{j}$$

$$\frac{\partial^2 \mathbf{v}}{\partial x^2} = 6y\mathbf{i} - 36x^2y^2\mathbf{k}$$

$$\frac{\partial^2 \mathbf{v}}{\partial x \partial z} = 2y\mathbf{j}$$

## Exercises 26.2

1 Given $\mathbf{v} = 2x\mathbf{i} + 3yz\mathbf{j} + 5xz^2\mathbf{k}$ find

(a) $\dfrac{\partial \mathbf{v}}{\partial x}$ (b) $\dfrac{\partial \mathbf{v}}{\partial y}$ (c) $\dfrac{\partial \mathbf{v}}{\partial z}$

2 If $\mathbf{f} = 2\mathbf{i} - xyz\mathbf{j} + 3x^2z\mathbf{k}$ find

(a) $\dfrac{\partial \mathbf{f}}{\partial x}$ (b) $\dfrac{\partial \mathbf{f}}{\partial y}$ (c) $\dfrac{\partial \mathbf{f}}{\partial z}$

(d) $\dfrac{\partial^2 \mathbf{f}}{\partial x^2}$ (e) $\dfrac{\partial^2 \mathbf{f}}{\partial y^2}$ (f) $\dfrac{\partial^2 \mathbf{f}}{\partial z^2}$

3 Given $\mathbf{E} = (x^2 + y)\mathbf{i} + (1 - z)\mathbf{j} + (x + 2z)\mathbf{k}$ find

(a) $\dfrac{\partial \mathbf{E}}{\partial x}$ (b) $\dfrac{\partial \mathbf{E}}{\partial y}$ (c) $\dfrac{\partial \mathbf{E}}{\partial z}$

(d) $\dfrac{\partial^2 \mathbf{E}}{\partial x^2}$ (e) $\dfrac{\partial^2 \mathbf{E}}{\partial y^2}$ (f) $\dfrac{\partial^2 \mathbf{E}}{\partial z^2}$

4 If $\mathbf{v} = 3xyz\mathbf{i} + (x^2 - y^2 + z^2)\mathbf{j} + (x + y^2)\mathbf{k}$ find $\dfrac{\partial \mathbf{v}}{\partial x}, \dfrac{\partial \mathbf{v}}{\partial y}, \dfrac{\partial \mathbf{v}}{\partial z}, \dfrac{\partial^2 \mathbf{v}}{\partial x^2}, \dfrac{\partial^2 \mathbf{v}}{\partial y^2}$, and $\dfrac{\partial^2 \mathbf{v}}{\partial z^2}$.

5 If $\mathbf{v} = \sin(xyz)\mathbf{i} + z\,e^{xy}\mathbf{j} - 2xy\mathbf{k}$ find $\dfrac{\partial \mathbf{v}}{\partial x}, \dfrac{\partial \mathbf{v}}{\partial y}, \dfrac{\partial \mathbf{v}}{\partial z}$.

6 If $\mathbf{v} = x\mathbf{i} + x^2y\mathbf{j} - 3x^3\mathbf{k}$, and $\phi = xyz$ find $\phi\mathbf{v}, \dfrac{\partial}{\partial x}(\phi\mathbf{v}), \dfrac{\partial \phi}{\partial x}, \dfrac{\partial \mathbf{v}}{\partial x}$. Deduce that

$$\frac{\partial}{\partial x}(\phi\mathbf{v}) = \phi\frac{\partial \mathbf{v}}{\partial x} + \frac{\partial \phi}{\partial x}\mathbf{v}$$

7 If $\mathbf{v} = \ln(xy)\mathbf{i} + 2xy\cos z\mathbf{j} - x^4yz\mathbf{k}$, find $\dfrac{\partial \mathbf{v}}{\partial x}, \dfrac{\partial \mathbf{v}}{\partial y}, \dfrac{\partial \mathbf{v}}{\partial z}, \dfrac{\partial^2 \mathbf{v}}{\partial x^2}, \dfrac{\partial^2 \mathbf{v}}{\partial y^2}$, and $\dfrac{\partial^2 \mathbf{v}}{\partial z^2}$.

## Solutions

1 (a) $2\mathbf{i} + 5z^2\mathbf{k}$ (b) $3z\mathbf{j}$

(c) $3y\mathbf{j} + 10xz\mathbf{k}$

2 (a) $-yz\mathbf{j} + 6xz\mathbf{k}$ (b) $-xz\mathbf{j}$

(c) $-xy\mathbf{j} + 3x^2\mathbf{k}$ (d) $6z\mathbf{k}$

(e) $\mathbf{0}$ (f) $\mathbf{0}$

3 (a) $2x\mathbf{i} + \mathbf{k}$ (b) $\mathbf{i}$

(c) $-\mathbf{j} + 2\mathbf{k}$ (d) $2\mathbf{i}$

(e) $\mathbf{0}$ (f) $\mathbf{0}$

4 $\dfrac{\partial \mathbf{v}}{\partial x} = 3yz\mathbf{i} + 2x\mathbf{j} + \mathbf{k}$

$\dfrac{\partial \mathbf{v}}{\partial y} = 3xz\mathbf{i} - 2y\mathbf{j} + 2y\mathbf{k}$

$\dfrac{\partial \mathbf{v}}{\partial z} = 3xy\mathbf{i} + 2z\mathbf{j}$

$\dfrac{\partial^2 \mathbf{v}}{\partial x^2} = 2\mathbf{j}$

$\dfrac{\partial^2 \mathbf{v}}{\partial y^2} = -2\mathbf{j} + 2\mathbf{k}$

$\dfrac{\partial^2 \mathbf{v}}{\partial z^2} = 2\mathbf{j}$

5 $\dfrac{\partial \mathbf{v}}{\partial x} = yz\cos(xyz)\mathbf{i} + yz\,e^{xy}\mathbf{j} - 2y\mathbf{k}$

$\dfrac{\partial \mathbf{v}}{\partial y} = xz\cos(xyz)\mathbf{i} + xz\,e^{xy}\mathbf{j} - 2x\mathbf{k}$

$\dfrac{\partial \mathbf{v}}{\partial z} = xy\cos(xyz)\mathbf{i} + e^{xy}\mathbf{j}$

6 $\phi\mathbf{v} = x^2yz\mathbf{i} + x^3y^2z\mathbf{j} - 3x^4yz\mathbf{k}$

$\dfrac{\partial(\phi\mathbf{v})}{\partial x} = 2xyz\mathbf{i} + 3x^2y^2z\mathbf{j} - 12x^3yz\mathbf{k}$

$\dfrac{\partial \phi}{\partial x} = yz$

$\dfrac{\partial \mathbf{v}}{\partial x} = \mathbf{i} + 2xy\mathbf{j} - 9x^2\mathbf{k}$

7 $\dfrac{\partial \mathbf{v}}{\partial x} = \dfrac{\mathbf{i}}{x} + 2y\cos z\mathbf{j} - 4x^3yz\mathbf{k}$

$\dfrac{\partial \mathbf{v}}{\partial y} = \dfrac{\mathbf{i}}{y} + 2x\cos z\mathbf{j} - x^4z\mathbf{k}$

$\dfrac{\partial \mathbf{v}}{\partial z} = -2xy\sin z\mathbf{j} - x^4y\mathbf{k}$

$\dfrac{\partial^2 \mathbf{v}}{\partial x^2} = -\dfrac{\mathbf{i}}{x^2} - 12x^2yz\mathbf{k}$

$\dfrac{\partial^2 \mathbf{v}}{\partial y^2} = -\dfrac{\mathbf{i}}{y^2}$

$\dfrac{\partial^2 \mathbf{v}}{\partial z^2} = -2xy\cos z\mathbf{j}$

## 26.3 The gradient of a scalar field

Given a scalar function of $x, y, z$

$$\phi = \phi(x, y, z)$$

we can differentiate it partially w.r.t. each of its independent variables to find $\frac{\partial \phi}{\partial x}, \frac{\partial \phi}{\partial y}$ and $\frac{\partial \phi}{\partial z}$. If we do this, the vector

$$\frac{\partial \phi}{\partial x}\mathbf{i} + \frac{\partial \phi}{\partial y}\mathbf{j} + \frac{\partial \phi}{\partial z}\mathbf{k}$$

turns out to be particularly important. We call this vector the **gradient** of $\phi$ and denote it by

$$\nabla \phi \qquad \text{or} \qquad \text{grad}\ \phi$$

An alternative form of writing $\nabla \phi$ is as three components

$$\left(\frac{\partial \phi}{\partial x}, \frac{\partial \phi}{\partial y}, \frac{\partial \phi}{\partial z}\right)$$

$$\text{grad}\ \phi = \nabla \phi = \frac{\partial \phi}{\partial x}\mathbf{i} + \frac{\partial \phi}{\partial y}\mathbf{j} + \frac{\partial \phi}{\partial z}\mathbf{k}$$

The process of forming a gradient applies only to a scalar field and the result is always a vector field.

It is often useful to write $\nabla \phi$ in the form

$$\left(\frac{\partial}{\partial x}, \frac{\partial}{\partial y}, \frac{\partial}{\partial z}\right)\phi$$

where the quantity in brackets is called a **vector operator** and is regarded as operating on the scalar $\phi$. Thus the vector operator, $\nabla$, is given by

$$\left(\frac{\partial}{\partial x}, \frac{\partial}{\partial y}, \frac{\partial}{\partial z}\right)$$

**Example 26.2** If $\phi = \phi(x, y, z) = 4x^3 y \sin z$, find $\nabla \phi$.

**Solution**

$$\phi(x, y, z) = 4x^3 y \sin z$$

so that by partial differentiation we obtain

$$\frac{\partial \phi}{\partial x} = 12x^2 y \sin z$$

$$\frac{\partial \phi}{\partial y} = 4x^3 \sin z$$

$$\frac{\partial \phi}{\partial z} = 4x^3 y \cos z$$

Therefore

$$\nabla\phi = 12x^2 y \sin z\mathbf{i} + 4x^3 \sin z\mathbf{j} + 4x^3 y \cos z\mathbf{k}$$

---

We often need to evaluate $\nabla\phi$ at a particular point, say, for example, at (4, 2, 3). We write $\nabla\phi|_{(4,2,3)}$ to denote the value of $\nabla\phi$ at the point (4, 2, 3).

**Example 26.3** If $\phi = x^3y + xy^2 + 3y$ find

(a) $\nabla\phi$

(b) $\nabla\phi|_{(0,0,0)}$

(c) $|\nabla\phi|$ at (1, 1, 1)

**Solution** (a) If $\phi = x^3y + xy^2 + 3y$ then

$$\frac{\partial\phi}{\partial x} = 3x^2y + y^2$$

$$\frac{\partial\phi}{\partial y} = x^3 + 2xy + 3$$

$$\frac{\partial\phi}{\partial z} = 0$$

so that

$$\nabla\phi = (3x^2y + y^2)\mathbf{i} + (x^3 + 2xy + 3)\mathbf{j} + 0\mathbf{k}$$

(b) At $(0, 0, 0)$, $\nabla\phi = 0\mathbf{i} + 3\mathbf{j} + 0\mathbf{k} = 3\mathbf{j}$.

(c) At $(1, 1, 1)$, $\nabla\phi = (3 \times 1^2 \times 1 + 1)\mathbf{i} + (1^3 + 2 \times 1 \times 1 + 3)\mathbf{j} + 0\mathbf{k} = 4\mathbf{i} + 6\mathbf{j} + 0\mathbf{k}$ so that $|\nabla\phi|$ at $(1, 1, 1)$ is equal to $\sqrt{4^2 + 6^2} = \sqrt{52}$.

---

So far we have been given $\phi$ and have calculated $\nabla\phi$. Sometimes we will be given $\nabla\phi$ and will need to find $\phi$. Consider Example 26.4.

**Example 26.4** If $\mathbf{F} = \nabla\phi$ find $\phi$ when $\mathbf{F} = (3x^2 + y^2)\mathbf{i} + (2xy + 5)\mathbf{j}$.

**Solution** Note that in this example $\mathbf{F}$ has only two components. Consequently $\nabla\phi$ will have two components, that is $\mathbf{F} = \nabla\phi = \dfrac{\partial\phi}{\partial x}\mathbf{i} + \dfrac{\partial\phi}{\partial y}\mathbf{j}$. Therefore

$$(3x^2 + y^2)\mathbf{i} + (2xy + 5)\mathbf{j} = \frac{\partial\phi}{\partial x}\mathbf{i} + \frac{\partial\phi}{\partial y}\mathbf{j}$$

Equating the **i** components we have

$$\frac{\partial \phi}{\partial x} = 3x^2 + y^2 \qquad (26.1)$$

Equating the **j** components we have

$$\frac{\partial \phi}{\partial y} = 2xy + 5 \qquad (26.2)$$

Integrating Equation (26.1) w.r.t. $x$ and treating $y$ as a constant we find

$$\phi = x^3 + xy^2 + f(y) \qquad (26.3)$$

where $f(y)$ is an arbitrary function of $y$ which plays the same role as the constant of integration does when there is only one independent variable. Note in particular that $\frac{\partial}{\partial x} f(y) = 0$. Check by partial differentiation that $\frac{\partial \phi}{\partial x} = 3x^2 + y^2$.

Integrating Equation (26.2) w.r.t. $y$ and treating $x$ as a constant we find

$$\phi = xy^2 + 5y + g(x) \qquad (26.4)$$

where $g(x)$ is an arbitrary function of $x$. Note that $\frac{\partial}{\partial y} g(x) = 0$. Check by partial differentiation that $\frac{\partial \phi}{\partial y} = 2xy + 5$. Comparing both forms for $\phi$ given in Equations (26.3) and (26.4) we see that by choosing $g(x) = x^3$ and $f(y) = 5y$ we have

$$\phi = x^3 + xy^2 + 5y$$

Check that **F** is indeed equal to $\nabla\phi$. Also check that by adding any constant to $\phi$ the same property holds, that is **F** is still equal to $\nabla\phi$.

---

### 26.3.1 Physical interpretation of $\nabla\phi$

Suppose we think of the scalar field $\phi(x, y, z)$ as describing the temperature throughout a region. This temperature will vary from point to point. At a particular point it can be shown that $\nabla\phi$ is a vector pointing in the direction in which the rate of temperature increase is greatest. $|\nabla\phi|$ is the magnitude of the rate of increase in that direction. Similarly, the rate of temperature decrease is greatest in the direction of $-\nabla\phi$. Analogous interpretations are possible for other scalar fields such as pressure and electrostatic potential.

**Example 26.5** **Electrostatic potential**

The electrostatic potential, $V$, in a region is given by

$$V = \frac{y}{(x^2 + y^2 + z^2)^{3/2}}$$

Suppose a unit charge is located in the region at the point with coordinates (2, 1, 0). Find the direction at this point, in which the rate of decrease in potential is greatest.

**Solution** The rate of decrease is greatest in the direction of $-\nabla V$.

We first calculate the first partial derivatives of $V$. Writing

$$V = y(x^2 + y^2 + z^2)^{-3/2}$$

we find

$$\frac{\partial V}{\partial x} = \left(-\frac{3}{2}\right)y(x^2 + y^2 + z^2)^{-5/2}(2x) = -3xy(x^2 + y^2 + z^2)^{-5/2}$$

$$\frac{\partial V}{\partial y} = \left(-\frac{3}{2}\right)y(x^2 + y^2 + z^2)^{-5/2}(2y) + (x^2 + y^2 + z^2)^{-3/2}$$

$$= -3y^2(x^2 + y^2 + z^2)^{-5/2} + (x^2 + y^2 + z^2)^{-3/2}$$

$$\frac{\partial V}{\partial z} = \left(-\frac{3}{2}\right)y(x^2 + y^2 + z^2)^{-5/2}(2z) = -3yz(x^2 + y^2 + z^2)^{-5/2}$$

These partial derivatives can each be evaluated at the point (2, 1, 0). That is,

$$\left.\frac{\partial V}{\partial x}\right|_{(2,1,0)} = -0.107 \qquad \left.\frac{\partial V}{\partial y}\right|_{(2,1,0)} = 0.036 \qquad \left.\frac{\partial V}{\partial z}\right|_{(2,1,0)} = 0$$

and so

$$\nabla V|_{(2,1,0)} = -0.107\mathbf{i} + 0.036\mathbf{j} + 0\mathbf{k}$$

Finally,

$$-\nabla V|_{(2,1,0)} = 0.107\mathbf{i} - 0.036\mathbf{j} - 0\mathbf{k}$$

At the point (2, 1, 0) this vector points in the direction of greatest rate of decrease in potential. This is also the direction of the electrostatic force experienced by the unit charge at that point.

## Exercises 26.3

1. If $\phi = x^2 - y^2 - 3xyz$, (a) find $\nabla\phi$, (b) evaluate $\nabla\phi$ at the point (0, 0, 0).

2. If $\phi = x^2yz^3$, find (a) $\nabla\phi$, (b) $\nabla\phi$ at (1, 2, 1), (c) $|\nabla\phi|$ at (1, 2, 1).

3. If $\mathbf{v} = \nabla\phi$, find $\phi$ when $\mathbf{v} = (2x - 4y^2)\mathbf{i} - 8xy\mathbf{j}$.

4. Given $\phi = xyz$ find (a) $\nabla\phi$, (b) $-\nabla\phi$, (c) $\nabla\phi$ evaluated at (3, 0, −1).

5. Find $\nabla V$ when

   (a) $V = x^2 + y^2 + z^2$

   (b) $V = z\sin^{-1}\left(\frac{y}{x}\right)$

   (c) $V = \mathrm{e}^{x+y+z}$.

6. An electrostatic potential is given by $V = x\,\mathrm{e}^{-\sqrt{y}}$. Find $\nabla V$ and deduce the direction in which the decrease of potential is greatest at the point with coordinates (1, 1, 1).

7. In the theory of fluid mechanics the scalar field $\phi$ is known as the **velocity potential** of a fluid flow. The fluid velocity vector, $\mathbf{v}$, at a point can be found from the equation $\mathbf{v} = \nabla\phi$. For a

particular type of flow $\phi = Ux$, where $U$ is a constant. Show that the corresponding fluid motion is entirely parallel to the $x$ axis, and at any point the fluid speed is $U$. Find a velocity potential for a similar flow which is entirely parallel to the $y$ axis.

8 Is $-\nabla\phi$ the same as $\nabla(-\phi)$? Explain your answer.

9 Given $\phi = 3x^2y + xz$,

(a) determine $\nabla\phi$

(b) determine $\nabla(7\phi)$

(c) determine $7\nabla\phi$

(d) Is $\nabla(7\phi)$ the same as $7\nabla\phi$?

10 For any scalar field $\phi$ and any constant $k$, is $\nabla(k\phi)$ the same as $k\nabla\phi$?

## Solutions

1 (a) $(2x - 3yz)\mathbf{i} - (2y + 3xz)\mathbf{j} - 3xy\mathbf{k}$

(b) $\mathbf{0}$

2 (a) $2xyz^3\mathbf{i} + x^2z^3\mathbf{j} + 3x^2yz^2\mathbf{k}$

(b) $4\mathbf{i} + \mathbf{j} + 6\mathbf{k}$

(c) $\sqrt{53}$

3 $\phi = x^2 - 4xy^2 + c$

4 (a) $yz\mathbf{i} + xz\mathbf{j} + xy\mathbf{k}$

(b) $-yz\mathbf{i} - xz\mathbf{j} - xy\mathbf{k}$

(c) $-3\mathbf{j}$

5 (a) $2x\mathbf{i} + 2y\mathbf{j} + 2z\mathbf{k}$

(b) $\dfrac{-zy}{x^2\sqrt{1 - y^2/x^2}}\mathbf{i} + \dfrac{z}{x\sqrt{1 - y^2/x^2}}\mathbf{j} + \sin^{-1}\left(\dfrac{y}{x}\right)\mathbf{k}$

(c) $e^{x+y+z}(\mathbf{i} + \mathbf{j} + \mathbf{k})$

6 $e^{-\sqrt{y}}\mathbf{i} - \dfrac{x\,e^{-\sqrt{y}}}{2\sqrt{y}}\mathbf{j}$, $-0.368\mathbf{i} + 0.184\mathbf{j}$

7 $\phi = Uy$

8 yes

9 (a) $(6xy + z)\mathbf{i} + 3x^2\mathbf{j} + x\mathbf{k}$

(b) $(42xy + 7z)\mathbf{i} + 21x^2\mathbf{j} + 7x\mathbf{k}$

(c) $(42xy + 7z)\mathbf{i} + 21x^2\mathbf{j} + 7x\mathbf{k}$

(d) yes

10 yes

## 26.4 The divergence of a vector field

Given a vector field $\mathbf{v} = \mathbf{v}(x, y, z)$ let us consider what happens when we differentiate its individual components. If

$$\mathbf{v} = v_x\mathbf{i} + v_y\mathbf{j} + v_z\mathbf{k}$$

we can take each component in turn and differentiate it partially w.r.t. $x$, $y$ and $z$, respectively; that is, we can evaluate

$$\frac{\partial v_x}{\partial x} \qquad \frac{\partial v_y}{\partial y} \qquad \frac{\partial v_z}{\partial z}$$

If we add the calculated quantities the result turns out to be a very useful scalar quantity known as the **divergence** of $\mathbf{v}$, that is

$$\text{divergence of } \mathbf{v} = \frac{\partial v_x}{\partial x} + \frac{\partial v_y}{\partial y} + \frac{\partial v_z}{\partial z}$$

This is usually abbreviated to div **v**. Alternatively, the notation $\nabla \cdot \mathbf{v}$ is often used. If we use the vector operator notation introduced in the previous section we have

$$\nabla \cdot \mathbf{v} = \left(\frac{\partial}{\partial x}, \frac{\partial}{\partial y}, \frac{\partial}{\partial z}\right) \cdot \mathbf{v}$$

$$= \left(\frac{\partial}{\partial x}, \frac{\partial}{\partial y}, \frac{\partial}{\partial z}\right) \cdot (v_x, v_y, v_z)$$

Interpreting the $\cdot$ as a scalar product we find

$$\nabla \cdot \mathbf{v} = \frac{\partial v_x}{\partial x} + \frac{\partial v_y}{\partial y} + \frac{\partial v_z}{\partial z}$$

as before, although this is not a scalar product in the usual sense because $\left(\frac{\partial}{\partial x}, \frac{\partial}{\partial y}, \frac{\partial}{\partial z}\right)$ is a vector operator. We note that the process of finding the divergence is always performed on a vector field and the result is always a scalar field.

$$\text{div}\,\mathbf{v} = \nabla \cdot \mathbf{v} = \frac{\partial v_x}{\partial x} + \frac{\partial v_y}{\partial y} + \frac{\partial v_z}{\partial z}$$

**Example 26.6** If $\mathbf{v} = x^2z\mathbf{i} + 2y^3z^2\mathbf{j} + xyz^2\mathbf{k}$ find div **v**.

**Solution** Partially differentiating the first component of **v** w.r.t. $x$ we find

$$\frac{\partial v_x}{\partial x} = 2xz$$

Similarly,

$$\frac{\partial v_y}{\partial y} = 6y^2z^2 \quad \text{and} \quad \frac{\partial v_z}{\partial z} = 2xyz$$

Adding these results we find

$$\text{div}\,\mathbf{v} = \nabla \cdot \mathbf{v} = 2xz + 6y^2z^2 + 2xyz$$

## 26.4.1 Physical interpretation of $\nabla \cdot \mathbf{v}$

If the vector field **v** represents a fluid velocity field, then, loosely speaking, the divergence of **v** evaluated at a point represents the rate at which fluid is flowing away from or towards that point. If fluid is flowing away from a point then either the fluid density must be decreasing there or there must be some source providing a supply of new fluid.

If the divergence of a flow is zero at all points then outflow from any point must be matched by an equal inflow to balance this. Such a vector field is said to be **solenoidal**.

**Example 26.7** Show that the vector field

$$\mathbf{v} = x\sin y\mathbf{i} + y\sin x\mathbf{j} - z(\sin x + \sin y)\mathbf{k}$$

is solenoidal.

**Solution** We have

$$v_x = x\sin y \qquad \text{so that} \qquad \frac{\partial v_x}{\partial x} = \sin y$$

Also,

$$v_y = y\sin x \qquad \text{so that} \qquad \frac{\partial v_y}{\partial y} = \sin x$$

Finally,

$$v_z = -z(\sin x + \sin y) \qquad \text{so that} \qquad \frac{\partial v_z}{\partial z} = -(\sin x + \sin y)$$

Therefore,

$$\nabla \cdot \mathbf{v} = \sin y + \sin x - (\sin x + \sin y) = 0$$

and hence $\mathbf{v}$ is solenoidal.

**Example 26.8** **Electric flux and Gauss's law**

We saw in Example 7.16 that electric charges produce an electric field, $\mathbf{E}$, around them which can be visualized by drawing lines of force. Suppose we surround a region containing charges with a surface $S$. If a small portion of this surface, $\delta S$, is chosen we can draw the field lines which pass through this portion as shown in Figure 26.1.

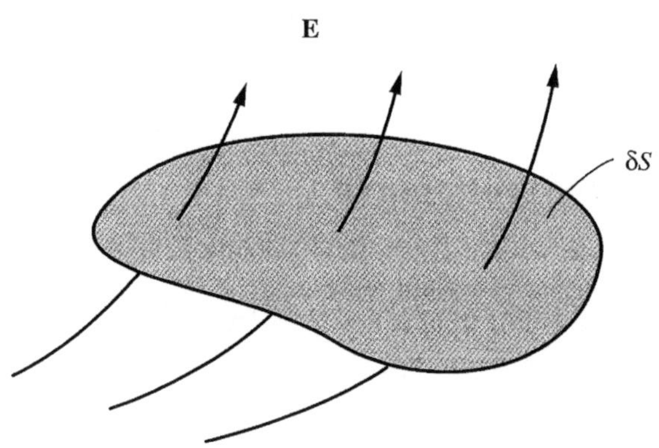


**Figure 26.1**
The flux of $\mathbf{E}$ through $\delta S$ is a measure of the number of lines of force passing through $\delta S$.

The **flux** of **E** through $\delta S$ is a measure of the number of lines of force passing through $\delta S$. Gauss's law states that the total flux out of any closed surface $S$ is proportional to the total charge enclosed. It is possible to show that this law can be expressed mathematically as

$$\nabla \cdot \mathbf{E} = \frac{\rho}{\varepsilon_0}$$

where $\rho$ is the charge density and $\varepsilon_0$ is a constant called the **permittivity of free space**. Note that in a charge-free region, $\rho = 0$, and so $\nabla \cdot \mathbf{E} = 0$. This means there is no net flux of **E**.

## Exercises 26.4

1 A vector field **v** is given by

$$\mathbf{v} = 3x^2y\mathbf{i} + 2y^3z\mathbf{j} + xz^3\mathbf{k}$$

Find

(a) $v_x, v_y, v_z$

(b) $\dfrac{\partial v_x}{\partial x}, \dfrac{\partial v_y}{\partial y}, \dfrac{\partial v_z}{\partial z}$

(c) $\nabla \cdot \mathbf{v}$

2 A vector field **F** is defined by

$$\mathbf{F} = (x + y^2)\mathbf{i} + (y^2 - z)\mathbf{j} + (y + z^2)\mathbf{k}$$

(a) Find $\nabla \cdot \mathbf{F}$.

(b) Calculate $\nabla \cdot \mathbf{F}$ at the point $(3, 2, -1)$.

3 If $\mathbf{A} = 3yz\mathbf{i} + 2xy\mathbf{j} + xyz\mathbf{k}$ find $\nabla \cdot \mathbf{A}$.

4 Find the divergence of each of the following vector fields.

(a) $\mathbf{v} = x^2\mathbf{i} + y^2\mathbf{j} + z^2\mathbf{k}$

(b) $\mathbf{v} = e^{xy}\mathbf{i} + 2z\sin(xy)\mathbf{j} + x^3z\mathbf{k}$

(c) $\mathbf{v} = xy\mathbf{i} - 2yz\mathbf{j} + \mathbf{k}$

(d) $\mathbf{v} = x^2y^2\mathbf{i} - y^2\mathbf{j} - xyz\mathbf{k}$

5 If $\mathbf{E} = x\mathbf{i} + z^2\mathbf{j} - yz\mathbf{k}$ find

(a) $\mathbf{E} \cdot \mathbf{i}$

(b) $\mathbf{E} \cdot \mathbf{j}$

(c) $\mathbf{E} \cdot \mathbf{k}$

(d) $\nabla \cdot \mathbf{E}$

6 A vector field is given by

$$\mathbf{F} = (3x^2 - z)\mathbf{i} + (2x + y)\mathbf{j} + (x + 3yz)\mathbf{k}$$

Find $\nabla \cdot \mathbf{F}$ at the point $(1, 2, 3)$.

7 Given the scalar field $\phi = x^2 + y^2 - 2z^2$, find $\nabla\phi$ and show that $\nabla \cdot (\nabla\phi) = 0$.

8 For any vector field **F** is $\nabla \cdot (-\mathbf{F})$ the same as $-(\nabla \cdot \mathbf{F})$?

9 The vector field **F** is given by

$$\mathbf{F} = xz^2\mathbf{i} + 2xy^2z\mathbf{j} + xz^3\mathbf{k}$$

(a) Find $\nabla \cdot \mathbf{F}$.

(b) State 4**F**.

(c) Find $\nabla \cdot (4\mathbf{F})$.

(d) Is $4(\nabla \cdot \mathbf{F})$ the same as $\nabla \cdot (4\mathbf{F})$?

10 For any vector field **F** and any scalar constant $k$ is $\nabla \cdot (k\mathbf{F})$ the same as $k\nabla \cdot \mathbf{F}$?

11 Give an example of a vector field $\mathbf{v} = v_x\mathbf{i} + v_y\mathbf{j} + v_z\mathbf{k}$ such that $\dfrac{\partial v_x}{\partial x} \neq 0$, $\dfrac{\partial v_y}{\partial y} \neq 0$, $\dfrac{\partial v_z}{\partial z} \neq 0$, but $\nabla \cdot \mathbf{v} = 0$.

## Solutions

1 (a) $3x^2y, 2y^3z, xz^3$ (b) $6xy, 6y^2z, 3xz^2$ (c) $6xy + 6y^2z + 3xz^2$T

2 (a) $1 + 2y + 2z$
(b) 3

3 $\nabla \cdot \mathbf{A} = 2x + xy$

4 (a) $2x + 2y + 2z$
(b) $y\,e^{xy} + 2xz\cos(xy) + x^3$
(c) $y - 2z$
(d) $2xy^2 - 2y - xy$

5 (a) $x$
(b) $z^2$
(c) $-yz$
(d) $1 - y$

6 13

7 $\nabla\phi = 2x\mathbf{i} + 2y\mathbf{j} - 4z\mathbf{k}$

8 yes

9 (a) $z^2 + 4xyz + 3xz^2$
(b) $4xz^2\mathbf{i} + 8xy^2z\mathbf{j} + 4xz^3\mathbf{k}$
(c) $4z^2 + 16xyz + 12xz^2$
(d) yes

10 yes

11 $\mathbf{v} = 2xy\mathbf{i} + y^2\mathbf{j} - 4yz\mathbf{k}$ for example

## 26.5 The curl of a vector field

A third differential operator is known as **curl**. It is defined rather like a vector product.

$$\begin{aligned}\text{curl}\,\mathbf{v} &= \nabla \times \mathbf{v}\\ &= \left(\frac{\partial}{\partial x}, \frac{\partial}{\partial y}, \frac{\partial}{\partial z}\right) \times (v_x, v_y, v_z)\\ &= \begin{vmatrix} \mathbf{i} & \mathbf{j} & \mathbf{k}\\ \dfrac{\partial}{\partial x} & \dfrac{\partial}{\partial y} & \dfrac{\partial}{\partial z}\\ v_x & v_y & v_z \end{vmatrix}\end{aligned}$$

This determinant is evaluated in the usual way except that we must regard $\frac{\partial}{\partial x}$, $\frac{\partial}{\partial y}$ and $\frac{\partial}{\partial z}$ as operators, not multipliers. Thus, for example,

$$\begin{vmatrix} \dfrac{\partial}{\partial x} & \dfrac{\partial}{\partial y}\\ v_x & v_y \end{vmatrix} \quad \text{means} \quad \frac{\partial v_y}{\partial x} - \frac{\partial v_x}{\partial y}$$

Explicitly we have

$$\text{curl}\,\mathbf{v} = \left(\frac{\partial v_z}{\partial y} - \frac{\partial v_y}{\partial z}\right)\mathbf{i} + \left(\frac{\partial v_x}{\partial z} - \frac{\partial v_z}{\partial x}\right)\mathbf{j} + \left(\frac{\partial v_y}{\partial x} - \frac{\partial v_x}{\partial y}\right)\mathbf{k}$$

**Example 26.9** If $\mathbf{v} = x^2yz\mathbf{i} - 2xy\mathbf{j} + yz\mathbf{k}$ find $\nabla \times \mathbf{v}$.

**Solution**

$$\nabla \times \mathbf{v} = \begin{vmatrix} \mathbf{i} & \mathbf{j} & \mathbf{k} \\ \dfrac{\partial}{\partial x} & \dfrac{\partial}{\partial y} & \dfrac{\partial}{\partial z} \\ x^2yz & -2xy & yz \end{vmatrix}$$

$$= \left[\frac{\partial(yz)}{\partial y} - \frac{\partial(-2xy)}{\partial z}\right]\mathbf{i} - \left[\frac{\partial(yz)}{\partial x} - \frac{\partial(x^2yz)}{\partial z}\right]\mathbf{j} + \left[\frac{\partial(-2xy)}{\partial x} - \frac{\partial(x^2yz)}{\partial y}\right]\mathbf{k}$$

$$= z\mathbf{i} + x^2y\mathbf{j} - (2y + x^2z)\mathbf{k}$$

---

Note that the curl operation is only performed on a vector field and the result is another vector field.

A detailed discussion of the physical interpretation of the curl of a vector field is beyond the scope of this book. However, if the vector field $\mathbf{v}$ under consideration represents a fluid flow then it may be shown that curl $\mathbf{v}$ is a vector which measures the extent to which individual particles of the fluid are spinning or rotating. For this reason, a vector field whose curl is zero for all values of $x$, $y$ and $z$ is said to be **irrotational**.

**Example 26.10** Show that the vector field

$$\mathbf{F} = y\,e^{xy}\mathbf{i} + x\,e^{xy}\mathbf{j} + 0\mathbf{k}$$

is irrotational.

**Solution**

$$\nabla \times \mathbf{F} = \begin{vmatrix} \mathbf{i} & \mathbf{j} & \mathbf{k} \\ \dfrac{\partial}{\partial x} & \dfrac{\partial}{\partial y} & \dfrac{\partial}{\partial z} \\ y\,e^{yx} & x\,e^{xy} & 0 \end{vmatrix}$$

$$= \left(\frac{\partial}{\partial y}0 - \frac{\partial}{\partial z}x\,e^{xy}\right)\mathbf{i} - \left(\frac{\partial}{\partial x}0 - \frac{\partial}{\partial z}y\,e^{xy}\right)\mathbf{j} + \left(\frac{\partial}{\partial x}x\,e^{xy} - \frac{\partial}{\partial y}y\,e^{xy}\right)\mathbf{k}$$

$$= 0\mathbf{i} + 0\mathbf{j} + ((xy\,e^{xy} + e^{xy}) - (yx\,e^{xy} + e^{xy}))\mathbf{k}$$

$$= 0 \qquad \text{for all } x, y \text{ and } z$$

The field is therefore irrotational.

---

## Exercises 26.5

1. Find the curl of the vector field $\mathbf{v} = x\mathbf{i} - 3xy\mathbf{j} + 4z\mathbf{k}$.

2. If $\mathbf{v} = 3x\mathbf{i} - 2y^2z\mathbf{j} + 3xyz\mathbf{k}$ find $\nabla \times \mathbf{v}$.

3. Suppose $\mathbf{F} = P(x, y)\mathbf{i} + Q(x, y)\mathbf{j}$ is a two-dimensional vector field. Show that $\mathbf{F}$ is irrotational if $\dfrac{\partial P}{\partial y} = \dfrac{\partial Q}{\partial x}$.

4. Find the divergence and curl of the vector field $\mathbf{E} = \cos x\mathbf{i} + \sin x\mathbf{j}$.

5. Find the curl of each of the following vector

fields:

(a) $\mathbf{E} = x^2y\mathbf{i} + 7xyz\mathbf{j} + 3x^2\mathbf{k}$

(b) $\mathbf{v} = y^2x\mathbf{i} + 4xz\mathbf{j} + y^2x\mathbf{k}$

(c) $\mathbf{F} = \sin x\mathbf{i} + \cos x\mathbf{j} + 3xyz\mathbf{k}$

6 A vector field **F** is given by

$$\mathbf{F} = x^3y\mathbf{i} + 2y^2\mathbf{j} + (x + z^2)\mathbf{k}$$

(a) Find $\nabla \times \mathbf{F}$.

(b) State $3\mathbf{F}$.

(c) Find $\nabla \times (3\mathbf{F})$.

(d) Is $3(\nabla \times \mathbf{F})$ the same as $\nabla \times (3\mathbf{F})$?

7 **F** is a vector field and $k$ is a constant. Is $\nabla \times (k\mathbf{F})$ the same as $k(\nabla \times \mathbf{F})$?

## Solutions

1 $-3y\mathbf{k}$

2 $(3xz + 2y^2)\mathbf{i} - 3yz\mathbf{j}$

4 $-\sin x$, $\cos x\mathbf{k}$

5 (a) $-7xy\mathbf{i} - 6x\mathbf{j} + (7yz - x^2)\mathbf{k}$

(b) $x(2y - 4)\mathbf{i} - y^2\mathbf{j} + (4z - 2xy)\mathbf{k}$

(c) $3xz\mathbf{i} - 3yz\mathbf{j} - \sin x\mathbf{k}$

6 (a) $-\mathbf{j} - x^3\mathbf{k}$

(b) $3x^3y\mathbf{i} + 6y^2\mathbf{j} + 3(x + z^2)\mathbf{k}$

(c) $-3\mathbf{j} - 3x^3\mathbf{k}$ (d) yes

7 yes

## 26.6 Combining the operators grad, div and curl

We have now met three vector operators; these are summarized in Table 26.1.

It is important to be able to combine the three operators grad, div and curl in sensible ways. For instance, because the gradient of a scalar is a vector we can consider evaluating its divergence, that is

$$\begin{aligned}
\nabla \cdot (\nabla\phi) &= \nabla \cdot \left(\frac{\partial\phi}{\partial x}, \frac{\partial\phi}{\partial y}, \frac{\partial\phi}{\partial z}\right) \\
&= \left(\frac{\partial}{\partial x}, \frac{\partial}{\partial y}, \frac{\partial}{\partial z}\right) \cdot \left(\frac{\partial\phi}{\partial x}, \frac{\partial\phi}{\partial y}, \frac{\partial\phi}{\partial z}\right) \\
&= \frac{\partial^2\phi}{\partial x^2} + \frac{\partial^2\phi}{\partial y^2} + \frac{\partial^2\phi}{\partial z^2}
\end{aligned}$$

**Table 26.1**
The three vector operators.

| Operator | Acts on | Result is a | Definition |
|---|---|---|---|
| grad | scalar field | vector field | $\nabla\phi = \text{grad}\,\phi = \frac{\partial\phi}{\partial x}\mathbf{i} + \frac{\partial\phi}{\partial y}\mathbf{j} + \frac{\partial\phi}{\partial z}\mathbf{k}$ |
| div | vector field | scalar field | $\nabla \cdot \mathbf{v} = \text{div}\,\mathbf{v} = \frac{\partial v_x}{\partial x} + \frac{\partial v_y}{\partial y} + \frac{\partial v_z}{\partial z}$ |
| curl | vector field | vector field | $\nabla \times \mathbf{v} = \text{curl}\,\mathbf{v} = \begin{vmatrix} \mathbf{i} & \mathbf{j} & \mathbf{k} \\ \frac{\partial}{\partial x} & \frac{\partial}{\partial y} & \frac{\partial}{\partial z} \\ v_x & v_y & v_z \end{vmatrix}$ |

This last expression is very important and is often abbreviated to simply

$$\nabla^2\phi$$

pronounced 'del-squared $\phi$', and occurs in Laplace's equation $\nabla^2\phi = 0$ and other partial differential equations.

**Example 26.11** If $\phi = 2x^2 - y^2 - z^2$, find $\nabla\phi$, $\nabla \cdot (\nabla\phi)$ and deduce that $\phi$ satisfies Laplace's equation.

**Solution**

$$\nabla\phi = 4x\mathbf{i} - 2y\mathbf{j} - 2z\mathbf{k}$$
$$\nabla \cdot (\nabla\phi) = 4 - 2 - 2 = 0$$

that is,

$$\nabla^2\phi = 0$$

Hence $\phi$ satisfies Laplace's equation.

**Example 26.12** If $\phi(x, y, z)$ is an arbitrary differentiable scalar field, show that $\text{curl}(\text{grad}\phi) = \nabla \times (\nabla\phi)$ is always zero.

**Solution** Given $\phi = \phi(x, y, z)$ we have, by definition,

$$\nabla\phi = \frac{\partial\phi}{\partial x}\mathbf{i} + \frac{\partial\phi}{\partial y}\mathbf{j} + \frac{\partial\phi}{\partial z}\mathbf{k}$$

Then

$$\begin{aligned}\text{curl}(\text{grad}\phi) &= \nabla \times (\nabla\phi)\\ &= \begin{vmatrix} \mathbf{i} & \mathbf{j} & \mathbf{k} \\ \dfrac{\partial}{\partial x} & \dfrac{\partial}{\partial y} & \dfrac{\partial}{\partial z} \\ \dfrac{\partial\phi}{\partial x} & \dfrac{\partial\phi}{\partial y} & \dfrac{\partial\phi}{\partial z} \end{vmatrix}\\ &= \left(\frac{\partial}{\partial y}\left(\frac{\partial\phi}{\partial z}\right) - \frac{\partial}{\partial z}\left(\frac{\partial\phi}{\partial y}\right)\right)\mathbf{i} - \left(\frac{\partial}{\partial x}\left(\frac{\partial\phi}{\partial z}\right) - \frac{\partial}{\partial z}\left(\frac{\partial\phi}{\partial x}\right)\right)\mathbf{j}\\ &\quad + \left(\frac{\partial}{\partial x}\left(\frac{\partial\phi}{\partial y}\right) - \frac{\partial}{\partial y}\left(\frac{\partial\phi}{\partial x}\right)\right)\mathbf{k}\end{aligned}$$

Now, since $\dfrac{\partial}{\partial x}\left(\dfrac{\partial\phi}{\partial y}\right) = \dfrac{\partial}{\partial y}\left(\dfrac{\partial\phi}{\partial x}\right)$ with similar results for the other mixed partial derivatives, it follows that

$$\nabla \times (\nabla\phi) = \mathbf{0}$$

for any scalar field $\phi$ whatsoever.

For an arbitrary differentiable scalar field $\phi$

$$\nabla \times (\nabla \phi) = \mathbf{0}$$

**Example 26.13** **Poisson's equation**

If $\mathbf{E}$ is an electric field and $V$ an electrostatic potential, then the two fields are related by

$$\mathbf{E} = -\nabla V$$

From Example 26.8 we know Gauss's law: $\nabla \cdot \mathbf{E} = \dfrac{\rho}{\varepsilon_0}$. Combining these two equations we can write

$$\nabla \cdot (-\nabla V) = \frac{\rho}{\varepsilon_0}$$

that is

$$\nabla^2 V = -\frac{\rho}{\varepsilon_0}$$

This partial differential equation is known as Poisson's equation and by solving it we could determine the electrostatic potential in a region occupied by charges. Note that in a charge-free region, $\rho = 0$ and Poisson's equation reduces to Laplace's equation $\nabla^2 V = 0$.

## Exercises 26.6

1. A scalar field $\phi$ is given by $\phi = 3x + y - y^2z^2$. Show that $\phi$ satisfies $\nabla^2\phi = -2(y^2 + z^2)$.

2. If $\phi = 2x^2y - xz^3$ show that $\nabla^2\phi = 4y - 6xz$.

3. If $\mathbf{v} = xy\mathbf{i} - yz\mathbf{j} + (y + 2z)\mathbf{k}$ find curl (curl ($\mathbf{v}$)).

4. If $\phi = xyz$ and $\mathbf{v} = 3x^2\mathbf{i} + 2y^3\mathbf{j} + xy\mathbf{k}$ find $\nabla\phi$, $\nabla \cdot \mathbf{v}$, and $\nabla \cdot (\phi\mathbf{v})$. Show that $\nabla \cdot (\phi\mathbf{v}) = (\nabla\phi) \cdot \mathbf{v} + \phi\nabla \cdot \mathbf{v}$.

5. Verify that $\phi = x^2y + y^2z + z^2x$ satisfies $\nabla \cdot (\nabla\phi) = 2(x + y + z)$.

6. If $\mathbf{A}$ is an arbitrary differentiable vector field show that the divergence of the curl of $\mathbf{A}$ is always 0.

7. Express each of the following in operator notation using '$\nabla$', '$\nabla\cdot$' and '$\nabla\times$'.

   (a) grad (div $\mathbf{F}$)

   (b) curl (grad $\phi$)

   (c) curl (curl $\mathbf{F}$)

   (d) div (curl $\mathbf{F}$)

   (e) div (grad $\phi$)

8. Scalar fields $\phi_1$ and $\phi_2$ are given by

$$\phi_1 = 2xy + y^2z \qquad \phi_2 = x^2z$$

   (a) Find $\nabla\phi_1$.

   (b) Find $\nabla\phi_2$.

   (c) State $\phi_1\phi_2$.

   (d) Find $\nabla(\phi_1\phi_2)$.

   (e) Find $\phi_1\nabla\phi_2 + \phi_2\nabla\phi_1$.

   (f) What do you conclude from (d) and (e)?

9. A scalar field $\phi$ and a vector field $\mathbf{F}$ are given by

$$\phi = xyz^2 \qquad \mathbf{F} = x^2\mathbf{i} + 2\mathbf{j} + z\mathbf{k}$$

   (a) Find $\nabla\phi$.

   (b) Find $\nabla \cdot \mathbf{F}$.

(c) Calculate $\phi(\nabla \cdot \mathbf{F}) + \mathbf{F} \cdot (\nabla\phi)$. [*Hint:* recall the dot product of two vectors.]

(d) State $\phi\mathbf{F}$.

(e) Calculate $\nabla \cdot (\phi\mathbf{F})$.

(f) What do you conclude from (c) and (e)?

## Solutions

3 $\mathbf{j} - \mathbf{k}$

4 $\nabla\phi = yz\mathbf{i} + xz\mathbf{j} + xy\mathbf{k}$

$\nabla \cdot \mathbf{v} = 6x + 6y^2$

$\nabla \cdot (\phi\mathbf{v}) = 9x^2yz + 8xy^3z + x^2y^2$

7 (a) $\nabla(\nabla \cdot \mathbf{F})$

(b) $\nabla \times (\nabla\phi)$

(c) $\nabla \times (\nabla \times \mathbf{F})$

(d) $\nabla \cdot (\nabla \times \mathbf{F})$

(e) $\nabla \cdot (\nabla\phi)$

8 (a) $2y\mathbf{i} + (2x + 2yz)\mathbf{j} + y^2\mathbf{k}$

(b) $2xz\mathbf{i} + x^2\mathbf{k}$

(c) $2x^3yz + y^2x^2z^2$

(d) $(6x^2yz + 2xy^2z^2)\mathbf{i} + (2x^3z + 2yx^2z^2)\mathbf{j} + (2x^3y + 2y^2x^2z)\mathbf{k}$

(e) same as (d)

(f) $\nabla(\phi_1\phi_2) = \phi_1\nabla\phi_2 + \phi_2\nabla\phi_1$

9 (a) $yz^2\mathbf{i} + xz^2\mathbf{j} + 2xyz\mathbf{k}$

(b) $2x + 1$

(c) $3x^2yz^2 + 2xz^2 + 3xyz^2$

(d) $x^3yz^2\mathbf{i} + 2xyz^2\mathbf{j} + xyz^3\mathbf{k}$

(e) same as (c)

(f) $\nabla \cdot (\phi\mathbf{F}) = \phi(\nabla \cdot \mathbf{F}) + \mathbf{F} \cdot (\nabla\phi)$

## 26.7 Vector calculus and electromagnetism

Vector calculus provides a useful mechanism for expressing the fundamental laws of electromagnetism in a concise manner. These laws can be summarized by means of four equations, known as Maxwell's equations. Much of electromagnetism is concerned with solving Maxwell's equations for different boundary conditions.

### Equation 1

$$\text{div}\,\mathbf{D} = \rho$$

where $\mathbf{D}$ = electric flux density, and $\rho$ = charge density. This equation is a general form of Gauss's theorem which states that the total electric flux flowing out of a closed surface is proportional to the electric charge enclosed by that surface.

### Equation 2

$$\text{div}\,\mathbf{B} = 0$$

where $\mathbf{B}$ is the magnetic flux density.

This equation arises from the observation that all magnetic poles occur in pairs and therefore magnetic field lines are continuous; that is, there are no isolated magnetic poles. In contrast, electric field lines originate on positive charges and terminate on negative charges and so a net positive charge in a region leads to an outflow of electric flux.

**Equation 3**

$$\text{curl } \mathbf{E} = -\frac{\partial \mathbf{B}}{\partial t}$$

where **E** is the electric field strength. This equation is a statement of Faraday's law. A time-varying magnetic field produces a space-varying electric field.

**Equation 4**

$$\text{curl } \mathbf{H} = \mathbf{J} + \frac{\partial \mathbf{D}}{\partial t}$$

where **H** is the magnetic field strength and **J** is the free current density. This equation states that a time-varying electric field gives rise to a space-varying magnetic field.

The derivation of these equations is beyond the scope of this text but can be found in many books on electromagnetism. The power of these equations lies in their generality. The brevity with which the main laws of electromagnetism can be expressed is a tribute to the utility of vector calculus.

## Review exercises 26

1 Find $\nabla\phi$ if

(a) $\phi = 3xyz$

(b) $\phi = x^2yz + xy^2z + xyz^2$

(c) $\phi = xy^2z^2 + x^2yz^2 + x^2y^2z$

2 If $\phi = 1/\sqrt{x^2 + y^2 + z^2}$, show that

$$\frac{\partial^2 \phi}{\partial x^2} + \frac{\partial^2 \phi}{\partial y^2} + \frac{\partial^2 \phi}{\partial z^2} = 0$$

3 Functions satisfying Laplace's equation are called **harmonic functions**. Show that the following functions are harmonic.

(a) $z = x^4 - 6x^2y^2 + y^4$

(b) $z = 4x^3y - 4xy^3$

4 If $\mathbf{A} = x\mathbf{i} + y\mathbf{j} + z\mathbf{k}$ and $\mathbf{B} = \cos x\mathbf{i} - \sin x\mathbf{j}$, find

(a) $\mathbf{A} \times \mathbf{B}$

(b) $\nabla \cdot (\mathbf{A} \times \mathbf{B})$

(c) $\nabla \times \mathbf{A}$

(d) $\nabla \times \mathbf{B}$

Verify that $\nabla \cdot (\mathbf{A} \times \mathbf{B}) = \mathbf{B} \cdot (\nabla \times \mathbf{A}) - \mathbf{A} \cdot (\nabla \times \mathbf{B})$.

5 For arbitrary differentiable scalar fields $\phi$ and $\psi$ show that $\nabla(\phi\psi) = \psi\nabla\phi + \phi\nabla\psi$.

6 If $\psi = x^2y$ and $\mathbf{a} = x\mathbf{i} + y\mathbf{j} + z\mathbf{k}$, find $\nabla\psi$, $\nabla \times \mathbf{a}$, $\nabla \times (\psi\mathbf{a})$. Show that $\nabla \times (\psi\mathbf{a}) = \psi\nabla \times \mathbf{a} + (\nabla\psi) \times \mathbf{a}$.

7 A scalar field $\phi$ is a function of $x$, $z$ and $t$ only. Vectors **E** and **H** are defined by

$$\mathbf{E} = \frac{1}{\varepsilon}\left(\frac{\partial \phi}{\partial z}\mathbf{i} - \frac{\partial \phi}{\partial x}\mathbf{k}\right) \qquad \mathbf{H} = -\frac{\partial \phi}{\partial t}\mathbf{j}$$

where $\varepsilon$ is a constant.

(a) Show that $\nabla \cdot \mathbf{E} = 0$.

(b) Show that $\nabla \cdot \mathbf{H} = 0$.

Given that $\nabla \times \mathbf{E} = -\mu\frac{\partial \mathbf{H}}{\partial t}$, where $\mu$ is a constant, show that $\phi$ satisfies the partial differential equation

$$\frac{\partial^2 \phi}{\partial x^2} + \frac{\partial^2 \phi}{\partial z^2} = \mu\varepsilon\frac{\partial^2 \phi}{\partial t^2}$$

8 If $\mathbf{v} = (2x^2y + 3x^5)\mathbf{i} + e^{xy}\mathbf{j} + xyz\mathbf{k}$ find $\frac{\partial \mathbf{v}}{\partial x}$ and $\frac{\partial^2 \mathbf{v}}{\partial x^2}$.

9 An electrostatic potential is given by $V = 5xyz$. Find

(a) the associated electric field **E**,

(b) $|\mathbf{E}|$ at the point $(1, 1, 1)$.

10 An electrostatic field is given by $\mathbf{E} = 3(x + y)\mathbf{i} + 2xy\mathbf{j}$. Find the direction of this field at

(a) the point $(2, 2)$

(b) the point $(3, 4)$.

11 Find the curl of $\mathbf{A} = y\mathbf{i} + 2xy\mathbf{j} + 3z\mathbf{k}$.

12 Find the curl of the vector field $\mathbf{F} = (x^2 - y)\mathbf{i} + (xy - 4y^2)\mathbf{j}$.

13 If $\phi = 5\,e^{x+2y}\cos z$ find $\nabla\phi$ at the point $(0, 0, 0)$.

14 The vector fields **A** and **B** are given by

$$\mathbf{A} = x^2y\mathbf{i} + 2xz\mathbf{j} + x\mathbf{k}$$
$$\mathbf{B} = yz\mathbf{i} + x^2y\mathbf{j} + 3\mathbf{k}$$

(a) Calculate the vector product $\mathbf{A} \times \mathbf{B}$.

(b) Calculate $\nabla \cdot (\mathbf{A} \times \mathbf{B})$.

(c) Calculate $\mathbf{B} \cdot (\nabla \times \mathbf{A}) - \mathbf{A} \cdot (\nabla \times \mathbf{B})$.

(d) What do you conclude from (b) and (c)?

(e) Can you prove this result is true for any two vector fields?

15 Given

$$\mathbf{F} = (3x, 2y, 4z) \qquad \mathbf{G} = (1, -1, 3)$$
$$\phi = x^2yz$$

find

(a) $\nabla \cdot \mathbf{F}$

(b) $\nabla\phi$

(c) $\nabla \times \mathbf{F}$

(d) $\nabla \cdot (\phi\mathbf{F})$

(e) $\nabla \times (\phi\mathbf{G})$

(f) $\nabla(\mathbf{F} \cdot \mathbf{G})$

(g) $\nabla \times (\mathbf{F} \times \mathbf{G})$

(h) $\nabla \cdot (\mathbf{F} + \mathbf{G})$

(i) $\nabla \times (3\mathbf{F} + 4\mathbf{G})$

## Solutions

1 (a) $3yz\mathbf{i} + 3xz\mathbf{j} + 3xy\mathbf{k}$

(b) $(2xyz + y^2z + yz^2)\mathbf{i} + (x^2z + 2xyz + xz^2)\mathbf{j} + (x^2y + xy^2 + 2xyz)\mathbf{k}$

(c) $(y^2z^2 + 2xyz^2 + 2xy^2z)\mathbf{i} + (2xyz^2 + x^2z^2 + 2x^2yz)\mathbf{j} + (2xy^2z + 2x^2yz + x^2y^2)\mathbf{k}$

4 (a) $z\sin x\mathbf{i} + z\cos x\mathbf{j} + (-y\cos x - x\sin x)\mathbf{k}$

(b) $z\cos x$

(c) $\mathbf{0}$

(d) $-\cos x\mathbf{k}$

6 $\nabla\psi = 2xy\mathbf{i} + x^2\mathbf{j}$

$\nabla \times \mathbf{a} = \mathbf{0}$

$\nabla \times (\psi\mathbf{a}) = x^2z\mathbf{i} - 2xyz\mathbf{j} + (2xy^2 - x^3)\mathbf{k}$

8 $(4xy + 15x^4)\mathbf{i} + y\,e^{xy}\mathbf{j} + yz\mathbf{k}$,

$(4y + 60x^3)\mathbf{i} + y^2\,e^{xy}\mathbf{j}$

9 (a) $\mathbf{E} = -\nabla V = -5yz\mathbf{i} - 5xz\mathbf{j} - 5xy\mathbf{k}$

(b) $\sqrt{75}$

10 (a) $12\mathbf{i} + 8\mathbf{j}$

(b) $21\mathbf{i} + 24\mathbf{j}$

11 $(2y - 1)\mathbf{k}$

12 $(y + 1)\mathbf{k}$

13 $5\mathbf{i} + 10\mathbf{j}$

14 (a) $(6xz - x^3y)\mathbf{i} + (xyz - 3x^2y)\mathbf{j} + (x^4y^2 - 2xyz^2)\mathbf{k}$

(b) $-3x^2(y + 1) - xz(4y - 1) + 6z$

(c) $-3x^2(y + 1) - xz(4y - 1) + 6z$

(d) $\nabla \cdot (\mathbf{A} \times \mathbf{B}) = \mathbf{B} \cdot (\nabla \times \mathbf{A}) - \mathbf{A} \cdot (\nabla \times \mathbf{B})$

15 (a) 9

(b) $2xyz\mathbf{i} + x^2z\mathbf{j} + x^2y\mathbf{k}$

(c) $\mathbf{0}$

(d) $21x^2yz$

(e) $x^2(y + 3z)\mathbf{i} + (x^2y - 6xyz)\mathbf{j} - (x^2z + 2xyz)\mathbf{k}$

(f) $3\mathbf{i} - 2\mathbf{j} + 12\mathbf{k}$

(g) $-6\mathbf{i} + 7\mathbf{j} - 15\mathbf{k}$

(h) 9

(i) $\mathbf{0}$

# Integration

# 13 Integration

## Chapter 13 Contents

## 13.1 Introduction

When a function, $f(x)$, is known we can differentiate it to obtain the derivative, $\frac{\mathrm{d}f}{\mathrm{d}x}$. The reverse process is to obtain the function $f(x)$ from knowledge of its derivative. This process is called **integration**. Thus, integration is the reverse of differentiation.

A problem related to integration is to find the area between a curve and the $x$ axis. At first sight it may not be clear that the calculation of area is connected to integration. This chapter aims to explain the connection. An area can have various interpretations. For example, the area under a graph of power used by a motor plotted against time represents the total energy used by the motor in a particular time period. The area under a graph of current flow into a capacitor against time represents the total charge stored by the capacitor.

Circuits to carry out integration are used extensively in electronics. For example, a circuit to display the total distance travelled by a car may have a speed signal as input and may integrate this signal to give the distance travelled as output. Integrator circuits are widely used in analog computers. These computers can be used to model a physical system and observe its response to a range of inputs. The advantage of this approach is that the system parameters can be varied in order to see what effect they have on system performance. This avoids the need to build the actual system and allows design ideas to be explored relatively quickly and cheaply by an engineer.

## 13.2 Elementary integration

Consider the following problem: given $\frac{\mathrm{d}y}{\mathrm{d}x} = 2x$, find $y(x)$. Differentiation of the function $y(x) = x^2 + c$, where $c$ is a constant, yields $\frac{\mathrm{d}y}{\mathrm{d}x} = 2x$ for any $c$. Therefore $y(x) = x^2 + c$ is a solution to the problem. As $c$ can be any constant, there are an infinite number of different solutions. The constant $c$ is known as a **constant of integration**. In this example, the function $y$ has been found from a knowledge of its derivative. We say $2x$ has been **integrated**, yielding $x^2 + c$. To indicate the process of integration the symbols $\int$ and $\mathrm{d}x$ are used. The $\int$ sign denotes that integration is to be performed and the $\mathrm{d}x$ indicates that $x$ is the independent variable. Returning to the previous problem, we write

$$\frac{\mathrm{d}y}{\mathrm{d}x} = 2x$$

$$y = \int 2x \, \mathrm{d}x = x^2 + c$$

$$\uparrow \quad \uparrow \qquad \quad \uparrow$$

symbols for integration    constant of integration

In general, if

$$\frac{dy}{dx} = f(x)$$

then

$$y = \int f(x)\,dx$$

Consider a simple example.

**Example 13.1** Given $\frac{dy}{dx} = \cos x - x$, find $y$.

**Solution** We need to find a function which, when differentiated, yields $\cos x - x$. Differentiating $\sin x$ yields $\cos x$, while differentiating $-x^2/2$ yields $-x$. Hence,

$$y = \int (\cos x - x)\,dx = \sin x - \frac{x^2}{2} + c$$

where $c$ is the constant of integration. Usually brackets are not used and the integral is written simply as $\int \cos x - x\,dx$.

---

The function to be integrated is known as the **integrand**. In Example 13.1 the integrand is $\cos x - x$.

**Example 13.2** Find $\frac{d}{dx}\left(\frac{x^{n+1}}{n+1} + c\right)$ and hence deduce that $\int x^n\,dx = \frac{x^{n+1}}{n+1} + c$.

**Solution** From Table 10.1 we find

$$\frac{d}{dx}\left(\frac{x^{n+1}}{n+1} + c\right) = \frac{d}{dx}\left(\frac{x^{n+1}}{n+1}\right) + \frac{d}{dx}(c) \quad \text{using the linearity of differentiation}$$

$$= \frac{1}{n+1}\frac{d}{dx}(x^{n+1}) + \frac{d}{dx}(c) \quad \text{again using the linearity of differentiation}$$

$$= \frac{1}{n+1}\{(n+1)x^n\} + 0 \quad \text{using Table 10.1.}$$

$$= x^n$$

Consequently, reversing the process we find

$$\int x^n\,dx = \frac{x^{n+1}}{n+1} + c$$

as required. Note that this result is invalid if $n = -1$ and so this result could not be applied to the integral $\int (1/x)\,dx$.

---

**Table 13.1**
The integrals of some common functions.

| $f(x)$ | $\int f(x)\,dx$ | $f(x)$ | $\int f(x)\,dx$ |
|---|---|---|---|
| $k$, constant | $kx + c$ | $\cos(ax+b)$ | $\dfrac{\sin(ax+b)}{a} + c$ |
| $x^n$ | $\dfrac{x^{n+1}}{n+1} + c \quad n \neq -1$ | $\tan x$ | $\ln\lvert\sec x\rvert + c$ |
| $x^{-1} = \dfrac{1}{x}$ | $\ln\lvert x\rvert + c$ | $\tan ax$ | $\dfrac{\ln\lvert\sec ax\rvert}{a} + c$ |
| $e^x$ | $e^x + c$ | $\tan(ax+b)$ | $\dfrac{\ln\lvert\sec(ax+b)\rvert}{a} + c$ |
| $e^{-x}$ | $-e^{-x} + c$ | $\mathrm{cosec}(ax+b)$ | $\dfrac{1}{a}\{\ln\lvert\mathrm{cosec}(ax+b) - \cot(ax+b)\rvert\} + c$ |
| $e^{ax}$ | $\dfrac{e^{ax}}{a} + c$ | | |
| $\sin x$ | $-\cos x + c$ | $\sec(ax+b)$ | $\dfrac{1}{a}\{\ln\lvert\sec(ax+b) + \tan(ax+b)\rvert\} + c$ |
| $\sin ax$ | $\dfrac{-\cos ax}{a} + c$ | | |
| $\sin(ax+b)$ | $\dfrac{-\cos(ax+b)}{a} + c$ | $\cot(ax+b)$ | $\dfrac{1}{a}\{\ln\lvert\sin(ax+b)\rvert\} + c$ |
| $\cos x$ | $\sin x + c$ | $\dfrac{1}{\sqrt{a^2 - x^2}}$ | $\sin^{-1}\dfrac{x}{a} + c$ |
| $\cos ax$ | $\dfrac{\sin ax}{a} + c$ | $\dfrac{1}{a^2 + x^2}$ | $\dfrac{1}{a}\tan^{-1}\dfrac{x}{a} + c$ |

Note that $a$, $b$, $n$ and $c$ are constants. When integrating trigonometric functions, angles must be in radians.

Table 13.1 lists several common functions and their integrals. Although the variable $x$ is used throughout Table 13.1, we can use this table to integrate functions of other variables, for example $t$ and $z$.

**Example 13.3** Use Table 13.1 to integrate the following functions:

(a) $x^4$

(b) $\cos kx$, where $k$ is a constant

(c) $\sin(3x + 2)$

(d) 5.9

(e) $\tan(6t - 4)$

(f) $e^{-3z}$

(g) $\dfrac{1}{x^2}$

(h) $\cos 100n\pi t$, where $n$ is a constant

**Solution** (a) From Table 13.1, we find $\int x^n \, dx = \dfrac{x^{n+1}}{n+1} + c, n \neq -1$. To find $\int x^4 \, dx$ let $n = 4$; we obtain

$$\int x^4 \, dx = \frac{x^5}{5} + c$$

(b) From Table 13.1, we find $\int \cos(ax) \, dx = \dfrac{\sin(ax)}{a} + c$. In this case $a = k$ and so

$$\int \cos kx \, dx = \frac{\sin kx}{k} + c$$

(c) From Table 13.1, we find $\int \sin(ax+b) \, dx = \dfrac{-\cos(ax+b)}{a} + c$. In this case $a = 3$ and $b = 2$, and so

$$\int \sin(3x+2) \, dx = \frac{-\cos(3x+2)}{3} + c$$

(d) From Table 13.1, we find that if $k$ is a constant then $\int k \, dx = kx + c$. Hence,

$$\int 5.9 \, dx = 5.9x + c$$

(e) In this example, the independent variable is $t$ but nevertheless from Table 13.1 we can deduce

$$\int \tan(at+b) \, dt = \frac{\ln|\sec(at+b)|}{a} + c$$

Hence with $a = 6$ and $b = -4$, we obtain

$$\int \tan(6t-4) \, dt = \frac{\ln|\sec(6t-4)|}{6} + c$$

(f) The independent variable is $z$ but from Table 13.1 we can deduce $\int e^{az} \, dz = \dfrac{e^{az}}{a} + c$. Hence, taking $a = -3$ we obtain

$$\int e^{-3z} \, dz = \frac{e^{-3z}}{-3} + c = -\frac{e^{-3z}}{3} + c$$

(g) Since $\dfrac{1}{x^2} = x^{-2}$, we find

$$\int \frac{1}{x^2} \, dx = \int x^{-2} \, dx = \frac{x^{-1}}{-1} + c = -\frac{1}{x} + c$$

(h) When integrating $\cos 100n\pi t$ with respect to $t$, note that $100n\pi$ is a constant. Hence, using part (b) we find

$$\int \cos 100n\pi t \, dt = \frac{\sin 100n\pi t}{100n\pi} + c$$

### 13.2.1 Integration as a linear operator

Integration, like differentiation, is a linear operator. If $f$ and $g$ are two functions of $x$, then

$$\int f + g \, \mathrm{d}x = \int f \, \mathrm{d}x + \int g \, \mathrm{d}x$$

This states that the integral of a sum of functions is the sum of the integrals of the individual functions. If $A$ is a constant and $f$ a function of $x$, then

$$\int Af \, \mathrm{d}x = A \int f \, \mathrm{d}x$$

Thus, constant factors can be taken through the integral sign.

If $A$ and $B$ are constants, and $f$ and $g$ are functions of $x$, then

$$\int Af + Bg \, \mathrm{d}x = A \int f \, \mathrm{d}x + B \int g \, \mathrm{d}x$$

These three properties are all consequences of the fact that integration is a linear operator. Note that the first two are special cases of the third. The properties are used in Example 13.4.

**Example 13.4** Use Table 13.1 and the properties of a linear operator to integrate the following expressions:

(a) $x^2 + 9$

(b) $3t^4 - \sqrt{t}$

(c) $\dfrac{1}{x}$

(d) $(t+2)^2$

(e) $\dfrac{1}{z} + z$

(f) $4\mathrm{e}^{2z}$

(g) $3 \sin 4t$

(h) $4 \cos(9x + 2)$

(i) $3\mathrm{e}^{2z}$

(j) $\dfrac{\sin x + \cos x}{2}$

(k) $2t - \mathrm{e}^t$

(l) $\tan\left(\dfrac{z-1}{2}\right)$

(m) $\mathrm{e}^t + \mathrm{e}^{-t}$

(n) $3 \sec(4x - 1)$

(o) $2 \cot 9x$

(p) $7 \operatorname{cosec}(\pi/3)$

**Solution** (a) $\displaystyle\int x^2 + 9 \, \mathrm{d}x = \int x^2 \, \mathrm{d}x + \int 9 \, \mathrm{d}x$ using linearity

$\displaystyle = \frac{x^3}{3} + 9x + c$ using Table 13.1

Note that only a single constant of integration is required.

(b) $\displaystyle\int 3t^4 - \sqrt{t} \, \mathrm{d}t = 3\int t^4 \, \mathrm{d}t - \int t^{1/2} \, \mathrm{d}t$ using linearity

$\displaystyle = 3\left(\frac{t^5}{5}\right) - \frac{t^{3/2}}{3/2} + c$ using Table 13.1

$\displaystyle = \frac{3t^5}{5} - \frac{2t^{3/2}}{3} + c$

(c) $\int \frac{1}{x}\,\mathrm{d}x = \ln|x| + c$ using Table 13.1.

Sometimes it is convenient to use the laws of logarithms to rewrite answers involving logarithms. For example, we can write $\ln|x| + c$ as $\ln|x| + \ln|A|$ where $c = \ln|A|$. This enables us to write the integral as

$$\int \frac{1}{x}\,\mathrm{d}x = \ln|Ax|$$

(d) $\int (t+2)^2\,\mathrm{d}t = \int t^2 + 4t + 4\,\mathrm{d}t = \frac{t^3}{3} + 2t^2 + 4t + c$

(e) $\int \frac{1}{z} + z\,\mathrm{d}z = \ln|z| + \frac{z^2}{2} + c$

(f) $\int 4\mathrm{e}^{2z}\,\mathrm{d}z = \frac{4\mathrm{e}^{2z}}{2} + c = 2\mathrm{e}^{2z} + c$

(g) $\int 3\sin(4t)\,\mathrm{d}t = -\frac{3\cos 4t}{4} + c$

(h) $\int 4\cos(9x+2)\,\mathrm{d}x = \frac{4\sin(9x+2)}{9} + c$

(i) $\int 3\mathrm{e}^{2z}\,\mathrm{d}z = \frac{3\mathrm{e}^{2z}}{2} + c$

(j) $\int \frac{\sin x + \cos x}{2}\,\mathrm{d}x = \frac{-\cos x + \sin x}{2} + c$

(k) $\int 2t - \mathrm{e}^t\,\mathrm{d}t = t^2 - \mathrm{e}^t + c$

(l) $\int \tan\left(\frac{z-1}{2}\right)\mathrm{d}z = 2\ln\left|\sec\left(\frac{z-1}{2}\right)\right| + c$

(m) $\int \mathrm{e}^t + \mathrm{e}^{-t}\,\mathrm{d}t = \mathrm{e}^t - \mathrm{e}^{-t} + c$

(n) $\int 3\sec(4x-1)\,\mathrm{d}x = \frac{3}{4}\ln|\sec(4x-1) + \tan(4x-1)| + c$

(o) $\int 2\cot 9x\,\mathrm{d}x = \frac{2}{9}\ln|\sin 9x| + c$

(p) $\int 7\,\mathrm{cosec}(\pi/3)\,\mathrm{d}x = \{7\,\mathrm{cosec}(\pi/3)\}x + c$ as $\mathrm{cosec}(\pi/3)$ is a constant

**Example 13.5** **Distance travelled by a particle**

The speed, $v$, of a particle is the rate of change of distance, $s$, with respect to time $t$, that is $v = \frac{ds}{dt}$. The speed at time $t$ is given by $3 + 2t$. Find the distance in terms of $t$.

**Solution** We are given that

$$v = \frac{ds}{dt} = 3 + 2t$$

and are required to find $s$. Therefore,

$$s = \int 3 + 2t \, dt = 3t + t^2 + c$$

**Example 13.6** **Voltage across a capacitor**

The current, $i$, through a capacitor depends upon time, $t$, and is given by

$$i = C\frac{dv}{dt}$$

where $v$ is the voltage across the capacitor and $C$ is the capacitance of the capacitor. Derive an expression for $v$.

**Solution** If

$$i = C\frac{dv}{dt} \quad \text{then} \quad \frac{dv}{dt} = \frac{i}{C}$$

Therefore,

$$v = \int \frac{i}{C} \, dt = \frac{1}{C}\int i \, dt \quad \text{using linearity}$$

Note that whereas the capacitance, $C$, is constant, the current, $i$, is not and so it cannot be taken through the integral sign. In order to perform the integration we need to know $i$ as a function of $t$.

---

## 13.2.2 Electronic integrators

Often there is a requirement in engineering to integrate electronic signals. Various circuits are available to carry out this task. One of the simplest circuits is shown in Figure 13.1. The input voltage is $v_i$, the output voltage is $v_o$, the voltage drop across the resistor is $v_R$ and the current flowing in the circuit is $i$. Applying Kirchhoff's voltage law yields

$$v_i = v_R + v_o \tag{13.1}$$

For the resistor with resistance, $R$,

$$v_R = iR \tag{13.2}$$

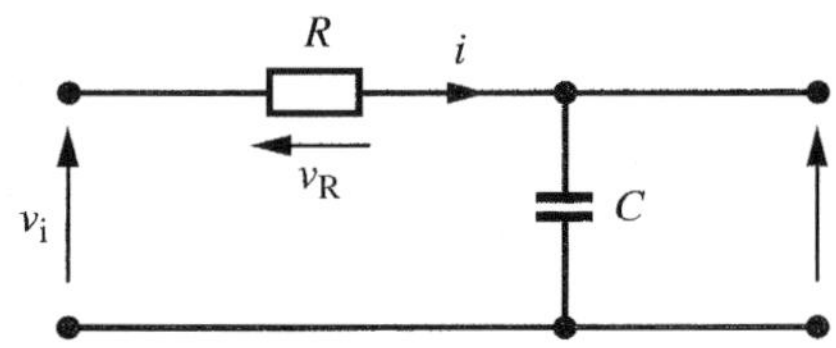


**Figure 13.1** Simple integrator.

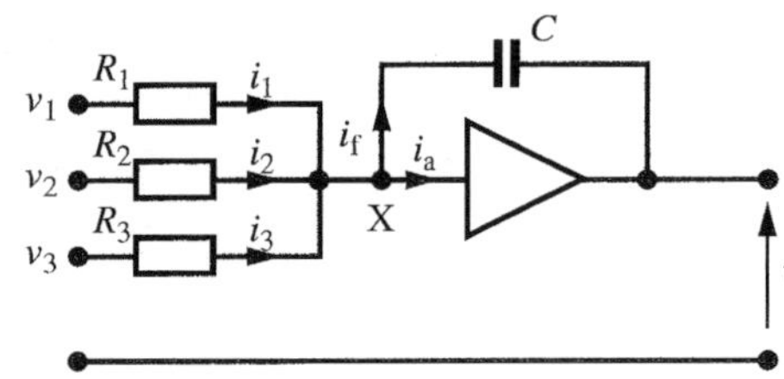


**Figure 13.2** Electronic integrator.

For the capacitor with capacitance, $C$,

$$i = C\frac{dv_o}{dt} \tag{13.3}$$

Combining Equations (13.1) to (13.3) yields

$$v_i = RC\frac{dv_o}{dt} + v_o \tag{13.4}$$

In general, $v_i$ will be an a.c. signal consisting of a range of frequencies. The a.c. resistance of a capacitor, known as the **capacitive reactance**, or **impedance**, $X_c$, is given by

$$X_c = \frac{1}{2\pi fC}$$

where $f$ = frequency of the signal (Hz). It can be seen that $X_c$ decreases with increasing frequency, $f$. For frequencies where $X_c$ is small compared with $R$, most of the voltage drop takes place across the resistor. In other words, $v_o$ is small compared with $v_R$. Examining Equation (13.1) for the case when $X_c$ is very much less than $R$ (written as $X_c \ll R$), and $v_o \ll v_R$, it can be seen that Equation (13.4) simplifies to

$$v_i = RC\frac{dv_o}{dt} \tag{13.5}$$

This equation is only valid for the range of frequencies for which $X_c \ll R$. Rearranging Equation (13.5) yields

$$\frac{dv_o}{dt} = \frac{v_i}{RC}$$

$$v_o = \frac{1}{RC}\int v_i \, dt$$

The output voltage from the circuit is an integrated version of the input voltage with a scaling factor $\frac{1}{RC}$.

A better electronic integrator, valid over a much greater range of frequencies, can be obtained using an operational amplifier circuit. Consider the circuit shown in Figure 13.2. One of the main characteristics of an operational amplifier is its extremely high voltage gain. This means that the input voltage must be much smaller than the output voltage if the amplifier is not to be driven into **saturation**. Saturation is a condition in which the output voltage reaches the supply voltage of the amplifier and cannot increase further. This means that point X in Figure 13.2 is virtually at a voltage of zero volts. For this reason it is known as a **virtual earth** point. For similar reasons the current drawn by the amplifier, $i_a$, is also very small. Using this information, it is now possible to analyse the circuit.

Assuming point X is at zero volts, and using Ohm's law, gives

$$i_1 = \frac{v_1}{R_1} \qquad i_2 = \frac{v_2}{R_2} \qquad i_3 = \frac{v_3}{R_3} \tag{13.6}$$

Assuming $i_a$ is negligible, then

$$i_f = i_1 + i_2 + i_3 \tag{13.7}$$

For the capacitor,

$$i_f = -C\frac{dv_o}{dt} \tag{13.8}$$

The negative sign is a result of the direction chosen for $i_f$. Combining Equations (13.6)–(13.8) yields

$$\frac{v_1}{R_1} + \frac{v_2}{R_2} + \frac{v_3}{R_3} = -C\frac{dv_o}{dt}$$

$$v_o = -\int \frac{v_1}{R_1C} + \frac{v_2}{R_2C} + \frac{v_3}{R_3C}\,dt$$

The circuit therefore acts as an integrator. An additional benefit is that it allows voltages to be summed before integration.

### 13.2.3 Integration of trigonometric functions

The trigonometric identities given in Table 3.1 together with Table 13.1 allow us to integrate a number of trigonometric functions.

**Example 13.7** Evaluate

(a) $\int \cos^2 t\,dt$

(b) $\int \sin^2 t\,dt$

**Solution** Powers of trigonometric functions, for example $\sin^2 t$, do not appear in the table of standard integrals. What we must attempt to do is rewrite the integrand to obtain a standard form.

(a) From Table 3.1

$$\cos^2 t = \frac{1 + \cos 2t}{2}$$

and so

$$\int \cos^2 t \, dt = \int \frac{1+\cos 2t}{2} \, dt$$

$$= \int \frac{1}{2} \, dt + \int \frac{\cos 2t}{2} \, dt$$

$$= \frac{t}{2} + \frac{\sin 2t}{4} + c$$

(b) $$\int \sin^2 t \, dt = \int 1 - \cos^2 t \, dt \qquad \text{using the trigonometric identities}$$

$$= \int 1 \, dt - \int \cos^2 t \, dt \qquad \text{using linearity}$$

$$= t - \left(\frac{t}{2} + \frac{\sin 2t}{4} + c\right) \qquad \text{using part (a)}$$

$$= \frac{t}{2} - \frac{\sin 2t}{4} + k$$

**Example 13.8** Find

(a) $\int \sin 2t \cos t \, dt$

(b) $\int \sin mt \sin nt \, dt$, where $m$ and $n$ are constants with $m \neq n$

**Solution** (a) Using the identities in Table 3.1 we find

$$2 \sin A \cos B = \sin(A+B) + \sin(A-B)$$

hence $\sin 2t \cos t$ can be written $\frac{1}{2}(\sin 3t + \sin t)$. Therefore,

$$\int \sin 2t \cos t \, dt = \int \frac{1}{2}(\sin 3t + \sin t) \, dt$$

$$= \frac{1}{2}\left(\frac{-\cos 3t}{3} - \cos t\right) + c$$

$$= -\frac{1}{6} \cos 3t - \frac{1}{2} \cos t + c$$

(b) Using the identity $2 \sin A \sin B = \cos(A-B) - \cos(A+B)$, we find

$$\sin mt \sin nt = \frac{1}{2}\{\cos(m-n)t - \cos(m+n)t\}$$

Therefore,

$$\int \sin mt \sin nt \, dt = \int \frac{1}{2}\{\cos(m-n)t - \cos(m+n)t\} \, dt$$
$$= \frac{1}{2}\left\{\frac{\sin(m-n)t}{m-n} - \frac{\sin(m+n)t}{m+n}\right\} + c$$

## Exercises 13.2

**1** Integrate the following expressions using Table 13.1.

(a) $x^{10}$ (b) $9$ (c) $x^{1.5}$

(d) $\sqrt{t}$ (e) $\frac{1}{z}$ (f) $-3.2$

(g) $\frac{1}{x^3}$ (h) $\frac{1}{\sqrt{t}}$ (i) $(x^2)^3$

(j) $x^{-2}$ (k) $t^{1/3}$

**2** Integrate the following expressions using Table 13.1.

(a) $e^{5x}$ (b) $e^{6x}$ (c) $e^{-3t}$

(d) $\frac{1}{e^x}$ (e) $e^{0.5t}$ (f) $e^{z/3}$

(g) $\frac{1}{e^{4t}}$ (h) $e^{-2.5x}$

**3** Integrate the following expressions using Table 13.1.

(a) $\sin 4x$ (b) $\sin 9t$

(c) $\sin\left(\frac{x}{2}\right)$ (d) $\sin\left(\frac{2t}{5}\right)$

(e) $\cos 7x$ (f) $\cos(-3x)$

(g) $\cos\left(\frac{5t}{3}\right)$ (h) $\tan 9x$

(i) $\operatorname{cosec} 2x$ (j) $\sec 5t$

(k) $\cot 8y$ (l) $\cos(5t+1)$

(m) $\tan(3x+4)$ (n) $\sin(3t-\pi)$

(o) $\operatorname{cosec}(5z+2)$ (p) $\sec\left(\frac{x}{2}+1\right)$

(q) $\sin\left(\frac{2t}{3}-1\right)$ (r) $\cot(5-x)$

(s) $\operatorname{cosec}(\pi-2x)$

**4** Use Table 13.1 to integrate the following expressions.

(a) $\frac{1}{1+x^2}$ (b) $\frac{1}{\sqrt{1-x^2}}$

(c) $\frac{1}{\sqrt{4-x^2}}$ (d) $\frac{1}{9+z^2}$

(e) $\frac{1}{\sqrt{0.25-x^2}}$ (f) $\frac{1}{0.01+v^2}$

(g) $\frac{1}{10^6+r^2}$ (h) $\frac{1}{10+t^2}$

(i) $\frac{1}{\sqrt{2-x^2}}$ (j) $\frac{1}{\frac{1}{9}+x^2}$

**5** Integrate the following expressions.

(a) $3+x+\frac{1}{x}$

(b) $e^{2x}-e^{-2x}$

(c) $2\sin 3x+\cos 3x$

(d) $\sec(2t+\pi)+\cot\left(\frac{t}{2}-\pi\right)$

(e) $\tan\left(\frac{t}{2}\right)+\operatorname{cosec}(3t-\pi)$

(f) $\sin x+\frac{x}{3}+\frac{1}{e^x}$

(g) $\frac{1}{\cos(3x)}$

(h) $\left(t+\frac{1}{t}\right)^2$

(i) $\frac{1}{3e^{2x}}$

(j) $\tan(4t - 3) + 2\sin(-t - 1)$

(k) $1 + 2\cot 3x$

(l) $\sin\left(\frac{t}{2}\right) - 3\cos\left(\frac{t}{2}\right)$

(m) $(t - 2)^2$

(n) $3e^{-t} - e^{-t/2}$

(o) $7 - 7x^6 + e^{-x}$

(p) $(k + t)^2$ $k$ constant

(q) $k\sin t - \cos kt$ $k$ constant

(r) $\dfrac{1}{25 + t^2}$

(s) $\dfrac{1}{\sqrt{25 - t^2}}$

(t) $\dfrac{6}{1 + x^2} + \dfrac{1 + x^2}{6}$

**6** The acceleration, $a$, of a particle is the rate of change of speed, $v$, with respect to time $t$, that is $a = \dfrac{dv}{dt}$. The speed of the particle is the rate of change of distance, $s$, that is $v = \dfrac{ds}{dt}$. If the acceleration is given by $1 + \dfrac{t}{2}$, find expressions for speed and distance.

**7** The speed, $v$, of a particle varies with time according to

$$v(t) = 2 - e^{-t}$$

(a) Obtain an expression for distance travelled by the particle.

(b) Calculate the distance travelled by the particle between $t = 0$ and $t = 3$.

**8** By writing $\sinh ax$ and $\cosh ax$ in terms of the exponential function find

(a) $\int \sinh ax \, dx$

(b) $\int \cosh ax \, dx$

(c) Use your results from (a) and (b) to find $\int 3\sinh 2x + \cosh 4x \, dx$.

**9** A capacitor of capacitance $10^{-2}$ F has a current $i(t)$ through it where

$$i(t) = 10 - e^{-t}$$

Find an expression for the voltage across the capacitor.

**10** Integrate the following:

(a) $\dfrac{1}{x^2 + 4}$ (b) $\dfrac{1}{2x^2 + 4}$

(c) $\dfrac{3}{2x^2 + 1}$ (d) $\dfrac{1}{\sqrt{9 - x^2}}$

(e) $\dfrac{2}{\sqrt{4 - x^2}}$ (f) $\dfrac{-7}{\sqrt{2 - 3x^2}}$

(g) $\dfrac{1}{\sqrt{1 - (x^2/2)}}$

**11** By writing $\dfrac{3 + x}{x}$ in the form $\dfrac{3}{x} + 1$, find $\displaystyle\int \frac{3 + x}{x} \, dx$.

**12** (a) Express

$$\frac{x^2 + 2x + 1}{x(x^2 + 1)}$$

as its partial fractions.

(b) Hence find $\displaystyle\int \frac{x^2 + 2x + 1}{x(x^2 + 1)} \, dx$

**13** The velocity, $v$, of a particle is given by

$$v = 2 + e^{-t/2}$$

(a) Given distance, $s$, and $v$ are related by $\dfrac{ds}{dt} = v$ find an expression for distance.

(b) Acceleration is the rate of change of velocity with respect to $t$. Determine the acceleration.

**14** (a) Use the product rule of differentiation to verify

$$\frac{d}{dx}(x\,e^{2x}) = e^{2x} + 2xe^{2x}$$

(b) Hence show

$$\int xe^{2x} \, dx = \frac{xe^{2x}}{2} - \frac{e^{2x}}{4} + c$$

**15** Integrate

(a) $\dfrac{2 - t^2}{t^3}$ (b) $\dfrac{4 + e^{2t}}{e^{3t}}$

(c) $\dfrac{\cos 4x}{\sin 4x}$ (d) $\dfrac{1}{2\sin 3x}$

(e) $\dfrac{2 + x^2}{1 + x^2}$ (f) $\sin^2 t + \cos^2 t$

## Solutions

**1** (a) $\frac{x^{11}}{11}+c$ (b) $9x+c$

(c) $\frac{2}{5}x^{2.5}+c$ (d) $\frac{2}{3}t^{1.5}+c$

(e) $\ln|z|+c$ (f) $-3.2x+c$

(g) $-\frac{1}{2x^2}+c$ (h) $2\sqrt{t}+c$

(i) $\frac{x^7}{7}+c$ (j) $-\frac{1}{x}+c$

(k) $\frac{3}{4}t^{4/3}+c$

**2** (a) $\frac{e^{5x}}{5}+c$ (b) $\frac{e^{6x}}{6}+c$

(c) $-\frac{e^{-3t}}{3}+c$ (d) $-e^{-x}+c$

(e) $2e^{0.5t}+c$ (f) $3e^{z/3}+c$

(g) $-\frac{e^{-4t}}{4}+c$ (h) $-\frac{2e^{-2.5x}}{5}+c$

**3** (a) $-\frac{\cos 4x}{4}+c$

(b) $-\frac{\cos 9t}{9}+c$

(c) $-2\cos\left(\frac{x}{2}\right)+c$

(d) $-\frac{5}{2}\cos\left(\frac{2t}{5}\right)+c$

(e) $\frac{\sin 7x}{7}+c$

(f) $-\frac{1}{3}\sin(-3x)+c$

(g) $\frac{3}{5}\sin\left(\frac{5t}{3}\right)+c$

(h) $\frac{\ln|\sec 9x|}{9}+c$

(i) $\frac{1}{2}(\ln|\operatorname{cosec} 2x-\cot 2x|)+c$

(j) $\frac{1}{5}(\ln|\sec 5t+\tan 5t|)+c$

(k) $\frac{1}{8}\ln|\sin 8y|+c$

(l) $\frac{1}{5}\sin(5t+1)+c$

(m) $\frac{1}{3}\ln|\sec(3x+4)|+c$

(n) $-\frac{1}{3}\cos(3t-\pi)+c$

(o) $\frac{1}{5}\ln|\operatorname{cosec}(5z+2)-\cot(5z+2)|+c$

(p) $2\ln\left|\sec\left(\frac{x}{2}+1\right)+\tan\left(\frac{x}{2}+1\right)\right|+c$

(q) $-\frac{3}{2}\cos\left(\frac{2t}{3}-1\right)+c$

(r) $-\ln|\sin(5-x)|+c$

(s) $-\frac{1}{2}\ln|\operatorname{cosec}(\pi-2x)-\cot(\pi-2x)|+c$

**4** (a) $\tan^{-1}x+c$

(b) $\sin^{-1}x+c$

(c) $\sin^{-1}\left(\frac{x}{2}\right)+c$

(d) $\frac{1}{3}\tan^{-1}\left(\frac{z}{3}\right)+c$

(e) $\sin^{-1}(2x)+c$

(f) $10\tan^{-1}(10v)+c$

(g) $10^{-3}\tan^{-1}\left(\frac{x}{10^3}\right)+c$

(h) $\frac{1}{\sqrt{10}}\tan^{-1}\left(\frac{t}{\sqrt{10}}\right)+c$

(i) $\sin^{-1}\left(\frac{x}{\sqrt{2}}\right)+c$

(j) $3\tan^{-1}(3x)+c$

**5** (a) $3x+\frac{x^2}{2}+\ln|x|+c$

(b) $\frac{e^{2x}}{2}+\frac{e^{-2x}}{2}+c$

(c) $-\frac{2}{3}\cos(3x)+\frac{\sin 3x}{3}+c$

(d) $0.5\ln|\sec(2t+\pi)+\tan(2t+\pi)|$
$+2\ln\left|\sin\left(\frac{t}{2}-\pi\right)\right|+c$

(e) $2\ln\left|\sec\left(\frac{t}{2}\right)\right|+\frac{1}{3}\ln|\operatorname{cosec}(3t-\pi)$
$-\cot(3t-\pi)|+c$

(f) $-\cos x+\frac{x^2}{6}-e^{-x}+c$

(g) $\frac{1}{3}\ln|\sec 3x + \tan 3x| + c$

(h) $\frac{t^3}{3} + 2t - \frac{1}{t} + c$

(i) $-\frac{e^{-2x}}{6} + c$

(j) $\frac{1}{4}\ln|\sec(4t-3)| + 2\cos(-t-1) + c$

(k) $x + \frac{2}{3}\ln|\sin 3x| + c$

(l) $-2\cos\left(\frac{t}{2}\right) - 6\sin\left(\frac{t}{2}\right) + c$

(m) $\frac{t^3}{3} - 2t^2 + 4t + c$

(n) $-3e^{-t} + 2e^{-t/2} + c$

(o) $7x - x^7 - e^{-x} + c$

(p) $k^2t + kt^2 + \frac{t^3}{3} + c$

(q) $-k\cos t - \frac{\sin kt}{k} + c$

(r) $\frac{1}{5}\tan^{-1}\left(\frac{t}{5}\right) + c$

(s) $\sin^{-1}\left(\frac{t}{5}\right) + c$

(t) $6\tan^{-1}x + \frac{x}{6} + \frac{x^3}{18} + c$

6 Speed: $t + \frac{t^2}{4} + c$, distance: $\frac{t^2}{2} + \frac{t^3}{12} + ct + d$

7 (a) $2t + e^{-t} + c$ (b) 5.0498

8 (a) $\frac{\cosh ax}{a} + c$

(b) $\frac{\sinh ax}{a} + c$

(c) $\frac{3}{2}\cosh 2x + \frac{1}{4}\sinh 4x + c$

9 $100(10t + e^{-t}) + c$

10 (a) $\frac{1}{2}\tan^{-1}\left(\frac{x}{2}\right) + c$

(b) $\frac{1}{2\sqrt{2}}\tan^{-1}\left(\frac{x}{\sqrt{2}}\right) + c$

(c) $\frac{3}{\sqrt{2}}\tan^{-1}(\sqrt{2}x) + c$

(d) $\sin^{-1}\left(\frac{x}{3}\right) + c$

(e) $2\sin^{-1}\left(\frac{x}{2}\right) + c$

(f) $\frac{-7}{\sqrt{3}}\sin^{-1}\left(\frac{\sqrt{3}}{\sqrt{2}}x\right) + c$

(g) $\sqrt{2}\sin^{-1}\left(\frac{x}{\sqrt{2}}\right) + c$

11 $3\ln|x| + x + c$

12 (a) $\frac{1}{x} + \frac{2}{x^2+1}$ (b) $\ln|x| + 2\tan^{-1}x + c$

13 (a) $2t - 2e^{-t/2} + c$ (b) $-\frac{1}{2}e^{-t/2}$

15 (a) $-t^{-2} - \ln|t| + c$

(b) $-\frac{4}{3}e^{-3t} - e^{-t} + c$

(c) $\frac{1}{4}\ln|\sin 4x| + c$

(d) $\frac{1}{6}\ln|\operatorname{cosec} 3x - \cot 3x| + c$

(e) $x + \tan^{-1}x + c$

(f) $t + c$

## 13.3 Definite and indefinite integrals

All the integration solutions so far encountered have contained a constant of integration. Such integrals are known as **indefinite integrals**. Integration can be used to determine the area under curves and this gives rise to **definite integrals**.

To estimate the area under $y(x)$, it is divided into thin rectangles. The sum of the rectangular areas is an approximation to the area under the curve. Several thin rectangles will give a better approximation than a few wide ones.

Consider Figure 13.3 where the area is approximated by a large number of rectangles. Suppose each rectangle has width $\delta x$. The area of rectangle 1 is $y(x_2)\delta x$, the area

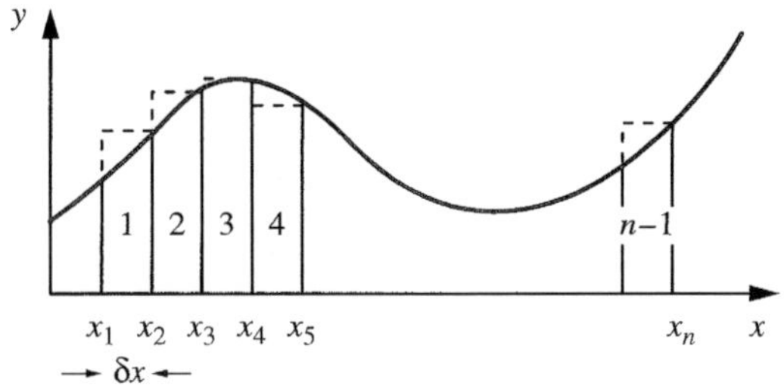


**Figure 13.3** The area is approximated by $(n-1)$ rectangles.

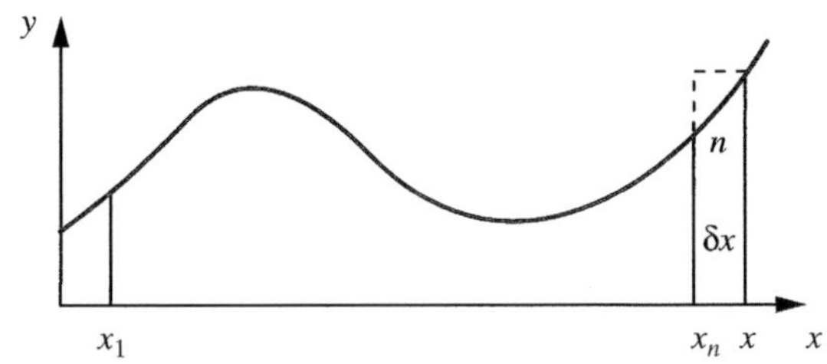


**Figure 13.4** The area is extended by adding an extra rectangle.

of rectangle 2 is $y(x_3)\delta x$ and so on. Let $A(x_n)$ denote the total area under the curve from $x_1$ to $x_n$. Then,

$$A(x_n) \approx \text{sum of the rectangular areas} = \sum_{i=2}^{n} y(x_i)\delta x$$

Let the area be increased by extending the base from $x_n$ to $x$. Then $A(x)$ is the total area under the curve from $x_1$ to $x$ (see Figure 13.4). Then,

$$\text{increase in area} = \delta A = A(x) - A(x_n) \approx y(x)\delta x$$

So,

$$\frac{\delta A}{\delta x} \approx y(x)$$

In the limit as $\delta x \to 0$, we get

$$\lim_{\delta x \to 0}\left(\frac{\delta A}{\delta x}\right) = \frac{\mathrm{d}A}{\mathrm{d}x} = y(x)$$

Since differentiation is the reverse of integration, we can write

$$A = \int y(x)\,\mathrm{d}x$$

To denote the limits of the area being considered we place values on the integral sign.

The area under the curve, $y(x)$, between $x = a$ and $x = b$ is denoted as

$$\int_{x=a}^{x=b} y\,\mathrm{d}x$$

or more compactly by

$$\int_{a}^{b} y\,\mathrm{d}x$$

The constants $a$ and $b$ are known as the **limits** of the integral: **lower** and **upper**, respectively. Since an area has a specific value, such an integral is called a definite integral. The area under the curve up to the vertical line $x = b$ is $A(b)$ (see Figure 13.5). Similarly $A(a)$ is the area up to the vertical line $x = a$. So the area between $x = a$ and $x = b$ is $A(b) - A(a)$, as shown in Figure 13.6.

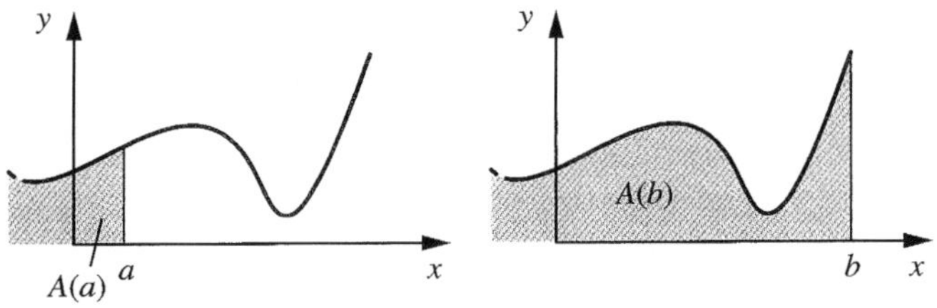


**Figure 13.5** The area depends on the limits $a$ and $b$.

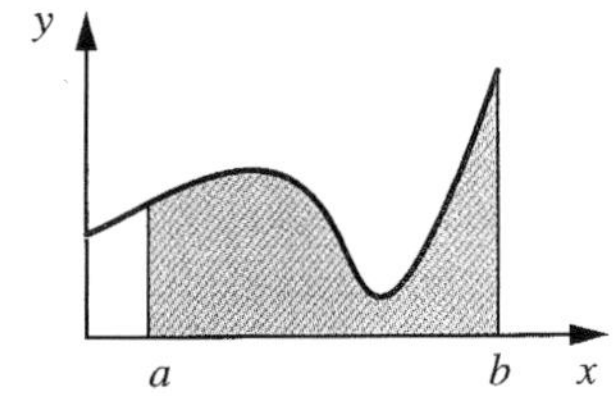


**Figure 13.6** The area between $x = a$ and $x = b$ is $A(b) - A(a)$.

The area between $x = a$ and $x = b$ is given by

$$\text{Area} = \int_a^b y \, dx = A(b) - A(a)$$

The integral is evaluated at the upper limit, $b$, and at the lower limit, $a$, and the difference between these gives the required area.

The expression $A(b) - A(a)$ is often written as $[A(x)]_a^b$. Similarly $[x^2 + 1]_2^3$ is the value of $x^2 + 1$ at $x = 3$ less the value of $x^2 + 1$ at $x = 2$. Thus

$$[x^2 + 1]_2^3 = (3^2 + 1) - (2^2 + 1) = 5$$

In general

$$[f(x)]_a^b = f(b) - f(a)$$

Note that since

$$\int_a^b y \, dx = A(b) - A(a)$$

then, interchanging upper and lower limits,

$$\int_b^a y \, dx = A(a) - A(b) = -\{A(b) - A(a)\}$$

that is,

$$\int_a^b y \, dx = -\int_b^a y \, dx$$

Interchanging the limits changes the sign of the integral.

The evaluation of definite integrals is illustrated in the following examples.

**Example 13.9** Evaluate

(a) $\displaystyle\int_1^2 x^2 + 1 \, dx$ (b) $\displaystyle\int_2^1 x^2 + 1 \, dx$ (c) $\displaystyle\int_0^{\pi} \sin x \, dx$

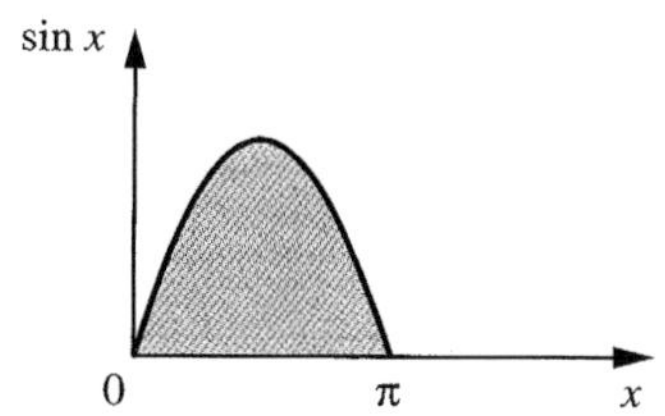


**Figure 13.7**
The area is given by a definite integral.

**Solution** (a) Let $I$ stand for $\int_1^2 x^2 + 1\,\mathrm{d}x$.

$$I = \int_1^2 x^2 + 1\,\mathrm{d}x = \left[\frac{x^3}{3} + x\right]_1^2$$

The integral is now evaluated at the upper and lower limits. The difference gives the value required.

$$I = \left(\frac{2^3}{3} + 2\right) - \left(\frac{1^3}{3} + 1\right) = \frac{8}{3} + 2 - \frac{4}{3} = \frac{10}{3}$$

(b) Because interchanging the limits of integration changes the sign of the integral, we find

$$\int_2^1 x^2 + 1\,\mathrm{d}x = -\int_1^2 x^2 + 1\,\mathrm{d}x = -\frac{10}{3}$$

(c) $\int_0^{\pi} \sin x\,\mathrm{d}x = [-\cos x]_0^{\pi} = (-\cos\pi) - (-\cos 0) = 1 - (-1) = 2$

Figure 13.7 illustrates this area.

---

Note that:

(1) The integrated function is evaluated at the upper and lower limits, and the difference found.

(2) No constant of integration is needed.

(3) Any angles are measured in radians.

**Example 13.10** Find the area under $z(t) = \mathrm{e}^{2t}$ from $t = 1$ to $t = 3$.

**Solution**

$$\text{area} = \int_1^3 z\,\mathrm{d}t = \int_1^3 \mathrm{e}^{2t}\,\mathrm{d}t = \left[\frac{\mathrm{e}^{2t}}{2}\right]_1^3$$

$$= \left[\frac{\mathrm{e}^6}{2}\right] - \left[\frac{\mathrm{e}^2}{2}\right] = 198$$

---

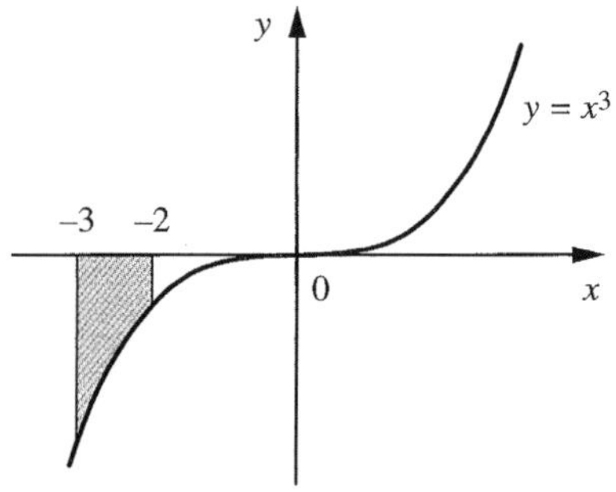


**Figure 13.8** Areas below the $x$ axis are classed as negative.

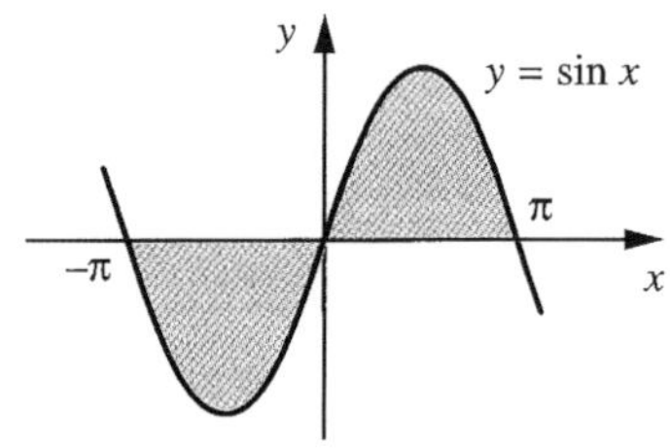


**Figure 13.9** The positive and negative areas cancel each other out.

If the evaluation of an area by integration yields a negative quantity this means that some or all of the corresponding area is below the horizontal axis. This is illustrated in Example 13.11.

**Example 13.11** Find the area bounded by $y = x^3$ and the $x$ axis from $x = -3$ to $x = -2$.

**Solution** Figure 13.8 illustrates the required area.

$$\int_{-3}^{-2} x^3 \, dx = \left[\frac{x^4}{4}\right]_{-3}^{-2}$$

$$= \left\{\frac{(-2)^4}{4}\right\} - \left\{\frac{(-3)^4}{4}\right\} = -\frac{65}{4}$$

The area is $65/4$ square units; the negative sign indicates that it is below the $x$ axis.

**Example 13.12**

(a) Sketch $y = \sin x$ for $x = -\pi$ to $x = \pi$.

(b) Calculate $\int_{-\pi}^{\pi} \sin x \, dx$ and comment on your findings.

(c) Calculate the area enclosed by $y = \sin x$ and the $x$ axis between $x = -\pi$ and $x = \pi$.

**Solution**

(a) A graph of $y = \sin x$ between $x = -\pi$ and $x = \pi$ is shown in Figure 13.9.

(b) $$\int_{-\pi}^{\pi} \sin x \, dx = [-\cos x]_{-\pi}^{\pi} = -\cos(\pi) + \cos(-\pi) = 0$$

Examining Figure 13.9 we see that the positive and negative contributions have cancelled each other out; that is, the area above the $x$ axis is equal in size to the area below the $x$ axis.

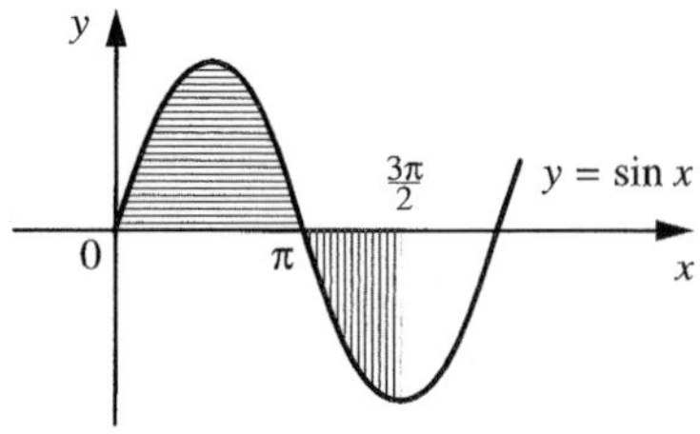


**Figure 13.10**
The positive and negative areas are calculated separately.

(c) From (b) the area above the $x$ axis is equal in size to the area below the $x$ axis. From Example 13.9(c) the area above the $x$ axis is 2. Hence the total area enclosed by $y = \sin x$ and the $x$ axis from $x = -\pi$ to $x = \pi$ is 4.

---

If an area contains parts both above and below the horizontal axis then calculating an integral will give the net area. If the total area is required, then the relevant limits must first be found. A sketch of the function often clarifies the situation.

**Example 13.13** Find the area contained by $y = \sin x$ from $x = 0$ to $x = 3\pi/2$.

**Solution** Figure 13.10 illustrates the required area. From this we see that there are parts both above and below the $x$ axis and the crossover point occurs when $x = \pi$.

$$\int_0^{\pi} \sin x \; dx = [-\cos x]_0^{\pi}$$

$$= -\cos\pi + \cos 0 = 2$$

$$\int_{\pi}^{3\pi/2} \sin x \; dx = [-\cos x]_{\pi}^{3\pi/2}$$

$$= -\cos\left(\frac{3\pi}{2}\right) + \cos\pi = -1$$

The total area is 3 square units. Note, however, that the single integral over 0 to $3\pi/2$ evaluates to 1; that is, it gives the net value of 2 and $-1$.

$$\int_0^{3\pi/2} \sin x \; dx = [-\cos x]_0^{3\pi/2} = -\cos\left(\frac{3\pi}{2}\right) + \cos 0 = 1$$

---

The need to evaluate the area under a curve is a common requirement in engineering. Often the rate of change of an engineering variable with time is known and it is required to calculate the value of the engineering variable. This corresponds to calculating the area under a curve.

**Example 13.14** **Energy used by an electric motor**

Consider a small d.c. electric motor being used to drive an electric screwdriver. The amount of power that is supplied to the motor by the batteries depends on the load on

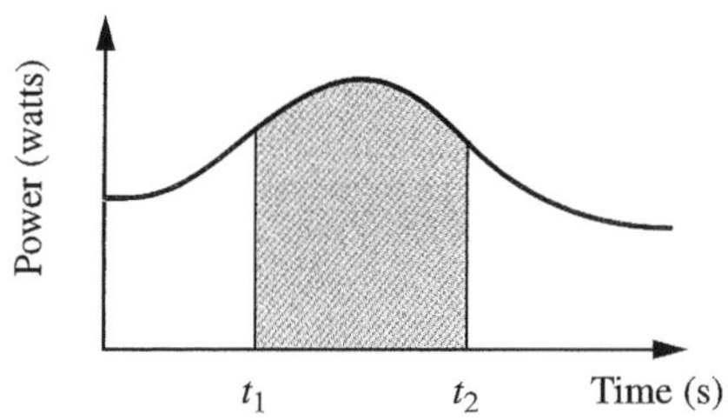


**Figure 13.11** Shaded area represents the energy used to drive the motor during the time interval $t_1 \leqslant t \leqslant t_2$.

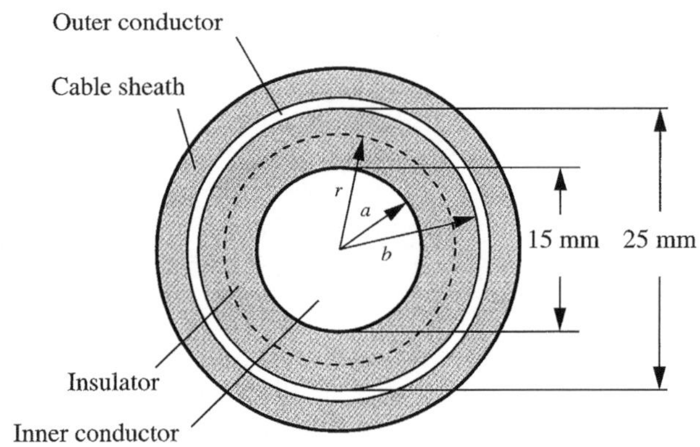


**Figure 13.12** Cross-section of a concentric cable.

the screwdriver. Therefore the power supplied to the screwdriver is a function that varies with time. Figure 13.11 shows a typical curve of power versus time. Now,

$$P = \frac{\mathrm{d}E}{\mathrm{d}t}$$

where $P =$ power (W), $E =$ energy (J). Therefore, to calculate the energy used by the motor between times $t_1$ and $t_2$, we can write

$$E = \int_{t_1}^{t_2} P \, \mathrm{d}t$$

This is equivalent to evaluating the area under the curve, $P(t)$, between $t_1$ and $t_2$, which is shown as the shaded region in Figure 13.11.

**Example 13.15**

### Capacitance of a concentric cable

A concentric cable has an inner conductor with a diameter of 15 mm and an outer conductor with an internal diameter of 25 mm, as shown in Figure 13.12. The insulator separating the two conductors has a relative permittivity of 2.5. Let us calculate the capacitance of the cable per metre length.

Before solving this problem it is instructive to derive the formula for the capacitance of a concentric cable. Imagine that the inner conductor has a charge of $+Q$ per metre length and that the outer conductor has a charge of $-Q$ per metre length. Further assume the cable is long and a central section is being analysed in order that end effects can be ignored.

Consider an imaginary cylindrical surface, radius $r$ and length $l$, within the insulator (or dielectric). Gauss's theorem states that the electric flux out of any closed surface is equal to the charge enclosed by the surface. In this case, because of symmetry, the electric flux points radially outwards and so no flux is directed through the ends of the imaginary cylinder; that is, end effects can be neglected. The curved surface area of the cylinder is $2\pi rl$. Therefore, using Gauss's theorem

$$D \times 2\pi rl = Ql$$

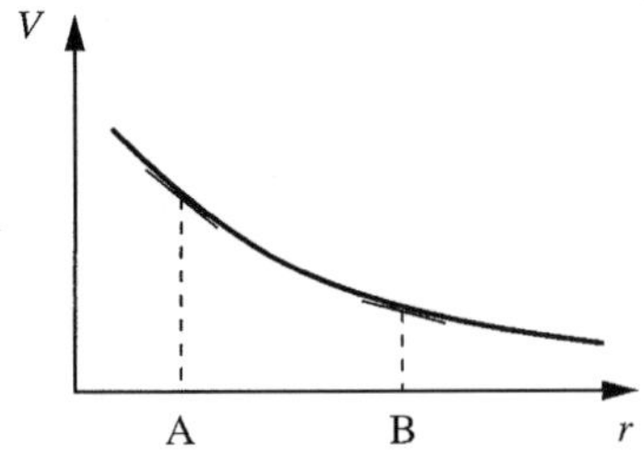


**Figure 13.13**
The gradient of the curve, $\frac{dV}{dr}$, is proportional to the magnitude of the electric field.

where $D$ = electric flux density.

When an insulator or dielectric is present then $D = \varepsilon_r \varepsilon_0 E$, where $E$ = electric field strength, $\varepsilon_r$ = relative permittivity, $\varepsilon_0$ = permittivity of free space = $8.854 \times 10^{-12}$ F m$^{-1}$. Therefore,

$$\varepsilon_r \varepsilon_0 E 2\pi r l = Ql$$

that is,

$$E = \frac{Q}{2\pi \varepsilon_r \varepsilon_0 r} \tag{13.9}$$

This equation gives a value for the electric field within the dielectric. In order to calculate the capacitance of the cable it is necessary to calculate the voltage difference between the two conductors. Let $V_a$ represent the voltage of the inner conductor and $V_b$ the voltage of the outer conductor.

The electric field is a measure of the rate of change of the voltage with position. In other words, if the voltage is changing rapidly with position then this corresponds to a large magnitude of the electric field. This is illustrated in Figure 13.13. The magnitude of the electric field at point A is larger than at point B. As a positive electric field, $E$, corresponds to a decrease in voltage, $V$, with position the relationship between $E$ and $V$, in general, is

$$E = -\frac{dV}{dr} \tag{13.10}$$

This expression can be used to calculate the voltage difference arising as a result of an electric field. In practice, this is a simplified equation and is only valid provided $r$ is in the same direction as the electric field. If this is not the case, then a modified vector form of Equation (13.10) is needed.

In the case of the concentric cable, $E$ is in the same direction as $r$ and so Equation (13.10) can be used to calculate the voltage difference between the two conductors. From Equation (13.10)

$$\frac{dV}{dr} = -E$$

Therefore the voltage at an arbitrary point, $r$, is given by

$$V = -\int E \, dr$$

Consequently, the voltage difference between points $r = b$ and $r = a$ is given by

$$V_b - V_a = -\int_a^b E\,\mathrm{d}r$$

$$= -\frac{Q}{2\pi\varepsilon_r\varepsilon_0}\int_a^b \frac{1}{r}\,\mathrm{d}r \qquad \text{using Equation (13.9)}$$

$$= -\frac{Q}{2\pi\varepsilon_r\varepsilon_0}[\ln r]_a^b$$

$$= -\frac{Q}{2\pi\varepsilon_r\varepsilon_0}\ln\left(\frac{b}{a}\right)$$

This gives the voltage of the outer conductor relative to the inner one. Thus the voltage of the inner conductor relative to the outer one is

$$V_a - V_b = \frac{Q}{2\pi\varepsilon_r\varepsilon_0}\ln\left(\frac{b}{a}\right)$$

More generally, capacitance is defined as $C = Q/V$, where $V$ is the voltage difference. Therefore

$$C = \frac{Q}{V_a - V_b} = \frac{2\pi\varepsilon_r\varepsilon_0}{\ln\left(\frac{b}{a}\right)}$$

Note that this is the capacitance per unit length of cable. Using $\varepsilon_r = 2.5$, $a = 7.5 \times 10^{-3}$ m, $b = 12.5 \times 10^{-3}$ m, we get

$$C = \frac{2\pi \times 2.5 \times 8.854 \times 10^{-12}}{\ln\left(\frac{12.5 \times 10^{-3}}{7.5 \times 10^{-3}}\right)} = 2.72 \times 10^{-10} = 272 \text{ pF m}^{-1}$$

---

### 13.3.1 Use of a dummy variable

Consider the following integrals, $I_1$ and $I_2$:

$$I_1 = \int_0^1 t^2\,\mathrm{d}t \qquad I_2 = \int_0^1 x^2\,\mathrm{d}x$$

Then,

$$I_1 = \left[\frac{t^3}{3}\right]_0^1 = \left(\frac{1}{3}\right) - (0) = \frac{1}{3}$$

$$I_2 = \left[\frac{x^3}{3}\right]_0^1 = \left(\frac{1}{3}\right) - (0) = \frac{1}{3}$$

So clearly $I_1 = I_2$. The value of $I_1$ does not depend upon $t$, and the value of $I_2$ does not depend upon $x$. In general,

$$I = \int_a^b f(t)\,\mathrm{d}t = \int_a^b f(x)\,\mathrm{d}x$$

Because the value of $I$ is the same, regardless of what the integrating variable may be, we say $x$ and $t$ are **dummy variables**. Indeed we could write

$$I = \int_a^b f(z)\, dz = \int_a^b f(r)\, dr = \int_a^b f(y)\, dy$$

Then $z$, $r$ and $y$ are dummy variables.

## Exercises 13.3

**1** Evaluate the following integrals.

(a) $\int_1^3 x^3\, dx$

(b) $\int_1^4 \frac{1}{x}\, dx$

(c) $\int_0^1 2\, dx$

(d) $\int_{-1}^1 e^x\, dx$

(e) $\int_0^{\pi/3} \sin t\, dt$

(f) $\int_0^{\pi} \sin(t+3)\, dt$

(g) $\int_0^{\pi/2} \cos 3t\, dt$

(h) $\int_1^2 \cos \pi t\, dt$

(i) $\int_1^{1.2} \tan x\, dx$

**2** Evaluate the following integrals.

(a) $\int_0^1 t^2 + 1\, dt$

(b) $\int_0^1 \frac{1}{1+t^2}\, dt$

(c) $\int_1^2 3e^{2x} - 2e^{3x}\, dx$

(d) $\int_1^2 (x+1)(x+2)\, dx$

(e) $\int_0^2 2 \sin 4t\, dt$

(f) $\int_0^{\pi} 4 \cos\left(\frac{t}{2}\right)\, dt$

**3** Evaluate the following integrals:

(a) $\int_0^1 t^2 + 0.5t - 6\, dt$

(b) $\int_2^3 \frac{3}{2x} + \frac{2x}{3}\, dx$

(c) $\int_1^2 e^{-2x} - 3e^{-x}\, dx$

(d) $\int_0^2 3 \sin(4t - \pi) + 5 \cos(3t + \pi/2)\, dt$

(e) $\int_0^1 2 \tan t\, dt$

(f) $\int_0^{1.5} \frac{2}{1+x^2} - \frac{1}{\sqrt{4-x^2}}\, dx$

**4** Calculate the area between $f(t) = \cos t$ and the $t$ axis as $t$ varies from

(a) 0 to $\frac{\pi}{4}$ (b) 0 to $\frac{\pi}{2}$

(c) $\frac{3\pi}{4}$ to $\pi$ (d) 0 to $\pi$

**5** Calculate the total area between $f(t) = \cos 2t$ and the $t$ axis as $t$ varies from

(a) 0 to $\frac{\pi}{4}$ (b) $\frac{\pi}{4}$ to $\frac{\pi}{2}$ (c) 0 to $\frac{\pi}{2}$

**6** Calculate the area enclosed by the curves $y = x^2$ and $y = x$.

**7** Calculate the area enclosed by the graphs of the functions $y = t^2 + 5$ and $y = 6$.

**8** Evaluate the following definite integrals:

(a) $\int_1^{1.5} \frac{1}{t} + \frac{1}{e^t} + \frac{1}{\sin t}\, dt$

(b) $\int_1^4 \frac{5}{8+3x^2}\, dx$

(c) $\int_{-1}^{1} \sinh x \, dx$

(d) $\int_{-1}^{1} \cosh x \, dx$

9 Calculate the area between $y = 2\tan t$ and the $t$ axis for $-1 \leqslant t \leqslant 1.4$.

10 Find the area between $y = \sin t$, $y = \cos t$ and the $y$ axis, for $t \geqslant 0$.

11 The velocity, $v$, of a particle is given by

$$v = (1+t)^2$$

Find the distance travelled by the particle from $t = 1$ to $t = 4$; that is, evaluate $\int_1^4 v \, dt$.

12 Evaluate the area under the function $x = 1/t$ for $1 \leqslant t \leqslant 10$.

13 Evaluate

(a) $\int_3^2 x^{1.4} \, dx$ (b) $\int_0^1 (e^t)^2 \, dt$

(c) $\int_0^{\pi} \sin x \cos x \, dx$ (d) $\int_1^2 \sinh^2 x \, dx$

## Solutions

1 (a) 20 (b) 1.3863 (c) 2
(d) 2.3504 (e) 0.5 (f) $-1.9800$
(g) $-\frac{1}{3}$ (h) 0 (i) 0.3995

2 (a) $\frac{4}{3}$ (b) $\frac{\pi}{4}$ (c) $-184.75$
(d) $\frac{53}{6}$ (e) 0.5728 (f) 8

3 (a) $-\frac{65}{12}$ (b) 2.275 (c) $-0.639$
(d) $-0.9255$ (e) 1.2313 (f) 1.1175

4 (a) 0.7071 (b) 1
(c) 0.7071 (d) 2

5 (a) $\frac{1}{2}$ (b) $\frac{1}{2}$ (c) 1

6 $\frac{1}{6}$

7 $\frac{4}{3}$

8 (a) 1.0839 (b) 0.6468
(c) 0 (d) 2.3504

9 4.7756

10 0.4142

11 39

12 2.3026

13 (a) $-3.6202$ (b) 3.1945
(c) 0 (d) 5.4158

## Review exercises 13

1 Find the following integrals:

(a) $\int 3x^2 + x \, dx$

(b) $\int \frac{2}{t} + 2t + 2 \, dt$

(c) $\int (1+z)(1-z) \, dz$

(d) $\int \sqrt{t} - \frac{1}{\sqrt{t}} \, dt$

(e) $\int x^{2/3} + 4x^3 \, dx$

2 Given

$$\frac{dy}{dx} = x^2 + \sin x + \cos 2x + 1$$

find an expression for $y(x)$.

3 Find the following integrals:

(a) $\int 3e^x + \frac{3}{e^x} \, dx$

(b) $\int (1+e^x)(1-e^{-x}) \, dx$

(c) $\int 2e^{4t} + 1 \, dt$

(d) $\int e^x(1+e^x) \, dx$

(e) $\int 4e^{-t} - e^{-2t} \, dt$

**4** Find the integrals

(a) $\int \sin 2x + \cos 2x \, dx$

(b) $\int 2 \sin t - \cos t \, dt$

(c) $\int 4 \tan\left(\frac{t}{2}\right) dt$

(d) $\int \sin(\pi - z) + \cos(\pi - 2z) \, dz$

(e) $\int \tan(t + \pi) \, dt$

(f) $\int 2 \sin 3t + 2 \sin\left(\frac{t}{3}\right) dt$

**5** Find the following integrals:

(a) $\int \text{cosec}(3t + \pi) \, dt$

(b) $\int \sec\left(\frac{x}{2} + 1\right) dx$

(c) $\int \cot\left(\frac{\pi + t}{2}\right) dt$

(d) $\int 3 \,\text{cosec}\left(\frac{y}{3} - 2\right) dy$

(e) $\int \frac{1}{2} \cot(\pi - 2z) \, dz$

(f) $\int \frac{2}{3} \sec(2t - \pi) \, dt$

**6** Find the following integrals:

(a) $\int \frac{4}{\sqrt{1 - v^2}} \, dv$

(b) $\int \frac{1}{2\sqrt{1 - v^2}} \, dv$

(c) $\int \frac{1}{49 + t^2} \, dt$

(d) $\int \frac{1}{50 + 2t^2} \, dt$

(e) $\int \frac{2}{\sqrt{1 - 4t^2}} \, dt$

(f) $\int \frac{1}{\sqrt{36 - 9x^2}} \, dx$

(g) $\int \frac{3}{x^2 + 3} \, dx$

**7** The speed, $v(t)$, of a particle is given by

$$v(t) = t + e^{-t}$$

(a) Find the distance travelled by the particle.

(b) Calculate the distance travelled between $t = 1$ and $t = 3$.

**8** The capacitance of a capacitor is 0.1 F. The current, $i(t)$, through the capacitor is given by

$$i(t) = 50 \sin \pi t$$

Derive an expression for the voltage across the capacitor.

**9** By using suitable trigonometric identities find

(a) $\int \sin^2 2t + \cos^2 2t \, dt$

(b) $\int \sin 2t \cos 2t \, dt$

(c) $\int \frac{1}{\sin 2t} \, dt$

(d) $\int \frac{\cos 2t}{\sin 2t} \, dt$

(e) $\int \frac{\sin 2t}{\cos 2t} \, dt$

**10** By expressing

$$\frac{2x^2 + x + 2}{x^3 + x}$$

as its partial fractions, find

$$\int \frac{2x^2 + x + 2}{x^3 + x} \, dx$$

**11** Evaluate the following definite integrals:

(a) $\int_0^1 2t^2 + t^3 \, dt$

(b) $\int_1^3 \frac{2}{x} - \frac{x}{2} \, dx$

(c) $\int_0^1 7 - t + 7t^2 \, dt$

(d) $\int_0^2 (z + 1)(z + 2) \, dz$

(e) $\int_1^4 \sqrt{x} \, dx$

(f) $\int_{-2}^{-1} \frac{x - 2}{x} \, dx$

12 Evaluate the following definite integrals:

(a) $\int_0^1 e^{3x+1}\,dx$

(b) $\int_{-1}^1 e^{2t} - e^t + 1\,dt$

(c) $\int_1^2 (e^z - 1)^2\,dz$

(d) $\int_0^1 e^{-2x} + e^{2x}\,dx$

(e) $\int_{-1}^0 x + e^x\,dx$

13 Evaluate the following integrals:

(a) $\int_0^{\pi/2} 2\sin 3t\,dt$

(b) $\int_{\pi/2}^{\pi} \sin 2t - \cos 2t\,dt$

(c) $\int_0^{\pi/4} \tan t + t\,dt$

(d) $\int_0^{\pi/4} \sin\left(\frac{t}{2}\right) + \cos\left(\frac{t}{2}\right)\,dt$

(e) $\int_0^{0.1} \tan 3t\,dt$

14 Evaluate the following definite integrals:

(a) $\int_0^{2\pi/k} \sin kt\,dt$

(b) $\int_0^{2\pi/k} \cos kt\,dt$

where $k$ is a constant.

15 Evaluate the following definite integrals:

(a) $\int_0^{0.5} \operatorname{cosec}(2x+1)\,dx$

(b) $\int_0^{0.1} \sec 3t\,dt$

(c) $\int_{-\pi/4}^{\pi/4} \tan(x+\pi)\,dx$

16 Evaluate the following definite integrals:

(a) $\int_0^2 \frac{3}{\sqrt{9-x^2}}\,dx$

(b) $\int_{-1}^1 \frac{2}{9+x^2}\,dx$

(c) $\int_0^1 \frac{1}{\sqrt{8-2x^2}}\,dx$

(d) $\int_1^3 \frac{1}{10+4t^2}\,dt$

17 (a) Calculate the area enclosed by the curve $y = x^3$, the $x$ axis and $x = 2$.

(b) Calculate the area enclosed by the curve $y = x^3$, the $y$ axis and $y = 8$.

18 Find the total area between $f(t) = t^2 - 4$ and the $t$ axis on the following intervals:

(a) $[-4, -3]$ (b) $[-3, -1]$
(c) $[0, 3]$ (d) $[-3, 3]$

19 Calculate the area enclosed by the curve $y = x^2 - x - 6$ and the $x$ axis.

20 Calculate the total area between $y = x^2 - 3x - 4$ and the $x$ axis on the following intervals:

(a) $[-2, -1]$ (b) $[-2, 1]$
(c) $[2, 4]$ (d) $[2, 5]$

21 Calculate the area enclosed by the curve $y = x^3$ and the line $y = x$.

22 Calculate the area enclosed by $y = x^2 + 4$ and $y = 12 - x^2$.

23 Calculate the area enclosed by $y = \sin x$ and $y = \frac{2x}{\pi}$.

## Solutions

1 (a) $x^3 + \frac{x^2}{2} + c$

(b) $2\ln|t| + t^2 + 2t + c$

(c) $z - \frac{z^3}{3} + c$

(d) $\frac{2}{3}t^{3/2} - 2t^{1/2} + c$

(e) $\frac{3}{5}x^{5/3} + x^4 + c$

**2** $\dfrac{x^3}{3} - \cos x + \dfrac{1}{2}\sin 2x + x + c$

**3** (a) $3e^x - 3e^{-x} + c$

(b) $e^x + e^{-x} + c$

(c) $\dfrac{e^{4t}}{2} + t + c$

(d) $e^x + \dfrac{e^{2x}}{2} + c$

(e) $-4e^{-t} + \dfrac{e^{-2t}}{2} + c$

**4** (a) $-\dfrac{1}{2}\cos 2x + \dfrac{1}{2}\sin 2x + c$

(b) $-2\cos t - \sin t + c$

(c) $8\ln\left|\sec\left(\dfrac{t}{2}\right)\right| + c$

(d) $\cos(\pi - z) - \frac{1}{2}\sin(\pi - 2z) + c$

(e) $\ln|\sec(t + \pi)| + c$

(f) $-\dfrac{2}{3}\cos 3t - 6\cos\left(\dfrac{t}{3}\right) + c$

**5** (a) $\frac{1}{3}\ln|\mathrm{cosec}(3t + \pi) - \cot(3t + \pi)| + c$

(b) $2\ln\left|\sec\left(\dfrac{x}{2} + 1\right) + \tan\left(\dfrac{x}{2} + 1\right)\right| + c$

(c) $2\ln\left|\sin\left(\dfrac{\pi + t}{2}\right)\right| + c$

(d) $9\ln\left|\mathrm{cosec}\left(\dfrac{y}{3} - 2\right) - \cot\left(\dfrac{y}{3} - 2\right)\right| + c$

(e) $-\frac{1}{4}\ln|\sin(\pi - 2z)| + c$

(f) $\frac{1}{3}\ln|\sec(2t - \pi) + \tan(2t - \pi)| + c$

**6** (a) $4\sin^{-1} v + c$

(b) $\frac{1}{2}\sin^{-1} v + c$

(c) $\dfrac{1}{7}\tan^{-1}\left(\dfrac{t}{7}\right) + c$

(d) $\frac{1}{10}\tan^{-1}\left(\dfrac{t}{5}\right) + c$

(e) $\sin^{-1}(2t) + c$

(f) $\dfrac{1}{3}\sin^{-1}\left(\dfrac{x}{2}\right) + c$

(g) $\sqrt{3}\tan^{-1}\left(\dfrac{x}{\sqrt{3}}\right) + c$

**7** (a) $\dfrac{t^2}{2} - e^{-t} + c$ (b) 4.3181

**8** $-\dfrac{500}{\pi}\cos \pi t + c$

**9** (a) $t + c$

(b) $-\dfrac{\cos 4t}{8} + c$

(c) $\frac{1}{2}\ln|\mathrm{cosec}\, 2t - \cot 2t| + c$

(d) $\frac{1}{2}\ln|\sin 2t| + c$

(e) $\frac{1}{2}\ln|\sec 2t| + c$

**10** $2\ln|x| + \tan^{-1} x + c$

**11** (a) $\frac{11}{12}$ (b) 0.1972 (c) $\frac{53}{6}$

(d) $\frac{38}{3}$ (e) $\frac{14}{3}$ (f) 2.3863

**12** (a) 17.2933 (b) 3.2765 (c) 15.2630

(d) 3.6269 (e) 0.1321

**13** (a) $\frac{2}{3}$ (b) $-1$ (c) 0.6550

(d) 0.9176 (e) 0.0152

**14** (a) 0 (b) 0

**15** (a) 0.5238 (b) 0.1015 (c) 0

**16** (a) 2.1892 (b) 0.4290

(c) 0.3702 (d) 0.0825

**17** (a) 4 (b) 12

**18** (a) $\frac{25}{3}$ (b) 4 (c) $\frac{23}{3}$ (d) $\frac{46}{3}$

**19** $\frac{125}{6}$

**20** (a) $\frac{17}{6}$ (b) $\frac{61}{6}$ (c) $\frac{22}{3}$ (d) $\frac{61}{6}$

**21** 0.5

**22** $\frac{64}{3}$

**23** 0.4292

# 14 Techniques of integration

| Chapter 14 | Contents |
|---|---|

## 14.1 Introduction

The previous chapter showed us how to integrate functions which matched the list of standard integrals given in Table 13.1. Clearly, it is impossible to list all possible functions in the table and so some general techniques are required. Integration techniques may be classified as **analytical**, that is exact, or **numerical**, that is approximate. We will now study three analytical techniques:

(1) integration by parts;

(2) integration by substitution;

(3) integration using partial fractions.

## 14.2 Integration by parts

This technique is used to integrate a product, and is derived from the product rule for differentiation. Let $u$ and $v$ be functions of $x$. Then the product rule of differentiation states:

$$\frac{\mathrm{d}}{\mathrm{d}x}(uv) = \frac{\mathrm{d}u}{\mathrm{d}x}v + u\frac{\mathrm{d}v}{\mathrm{d}x}$$

Rearranging we have

$$u\frac{\mathrm{d}v}{\mathrm{d}x} = \frac{\mathrm{d}}{\mathrm{d}x}(uv) - v\frac{\mathrm{d}u}{\mathrm{d}x}$$

Integrating this equation yields

$$\int u\frac{\mathrm{d}v}{\mathrm{d}x}\,\mathrm{d}x = \int \frac{\mathrm{d}}{\mathrm{d}x}(uv)\,\mathrm{d}x - \int v\frac{\mathrm{d}u}{\mathrm{d}x}\,\mathrm{d}x$$

Recognizing that integration and differentiation are inverse processes allows

$$\int \frac{\mathrm{d}(uv)}{\mathrm{d}x}\,\mathrm{d}x$$

to be simplified to $uv$. Hence,

$$\int u\left(\frac{\mathrm{d}v}{\mathrm{d}x}\right)\mathrm{d}x = uv - \int v\left(\frac{\mathrm{d}u}{\mathrm{d}x}\right)\mathrm{d}x$$

This is the formula for integration by parts.

**Example 14.1** Find $\int x \sin x \,\mathrm{d}x$.

**Solution** We recognize the integrand as a product of the functions $x$ and $\sin x$. Let $u = x$, $\frac{dv}{dx} = \sin x$. Then $\frac{du}{dx} = 1$, $v = -\cos x$. Using the integration by parts formula we get

$$\int x \sin x \, dx = x(-\cos x) - \int (-\cos x)1 \, dx$$

$$= -x \cos x + \sin x + c$$

---

When dealing with definite integrals the corresponding formula for integration by parts is

$$\int_a^b u\left(\frac{dv}{dx}\right)dx = [uv]_a^b - \int_a^b v\left(\frac{du}{dx}\right)dx$$

**Example 14.2** Evaluate

$$\int_0^2 xe^x \, dx$$

**Solution** We let

$$u = x \quad \text{and} \quad \frac{dv}{dx} = e^x$$

Then

$$\frac{du}{dx} = 1 \quad \text{and} \quad v = e^x$$

Using the integration by parts formula for definite integrals we have

$$\int_0^2 xe^x \, dx = [xe^x]_0^2 - \int_0^2 e^x \cdot 1 \, dx$$

$$= 2e^2 - [e^x]_0^2$$

$$= 2e^2 - [e^2 - 1]$$

$$= e^2 + 1$$

---

Sometimes integration by parts needs to be used twice, as the next example illustrates.

**Example 14.3** Evaluate

$$\int_0^2 x^2 e^x \, dx$$

**Solution** We let

$$u = x^2 \qquad \text{and} \qquad \frac{dv}{dx} = e^x$$

Then

$$\frac{du}{dx} = 2x \qquad \text{and} \qquad v = e^x$$

Using the integration by parts formula we have

$$\int_0^2 x^2 e^x \, dx = [x^2 e^x]_0^2 - \int_0^2 2xe^x \, dx$$
$$= 4e^2 - 2\int_0^2 xe^x \, dx$$

Now $\int_0^2 xe^x \, dx$ has been evaluated using integration by parts in Example 14.2. So

$$\int_0^2 x^2 e^x \, dx = 4e^2 - 2[e^2 + 1] = 2e^2 - 2 = 12.78$$

---

The next example illustrates a case in which the integral to be found reappears after repeated application of integration by parts.

**Example 14.4** Find

$$\int e^t \sin t \, dt$$

**Solution** We let

$$u = e^t \qquad \text{and} \qquad \frac{dv}{dt} = \sin t$$

and so

$$\frac{du}{dt} = e^t \qquad \text{and} \qquad v = -\cos t$$

Applying integration by parts yields

$$\int e^t \sin t \, dt = -e^t \cos t - \int (-\cos t)e^t \, dt + c$$

$$= -e^t \cos t + \int e^t \cos t \, dt + c \qquad (14.1)$$

We now apply integration by parts to $\int e^t \cos t \, dt$. We let

$$u = e^t \qquad \text{and} \qquad \frac{dv}{dt} = \cos t$$

Then

$$\frac{du}{dt} = e^t \qquad \text{and} \qquad v = \sin t$$

So

$$\int e^t \cos t \, dt = e^t \sin t - \int e^t \sin t \, dt \tag{14.2}$$

Substituting Equation (14.2) into Equation (14.1) yields

$$\int e^t \sin t \, dt = -e^t \cos t + e^t \sin t - \int e^t \sin t \, dt + c$$

Rearranging the equation gives

$$2 \int e^t \sin t \, dt = -e^t \cos t + e^t \sin t + c$$

from which we see that

$$\int e^t \sin t \, dt = \frac{-e^t \cos t + e^t \sin t + c}{2}$$

**Example 14.5** Evaluate

$$\int_0^2 x^n e^x \, dx$$

for $n = 3, 4, 5$.

**Solution** The integral may be evaluated by using integration by parts repeatedly. However, this is slow and cumbersome. Instead it is useful to develop a **reduction formula** as is now illustrated.

Let $u = x^n$ and $\frac{dv}{dx} = e^x$. Then $\frac{du}{dx} = nx^{n-1}$ and $v = e^x$.

Using integration by parts we have

$$\begin{aligned}\int_0^2 x^n e^x \, dx &= [x^n e^x]_0^2 - \int_0^2 nx^{n-1} e^x \, dx \\ &= 2^n e^2 - n \int_0^2 x^{n-1} e^x \, dx\end{aligned}$$

Writing

$$I_n = \int_0^2 x^n e^x \, dx$$

we see that

$$I_{n-1} = \int_0^2 x^{n-1} e^x \, dx$$

Hence

$$I_n = 2^n e^2 - nI_{n-1} \tag{14.3}$$

Equation (14.3) is called a **reduction formula**.

We have already evaluated $I_1$, that is $\int_0^2 xe^x\, dx$ in Example 14.2, and found

$$I_1 = e^2 + 1$$

Using the reduction formula with $n = 2$ gives

$$\begin{aligned}\int_0^2 x^2 e^x\, dx = I_2 &= 2^2 e^2 - 2I_1 \\ &= 4e^2 - 2(e^2 + 1) \\ &= 2e^2 - 2\end{aligned}$$

Note that this is in agreement with Example 14.3.

With $n = 3$ the reduction formula yields

$$\begin{aligned}\int_0^2 x^3 e^x\, dx = I_3 &= 2^3 e^2 - 3I_2 \\ &= 8e^2 - 3(2e^2 - 2) \\ &= 2e^2 + 6\end{aligned}$$

With $n = 4$ we have

$$\begin{aligned}\int_0^2 x^4 e^x\, dx = I_4 &= 2^4 e^2 - 4I_3 \\ &= 16e^2 - 4(2e^2 + 6) \\ &= 8e^2 - 24\end{aligned}$$

With $n = 5$ we have

$$\begin{aligned}\int_0^2 x^5 e^x\, dx = I_5 &= 2^5 e^2 - 5I_4 \\ &= 32e^2 - 5(8e^2 - 24) \\ &= 120 - 8e^2\end{aligned}$$

## Exercises 14.2

1 Use integration by parts to find the following:

(a) $\int x \sin(2x)\, dx$

(b) $\int te^{3t}\, dt$

(c) $\int x \cos x\, dx$

(d) $\int 2v \sin\left(\frac{v}{2}\right) dv$

(e) $\int \frac{x}{e^x}\, dx$

**2** Use integration by parts to find

(a) $\int t \ln t \, dt$

(b) $\int \ln t \, dt$

(c) $\int t^n \ln t \, dt \qquad (n \neq -1)$

(d) $\int t \sin(at + b) \, dt \qquad a, b$ constants

(e) $\int t e^{at+b} \, dt \qquad a, b$ constants

**3** Evaluate the following definite integrals:

(a) $\int_0^1 x \cos 2x \, dx$

(b) $\int_0^{\pi/2} x \sin 2x \, dx$

(c) $\int_{-1}^1 t e^{2t} \, dt$

(d) $\int_1^3 t^2 \ln t \, dt$

(e) $\int_0^2 \frac{2x}{e^{2x}} \, dx$

**4** Find

(a) $\int t^2 e^{2t} \, dt$

(b) $\int t^2 \cos 3t \, dt$

(c) $\int t^2 \sin\left(\frac{t}{2}\right) dt$

**5** Evaluate the following definite integrals:

(a) $\int_0^2 t^2 e^t \, dt$

(b) $\int_{-1}^1 t^2 \sin t \, dt$

(c) $\int_0^1 t^2 \cos 3t \, dt$

**6** Obtain a reduction formula for

$$I_n = \int t^n e^{kt} \, dt \qquad n, k \text{ constants}$$

Hence find $\int t^2 e^{3t} \, dt$, $\int t^3 e^{3t} \, dt$ and $\int t^4 e^{3t} \, dt$.

**7** Use integration by parts twice to obtain a reduction formula for

$$I_n = \int_0^{\pi/2} t^n \sin t \, dt$$

Hence find $\int_0^{\pi/2} t^3 \sin t \, dt$, $\int_0^{\pi/2} t^5 \sin t \, dt$ and $\int_0^{\pi/2} t^7 \sin t \, dt$.

**8** Use integration by parts to find

$$\int_0^{\pi/2} e^{2x} \cos x \, dx$$

## Solutions

**1** (a) $\frac{\sin 2x}{4} - \frac{x \cos 2x}{2} + c$

(b) $e^{3t}\left(\frac{t}{3} - \frac{1}{9}\right) + c$

(c) $\cos x + x \sin x + c$

(d) $8 \sin\left(\frac{v}{2}\right) - 4v \cos\left(\frac{v}{2}\right) + c$

(e) $-e^{-x}(x + 1) + c$

**2** (a) $\frac{t^2 \ln t}{2} - \frac{t^2}{4} + c$

(b) $t \ln t - t + c$

(c) $\frac{(\ln t)t^{n+1}}{n+1} - \frac{t^{n+1}}{(n+1)^2} + c$

(d) $\frac{\sin(at + b)}{a^2} - \frac{t \cos(at + b)}{a} + c$

(e) $e^{at+b}\left(\frac{t}{a} - \frac{1}{a^2}\right) + c$

**3** (a) 0.1006 (b) 0.7854 (c) 1.9488
(d) 6.9986 (e) 0.4542

4 (a) $\dfrac{e^{2t}(2t^2-2t+1)}{4}+c$

(b) $\dfrac{2}{9}t\cos 3t+\left(\dfrac{t^2}{3}-\dfrac{2}{27}\right)\sin 3t+c$

(c) $8t\sin\left(\dfrac{t}{2}\right)-2(t^2-8)\cos\left(\dfrac{t}{2}\right)+c$

5 (a) 12.7781 (b) 0 (c) −0.1834

6 $I_n=\dfrac{t^n e^{kt}}{k}-\dfrac{n}{k}I_{n-1}$, $\dfrac{e^{3t}(9t^2-6t+2)}{27}$, $\dfrac{e^{3t}(9t^3-9t^2+6t-2)}{27}$, $\dfrac{e^{3t}(27t^4-36t^3+36t^2-24t+8)}{81}$

7 $I_n=n\left\{\left(\dfrac{\pi}{2}\right)^{n-1}-(n-1)I_{n-2}\right\}$

1.4022, 2.3963, 4.5084

8 4.2281

## 14.3 Integration by substitution

This technique is the integral equivalent of the chain rule. It is best illustrated by examples.

**Example 14.6** Find $\int (3x+1)^{2.7}\,dx$.

**Solution** Let $z=3x+1$, so that $\dfrac{dz}{dx}=3$, that is $dx=\dfrac{dz}{3}$. Writing the integral in terms of $z$, it becomes

$$\int z^{2.7}\frac{1}{3}\,dz=\frac{1}{3}\int z^{2.7}dz=\frac{1}{3}\left(\frac{z^{3.7}}{3.7}\right)+c=\frac{1}{3}\frac{(3x+1)^{3.7}}{3.7}+c$$

**Example 14.7** Evaluate $\int_2^3 t\sin(t^2)\,dt$.

**Solution** Let $v=t^2$ so $\dfrac{dv}{dt}=2t$, that is

$$dt=\frac{1}{2t}\,dv$$

When changing the integral from one in terms of $t$ to one in terms of $v$, the limits must also be changed. When $t=2$, $v=4$; when $t=3$, $v=9$. Hence, the integral becomes

$$\int_4^9 \frac{\sin v}{2}\,dv=\frac{1}{2}[-\cos v]_4^9=\frac{1}{2}[-\cos 9+\cos 4]=0.129$$

Sometimes the substitution can involve a trigonometric function.

**Example 14.8** Evaluate $\int_1^2 \sin t\,\cos^2 t\,dt$.

**Solution** Put $z = \cos t$ so that $\dfrac{dz}{dt} = -\sin t$, that is $\sin t\, dt = -dz$. When $t = 1$, $z = \cos 1$; when $t = 2$, $z = \cos 2$. Hence

$$\int_1^2 \sin t \cos^2 t \, dt = -\int_{\cos 1}^{\cos 2} z^2 \, dz = -\left[\frac{z^3}{3}\right]_{\cos 1}^{\cos 2}$$

$$= \frac{\cos^3 1 - \cos^3 2}{3} = 0.0766$$

**Example 14.9** Find $\displaystyle\int \frac{e^{\tan x}}{\cos^2 x} \, dx$.

**Solution** Put $z = \tan x$. Then $\dfrac{dz}{dx} = \sec^2 x$, $dz = \dfrac{dx}{\cos^2 x}$. Hence,

$$\int \frac{e^{\tan x}}{\cos^2 x} \, dx = \int e^z \, dz = e^z + c = e^{\tan x} + c$$

---

Integration by substitution allows functions of the form $\dfrac{df/dx}{f}$ to be integrated.

**Example 14.10** Find $\displaystyle\int \frac{3x^2 + 1}{x^3 + x + 2} \, dx$.

**Solution** Put $z = x^3 + x + 2$, then $\dfrac{dz}{dx} = 3x^2 + 1$, that is $dz = (3x^2 + 1)\, dx$. Hence,

$$\int \frac{3x^2 + 1}{x^3 + x + 2} \, dx = \int \frac{dz}{z} = \ln|z| + c = \ln|x^3 + x + 2| + c$$

**Example 14.11** Find $\displaystyle\int \frac{df/dx}{f} \, dx$.

**Solution** Put $z = f$. Then $\dfrac{dz}{dx} = \dfrac{df}{dx}$, that is

$$dz = \frac{df}{dx} \, dx.$$

Hence,

$$\int \frac{df/dx}{f} \, dx = \int \frac{dz}{z} = \ln|z| + c = \ln|f| + c$$

and so

$$\int \frac{df/dx}{f} \, dx = \ln|f| + c$$

---

The result of Example 14.11 is particularly important.

$$\int \frac{\mathrm{d}f/\mathrm{d}x}{f}\,\mathrm{d}x = \ln|f| + c$$

**Example 14.12** Evaluate $\displaystyle\int_2^4 \frac{3t^2+2t}{t^3+t^2+1}\,\mathrm{d}t$.

**Solution** The numerator is the derivative of the denominator and so

$$\int_2^4 \frac{3t^2+2t}{t^3+t^2+1}\,\mathrm{d}t = [\ln|t^3+t^2+1|]_2^4 = \ln 81 - \ln 13 = 1.83$$

**Example 14.13** Find

(a) $\displaystyle\int \frac{4}{5x-7}\,\mathrm{d}x$

(b) $\displaystyle\int \frac{t}{t^2+1}\,\mathrm{d}t$

(c) $\displaystyle\int \frac{\mathrm{e}^{t/2}}{\mathrm{e}^{t/2}+1}\,\mathrm{d}t$

**Solution** The integrands are rewritten so that the numerator is the derivative of the denominator.

(a) $\displaystyle\int \frac{4}{5x-7}\,\mathrm{d}x = \frac{4}{5}\int \frac{5}{5x-7}\,\mathrm{d}x = \frac{4}{5}\ln|5x-7| + c$

(b) $\displaystyle\int \frac{t}{t^2+1}\,\mathrm{d}t = \frac{1}{2}\int \frac{2t}{t^2+1}\,\mathrm{d}t$

$$= \frac{1}{2}\ln|t^2+1| + c$$

(c) $\displaystyle\int \frac{\mathrm{e}^{t/2}}{\mathrm{e}^{t/2}+1}\,\mathrm{d}t = 2\int \frac{\frac{1}{2}\mathrm{e}^{t/2}}{\mathrm{e}^{t/2}+1}\,\mathrm{d}t = 2\ln|\mathrm{e}^{t/2}+1| + c$

## Exercises 14.3

1 Use the given substitutions to find the following integrals:

(a) $\displaystyle\int (4x+1)^7\,\mathrm{d}x$, $\quad z = 4x+1$

(b) $\displaystyle\int t^2\sin(t^3+1)\,\mathrm{d}t$, $\quad z = t^3+1$

(c) $\displaystyle\int 4t\mathrm{e}^{-t^2}\,\mathrm{d}t$, $\quad z = t^2$

(d) $\displaystyle\int (1-z)^{1/3}\,\mathrm{d}z$, $\quad t = 1-z$

(e) $\displaystyle\int \cos t(\sin^5 t)\,\mathrm{d}t$, $\quad z = \sin t$

**2** Evaluate the following definite integrals:

(a) $\int_1^2 (2t+3)^7 \, dt$

(b) $\int_0^{\pi/2} \sin 2t \cos^4 2t \, dt$

(c) $\int_0^1 3t^2 e^{t^3} \, dt$

(d) $\int_0^2 \sqrt{4+3x} \, dx$

(e) $\int_1^2 \frac{\sin(\sqrt{x})}{\sqrt{x}} \, dx$

**3** Find the area between $y = x(3x^2+2)^4$ and the $x$ axis from $x = 0$ to $x = 1$.

**4** Find

(a) $\int \frac{4x+1}{2x^2+x+3} \, dx$

(b) $\int \frac{2 \sin 2x}{\cos 2x + 7} \, dx$

(c) $\int \frac{3}{9-2x} \, dx$

(d) $\int \frac{t}{t^2+1} \, dt$

(e) $\int \frac{1}{t \ln t} \, dt$

**5** Evaluate the following:

(a) $\int_0^1 \frac{2}{(1+3x)^2} \, dx$

(b) $\int_0^{\pi/2} \sin t \sqrt{\cos t} \, dt$

(c) $\int_1^2 \frac{3+x}{x^2+6x+1} \, dx$

(d) $\int_1^2 \frac{e^{\sqrt{t}}}{\sqrt{t}} \, dt$

(e) $\int_0^2 x \sin(\pi - x^2) \, dx$

## Solutions

**1** (a) $\frac{(4x+1)^8}{32} + c$

(b) $-\frac{\cos(t^3+1)}{3} + c$

(c) $-2e^{-t^2} + c$

(d) $-\frac{3}{4}(1-z)^{4/3} + c$

(e) $\frac{1}{6} \sin^6 t + c$

**2** (a) $3.3588 \times 10^5$

(b) 0.2

(c) 1.7183

(d) 5.2495

(e) 0.7687

**3** 103.098

**4** (a) $\ln(2x^2+x+3) + c$

(b) $-\ln(\cos 2x + 7) + c$

(c) $-\frac{3}{2} \ln(9-2x) + c$

(d) $\frac{1}{2} \ln(t^2+1) + c$

(e) $\ln(\ln t) + c$

**5** (a) 0.5

(b) 0.6667

(c) 0.3769

(d) 2.7899

(e) 0.8268

## 14.4 Integration using partial fractions

The technique of expressing a rational function as the sum of its partial fractions has been covered in Section 1.6. Some expressions which at first sight look impossible to integrate may in fact be integrated when expressed as their partial fractions.

**Example 14.14** Find

(a) $\displaystyle\int \frac{1}{x^3+x}\,dx$

(b) $\displaystyle\int \frac{13x-4}{6x^2-x-2}\,dx$

**Solution** (a) First express the integrand in partial fractions:

$$\frac{1}{x^3+x} = \frac{1}{x(x^2+1)} = \frac{A}{x} + \frac{Bx+C}{x^2+1}$$

Then,

$$1 = A(x^2+1) + x(Bx+C)$$

Equating the constant terms: $1 = A$ so that $A = 1$.

Equating the coefficients of $x$: $0 = C$ so that $C = 0$.

Equating the coefficients of $x^2$: $0 = A + B$ and hence $B = -1$.

Then,

$$\int \frac{1}{x^3+x}\,dx = \int \frac{1}{x} - \frac{x}{x^2+1}\,dx$$

$$= \ln|x| - \frac{1}{2}\ln|x^2+1| + c = \ln\left|\frac{x}{\sqrt{x^2+1}}\right| + c$$

(b)

$$\int \frac{13x-4}{6x^2-x-2}\,dx = \int \frac{13x-4}{(2x+1)(3x-2)}\,dx$$

$$= \int \frac{3}{2x+1} + \frac{2}{3x-2}\,dx \qquad \text{using partial fractions}$$

$$= \frac{3}{2}\int \frac{2}{2x+1}\,dx + \frac{2}{3}\int \frac{3}{3x-2}\,dx$$

$$= \frac{3}{2}\ln|2x+1| + \frac{2}{3}\ln|3x-2| + c$$

**Example 14.15** Evaluate $\displaystyle\int_0^1 \frac{4t^3-2t^2+3t-1}{2t^2+1}\,dt$.

**Solution** Using partial fractions we may write

$$\frac{4t^3-2t^2+3t-1}{2t^2+1} = 2t - 1 + \frac{t}{2t^2+1}$$

Hence,

$$\int_0^1 \frac{4t^3 - 2t^2 + 3t - 1}{2t^2 + 1}\,dt = \int_0^1 2t - 1 + \frac{t}{2t^2 + 1}\,dt = \left[t^2 - t + \frac{1}{4}\ln|2t^2 + 1|\right]_0^1$$

$$= \left[1 - 1 + \frac{1}{4}\ln 3\right] - \left[0 - 0 + \frac{1}{4}\ln 1\right] = 0.275$$

## Exercises 14.4

1 By writing the integrand as its partial fractions find

(a) $\int \frac{x + 3}{x^2 + x}\,dx$

(b) $\int \frac{t - 3}{t^2 - 1}\,dt$

(c) $\int \frac{8x + 10}{4x^2 + 8x + 3}\,dx$

(d) $\int \frac{2t^2 + 3t + 3}{2(t + 1)}\,dt$

(e) $\int \frac{2x^2 + x + 1}{x^3 + x^2}\,dx$

2 Evaluate the following integrals:

(a) $\int_1^3 \frac{5x + 6}{2x^2 + 4x}\,dx$

(b) $\int_0^1 \frac{3x + 5}{(x + 1)(x + 2)}\,dx$

(c) $\int_1^2 \frac{3 - 3x}{2x^2 + 6x}\,dx$

(d) $\int_{-1}^0 \frac{4x + 1}{2x^2 + x - 6}\,dx$

(e) $\int_2^3 \frac{x^2 + 2x - 1}{(x^2 + 1)(x - 1)}\,dx$

3 Find the area between $y = \frac{4x + 7}{4x^2 + 8x + 3}$ and the $x$ axis from $x = 0$ to $x = 1$.

4 Use partial fractions to find

(a) $\int_2^3 \frac{3x + 2}{x^2 - 1}\,dx$

(b) $\int \frac{t + 3}{t^2 + 2t + 1}\,dt$

(c) $\int \frac{2t^2 + 3t + 1}{t^3 + t}\,dt$

(d) $\int \frac{6t + 3}{2t^2 - 5t + 2}\,dt$

## Solutions

1 (a) $3\ln x - 2\ln(x + 1) + c$

(b) $2\ln(t + 1) - \ln(t - 1) + c$

(c) $\frac{1}{2}\ln(2x + 3) + \frac{3}{2}\ln(2x + 1) + c$

(d) $\ln(t + 1) + \frac{t(t + 1)}{2} + c$

(e) $2\ln(x + 1) - \frac{1}{x} + c$

2 (a) 2.1587

(b) 1.7918

(c) −0.09971

(d) 0.1823

(e) 0.9769

3 1.2456

4 (a) 1.8767

(b) $\ln(t + 1) - \frac{2}{t + 1} + c$

(c) $3\tan^{-1} t + \frac{1}{2}\ln(t^2 + 1) + \ln t + c$

(d) $5\ln(t - 2) - 2\ln(2t - 1) + c$

## Review exercises 14

**1** Use the given substitution to find the following integrals:

(a) $\int_0^1 (9t+2)^{10}\,dt$ $\quad z = 9t+2$

(b) $\int_3^5 (-t+1)^6\,dt$ $\quad z = -t+1$

(c) $\int_6^3 (4x-1)^{27}\,dx$ $\quad z = 4x-1$

(d) $\int \sqrt{3t+1}\,dt$ $\quad z = 3t+1$

(e) $\int (9y-2)^{17}\,dy$ $\quad z = 9y-2$

(f) $\int_0^2 \frac{3}{(2z+5)^6}\,dz$ $\quad y = 2z+5$

(g) $\int t^2 \sin(t^3)\,dt$ $\quad z = t^3$

(h) $\int x^2 e^{x^3+1}\,dx$ $\quad z = x^3+1$

(i) $\int_0^{0.5} \sin(2t)e^{\cos(2t)}\,dt$ $\quad z = \cos(2t)$

(j) $\int_0^{\pi} \sin t \cos^2 t\,dt$ $\quad z = \cos t$

(k) $\int \cos t \sqrt{\sin t}\,dt$ $\quad z = \sin t$

**2** Use integration by parts to find

(a) $\int_0^{\pi/2} e^{2x} \cos x\,dx$

(b) $\int_0^{\pi/2} e^{2x} \sin x\,dx$

**3** Find

$$\int \frac{\ln t}{t}\,dt$$

using

(a) integration by parts

(b) the substitution $z = \ln t$.

**4** The integral $I_n$ is given by

$$I_n = \int_0^{\pi/2} \sin^n \theta\,d\theta$$

(a) State $I_{n-2}$.

(b) Show

$$I_n = \frac{n-1}{n} I_{n-2}$$

(c) Evaluate $I_0$, $I_1$, $I_2$ and $I_3$.

**5** Evaluate

(a) $\int \frac{t^2}{t^3+1}\,dt$

(b) $\int_0^{\pi/3} \sin t \cos t\,dt$

(c) $\int_1^3 \frac{4}{e^{2t}}\,dt$

(d) $\int \frac{3x-7}{(x-2)(x-3)(x-4)}\,dx$

(e) $\int \frac{e^x}{e^x+1}\,dx$

**6** Evaluate

(a) $\int_0^1 \frac{3}{(e^t)^2} + \sin t \cos^2 t\,dt$

(b) $\int_0^1 4t^2 e^{t^3} + t(1+t^2)^{12}\,dt$

(c) $\int_0^{\pi} \sin^2 \omega t + \cos^2 \omega t + \omega\,dt$
$\omega$ constant

(d) $\int_1^2 \frac{1+t+t^2}{t(1+t^2)}\,dt$

(e) $\int_0^1 (t+e^t)\sin t\,dt$

(f) $\int_1^3 \frac{1+4x}{2x+4x^2}\,dx$

**7** Calculate the area under $y(x) = \frac{1+2e^{2x}}{x+e^{2x}}$ from $x = 1$ to $x = 3$.

**8** Evaluate the following integrals:

(a) $\int (-2t+0.1)^4\,dt$

(b) $\int (1+x)\sin x\,dx$

(c) $\int_1^2 x\sin(1+x)\,dx$

(d) $\int_3^6 \frac{t}{\sqrt{t^2+1}}\,dt$

(e) $\int \frac{1}{t^3+2t^2+t}\,dt$

(f) $\int_1^5 \frac{1}{1+e^t}\,dt$

9 Find

(a) $\int \frac{\cos t}{10+\sin t}\,dt$

(b) $\int \frac{2\sin t\cos t}{1+\sin^2 t}\,dt$

(c) $\int \frac{1}{t(1+\ln t)}\,dt$

(d) $\int \frac{1}{e^t(1+e^{-t})}\,dt$

(e) $\int \frac{1+\ln x}{x\ln x}\,dx$

10 Find $\int x^3 e^{x^2}\,dx$.

## Solutions

1 (a) $2.8819\times 10^9$

(b) 2322

(c) $-1.2\times 10^{36}$

(d) $\frac{2}{9}(3t+1)^{3/2}+c$

(e) $\frac{(9y-2)^{18}}{162}+c$

(f) $9.092\times 10^{-5}$

(g) $-\frac{1}{3}\cos(t^3)+c$

(h) $\frac{e^{x^3+1}}{3}+c$

(i) 0.5009

(j) $\frac{2}{3}$

(k) $\frac{2}{3}(\sin t)^{3/2}+c$

2 (a) 4.2281 (b) 9.4563

3 $\frac{(\ln t)^2}{2}+c$

4 (a) $I_{n-2}=\int_0^{\pi/2}\sin^{n-2}\theta\,d\theta$

(c) $\frac{\pi}{2}$, 1, 0.7854, 0.6667

5 (a) $\frac{1}{3}\ln|t^3+1|+c$

(b) $\frac{3}{8}$

(c) 0.2657

(d) $-\frac{1}{2}\ln|x-2|-2\ln|x-3|+\frac{5}{2}\ln|x-4|+c$

(e) $\ln|e^x+1|+c$

6 (a) 1.5778 (b) 317.3 (c) $\pi(1+\omega)$

(d) 1.0149 (e) 1.2105 (f) 0.9730

7 3.8805

8 (a) $-\frac{(-2t+0.1)^5}{10}+c$

(b) $-(1+x)\cos x+\sin x+c$

(c) 0.7957

(d) 2.9205

(e) $\ln|t|-\ln|t+1|+\frac{1}{t+1}+c$

(f) 0.3066

9 (a) $\ln(\sin t+10)+c$

(b) $\ln(\sin^2 t+1)+c$

(c) $\ln(1+\ln t)+c$

(d) $-\ln(1+e^{-t})+c$

(e) $\ln(x\ln x)+c$

10 $\frac{e^{x^2}(x^2-1)}{2}+c$

# 27 Line integrals and multiple integrals

| Chapter 27 | Contents |
| --- | --- |

## 27.1 Introduction

In this chapter a number of new sorts of integral are introduced. These are intimately connected with the developments of the previous chapter on differential vector calculus. The chapter starts by explaining the physical significance of line integrals and how these are evaluated. This leads naturally into the topics of conservative vector fields and potential functions. These are important in the study of electrostatics. Double and triple integrals are then introduced; these generalize the earlier work on integration to integrands which contain two and three independent variables.

Finally some simple volume and surface integrals are introduced, together with the divergence theorem and Stokes' theorem. These enable Maxwell's equations to be expressed in integral form.

## 27.2 Line integrals

Consider an object of mass $m$ placed in a gravitational field. Because the force of gravity is a vector the gravitational field is an example of a **vector field**. The gravitational force on the mass is known as its weight and is given by $m\mathbf{g}$ where $\mathbf{g}$ is a constant vector called **the acceleration due to gravity**. Suppose we release the mass and allow it to fall from point A in Figure 27.1. The vertical displacement measured downwards from A is $s$.

Work is being done by the gravitational force in order to make the mass accelerate. We wish to calculate the work done by the field in moving the mass from A to B. Suppose we consider the amount of work done as the mass moves from point M to point N, a distance $\delta s$. Elementary physics tells us that the work done is equal to the product of the magnitude of the force and the distance moved in the direction of the force. In this case the magnitude of the force is $mg$, and so the small amount of work done, $\delta W$, in moving from M to N, is

$$\delta W = mg\ \delta s$$

from which we have $\dfrac{\delta W}{\delta s} = mg$. As $\delta s \to 0$ we obtain

$$\lim_{\delta s \to 0} \frac{\delta W}{\delta s} = \frac{\mathrm{d}W}{\mathrm{d}s} = mg$$

To find the total work done as the mass falls from A to B we must add up, or integrate, the contributions over the whole interval of interest, that is

$$\text{total work done} = W = \int_{\mathrm{A}}^{\mathrm{B}} mg\ \mathrm{d}s$$

This is an elementary example of a **line integral**, so called because we are integrating along the line from A to B. In this case it is straightforward to evaluate. Since both $g$ and $m$ are constants the integral becomes

$$W = mg \int_{\mathrm{A}}^{\mathrm{B}} \mathrm{d}s$$

which equals $mg\times$ (distance from A to B).

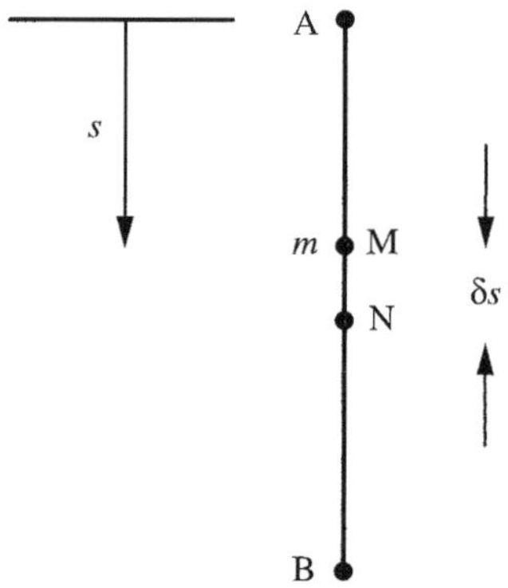


**Figure 27.1** An object of mass $m$ falls from A to B.

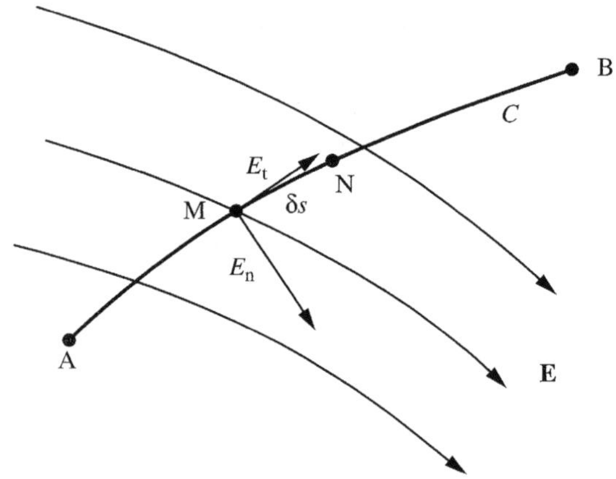


**Figure 27.2** As a charge moves from M to N, the field **E** does work $E_t\delta s$.

**Example 27.1**

## The work done by the gravitational field

An object of mass $m$ falls vertically from A to B. If A is the point where $s = 0$ and B where $s = 10$ find the total work done by gravity as the mass falls from A to B.

**Solution** The work done by gravity is found by evaluating the line integral

$$W = mg \int_{s=0}^{s=10} \mathrm{d}s = mg[s]_0^{10} = 10mg$$

Note that this is also the potential energy lost by $m$ in falling a distance of 10 units.

---

In the previous example the path along which we integrated was a straight line, but this need not always be the case. Consider the following example.

**Example 27.2**

## The work done by an electric field

Figure 27.2 shows a unit charge moving along a curve $C$ from point A to point B in an electric field **E**.

At the particular point of interest, M, we have resolved the electric field vector into two components. Resolving a vector into perpendicular components has been described in Example 7.3. One component is tangent to $C$, namely $E_t$, and one is normal to $C$, namely $E_n$. As a unit charge moves from M to N, a distance $\delta s$ along the curve, the work done by the electric field is $E_t\delta s$. The component $E_n$ does no work since there is no motion perpendicular to the curve $C$. To find the total work done we must add up all contributions, resulting in the integral

$$\text{total work done} = \int_A^B E_t \, \mathrm{d}s$$

This is a second example of a line integral, the line being the curve, $C$, joining A and B.

It is usual to denote this by

$$\text{total work done} = \int_C E_t \, ds$$

where the symbol $\int_C$ tells us to integrate along the curve $C$.

---

If the coordinates of the end-points of the curve $C$ are known, say $(x_1, y_1)$ and $(x_2, y_2)$, we often write $\int_{(x_1,y_1)}^{(x_2,y_2)}$ to show this, but care must then be taken to define the intended route from A to B.

We now explain how to integrate a function along a curve. Consider a vector field, **F**, through which runs a curve, $C$, as shown in Figure 27.3.

Suppose we restrict ourselves to two-dimensional situations. In the general case the vector field will vary as $x$ and $y$ vary, that is $\mathbf{F} = \mathbf{F}(x, y)$. Consider the small element of $C$ joining points M and N. Let $\theta$ be the angle between the tangent to the curve at M and the direction of the field there. We shall denote the vector joining M and N (i.e. $\overrightarrow{MN}$) by $\delta\mathbf{s}$. Consider the quantity

$$\mathbf{F} \cdot \delta\mathbf{s}$$

where $\cdot$ represents the scalar product. When **F** represents a gravitational force field, $\mathbf{F} \cdot \delta\mathbf{s}$ represents the small amount of work done by the field in moving a particle of unit mass from M to N. The appropriate integral along the whole curve represents the total work done. From the definition of the scalar product we note that

$$\mathbf{F} \cdot \delta\mathbf{s} = |\mathbf{F}||\delta\mathbf{s}| \cos\theta$$

Writing the modulus of **F** as simply $F$, and the modulus of $\delta\mathbf{s}$, as $\delta s$, we have

$$\begin{aligned} \mathbf{F} \cdot \delta\mathbf{s} &= F\delta s \cos\theta \\ &= (F \cos\theta)\delta s \\ &= F_t \delta s \end{aligned}$$

where $F_t$ is the component of **F** tangential to $C$. This result is of the same form as the expressions for work done obtained previously. We are therefore interested in integrals of the form

$$\int_C \mathbf{F}(x, y) \cdot d\mathbf{s}$$

Since **F** is a vector function of $x$ and $y$ it will have Cartesian components $P(x, y)$ and $Q(x, y)$ and so we can write **F** in the form

$$\mathbf{F}(x, y) = P(x, y)\mathbf{i} + Q(x, y)\mathbf{j}$$

Similarly, referring to Figure 27.4, we can write the vector $d\mathbf{s}$ as $d\mathbf{s} = dx\mathbf{i} + dy\mathbf{j}$. Hence

$$\int_C \mathbf{F}(x, y) \cdot d\mathbf{s} = \int_C (P(x, y)\mathbf{i} + Q(x, y)\mathbf{j}) \cdot (dx\mathbf{i} + dy\mathbf{j})$$

Taking the scalar product gives

$$\int_C P(x, y)\, dx + Q(x, y)\, dy$$

and this is the line integral in Cartesian form.

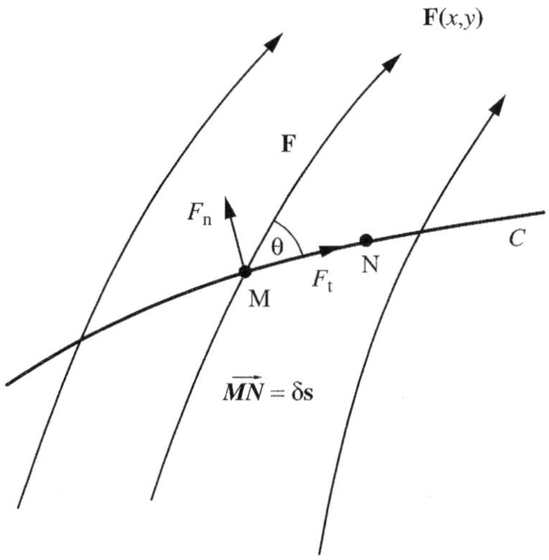


**Figure 27.3** The integral $\int_C \mathbf{F} \cdot d\mathbf{s}$ is equal to the work done by **F** as the particle moves along $C$.

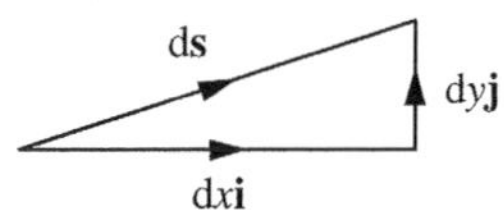


**Figure 27.4** The vector ds can be written as $dx\mathbf{i} + dy\mathbf{j}$.

If $\mathbf{F}(x, y) = P(x, y)\mathbf{i} + Q(x, y)\mathbf{j}$ then

$$\int_C \mathbf{F}(x, y) \cdot d\mathbf{s} = \int_C (P(x, y)\mathbf{i} + Q(x, y)\mathbf{j}) \cdot (dx\mathbf{i} + dy\mathbf{j})$$
$$= \int_C P(x, y)\, dx + Q(x, y)\, dy$$

In order to proceed further we now need to explore how such integrals are evaluated in practice. This is the topic of the next section.

## 27.3 Evaluation of line integrals in two dimensions

**Example 27.3** Evaluate

$$\int_C \mathbf{F} \cdot d\mathbf{s}$$

where $\mathbf{F} = 5y^2\mathbf{i} + 2xy\mathbf{j}$ and $C$ is the straight line joining the origin and the point $(1, 1)$.

**Solution** We compare the integrand with the standard form and recognize that in this case $P(x, y) = 5y^2$ and $Q(x, y) = 2xy$. The integral becomes

$$\int_C 5y^2\, dx + 2xy\, dy$$

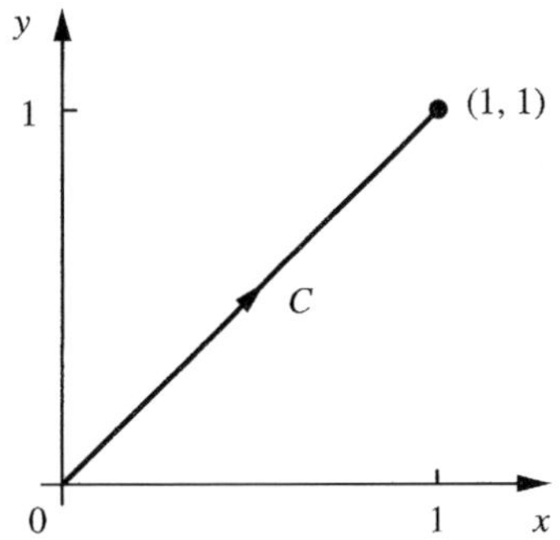


**Figure 27.5** The path of integration joins (0, 0) and (1, 1) and has equation $y = x$.

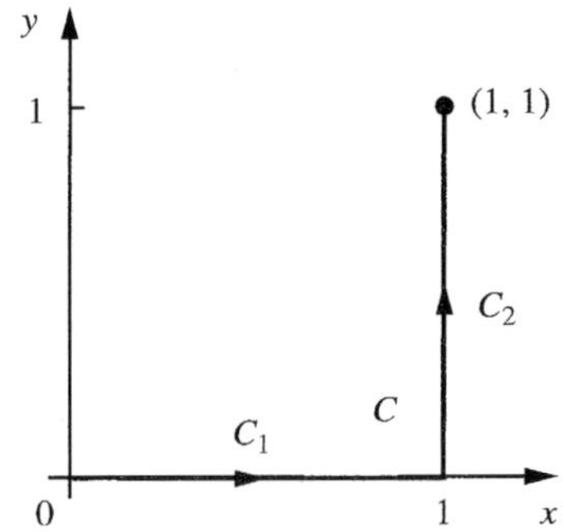


**Figure 27.6** The path $C$ is made up of two distinct parts. Integration is performed separately on each part.

The curve of interest, in this case a straight line, is shown in Figure 27.5. Along this curve it is clear that $y = x$ at all points. We use this fact to simplify the integral by writing everything in terms of $x$. We could equally well choose to write everything in terms of $y$. If $y = x$ then $\dfrac{dy}{dx} = 1$, that is $dy = dx$. As we move along the curve $C$, $x$ ranges from 0 to 1, and the integral reduces to

$$\int_C 5x^2\,dx + 2x^2\,dx = \int_C 7x^2\,dx = \int_{x=0}^{x=1} 7x^2\,dx = \left[\frac{7x^3}{3}\right]_0^1 = \frac{7}{3}$$

---

Let us now see what happens when we choose to evaluate the integral of Example 27.3 along a different path joining (0, 0) and (1, 1).

**Example 27.4** Evaluate the integral $\int_C 5y^2\,dx + 2xy\,dy$ along the curve, $C$, consisting of the $x$ axis between $x = 0$ and $x = 1$ and the line $x = 1$ as shown in Figure 27.6.

**Solution** We evaluate this integral in two parts because the curve $C$ is made up of two pieces. The first piece $C_1$ is horizontal, and the second $C_2$ is vertical. The required integral is the sum of the two separate ones. Along the $x$ axis, $y = 0$ and $dy = 0$. This means that both the terms $5y^2\,dx$ and $2xy\,dy$ are zero, and so the integral reduces to

$$\int_{x=0}^{x=1} 0\,dx = 0$$

and so there is zero contribution to the final answer from this part of the curve $C$. Along the line $x = 1$, the quantity $dx$ equals zero. Hence $5y^2\,dx$ also equals zero, and $2xy\,dy$ equals $2y\,dy$. Because $y$ ranges from 0 to 1 the integral becomes

$$\int_{y=0}^{y=1} 2y\,dy = [y^2]_0^1 = 1$$

Note that this is a different answer from that obtained in Example 27.3.

---

As we have seen from Examples 27.3 and 27.4 the value of a line integral can depend upon the path taken. It is therefore essential to specify this path clearly.

**Example 27.5** Evaluate the integral $\int_C \mathbf{F}(x, y) \cdot \mathbf{ds}$ where $\mathbf{F}(x, y) = (3x^2 + y)\mathbf{i} + (5x - y)\mathbf{j}$ and $C$ is the portion of the curve $y = 2x^2$ between A(2, 8) and B(3, 18).

**Solution**

$$\int_C \mathbf{F}(x, y) \cdot \mathbf{ds} = \int_C (3x^2 + y)\,dx + (5x - y)\,dy$$

The curve $C$ has equation $y = 2x^2$ for $2 \leqslant x \leqslant 3$. Along this curve we can replace $y$ by $2x^2$. Note also that $\dfrac{dy}{dx} = 4x$ and so we can replace $dy$ with $4x\,dx$. This will produce an integral entirely in terms of the variable $x$ which is then integrated between $x = 2$ and $x = 3$. Thus

$$\begin{aligned}\int_C (3x^2 + y)\,dx + (5x - y)\,dy &= \int_2^3 (3x^2 + 2x^2)\,dx + (5x - 2x^2)(4x\,dx) \\ &= \int_2^3 25x^2 - 8x^3\,dx \\ &= \left[\frac{25x^3}{3} - 2x^4\right]_2^3 \\ &= 28.333\end{aligned}$$

## Exercises 27.3

1. Evaluate $\int_C 3y\,dx + 2x\,dy$ along the straight line $C$ between (1, 1) and (3, 3).

2. Evaluate $\int_C 2yx\,dx + x^2\,dy$ along the straight line $y = 4x$ from (0, 0) to (3, 12).

3. Evaluate $\int_C (7x + 3y)\,dx + 2y\,dy$ along the curve $y = x^2$ between(0, 0) and (2, 4).

4. If $\mathbf{E} = (x + 2y)\mathbf{i} + (x - 3y)\mathbf{j}$, A is the point (0, 0) and B is the point (3, 2), evaluate

$$\int_A^B \mathbf{E} \cdot \mathbf{ds}$$

(a) along the straight line joining A and B,

(b) horizontally along the $x$ axis from $x = 0$ to $x = 3$ and then vertically from $y = 0$ to $y = 2$.

5. If $\mathbf{F} = (2xy - y^4 + 3)\mathbf{i} + (x^2 - 4xy^3)\mathbf{j}$ evaluate $\int_C \mathbf{F} \cdot \mathbf{ds}$ where $C$ is the straight line joining A(1, 3) and B(2, 5).

6. Evaluate the integral

$$\int_C (3x^2 + 2y)\,dx + (7x + y^2)\,dy$$

from A(0, 1) to B(2, 5) along the curve $C$ defined by $y = 2x + 1$.

## Solutions

1. 20
2. 108
3. 38
4. (a) $\frac{15}{2}$ (b) $\frac{9}{2}$
5. −1149
6. $\frac{268}{3}$

## 27.4 Evaluation of line integrals in three dimensions

Evaluation of line integrals along curves lying in three-dimensional space is performed in a similar way. It is often helpful in this case to express the independent variables $x$, $y$ and $z$ in terms of a single parameter. Consider the following example.

**Example 27.6** A curve, $C$, is defined parametrically by

$$x = 4 \qquad y = t^3 \qquad z = 5 + t$$

and is located within a vector field $\mathbf{F} = y\mathbf{i} + x^2\mathbf{j} + (z + x)\mathbf{k}$.

(a) Find the coordinates of the point P on the curve where the parameter $t$ takes the value 1.

(b) Find the coordinates of the point Q where the parameter $t$ takes the value 3.

(c) By expressing the line integral $\int_C \mathbf{F} \cdot \mathbf{ds}$ entirely in terms of $t$ find the value of the line integral from P to Q. Note that $\mathbf{ds} = \mathrm{d}x\mathbf{i} + \mathrm{d}y\mathbf{j} + \mathrm{d}z\mathbf{k}$.

**Solution** (a) When $t = 1$, $x = 4$, $y = 1$, and $z = 6$, and so P has coordinates (4, 1, 6).

(b) When $t = 3$, $x = 4$, $y = 27$ and $z = 8$, and so Q has coordinates (4, 27, 8).

(c) To express the line integral entirely in terms of $t$ we note that if $x = 4$, $\dfrac{\mathrm{d}x}{\mathrm{d}t} = 0$ so that $\mathrm{d}x$ is also zero. If $y = t^3$ then $\dfrac{\mathrm{d}y}{\mathrm{d}t} = 3t^2$ so that $\mathrm{d}y = 3t^2\,\mathrm{d}t$. Similarly since $z = 5 + t$, $\dfrac{\mathrm{d}z}{\mathrm{d}t} = 1$ so that $\mathrm{d}z = \mathrm{d}t$. The line integral becomes

$$\begin{aligned}
\int_C \mathbf{F} \cdot \mathbf{ds} &= \int_C (y\mathbf{i} + x^2\mathbf{j} + (z + x)\mathbf{k}) \cdot (\mathrm{d}x\mathbf{i} + \mathrm{d}y\mathbf{j} + \mathrm{d}z\mathbf{k}) \\
&= \int_C y\,\mathrm{d}x + x^2\mathrm{d}y + (z + x)\,\mathrm{d}z \\
&= \int_{t=1}^{t=3} 0 + 16(3t^2)\,\mathrm{d}t + (9 + t)\,\mathrm{d}t \\
&= \int_1^3 48t^2 + 9 + t\,\mathrm{d}t \\
&= \left[\frac{48t^3}{3} + 9t + \frac{t^2}{2}\right]_1^3 \\
&= \left(\frac{48(3^3)}{3} + (9)(3) + \frac{3^2}{2}\right) - \left(\frac{48}{3} + 9 + \frac{1}{2}\right) \\
&= 438
\end{aligned}$$

## Exercises 27.4

1 You are required to evaluate the line integral $\int_C \mathbf{F} \cdot \mathrm{d}\mathbf{s}$ where $\mathbf{F}$ is the vector field $\mathbf{F} = (2y + 3x)\mathbf{i} + (yz + x)\mathbf{j} + 3xy\mathbf{k}$ and $\mathrm{d}\mathbf{s} = \mathrm{d}x\mathbf{i} + \mathrm{d}y\mathbf{j} + \mathrm{d}z\mathbf{k}$. The curve $C$ is defined parametrically by $x = t^2$, $y = 3t$ and $z = 2t$ for values of $t$ between 0 and 1.

(a) Find the coordinates of the point A, where $t = 0$.

(b) Find the coordinates of the point B, where $t = 1$.

(c) By expressing the line integral entirely in terms of $t$, evaluate the line integral from A to B along the curve $C$.

## Solutions

1 (a) (0, 0, 0) (b) (1, 3, 2) (c) 17

## 27.5 Conservative fields and potential functions

We have seen that, in general, the value of a line integral depends upon the particular path chosen. However, in special cases, the integral of a given vector field $\mathbf{F}$ turns out to be the same on any path with the same end-points; that is, it is independent of the path chosen. In these cases the vector field $\mathbf{F}$ is said to be **conservative**. There is a simple test which tells us whether or not $\mathbf{F}$ is conservative:

> $\mathbf{F}$ is a conservative vector field if
>
> $\text{curl}\,\mathbf{F} = \mathbf{0}$ everywhere

If we are dealing with a two-dimensional vector field $\mathbf{F}(x, y) = P(x, y)\mathbf{i} + Q(x, y)\mathbf{j}$ then this test becomes: $\mathbf{F}$ is conservative if $\dfrac{\partial P}{\partial y} = \dfrac{\partial Q}{\partial x}$. (See Question 7 in Exercises 27.5).

**Example 27.7** Show that the vector field

$$\mathbf{F} = z\mathrm{e}^x \sin y\mathbf{i} + z\mathrm{e}^x \cos y\mathbf{j} + \mathrm{e}^x \sin y\mathbf{k}$$

is a conservative field.

**Solution** We find curl $\mathbf{F}$.

$$\nabla \times \mathbf{F} = \begin{vmatrix} \mathbf{i} & \mathbf{j} & \mathbf{k} \\ \dfrac{\partial}{\partial x} & \dfrac{\partial}{\partial y} & \dfrac{\partial}{\partial z} \\ z\mathrm{e}^x \sin y & z\mathrm{e}^x \cos y & \mathrm{e}^x \sin y \end{vmatrix}$$

$$= (\mathrm{e}^x \cos y - \mathrm{e}^x \cos y)\mathbf{i} - (\mathrm{e}^x \sin y - \mathrm{e}^x \sin y)\mathbf{j} + (z\mathrm{e}^x \cos y - z\mathrm{e}^x \cos y)\mathbf{k}$$

$$= \mathbf{0}$$

We have shown that $\nabla \times \mathbf{F} = \mathbf{0}$ and so the field is conservative. Note from Section 26.5 that such a field is also said to be irrotational.

---

There are two important properties of conservative vector fields which we now discuss.

### 27.5.1 The potential function

It can be shown that any conservative vector field, **F**, can be expressed as the gradient of some scalar field $\phi$. That is, we can find a scalar field $\phi$ such that $\mathbf{F} = \nabla\phi$. The scalar field $\phi$ is said to be a **potential function** and **F** is said to be **derivable from a potential**. In three dimensions, if

$$\mathbf{F} = P(x, y, z)\mathbf{i} + Q(x, y, z)\mathbf{j} + R(x, y, z)\mathbf{k}$$

is conservative, we can write

$$\begin{aligned}\mathbf{F} &= \nabla\phi \\ &= \frac{\partial\phi}{\partial x}\mathbf{i} + \frac{\partial\phi}{\partial y}\mathbf{j} + \frac{\partial\phi}{\partial z}\mathbf{k}\end{aligned}$$

So

$$P = \frac{\partial\phi}{\partial x} \qquad Q = \frac{\partial\phi}{\partial y} \qquad R = \frac{\partial\phi}{\partial z}$$

You should refer back to Example 26.4 where this idea was introduced.

**Example 27.8** The vector field **v** is derivable from the potential $\phi = 2xy + zx$. Find **v**.

**Solution** If **v** is derivable from the potential $\phi$, then $\mathbf{v} = \nabla\phi$ and so

$$\mathbf{v} = \nabla\phi = (2y + z)\mathbf{i} + 2x\mathbf{j} + x\mathbf{k}$$

This vector field is conservative as is easily verified by finding curl **v**. In fact,

$$\begin{aligned}\nabla \times \mathbf{v} &= \begin{vmatrix} \mathbf{i} & \mathbf{j} & \mathbf{k} \\ \dfrac{\partial}{\partial x} & \dfrac{\partial}{\partial y} & \dfrac{\partial}{\partial z} \\ 2y + z & 2x & x \end{vmatrix} \\ &= 0\mathbf{i} - (1 - 1)\mathbf{j} + (2 - 2)\mathbf{k} \\ &= \mathbf{0}\end{aligned}$$

Indeed, recall from Example 26.12 that curl(grad $\phi$) is identically zero for any $\phi$.

---

When the vector field $\mathbf{F}$ is conservative there is an alternative method of evaluating the line integral $\int_C \mathbf{F} \cdot \mathbf{ds}$ which involves the use of the potential function $\phi$. Consider the following example.

**Example 27.9** The two-dimensional vector field $\mathbf{F} = \mathbf{i} + 2\mathbf{j}$ is conservative.

(a) Find a suitable potential function $\phi$ such that $\mathbf{F} = \nabla\phi = \dfrac{\partial\phi}{\partial x}\mathbf{i} + \dfrac{\partial\phi}{\partial y}\mathbf{j}$.

(b) Evaluate $\int_{(0,0)}^{(3,2)} \mathbf{F} \cdot \mathbf{ds}$ along any convenient path.

(c) Find the value of $\phi$ at B(3, 2), and the value of $\phi$ at A(0, 0), and show that the difference between these is equal to the value of the line integral obtained in part (b).

**Solution** (a) We are given that $\dfrac{\partial\phi}{\partial x} = 1$ so that $\phi = x + f(y)$ where $f$ is an arbitrary function of $y$. We are also given that $\dfrac{\partial\phi}{\partial y} = 2$ so that $\phi = 2y + g(x)$ where $g$ is an arbitrary function of $x$. It is easy to verify that $\phi = x + 2y$ is a suitable potential function.

(b) To find the line integral we shall choose the straight line path, $C$, joining (0, 0) and (3, 2). This has equation $y = \frac{2}{3}x$. The line integral becomes

$$\begin{aligned}
\int_{(0,0)}^{(3,2)} \mathbf{F} \cdot \mathbf{ds} &= \int_{(0,0)}^{(3,2)} (\mathbf{i} + 2\mathbf{j}) \cdot (\mathrm{d}x\mathbf{i} + \mathrm{d}y\mathbf{j}) \\
&= \int_{(0,0)}^{(3,2)} \mathrm{d}x + 2\,\mathrm{d}y \\
&= \int_{(0,0)}^{(3,2)} \mathrm{d}x + \frac{4}{3}\,\mathrm{d}x \qquad \text{since } \mathrm{d}y = \frac{2}{3}\,\mathrm{d}x \text{ on } C \\
&= \int_{x=0}^{x=3} \frac{7}{3}\,\mathrm{d}x \\
&= \left[\frac{7}{3}x\right]_0^3 \\
&= 7
\end{aligned}$$

(c) The value of $\phi$ at B(3, 2) is $3 + 2(2) = 7$. The value of $\phi$ at A(0, 0) is 0. Clearly the difference between these values is 7, the same as the value of the line integral obtained in part (b).

The result obtained in the previous example is important:

If **F** is a conservative vector field such that $\mathbf{F} = \nabla\phi$ then, for any points A and B,

$$\int_A^B \mathbf{F}\cdot d\mathbf{s} = \phi(B) - \phi(A)$$

## 27.5.2 The line integral around a closed loop

A second important property of conservative fields arises when the curve $C$ of integration forms a closed loop. Suppose we evaluate a line integral from A to B firstly along the curve $C_1$ and secondly along $C_2$ as shown in Figure 27.7.

If the field, **F**, is conservative both integrals will yield the same answer, that is

$$\int_{C_1} \mathbf{F}\cdot d\mathbf{s} = \int_{C_2} \mathbf{F}\cdot d\mathbf{s}$$

But

$$\int \mathbf{F}\cdot d\mathbf{s} \text{ from A to B } = -\int \mathbf{F}\cdot d\mathbf{s} \text{ from B to A}$$

Consequently, the line integral around the closed curve A to B and back to A must equal zero. When the path of integration is a closed curve we use the symbol

$$\oint$$

to represent the integral. So, for a conservative field we have the result

$$\oint_C \mathbf{F}\cdot d\mathbf{s} = 0$$

for any closed curve $C$.

In summary we have the following results:

For a conservative field, **F**, all the following statements are equivalent:

$$\nabla \times \mathbf{F} = \mathbf{0}$$

$$\oint \mathbf{F}\cdot d\mathbf{s} = 0$$

$\int_A^B \mathbf{F}\cdot d\mathbf{s}$ is independent of the path between A and B

**F** is derivable from a scalar potential, that is $\mathbf{F} = \nabla\phi$

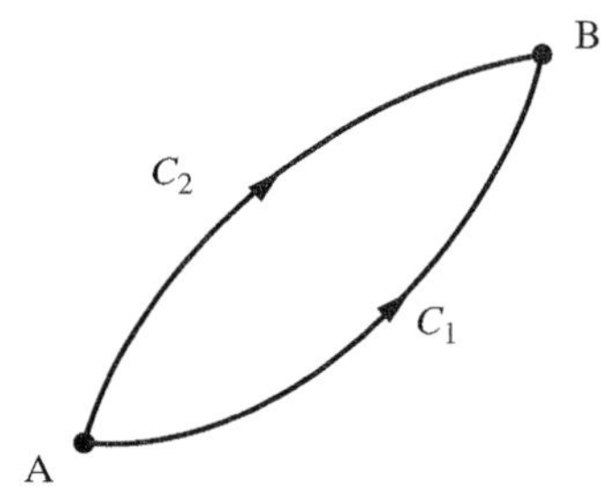


**Figure 27.7** The line integral $\int \mathbf{F} \cdot \mathbf{ds}$ can be evaluated along different paths between A and B.

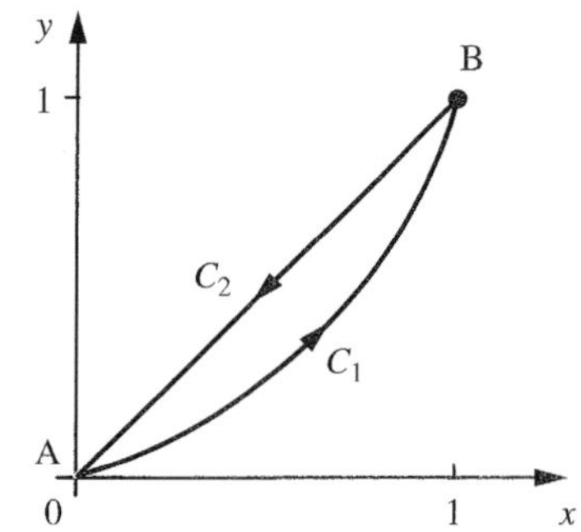


**Figure 27.8** The path of integration is the curve $C_1$ followed by the line $C_2$.

**Example 27.10** Evaluate

$$\int_C \mathbf{F} \cdot \mathbf{ds}$$

where $\mathbf{F}$ is the vector field $y^2\mathbf{i} + 2xy\mathbf{j}$ and where

(a) $C = C_1$ is the curve $y = x^2$ going from A(0, 0) to B(1, 1).

(b) $C = C_2$ is the straight line going from B(1, 1) to A(0, 0).

(c) Deduce that $\oint \mathbf{F} \cdot \mathbf{ds} = 0$ where the closed line integral is taken around the path $C_1$ and then $C_2$.

**Solution** The situation is depicted in Figure 27.8.

(a) $C_1$ has equation $y = x^2$ and so $\mathrm{d}y = 2x\,\mathrm{d}x$. Note that we are integrating from A to B.

Therefore

$$\int_{C_1} \mathbf{F} \cdot \mathbf{ds} = \int_{C_1} (y^2\mathbf{i} + 2xy\mathbf{j}) \cdot (\mathrm{d}x\mathbf{i} + \mathrm{d}y\mathbf{j}) = \int_{C_1} y^2\,\mathrm{d}x + 2xy\,\mathrm{d}y$$

Substituting $y = x^2$ and $\mathrm{d}y = 2x\,\mathrm{d}x$ we have

$$\int_{C_1} \mathbf{F} \cdot \mathbf{ds} = \int_{C_1} x^4\mathrm{d}x + (2x)x^2(2x\,\mathrm{d}x)$$

$$= \int_{x=0}^{x=1} 5x^4\,\mathrm{d}x = [x^5]_0^1 = 1$$

(b) $C_2$ has equation $y = x$ and so $\mathrm{d}y = \mathrm{d}x$. Note that this time we are integrating from B to A. Therefore

$$\int_{C_2} \mathbf{F} \cdot \mathrm{d}\mathbf{s} = \int_{C_2} (y^2\mathbf{i} + 2xy\mathbf{j}) \cdot (\mathrm{d}x\mathbf{i} + \mathrm{d}y\mathbf{j}) = \int_{C_2} y^2\,\mathrm{d}x + 2xy\,\mathrm{d}y$$

Substituting $y = x$ and $\mathrm{d}y = \mathrm{d}x$ we have

$$\int_{C_2} \mathbf{F} \cdot \mathrm{d}\mathbf{s} = \int_{x=1}^{x=0} x^2\,\mathrm{d}x + 2x^2\,\mathrm{d}x = \int_1^0 3x^2\,\mathrm{d}x = [x^3]_1^0 = -1$$

(c) Now

$$\oint \mathbf{F} \cdot \mathrm{d}\mathbf{s} = \int_{C_1} \mathbf{F} \cdot \mathrm{d}\mathbf{s} + \int_{C_2} \mathbf{F} \cdot \mathrm{d}\mathbf{s} = 1 - 1 = 0$$

The line integral around the closed path is zero because the field is conservative. You should check that $\nabla \times \mathbf{F} = \mathbf{0}$ and that a suitable potential function is $\phi = y^2x$.

## Exercises 27.5

1 Verify that the vector field $\mathbf{F} = (4x^3 + y)\mathbf{i} + x\mathbf{j}$ is conservative.

2 For the vector field $\mathbf{F} = y\cos xy\mathbf{i} + x\cos xy\mathbf{j} + 2z\mathbf{k}$ find $\nabla \times \mathbf{F}$ and verify that the field is conservative.

3 Consider the field $\mathbf{F} = y\mathbf{i} + x\mathbf{j}$.

(a) Show that $\mathbf{F}$ is a conservative field.

(b) Find a function $\phi$ such that $\dfrac{\partial \phi}{\partial x} = y$ and $\dfrac{\partial \phi}{\partial y} = x$.

(c) Find a suitable potential function $\phi$ for $\mathbf{F}$.

(d) If A is the point (2, 1) and B is the point (5, 8) evaluate $\int_A^B \mathbf{F} \cdot \mathrm{d}\mathbf{s}$.

(e) Find $\phi$ at B and $\phi$ at A and show that the value of the line integral calculated in part (d) is equal to the difference between the values of $\phi$ at B and A.

4 Show that the vector field, $\mathbf{F} = (2xy - y^4 + 3)\mathbf{i} + (x^2 - 4xy^3)\mathbf{j}$, of Question 5 in Exercises 27.3, is conservative and find a suitable potential function $\phi$ from which $\mathbf{F}$ can be derived. Show that the difference between $\phi$ evaluated at B(2, 1) and at A(1, 0) is equal to the value of the line integral $\int_A^B \mathbf{F} \cdot \mathrm{d}\mathbf{s}$.

5 Show that

$$I = \int_{(-1,-1)}^{(1,1)} 3x^2y^2\,\mathrm{d}x + 2x^3y\,\mathrm{d}y$$

is independent of the path of integration, and evaluate the integral.

6 The function $\phi = 4xy$ is a potential function for which $\mathbf{F} = \nabla\phi$.

(a) Find $\mathbf{F}$.

(b) Evaluate $\int \mathbf{F} \cdot \mathrm{d}\mathbf{s}$ along the curve $y = x^3$ from A(0, 0) to B(2, 8).

(c) Evaluate $\phi$ at B and at A and show that the difference between these values is equal to the value of the line integral obtained in part (b).

7 If $\mathbf{F} = P(x, y)\mathbf{i} + Q(x, y)\mathbf{j} + 0\mathbf{k}$, show that $\nabla \times \mathbf{F} = \left(\dfrac{\partial Q}{\partial x} - \dfrac{\partial P}{\partial y}\right)\mathbf{k}$. Deduce that if $\mathbf{F}$ is conservative then $\dfrac{\partial Q}{\partial x} = \dfrac{\partial P}{\partial y}$.

## Solutions

3 (b) $\phi = xy + c$ (c) $xy + c$ (d) 38

4 $\phi = x^2y - y^4x + 3x + c, 5$

5 2

6 (a) $\mathbf{F} = 4y\mathbf{i} + 4x\mathbf{j}$ (b) 64 (c) 64

# 27.6 Double and triple integrals

## 27.6.1 Double integrals

Expressions such as

$$\int_{y=y_1}^{y=y_2} \int_{x=x_1}^{x=x_2} f(x, y)\,dx\,dy$$

are known as **double integrals**. What is meant by the above is

$$\int_{y=y_1}^{y=y_2} \left( \int_{x=x_1}^{x=x_2} f(x, y)\,dx \right) dy$$

where firstly the inner integral is performed by integrating $f$ with respect to $x$, treating $y$ as if it were a constant. The limits of integration are inserted as usual and then the whole expression is integrated with respect to $y$ between the limits $y_1$ and $y_2$.

It is important that you can distinguish between double integrals and line integrals. Physically they mean quite different things, and they are evaluated in different ways. Whilst both types of integral contain terms involving $x$, $y$, $dx$ and $dy$, in a double integral $dx$ and $dy$ always occur as a product, that is as $dx\,dy$. In a line integral they occur separately. When evaluating a line integral we integrate along a curve. When evaluating a double integral we integrate over a two-dimensional region.

Double integrals may also be written in the form

$$\iint_R f(x, y)\,dx\,dy$$

where $R$ is called the **region of integration**. The region $R$ must be described mathematically. In the integral

$$\int_{y=y_1}^{y=y_2} \int_{x=x_1}^{x=x_2} f(x, y)\,dx\,dy$$

$R$ is the rectangular region defined by $x_1 \leqslant x \leqslant x_2$, $y_1 \leqslant y \leqslant y_2$. Non-rectangular regions are also common.

**Example 27.11** Sketch the region $R$ defined by $1 \leqslant x \leqslant 4$ and $0 \leqslant y \leqslant 2$.

**Solution** The region is shown in Figure 27.9. We see that $x$ lies between 1 and 4, and $y$ lies between 0 and 2. Consequently the region is rectangular.

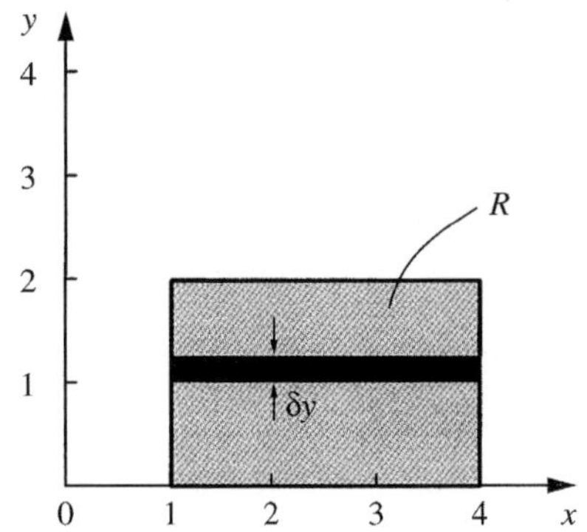


**Figure 27.9** The rectangular region over which the integration in Example 27.12 is performed.

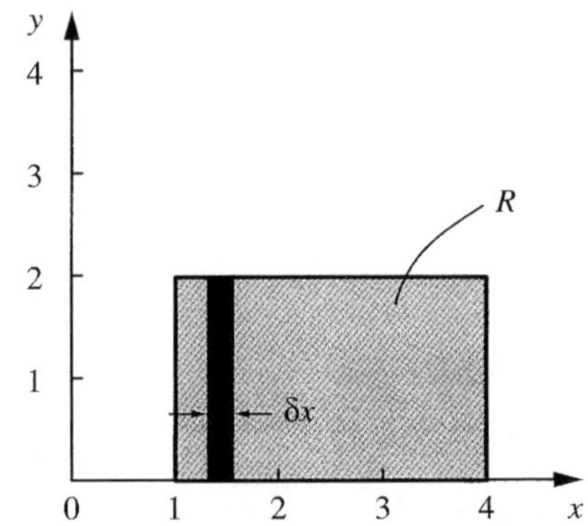


**Figure 27.10** The integral could have been found by first integrating over a vertical strip such as that shown.

**Example 27.12** Evaluate

$$\int_{y=0}^{y=2} \int_{x=1}^{x=4} x + 2y \, dx \, dy$$

over the region, $R$, given in Example 27.11 and defined by $1 \leqslant x \leqslant 4$ and $0 \leqslant y \leqslant 2$.

**Solution** The inner integral is found first by integrating with respect to $x$, keeping $y$ fixed, that is constant.

$$\int_{x=1}^{x=4} x + 2y \, dx = \left[\frac{x^2}{2} + 2xy\right]_{x=1}^{x=4} = 8 + 8y - \frac{1}{2} - 2y = \frac{15}{2} + 6y$$

Then the outer integral is found by integrating the result with respect to $y$:

$$\int_{y=0}^{y=2} \frac{15}{2} + 6y \, dy = \left[\frac{15}{2}y + 3y^2\right]_0^2 = 15 + 12 = 27$$

---

Now consider again Example 27.12. By performing the inner integral first,

$$\int_{x=1}^{x=4} x + 2y \, dx$$

we are effectively singling out a horizontal strip, such as that shown in Figure 27.9, and integrating along it from $x = 1$ to $x = 4$. When we then integrate the result from $y = 0$ to $y = 2$ we are effectively adding up contributions from all such horizontal strips.

The integral over the same region could also have been performed by integrating first over vertical strips for $0 \leqslant y \leqslant 2$ (Figure 27.10) yielding

$$\int_{y=0}^{y=2} x + 2y \, dy = [xy + y^2]_{y=0}^{y=2} = 2x + 4$$

The result is then integrated from $x = 1$ to $x = 4$ effectively adding up contributions from each vertical strip:

$$\int_{x=1}^{x=4} 2x + 4\,\mathrm{d}x = [x^2 + 4x]_1^4 = 32 - 5 = 27$$

as expected. We note that

$$\int_{y=0}^{y=2} \int_{x=1}^{x=4} x + 2y\,\mathrm{d}x\,\mathrm{d}y = \int_{x=1}^{x=4} \int_{y=0}^{y=2} x + 2y\,\mathrm{d}y\,\mathrm{d}x \tag{27.1}$$

In particular, note the order of $\mathrm{d}x$ and $\mathrm{d}y$ in Equation (27.1). The simple interchange of limits is only possible because in this example the region $R$ is a rectangle.

When evaluating a double integral over a *rectangular* region $R$, the integration may be carried out in any order, that is

$$\iint_R f(x, y)\,\mathrm{d}x\,\mathrm{d}y = \iint_R f(x, y)\,\mathrm{d}y\,\mathrm{d}x$$

The double integral in Example 27.12 could have the following interpretation. Consider the surface $z = x + 2y$, for $0 \leqslant y \leqslant 2$, $1 \leqslant x \leqslant 4$, as shown in Figure 27.11. In this example the surface is a plane but the theory applies to more general surfaces. The variable $z$ represents the height of the surface above the point $(x, y)$ in the $x$–$y$ plane. For example, consider a point in the $x$–$y$ plane, say (2, 3), that is $x = 2$, $y = 3$. Then at (2, 3), $z = x + 2y = 2 + 2(3) = 8$. Thus the point on the surface directly above (2, 3) is 8 units from (2, 3).

Let us now consider $\mathrm{d}x\,\mathrm{d}y$. We call $\mathrm{d}x\,\mathrm{d}y$ an **element of area**. It is a rectangle with dimensions $\mathrm{d}x$ and $\mathrm{d}y$ and area $\mathrm{d}x\,\mathrm{d}y$. Hence $z\,\mathrm{d}x\,\mathrm{d}y$ represents the volume of a rectangular column of base $\mathrm{d}x\,\mathrm{d}y$. As we integrate with respect to $x$ for $1 \leqslant x \leqslant 4$ and integrate with respect to $y$ for $0 \leqslant y \leqslant 2$ we are effectively summing all such volumes. Thus

$$\int_{y=0}^{y=2} \int_{x=1}^{x=4} x + 2y\,\mathrm{d}x\,\mathrm{d}y$$

represents the volume bounded by the surface $z = x + 2y$ and the region $R$ in the $x$–$y$ plane.

**Example 27.13** Sketch the region $R$ over which we would evaluate the integral

$$\int_{y=0}^{y=1} \int_{x=0}^{x=2-2y} f(x, y)\,\mathrm{d}x\,\mathrm{d}y$$

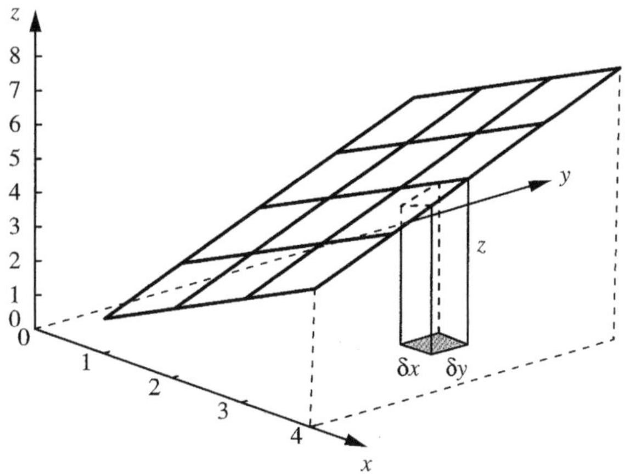


**Figure 27.11** The surface $z = x + 2y$, $0 \leqslant y \leqslant 2$, $1 \leqslant x \leqslant 4$; the quantity $z\,\mathrm{d}x\,\mathrm{d}y$ is the volume of the rectangular column with base area $\mathrm{d}x\,\mathrm{d}y$.

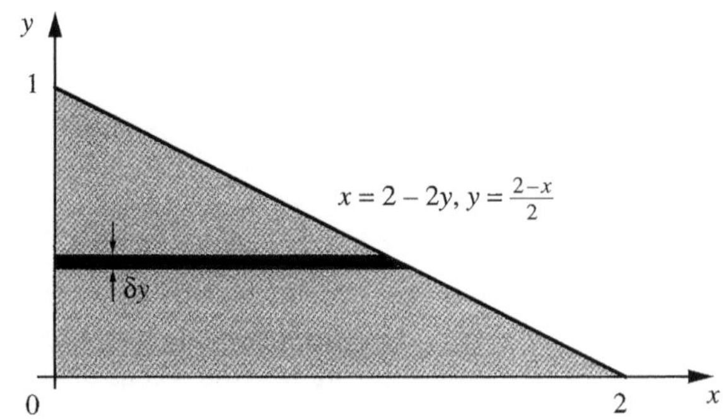


**Figure 27.12** The region over which the integration in Example 27.14 is performed.

**Solution** First consider the outer integral. The restriction on $y$ means that interest can be confined to the horizontal strip $0 \leqslant y \leqslant 1$. Then examine the inner integral. The lower limit on $x$ means that we need only consider values of $x$ greater than or equal to 0. The upper $x$ limit depends upon the value of $y$. If $y = 0$ this upper limit is $x = 2 - 2y = 2$. If $y = 1$ the upper limit is $x = 2 - 2y = 0$. At any other intermediate value of $y$ we can calculate the corresponding upper $x$ limit. This upper limit will lie on the straight line $x = 2 - 2y$. With this information the region of integration can be sketched. The region is shown in Figure 27.12 and is seen to be triangular.

**Example 27.14** Evaluate

$$\int_{y=0}^{y=1} \int_{x=0}^{x=2-2y} 4x + 5\,\mathrm{d}x\,\mathrm{d}y$$

over the region described in Example 27.13.

**Solution** We first perform the inner integral

$$\int_{x=0}^{x=2-2y} 4x + 5\,\mathrm{d}x$$

integrating with respect to $x$. This gives

$$\begin{aligned}[2x^2 + 5x]_{x=0}^{x=2-2y} &= 2(2-2y)^2 + 5(2-2y) - 0 \\ &= 8y^2 - 26y + 18\end{aligned}$$

Next we perform the outer integral

$$\int_{y=0}^{y=1} 8y^2 - 26y + 18\,\mathrm{d}y = \left[\frac{8y^3}{3} - \frac{26y^2}{2} + 18y\right]_0^1$$

$$= \frac{8}{3} - \frac{26}{2} + 18$$

$$= 7.667$$

The region of integration is shown in Figure 27.12. The first integral, with respect to $x$, corresponds to integrating along the horizontal strip from $x = 0$ to $x = 2 - 2y$. Then as $y$ varies from 0 to 1 in the second integral, the horizontal strips will cover the entire region.

---

If we wish to change the order in which the integration is carried out, care must be taken with the limits of a non-rectangular region. Consider again Figure 27.12. The line $x = 2 - 2y$ can be written as $y = \dfrac{2-x}{2}$. We can describe the region $R$ by restricting attention to the vertical strip $0 \leqslant x \leqslant 2$, and then letting $y$ vary from 0 up to $\dfrac{2-x}{2}$, that is

$$\int_{x=0}^{x=2} \int_{y=0}^{y=(2-x)/2} 4x + 5\,\mathrm{d}y\,\mathrm{d}x$$

You should check by evaluating this integral that the same result is obtained as in Example 27.14.

**Example 27.15** Evaluate the double integral of $f(x, y) = x^2 + 3xy$ over the region $R$ indicated in Figure 27.13 by

(a) integrating first with respect to $x$, and then with respect to $y$,

(b) integrating first with respect to $y$, and then with respect to $x$.

**Solution** (a) If we integrate first with respect to $x$ we must select an arbitrary horizontal strip as shown in Figure 27.13 and integrate in the $x$ direction. On OB $y = x$ so that the lower limit of the $x$ integration is $x = y$. On AB, $x = 1$ so the upper limit is $x = 1$. Therefore

$$\int_{x=y}^{x=1} x^2 + 3xy\,\mathrm{d}x = \left[\frac{x^3}{3} + \frac{3x^2y}{2}\right]_y^1$$

$$= \left(\frac{1}{3} + \frac{3y}{2}\right) - \left(\frac{y^3}{3} + \frac{3y^3}{2}\right)$$

$$= \frac{1}{3} + \frac{3y}{2} - \frac{11y^3}{6}$$

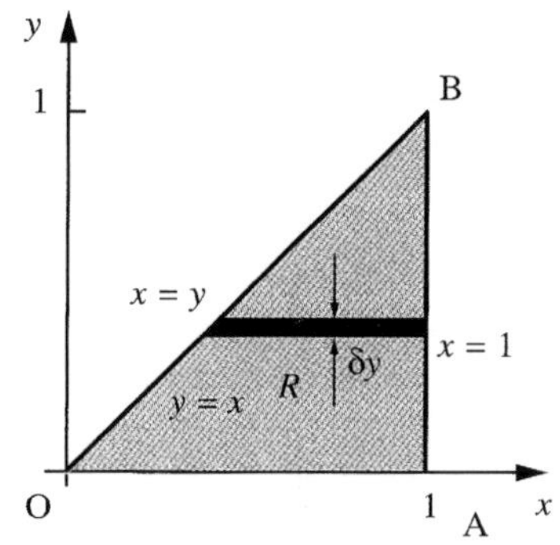


Figure 27.13 The integral with respect to $x$ has limits $x = y$ and $x = 1$.

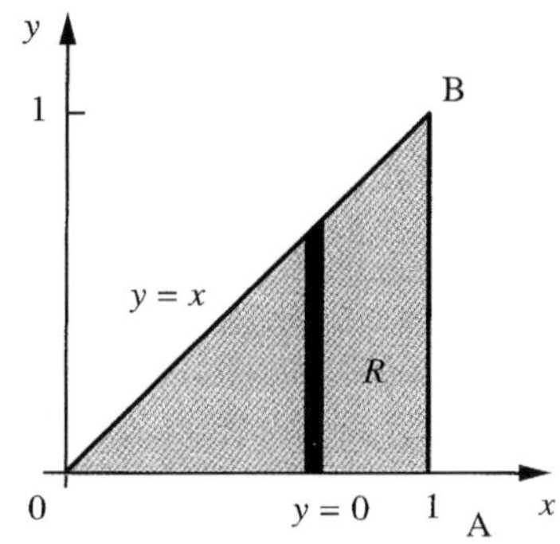


Figure 27.14 We integrate along a vertical strip from $y = 0$ to $y = x$.

As $y$ varies from 0 to 1 the horizontal strips will cover the entire region. Hence the limits of integration of the $y$ integral are 0 and 1. So

$$\int_{y=0}^{y=1} \frac{1}{3} + \frac{3y}{2} - \frac{11}{6}y^3 \, dy = \left[\frac{1}{3}y + \frac{3}{4}y^2 - \frac{11y^4}{24}\right]_0^1$$

$$= \frac{1}{3} + \frac{3}{4} - \frac{11}{24}$$

$$= \frac{15}{24}$$

$$= \frac{5}{8}$$

that is,

$$\int_{y=0}^{y=1} \int_{x=y}^{x=1} x^2 + 3xy \, dx \, dy = \frac{5}{8}$$

(b) If we choose to integrate with respect to $y$ first we must select an arbitrary vertical strip as shown in Figure 27.14. At the lower end of the strip $y = 0$. At the upper end $y = x$.

To integrate along the strip we evaluate

$$\int_{y=0}^{y=x} x^2 + 3xy \, dy = \left[x^2 y + \frac{3xy^2}{2}\right]_0^x = x^3 + \frac{3x^3}{2} = \frac{5x^3}{2}$$

We add contributions of all such vertical strips by integrating with respect to $x$ from $x = 0$ to $x = 1$:

$$\int_0^1 \frac{5x^3}{2} \, dx = \left[\frac{5x^4}{8}\right]_0^1 = \frac{5}{8}$$

We see that the prudent selection of the order of integration can yield substantial savings in the effort required.

### 27.6.2 Triple integrals

The techniques we have used for evaluating double integrals can be generalized naturally to **triple integrals**. Whereas double integrals are evaluated over two-dimensional regions, triple integrals are evaluated over volumes.

**Example 27.16** Evaluate

$$I = \int_{x=0}^{x=1} \int_{y=0}^{y=1} \int_{z=0}^{z=1} x + y + z \, dz \, dy \, dx$$

**Solution** What is meant by this expression is

$$I = \int_{x=0}^{x=1} \left( \int_{y=0}^{y=1} \left( \int_{z=0}^{z=1} x + y + z \, dz \right) dy \right) dx$$

where, as before, the inner integral is performed first, integrating with respect to $z$, with $x$ and $y$ being treated as constants. So

$$\begin{aligned}
I &= \int_{x=0}^{x=1} \left( \int_{y=0}^{y=1} \left[ xz + yz + \frac{z^2}{2} \right]_0^1 dy \right) dx \\
&= \int_{x=0}^{x=1} \left( \int_{y=0}^{y=1} x + y + \frac{1}{2} dy \right) dx \\
&= \int_{x=0}^{x=1} \left[ xy + \frac{y^2}{2} + \frac{1}{2} y \right]_0^1 dx \\
&= \int_{x=0}^{x=1} x + \frac{1}{2} + \frac{1}{2} dx \\
&= \left[ \frac{x^2}{2} + x \right]_0^1 \\
&= \frac{3}{2}
\end{aligned}$$

Consideration of the limits of integration shows that the integral is evaluated over a unit cube.

---

### 27.6.3 Green's theorem

There is an important relationship between line and double integrals expressed in **Green's theorem in the plane**:

If the functions $P(x, y)$ and $Q(x, y)$ are finite and continuous in a region of the $x$–$y$ plane, $R$, and on its boundary, the closed curve $C$, provided the relevant partial derivatives exist and are continuous in and on $C$, then

$$\oint_C P\,dx + Q\,dy = \iint_R \left(\frac{\partial Q}{\partial x} - \frac{\partial P}{\partial y}\right) dx\,dy$$

where the direction of integration along $C$ is such that the region $R$ is always to the left.

The conditions given in the theorem are present for mathematical completeness. Most of the functions that engineers deal with satisfy these conditions, and so we will not consider these further. The important thing to note is that this relationship states that a line integral around a closed curve can be expressed in terms of a double integral over the region, $R$, enclosed by $C$.

**Example 27.17**

(a) Evaluate $\oint_C xy\,dx + x^2\,dy$ around the sides of the square with vertices D(0, 0), E(1, 0), F(1, 1) and G(0, 1).

(b) Convert the line integral to a double integral and verify Green's theorem.

**Solution**

(a) The path of integration is shown in Figure 27.15. To apply Green's theorem the path of integration should be followed in such a way that the region of integration is always to its left. We must therefore travel anticlockwise around $C$.

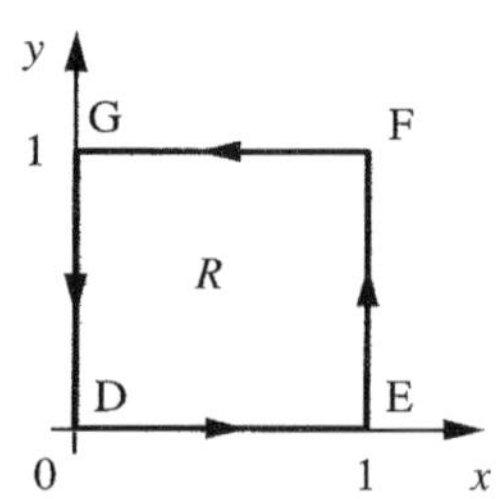

**Figure 27.15** The path $C$ is chosen so that the region $R$ is always to its left.

On DE, $y = 0$, $dy = 0$ and $0 \leqslant x \leqslant 1$.
On EF, $x = 1$, $dx = 0$ and $0 \leqslant y \leqslant 1$.
On FG, $y = 1$, $dy = 0$ and $x$ decreases from 1 to 0.
On GD, $x = 0$, $dx = 0$ and $y$ decreases from 1 to 0.

The integral around the curve $C$ can then be written as

$$\oint_C = \int_D^E + \int_E^F + \int_F^G + \int_G^D$$

Therefore

$$\oint_C xy\,dx + x^2\,dy = 0 + \int_0^1 1\,dy + \int_1^0 x\,dx + 0$$

$$= [y]_0^1 + \left[\frac{x^2}{2}\right]_1^0$$

$$= 1 - \frac{1}{2}$$

$$= \frac{1}{2}$$

(b) Applying Green's theorem with $P(x, y) = xy$ and $Q(x, y) = x^2$ we can convert the line integral into a double integral. Note that $\dfrac{\partial Q}{\partial x} = 2x$ and $\dfrac{\partial P}{\partial y} = x$. Clearly the region of integration is the square $R$. We find

$$\oint_C xy\,dx + x^2\,dy = \iint_R (2x - x)\,dx\,dy$$
$$= \int_0^1 \int_0^1 x\,dx\,dy$$
$$= \int_0^1 \left[\frac{x^2}{2}\right]_0^1 dy$$
$$= \int_0^1 \frac{1}{2}\,dy$$
$$= \left[\frac{1}{2}y\right]_0^1$$
$$= \frac{1}{2}$$

We see that the same result as that in part (a) is obtained and so Green's theorem has been verified.

---

## Exercises 27.6

1. Evaluate

(a) $\displaystyle\int_0^1 \int_0^3 z^2\,dx\,dz$

(b) $\displaystyle\int_0^4 \int_0^2 x\,dy\,dz$

(c) $\displaystyle\int_1^2 \int_2^3 x^2y + 1\,dx\,dy$

(d) $\displaystyle\int_{-1}^1 \int_2^3 \frac{y}{x}\,dx\,dy$

2. $R$ is the shaded region shown in Figure 27.16. Evaluate $\iint_R x + \sqrt{y}\,dx\,dy$

(a) performing the integration with respect to $x$ first,

(b) performing the integration with respect to $y$ first.

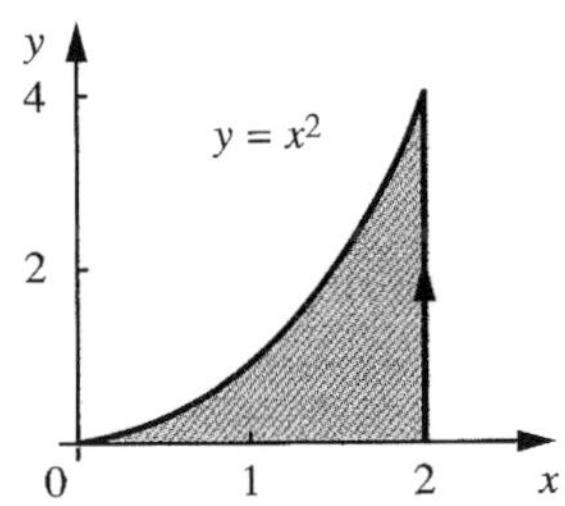


**Figure 27.16** The region of integration for Question 2.

3. Evaluate $\iint_R (5x^2 + 2y^2)\,dx\,dy$ where $R$ is the interior of the triangular region bounded by A(1, 1), B(2, 0) and C(2, 2).

4. (a) Sketch the region of integration of the double integral

$$\int_1^3 \int_1^{\sqrt{4-y}} y\,dx\,dy$$

(b) Evaluate the integral by first reversing the order of integration.

5 Evaluate

$$\int_{-1}^{1}\int_{1}^{5}(x^2+y^2)\,dx\,dy$$

6 Evaluate

$$\iint_R (x^2+y^2)\,dx\,dy$$

over the triangular region $R$ with vertices at (0, 0), (2, 0) and (1, 1).

7 Evaluate

$$\int_R (x+2y)^{-1/2}\,dx\,dy$$

over the region $R$ given by $x - 2y \leqslant 1$ and $x \geqslant y^2 + 1$.

8 Evaluate $\oint_C (\sin x + \cos y)\,dx + 4e^x\,dy$ where $C$ is the boundary of the triangle formed by the points (1, 0), (3, 0) and (3, 2). By converting this line integral into a double integral, verify Green's theorem.

9 Evaluate the line integral

$$\oint_C (x+y)\,dx + 3xy\,dy$$

where $C$ is the boundary of the triangle formed by the points (0, 0), (2, 0) and (0, 5). Express the line integral in terms of an appropriate double integral and evaluate this. Verify Green's theorem.

## Solutions

1 (a) 1

(b) $8x$

(c) 10.5

(d) 0

2 (a) $\frac{20}{3}$

(b) $\frac{20}{3}$

3 $\frac{33}{2}$

4 (b) 1.35435

5 $\frac{256}{3}$

6 $\frac{4}{3}$

7 $\frac{2}{3}$. The region $R$ is shown in Figure S.21.

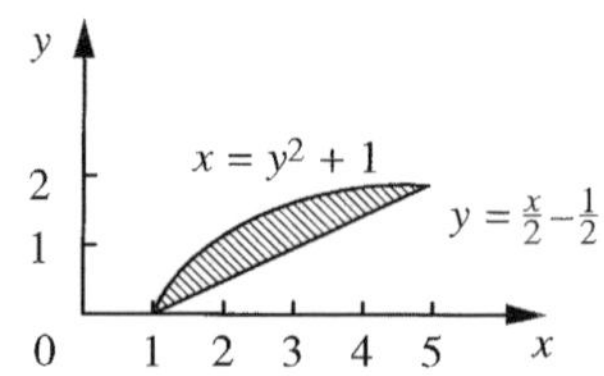


**Figure S.21**

8 92.306

9 20

# 27.7 Some simple volume and surface integrals

Volume and surface integrals arise frequently in electromagnetism and fluid mechanics. We will illustrate these concepts through some simple examples. For a thorough treatment of more general cases you will need to refer to a more advanced text.

**Example 27.18** **The mass of a solid object**

Consider a solid object such as that shown in Figure 27.17. The density, $\rho$, of this object may vary from point to point. So, at any point $P$ with coordinates $(x, y, z)$, the density is a function of position, that is $\rho = \rho(x, y, z)$. Since density is a scalar, this is an example of a scalar field, like those discussed in Section 7.4.

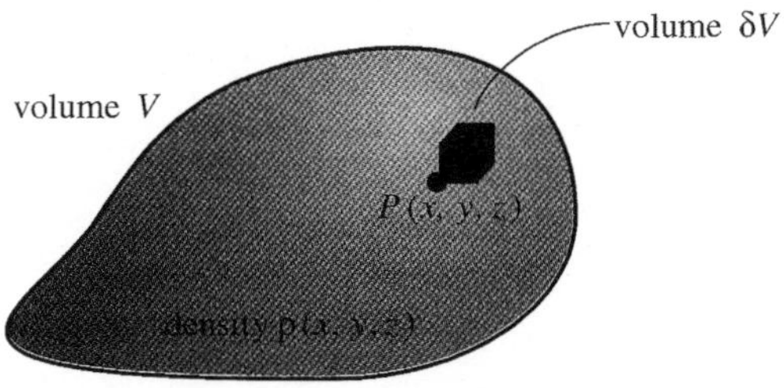


**Figure 27.17** The total mass of a body is found by summing, or integrating, throughout the whole volume.

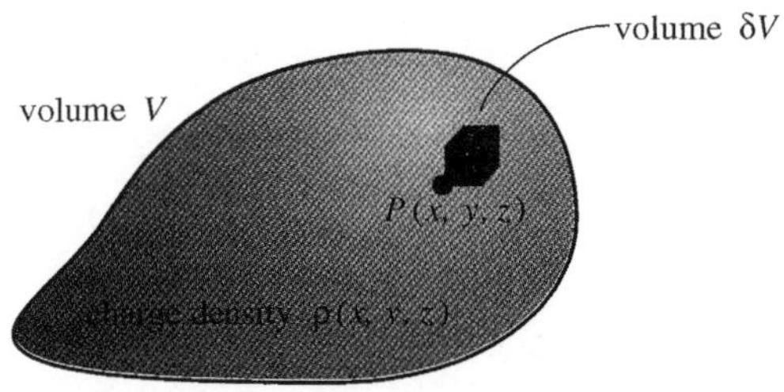


**Figure 27.18** The total charge enclosed is found by summing, or integrating, throughout the whole volume.

Suppose we select a very small piece of this object having volume $\delta V$ and located at $P(x, y, z)$. Recall from elementary physics that

$$\text{density} = \frac{\text{mass}}{\text{volume}}$$

Then the mass of this small piece, $\delta m$, is given by

$$\delta m = \rho\,\delta V$$

If we wish to calculate the total mass, $M$, of the object we must sum all such contributions from the entire volume. This is found by integrating throughout the volume. We write this as

$$\text{total mass, } M = \int_V \rho\,\mathrm{d}V$$

This is an example of a **volume integral**, so called because the integration is performed throughout the volume. It will usually take the form of a triple integral such as those discussed in Section 27.6.2. Technically, there are three integral signs, but for brevity these have been replaced by the single $\int_V$ where it is to be understood that the integral is to be performed over a volume. In any specific problem care must be taken to ensure that the entire volume is included when the integration is performed.

For example, consider the case of a solid cube with sides of length 1 unit. Let one corner be positioned at the origin and let the edges coincide with the positive $x$, $y$ and $z$ axes. Suppose the density of the cube varies from point to point, and is given by $\rho(x, y, z) = x + y + z$. Then the integral which gives the mass of the cube is $\int_V (x + y + z)\,\mathrm{d}V$, where the volume $V$ is the region occupied by the cube. This integral has been evaluated in Example 27.16 and found to be $\frac{3}{2}$, representing the mass of the cube.

**Example 27.19** **The electric charge enclosed in a region**

Suppose electric charge is distributed throughout a volume, $V$, and at any point has charge density $\rho(x, y, z)$. Charge density is a scalar field.

Suppose we select a very small portion having volume $\delta V$ and located at $P(x, y, z)$ as shown in Figure 27.18. The charge in this portion, $\delta Q$, is given by

$$\delta Q = \rho\,\delta V$$

**Figure 27.19**
The vector field **v** represents fluid velocity and $S$ is an imaginary surface through which the fluid flows.

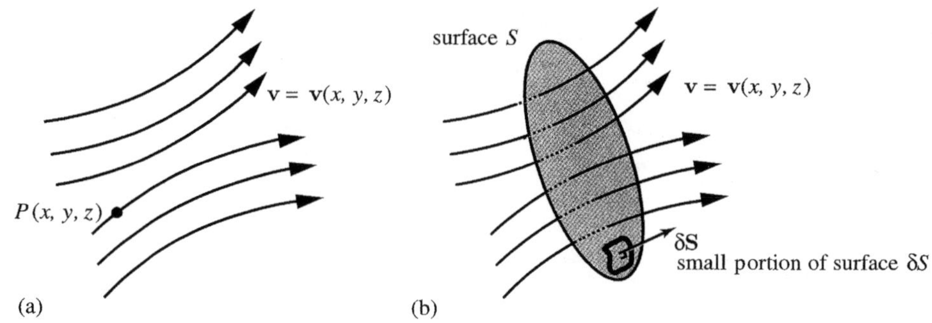


If we wish to calculate the total charge enclosed within the volume, we must sum all such contributions from the entire volume. This is found by integrating throughout the volume. We write this as

$$\text{total charge, } Q = \int_V \rho \, \mathrm{d}V$$

This is another example of a volume integral.

**Example 27.20**

## Fluid flow across a surface

Figure 27.19(a) represents the motion of a body of fluid throughout a region. At any point $P(x, y, z)$ fluid will be moving with a certain speed in a certain direction. So, each small fluid element has a particular velocity **v**, which varies with position, that is $\mathbf{v} = \mathbf{v}(x, y, z)$. This is an example of a vector field, as discussed in Section 7.4.

In Figure 27.19(b) we have placed an imaginary surface, $S$, within the flow and it is reasonable to ask 'what is the volume of fluid which crosses this surface in any given time?' Suppose we select a very small portion of the surface having area $\delta S$. Note that $\delta S$ is a scalar. We can also define an associated vector $\delta\mathbf{S}$, which has magnitude $\delta S$ and whose direction is normal to this portion of the surface. The component of fluid velocity in the direction of $\delta\mathbf{S}$ is given by the scalar product $\mathbf{v} \cdot \widehat{\delta\mathbf{S}}$ where $\widehat{\delta\mathbf{S}}$ is a unit vector in the direction of $\delta\mathbf{S}$. The volume of fluid crossing this portion each second is $\mathbf{v} \cdot \delta\mathbf{S}$. This is also known as the **flux** of **v**. If we wish to calculate the total flux through the surface $S$ we must sum all such contributions over the entire surface. This is found by integrating over the surface. We write this as

$$\text{volume flow per second} = \text{total flux} = \int_S \mathbf{v} \cdot \mathrm{d}\mathbf{S}$$

This is an example of a **surface integral**, so called because we must integrate over a surface. It will usually take the form of a double integral such as those discussed in Section 27.6.1. Technically, there are two integral signs, but for brevity these have been replaced by the single $\int_S$ where it is to be understood that the integral is to be performed over the surface $S$. In any specific problem care must be taken to ensure that the entire surface is included when the integration is performed. The double integrals evaluated in Section 27.6 are special cases of surface integrals, in which the surface is a plane region (the $x$–$y$ plane).

For example, suppose the velocity field is given by $\mathbf{v} = (x + 2y)\mathbf{k}$. This represents a flow in the $z$ direction whose magnitude varies with $x$ and $y$. Suppose $S$ is the plane

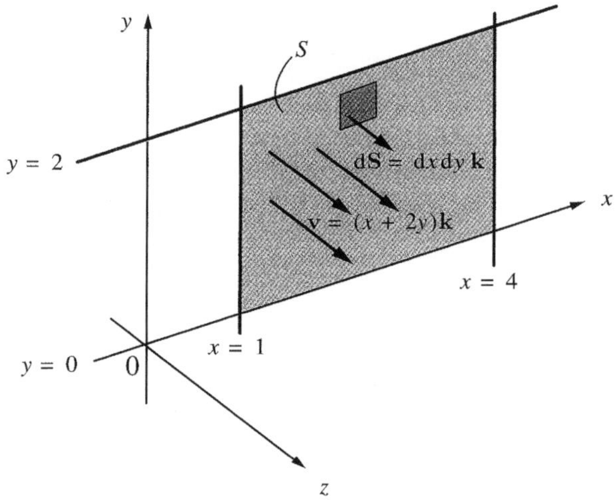


**Figure 27.20** The vector field **v** represents fluid flowing across the surface $S$. The integral over the surface of $\mathbf{v} \cdot \mathrm{d}\mathbf{S}$ gives the volume flow per second across $S$.

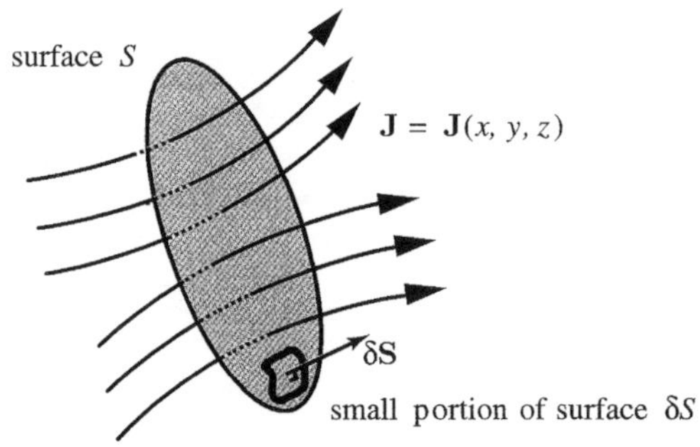


**Figure 27.21** The electric current through a surface is obtained using a surface integral.

surface defined by $1 \leqslant x \leqslant 4$, $0 \leqslant y \leqslant 2$, $z = 0$. This surface is shown in Figure 27.20. Note that the normal to this surface is parallel to the $z$ axis and so we can write $\mathrm{d}\mathbf{S} = \mathrm{d}x\,\mathrm{d}y\,\mathbf{k}$. Then

$$\begin{aligned}\mathbf{v} \cdot \mathrm{d}\mathbf{S} &= (x + 2y)\mathbf{k} \cdot \mathrm{d}x\,\mathrm{d}y\,\mathbf{k} \\ &= (x + 2y)\,\mathrm{d}x\,\mathrm{d}y\end{aligned}$$

The surface integral which gives the flux of **v** through $S$ is

$$\int_{y=0}^{y=2} \int_{x=1}^{x=4} (x + 2y)\,\mathrm{d}x\,\mathrm{d}y$$

Note how the limits of integration are chosen so that contributions from the whole surface are included. This integral has already been evaluated in Example 27.12 and found to be 27. This represents the volume flow per second through $S$.

**Example 27.21** **Electric current density**

Electric current is the flow of electric charges. Figure 27.21 represents an electric current flowing across a surface $S$.

If $\rho(x, y, z)$ is the charge density at a point, and $\mathbf{v}(x, y, z)$ is the velocity of the charges, then the quantity **J** defined as

$$\mathbf{J} = \rho\mathbf{v}$$

is called the current density. Suppose we select a very small portion of the surface having area $\delta S$. Note that $\delta S$ is a scalar. Suppose we define a vector, $\delta\mathbf{S}$, which has magnitude $\delta S$ and which is normal to this portion of surface. The component of current density in the direction of $\delta\mathbf{S}$ is given by the scalar product $\mathbf{J} \cdot \widehat{\delta\mathbf{S}}$. The current crossing this portion is $\mathbf{J} \cdot \delta\mathbf{S}$. If we wish to calculate the total current, $I$, through the surface $S$ we must sum all such contributions over the entire surface. This is found by integrating over the surface. We write this as

$$\text{current, } I = \int_S \mathbf{J} \cdot \mathrm{d}\mathbf{S}$$

This is an example of a **surface integral**.

**Example 27.22** **Electric flux and Gauss's law**

Electric charges produce an electric field, $\mathbf{E}$, which can be visualized by drawing lines of force. Suppose we surround a region containing charges with a surface $S$. The flux of $\mathbf{E}$ through $S$ is a measure of the number of lines of force passing through it. The flux is given by

$$\text{flux} = \int_S \mathbf{E} \cdot \mathrm{d}\mathbf{S}$$

Gauss's law states that the total flux out of any closed surface is proportional to the total charge enclosed. So consider a closed surface in free space, enclosing a volume $V$. The total charge enclosed in $V$ is given by the volume integral

$$\text{total charge} = \int_V \rho \, \mathrm{d}V$$

Gauss's law then states:

$$\oint_S \mathbf{E} \cdot \mathrm{d}\mathbf{S} = \frac{1}{\varepsilon_0} \int_V \rho \, \mathrm{d}V$$

where $\varepsilon_0$ is the permittivity of free space. The notation $\oint$ indicates that the surface is a closed surface. Note how a surface integral can be expressed as a volume integral. This relationship is generalized in the divergence theorem in the following section.

**Example 27.23** A vector field is given by $\mathbf{v} = x^2\mathbf{i} + \frac{1}{2}y^2\mathbf{j} + \frac{1}{2}z^2\mathbf{k}$.

(a) Find div $\mathbf{v}$.

(b) Evaluate $\int_V \operatorname{div} \mathbf{v} \, \mathrm{d}V$ where $V$ is the unit cube $0 \leqslant x \leqslant 1, 0 \leqslant y \leqslant 1, 0 \leqslant z \leqslant 1$.

**Solution** (a) $\operatorname{div} \mathbf{v} = 2x + y + z$.

(b) We seek $\int_V (2x + y + z) \, \mathrm{d}V$ where $V$ is the given unit cube. The small element of volume $\mathrm{d}V$ is equal to $\mathrm{d}z \, \mathrm{d}y \, \mathrm{d}x$. With appropriate limits of integration the integral becomes

$$\int_{x=0}^{x=1} \int_{y=0}^{y=1} \int_{z=0}^{z=1} (2x + y + z) \, \mathrm{d}z \, \mathrm{d}y \, \mathrm{d}x$$

This is a triple integral of the kind evaluated in Section 27.6.2.

$$\int_{x=0}^{x=1}\int_{y=0}^{y=1}\int_{z=0}^{z=1}(2x+y+z)\,\mathrm{d}z\,\mathrm{d}y\,\mathrm{d}x = \int_{x=0}^{x=1}\int_{y=0}^{y=1}\left[2xz+yz+\frac{z^2}{2}\right]_0^1\mathrm{d}y\,\mathrm{d}x$$

$$= \int_{x=0}^{x=1}\int_{y=0}^{y=1}\left(2x+y+\tfrac{1}{2}\right)\mathrm{d}y\,\mathrm{d}x$$

$$= \int_{x=0}^{x=1}\left[2xy+\frac{y^2}{2}+\frac{y}{2}\right]_0^1\mathrm{d}x$$

$$= \int_{x=0}^{x=1} 2x+1\,\mathrm{d}x$$

$$= [x^2+x]_0^1$$

$$= 2$$

**Example 27.24** Evaluate $\oint_S \mathbf{v}\cdot\mathrm{d}\mathbf{S}$ where $\mathbf{v} = x^2\mathbf{i}+\frac{1}{2}y^2\mathbf{j}+\frac{1}{2}z^2\mathbf{k}$ and where $S$ is the surface of the unit cube $0 \leqslant x \leqslant 1$, $0 \leqslant y \leqslant 1$, $0 \leqslant z \leqslant 1$. The vector $\mathrm{d}\mathbf{S}$ should be drawn on each of the six faces in an outward sense.

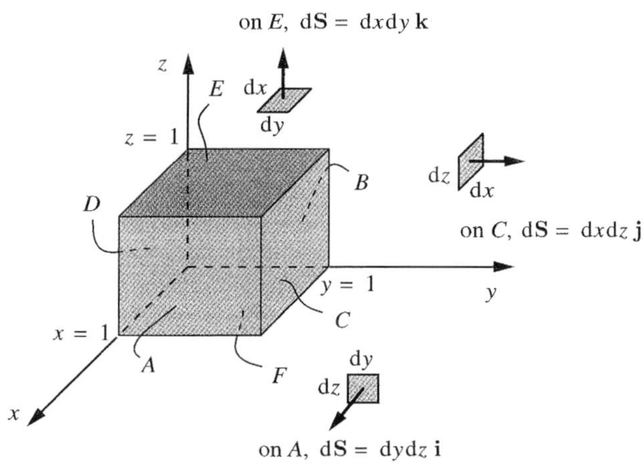


**Figure 27.22** The integral is evaluated over all six surfaces.

**Solution** The cube is shown in Figure 27.22. We evaluate the surface integral over each of the six faces separately and then add the results.

On surface $A$, $x = 1$ and $0 \leqslant y \leqslant 1$, $0 \leqslant z \leqslant 1$. $\mathrm{d}\mathbf{S}$ is a vector normal to this surface, drawn in an outward sense, and so we can write it as $\mathrm{d}y\,\mathrm{d}z\,\mathbf{i}$. Then

$$\mathbf{v}\cdot\mathrm{d}\mathbf{S} = \left(x^2\mathbf{i}+\tfrac{1}{2}y^2\mathbf{j}+\tfrac{1}{2}z^2\mathbf{k}\right)\cdot\mathrm{d}y\,\mathrm{d}z\,\mathbf{i}$$

$$= x^2\,\mathrm{d}y\,\mathrm{d}z$$

$$= \mathrm{d}y\,\mathrm{d}z \qquad \text{since on } A,\ x = 1$$

The required surface integral over $A$ is then

$$\int_{z=0}^{z=1}\int_{y=0}^{y=1} 1\,\mathrm{d}y\,\mathrm{d}z = \int_{z=0}^{z=1} [y]_0^1\,\mathrm{d}z$$
$$= 1$$

On surface $B$, $x = 0$ and $0 \leqslant y \leqslant 1$, $0 \leqslant z \leqslant 1$. $\mathbf{dS}$ is a vector normal to this surface and so we can write it as $-\mathrm{d}y\,\mathrm{d}z\,\mathbf{i}$. Then $\mathbf{v}\cdot\mathbf{dS}$ becomes $-x^2\,\mathrm{d}y\,\mathrm{d}z = 0$ since $x = 0$. Over this surface, the integral is zero.

You should verify in a similar manner that over each of $C$ and $E$ the integral is $\frac{1}{2}$, whilst integrals over $D$ and $F$ are zero. The total surface integral is then 2.

## Exercises 27.7

1. Given $\mathbf{F} = -y\mathbf{i} - x\mathbf{k}$ evaluate $\oint_S \mathbf{F}\cdot\mathbf{dS}$ where $S$ is the surface of a unit cube $0 \leqslant x \leqslant 1$, $0 \leqslant y \leqslant 1$, $0 \leqslant z \leqslant 1$.

2. Given $\mathbf{F} = 6xy^2z^2\mathbf{k}$ evaluate $\int_S \mathbf{F}\cdot\mathbf{dS}$ where $S$ is the plane surface $z = 2$, $0 \leqslant x \leqslant 2$, $0 \leqslant y \leqslant 2$. Take the direction of the vector element of area to be $\mathbf{k}$.

3. Evaluate the volume integral $\int_V 6x\,\mathrm{d}V$ where $V$ is the parallelepiped $0 \leqslant z \leqslant 2$, $0 \leqslant x \leqslant 1$, $0 \leqslant y \leqslant 3$.

4. Evaluate $\int_V 1 + z\,\mathrm{d}V$ where $V$ is a unit cube $0 \leqslant x \leqslant 1$, $0 \leqslant y \leqslant 1$, $0 \leqslant z \leqslant 1$.

### Solutions

1. 0
2. 128
3. 18
4. $\frac{3}{2}$

## 27.8 The divergence theorem and Stokes' theorem

There are a number of theorems in vector calculus which allow line, surface and volume integrals to be expressed in alternative forms. One of these, Green's theorem, has been described in Section 27.6.3. This allows a line integral to be written in terms of a double integral. Now we give details of the divergence theorem and Stokes' theorem.

### 27.8.1 The divergence theorem

The divergence theorem relates the integral over a volume, $V$, to an integral over the closed surface, $S$, which surrounds that volume, as illustrated in Figure 27.23.

When calculating such surface integrals vectors drawn normal to the surface should always be drawn in an outward sense, that is away from the enclosed volume. Recall that when a surface is closed the symbol for a surface integral is $\oint_S$.

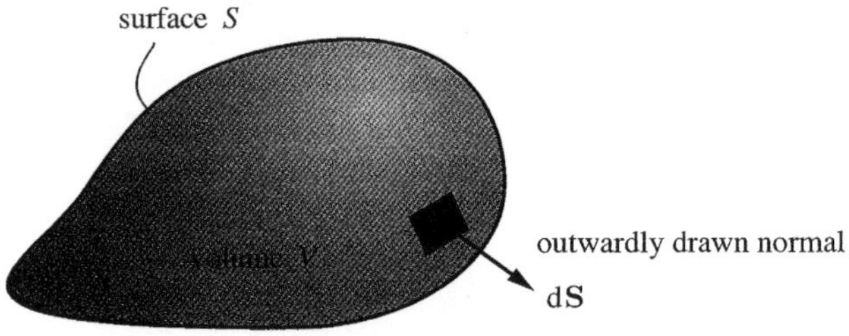


**Figure 27.23** The divergence theorem relates a volume integral to a surface integral.

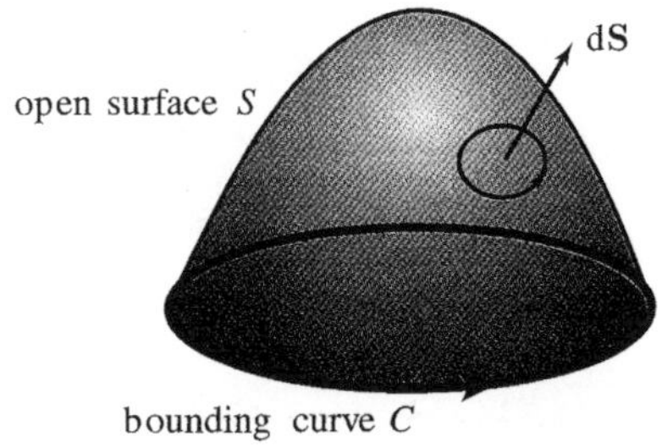


**Figure 27.24** An open surface $S$ with bounding curve $C$.

The **divergence theorem**:

$$\oint_S \mathbf{v} \cdot d\mathbf{S} = \int_V \operatorname{div} \mathbf{v} \, dV$$

**Example 27.25** Verify the divergence theorem for the vector field $\mathbf{v} = x^2\mathbf{i} + \frac{1}{2}y^2\mathbf{j} + \frac{1}{2}z^2\mathbf{k}$ over the unit cube $0 \leqslant x \leqslant 1, 0 \leqslant y \leqslant 1, 0 \leqslant z \leqslant 1$.

**Solution** Firstly we need to evaluate $\oint_S \mathbf{v} \cdot d\mathbf{S}$ where $S$ is the surface of the cube. This integral has been calculated in Example 27.24 and shown to be 2.

Secondly we need to calculate $\int_V \operatorname{div} \mathbf{v} \, dV$ over the volume of the cube. This has been done in Example 27.23 and again the result is 2.

We have verified the divergence theorem that $\oint_S \mathbf{v} \cdot d\mathbf{S} = \int_V \operatorname{div} \mathbf{v} \, dV$.

### 27.8.2 Stokes' theorem

Stokes' theorem relates the integral over an open surface, $S$, to a line integral around a closed curve, $C$, which bounds that surface such as that shown in Figure 27.24.

When a surface is open we adopt the following convention when drawing vectors normal to the surface. When the direction of the normal vector has been specified, use the right-hand screw rule to obtain a sense of turning around the normal vector, as shown in Figure 27.24. Imagine now moving the circle which surrounds the normal vector along the surface until it just meets the curve $C$. Transfer its sense of turning to the curve $C$. When calculating the line integral around the curve $C$, it should be traversed in the same sense.

Specifically consider the two open surfaces shown in Figure 27.25. In both cases we are considering cubes. In the first case the cube has no top face. In the second case the cube has no bottom face. Drawing vector $dx\,dz\,\mathbf{j}$ note that the sense of turning required by the right-hand screw rule is that shown. The curve $C$ must be traversed in the directions shown.

Recall that when a curve is closed the symbol for a line integral is $\oint_C$.

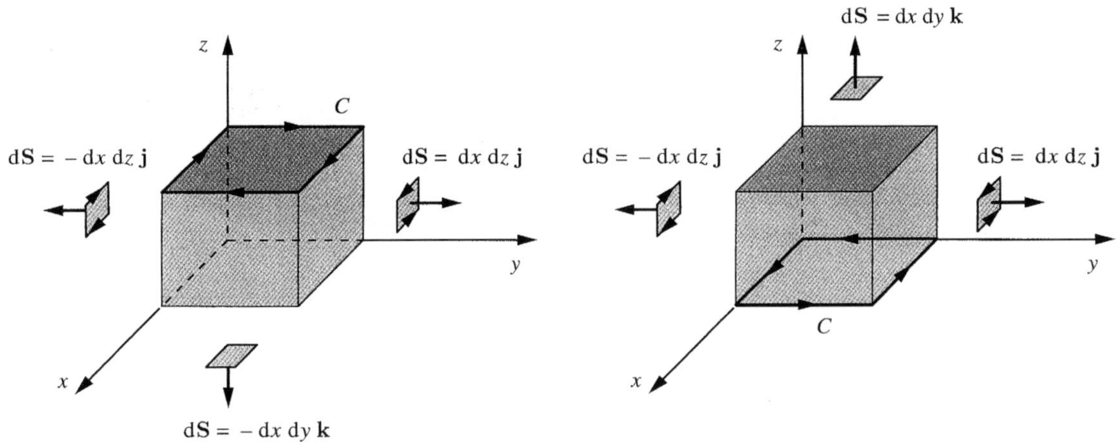


**Figure 27.25** The right-hand screw rule gives the direction in which $C$ must be traversed.

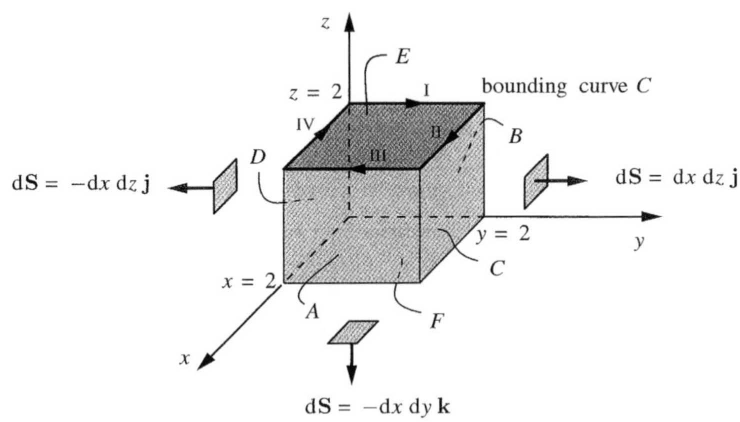


**Figure 27.26** A cubical box with open top bounded by curve $C$.

**Stokes' theorem:**

$$\oint_C \mathbf{v} \cdot d\mathbf{r} = \int_S \text{curl}\,\mathbf{v} \cdot d\mathbf{S}$$

Here $d\mathbf{r}$ is an element of length along the curve $C$. Recall that $d\mathbf{r} = dx\mathbf{i} + dy\mathbf{j} + dz\mathbf{k}$. We have used the symbol $d\mathbf{r}$ rather than $d\mathbf{s}$ as we did in Section 27.2 to avoid confusion with the element of area $d\mathbf{S}$.

**Example 27.26**

A cube of side 2 units is constructed with five solid faces and one open face. It is located in the region defined by $0 \leqslant x \leqslant 2$, $0 \leqslant y \leqslant 2$, $0 \leqslant z \leqslant 2$ and its open face is its top face, bounded by the curve $C$, lying in the plane $z = 2$, as shown in Figure 27.26.

Throughout this region a vector field is given by

$$\mathbf{v} = (x + y)\mathbf{i} + (y + z)\mathbf{j} + (x + z)\mathbf{k}$$

(a) Evaluate $\oint_C \mathbf{v} \cdot d\mathbf{r}$.

(b) Evaluate curl $\mathbf{v}$.

(c) Evaluate $\int_S \text{curl}\,\mathbf{v}\,d\mathbf{S}$, and verify Stokes' theorem.

**Solution** (a) The open face is highlighted in Figure 27.26. It is bounded by the curve $C$ around which the line integral $\oint_C \mathbf{v} \cdot d\mathbf{r}$ must be performed in the sense shown. In this plane $z = 2$ and $dz = 0$, and hence

$$\mathbf{v} \cdot d\mathbf{r} = (x + y)\,dx + (y + 2)\,dy$$

We perform the line integral around $C$ in four stages.

On I, $x = 0$, $dx = 0$ and hence $\mathbf{v} \cdot d\mathbf{r} = (y + 2)\,dy$. Noting that $y$ varies from 0 to 2, the contribution to the line integral is

$$\int_0^2 y + 2\,dy = \left[\frac{y^2}{2} + 2y\right]_0^2 = 6$$

On II, $y = 2$, $dy = 0$ and hence $\mathbf{v} \cdot d\mathbf{r} = (x + 2)\,dx$. Noting that $x$ varies from 0 to 2, the contribution to the line integral is

$$\int_0^2 x + 2\,dx = \left[\frac{x^2}{2} + 2x\right]_0^2 = 6$$

On III, $x = 2$, $dx = 0$ and hence $\mathbf{v} \cdot d\mathbf{r} = (y + 2)\,dy$. Here $y$ varies from 2 to 0. This contribution to the line integral is

$$\int_2^0 y + 2\,dy = \left[\frac{y^2}{2} + 2y\right]_2^0 = -6$$

On IV, $y = 0$, $dy = 0$ and hence $\mathbf{v} \cdot d\mathbf{r} = x\,dx$. Here $x$ varies from 2 to 0. The contribution to the line integral is

$$\int_2^0 x\,dx = \left[\frac{x^2}{2}\right]_2^0 = -2$$

Putting all these results together we find

$$\oint_C \mathbf{v} \cdot d\mathbf{r} = 6 + 6 - 6 - 2 = 4$$

(b)

$$\text{curl}\,\mathbf{v} = \begin{vmatrix} \mathbf{i} & \mathbf{j} & \mathbf{k} \\ \dfrac{\partial}{\partial x} & \dfrac{\partial}{\partial y} & \dfrac{\partial}{\partial z} \\ x + y & y + z & x + z \end{vmatrix} = -\mathbf{i} - \mathbf{j} - \mathbf{k}$$

(c) Now we calculate the surface integral which must be performed over the five solid surfaces separately. Refer to Figure 27.26. On surface $A$, the front face lying in the plane $x = 2$, $\mathrm{d}\mathbf{S} = \mathrm{d}y\,\mathrm{d}z\,\mathbf{i}$. Hence $\mathrm{curl}\,\mathbf{v} \cdot \mathrm{d}\mathbf{S} = -\mathrm{d}y\,\mathrm{d}z$. Then

$$\begin{aligned}\int_A \mathrm{curl}\,\mathbf{v} \cdot \mathrm{d}\mathbf{S} &= \int_{z=0}^{z=2} \int_{y=0}^{y=2} -\mathrm{d}y\,\mathrm{d}z \\ &= \int_{z=0}^{z=2} [-y]_0^2\,\mathrm{d}z \\ &= \int_{z=0}^{z=2} -2\,\mathrm{d}z \\ &= [-2z]_0^2 \\ &= -4\end{aligned}$$

On $B$, the back face lying in the plane $x = 0$, $\mathrm{d}\mathbf{S} = -\mathrm{d}y\,\mathrm{d}z\,\mathbf{i}$. It follows that $\mathrm{curl}\,\mathbf{v} \cdot \mathrm{d}\mathbf{S} = \mathrm{d}y\,\mathrm{d}z$. The required integral over $B$ is

$$\int_{z=0}^{z=2} \int_{y=0}^{y=2} \mathrm{d}y\,\mathrm{d}z = 4$$

On $C$, the right-hand face, $\mathrm{d}\mathbf{S} = \mathrm{d}x\,\mathrm{d}z\,\mathbf{j}$. Hence $\mathrm{curl}\,\mathbf{v} \cdot \mathrm{d}\mathbf{S} = -\mathrm{d}x\,\mathrm{d}z$. The required integral over $C$ is

$$\int_{z=0}^{z=2} \int_{x=0}^{x=2} -\mathrm{d}x\,\mathrm{d}z = -4$$

Similarly, on $D$, the left-hand face, $\mathrm{d}\mathbf{S} = -\mathrm{d}x\,\mathrm{d}z\,\mathbf{j}$. Hence $\mathrm{curl}\,\mathbf{v} \cdot \mathrm{d}\mathbf{S} = \mathrm{d}x\,\mathrm{d}z$. The required integral over $D$ is

$$\int_{z=0}^{z=2} \int_{x=0}^{x=2} \mathrm{d}x\,\mathrm{d}z = 4$$

On surface $F$, the base, $z = 0$ and $\mathrm{d}\mathbf{S} = -\mathrm{d}x\,\mathrm{d}y\,\mathbf{k}$. Hence $\mathrm{curl}\,\mathbf{v} \cdot \mathrm{d}\mathbf{S} = \mathrm{d}x\,\mathrm{d}y$. The required integral over $F$ is

$$\int_{y=0}^{y=2} \int_{x=0}^{x=2} \mathrm{d}x\,\mathrm{d}y = 4$$

Recall that the top surface $E$ is open, and so we have completed the surface integrals. Finally, putting these results together,

$$\int_S \mathrm{curl}\,\mathbf{v} \cdot \mathrm{d}\mathbf{S} = -4 + 4 - 4 + 4 + 4 = 4$$

Note from part (a) that this equals $\oint \mathbf{v} \cdot \mathrm{d}\mathbf{r}$ and so we have verified Stokes' theorem.

## Exercises 27.8

1 Verify Stokes' theorem for the field $\mathbf{v} = xy\mathbf{i} + yz\mathbf{j}$ where $S$ is the surface of the cube $0 \leqslant x \leqslant 1, 0 \leqslant y \leqslant 1, 0 \leqslant z \leqslant 1$ and the face $z = 0$ is open.

2 If $\mathbf{v} = 3x^2\mathbf{i} + xyz\mathbf{j} - 5z\mathbf{k}$ verify Stokes' theorem where $S$ is the surface of the cube $0 \leqslant x \leqslant 1, 0 \leqslant y \leqslant 1, 0 \leqslant z \leqslant 1$ and the face $z = 0$ is open.

3 Suppose $\mathbf{v} = x^3\mathbf{i} - 3x^2y^2z^2\mathbf{j} + (7x + z)\mathbf{k}$ and $S$ is the surface of a cube of side 2 units lying in the region $0 \leqslant x \leqslant 2, 0 \leqslant y \leqslant 2, 0 \leqslant z \leqslant 2$ with an open top in the plane $z = 2$. Verify Stokes' theorem for this field.

4 Consider a cube given by $0 \leqslant x \leqslant 1$, $0 \leqslant y \leqslant 1, 1 \leqslant z \leqslant 2$, above the surface $z = 1$. Suppose the surface $z = 1$ is the only open face. Let $S$ be the surface of this cube. Verify Stokes' theorem for the field $\mathbf{v} = y\mathbf{i} + (x - 2xz)\mathbf{j} - xy\mathbf{k}$. Take $C$ as the square with corners $(0, 0, 1)$, $(1, 0, 1)$, $(1, 1, 1)$, $(0, 1, 1)$ in the plane $z = 1$.

5 Consider that part of the positive octant, that is where $x$, $y$ and $z$ are all positive, bounded by the planes $x = 0$, $y = 0$, $z = 0$ and $x + y + 2z = 2$. Assume that the tetrahedron so formed has three solid faces, and one open face on the plane $x + y + 2z = 2$. Verify Stokes' theorem for the field $\mathbf{v} = x^2\mathbf{i} - 2xz\mathbf{k}$. Take $C$ as the triangle $(2, 0, 0)$, $(0, 2, 0)$, and $(0, 0, 1)$.

## Solutions

When calculating the relevant line and surface integrals the sign of the result depends upon the orientation of the curve $C$.

1 $\oint \mathbf{v} \cdot d\mathbf{r} = \pm\frac{1}{2}$

2 $\oint \mathbf{v} \cdot d\mathbf{r} = 0$

3 $\oint \mathbf{v} \cdot d\mathbf{r} = \pm 128$

4 $\pm 2$

5 $\pm\frac{2}{3}$

## 27.9 Maxwell's equations in integral form

In Section 26.7 Maxwell's equations were stated as examples of the application of vector calculus. In fact, alternative integral forms of these equations are often more useful and these are given here for completeness.

### Equation 1

$$\oint_S \mathbf{D} \cdot d\mathbf{S} = \int_V \rho \, dV$$

where $\mathbf{D}$ = electric flux density, and $\rho$ is electric charge density. Note that the r.h.s. is the total charge enclosed by the volume $V$. This equation states that the total flux crossing a closed surface $S$ which encloses a volume $V$ is equal to the total charge enclosed by the surface. This is also the integral form of Gauss's law. (See Example 27.22 which is obtained by letting $\mathbf{D} = \varepsilon_0\mathbf{E}$.)

### Equation 2

$$\oint_S \mathbf{B} \cdot d\mathbf{S} = 0$$

where $\mathbf{B}$ = magnetic flux density. This law states that the net magnetic flux crossing any closed surface is zero. So whilst charges can be thought of as sources or sinks of electric flux, there are no equivalent sources or sinks of magnetic flux.

**Equation 3**

$$\oint_C \mathbf{E} \cdot \mathbf{dr} = -\frac{\partial}{\partial t}\int_S \mathbf{B} \cdot \mathbf{dS}$$

Note that in the theory of electrostatics, differentiating partially with respect to time always yields zero, and so this equation reduces to $\oint_C \mathbf{E} \cdot \mathbf{dr} = 0$. This is a condition discussed in Section 27.5 and confirms that an electrostatic field is a conservative field.

**Equation 4**

$$\oint_C \mathbf{H} \cdot \mathbf{dr} = \frac{\partial}{\partial t}\int_S \mathbf{D} \cdot \mathbf{dS} + \int_S \mathbf{J} \cdot \mathbf{dS}$$

This is the integral form of Ampère's circuital law. The closed curve $C$ bounds an open surface $S$. A current with density $\frac{\partial \mathbf{D}}{\partial t} + \mathbf{J}$ flows through the surface $S$.

## Exercises 27.9

1. Starting with Maxwell's equation $\nabla \cdot \mathbf{D} = \rho$, by integrating both sides over an arbitrary volume $V$ and using the divergence theorem obtain Equation 1 above.

2. Starting with Maxwell's equation $\nabla \cdot \mathbf{B} = 0$, by integrating both sides over an arbitrary volume $V$ and using the divergence theorem obtain Equation 2 above.

3. Starting with the equation $\nabla \times \mathbf{E} = \mathbf{0}$ for static electric fields, use Stokes' theorem to show that $\oint \mathbf{E} \cdot \mathbf{dr} = 0$.

4. Starting from $\nabla \times \mathbf{H} = \frac{\partial \mathbf{D}}{\partial t} + \mathbf{J}$ and using Stokes' theorem obtain Equation 4.

5. In magnetostatics $\left(\frac{\partial}{\partial t} = 0\right)$, Ampère's law (or the magnetic circuit law) states:

$$\oint_C \mathbf{H} \cdot \mathbf{dr} = I$$

where $I$ is the current enclosed by the closed path $C$. Obtain this law from Equation 4 and using $\int_S \mathbf{J} \cdot \mathbf{dS} = I$.

## Review exercises 27

1. Find $\int_C (2x - y)\,\mathrm{d}x + xy\,\mathrm{d}y$ along the straight line joining $(-1, -1)$ and $(1, 1)$.

2. Find $\int_C (2x + y)\,\mathrm{d}x + y^3\,\mathrm{d}y$

   (a) along the curve $y = x^3$ between $(1, 1)$ and $(2, 8)$, and

   (b) along the straight line joining these points.

3. If $\mathbf{F} = 3xy\mathbf{i} + 2e^x y\mathbf{j}$ find $\int_C \mathbf{F} \cdot \mathbf{ds}$ where $C$ is the straight line $y = 2x + 1$ between $(1, 3)$ and $(4, 9)$.

4. Show that the field $\mathbf{F} = (2x + 1)y\mathbf{i} + (x^2 + x + 1)\mathbf{j}$ is conservative and find a suitable potential function $\phi$.

5. Find $\oint_C (x^2\mathbf{i} + 4xy\mathbf{j}) \cdot \mathbf{ds}$ where $C$ is a closed path in the form of a triangle with vertices at $(0, 0)$, $(3, 0)$ and $(3, 5)$.

6 Find $\int_{y=0}^{y=3}\int_{x=1}^{x=2}(3x-5y)\,dx\,dy$.

7 Find $\int_{y=0}^{y=2}\int_{x=0}^{x=1+y}(2y+5x)\,dx\,dy$.

8 Find
$\int_{x=0}^{x=2}\int_{y=0}^{y=1}\int_{z=0}^{z=3}(x^2+y^2+z^2)\,dz\,dy\,dx$.

9 Evaluate $\iint_R(4y+x^2)\,dx\,dy$ where $R$ is the interior of the square with vertices at (0, 0), (4, 4), (0, 4) and (4, 0).

10 Evaluate $\oint_C e^y\,dx+e^x\,dy$ where $C$ is the boundary of the triangle formed by the lines $y=x$, $y=5$ and $x=0$. By converting this line integral into a double integral verify Green's theorem in the plane.

11 The region $R$ is bounded by the $y$ axis and the lines $y=x$ and $y=3-2x$.

(a) Sketch the region $R$.

(b) Find the volume between the surface $z=xy+1$ and the region $R$.

12 The region $R$ is shown in Figure 27.27. The vector field $\mathbf{F}$ is given by

$$\mathbf{F}=y^2\mathbf{i}+3xy\mathbf{j}$$

(a) Evaluate $\oint_C \mathbf{F}\cdot d\mathbf{s}$ where $C$ is the curve enclosing the region $R$.

(b) Verify Green's theorem in the plane.

(c) The surface, $z(x, y)$, is given by $z=1+x+xy$. Calculate the volume under the surface and above the region $R$.

13 The region $R$ is bounded by the $x$ axis and the curve $y=8+2x-x^2$.

(a) Sketch $R$.

(b) Evaluate $\iint_R 3x+2y\,dx\,dy$

14 Evaluate

(a) $\int_{-1}^{0}\int_{3}^{4}3xy\,dx\,dy$

(b) $\int_{2}^{3}\int_{0}^{2}4+x-y\,dy\,dx$

(c) $\int_{0}^{1}\int_{2y}^{4}x^2+y^2\,dx\,dy$

(d) $\int_{-2}^{-1}\int_{0}^{x^3}1\,dy\,dx$

15 Sketch the regions of integration of the double integrals in Question 14.

16 If $a$, $b$, $c$ and $d$ are constants show that

$$\int_c^d\int_a^b f(x)g(y)\,dx\,dy$$

is identical to

$$\left[\int_a^b f(x)\,dx\right]\left[\int_c^d g(y)\,dy\right]$$

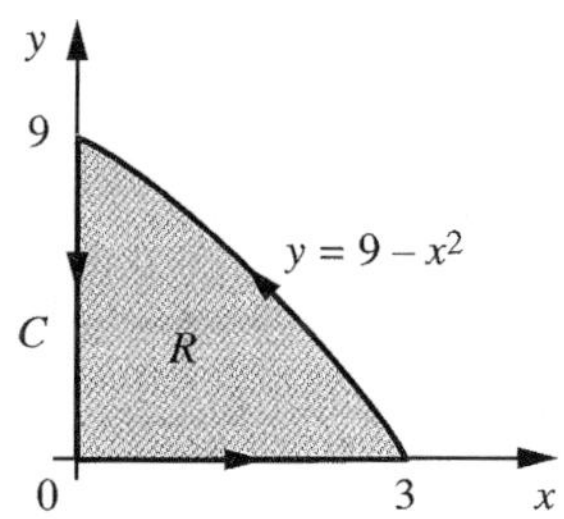


**Figure 27.27** The region $R$ for Question 12.

## Solutions

1 $\frac{2}{3}$

2 (a) 1030.5 (b) 1031.25

3 1666.37

4 $\phi=x^2y+yx+y+c$

5 50

6 −9

7 31

8 28

9 $\frac{640}{3}$

10 −452.239

11 (b) $\frac{17}{8}$

12 (a) 64.8 (c) 99

13 (b) 367.2

14 (a) $-\frac{21}{4}$ (b) 11 (c) 21.5

(d) $-\frac{15}{4}$

# Matrices

# 5 Matrix Algebra

| Chapter 5 | Contents |
|---|---|

## 5.1 Introduction

The solution of simultaneous equations is part of elementary algebra. Many engineering problems can be formulated in terms of simultaneous equations, but in most practical situations the number of equations is extremely large and traditional methods of solution are not feasible. Even the question of whether solutions exist is not easy to answer. Setting the equations up in matrix form provides a systematic way of answering this question and also suggests practical methods of solution. Over the past 150 years or so, a large number of matrix techniques have been developed, and many have been applied to the solution of engineering and scientific problems. The advent of quantum mechanics and the matrix representation developed by Heisenberg did much to stimulate their popularity, since scientists and engineers were then able to appreciate the convenience and economy of matrix formulations.

In many problems the relationships between vector quantities can be represented by matrices. We saw in Chapter 4 that vectors in three dimensions are represented by three numbers $(x_1, x_2, x_3)$ with respect to some coordinate system. If the coordinate system is changed, the representation of the vector changes to another triple $(x'_1, x'_2, x'_3)$, related to the original through a matrix. In this three-dimensional case the matrix is a $3 \times 3$ array of numbers. Such matrices satisfy various addition and multiplication properties, which we shall develop in this chapter, and indeed it is change of axes that provides the most natural way of introducing the matrix product.

In the previous chapter we noted that forces provide an excellent example of vectors and that they have wide use in engineering. When we are dealing with a continuous medium – for instance when we try to specify the forces in a beam or an aircraft wing or the forces due to the flow of a fluid – we have to extend our ideas and define the **stress** at a point. This can be represented by a $3 \times 3$ matrix, and matrix algebra is therefore required for a better understanding of the mathematical manipulations involved.

Perhaps the major impact on engineering applications came with the advent of computers since these are ideally set up to deal with vectors and arrays (matrices), and matrix formulations of problems are therefore already in a form highly suitable for computation. Indeed, all of the widely used aspects of matrices are incorporated into most computer packages, either just for calculation or for the algebraic manipulation of matrices. Packages that are currently popular with students include MATLAB which is highly suitable for numerical computation, and either, MAPLE or the Symbolic Math Toolbox in MATLAB, for algebraic manipulation. These packages are used throughout this chapter.

Many physical problems can be modelled using differential equations, and such models form the basis of much modern science and technology. Most of these equations cannot be solved analytically because of their complexity, and it is necessary to revert to numerical solution. This almost always involves convenient vector and matrix formulations. For instance, a popular method of analysing structures is in terms of finite elements. Finite-element packages have been developed over the past 30 years or so to deal with problems having $10^5$ or more variables. A major part of such packages involves setting up the data in matrix form and then solving the resulting matrix equations. They are now used to design large buildings, to stress aircraft, to determine the flow through a turbine, to study waveguides and in many other situations of great interest to engineers and scientists.

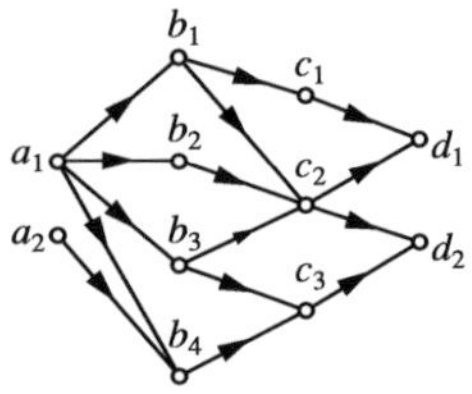


**Figure 5.1**
Simple electrical network.

The analysis of circuits can be very complex. In modern VLSI (Very Large Scale Integration) systems there can be many hundreds of connections. Circuit simulation programs use matrix theory, and have proved to be a most important tool for the analysis of the electrical performance of integrated circuits. Such systems have wide use in CAD (Computer Aided Design) work. The detailed structure of the matrices gives information about the characteristics of the system and provides an indication of how to tackle the solution of the matrix equations. To give an example of a simple electrical network (or road system for that matter) we consider the connections in the situation illustrated in Figure 5.1. They can be represented by arrays with entries of one if a link exists and zero otherwise, thus:

$$\begin{array}{c|cccc} & b_1 & b_2 & b_3 & b_4 \\ a_1 & 1 & 1 & 1 & 1 \\ a_2 & 0 & 0 & 0 & 1 \end{array} \qquad \boldsymbol{P} = \begin{bmatrix} 1 & 1 & 1 & 1 \\ 0 & 0 & 0 & 1 \end{bmatrix}$$

$$\begin{array}{c|ccc} & c_1 & c_2 & c_3 \\ b_1 & 1 & 1 & 0 \\ b_2 & 0 & 1 & 0 \\ b_3 & 0 & 1 & 1 \\ b_4 & 0 & 0 & 1 \end{array} \qquad \boldsymbol{Q} = \begin{bmatrix} 1 & 1 & 0 \\ 0 & 1 & 0 \\ 0 & 1 & 1 \\ 0 & 0 & 1 \end{bmatrix}$$

$$\begin{array}{c|cc} & d_1 & d_2 \\ c_1 & 1 & 0 \\ c_2 & 1 & 1 \\ c_3 & 0 & 1 \end{array} \qquad \boldsymbol{R} = \begin{bmatrix} 1 & 0 \\ 1 & 1 \\ 0 & 1 \end{bmatrix}$$

We now have a concise numerical way of representing the diagram in Figure 5.1. The arrays can be written in matrix form as $\boldsymbol{P}$, $\boldsymbol{Q}$ and $\boldsymbol{R}$, and we can perform algebraic operations on them. The product of matrices will be defined in Section 5.2.4; it is found that the entries in the product $\boldsymbol{PQ}$ give the number of different paths from $a_i$ to $c_j$, and those in $\boldsymbol{PQR}$ the numbers of different paths from $a_i$ to $d_k$.

The matrix product is the most interesting property in the theory, since it enables complicated sets of equations to be written in a convenient and compact way. For instance, three ores are known to contain fractions of Pb, Fe, Cu and Mn as indicated in Figure 5.2. If we mix the ores so that there are $x_1$ kg of ore 1, $x_2$ kg of ore 2 and $x_3$ kg of ore 3 then we can compute the amount of each element as

**Figure 5.2**
Table of fractions in each kilogram of ore.

| | *Ore 1* | *Ore 2* | *Ore 3* |
|---|---|---|---|
| Pb | 0.1 | 0.2 | 0.3 |
| Fe | 0.2 | 0.3 | 0.3 |
| Cu | 0.6 | 0.2 | 0.2 |
| Mn | 0.1 | 0.3 | 0.2 |

$$\left.\begin{aligned}\text{amount of Pb} &= A_{\text{Pb}} = 0.1x_1 + 0.2x_2 + 0.3x_3\\ \text{amount of Fe} &= A_{\text{Fe}} = 0.2x_1 + 0.3x_2 + 0.3x_3\\ \text{amount of Cu} &= A_{\text{Cu}} = 0.6x_1 + 0.2x_2 + 0.2x_3\\ \text{amount of Mn} &= A_{\text{Mn}} = 0.1x_1 + 0.3x_2 + 0.2x_3\end{aligned}\right\} \tag{5.1}$$

We can rewrite the array in Figure 5.2 as a matrix

$$\boldsymbol{A} = \begin{bmatrix} 0.1 & 0.2 & 0.3 \\ 0.2 & 0.3 & 0.3 \\ 0.6 & 0.2 & 0.2 \\ 0.1 & 0.3 & 0.2 \end{bmatrix}$$

and if we define the vectors

$$\boldsymbol{M} = \begin{bmatrix} A_{\text{Pb}} \\ A_{\text{Fe}} \\ A_{\text{Cu}} \\ A_{\text{Mn}} \end{bmatrix} \quad \text{and} \quad \boldsymbol{X} = \begin{bmatrix} x_1 \\ x_2 \\ x_3 \end{bmatrix}$$

then the equations can be written in matrix form

$$\boldsymbol{M} = \boldsymbol{A}\boldsymbol{X}$$

with the product interpreted as in (5.1). The matrix $\boldsymbol{A}$ has 4 rows and 3 columns, so it is called a $4 \times 3$ (read '4 by 3') matrix. $\boldsymbol{M}$ and $\boldsymbol{X}$ are called column vectors; they are $4 \times 1$ and $3 \times 1$ matrices respectively.

## 5.2 Definitions and properties

We can look at the 'ore' problem in a different context. In Section 4.3.2 of Chapter 4, we saw that the equation of a plane can be written in the form

$$\alpha x + \beta y + \gamma z = p$$

where $\alpha$, $\beta$, $\gamma$ and $p$ are constants. The four planes

$$\left.\begin{aligned} 4x + 2y + z &= 7 \\ 2x + y - z &= 5 \\ x + 2y + 2z &= 3 \\ 3x - 2y - z &= 0 \end{aligned}\right\} \tag{5.2}$$

meet in a single point. What are the coordinates of that point? Obviously they are those values of $x$, $y$ and $z$ that satisfy all four of (5.2) simultaneously.

Equations (5.2) provide an example of a mathematical problem that arises in a wide range of engineering problems: the simultaneous solution of a set of linear equations, as mentioned in the introduction. The general form of a linear equation is the sum of a set of variables, each multiplied only by a numerical factor, set equal to a constant. No variable is raised to any power or multiplied by any other variable. In this case we have four linear equations in three variables $x$, $y$ and $z$. We shall see that there is a large body of mathematical theory concerning the solution of such equations.

As is common in mathematics, one of the first stages in solving the problem is to introduce a better notation to represent the problem. In this case we introduce the idea of an array of numbers called a **matrix**. We write

$$\boldsymbol{A} = \begin{bmatrix} 4 & 2 & 1 \\ 2 & 1 & -1 \\ 1 & 2 & 2 \\ 3 & -2 & -1 \end{bmatrix}$$

and call $\boldsymbol{A}$ a $4 \times 3$ matrix; that is, a matrix with four rows and three columns. We also introduce an alternative notation for a vector, writing

$$\boldsymbol{X} = \begin{bmatrix} x \\ y \\ z \end{bmatrix} \quad \text{and} \quad \boldsymbol{b} = \begin{bmatrix} 7 \\ 5 \\ 3 \\ 0 \end{bmatrix}$$

We call these column vectors. Equations (5.2) can then be expressed in the form

$$\boldsymbol{AX} = \boldsymbol{b}$$

where the product of the matrix $\boldsymbol{A}$ and the vector $\boldsymbol{X}$ is understood to produce the left-hand sides of (5.2).

As another example let us seek the relationship between the coordinates of P in the O$xy$ system and the O$x'y'$ system in Figure 5.3. Trigonometry gives

$$x = r\cos\phi, \quad y = r\sin\phi$$

and

$$x' = r\cos(\phi - \theta), \quad y' = r\sin(\phi - \theta)$$

**Figure 5.3**
Change of axes from O$xy$ to O$x'y'$.

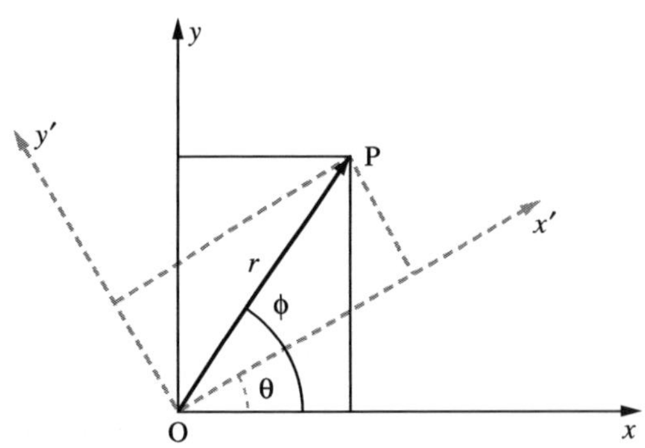

Expanding the trigonometrical expressions gives

$$x' = r\cos\phi\cos\theta + r\sin\phi\sin\theta = x\cos\theta + y\sin\theta \qquad (5.3)$$

$$y' = r\sin\phi\cos\theta - r\cos\phi\sin\theta = y\cos\theta - x\sin\theta$$

If we take

$$\boldsymbol{B} = \begin{bmatrix} \cos\theta & \sin\theta \\ -\sin\theta & \cos\theta \end{bmatrix}, \quad \boldsymbol{X} = \begin{bmatrix} x \\ y \end{bmatrix}, \quad \boldsymbol{X}' = \begin{bmatrix} x' \\ y' \end{bmatrix}$$

then (5.3) can be written as

$$\boldsymbol{X}' = \boldsymbol{BX}$$

We see that a change of axes can be written in a natural manner in matrix form, with $\boldsymbol{B}$ containing all the information about the transformation.

In each of these examples arrays $\boldsymbol{A}$ and $\boldsymbol{B}$ and vectors $\boldsymbol{X}$ and $\boldsymbol{X}'$ appear in a natural way, and the method of multiplication of the arrays and vectors is consistent. We build on this idea to define matrices generally.

## 5.2.1 Definitions

An array of real numbers

$$\boldsymbol{A} = \begin{bmatrix} a_{11} & a_{12} & a_{13} & \dots & a_{1n} \\ a_{21} & a_{22} & a_{23} & \dots & a_{2n} \\ \vdots & \vdots & \vdots & & \vdots \\ a_{m1} & a_{m2} & a_{m3} & \dots & a_{mn} \end{bmatrix} \qquad \textbf{(5.4)}$$

is called an $m \times n$ **matrix**, with $m$ rows and $n$ columns. The entry $a_{ij}$ denotes the **element** in the $i$th row and $j$th column. The element can be real or complex (but in this chapter we deal mainly with real matrices). If $m = n$ then the array is square, and $\boldsymbol{A}$ is then called a **square matrix** of order $n$. If the matrix has one column or one row

$$\boldsymbol{b} = \begin{bmatrix} b_1 \\ b_2 \\ \vdots \\ b_m \end{bmatrix} \quad \text{or} \quad \boldsymbol{c} = [c_1 \quad c_2 \quad \dots \quad c_n] \qquad \textbf{(5.5)}$$

then it is called a **column vector** or a **row vector** respectively. The row vector was used in Chapter 4, Section 4.2.2, as the basic definition of a vector, but in matrix theory a vector is normally taken to be a column vector unless otherwise stated. This slight inconsistency in the notation between vector theory and matrix theory can be inconvenient, but it is so standard in the literature that we must accept it. We have to get used to vectors appearing in several different notations. It is also a common convention to use upper-case letters to represent matrices and lower-case ones for vectors. We shall adopt this convention in this chapter with one exception: the vectors

$$\begin{bmatrix} x \\ y \\ z \end{bmatrix} \quad \text{and} \quad \begin{bmatrix} x \\ y \end{bmatrix}$$

will be denoted by $\boldsymbol{X}$. (Vectors and matrices are further distinguished here by the use of a 'serif' bold face for the former (e.g. $\boldsymbol{b}$) and a 'sans serif' bold face for the latter (e.g. $\mathsf{\mathbf{A}}$).) As an example of the notation used consider the matrix $\mathsf{\mathbf{A}}$ and vector $\boldsymbol{b}$

$$\mathsf{\mathbf{A}} = \begin{bmatrix} 0 & -1 & 2 \\ 3 & 0 & 1 \end{bmatrix} \quad \text{and} \quad \boldsymbol{b} = \begin{bmatrix} 0.15 \\ 1.11 \\ -3.01 \end{bmatrix}$$

The matrix $\mathsf{\mathbf{A}}$ is a $2 \times 3$ matrix with elements $a_{11} = 0$, $a_{12} = -1$, $a_{13} = 2$, $a_{21} = 3$ and so on. The vector $\boldsymbol{b}$ is a column vector with elements $b_1 = 0.15$, $b_2 = 1.11$ and $b_3 = -3.01$.

In a square matrix of order $n$ the diagonal containing the elements $a_{11}, a_{22}, \ldots, a_{nn}$ is called the **principal**, **main** or **leading** diagonal. The sum of the elements of the leading diagonal is called the **trace** of the square matrix $\mathsf{\mathbf{A}}$, that is

$$\text{trace } \mathsf{\mathbf{A}} = a_{11} + a_{22} + \ldots + a_{nn} = \sum_{i=1}^{n} a_{ii}$$

A **diagonal matrix** is a square matrix that has its only non-zero elements along the leading diagonal. (It may have zeros on the leading diagonal also.)

$$\begin{bmatrix} a_{11} & 0 & 0 & \ldots & 0 \\ 0 & a_{22} & 0 & \ldots & 0 \\ 0 & 0 & a_{33} & \ldots & 0 \\ \vdots & \vdots & \vdots & & \vdots \\ 0 & 0 & 0 & \ldots & a_{nn} \end{bmatrix}$$

An important special case of a diagonal matrix is the **unit matrix** or **identity matrix** $\mathsf{\mathbf{I}}$, for which $a_{11} = a_{22} = \ldots = a_{nn} = 1$.

$$\mathsf{\mathbf{I}} = \begin{bmatrix} 1 & 0 & 0 & \ldots & 0 \\ 0 & 1 & 0 & \ldots & 0 \\ 0 & 0 & 1 & \ldots & 0 \\ \vdots & \vdots & \vdots & & \vdots \\ 0 & 0 & 0 & \ldots & 1 \end{bmatrix}$$

The unit matrix can be written conveniently in terms of the Kronecker delta. This is defined as

$$\delta_{ij} = \begin{cases} 1 & \text{if} \quad i = j \\ 0 & \text{if} \quad i \neq j \end{cases}$$

The unit matrix thus has elements $\delta_{ij}$. The notation $\boldsymbol{I}_n$ is sometimes used to denote the $n \times n$ unit matrix where its size is important or not clear.

The **zero** or **null matrix** is the matrix with every element zero, and is written as either 0 or **0**. Sometimes a zero matrix of order $m \times n$ is written $\mathbf{O}_{m \times n}$.

The **transposed matrix** $\boldsymbol{A}^{\mathrm{T}}$ of (5.4) is the matrix with elements $b_{ij} = a_{ji}$ and is written in full as the $n \times m$ matrix

$$\boldsymbol{A}^{\mathrm{T}} = \begin{bmatrix} a_{11} & a_{21} & a_{31} & \dots & a_{m1} \\ a_{12} & a_{22} & a_{32} & \dots & a_{m2} \\ \vdots & \vdots & \vdots & & \vdots \\ a_{1n} & a_{2n} & a_{3n} & \dots & a_{mn} \end{bmatrix}$$

This is just the matrix in (5.4) with rows and columns interchanged. We may note from (5.5) that

$$\boldsymbol{b}^{\mathrm{T}} = [b_1 \quad b_2 \quad \dots \quad b_m] \quad \text{and} \quad \mathbf{c}^{\mathrm{T}} = \begin{bmatrix} c_1 \\ c_2 \\ \vdots \\ c_n \end{bmatrix}$$

so that a column vector is transposed to a row vector and vice versa.

If a square matrix is such that $\boldsymbol{A}^{\mathrm{T}} = \boldsymbol{A}$ then $a_{ij} = a_{ji}$, and the elements are therefore symmetric about the diagonal. Such a matrix is called a **symmetric matrix**; symmetric matrices play important roles in many computations. If $\boldsymbol{A}^{\mathrm{T}} = -\boldsymbol{A}$, so that $a_{ij} = -a_{ji}$, the matrix is called **skew-symmetric** or **antisymmetric**. Obviously the diagonal elements of a skew-symmetric matrix satisfy $a_{ii} = -a_{ii}$ and so must all be zero.

A few examples will illustrate these definitions:

$$\boldsymbol{A} = \begin{bmatrix} 2 & 3 \\ 1 & 2 \\ 4 & 5 \end{bmatrix} \text{ is a } 3 \times 2 \text{ matrix}$$

$$\boldsymbol{A}^{\mathrm{T}} = \begin{bmatrix} 2 & 1 & 4 \\ 3 & 2 & 5 \end{bmatrix} \text{ is a } 2 \times 3 \text{ matrix}$$

$$\boldsymbol{B} = \begin{bmatrix} 1 & 2 & 3 \\ 2 & 3 & 4 \\ 3 & 4 & 5 \end{bmatrix} \text{ is a symmetric } 3 \times 3 \text{ matrix}$$

trace $\boldsymbol{B} = 1 + 3 + 5 = 9$

$$\boldsymbol{C} = \begin{bmatrix} 0 & 7 & -1 \\ -7 & 0 & 4 \\ 1 & -4 & 0 \end{bmatrix} \text{ and } \boldsymbol{C}^{\mathrm{T}} = \begin{bmatrix} 0 & -7 & 1 \\ 7 & 0 & -4 \\ -1 & 4 & 0 \end{bmatrix} \text{ are skew-symmetric } 3 \times 3 \text{ matrices}$$

$$\boldsymbol{D} = \begin{bmatrix} 2 & 0 & 0 \\ 0 & 3 & 0 \\ 0 & 0 & 4 \end{bmatrix} \text{ is a } 3 \times 3 \text{ diagonal matrix}$$

trace $\boldsymbol{D} = 2 + 3 + 4 = 9$

$$\boldsymbol{I} = \begin{bmatrix} 1 & 0 & 0 & 0 \\ 0 & 1 & 0 & 0 \\ 0 & 0 & 1 & 0 \\ 0 & 0 & 0 & 1 \end{bmatrix} \text{ is the } 4 \times 4 \text{ unit matrix (sometimes written } \boldsymbol{I}_4\text{)}$$

## 5.2.2 Basic operations of matrices

### (a) Equality

Two matrices $\boldsymbol{A}$ and $\boldsymbol{B}$ are said to be **equal** if and only if all their elements are the same, $a_{ij} = b_{ij}$ for $1 \leqslant i \leqslant m$, $1 \leqslant j \leqslant n$, and this equality is written as

$$\boldsymbol{A} = \boldsymbol{B}$$

Note that this requires the two matrices to be of the same order $m \times n$.

### (b) Addition and subtraction

Addition of matrices is straightforward; we can only add an $m \times n$ matrix to another $m \times n$ matrix, and an element of the sum is the sum of the corresponding elements. If $\boldsymbol{A}$ has elements $a_{ij}$ and $\boldsymbol{B}$ has elements $b_{ij}$ then $\boldsymbol{A} + \boldsymbol{B}$ has elements $a_{ij} + b_{ij}$.

$$\begin{bmatrix} a_{11} & a_{12} & a_{13} & \cdots \\ a_{21} & a_{22} & a_{23} & \cdots \\ \vdots & \vdots & \vdots & \end{bmatrix} + \begin{bmatrix} b_{11} & b_{12} & b_{13} & \cdots \\ b_{21} & b_{22} & b_{23} & \cdots \\ \vdots & \vdots & \vdots & \end{bmatrix}$$

$$= \begin{bmatrix} a_{11} + b_{11} & a_{12} + b_{12} & a_{13} + b_{13} & \cdots \\ a_{21} + b_{21} & a_{22} + b_{22} & a_{23} + b_{23} & \cdots \\ \vdots & \vdots & \vdots & \end{bmatrix}$$

Similarly for subtraction, $\boldsymbol{A} - \boldsymbol{B}$ has elements $a_{ij} - b_{ij}$.

### (c) Multiplication by a scalar

The matrix $\lambda\boldsymbol{A}$ has elements $\lambda a_{ij}$; that is, we just multiply each element by the scalar $\lambda$

$$\lambda\begin{bmatrix} a_{11} & a_{12} & a_{13} & \dots \\ a_{21} & a_{22} & a_{23} & \dots \\ \vdots & \vdots & \vdots & \end{bmatrix} = \begin{bmatrix} \lambda a_{11} & \lambda a_{12} & \lambda a_{13} & \dots \\ \lambda a_{21} & \lambda a_{22} & \lambda a_{23} & \dots \\ \vdots & \vdots & \vdots & \end{bmatrix}$$

### (d) Properties of the transpose

From the definition, the transpose of a matrix is such that

$$(\boldsymbol{A} + \boldsymbol{B})^{\mathrm{T}} = \boldsymbol{A}^{\mathrm{T}} + \boldsymbol{B}^{\mathrm{T}}$$

Similarly, we observe that

$$(\boldsymbol{A}^{\mathrm{T}})^{\mathrm{T}} = \boldsymbol{A}$$

so that transposing twice gives back the original matrix.

We may note as a special case of this result that for a square matrix $\boldsymbol{A}$

$$(\boldsymbol{A}^{\mathrm{T}} + \boldsymbol{A})^{\mathrm{T}} = (\boldsymbol{A}^{\mathrm{T}})^{\mathrm{T}} + \boldsymbol{A}^{\mathrm{T}} = \boldsymbol{A} + \boldsymbol{A}^{\mathrm{T}}$$

and hence $\boldsymbol{A}^{\mathrm{T}} + \boldsymbol{A}$ must be a symmetric matrix. This proves to be a very useful result, which we shall see used in several places. Similarly, $\boldsymbol{A} - \boldsymbol{A}^{\mathrm{T}}$ is a skew-symmetric matrix, so that any square matrix $\boldsymbol{A}$ may be expressed as the sum of a symmetric and a skew-symmetric matrix:

$$\boldsymbol{A} = \tfrac{1}{2}(\boldsymbol{A} + \boldsymbol{A}^{\mathrm{T}}) + \tfrac{1}{2}(\boldsymbol{A} - \boldsymbol{A}^{\mathrm{T}})$$

### (e) Basic rules of addition

Because the usual rules of arithmetic are followed in the definitions of the sum of matrices and of multiplication by scalars, the

**commutative law** $\boldsymbol{A} + \boldsymbol{B} = \boldsymbol{B} + \boldsymbol{A}$

**associative law** $(\boldsymbol{A} + \boldsymbol{B}) + \boldsymbol{C} = \boldsymbol{A} + (\boldsymbol{B} + \boldsymbol{C})$

and

**distributive law** $\lambda(\boldsymbol{A} + \boldsymbol{B}) = \lambda\boldsymbol{A} + \lambda\boldsymbol{B}$

all hold for matrices.

**Example 5.1** Let

$$\boldsymbol{A} = \begin{bmatrix} 1 & 2 & 1 \\ 1 & 1 & 2 \\ 1 & 1 & 1 \end{bmatrix}, \quad \boldsymbol{B} = \begin{bmatrix} 2 & 1 \\ 1 & 0 \\ 1 & 1 \end{bmatrix}, \quad \boldsymbol{C} = \begin{bmatrix} 0 & 1 & 1 \\ 0 & 0 & 1 \\ 1 & 0 & 0 \end{bmatrix}$$

Find, where possible, (a) $\boldsymbol{A} + \boldsymbol{B}$, (b) $\boldsymbol{A} + \boldsymbol{C}$, (c) $\boldsymbol{C} - \boldsymbol{A}$, (d) $3\boldsymbol{A}$, (e) $4\boldsymbol{B}$, (f) $\boldsymbol{C} + \boldsymbol{B}$, (g) $3\boldsymbol{A} + 2\boldsymbol{C}$, (h) $\boldsymbol{A}^{\mathrm{T}} + \boldsymbol{A}$ and (i) $\boldsymbol{A} + \boldsymbol{C}^{\mathrm{T}} + \boldsymbol{B}^{\mathrm{T}}$.

**Solution** (a) $\boldsymbol{A} + \boldsymbol{B}$ is not possible.

(b) $$\boldsymbol{A} + \boldsymbol{C} = \begin{bmatrix} 1+0 & 2+1 & 1+1 \\ 1+0 & 1+0 & 2+1 \\ 1+1 & 1+0 & 1+0 \end{bmatrix} = \begin{bmatrix} 1 & 3 & 2 \\ 1 & 1 & 3 \\ 2 & 1 & 1 \end{bmatrix}$$

(c) $$\boldsymbol{C} - \boldsymbol{A} = \begin{bmatrix} 0-1 & 1-2 & 1-1 \\ 0-1 & 0-1 & 1-2 \\ 1-1 & 0-1 & 0-1 \end{bmatrix} = \begin{bmatrix} -1 & -1 & 0 \\ -1 & -1 & -1 \\ 0 & -1 & -1 \end{bmatrix}$$

(d) $$3\boldsymbol{A} = \begin{bmatrix} 3 & 6 & 3 \\ 3 & 3 & 6 \\ 3 & 3 & 3 \end{bmatrix}$$

(e) $$4\boldsymbol{B} = \begin{bmatrix} 8 & 4 \\ 4 & 0 \\ 4 & 4 \end{bmatrix}$$

(f) $\boldsymbol{C} + \boldsymbol{B}$ is not possible.

(g) $$3\boldsymbol{A} + 2\boldsymbol{C} = \begin{bmatrix} 3 & 6 & 3 \\ 3 & 3 & 6 \\ 3 & 3 & 3 \end{bmatrix} + \begin{bmatrix} 0 & 2 & 2 \\ 0 & 0 & 2 \\ 2 & 0 & 0 \end{bmatrix} = \begin{bmatrix} 3 & 8 & 5 \\ 3 & 3 & 8 \\ 5 & 3 & 3 \end{bmatrix}$$

(h) $$\boldsymbol{A}^{\mathrm{T}} + \boldsymbol{A} = \begin{bmatrix} 1 & 1 & 1 \\ 2 & 1 & 1 \\ 1 & 2 & 1 \end{bmatrix} + \begin{bmatrix} 1 & 2 & 1 \\ 1 & 1 & 2 \\ 1 & 1 & 1 \end{bmatrix} = \begin{bmatrix} 2 & 3 & 2 \\ 3 & 2 & 3 \\ 2 & 3 & 2 \end{bmatrix}$$

(Note that this matrix is symmetric.)

(i) $\boldsymbol{A} + \boldsymbol{C}^{\mathrm{T}} + \boldsymbol{B}^{\mathrm{T}}$ is not possible.

**Example 5.2** A local roadside cafe serves beefburgers, eggs, chips and beans in four combination meals:

| | | | | |
|---|---|---|---|---|
| *Slimmers* | – | 150 g chips | 100 g beans | 1 burger |
| *Normal* | 1 egg | 250 g chips | 150 g beans | 1 burger |
| *Jumbo* | 2 eggs | 350 g chips | 200 g beans | 2 burgers |
| *Veggie* | 1 egg | 200 g chips | 150 g beans | – |

A party orders 1 slimmer, 4 normal, 2 jumbo and 2 veggie meals. What is the total amount of materials that the kitchen staff need to cook? One of the customers sees the size of a jumbo meal and changes his order to a normal meal. How much less material will the kitchen staff need?

**Solution** The meals written in matrix form are

$$\boldsymbol{s} = \begin{bmatrix} 0 \\ 150 \\ 100 \\ 1 \end{bmatrix}, \quad \boldsymbol{n} = \begin{bmatrix} 1 \\ 250 \\ 150 \\ 1 \end{bmatrix},$$

$$\boldsymbol{j} = \begin{bmatrix} 2 \\ 350 \\ 200 \\ 2 \end{bmatrix}, \quad \boldsymbol{v} = \begin{bmatrix} 1 \\ 200 \\ 150 \\ 0 \end{bmatrix}$$

and hence the kitchen requirements are

$$\boldsymbol{s} + 4\boldsymbol{n} + 2\boldsymbol{j} + 2\boldsymbol{v} = \begin{bmatrix} 10 \\ 2250 \\ 1400 \\ 9 \end{bmatrix}$$

The change in requirements is

$$\boldsymbol{j} - \boldsymbol{n} = \begin{bmatrix} 2 \\ 350 \\ 200 \\ 2 \end{bmatrix} - \begin{bmatrix} 1 \\ 250 \\ 150 \\ 1 \end{bmatrix} = \begin{bmatrix} 1 \\ 100 \\ 50 \\ 1 \end{bmatrix}$$

less materials needed.

Although this may appear to be a rather trivial example, the basic problem is identical to any production process that requires a supply of parts.

All the basic matrix operations may be implemented in MATLAB and MAPLE using simple commands.

MATLAB

A matrix is entered as an array, with row elements separated by a space (or a comma) and each row of elements separated by a semicolon. Thus for example

```
A = [1 2 3; 4 0 5; 7 6 2]
```

gives A as

```
A =
     1  2  3
     4  0  5
     7  6  2
```

The transpose of a matrix is written `A'`, with an apostrophe.

```
A' =
      1  4  7
      2  0  6
      3  5  2
```

and `trace(A)` produces the obvious answer = 3.

Having specified two matrices $\boldsymbol{A}$ and $\boldsymbol{B}$ the usual operations are written

```
C = A + B, C = A - B
```

and multiplication with a scalar as

```
C = 2*A + 3*B
```

MAPLE

There are several ways of setting up arrays in MAPLE the simplest is to use the linear algebra package

```
with (linalg):
array([list of elements]);
```

Thus for example

```
A:=array([[1,2,3],[4,0,5],
[7,6,2]]);
```

produces

```
        1  2  3
A  =    4  0  5
        7  6  2
```

The transpose and trace are obtained from

`transpose(A);` and `trace(A);`

Having specified two matrices $\boldsymbol{A}$ and $\boldsymbol{B}$ the usual operations are written

`C := A + B;` and `C := A - B;`

Because MAPLE is a symbolic package, the *evaluation* of the multiplication of a matrix by a scalar requires the command

```
C:= evalm(2*A + 3*B);
```

## 5.2.3 Exercises

Check your answers using MATLAB or MAPLE whenever possible.

1 Given the matrices

$$\boldsymbol{a} = \begin{bmatrix} 1 \\ 2 \\ 0 \end{bmatrix}, \quad \boldsymbol{b} = [0 \quad 1 \quad 1],$$

$$\boldsymbol{C} = \begin{bmatrix} 3 & 2 & 1 \\ 1 & 2 & -1 \end{bmatrix}, \quad \boldsymbol{D} = \begin{bmatrix} 5 & 6 \\ 7 & 8 \\ 9 & 10 \end{bmatrix}$$

evaluate, where possible, (a) $\boldsymbol{a} + \boldsymbol{b}$, (b) $\boldsymbol{b}^{\mathrm{T}} + \boldsymbol{a}$, (c) $\boldsymbol{b} + \boldsymbol{C}^{\mathrm{T}}$, (d) $\boldsymbol{C} + \boldsymbol{D}$, (e) $\boldsymbol{D}^{\mathrm{T}} + \boldsymbol{C}$.

2 Given the matrices

$$\boldsymbol{A} = \begin{bmatrix} 1 & 0 & 1 \\ 2 & 2 & 0 \\ 0 & 1 & 2 \end{bmatrix} \quad \text{and}$$

$$\boldsymbol{B} = \begin{bmatrix} -1 & 1 & 0 \\ 1 & 0 & -1 \\ 0 & -1 & 1 \end{bmatrix}$$

evaluate $\boldsymbol{C}$ in the three cases.

(a) $\boldsymbol{C} = \boldsymbol{A} + \boldsymbol{B}$ (b) $2\boldsymbol{A} + 3\boldsymbol{C} = 4\boldsymbol{B}$

(c) $\boldsymbol{A} - \boldsymbol{C} = \boldsymbol{B} + \boldsymbol{C}$

**3** Solve for the matrix $\boldsymbol{X}$

$$\boldsymbol{X} - 2\begin{bmatrix} 3 & 2 & -1 \\ 7 & 2 & 6 \end{bmatrix} = \begin{bmatrix} -2 & 3 & 1 \\ 4 & 6 & 2 \end{bmatrix}$$

**4** If

$$\boldsymbol{A} = \begin{bmatrix} 1 & 2 & -3 \\ 5 & 0 & 2 \\ 1 & -1 & 1 \end{bmatrix}, \quad \boldsymbol{B} = \begin{bmatrix} 3 & -1 & 2 \\ 4 & 2 & 5 \\ 2 & 0 & 5 \end{bmatrix}$$

$$\text{and} \quad \boldsymbol{C} = \begin{bmatrix} 4 & 0 & -2 \\ 5 & 3 & 1 \\ 2 & 5 & 4 \end{bmatrix}$$

(a) show that

$$\text{trace}(\boldsymbol{A} + \boldsymbol{B}) = \text{trace}\,\boldsymbol{A} + \text{trace}\,\boldsymbol{B}$$

(b) find $\boldsymbol{D}$ so that $\boldsymbol{A} + \boldsymbol{D} = \boldsymbol{C}$.

(c) verify the associative law

$$(\boldsymbol{A} + \boldsymbol{B}) + \boldsymbol{C} = \boldsymbol{A} + (\boldsymbol{B} + \boldsymbol{C})$$

**5** Find the values of $x$, $y$, $z$ and $t$ from the equation

$$\begin{bmatrix} x & y - x + t \\ t - z & z - 1 \end{bmatrix} = \begin{bmatrix} 1 & 2 \\ 0 & 1 \end{bmatrix}$$

**6** Find the values of $\alpha$, $\beta$, $\gamma$ that satisfy

$$\alpha\begin{bmatrix} 1 \\ 0 \\ 0 \end{bmatrix} + \beta\begin{bmatrix} 1 \\ -1 \\ 0 \end{bmatrix} + \gamma\begin{bmatrix} 0 \\ 1 \\ -1 \end{bmatrix} = \begin{bmatrix} 0 \\ 3 \\ -2 \end{bmatrix}$$

**7** Given the matrix

$$\boldsymbol{A} = \lambda\begin{bmatrix} 1 & 0 \\ 0 & 1 \end{bmatrix} + \mu\begin{bmatrix} 1 & 1 \\ 0 & 1 \end{bmatrix} + v\begin{bmatrix} 0 & 0 \\ 0 & 1 \end{bmatrix}$$

(a) find the value of $\lambda$, $\mu$, $v$ so that $\boldsymbol{A} = \begin{bmatrix} 0 & -1 \\ 0 & 3 \end{bmatrix}$;

(b) show that no solution is possible if

$$\boldsymbol{A} = \begin{bmatrix} 1 & -1 \\ 1 & 0 \end{bmatrix}$$

**8** Market researchers are testing customers' preferences for five products. There are four researchers who are allocated to different groups: researcher $R_1$ deals with men under 40, $R_2$ deals with men over 40, $R_3$ deals with women under 40 and $R_4$ deals with women over 40. They return their findings as a vector giving the number of customers with first preference for a particular product.

| Product | $R_1$ | $R_2$ | $R_3$ | $R_4$ |
|---|---|---|---|---|
| ***a*** | 23 | 32 | 28 | 39 |
| ***b*** | 34 | 22 | 33 | 21 |
| ***c*** | 18 | 21 | 22 | 17 |
| ***d*** | 9 | 15 | 10 | 12 |
| ***e*** | 16 | 10 | 7 | 11 |

Find the average over the whole sample. The company decides that their main target is older women so they weight the returns in the ratio 1 : 1 : 2 : 3; find the weighted average.

**9** A newspaper shop has sales organized in matrix form as

| | Mon | Tues | Weds | Thur | Fri |
|---|---|---|---|---|---|
| Post | 272 | 331 | 309 | 284 | 348 |
| News | 356 | 402 | 389 | 312 | 458 |
| Bulletin | 157 | 200 | 179 | 196 | 110 |

and wishes to increase the sales by 15%. Find the additional number of papers required, rounded down to the nearest integer and the projected total sales.

**10** A builder's yard organizes its stock in the form of a vector

Bricks – type A
Bricks – type B
Bricks – type C
Bags of cement
Tons of sand

The current stock, $\boldsymbol{S}$, and the minimum stock, $\boldsymbol{M}$, required to avoid running out of materials, are given as

$$\boldsymbol{S} = \begin{bmatrix} 45\,750 \\ 23\,600 \\ 17\,170 \\ 462 \\ 27 \end{bmatrix} \quad \text{and} \quad \boldsymbol{M} = \begin{bmatrix} 5000 \\ 4000 \\ 3500 \\ 100 \\ 10 \end{bmatrix}$$

The firm has five lorries which take materials from stock for deliveries; Lorry1 makes three deliveries in the day with the same load each time; Lorry2 makes two deliveries in the day with the same load each time; the other lorries make one delivery. The loads are

$$\boldsymbol{L}_1 = \begin{bmatrix} 5500 \\ 0 \\ 3800 \\ 75 \\ 3 \end{bmatrix} \quad \boldsymbol{L}_2 = \begin{bmatrix} 2500 \\ 1500 \\ 0 \\ 40 \\ 2 \end{bmatrix} \quad \boldsymbol{L}_3 = \begin{bmatrix} 7500 \\ 2000 \\ 1500 \\ 0 \\ 3 \end{bmatrix}$$

$$\boldsymbol{L}_4 = \begin{bmatrix} 0 \\ 4000 \\ 2500 \\ 20 \\ 2 \end{bmatrix} \quad \boldsymbol{L}_5 = \begin{bmatrix} 2000 \\ 0 \\ 1500 \\ 15 \\ 0 \end{bmatrix}$$

How much material has gone from stock, what is the current stock position and has any element gone below the minimum?

## 5.2.4 Matrix multiplication

The most important property of matrices as far as their practical applications are concerned is the multiplication of one matrix by another. We saw informally in Section 5.2 how multiplication arose and how to define multiplication of a matrix and a vector. The idea can be extended further by looking again at change of axes. Take

$$z_1 = a_{11}y_1 + a_{12}y_2, \quad y_1 = b_{11}x_1 + b_{12}x_2$$
$$z_2 = a_{21}y_1 + a_{22}y_2, \quad y_2 = b_{21}x_1 + b_{22}x_2$$

Then we can ask for the transformation from the $z$s to the $x$s. This we can do by straight substitution:

$$z_1 = (a_{11}b_{11} + a_{12}b_{21})x_1 + (a_{11}b_{12} + a_{12}b_{22})x_2$$
$$z_2 = (a_{21}b_{11} + a_{22}b_{21})x_1 + (a_{21}b_{12} + a_{22}b_{22})x_2$$

If we write the first two transformations as

$$\boldsymbol{A} = \begin{bmatrix} a_{11} & a_{12} \\ a_{21} & a_{22} \end{bmatrix} \quad \text{and} \quad \boldsymbol{B} = \begin{bmatrix} b_{11} & b_{12} \\ b_{21} & b_{22} \end{bmatrix}$$

then the composite transformation is written

$$\boldsymbol{AB} = \begin{bmatrix} a_{11}b_{11} + a_{12}b_{21} & a_{11}b_{12} + a_{12}b_{22} \\ a_{21}b_{11} + a_{22}b_{21} & a_{21}b_{12} + a_{22}b_{22} \end{bmatrix}$$

and this is precisely how we define the matrix product.

**Illustration**

$z_1 = y_1 + 3y_2$
$z_2 = 2y_1 - y_2$

$y_1 = -x_1 + 2x_2$
$y_2 = 2x_1 - x_2$

Substitute to get

$z_1 = 5x_1 - x_2$
$z_2 = -4x_1 + 5x_2$

In matrix form

$$\boldsymbol{A} = \begin{bmatrix} 1 & 3 \\ 2 & -1 \end{bmatrix}$$

$$\boldsymbol{B} = \begin{bmatrix} -1 & 2 \\ 2 & -1 \end{bmatrix}$$

$$\boldsymbol{AB} = \begin{bmatrix} 5 & -1 \\ -4 & 5 \end{bmatrix}$$

### *Definition*

If $\boldsymbol{A}$ is an $m \times p$ matrix with elements $a_{ij}$ and $\boldsymbol{B}$ a $p \times n$ matrix with elements $b_{ij}$ then we define the **product** $\boldsymbol{C} = \boldsymbol{AB}$ as the $m \times n$ matrix with components

$$c_{ij} = \sum_{k=1}^{p} a_{ik} b_{kj} \quad \text{for } i = 1, \ldots, m \quad \text{and} \quad j = 1, \ldots, n$$

In pictorial form, the $i$th row of $\boldsymbol{A}$ is multiplied term by term with the $j$th column of $\boldsymbol{B}$ and the products are added to form the $ij$th component of $\boldsymbol{C}$. This is commonly referred to as the 'row-by-column' method of multiplication. Clearly, in order for multiplication to be possible, $\boldsymbol{A}$ must have $p$ columns and $\boldsymbol{B}$ must have $p$ rows otherwise the product $\boldsymbol{AB}$ is not defined.

$$
\begin{array}{cc}
 & \begin{array}{ccc} & j & \\ & \downarrow & \end{array} \\
i \rightarrow & \begin{bmatrix} & \vdots & \\ \cdots & c_{ij} & \cdots \\ & \vdots & \end{bmatrix}
\end{array}
= i \rightarrow \begin{bmatrix} & & & \\ a_{i1} & a_{i2} & \cdots & a_{ip} \\ & & & \end{bmatrix}
\begin{array}{c} j \\ \downarrow \\ \begin{bmatrix} & b_{1j} & \\ & b_{2j} & \\ & \vdots & \\ & b_{pj} & \end{bmatrix} \end{array}
$$

**Example 5.3** Given

$$\boldsymbol{A} = \begin{bmatrix} 1 & 1 & 0 \\ 2 & 0 & 1 \end{bmatrix}, \quad \boldsymbol{B} = \begin{bmatrix} 2 & 0 \\ 0 & 1 \\ 1 & 3 \end{bmatrix},$$

$$\boldsymbol{b} = \begin{bmatrix} -1 \\ 2 \end{bmatrix}, \quad \boldsymbol{c} = \begin{bmatrix} 1 \\ 1 \\ -1 \end{bmatrix} \quad \text{and} \quad \boldsymbol{C} = \begin{bmatrix} 1 & -2 \\ -1 & 2 \\ -2 & 4 \end{bmatrix}$$

find (a) $\boldsymbol{AB}$, (b) $\boldsymbol{BA}$, (c) $\boldsymbol{Bb}$, (d) $\boldsymbol{A}^{\mathrm{T}}\boldsymbol{b}$, (e) $\boldsymbol{c}^{\mathrm{T}}(\boldsymbol{A}^{\mathrm{T}}\boldsymbol{b})$ and (f) $\boldsymbol{AC}$.

**Solution**

(a) $$\boldsymbol{AB} = \begin{bmatrix} 1 & 1 & 0 \\ 2 & 0 & 1 \end{bmatrix}\begin{bmatrix} 2 & 0 \\ 0 & 1 \\ 1 & 3 \end{bmatrix} = \begin{bmatrix} \text{row}\,1 \times \text{col}\,1 & \text{row}\,1 \times \text{col}\,2 \\ \text{row}\,2 \times \text{col}\,1 & \text{row}\,2 \times \text{col}\,2 \end{bmatrix}$$

$$= \begin{bmatrix} (1)(2) + (1)(0) + (0)(1) & (1)(0) + (1)(1) + (0)(3) \\ (2)(2) + (0)(0) + (1)(1) & (2)(0) + (0)(1) + (1)(3) \end{bmatrix} = \begin{bmatrix} 2 & 1 \\ 5 & 3 \end{bmatrix}$$

(b) $$\boldsymbol{BA} = \begin{bmatrix} 2 & 0 \\ 0 & 1 \\ 1 & 3 \end{bmatrix}\begin{bmatrix} 1 & 1 & 0 \\ 2 & 0 & 1 \end{bmatrix} = \begin{bmatrix} 2+0 & 2+0 & 0+0 \\ 0+2 & 0+0 & 0+1 \\ 1+6 & 1+0 & 0+3 \end{bmatrix} = \begin{bmatrix} 2 & 2 & 0 \\ 2 & 0 & 1 \\ 7 & 1 & 3 \end{bmatrix}$$

(Note that $\boldsymbol{BA}$ is not equal to $\boldsymbol{AB}$.)

(c) $$\boldsymbol{Bb} = \begin{bmatrix} 2 & 0 \\ 0 & 1 \\ 1 & 3 \end{bmatrix}\begin{bmatrix} -1 \\ 2 \end{bmatrix} = \begin{bmatrix} -2 \\ 2 \\ 5 \end{bmatrix}$$

(d) $A^{\mathrm{T}}b = \begin{bmatrix} 1 & 2 \\ 1 & 0 \\ 0 & 1 \end{bmatrix} \begin{bmatrix} -1 \\ 2 \end{bmatrix} = \begin{bmatrix} 3 \\ -1 \\ 2 \end{bmatrix}$

(e) $c^{\mathrm{T}}(A^{\mathrm{T}}b) = [1 \quad 1 \quad -1] \begin{bmatrix} 3 \\ -1 \\ 2 \end{bmatrix} = [0] = 0$

(Note that this matrix is the zero $1 \times 1$ matrix, which can just be written 0.)

(f) $AC = \begin{bmatrix} 1 & 1 & 0 \\ 2 & 0 & 1 \end{bmatrix} \begin{bmatrix} 1 & -2 \\ -1 & 2 \\ -2 & 4 \end{bmatrix} = \begin{bmatrix} 0 & 0 \\ 0 & 0 \end{bmatrix} = 0$

(Note that the product $AC$ is zero even though neither $A$ nor $C$ is zero.)

**Example 5.4** If

$$A = \begin{bmatrix} 1 & 2 & 0 \\ 1 & 1 & 0 \\ 2 & 1 & 1 \end{bmatrix} \quad \text{and} \quad X = \begin{bmatrix} x \\ y \\ z \end{bmatrix}$$

evaluate (a) $X^{\mathrm{T}}X$, (b) $AX$, (c) $X^{\mathrm{T}}(AX)$ and (d) $\frac{1}{2}X^{\mathrm{T}}[(A^{\mathrm{T}} + A)X]$.

**Solution**

(a) $X^{\mathrm{T}}X = [x \quad y \quad z] \begin{bmatrix} x \\ y \\ z \end{bmatrix} = x^2 + y^2 + z^2$

(b) $AX = \begin{bmatrix} 1 & 2 & 0 \\ 1 & 1 & 0 \\ 2 & 1 & 1 \end{bmatrix} \begin{bmatrix} x \\ y \\ z \end{bmatrix} = \begin{bmatrix} x + 2y \\ x + y \\ 2x + y + z \end{bmatrix}$

(c) $X^{\mathrm{T}}(AX) = [x \quad y \quad z] \begin{bmatrix} x + 2y \\ x + y \\ 2x + y + z \end{bmatrix} = (x^2 + 2xy) + (yx + y^2) + (2xz + yz + z^2)$

$$= x^2 + y^2 + z^2 + 3xy + 2xz + yz$$

(d) $\frac{1}{2}(A^{\mathrm{T}} + A) = \begin{bmatrix} 1 & \frac{3}{2} & 1 \\ \frac{3}{2} & 1 & \frac{1}{2} \\ 1 & \frac{1}{2} & 1 \end{bmatrix}$

and

$$\tfrac{1}{2}(\boldsymbol{A}^{\mathrm{T}} + \boldsymbol{A})\boldsymbol{X} = \begin{bmatrix} 1 & \frac{3}{2} & 1 \\ \frac{3}{2} & 1 & \frac{1}{2} \\ 1 & \frac{1}{2} & 1 \end{bmatrix}\begin{bmatrix} x \\ y \\ z \end{bmatrix} = \begin{bmatrix} x + \frac{3}{2}y + z \\ \frac{3}{2}x + y + \frac{1}{2}z \\ x + \frac{1}{2}y + z \end{bmatrix}$$

Therefore

$$\tfrac{1}{2}\boldsymbol{X}^{\mathrm{T}}[(\boldsymbol{A}^{\mathrm{T}} + \boldsymbol{A})\boldsymbol{X}] = [x \quad y \quad z]\begin{bmatrix} x + \frac{3}{2}y + z \\ \frac{3}{2}x + y + \frac{1}{2}z \\ x + \frac{1}{2}y + z \end{bmatrix}$$

$$= x^2 + y^2 + z^2 + 3xy + 2xz + yz$$

(Note that this is the same as the result of part (c).)

---

There are several points to note from the preceding examples. One-by-one matrices are just numbers, so the square brackets become redundant and are usually omitted. The expression $\boldsymbol{X}^{\mathrm{T}}\boldsymbol{X}$ just gives the square of the length of the vector $\boldsymbol{X}$ in the usual sense, namely $\boldsymbol{X}^{\mathrm{T}}\boldsymbol{X} = x^2 + y^2 + z^2$. Similarly,

$$\boldsymbol{X}^{\mathrm{T}}\boldsymbol{X}' = [x \quad y \quad z]\begin{bmatrix} x' \\ y' \\ z' \end{bmatrix} = xx' + yy' + zz'$$

which is the usual **scalar** or **inner product**, here written in matrix form. The expression $\boldsymbol{AX}$ gives a column vector with linear expressions as its elements. Using Example 5.4(b), we can rewrite the linear equations

$$\begin{aligned} x + 2y \quad &= 3 \\ x + y \quad &= 4 \\ 2x + y + z &= 5 \end{aligned}$$

as

$$\begin{bmatrix} 1 & 2 & 0 \\ 1 & 1 & 0 \\ 2 & 1 & 1 \end{bmatrix}\begin{bmatrix} x \\ y \\ z \end{bmatrix} = \begin{bmatrix} 3 \\ 4 \\ 5 \end{bmatrix}$$

which may be written in the standard matrix form for linear equations as

$$\boldsymbol{AX} = \boldsymbol{b}$$

It is also important to realize that if $\boldsymbol{AB} = 0$ it does not follow that either $\boldsymbol{A}$ or $\boldsymbol{B}$ is zero. In Example 5.3(f) we saw that the product $\boldsymbol{AC} = 0$, but neither $\boldsymbol{A}$ nor $\boldsymbol{C}$ is the zero matrix.

Matrix multiplication is an important part of computer packages and is easily implemented.

MATLAB

If $\boldsymbol{A}$ and $\boldsymbol{B}$ have been defined and have the correct dimensions then

```
A * B and A^2
```

have the usual meaning of matrix multiplication and squaring.

For matrices involving algebraic quantities, or when exact arithmetic is desirable, use of the Symbolic Math Toolbox is required; in which case the matrices $\boldsymbol{A}$ and $\boldsymbol{B}$ must be expressed in symbolic form using the *sym* command, that is

```
A = sym(A); B = sym(B)
```

MAPLE

If $\boldsymbol{A}$ and $\boldsymbol{B}$ have been defined and have the correct dimensions then it is best first to invoke the linalg package

```
with(linalg):
multiply(A,B);
evalm(A &* B);
```

both produce the product of the two matrices.

```
evalm(A&^2);
```

squares the matrix $\boldsymbol{A}$.

Because MAPLE is a symbolic package all variables are assumed to be symbols and there is no need to declare them to be so.

## 5.2.5 Exercises

Most of these exercises can be checked using MATLAB. For non-numerical exercises use either MAPLE or the Symbolic Math Toolbox of MATLAB.

**11** Given the matrices

$$\boldsymbol{A} = \begin{bmatrix} 1 & 1 & 1 \\ 1 & 1 & 1 \end{bmatrix}, \quad \boldsymbol{B} = \begin{bmatrix} 1 & 1 & 0 \\ 1 & 1 & 0 \\ 0 & 0 & -1 \end{bmatrix}$$

and

$$\boldsymbol{C} = \begin{bmatrix} 0 & 2 \\ 1 & 1 \\ -1 & -1 \end{bmatrix}$$

evaluate $\boldsymbol{AB}$, $\boldsymbol{AC}$, $\boldsymbol{BC}$, $\boldsymbol{CA}$ and $\boldsymbol{BA}^{\mathrm{T}}$. Which if any of these are diagonal, unit or symmetric?

**12** The matrices

$$\boldsymbol{A} = \begin{bmatrix} 1 & 2 & 1 \\ 3 & 0 & 2 \end{bmatrix}, \quad \boldsymbol{B} = \begin{bmatrix} 4 & 1 & 3 \\ 0 & 2 & 1 \end{bmatrix}$$

and

$$\boldsymbol{C} = \begin{bmatrix} 1 & 2 \\ 3 & 1 \\ 2 & 3 \end{bmatrix}$$

are given.

(a) Which of the following make sense: $\boldsymbol{AB}$, $\boldsymbol{AC}$, $\boldsymbol{BC}$, $\boldsymbol{AB}^{\mathrm{T}}$, $\boldsymbol{AC}^{\mathrm{T}}$ and $\boldsymbol{BC}^{\mathrm{T}}$?

(b) Evaluate those products that do exist.

(c) Evaluate $(\boldsymbol{A}^{\mathrm{T}}\boldsymbol{B})\boldsymbol{C}$ and $\boldsymbol{A}^{\mathrm{T}}(\boldsymbol{BC})$ and show that they are equal.

**13** Given

$$\boldsymbol{A} = \begin{bmatrix} 3 & 2 \\ 5 & 4 \end{bmatrix} \quad \text{and} \quad \boldsymbol{B} = \begin{bmatrix} 4 & -2 \\ -5 & 3 \end{bmatrix}$$

evaluate $\boldsymbol{AB}$ and $\boldsymbol{BA}$ and hence show that these two matrices commute. Solve the equation

$$AX = \begin{bmatrix} 1 \\ 0 \end{bmatrix}$$

for the vector $X$ by multplying both sides by $B$.

14 Show that for any $x$ the matrix

$$A = \begin{bmatrix} \cos(2x) & \sin(2x) \\ \sin(2x) & -\cos(2x) \end{bmatrix}$$

satisfies the relation $A^2 = I$.

15 If

$$A = \begin{bmatrix} a & b \\ -b & a \end{bmatrix} \quad \text{and} \quad B = \begin{bmatrix} c & d \\ -d & c \end{bmatrix}$$

show that the product $AB$ has exactly the same form.

16 Given

$$A = \begin{bmatrix} 1 & 2 & 3 \\ 3 & 4 & 5 \\ 5 & 6 & 7 \end{bmatrix}, \quad X = \begin{bmatrix} x \\ y \\ z \end{bmatrix} \quad \text{and} \quad b = \begin{bmatrix} 2 \\ 3 \\ 4 \end{bmatrix}$$

evaluate $X^TX$ and $X^TAX$ and write out the equations given by $AX = b$.

### 5.2.6 Properties of matrix multiplication

We now consider the basic properties of matrix multiplication. These may be proved using the definition of matrix multiplication and this is left as an exercise for the reader.

*(a) Commutative law*

Matrices *do not commute in general*, although they may do in special cases. In Example 5.3 we saw that $AB \neq BA$, and a further example illustrates the same result:

$$A = \begin{bmatrix} 1 & 0 \\ 0 & 0 \end{bmatrix}, \quad B = \begin{bmatrix} 1 & 2 \\ 1 & 0 \end{bmatrix}$$

$$AB = \begin{bmatrix} 1 & 2 \\ 0 & 0 \end{bmatrix}, \quad BA = \begin{bmatrix} 1 & 0 \\ 1 & 0 \end{bmatrix}$$

so again $AB \neq BA$. The products do not necessarily have the same size, as shown in Example 5.3(a and b), where $AB$ is a $2 \times 2$ matrix while $BA$ is $3 \times 3$. In fact, even if $AB$ exists, it does not follow that $BA$ does. Take, for example, the matrices

$a = [1 \quad 1 \quad 1]$ and $B = \begin{bmatrix} 1 & 2 \\ 2 & 1 \\ 1 & 1 \end{bmatrix}$. The product $aB = [4 \quad 4]$ is well defined but $Ba$ cannot be computed since a $3 \times 2$ matrix cannot be multiplied on the right by a $1 \times 3$ matrix. Thus order matters, and we need to distinguish between $AB$ and $BA$. To do this, we talk of **pre-multiplication** of $B$ by $A$ to form $AB$, and **post-multiplication** of $B$ by $A$ to form $BA$.

*(b) Associative law*

It can be shown that

$$A(BC) = (AB)C$$

where $A$ is $m \times p$, $B$ is $p \times q$ and $C$ is $q \times n$.

Matrix multiplication is associative and we can therefore omit the brackets.

*(c) Distributive law over multiplication by a scalar*

$(m\boldsymbol{A})\boldsymbol{B} = \boldsymbol{A}(m\boldsymbol{B}) = m\boldsymbol{AB}$ holds

*(d) Distributive law over addition*

$(\boldsymbol{A}+\boldsymbol{B})\boldsymbol{C} = \boldsymbol{AC}+\boldsymbol{BC}$ and $\boldsymbol{A}(\boldsymbol{B}+\boldsymbol{C}) = \boldsymbol{AB}+\boldsymbol{AC}$

so we can multiply out brackets in the usual way, but making sure that the order of the products is maintained.

*(e) Multiplication by unit matrices*

If $\boldsymbol{A}$ is an $m \times n$ matrix and if $\boldsymbol{I}_m$ and $\boldsymbol{I}_n$ are the unit matrices of orders $m$ and $n$ then

$\boldsymbol{I}_m\boldsymbol{A} = \boldsymbol{A}\boldsymbol{I}_n = \boldsymbol{A}$

Thus pre- or post-multiplication by the appropriate unit matrix leaves $\boldsymbol{A}$ unchanged.

*(f) Transpose of a product*

$(\boldsymbol{AB})^{\mathrm{T}} = \boldsymbol{B}^{\mathrm{T}}\boldsymbol{A}^{\mathrm{T}}$

where $\boldsymbol{A}$ is an $m \times p$ matrix and $\boldsymbol{B}$ a $p \times n$ matrix. The proof is straightforward but requires careful treatment of summation signs. Thus the transpose of the product of matrices is the product of the transposed matrices in the reverse order.

**Example 5.5** Given the matrices

$$\boldsymbol{A} = \begin{bmatrix} 1 & 2 & 2 \\ 0 & 1 & 1 \\ 1 & 0 & 1 \end{bmatrix}, \quad \boldsymbol{B} = \begin{bmatrix} 1 & -2 & 0 \\ 1 & -1 & -1 \\ -1 & 2 & 1 \end{bmatrix}, \quad \boldsymbol{X} = \begin{bmatrix} x \\ y \\ z \end{bmatrix} \quad \text{and} \quad \boldsymbol{c} = \begin{bmatrix} 1 \\ 0 \\ 1 \end{bmatrix}$$

(a) find (i) $\boldsymbol{AB}$, (ii) $(\boldsymbol{AB})^{\mathrm{T}}$ and (iii) $\boldsymbol{B}^{\mathrm{T}}\boldsymbol{A}^{\mathrm{T}}$.

(b) Pre-multiply each side of the equation $\boldsymbol{BX} = \boldsymbol{c}$ by $\boldsymbol{A}$.

**Solution** (a) It would be a useful exercise to check these products using MATLAB or MAPLE.

$$\text{(i) } \boldsymbol{AB} = \begin{bmatrix} 1 & 2 & 2 \\ 0 & 1 & 1 \\ 1 & 0 & 1 \end{bmatrix}\begin{bmatrix} 1 & -2 & 0 \\ 1 & -1 & -1 \\ -1 & 2 & 1 \end{bmatrix} = \begin{bmatrix} 1 & 0 & 0 \\ 0 & 1 & 0 \\ 0 & 0 & 1 \end{bmatrix} = \boldsymbol{I}$$

The MATLAB commands

```
A = [1 2 2; 0 1 1; 1 0 1];
B = [1 -2 0; 1 -1 -1; -1 2 1]; A*B
```

produce the correct unit matrix.

(ii) $(\mathbf{AB})^{\mathrm{T}} = \begin{bmatrix} 1 & 0 & 0 \\ 0 & 1 & 0 \\ 0 & 0 & 1 \end{bmatrix} = \mathbf{I}$

(iii) $\mathbf{B}^{\mathrm{T}}\mathbf{A}^{\mathrm{T}} = \begin{bmatrix} 1 & 1 & -1 \\ -2 & -1 & 2 \\ 0 & -1 & 1 \end{bmatrix}\begin{bmatrix} 1 & 0 & 1 \\ 2 & 1 & 0 \\ 2 & 1 & 1 \end{bmatrix} = \begin{bmatrix} 1 & 0 & 0 \\ 0 & 1 & 0 \\ 0 & 0 & 1 \end{bmatrix} = \mathbf{I}$

(b) The equation $\mathbf{B}X = \mathbf{c}$ can be rewritten as

$$\begin{bmatrix} 1 & -2 & 0 \\ 1 & -1 & -1 \\ -1 & 2 & 1 \end{bmatrix}\begin{bmatrix} x \\ y \\ z \end{bmatrix} = \begin{bmatrix} 1 \\ 0 \\ 1 \end{bmatrix} \quad \text{or} \quad \begin{aligned} x - 2y \quad &= 1 \\ x - y - z &= 0 \\ -x + 2y + z &= 1 \end{aligned}$$

If we now pre-multiply the equation by $\mathbf{A}$ we obtain

$$\mathbf{AB}X = \mathbf{A}\mathbf{c}$$

and since $\mathbf{AB} = \mathbf{I}$, we obtain

$$\mathbf{I}X = \begin{bmatrix} 1 & 2 & 2 \\ 0 & 1 & 1 \\ 1 & 0 & 1 \end{bmatrix}\begin{bmatrix} 1 \\ 0 \\ 1 \end{bmatrix} = \begin{bmatrix} 3 \\ 1 \\ 2 \end{bmatrix} \quad \text{or} \quad \begin{bmatrix} x \\ y \\ z \end{bmatrix} = \begin{bmatrix} 3 \\ 1 \\ 2 \end{bmatrix}$$

and we see that we have a solution to our set of linear equations.

In MATLAB the solution $X$ to the set of linear equations $\mathbf{B}X = \mathbf{c}$ is determined by the command `B\c`. Check that the commands

```
B = [1 -2 0; 1 -1 -1; -1 2 1];
c = [1;0;1];
B\c
```

return the given answer.

**Example 5.6** Given the three matrices

$$\mathbf{A} = \begin{bmatrix} 1 & -1 & 1 \\ -2 & 0 & 3 \\ 0 & 1 & -2 \end{bmatrix}, \quad \mathbf{B} = \begin{bmatrix} 0 & 0 & 1 \\ 0 & 2 & 3 \\ 1 & 2 & 3 \end{bmatrix} \quad \text{and} \quad \mathbf{C} = \begin{bmatrix} 2 & 3 \\ -1 & 2 \\ -3 & 1 \end{bmatrix}$$

verify the associative law and the distributive law over addition.

**Solution**

$$\text{Now } \boldsymbol{BC} = \begin{bmatrix} 0 & 0 & 1 \\ 0 & 2 & 3 \\ 1 & 2 & 3 \end{bmatrix}\begin{bmatrix} 2 & 3 \\ -1 & 2 \\ -3 & 1 \end{bmatrix} = \begin{bmatrix} -3 & 1 \\ -11 & 7 \\ -9 & 10 \end{bmatrix} \text{ and}$$

$$\boldsymbol{A}(\boldsymbol{BC}) = \begin{bmatrix} 1 & -1 & 1 \\ -2 & 0 & 3 \\ 0 & 1 & -2 \end{bmatrix}\begin{bmatrix} -3 & 1 \\ -11 & 7 \\ -9 & 10 \end{bmatrix} = \begin{bmatrix} -1 & 4 \\ -21 & 28 \\ 7 & -13 \end{bmatrix}$$

$$\text{Likewise } \boldsymbol{AB} = \begin{bmatrix} 1 & -1 & 1 \\ -2 & 0 & 3 \\ 0 & 1 & -2 \end{bmatrix}\begin{bmatrix} 0 & 0 & 1 \\ 0 & 2 & 3 \\ 1 & 2 & 3 \end{bmatrix} = \begin{bmatrix} 1 & 0 & 1 \\ 3 & 6 & 7 \\ -2 & -2 & -3 \end{bmatrix} \text{ and}$$

$$(\boldsymbol{AB})\boldsymbol{C} = \begin{bmatrix} 1 & 0 & 1 \\ 3 & 6 & 7 \\ -2 & -2 & -3 \end{bmatrix}\begin{bmatrix} 2 & 3 \\ -1 & 2 \\ -3 & 1 \end{bmatrix} = \begin{bmatrix} -1 & 4 \\ -21 & 28 \\ 7 & -13 \end{bmatrix}$$

Thus the associative law is satisfied for these three matrices. For the distributive law we need to evaluate

$$(\boldsymbol{A} + \boldsymbol{B})\boldsymbol{C} = \begin{bmatrix} 1 & -1 & 2 \\ -2 & 2 & 6 \\ 1 & 3 & 1 \end{bmatrix}\begin{bmatrix} 2 & 3 \\ -1 & 2 \\ -3 & 1 \end{bmatrix} = \begin{bmatrix} -3 & 3 \\ -24 & 4 \\ -4 & 10 \end{bmatrix}$$

and

$$\boldsymbol{AC} + \boldsymbol{BC} = \begin{bmatrix} 1 & -1 & 1 \\ -2 & 0 & 3 \\ 0 & 1 & -2 \end{bmatrix}\begin{bmatrix} 2 & 3 \\ -1 & 2 \\ -3 & 1 \end{bmatrix} + \begin{bmatrix} 0 & 0 & 1 \\ 0 & 2 & 3 \\ 1 & 2 & 3 \end{bmatrix}\begin{bmatrix} 2 & 3 \\ -1 & 2 \\ -3 & 1 \end{bmatrix}$$

$$= \begin{bmatrix} 0 & 2 \\ -13 & -3 \\ 5 & 0 \end{bmatrix} + \begin{bmatrix} -3 & 1 \\ -11 & 7 \\ -9 & 10 \end{bmatrix} = \begin{bmatrix} -3 & 3 \\ -24 & 4 \\ -4 & 10 \end{bmatrix}$$

The two matrices are equal so the distributive law is verified for the three given matrices.

**Example 5.7**

Show that the transformation

$$\begin{bmatrix} x' \\ y' \end{bmatrix} = \begin{bmatrix} \cos\theta & \sin\theta \\ -\sin\theta & \cos\theta \end{bmatrix}\begin{bmatrix} x \\ y \end{bmatrix}$$

with $\theta = 60°$, maps the square with corners $\begin{bmatrix} 1 \\ 1 \end{bmatrix}, \begin{bmatrix} 1 \\ 2 \end{bmatrix}, \begin{bmatrix} 2 \\ 2 \end{bmatrix}$ and $\begin{bmatrix} 2 \\ 1 \end{bmatrix}$ on to a square.

**Solution** Substituting the given vectors in turn for $\begin{bmatrix} x \\ y \end{bmatrix}$ into the equation

$$\begin{bmatrix} x' \\ y' \end{bmatrix} = \begin{bmatrix} 0.5 & 0.8660 \\ -0.8660 & 0.5 \end{bmatrix} \begin{bmatrix} x \\ y \end{bmatrix}$$

we find the following vectors for $\begin{bmatrix} x' \\ y' \end{bmatrix}$

$$\begin{bmatrix} 1.366 \\ -0.366 \end{bmatrix}, \begin{bmatrix} 2.232 \\ 0.134 \end{bmatrix}, \begin{bmatrix} 2.732 \\ -0.732 \end{bmatrix} \text{ and } \begin{bmatrix} 1.866 \\ -1.232 \end{bmatrix}$$

Plotting these points on the plane as in Figure 5.4, we see that the square has been rotated through an angle of 60° about the origin. It is left as an exercise for the reader to verify the result.

This type of analysis forms the basis of manipulation of diagrams on a computer screen, and is used in many CAD/CAM situations.

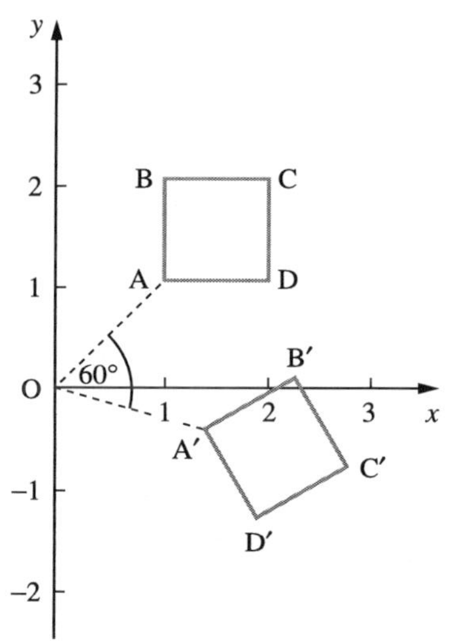


**Figure 5.4** Transformation of a square in Example 5.7.

**Example 5.8**

In quantum mechanics the components of the spin of an electron can be repesented by the Pauli matrices

$$\boldsymbol{A} = \begin{bmatrix} 0 & 1 \\ 1 & 0 \end{bmatrix}, \quad \boldsymbol{B} = \begin{bmatrix} 0 & -\mathrm{j} \\ \mathrm{j} & 0 \end{bmatrix}, \quad \boldsymbol{C} = \begin{bmatrix} 1 & 0 \\ 0 & -1 \end{bmatrix}$$

Show that

(a) the matrices anticommute

$$\boldsymbol{AB} + \boldsymbol{BA} = 0, \quad \boldsymbol{BC} + \boldsymbol{CB} = 0, \quad \boldsymbol{CA} + \boldsymbol{AC} = 0$$

(b) $\boldsymbol{AB} - \boldsymbol{BA} = 2\mathrm{j}\boldsymbol{C}$, $\boldsymbol{BC} - \boldsymbol{CB} = 2\mathrm{j}\boldsymbol{A}$, $\boldsymbol{CA} - \boldsymbol{AC} = 2\mathrm{j}\boldsymbol{B}$

(c) $\boldsymbol{AB} = \mathrm{j}\boldsymbol{C}$, $\boldsymbol{BC} = \mathrm{j}\boldsymbol{A}$, $\boldsymbol{CA} = \mathrm{j}\boldsymbol{B}$

**Solution** (a) $\boldsymbol{AB} = \begin{bmatrix} 0 & 1 \\ 1 & 0 \end{bmatrix}\begin{bmatrix} 0 & -\mathrm{j} \\ \mathrm{j} & 0 \end{bmatrix} = \begin{bmatrix} \mathrm{j} & 0 \\ 0 & -\mathrm{j} \end{bmatrix}$ and $\boldsymbol{BA} = \begin{bmatrix} 0 & -\mathrm{j} \\ \mathrm{j} & 0 \end{bmatrix}\begin{bmatrix} 0 & 1 \\ 1 & 0 \end{bmatrix} = \begin{bmatrix} -\mathrm{j} & 0 \\ 0 & \mathrm{j} \end{bmatrix}$

so

$$\boldsymbol{AB} + \boldsymbol{BA} = 0$$

and the other two results follow similarly.

(b) From part (a)

$$\boldsymbol{AB} - \boldsymbol{BA} = \begin{bmatrix} \mathrm{j} & 0 \\ 0 & -\mathrm{j} \end{bmatrix} - \begin{bmatrix} -\mathrm{j} & 0 \\ 0 & \mathrm{j} \end{bmatrix} = \begin{bmatrix} 2\mathrm{j} & 0 \\ 0 & -2\mathrm{j} \end{bmatrix} = 2\mathrm{j}\boldsymbol{C}$$

and again the other two results follow similarly.

(c) These results can be obtained directly from part (a) since $\boldsymbol{AB}$ has already been calculated, similarly for $\boldsymbol{BC}$ and $\boldsymbol{CA}$.

*Note*: that this example illustrates the use of matrices that have complex elements. Pauli discovered that the matrices $\boldsymbol{A}$, $\boldsymbol{B}$ and $\boldsymbol{C}$ have the properties (a), (b) and (c) required of the components of the spin of an electron.

**Example 5.9** A rectangular site is to be levelled, and the amount of earth that needs to be removed must be determined. A survey of the site at a regular mesh of points 10 m apart is made. The heights in metres above the level required are given in the following table.

| | | | | | |
|---|---|---|---|---|---|
| 0 | 0.31 | 0.40 | 0.45 | 0.51 | 0.60 |
| 0.12 | 0.33 | 0.51 | 0.58 | 0.66 | 0.75 |
| 0.19 | 0.38 | 0.60 | 0.69 | 0.78 | 0.86 |
| 0.25 | 0.46 | 0.68 | 0.77 | 0.89 | 0.97 |

It is known that the approximate volume of a cell of side $x$ and with corner heights of $a$, $b$, $c$ and $d$ is

$$V = \tfrac{1}{4}x^2(a + b + c + d)$$

Write the total approximate volume in matrix form and hence estimate the volume to be removed.

**Solution** Note that for the first row of cells the volume is

$$\begin{aligned} 25(\,0 + 0.31 \quad &+0.31 + 0.40 \quad +0.40 + 0.45 \quad +0.45 + 0.51 \quad +0.51 + 0.60 \\ +0.12 + 0.33 \quad &+0.33 + 0.51 \quad +0.51 + 0.58 \quad +0.58 + 0.66 \quad +0.66 + 0.75) \end{aligned}$$

$$\begin{aligned} &= 25[0 + 2(0.31 + 0.40 + 0.45 + 0.51) + 0.60] \\ &\quad + 25[0.12 + 2(0.33 + 0.51 + 0.58 + 0.66) + 0.75] \end{aligned}$$

The second and third rows of cells are dealt with in a similar manner, so that, when we compute the total volume, we need to multiply the corner values by 1, the other side values by 2 and the centre values by 4. In matrix form this multiplication can be performed as

$$[1 \quad 2 \quad 2 \quad 1]\begin{bmatrix} 0 & 0.31 & 0.40 & 0.45 & 0.51 & 0.60 \\ 0.12 & 0.33 & 0.51 & 0.58 & 0.66 & 0.75 \\ 0.19 & 0.38 & 0.60 & 0.69 & 0.78 & 0.86 \\ 0.25 & 0.46 & 0.68 & 0.77 & 0.86 & 0.97 \end{bmatrix}\begin{bmatrix} 1 \\ 2 \\ 2 \\ 2 \\ 2 \\ 1 \end{bmatrix}$$

This can be checked by multiplying the matrices out. The checking can be done on one of the symbolic manipulation packages, such as MAPLE or the Symbolic Math Toolbox of MATLAB, by putting in general symbols for the matrix and verifying that, after the matrix multiplications, the elements are multiplied by the stated factors. Performing the calculation and multiplying by the 25 gives the total volume as $816.5\,\text{m}^3$.

A similar analysis can be applied to other situations – all that is needed is measured heights and a matrix multiplication routine on a computer to deal with the large amount of data that would be required. For other mesh shapes, or even irregular meshes, the method is similar, but the multiplying vectors will need careful calculation.

**Example 5.10**

A contractor makes two products $P_1$ and $P_2$. The four components required to make the products are subcontracted out and each of the components is made up from three ingredients $A$, $B$ and $C$ as follows:

| *Component* | *Units of A* | *Units of B* | *Units of C* | *Make-up cost and profit for subcontractor* |
|---|---|---|---|---|
| 1 requires | 5 | 4 | 3 | 10 |
| 2 requires | 2 | 1 | 1 | 7 |
| 3 requires | 0 | 1 | 3 | 5 |
| 4 requires | 3 | 4 | 1 | 2 |

The cost per unit of the ingredients $A$, $B$ and $C$ are $a$, $b$ and $c$ respectively. The contractor makes the product $P_1$ with 2 of component 1, 3 of component 2 and 4 of component 4, the make-up cost is 15; product $P_2$ requires 1 of component 1, 1 of component 2, 1 of component 3 and 2 of component 4, the make-up cost is 12. Find the cost to the contractor for $P_1$ and $P_2$. What is the change in costs if $a$ increases to $(a + 1)$? It is found that the 5 units of $A$ required for component 1 can be reduced to 4. What is the effect on the costs?

**Solution** The information presented can be written naturally in matrix form. Let $C_1$, $C_2$, $C_3$ and $C_4$ be the cost the subcontractor charges the contractor for the four components, then the cost $C_1$ is computed as $C_1 = 5a + 4b + 3c + 10$. This expression is the first row of the matrix equation

$$\begin{bmatrix} C_1 \\ C_2 \\ C_3 \\ C_4 \end{bmatrix} = \begin{bmatrix} 5 & 4 & 3 \\ 2 & 1 & 1 \\ 0 & 1 & 3 \\ 3 & 4 & 1 \end{bmatrix} \begin{bmatrix} a \\ b \\ c \end{bmatrix} + \begin{bmatrix} 10 \\ 7 \\ 5 \\ 2 \end{bmatrix}$$

and the other three costs follow in a similar manner. Now let $p_1$, $p_2$ be the costs of producing the final products. The costs are constructed in exactly the same way as

$$\begin{bmatrix} p_1 \\ p_2 \end{bmatrix} = \begin{bmatrix} 2 & 3 & 0 & 4 \\ 1 & 1 & 1 & 2 \end{bmatrix} \begin{bmatrix} C_1 \\ C_2 \\ C_3 \\ C_4 \end{bmatrix} + \begin{bmatrix} 15 \\ 12 \end{bmatrix}$$

Substituting gives

$$\begin{bmatrix} p_1 \\ p_2 \end{bmatrix} = \begin{bmatrix} 2 & 3 & 0 & 4 \\ 1 & 1 & 1 & 2 \end{bmatrix} \begin{bmatrix} 5 & 4 & 3 \\ 2 & 1 & 1 \\ 0 & 1 & 3 \\ 3 & 4 & 1 \end{bmatrix} \begin{bmatrix} a \\ b \\ c \end{bmatrix} + \begin{bmatrix} 2 & 3 & 0 & 4 \\ 1 & 1 & 1 & 2 \end{bmatrix} \begin{bmatrix} 10 \\ 7 \\ 5 \\ 2 \end{bmatrix} + \begin{bmatrix} 15 \\ 12 \end{bmatrix}$$

or

$$\begin{bmatrix} p_1 \\ p_2 \end{bmatrix} = \begin{bmatrix} 28 & 27 & 13 \\ 13 & 14 & 9 \end{bmatrix} \begin{bmatrix} a \\ b \\ c \end{bmatrix} + \begin{bmatrix} 64 \\ 38 \end{bmatrix}$$

Thus a simple matrix formulation gives a convenient way of coding the data. If $a$ is increased to $(a + 1)$ then multiplying out shows that $p_1$ increases by 28 and $p_2$ by 13. If the 5 in the first matrix is reduced to 4 then the costs will be

$$\begin{bmatrix} p_1 \\ p_2 \end{bmatrix} = \begin{bmatrix} 26 & 27 & 13 \\ 12 & 14 & 9 \end{bmatrix} \begin{bmatrix} a \\ b \\ c \end{bmatrix} + \begin{bmatrix} 64 \\ 38 \end{bmatrix}$$

so $p_1$ is reduced by $2a$ and $p_2$ by $a$.

---

A similar approach can be used in more complicated, realistic situations. Storing and processing the information is convenient, particularly in conjunction with a computer package or spreadsheet.

**Example 5.11** The tape of a tape recorder passes the reading head at a constant speed $v$. On the feed reel there is a length of tape $L$ left and it has radius $R$. If the rev counter is set to zero and the thickness of the tape is $h$ find how the radius and the length of the reel vary with the number of revolutions $n$.

**Solution** Let $t_n$, $R_n$ and $L_n$ denote the time, radius and length after $n$ revolutions. It is given that $t_0 = 0$, $R_0 = R$ and $L_0 = L$. At stage $n$ after one further revolution a thickness $h$ is peeled off the radius, the length is reduced by $2\pi R_n$ and the time has advanced by $2\pi R_n/v$. A table summarizes these remarks.

| *Revs* (*n*) | *Time* ($t_n$) | *Radius* ($R_n$) | *Length remaining* ($L_n$) |
|---|---|---|---|
| 0 | $t_0 = 0$ | $R_0 = R$ | $L_0 = L$ |
| 1 | $t_1 = 2\pi R_0/v + t_0$ | $R_1 = R_0 - h$ | $L_1 = L_0 - 2\pi R_0$ |
| 2 | $t_2 = 2\pi R_1/v + t_1$ | $R_2 = R_1 - h$ | $L_2 = L_1 - 2\pi R_1$ |
| … | … | … | … |
| … | … | … | … |
| $n + 1$ | $t_{n+1} = 2\pi R_n/v + t_n$ | $R_{n+1} = R_n - h$ | $L_{n+1} = L_n - 2\pi R_n$ |

This data can be written conveniently in matrix notation as

$$\begin{bmatrix} t_{n+1} \\ R_{n+1} \\ L_{n+1} \end{bmatrix} = \begin{bmatrix} 1 & 2\pi/v & 0 \\ 0 & 1 & 0 \\ 0 & -2\pi & 1 \end{bmatrix} \begin{bmatrix} t_n \\ R_n \\ L_n \end{bmatrix} - \begin{bmatrix} 0 \\ h \\ 0 \end{bmatrix}$$

or identifying the matrices in an obvious manner as

$$\boldsymbol{X}_{n+1} = \boldsymbol{A}\boldsymbol{X}_n - \boldsymbol{\Delta}$$

Successive substitution gives

$$\begin{aligned} \boldsymbol{X}_{n+1} &= \boldsymbol{A}(\boldsymbol{A}\boldsymbol{X}_{n-1} - \Delta) - \Delta = \boldsymbol{A}^2\boldsymbol{X}_{n-1} - (\boldsymbol{A} + \boldsymbol{I})\Delta \\ &= \boldsymbol{A}^2(\boldsymbol{A}\boldsymbol{X}_{n-2} - \Delta) - (\boldsymbol{A} + \boldsymbol{I})\Delta = \boldsymbol{A}^3\boldsymbol{X}_{n-2} - (\boldsymbol{A}^2 + \boldsymbol{A} + \boldsymbol{I})\Delta \\ &\dots \\ &= \boldsymbol{A}^{n+1}\boldsymbol{X}_0 - (\boldsymbol{A}^n + \boldsymbol{A}^{n-1} + \dots + \boldsymbol{A} + \boldsymbol{I})\Delta \end{aligned} \tag{5.6}$$

The required values can now be determined by evaluating the right-hand side of this equation. Repeated products of $\boldsymbol{A}$ gives

$$\boldsymbol{A}^n = \begin{bmatrix} 1 & 2\pi n/v & 0 \\ 0 & 1 & 0 \\ 0 & -2\pi n & 1 \end{bmatrix}$$

and the sum

$$\boldsymbol{A}^n + \boldsymbol{A}^{n-1} + \ldots + \boldsymbol{A} + \boldsymbol{I} = \begin{bmatrix} n+1 & 2\pi S/v & 0 \\ 0 & n+1 & 0 \\ 0 & -2\pi S & n+1 \end{bmatrix}$$

can be computed, where

$$S = 1 + 2 + 3 + \ldots + n = \tfrac{1}{2}n(n+1)$$

Writing out equation (5.6) in full gives

$$\begin{bmatrix} t_{n+1} \\ R_{n+1} \\ L_{n+1} \end{bmatrix} = \begin{bmatrix} 1 & 2\pi(n+1)/v & 0 \\ 0 & 1 & 0 \\ 0 & -2\pi(n+1) & 1 \end{bmatrix} \begin{bmatrix} 0 \\ R \\ L \end{bmatrix} - \begin{bmatrix} n+1 & \pi n(n+1)/v & 0 \\ 0 & n+1 & 0 \\ 0 & -\pi n(n+1) & n+1 \end{bmatrix} \begin{bmatrix} 0 \\ h \\ 0 \end{bmatrix}$$

Thus

$$R_{n+1} = R - (n+1)h$$

$$t_{n+1} = \frac{2\pi}{v}(n+1)(R - \tfrac{1}{2}nh)$$

$$L_{n+1} = L - 2\pi(n+1)(R - \tfrac{1}{2}nh)$$

which gives the required result.

Note that the length depends on time in a linear fashion but that the relation between the radius and the time is quadratic

$$t_{n+1} = \frac{\pi}{vh}(R - R_{n+1})(R + R_{n+1} + h)$$

**Example 5.12** Find the values of $x$ that make the matrix $\boldsymbol{Z}^5$ a diagonal matrix, where

$$\boldsymbol{Z} = \begin{bmatrix} x & 0 & 0 \\ 0 & x & 1 \\ 0 & -1 & 0 \end{bmatrix}$$

**Solution** Although this problem can be done by hand it is tedious and a MAPLE solution is given.

```
with (linalg):
Z:= array ([[x, 0, 0], [0, x, 1], [0, -1, 0]]):
Z5:= simplify (multiply (Z, Z, Z, Z, Z));
```

$$Z5 := \begin{bmatrix} x^5 & 0 & 0 \\ 0 & 3x - 4x^3 + x^5 & 1 - 3x^2 + x^4 \\ 0 & -1 + 3x^2 - x^4 & 2x - x^3 \end{bmatrix}$$

```
evalf (solve ({Z5 [2, 3] = 0}, {x}));
{x = 1.618}, {x =-0.618}, {x = 0.618}, {x =-1.618}
```

Using MATLAB's Symbolic Math Toolbox the commands

```
syms x
Z = syms([x 0 0; 0 x 1; 0 -1 0]);
Z5 = Z^5; simplify(Z5);
pretty(ans)
```

produce the same matrix as above. The additional commands

```
solve(1 - 3*x^2 + x^4); double(ans)
```

produce the same values of $x$.

## 5.2.7 Exercises

Check the answers to the exercises using MATLAB or MAPLE whenever possible.

17 Given the matrices

$$\boldsymbol{A} = \begin{bmatrix} 1 & 0 & 1 \\ 2 & 1 & 2 \end{bmatrix}, \quad \boldsymbol{B} = \begin{bmatrix} 0 & 1 \\ 1 & 0 \\ 0 & 1 \end{bmatrix},$$

$$\boldsymbol{C} = \begin{bmatrix} 2 & 1 \\ -1 & 2 \end{bmatrix}$$

evaluate where possible

$$\boldsymbol{AB}, \boldsymbol{BA}, \boldsymbol{BC}, \boldsymbol{CB}, \boldsymbol{CA}, \boldsymbol{AC}$$

18 For the matrices

$$\boldsymbol{A} = \begin{bmatrix} 1 & 1 \\ 0 & 1 \end{bmatrix} \quad \text{and} \quad \boldsymbol{B} = \begin{bmatrix} 0 & 1 \\ 1 & 0 \end{bmatrix}$$

(a) evaluate $(\boldsymbol{A} + \boldsymbol{B})^2$ and $\boldsymbol{A}^2 + 2\boldsymbol{AB} + \boldsymbol{B}^2$

(b) evaluate $(\boldsymbol{A} + \boldsymbol{B})(\boldsymbol{A} - \boldsymbol{B})$ and $\boldsymbol{A}^2 - \boldsymbol{B}^2$

Repeat the calculations with the matrices

$$\boldsymbol{A} = \begin{bmatrix} 1 & 2 \\ 5 & 2 \end{bmatrix} \quad \text{and} \quad \boldsymbol{B} = \begin{bmatrix} 2 & -2 \\ -5 & 1 \end{bmatrix}$$

and explain the differences between the results for the two sets.

19 Show that for a square matrix $(\boldsymbol{A}^2)^{\mathrm{T}} = (\boldsymbol{A}^{\mathrm{T}})^2$.

20 Show that $\boldsymbol{AA}^{\mathrm{T}}$ is a symmetric matrix.

21 Find all the $2 \times 2$ matrices that commute (that is $\boldsymbol{AB} = \boldsymbol{BA}$) with $\begin{bmatrix} 1 & -1 \\ 0 & 2 \end{bmatrix}$.

22 A matrix with $m$ rows and $n$ columns is said to be of type $m \times n$. Give simple examples of matrices $\boldsymbol{A}$ and $\boldsymbol{B}$ to illustrate the following situations:

(a) $\boldsymbol{AB}$ is defined but $\boldsymbol{BA}$ is not,

(b) $\boldsymbol{AB}$ and $\boldsymbol{BA}$ are both defined but have different type,

(c) $\boldsymbol{AB}$ and $\boldsymbol{BA}$ are both defined and have the same type but are unequal.

23 Given

$$\boldsymbol{A} = \begin{bmatrix} 1 & 3 & 2 \\ 2 & -1 & 0 \\ 1 & 4 & 1 \end{bmatrix}$$

determine a symmetric matrix $\boldsymbol{C}$ and a skew-symmetric matrix $\boldsymbol{D}$ such that

$$\boldsymbol{A} = \boldsymbol{C} + \boldsymbol{D}$$

24 Given the matrices

$$\boldsymbol{a} = [3 \quad 2 \quad -1], \quad \boldsymbol{b} = \begin{bmatrix} 11 \\ 0 \\ 2 \end{bmatrix} \quad \text{and}$$

$$\boldsymbol{C} = \begin{bmatrix} 4 & 1 & 1 \\ -1 & 7 & -3 \\ -1 & 3 & 5 \end{bmatrix}$$

determine the elements of $\boldsymbol{G}$ where

$$(ab)\boldsymbol{I} + \boldsymbol{C}^2 = \boldsymbol{C}^{\mathrm{T}} + \boldsymbol{G}$$

and $\boldsymbol{I}$ is the unit matrix.

25 A firm allocates staff into four categories: welders, fitters, designers and administrators. It is estimated that for their three main products the time spent, in hours, on each item is given in the following matrix.

| | Boiler | Water tank | Holding frame |
|---|---|---|---|
| Welder | 2 | 0.75 | 1.25 |
| Fitter | 1.4 | 0.5 | 1.75 |
| Designer | 0.3 | 0.1 | 0.1 |
| Admin | 0.1 | 0.25 | 0.3 |

The wages, pension contributions and overheads, in £ per hour, are known to be

| | Welder | Fitter | Designer | Administrator |
|---|---|---|---|---|
| Wages | 12 | 8 | 20 | 10 |
| Pension | 1 | 0.5 | 2 | 1 |
| O/heads | 0 | 0 | 1 | 3 |

Write the problem in matrix form and use matrix products to find the total cost of producing 10 boilers, 25 water tanks and 35 frames.

26 Given

$$\boldsymbol{A} = \begin{bmatrix} 1 & 1 & 1 \\ 2 & 1 & 2 \\ -2 & 1 & -1 \end{bmatrix}$$

evaluate $\boldsymbol{A}^2$ and $\boldsymbol{A}^3$. Verify that

$$\boldsymbol{A}^3 - \boldsymbol{A}^2 - 3\boldsymbol{A} + \boldsymbol{I} = 0$$

27 Given

$$\boldsymbol{A} = \begin{bmatrix} 5 & -2 & 0 \\ -2 & 6 & 2 \\ 0 & 2 & 7 \end{bmatrix} \quad \text{and} \quad \boldsymbol{X} = \begin{bmatrix} x_1 \\ x_2 \\ x_3 \end{bmatrix}$$

show that

$$\boldsymbol{X}^{\mathrm{T}}\boldsymbol{A}\boldsymbol{X} = 27 \qquad \textbf{(5.7)}$$

implies that

$$5x_1^2 + 6x_2^2 + 7x_3^2 - 4x_1x_2 + 4x_2x_3 = 27$$

Under the transformation

$$\boldsymbol{X} = \boldsymbol{B}\boldsymbol{Y}$$

show that (5.7) becomes

$$\boldsymbol{Y}^{\mathrm{T}}(\boldsymbol{B}^{\mathrm{T}}\boldsymbol{A}\boldsymbol{B})\boldsymbol{Y} = 27$$

If

$$\boldsymbol{B} = \begin{bmatrix} 2 & 2 & -1 \\ 2 & -1 & 2 \\ -1 & 2 & 2 \end{bmatrix} \quad \text{and} \quad \boldsymbol{Y} = \begin{bmatrix} y_1 \\ y_2 \\ y_3 \end{bmatrix}$$

evaluate $\boldsymbol{B}^{\mathrm{T}}\boldsymbol{A}\boldsymbol{B}$, and hence show that

$$y_1^2 + 2y_2^2 + 3y_3^2 = 1$$

28 Figure 5.5 shows a Wheatstone bridge circuit. Kirchhoff's law states that the total current entering a junction is equal to the total current leaving it. Ohm's law in a circuit states that the imposed voltage in the circuit is the sum of current times resistance in the sections of the circuit. Write down the equations for the system and put them into the matrix form

$$\boldsymbol{A}\begin{bmatrix} i_1 \\ i_2 \\ \vdots \\ i_6 \end{bmatrix} = \boldsymbol{b}$$

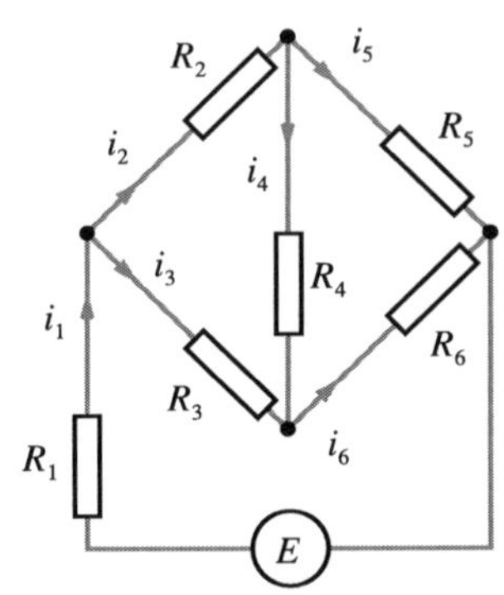


**Figure 5.5** Wheatstone bridge circuit

29 A well-known problem concerns a mythical country that has three cities, A, B and C, with a total population of 2400. At the end of each year it is decreed that all people must move to another city, half to one and half to the other. If $a$, $b$ and $c$ are the populations in the cities A, B and C respectively, show that in the next year the populations are given by

$$\begin{bmatrix} a' \\ b' \\ c' \end{bmatrix} = \begin{bmatrix} 0 & \frac{1}{2} & \frac{1}{2} \\ \frac{1}{2} & 0 & \frac{1}{2} \\ \frac{1}{2} & \frac{1}{2} & 0 \end{bmatrix} \begin{bmatrix} a \\ b \\ c \end{bmatrix}$$

Supposing that the three cities have initial populations of 600, 800 and 1000, what are the populations after 10 years and after a very long time (a package such as MATLAB is ideal for the calculations)? (Note that this example is a version of a **Markov chain** problem. Markov chains have applications in many areas of science and engineering.)

30 Find values of $h$, $k$, $l$ and $m$ so that $\boldsymbol{A} \neq 0$, $\boldsymbol{B} \neq 0$, $\boldsymbol{A}^2 = \boldsymbol{A}$, $\boldsymbol{B}^2 = \boldsymbol{B}$ and $\boldsymbol{AB} = 0$, where

$$\boldsymbol{A} = h \begin{bmatrix} 1 & 1 & 1 \\ 1 & 1 & 1 \\ 1 & 1 & 1 \end{bmatrix} \quad \text{and}$$

$$\boldsymbol{B} = \begin{bmatrix} k & -l & -l \\ -l & m & m \\ -l & m & m \end{bmatrix}$$

31 The Königsberg bridge problem concerns trying to follow a path across all the bridges to the islands in a river, as shown in Figure 5.6, without going over any bridge twice. Defining three matrices in an obvious way,

the adjacency matrix $\boldsymbol{A} = \begin{bmatrix} 0 & 2 & 0 & 1 \\ 2 & 0 & 2 & 1 \\ 0 & 2 & 0 & 1 \\ 1 & 1 & 1 & 0 \end{bmatrix}$

the degree matrix $\boldsymbol{D} = \begin{bmatrix} 3 & 0 & 0 & 0 \\ 0 & 5 & 0 & 0 \\ 0 & 0 & 3 & 0 \\ 0 & 0 & 0 & 3 \end{bmatrix}$

and the vertex-arc matrix

$$\boldsymbol{B} = \begin{bmatrix} 1 & 1 & 0 & 0 & 0 & 1 & 0 \\ 1 & 1 & 1 & 1 & 1 & 0 & 0 \\ 0 & 0 & 1 & 1 & 0 & 0 & 1 \\ 0 & 0 & 0 & 0 & 1 & 1 & 1 \end{bmatrix}$$

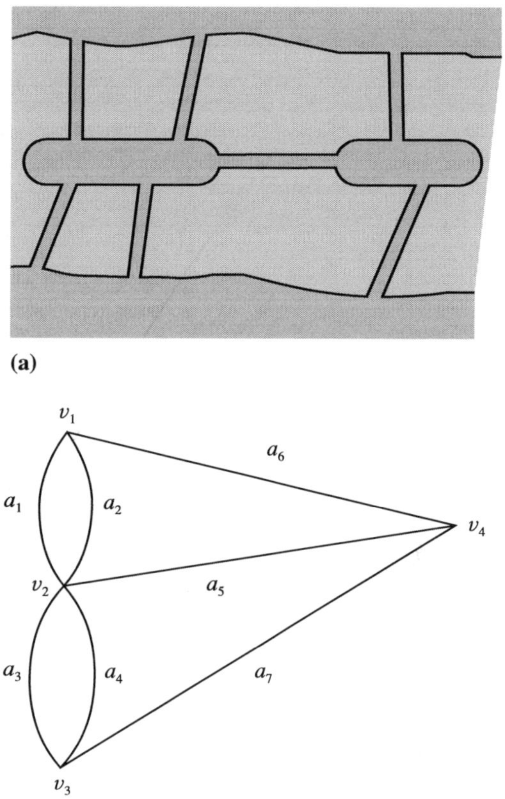


**Figure 5.6** The Königsberg bridge problem.

part of the solution involves showing that

$$\boldsymbol{BB}^{\mathrm{T}} = \boldsymbol{A} + \boldsymbol{D}$$

Verify this result.

32 A computer screen has dimensions 20 cm × 30 cm. Axes are set up at the centre of the screen as illustrated in Figure 5.7. A box containing an arrow

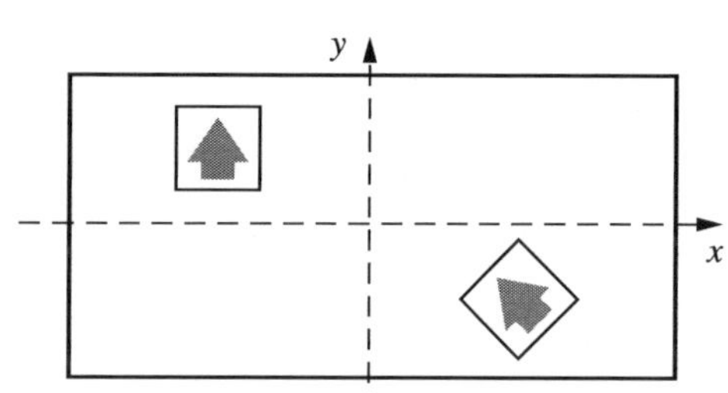


**Figure 5.7** Manipulation of a computer screen in Question 32.

has dimensions 2 cm × 2 cm and is situated with its centre at the point (−16, 10). It is first to be rotated through 45° in an anticlockwise direction. Find this transformation in the form

$$\begin{bmatrix} x' + 16 \\ y' - 10 \end{bmatrix} = \boldsymbol{A}\begin{bmatrix} x + 16 \\ y - 10 \end{bmatrix}$$

The rotated box is now moved to a new position with its centre at (16, −10). Find the overall transformation in the form

$$\begin{bmatrix} x'' \\ y'' \end{bmatrix} = \begin{bmatrix} a \\ b \end{bmatrix} + \boldsymbol{B}\begin{bmatrix} x \\ y \end{bmatrix}$$

33 Given the matrix

$$\boldsymbol{A} = \begin{bmatrix} 0 & 1 & 0 & 0 & 0 & 0 & 0 & 0 \\ 0 & 0 & 0 & 1 & 0 & 0 & 0 & 0 \\ 0 & 0 & 1 & 0 & 0 & 0 & 0 & 0 \\ 1 & 0 & 0 & 0 & 0 & 0 & 0 & 0 \\ 0 & 0 & 0 & 0 & 0 & 0 & 0 & 1 \\ 0 & 0 & 0 & 0 & 1 & 0 & 0 & 0 \\ 0 & 0 & 0 & 0 & 0 & 0 & 1 & 0 \\ 0 & 0 & 0 & 0 & 0 & 1 & 0 & 0 \end{bmatrix}$$

it is known that $\boldsymbol{A}^n = \boldsymbol{I}$, the unit matrix, for some $n$; find this value.

## 5.3 Determinants

The idea of a determinant is closely related to that of a square matrix and is crucial to the solution of linear equations. We shall deal here mainly with 2 × 2 and 3 × 3 determinants.

Given the square matrices

$$\boldsymbol{A} = \begin{bmatrix} a_{11} & a_{12} \\ a_{21} & a_{22} \end{bmatrix} \quad \text{and} \quad \boldsymbol{B} = \begin{bmatrix} a_{11} & a_{12} & a_{13} \\ a_{21} & a_{22} & a_{23} \\ a_{31} & a_{32} & a_{33} \end{bmatrix}$$

the **determinant** of $\boldsymbol{A}$, denoted by det $\boldsymbol{A}$ or $|\boldsymbol{A}|$, is given by

$$|\boldsymbol{A}| = a_{11}a_{22} - a_{12}a_{21} \tag{5.8}$$

For the 3 × 3 matrix $\boldsymbol{B}$

$$|\boldsymbol{B}| = a_{11}\begin{vmatrix} a_{22} & a_{23} \\ a_{32} & a_{33} \end{vmatrix} - a_{12}\begin{vmatrix} a_{21} & a_{23} \\ a_{31} & a_{33} \end{vmatrix} + a_{13}\begin{vmatrix} a_{21} & a_{22} \\ a_{31} & a_{32} \end{vmatrix} \tag{5.9}$$

This is known as the expansion of the determinant along the first row.

The determinant of a 1 × 1 matrix, $\boldsymbol{A} = [a]$, having a single entry $a$ is simply its entry. Thus

$$|\boldsymbol{A}| = a$$

It is important that this be distinguished from mod $a$ which is also written as $|a|$.

**Example 5.13** Evaluate the third-order determinant

$$\begin{vmatrix} 1 & 2 & 4 \\ -1 & 0 & 3 \\ 3 & 1 & -2 \end{vmatrix}$$

**Solution** Expanding along the first row as in (5.9), we have

$$\begin{vmatrix} 1 & 2 & 4 \\ -1 & 0 & 3 \\ 3 & 1 & -2 \end{vmatrix} = 1\begin{vmatrix} 0 & 3 \\ 1 & -2 \end{vmatrix} - 2\begin{vmatrix} -1 & 3 \\ 3 & -2 \end{vmatrix} + 4\begin{vmatrix} -1 & 0 \\ 3 & 1 \end{vmatrix}$$

$$\begin{aligned} &= 1[(0)(-2) - (1)(3)] - 2[(-1)(-2) - (3)(3)] \\ &\quad + 4[(-1)(1) - (3)(0)] \quad \text{(using (5.8))} \\ &= 1(-3) - 2(-7) + 4(-1) \\ &= 7 \end{aligned}$$

---

If we take a determinant and delete row $i$ and column $j$ then the determinant remaining is called the **minor** $M_{ij}$. In general we can take *any* row (or column) and evaluate an $n \times n$ determinant $|\boldsymbol{A}|$ as

$$|\boldsymbol{A}| = \sum_{j=1}^{n} (-1)^{i+j} a_{ij} M_{ij} \tag{5.10}$$

The fact that the determinant is the same for *any* $i$ requires detailed proof.

The sign associated with a minor is given in the array

$$\begin{vmatrix} + & - & + & - & + & \dots \\ - & + & - & + & - & \dots \\ + & - & + & - & + & \dots \\ \vdots & \vdots & \vdots & \vdots & \vdots & \end{vmatrix}$$

A minor multiplied by the appropriate sign is called the **cofactor** $A_{ij}$ of the element, so

$$A_{ij} = (-1)^{i+j} M_{ij}$$

and thus

$$|\boldsymbol{A}| = \sum_{j} a_{ij} A_{ij}$$

**Example 5.14** Evaluate the minors and cofactors of the determinant

$$|\mathbf{A}| = \begin{vmatrix} 3 & 4 & 5 \\ 6 & -4 & 2 \\ 2 & -1 & 1 \end{vmatrix}$$

associated with the first row, and hence evaluate the determinant.

**Solution**

$$\begin{vmatrix} 3 & 4 & 5 \\ 6 & -4 & 2 \\ 2 & -1 & 1 \end{vmatrix} \rightarrow \begin{vmatrix} -4 & 2 \\ -1 & 1 \end{vmatrix} = -4 - (-2) = -2$$

Element $a_{11}$ has minor $M_{11} = -2$ and cofactor $A_{11} = -2$.

$$\begin{vmatrix} 3 & 4 & 5 \\ 6 & -4 & 2 \\ 2 & -1 & 1 \end{vmatrix} \rightarrow \begin{vmatrix} 6 & 2 \\ 2 & 1 \end{vmatrix} = 2$$

Element $a_{12}$ has minor $M_{12} = 2$ and cofactor $A_{12} = -2$.

$$\begin{vmatrix} 3 & 4 & 5 \\ 6 & -4 & 2 \\ 2 & -1 & 1 \end{vmatrix} \rightarrow \begin{vmatrix} 6 & -4 \\ 2 & -1 \end{vmatrix} = 2$$

Element $a_{13}$ has minor $M_{13} = 2$ and cofactor $A_{13} = 2$. Thus the determinant is

$$|\mathbf{A}| = 3 \times (-2) + 4 \times (-2) + 5 \times 2 = -4$$

It may be checked that the same result is obtained by expanding along any row (or column), care being taken to incorporate the correct signs.

---

The properties of determinants are not always obvious, and are often quite difficult to prove in full generality. The commonly useful row operations are as follows.

*(a) Two rows (or columns) equal*

$$|\mathbf{A}| = \begin{vmatrix} a_{11} & a_{12} & a_{13} \\ a_{21} & a_{22} & a_{23} \\ a_{21} & a_{22} & a_{23} \end{vmatrix} = a_{11}\begin{vmatrix} a_{22} & a_{23} \\ a_{22} & a_{23} \end{vmatrix} - a_{12}\begin{vmatrix} a_{21} & a_{23} \\ a_{21} & a_{23} \end{vmatrix} + a_{13}\begin{vmatrix} a_{21} & a_{22} \\ a_{21} & a_{22} \end{vmatrix} = 0$$

Thus if two rows (or columns) are the same, the determinant is zero.

### *(b) Multiple of a row by a scalar*

$$|\boldsymbol{B}| = \begin{vmatrix} \lambda a_{11} & \lambda a_{12} & \lambda a_{13} \\ a_{21} & a_{22} & a_{23} \\ a_{31} & a_{32} & a_{33} \end{vmatrix} = \lambda|\boldsymbol{A}|$$

The proof of this follows immediately from the definition. A consequence of (a) and (b) is that if any row (or column) is a multiple of another row (or column) then the determinant is zero.

### *(c) Interchange of two rows (or columns)*

Consider $|\boldsymbol{A}|$ and $|\boldsymbol{B}|$ in which rows 1 and 2 are interchanged

$$|\boldsymbol{A}| = \begin{vmatrix} a_{11} & a_{12} & a_{13} \\ a_{21} & a_{22} & a_{23} \\ a_{31} & a_{32} & a_{33} \end{vmatrix} \quad \text{and} \quad |\boldsymbol{B}| = \begin{vmatrix} a_{21} & a_{22} & a_{23} \\ a_{11} & a_{12} & a_{13} \\ a_{31} & a_{32} & a_{33} \end{vmatrix}$$

Expanding $|\boldsymbol{A}|$ by the first row,

$$|\boldsymbol{A}| = a_{11}\begin{vmatrix} a_{22} & a_{23} \\ a_{32} & a_{33} \end{vmatrix} - a_{12}\begin{vmatrix} a_{21} & a_{23} \\ a_{31} & a_{33} \end{vmatrix} + a_{13}\begin{vmatrix} a_{21} & a_{22} \\ a_{31} & a_{32} \end{vmatrix}$$

and $|\boldsymbol{B}|$ by the second row

$$|\boldsymbol{B}| = -a_{11}\begin{vmatrix} a_{22} & a_{23} \\ a_{32} & a_{33} \end{vmatrix} + a_{12}\begin{vmatrix} a_{21} & a_{23} \\ a_{31} & a_{33} \end{vmatrix} - a_{13}\begin{vmatrix} a_{21} & a_{22} \\ a_{31} & a_{32} \end{vmatrix}$$

Thus

$$|\boldsymbol{A}| = -|\boldsymbol{B}|$$

so that interchanging two rows changes the sign of the determinant. Entirely similar results apply changing two columns.

### *(d) Addition rule*

Expanding by the first row

$$\begin{vmatrix} a_{11}+b_{11} & a_{12}+b_{12} & a_{13}+b_{13} \\ a_{21} & a_{22} & a_{23} \\ a_{31} & a_{32} & a_{33} \end{vmatrix}$$

$$= (a_{11}+b_{11})A_{11} + (a_{12}+b_{12})A_{12} + (a_{13}+b_{13})A_{13}$$

$$= (a_{11}A_{11} + a_{12}A_{12} + a_{13}A_{13}) + (b_{11}A_{11} + b_{12}A_{12} + b_{13}A_{13})$$

$$= \begin{vmatrix} a_{11} & a_{12} & a_{13} \\ a_{21} & a_{22} & a_{23} \\ a_{31} & a_{32} & a_{33} \end{vmatrix} + \begin{vmatrix} b_{11} & b_{12} & b_{13} \\ a_{21} & a_{22} & a_{23} \\ a_{31} & a_{32} & a_{33} \end{vmatrix}$$

It should be noted that $|\boldsymbol{A} + \boldsymbol{B}|$ is *not* equal to $|\boldsymbol{A}| + |\boldsymbol{B}|$ in *general.*

*(e) Adding multiples of rows (or columns)*
Consider

$$|\boldsymbol{A}| = \begin{vmatrix} a_{11} & a_{12} & a_{13} \\ a_{21} & a_{22} & a_{23} \\ a_{31} & a_{32} & a_{33} \end{vmatrix}$$

Then

$$|\boldsymbol{B}| = \begin{vmatrix} a_{11} + \lambda a_{21} & a_{12} + \lambda a_{22} & a_{13} + \lambda a_{23} \\ a_{21} & a_{22} & a_{23} \\ a_{31} & a_{32} & a_{33} \end{vmatrix}$$

$$= \begin{vmatrix} a_{11} & a_{12} & a_{13} \\ a_{21} & a_{22} & a_{23} \\ a_{31} & a_{32} & a_{33} \end{vmatrix} + \lambda \begin{vmatrix} a_{21} & a_{22} & a_{23} \\ a_{21} & a_{22} & a_{23} \\ a_{31} & a_{32} & a_{33} \end{vmatrix} \quad \text{(using (d) and then (b))}$$

$$= |\boldsymbol{A}| \quad \text{(since, by (a), the second determinant is zero)}$$

This means that adding multiples of rows (or columns) together makes no difference to the determinant.

*(f) Transpose*

$$|\boldsymbol{A}^{\mathrm{T}}| = |\boldsymbol{A}|$$

This just states that expanding by the first row or the first column gives the same result.

*(g) Product*

$$|\boldsymbol{AB}| = |\boldsymbol{A}||\boldsymbol{B}|$$

This result is difficult to prove generally, but it can be verified rather tediously for the $2 \times 2$ or $3 \times 3$ cases. For the $2 \times 2$ case

$$|\boldsymbol{A}||\boldsymbol{B}| = (a_{11}a_{22} - a_{12}a_{21})(b_{11}b_{22} - b_{12}b_{21})$$

$$= a_{11}a_{22}b_{11}b_{22} - a_{11}a_{22}b_{12}b_{21} - a_{12}a_{21}b_{11}b_{22} + a_{12}a_{21}b_{12}b_{21}$$

and

$$|\boldsymbol{AB}| = \begin{vmatrix} a_{11}b_{11} + a_{12}b_{21} & a_{11}b_{12} + a_{12}b_{22} \\ a_{21}b_{11} + a_{22}b_{21} & a_{21}b_{12} + a_{22}b_{22} \end{vmatrix}$$

$$= (a_{11}b_{11} + a_{12}b_{21})(a_{21}b_{12} + a_{22}b_{22}) - (a_{11}b_{12} + a_{12}b_{22})(a_{21}b_{11} + a_{22}b_{21})$$

$$= a_{11}a_{22}b_{11}b_{22} - a_{11}a_{22}b_{12}b_{21} - a_{12}a_{21}b_{11}b_{22} + a_{12}a_{21}b_{12}b_{21}$$

**Example 5.15** Evaluate the $3 \times 3$ determinants

$$\text{(a)}\ \begin{vmatrix} 1 & 0 & 1 \\ 0 & 1 & 2 \\ 1 & 1 & 0 \end{vmatrix},\quad \text{(b)}\ \begin{vmatrix} 1 & 0 & 1 \\ 1 & 1 & 0 \\ 0 & 1 & 2 \end{vmatrix},\quad \text{(c)}\ \begin{vmatrix} 1 & 1 & 0 \\ 0 & 1 & 1 \\ 1 & 0 & 2 \end{vmatrix},\quad \text{(d)}\ \begin{vmatrix} 1 & 0 & 1 \\ 0 & 2 & 4 \\ 3 & 3 & 0 \end{vmatrix}$$

**Solution** (a) Expand by the first row:

$$\begin{vmatrix} 1 & 0 & 1 \\ 0 & 1 & 2 \\ 1 & 1 & 0 \end{vmatrix} = 1\begin{vmatrix} 1 & 2 \\ 1 & 0 \end{vmatrix} - 0\begin{vmatrix} 0 & 2 \\ 1 & 0 \end{vmatrix} + 1\begin{vmatrix} 0 & 1 \\ 1 & 1 \end{vmatrix} = -2 - 0 - 1 = -3$$

(b) Expand by the first column:

$$\begin{vmatrix} 1 & 0 & 1 \\ 1 & 1 & 0 \\ 0 & 1 & 2 \end{vmatrix} = 1\begin{vmatrix} 1 & 0 \\ 1 & 2 \end{vmatrix} - 1\begin{vmatrix} 0 & 1 \\ 1 & 2 \end{vmatrix} + 0\begin{vmatrix} 0 & 1 \\ 1 & 0 \end{vmatrix} = 2 + 1 + 0 = 3$$

Note that (a) and (b) are the same determinant, but with two rows interchanged. The result confirms property (c) just stated above.

(c) Expand by the third row:

$$\begin{vmatrix} 1 & 1 & 0 \\ 0 & 1 & 1 \\ 1 & 0 & 2 \end{vmatrix} = 1\begin{vmatrix} 1 & 0 \\ 1 & 1 \end{vmatrix} - 0\begin{vmatrix} 1 & 0 \\ 0 & 1 \end{vmatrix} + 2\begin{vmatrix} 1 & 1 \\ 0 & 1 \end{vmatrix} = 1 - 0 + 2 = 3$$

Note that the matrix associated with the determinant in (c) is just the transpose of the matrix associated with the determinant in (b).

$$\text{(d)}\quad \begin{vmatrix} 1 & 0 & 1 \\ 0 & 2 & 4 \\ 3 & 3 & 0 \end{vmatrix} = 2\begin{vmatrix} 1 & 0 & 1 \\ 0 & 1 & 2 \\ 3 & 3 & 0 \end{vmatrix} = 6\begin{vmatrix} 1 & 0 & 1 \\ 0 & 1 & 2 \\ 1 & 1 & 0 \end{vmatrix} = -18$$

Note that we have used the multiple of a row rule on two occasions; the final determinant is the same as (a).

In MATLAB and MAPLE the determinant of a matrix $\boldsymbol{A}$ is given by the command `det(A)`. Considering Example 5.15(d) the MATLAB commands

```
A = [1 0 1; 0 2 4; 3 3 0];
det(A)
```

return the answer `-18`.

**Example 5.16** Given the matrices

$$\mathbf{A} = \begin{bmatrix} 1 & 2 & 3 \\ 2 & 3 & 4 \\ 4 & 5 & 6 \end{bmatrix} \quad \text{and} \quad \mathbf{B} = \begin{bmatrix} 1 & 0 & 1 \\ 1 & 1 & 1 \\ 1 & 2 & 3 \end{bmatrix}$$

evaluate (a) $|\mathbf{A}|$, (b) $|\mathbf{B}|$ and (c) $|\mathbf{AB}|$.

**Solution**

(a) $$|\mathbf{A}| = 1\begin{vmatrix} 3 & 4 \\ 5 & 6 \end{vmatrix} - 2\begin{vmatrix} 2 & 4 \\ 4 & 6 \end{vmatrix} + 3\begin{vmatrix} 2 & 3 \\ 4 & 5 \end{vmatrix}$$

$$= 1 \times (-2) - 2 \times (-4) + 3 \times (-2) = 0$$

(b) $$|\mathbf{B}| = \begin{vmatrix} 1 & 0 & 1 \\ 1 & 1 & 1 \\ 1 & 2 & 3 \end{vmatrix}$$

$$= \begin{vmatrix} 1 & 0 & 0 \\ 1 & 1 & 0 \\ 1 & 2 & 2 \end{vmatrix} \quad \text{(subtracting column 1 from column 3)}$$

$$= 1\begin{vmatrix} 1 & 0 \\ 2 & 2 \end{vmatrix} = 2 \quad \text{(expanding by first row)}$$

(c) $$|\mathbf{AB}| = \begin{vmatrix} 6 & 8 & 12 \\ 9 & 11 & 17 \\ 15 & 17 & 27 \end{vmatrix}$$

$$= 6[(11)(27) - (17)(17)] - 8[(9)(27) - (17)(15)] + 12[(9)(17) - (11)(15)]$$

$$= 48 + 96 - 144 = 0$$

---

We can use properties (a)–(e) to reduce the amount of computation involved in evaluating a determinant. We introduce as many zeros as possible into a row or column, and then expand along that row or column.

**Example 5.17** Evaluate

$$D = \begin{vmatrix} 1 & 1 & 1 & 1 \\ 1 & 1+a & 1 & 1 \\ 1 & 1 & 1+b & 1 \\ 1 & 1 & 1 & 1+c \end{vmatrix}$$

**Solution**

$$D = \begin{vmatrix} 1 & 0 & 0 & 0 \\ 1 & a & 0 & 0 \\ 1 & 0 & b & 0 \\ 1 & 0 & 0 & c \end{vmatrix} \quad \text{(by subtracting col. 1 from col. 2, col. 3 and col. 4)}$$

$$= 1\begin{vmatrix} a & 0 & 0 \\ 0 & b & 0 \\ 0 & 0 & c \end{vmatrix} \quad \text{(by expanding by the top row)}$$

$$= a\begin{vmatrix} b & 0 \\ 0 & c \end{vmatrix} = abc$$

A solution using MAPLE is given by the commands

```
with (linalg):
E:= array ([[1, 1, 1, 1], [1, 1+a, 1, 1],
[1, 1, 1+b, 1], [1, 1, 1, 1+c]]):
det(E);
```

Using MATLAB's Symbolic Math Toolbox the commands

```
syms a b c
E = sym([1 1 1 1; 1 1+a 1 1; 1 1 1+b 1; 1 1 1 1+c]);
det(E);
pretty(ans)
```

return the answer `abc`.

---

A point that should be carefully noted concerns large determinants; they are extremely difficult and time-consuming to evaluate (using the basic definition (5.10) for an $n \times n$ determinant involves $n!(n-1)$ multiplications). This is a problem even with computers – which in fact use alternative methods. If at all possible, evaluation of large determinants should be avoided. They do, however, play a central role in matrix theory.

The cofactors $A_{11}$, $A_{12}$, … defined earlier have the property that

$$|\boldsymbol{A}| = a_{11}A_{11} + a_{12}A_{12} + a_{13}A_{13}$$

Consider the expression $a_{21}A_{11} + a_{22}A_{12} + a_{23}A_{13}$. In determinant form we have

$$a_{21}A_{11} + a_{22}A_{12} + a_{23}A_{13} = \begin{vmatrix} a_{21} & a_{22} & a_{23} \\ a_{21} & a_{22} & a_{23} \\ a_{31} & a_{32} & a_{33} \end{vmatrix} = 0$$

since two rows are identical. Similarly,

$$a_{31}A_{11} + a_{32}A_{12} + a_{33}A_{13} = 0$$

In general it can be shown

$$\sum_k a_{ik}A_{jk} = \begin{cases} |\mathbf{A}| & \text{if } i = j \\ 0 & \text{if } i \neq j \end{cases} \quad \textbf{(5.11)}$$

and, expanding by columns,

$$\sum_k a_{ki}A_{kj} = \begin{cases} |\mathbf{A}| & \text{if } i = j \\ 0 & \text{if } i \neq j \end{cases} \quad \textbf{(5.12)}$$

A numerical example illustrates these points.

**Example 5.18** Illustrate the use of cofactors in the expansion of determinants on the matrix

$$\mathbf{A} = \begin{bmatrix} 1 & 2 & 3 \\ 6 & 5 & 4 \\ 7 & 8 & 1 \end{bmatrix}$$

**Solution** The cofactors are evaluated as

$$A_{11} = \begin{vmatrix} 5 & 4 \\ 8 & 1 \end{vmatrix} = -27, \quad A_{12} = -\begin{vmatrix} 6 & 4 \\ 7 & 1 \end{vmatrix} = 22, \quad A_{13} = \begin{vmatrix} 6 & 5 \\ 7 & 8 \end{vmatrix} = 13$$

and continuing in the same way

$$A_{21} = 22, A_{22} = -20, A_{23} = 6, A_{31} = -7, A_{32} = 14 \text{ and } A_{33} = -7$$

A selection of the evaluations in equation (5.11), that is expansion by rows, is

$$a_{11}A_{11} + a_{12}A_{12} + a_{13}A_{13} = 1 \times (-27) + 2 \times 22 + 3 \times 13 = 56$$

$$a_{21}A_{11} + a_{22}A_{12} + a_{23}A_{13} = 6 \times (-27) + 5 \times 22 + 4 \times 13 = 0$$

$$a_{31}A_{21} + a_{32}A_{22} + a_{33}A_{23} = 7 \times 22 + 8 \times (-20) + 1 \times 6 = 0$$

and in equation (5.12), that is expansion by columns, is

$$a_{11}A_{12} + a_{21}A_{22} + a_{31}A_{32} = 1 \times 22 + 6 \times (-20) + 7 \times 14 = 0$$

$$a_{12}A_{12} + a_{22}A_{22} + a_{32}A_{32} = 2 \times 22 + 5 \times (-20) + 8 \times 14 = 56$$

$$a_{13}A_{11} + a_{23}A_{21} + a_{33}A_{31} = 3 \times (-27) + 4 \times 22 + 1 \times (-7) = 0$$

The other expansions in equations (5.11) and (5.12) can be verified on this example. It may be noted that the determinant of the matrix is 56.

---

A matrix with particularly interesting properties is the **adjoint** or **adjugate matrix**, which is defined as the transpose of the matrix of cofactors; that is,

$$\text{adj}\,\boldsymbol{A} = \begin{bmatrix} A_{11} & A_{12} & A_{13} \\ A_{21} & A_{22} & A_{23} \\ A_{31} & A_{32} & A_{33} \end{bmatrix}^{\mathrm{T}} \tag{5.13}$$

If we now calculate $\boldsymbol{A}$ (adj $\boldsymbol{A}$), we have

$$[\boldsymbol{A}\,(\text{adj}\,\boldsymbol{A})]_{ij} = \sum_k a_{ik}(\text{adj}\,\boldsymbol{A})_{kj} = \sum_k a_{ik}A_{jk}$$

$$= \begin{cases} |\boldsymbol{A}| & \text{if } i = j \quad (\text{from (5.11)}) \\ 0 & \text{if } i \neq j \end{cases}$$

So

$$\boldsymbol{A}(\text{adj}\,\boldsymbol{A}) = \begin{bmatrix} |\boldsymbol{A}| & 0 & 0 \\ 0 & |\boldsymbol{A}| & 0 \\ 0 & 0 & |\boldsymbol{A}| \end{bmatrix} = |\boldsymbol{A}|\boldsymbol{I} \tag{5.14}$$

and we have thus discovered a matrix that when multiplied by $\boldsymbol{A}$ gives a scalar times the unit matrix.

If $\boldsymbol{A}$ is a square matrix of order $n$ then, taking determinants on both sides of (5.14),

$$|\boldsymbol{A}|\,|\text{adj}\,\boldsymbol{A}| = |\boldsymbol{A}(\text{adj}\,\boldsymbol{A})| = ||\boldsymbol{A}|\boldsymbol{I}_n| = |\boldsymbol{A}|^n$$

If $|\boldsymbol{A}| \neq 0$, it follows that

$$|\text{adj}\,\boldsymbol{A}| = |\boldsymbol{A}|^{n-1} \tag{5.15}$$

a result known as **Cauchy's theorem**.

It is also the case that

$$\text{adj}(\boldsymbol{AB}) = (\text{adj}\,\boldsymbol{B})(\text{adj}\,\boldsymbol{A}) \tag{5.16}$$

so in taking the adjoint of a product the order is reversed.

An important piece of notation that has significant implications for the solution of sets of linear equations concerns whether or not a matrix has zero determinant. A square matrix $\boldsymbol{A}$ is called **non-singular** if $|\boldsymbol{A}| \neq 0$ and **singular** if $|\boldsymbol{A}| = 0$.

**Example 5.19**

Derive the adjoint of the $2 \times 2$ matrices

$$\boldsymbol{A} = \begin{bmatrix} 1 & 3 \\ 2 & 8 \end{bmatrix} \quad \text{and} \quad \boldsymbol{B} = \begin{bmatrix} -1 & 2 \\ -3 & -4 \end{bmatrix}$$

and verify the results in equations (5.14), (5.15) and (5.16).

**Solution** The cofactors are very easy to evaluate in the $2 \times 2$ case: for the matrix $\boldsymbol{A}$

$$A_{11} = 8, A_{12} = -2, A_{21} = -3 \quad \text{and} \quad A_{22} = 1$$

and for the matrix $\boldsymbol{B}$

$$B_{11} = -4, B_{12} = 3, B_{21} = -2 \quad \text{and} \quad B_{22} = -1$$

The adjoint or adjugate matrices can be written down immediately as

$$\text{adj}\,\boldsymbol{A} = \begin{bmatrix} 8 & -3 \\ -2 & 1 \end{bmatrix} \quad \text{and} \quad \text{adj}\,\boldsymbol{B} = \begin{bmatrix} -4 & -2 \\ 3 & -1 \end{bmatrix}$$

Now (5.14) gives

$$\boldsymbol{A}(\text{adj}\,\boldsymbol{A}) = \begin{bmatrix} 1 & 3 \\ 2 & 8 \end{bmatrix}\begin{bmatrix} 8 & -3 \\ -2 & 1 \end{bmatrix} = \begin{bmatrix} 2 & 0 \\ 0 & 2 \end{bmatrix} = 2\boldsymbol{I}$$

$$\boldsymbol{B}(\text{adj}\,\boldsymbol{B}) = \begin{bmatrix} -1 & 2 \\ -3 & -4 \end{bmatrix}\begin{bmatrix} -4 & -2 \\ 3 & -1 \end{bmatrix} = \begin{bmatrix} 10 & 0 \\ 0 & 10 \end{bmatrix} = 10\boldsymbol{I}$$

so the property is satisfied and the determinants are 2 and 10 respectively. For equation (5.15) we have $n = 2$ so

$$|\text{adj}\,\boldsymbol{A}| = \begin{vmatrix} 8 & -3 \\ -2 & 1 \end{vmatrix} = 2 \quad \text{and} \quad |\text{adj}\,\boldsymbol{B}| = \begin{vmatrix} -4 & -2 \\ 3 & -1 \end{vmatrix} = 10$$

as required.

Evaluating the matrices in (5.16)

$$\text{adj}(\boldsymbol{AB}) = \text{adj}\begin{bmatrix} -10 & -10 \\ -26 & -28 \end{bmatrix} = \begin{bmatrix} -28 & 10 \\ 26 & -10 \end{bmatrix}$$

and

$$\text{adj}\,\boldsymbol{B}\;\text{adj}\,\boldsymbol{A} = \begin{bmatrix} -4 & -2 \\ 3 & -1 \end{bmatrix}\begin{bmatrix} 8 & -3 \\ -2 & 1 \end{bmatrix} = \begin{bmatrix} -28 & 10 \\ 26 & -10 \end{bmatrix}$$

and the statement is clearly verified. It is left as an exercise to show that the product of the matrices the other way round, adj $\boldsymbol{A}$ adj $\boldsymbol{B}$, gives a totally different matrix.

**Example 5.20** Given

$$\boldsymbol{A} = \begin{bmatrix} 1 & 1 & 2 \\ 2 & 0 & 1 \\ 3 & 1 & 1 \end{bmatrix}$$

determine adj $\boldsymbol{A}$ and show that $\boldsymbol{A}(\text{adj}\,\boldsymbol{A}) = (\text{adj}\,\boldsymbol{A})\boldsymbol{A} = |\boldsymbol{A}|\boldsymbol{I}$.

**Solution** The matrix of cofactors is

$$\begin{bmatrix} \begin{vmatrix} 0 & 1 \\ 1 & 1 \end{vmatrix} & -\begin{vmatrix} 2 & 1 \\ 3 & 1 \end{vmatrix} & \begin{vmatrix} 2 & 0 \\ 3 & 1 \end{vmatrix} \\ -\begin{vmatrix} 1 & 2 \\ 1 & 1 \end{vmatrix} & \begin{vmatrix} 1 & 2 \\ 3 & 1 \end{vmatrix} & -\begin{vmatrix} 1 & 1 \\ 3 & 1 \end{vmatrix} \\ \begin{vmatrix} 1 & 2 \\ 0 & 1 \end{vmatrix} & -\begin{vmatrix} 1 & 2 \\ 2 & 1 \end{vmatrix} & \begin{vmatrix} 1 & 1 \\ 2 & 0 \end{vmatrix} \end{bmatrix} = \begin{bmatrix} -1 & 1 & 2 \\ 1 & -5 & 2 \\ 1 & 3 & -2 \end{bmatrix}$$

so, from (5.13)

$$\text{adj}\,\boldsymbol{A} = \begin{bmatrix} -1 & 1 & 2 \\ 1 & -5 & 2 \\ 1 & 3 & -2 \end{bmatrix}^{\mathrm{T}} = \begin{bmatrix} -1 & 1 & 1 \\ 1 & -5 & 3 \\ 2 & 2 & -2 \end{bmatrix}$$

$$\boldsymbol{A}(\text{adj}\,\boldsymbol{A}) = \begin{bmatrix} 1 & 1 & 2 \\ 2 & 0 & 1 \\ 3 & 1 & 1 \end{bmatrix}\begin{bmatrix} -1 & 1 & 1 \\ 1 & -5 & 3 \\ 2 & 2 & -2 \end{bmatrix} = \begin{bmatrix} 4 & 0 & 0 \\ 0 & 4 & 0 \\ 0 & 0 & 4 \end{bmatrix}$$

$$(\text{adj}\,\boldsymbol{A})\boldsymbol{A} = \begin{bmatrix} -1 & 1 & 1 \\ 1 & -5 & 3 \\ 2 & 2 & -2 \end{bmatrix}\begin{bmatrix} 1 & 1 & 2 \\ 2 & 0 & 1 \\ 3 & 1 & 1 \end{bmatrix} = \begin{bmatrix} 4 & 0 & 0 \\ 0 & 4 & 0 \\ 0 & 0 & 4 \end{bmatrix}$$

Since $|\boldsymbol{A}| = 4$ the last result then follows.

---

In MAPLE the adjoint of a matrix $\boldsymbol{A}$ is determined by the command *adj*(A). There appears to be no equivalent command in either MATLAB or its Symbolic Math Toolbox. However, the `maple` command in the Toolbox may be used to access the command in MAPLE, having first expressed the matrix $\boldsymbol{A}$ in symbolic form using the *sym* command. Consequently in MATLAB's Symbolic Math Toolbox the adjoint is determined by the commands

```
A = sym(A);
adjA = maple('adj', A)
```

Check that in MATLAB the commands

```
A = [1 1 2; 2 0 1; 3 1 1];
A = sym(A);
adjA = maple('adj',A)
```

return the first answer in Example 5.20.

## 5.3.1 Exercises

Check your answers using MATLAB or MAPLE whenever possible.

**34** Find all the minors and cofactors of the determinant

$$\begin{vmatrix} 1 & 2 & 3 \\ 1 & 0 & 1 \\ 1 & 1 & 1 \end{vmatrix}$$

Hence evaluate the determinant.

**35** Evaluate the determinants of the following matrices:

(a) $\begin{bmatrix} 1 & 7 \\ 4 & 9 \end{bmatrix}$ (b) $\begin{bmatrix} 1 & 4 & 3 \\ 2 & -4 & 1 \\ 3 & 2 & -6 \end{bmatrix}$

(c) $\begin{bmatrix} 2 & -1 & 3 \\ 4 & 2 & 9 \\ 1 & 3 & -4 \end{bmatrix}$ (d) $\begin{bmatrix} 1 & 0 & 1 \\ 0 & 1 & 0 \\ 1 & 0 & 2 \end{bmatrix}$

(e) $\begin{bmatrix} 1 & -1 & 0 \\ 1 & 1 & 1 \\ 0 & 1 & -1 \end{bmatrix}$

**36** Given the matrix

$$\boldsymbol{A} = \begin{bmatrix} 1 & 0 & -1 \\ 1 & 0 & 1 \\ 2 & 2 & 2 \end{bmatrix}$$

determine $|\boldsymbol{A}|$, $|\boldsymbol{A}\boldsymbol{A}^{\mathrm{T}}|$, $|\boldsymbol{A}^2|$ and $|\boldsymbol{A} + \boldsymbol{A}|$.

**37** Find a series of row manipulations that takes $\begin{vmatrix} 1 & 0 & 1 \\ 2 & 1 & 0 \\ 0 & 1 & 1 \end{vmatrix}$ to $-\begin{vmatrix} 2 & 1 & 0 \\ 0 & -\frac{1}{2} & 1 \\ 0 & 0 & 3 \end{vmatrix}$ and hence evaluate the determinant.

**38** Determine adj $\boldsymbol{A}$ when

$$\boldsymbol{A} = \begin{bmatrix} a & b \\ c & d \end{bmatrix}$$

**39** Determine adj $\boldsymbol{A}$ when

$$\boldsymbol{A} = \begin{bmatrix} 2 & 1 & 1 \\ 3 & 2 & 2 \\ 1 & 1 & 2 \end{bmatrix}$$

Check that $\boldsymbol{A}(\text{adj}\,\boldsymbol{A}) = (\text{adj}\,\boldsymbol{A})\boldsymbol{A} = |\boldsymbol{A}|\boldsymbol{I}$.

**40** For the matrix

$$\boldsymbol{A} = \begin{bmatrix} 2 & 0 \\ 3 & 1 \end{bmatrix}$$

evaluate $|\boldsymbol{A}|$, adj($\boldsymbol{A}$), $\boldsymbol{B} = \dfrac{\text{adj}(\boldsymbol{A})}{|\boldsymbol{A}|}$ and $\boldsymbol{AB}$.

**41** Show that the matrix

$$\boldsymbol{B} = \begin{bmatrix} 1 & 0 & 2 \\ 3 & 4 & 0 \\ 6 & -2 & 1 \end{bmatrix}$$

is non-singular and verify Cauchy's theorem, namely $|\text{adj}\,\boldsymbol{B}| = |\boldsymbol{B}|^2$.

**42** If $|\boldsymbol{A}| = 0$ deduce that $|\boldsymbol{A}^n| = 0$ for any integer $n$.

**43** Given

$$\boldsymbol{A} = \begin{bmatrix} 2 & -1 & 0 \\ -4 & 3 & -1 \\ 1 & -1 & 1 \end{bmatrix} \quad \text{and}$$

$$\boldsymbol{B} = \begin{bmatrix} 1 & 0 & 2 \\ 3 & 4 & 0 \\ 6 & -2 & 1 \end{bmatrix}$$

verify that adj($\boldsymbol{AB}$) = (adj $\boldsymbol{B}$)(adj $\boldsymbol{A}$).

**44** Find the values of $\lambda$ that make the following determinants zero:

(a) $\begin{vmatrix} 2-\lambda & 7 \\ 4 & 6-\lambda \end{vmatrix}$

(b) $\begin{vmatrix} 1 & 3-\lambda & 4 \\ 4-\lambda & 2 & -1 \\ 1 & \lambda-6 & 2 \end{vmatrix}$

(c) $\begin{vmatrix} 0 & 2-\lambda & 0 \\ 2-\lambda & 4 & 1 \\ 2 & -3 & \lambda-4 \end{vmatrix}$

45 Evaluate the determinants of the square matrices

(a) $\begin{bmatrix} 0.42 & 0.31 & -0.16 \\ 0.17 & -0.22 & 0.63 \\ 0.89 & 0.93 & 0.41 \end{bmatrix}$

(b) $\begin{bmatrix} 5 & 4 & 1 & 1 \\ 4 & 5 & 1 & 1 \\ 1 & 1 & 4 & 2 \\ 1 & 1 & 2 & 4 \end{bmatrix}$

46 Show that the area of a triangle with vertices $(x_1, y_1)$, $(x_2, y_2)$ and $(x_3, y_3)$ is given by the absolute value of

$$\frac{1}{2}\begin{vmatrix} 1 & x_1 & y_1 \\ 1 & x_2 & y_2 \\ 1 & x_3 & y_3 \end{vmatrix}$$

Refer to Question 32 in Exercises (4.2.10) and the definition of the vector product in Section 4.2.9.

47 Show that $x + x^2 - 2x^3$ is a factor of the determinant $D$ where

$$D = \begin{vmatrix} 0 & x & 2 & x^2 \\ -x & 0 & 1 & x^3 \\ -2 & -1 & 0 & 1 \\ -x^2 & -x^3 & -1 & 0 \end{vmatrix}$$

and hence express $D$ as a product of linear factors.

48 Show that

$$\begin{vmatrix} x & a & b \\ x^2 & a^2 & b^2 \\ a+b & x+b & x+a \end{vmatrix}$$

$$= (b-a)(x-a)(x-b)(x+a+b)$$

Such an exercise can be solved in two lines of code of a symbolic manipulation package such as MAPLE or MATLAB's Symbolic Math Toolbox.

49 Verify that if $\boldsymbol{A}$ is a symmetric matrix then so is adj $\boldsymbol{A}$.

50 If $\boldsymbol{A}$ is a skew-symmetric $n \times n$ matrix, verify that adj $\boldsymbol{A}$ is symmetric or skew-symmetric according to whether $n$ is odd or even.

## 5.4 The inverse matrix

In Section 5.3 we constructed adj $\boldsymbol{A}$ and saw that it had interesting properties in relation to the unit matrix. We also saw, in Example 5.5, that we had a method of solving linear equations if we could construct $\boldsymbol{B}$ such that $\boldsymbol{AB} = \boldsymbol{I}$. These ideas can be brought together to provide a comprehensive theory of the solution of linear equations, which we will consider in Section 5.5.

Given a square matrix $\boldsymbol{A}$, if we can construct a matrix $\boldsymbol{B}$ such that

$$\boldsymbol{BA} = \boldsymbol{AB} = \boldsymbol{I}$$

then **we call $\boldsymbol{B}$ the inverse of $\boldsymbol{A}$ and write it as $\boldsymbol{A}^{-1}$**. From (5.14)

$$\boldsymbol{A}(\text{adj } \boldsymbol{A}) = |\boldsymbol{A}|\boldsymbol{I}$$

so that we have gone a long way to constructing the inverse. We have two cases:

- If $\boldsymbol{A}$ is non-singular then $|\boldsymbol{A}| \neq 0$ and

$$\boldsymbol{A}^{-1} = \frac{\text{adj}\,\boldsymbol{A}}{|\boldsymbol{A}|}$$

- If $\boldsymbol{A}$ is singular then $|\boldsymbol{A}| = 0$ and it can be shown that the inverse $\boldsymbol{A}^{-1}$ does not exist.

If the inverse exists then it is unique. Suppose for a given $\boldsymbol{A}$ we have two inverses $\boldsymbol{B}$ and $\boldsymbol{C}$. Then

$$\boldsymbol{AB} = \boldsymbol{BA} = \boldsymbol{I}, \quad \boldsymbol{AC} = \boldsymbol{CA} = \boldsymbol{I}$$

and therefore

$$\boldsymbol{AB} = \boldsymbol{AC}$$

Pre-multiplying by $\boldsymbol{C}$, we have

$$\boldsymbol{C}(\boldsymbol{AB}) = \boldsymbol{C}(\boldsymbol{AC})$$

But matrix multiplication is associative, so we can write this as

$$(\boldsymbol{CA})\boldsymbol{B} = (\boldsymbol{CA})\boldsymbol{C}$$

Hence

$$\boldsymbol{IB} = \boldsymbol{IC} \quad (\text{since } \boldsymbol{CA} = \boldsymbol{I})$$

and so

$$\boldsymbol{B} = \boldsymbol{C}$$

The inverse is therefore unique.

It should be noted that if both $\boldsymbol{A}$ and $\boldsymbol{B}$ are square matrices then $\boldsymbol{AB} = \boldsymbol{I}$ if and only if $\boldsymbol{BA} = \boldsymbol{I}$.

**Example 5.21** Find $\boldsymbol{A}^{-1}$ and $\boldsymbol{B}^{-1}$ for the matrices

$$\text{(a) } \boldsymbol{A} = \begin{bmatrix} 1 & 2 \\ 2 & 3 \end{bmatrix} \quad \text{and} \quad \text{(b) } \boldsymbol{B} = \begin{bmatrix} 5 & 2 & 4 \\ 3 & -1 & 2 \\ 1 & 4 & -3 \end{bmatrix}$$

**Solution**

$$\text{(a) adj}\,\boldsymbol{A} = \begin{bmatrix} 3 & -2 \\ -2 & 1 \end{bmatrix}^{\mathrm{T}} = \begin{bmatrix} 3 & -2 \\ -2 & 1 \end{bmatrix} \quad \text{and} \quad |\boldsymbol{A}| = -1$$

so that

$$\boldsymbol{A}^{-1} = \frac{\text{adj}\,\boldsymbol{A}}{|\boldsymbol{A}|} = \begin{bmatrix} -3 & 2 \\ 2 & -1 \end{bmatrix}$$

$$\text{(b) adj}\boldsymbol{B} = \begin{bmatrix} -5 & 11 & 13 \\ 22 & -19 & -18 \\ 8 & 2 & -11 \end{bmatrix}^{\mathrm{T}} = \begin{bmatrix} -5 & 22 & 8 \\ 11 & -19 & 2 \\ 13 & -18 & -11 \end{bmatrix} \quad \text{and} \quad |\boldsymbol{B}| = 49$$

so that

$$\boldsymbol{B}^{-1} = \frac{1}{49}\begin{bmatrix} -5 & 22 & 8 \\ 11 & -19 & 2 \\ 13 & -18 & -11 \end{bmatrix}$$

In both cases it can be checked that $\boldsymbol{AA}^{-1} = \boldsymbol{I}$ and $\boldsymbol{BB}^{-1} = \boldsymbol{I}$.

---

Finding the inverse of a $2 \times 2$ matrix is very easy, since for

$$\boldsymbol{A} = \begin{bmatrix} a & b \\ c & d \end{bmatrix}$$

$$\boldsymbol{A}^{-1} = \frac{1}{ad - bc}\begin{bmatrix} d & -b \\ -c & a \end{bmatrix} \quad \text{(provided that } ad - bc \neq 0\text{)}$$

Unfortunately there is no simple extension of this result to higher-order matrices. On the other hand, in most practical situations the inverse itself is rarely required – it is the solution of the corresponding linear equations that is important. To understand the power and applicability of the various methods of solution of linear equations, the role of the inverse is essential. The consideration of the adjoint matrix provides a theoretical framework for this study, but as a practical method for finding the inverse of a matrix it is virtually useless, since, as we saw earlier, it is so time-consuming to compute determinants.

To find the inverse of a product of two matrices, the order is reversed:

$$(\boldsymbol{AB})^{-1} = \boldsymbol{B}^{-1}\boldsymbol{A}^{-1} \tag{5.17}$$

(provided that $\boldsymbol{A}$ and $\boldsymbol{B}$ are invertible). To prove this, let $\boldsymbol{C} = \boldsymbol{B}^{-1}\boldsymbol{A}^{-1}$. Then

$$\boldsymbol{C}(\boldsymbol{AB}) = (\boldsymbol{B}^{-1}\boldsymbol{A}^{-1})(\boldsymbol{AB}) = \boldsymbol{B}^{-1}(\boldsymbol{A}^{-1}\boldsymbol{A})\boldsymbol{B} = \boldsymbol{B}^{-1}\boldsymbol{IB} = \boldsymbol{B}^{-1}\boldsymbol{B} = \boldsymbol{I}$$

and thus

$$\boldsymbol{C} = \boldsymbol{B}^{-1}\boldsymbol{A}^{-1} = (\boldsymbol{AB})^{-1}$$

Since matrices do not commute in general $\boldsymbol{A}^{-1}\boldsymbol{B}^{-1} \neq \boldsymbol{B}^{-1}\boldsymbol{A}^{-1}$.

In MATLAB the inverse of a matrix $\boldsymbol{A}$ is determined by the command `inv(A)`; first expressing $\boldsymbol{A}$ in symbolic form using the `sym` command if the Symbolic Math Toolbox is used. In MAPLE the corresponding command is `inverse(A)`.

**Example 5.22** Given

$$\boldsymbol{A} = \begin{bmatrix} 1 & 2 \\ 2 & 1 \end{bmatrix} \quad \text{and} \quad \boldsymbol{B} = \begin{bmatrix} 0 & 1 \\ 1 & 1 \end{bmatrix}$$

evaluate $(\boldsymbol{AB})^{-1}$, $\boldsymbol{A}^{-1}\boldsymbol{B}^{-1}$, $\boldsymbol{B}^{-1}\boldsymbol{A}^{-1}$ and show that $(\boldsymbol{AB})^{-1} = \boldsymbol{B}^{-1}\boldsymbol{A}^{-1}$.

**Solution**

$$\boldsymbol{A}^{-1} = \begin{bmatrix} -\frac{1}{3} & \frac{2}{3} \\ \frac{2}{3} & -\frac{1}{3} \end{bmatrix}, \quad \boldsymbol{B}^{-1} = \begin{bmatrix} -1 & 1 \\ 1 & 0 \end{bmatrix}$$

$$\boldsymbol{AB} = \begin{bmatrix} 2 & 3 \\ 1 & 3 \end{bmatrix}, \quad (\boldsymbol{AB})^{-1} = \begin{bmatrix} 1 & -1 \\ -\frac{1}{3} & \frac{2}{3} \end{bmatrix}$$

$$\boldsymbol{A}^{-1}\boldsymbol{B}^{-1} = \begin{bmatrix} -\frac{1}{3} & \frac{2}{3} \\ \frac{2}{3} & -\frac{1}{3} \end{bmatrix}\begin{bmatrix} -1 & 1 \\ 1 & 0 \end{bmatrix} = \begin{bmatrix} 1 & -\frac{1}{3} \\ -1 & \frac{2}{3} \end{bmatrix}$$

$$\boldsymbol{B}^{-1}\boldsymbol{A}^{-1} = \begin{bmatrix} -1 & 1 \\ 1 & 0 \end{bmatrix}\begin{bmatrix} -\frac{1}{3} & \frac{2}{3} \\ \frac{2}{3} & -\frac{1}{3} \end{bmatrix} = \begin{bmatrix} 1 & -1 \\ -\frac{1}{3} & \frac{2}{3} \end{bmatrix} = (\boldsymbol{AB})^{-1}$$

**Example 5.23** Given the two matrices

$$\boldsymbol{A} = \begin{bmatrix} 0 & -\frac{3}{5} & 0 \\ \frac{5}{3} & 0 & -\frac{5}{3} \\ 0 & 6 & -6 \end{bmatrix} \quad \text{and} \quad \boldsymbol{T} = \begin{bmatrix} 0.6 & 0.3 & 0.1 \\ 1 & 1 & 0.5 \\ 1.2 & 1.5 & 1 \end{bmatrix}$$

show that the matrix $\boldsymbol{T}^{-1}\boldsymbol{AT}$ is diagonal.

**Solution** The inverse is best computed using MATLAB or a similar package. It may be verified by direct multiplication that

$$\boldsymbol{T}^{-1} = \frac{1}{6}\begin{bmatrix} 25 & -15 & 5 \\ -40 & 48 & -20 \\ 30 & -54 & 30 \end{bmatrix}$$

The further multiplications give

$$\frac{1}{6}\begin{bmatrix} 25 & -15 & 5 \\ -40 & 48 & -20 \\ 30 & -54 & 30 \end{bmatrix}\begin{bmatrix} 0 & -\frac{3}{5} & 0 \\ \frac{5}{3} & 0 & -\frac{5}{3} \\ 0 & 6 & -6 \end{bmatrix}\begin{bmatrix} 0.6 & 0.3 & 0.1 \\ 1 & 1 & 0.5 \\ 1.2 & 1.5 & 1 \end{bmatrix} = \begin{bmatrix} -1 & 0 & 0 \\ 0 & -2 & 0 \\ 0 & 0 & -3 \end{bmatrix}$$

This technique is an important one mathematically (see the companion text *Advanced Modern Engineering Mathematics*) since it provides a method of uncoupling a system of coupled equations. Practically it is the process used to reduce a physical system to principal axes; in elasticity it provides the principal stresses in a body.

Check that in MATLAB the commands

```
T = [0.6 0.3 0.1; 1 1 0.5; 1.2 1.5 1];
inv(T)
```

return the inverse $\boldsymbol{T}^{-1}$ in the numeric form

$$\begin{bmatrix} 4.1667 & -2.5000 & 0.8333 \\ -6.6667 & 8.0000 & -3.3333 \\ 5.0000 & -9.0000 & 5.0000 \end{bmatrix}$$

Check also that, using the Symbolic Math Toolbox, the exact form given in the solution is obtained using the commands

```
T = [0.6 0.3 0.1; 1 1 0.5; 1.2 1.5 1];
T = sym(T);
inv(T)
```

## 5.4.1 Exercises

Check your answers to the exercises using MATLAB.

51 Determine whether the following matrices are singular or non-singular *and* find the inverse of the non-singular matrices:

(a) $\begin{bmatrix} 1 & 2 \\ 2 & 1 \end{bmatrix}$ (b) $\begin{bmatrix} 1 & 2 & 3 \\ 2 & 2 & 1 \\ 5 & 6 & 5 \end{bmatrix}$

(c) $\begin{bmatrix} 1 & 0 & 0 & 1 \\ 0 & 1 & 0 & 1 \\ 0 & 0 & 1 & 1 \\ 0 & 0 & 0 & 1 \end{bmatrix}$ (d) $\begin{bmatrix} 1 & 0 & 1 \\ 0 & 1 & 0 \\ 1 & 0 & 1 \end{bmatrix}$

52 Find the inverses of the matrices

(a) $\begin{bmatrix} 1 & 1 & 1 \\ 0 & 1 & 0 \\ 0 & 0 & 1 \end{bmatrix}$ (b) $\begin{bmatrix} 1 & 0 & 0 & 0 \\ 0 & 2 & 0 & 0 \\ 0 & 0 & 3 & 0 \\ 0 & 0 & 0 & 4 \end{bmatrix}$

(c) $\begin{bmatrix} 1 & j \\ -j & 2 \end{bmatrix}$ (d) $\begin{bmatrix} 1 & 2 & 3 \\ 0 & 1 & 2 \\ 2 & 3 & 1 \end{bmatrix}$

53 Verify that

$$\boldsymbol{A} = \begin{bmatrix} 0 & 1 & -3 \\ 2 & 1 & 0 \\ 1 & -2 & 1 \end{bmatrix}$$

has an inverse

$$\boldsymbol{A}^{-1} = \frac{1}{13}\begin{bmatrix} 1 & 5 & 3 \\ -2 & 3 & -6 \\ -5 & 1 & -2 \end{bmatrix}$$

and hence solve the equation

$$\boldsymbol{ACA} = \begin{bmatrix} 2 & 1 & 1 \\ 0 & 2 & 3 \\ 2 & 1 & 0 \end{bmatrix}$$

**54** (a) If a square matrix $\boldsymbol{A}$ satisfies $\boldsymbol{A}^2 = \boldsymbol{A}$ and has an inverse show that $\boldsymbol{A}$ is the unit matrix.

(b) Show that $\boldsymbol{A} = \begin{bmatrix} 1 & 0 \\ 0 & 0 \end{bmatrix}$ satisfies $\boldsymbol{A}^2 = \boldsymbol{A}$.

(*Note*: matrices that satisfy $\boldsymbol{A}^2 = \boldsymbol{A}$ are called idempotent.)

**55** If

$$\boldsymbol{A} = \begin{bmatrix} 1 & 0 & 0 \\ 1 & 1 & 0 \\ 0 & 2 & 1 \end{bmatrix}, \quad \boldsymbol{B} = \begin{bmatrix} 1 & 4 & -1 \\ 0 & 2 & 1 \\ 0 & 0 & 2 \end{bmatrix}$$

$$\text{and} \quad \boldsymbol{C} = \begin{bmatrix} 1 & 4 & -1 \\ 1 & 6 & 0 \\ 0 & 4 & 4 \end{bmatrix}$$

show that $\boldsymbol{AB} = \boldsymbol{C}$. Find the inverse of $\boldsymbol{A}$ and $\boldsymbol{B}$ and hence of $\boldsymbol{C}$.

(*Note*: this is an example of a powerful method called **LU** decomposition.)

**56** Given the matrix

$$\boldsymbol{A} = \begin{bmatrix} 1 & 1 & 0 \\ 0 & 1 & 2 \\ 1 & 2 & 3 \end{bmatrix}$$

and the elementary matrices

$$\boldsymbol{E}_1 = \begin{bmatrix} 1 & 0 & 0 \\ 0 & 1 & 0 \\ -1 & 0 & 1 \end{bmatrix} \quad \boldsymbol{E}_2 = \begin{bmatrix} 1 & 0 & 0 \\ 0 & 1 & 0 \\ 0 & -1 & 1 \end{bmatrix}$$

$$\boldsymbol{E}_3 = \begin{bmatrix} 1 & 0 & 0 \\ 0 & 1 & -2 \\ 0 & 0 & 1 \end{bmatrix} \quad \boldsymbol{E}_4 = \begin{bmatrix} 1 & -1 & 0 \\ 0 & 1 & 0 \\ 0 & 0 & 1 \end{bmatrix}$$

evaluate $\boldsymbol{E}_1\boldsymbol{A}$, $\boldsymbol{E}_2\boldsymbol{E}_1\boldsymbol{A}$, $\boldsymbol{E}_3\boldsymbol{E}_2\boldsymbol{E}_1\boldsymbol{A}$ and $\boldsymbol{E}_4\boldsymbol{E}_3\boldsymbol{E}_2\boldsymbol{E}_1\boldsymbol{A}$ and hence find the inverse of $\boldsymbol{A}$.

(*Note*: the elementary matrices manipulate the rows of the matrix $\boldsymbol{A}$.)

**57** For the matrix

$$\boldsymbol{A} = \begin{bmatrix} 1 & 2 & 2 \\ 2 & 1 & 2 \\ 2 & 2 & 1 \end{bmatrix}$$

show that $\boldsymbol{A}^2 - 4\boldsymbol{A} - 5\boldsymbol{I} = 0$ and hence that $\boldsymbol{A}^{-1} = \frac{1}{5}(\boldsymbol{A} - 4\boldsymbol{I})$. Calculate $\boldsymbol{A}^{-1}$ from this result. Further show that the inverse of $\boldsymbol{A}^2$ is given by $\frac{1}{25}(21\boldsymbol{I} - 4\boldsymbol{A})$ and evaluate.

**58** Given

$$\boldsymbol{A} = \begin{bmatrix} 1 & 0 & 2 \\ 6 & 4 & 0 \\ 6 & -2 & 1 \end{bmatrix} \quad \text{and} \quad \boldsymbol{B} = \begin{bmatrix} 5 & 2 & 4 \\ 3 & -1 & 2 \\ 1 & 4 & -3 \end{bmatrix}$$

find $\boldsymbol{A}^{-1}$ and $\boldsymbol{B}^{-1}$. Verify that $(\boldsymbol{AB})^{-1} = \boldsymbol{B}^{-1}\boldsymbol{A}^{-1}$.

**59** Given the matrices

$$\boldsymbol{A} = \begin{bmatrix} 1 & 0 & 0 & 0 \\ 0 & 0 & 1 & 0 \\ 0 & 1 & 0 & 0 \\ 0 & 0 & 0 & 1 \end{bmatrix} \quad \text{and} \quad \boldsymbol{B} = \begin{bmatrix} 1 & 0 & 0 & 0 \\ 0 & 0 & 1 & 0 \\ 0 & 0 & 0 & 1 \\ 0 & 1 & 0 & 0 \end{bmatrix}$$

show that $\boldsymbol{A}^2 = \boldsymbol{I}$ and $\boldsymbol{B}^3 = \boldsymbol{I}$, and hence find $\boldsymbol{A}^{-1}$, $\boldsymbol{B}^{-1}$ and $(\boldsymbol{AB})^{-1}$.

(*Note*: the matrices $\boldsymbol{A}$ and $\boldsymbol{B}$ in this exercise are examples of **permutation matrices**, since

$$\boldsymbol{A}\begin{bmatrix} a_1 \\ a_2 \\ a_3 \\ a_4 \end{bmatrix} = \begin{bmatrix} a_1 \\ a_3 \\ a_2 \\ a_4 \end{bmatrix}$$

and the suffixes are just permuted; $\boldsymbol{B}$ has similar properties.)

# 5.5 Linear equations

Although matrices are of great importance in themselves, their practical importance lies in the solution of sets of linear equations. Such sets of equations occur in a wide range of scientific and engineering problems. In the first part of this section we shall consider whether or not a solution exists, and then in Sections 5.5.2 and 5.5.4 we shall look at practical methods of solution.

We now make some definitive statements about the solution of the system of simultaneous linear equations.

$$\left.\begin{aligned} a_{11}x_1 + a_{12}x_2 + \ldots + a_{1n}x_n &= b_1 \\ a_{21}x_1 + a_{22}x_2 + \ldots + a_{2n}x_n &= b_2 \\ \vdots \qquad\qquad & \vdots \\ a_{n1}x_1 + a_{n2}x_2 + \ldots + a_{nn}x_n &= b_n \end{aligned}\right\} \tag{5.18}$$

or, in matrix notation,

$$\begin{bmatrix} a_{11} & a_{12} & \ldots & a_{1n} \\ a_{21} & a_{22} & \ldots & a_{2n} \\ \vdots & & & \\ a_{n1} & a_{n2} & \ldots & a_{nn} \end{bmatrix} \begin{bmatrix} x_1 \\ x_2 \\ \vdots \\ x_n \end{bmatrix} = \begin{bmatrix} b_1 \\ b_2 \\ \vdots \\ b_n \end{bmatrix}$$

that is,

$$\boldsymbol{AX} = \boldsymbol{b} \tag{5.19}$$

where $\boldsymbol{A}$ is the matrix of coefficients and $\boldsymbol{X}$ the vector of unknowns. If $\boldsymbol{b} = 0$ the equations are called **homogeneous**, while if $\boldsymbol{b} \neq 0$ they are called **nonhomogeneous** (or **inhomogeneous**). There are several cases to consider.

*Case (a)* $\boldsymbol{b} \neq 0$ *and* $|\boldsymbol{A}| \neq 0$

We know that $\boldsymbol{A}^{-1}$ exists, and hence

$$\boldsymbol{A}^{-1}\boldsymbol{AX} = \boldsymbol{A}^{-1}\boldsymbol{b}$$

so that

$$\boldsymbol{X} = \boldsymbol{A}^{-1}\boldsymbol{b} \tag{5.20}$$

and we have a unique solution to (5.18) and (5.19).

*Case (b)* $\boldsymbol{b} = 0$ *and* $|\boldsymbol{A}| \neq 0$

Again $\boldsymbol{A}^{-1}$ exists, and the homogeneous equations

$$\boldsymbol{AX} = 0$$

give

$$\boldsymbol{A}^{-1}\boldsymbol{A}\boldsymbol{X} = \boldsymbol{A}^{-1}0 \quad \text{or} \quad \boldsymbol{X} = 0$$

We therefore only have the **trivial solution** $\boldsymbol{X} = 0$.

### *Case (c) $b \neq 0$ and $|\boldsymbol{A}| = 0$*

The inverse matrix does not exist, and this is perhaps the most complicated case. We have two possibilities: either we have no solution or we have infinitely many solutions. A simple example will illustrate the situation. The equations

$$\left.\begin{aligned} 3x + 2y &= 2 \\ 3x + 2y &= 6 \end{aligned}\right\}, \quad \text{or} \quad \begin{bmatrix} 3 & 2 \\ 3 & 2 \end{bmatrix}\begin{bmatrix} x \\ y \end{bmatrix} = \begin{bmatrix} 2 \\ 6 \end{bmatrix}$$

are clearly inconsistent, and no solution exists. However, in the case of

$$\left.\begin{aligned} 3x + 2y &= 2 \\ 6x + 4y &= 4 \end{aligned}\right\}, \quad \text{or} \quad \begin{bmatrix} 3 & 2 \\ 6 & 4 \end{bmatrix}\begin{bmatrix} x \\ y \end{bmatrix} = \begin{bmatrix} 2 \\ 4 \end{bmatrix}$$

where one equation is a multiple of the other, we have infinitely many solutions: $x = \lambda$, $y = 1 - \frac{3}{2}\lambda$ is a solution for any value of $\lambda$.

The same behaviour is observed for problems involving more than two variables, but the situation is then much more difficult to analyse. The problem of determining whether or not a set of equations has a solution will be discussed in Section 5.6.

### *Case (d) $b = 0$ and $|\boldsymbol{A}| = 0$*

As in case (c), we have infinitely many solutions. For instance, the case of two equations takes the form

$$\begin{aligned} px + qy &= 0 \\ \alpha px + \alpha qy &= 0 \end{aligned}$$

so that $|\boldsymbol{A}| = 0$ and we find a solution $x = \lambda$, $y = -p\lambda/q$ if $q \neq 0$. If $q = 0$ then $x = 0$, $y = \lambda$ is a solution.

This case is one of the most important, since we can deduce the important general result that *the equation*

$$\boldsymbol{A}\boldsymbol{X} = 0$$

*has a non-trivial solution if and only if* $|\boldsymbol{A}| = 0$.

**Example 5.24**

Write the five sets of equations in matrix form and decide whether they have or do not have a solution.

(a) $2x + y = 5$, $x - 2y = -5$

(b) $2x + y = 0$, $x - 2y = 0$

(c) $-3x + 6y = 15$, $x - 2y = -5$

(d) $-3x + 6y = 10$, $x - 2y = -5$

(e) $-3x + 6y = 0$, $x - 2y = 0$

**Solution** (a) In matrix form the equations are $\begin{bmatrix} 2 & 1 \\ 1 & -2 \end{bmatrix}\begin{bmatrix} x \\ y \end{bmatrix} = \begin{bmatrix} 5 \\ -5 \end{bmatrix}$. The determinant of the matrix has the value –5 and the right-hand side is non-zero so the problem is of the type **Case (a)** and hence has a unique solution, namely $x = 1$, $y = 3$.

(b) In matrix form the equations are $\begin{bmatrix} 2 & 1 \\ 1 & -2 \end{bmatrix}\begin{bmatrix} x \\ y \end{bmatrix} = \begin{bmatrix} 0 \\ 0 \end{bmatrix}$. The determinant of the matrix has the value –5 and the right-hand side is now zero so the problem is of the type **Case (b)** and hence only has the trivial solution, namely $x = 0$, $y = 0$.

(c) In matrix form the equations are $\begin{bmatrix} -3 & 6 \\ 1 & -2 \end{bmatrix}\begin{bmatrix} x \\ y \end{bmatrix} = \begin{bmatrix} 15 \\ -5 \end{bmatrix}$. The determinant of the matrix matrix is now zero and the right-hand side is non-zero so the problem is of the type **Case (c)** and hence the solution is not so easy. Essentially the first equation is just (–3) times the second equation so a solution can be computed. A bit of rearrangement soon gives $x = 2t - 5$, $y = t$ for any $t$, and thus there are infinitely many solutions to this set of equations.

(d) In matrix form the equations are $\begin{bmatrix} -3 & 6 \\ 1 & -2 \end{bmatrix}\begin{bmatrix} x \\ y \end{bmatrix} = \begin{bmatrix} 10 \\ -5 \end{bmatrix}$. The determinant of the matrix is zero again and the right-hand side is non-zero so the problem is once more of the type **Case (c)** and hence the solution is not so easy. The left-hand side of the first equation is (–3) times the second equation but the right-hand side is only (–2) times the second equation so the equations are inconsistent and there is no solution to this set of equations.

(e) In matrix form the equations are $\begin{bmatrix} -3 & 6 \\ 1 & -2 \end{bmatrix}\begin{bmatrix} x \\ y \end{bmatrix} = \begin{bmatrix} 0 \\ 0 \end{bmatrix}$. The determinant of the matrix is zero again and the right-hand side is also zero so the problem is of the type **Case (d)** and hence a non-trivial solution can be found. It can be seen that $x = 2s$ and $y = s$ gives the solution for any $s$.

**Example 5.25** Find a solution of

$$\begin{aligned} x + y + z &= 6 \\ x + 2y + 3z &= 14 \\ x + 4y + 9z &= 36 \end{aligned}$$

**Solution** Expressing the equations in matrix form $\boldsymbol{AX} = \boldsymbol{b}$

$$\begin{bmatrix} 1 & 1 & 1 \\ 1 & 2 & 3 \\ 1 & 4 & 9 \end{bmatrix}\begin{bmatrix} x \\ y \\ z \end{bmatrix} = \begin{bmatrix} 6 \\ 14 \\ 36 \end{bmatrix}$$

we have

$$|\boldsymbol{A}| = \begin{vmatrix} 1 & 1 & 1 \\ 1 & 2 & 3 \\ 1 & 4 & 9 \end{vmatrix} = \begin{vmatrix} 1 & 0 & 0 \\ 1 & 1 & 2 \\ 1 & 3 & 8 \end{vmatrix} = 2 \neq 0$$ (subtracting column 1 from columns 2 and 3)

so that a solution does exist and is unique. The inverse of $\boldsymbol{A}$ can be computed as

$$\boldsymbol{A}^{-1} = \begin{bmatrix} 3 & -\frac{5}{2} & \frac{1}{2} \\ -3 & 4 & -1 \\ 1 & -\frac{3}{2} & \frac{1}{2} \end{bmatrix}$$

and hence, from (5.20),

$$\boldsymbol{X} = \begin{bmatrix} x \\ y \\ z \end{bmatrix} = \boldsymbol{A}^{-1} \begin{bmatrix} 6 \\ 14 \\ 36 \end{bmatrix} = \begin{bmatrix} 1 \\ 2 \\ 3 \end{bmatrix}$$

so the solution is $x = 1$, $y = 2$ and $z = 3$.

**Example 5.26** Find the values of $k$ for which the equations

$$x + 5y + 3z = 0$$
$$5x + y - kz = 0$$
$$x + 2y + kz = 0$$

have a non-trivial solution.

**Solution** The matrix of coefficients is

$$\boldsymbol{A} = \begin{bmatrix} 1 & 5 & 3 \\ 5 & 1 & -k \\ 1 & 2 & k \end{bmatrix}$$

For a non-zero solution, $|\boldsymbol{A}| = 0$. Hence

$$0 = |\boldsymbol{A}| = \begin{vmatrix} 1 & 5 & 3 \\ 5 & 1 & -k \\ 1 & 2 & k \end{vmatrix} = 27 - 27k$$

Thus the equations have a non-trivial solution if $k = 1$; if $k \neq 1$, the only solution is $x = y = z = 0$. For $k = 1$ a simple calculation gives $x = \lambda$, $y = -2\lambda$ and $z = 3\lambda$ for any $\lambda$.

**Example 5.27** Find the values of $\lambda$ and the corresponding column vector $\boldsymbol{X}$ such that

$$(\boldsymbol{A} - \lambda \boldsymbol{I})\boldsymbol{X} = 0$$

has a non-trivial solution, given

$$\boldsymbol{A} = \begin{bmatrix} 3 & 1 \\ -2 & 0 \end{bmatrix}$$

**Solution** We require

$$0 = |\boldsymbol{A} - \lambda \boldsymbol{I}| = \begin{vmatrix} 3-\lambda & 1 \\ -2 & -\lambda \end{vmatrix}$$

$$= -3\lambda + \lambda^2 + 2 = (\lambda - 2)(\lambda - 1)$$

Non-trivial solutions occur only if $\lambda = 1$ or 2.

If $\lambda = 1$,

$$\begin{bmatrix} 2 & 1 \\ -2 & -1 \end{bmatrix}\begin{bmatrix} x \\ y \end{bmatrix} = 0, \quad \text{so } \boldsymbol{X} = \begin{bmatrix} x \\ y \end{bmatrix} = \alpha\begin{bmatrix} 1 \\ -2 \end{bmatrix} \quad \text{for any } \alpha$$

If $\lambda = 2$,

$$\begin{bmatrix} 1 & 1 \\ -2 & -2 \end{bmatrix}\begin{bmatrix} x \\ y \end{bmatrix} = 0, \quad \text{so } \boldsymbol{X} = \begin{bmatrix} x \\ y \end{bmatrix} = \beta\begin{bmatrix} 1 \\ -1 \end{bmatrix} \quad \text{for any } \beta$$

(Note that the problem described here is an important one. The $\lambda$ and $\boldsymbol{X}$ are called **eigenvalues** and **eigenvectors**, which are introduced in Section 5.7.)

---

It is possible to write down the solution of a set of equations explicitly in terms of the cofactors of a matrix. However, as a method for computing the solution, this is extremely inefficient; a set of ten equations, for example, will require $4 \times 10^8$ multiplications – which takes a long time even on modern computers. The method is of great theoretical interest though. Consider the set of equations

$$\left.\begin{aligned} a_{11}x_1 + a_{12}x_2 + a_{13}x_3 &= b_1 \\ a_{21}x_1 + a_{22}x_2 + a_{23}x_3 &= b_2 \\ a_{31}x_1 + a_{32}x_2 + a_{33}x_3 &= b_3 \end{aligned}\right\} \tag{5.21}$$

Denoting the matrix of coefficients by $\boldsymbol{A}$ and recalling the definitions of the cofactors in Section 5.3, we multiply the equations by $A_{11}$, $A_{21}$ and $A_{31}$ respectively, and add to give

$$\begin{aligned} (a_{11}A_{11} + a_{21}A_{21} + a_{31}A_{31})x_1 + (a_{12}A_{11} + a_{22}A_{21} + a_{32}A_{31})x_2 \\ + (a_{13}A_{11} + a_{23}A_{21} + a_{33}A_{31})x_3 \\ = b_1A_{11} + b_2A_{21} + b_3A_{31} \end{aligned}$$

Using (5.12), we obtain

$$|\boldsymbol{A}|x_1 + 0x_2 + 0x_3 = b_1A_{11} + b_2A_{21} + b_3A_{31}$$

The right-hand side can be written as a determinant, so

$$|\boldsymbol{A}|x_1 = \begin{vmatrix} b_1 & a_{12} & a_{13} \\ b_2 & a_{22} & a_{23} \\ b_3 & a_{32} & a_{33} \end{vmatrix}$$

The other $x_i$ follow similarly, and we derive **Cramer's rule** that a solution of (5.21) is

$$x_1 = |\boldsymbol{A}|^{-1}\begin{vmatrix} b_1 & a_{12} & a_{13} \\ b_2 & a_{22} & a_{23} \\ b_3 & a_{32} & a_{33} \end{vmatrix},$$

$$x_2 = |\boldsymbol{A}|^{-1}\begin{vmatrix} a_{11} & b_1 & a_{13} \\ a_{21} & b_2 & a_{23} \\ a_{31} & b_3 & a_{33} \end{vmatrix},$$

$$x_3 = |\boldsymbol{A}|^{-1}\begin{vmatrix} a_{11} & a_{12} & b_1 \\ a_{21} & a_{22} & b_2 \\ a_{31} & a_{32} & b_3 \end{vmatrix}$$

Again it should be stressed that this rule should not be used as a computational method because of the large effort required to evaluate determinants.

**Example 5.28**

A function $u(x, y)$ is known to take values $u_1$, $u_2$ and $u_3$ at the points $(x_1, y_1)$, $(x_2, y_2)$ and $(x_3, y_3)$ respectively. Find the linear interpolating function

$$u = a + bx + cy$$

within the triangle having its vertices at these three points.

**Solution**

To fit the data to the linear interpolating function

$$\begin{aligned} u_1 &= a + bx_1 + cy_1 \\ u_2 &= a + bx_2 + cy_2 \\ u_3 &= a + bx_3 + cy_3 \end{aligned} \quad \text{or in matrix form} \quad \begin{bmatrix} u_1 \\ u_2 \\ u_3 \end{bmatrix} = \begin{bmatrix} 1 & x_1 & y_1 \\ 1 & x_2 & y_2 \\ 1 & x_3 & y_3 \end{bmatrix}\begin{bmatrix} a \\ b \\ c \end{bmatrix}$$

The values of $a$, $b$ and $c$ can be obtained from Cramer's rule as

$$a = \begin{vmatrix} u_1 & x_1 & y_1 \\ u_2 & x_2 & y_2 \\ u_3 & x_3 & y_3 \end{vmatrix} / \det(\boldsymbol{A}), \quad b = \begin{vmatrix} 1 & u_1 & y_1 \\ 1 & u_2 & y_2 \\ 1 & u_3 & y_3 \end{vmatrix} / \det(\boldsymbol{A}) \quad \text{and}$$

$$c = \begin{vmatrix} 1 & x_1 & u_1 \\ 1 & x_2 & u_2 \\ 1 & x_3 & u_3 \end{vmatrix} / \det(\boldsymbol{A})$$

where $\boldsymbol{A}$ is the matrix of coefficients. The interpolation formula is now known. In finite-element analysis the evaluation of interpolation functions, such as the one described, is of great importance. Finite elements are central to many large-scale calculations in all branches of engineering; an introduction is given in Chapter 9 of the companion text *Advanced Modern Engineering Mathematics*.

**Example 5.29** Solve the matrix equation $\boldsymbol{AX} = \boldsymbol{c}$ where

$$\boldsymbol{A} = \begin{bmatrix} 4 & 1 & 0 & 0 & 0 & 0 & 0 & 0 & 0 & 0 \\ 1 & 4 & 1 & 0 & 0 & 0 & 0 & 0 & 0 & 0 \\ 1 & 0 & 4 & 1 & 0 & 0 & 0 & 0 & 0 & 0 \\ 1 & 0 & 0 & 4 & 1 & 0 & 0 & 0 & 0 & 0 \\ 1 & 0 & 0 & 0 & 4 & 1 & 0 & 0 & 0 & 0 \\ 1 & 0 & 0 & 0 & 0 & 4 & 1 & 0 & 0 & 0 \\ 1 & 0 & 0 & 0 & 0 & 0 & 4 & 1 & 0 & 0 \\ 1 & 0 & 0 & 0 & 0 & 0 & 0 & 4 & 1 & 0 \\ 1 & 0 & 0 & 0 & 0 & 0 & 0 & 0 & 4 & 1 \\ 1 & 0 & 0 & 0 & 0 & 0 & 0 & 0 & 0 & 4 \end{bmatrix} \quad \text{and} \quad \boldsymbol{c} = \begin{bmatrix} 1 \\ 2 \\ 3 \\ 4 \\ 5 \\ 5 \\ 4 \\ 3 \\ 2 \\ 1 \end{bmatrix}$$

**Solution** The solution of such a problem is beyond the scope of hand computation; Cramer's rule, evaluation of the adjoint and direct evaluation of the inverse are all impracticable. Even the more practical methods in the next sections struggle with this size of problem if hand computation is tried. A computer package must be used. In MATLAB the relevant instructions are given.

```
b = zeros (10, 10);
for i = 1 : 9, b (i, i) = 4; b (i, i + 1) = 1; b (i + 1, 1)
= 1; end
b (10, 10) = 4;
c = [1; 2; 3; 4; 5; 5; 4; 3; 2; 1];
b\c
```

gives the solution

```
0.1685 0.3258 0.5282 0.7188 0.9563 1.0063 0.8063
0.6064 0.4059 0.2079
```

## 5.5.1 Exercises

Check your answers using MATLAB or MAPLE whenever possible.

**60** Solve the matrix equation $\boldsymbol{AX} = \boldsymbol{b}$ for the vector $\boldsymbol{X}$ in the following:

(a) $\boldsymbol{A} = \begin{bmatrix} 2 & 3 \\ 5 & -2 \end{bmatrix} \quad \boldsymbol{b} = \begin{bmatrix} 8 \\ 1 \end{bmatrix}$

(b) $\boldsymbol{A} = \begin{bmatrix} 1 & 0 & 0 \\ 2 & -1 & 0 \\ 2 & 2 & 2 \end{bmatrix} \quad \boldsymbol{b} = \begin{bmatrix} 1 \\ 6 \\ -6 \end{bmatrix}$

(c) $\boldsymbol{A} = \begin{bmatrix} 2 & 1 \\ 0 & 1 \end{bmatrix}\begin{bmatrix} 1 & 0 \\ 3 & 1 \end{bmatrix} \quad \boldsymbol{b} = -\begin{bmatrix} 3 \\ 1 \end{bmatrix}$

(d) $\boldsymbol{A} = \begin{bmatrix} 1 & 0 & 0 & 0 \\ 0 & 3 & 1 & 0 \\ 0 & 1 & 2 & 0 \\ 0 & 0 & 0 & 1 \end{bmatrix} \quad \boldsymbol{b} = \begin{bmatrix} 4 \\ 11 \\ 7 \\ 1 \end{bmatrix}$

**61** If

$$\boldsymbol{A} = \begin{bmatrix} \cos\alpha & -\sin\alpha \\ \sin\alpha & \cos\alpha \end{bmatrix}$$

show that

$$\boldsymbol{A}^{-1} = \begin{bmatrix} \cos\alpha & \sin\alpha \\ -\sin\alpha & \cos\alpha \end{bmatrix}$$

and hence solve for the vector $\boldsymbol{X}$ in the equation

$$\begin{bmatrix} \cos\frac{\pi}{8} & -\sin\frac{\pi}{8} \\ \sin\frac{\pi}{8} & \cos\frac{\pi}{8} \end{bmatrix}\boldsymbol{X} = \begin{bmatrix} \cos\frac{\pi}{4} \\ \sin\frac{\pi}{4} \end{bmatrix}$$

**62** Solve the complex matrix equation

$$\begin{bmatrix} 1 & \mathrm{j} & 0 \\ 0 & 1 & 0 \\ \mathrm{j} & 0 & \mathrm{j} \end{bmatrix}\boldsymbol{X} = \begin{bmatrix} 0 \\ 1 \\ 0 \end{bmatrix}$$

**63** Find the inverse of the matrix

$$\boldsymbol{A} = \begin{bmatrix} -1 & 2 & 1 \\ 0 & 1 & -2 \\ 1 & 4 & -1 \end{bmatrix}$$

and hence solve the equations

$$\begin{aligned} -x + 2y + \quad z &= 2 \\ y - 2z &= -3 \\ x + 4y - \quad z &= 4 \end{aligned}$$

**64** Show that there are two values of $\alpha$ for which the equations

$$\begin{aligned} \alpha x - 3y + (1+\alpha)z &= 0 \\ 2x + \quad y - \quad \alpha z &= 0 \\ (\alpha+2)x - 2y + \quad \alpha z &= 0 \end{aligned}$$

have non-trivial solutions. Find the solutions corresponding to these two values of $\alpha$.

**65** If

$$\boldsymbol{A} = \begin{bmatrix} -3 & 1 & -1 \\ 1 & -5 & 1 \\ -1 & 1 & -3 \end{bmatrix}$$

find the values of $\lambda$ for which the equation $\boldsymbol{AX} = \lambda\boldsymbol{X}$ has non-trivial solutions.

**66** Given the matrix

$$\boldsymbol{A} = \begin{bmatrix} 1 & a & -1 \\ a & -2 & 2 \\ -1 & 1 & a \end{bmatrix}$$

(a) solve $|\boldsymbol{A}| = 0$ for real $a$;

(b) if $a = 2$, find $\boldsymbol{A}^{-1}$ and hence solve

$$\boldsymbol{A}\begin{bmatrix} x \\ y \\ z \end{bmatrix} = \begin{bmatrix} 1 \\ 0 \\ 2 \end{bmatrix}$$

(c) if $a = 0$, find the general solution of

$$\mathbf{A}\begin{bmatrix} x \\ y \\ z \end{bmatrix} = \begin{bmatrix} 0 \\ 0 \\ 0 \end{bmatrix}$$

(d) if $a = 1$, show that

$$\mathbf{A}\begin{bmatrix} x \\ y \\ z \end{bmatrix} = 2\begin{bmatrix} x \\ y \\ z \end{bmatrix}$$

can be solved for non-zero $x$, $y$ and $z$.

67 Use MATLAB or a similar package to find the inverse of the matrix

$$\begin{bmatrix} 6 & 2 & 1 & 0 & 0 & 0 \\ 2 & 6 & 2 & 1 & 0 & 0 \\ 1 & 2 & 6 & 2 & 1 & 0 \\ 0 & 1 & 2 & 6 & 2 & 1 \\ 0 & 0 & 1 & 2 & 6 & 2 \\ 0 & 0 & 0 & 1 & 2 & 6 \end{bmatrix}$$

and hence solve the matrix equation

$$\mathbf{AX} = \mathbf{c}$$

where $\mathbf{c}^{\mathrm{T}} = [1\ 0\ 0\ 0\ 0\ 1]$.

68 In finite-element calculations the bilinear function

$$u(x, y) = a + bx + cy + dxy$$

is commonly used for interpolation over a quadrilateral and data is always stored in matrix form. If the function fits the data $u(0, 0) = u_1$, $u(p, 0) = u_2$, $u(0, q) = u_3$ and $u(p, q) = u_4$ at the four corners of a rectangle, use matrices to find the coefficients $a$, $b$, $c$ and $d$.

69 In an industrial process water flows through three tanks in succession as illustrated in Figure 5.8.

The tanks have unit cross-section and have heads of water $x$, $y$ and $z$ respectively. The rate of inflow into the first tank is $u$, the flowrate in the tube connecting tanks 1 and 2 is $6(x - y)$, the flowrate in the tube connecting tanks 2 and 3 is $5(y - z)$ and the rate of outflow from tank 3 is $4.5z$.

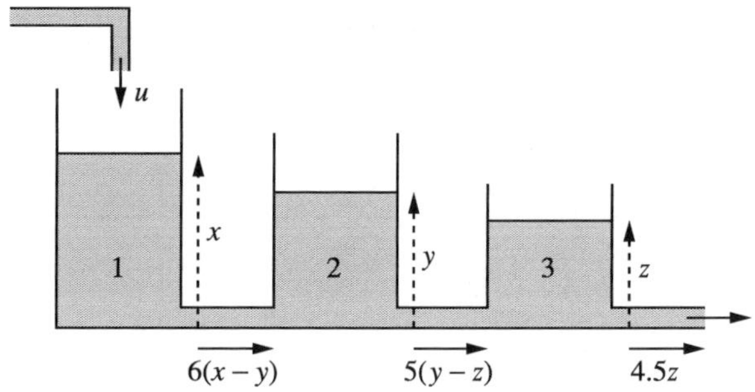


**Figure 5.8** Flow through three tanks in Question 69.

Show that the equations of the system in the steady flow situation are

$$u = 6x - 6y$$
$$0 = 6x - 11y + 5z$$
$$0 = 5y - 9.5z$$

and hence find $x$, $y$ and $z$.

70 A function is known to fit closely to the approximate function

$$f(z) = \frac{az + b}{cz + 1}$$

It is fitted to the three points ($z = 0, f = 1$), ($z = 0.5$, $f = 1.128$) and ($z = 1.3, f = 1.971$). Show that the parameters satisfy

$$\begin{bmatrix} 1 \\ 1.128 \\ 1.971 \end{bmatrix} = \begin{bmatrix} 0 & 1 & 0 \\ 0.5 & 1 & -0.5640 \\ 1.3 & 1 & -2.562 \end{bmatrix}\begin{bmatrix} a \\ b \\ c \end{bmatrix}$$

Find $a$, $b$ and $c$ and hence the approximating function (use of MATLAB is recommended). Check the value $f(1) = 1.543$. (Note that the values were chosen from tables of cosh $z$.)

The method described here is a simple example of a powerful approximation method.

71 A cantilever beam bends under a uniform load $w$ per unit length and is subject to an axial force $P$ at its free end. For small deflections a numerical approximation to the shape of the beam is given by the set of equations

$$\begin{aligned} -vy_1 + y_2 \qquad\qquad &= -u \\ y_1 - vy_2 + y_3 \qquad &= -4u \\ y_2 - vy_3 + y_4 &= -9u \\ 2y_3 - vy_4 &= -16u \end{aligned}$$

The deflections are indicated on Figure 5.9. The parameter $\upsilon$ is defined as

$$\upsilon = 2 + \frac{PL^2}{16EI}$$

where $EI$ is the flexural rigidity and $L$ is the length of the beam. The parameter $u = wL^4/32EI$.

Use either Cramer's rule or the adjoint matrix to solve the equations when $\upsilon = 3$ and $u = 1$.

Note the immense effort required to solve this very simple problem using these methods. In later sections much more efficient methods will be described. A computer package such as MATLAB should be used to check the results.

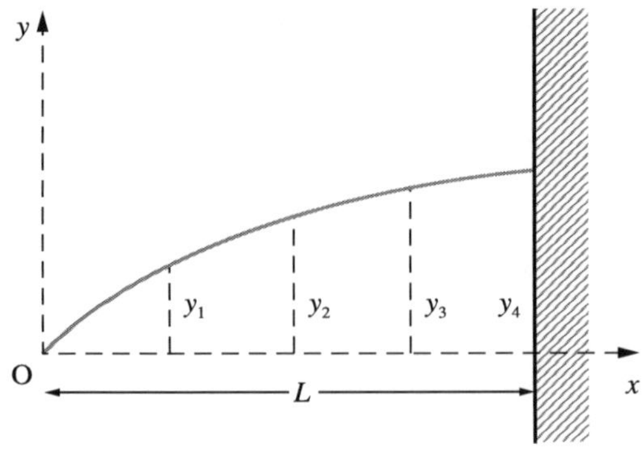


**Figure 5.9** Cantilever beam in Question 71.

## 5.5.2 The solution of linear equations: elimination methods

The idea behind elimination techniques can be seen by considering the solution of two simultaneous equations

$$x + 2y = 4$$

$$2x + y = 5$$

Subtract 2 × (equation 1) from (equation 2) to give

$$x + 2y = 4$$

$$-3y = -3$$

Divide the second equation by −3

$$x + 2y = 4$$

$$y = 1$$

From the second of these equations $y = 1$ and substituting into the first equation gives $x = 2$.

This example illustrates the basic technique for the solution of a set of linear equations by Gaussian elimination, which is very straightforward in principle. However, it needs considerable care to ensure that the calculations are carried out efficiently. Given $n$ linear equations in the variables $x_1, x_2, \ldots, x_n$, we solve in a series of steps:

(1) We solve the first equation for $x_1$ in terms of $x_2, \ldots, x_n$, and eliminate $x_1$ from the remaining equations.

(2) We then solve the second equation of the remaining set for $x_2$ in terms of $x_3, \ldots, x_n$ and eliminate $x_2$ from the remaining equations.

(3) We repeat the process in turn on $x_3, x_4, \ldots$ until we arrive at a final equation for $x_n$, which we can then solve.

(4) We substitute back to get in turn $x_{n-1}, x_{n-2}, \ldots, x_1$.

For a small number of variables, say two, three or four, the method is easy to apply, and efficiency is not of the highest priority. In most science and engineering problems we are normally dealing with a large number of variables – a simple stability analysis of a vibrating system can lead to seven or eight variables, and a plate-bending problem could easily give rise to several hundred variables.

As a further example of the basic technique, we solve

$$x_1 + x_2 = 3 \tag{5.22}$$

$$2x_1 + x_2 + x_3 = 7 \tag{5.23}$$

$$x_1 + 2x_2 + 3x_3 = 14 \tag{5.24}$$

First, we eliminate $x_1$:

(5.22) gives $\quad x_1 = 3 - x_2$ **(5.22′)**

(5.23) gives $\quad 2(3 - x_2) + x_2 + x_3 = 7, \quad \text{or} \quad -x_2 + x_3 = 1$ **(5.23′)**

(5.24) gives $\quad (3 - x_2) + 2x_2 + 3x_3 = 14, \quad \text{or} \quad x_2 + 3x_3 = 11$ **(5.24′)**

Secondly we eliminate $x_2$:

(5.23′) gives $\quad x_2 = x_3 - 1$ **(5.23″)**

(5.24′) gives $\quad (x_3 - 1) + 3x_3 = 11, \quad \text{or} \quad 4x_3 = 12$ **(5.24″)**

Equation (5.24″) gives $x_3 = 3$; we put this into (5.23″) to obtain $x_2 = 2$; we then put this into (5.22′) to obtain $x_1 = 1$. Thus the values $x_1 = 1$, $x_2 = 2$ and $x_3 = 3$ give a solution to the original problem.

Equations (5.22)–(5.24) in matrix form become

$$\begin{bmatrix} 1 & 1 & 0 \\ 2 & 1 & 1 \\ 1 & 2 & 3 \end{bmatrix} \begin{bmatrix} x_1 \\ x_2 \\ x_3 \end{bmatrix} = \begin{bmatrix} 3 \\ 7 \\ 14 \end{bmatrix}$$

The elimination procedure has reduced the equations to (5.22), (5.23′) and (5.24″), which in matrix form become

$$\begin{bmatrix} 1 & 1 & 0 \\ 0 & -1 & 1 \\ 0 & 0 & 4 \end{bmatrix} \begin{bmatrix} x_1 \\ x_2 \\ x_3 \end{bmatrix} = \begin{bmatrix} 3 \\ 1 \\ 12 \end{bmatrix}$$

Essentially the elimination has brought the equations to **upper-triangular** form (that is, a form in which the matrix of coefficients has zeros in every position below the diagonal), which are then very easy to solve.

Elimination procedures rely on the manipulation of equations or, equivalently, the rows of the matrix equation. There are various **elementary row operations** used which do not alter the solution of the equations:

(a) multiply a row by a constant,
(b) interchange any two rows,
(c) add or subtract one row from another.

To illustrate these, we take the matrix equation

$$\begin{bmatrix} 1 & 1 & 0 \\ 2 & 1 & 1 \\ -1 & 2 & 3 \end{bmatrix} \begin{bmatrix} x_1 \\ x_2 \\ x_3 \end{bmatrix} = \begin{bmatrix} 3 \\ 7 \\ 12 \end{bmatrix}$$

which has the solution $x_1 = 1$, $x_2 = 2$, $x_3 = 3$.

Multiplying the first row by 2 (a row operation of type (a)) yields

$$\begin{bmatrix} 2 & 2 & 0 \\ 2 & 1 & 1 \\ -1 & 2 & 3 \end{bmatrix}\begin{bmatrix} x_1 \\ x_2 \\ x_3 \end{bmatrix} = \begin{bmatrix} 6 \\ 7 \\ 12 \end{bmatrix}$$

Interchanging rows 1 and 3 (a row operation of type (b)) yields

$$\begin{bmatrix} -1 & 2 & 3 \\ 2 & 1 & 1 \\ 1 & 1 & 0 \end{bmatrix}\begin{bmatrix} x_1 \\ x_2 \\ x_3 \end{bmatrix} = \begin{bmatrix} 12 \\ 7 \\ 3 \end{bmatrix}$$

Subtracting row 1 from row 2 (a row operation of type (c)) yields

$$\begin{bmatrix} 1 & 1 & 0 \\ 1 & 0 & 1 \\ -1 & 2 & 3 \end{bmatrix}\begin{bmatrix} x_1 \\ x_2 \\ x_3 \end{bmatrix} = \begin{bmatrix} 3 \\ 4 \\ 12 \end{bmatrix}$$

In each case we see that the solution of the modified equations is still $x_1 = 1$, $x_2 = 2$, $x_3 = 3$.

Elimination procedures use repeated applications of (a), (b) and (c) in some systematic manner until the equations are processed into a required form such as the upper-triangular equations

$$\begin{bmatrix} a_{11} & a_{12} & a_{13} & \dots & a_{1n} \\ 0 & a_{22} & a_{23} & \dots & a_{2n} \\ 0 & 0 & a_{33} & \dots & a_{3n} \\ \vdots & \vdots & \vdots & & \vdots \\ 0 & 0 & 0 & \dots & a_{nn} \end{bmatrix}\begin{bmatrix} x_1 \\ x_2 \\ x_3 \\ \vdots \\ x_n \end{bmatrix} = \begin{bmatrix} b_1 \\ b_2 \\ b_3 \\ \vdots \\ b_n \end{bmatrix} \quad \textbf{(5.25)}$$

The solution of the equations in upper-triangular form can be written as

$$x_n = b_n / a_{nn}$$

$$x_{n-1} = (b_{n-1} - a_{n-1,n}x_n)/a_{n-1,n-1}$$

$$x_{n-2} = (b_{n-2} - a_{n-2,n}x_n - a_{n-2,n-1}x_{n-1})/a_{n-2,n-2}$$

$$\vdots$$

$$x_1 = (b_1 - a_{1n}x_n - a_{1,n-1}x_{n-1} - \dots - a_{12}x_2)/a_{11}$$

A pseudocode procedure implementing these equations is shown in Figure 5.10. The elementary row operations and the elimination technique are illustrated in Example 5.30.

**Figure 5.10**
Procedure to solve the upper-triangular system (5.25).

```
procedure uppertriangular (A, b, n → x)
{A is an n × n matrix, b and x are vectors with n elements}
  x(n)←b(n)/A(n, n)
  for j is n – 1  to 1 by –1 do
    sum←b(j)
    for i is n  to j + 1 by –1 do
      sum←sum – A(j, i) * x(i)
    endfor
    x(j)←sum/A(j, j)
  endfor
endprocedure
```

**Example 5.30** Use elementary row operations and elimination to solve the set of linear equations

$$x + 2y + 3z = 10$$

$$-x + y + z = 0$$

$$y - z = 1$$

**Solution** In matrix form the equations are: $\begin{bmatrix} 1 & 2 & 3 \\ -1 & 1 & 1 \\ 0 & 1 & -1 \end{bmatrix}\begin{bmatrix} x \\ y \\ z \end{bmatrix} = \begin{bmatrix} 10 \\ 0 \\ 1 \end{bmatrix}$

Add row 1 to row 2: $\begin{bmatrix} 1 & 2 & 3 \\ 0 & 3 & 4 \\ 0 & 1 & -1 \end{bmatrix}\begin{bmatrix} x \\ y \\ z \end{bmatrix} = \begin{bmatrix} 10 \\ 10 \\ 1 \end{bmatrix}$

Divide row 2 by 3: $\begin{bmatrix} 1 & 2 & 3 \\ 0 & 1 & \frac{4}{3} \\ 0 & 1 & -1 \end{bmatrix}\begin{bmatrix} x \\ y \\ z \end{bmatrix} = \begin{bmatrix} 10 \\ \frac{10}{3} \\ 1 \end{bmatrix}$

Subtract row 2 from row 3: $\begin{bmatrix} 1 & 2 & 3 \\ 0 & 1 & \frac{4}{3} \\ 0 & 0 & -\frac{7}{3} \end{bmatrix}\begin{bmatrix} x \\ y \\ z \end{bmatrix} = \begin{bmatrix} 10 \\ \frac{10}{3} \\ -\frac{7}{3} \end{bmatrix}$

Divide row 3 by $(-\frac{7}{3})$: $\begin{bmatrix} 1 & 2 & 3 \\ 0 & 1 & \frac{4}{3} \\ 0 & 0 & 1 \end{bmatrix}\begin{bmatrix} x \\ y \\ z \end{bmatrix} = \begin{bmatrix} 10 \\ \frac{10}{3} \\ 1 \end{bmatrix}$

The equations are now in a standard upper-triangular form for the application of the back substitution procedure described formally in Figure 5.10.

From the third row $z = 1$

From the second row $y = \frac{10}{3} - \frac{4}{3}z = 2$

From the first row $x = 10 - 2y - 3z = 3$

---

It remains to undertake the operations in the example in a routine and logical manner to make the method into one of the most powerful techniques, called **elimination methods**, available for the solution of sets of linear equations. The method is available on all computer packages. Such packages are excellent at undertaking the rather tedious arithmetic and some will even illustrate the computational detail also. They are well worth mastering. However, writing and checking your own procedures, following the pseudocode in Figure 5.10 for instance, is a powerful learning tool and gives great understanding of the method, the difficulties and errors involved in a method.

### Tridiagonal or Thomas algorithm

Because of the ease of solution of upper-triangular systems, many methods use the general strategy of reducing the equations to this form. As an example of this strategy, we shall look at a **tridiagonal system**, which takes the form

$$\begin{bmatrix} a_1 & b_1 & 0 & 0 & 0 & 0 & \dots & 0 \\ c_2 & a_2 & b_2 & 0 & 0 & 0 & \dots & 0 \\ 0 & c_3 & a_3 & b_3 & 0 & 0 & \dots & 0 \\ 0 & 0 & c_4 & a_4 & b_4 & 0 & \dots & 0 \\ & & & & & & & \vdots \\ \vdots & & & & & & & 0 \\ 0 & & \dots & 0 & c_{n-1} & a_{n-1} & b_{n-1} \\ 0 & & \dots & 0 & 0 & c_n & a_n \end{bmatrix} \begin{bmatrix} x_1 \\ x_2 \\ \vdots \\ x_{n-1} \\ x_n \end{bmatrix} = \begin{bmatrix} d_1 \\ d_2 \\ \vdots \\ d_{n-1} \\ d_n \end{bmatrix} \qquad \textbf{(5.26)}$$

or

$$\begin{aligned} a_1x_1 + b_1x_2 \quad &= d_1 \\ c_2x_1 + a_2x_2 + b_2x_3 \quad &= d_2 \\ c_3x_2 + a_3x_3 + b_3x_4 \quad &= d_3 \\ \ddots \qquad \ddots \quad &\quad \vdots \\ c_nx_{n-1} + a_nx_n \quad &= d_n \end{aligned}$$

First we eliminate $x_1$:

$$\begin{aligned} x_1 + b_1'x_2 \quad &= d_1' \\ a_2'x_2 + b_2x_3 \quad &= d_2' \\ c_3x_2 + a_3x_3 + b_3x_4 \quad &= d_3 \end{aligned}$$

and so on

**Figure 5.11**
Tridiagonal or Thomas algorithm for the solution of (5.26).

```
procedure tridiagonal (a, b, c, d, n→a, b, d, x)
  {a, b, c, d and x are vectors with n elements}
  for i is 1 to n – 1 do
  b(i)←b(i)/a(i)
  d(i)←d(i)/a(i)
  a(i + 1)←a(i + 1) – c(i + 1) * b(i)
  d(i + 1)←d(i + 1) – c(i + 1) * d(i)
  endfor {elimination stage}
    x(n)←d(n)/a(n)
    for i is n – 1 to 1 by –1 do
      x(i)←d(i) – b(i) * x(i + 1)
    endfor {back substitution}
endprocedure
```

where

$$b_1' = \frac{b_1}{a_1}, \quad d_1' = \frac{d_1}{a_1}, \quad a_2' = a_2 - c_2 b_1' \quad \text{and} \quad d_2' = d_2 - c_2 d_1'$$

Next we eliminate $x_2$:

$$\begin{aligned} x_1 + b_1' x_2 \qquad\qquad\qquad\qquad &= d_1' \\ x_2 + b_2'' x_3 \qquad\qquad\quad &= d_2'' \\ a_3'' x_3 + b_3 x_4 \qquad &= d_3'' \\ c_4 x_3 + a_4 x_4 + b_4 x_5 &= d_4 \end{aligned}$$

and so on

where

$$b_2'' = \frac{b_2}{a_2'}, \quad d_2'' = \frac{d_2'}{a_2'}, \quad a_3'' = a_3 - c_3 b_2'' \quad \text{and} \quad d_3'' = d_3 - c_3 d_2''$$

We can proceed to eliminate all the variables down to the $n$th. We have then converted the problem to an upper-triangular form, which can be solved by the procedure in Figure 5.10. A pseudocode procedure to solve (5.26) called the **tridiagonal or Thomas algorithm** is shown in Figure 5.11. The algorithm is written so that each primed value, when it is computed, replaces the previous value. Similarly the double-primed values replace the primed values. This is called **overwriting**, and reduces the storage required to implement the algorithm on a computer. It should be noted, however, that the algorithm is written for clarity and not minimum storage or maximum efficiency. The algorithm is very widely used; it is exceptionally fast and requires very little storage. Again writing your own procedure from Figure 5.11 can greatly enhance the understanding of the method.

**Example 5.31** Use the tridiagonal procedure to solve

$$\begin{bmatrix} 2 & 1 & 0 & 0 \\ 1 & 2 & 1 & 0 \\ 0 & 1 & 2 & 1 \\ 0 & 0 & 1 & 2 \end{bmatrix} \begin{bmatrix} x \\ y \\ z \\ t \end{bmatrix} = \begin{bmatrix} 1 \\ 1 \\ 1 \\ -2 \end{bmatrix}$$

**Solution** The sequence of matrices is given by

$$\begin{bmatrix} 1 & \frac{1}{2} & 0 & 0 \\ 0 & \frac{3}{2} & 1 & 0 \\ 0 & 1 & 2 & 1 \\ 0 & 0 & 1 & 2 \end{bmatrix}\begin{bmatrix} x \\ y \\ z \\ t \end{bmatrix} = \begin{bmatrix} \frac{1}{2} \\ \frac{1}{2} \\ 1 \\ -2 \end{bmatrix}, \quad \begin{bmatrix} 1 & \frac{1}{2} & 0 & 0 \\ 0 & 1 & \frac{2}{3} & 0 \\ 0 & 0 & \frac{4}{3} & 1 \\ 0 & 0 & 1 & 2 \end{bmatrix}\begin{bmatrix} x \\ y \\ z \\ t \end{bmatrix} = \begin{bmatrix} \frac{1}{2} \\ \frac{1}{3} \\ \frac{2}{3} \\ -2 \end{bmatrix}$$

$$\begin{bmatrix} 1 & \frac{1}{2} & 0 & 0 \\ 0 & 1 & \frac{2}{3} & 0 \\ 0 & 0 & 1 & \frac{3}{4} \\ 0 & 0 & 0 & \frac{5}{4} \end{bmatrix}\begin{bmatrix} x \\ y \\ z \\ t \end{bmatrix} = \begin{bmatrix} \frac{1}{2} \\ \frac{1}{3} \\ \frac{1}{2} \\ -\frac{5}{2} \end{bmatrix}$$

The elimination stage is now complete, and we substitute back to give

$$t = -2,\ z = \tfrac{1}{2} - \tfrac{3}{4}t = 2,\ y = \tfrac{1}{3} - \tfrac{2}{3}z = -1 \quad \text{and} \quad x = \tfrac{1}{2} - \tfrac{1}{2}y = 1$$

so that the complete solution is $x = 1$, $y = -1$, $z = 2$, $t = -2$.

---

Although the Thomas algorithm is efficient, the procedure in Figure 5.11 is not fool-proof, as illustrated by the simple example

$$\begin{bmatrix} -1 & 1 & 0 \\ 1 & -1 & 1 \\ 0 & 1 & -1 \end{bmatrix}\begin{bmatrix} x \\ y \\ z \end{bmatrix} = \begin{bmatrix} -1 \\ 2 \\ 1 \end{bmatrix}$$

After the first step we have

$$\begin{bmatrix} 1 & -1 & 0 \\ 0 & 0 & 1 \\ 0 & 1 & -1 \end{bmatrix}\begin{bmatrix} x \\ y \\ z \end{bmatrix} = \begin{bmatrix} 1 \\ 1 \\ 1 \end{bmatrix}$$

The next step divides by the diagonal element $a_{22}$. Since this element is zero, the method crashes to a halt. There is a perfectly good solution, however, since simply interchanging the last two rows,

$$\begin{bmatrix} 1 & -1 & 0 \\ 0 & 1 & -1 \\ 0 & 0 & 1 \end{bmatrix}\begin{bmatrix} x \\ y \\ z \end{bmatrix} = \begin{bmatrix} 1 \\ 1 \\ 1 \end{bmatrix}$$

gives an upper-triangular matrix with the obvious solution $z = 1$, $y = 2$, $x = 3$. It is clear that checks must be put into the algorithm to prevent such failures.

### Gaussian elimination

Since most matrix equations are not tridiagonal, we should like to extend the idea to a general matrix

$$\begin{bmatrix} a_{11} & a_{12} & a_{13} & \dots & a_{1n} \\ a_{21} & a_{22} & a_{23} & \dots & a_{2n} \\ \vdots & \vdots & \vdots & & \vdots \\ a_{n1} & a_{n2} & a_{n3} & \dots & a_{nn} \end{bmatrix} \begin{bmatrix} x_1 \\ x_2 \\ \vdots \\ x_n \end{bmatrix} = \begin{bmatrix} b_1 \\ b_2 \\ \vdots \\ b_n \end{bmatrix} \tag{5.27}$$

The result of doing this is a method known as **Gaussian elimination**. It is a little more involved than the Thomas algorithm. First we eliminate $x_1$:

$$\begin{bmatrix} 1 & a'_{12} & a'_{13} & \dots & a'_{1n} \\ 0 & a'_{22} & a'_{23} & \dots & a'_{2n} \\ 0 & a'_{32} & a'_{33} & \dots & a'_{3n} \\ \vdots & \vdots & \vdots & & \vdots \\ 0 & a'_{n2} & a'_{n3} & \dots & a'_{nn} \end{bmatrix} \begin{bmatrix} x_1 \\ x_2 \\ \\ \vdots \\ x_n \end{bmatrix} = \begin{bmatrix} b'_1 \\ b'_2 \\ \\ \vdots \\ b'_n \end{bmatrix}$$

where

$$a'_{12} = \frac{a_{12}}{a_{11}}, \quad a'_{13} = \frac{a_{13}}{a_{11}}, \quad \dots, \quad a'_{1n} = \frac{a_{1n}}{a_{11}}, \quad b'_1 = \frac{b_1}{a_{11}}$$

$$a'_{22} = a_{22} - a_{21}a'_{12}, \quad a'_{23} = a_{23} - a_{21}a'_{13}, \quad \dots, \quad b'_2 = b_2 - a_{21}b'_1$$

$$a'_{32} = a_{32} - a_{31}a'_{12}, \quad a'_{33} = a_{33} - a_{31}a'_{13}, \quad \dots, \quad b'_3 = b_3 - a_{31}b'_1$$

and so on.

Generally these can be written as

$$a'_{1j} = \frac{a_{1j}}{a_{11}}, \quad j = 1, \dots, n \quad b'_1 = \frac{b_1}{a_{11}}$$

$$\left.\begin{aligned} a'_{ij} &= a_{ij} - a_{i1}a'_{ij} \\ b'_i &= b_i - a_{i1}b'_1 \end{aligned}\right\}, \quad i = 2, \dots, n \quad \text{and} \quad j = 2, \dots, n$$

We now operate in an identical manner on the $(n - 1) \times (n - 1)$ submatrix, formed by ignoring row 1 and column 1, and repeat the process until the equations are of upper-triangular form. At the general step in the algorithm the equations will take the form

$$\begin{bmatrix} 1 & * & * & * & & & \dots & * \\ 0 & 1 & * & * & & & \dots & * \\ 0 & 0 & 1 & * & & & \dots & * \\ 0 & 0 & & \ddots & & & & \vdots \\ \vdots & \vdots & & \ddots & & & & \\ 0 & \dots & & 0 & 1 & * & \dots & * \\ 0 & \dots & & & 0 & a_{ii} & \dots & a_{in} \\ \vdots & & & & 0 & \vdots & \ddots & \vdots \\ & & & & \vdots & & & \\ 0 & \dots & & & 0 & a_{ni} & \dots & a_{nn} \end{bmatrix} \begin{bmatrix} x_1 \\ x_2 \\ \\ \\ \vdots \\ \\ \\ \\ \\ x_n \end{bmatrix} = \begin{bmatrix} * \\ * \\ \\ \\ \vdots \\ \\ \\ \\ \\ * \end{bmatrix} \tag{5.28}$$

**Figure 5.12**
Elimination procedure for (5.27).

```
procedure eliminate (A, b, n→A, b)
  {A is an n × n matrix and b is a vector with n elements}
  for i is 1 to n − 1 do
    {a segment will be inserted here later}
    b(i)←b(i)/A(i, i)
    for j is i to n do
      A(i, j)←A(i, j)/A(i, i)
      for k is i + 1 to n do
        A(k, j)←A(k, j) − A(k, i)*A(i, j)
      endfor
    endfor
    for k is i + 1 to n do
      b(k)←b(k) − A(k, i)*b(i)
    endfor
  endfor
endprocedure
```

Again overwriting avoids the need for introducing primed symbols; the algorithm is shown in Figure 5.12.

The general Gaussian elimination procedure would then put the eliminate and uppertriangular procedures together in a program

```
read (file, A, b, n)
    eliminate (A, b, n→A, b)
    uppertriangular (A, b, n→x)
write (vdu, x)
```

This algorithm, sharing the merits of the Thomas algorithm, is very widely used by engineers to solve linear equations.

In Example 5.30 the basic elimination technique was illustrated but now the two procedures *eliminate* and *uppertriangular* have reduced the method to one of routine. The major problem is to perform the arithmetic accurately.

**Example 5.32** Using elimination and back substitution solve the equations

$$\begin{bmatrix} 2 & 3 & 4 \\ 1 & 2 & 3 \\ 1 & 4 & 5 \end{bmatrix}\begin{bmatrix} x \\ y \\ z \end{bmatrix} = \begin{bmatrix} 1 \\ 1 \\ 2 \end{bmatrix}$$

**Solution** From the method in Figure 5.12 the steps are

Divide first row by 2: $\begin{bmatrix} 1 & \frac{3}{2} & 2 \\ 1 & 2 & 3 \\ 1 & 4 & 5 \end{bmatrix}\begin{bmatrix} x \\ y \\ z \end{bmatrix} = \begin{bmatrix} \frac{1}{2} \\ 1 \\ 2 \end{bmatrix}$

Subtract row 1 from row 2 and row 3: $\begin{bmatrix} 1 & \frac{3}{2} & 2 \\ 0 & \frac{1}{2} & 1 \\ 0 & \frac{5}{2} & 3 \end{bmatrix} \begin{bmatrix} x \\ y \\ z \end{bmatrix} = \begin{bmatrix} \frac{1}{2} \\ \frac{1}{2} \\ \frac{3}{2} \end{bmatrix}$

Divide second row by $\frac{1}{2}$: $\begin{bmatrix} 1 & \frac{3}{2} & 2 \\ 0 & 1 & 2 \\ 0 & \frac{5}{2} & 3 \end{bmatrix} \begin{bmatrix} x \\ y \\ z \end{bmatrix} = \begin{bmatrix} \frac{1}{2} \\ 1 \\ \frac{3}{2} \end{bmatrix}$

Subtract $\frac{5}{2}$ × (row 2) from row 3: $\begin{bmatrix} 1 & \frac{3}{2} & 2 \\ 0 & 1 & 2 \\ 0 & 0 & -2 \end{bmatrix} \begin{bmatrix} x \\ y \\ z \end{bmatrix} = \begin{bmatrix} \frac{1}{2} \\ 1 \\ -1 \end{bmatrix}$

Divide row 3 by (−2): $\begin{bmatrix} 1 & \frac{3}{2} & 2 \\ 0 & 1 & 2 \\ 0 & 0 & 1 \end{bmatrix} \begin{bmatrix} x \\ y \\ z \end{bmatrix} = \begin{bmatrix} \frac{1}{2} \\ 1 \\ \frac{1}{2} \end{bmatrix}$

The elimination procedure is now complete and the back substitution (from Figure 5.10) is applied to the upper-triangular matrix.

From the third row $z = \frac{1}{2}$

From the second row $y = 1 - 2z = 0$

From the first row $x = \frac{1}{2} - \frac{3}{2}y - 2z = -\frac{1}{2}$

so the solution is $x = -\frac{1}{2}$, $y = 0$, $z = \frac{1}{2}$.

**Example 5.33** Solve

$$\begin{bmatrix} 1 & 2 & 3 & 1 \\ 2 & 1 & 1 & 1 \\ 1 & 2 & 1 & 0 \\ 0 & 1 & 1 & 2 \end{bmatrix} \begin{bmatrix} x \\ y \\ z \\ t \end{bmatrix} = \begin{bmatrix} 5 \\ 3 \\ 4 \\ 0 \end{bmatrix}$$

**Solution** The elimination sequence is

$$\begin{bmatrix} 1 & 2 & 3 & 1 \\ 0 & -3 & -5 & -1 \\ 0 & 0 & -2 & -1 \\ 0 & 1 & 1 & 2 \end{bmatrix} \begin{bmatrix} x \\ y \\ z \\ t \end{bmatrix} = \begin{bmatrix} 5 \\ -7 \\ -1 \\ 0 \end{bmatrix}, \quad \begin{bmatrix} 1 & 2 & 3 & 1 \\ 0 & 1 & \frac{5}{3} & \frac{1}{3} \\ 0 & 0 & -2 & -1 \\ 0 & 0 & -\frac{2}{3} & \frac{5}{3} \end{bmatrix} \begin{bmatrix} x \\ y \\ z \\ t \end{bmatrix} = \begin{bmatrix} 5 \\ \frac{7}{3} \\ -1 \\ -\frac{7}{3} \end{bmatrix}$$

$$\begin{bmatrix} 1 & 2 & 3 & 1 \\ 0 & 1 & \frac{5}{3} & \frac{1}{3} \\ 0 & 0 & 1 & \frac{1}{2} \\ 0 & 0 & 0 & 2 \end{bmatrix} \begin{bmatrix} x \\ y \\ z \\ t \end{bmatrix} = \begin{bmatrix} 5 \\ \frac{7}{3} \\ \frac{1}{2} \\ -2 \end{bmatrix}$$

and application of the upper-triangular procedure gives $t = -1$, $z = 1$, $y = 1$ and $x = 1$.

It is clear again that if, in the algorithm shown in Figure 5.12, A(i, i) is zero at any time, the method will fail. It is, in fact, also found to be beneficial to the stability of the method to have A(i, i) as large as possible. Thus in (5.28) it is usual to perform a 'partial pivoting' so that the largest value in the column, $\max_{i \leq p \leq n} |A(p, i)|$, is chosen and the equations are swapped around to make this element the pivot. In Figure 5.12 the following segment of program would need to be inserted at the point indicated:

```
{find max_{i≤p≤n} |A(p, i)|}

{interchange row i with row p_max}
```

In practical computer implementations of the algorithm the elements of the rows would not be swapped explicitly. Instead, a pointer system would be used to implement a technique known as **indirect addressing**, which allows much faster computations. The interested reader is referred to texts on computer programming techniques for a full explanation of this method.

In a hand-computation version of this elimination procedure there are methods that maintain running checks and minimize the amount of writing. In this book the emphasis is on a computer implementation, and the hand computations are provided to illustrate the principle of the method. It is a powerful learning technique to write your own programs, but the practising professional engineer will normally use procedures from a computer software library, where these are available.

In MATLAB the instruction `[L, U] = lu(A)` provides in ***U*** the eliminated matrix. However the method used in MATLAB always uses partial pivoting and the method only works for a square matrix. The instruction `A\b` will give the solution to the matrix equation in one step. The MAPLE package can deal with any size matrix, so the right-hand side of the matrix equation should be appended to ***A*** and hence included in the elimination, and the instruction `gausselim(A);` provides the elimination but without partial pivoting. The instruction `gaussjord(A);` uses a much more subtle elimination process – see any advanced textbook on numerical linear algebra – and gives the solution in the most convenient form. The instruction `backsub(B)` is also available for the back substitution.

**Example 5.34** Solve the matrix equation

$$\begin{bmatrix} 1 & 2 & 3 & 1 \\ 2 & 1 & 1 & 1 \\ 1 & 3 & 1 & 0 \\ 0 & 1 & 1 & 2 \end{bmatrix} \begin{bmatrix} x \\ y \\ z \\ t \end{bmatrix} = \begin{bmatrix} 4 \\ 3 \\ 2 \\ 1 \end{bmatrix}$$

by Gaussian elimination with partial pivoting.

**Solution** The sequence is as follows. We first interchange rows 1 and 2 and eliminate:

$$\begin{bmatrix} 2 & 1 & 1 & 1 \\ 1 & 2 & 3 & 1 \\ 1 & 3 & 1 & 0 \\ 0 & 1 & 1 & 2 \end{bmatrix}\begin{bmatrix} x \\ y \\ z \\ t \end{bmatrix} = \begin{bmatrix} 3 \\ 4 \\ 2 \\ 1 \end{bmatrix} \to \begin{bmatrix} 1 & \frac{1}{2} & \frac{1}{2} & \frac{1}{2} \\ 0 & \frac{3}{2} & \frac{5}{2} & \frac{1}{2} \\ 0 & \frac{5}{2} & \frac{1}{2} & -\frac{1}{2} \\ 0 & 1 & 1 & 2 \end{bmatrix}\begin{bmatrix} x \\ y \\ z \\ t \end{bmatrix} = \begin{bmatrix} \frac{3}{2} \\ \frac{5}{2} \\ \frac{1}{2} \\ 1 \end{bmatrix}$$

We then interchange rows 2 and 3 and eliminate:

$$\begin{bmatrix} 1 & \frac{1}{2} & \frac{1}{2} & \frac{1}{2} \\ 0 & \frac{5}{2} & \frac{1}{2} & -\frac{1}{2} \\ 0 & \frac{3}{2} & \frac{5}{2} & \frac{1}{2} \\ 0 & 1 & 1 & 2 \end{bmatrix}\begin{bmatrix} x \\ y \\ z \\ t \end{bmatrix} = \begin{bmatrix} \frac{3}{2} \\ \frac{1}{2} \\ \frac{5}{2} \\ 1 \end{bmatrix} \to \begin{bmatrix} 1 & \frac{1}{2} & \frac{1}{2} & \frac{1}{2} \\ 0 & 1 & \frac{1}{5} & -\frac{1}{5} \\ 0 & 0 & \frac{11}{5} & \frac{4}{5} \\ 0 & 0 & \frac{4}{5} & \frac{11}{5} \end{bmatrix}\begin{bmatrix} x \\ y \\ z \\ t \end{bmatrix} = \begin{bmatrix} \frac{3}{2} \\ \frac{1}{5} \\ \frac{11}{5} \\ \frac{4}{5} \end{bmatrix}$$

There is no need to interchange rows at this stage, and the elimination proceeds immediately:

$$\begin{bmatrix} 1 & \frac{1}{2} & \frac{1}{2} & \frac{1}{2} \\ 0 & 1 & \frac{1}{5} & -\frac{1}{5} \\ 0 & 0 & 1 & \frac{4}{11} \\ 0 & 0 & 0 & \frac{21}{11} \end{bmatrix}\begin{bmatrix} x \\ y \\ z \\ t \end{bmatrix} = \begin{bmatrix} \frac{3}{2} \\ \frac{1}{5} \\ 1 \\ 0 \end{bmatrix}$$

Back substitution now gives $t = 0$, $z = 1$, $y = 0$ and $x = 1$.

---

### Ill-conditioning

Elimination methods are not without their difficulties, and the following example will highlight some of them.

**Example 5.35** Solve, by elimination, the equations

(a) $\begin{bmatrix} 2 & 1 \\ 1 & 0.5001 \end{bmatrix}\begin{bmatrix} x \\ y \end{bmatrix} = \begin{bmatrix} 0.3 \\ 0.6 \end{bmatrix}$ (b) $\begin{bmatrix} 2 & 1 \\ 1 & 0.4999 \end{bmatrix}\begin{bmatrix} x \\ y \end{bmatrix} = \begin{bmatrix} 0.3 \\ 0.6 \end{bmatrix}$

**Solution** Keeping the calculations parallel,

(a) $\begin{bmatrix} 1 & 0.5 \\ 1 & 0.5001 \end{bmatrix}\begin{bmatrix} x \\ y \end{bmatrix} = \begin{bmatrix} 0.15 \\ 0.6 \end{bmatrix}$ (b) $\begin{bmatrix} 1 & 0.5 \\ 1 & 0.4999 \end{bmatrix}\begin{bmatrix} x \\ y \end{bmatrix} = \begin{bmatrix} 0.15 \\ 0.6 \end{bmatrix}$

$\begin{bmatrix} 1 & 0.5 \\ 0 & 0.0001 \end{bmatrix}\begin{bmatrix} x \\ y \end{bmatrix} = \begin{bmatrix} 0.15 \\ 0.45 \end{bmatrix}$ $\begin{bmatrix} 1 & 0.5 \\ 0 & -0.0001 \end{bmatrix}\begin{bmatrix} x \\ y \end{bmatrix} = \begin{bmatrix} 0.15 \\ 0.45 \end{bmatrix}$

with solution (a)

$y = 4500$, $x = -2249.85$

with solution (b)

$y = -4500$, $x = 2250.15$

---

In Example 5.35 simple equations that have only marginally different coefficients have wildly different solutions. This situation is likely to cause problems so it must be analysed carefully. To do so in full detail is not appropriate here, but the problem is clearly connected with taking differences of numbers that are almost equal: $0.5001 - 0.5 = 0.0001$.

Systems of equations that exhibit such awkward behaviour are called **ill-conditioned**. It is not straightforward to identify ill-conditioning in matrices involving many variables, but an example will illustrate the difficulties in the two-variable case. Suppose we solve

$$\begin{aligned} 2x + \quad y &= 0.3 \\ x - \alpha y &= 0 \end{aligned}$$

where $\alpha = 1 \pm 0.05$ has some error in its value. We easily obtain $x = 0.3\alpha/(1 + 2\alpha)$ and $y = 0.3/(1 + 2\alpha)$, and putting in the range of $\alpha$ values we get $0.0983 \leqslant x \leqslant 0.1016$ and $0.0968 \leqslant y \leqslant 0.1034$. Thus an error of $\pm 5\%$ in the value of $\alpha$ produces an error of $\pm 2\%$ in $x$ and an error of $\pm 3\%$ in $y$.

If we now try to solve

$$\begin{aligned} 2x + \quad y &= 0.3 \\ x + \alpha y &= 0.3 \end{aligned}$$

where $\alpha = 0.4 \pm 0.05$, then we get the solution $x = 0.3(1 - \alpha)/(1 - 2\alpha)$, $y = -0.3/(1 - 2\alpha)$. Putting in the range of $\alpha$ values now gives $0.65 \leqslant x \leqslant 1.65$ and $-3 \leqslant y \leqslant -1$, and an error of $\pm 12\%$ in the value of $\alpha$ produces errors in $x$ and $y$ of up to 100%.

Figure 5.13 illustrates these equations geometrically. We see that a small change in the slope of the line $x - \alpha y = 0$ makes only a small difference in the solution. However, changing the slope of the line $x + \alpha y = 0.3$ makes a large difference, because the lines are nearly parallel. Identifying such behaviour for higher-dimensional problems is not at all easy. Sets of equations of this kind do occur in engineering contexts, so the difficulties outlined here should be appreciated. In each of the ill-conditioned cases we have studied, the determinant of the system is 'small':

$$\begin{vmatrix} 2 & 1 \\ 1 & 0.5001 \end{vmatrix} = 0.0002,$$

$$\begin{vmatrix} 2 & 1 \\ 1 & 0.4999 \end{vmatrix} = -0.0002$$

$$\begin{vmatrix} 2 & 1 \\ 1 & 0.4 \pm 0.05 \end{vmatrix} = -0.2 \pm 0.1$$

Thus the equations are 'nearly singular' – and this is one means of identifying the problem. However, the reader should refer to a more advanced book on numerical analysis to see how to identify and deal with ill-conditioning in the general case.

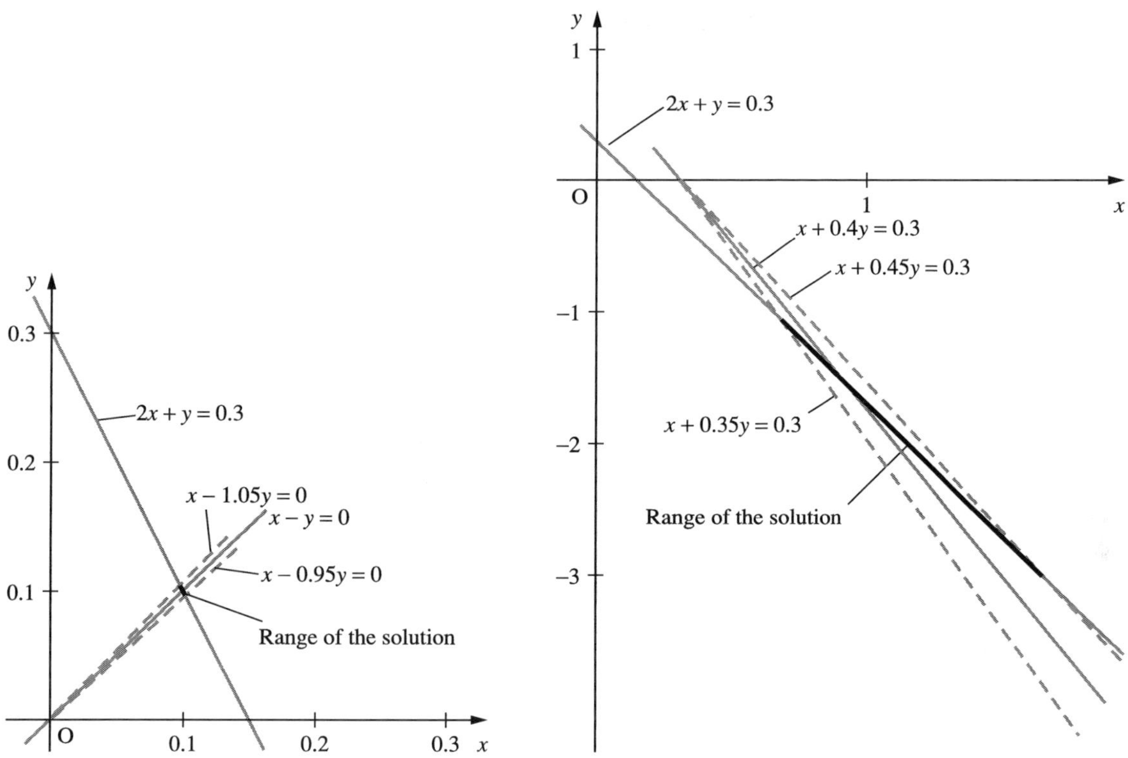


**(a)** **(b)**

**Figure 5.13** Solution of (a) $2x + y = 0.3$, $x - \alpha y = 0$ with $\alpha = 1 \pm 0.05$; and (b) $2x + y = 0.3$, $x + \alpha y = 0.3$ with $\alpha = 0.4 \pm 0.05$. The heavy black lines indicate the ranges of the solutions.

## 5.5.3 Exercises

Most of these exercises will require MATLAB or MAPLE for their solution. To appreciate the elimination method, hand computation should be tried on the first few exercises.

**72** Use elimination with and/or without partial pivoting, to solve the equations

(a) $$\begin{bmatrix} 1 & 3 & 2 \\ 2 & 1 & 4 \\ 3 & -1 & 5 \end{bmatrix} \begin{bmatrix} x \\ y \\ z \end{bmatrix} = \begin{bmatrix} 1 \\ 2 \\ 1 \end{bmatrix}$$

(b) $$\begin{bmatrix} 0 & 1 & 1 \\ 3 & -1 & 1 \\ 1 & 1 & -3 \end{bmatrix} \begin{bmatrix} x \\ y \\ z \end{bmatrix} = \begin{bmatrix} 6 \\ -7 \\ -13 \end{bmatrix}$$

(c) $$\begin{bmatrix} 1 & 2 & 4 \\ -6 & 2 & 10 \\ 2 & 8 & 7 \end{bmatrix} \begin{bmatrix} x \\ y \\ z \end{bmatrix} = \begin{bmatrix} 0 \\ 1 \\ 0 \end{bmatrix}$$

**73** Solve the equations

$$\begin{aligned} 4x - y \quad &= 2 \\ -x + 4y - z \quad &= 5 \\ -y + 4z - t &= 3 \\ -z + 4t &= 10 \end{aligned}$$

using the tridiagonal algorithm.

**74** Solve the equations

$$\begin{aligned} 4x - y \quad\quad - t &= -4 \\ -x + 4y - z \quad\quad &= 1 \\ -y + 4z - t &= 4 \\ -x \quad\quad - z + 4t &= 10 \end{aligned}$$

using Gaussian elimination.

**75** Solve, using Gaussian elimination with partial pivoting, the following equations:

(a) $\begin{bmatrix} 1.17 & 2.64 & 7.41 \\ 3.37 & 1.22 & 9.64 \\ 4.10 & 2.89 & 3.37 \end{bmatrix}\begin{bmatrix} x \\ y \\ z \end{bmatrix} = \begin{bmatrix} 1.27 \\ 3.91 \\ 4.63 \end{bmatrix}$

(b) $\begin{bmatrix} 3.21 & 4.18 & -2.31 \\ -4.17 & 3.63 & 4.20 \\ 1.88 & -8.14 & 0.01 \end{bmatrix}\begin{bmatrix} x \\ y \\ z \end{bmatrix} = \begin{bmatrix} 3.27 \\ -1.21 \\ 4.88 \end{bmatrix}$

(c) $\begin{bmatrix} 1 & 7 & 2 & -1 \\ 11 & 4 & -3 & 9 \\ 7 & 6 & 4 & -2 \\ 5 & 8 & -5 & 3 \end{bmatrix}\begin{bmatrix} x \\ y \\ z \\ t \end{bmatrix} = \begin{bmatrix} 12 \\ -12 \\ 7 \\ -7 \end{bmatrix}$

**76** The two almost identical matrix equations are given

$$\begin{bmatrix} 0.11 & 0.19 & 0.10 \\ 0.49 & -0.31 & 0.21 \\ 1.55 & -0.70 & 0.70 \end{bmatrix}\begin{bmatrix} x \\ y \\ z \end{bmatrix} = \begin{bmatrix} 1 \\ 1 \\ 1 \end{bmatrix} \quad \text{and}$$

$$\begin{bmatrix} 0.11 & 0.19 & 0.10 \\ 0.49 & -0.31 & 0.21 \\ 1.55 & -0.70 & 0.71 \end{bmatrix}\begin{bmatrix} x \\ y \\ z \end{bmatrix} = \begin{bmatrix} 1 \\ 1 \\ 1 \end{bmatrix}$$

Use MATLAB or MAPLE to show that the solutions are wildly different. Evaluate the determinants of the two $3 \times 3$ matrices.

**77** Show that a tridiagonal matrix can be written in the form

$$\begin{bmatrix} a_1 & b_1 & & & & 0 \\ c_2 & a_2 & b_2 & & & \\ & c_3 & a_3 & b_3 & & \\ & & \ddots & \ddots & \ddots & \\ & 0 & & c_{n-1} & a_{n-1} & b_{n-1} \\ & & & & c_n & a_n \end{bmatrix}$$

$$= \begin{bmatrix} l_{11} & & & & 0 \\ l_{21} & l_{22} & & & \\ & l_{32} & l_{33} & & \\ & & \ddots & \ddots & \\ & 0 & & l_{n,n-1} & l_{nn} \end{bmatrix}$$

$$\times \begin{bmatrix} 1 & u_{12} & & & & 0 \\ & 1 & u_{23} & & & \\ & & 1 & u_{34} & & \\ & & & \ddots & \ddots & \\ & & & & 1 & u_{n-1,n} \\ & 0 & & & & 1 \end{bmatrix}$$

A matrix that has zeros in every position below the diagonal is called an **upper-triangular matrix** and one with zeros everywhere above the diagonal is called a **lower-triangular matrix**. A matrix that only has non-zero elements in certain diagonal lines is called a **banded matrix**. In this case we have shown that a tridiagonal matrix can be written as the product of a lower-triangular banded matrix and an upper-triangular banded matrix.

**78** The cantilever beam in Question 71 (Exercises 5.5.1) and illustrated in Figure 5.9 was solved using very inefficient methods. Solve the same equations using the Thomas algorithm.

If the displacements are not small then the equations are more complicated. They take the form

$$\left.\begin{aligned} -v_1y_1 + y_2 \quad\quad &= -uw_1 \\ y_1 - v_2y_2 + y_3 \quad\quad &= -4uw_2 \\ y_2 - v_3y_3 + y_4 &= -9uw_3 \\ 2y_3 - v_4y_4 &= -16u \end{aligned}\right\} \quad \textbf{(5.29)}$$

where

$$w_1 = \left[1 + 4\left(\frac{y_2}{L}\right)^2\right]^{3/2}$$

$$w_2 = \left[1 + 4\left(\frac{y_3 - y_1}{L}\right)^2\right]^{3/2}$$

and

$$w_3 = \left[1 + 4\left(\frac{y_4 - y_2}{L}\right)^2\right]^{3/2}$$

and putting $k = PL^2/16EI$

$$v_1 = 2 + kw_1, \quad v_2 = 2 + kw_2$$

$$v_3 = 2 + kw_3, \quad v_4 = 2 + k$$

Solve the equations iteratively, calculating $w_i$ and $v_i$ from the previous iteration and then solving the tridiagonal scheme. Use the same values as before, namely $k = 1$ and $u = 1$, and take $L = 2$. A full solution of this exercise will require the use of a computer package such as MATLAB.

79 A wire is loaded with equal weights $W$ at nine uniformly spaced points as illustrated in Figure 5.14. The wire is sufficiently taut that the tension $T$ may be considered to be constant. The end points are at the same level, so that $u_0 = u_{10} = 0$ and the system is symmetrical about its midpoint. The equations to determine the displacements $u_i$ are

$$\begin{aligned}
W &= (T/d)(2u_1 - u_2) \\
W &= (T/d)(-u_1 + 2u_2 - u_3) \\
W &= (T/d)(-u_2 + 2u_3 - u_4) \\
W &= (T/d)(-u_3 + 2u_4 - u_5) \\
W &= (T/d)(-2u_4 + 2u_5)
\end{aligned}$$

Taking $Wd/T = l$, calculate $u_i/l$ for $i = 1, \ldots, 5$.

80 A ladder network is shown in Figure 5.15. The driver is an a.c. voltage of $E = E_0 e^{j\omega t}$ and the currents are taken to be $I_p = Z_p e^{j\omega t}$. The equations satisfied by the $Z_p$ are

$$jE_0\omega = -\tfrac{1}{2}LZ_0\omega^2 + \frac{1}{C}(Z_0 - Z_1)$$

$$0 = -LZ_p\omega^2 + \frac{1}{C}(-Z_{p-1} + 2Z_p - Z_{p+1})$$

$$\text{for } p = 1, \ldots, n-1$$

$$0 = -\tfrac{1}{2}LZ_n\omega^2 + \frac{1}{C}(Z_n - Z_{n-1})$$

Take $n = 3$ and solve for $Z_3$. Evaluate the effective resistance in the final circuit as $|E_0/Z_3|$. Plot this resistance against $\omega$ and interpret the graph obtained. Note that the matrices contain complex numbers. (See Review exercises 7.12, Question 21.) Although it is possible to solve this exercise by hand, the use of MATLAB's Symbolic Math Toolbox or MAPLE, is recommended.

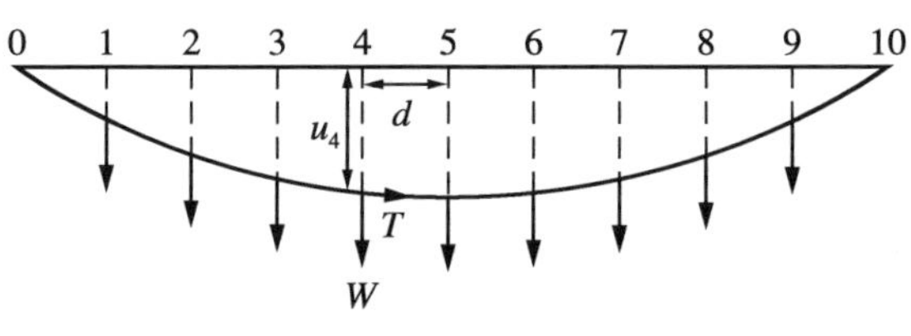


**Figure 5.14** Loaded wire.

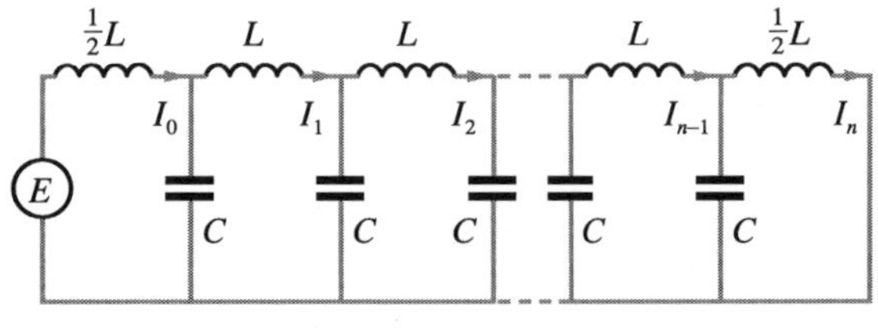


**Figure 5.15** Ladder network.

## 5.5.4 The solution of linear equations: iterative methods

An alternative and very popular way of solving linear equations is by iteration. This has the attraction of being easy to program. In practice, the availability of efficient procedures in computer libraries means that elimination methods are usually preferred for small problems. However, when the number of variables gets large, say several hundred, elimination methods struggle because the matrices can contain $10^6$ or more elements. Problems of such size commonly occur in those scientific and engineering computations that require numerical solution on a mesh. Typically, in a turbine flow, we have a three-dimensional fluid flow problem that would need to be solved for three velocities and pressure on a $30 \times 30 \times 30$ mesh. The problem would require the solution of a $27\,000 \times 27\,000$ matrix equation. The saving feature of such problems is that it is very common for almost all the entries in the matrix to be zero. Matrices in which the large majority of elements are zero are called **sparse matrices**. Unless there is special structure to the equations, elimination will quickly destroy the sparseness. On the other hand, iterative methods only have to deal with the non-zero terms, so there is considerable computational saving. As usual, there is a price to pay:

(a) it is not always easy to decide when the method has converged;
(b) if the method takes a very large number of iterations to converge, any savings are quickly consumed.

A simple example will illustrate the way the method proceeds; in this example exact fractions will be used.

To solve the equations

$$4x + y = 2$$

$$x + 4y = -7$$

we first rearrange them as

$$x = \tfrac{1}{4}(2 - y)$$

$$y = \tfrac{1}{4}(-7 - x)$$

and start with $x = 0$, $y = 0$.

Putting these values into the right-hand side gives $x = \frac{1}{2}$, $y = -\frac{7}{4}$

Putting these new values into the right-hand side gives $x = \frac{15}{16}$, $y = -\frac{15}{8}$

Putting these new values into the right-hand side gives $x = \frac{31}{32}$, $y = -\frac{127}{64}$

Putting these new values into the right-hand side gives $x = \frac{255}{256}$, $y = -\frac{255}{128}$

Putting these new values into the right-hand side gives $x = \frac{511}{512}$, $y = -\frac{2047}{1024}$

Performing the same procedure repeatedly, normally called **iteration**, gives a set of numbers that appear to be tending to the solution $x = 1$, $y = -2$.

This particular example shows the strength of the method but we are not always so fortunate, as illustrated in the next example.

Consider the tridiagonal equations in Example 5.31:

$$\begin{aligned} 2x + y \qquad\quad &= 1 \\ x + 2y + z \qquad &= 1 \\ y + 2z + t &= 1 \\ z + 2t &= -2 \end{aligned}$$

| *Iteration* | *0* | *1* | *2* | *3* | *4* | *5* | *6* | *7* | *8* | *9* | *10* |
|---|---|---|---|---|---|---|---|---|---|---|---|
| $x$ | 0 | 0.5 | 0.25 | 0.5 | 0.5 | 0.6562 | 0.6719 | 0.7734 | 0.7852 | 0.8516 | 0.8594 |
| $y$ | 0 | 0.5 | 0 | 0 | −0.3125 | −0.3437 | −0.5469 | −0.5703 | −0.7031 | −0.7187 | −0.8057 |
| $z$ | 0 | 0.5 | 0.75 | 1.1250 | 1.1875 | 1.4375 | 1.4687 | 1.6328 | 1.6523 | 1.7598 | 1.7725 |
| $t$ | 0 | −1 | −1.25 | −1.3750 | −1.5625 | −1.5937 | −1.7187 | −1.7344 | −1.8164 | −1.8262 | −1.8799 |

**Figure 5.16** Iterative solution of (5.30) using Jacobi iteration.

We can rearrange these as

$$\begin{aligned} x &= \tfrac{1}{2}(1 - y) \\ y &= \tfrac{1}{2}(1 - x - z) \\ z &= \tfrac{1}{2}(1 - y - t) \\ t &= \tfrac{1}{2}(-2 - z) \end{aligned} \quad \text{or} \quad \begin{bmatrix} x \\ y \\ z \\ t \end{bmatrix} = \frac{1}{2}\begin{bmatrix} 0 & -1 & 0 & 0 \\ -1 & 0 & -1 & 0 \\ 0 & -1 & 0 & -1 \\ 0 & 0 & -1 & 0 \end{bmatrix}\begin{bmatrix} x \\ y \\ z \\ t \end{bmatrix} + \frac{1}{2}\begin{bmatrix} 1 \\ 1 \\ 1 \\ -2 \end{bmatrix} \quad \textbf{(5.30)}$$

Suppose we start with $x = y = z = t = 0$. We substitute these into the right-hand side and evaluate the new $x$, $y$, $z$ and $t$; we then substitute the new values back in and repeat the process. Such iteration gives the results shown in Figure 5.16. This shows values going depressingly slowly to the solution 1, −1, 2, −2: even after 20 iterations the values are 0.9381, −0.9767, 1.9727, −1.9856. The method just described is called the **Jacobi method**, and can be written, using superscripts as iteration counters, in the form

$$\begin{aligned} x^{(r+1)} &= \tfrac{1}{2}(1 - y^{(r)}) \\ y^{(r+1)} &= \tfrac{1}{2}(1 - x^{(r)} - z^{(r)}) \\ z^{(r+1)} &= \tfrac{1}{2}(1 - y^{(r)} - t^{(r)}) \\ t^{(r+1)} &= \tfrac{1}{2}(-2 - z^{(r)}) \end{aligned}$$

An obvious step is to use the new values as soon as they are available. In the two-variable example the same equations

$$\begin{aligned} x &= \tfrac{1}{4}(2 - y) \\ y &= \tfrac{1}{4}(-7 - x) \end{aligned}$$

are used and the same starting point $x = 0$, $y = 0$ is used. The iteration proceeds slightly differently:

Put the values 0, 0 in the first equation $\Rightarrow x = \frac{1}{2}$

Put the values $\frac{1}{2}$, 0 in the second equation $\Rightarrow y = -\frac{15}{8}$

Put the values $\frac{1}{2}$, $-\frac{15}{8}$ in the first equation $\Rightarrow x = \frac{31}{32}$

Put the values $\frac{31}{32}$, $-\frac{15}{8}$ in the second equation $\Rightarrow y = -\frac{255}{128}$

Put the values $\frac{31}{32}$, $-\frac{255}{128}$ in the first equation $\Rightarrow x = \frac{511}{512}$

and continue in the same way. It can be seen that already the convergence is very much faster.

| *Iteration* | *0* | *1* | *2* | *3* | *4* | *5* | *6* | *7* | *8* | *9* | *10* |
|---|---|---|---|---|---|---|---|---|---|---|---|
| $x$ | 0 | 0.5 | 0.375 | 0.4375 | 0.6172 | 0.7480 | 0.8350 | 0.8920 | 0.9293 | 0.9537 | 0.9697 |
| $y$ | 0 | 0.25 | 0.125 | −0.2344 | −0.4961 | −0.6699 | −0.7839 | −0.8586 | −0.9074 | −0.9394 | −0.9603 |
| $z$ | 0 | 0.375 | 1.0312 | 1.3750 | 1.5918 | 1.7329 | 1.8252 | 1.8856 | 1.9251 | 1.9510 | 1.9679 |
| $t$ | 0 | −1.1875 | −1.5156 | −1.6875 | −1.7959 | −1.8665 | −1.9126 | −1.9426 | −1.9626 | −1.9755 | −1.9840 |

**Figure 5.17** Iterative solution of (5.30) using Gauss–Seidel iteration.

In the second example we use the new values of $x$, $y$, $z$ and $t$ as soon as they are calculated: the method is called **Gauss–Seidel iteration**. This can be written as

$$\begin{aligned} x^{(r+1)} &= \tfrac{1}{2}(1 - y^{(r)}) \\ y^{(r+1)} &= \tfrac{1}{2}(1 - x^{(r+1)} - z^{(r)}) \\ z^{(r+1)} &= \tfrac{1}{2}(1 - y^{(r+1)} - t^{(r)}) \\ t^{(r+1)} &= \tfrac{1}{2}(-2 - z^{(r+1)}) \end{aligned}$$

The calculation now yields the results shown in Figure 5.17. We see that, after the ten iterations quoted, the solution obtained by Gauss–Seidel iteration is within 4% of the actual solution whereas that obtained by Jacobi iteration still has an error of about 20%. The Gauss–Seidel method is both faster and more convenient for computer implementation. Within 20 iterations the Gauss–Seidel solution is accurate to three decimal places. A pseudocode algorithm for this method applied to the present problem is shown in Figure 5.18 and is easily implemented in MATLAB.

Although the two iteration methods have been described in terms of a particular example, the method is quite general. To solve

$$\boldsymbol{AX} = \boldsymbol{b}$$

we rewrite

$$\boldsymbol{A} = \boldsymbol{D} + \boldsymbol{L} + \boldsymbol{U}$$

where $\boldsymbol{D}$ is diagonal, $\boldsymbol{L}$ only has non-zero elements below the diagonal and $\boldsymbol{U}$ only has non-zero elements above the diagonal, so that

**Figure 5.18** Algorithm to implement the Gauss–Seidel iteration.

```
read(vdu,eps,kmax)
k←0
x←0;y←0;z←0;t←0
repeat
  k←k + 1
  xold←x;  x←(1 − y)/2
  yold←y;     y←(1 − x − z)/2
  zold←z;     z←(1 − y − t)/2
  told←t;   t←(−2 − z)/2
until ((abs(x − xold) < eps)and(abs(y − yold) < eps)and(abs(z − zold) < eps)
    and(abs(t − told) < eps))or (k > kmax)
```

$$
\boldsymbol{A} = \begin{bmatrix} a_{11} & & & & \\ & a_{22} & & 0 & \\ & & a_{33} & & \\ & 0 & & \ddots & \\ & & & & a_{nn} \end{bmatrix} + \begin{bmatrix} 0 & & & & \\ a_{21} & 0 & & 0 & \\ a_{31} & a_{32} & 0 & & \\ \vdots & \vdots & & \ddots & \\ a_{n1} & a_{n2} & \dots & a_{n,n-1} & 0 \end{bmatrix}
$$

$$
+ \begin{bmatrix} 0 & a_{12} & a_{13} & \dots & a_{1n} \\ & 0 & a_{23} & \dots & a_{2n} \\ & & & \ddots & \vdots \\ & & 0 & 0 & a_{n-1,n} \\ & & & & 0 \end{bmatrix}
$$

The Jacobi method is written in this notation as

$$\boldsymbol{DX}^{(r+1)} = -(\boldsymbol{L} + \boldsymbol{U})\boldsymbol{X}^{(r)} + \boldsymbol{b}$$

and the Gauss–Seidel method as

$$\boldsymbol{DX}^{(r+1)} = -\boldsymbol{LX}^{(r+1)} - \boldsymbol{UX}^{(r)} + \boldsymbol{b}$$

(Remember that $\boldsymbol{X}^{(r)}$ denotes the $r$th iteration of $\boldsymbol{X}$, not $\boldsymbol{X}$ raised to the power $r$.)

By changing the method slightly, we have been able to speed up the method, so it is natural to ask if it can be speeded up even further. A popular method for doing this is **successive over-relaxation (SOR)**. This anticipates what the $x_i$ values might be and overshoots the values obtained by Gauss–Seidel iteration. The new value of each component of the vector $\boldsymbol{X}^{(r+1)}$ is taken to be

$$wx_i^{(r+1)} + (1 - w)x_i^{(r)} \qquad \textbf{(5.31)}$$

which is the weighted average of the previous value and the new value given by Gauss–Seidel iteration. In the two-variable example the weighted average rearranges the equations as

$$x = w[\tfrac{1}{4}(2 - y)] + (1 - w)x = x + w[\tfrac{1}{4}(2 - y - 4x)]$$

$$y = w[\tfrac{1}{4}(-7 - x)] + (1 - w)y = y + w[\tfrac{1}{4}(-7 - x - 4y)]$$

The convergence for this example is so rapid that the enhanced convergence of SOR is hardly worth the effort; an optimum value of $w = 1.05$ reduces the convergence, to six significant figures, from seven to six iterations. However, for most problems the improved convergence is significant. Note that $w = 1$ gives the Gauss–Seidel method.

If we repeat the calculation for (5.30) including (5.31) with $w = 1.4$, we obtain the results shown in Figure 5.19. It may be noted that the iterations converge even faster than the two previous methods, with a solution accurate to about 0.1% after ten steps. The optimum value of $w$ is of great interest, and specialist books on numerical analysis

| *Iteration* | *0* | *1* | *2* | *3* | *4* | *5* | *6* | *7* | *8* | *9* | *10* |
|---|---|---|---|---|---|---|---|---|---|---|---|
| $x$ | 0 | 0.7 | 0.273 | 0.5643 | 1.1060 | 1.0195 | 1.0226 | 1.0055 | 0.9956 | 0.9995 | 0.9995 |
| $y$ | 0 | 0.21 | 0.0378 | −0.9025 | −1.0885 | −1.0434 | −1.0208 | −0.9969 | −0.9967 | −0.9990 | −0.9997 |
| $z$ | 0 | 0.553 | 1.7033 | 1.9646 | 2.0930 | 2.0320 | 2.0019 | 1.9979 | 1.9971 | 1.9996 | 2.0001 |
| $t$ | 0 | −1.7871 | −1.8775 | −2.0242 | −2.0554 | −2.0002 | −2.0013 | −1.9981 | −1.9988 | −2.0002 | −2.0000 |

**Figure 5.19** Iterative solution of (5.30) with SOR factor $w = 1.4$ in (5.31).

| | | | | | | | | | |
|---|---|---|---|---|---|---|---|---|---|
| *SOR factor w* | 0.2 | 0.4 | 0.6 | 0.8 | 1.0 | 1.2 | 1.4 | 1.6 | 1.8 |
| *Iterations required for convergence* | >50 | >50 | 47 | 34 | 26 | 21 | 17 | 29 | >50 |

**Figure 5.20** Variation of rate of convergence with SOR factor $w$.

give details of how this can be computed (for example, *Applied Linear Algebra*, Peter Olver and Cheri Shakiban (2005), Pearson). Usually the best approach is a heuristic one – experiment with $w$ to find a value that gives the fastest convergence. For 'one-off' problems this is hardly worth the effort so long as convergence is achieved, but in many scientific and engineering problems the same calculation may be done many hundreds of times, so the optimum value of $w$ can reduce calculation time by half or more. For the current problem the number of iterations required to give four-decimal-place accuracy is shown in Figure 5.20.

It can be shown that outside the region $0 < w < 2$ the method will diverge but that inside it may or may not converge. The case $w < 1$ is called **under-relaxation** and $w > 1$ is called **over-relaxation**. In straightforward problems $w$ in the range 1.2–1.8 usually gives the most rapid convergence, and this is normally the region to explore as a first guess. In the problem studied a value of $w = 1.4$ gives just about the fastest convergence, requiring only about two-thirds of the iterations required for the Gauss–Seidel method. In some physical problems, however, under-relaxation is required in order to avoid too rapid variation from iteration to iteration.

Great care must be taken with iterative methods, and convergence for some equations can be particularly difficult. Considerable experience is needed in looking at sets of equations to decide whether or not convergence can be expected, and often – even for the experienced mathematician – the answer is 'try it and see'. One simple test that will guarantee convergence is to test whether the matrix is **diagonally dominant**. This means that the magnitude of a diagonal element is larger than or equal to the sum of the magnitudes of the off-diagonal elements in that row, or $|a_{ii}| \geqslant \sum_{\substack{j=1 \\ i \neq j}}^{n} |a_{ij}|$ for each $i$. If the system is not diagonally dominant, the iteration method may or may not converge.

A detailed analysis of the convergence of iterative methods is not possible without a study of eigenvalues, and can be found in specialist numerical analysis books.

Iterative methods described in this section are fairly easy to program and an implementation in MATLAB, or similar package, is highly suitable.

## 5.5.5 Exercises

(*Note*: All of these exercises are best solved using a computer matrix package such as MATLAB.)

81 Solve the equations in Question 73 (Exercises 5.5.3) using Jacobi iteration starting from the estimate $\boldsymbol{X} = [1 \quad 1 \quad 1 \quad 1]^{\mathrm{T}}$. How accurate is the solution obtained after five iterations?

82 Solve the equations in Question 74 (Exercises 5.5.3) using Gauss–Seidel iteration, starting from the estimate $\boldsymbol{X} = [1 \quad 0 \quad 0 \quad 0]^{\mathrm{T}}$. How accurate is the solution obtained after three iterations?

83 Write a computer program in MATLAB or similar package to obtain the solution, by SOR, to the equations in Question 75 (Exercises 5.5.3). Determine the optimum SOR factor for each equation.

84 Use an SOR program to solve the equations

$$\begin{aligned} x - 0.7y \phantom{+ z} &= -4 \\ -0.7x + y - 0.7z &= 34 \\ -0.7y + z &= -44 \end{aligned}$$

so that successive iterations differ by no more than 1 in the fourth decimal place. Find an SOR factor that produces this convergence in less than 50 iterations.

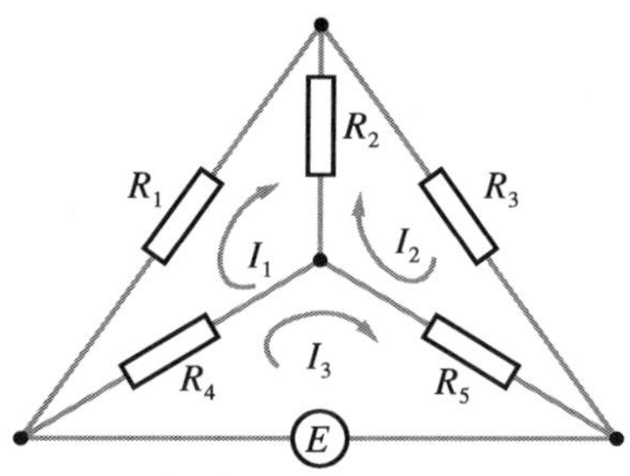


**Figure 5.21** Circuit for Question 85.

85 Show that the circuit in Figure 5.21 has equations

$$\begin{bmatrix} R_1 + R_2 + R_4 & -R_2 & -R_4 \\ -R_2 & R_3 + R_5 + R_2 & -R_5 \\ -R_4 & -R_5 & R_4 + R_5 \end{bmatrix} \begin{bmatrix} I_1 \\ I_2 \\ I_3 \end{bmatrix} = \begin{bmatrix} 0 \\ 0 \\ E \end{bmatrix}$$

Take $R_1 = 1$, $R_2 = 2$, $R_3 = 2$, $R_4 = 2$ and $R_5 = 3$ (all in $\Omega$) and $E = 1.5$ V. Show that the equations are diagonally dominant, and hence solve the equations by an iterative method.

86 Solve the $10 \times 10$ matrix equation in Example 5.29 using an iterative method starting from $\boldsymbol{X} = [1 \quad 1 \quad 1 \quad 1 \quad 1 \quad 1 \quad 1 \quad 1 \quad 1 \quad 1]^{\mathrm{T}}$. Verify that a solution to four-figure accuracy can be obtained in less than ten iterations.

## 5.6 Rank

The solution of sets of linear equations has been considered in Section 5.5. Provided the determinant of a matrix is non-zero, we can obtain explicit solutions in terms of the inverse matrix. However, when we looked at cases with zero determinant the results were much less clear. The idea of the **rank** of a matrix helps to make these results more precise. Unfortunately, rank is not an easy concept, and it is usually difficult to compute. We shall take an informal approach that is not fully general but is sufficient to deal with the cases (c) and (d) of Section 5.5. The method we shall use is to take the Gaussian elimination procedure described in Figure 5.12 (Section 5.5.2) and examine the consequences for a zero-determinant situation.

If we start with the equations

$$\begin{bmatrix} 1 & 0 & 1 & 1 & 0 & 0 \\ 0 & 1 & 1 & 0 & 1 & 2 \\ 1 & 1 & 2 & 1 & 1 & 2 \\ 1 & 0 & 1 & 0 & 1 & 3 \\ 0 & 0 & 0 & 0 & 1 & 3 \\ 1 & 1 & 2 & 0 & 2 & 5 \end{bmatrix} \begin{bmatrix} x_1 \\ x_2 \\ . \\ . \\ . \\ x_6 \end{bmatrix} = \begin{bmatrix} 1 \\ 1 \\ 2 \\ 0 \\ 0 \\ 1 \end{bmatrix} \tag{5.32}$$

and proceed with the elimination, the first and second steps are quite normal:

$$\begin{bmatrix} 1 & 0 & 1 & 1 & 0 & 0 \\ 0 & 1 & 1 & 0 & 1 & 2 \\ 0 & 1 & 1 & 0 & 1 & 2 \\ 0 & 0 & 0 & -1 & 1 & 3 \\ 0 & 0 & 0 & 0 & 1 & 3 \\ 0 & 1 & 1 & -1 & 2 & 5 \end{bmatrix} \begin{bmatrix} x_1 \\ x_2 \\ . \\ . \\ . \\ x_6 \end{bmatrix} = \begin{bmatrix} 1 \\ 1 \\ 1 \\ -1 \\ 0 \\ 0 \end{bmatrix}, \begin{bmatrix} 1 & 0 & 1 & 1 & 0 & 0 \\ 0 & 1 & 1 & 0 & 1 & 2 \\ 0 & 0 & 0 & 0 & 0 & 0 \\ 0 & 0 & 0 & -1 & 1 & 3 \\ 0 & 0 & 0 & 0 & 1 & 3 \\ 0 & 0 & 0 & -1 & 1 & 3 \end{bmatrix} \begin{bmatrix} x_1 \\ x_2 \\ . \\ . \\ . \\ x_6 \end{bmatrix} = \begin{bmatrix} 1 \\ 1 \\ 0 \\ -1 \\ 0 \\ -1 \end{bmatrix}$$

The next step in the elimination procedure looks for a non-zero entry in the third column on or below the diagonal element. All the entries are zero – so the procedure, as it stands, fails. To overcome the problem, we just proceed to the next column and repeat the normal sequence of operations. We interchange the third and fourth rows and perform the elimination on column 4. Finally we interchange rows 4 and 5 to give

$$\begin{bmatrix} 1 & 0 & 1 & 1 & 0 & 0 \\ 0 & 1 & 1 & 0 & 1 & 2 \\ 0 & 0 & 0 & 1 & -1 & -3 \\ 0 & 0 & 0 & 0 & 1 & 3 \\ 0 & 0 & 0 & 0 & 0 & 0 \\ 0 & 0 & 0 & 0 & 0 & 0 \end{bmatrix} \begin{bmatrix} x_1 \\ x_2 \\ . \\ . \\ . \\ x_6 \end{bmatrix} = \begin{bmatrix} 1 \\ 1 \\ 1 \\ 0 \\ 0 \\ 0 \end{bmatrix} \tag{5.33}$$

To perform the back substitution we put $x_6 = \mu$. Then

row 4 gives $x_5 = -3x_6 = -3\mu$

row 3 gives $x_4 = 1 + x_5 + 3x_6 = 1$

put $x_3 = \lambda$

row 2 gives $x_2 = 1 - x_3 - x_5 - 2x_6 = 1 - \lambda + \mu$

row 1 gives $x_1 = 1 - x_3 - x_4 = -\lambda$

Thus our solution is

$$x_1 = -\lambda, \quad x_2 = 1 - \lambda + \mu, \quad x_3 = \lambda, \quad x_4 = 1, \quad x_5 = -3\mu, \quad x_6 = \mu$$

The equations have been reduced to **echelon form**, and it is clear that the same process can be followed for any matrix.

In general we use the elementary row operations, introduced in Section 5.5.2, to manipulate the equation or matrix to **echelon form**:

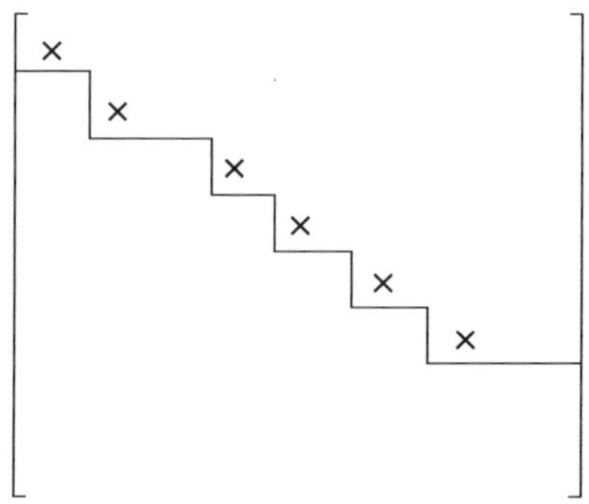

Below the line all the entries are zero, and the leading element, marked ×, in each row above the line is non-zero. The row operations do not change the solution to the set of equations corresponding to the matrix.

When this procedure is applied to a non-singular matrix, the method reduces to that shown in Figure 5.12, the final matrix has non-zero diagonal elements, and back substitution gives a unique solution. When the determinant is zero, as in (5.32), the elimination gives a matrix with some zeros in the diagonal and some zero rows, as in (5.33). The number of non-zero rows in the echelon form is called the **rank** of the matrix, rank $\boldsymbol{A}$; in the case of the matrix in (5.32) and that derived from it by row manipulation (5.33), we have rank $\boldsymbol{A} = 4$.

**Example 5.36**

Find the rank of the matrices

$$\text{(a)} \begin{bmatrix} 1 & 1 & -1 \\ 2 & -1 & 2 \\ 0 & -3 & 4 \end{bmatrix} \quad \text{(b)} \begin{bmatrix} 1 & -1 & 1 \\ -2 & 2 & -2 \\ -1 & 1 & -1 \end{bmatrix} \quad \text{(c)} \begin{bmatrix} 1 & 0 & 0 \\ 0 & 1 & 1 \\ 2 & 0 & 1 \end{bmatrix}$$

**Solution**

Using the usual elimination method gives in each case

$$\text{(a)} \begin{bmatrix} 1 & 1 & -1 \\ 2 & -1 & 2 \\ 0 & -3 & 4 \end{bmatrix} \rightarrow \begin{bmatrix} 1 & 1 & -1 \\ 0 & -3 & 4 \\ 0 & -3 & 4 \end{bmatrix} \rightarrow \begin{bmatrix} 1 & 1 & -1 \\ 0 & -3 & 4 \\ 0 & 0 & 0 \end{bmatrix} \Rightarrow \text{rank } 2$$

$$\text{(b)} \begin{bmatrix} 1 & -1 & 1 \\ -2 & 2 & -2 \\ -1 & 1 & -1 \end{bmatrix} \rightarrow \begin{bmatrix} 1 & -1 & 1 \\ 0 & 0 & 0 \\ 0 & 0 & 0 \end{bmatrix} \Rightarrow \text{rank } 1$$

$$\text{(c)} \quad \begin{bmatrix} 1 & 0 & 0 \\ 0 & 1 & 1 \\ 2 & 0 & 1 \end{bmatrix} \rightarrow \begin{bmatrix} 1 & 0 & 0 \\ 0 & 1 & 1 \\ 0 & 0 & 1 \end{bmatrix} \Rightarrow \text{rank } 3$$

---

The more common definition of rank is given by the order of the largest square submatrix with non-zero determinant. A square submatrix is formed by deleting rows and columns to form a square matrix. In (5.32) the $6 \times 6$ determinant is zero and all the $5 \times 5$ submatrices have zero determinant; however, if we delete columns 3 and 6 and rows 3 and 4, we obtain

$$\begin{bmatrix} 1 & 0 & 1 & 0 \\ 0 & 1 & 0 & 1 \\ 0 & 0 & 0 & 1 \\ 1 & 1 & 0 & 2 \end{bmatrix}$$

which has determinant equal to one, hence confirming that the matrix is of rank 4. To show equivalence of the two definitions is not straightforward and is omitted here. To determine the rank of a matrix, it is very much easier to look at the echelon form.

If we find any of the rows of the echelon matrix to be zero then, for consistency, the corresponding right-hand sides of the matrix equation must also be zero. The elementary row operations reduce the equation to echelon form, so that the equations take the form

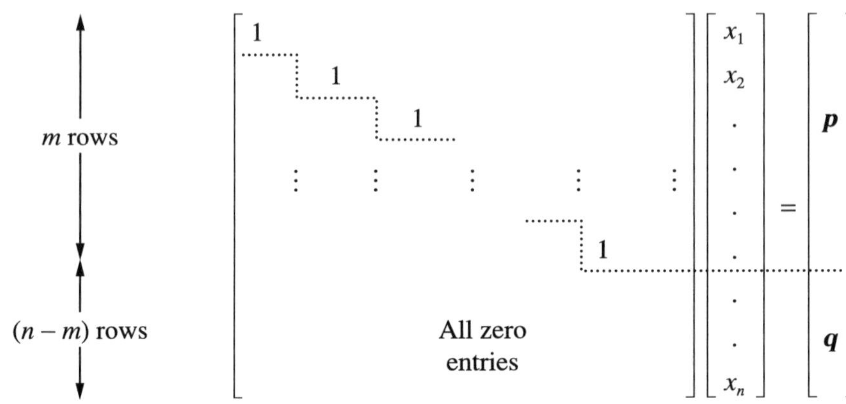


where $\boldsymbol{p}$ is a vector with $m$ elements and $\boldsymbol{q}$ is a vector with $(n - m)$ elements. Note that each of the $m$ non-zero rows will have a leading non-zero entry of 1 but this entry will not necessarily be on a diagonal, as illustrated for example in (5.33). Three statements follow from this reduction.

(i) The matrix has rank $(\boldsymbol{A}) = m$.
(ii) If $\boldsymbol{q} \neq 0$ then the equations are inconsistent.
(iii) If $\boldsymbol{q} = 0$ then the equations are consistent and have a solution. In addition it can be shown that the solution has $(n - m)$ free parameters.

Writing the equations as

$$\boldsymbol{AX} = \boldsymbol{b} \qquad \textbf{(5.34)}$$

we define the **augmented matrix** $(\boldsymbol{A} : \boldsymbol{b})$ as the matrix $\boldsymbol{A}$ with the $\boldsymbol{b}$ column added to it. When reduced to echelon form the matrix and the augmented matrix take the form

$\boldsymbol{A} =$ 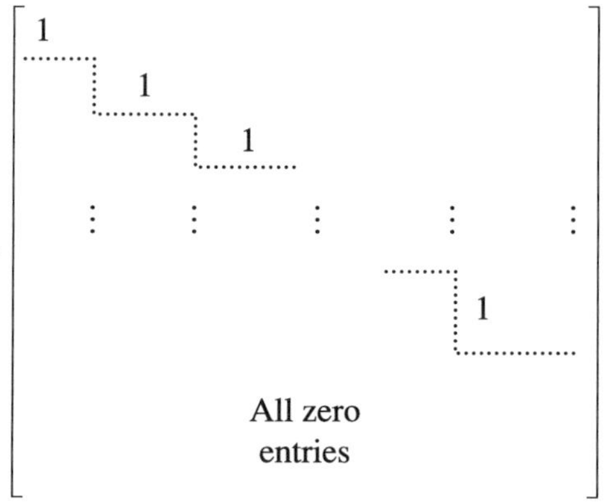


and $(\boldsymbol{A} : \boldsymbol{b}) =$ 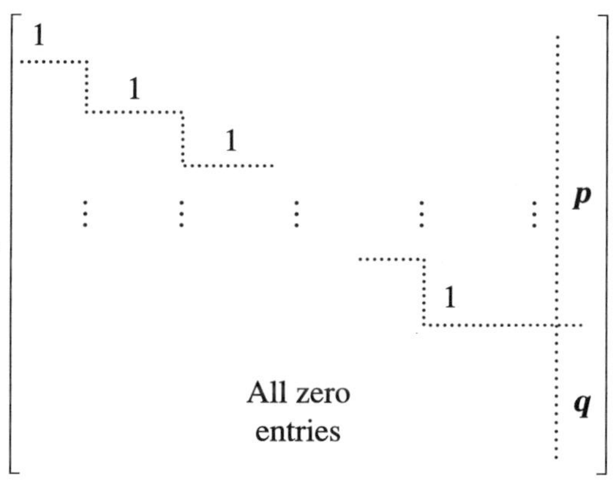


and the solution of the equations can be written in terms of *rank*. It is easy to see from the echelon form that $\boldsymbol{A}$ and $(\boldsymbol{A} : \boldsymbol{b})$ must have the same rank to ensure consistency. The original equations must have the same property, so we can state the results (c) and (d) of Section 5.5 more clearly in terms of rank.

> If $\boldsymbol{A}$ and the augmented matrix $(\boldsymbol{A} : \boldsymbol{b})$ have different rank then we have no solution to the equations (5.34). If the two matrices have the same rank then a solution exists, and furthermore it can be shown that the solution will contain a number of free parameters equal to $n - \text{rank}\, \boldsymbol{A}$.

The calculation of rank is not easy, so, while the result is rigorous, it is not simple to apply. Reducing equations to echelon form tells us immediately the rank of the associated matrix, and gives a constructive method of solution. There is a large amount of arithmetic in the reduction, but if the solution is required then this is inevitable anyway. The numerical calculation of rank does not normally entail reduction to echelon form; rather more advanced methods such as singular value decomposition are used.

> The instruction `rank(A)` evaluates the rank of an $m \times n$ matrix $\boldsymbol{A}$ in both MATLAB and MAPLE.

**Example 5.37** Reduce the following equations to echelon form, calculate the rank of the matrices and find the solutions of the equations (if they exist):

$$\text{(a)}\quad \begin{bmatrix} 0 & 1 & 1 & 0 \\ 1 & 0 & 3 & 2 \\ 2 & 1 & 5 & 4 \\ 1 & -2 & 0 & 2 \end{bmatrix} \begin{bmatrix} x_1 \\ x_2 \\ x_3 \\ x_4 \end{bmatrix} = \begin{bmatrix} 1 \\ 3 \\ 7 \\ 2 \end{bmatrix} \qquad \text{(b)}\quad \begin{bmatrix} 1 & 0 & -1 & 1 & -1 \\ 0 & 1 & 1 & -1 & 1 \\ 1 & 1 & 0 & 0 & 0 \\ 2 & 3 & 1 & -1 & 1 \\ 2 & 2 & 0 & 0 & 0 \end{bmatrix} \begin{bmatrix} x_1 \\ x_2 \\ x_3 \\ x_4 \\ x_5 \end{bmatrix} = \begin{bmatrix} 0 \\ 1 \\ 1 \\ 3 \\ 2 \end{bmatrix}$$

**Solution** (a) Rows 1 and 3 are interchanged, and the elimination then proceeds as follows:

$$\begin{bmatrix} 2 & 1 & 5 & 4 \\ 1 & 0 & 3 & 2 \\ 0 & 1 & 1 & 0 \\ 1 & -2 & 0 & 2 \end{bmatrix} \begin{bmatrix} x_1 \\ x_2 \\ x_3 \\ x_4 \end{bmatrix} = \begin{bmatrix} 7 \\ 3 \\ 1 \\ 2 \end{bmatrix} \to \begin{bmatrix} 1 & \frac{1}{2} & \frac{5}{2} & 2 \\ 0 & -\frac{1}{2} & \frac{1}{2} & 0 \\ 0 & 1 & 1 & 0 \\ 0 & -\frac{5}{2} & -\frac{5}{2} & 0 \end{bmatrix} \begin{bmatrix} x_1 \\ x_2 \\ x_3 \\ x_4 \end{bmatrix} = \begin{bmatrix} \frac{7}{2} \\ -\frac{1}{2} \\ 1 \\ -\frac{3}{2} \end{bmatrix}$$

interchange row 2 and row 4

$$\to \begin{bmatrix} 1 & \frac{1}{2} & \frac{5}{2} & 2 \\ 0 & -\frac{5}{2} & -\frac{5}{2} & 0 \\ 0 & 1 & 1 & 0 \\ 0 & -\frac{1}{2} & \frac{1}{2} & 0 \end{bmatrix} \begin{bmatrix} x_1 \\ x_2 \\ x_3 \\ x_4 \end{bmatrix} = \begin{bmatrix} \frac{7}{2} \\ -\frac{3}{2} \\ 1 \\ -\frac{1}{2} \end{bmatrix}$$

eliminate elements in column 2

$$\to \begin{bmatrix} 1 & \frac{1}{2} & \frac{5}{2} & 2 \\ 0 & 1 & 1 & 0 \\ 0 & 0 & 0 & 0 \\ 0 & 0 & 1 & 0 \end{bmatrix} \begin{bmatrix} x_1 \\ x_2 \\ x_3 \\ x_4 \end{bmatrix} = \begin{bmatrix} \frac{7}{2} \\ \frac{3}{5} \\ \frac{2}{5} \\ -\frac{1}{5} \end{bmatrix}$$

interchange row 3 and row 4

$$\to \begin{bmatrix} 1 & \frac{1}{2} & \frac{5}{2} & 2 \\ 0 & 1 & 1 & 0 \\ 0 & 0 & 1 & 0 \\ 0 & 0 & 0 & 0 \end{bmatrix} \begin{bmatrix} x_1 \\ x_2 \\ x_3 \\ x_4 \end{bmatrix} = \begin{bmatrix} \frac{7}{2} \\ \frac{3}{5} \\ -\frac{1}{5} \\ \frac{2}{5} \end{bmatrix}$$

The rank of the matrix is 3 while that of the augmented matrix ($\boldsymbol{A} : \boldsymbol{b}$) is 4, so the equations represented by the matrix equation (a) are not consistent. Note that the last row cannot be satisfied and hence the equations have no solution.

(b) Interchanging the first and last rows, making the pivot 1 and performing the first elimination, we obtain

$$\begin{bmatrix} 1 & 1 & 0 & 0 & 0 \\ 0 & 1 & 1 & -1 & 1 \\ 0 & 0 & 0 & 0 & 0 \\ 0 & 1 & 1 & -1 & 1 \\ 0 & -1 & -1 & 1 & -1 \end{bmatrix} \begin{bmatrix} x_1 \\ . \\ . \\ . \\ x_5 \end{bmatrix} = \begin{bmatrix} 1 \\ 1 \\ 0 \\ 1 \\ -1 \end{bmatrix} \rightarrow \begin{bmatrix} 1 & 1 & 0 & 0 & 0 \\ 0 & 1 & 1 & -1 & 1 \\ 0 & 0 & 0 & 0 & 0 \\ 0 & 0 & 0 & 0 & 0 \\ 0 & 0 & 0 & 0 & 0 \end{bmatrix} \begin{bmatrix} x_1 \\ . \\ . \\ . \\ x_5 \end{bmatrix} = \begin{bmatrix} 1 \\ 1 \\ 0 \\ 0 \\ 0 \end{bmatrix}$$

The matrix and the augmented matrix both have rank 2, so the equations are consistent and we can compute the solution

$$x_1 = 1 - \lambda, \quad x_2 = \lambda, \quad x_3 = 1 - \lambda + \mu - \upsilon, \quad x_4 = \mu, \quad x_5 = \upsilon$$

As expected, the solution contains three free parameters, since the order of the equation is 5 and the rank is 2.

---

In most practical problems that reduce to the solution of linear equations, it is usual that there are $n$ independent variables to be computed from $n$ equations. This is not always the case and the resulting matrix form is *not* square. A geometrical example of four equations and three unknowns was described in equation (5.2). The idea of a determinant is only sensible if matrices are square so the simple results about the solution of the equations cannot be used. However, the ideas of elementary row operations, reduction to echelon form and rank still hold and the existence or non-existence of solutions can be written in terms of these concepts. Some examples will illustrate the possible situations that can occur.

### Underspecified sets of equations

Here there are more variables than equations.

#### *Case (a)*

Solve $\begin{bmatrix} 1 & 1 & 1 \\ 1 & 2 & 3 \end{bmatrix} \begin{bmatrix} x \\ y \\ z \end{bmatrix} = \begin{bmatrix} 1 \\ 2 \end{bmatrix}$

Subtract row 1 from row 2: $\begin{bmatrix} 1 & 1 & 1 \\ 0 & 1 & 2 \end{bmatrix} \begin{bmatrix} x \\ y \\ z \end{bmatrix} = \begin{bmatrix} 1 \\ 1 \end{bmatrix}$

The elimination is now complete and the back substitution starts

Put $z = t$

From row 2 $\quad y = 1 - 2t$

From row 1 $\quad x = 1 - y - z = t$

so the full solution is

$$x = t, \quad y = 1 - 2t, \quad z = t$$

for any $t$. Note that rank $(\boldsymbol{A})$ = rank $(\boldsymbol{A} : \boldsymbol{b}) = 2$ and $n = 3$ so the solution has one free parameter.

### *Case (b)*

Solve $\begin{bmatrix} 1 & 1 & 1 \\ 2 & 2 & 2 \end{bmatrix} \begin{bmatrix} x \\ y \\ z \end{bmatrix} = \begin{bmatrix} 1 \\ 1 \end{bmatrix}$

Subtract 2 × (row 1) from row 2: $\begin{bmatrix} 1 & 1 & 1 \\ 0 & 0 & 0 \end{bmatrix} \begin{bmatrix} x \\ y \\ z \end{bmatrix} = \begin{bmatrix} 1 \\ -1 \end{bmatrix}$

and it is clear that rank $(\boldsymbol{A}) = 1$ and rank $(\boldsymbol{A} : \boldsymbol{b}) = 2$ so there is no solution. Obviously the last row is inconsistent. Although this example may be seen to be almost trivial since the equations are obviously inconsistent [$x + y + z = 1$ and $2(x + y + z) = 1$], in larger systems the situation is hardly ever obvious.

## Overspecified sets of equations

Here there are more equations than variables.

### *Case (c)*

Solve $\begin{bmatrix} 1 & 1 \\ 1 & 2 \\ 1 & 3 \end{bmatrix} \begin{bmatrix} x \\ y \end{bmatrix} = \begin{bmatrix} -1 \\ 0 \\ 1 \end{bmatrix}$

Subtract row 1 from rows 2 and 3: $\begin{bmatrix} 1 & 1 \\ 0 & 1 \\ 0 & 2 \end{bmatrix} \begin{bmatrix} x \\ y \end{bmatrix} = \begin{bmatrix} -1 \\ 1 \\ 2 \end{bmatrix}$

Subtract 2 × (row 2) from row 3: $\begin{bmatrix} 1 & 1 \\ 0 & 1 \\ 0 & 0 \end{bmatrix} \begin{bmatrix} x \\ y \end{bmatrix} = \begin{bmatrix} -1 \\ 1 \\ 0 \end{bmatrix}$

It can be observed that rank $(\boldsymbol{A})$ = rank $(\boldsymbol{A} : \boldsymbol{b}) = 2$ and that the equations are consistent since the last row contains all zeros. Since $n = 2$ a unique solution is obtained as $x = -2$ and $y = 1$ using back substitution.

However, for overspecified equations the more common situation is that no solution is possible.

*Case (d)*

Solve $\begin{bmatrix} 1 & 1 \\ 1 & 2 \\ 1 & 3 \end{bmatrix} \begin{bmatrix} x \\ y \end{bmatrix} = \begin{bmatrix} 0 \\ 1 \\ -2 \end{bmatrix}$

Subtract row 1 from rows 2 and 3: $\begin{bmatrix} 1 & 1 \\ 0 & 1 \\ 0 & 2 \end{bmatrix} \begin{bmatrix} x \\ y \end{bmatrix} = \begin{bmatrix} 0 \\ 1 \\ -2 \end{bmatrix}$

Subtract 2 × (row 2) from row 3: $\begin{bmatrix} 1 & 1 \\ 0 & 1 \\ 0 & 0 \end{bmatrix} \begin{bmatrix} x \\ y \end{bmatrix} = \begin{bmatrix} 0 \\ 1 \\ -4 \end{bmatrix}$

The equations are now clearly inconsistent since the last row says $0 = -4$ and rank $(\boldsymbol{A}) = 2$, rank $(\boldsymbol{A} : \boldsymbol{b}) = 3$ confirms this observation.

The existence or non-existence of solutions can be deduced from the echelon form and hence the idea of rank, and we can understand the solution of matrix equations involving non-square matrices. If $\boldsymbol{A}$ is a $p \times q$ matrix and $\boldsymbol{b}$ a $p \times 1$ *column vector, the matrix equation* $\boldsymbol{AX} = \boldsymbol{b}$ represents $p$ linear equations in $q$ variables. The rank of a matrix, being the number of non-zero rows in the echelon form of the matrix, cannot exceed $p$. On the other hand, the row reduction process will produce an echelon form with at most $q$ non-zero rows. Hence the rank of a $p \times q$ matrix cannot exceed the smaller of $p$ and $q$. There are two possible cases:

(i) $p < q$: Here there are more variables than equations. The rank of $\boldsymbol{A}$ must be less than the number of variables. If rank $(\boldsymbol{A} : \boldsymbol{b}) >$ rank $\boldsymbol{A}$, the equations are inconsistent and there is no solution, as in case (b). If rank $(\boldsymbol{A} : \boldsymbol{b}) =$ rank $\boldsymbol{A}$, as in case (a), there is a solution, which must contain $q -$ rank $\boldsymbol{A}$ free parameters.

(ii) $p > q$: Here there are more equations than variables. The rank of $\boldsymbol{A}$ cannot exceed the number of variables. If rank $(\boldsymbol{A} : \boldsymbol{b}) >$ rank $\boldsymbol{A}$, as in case (d), the equations are inconsistent and there is no solution. If rank $(\boldsymbol{A} : \boldsymbol{b}) =$ rank $\boldsymbol{A}$, as in case (c), some of the equations are redundant and there is a solution containing $q -$ rank $\boldsymbol{A}$ free parameters.

## 5.6.1 Exercises

Check your answers using MATLAB or MAPLE whenever possible.

87 Find the rank of $\boldsymbol{A}$ and of the augmented matrix $(\boldsymbol{A} : \boldsymbol{b})$. Solve $\boldsymbol{AX} = \boldsymbol{b}$ where possible and check that there are $(n - \text{rank}(\boldsymbol{A}))$ free parameters.

(a) $\boldsymbol{A} = \begin{bmatrix} 1 & 2 \\ 2 & 1 \end{bmatrix}$ $\boldsymbol{b} = \begin{bmatrix} 0 \\ 1 \end{bmatrix}$

(b) $\boldsymbol{A} = \begin{bmatrix} 1 & 0 \\ 0 & 0 \end{bmatrix}$ $\boldsymbol{b} = \begin{bmatrix} 0 \\ 1 \end{bmatrix}$

(c) $\boldsymbol{A} = \begin{bmatrix} 1 & 0 & 0 \\ 0 & 1 & 1 \\ 0 & 1 & 1 \end{bmatrix}$ $\boldsymbol{b} = \begin{bmatrix} 1 \\ 0 \\ 0 \end{bmatrix}$

(d) $\boldsymbol{A} = \begin{bmatrix} 1 & 0 & 1 \\ 0 & 1 & 0 \end{bmatrix} \quad \boldsymbol{b} = \begin{bmatrix} 2 \\ 1 \end{bmatrix}$

(e) $\boldsymbol{A} = \begin{bmatrix} 1 & 0 \\ 0 & 1 \\ 1 & 0 \end{bmatrix} \quad \boldsymbol{b} = \begin{bmatrix} 1 \\ 0 \\ 0 \end{bmatrix}$

(f) $\boldsymbol{A} = \begin{bmatrix} 0 & 0 & 0 & 1 \\ 0 & 0 & 2 & 0 \\ 0 & 3 & 0 & 0 \\ 4 & 0 & 0 & 0 \end{bmatrix} \quad \boldsymbol{b} = \begin{bmatrix} 1 \\ 0 \\ 1 \\ 0 \end{bmatrix}$

**88** Find the rank of the coefficient matrix and of the augmented matrix in the matrix equation

$$\begin{bmatrix} 1 & 1-\alpha \\ \alpha & -2 \end{bmatrix}\begin{bmatrix} x \\ y \end{bmatrix} = \begin{bmatrix} \alpha^2 \\ \alpha \end{bmatrix}$$

For each value of $\alpha$, find, where possible, the solution of the equation.

**89** Find the rank of the matrices

(a) $\begin{bmatrix} 2 & 1 & 1 & 1 \\ 4 & 2 & 2 & 3 \\ 0 & 0 & 0 & 1 \\ -2 & -1 & -1 & 0 \end{bmatrix}$, (b) $\begin{bmatrix} 1 & 1 & 1 & 1 \\ 2 & 1 & 2 & 1 \\ 0 & 1 & 0 & 1 \\ 1 & 0 & 1 & 1 \end{bmatrix}$

**90** Reduce the matrices in the following equations to echelon form, determine their ranks and solve the equations, if a solution exists:

(a) $\begin{bmatrix} 1 & 2 & 3 \\ 3 & 2 & 1 \\ 1 & 1 & 1 \end{bmatrix}\begin{bmatrix} x \\ y \\ z \end{bmatrix} = \begin{bmatrix} 8 \\ 4 \\ 3 \end{bmatrix}$

(b) $\begin{bmatrix} 1 & 2 & -1 & 1 \\ 1 & 1 & 0 & 0 \\ 0 & 1 & -1 & 1 \\ 1 & 0 & 1 & -1 \end{bmatrix}\begin{bmatrix} x \\ y \\ z \\ t \end{bmatrix} = \begin{bmatrix} 0 \\ 1 \\ -1 \\ 1 \end{bmatrix}$

**91** By obtaining the order of the largest square submatrix with non-zero determinant determine the rank of the matrix

$$\boldsymbol{A} = \begin{bmatrix} 1 & 1 & 0 & 1 \\ 1 & 0 & 0 & 1 \\ 0 & 1 & 0 & 0 \\ 1 & 1 & 1 & 1 \end{bmatrix}$$

Reduce the matrix to echelon form and confirm your result. Check the rank of the augmented matrix $(\boldsymbol{A} : \boldsymbol{b})$, where $\boldsymbol{b}^{\mathrm{T}} = [-1 \quad 0 \quad -1 \quad 0]$. Does the equation $\boldsymbol{AX} = \boldsymbol{b}$ have a solution?

**92** Solve, where possible, the following matrix equations:

(a) $\begin{bmatrix} 1 & 3 & 4 \\ -1 & 3 & 4 \end{bmatrix}\begin{bmatrix} x \\ y \\ z \end{bmatrix} = \begin{bmatrix} 1 \\ 3 \end{bmatrix}$

(b) $\begin{bmatrix} 2 & 1 \\ 4 & 6 \\ 3 & 5 \end{bmatrix}\begin{bmatrix} x \\ y \end{bmatrix} = \begin{bmatrix} 1 \\ 4 \\ -2 \end{bmatrix}$

(c) $\begin{bmatrix} 1 & 4 & 7 & -3 \\ -2 & 3 & -6 & 1 \\ 0 & 11 & 8 & -5 \end{bmatrix}\begin{bmatrix} x \\ y \\ z \\ t \end{bmatrix} = \begin{bmatrix} 1 \\ 3 \\ 5 \end{bmatrix}$

(d) $\begin{bmatrix} 2 & 1 & 4 \\ 3 & 2 & 9 \\ 4 & 1 & 3 \\ 3 & 3 & 3 \end{bmatrix}\begin{bmatrix} x \\ y \\ z \end{bmatrix} = \begin{bmatrix} 1 \\ 4 \\ -2 \\ -3 \end{bmatrix}$

**93** In a fluid flow problem there are five natural parameters. These have dimensions in terms of length L, mass M and time T as follows:

velocity $= V = \mathrm{LT}^{-1}$, density $= \rho = \mathrm{ML}^{-3}$

distance $= D = \mathrm{L}$, gravity $= g = \mathrm{LT}^{-2}$

and

viscosity $= \mu = \mathrm{ML}^{-1}\mathrm{T}^{-1}$

To determine how many non-dimensional parameters can be constructed, seek values of $p$, $q$, $r$, $s$ and $t$ so that

$$V^p \rho^q D^r g^s \mu^t$$

is dimensionless. Write the equations for $p$, $q$, $r$, $s$ and $t$ in matrix form and show that the resulting $3 \times 5$ matrix has rank 3. Thus there are two parameters that can be chosen independently.

By choosing these appropriately, show that they correspond to the Reynolds number $Re = V\rho D/\mu$ and the Froude number $Fr = Dg/V^2$.

Repeat a similar dimensional analysis when heat transfer is included.

94 Four points in a three-dimensional space have coordinates $(x_i, y_i, z_i)$ for $i = 1, \ldots, 4$. From the rank of the matrix

$$\begin{bmatrix} x_1 & y_1 & z_1 & 1 \\ x_2 & y_2 & z_2 & 1 \\ x_3 & y_3 & z_3 & 1 \\ x_4 & y_4 & z_4 & 1 \end{bmatrix}$$

determine whether the points lie on a plane or a line or whether there are other possibilities.

95 A popular method of numerical integration – see the work in Chapter 8 – involves Gaussian integration; it is used in finite-element calculations which are well used in most of engineering. As a simple example, the numerical integral over the interval $-1 \leqslant x \leqslant 1$ is written

$$\int_{-1}^{1} f(x)\mathrm{d}x = C_1 f(x_1) + C_2 f(x_2)$$

and the formula is made exact for the four functions $f = 1, f = x, f = x^2$ and $f = x^3$, so it must be accurate for all cubics. This leads to the four equations

$$C_1 + C_2 \quad = 2$$
$$C_1 x_1 + C_2 x_2 = 0$$
$$C_1 x_1^2 + C_2 x_2^2 = \tfrac{2}{3}$$
$$C_1 x_1^3 + C_2 x_2^3 = 0$$

Use Gaussian elimination to reduce the equations and hence deduce that the equations are only consistent if $x_1$ and $x_2$ are chosen at the 'Gauss' points $\pm\frac{1}{\sqrt{3}}$.

## 5.7 The eigenvalue problem

A problem that leads to a concept of crucial importance in many branches of mathematics and its applications is that of seeking non-trivial solutions $X \neq 0$ to the matrix equation

$$\boldsymbol{A}X = \lambda X$$

This is referred to as the eigenvalue problem; values of the scalar $\lambda$ for which non-trivial solutions exist are called **eigenvalues** and the corresponding solutions $X \neq 0$ are called the **eigenvectors**. We saw an example of eigenvalues in Example 5.27. Such problems arise naturally in many branches of engineering. For example, in vibrations the eigenvalues and eigenvectors describe the frequency and mode of vibration respectively, while in mechanics they represent principal stresses and the principal axes of stress in bodies subjected to external forces. Eigenvalues also play an important role in the stability analysis of dynamical systems and are central to the evaluation of energy levels in quantum mechanics.

### 5.7.1 The characteristic equation

The set of simultaneous equations

$$\boldsymbol{A}X = \lambda X \qquad \textbf{(5.35)}$$

where $\boldsymbol{A}$ is an $n \times n$ matrix and $X = [x_1 \quad x_2 \quad \ldots \quad x_n]^{\mathrm{T}}$ is an $n \times 1$ column vector can be written in the form

$$(\lambda \boldsymbol{I} - \boldsymbol{A})X = 0 \qquad \textbf{(5.36)}$$

where $\boldsymbol{I}$ is the identity matrix. The matrix equation (5.36) represents simply a set of homogeneous equations, and we know that a non-trivial solution exists if

$$c(\lambda) = |\lambda \boldsymbol{I} - \boldsymbol{A}| = 0 \tag{5.37}$$

Here $c(\lambda)$ is the expansion of the determinant and is a polynomial of degree $n$ in $\lambda$, called the **characteristic polynomial** of $\boldsymbol{A}$. Thus

$$c(\lambda) = \lambda^n + c_{n-1}\lambda^{n-1} + c_{n-2}\lambda^{n-2} + \ldots + c_1\lambda + c_0$$

and the equation $c(\lambda) = 0$ is called the **characteristic equation** of $\boldsymbol{A}$. We note that this equation can be obtained just as well by evaluating $|\boldsymbol{A} - \lambda \boldsymbol{I}| = 0$; however, the form (5.37) is preferred for the definition of the characteristic equation, since the coefficient of $\lambda^n$ is then always +1.

In many areas of engineering, particularly in those involving vibration or the control of processes, the determination of those values of $\lambda$ for which (5.36) has a non-trivial solution (that is, a solution for which $\boldsymbol{x} \neq 0$) is of vital importance. These values of $\lambda$ are precisely the values that satisfy the characteristic equation, and are called the eigenvalues of $\boldsymbol{A}$.

**Example 5.38** Find the characteristic equation and the eigenvalues of the matrix

$$\boldsymbol{A} = \begin{bmatrix} -2 & 1 \\ 1 & -2 \end{bmatrix}$$

**Solution** Equation (5.37) gives

$$0 = |\lambda \boldsymbol{I} - \boldsymbol{A}| = \begin{vmatrix} \lambda + 2 & -1 \\ -1 & \lambda + 2 \end{vmatrix} = (\lambda + 2)^2 - 1$$

so the characteristic equation is

$$\lambda^2 + 4\lambda + 3 = 0$$

The roots of this equation, namely $\lambda = -1$ and $-3$, give the eigenvalues.

**Example 5.39** Find the characteristic equation for the matrix

$$\boldsymbol{A} = \begin{bmatrix} 1 & 1 & -2 \\ -1 & 2 & 1 \\ 0 & 1 & -1 \end{bmatrix}$$

**Solution** By (5.37), the characteristic equation for $\boldsymbol{A}$ is the cubic equation

$$c(\lambda) = \begin{vmatrix} \lambda - 1 & -1 & 2 \\ 1 & \lambda - 2 & -1 \\ 0 & -1 & \lambda + 1 \end{vmatrix} = 0$$

Expanding the determinant along the first column gives

$$c(\lambda) = (\lambda - 1)\begin{vmatrix} \lambda - 2 & -1 \\ -1 & \lambda + 1 \end{vmatrix} - \begin{vmatrix} -1 & 2 \\ -1 & \lambda + 1 \end{vmatrix}$$

$$= (\lambda - 1)[(\lambda - 2)(\lambda + 1) - 1] - [2 - (\lambda + 1)]$$

Thus

$$c(\lambda) = \lambda^3 - 2\lambda^2 - \lambda + 2 = 0$$

is the required characteristic equation.

---

For matrices of large order, determining the characteristic polynomial by direct expansion of $|\lambda \boldsymbol{I} - \boldsymbol{A}|$ is unsatisfactory in view of the large number of terms involved in the determinant expansion but alternative procedures are available.

## 5.7.2 Eigenvalues and eigenvectors

The roots of the characteristic equation (5.37) are called the eigenvalues of the matrix $\boldsymbol{A}$ (the terms latent roots, proper roots and characteristic roots are also sometimes used). By the Fundamental Theorem of Algebra, a polynomial equation of degree $n$ has exactly $n$ roots, so that the matrix $\boldsymbol{A}$ has exactly $n$ eigenvalues $\lambda_i$, $i = 1, 2, \dots, n$. These eigenvalues may be real or complex, and not necessarily distinct. Corresponding to each eigenvalue $\lambda_i$, there is a non-zero solution $\boldsymbol{x} = \boldsymbol{e}_i$ of (5.36); $\boldsymbol{e}_i$ is called the eigenvector of $\boldsymbol{A}$ corresponding to the eigenvalue $\lambda_i$. (Again the terms latent vector, proper vector and characteristic vector are sometimes seen, but are generally obsolete.) We note that if $\boldsymbol{x} = \boldsymbol{e}_i$ satisfies (5.36) then any scalar multiple $\beta_i\boldsymbol{e}_i$ of $\boldsymbol{e}_i$ also satisfies (5.36), so that the eigenvector $\boldsymbol{e}_i$ may only be determined to within a scalar multiple.

**Example 5.40** Verify that $\begin{bmatrix} 1 \\ 1 \end{bmatrix}$ and $\begin{bmatrix} 1 \\ -1 \end{bmatrix}$ are eigenvectors of the matrix

$$\boldsymbol{A} = \begin{bmatrix} -2 & 1 \\ 1 & -2 \end{bmatrix}$$

**Solution** The matrix is the same as the one given in Example 5.38 so we would expect that these eigenvectors correspond to the eigenvalues −1 and −3. To verify the fact we must check that equation (5.35) is satisfied. Now for the first column vector

$$\begin{bmatrix} -2 & 1 \\ 1 & -2 \end{bmatrix}\begin{bmatrix} 1 \\ 1 \end{bmatrix} = \begin{bmatrix} -1 \\ -1 \end{bmatrix} = -1\begin{bmatrix} 1 \\ 1 \end{bmatrix}$$

so $\begin{bmatrix} 1 \\ 1 \end{bmatrix}$ is an eigenvector corresponding to the eigenvector −1.

For the second column vector

$$\begin{bmatrix}-2 & 1\\ 1 & -2\end{bmatrix}\begin{bmatrix}1\\ -1\end{bmatrix}=\begin{bmatrix}-3\\ 3\end{bmatrix}=-3\begin{bmatrix}1\\ -1\end{bmatrix}$$

so $\begin{bmatrix}1\\ -1\end{bmatrix}$ is an eigenvector corresponding to the eigenvector −3.

**Example 5.41** Find the eigenvalues and eigenvectors of the matrix $\boldsymbol{A}=\begin{bmatrix}0 & -1\\ 1 & 0\end{bmatrix}$.

**Solution** To find the eigenvalues use equation (5.37)

$$0=|\lambda \boldsymbol{I}-\boldsymbol{A}|=\begin{vmatrix}\lambda & 1\\ -1 & \lambda\end{vmatrix}=\lambda^2+1$$

This characteristic equation has two roots $\lambda = +\mathrm{j}$ and $-\mathrm{j}$ which are the eigenvalues, in this case complex. Note that in general eigenvalues are complex although in most of the remaining examples in this section they have been constructed to be real.

To obtain the eigenvectors use equation (5.36).

For the eigenvalue $\lambda = \mathrm{j}$ then (5.36) gives

$$(\lambda \boldsymbol{I}-\boldsymbol{A})\begin{bmatrix}a\\ b\end{bmatrix}=\begin{bmatrix}\mathrm{j} & 1\\ -1 & \mathrm{j}\end{bmatrix}\begin{bmatrix}a\\ b\end{bmatrix}=0$$

or in expanded form

$$\begin{aligned}\mathrm{j}a+b&=0\\ -a+\mathrm{j}b&=0\end{aligned}\quad \text{with solution } a=\mathrm{j} \text{ and } b=1$$

and hence the eigenvector corresponding to $\lambda = \mathrm{j}$ is $\begin{bmatrix}\mathrm{j}\\ 1\end{bmatrix}$.

For the eigenvalue $\lambda = -\mathrm{j}$ then (5.36) gives

$$(\lambda \boldsymbol{I}-\boldsymbol{A})\begin{bmatrix}c\\ d\end{bmatrix}=\begin{bmatrix}-\mathrm{j} & 1\\ -1 & -\mathrm{j}\end{bmatrix}\begin{bmatrix}c\\ d\end{bmatrix}=0$$

or in expanded form

$$\begin{aligned}-\mathrm{j}c+d&=0\\ -c-\mathrm{j}d&=0\end{aligned}\quad \text{with solution } c=1 \text{ and } d=\mathrm{j}$$

and hence the eigenvector corresponding to $\lambda = -\mathrm{j}$ is $\begin{bmatrix}1\\ \mathrm{j}\end{bmatrix}$.

**Example 5.42** Determine the eigenvalues and eigenvectors for the matrix $\boldsymbol{A}$ of Example 5.39.

**Solution**

$$\boldsymbol{A} = \begin{bmatrix} 1 & 1 & -2 \\ -1 & 2 & 1 \\ 0 & 1 & -1 \end{bmatrix}$$

The eigenvalues $\lambda_i$ of $\boldsymbol{A}$ satisfy the characteristic equation $c(\lambda) = 0$, and this has been obtained in Example 5.39 as the cubic

$$\lambda^3 - 2\lambda^2 - \lambda + 2 = 0$$

which can be solved to obtain the eigenvalues $\lambda_1$, $\lambda_2$ and $\lambda_3$.

Alternatively, it may be possible, using the determinant form $|\boldsymbol{A} - \lambda\boldsymbol{I}|$, to carry out suitable row and/or column operations to factorize the determinant.

In this case

$$|\boldsymbol{A} - \lambda\boldsymbol{I}| = \begin{vmatrix} 1-\lambda & 1 & -2 \\ -1 & 2-\lambda & 1 \\ 0 & 1 & -1-\lambda \end{vmatrix}$$

and adding column 1 to column 3 gives

$$\begin{vmatrix} 1-\lambda & 1 & -1-\lambda \\ -1 & 2-\lambda & 0 \\ 0 & 1 & -1-\lambda \end{vmatrix} = -(1+\lambda)\begin{vmatrix} 1-\lambda & 1 & 1 \\ -1 & 2-\lambda & 0 \\ 0 & 1 & 1 \end{vmatrix}$$

Subtracting row 3 from row 1 gives

$$-(1+\lambda)\begin{vmatrix} 1-\lambda & 0 & 0 \\ -1 & 2-\lambda & 0 \\ 0 & 1 & 1 \end{vmatrix} = -(1+\lambda)(1-\lambda)(2-\lambda)$$

Setting $|\boldsymbol{A} - \lambda\boldsymbol{I}| = 0$ gives the eigenvalues as $\lambda_1 = 2$, $\lambda_2 = 1$ and $\lambda_3 = -1$. The order in which they are written is arbitrary, but for consistency we shall adopt the convention of taking $\lambda_1, \lambda_2, \dots, \lambda_n$ in decreasing order.

Having obtained the eigenvalues $\lambda_i$ $(i = 1, 2, 3)$, the corresponding eigenvectors $\boldsymbol{e}_i$ are obtained by solving the appropriate homogeneous equations

$$(\boldsymbol{A} - \lambda_i\boldsymbol{I})\boldsymbol{e}_i = 0 \tag{5.38}$$

When $i = 1$, $\lambda_1 = 2$ and (5.38) is

$$\begin{bmatrix} -1 & 1 & -2 \\ -1 & 0 & 1 \\ 0 & 1 & -3 \end{bmatrix}\begin{bmatrix} e_{11} \\ e_{12} \\ e_{13} \end{bmatrix} \equiv 0$$

that is,

$$-e_{11} + e_{12} - 2e_{13} = 0$$

$$-e_{11} + 0e_{12} + e_{13} = 0$$

$$0e_{11} + e_{12} - 3e_{13} = 0$$

leading to the solution

$$\frac{e_{11}}{-1} = \frac{-e_{12}}{3} = \frac{e_{13}}{-1} = \beta_1$$

where $\beta_1$ is an arbitrary non-zero scalar. Thus the eigenvector $\boldsymbol{e}_1$ corresponding to the eigenvalue $\lambda_1 = 2$ is

$$\boldsymbol{e}_1 = \beta_1[1 \quad 3 \quad 1]^{\mathrm{T}}$$

As a check, we can compute

$$\boldsymbol{Ae}_1 = \beta_1\begin{bmatrix} 1 & 1 & -2 \\ -1 & 2 & 1 \\ 0 & 1 & -1 \end{bmatrix}\begin{bmatrix} 1 \\ 3 \\ 1 \end{bmatrix} = \beta_1\begin{bmatrix} 2 \\ 6 \\ 2 \end{bmatrix} = 2\beta_1\begin{bmatrix} 1 \\ 3 \\ 1 \end{bmatrix} = \lambda_1\boldsymbol{e}_1$$

and thus conclude that our calculation was correct.

When $i = 2$, $\lambda_2 = 1$ and we have to solve

$$\begin{bmatrix} 0 & 1 & -2 \\ -1 & 1 & 1 \\ 0 & 1 & -2 \end{bmatrix}\begin{bmatrix} e_{21} \\ e_{22} \\ e_{23} \end{bmatrix} = 0$$

that is,

$$0e_{21} + e_{22} - 2e_{23} = 0$$

$$-e_{21} + e_{22} + e_{23} = 0$$

$$0e_{21} + e_{22} - 2e_{23} = 0$$

leading to the solution

$$\frac{e_{21}}{-3} = \frac{-e_{22}}{2} = \frac{e_{23}}{-1} = \beta_2$$

where $\beta_2$ is an arbitrary scalar. Thus the eigenvector $\boldsymbol{e}_2$ corresponding to the eigenvalue $\lambda_2 = 1$ is

$$\boldsymbol{e}_2 = \beta_2[3 \quad 2 \quad 1]^{\mathrm{T}}$$

Again a check could be made by computing $\boldsymbol{Ae}_2$.

Finally, when $i = 3$, $\lambda_3 = -1$ and we obtain from (5.38)

$$\begin{bmatrix} 2 & 1 & -2 \\ -1 & 3 & 1 \\ 0 & 1 & 0 \end{bmatrix}\begin{bmatrix} e_{31} \\ e_{32} \\ e_{33} \end{bmatrix} = 0$$

that is,

$$2e_{31} + \phantom{3}e_{32} - 2e_{33} = 0$$

$$-e_{31} + 3e_{32} + \phantom{2}e_{33} = 0$$

$$0e_{31} + \phantom{3}e_{32} + 0e_{33} = 0$$

and hence

$$\frac{e_{31}}{-1} = \frac{e_{32}}{0} = \frac{e_{33}}{-1} = \beta_3$$

Here again $\beta_3$ is an arbitrary scalar, and the eigenvector $\boldsymbol{e}_3$ corresponding to the eigenvalue $\lambda_3$ is

$$\boldsymbol{e}_3 = \beta_3[1 \quad 0 \quad 1]^{\mathrm{T}}$$

The calculation can be checked as before. Thus we have found that the eigenvalues of the matrix $\boldsymbol{A}$ are 2, 1 and −1, with corresponding eigenvectors

$$\beta_1[1 \quad 3 \quad 1]^{\mathrm{T}}, \quad \beta_2[3 \quad 2 \quad 1]^{\mathrm{T}} \quad \text{and} \quad \beta_3[1 \quad 0 \quad 1]^{\mathrm{T}}$$

respectively.

---

Since in Example 5.42 the $\beta_i$, $i = 1, 2, 3$, are arbitrary, it follows that there are an infinite number of eigenvectors, scalar multiples of each other, corresponding to each eigenvalue. Sometimes it is convenient to scale the eigenvectors according to some convention. A convention frequently adopted is to **normalize** the eigenvectors so that they are uniquely determined up to a scale factor of ±1. The normalized form of an eigenvector $\boldsymbol{e} = [e_1 \quad e_2 \quad \dots \quad e_n]^{\mathrm{T}}$ is denoted by $\hat{\boldsymbol{e}}$ and is given by

$$\hat{\boldsymbol{e}} = \frac{\boldsymbol{e}}{|\boldsymbol{e}|}$$

where

$$|\boldsymbol{e}| = \sqrt{(e_1^2 + e_2^2 + \dots + e_n^2)}$$

For example, for the matrix $\boldsymbol{A}$ of Example 5.42, the normalized forms of the eigenvectors are

$$\hat{\boldsymbol{e}}_1 = [1/\sqrt{11} \quad 3/\sqrt{11} \quad 1/\sqrt{11}]^{\mathrm{T}}, \quad \hat{\boldsymbol{e}}_2 = [3/\sqrt{14} \quad 2/\sqrt{14} \quad 1/\sqrt{14}]^{\mathrm{T}}$$

and

$$\hat{\boldsymbol{e}}_3 = [1/\sqrt{2} \quad 0 \quad 1/\sqrt{2}]^{\mathrm{T}}$$

However, throughout the text, unless otherwise stated, the eigenvectors will always be presented in their 'simplest' form, so that for the matrix of Example 5.42 we take $\beta_1 = \beta_2 = \beta_3 = 1$ and write

$$\boldsymbol{e}_1 = [1 \quad 3 \quad 1]^T, \quad \boldsymbol{e}_2 = [3 \quad 2 \quad 1]^T \quad \text{and} \quad \boldsymbol{e}_3 = [1 \quad 0 \quad 1]^T$$

**Example 5.43** Find the eigenvalues and eigenvectors of

$$\boldsymbol{A} = \begin{bmatrix} \cos\theta & -\sin\theta \\ \sin\theta & \cos\theta \end{bmatrix}$$

**Solution** Now

$$|\lambda \boldsymbol{I} - \boldsymbol{A}| = \begin{vmatrix} \lambda - \cos\theta & \sin\theta \\ -\sin\theta & \lambda - \cos\theta \end{vmatrix}$$

$$= \lambda^2 - 2\lambda\cos\theta + \cos^2\theta + \sin^2\theta = \lambda^2 - 2\lambda\cos\theta + 1$$

So the eigenvalues are the roots of

$$\lambda^2 - 2\lambda\cos\theta + 1 = 0$$

that is,

$$\lambda = \cos\theta \pm \mathrm{j}\sin\theta$$

Solving for the eigenvectors as in Example 5.42, we obtain

$$\boldsymbol{e}_1 = [1 \quad -\mathrm{j}]^T \quad \text{and} \quad \boldsymbol{e}_2 = [1 \quad \mathrm{j}]^T$$

---

In Examples 5.41 and 5.43 we see that eigenvalues can be complex numbers, and that the eigenvectors may have complex components. This situation arises when the characteristic equation has complex (conjugate) roots.

For a $n \times n$ matrix $\boldsymbol{A}$ the MATLAB command `p=poly(A)` generates an $n + 1$ element row vector whose elements are the coefficients of the characteristic polynomial of $\boldsymbol{A}$, the coefficients being ordered in descending powers. The eigenvalues of $\boldsymbol{A}$ are the roots of the polynomial and are generated using the command `roots(p)`. The command

```
[M,S]=eig(A)
```

generates the normalized eigenvectors of $\boldsymbol{A}$ as the columns of the matrix $\boldsymbol{M}$ and its corresponding eigenvalues as the diagonal elements of the diagonal matrix $\boldsymbol{S}$ ($\boldsymbol{M}$ and $\boldsymbol{S}$ are called respectively the modal and spectral matrices of $\boldsymbol{A}$). In the absence of the left-hand arguments, the command `eig(A)` by itself simply generates the eigenvalues of $\boldsymbol{A}$.

For the matrix $\boldsymbol{A}$ of Example 5.42 the commands

```
A=[1 1 -2; -1 2 1; 0 1 -1];
[M,S]=eig(A)
```

generate the output

```
  0.3015   -0.8018   0.7071        2.0000  0        0
M=0.9045   -0.5345   0.0000     S=0         1.0000  0
  0.3015   -0.2673   0.7071        0        0       -1.0000
```

These concur with our calculated answers, with $\beta_1 = 0.3015$, $\beta_2 = -0.2673$ and $\beta_3 = 0.7071$.

Using the Symbolic Math Toolbox in MATLAB the matrix $\boldsymbol{A}$ may be converted from numeric into symbolic form using the command `A=sym(A)`. Then its symbolic eigenvalues and eigenvectors are generated using the sequence of commands

```
A=[1 1 -2; -1 2 1; 0 1 -1];
A=sym(A);
[M, S]=eig(A)
```

as

```
M=[3, 1, 1]    S=[1, 0, 0]
  [2, 3, 0]      [0, 2, 0]
  [1, 1, 1]      [0, 0, -1]
```

In MAPLE `eigenvectors(A);` produces the corresponding results using the linalg package.

## 5.7.3 Exercises

Check your answers using MATLAB or MAPLE.

**96** Obtain the characteristic polynomials of the matrices

(a) $\begin{bmatrix} 2 & -1 \\ -1 & 2 \end{bmatrix}$ (b) $\begin{bmatrix} 2 & 1 \\ 1 & 1 \end{bmatrix}$

(c) $\begin{bmatrix} 1 & 2 & 3 \\ 0 & 2 & 3 \\ 0 & 0 & 3 \end{bmatrix}$ (d) $\begin{bmatrix} 1 & 2 & 0 \\ 0 & 2 & 2 \\ 0 & 1 & 3 \end{bmatrix}$

(e) $\begin{bmatrix} 3 & 2 & 1 \\ 4 & 5 & -1 \\ 2 & 3 & 4 \end{bmatrix}$ (f) $\begin{bmatrix} 2 & 1 \\ -1 & a \end{bmatrix}$

and hence evaluate the eigenvalues of the matrices.

**97** Find the eigenvalues and corresponding eigenvectors of the matrices

(a) $\begin{bmatrix} 1 & 1 \\ 1 & 1 \end{bmatrix}$ (b) $\begin{bmatrix} 1 & 2 \\ 3 & 2 \end{bmatrix}$

(c) $\begin{bmatrix} 1 & 0 & -4 \\ 0 & 5 & 4 \\ -4 & 4 & 3 \end{bmatrix}$ (d) $\begin{bmatrix} 1 & 1 & 2 \\ 0 & 2 & 2 \\ -1 & 1 & 3 \end{bmatrix}$

(e) $\begin{bmatrix} 5 & 0 & 6 \\ 0 & 11 & 6 \\ 6 & 6 & -2 \end{bmatrix}$ (f) $\begin{bmatrix} 1 & -1 & 0 \\ 1 & 2 & 1 \\ -2 & 1 & -1 \end{bmatrix}$

(g) $\begin{bmatrix} 4 & 1 & 1 \\ 2 & 5 & 4 \\ -1 & -1 & 0 \end{bmatrix}$ (h) $\begin{bmatrix} 1 & -4 & -2 \\ 0 & 3 & 1 \\ 1 & 2 & 4 \end{bmatrix}$

### 5.7.4 Repeated eigenvalues

In the examples considered so far the eigenvalues $\lambda_i$ ($i = 1, 2, \ldots$) of the matrix $\boldsymbol{A}$ have been distinct, and in such cases the corresponding eigenvectors can be found. The matrix $\boldsymbol{A}$ is then said to have a full set of independent eigenvectors. It is clear that the roots of the characteristic equation $c(\lambda)$ may not all be distinct; and when $c(\lambda)$ has $p \leq n$ distinct roots, $c(\lambda)$ may be factorized as

$$c(\lambda) = (\lambda - \lambda_1)^{m_1}(\lambda - \lambda_2)^{m_2} \ldots (\lambda - \lambda_p)^{m_p}$$

indicating that the root $\lambda = \lambda_i$, $i = 1, 2, \ldots, p$, is a root of order $m_i$, where the integer $m_i$ is called the **algebraic multiplicity** of the eigenvalue $\lambda_i$. Clearly $m_1 + m_2 + \ldots + m_p = n$. When a matrix $\boldsymbol{A}$ has repeated eigenvalues, the question arises as to whether it is possible to obtain a full set of independent eigenvectors for $\boldsymbol{A}$. We first consider some examples to illustrate the situation.

**Example 5.44** Determine the eigenvalues and corresponding eigenvectors of the matrices

(a) $\boldsymbol{A} = \begin{bmatrix} 1 & 0 \\ 0 & 1 \end{bmatrix}$ (b) $\boldsymbol{B} = \begin{bmatrix} 1 & 1 \\ 0 & 1 \end{bmatrix}$

**Solution** (a) The eigenvalues of $\boldsymbol{A}$ are obtained from

$$0 = |\lambda \boldsymbol{I} - \boldsymbol{A}| = \begin{vmatrix} \lambda - 1 & 0 \\ 0 & \lambda - 1 \end{vmatrix} = (\lambda - 1)^2$$

giving the value 1 repeated twice.

The eigenvectors we calculate from

$$0 = (\boldsymbol{I} - \boldsymbol{A})\begin{bmatrix} a \\ b \end{bmatrix} = \begin{bmatrix} 0 & 0 \\ 0 & 0 \end{bmatrix}\begin{bmatrix} a \\ b \end{bmatrix}$$

which is clearly satisfied by any values of $a$ and $b$. Thus taking

$$\begin{bmatrix} a \\ b \end{bmatrix} = a\begin{bmatrix} 1 \\ 0 \end{bmatrix} + b\begin{bmatrix} 0 \\ 1 \end{bmatrix}$$

it can be seen that there are two independent eigenvectors $\begin{bmatrix} 1 \\ 0 \end{bmatrix}$ and $\begin{bmatrix} 0 \\ 1 \end{bmatrix}$. Any linear combination of the two vectors is also an eigenvector. Geometrically this corresponds to the fact that the unit matrix maps *every* vector on to itself.

(b) The eigenvalues of $\boldsymbol{B}$ are obtained from

$$0 = |\lambda \boldsymbol{I} - \boldsymbol{B}| = \begin{vmatrix} \lambda - 1 & -1 \\ 0 & \lambda - 1 \end{vmatrix} = (\lambda - 1)^2$$

giving the value 1 repeated twice.

The eigenvectors we calculate from

$$0 = (\boldsymbol{I} - \boldsymbol{B})\begin{bmatrix} c \\ d \end{bmatrix} = \begin{bmatrix} 0 & -1 \\ 0 & 0 \end{bmatrix}\begin{bmatrix} c \\ d \end{bmatrix} = \begin{bmatrix} -d \\ 0 \end{bmatrix}$$

Thus $d = 0$ and there is *only one* eigenvector $\begin{bmatrix} 1 \\ 0 \end{bmatrix}$ and, of course, any multiple of this vector.

---

We note from Example 5.44 that the evaluation of eigenvectors is much more complicated when there are multiple eigenvalues. The idea of rank, introduced in Section 5.6, is required to sort out the complications but the details are left to the companion text *Advanced Modern Engineering Mathematics*.

The following two 3 × 3 examples illustrate similar points.

**Example 5.45** Determine the eigenvalues and corresponding eigenvectors of the matrix

$$\boldsymbol{A} = \begin{bmatrix} 3 & -3 & 2 \\ -1 & 5 & -2 \\ -1 & 3 & 0 \end{bmatrix}$$

**Solution** We find the eigenvalues from

$$\begin{vmatrix} 3-\lambda & -3 & 2 \\ -1 & 5-\lambda & -2 \\ -1 & 3 & -\lambda \end{vmatrix} = 0$$

as $\lambda_1 = 4$, $\lambda_2 = \lambda_3 = 2$.

The eigenvectors are obtained from

$$(\boldsymbol{A} - \lambda\boldsymbol{I})\boldsymbol{e}_i = 0 \qquad \textbf{(5.39)}$$

and when $\lambda = \lambda_1 = 4$, we obtain from (5.39)

$$\boldsymbol{e}_1 = [1 \quad -1 \quad -1]^{\mathrm{T}}$$

When $\lambda = \lambda_2 = \lambda_3 = 2$, (5.39) becomes

$$\begin{bmatrix} 1 & -3 & 2 \\ -1 & 3 & -2 \\ -1 & 3 & -2 \end{bmatrix}\begin{bmatrix} e_{21} \\ e_{22} \\ e_{23} \end{bmatrix} = 0$$

so that the corresponding eigenvector is obtained from the single equation

$$e_{21} - 3e_{22} + 2e_{23} = 0 \qquad \textbf{(5.40)}$$

Clearly we are free to choose any two of the components $e_{21}$, $e_{22}$ or $e_{23}$ at will, with the remaining one determined by (5.40). Suppose we set $e_{22} = \alpha$ and $e_{23} = \beta$; then (5.41) means that $e_{21} = 3\alpha - 2\beta$, and thus

$$\begin{aligned} \boldsymbol{e}_2 &= [3\alpha - 2\beta \quad \alpha \quad \beta]^{\mathrm{T}} \\ &= \alpha \begin{bmatrix} 3 \\ 1 \\ 0 \end{bmatrix} + \beta \begin{bmatrix} -2 \\ 0 \\ 1 \end{bmatrix} \end{aligned} \qquad \textbf{(5.41)}$$

Now $\lambda = 2$ is an eigenvalue of multiplicity 2, and we seek, if possible, two independent eigenvectors defined by (5.41). Setting $\alpha = 1$ and $\beta = 0$ yields

$$\boldsymbol{e}_2 = [3 \quad 1 \quad 0]^{\mathrm{T}}$$

and setting $\alpha = 0$ and $\beta = 1$ gives a second vector

$$\boldsymbol{e}_3 = [-2 \quad 0 \quad 1]^{\mathrm{T}}$$

These two vectors are independent and of the form defined by (5.41), and it is clear that many other choices are possible. However, any other choices of the form (5.41) will be linear combinations of $\boldsymbol{e}_2$ and $\boldsymbol{e}_3$ as chosen above. For example, $\boldsymbol{e} = [1 \quad 1 \quad 1]$ satisfies (5.41), but $\boldsymbol{e} = \boldsymbol{e}_2 + \boldsymbol{e}_3$.

In this example, although there was a repeated eigenvalue of algebraic multiplicity 2, it was possible to construct two independent eigenvectors corresponding to this eigenvalue. Thus the matrix $\boldsymbol{A}$ has three and only three independent eigenvectors.

The MATLAB commands for Example 5.45

```
A=[3 -3 2; -1 5 -2; -1 3 0];
[M, S]=eig(A)
```

generate

```
    0.5774   -0.5774   -0.7513         4.0000   0         0
M=-0.5774   -0.5774    0.1735      S=0        2.0000    0
   -0.5774   -0.5774    0.6361         0        0         2.0000
```

Clearly the first column of $\boldsymbol{M}$ (corresponding to the eighenvalue $\lambda_1 = 4$) is a scalar multiple of $\boldsymbol{e}_1$. The second and third columns of $\boldsymbol{M}$ (corresponding to the repeated eigenvalue $\lambda_2 = \lambda_3 = 2$) are not scalar multiples of $\boldsymbol{e}_2$ and $\boldsymbol{e}_3$. However, both satisfy (5.39) and are equally acceptable as a pair of linearly independent eigenvectors corresponding to the repeated eigenvalue. It is left as an exercise to show that both are linear combinations of $\boldsymbol{e}_2$ and $\boldsymbol{e}_3$.

Check that in symbolic form the commands

```
A=sym(A);
[M, S]=eig(A)
```

generate

```
M=[-1, 3, -2]     S=[4, 0, 0]
  [1, 1, 0]         [0, 2, 0]
  [1, 0, 1]         [0, 0, 2]
```

In the linalg package of MAPLE, `eigenvectors(A);` produces the corresponding results.

**Example 5.46** Determine the eigenvalues and corresponding eigenvectors of the matrix

$$A = \begin{bmatrix} 1 & 2 & 2 \\ 0 & 2 & 1 \\ -1 & 2 & 2 \end{bmatrix}$$

**Solution** Solving $|A - \lambda I| = 0$ gives the eigenvalues as $\lambda_1 = \lambda_2 = 2$, $\lambda_3 = 1$. The eigenvector corresponding to the non-repeated or simple eigenvalue $\lambda_3 = 1$ is easily found as

$$e_3 = [1 \quad 1 \quad -1]^T$$

When $\lambda = \lambda_1 = \lambda_2 = 2$, the corresponding eigenvector is given by

$$(A - 2I)e_1 = 0$$

that is, as the solution of

$$-e_{11} + 2e_{12} + 2e_{13} = 0 \qquad \text{(i)}$$

$$e_{13} = 0 \qquad \text{(ii)}$$

$$-e_{11} + 2e_{12} \quad = 0 \qquad \text{(iii)}$$

From (ii) we have $e_{13} = 0$, and from both (i) and (iii) it follows that $e_{11} = 2e_{12}$. We deduce that there is only one independent eigenvector corresponding to the repeated eigenvalue $\lambda = 2$, namely

$$e_1 = [2 \quad 1 \quad 0]^T$$

and in this case the matrix $A$ does not possess a full set of independent eigenvectors.

---

We see from Examples 5.44–5.46 that if an $n \times n$ matrix $A$ has repeated eigenvalues then a full set of $n$ independent eigenvectors may or may not exist.

## 5.7.5 Exercises

Check your answers using MATLAB or MAPLE whenever possible.

98 Find the eigenvalues and eigenvectors of the matrices

$$\begin{bmatrix} 3 & 0 \\ 0 & 3 \end{bmatrix}, \begin{bmatrix} 2 & 0 \\ 1 & 2 \end{bmatrix}, \begin{bmatrix} 3 & \frac{1}{4} \\ -1 & 2 \end{bmatrix}, \begin{bmatrix} \frac{1}{2} & \frac{1}{4} \\ -1 & -\frac{1}{2} \end{bmatrix}$$

99 Obtain the eigenvalues and corresponding eigenvectors of the matrices

(a) $\begin{bmatrix} 2 & 2 & 1 \\ 1 & 3 & 1 \\ 1 & 2 & 2 \end{bmatrix}$ (b) $\begin{bmatrix} 0 & -2 & -2 \\ -1 & 1 & 2 \\ -1 & -1 & 2 \end{bmatrix}$

(c) $\begin{bmatrix} 4 & 6 & 6 \\ 1 & 3 & 2 \\ -1 & -5 & -2 \end{bmatrix}$ (d) $\begin{bmatrix} 7 & -2 & -4 \\ 3 & 0 & -2 \\ 6 & -2 & -3 \end{bmatrix}$

100 Given that $\lambda = 1$ is a three-times repeated eigenvalue of the matrix

$$\boldsymbol{A} = \begin{bmatrix} -3 & -7 & -5 \\ 2 & 4 & 3 \\ 1 & 2 & 2 \end{bmatrix}$$

determine how many independent eigenvectors correspond to this value of $\lambda$. Determine a corresponding set of independent eigenvectors.

101 Given that $\lambda = 1$ is a twice-repeated eigenvalue of the matrix

$$\boldsymbol{A} = \begin{bmatrix} 2 & 1 & -1 \\ -1 & 0 & 1 \\ -1 & -1 & 2 \end{bmatrix}$$

determine a set of independent eigenvectors.

102 Find all the eigenvalues and eigenvectors of the matrix

$$\begin{bmatrix} 1 & 0 & 0 & 2 \\ 0 & 2 & 0 & 0 \\ 0 & 0 & 2 & 0 \\ 2 & 0 & 0 & 1 \end{bmatrix}$$

### 5.7.6 Some useful properties of eigenvalues

The following basic properties of the eigenvalues $\lambda_1, \lambda_2, \ldots, \lambda_n$ of an $n \times n$ matrix $\boldsymbol{A}$ are sometimes useful. The results are readily proved from either the definition of eigenvalues as the values of $\lambda$ satisfying (5.35), or by comparison of corresponding characteristic polynomials (5.37). Consequently, the proofs are left to Exercise 103.

**Property 1**

The sum of the eigenvalues of $\boldsymbol{A}$ is

$$\sum_{i=1}^{n} \lambda_i = \text{trace}\,\boldsymbol{A} = \sum_{i=1}^{n} a_{ii}$$

### Property 2

The product of the eigenvalues of $\boldsymbol{A}$ is

$$\prod_{i=1}^{n} \lambda_i = \det \boldsymbol{A}$$

where det $\boldsymbol{A}$ denotes the determinant of the matrix $\boldsymbol{A}$.

### Property 3

The eigenvalues of the inverse matrix $\boldsymbol{A}^{-1}$, provided it exists, are

$$\frac{1}{\lambda_1}, \quad \frac{1}{\lambda_2}, \quad \ldots, \quad \frac{1}{\lambda_n}$$

### Property 4

The eigenvalues of the transposed matrix $\boldsymbol{A}^{\mathrm{T}}$ are

$$\lambda_1, \quad \lambda_2, \quad \ldots, \quad \lambda_n$$

as for the matrix $\boldsymbol{A}$.

### Property 5

If $k$ is a scalar then the eigenvalues of $k\boldsymbol{A}$ are

$$k\lambda_1, \quad k\lambda_2, \quad \ldots, \quad k\lambda_n$$

### Property 6

If $k$ is a scalar and $\boldsymbol{I}$ the $n \times n$ identity (unit) matrix then the eigenvalues of $\boldsymbol{A} \pm k\boldsymbol{I}$ are respectively

$$\lambda_1 \pm k, \quad \lambda_2 \pm k, \quad \ldots, \quad \lambda_n \pm k$$

### Property 7

If $k$ is a positive integer then the eigenvalues of $\boldsymbol{A}^k$ are

$$\lambda_1^k, \quad \lambda_2^k, \quad \ldots, \quad \lambda_n^k$$

**Property 8**

As a consequence of Properties 5 and 7, any polynomial in $\boldsymbol{A}$

$$\boldsymbol{A}^m + \alpha_{m-1}\boldsymbol{A}^{m-1} + \ldots + \alpha_1\boldsymbol{A} + \alpha_0\boldsymbol{I}$$

has eigenvalues

$$\lambda_i^m + \alpha_{m-1}\lambda_i^{m-1} + \ldots + \alpha_1\lambda_i + \alpha_0 \quad \text{for} \quad i = 1, 2, \ldots, n$$

### 5.7.7 Symmetric matrices

A square matrix $\boldsymbol{A}$ is said to be **symmetric** if $\boldsymbol{A}^{\mathrm{T}} = \boldsymbol{A}$. Such matrices form an important class and arise in a variety of practical situations. Two important results concerning the eigenvalues and eigenvectors of such matrices can be proved:

(i) The eigenvalues of a real symmetric matrix are real.
(ii) For an $n \times n$ real symmetric matrix it is always possible to find $n$ independent eigenvectors $\boldsymbol{e}_1, \boldsymbol{e}_2, \ldots, \boldsymbol{e}_n$ that are mutually orthogonal so that $\boldsymbol{e}_i^{\mathrm{T}}\boldsymbol{e}_j = 0$ for $i \neq j$.

If the orthogonal eigenvectors of a symmetric matrix are normalized as

$$\hat{\boldsymbol{e}}_1, \hat{\boldsymbol{e}}_2, \ldots, \hat{\boldsymbol{e}}_n$$

then the **inner (scalar) product** is

$$\hat{\boldsymbol{e}}_i^{\mathrm{T}}\hat{\boldsymbol{e}}_j = \delta_{ij} \quad (i, j = 1, 2, \ldots, n)$$

where $\delta_{ij}$ is the Kronecker delta defined in Section 5.2.1.

The set of normalized eigenvectors of a symmetric matrix therefore form an orthonormal set (that is, they form a mutually orthogonal normalized set of vectors).

**Example 5.47**

Obtain the eigenvalues and corresponding orthogonal eigenvectors of the symmetric matrix

$$\boldsymbol{A} = \begin{bmatrix} 2 & 2 & 0 \\ 2 & 5 & 0 \\ 0 & 0 & 3 \end{bmatrix}$$

and show that the normalized eigenvectors form an orthonormal set.

**Solution**

The eigenvalues of $\boldsymbol{A}$ are $\lambda_1 = 6$, $\lambda_2 = 3$ and $\lambda_3 = 1$, with corresponding eigenvectors

$$\boldsymbol{e}_1 = [1 \quad 2 \quad 0]^{\mathrm{T}}, \quad \boldsymbol{e}_2 = [0 \quad 0 \quad 1]^{\mathrm{T}}, \quad \boldsymbol{e}_3 = [-2 \quad 1 \quad 0]^{\mathrm{T}}$$

which in normalized form are

$$\hat{\boldsymbol{e}}_1 = [1 \quad 2 \quad 0]^{\mathrm{T}}/\sqrt{5}, \quad \hat{\boldsymbol{e}}_2 = [0 \quad 0 \quad 1]^{\mathrm{T}}, \quad \hat{\boldsymbol{e}}_3 = [-2 \quad 1 \quad 0]^{\mathrm{T}}/\sqrt{5}$$

Evaluating the inner products, we see that, for example,

$$\hat{e}_1^T\hat{e}_1 = \tfrac{1}{5} + \tfrac{4}{5} + 0 = 1, \quad \hat{e}_1^T\hat{e}_3 = -\tfrac{2}{5} + \tfrac{2}{5} + 0 = 0$$

and that

$$\hat{e}_i^T\hat{e}_j = \delta_{ij} \quad (i, j = 1, 2, 3)$$

confirming that the eigenvectors form an orthonormal set.

### 5.7.8 Exercises

Check your answers using MATLAB or MAPLE whenever possible.

**103** Verify Properties 1–8 of Section 5.7.6.

**104** Given that the eigenvalues of the matrix

$$A = \begin{bmatrix} 4 & 1 & 1 \\ 2 & 5 & 4 \\ -1 & -1 & 0 \end{bmatrix}$$

are 5, 3 and 1:

(a) confirm Properties 1–4 of Section 5.7.6;

(b) taking $k = 2$, confirm Properties 5–8 of Section 5.7.6.

**105** Determine the eigenvalues and corresponding eigenvectors of the symmetric matrix

$$A = \begin{bmatrix} -3 & -3 & -3 \\ -3 & 1 & -1 \\ -3 & -1 & 1 \end{bmatrix}$$

and verify that the eigenvectors are mutually orthogonal.

**106** The $3 \times 3$ symmetric matrix $\boldsymbol{A}$ has eigenvalues 6, 3 and 2. The eigenvectors corresponding to the eigenvalues 6 and 3 are $[1 \quad 1 \quad 2]^T$ and $[1 \quad 1 \quad -1]^T$ respectively. Find an eigenvector corresponding to the eigenvalue 2.

**107** Verify that the matrix

$$A = \begin{bmatrix} -\frac{3}{20} & \frac{1}{5} \\ \frac{1}{5} & \frac{3}{20} \end{bmatrix}$$

has eigenvalues $\pm\frac{1}{4}$ and corresponding eigenvectors $X = \begin{bmatrix} 2 \\ -1 \end{bmatrix}$ and $Y = \begin{bmatrix} 1 \\ 2 \end{bmatrix}$. What are the eigenvalues of $\boldsymbol{A}^n$? Show that any vector $Z = \begin{bmatrix} a \\ b \end{bmatrix}$ can be written as $Z = \alpha X + \beta Y$ and hence deduce that $\boldsymbol{A}^n Z \to \mathbf{0}$ as $n \to \infty$.

## 5.8 Engineering application: spring systems

The vibration of many mechanical systems can be modelled very satisfactorily by spring and damper systems. The shock absorbers and springs of a motor car give one of the simplest practical examples. On a more fundamental level, the vibration of the atoms or molecules of a solid can be modelled by a lattice containing atoms or molecules that interact with each other through spring forces. The model gives a detailed understanding of the structure of the solid and the strength of interactions and has practical applications in such areas as the study of impurities or 'doped' materials in semiconductor physics.

The motion of these systems demands the use of Newton's equations, which in turn require the calculus. We shall look at methods of solution in Chapters 10 and 11. In this case study we shall not consider vibrations but shall restrict our attention to the static situation. This is the first step in the solution of vibrational systems. Even here, we shall see that matrices and vectors allow a systematic approach to the more complicated situation.

### 5.8.1 A two-particle system

We start with the very simple situation illustrated in Figure 5.22. Two masses are connected by springs of stiffnesses $k_1$, $k_2$ and $k_3$ and of natural lengths $l_1$, $l_2$ and $l_3$ that are fixed to the walls at A and B, with distance AB $= L$. It is required to calculate the equilibrium values of $x_1$ and $x_2$. We use Hooke's law – that force is proportional to extension – to calculate the tension:

$$T_1 = k_1(x_1 - l_1)$$
$$T_2 = k_2(x_2 - x_1 - l_2)$$
$$T_3 = k_3(L - x_2 - l_3)$$

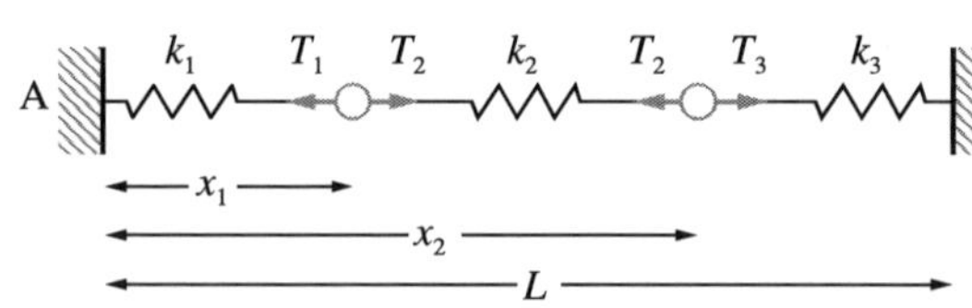


**Figure 5.22**
Two-particle system.

Since the forces are in equilibrium,

$$k_1(x_1 - l_1) = k_2(x_2 - x_1 - l_2)$$
$$k_2(x_2 - x_1 - l_2) = k_3(L - x_2 - l_3)$$

We have two simultaneous equations in the two unknowns, which can be written in matrix form as

$$\begin{bmatrix} k_1 + k_2 & -k_2 \\ -k_2 & k_2 + k_3 \end{bmatrix} \begin{bmatrix} x_1 \\ x_2 \end{bmatrix} = \begin{bmatrix} k_1 l_1 - k_2 l_2 \\ k_2 l_2 - k_3 l_3 + k_3 L \end{bmatrix}$$

It is easy to invert $2 \times 2$ matrices, so we can compute the solution as

$$\begin{bmatrix} x_1 \\ x_2 \end{bmatrix} = \frac{1}{(k_1 + k_2)(k_2 + k_3) - k_2^2} \begin{bmatrix} k_2 + k_3 & k_2 \\ k_2 & k_1 + k_2 \end{bmatrix} \begin{bmatrix} k_1 l_1 - k_2 l_2 \\ k_2 l_2 - k_3 l_3 + k_3 L \end{bmatrix}$$

If we take the simplest situation when $k_1 = k_2 = k_3$ and $l_1 = l_2 = l_3$ then we obtain the obvious solution $x_1 = \frac{1}{3}L$, $x_2 = \frac{2}{3}L$.

### 5.8.2 An $n$-particle system

In the simplest situation, described in Section 5.8.1, matrix notation is convenient but not really necessary. If we try to extend the problem to many particles and many springs

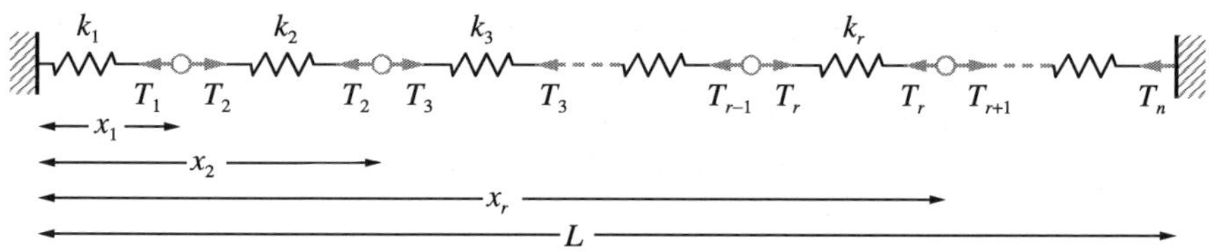


**Figure 5.23**
$n$-particle system.

then such notation simplifies the statement of the problem considerably. Consider the problem illustrated in Figure 5.23. From Hooke's law

$$
\begin{aligned}
T_1 &= k_1(x_1 - l_1)\\
T_2 &= k_2(x_2 - x_1 - l_2)\\
T_3 &= k_3(x_3 - x_2 - l_3)\\
&\vdots\\
T_r &= k_r(x_r - x_{r-1} - l_r)\\
&\vdots\\
T_n &= k_n(L - x_{n-1} - l_n)
\end{aligned}
$$

The equilibrium equations for each 'unit' are

$$
\begin{aligned}
k_1(x_1 - l_1) &= k_2(x_2 - x_1 - l_2)\\
k_2(x_2 - x_1 - l_2) &= k_3(x_3 - x_2 - l_3)\\
&\vdots\\
k_r(x_r - x_{r-1} - l_r) &= k_{r+1}(x_{r+1} - x_r - l_{r+1})\\
&\vdots\\
k_{n-1}(x_{n-1} - x_{n-2} - l_{n-1}) &= k_n(L - x_{n-1} - l_n)
\end{aligned}
$$

In matrix form, these become

$$
\begin{bmatrix}
k_1 + k_2 & -k_2 & & & & & \\
-k_2 & k_2 + k_3 & -k_3 & & \mathbf{0} & & \\
 & -k_3 & k_3 + k_4 & -k_4 & & & \\
 & \ddots & \ddots & & \ddots & & \\
 & \mathbf{0} & & -k_{n-2} & k_{n-2} + k_{n-1} & -k_{n-1} \\
 & & & & -k_{n-1} & k_{n-1} + k_n
\end{bmatrix}
\begin{bmatrix}
x_1\\ x_2\\ \\ \vdots\\ \\ x_{n-1}
\end{bmatrix}
$$

$$
= \begin{bmatrix}
k_1 l_1 - k_2 l_2\\
k_2 l_2 - k_3 l_3\\
\\
\vdots\\
\\
k_{n-2} l_{n-2} - k_{n-1} l_{n-1}\\
k_{n-1} l_{n-1} - k_n l_n + k_n L
\end{bmatrix}
$$

We recognize the form of these equations immediately, since they constitute a tridiagonal system studied in Section 5.5.2, and we can use the Thomas algorithm (Figure 5.11) to solve them. Thus, by writing the equations in matrix form, we are immediately able to identify an efficient method of solution.

In some special cases the solution can be obtained by a mixture of insight and physical intuition. If we take $k_1 = k_2 = \dots = k_n$ and $l_1 = l_2 = \dots = l_n$ and the couplings are all the same then the equations become

$$\begin{bmatrix} 2 & -1 & & & & & \\ -1 & 2 & -1 & & & \mathbf{0} & \\ & -1 & 2 & -1 & & & \\ & & -1 & 2 & & & \\ & & \ddots & & \ddots & \ddots & \\ & \mathbf{0} & & & -1 & 2 & -1 \\ & & & & & -1 & 2 \end{bmatrix} \begin{bmatrix} x_1 \\ x_2 \\ \\ \vdots \\ \\ \\ x_{n-1} \end{bmatrix} = \begin{bmatrix} 0 \\ 0 \\ \\ \vdots \\ \\ 0 \\ L \end{bmatrix}$$

We should expect all the spacings to be uniform, so we seek a solution $x_1 = \alpha$, $x_2 = 2\alpha$, $x_3 = 3\alpha, \dots$ . The first $n - 2$ equations are satisfied identically, as expected, and the final equation in matrix formulation gives $[-(n-2) + 2(n-1)]\alpha = L$. Thus $\alpha = L/n$, and our intuitive solution is justified.

In a second special case where a simple solution is possible, we assume one of the couplings to be a 'rogue'. We take $k_1 = k_2 = \dots = k_{r-1} = k_{r+1} = \dots = k_n = k$, $k_r = k'$ and $l_1 = l_2 = \dots = l_n = l$. If we divide all the equations in the matrix by $k$ and write $\lambda = k'/k$ then the matrix takes the form

$$\begin{bmatrix} 2 & -1 & & & & & & & & \\ -1 & 2 & -1 & & & & \mathbf{0} & & & \\ & -1 & 2 & -1 & & & & & & \\ & \ddots & & \ddots & & \ddots & & & & \\ & & & -1 & 2 & -1 & & & & \\ & & & & -1 & 1+\lambda & -\lambda & & & \\ & & & & & -\lambda & 1+\lambda & -1 & & \\ & & & & & & -1 & 2 & -1 & \\ & & & & & & & \ddots & \ddots & \ddots \\ & \mathbf{0} & & & & & & & & -1 \\ & & & & & & & & -1 & 2 \end{bmatrix} \begin{bmatrix} x_1 \\ x_2 \\ \vdots \\ \\ \\ x_{r-1} \\ x_r \\ \vdots \\ \\ \\ x_{n-1} \end{bmatrix} = \begin{bmatrix} 0 \\ 0 \\ \\ \\ 0 \\ l(1-\lambda) \\ l(\lambda-1) \\ \\ 0 \\ \vdots \\ L \end{bmatrix}$$

A reasonable assumption is that the spacings between 'good' links are all the same. Thus we try a solution of the form

$$x_1 = a, \quad x_2 = 2a, \quad \dots, \quad x_{r-1} = (r-1)a, \quad x_r = b$$

$$x_{r+1} = b + a, \quad x_{r+2} = b + 2a, \quad \dots, \quad x_{n-1} = b + (n-1-r)a$$

It can be checked that the matrix equation is satisfied except for the $(r-1)$th, $r$th and $(n-1)$th rows. These give respectively

$$-\lambda b + a(-\lambda + 1 + \lambda r) = l(1 - \lambda)$$

$$\lambda b \ + a(\lambda - 1 - \lambda r) \ = l(\lambda - 1)$$

and

$$b \ + a(n - r) \ = L$$

The first two of these are identical, so we have two equations in the two unknowns, $a$ and $b$, to solve. We obtain

$$a = \frac{L - l(1 - \lambda^{-1})}{n - (1 - \lambda^{-1})}, \quad b = \frac{rL - (1 - \lambda^{-1})[L - (n - r)l]}{n - (1 - \lambda^{-1})}$$

We note that if $\lambda = 1$ then the solution reduces to the previous one, as expected.

The solution just obtained gives the deformation due to a single rogue coupling. Although this problem is of limited interest, its two- and three-dimensional extensions are of great interest in the theory of crystal lattices. It is possible to determine the deformation due to a single impurity, to compute the effect of two or more impurities and how close they have to be to interact with each other. These are problems with considerable application in materials science.

## 5.9 Engineering application: steady heat transfer through composite materials

### 5.9.1 Introduction

In many practical situations heat is transferred through several layers of different materials. Perhaps the simplest example is a double glazing unit, which comprises a layer of glass, a layer of air and another layer of glass. The thermal properties and the thicknesses of the individual layers are known but what is required is the overall thermal properties of the composite unit. How do the overall properties depend on the components? Which parameters are the most important? How sensitive is the overall heat transfer to changes in each of the components?

A second example looks at the thickness of a furnace wall. A furnace wall will comprise three layers: refractory bricks for heat resistance, insulating bricks for heat insulation and steel casing for mechanical protection. Such a furnace is enormously expensive to construct so it is important that the thickness of the wall is minimized subject to acceptable heat losses, working within the serviceable temperatures and known thickness constraints. The basic problem is again to construct a model that will give some idea how heat is transferred through such a composite material.

The basic properties of heat conduction will be discussed, and it will then be seen that matrices give a natural method of solving the theoretical equations of composite layers.

## 5.9.2 Heat conduction

In its full generality heat conduction forms a part of partial differential equations (see Chapter 9 of *Advanced Modern Engineering Mathematics* 3rd edition). However, for current purposes a simplified one-dimensional version is sufficient. The theory is based on the well-established **Fourier law**:

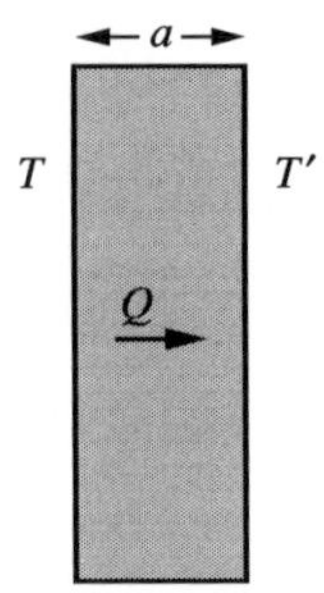


**Figure 5.24** Heat transfer through layers.

> Heat transferred per unit area is proportional to the temperature gradient.

Provided a layer is not too thick and the thermal properties do not vary, then the temperature varies linearly across the solid. If $Q$ is the amount of heat transferred per unit area from left, at temperature $T$, to right, at temperature $T'$, as shown in Figure 5.24, then this law can be written mathematically

$$Q = -k\frac{T' - T}{a}$$

where $k$ is the proportionality constant, called the thermal conductivity, $a$ is the thickness of the layer and the minus sign is to ensure that heat is transferred from hot to cold.

For the conduction *through* an interface between two solids with good contact, as in the situation of the furnace wall, it is assumed that

(i) The temperatures at each side of the interface are equal.
(ii) The heat transferred out of the left side is equal to the heat transferred into the right side.

With the Fourier law and these interface conditions the multilayer situation can be analysed satisfactorily, provided, of course, the heat flow remains one-dimensional and steady.

## 5.9.3 The three-layer situation

Let the three layers have thicknesses $a_1$, $a_2$ and $a_3$ and thermal conductivities $k_1$, $k_2$ and $k_3$, as illustrated in Figure 5.25. At the interfaces the temperatures are taken to be $T_1$, $T_2$, $T_3$ and $T_4$. The simplest problem to study is to fix the temperatures $T_1$ and $T_4$ at the edges and determine how the temperatures $T_2$ and $T_3$ depend on the known parameters.

From the specification of the problem the temperatures at the interfaces are specified so it only remains to satisfy the heat transfer condition across the interface.

At the first interface:

$$\frac{k_1}{a_1}(T_2 - T_1) = \frac{k_2}{a_2}(T_3 - T_2)$$

and at the second interface:

$$\frac{k_2}{a_2}(T_3 - T_2) = \frac{k_3}{a_3}(T_4 - T_3)$$

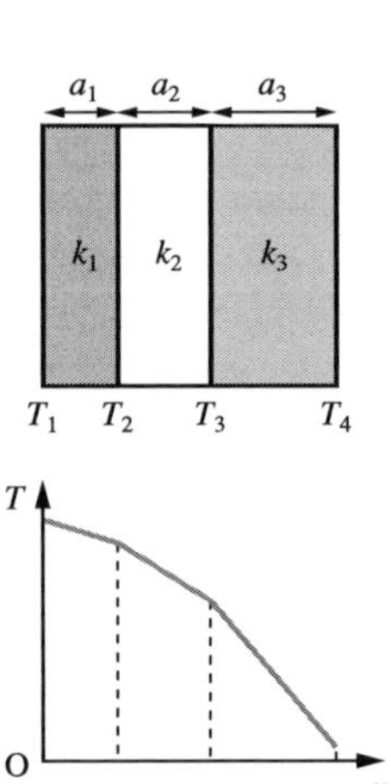


**Figure 5.25** Temperature distribution across three layers.

It turns out to be convenient to let $u_1 = \frac{a_1}{k_1}$, $u_2 = \frac{a_2}{k_2}$ and so on. The equations then become

$$u_2(T_2 - T_1) = u_1(T_3 - T_2)$$
$$u_3(T_3 - T_2) = u_2(T_4 - T_3)$$

or in matrix form

$$\begin{bmatrix} (u_1 + u_2) & -u_1 \\ -u_3 & (u_2 + u_3) \end{bmatrix} \begin{bmatrix} T_2 \\ T_3 \end{bmatrix} = u_2 \begin{bmatrix} T_1 \\ T_4 \end{bmatrix}$$

The determinant of the matrix is easily calculated as $u_2(u_1 + u_2 + u_3)$, which is non-zero so a solution can be computed as

$$\begin{bmatrix} T_2 \\ T_3 \end{bmatrix} = \frac{1}{(u_1 + u_2 + u_3)} \begin{bmatrix} (u_2 + u_3) & u_1 \\ u_3 & (u_1 + u_2) \end{bmatrix} \begin{bmatrix} T_1 \\ T_4 \end{bmatrix}$$

Thus the temperatures $T_2$ and $T_3$ are now known, and any required properties can be deduced.

For the furnace problem described in Section 5.9.1 the following data is known:

$T_1 = 1650$ K and $T_4 = 300$ K

and

| | ***Maximum working temperature (K)*** | ***Thermal conductivity at 100 K ($W\,m^{-1}K^{-1}$)*** | ***Thermal conductivity at 2000 K ($W\,m^{-1}K^{-1}$)*** |
|---|---|---|---|
| *Refractory brick* | 1700 | 3.1 | 6.2 |
| *Insulating brick* | 1400 | 1.6 | 3.1 |
| *Steel* | – | 45.2 | 45.2 |

It may be noted that the thermal conductivity depends on the temperature but in these calculations it is assumed constant (a more sophisticated analysis is required to take these variations into account). Average values $k_1 = 5$, $k_2 = 2.5$ and $k_3 = 45.2$ are chosen. The required temperatures are evaluated as

$$T_2 = \frac{(0.4a_2 + 0.022a_3)1650 + (0.2a_1)300}{0.2a_1 + 0.4a_2 + 0.022a_3}$$

$$T_3 = \frac{(0.022a_3)1650 + (0.2a_1 + 0.4a_2)300}{0.2a_1 + 0.4a_2 + 0.022a_3}$$

A typical question that would be asked is how to minimize the thickness (or perhaps the cost) subject to appropriate constraints. For instance find

$$\min(a_1 + a_2 + a_3)$$

subject to

$\frac{k_3}{a_3}(300 - T_3) < 50\,000$ (allowable heat loss at the right-hand boundary)

$T_2 < 1400$ (below the maximum working temperature)

$a_1 > 0.1$ (must have a minimum refractory thickness)

The problem is beyond the scope of the present book, but it illustrates the type of question that can be answered.

A more straightforward question is to evaluate the effective conductivity of the composite. It may be noted that in the general case, the heat flow is

$$Q = -\frac{1}{u_1}(T_2 - T_1) \quad \text{which on substitution gives } Q = -\frac{T_4 - T_1}{u_1 + u_2 + u_3}$$

so the effective conductivity over the whole region is

$$k = \frac{a_1 + a_2 + a_3}{u_1 + u_2 + u_3} \quad \text{or} \quad \frac{a_1 + a_2 + a_3}{k} = \frac{a_1}{k_1} + \frac{a_2}{k_2} + \frac{a_3}{k_3}$$

## 5.9.4 Many-layer situation

Although matrix theory was used to solve the three-layer problem, it was unnecessary since the mathematics reduced to the solution of a pair of simultaneous equations. However, for the many-layer system it is important to approach the problem in a logical and systematic manner, and matrix theory proves to be the ideal mathematical method to use.

Consider the successive interfaces in turn and construct the heat flow equation for each of them (Figure 5.26).

$$\frac{k_1}{a_1}(T_2 - T_1) = \frac{k_2}{a_2}(T_3 - T_2)$$

$$\frac{k_2}{a_2}(T_3 - T_2) = \frac{k_3}{a_3}(T_4 - T_3)$$

$$\vdots$$

$$\frac{k_{n-1}}{a_{n-1}}(T_n - T_{n-1}) = \frac{k_n}{a_n}(T_{n+1} - T_n)$$

As in the three-layer case, it is convenient to define $u_1 = \frac{a_1}{k_1}$, $u_2 = \frac{a_2}{k_2}$ and so on. The equations then become

$$u_2(T_2 - T_1) = u_1(T_3 - T_2)$$

$$u_3(T_3 - T_2) = u_2(T_4 - T_3)$$

$$u_4(T_4 - T_3) = u_3(T_5 - T_4)$$

$$\vdots$$

$$u_n(T_n - T_{n-1}) = u_{n-1}(T_{n+1} - T_n)$$

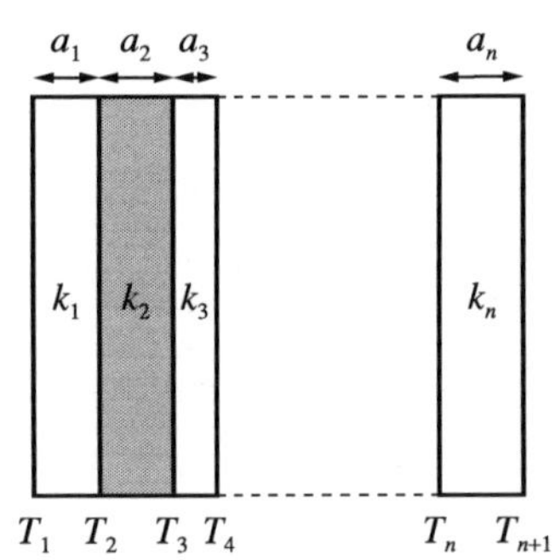


**Figure 5.26**
$n$-layered problem.

or in matrix form

$$\begin{bmatrix} (u_1+u_2) & -u_1 & 0 & . & . & . & . & 0 \\ -u_3 & (u_2+u_3) & -u_2 & 0 & . & . & . & 0 \\ 0 & -u_4 & (u_3+u_4) & -u_3 & 0 & . & . & 0 \\ . & . & . & . & . & . & . & . \\ . & . & . & . & . & . & . & . \\ . & . & . & . & . & . & . & . \\ 0 & 0 & 0 & . & . & 0 & -u_n & (u_{n-1}+u_n) \end{bmatrix} \begin{bmatrix} T_2 \\ . \\ . \\ . \\ . \\ T_n \end{bmatrix}$$

$$= \begin{bmatrix} u_2T_1 \\ 0 \\ 0 \\ . \\ . \\ 0 \\ u_{n-1}T_{n+1} \end{bmatrix}$$

The matrix equation is of tridiagonal form, hence we know that there is an efficient algorithm for solution. An explicit solution, as in the three-layer case, is not so easy and requires a lot of effort. However, it is a comparatively easy exercise to prove that the effective conductivity ($k$) of the whole composite is obtained from the equivalent formula

$$\frac{\Sigma a_i}{k} = \frac{a_1}{k_1} + \frac{a_2}{k_2} + \ldots + \frac{a_n}{k_n}$$

## 5.10 Review exercises (1–26)

Check your answers using MATLAB or MAPLE whenever possible.

1 Given

$$\boldsymbol{P} = \begin{bmatrix} 2 & 4 & 1 \\ 0 & 2 & 1 \\ 0 & 0 & 4 \end{bmatrix} \quad \boldsymbol{Q} = \begin{bmatrix} 6 & 2 & -1 \\ 0 & 2 & -2 \\ 0 & 0 & 4 \end{bmatrix}$$

and

$$\boldsymbol{R} = \begin{bmatrix} 2 & 7 & -6 \\ 0 & 0 & 2 \\ 0 & 0 & 1 \end{bmatrix}$$

(a) calculate $\boldsymbol{RQ}$ and $\boldsymbol{Q}^{\mathrm{T}}\boldsymbol{R}^{\mathrm{T}}$;

(b) calculate $\boldsymbol{Q}+\boldsymbol{R}$, $\boldsymbol{PQ}$ and $\boldsymbol{PR}$, and hence verify that in this particular case

$$\boldsymbol{P}(\boldsymbol{Q}+\boldsymbol{R}) = \boldsymbol{PQ}+\boldsymbol{PR}$$

2 Let

$$\boldsymbol{A} = \begin{bmatrix} -1 & 2 \\ 4 & 1 \end{bmatrix} \quad \text{and} \quad \boldsymbol{B} = \begin{bmatrix} 1 & 1 \\ \lambda & \mu \end{bmatrix}$$

where $\lambda \neq \mu$. Find all pairs of values $\lambda$, $\mu$ such that $\boldsymbol{B}^{-1}\boldsymbol{AB}$ is a diagonal matrix.

3 At a point in an elastic continuum the matrix representation of the infinitesimal strain tensor referred to axes $Ox_1x_2x_3$ is

$$\boldsymbol{E} = \begin{bmatrix} 1 & -3 & \sqrt{2} \\ -3 & 1 & -\sqrt{2} \\ \sqrt{2} & -\sqrt{2} & 4 \end{bmatrix}$$

If $\boldsymbol{i}, \boldsymbol{j}$ and $\boldsymbol{k}$ are unit vectors in the direction of the $Ox_1x_2x_3$ coordinate axes, determine the normal strain in the direction of

$$\boldsymbol{n} = \tfrac{1}{2}(\boldsymbol{i} - \boldsymbol{j} + \sqrt{2}\boldsymbol{k})$$

and the shear strain between the directions $\boldsymbol{n}$ and

$$\boldsymbol{m} = \tfrac{1}{2}(-\boldsymbol{i} + \boldsymbol{j} + \sqrt{2}\boldsymbol{k})$$

(Note that, using matrix notation, the normal strain is $\boldsymbol{En}$, and the shear strain between two directions is $\boldsymbol{m}^{\mathrm{T}}\boldsymbol{En}$.)

4 Express the determinant

$$\begin{vmatrix} \alpha & \beta & \gamma \\ \beta\gamma & \gamma\alpha & \alpha\beta \\ -\alpha + \beta + \gamma & \alpha - \beta + \gamma & \alpha + \beta - \gamma \end{vmatrix}$$

as a product of linear factors.

5 Determine the values of $\theta$ for which the system of equations

$$x + y + z = 1$$
$$x + 2y + 4z = \theta$$
$$x + 4y + 10z = \theta^2$$

possesses a solution, and for each such value find all solutions.

6 Given

$$\boldsymbol{A} = \begin{bmatrix} 1 & 1 & 1 \\ 2 & 1 & 2 \\ -2 & 1 & -1 \end{bmatrix}$$

evaluate $\boldsymbol{A}^2$ and $\boldsymbol{A}^3$. Verify that

$$\boldsymbol{A}^3 - \boldsymbol{A}^2 - 3\boldsymbol{A} + \boldsymbol{I} = 0$$

where $\boldsymbol{I}$ is the unit matrix of order 3. Using this result, or otherwise, find the inverse $\boldsymbol{A}^{-1}$ of $\boldsymbol{A}$, and hence solve the equations

$$x + y + z = 3$$
$$2x + y + 2z = 7$$
$$-2x + y - z = 6$$

7 (a) If $\boldsymbol{P} = \dfrac{1}{3}\begin{bmatrix} 2 & 1 & 2 \\ -2 & 2 & 1 \\ -1 & -2 & 2 \end{bmatrix}$ write down the transpose matrix $\boldsymbol{P}^{\mathrm{T}}$. Calculate $\boldsymbol{PP}^{\mathrm{T}}$ and hence show that $\boldsymbol{P}^{\mathrm{T}} = \boldsymbol{P}^{-1}$. What does this mean about the solution of the matrix equation $\boldsymbol{Px} = \boldsymbol{b}$?

(b) The matrix $\boldsymbol{F} = \begin{bmatrix} I_x & I_{xy} & Q_x \\ I_{xy} & I_y & Q_y \\ Q_x & Q_y & A \end{bmatrix}$ occurs in the structural analysis of an arch. If

$$\boldsymbol{B} = \begin{bmatrix} 1 & 0 & -Q_x/A \\ 0 & 1 & -Q_y/A \\ 0 & 0 & 1 \end{bmatrix}$$

find $\boldsymbol{E} = \boldsymbol{BFB}^{\mathrm{T}}$ and show that it is a symmetric matrix.

8 (a) If the matrix $\boldsymbol{A} = \begin{bmatrix} 1 & 0 & 0 \\ 1 & -1 & 0 \\ 1 & -2 & 1 \end{bmatrix}$ show that $\boldsymbol{A}^2 = \boldsymbol{I}$ and derive the elements of a square matrix $\boldsymbol{B}$ which satisfies

$$\boldsymbol{BA} = \begin{bmatrix} 1 & 4 & 3 \\ 0 & 2 & 1 \\ -1 & 0 & 0 \end{bmatrix}$$

(b) Find suitable values for $k$ in order that the following system of linear simultaneous equations are consistent:

$$6x + (k - 6)y = 3$$
$$2x + y = 5$$
$$(2k + 1)x + 6y = 1$$

9 Express the system of linear equations

$$\begin{aligned} 3x - y + 4z &= 13 \\ 5x + y - 3z &= 5 \\ x - y + z &= 3 \end{aligned}$$

in the form $\boldsymbol{AX} = \boldsymbol{b}$, where $\boldsymbol{A}$ is a $3 \times 3$ matrix and $\boldsymbol{X}$, $\boldsymbol{b}$ are appropriate column matrices.

(a) Find adj $\boldsymbol{A}$, $|\boldsymbol{A}|$ and $\boldsymbol{A}^{-1}$ and hence solve the system of equations.

(b) Find a matrix $\boldsymbol{Y}$ which satisfies the equation

$$\boldsymbol{AYA}^{-1} = 22\boldsymbol{A}^{-1} + 2\boldsymbol{A}$$

(c) Find a matrix $\boldsymbol{Z}$ which satisfies the equation

$$\boldsymbol{AZ} = 44\boldsymbol{I}_3 - \boldsymbol{A} + \boldsymbol{AA}^{\mathrm{T}}$$

where $\boldsymbol{I}_3$ is the $3 \times 3$ identity matrix.

10 (a) Using the method of Gaussian elimination, find the solution of the equation

$$\begin{bmatrix} 1 & 2 & 4 & 8 \\ 2 & 7 & 13 & 25 \\ -1 & 1 & 5 & 9 \\ 2 & 1 & 11 & 24 \end{bmatrix} \begin{bmatrix} x_1 \\ x_2 \\ x_3 \\ x_4 \end{bmatrix} = \begin{bmatrix} 19 \\ 57 \\ 16 \\ 52 \end{bmatrix}$$

Hence evaluate the determinant of the matrix in the equation.

(b) Solve by the method of Gaussian elimination

$$\begin{bmatrix} 1 & 1 & -1 & 1 \\ 2 & 3 & -3 & 3 \\ -1 & 1 & 0 & 0 \\ 2 & 3 & -1 & 2 \end{bmatrix} \begin{bmatrix} x_1 \\ x_2 \\ x_3 \\ x_4 \end{bmatrix} = \begin{bmatrix} 4 \\ 11 \\ 1 \\ 13 \end{bmatrix}$$

with partial pivoting.

11 Rearrange the equations

$$\begin{aligned} x_1 - x_2 + 3x_3 &= 8 \\ 4x_1 + x_2 - x_3 &= 3 \\ x_1 + 2x_2 + x_3 &= 8 \end{aligned}$$

so that they are diagonally dominant to ensure convergence of the Gauss–Seidel method. Write a MATLAB program to obtain the solution of these equations using this method, starting from (0, 0, 0). Compare your solution with that from a program when the equations are not rearranged. Use SOR, with $\omega = 1.3$, to solve the equations. Is there any improvement?

12 Find the rank of the matrix

$$\begin{bmatrix} 0 & c & b & a \\ -c & 0 & a & b \\ -b & -a & 0 & c \\ -a & -b & -c & 0 \end{bmatrix}$$

where $b \neq 0$ and $a^2 + c^2 = b^2$.

13 For a given set of discrete data points $(x_i, f_i)$ $(i = 0, 1, 2, \dots, n)$, show that the coefficients $a_k$ $(k = 0, 1, \dots, n)$ fitted to the polynomial

$$y(x) = \sum_{k=0}^{n} a_k x^k$$

are given by the solution of the equations written in the matrix form as

$$\boldsymbol{Aa} = \boldsymbol{f}$$

where

$$\boldsymbol{A} = \begin{bmatrix} 1 & x_0 & x_0^2 & \dots & x_0^n \\ 1 & x_1 & x_1^2 & \dots & x_1^n \\ \vdots & \vdots & & & \vdots \\ 1 & x_n & x_n^2 & \dots & x_n^n \end{bmatrix}$$

$$\boldsymbol{a} = [a_0 \ a_1 \ \dots \ a_n]^{\mathrm{T}}$$

$$\boldsymbol{f} = [f_0 \ f_1 \ \dots \ f_n]^{\mathrm{T}}$$

(See Question 102 in Exercises 2.9.2 of Chapter 2 for the Lagrange interpolation solution of these equations for the case $n = 3$.)

The following data is taken from the tables of the Airy function $f(x) = \mathrm{Ai}(-x)$:

| $x$ | 1 | 1.5 | 2.3 | 3.0 | 3.9 |
|---|---|---|---|---|---|
| $f(x)$ | 0.535 56 | 0.464 26 | 0.026 70 | −0.378 81 | −0.147 42 |

Estimate from the polynomial approximation the values of $f(2.0)$ and $f(3.5)$.

14 Data is fitted to a cubic

$$f = ax^3 + bx^2 + cx + d$$

with the slope of the curve given by

$$f' = 3ax^2 + 2bx + c$$

If $f_1 = f(x_1), f_2 = f(x_2), f'_1 = f'(x_1)$ and $f'_2 = f'(x_2)$, show that fitting the data gives the matrix equation for $a$, $b$, $c$ and $d$ as

$$\begin{bmatrix} f_1 \\ f_2 \\ f'_1 \\ f'_2 \end{bmatrix} = \begin{bmatrix} x_1^3 & x_1^2 & x_1 & 1 \\ x_2^3 & x_2^2 & x_2 & 1 \\ 3x_1^2 & 2x_1 & 1 & 0 \\ 3x_2^2 & 2x_2 & 1 & 0 \end{bmatrix} \begin{bmatrix} a \\ b \\ c \\ d \end{bmatrix}$$

Use Gaussian elimination to evaluate $a$, $b$, $c$ and $d$. For the case

| $x$ | $f$ | $f'$ |
|---|---|---|
| 0.4 | 0.327 54 | 0.511 73 |
| 0.8 | 0.404 90 | −0.054 14 |

evaluate $a$, $b$, $c$ and $d$. Plot the cubic and estimate the maximum value of $f$ in the region $0 < x < 1$. Note that this exercise forms the basis of one of the standard methods for finding the maximum of a function $f(x)$ numerically.

15 The transformation $\boldsymbol{y} = \boldsymbol{AX}$ where

$$\boldsymbol{A} = \frac{1}{9}\begin{bmatrix} 8 & -1 & -4 \\ 4 & 4 & 7 \\ 1 & -8 & 4 \end{bmatrix}$$

$$\boldsymbol{y} = \begin{bmatrix} y_1 \\ y_2 \\ y_3 \end{bmatrix} \quad \text{and} \quad \boldsymbol{X} = \begin{bmatrix} x_1 \\ x_2 \\ x_3 \end{bmatrix}$$

takes a point with coordinates $(x_1, x_2, x_3)$ into a point with coordinates $(y_1, y_2, y_3)$. Show that the coordinates of the points that transform into themselves satisfy the matrix equation $\boldsymbol{BX} = 0$, where $\boldsymbol{B} = \boldsymbol{A} - \boldsymbol{I}$, with $\boldsymbol{I}$ the identity matrix. Find the rank of $\boldsymbol{B}$ and hence deduce that for points which transform into themselves

$$[x_1 \quad x_2 \quad x_3] = \alpha[-3 \quad -1 \quad 1]$$

where $\alpha$ is a parameter.

Find $\boldsymbol{AA}^{\mathrm{T}}$. What is the inverse of $\boldsymbol{A}$?

If $y_1 = 3$, $y_2 = -1$ and $y_3 = 2$, determine the values of $x_1$, $x_2$ and $x_3$ under this transformation.

16 (a) If

$$\boldsymbol{A} = \begin{bmatrix} 1 & 0 & 1 & 0 \\ 2 & 1 & 2 & 1 \\ 1 & -2 & 2 & -2 \\ 2 & 0 & 3 & 1 \end{bmatrix}$$

verify that

$$\boldsymbol{A}^{-1} = \begin{bmatrix} 6 & -2 & -1 & 0 \\ -5 & 3 & 1 & -1 \\ -5 & 2 & 1 & 0 \\ 3 & -2 & -1 & 1 \end{bmatrix}$$

(b) Use the inverse matrix given in (a) to solve the system of linear equations $\boldsymbol{AX} = \boldsymbol{b}$ in which

$$\boldsymbol{b}^{\mathrm{T}} = [5 \quad -5 \quad -4 \quad 4]$$

17 When a body is deformed in a certain manner, the particle at point $\boldsymbol{x}$ moves to $\boldsymbol{AX}$, where

$$\boldsymbol{X} = \begin{bmatrix} x \\ y \\ z \end{bmatrix} \quad \text{and} \quad \boldsymbol{A} = \begin{bmatrix} 1 & -2 & 0 \\ -2 & 3 & 0 \\ 0 & 0 & 2 \end{bmatrix}$$

(a) Where would the point $\begin{bmatrix} 2 \\ 1 \\ 1 \end{bmatrix}$ move to?

(b) Find the point from which the particle would move to the point $\begin{bmatrix} 2 \\ 1 \\ 1 \end{bmatrix}$.

18 Find the eigenvalues and the normalized eigenvectors of the matrices

(a) $\begin{bmatrix} 4 & 1 & 1 \\ 2 & 1 & -1 \\ -2 & 2 & 4 \end{bmatrix}$ (b) $\begin{bmatrix} 1 & -1 & 2 \\ -2 & 0 & 5 \\ 6 & -3 & 6 \end{bmatrix}$

(c) $\begin{bmatrix} 5 & -2 & 0 \\ -2 & 6 & 2 \\ 0 & 2 & 7 \end{bmatrix} = \boldsymbol{C}$

In (c) write the normalized eigenvectors as the columns of the matrix $\boldsymbol{U}$ and show that $\boldsymbol{U}^{\mathrm{T}}\boldsymbol{C}\boldsymbol{U}$ is a diagonal matrix with the eigenvalues in the diagonal.

19 The vector $[1 \quad 0 \quad 1]^{\mathrm{T}}$ is an eigenvector of the symmetric matrix

$$\begin{bmatrix} 6 & -1 & 3 \\ -1 & 7 & \alpha \\ 3 & \alpha & \beta \end{bmatrix}$$

Find the values of $\alpha$ and $\beta$ and find the corresponding eigenvalue.

20 Show that the matrix $\begin{bmatrix} -1 & 0 & 2 \\ 0 & 1 & 0 \\ 2 & 0 & -1 \end{bmatrix}$ has eigenvalues 1, 1 and $-3$. Find the corresponding eigenvectors. Is there a full set of three independent eigenvectors?

21 A colony of insects is observed at regular intervals and comprises four age groups containing $n_1$, $n_2$, $n_3$, $n_4$ insects in the groups. At the end of an interval, of the $n_1$ in group 1 some have died and $(1 - \beta_1)n_1$ become the new group 2. Similarly $(1 - \beta_2)n_2$ of group 2 become the new group 3 and $(1 - \beta_3)n_3$ of group 3 become the new group 4. All group 4 die out at the end of the interval. Groups 2, 3 and 4 produce $\alpha_2 n_2$, $\alpha_3 n_3$ and $\alpha_4 n_4$ infant insects that enter group 1. Show that the changes from one interval to the next can be written

$$\begin{bmatrix} n_1 \\ n_2 \\ n_3 \\ n_4 \end{bmatrix}_{\text{new}} = \begin{bmatrix} 0 & \alpha_2 & \alpha_3 & \alpha_4 \\ 1-\beta_1 & 0 & 0 & 0 \\ 0 & 1-\beta_2 & 0 & 0 \\ 0 & 0 & 1-\beta_3 & 0 \end{bmatrix} \begin{bmatrix} n_1 \\ n_2 \\ n_3 \\ n_4 \end{bmatrix}_{\text{old}}$$

Take $\alpha_3 = 0.5$, $\alpha_4 = 0.25$, $\beta_1 = 0.2$, $\beta_2 = 0.25$ and $\beta_3 = 0.5$. Try the values $\alpha_2 = 0.77, 0.78, 0.79$ and check whether the population grows or dies out over many intervals starting from an initial population $\begin{bmatrix} 100 \\ 90 \\ 50 \\ 30 \end{bmatrix}$.

Find the eigenvalues in the three cases and check the magnitudes of the eigenvalues. Is there any connection between survival and eigenvalues?

Realistic populations can be modelled using this approach, the matrices are called Leslie matrices.

22 (a) Find the eigenvalues $\lambda_1$, $\lambda_2$ and the normalized eigenvectors $\boldsymbol{X}_1$, $\boldsymbol{X}_2$ of the matrix $\boldsymbol{A} = \begin{bmatrix} 2 & 1 \\ 1 & 2 \end{bmatrix}$. Check that

$$\boldsymbol{A} = \lambda_1 \boldsymbol{X}_1 \boldsymbol{X}_1^{\mathrm{T}} + \lambda_2 \boldsymbol{X}_2 \boldsymbol{X}_2^{\mathrm{T}}$$

(b) Use MATLAB or MAPLE to repeat a similar calculation for the three eigenvalues and normalized eigenvectors of

$$\boldsymbol{B} = \begin{bmatrix} -1 & 1 & 0 \\ 1 & 0 & 1 \\ 0 & 1 & -2 \end{bmatrix}$$

(*Note*: The process described in this question calculates the spectral decomposition of a symmetric matrix.)

23 In Section 5.7.7 it was stated that a symmetric matrix $\boldsymbol{A}$ has real eigenvalues $\lambda_1, \lambda_2, \dots, \lambda_n$ (written in descending order) and corresponding orthonormal eigenvectors $\mathbf{e}_1, \mathbf{e}_2, \dots, \mathbf{e}_n$, that is $\mathbf{e}_i^{\mathrm{T}}\mathbf{e}_j = \delta_{ij}$. In consequence any vector can be written as

$$\boldsymbol{X} = c_1\mathbf{e}_1 + c_2\mathbf{e}_2 + \dots + c_n\mathbf{e}_n$$

Deduce that

$$\frac{\boldsymbol{X}^{\mathrm{T}}\boldsymbol{A}\boldsymbol{X}}{\boldsymbol{X}^{\mathrm{T}}\boldsymbol{X}} \leqslant \lambda_1 \qquad \textbf{(5.42)}$$

so that a lower bound of the largest eigenvalue has been found. The left-hand side of (5.42) is called the Rayleigh quotient.

It is known that the matrix $\begin{bmatrix} 0 & 1 & 0 & 0 \\ 1 & 0 & 1 & 0 \\ 0 & 1 & 0 & 1 \\ 0 & 0 & 1 & 0 \end{bmatrix}$ has a largest eigenvalue of $\frac{1}{2}(1+\sqrt{5})$. Check that the result (5.42) holds for any vector of your choice.

24 A rotation of a set of rectangular cartesian axes $\Phi(Ox_1x_2x_3)$ to a set $\Phi'(Ox_1'x_2'x_3')$ is described by the matrix $\boldsymbol{L} = (l_{ij})$ $(i, j = 1, 2, 3)$, where $l_{ij}$ is the cosine of the angle between $Ox_i'$ and $Ox_j$. Show that $\boldsymbol{L}$ is such that

$$\boldsymbol{L}\boldsymbol{L}^{\mathrm{T}} = \boldsymbol{I}$$

and that the coordinates of a point in space referred to the two sets of axes are related by

$$\boldsymbol{X}' = \boldsymbol{L}\boldsymbol{X}$$

where $\boldsymbol{X}' = [x_1' \quad x_2' \quad x_3']^{\mathrm{T}}$ and $\boldsymbol{X} = [x_1 \quad x_2 \quad x_3]^{\mathrm{T}}$.

Prove that

$$x_1'^2 + x_2'^2 + x_3'^2 = x_1^2 + x_2^2 + x_3^2$$

Describe the relationship between the axes $\Phi$ and $\Phi'$, given that

$$\boldsymbol{L} = \begin{bmatrix} \frac{1}{2} & 0 & \frac{1}{2}\sqrt{3} \\ 0 & 1 & 0 \\ -\frac{1}{2}\sqrt{3} & 0 & \frac{1}{2} \end{bmatrix}$$

The axes $\Phi'$ are now rotated through 45° about $Ox_3'$ in the sense from $Ox_1'$ to $Ox_2'$ to form a new set $\Phi''$. Show that the angle $\theta$ between the line OP and the axis $Ox_1''$, where P is the point with coordinates $(1, 2, -1)$ referred to the original system $\Phi$, is

$$\theta = \cos^{-1}\left(\frac{5\sqrt{3}-3}{12}\right)$$

25 A car is at rest on horizontal ground as shown in Figure 5.27. The weight $W$ acts through the centre of gravity, and the springs have stiffness constants $k_1$ and $k_2$ and natural lengths $a_1$ and $a_2$. Show that the height $z$ and the angle $\theta$ (assumed too small) satisfy the matrix equation

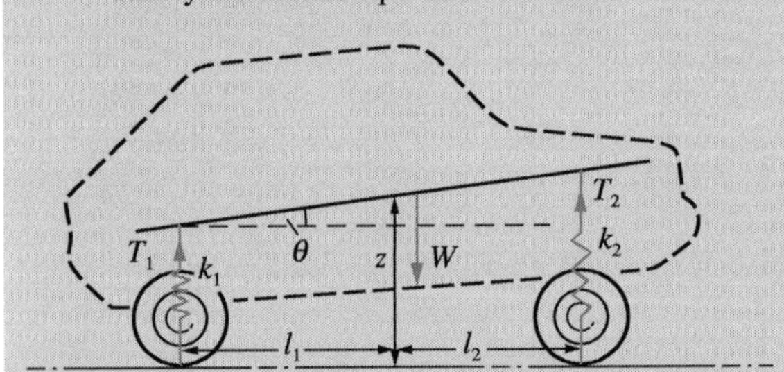


**Figure 5.27** Car at rest on horizontal ground.

$$\begin{bmatrix} -W + a_1k_1 + a_2k_2 \\ l_1k_1a_1 - l_2k_2a_2 \end{bmatrix} = \begin{bmatrix} k_1 + k_2 & -l_1k_1 + l_2k_2 \\ l_1k_1 - l_2k_2 & -l_1^2k_1 - l_2^2k_2 \end{bmatrix} \begin{bmatrix} z \\ \theta \end{bmatrix}$$

Obtain reasonable values for the various parameters to ensure that $\theta = 0$.

26 In the circuit in Figure 5.28(a) show that the equations can be written

$$\begin{bmatrix} E_1 \\ I_1 \end{bmatrix} = \begin{bmatrix} 1 & Z_1 \\ 0 & 1 \end{bmatrix} \begin{bmatrix} E_2 \\ I_2 \end{bmatrix}$$

and that in Figure 5.28(b) they take the form

$$\begin{bmatrix} E_1 \\ I_1 \end{bmatrix} = \begin{bmatrix} 1 & 0 \\ 1/Z_2 & 1 \end{bmatrix} \begin{bmatrix} E_2 \\ I_2 \end{bmatrix}$$

Dividing the circuit in Figure 5.28(c) into blocks, with the output from one block inputting to the next block, analyse the relation between $I_1$, $E_1$ and $I_2$, $E_2$.

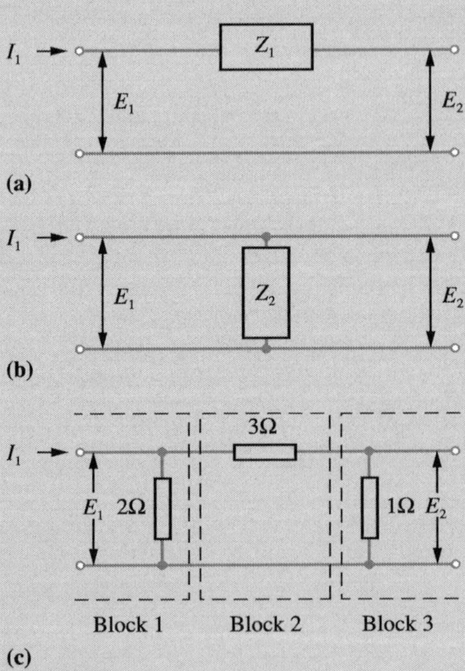


**Figure 5.28**

## CHAPTER 5

### Exercises

**1** (a) not possible (b) $\begin{bmatrix}1\\3\\1\end{bmatrix}$ (c) not possible

(d) not possible (e) $\begin{bmatrix}8 & 9 & 10\\7 & 10 & 9\end{bmatrix}$

**2** (a) $\begin{bmatrix}0 & 1 & 1\\3 & 2 & -1\\0 & 0 & 3\end{bmatrix}$ (b) $\begin{bmatrix}-2 & \frac{4}{3} & -\frac{2}{3}\\0 & -\frac{4}{3} & -\frac{4}{3}\\0 & -2 & 0\end{bmatrix}$

(c) $\begin{bmatrix}1 & -\frac{1}{2} & \frac{1}{2}\\\frac{1}{2} & 1 & \frac{1}{2}\\0 & 1 & \frac{1}{2}\end{bmatrix}$

**3** $\begin{bmatrix}4 & 7 & -1\\18 & 10 & 14\end{bmatrix}$

**4** (b) $\begin{bmatrix}3 & -2 & 1\\0 & 3 & -1\\1 & 6 & 3\end{bmatrix}$

**5** 1, 1, 2, 2,

**6** $\alpha = 1 \quad \beta = -1 \quad \gamma = 2$

**7** (a) $\lambda = 1 \quad \mu = -1 \quad \nu = 3$

**8** Average = $\begin{bmatrix}30.5\\27.5\\19.5\\11.5\\11.0\end{bmatrix}$ Weighted average = $\begin{bmatrix}32.57\\26.43\\19.14\\11.43\\10.43\end{bmatrix}$

**9** $\begin{bmatrix}40 & 49 & 46 & 42 & 52\\53 & 60 & 58 & 46 & 68\\23 & 30 & 26 & 29 & 16\end{bmatrix}$

*312 380 355 326 400*
*409 462 447 358 526*
*180 230 205 225 126*

**10** $\begin{bmatrix}31\,000\\9000\\16\,900\\340\\18\end{bmatrix}$ $\begin{bmatrix}14\,750\\14\,600\\270\\122\\9\end{bmatrix}$ Bricks – type C and sand

**11** $\begin{bmatrix}2 & 2 & -1\\2 & 2 & -1\end{bmatrix}\begin{bmatrix}0 & 2\\0 & 2\end{bmatrix}$

$\begin{bmatrix}1 & 3\\1 & 3\\1 & 1\end{bmatrix}\begin{bmatrix}2 & 2 & 2\\2 & 2 & 2\\-2 & -2 & -2\end{bmatrix}$

$\begin{bmatrix}2 & 2\\2 & 2\\-1 & -1\end{bmatrix}$

**12** (a) No, yes, yes, yes, no, no

(b) $\begin{bmatrix}9 & 7\\7 & 12\end{bmatrix}\begin{bmatrix}13 & 18\\8 & 5\end{bmatrix}\begin{bmatrix}9 & 5\\18 & 2\end{bmatrix}$

(c) $\begin{bmatrix}37 & 33\\26 & 36\\29 & 28\end{bmatrix}$

**13** $\boldsymbol{AB} = \boldsymbol{BA} = \begin{bmatrix}2 & 0\\0 & 2\end{bmatrix}, \boldsymbol{X} = \begin{bmatrix}2\\-\frac{5}{2}\end{bmatrix}$

**16** $x^2 + y^2 + z^2$
$x^2 + 4y^2 + 7z^2 + 5xy + 8xz + 11yz$

$$\left.\begin{aligned}x + 2y + 3z &= 2\\3x + 4y + 5z &= 3\\5x + 6y + 7z &= 4\end{aligned}\right\}$$

**17** $\boldsymbol{AB} = \begin{bmatrix}0 & 2\\1 & 4\end{bmatrix}$, $\boldsymbol{BA} = \begin{bmatrix}2 & 1 & 2\\1 & 0 & 1\\2 & 1 & 2\end{bmatrix}$, $\boldsymbol{BC} = \begin{bmatrix}-1 & 2\\2 & 1\\-1 & 2\end{bmatrix}$

$\boldsymbol{CB}$ not defined, $\boldsymbol{CA} = \begin{bmatrix}4 & 1 & 4\\3 & 2 & 3\end{bmatrix}$, $\boldsymbol{AC}$ not defined

**18** (a) $\begin{bmatrix}3 & 4\\2 & 3\end{bmatrix}$, $\begin{bmatrix}4 & 4\\2 & 2\end{bmatrix}$ (b) $\begin{bmatrix}-1 & 2\\0 & 1\end{bmatrix}$, $\begin{bmatrix}0 & 2\\0 & 0\end{bmatrix}$

both $\begin{bmatrix}9 & 0\\0 & 9\end{bmatrix}$ both $\begin{bmatrix}-3 & 12\\30 & 3\end{bmatrix}$

First set does not commute, second set commutes

**21** $\begin{bmatrix}b + d & b\\o & d\end{bmatrix}$

**22** (a) $\boldsymbol{A} = \begin{bmatrix}1 & 1 & 1\\1 & 1 & 1\end{bmatrix}$ $\boldsymbol{B} = \begin{bmatrix}1\\1\\1\end{bmatrix}$

(b) $\boldsymbol{A} = \begin{bmatrix} 1 & 1 & 1 \end{bmatrix}$ $\boldsymbol{B} = \begin{bmatrix} 1 \\ 1 \\ 1 \end{bmatrix}$

(c) $\boldsymbol{A} = \begin{bmatrix} 1 & 0 \\ 0 & 0 \end{bmatrix}$ $\boldsymbol{B} = \begin{bmatrix} 0 & 0 \\ 1 & 1 \end{bmatrix}$

**23** $\boldsymbol{A} = \begin{bmatrix} 1 & \frac{5}{2} & \frac{3}{2} \\ \frac{5}{2} & -1 & 2 \\ \frac{3}{2} & 2 & 1 \end{bmatrix} + \begin{bmatrix} 0 & \frac{1}{2} & \frac{1}{2} \\ -\frac{1}{2} & 0 & -2 \\ -\frac{1}{2} & 2 & 0 \end{bmatrix}$

**24** $\begin{bmatrix} 41 & 15 & 7 \\ -9 & 63 & -40 \\ -13 & 38 & 41 \end{bmatrix}$

**25** £2273.88

**26** $\begin{bmatrix} 1 & 3 & 2 \\ 0 & 5 & 2 \\ 2 & -2 & 1 \end{bmatrix} \begin{bmatrix} 3 & 6 & 5 \\ 6 & 7 & 8 \\ -4 & 1 & -3 \end{bmatrix}$

**28** $\begin{bmatrix} R_1 & R_2 & 0 & 0 & R_5 & 0 \\ 0 & R_2 & -R_3 & R_4 & 0 & 0 \\ 0 & 0 & 0 & R_4 & -R_5 & R_6 \\ 1 & -1 & -1 & 0 & 0 & 0 \\ 0 & 1 & 0 & -1 & -1 & 0 \\ 0 & 0 & -1 & -1 & 0 & 1 \end{bmatrix} \begin{bmatrix} i_1 \\ i_2 \\ i_3 \\ i_4 \\ i_5 \\ i_6 \end{bmatrix} = \begin{bmatrix} E \\ 0 \\ 0 \\ 0 \\ 0 \\ 0 \end{bmatrix}$

**29** $\begin{bmatrix} 799.8 \\ 800 \\ 800.2 \end{bmatrix} \begin{bmatrix} 800 \\ 800 \\ 800 \end{bmatrix}$

**30** $h = \frac{1}{3}, k = \frac{2}{3}, l = \frac{1}{3}, m = \frac{1}{6}$

**32** $\boldsymbol{A} = \begin{bmatrix} \sqrt{\frac{1}{2}} & -\sqrt{\frac{1}{2}} \\ \sqrt{\frac{1}{2}} & \sqrt{\frac{1}{2}} \end{bmatrix}$

$\begin{bmatrix} a \\ b \end{bmatrix} = \begin{bmatrix} 16 \\ -10 \end{bmatrix} + \boldsymbol{A} \begin{bmatrix} 16 \\ -10 \end{bmatrix}$ and $\boldsymbol{B} = \boldsymbol{A}$

**33** $n = 3$

**34** Minors $= \begin{matrix} -1 & 0 & 1 \\ -1 & -2 & -1 \\ 2 & -2 & -2 \end{matrix}$

Cofactors $= \begin{matrix} -1 & 0 & 1 \\ 1 & -2 & 1 \\ 2 & 2 & -2 \end{matrix}$

$|\boldsymbol{A}| = 2$

**35** (a) −19 (b) 130 (c) −65
(d) 1 (e) −3

**36** −4, 16, 16, −32

**37** 3

**38** $\begin{bmatrix} d & -b \\ -c & a \end{bmatrix}$

**39** $\begin{bmatrix} 2 & -1 & 0 \\ -4 & 3 & -1 \\ 1 & -1 & 1 \end{bmatrix}$

**40** $2, \begin{bmatrix} 1 & 0 \\ -3 & 2 \end{bmatrix}, \frac{1}{2}\begin{bmatrix} 1 & 0 \\ -3 & 2 \end{bmatrix}, \begin{bmatrix} 1 & 0 \\ 0 & 1 \end{bmatrix}$

**44** (a) −1.6569, 9.6569
(b) $4.6667 \pm j0.623\,61$
(c) $2, 3 \pm j$

**45** (a) −0.1884 (b) 100

**47** $x^2(2x + 1)^2(x - 1)^2$

**51** Non-singular, singular, non-singular, singular

$\begin{bmatrix} -\frac{1}{3} & \frac{2}{3} \\ \frac{2}{3} & -\frac{1}{3} \end{bmatrix} \begin{bmatrix} 1 & 0 & 0 & -1 \\ 0 & 1 & 0 & -1 \\ 0 & 0 & 1 & -1 \\ 0 & 0 & 0 & 1 \end{bmatrix}$

**52** $\begin{bmatrix} 1 & -1 & -1 \\ 0 & 1 & 0 \\ 0 & 0 & 1 \end{bmatrix}, \begin{bmatrix} 1 & 0 & 0 & 0 \\ 0 & \frac{1}{2} & 0 & 0 \\ 0 & 0 & \frac{1}{3} & 0 \\ 0 & 0 & 0 & \frac{1}{4} \end{bmatrix},$

$\begin{bmatrix} 2 & -j \\ j & 1 \end{bmatrix}, \frac{1}{3}\begin{bmatrix} 5 & -7 & -1 \\ -4 & 5 & 2 \\ 2 & -1 & -1 \end{bmatrix}$

**53** $\frac{1}{169}\begin{bmatrix} -100 & 98 & -92 \\ -47 & -79 & -50 \\ 6 & -87 & -8 \end{bmatrix}$

**55** $\begin{bmatrix} 1 & 0 & 0 \\ -1 & 1 & 0 \\ 2 & -2 & 1 \end{bmatrix}, \frac{1}{4}\begin{bmatrix} 4 & -8 & 6 \\ 0 & 2 & -1 \\ 0 & 0 & 2 \end{bmatrix}, \frac{1}{4}\begin{bmatrix} 24 & -20 & 3 \\ -4 & 4 & -1 \\ 4 & -4 & 2 \end{bmatrix}$

**56** $\begin{bmatrix} 1 & 1 & 0 \\ 0 & 1 & 2 \\ 0 & 1 & 3 \end{bmatrix}, \begin{bmatrix} 1 & 1 & 0 \\ 0 & 1 & 2 \\ 0 & 0 & 1 \end{bmatrix}, \begin{bmatrix} 1 & 1 & 0 \\ 0 & 1 & 0 \\ 0 & 0 & 1 \end{bmatrix},$

$\begin{bmatrix} 1 & 0 & 0 \\ 0 & 1 & 0 \\ 0 & 0 & 1 \end{bmatrix}, \begin{bmatrix} -1 & -3 & 2 \\ 2 & 3 & -2 \\ -1 & -1 & 1 \end{bmatrix}$

**57** $\frac{1}{5}\begin{bmatrix} -3 & 2 & 2 \\ 2 & -3 & 2 \\ 2 & 2 & -3 \end{bmatrix}, \begin{bmatrix} 0.68 & -0.32 & -0.32 \\ -0.32 & 0.68 & -0.32 \\ -0.32 & -0.32 & 0.68 \end{bmatrix}$

**58** $\frac{1}{68}\begin{bmatrix} -4 & 4 & 8 \\ 6 & 11 & -12 \\ 36 & -2 & -4 \end{bmatrix} \quad \frac{1}{49}\begin{bmatrix} -5 & 22 & 8 \\ 11 & -19 & 2 \\ 13 & -18 & -11 \end{bmatrix}$

**59** $\boldsymbol{A} = \boldsymbol{A}^{-1}, \boldsymbol{B}^{-1} = \begin{bmatrix} 1 & 0 & 0 & 0 \\ 0 & 0 & 0 & 1 \\ 0 & 1 & 0 & 0 \\ 0 & 0 & 1 & 0 \end{bmatrix}$

$(\boldsymbol{AB})^{-1} = \begin{bmatrix} 1 & 0 & 0 & 0 \\ 0 & 0 & 0 & 1 \\ 0 & 0 & 1 & 0 \\ 0 & 1 & 0 & 0 \end{bmatrix}$

**60** (a) $\begin{bmatrix} 1 \\ 2 \end{bmatrix}$ (b) $\begin{bmatrix} 1 \\ -4 \\ 0 \end{bmatrix}$ (c) $\begin{bmatrix} -1 \\ 2 \end{bmatrix}$ (d) $\begin{bmatrix} 4 \\ 3 \\ 2 \\ 1 \end{bmatrix}$

**61** $\begin{bmatrix} \cos(-\frac{\pi}{8}) \\ -\sin(-\frac{\pi}{8}) \end{bmatrix}$

**62** $\begin{bmatrix} -\mathrm{j} \\ 1 \\ \mathrm{j} \end{bmatrix}$

**63** $\frac{1}{12}\begin{bmatrix} -7 & -6 & 5 \\ 2 & 0 & 2 \\ 1 & -6 & 1 \end{bmatrix}$

$x = 2, y = 1, z = 2$

**64** $\alpha = 1 \quad x = \lambda \quad y = 5\lambda \quad z = 7\lambda$
$\alpha = -6 \quad x = \mu \quad y = -2\mu \quad z = 0$

**65** $-6, -3, -2$

**66** (a) $a = 0$ (b) $\frac{1}{9}\begin{bmatrix} 1 \\ 7 \\ 6 \end{bmatrix}$ (c) $\begin{bmatrix} \lambda \\ \lambda \\ \lambda \end{bmatrix}$ (d) $\begin{bmatrix} -2 \\ 1 \\ 3 \end{bmatrix}$

**67** $\begin{bmatrix} 0.1896 & -0.0604 & -0.0167 & 0.0167 & -0.0021 & -0.0021 \\ -0.0604 & 0.2088 & -0.0551 & -0.0218 & 0.0171 & -0.0021 \\ -0.0167 & -0.0551 & 0.2103 & -0.0564 & -0.0218 & 0.0167 \\ 0.0167 & -0.0218 & -0.0564 & 0.2103 & -0.0551 & -0.0167 \\ -0.0021 & 0.0171 & -0.0218 & -0.0551 & 0.2088 & -0.0604 \\ -0.0021 & -0.0021 & 0.0167 & -0.0167 & -0.0604 & 0.1896 \end{bmatrix}$

$\begin{bmatrix} 0.1875 \\ -0.0625 \\ 0 \\ 0 \\ -0.0625 \\ 0.1875 \end{bmatrix}$

**68** $a = u_1 \quad b = (-u_1 + u_2)/p \quad c = (-u_1 + u_3)/q$
$d = (u_1 - u_2 - u_3 + u_4)/pq$

**69** $x = 0.5889u \quad y = 0.4222u \quad z = 0.2222u$

**70** $a = -0.4011 \quad b = 1 \quad c = -0.5825$
$f(1) = 1.4345$

**71** $y_1 = 1.8936 \quad y_2 = 4.6809 \quad y_3 = 8.1489 \quad y_4 = 10.7660$

**72** (a) $\begin{bmatrix} -3 \\ 0 \\ 2 \end{bmatrix}$ (b) $\begin{bmatrix} -3 \\ 2 \\ 4 \end{bmatrix}$ (c) $\begin{bmatrix} -\frac{3}{25} \\ \frac{1}{150} \\ \frac{2}{75} \end{bmatrix}$

**73** $x = 1 \quad y = 2 \quad z = 2 \quad t = 3$

**74** $x = -0.0833 \quad y = 0.7083 \quad z = 1.9167 \quad t = 2.9583$

**75** (a) $\begin{bmatrix} 1.1602 \\ -0.0515 \\ 0.0065 \end{bmatrix}$ (b) $\begin{bmatrix} 2.6844 \\ 0.0234 \\ 2.3569 \end{bmatrix}$ (c) $\begin{bmatrix} -1.3424 \\ 1.2860 \\ 2.4458 \\ 0.5511 \end{bmatrix}$

**76** $\begin{bmatrix} -74.17 \\ -25.54 \\ 140.11 \end{bmatrix}$, det = 0.002 725 $\quad \begin{bmatrix} -142.53 \\ -50.52 \\ 262.77 \end{bmatrix}$, det = 0.001 453

**78** $y_1 = 1.028 \quad y_2 = 4.004 \quad y_3 = 8.993 \quad y_4 = 11.329$

**79** 4.5, 8, 10.5, 12, 12.5

**80** $$\left|\frac{E_0}{Z_3}\right| = \sqrt{\left(\frac{L}{C}\right)\frac{1}{\alpha}[(2-\alpha^2)^2(1-\tfrac{1}{2}\alpha^2)^2 - 2(2-\alpha^2)(1-\tfrac{1}{2}\alpha^2) - (1-\tfrac{1}{2}\alpha^2)^2 + 1]}$$
where $\alpha^2 = LC\omega^2$

**81** Solution: 1, 2, 2, 3
After 5 iterations: 0.989, 1.99, 1.98, 3.00

**82** Solution: −0.083, 0.708, 1.917, 2.958
After 3 iterations: −0.189, 0.634, 1.868, 2.920

**83** (a) 0.8 (b) 1.1 (c) no convergence

**84** $\begin{bmatrix} 10 \\ 20 \\ -30 \end{bmatrix}$

There is no convergence in 50 iterations, even from a starting value of $\begin{bmatrix} 10.1 \\ 19.9 \\ -29.9 \end{bmatrix}$

**85** $I_1 = 0.5172$, $I_2 = 0.4914$, $I_3 = 0.8017$

**86** 0.1685, 0.3258, 0.5282, 0.7188, 0.9563, 1.0063, 0.8063, 0.6064, 0.4059, 0.2079

**87** (a) 2, 2, [2/3, −1/3] (b) 1, 2, inconsistent
(c) 2, 2, [1, −*t*, *t*] (d) 2, 2, [2 − *t*, 1, *t*]
(e) 2, 3, inconsistent (f) 4, 4, [0, 1/3, 0, 1]

**88** $\alpha = 2$ gives 1, 2 and inconsistent equations; $\alpha = -1$ gives 1, 1 solution $[1 - 2t, t]$; otherwise solution is $\left[\dfrac{-\alpha}{\alpha - 2}, \dfrac{(\alpha - 1)\alpha}{\alpha - 2}\right]$

**89** (a) 2 (b) 3

**90** (a) Rank = 2, $(-2 + t, 5 - 2t, t)$
(b) Rank = 2, no solution

**91** Rank = 3, rank = 3; $(\mu, -1, 1, -\mu)$

**92** (a) $x = -1$, $y = \frac{1}{3}(2 - 4\mu)$, $z = \mu$
(b) No solution
(c) $x = \frac{1}{11}(-9 - 45\lambda + 13\mu)$, $y = \frac{1}{11}(5 - 8\lambda + 5\mu)$
$z = \lambda$, $t = \mu$
(d) Unique solution $x = -1$, $y = -1$, $z = 1$

**94** Rank = 4 implies points not coplanar; rank = 3 implies the points lie on a plane; rank = 2 implies the points lie on a line; rank = 1 implies the four points are identical

**96** (a) $\lambda^2 - 4\lambda + 3$, eigenvalues 3, 1
(b) $\lambda^2 - 3\lambda + 1$, eigenvalues 2.618, 0.382
(c) $\lambda^3 - 6\lambda^2 + 11\lambda - 6$, eigenvalues 3, 2, 1
(d) $\lambda^3 - 6\lambda^2 + 9\lambda - 4$, eigenvalues 4, 1, 1
(e) $\lambda^3 - 12\lambda^2 + 40\lambda - 35$, eigenvalues 7, 3.618, 1.382
(f) $\lambda^2 - (2 + a)\lambda + 1 + 2a$, eigenvalues $1 + \frac{1}{2}a \pm \frac{1}{2}\sqrt{(a^2 - 4a)}$

**97** (a) 2, 0; $\begin{bmatrix} 1 \\ 1 \end{bmatrix}, \begin{bmatrix} 1 \\ -1 \end{bmatrix}$ (b) 4, −1; $\begin{bmatrix} 2 \\ 3 \end{bmatrix}, \begin{bmatrix} -1 \\ 1 \end{bmatrix}$

(c) 9, 3, −3; $\begin{bmatrix} -1 \\ 2 \\ 2 \end{bmatrix}, \begin{bmatrix} 2 \\ 2 \\ -1 \end{bmatrix}, \begin{bmatrix} 2 \\ -1 \\ 2 \end{bmatrix}$

(d) 3, 2, 1; $\begin{bmatrix} 2 \\ 2 \\ 1 \end{bmatrix}, \begin{bmatrix} 1 \\ 1 \\ 0 \end{bmatrix}, \begin{bmatrix} 0 \\ 2 \\ -1 \end{bmatrix}$

(e) 14, 7, −7; $\begin{bmatrix} 2 \\ 6 \\ 3 \end{bmatrix}, \begin{bmatrix} 6 \\ -3 \\ 2 \end{bmatrix}, \begin{bmatrix} 3 \\ 2 \\ -6 \end{bmatrix}$

(f) 2, 1, −1; $\begin{bmatrix} 1 \\ -1 \\ -1 \end{bmatrix}, \begin{bmatrix} 1 \\ 0 \\ -1 \end{bmatrix}, \begin{bmatrix} 1 \\ 2 \\ -7 \end{bmatrix}$

(g) 5, 3, 1; $\begin{bmatrix} -2 \\ -3 \\ 1 \end{bmatrix}, \begin{bmatrix} 1 \\ -1 \\ 0 \end{bmatrix}, \begin{bmatrix} 0 \\ -1 \\ 1 \end{bmatrix}$

(h) 4, 3, 1; $\begin{bmatrix} 2 \\ -1 \\ -1 \end{bmatrix}, \begin{bmatrix} 2 \\ -1 \\ 0 \end{bmatrix}, \begin{bmatrix} 4 \\ 1 \\ -2 \end{bmatrix}$

**98** Eigenvalues 3, 3 eigenvectors [1, 0], [0, 1]
Eigenvalues 3, 3 eigenvector [0, 1]
Eigenvalues 5/2, 5/2 eigenvector [1, −2]
Eigenvalues 0, 0 eigenvector [1, −2]

**99** (a) 5, 1, 1; $\begin{bmatrix} 1 \\ 1 \\ 1 \end{bmatrix}, \begin{bmatrix} -2 \\ 1 \\ 0 \end{bmatrix}, \begin{bmatrix} -1 \\ 0 \\ 1 \end{bmatrix}$

(b) 2, 2, −1; $\begin{bmatrix} -1 \\ 1 \\ 0 \end{bmatrix}, \begin{bmatrix} 8 \\ 1 \\ 3 \end{bmatrix}$

(c) 2, 2, 1; $\begin{bmatrix} 3 \\ 1 \\ -2 \end{bmatrix}, \begin{bmatrix} 4 \\ 1 \\ -3 \end{bmatrix}$

(d) 2, 1, 1; $\begin{bmatrix} 2 \\ 1 \\ 2 \end{bmatrix}, \begin{bmatrix} 0 \\ -2 \\ 1 \end{bmatrix}, \begin{bmatrix} 1 \\ 3 \\ 0 \end{bmatrix}$

**100** One eigenvector $\begin{bmatrix} -3 \\ 1 \\ 1 \end{bmatrix}$

**101** 2, 1, 1; $\begin{bmatrix} -1 \\ 1 \\ 1 \end{bmatrix}, \begin{bmatrix} -1 \\ 1 \\ 0 \end{bmatrix}, \begin{bmatrix} 1 \\ 0 \\ 1 \end{bmatrix}$

**102** 3, [1, 0, 0, 1]; 2, [0, 1, 0, 0] and [0, 0, 1, 0]; −1, [−1, 0, 0, 1]

**105** 3, 2, −6; $\begin{bmatrix} -1 \\ 1 \\ 1 \end{bmatrix}, \begin{bmatrix} 0 \\ 1 \\ -1 \end{bmatrix}, \begin{bmatrix} 2 \\ 1 \\ 1 \end{bmatrix}$

**106** $\begin{bmatrix} 1 \\ -1 \\ 0 \end{bmatrix}$

## 5.9 Review exercises

**1** (a) $\begin{bmatrix} 12 & 18 & -40 \\ 0 & 0 & 8 \\ 0 & 0 & 4 \end{bmatrix}\begin{bmatrix} 12 & 0 & 0 \\ 18 & 0 & 0 \\ -40 & 8 & 4 \end{bmatrix}$

(b) $\begin{bmatrix} 8 & 9 & -7 \\ 0 & 2 & 0 \\ 0 & 0 & 5 \end{bmatrix}\begin{bmatrix} 12 & 12 & -6 \\ 0 & 4 & 0 \\ 0 & 0 & 16 \end{bmatrix}$

$\begin{bmatrix} 4 & 14 & -3 \\ 0 & 0 & 5 \\ 0 & 0 & 4 \end{bmatrix}$

**2** $\lambda = -1, \mu = 2$
$\lambda = 2, \mu = -1$

**3** Normal strain $= \begin{bmatrix} 3 \\ -3 \\ 3\sqrt{2} \end{bmatrix}$

Shear strain = 0

**4** $(\alpha - \beta)(\beta - \gamma)(\gamma - \alpha)(\alpha + \beta + \gamma)$

**5** $\theta = 1$: $(1 + 2\alpha, -3\alpha, \alpha)$
$\theta = 2$: $(2\alpha, 1 - 3\alpha, \alpha)$

**6** $\boldsymbol{A}^2 = \begin{bmatrix} 1 & 3 & 2 \\ 0 & 5 & 2 \\ 2 & -2 & 1 \end{bmatrix}$ $\boldsymbol{A}^3 = \begin{bmatrix} 3 & 6 & 5 \\ 6 & 7 & 8 \\ -4 & 1 & -3 \end{bmatrix}$

$\boldsymbol{A}^{-1} = \begin{bmatrix} 3 & -2 & -1 \\ 2 & -1 & 0 \\ -4 & 3 & 1 \end{bmatrix}$ $X = \begin{bmatrix} -11 \\ -1 \\ 15 \end{bmatrix}$

**7** (a) $\boldsymbol{P}^{\mathrm{T}} = \frac{1}{3}\begin{bmatrix} 2 & -2 & -1 \\ 1 & 2 & -2 \\ 2 & 1 & 2 \end{bmatrix}$, the solution $\boldsymbol{x} = \boldsymbol{P}^{-1}\boldsymbol{b}$ exists

(b) $\boldsymbol{E} = \begin{bmatrix} I_x - \dfrac{Q_x^2}{A} & I_{xy} - \dfrac{Q_xQ_y}{A} & 0 \\ I_{xy} - \dfrac{Q_xQ_y}{A} & I_y - \dfrac{Q_y^2}{A} & 0 \\ 0 & 0 & A \end{bmatrix}$

**8** (a) $\boldsymbol{B} = \begin{bmatrix} 8 & -10 & 3 \\ 3 & -4 & 1 \\ -1 & 0 & 0 \end{bmatrix}$

(b) $k = 8.2316$, $k = -1.9316$

**9** (a) $\begin{bmatrix} -2 & -3 & -1 \\ -8 & -1 & 29 \\ -6 & 2 & 8 \end{bmatrix}, -22, \frac{1}{22}\begin{bmatrix} 2 & 3 & 1 \\ 8 & 1 & -29 \\ 6 & -2 & -8 \end{bmatrix},$

$z = 2, y = 1, x = 2$

(b) $\boldsymbol{Y} = \begin{bmatrix} 8 & 1 & 9 \\ 18 & 3 & -35 \\ 8 & -4 & -6 \end{bmatrix}$

(c) $\boldsymbol{Z} = \begin{bmatrix} 6 & 11 & 3 \\ 15 & 2 & -59 \\ 16 & -7 & -16 \end{bmatrix}$

**10** (a) 3, 0, 2, 1; det = 12
(b) 1, 2, 3, 4

**11** 1, 2, 3

**12** If $c \neq 0$ then rank = 2
if $c = 0$ then rank = 1

**13** $\boldsymbol{a} = \begin{bmatrix} 0.0051 \\ 0.9712 \\ -0.3931 \\ -0.0760 \\ 0.0283 \end{bmatrix}$ $f(2) = 0.2200$ $f(3.5) = -0.4228$

**14** $a = 0.4424, b = -1.5037, c = 1.5023, d = -0.0611$
max at $x = 0.74, f = 0.4065$

**15** rank $\boldsymbol{B} = 2$, $\boldsymbol{AA}^{\mathrm{T}} = \boldsymbol{I}$, $\boldsymbol{A}^{-1} = \boldsymbol{A}^{\mathrm{T}}$
$x_1 = 2.444$, $x_2 = -2.556$, $x_3 = -1.222$

**16** (b) $x_1 = 44$, $x_2 = -48$, $x_3 = -39$, $x_4 = 33$

**17** (a) $\begin{bmatrix} 0 \\ -1 \\ 2 \end{bmatrix}$ (b) $\begin{bmatrix} -8 \\ -5 \\ \frac{1}{2} \end{bmatrix}$

**18** (a) 4, 3, 2; $\begin{bmatrix} 0.5774 \\ 0.5774 \\ -0.5774 \end{bmatrix}, \begin{bmatrix} 0.1961 \\ 0.5883 \\ -0.7845 \end{bmatrix}, \begin{bmatrix} 0 \\ 0.7071 \\ -0.7071 \end{bmatrix}$

(b) 5, 3, −1; $\begin{bmatrix} 0.2033 \\ 0.6505 \\ 0.7318 \end{bmatrix}, \begin{bmatrix} 0.1374 \\ 0.8242 \\ 0.5494 \end{bmatrix}, \begin{bmatrix} -0.4472 \\ -0.8944 \\ 0 \end{bmatrix}$

(c) 9, 6, 3; $\frac{1}{3}\begin{bmatrix} -1 \\ 2 \\ 2 \end{bmatrix}, \frac{1}{3}\begin{bmatrix} 2 \\ -1 \\ 2 \end{bmatrix}, \frac{1}{3}\begin{bmatrix} 2 \\ 2 \\ -1 \end{bmatrix}$

**19** $\lambda = 9$ $\alpha = 1$ $\beta = 6$

**20** $\begin{bmatrix} 1 \\ 0 \\ 1 \end{bmatrix}, \begin{bmatrix} 0 \\ 1 \\ 0 \end{bmatrix}, \begin{bmatrix} -1 \\ 0 \\ 1 \end{bmatrix}$

**21** After 100 iterations rounded down to the nearest integer

| | | |
|---|---|---|
| 70 | 98 | 136 |
| 56 | 78 | 109 |
| 42 | 59 | 81 |
| 21 | 29 | 40 |

and the largest eigenvalues are 0.9963, 0.9996, 1.0029

**22** (a) 3, 1; $\begin{bmatrix} 0.7071 \\ 0.7071 \end{bmatrix}, \begin{bmatrix} 0.7071 \\ -0.7071 \end{bmatrix}$

(b) 0.8794, −1.3473, −2.5321;
$\begin{bmatrix} 0.4491 \\ 0.8440 \\ 0.2931 \end{bmatrix}, \begin{bmatrix} 0.8440 \\ -0.2931 \\ -0.4491 \end{bmatrix}, \begin{bmatrix} 0.2931 \\ -0.4491 \\ 0.8440 \end{bmatrix}$

**26** $E_1 = 4E_2 + 3I_2$; $I_1 = 3E_2 + \frac{5}{2}I_2$

# Fourier Series

# 23 Fourier series

| Chapter 23 | Contents |
|---|---|

## 23.1 Introduction

The ability to analyse waveforms of various types is an important engineering skill. Fourier analysis provides a set of mathematical tools which enable the engineer to break down a wave into its various frequency components. It is then possible to predict the effect a particular waveform may have from knowledge of the effects of its individual frequency components. Often an engineer finds it useful to think of a signal in terms of its frequency components rather than in terms of its time domain representation. This alternative view is called a frequency domain representation. It is particularly useful when trying to understand the effect of a filter on a signal. Filters are used extensively in many areas of engineering. In particular, communication engineers use them in signal reception equipment for filtering out unwanted frequencies in the received signal; that is, removing the transmission signal to leave the audio signal. We shall begin this chapter by reviewing the essential properties of waves before describing how breaking down into frequency components is achieved.

## 23.2 Periodic waveforms

In this chapter we shall be concerned with periodic functions, especially sine and cosine functions. Let us recall some important definitions and properties already discussed in Section 3.6. The function $f(t) = A\sin(\omega t + \phi) = A\sin\omega\left(t + \frac{\phi}{\omega}\right)$ is a sine wave of amplitude $A$, angular frequency $\omega$, frequency $\frac{\omega}{2\pi}$, period $T = \frac{2\pi}{\omega}$ and phase angle $\phi$. The time displacement is defined to be $\frac{\phi}{\omega}$. These quantities are shown in Figure 23.1.

Similar remarks can be made about the function $A\cos(\omega t + \phi)$ and together the sine and cosine functions form a class of functions known as **sinusoids** or **harmonics**. It will be particularly important for what follows that you have mastered the skills of integrating these functions. The following results can be found in Table 13.1:

$$\int \sin n\omega t \, dt = -\frac{\cos n\omega t}{n\omega} + c \qquad \int \cos n\omega t \, dt = \frac{\sin n\omega t}{n\omega} + c$$

for $n = \pm 1, \pm 2, \ldots$

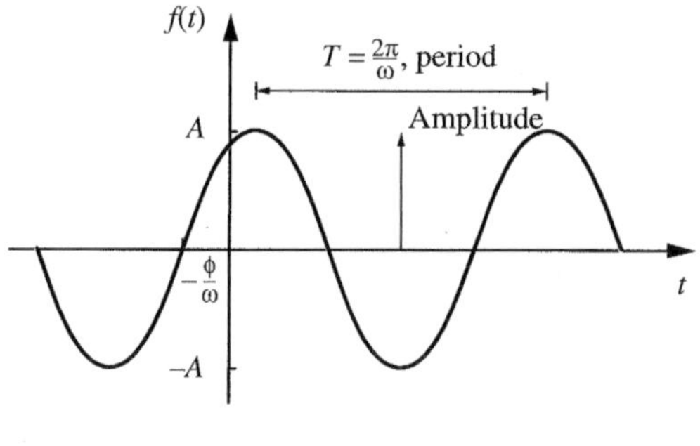


**Figure 23.1**
The function:
$f(t) = A\sin(\omega t + \phi)$.

Sometimes a function occurs as the sum of a number of different sine or cosine components such as

$$f(t) = 2\sin\omega_1 t + 0.8\sin 2\omega_1 t + 0.7\sin 4\omega_1 t \tag{23.1}$$

The r.h.s. of Equation (23.1) is a **linear combination** of sinusoids.

Note in particular that the angular frequencies of all components in Equation (23.1) are integer multiples of the angular frequency $\omega_1$. Functions like these can easily be plotted using a graphics calculator or computer graph plotting package. The component with the lowest frequency, or largest period, is $2\sin\omega_1 t$. The quantity $\omega_1$ is called the **fundamental angular frequency** and this component is called the **fundamental** or **first harmonic**. The component with angular frequency $2\omega_1$ is called the second harmonic and so on. In what follows all angular frequencies are integer multiples of the fundamental angular frequency as in Equation (23.1). A consequence of this is that the resulting function, $f(t)$, is periodic and has the same frequency as the fundamental. Some harmonics may be missing. For example, in Equation (23.1) the third harmonic is missing. In some cases the first harmonic may be missing. For example, if

$$f(t) = \cos 2\omega_1 t + 0.5\cos 3\omega_1 t + 0.4\cos 4\omega_1 t + \cdots$$

all angular frequencies are integer multiples of the fundamental angular frequency $\omega_1$, which is missing. Nevertheless, $f(t)$ has the same angular frequency as the fundamental. A common value for $\omega_1$ is $100\pi$ as this corresponds to a frequency of 50 Hz, the frequency of the UK mains supply.

**Example 23.1** Describe the frequency and amplitude characteristics of the different harmonic components of the function

$$f(t) = \cos 20\pi t + 0.6\cos 60\pi t - 0.2\sin 140\pi t$$

**Solution** The fundamental angular frequency is $20\pi$ arising through the term $\cos 20\pi t$. This corresponds to a frequency of 10 Hz. This term has amplitude 1. The second, fourth, fifth and sixth harmonics are missing, while the third and seventh have amplitudes 0.6 and 0.2, respectively.

**Example 23.2** If $f(t) = 2\sin t + 3\cos t$, express $f(t)$ as a single sinusoid and hence determine its amplitude and phase.

**Solution** Both terms have angular frequency $\omega = 1$. Recalling the trigonometric identity (Section 3.5)

$$R\cos(\omega t - \theta) = a\cos\omega t + b\sin\omega t$$

where $R = \sqrt{a^2 + b^2}$, $\tan\theta = \dfrac{b}{a}$, we see that in this case $R = \sqrt{3^2 + 2^2} = \sqrt{13}$ and $\tan\theta = \frac{2}{3}$, that is $\theta = 0.59$ radians. Therefore we can express $f(t)$ in the form

$$f(t) = \sqrt{13}\cos(t - 0.59)$$

We see immediately that this is a sinusoid of amplitude $\sqrt{13}$ and phase angle $-0.59$ radians.

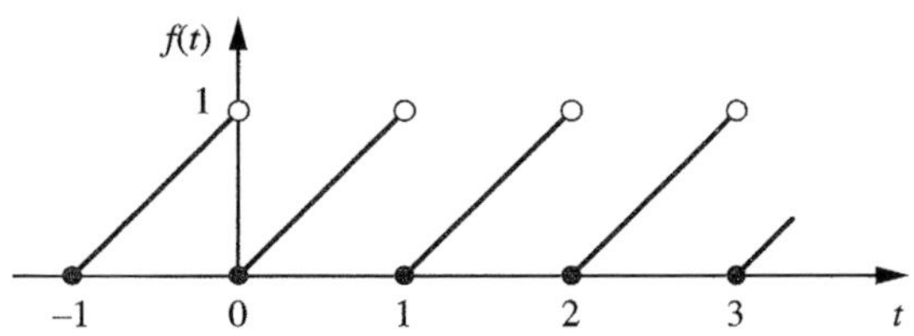


**Figure 23.2** Graph for Example 23.4.

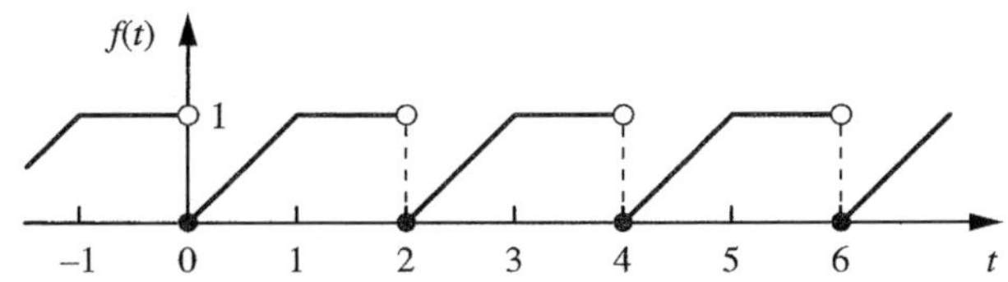


**Figure 23.3** Graph for Example 23.5.

**Example 23.3** Find the amplitude and phase of the fundamental component of the function

$$f(t) = 0.5 \sin \omega_1 t + 1.5 \cos \omega_1 t + 3.5 \sin 2\omega_1 t - 3 \cos 3\omega_1 t$$

**Solution** Contributions to the fundamental component – that is, that with the lowest frequency – come from the terms $0.5 \sin \omega_1 t$ and $1.5 \cos \omega_1 t$ only. To find the amplitude and phase we must express these as a single component. Using the trigonometric identity

$$R \cos(\omega t - \theta) = a \cos \omega t + b \sin \omega t$$

where $R = \sqrt{a^2 + b^2}$, $\tan \theta = \dfrac{b}{a}$, we find

$$R = \sqrt{1.5^2 + 0.5^2} = 1.58$$

$$\tan \theta = \frac{0.5}{1.5} = \frac{1}{3} \qquad \text{that is, } \theta = 0.32 \text{ radians}$$

Therefore the fundamental can be written $1.58 \cos(\omega_1 t - 0.32)$ and has amplitude 1.58 and phase angle $-0.32$ radians.

---

Many other periodic functions arise in engineering applications as well as the more familiar harmonic waves. Remember, to be periodic the function values must repeat at regular intervals known as the period, $T$. The angular frequency $\omega$ is given by $\omega = \dfrac{2\pi}{T}$. To describe a periodic function mathematically it is sufficient to give its equation over one full period and state that period. From this information the complete graph can be drawn as Examples 23.4 and 23.5 show.

**Example 23.4** Sketch the graph of the periodic function defined by

$$f(t) = t \qquad 0 \leqslant t < 1 \qquad \text{period } 1$$

**Solution** To proceed we first sketch the graph on the given interval $0 \leqslant t < 1$ (Figure 23.2), and then use the fact that the function repeats regularly with period 1 to complete the picture.

**Example 23.5** Write down a mathematical expression for the function whose graph is shown in Figure 23.3.

**Solution** We first note that the interval over which the function repeats itself is 2; that is, period $= 2$. It is then sufficient to describe the function over any interval of length 2. The simplest interval to take is $0 \leqslant t < 2$. We note in this example that a single formula is insufficient to describe the function for $0 \leqslant t < 2$ since different behaviour is exhibited in the two intervals $0 \leqslant t < 1$ and $1 \leqslant t < 2$. For $0 \leqslant t < 1$ the function is a ramp with slope 1 and passes through the origin, that is it has equation $f(t) = t$. For $1 \leqslant t < 2$ the function value remains constant at 1. Therefore this periodic function can be described by the expression

$$f(t) = \begin{cases} t & 0 \leqslant t < 1 \\ 1 & 1 \leqslant t < 2 \end{cases} \qquad \text{period } 2$$

## Exercises 23.2

1 Describe the frequency and amplitude characteristics of the different harmonic components of the following waveforms:

(a) $f(t) = 3\sin 100\pi t - 4\sin 200\pi t + 0.7\sin 300\pi t$

(b) $f(t) = \sin 40t - 0.5\cos 120t + 0.3\cos 240t$

Use a graph plotting computer package or graphics calculator to graph these waveforms.

2 Express each of the following functions as a single sinusoid and hence find their amplitudes and phases.

(a) $f(t) = 2\cos t - 3\sin t$

(b) $f(t) = 0.5\cos t + 3.2\sin t$

(c) $f(t) = 3\cos 3t$

(d) $f(t) = 2\cos 2t + 3\sin 2t$

3 Sketch the graphs of the following functions.

(a) $f(t) = t^2$, $-1 \leqslant t \leqslant 1$, period 2

(b) $f(t) = \begin{cases} 0 & 0 \leqslant t < \pi/2 \\ \sin t & \pi/2 \leqslant t \leqslant \pi \end{cases}$ period $\pi$

(c) $f(t) = \begin{cases} -t & -2 \leqslant t < 0 \\ t & 0 \leqslant t < 1 \end{cases}$ period 3

4 Write down mathematical expressions to describe the functions whose graphs are shown in Figure 23.4.

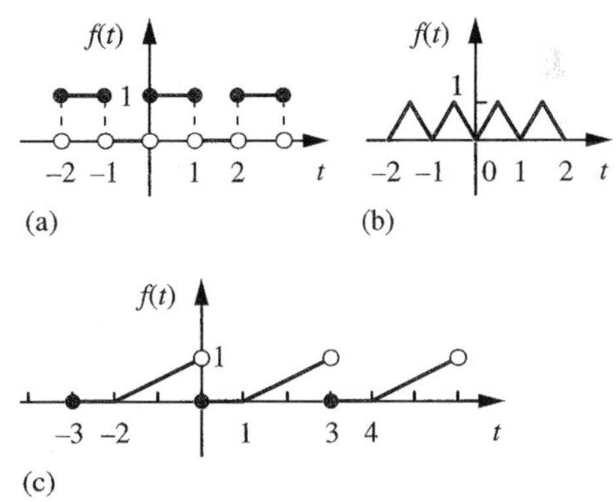


**Figure 23.4**

## Solutions

1 (a) Fundamental frequency is 50 Hz, amplitude 3. Second harmonic has frequency of 100 Hz, amplitude 4. Third harmonic has frequency of 150 Hz, amplitude 0.7.

(b) Fundamental frequency is $\frac{20}{\pi}$Hz, amplitude 1. Second harmonic is missing. Third harmonic has frequency of $\frac{60}{\pi}$Hz, amplitude 0.5. Fourth and fifth harmonics are missing. Sixth harmonic has frequency of $\frac{120}{\pi}$Hz, amplitude 0.3.

2 (a) $\sqrt{13}\cos(t + 0.983)$; amplitude $= \sqrt{13}$, phase $= 0.983$

(b) $3.24\cos(t + 4.867)$; amplitude $= 3.24$, phase $= 4.867$

(c) $3\cos 3t$; amplitude $= 3$, phase $= 0$

(d) $\sqrt{13}\cos(2t - 0.983)$; amplitude $= \sqrt{13}$, phase $= -0.983$

4 (a) $f(t) = \begin{cases} 1 & 0 \leqslant t \leqslant 1 \\ 0 & 1 < t < 2 \end{cases}$ period $= 2$

(b) $f(t) = \begin{cases} 2t & 0 \leqslant t \leqslant 1/2 \\ 2 - 2t & 1/2 < t < 1 \end{cases}$

period $=1$

(c) $f(t) = \begin{cases} 0 & 0 \leqslant t \leqslant 1 \\ t/2 - 1/2 & 1 < t < 3 \end{cases}$

period $=3$

## 23.3 Odd and even functions

The functions $\sin t$ and $\cos t$ each possess certain properties which can be generalized to other functions. Figure 23.5 shows the graph of $f(t) = \cos t$. It is obvious from the graph that the function value at a negative $t$ value, say $-\frac{\pi}{4}$, will be the same as the function value at the corresponding positive $t$ value, in this case $+\frac{\pi}{4}$. This is true because the graph is symmetrical about the vertical axis. We can therefore state that for any value of $t$, $\cos(-t) = \cos t$.

More generally, any function with the property that $f(t) = f(-t)$ for any value of its argument, $t$, is said to be an **even** function.

If $f(t) = f(-t)$ then $f$ is an even function.

In particular, the set of functions $\cos n\omega t$, for any integer $n$, is even. The graphs of all

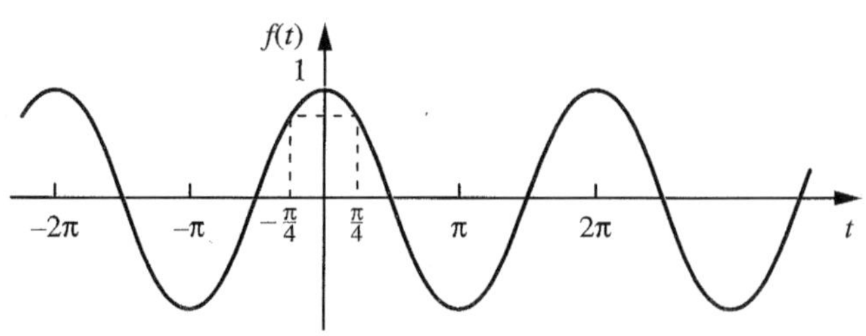


**Figure 23.5** The function: $f(t) = \cos t$.

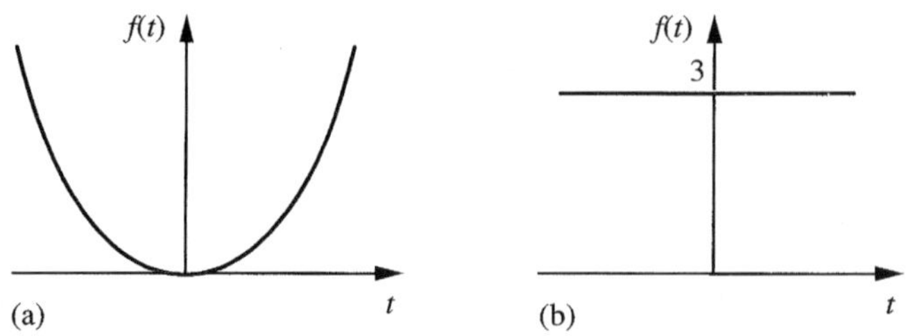


**Figure 23.6** Examples of even functions: (a) $f(t) = t^2$; (b) $f(t) = 3$.

even functions are symmetrical about the vertical axis – or equivalently, the graph on the left of the origin can be obtained by reflecting in the vertical axis that on the right. Some other examples of even functions are shown in Figure 23.6.

Sketching a graph shows up the required symmetry immediately. However, even functions can be identified by an algebraic approach as shown in Example 23.6. Given any function $f(t)$, we examine $f(-t)$ to see if $f(t) = f(-t)$.

**Example 23.6** Show that $f(t) = t^2$ is even.

**Solution** We can argue as follows. If

$$f(t) = t^2$$

then

$$\begin{aligned} f(-t) &= (-t)^2 \\ &= t^2 \\ &= f(t) \end{aligned}$$

so that $f(t)$ is even, by definition.

**Example 23.7** Test whether or not the function $f(t) = 4t^3$ is even.

**Solution** If

$$f(t) = 4t^3$$

then

$$\begin{aligned} f(-t) &= 4(-t)^3 \\ &= -4t^3 \\ &= -f(t) \end{aligned}$$

so that $f(-t)$ is not equal to $f(t)$ and therefore the given function is not even.

---

Let us turn now to the graph of $f(t) = \sin t$ in Figure 23.7. It is obvious from the graph that the function value at a negative $t$ value, say $-\frac{\pi}{4}$, will not be the same as the function value at the corresponding positive $t$ value, in this case $+\frac{\pi}{4}$. This graph is not symmetrical about the vertical axis. However, we can state something else. The function value at a negative $t$ value is minus the function value at the corresponding positive $t$ value. For example, $\sin\left(-\frac{\pi}{4}\right) = -\sin\left(\frac{\pi}{4}\right)$. In fact, for all values of $t$ we

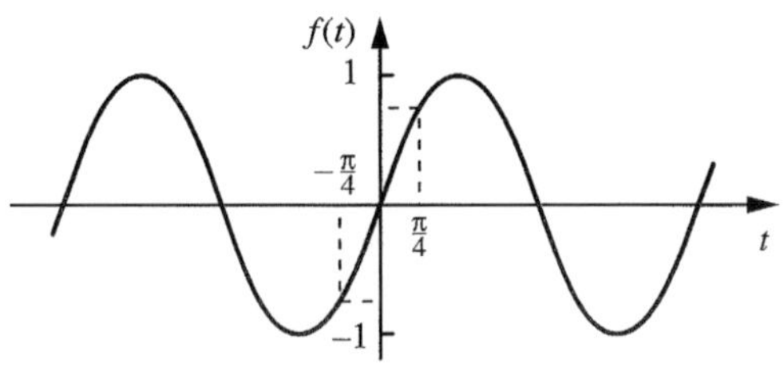


**Figure 23.7** The function: $f(t) = \sin t$.

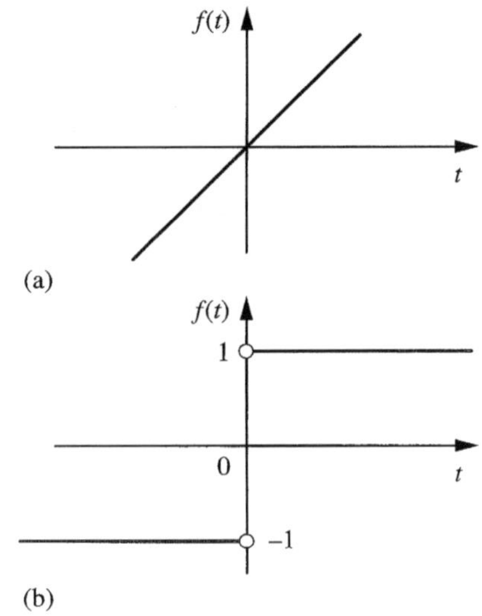


**Figure 23.8** Examples of odd functions: (a) $f(t) = t$; (b) $f(t) = \begin{cases} 1 & t > 0 \\ -1 & t < 0. \end{cases}$

can state that $\sin(-t) = -\sin t$. More generally, any function with the property that $f(-t) = -f(t)$ for all values of its argument, $t$, is said to be an **odd** function.

If $f(-t) = -f(t)$ then $f$ is an odd function.

In particular, the set of functions $\sin n\omega t$, for any integer $n$, is odd. In Example 23.7, $f(t) = 4t^3$, we found that $f(-t) = -f(t)$ so this function is odd. The graph of an odd function can be obtained by reflection first in the horizontal axis and then in the vertical axis. Some more examples of odd functions are shown in Figure 23.8.

There are some functions that are neither odd nor even – for example, the exponential function (see Chapter 2).

**Example 23.8** Show that any function, $f(t)$, can be expressed as the sum of an odd component and an even component.

**Solution** We can write

$$f(t) = f(t) + \frac{f(-t)}{2} - \frac{f(-t)}{2}$$
$$= \frac{f(t)}{2} + \frac{f(t)}{2} + \frac{f(-t)}{2} - \frac{f(-t)}{2}$$

Rearranging gives

$$f(t) = \frac{f(t) + f(-t)}{2} + \frac{f(t) - f(-t)}{2}$$

Now it is easy to check that the first term on the r.h.s. is even and the second term is odd, so that we have expressed $f(t)$ as the sum of an even and an odd component as required.

**Example 23.9** Show that the product of two even functions is itself an even function. Determine whether the product of two odd functions is even or odd. Is the product of an even function and an odd function even or odd?

**Solution** If $f(t)$ and $g(t)$ are even then $f(-t) = f(t)$ and $g(-t) = g(t)$. Let $P(t) = f(t)g(t)$ be the product of $f$ and $g$. Then

$$\begin{aligned} P(-t) &= f(-t)g(-t) && \text{by definition} \\ &= f(t)g(t) && \text{since } f \text{ and } g \text{ are even} \\ &= P(t) \end{aligned}$$

Therefore, $P(-t) = P(t)$ and so the product $f(t)g(t)$ is itself an even function. On the other hand, if $f(t)$ and $g(t)$ are both odd we find

$$\begin{aligned} P(-t) &= f(-t)g(-t) \\ &= (-f(t))(-g(t)) \\ &= f(t)g(t) \\ &= P(t) \end{aligned}$$

so that the product $f(t)g(t)$ is even.

If $f(t)$ is even and $g(t)$ is odd, we find

$$\begin{aligned} P(-t) &= f(-t)g(-t) \\ &= f(t)(-g(t)) \\ &= -f(t)g(t) \\ &= -P(t) \end{aligned}$$

so the product is an odd function. These rules are obviously analogous to the rules for multiplying positive and negative numbers.

---

The results of Example 23.9 are summarized thus:

(even) × (even) = even
(odd) × (odd) = even
(even) × (odd) = odd

## 23.3.1 Integral properties of even and odd functions

Consider a typical odd function, $f(t)$, such as that shown in Figure 23.9. Suppose we wish to evaluate $\int_{-a}^{a} f(t)\,dt$ where the interval of integration $[-a, a]$ is symmetrical about the vertical axis. Recall from Chapter 13 that a definite integral can be regarded as the area bounded by the graph of the integrand and the horizontal axis. Areas above the

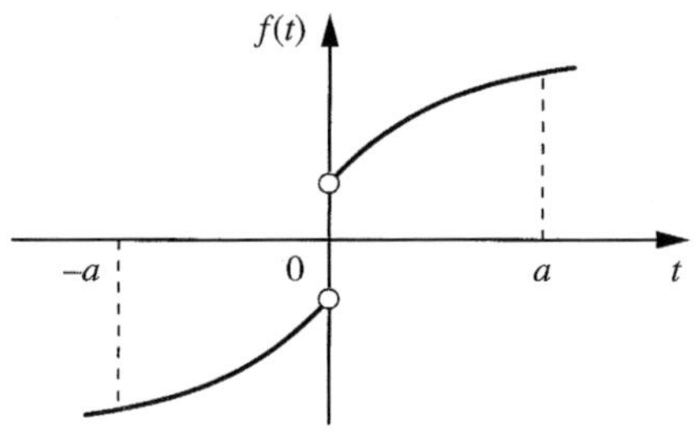


**Figure 23.9** A typical odd function, $f(t)$.

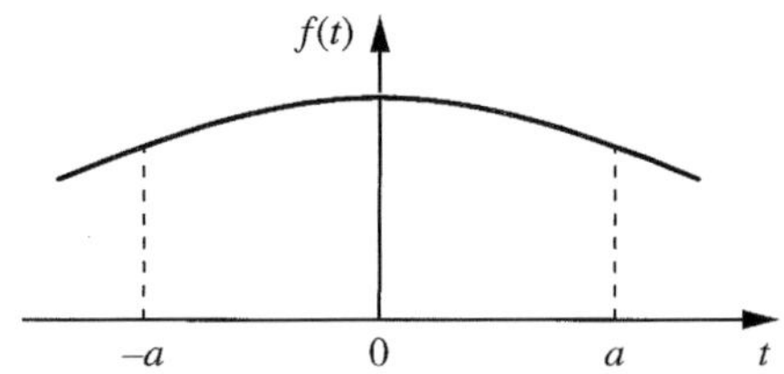


**Figure 23.10** A typical even function, $f(t)$.

horizontal axis are positive while those below are negative. We see that because positive and negative contributions cancel, the integral of an odd function over an interval which is symmetrical about the vertical axis will be 0.

**Example 23.10** Evaluate $\int_{-\pi}^{\pi} t \cos n\omega t \, dt$.

**Solution** The function $t$ is odd. The function $\cos n\omega t$ is even and hence the product $t \cos n\omega t$ is odd. The interval $[-\pi, \pi]$ is symmetrical about the vertical axis and hence the required integral is zero.

---

Consider now a typical even function, $f(t)$, such as that shown in Figure 23.10. Suppose we wish to evaluate $\int_{-a}^{a} f(t) \, dt$. Clearly the area bounded by the graph and the $t$ axis in the interval $[-a, 0]$ is the same as the corresponding area in the interval $[0, a]$. Hence we can write

$$\int_{-a}^{a} f(t) \, dt = 2 \int_{0}^{a} f(t) \, dt$$

**Example 23.11** Evaluate $\int_{-\pi}^{\pi} t \sin t \, dt$.

**Solution** The functions $t$ and $\sin t$ are both odd, and hence their product is even. Therefore, using the fact that the integrand is even we can write

$$\int_{-\pi}^{\pi} t \sin t \, dt = 2 \int_{0}^{\pi} t \sin t \, dt$$

So, integrating by parts,

$$\begin{aligned} 2 \int_{0}^{\pi} t \sin t \, dt &= 2\left( [-t \cos t]_0^{\pi} + \int_{0}^{\pi} \cos t \, dt \right) \\ &= 2((-\pi \cos \pi) - (0) + [\sin t]_0^{\pi}) \\ &= 2\pi \end{aligned}$$

---

## Exercises 23.3

1 Determine by inspection whether each of the functions in Figure 23.11 is odd, even or neither.

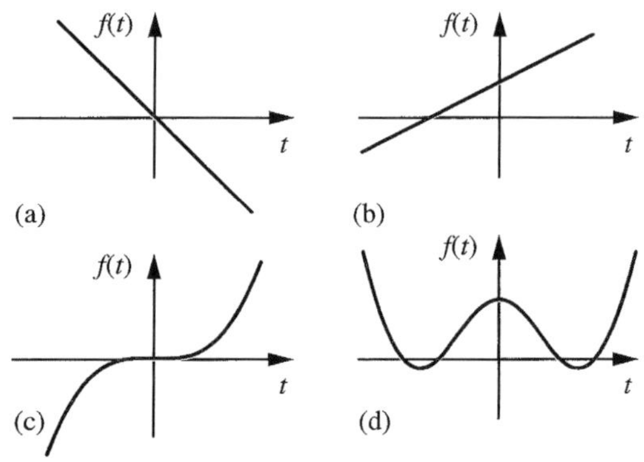


**Figure 23.11** (a) The function: $f(t) = -t$; (b) $f(t) = \frac{t}{2} + 1$; (c) $f(t) = t^3$; (d) $f(t) = \cos t + 0.1t^2$.

2 By using the properties of odd and even functions developed in Example 23.9 state whether the following are odd, even or neither.

(a) $t^3 \sin \omega t$

(b) $t \cos 2t$

(c) $\sin t \, \sin 4t$

(d) $\cos \omega t \, \sin 2\omega t$

(e) $e^t \, \sin t$

3 Evaluate the following integrals using the integral properties of odd and even functions where appropriate.

(a) $\int_{-5}^{5} t^3 \, dt$

(b) $\int_{-5}^{5} t^3 \cos 3t \, dt$

(c) $\int_{-\pi}^{\pi} t^2 \sin t \, dt$

(d) $\int_{-2}^{2} t \cosh 3t \, dt$

(e) $\int_{-1}^{1} |t| \, dt$

(f) $\int_{-1}^{1} t|t| \, dt$

## Solutions

1 (a) odd (b) neither
(c) odd (d) even

2 (a) even (b) odd (c) even
(d) odd (e) neither

3 (a) 0 (b) 0
(c) 0 (d) 0
(e) 1 (f) 0

# 23.4 Orthogonality relations and other useful identities

Recall from Chapter 16 that two functions $f(t)$ and $g(t)$ are said to be orthogonal on the interval $a \leqslant t \leqslant b$ if

$$\int_a^b f(t)g(t) \, dt = 0$$

**Example 23.12** Show that the functions $\cos m\omega t$ and $\cos n\omega t$ with $m, n$ positive integers and $m \neq n$ are orthogonal on the interval $-\frac{\pi}{\omega} \leqslant t \leqslant \frac{\pi}{\omega}$.

**Solution** We must evaluate

$$\int_{-\pi/\omega}^{\pi/\omega} \cos m\omega t \, \cos n\omega t \, dt$$

Using the trigonometric identity $2\cos A \cos B = \cos(A+B) + \cos(A-B)$, we find the integral becomes

$$\frac{1}{2}\int_{-\pi/\omega}^{\pi/\omega} \cos(m+n)\omega t + \cos(m-n)\omega t \, dt$$

$$= \frac{1}{2}\left[\frac{\sin(m+n)\omega t}{(m+n)\omega} + \frac{\sin(m-n)\omega t}{(m-n)\omega}\right]_{-\pi/\omega}^{\pi/\omega}$$

$$= 0$$

since $\sin(m \pm n)\pi = 0$ for all integers $m$, $n$. It was necessary to require $m \neq n$ since otherwise the second quantity in brackets becomes undefined.

Hence $\cos m\omega t$ and $\cos n\omega t$ are orthogonal on the given interval.

---

A number of other functions regularly appearing in work connected with Fourier analysis are orthogonal. The main results together with some other useful integral identities are given in Table 23.1.

**Table 23.1**
Some useful integral identities.

$$\int_0^T \sin\frac{2n\pi t}{T}\, dt = 0 \qquad \text{for all integers } n$$

$$\int_0^T \cos\frac{2n\pi t}{T}\, dt = 0 \qquad n = 1, 2, 3, \ldots$$

$$\int_0^T \cos\frac{2n\pi t}{T}\, dt = T \qquad n = 0$$

$$\int_0^T \cos\frac{2m\pi t}{T}\cos\frac{2n\pi t}{T}\, dt = \begin{cases} 0 & m \neq n \\ T/2 & m = n \neq 0 \end{cases}$$

$$\int_0^T \sin\frac{2m\pi t}{T}\sin\frac{2n\pi t}{T}\, dt = \begin{cases} 0 & m \neq n \\ T/2 & m = n \neq 0 \end{cases}$$

$$\int_0^T \sin\frac{2m\pi t}{T}\cos\frac{2n\pi t}{T}\, dt = 0 \qquad \text{for all integers } m \text{ and } n$$

## 23.5 Fourier series

We have seen that the functions $\sin\omega t$, $\sin 2\omega t$, $\sin 3\omega t, \ldots, \cos\omega t$, $\cos 2\omega t, \ldots$ are periodic. Furthermore, linear combinations of them are also periodic. They are also convenient functions to deal with because they can be easily differentiated, integrated, etc. They also possess another very useful property – that of **completeness**. This means that almost any periodic function can be expressed as a linear combination of them and no additional functions are required to do this. In other words, they can be used as building blocks to construct periodic functions simply by adding particular multiples of them together.

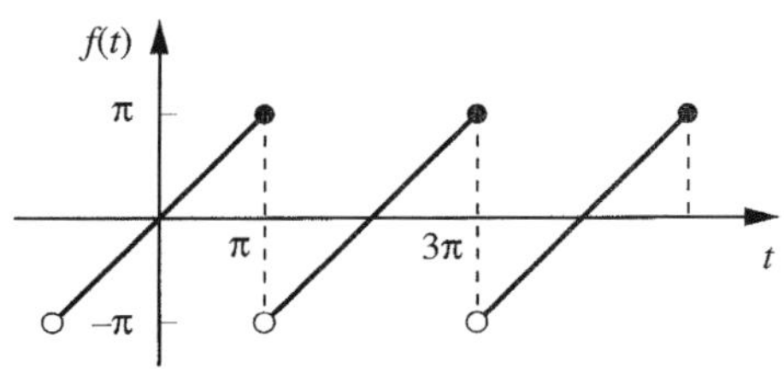


**Figure 23.12**
Sawtooth waveform.

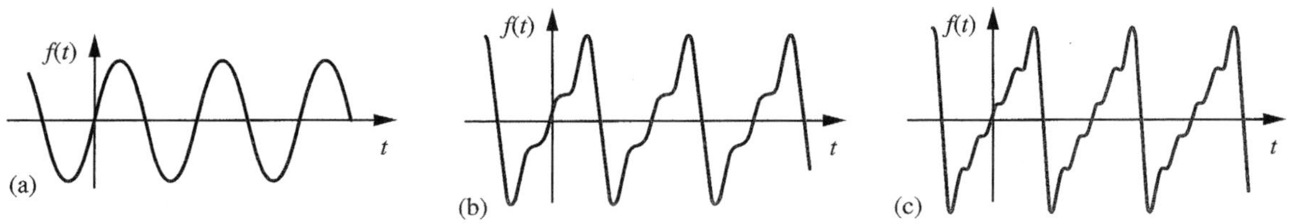


**Figure 23.13** Fourier synthesis of a sawtooth waveform: (a) $f(t) = 2\sin t$; (b) $f(t) = 2(\sin t - \frac{1}{2}\sin 2t + \frac{1}{3}\sin 3t)$; (c) $f(t) = 2(\sin t - \frac{1}{2}\sin 2t + \frac{1}{3}\sin 3t - \frac{1}{4}\sin 4t + \frac{1}{5}\sin 5t)$.

We shall see, for example, that the sawtooth waveform with period $2\pi$, shown in Figure 23.12, is given by the particular combination

$$f(t) = 2\left(\sin t - \tfrac{1}{2}\sin 2t + \tfrac{1}{3}\sin 3t - \tfrac{1}{4}\sin 4t + \tfrac{1}{5}\sin 5t - \cdots\right)$$

This is an infinite series which can be shown to converge for almost all values of $t$ to the function $f$. This means that if any value of $t$ is substituted into the infinite series and the series is summed, the result will be the same as the value of the sawtooth function at that value of $t$. There is an exception: if $t$ is one of the points of discontinuity the infinite series will converge to the mean of the values to its left and right, that is 0.

To obtain a feel for what is happening consider Figure 23.13. Graphs (a), (b) and (c) show the effect of including more and more terms in the series. As more terms are taken we see that the series approaches the desired sawtooth waveform. The process of adding together sinusoids to form a new periodic function is called **Fourier synthesis**. We see that the sawtooth waveform has been expressed as an infinite series of harmonic waves, $\sin t$ being the fundamental or first harmonic, and the rest being waves with frequencies that are integer multiples of the fundamental frequency. This infinite series is called the **Fourier series** representation of $f(t)$ and what we have succeeded in doing is to break down $f(t)$ into its component harmonic waveforms. In this example, only sine waves were required to construct the function. More generally we shall need both sine and cosine waves.

Suppose the function $f(t)$ is defined in the interval $0 < t < T$ and is periodic with period $T$. Then, under certain conditions, its Fourier series is given by

$$f(t) = \frac{a_0}{2} + \sum_{n=1}^{\infty}\left(a_n \cos\frac{2n\pi t}{T} + b_n \sin\frac{2n\pi t}{T}\right) \qquad (23.2)$$

or equivalently

$$f(t) = \frac{a_0}{2} + \sum_{n=1}^{\infty}(a_n \cos n\omega t + b_n \sin n\omega t)$$

where $a_n$ and $b_n$ are constants called the **Fourier coefficients**. These are given by the formulae

$$a_0 = \frac{2}{T}\int_0^T f(t)\,\mathrm{d}t \qquad (23.3)$$

$$a_n = \frac{2}{T}\int_0^T f(t)\cos\frac{2n\pi t}{T}\,\mathrm{d}t \quad \text{for } n \text{ a positive integer} \qquad (23.4)$$

$$b_n = \frac{2}{T}\int_0^T f(t)\sin\frac{2n\pi t}{T}\,\mathrm{d}t \quad \text{for } n \text{ a positive integer} \qquad (23.5)$$

The term $\frac{a_0}{2}$ represents the mean value or d.c. component of the waveform (see Section 15.2). The derivation of these formulae appears in Example 23.16. It is important to point out that the integrals in Equations (23.3), (23.4) and (23.5) can be evaluated over any complete period, for example from $t = -\frac{T}{2}$ to $t = \frac{T}{2}$. Prudent choice of the interval of integration can often save effort. The expression appearing in the r.h.s. of the Fourier representation, Equation (23.2), is an infinite series. We list conditions, often called the Dirichlet conditions, sufficient for the series to converge to the value of the function $f(t)$. The integral $\int |f(t)|\,\mathrm{d}t$ over a complete period must be finite, and $f(t)$ may have no more than a finite number of discontinuities in any finite interval. Fortunately, most signals of interest to engineers satisfy these conditions. At a point of discontinuity the Fourier series converges to the average of the two function values at either side of the discontinuity.

**Example 23.13** Find the Fourier series representation of the function with period $T = \frac{1}{50}$ given by

$$f(t) = \begin{cases} 1 & 0 \leqslant t < 0.01 \\ 0 & 0.01 \leqslant t < 0.02 \end{cases}$$

**Solution** The function $f(t)$ is shown in Figure 23.14. Note that $f(t)$ is defined to be zero between $t = 0.01$ and $t = 0.02$. This means we need only consider $0 \leqslant t < 0.01$. Using

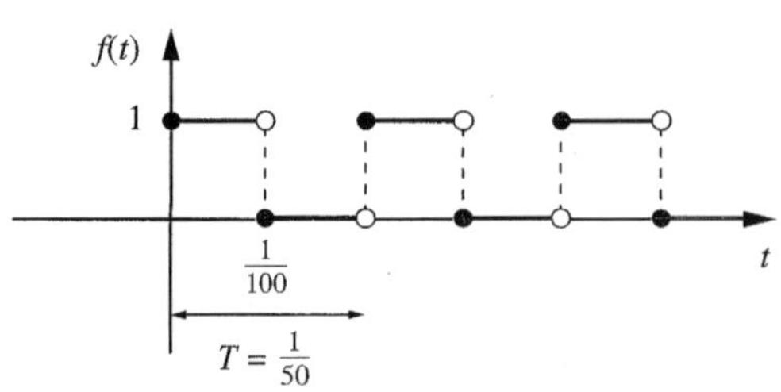


**Figure 23.14** Graph for Example 23.13.

Equations (23.3)–(23.5) we find

$$a_0 = 100\int_0^{0.02} f(t)\,dt = 100\int_0^{0.01} 1\,dt + 100\int_{0.01}^{0.02} 0\,dt$$

$$= 100[t]_0^{0.01} = 1$$

$$a_n = 100\int_0^{0.01} \cos 100n\pi t\,dt = 100\left[\frac{\sin 100n\pi t}{100n\pi}\right]_0^{0.01}$$

$$= 0$$

$$b_n = 100\int_0^{0.01} \sin 100\,n\pi t\,dt = 100\left[\frac{-\cos 100n\pi t}{100n\pi}\right]_0^{0.01}$$

$$= -\frac{1}{n\pi}(\cos n\pi - \cos 0)$$

Noting that $\cos n\pi = (-1)^n$ we find

$$b_n = \frac{1}{n\pi}(1 - (-1)^n)$$

If $n$ is even $b_n = 0$. If $n$ is odd $b_n = \frac{2}{n\pi}$. Therefore the Fourier series representation of $f(t)$ is

$$f(t) = \frac{1}{2} + \frac{2}{\pi}\left(\sin 100\pi t + \frac{\sin 300\pi t}{3} + \frac{\sin 500\pi t}{5} + \cdots\right)$$

The average value of the waveform is $\frac{1}{2}$. This is the zero frequency component or d.c. value. We note that in this example only odd harmonics are present.

**Example 23.14** Find the Fourier series representation of $f(t) = 1 + t$, $-\pi < t \leqslant \pi$, period $2\pi$.

**Solution** As usual we sketch $f(t)$ first as this often provides insight into what follows (see Figure 23.15). Here $T = 2\pi$, $\omega = 1$, and for convenience we shall consider the period

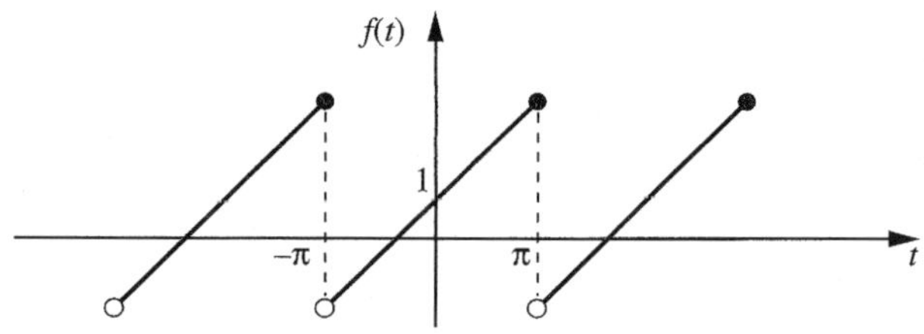


**Figure 23.15** Graph for Example 23.14.

of integration to be $[-\pi, \pi]$. Using Equation (23.3) we find

$$
\begin{aligned}
a_0 &= \frac{1}{\pi}\int_{-\pi}^{\pi} 1 + t \,\mathrm{d}t = \frac{1}{\pi}\left[t + \frac{t^2}{2}\right]_{-\pi}^{\pi} \\
&= \frac{1}{\pi}\left(\left(\pi + \frac{\pi^2}{2}\right) - \left(-\pi + \frac{\pi^2}{2}\right)\right) \\
&= \frac{1}{\pi}(2\pi) \\
&= 2
\end{aligned}
$$

Similarly, using Equation (23.4) we find

$$
a_n = \frac{1}{\pi}\int_{-\pi}^{\pi} (1 + t)\cos nt \,\mathrm{d}t
$$

Integrating by parts gives

$$
\begin{aligned}
a_n &= \frac{1}{\pi}\left(\left[(1+t)\frac{\sin nt}{n}\right]_{-\pi}^{\pi} - \int_{-\pi}^{\pi} \frac{\sin nt}{n}\,\mathrm{d}t\right) \\
&= \frac{1}{\pi}\left(0 + \left[\frac{\cos nt}{n^2}\right]_{-\pi}^{\pi}\right) \qquad \text{since } \sin \pm n\pi = 0 \\
&= \frac{1}{\pi n^2}(\cos n\pi - \cos(-n\pi))
\end{aligned}
$$

but $\cos(-n\pi) = \cos n\pi$ and hence $a_n = 0$, for all positive integers $n$. Using Equation (23.5) we find

$$
\begin{aligned}
b_n &= \frac{1}{\pi}\int_{-\pi}^{\pi} (1 + t)\sin nt \,\mathrm{d}t \\
&= \frac{1}{\pi}\left(\left[-(1+t)\frac{\cos nt}{n}\right]_{-\pi}^{\pi} + \int_{-\pi}^{\pi} \frac{\cos nt}{n}\,\mathrm{d}t\right) \\
&= \frac{1}{\pi}\left(-(1+\pi)\frac{\cos n\pi}{n} + (1-\pi)\frac{\cos(-n\pi)}{n} + \left[\frac{\sin nt}{n^2}\right]_{-\pi}^{\pi}\right) \\
&= \frac{1}{\pi n}(-2\pi \cos n\pi)
\end{aligned}
$$

since $\sin \pm n\pi = 0$. Hence,

$$
b_n = -\frac{2}{n}\cos n\pi = -\frac{2}{n}(-1)^n
$$

We find $b_1 = 2, b_2 = -1, b_3 = \frac{2}{3}, \ldots$. Thus the Fourier series representation is given from Equation (23.2) as

$$f(t) = 1 + 2\sin t - \sin 2t + \tfrac{2}{3}\sin 3t + \cdots$$

which we can write concisely as

$$f(t) = 1 - \sum_{n=1}^{\infty} \frac{2}{n}(-1)^n \sin nt$$

**Example 23.15** Find the Fourier series representation of the function with period $2\pi$ defined by $f(t) = t^2, 0 < t \leqslant 2\pi$.

**Solution** As usual we sketch $f(t)$, as shown in Figure 23.16. Here $T = 2\pi$ and we shall integrate, for convenience, over the interval $[0, 2\pi]$. Using Equation (23.3) we find

$$a_0 = \frac{1}{\pi}\int_0^{2\pi} t^2 \, dt = \frac{1}{\pi}\left[\frac{t^3}{3}\right]_0^{2\pi} = \frac{8\pi^2}{3}$$

Using Equation (23.4) we have

$$a_n = \frac{1}{\pi}\int_0^{2\pi} t^2 \cos nt \, dt$$

Integrating by parts, we find

$$\begin{aligned} a_n &= \frac{1}{\pi}\left(\left[t^2\frac{\sin nt}{n}\right]_0^{2\pi} - \int_0^{2\pi} 2t\frac{\sin nt}{n}\,dt\right) \\ &= -\frac{2}{n\pi}\int_0^{2\pi} t\sin nt\,dt \\ &= -\frac{2}{n\pi}\left(\left[-t\frac{\cos nt}{n}\right]_0^{2\pi} + \int_0^{2\pi}\frac{\cos nt}{n}\,dt\right) \\ &= -\frac{2}{n\pi}\left(\frac{-2\pi\cos 2n\pi}{n} + \left[\frac{\sin nt}{n^2}\right]_0^{2\pi}\right) \\ &= \frac{4}{n^2} \end{aligned}$$

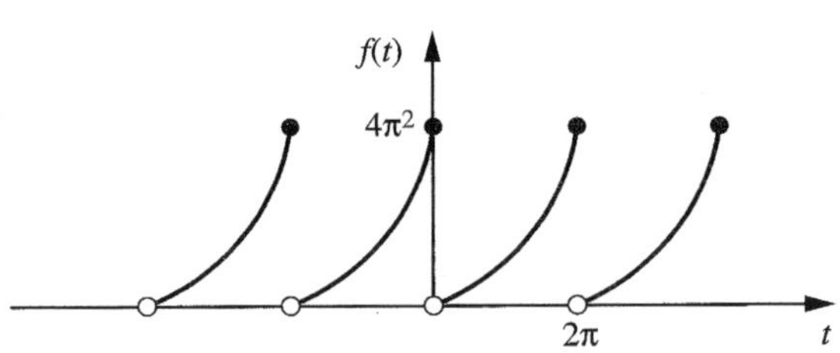


**Figure 23.16** Graph for Example 23.15.

Hence $a_1 = 4$, $a_2 = 1$, $a_3 = \frac{4}{9}, \dots$. Similarly,

$$
\begin{aligned}
b_n &= \frac{1}{\pi}\int_0^{2\pi} t^2 \sin nt \, \mathrm{d}t \\
&= \frac{1}{\pi}\left(\left[-t^2\frac{\cos nt}{n}\right]_0^{2\pi} + \int_0^{2\pi} 2t\frac{\cos nt}{n}\,\mathrm{d}t\right) \\
&= \frac{1}{\pi}\left(-\frac{4\pi^2}{n}\cos 2n\pi + \frac{2}{n}\int_0^{2\pi} t\cos nt\,\mathrm{d}t\right) \\
&= \frac{1}{\pi}\left(-\frac{4\pi^2}{n} + \frac{2}{n}\left(\left[\frac{t\sin nt}{n}\right]_0^{2\pi} - \int_0^{2\pi}\frac{\sin nt}{n}\,\mathrm{d}t\right)\right) \\
&= \frac{1}{\pi}\left(-\frac{4\pi^2}{n} - \frac{2}{n^2}\left[-\frac{\cos nt}{n}\right]_0^{2\pi}\right) \\
&= -\frac{4\pi}{n}
\end{aligned}
$$

Thus $b_1 = -4\pi$, $b_2 = -2\pi, \dots$. Finally, the required Fourier series representation is given by

$$
\begin{aligned}
f(t) = &\frac{4\pi^2}{3} + \left(4\cos t + \cos 2t + \frac{4}{9}\cos 3t + \cdots\right) \\
&- \pi\left(4\sin t + 2\sin 2t + \frac{4\sin 3t}{3} + \cdots\right)
\end{aligned}
$$

**Example 23.16** Obtain the expressions for the Fourier coefficients $a_0$, $a_n$ and $b_n$ in Equations (23.3), (23.4) and (23.5).

**Solution** Assume that $f(t)$ can be expressed in the form

$$f(t) = \frac{a_0}{2} + \sum_{n=1}^{\infty}\left(a_n\cos\frac{2n\pi t}{T} + b_n\sin\frac{2n\pi t}{T}\right) \tag{23.6}$$

Multiplying Equation (23.6) through by $\cos\dfrac{2m\pi t}{T}$ and integrating from 0 to $T$ we find

$$
\begin{aligned}
\int_0^T f(t)\cos\frac{2m\pi t}{T}\,\mathrm{d}t = &\int_0^T \frac{a_0}{2}\cos\frac{2m\pi t}{T}\,\mathrm{d}t \\
&+ \int_0^T \sum_{n=1}^{\infty}\left(a_n\cos\frac{2n\pi t}{T} + b_n\sin\frac{2n\pi t}{T}\right)\cos\frac{2m\pi t}{T}\,\mathrm{d}t
\end{aligned}
$$

If we now assume that it is legitimate to interchange the order of integration and summation we obtain

$$\int_0^T f(t)\cos\frac{2m\pi t}{T}\,\mathrm{d}t = \int_0^T \frac{a_0}{2}\cos\frac{2m\pi t}{T}\,\mathrm{d}t + \sum_{n=1}^{\infty}\int_0^T\left(a_n\cos\frac{2n\pi t}{T} + b_n\sin\frac{2n\pi t}{T}\right)\cos\frac{2m\pi t}{T}\,\mathrm{d}t$$

The first integral on the r.h.s. is easily shown to be zero unless $m = 0$. Furthermore, we can use the previously found orthogonality properties (Table 23.1) to show that the rest of the integrals on the r.h.s. vanish except for the case when $n = m$, in which case the r.h.s. reduces to $\frac{a_m T}{2}$. Consequently,

$$a_m = \frac{2}{T}\int_0^T f(t)\cos\frac{2m\pi t}{T}\,\mathrm{d}t \qquad \text{for all positive integers } m$$

as required. When $m = 0$ all terms on the r.h.s. except the first vanish and we obtain

$$\int_0^T f(t)\,\mathrm{d}t = \int_0^T \frac{a_0}{2}\,\mathrm{d}t = \frac{a_0 T}{2}$$

so that

$$a_0 = \frac{2}{T}\int_0^T f(t)\,\mathrm{d}t$$

To obtain the formula for the $b_n$ multiply Equation (23.6) through by $\sin\frac{2m\pi t}{T}$ and integrate from 0 to $T$.

$$\int_0^T f(t)\sin\frac{2m\pi t}{T}\,\mathrm{d}t = \int_0^T \frac{a_0}{2}\sin\frac{2m\pi t}{T}\,\mathrm{d}t + \int_0^T\sum_{n=1}^{\infty}\left(a_n\cos\frac{2n\pi t}{T} + b_n\sin\frac{2n\pi t}{T}\right)\sin\frac{2m\pi t}{T}\,\mathrm{d}t$$

Again assuming that it is legitimate to interchange the order of integration and summation, we obtain

$$\int_0^T f(t)\sin\frac{2m\pi t}{T}\,\mathrm{d}t = \int_0^T \frac{a_0}{2}\sin\frac{2m\pi t}{T}\,\mathrm{d}t + \sum_{n=1}^{\infty}\int_0^T\left(a_n\cos\frac{2n\pi t}{T} + b_n\sin\frac{2n\pi t}{T}\right)\sin\frac{2m\pi t}{T}\,\mathrm{d}t$$

The first integral on the r.h.s. is easily shown to be zero. Furthermore, we can use the properties given in Table 23.1 to show that the rest of the integrals on the r.h.s. vanish except for the case when $n = m$, in which case the r.h.s. reduces to $\frac{b_m T}{2}$. Hence we find

$$b_m = \frac{2}{T}\int_0^T f(t)\sin\frac{2m\pi t}{T}\,\mathrm{d}t$$

as required.

### 23.5.1 Fourier series of odd and even functions

Let us now consider what happens when we determine Fourier series of functions which are either odd or even.

**Example 23.17** Find the Fourier series for the function with period $2\pi$ defined by

$$f(t) = \begin{cases} 0 & -\pi < t < -\pi/2 \\ 4 & -\pi/2 \leqslant t \leqslant \pi/2 \\ 0 & \pi/2 < t < \pi \end{cases}$$

**Solution** As usual we sketch the function first (Figure 23.17). Inspection of Figure 23.17 shows that the Dirichlet conditions (page 708) are satisfied. We note from the graph that the function is symmetrical about the vertical axis; that is, it is an even function. We shall see shortly that this fact has important implications for the Fourier series representation. For convenience we consider the period of integration to be $\left[-\frac{T}{2}, \frac{T}{2}\right]$. Hence Equation (23.4) becomes

$$a_n = \frac{2}{T}\int_{-T/2}^{T/2} f(t)\cos\frac{2n\pi t}{T}\,dt \qquad \text{for all positive integers } n$$

In this example the period $T$ equals $2\pi$. The formula for $a_n$ then simplifies to

$$a_n = \frac{1}{\pi}\int_{-\pi}^{\pi} f(t)\cos nt\,dt$$

The interval of integration is from $t = -\pi$ to $t = \pi$. However, a glance at the graph shows that the function is zero outside the interval $-\frac{\pi}{2} \leqslant t \leqslant \frac{\pi}{2}$, and takes the value 4 inside. The integral thus reduces to

$$\begin{aligned} a_n &= \frac{1}{\pi}\int_{-\pi/2}^{\pi/2} 4\cos nt\,dt \\ &= \frac{4}{\pi}\int_{-\pi/2}^{\pi/2} \cos nt\,dt \\ &= \frac{4}{\pi}\left[\frac{\sin nt}{n}\right]_{-\pi/2}^{\pi/2} \\ &= \frac{4}{n\pi}\left[\sin\frac{n\pi}{2} - \sin\left(-\frac{n\pi}{2}\right)\right] \\ &= \frac{8}{n\pi}\sin\frac{n\pi}{2} \end{aligned}$$

We obtain $a_1 = \frac{8}{\pi}$, $a_2 = 0$, $a_3 = -\frac{8}{3\pi}$, etc. We find $a_0$ using Equation (23.3), again

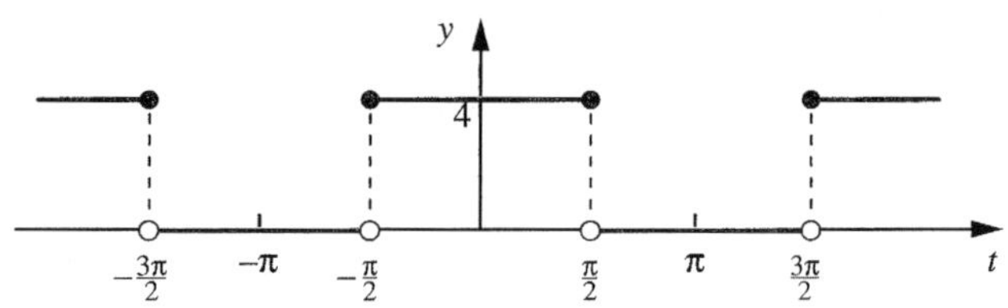


**Figure 23.17** Graph for Example 23.17.

integrating over $\left[-\frac{T}{2}, \frac{T}{2}\right]$:

$$a_0 = \frac{2}{T}\int_{-T/2}^{T/2} f(t)\,\mathrm{d}t$$

$$= \frac{1}{\pi}\int_{-\pi/2}^{\pi/2} 4\,\mathrm{d}t = \frac{4}{\pi}[t]_{-\pi/2}^{\pi/2}$$

$$= 4$$

Similarly, to find the Fourier coefficients, $b_n$, we use Equation (23.5):

$$b_n = \frac{2}{T}\int_{-T/2}^{T/2} f(t)\sin\frac{2n\pi t}{T}\,\mathrm{d}t$$

which reduces to

$$b_n = \frac{1}{\pi}\int_{-\pi/2}^{\pi/2} 4\sin nt\,\mathrm{d}t$$

$$= \frac{4}{\pi}\left[\frac{-\cos nt}{n}\right]_{-\pi/2}^{\pi/2}$$

$$= \frac{4}{n\pi}\left[-\cos\frac{n\pi}{2} + \cos\frac{n\pi}{2}\right]$$

$$= 0$$

that is, all the Fourier coefficients, $b_n$, are zero. Finally we can gather together all our results and write down the Fourier series representation of $f(t)$:

$$f(t) = 2 + \frac{8}{\pi}\cos t - \frac{8}{3\pi}\cos 3t + \frac{8}{5\pi}\cos 5t - \cdots$$

---

In this example we see that there are no sine terms at all. In fact, whenever a function is even its Fourier series will possess no sine terms. To see this we note that $b_n$ can be found from

$$b_n = \frac{2}{T}\int_{-T/2}^{T/2} f(t)\sin\frac{2n\pi t}{T}\,\mathrm{d}t$$

Since $f(t)$ is even and $\sin\dfrac{2n\pi t}{T}$ is odd, the product $f(t)\sin\dfrac{2n\pi t}{T}$ is odd also. Now the integral of an odd function on an interval which is symmetrical about the vertical axis was shown in Section 23.3 to be zero. Hence whenever $f(t)$ is even we can immediately assume $b_n = 0$ for all $n$.

Correspondingly, when a function is odd its Fourier series will contain no cosine or constant terms. This is because the product

$$f(t)\cos\frac{2n\pi t}{T}$$

is odd also and so the integral

$$a_n = \frac{2}{T}\int_{-T/2}^{T/2} f(t)\cos\frac{2n\pi t}{T}\,\mathrm{d}t$$

will equal zero. We conclude that when $f(t)$ is odd, $a_n = 0$ for all $n$. These facts can often be used to save time and effort. Knowing the function in Example 23.17 was even before we started the Fourier analysis, we could have assumed that the $b_n$ would all be zero.

**Example 23.18** Find the Fourier series representation of the sawtooth waveform described at the beginning of this section (see Figure 23.12).

**Solution** This function is defined by $f(t) = t$, $-\pi < t < \pi$, and has period $T = 2\pi$. It is an odd function and hence $a_n = 0$ for all $n$. To find the $b_n$ we must evaluate

$$\begin{aligned} b_n &= \frac{1}{\pi}\int_{-\pi}^{\pi} t\sin nt\,\mathrm{d}t \\ &= \frac{1}{\pi}\left\{\left[\frac{-t\cos nt}{n}\right]_{-\pi}^{\pi} + \int_{-\pi}^{\pi}\frac{\cos nt}{n}\,\mathrm{d}t\right\} \\ &= \frac{1}{n\pi}\{-\pi\cos n\pi - \pi\cos n\pi\} \end{aligned}$$

since the last integral vanishes. Therefore,

$$b_n = -\frac{2}{n}\cos n\pi = -\frac{2}{n}(-1)^n$$

We conclude that $b_1 = 2$, $b_2 = -1$, $b_3 = \frac{2}{3}, \ldots$. Therefore $f(t)$ has Fourier series

$$f(t) = 2\{\sin t - \tfrac{1}{2}\sin 2t + \tfrac{1}{3}\sin 3t - \tfrac{1}{4}\sin 4t + \tfrac{1}{5}\sin 5t - \cdots\}$$

## Exercises 23.5

1 Find the Fourier series representation of the function

$$f(t) = \begin{cases} 0 & -5 < t < 0 \quad \text{period } 10 \\ 1 & 0 < t < 5 \end{cases}$$

2 Find the Fourier series representation of the function

$$f(t) = \begin{cases} -t & -\pi < t < 0 \quad \text{period } 2\pi \\ 0 & 0 < t < \pi \end{cases}$$

3 Find the Fourier series representation of the function

$$f(t) = t^2 + \pi t \qquad -\pi < t < \pi \quad \text{period } 2\pi$$

4 Find the Fourier series representation of the function

$$f(t) = \begin{cases} -4 & -\pi < t \leqslant 0 \quad \text{period } 2\pi \\ 4 & 0 < t < \pi \end{cases}$$

5 Find the Fourier series representation of the function

$$f(t) = \begin{cases} 2(1+t) & -1 < t \leqslant 0 \quad \text{period } 2 \\ 0 & 0 < t < 1 \end{cases}$$

6 Find the Fourier series representation of the function with period $2\pi$ given by

$$f(t) = \begin{cases} t^2 & 0 \leqslant t < \pi \\ 0 & \pi \leqslant t < 2\pi \end{cases}$$

7 Find the Fourier series representation of the function

$$f(t) = 2 \sin t \quad 0 < t < 2\pi \quad \text{period } 2\pi$$

## Solutions

1 $\frac{1}{2} + \frac{2}{\pi} \sin \frac{\pi t}{5} + \frac{2}{3\pi} \sin \frac{3\pi t}{5} + \frac{2}{5\pi} \sin \frac{5\pi t}{5} + \frac{2}{7\pi} \sin \frac{7\pi t}{5} \cdots$

2 $\frac{\pi}{4} - \frac{2}{\pi} \cos t - \sin t + \frac{1}{2} \sin 2t - \frac{2}{9\pi} \cos 3t - \frac{1}{3} \sin 3t \ldots$

3 $\frac{\pi^2}{3} + 2\pi \sin t - 4 \cos t - \pi \sin 2t + \cos 2t + \frac{2\pi}{3} \sin 3t - \frac{4}{9} \cos 3t \cdots$

4 $\frac{8\left(2 \sin t + \frac{2}{3} \sin 3t + \frac{2}{5} \sin 5t + \cdots\right)}{\pi}$

5 $\frac{1}{2} + \frac{2\{(2/\pi) \cos \pi t - \sin \pi t - \frac{1}{2} \sin 2\pi t + (2/9\pi) \cos 3\pi t - \frac{1}{3} \sin 3\pi t + \cdots\}}{\pi}$

6 $\frac{\pi^2}{6} + \frac{\pi^2 - 4}{\pi} \sin t - 2 \cos t - \frac{\pi}{2} \sin 2t + \frac{1}{2} \cos 2t + \frac{9\pi^2 - 4}{27\pi} \sin 3t - \frac{2}{9} \cos 3t + \cdots$

7 $2 \sin t$

## 23.6 Half-range series

Sometimes an engineering function is not periodic but is only defined over a finite interval, $0 < t < \frac{T}{2}$ say, as shown in Figure 23.18. In cases like this Fourier analysis can still be useful. Because the region of interest is only that between $t = 0$ and $t = \frac{T}{2}$ we may choose to define the function arbitrarily outside the interval. In particular, we can make our choice so that the resulting function is periodic, with period $T$. There is more than one way to proceed. For example, we can reflect the above function in the vertical axis and then repeat it periodically so that the result is the periodic even function shown in Figure 23.19. We have performed what is called a **periodic extension** of the given function. Note that within the interval of interest nothing has altered but we have now achieved our objective of finding a periodic function. We can find the Fourier series of this periodic function and within the interval of interest this will converge to the required function. What happens outside this interval is not important. Moreover, since the periodic function is even the Fourier series will contain no sine terms.

An alternative periodic extension is that shown in Figure 23.20, which has been obtained by reflecting in both the vertical and $t$ axes before repeating it periodically to give a periodic odd function. Its Fourier series will contain no cosine terms and within the interval of interest will converge to the function required.

A third alternative periodic extension is shown in Figure 23.21. However, this extension is neither odd nor even and so it has none of the desirable properties of the other two. Whichever extension we choose, the resulting Fourier series only gives a representation of the original function in the interval $0 < t < \frac{T}{2}$ and as such is termed a **half-range** Fourier series. Similarly we have the terminology **half-range sine series** for a series containing only sine terms and **half-range cosine series** for a series containing only cosine terms. The Fourier series formulae then simplify to give the following half-range formulae:

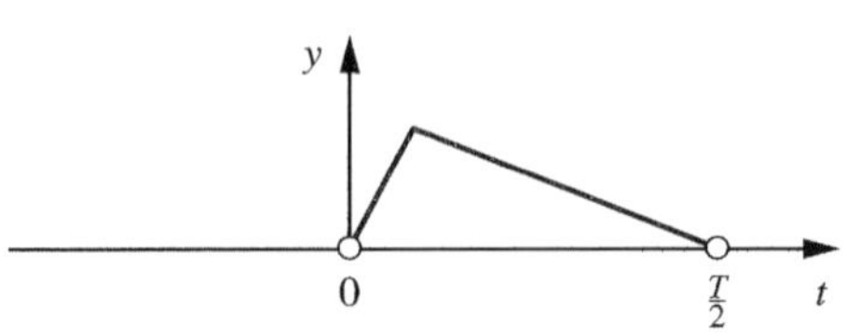


**Figure 23.18** Function defined over interval $0 < t < \frac{T}{2}$.

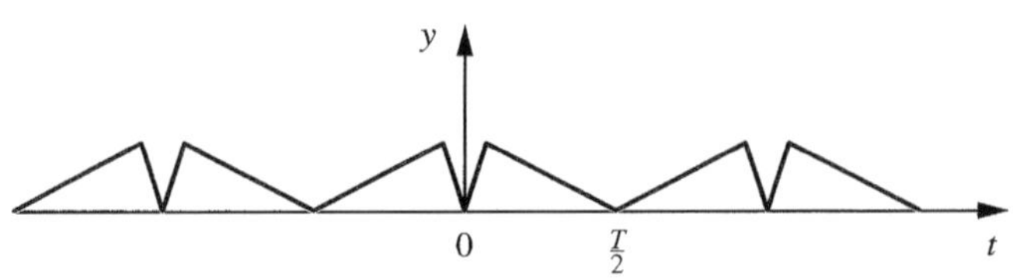


**Figure 23.19** An even periodic extension.

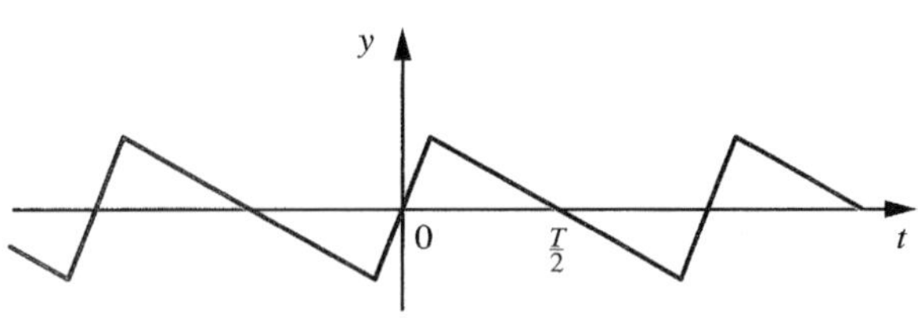


**Figure 23.20** An odd periodic extension.

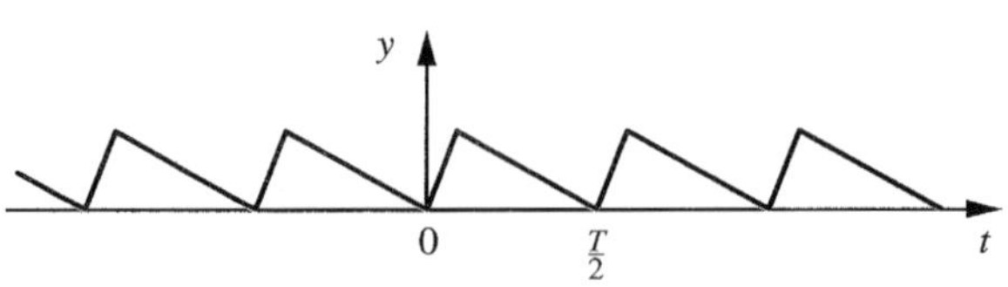


**Figure 23.21** A periodic extension that is neither even nor odd.

Half-range sine series:

$$a_0 = 0,\ a_n = 0 \qquad \text{for } n \text{ a positive integer}$$

$$b_n = \frac{4}{T}\int_0^{T/2} f(t)\sin\frac{2n\pi t}{T}\,dt \qquad \text{for } n \text{ a positive integer} \qquad (23.7)$$

and $f(t)$ is given by

$$f(t) = \sum_{n=1}^{\infty} b_n \sin\frac{2n\pi t}{T}$$

Half-range cosine series:

$$a_0 = \frac{4}{T}\int_0^{T/2} f(t)\,dt \qquad (23.8)$$

$$a_n = \frac{4}{T}\int_0^{T/2} f(t)\cos\frac{2n\pi t}{T}\,dt \qquad \text{for } n \text{ a positive integer} \qquad (23.9)$$

$$b_n = 0 \qquad \text{for } n \text{ a positive integer}$$

and then $f(t)$ is given by

$$f(t) = \frac{a_0}{2} + \sum_{n=1}^{\infty} a_n \cos\frac{2n\pi t}{T}$$

**Example 23.19** By defining an appropriate periodic extension of the function illustrated in Figure 23.22, find the half-range cosine series representation.

**Solution** The function illustrated in Figure 23.22 is given by the formula $f(t) = t$ for $0 < t < \pi$ and is undefined outside this interval. Since the cosine series is required an even periodic extension must be formed. This is illustrated in Figure 23.23. Taking $T = 2\pi$ in Equations (23.8) and (23.9), we find $a_0$ and $a_n$.

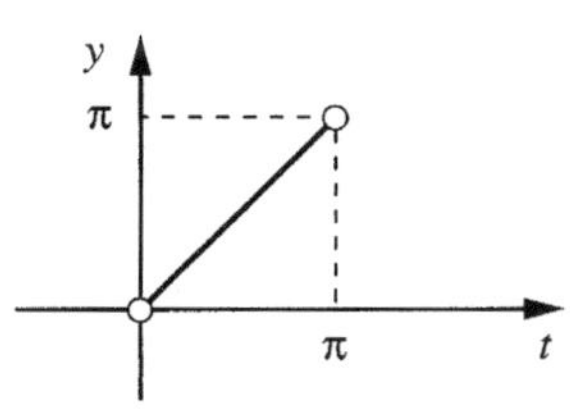


**Figure 23.22** Graph for Example 23.19.

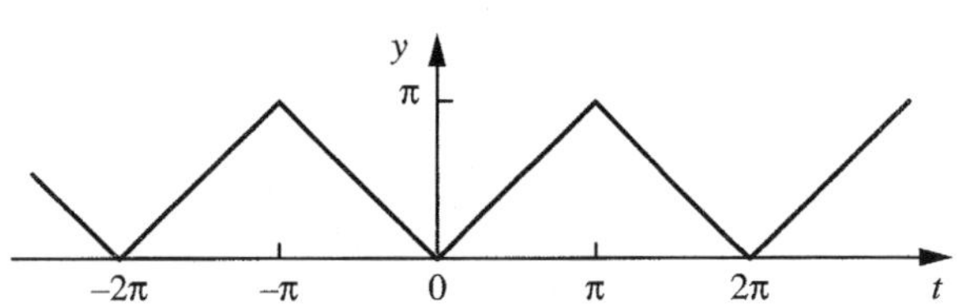


**Figure 23.23** Graph for Example 23.19.

$$a_0 = \frac{2}{\pi}\int_0^{\pi} t \, dt$$

$$= \frac{2}{\pi}\left[\frac{t^2}{2}\right]_0^{\pi}$$

$$= \pi$$

$$a_n = \frac{2}{\pi}\int_0^{\pi} t \cos nt \, dt$$

$$= \frac{2}{\pi}\left\{\left[\frac{t \sin nt}{n}\right]_0^{\pi} - \int_0^{\pi} \frac{\sin nt}{n} \, dt\right\}$$

$$= \frac{2}{\pi}\left[\frac{\cos nt}{n^2}\right]_0^{\pi}$$

Now $\cos n\pi = (-1)^n$, so that

$$a_n = \frac{2}{\pi}\left(\frac{(-1)^n}{n^2} - \frac{1}{n^2}\right) \qquad n = 1, 2, \ldots$$

Of course, all the $b_n$ are zero. Therefore the half-range cosine series is

$$f(t) = \frac{\pi}{2} - \frac{4}{\pi}\cos t - \frac{4}{9\pi}\cos 3t \ldots$$

and this series converges to the given function within the interval $0 < t < \pi$.

---

## Exercises 23.6

1 Graph an appropriate periodic extension of

$$f(t) = 3t \qquad 0 < t < \pi$$

and hence find its half-range cosine series representation.

2 Find the half-range sine series representation of the function given in Example 23.19.

3 Find the half-range cosine series representing the function

$$f(t) = \sin t \qquad 0 < t < \pi$$

4 Graph an appropriate periodic extension of

$$f(t) = e^t \qquad 0 < t < 1$$

and find its half-range cosine series.

5 Find the half-range sine series representation of $f(t) = 2 - t, 0 \leqslant t \leqslant 2$.

## Solutions

1 $\dfrac{3\pi}{2} + \dfrac{6}{\pi}\sum_1^{\infty}\left(\dfrac{\cos n\pi - 1}{n^2}\right)\cos nt$

2 $-2\sum_1^{\infty}\left(\dfrac{\cos n\pi}{n}\right)\sin nt$

3 $\frac{2}{\pi} - \frac{2}{\pi}\sum_{2}^{\infty}\left(\frac{\cos n\pi + 1}{n^2 - 1}\right)\cos nt$

4 $\mathrm{e} - 1 + 2\sum_{1}^{\infty}\left(\frac{\mathrm{e}\cos n\pi - 1}{n^2\pi^2 + 1}\right)\cos n\pi t$

5 $\frac{4}{\pi}\sum_{1}^{\infty}\frac{\sin(n\pi t/2)}{n}$

## 23.7 Parseval's theorem

If the function $f(t)$ is periodic with period $T$ and has Fourier coefficients $a_n$ and $b_n$, then Parseval's theorem states:

$$\frac{2}{T}\int_0^T (f(t))^2\,\mathrm{d}t = \tfrac{1}{2}a_0^2 + \sum_{n=1}^{\infty}(a_n^2 + b_n^2)$$

It is frequently useful in power calculations as the following example shows.

### Example 23.20 Average power of a signal

Find the average power developed across a 1 Ω resistor by a voltage signal with period $2\pi$ given by

$$v(t) = \cos t - \frac{1}{3}\sin 2t + \frac{1}{2}\cos 3t$$

**Solution** We note that $v(t)$ is periodic with period $T = 2\pi$; $v(t)$ is already expressed as a Fourier series with $a_1 = 1$, $a_3 = \frac{1}{2}$ and $b_2 = -\frac{1}{3}$. All other Fourier coefficients are 0. The instantaneous power is $(v(t))^2$ and hence the average power over one period is given by

$$P_{\mathrm{av}} = \frac{1}{2\pi}\int_0^{2\pi}(v(t))^2\,\mathrm{d}t$$

Therefore, using Parseval's theorem we find

$$P_{\mathrm{av}} = \frac{1}{2}\left(1^2 + \left(-\frac{1}{3}\right)^2 + \left(\frac{1}{2}\right)^2\right) = 0.68\ \mathrm{W}$$

---

## 23.8 Complex notation

An alternative notation for Fourier series involving complex numbers is available which leads naturally into the more general topic of Fourier transforms. Recall from Chapter 9 the Euler relations

$$\mathrm{e}^{\pm \mathrm{j}\theta} = \cos\theta \pm \mathrm{j}\sin\theta$$

from which we can obtain expressions for $\cos\theta$ and $\sin\theta$:

$$\cos\theta = \frac{e^{j\theta} + e^{-j\theta}}{2} \qquad \sin\theta = \frac{e^{j\theta} - e^{-j\theta}}{2j}$$

which enable us to rewrite the Fourier representation

$$f(t) = \frac{a_0}{2} + \sum_{n=1}^{\infty}\left(a_n \cos\frac{2n\pi t}{T} + b_n \sin\frac{2n\pi t}{T}\right)$$

as

$$f(t) = \frac{a_0}{2} + \sum_{n=1}^{\infty}\left(a_n \frac{e^{j2n\pi t/T} + e^{-j2n\pi t/T}}{2} + b_n \frac{e^{j2n\pi t/T} - e^{-j2n\pi t/T}}{2j}\right)$$

$$= \frac{a_0}{2} + \sum_{n=1}^{\infty}\left(\frac{a_n - jb_n}{2} e^{j2n\pi t/T} + \frac{a_n + jb_n}{2} e^{-j2n\pi t/T}\right)$$

which we can write equivalently as

$$f(t) = \sum_{n=-\infty}^{\infty} c_n e^{j2n\pi t/T}$$

where

$$c_n = \frac{a_n - jb_n}{2} \qquad c_{-n} = \frac{a_n + jb_n}{2} \qquad n = 1, 2, \ldots$$

and $c_0 = a_0/2$. It can be shown that the Fourier coefficients, $c_n$, are then given by

$$c_n = \frac{1}{T}\int_{-T/2}^{T/2} f(t)\, e^{-j2n\pi t/T}\, dt$$

The integral can also be evaluated over any complete period as convenient. Further, if we write $T = \frac{2\pi}{\omega_1}$ then this complex form can be expressed as

$$f(t) = \sum_{n=-\infty}^{\infty} c_n e^{jn\omega_1 t}$$

where

$$c_n = \frac{\omega_1}{2\pi}\int_{-\pi/\omega_1}^{\pi/\omega_1} f(t)\, e^{-jn\omega_1 t}\, dt$$

**Example 23.21** Find the complex Fourier series representation of the function with period $T$ defined by

$$f(t) = \begin{cases} 1 & -T/4 < t < T/4 \\ 0 & \text{otherwise} \end{cases}$$

**Solution** We find

$$c_n = \frac{1}{T}\int_{-T/4}^{T/4} 1\mathrm{e}^{-\mathrm{j}2n\pi t/T}\,\mathrm{d}t$$

$$= \frac{1}{T}\left[\frac{\mathrm{e}^{-\mathrm{j}2n\pi t/T}}{-\mathrm{j}2n\pi/T}\right]_{-T/4}^{T/4}$$

$$= \frac{-1}{2n\pi j}(\mathrm{e}^{-\mathrm{j}n\pi/2} - \mathrm{e}^{\mathrm{j}n\pi/2})$$

$$= \frac{1}{n\pi}\left(\frac{\mathrm{e}^{\mathrm{j}n\pi/2} - \mathrm{e}^{-\mathrm{j}n\pi/2}}{2\mathrm{j}}\right)$$

$$= \frac{1}{n\pi}\sin\frac{n\pi}{2}$$

Therefore,

$$f(t) = \sum_{n=-\infty}^{\infty} \frac{1}{n\pi}\sin\frac{n\pi}{2}\,\mathrm{e}^{\mathrm{j}2n\pi t/T}$$

The observant reader will note that the expressions for $c_n$ appear invalid when $n = 0$, since the denominator is then zero. We can compute $c_0$ in either of two ways. Using an integral expression we see that

$$c_0 = \frac{1}{T}\int_{-T/4}^{T/4} 1\,\mathrm{d}t = \frac{1}{2}$$

Also, using a Taylor series expansion it is possible to show

$$\lim_{n\to 0}\frac{1}{T}\left[\frac{\mathrm{e}^{-\mathrm{j}2n\pi t/T}}{-\mathrm{j}2n\pi/T}\right]_{-T/4}^{T/4} = \frac{1}{2}$$

giving a consistent result.

---

## Exercises 23.8

1. Find the complex Fourier series representation of

(a) $f(t) = \begin{cases} 1 & 0 < t < 2 \\ 0 & 2 < t < 4 \end{cases}$ period 4

(b) $f(t) = \mathrm{e}^t \quad -1 < t < 1$ period 2

(c) $f(t) = \begin{cases} A\sin\omega t & 0 < t < \pi/\omega \\ 0 & \pi/\omega < t < 2\pi/\omega \end{cases}$ period $2\pi/\omega$

2. If

$$f(t) = \sum_{-\infty}^{\infty} c_n\,\mathrm{e}^{\mathrm{j}2n\pi t/T},$$

show that the coefficients, $c_n$, are given by

$$c_n = \frac{1}{T}\int_0^T f(t)\,\mathrm{e}^{-\mathrm{j}2n\pi t/T}\,\mathrm{d}t$$

[*Hint:* multiply both sides by $\mathrm{e}^{-\mathrm{j}2m\pi t/T}$ and integrate over $[0, T]$.]

## Solutions

1 (a) $\sum_{-\infty}^{\infty} \frac{j}{2n\pi}(\cos n\pi - 1)\,e^{jn\pi t/2}$

(b) $\frac{1}{2}\sum_{-\infty}^{\infty}\left(\frac{e^{-jn\pi+1} - e^{-1+jn\pi}}{1 - jn\pi}\right)e^{jn\pi t}$

(c) $\sum_{-\infty}^{\infty} \frac{A(1 + e^{-jn\pi})\,e^{jn\omega t}}{2\pi(1 - n^2)}$

# 23.9 Frequency response of a linear system

We have already examined some of the basic features of linear systems in Section 18.2. Linear systems have the property that the response to several inputs being applied to the system can be obtained by adding the effects of the individual inputs. Another useful property of linear systems is that if a sinusoidal input is applied to the system then the output will also be a sinusoid of the same frequency but with modified amplitude and phase. This is illustrated in Figure 23.24.

In Section 9.7 we saw that sinusoidal signals can be represented by complex numbers and that an a.c. electrical circuit can be analysed using complex numbers. This is true for linear systems in general. It is possible to define a **complex frequency function**, $G(j\omega)$, where $\omega$ is the frequency of the input; $G$ relates the output and the input of a linear system.

If a sine wave of amplitude $A_i$ is applied to the system then the amplitude, $A_o$, of the output is given by

$$A_o = |G(j\omega)|A_i$$

The phase shift, $\phi$, is given by

$$\phi = \angle G(j\omega)$$

Note that $A_o$ and $\phi$ depend upon $\omega$. It is important to note that $G(j\omega)$ is a frequency-dependent function. Although the notation for $G(j\omega)$ may seem slightly odd it arises because one method of obtaining the frequency function for a linear system is to substitute $s = j\omega$ in the Laplace transform transfer function, $G(s)$, of the system.

It is now possible to analyse the effect of applying a generalized periodic waveform to a linear system. The first stage is to calculate the Fourier components of the input waveform. The amplitude and phase shift of each of the output components is then calculated using $G(j\omega)$. Finally, the output components are added to obtain the output waveform. This is only possible because of the additive nature of linear systems. An example will help to clarify these points.

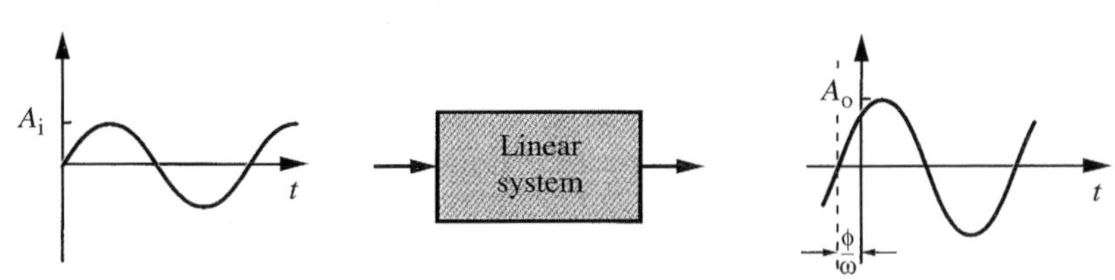


**Figure 23.24**
The response of a linear system to a sinusoidal input is also sinusoidal.

**Example 23.22** **Low-pass filter**

Consider the circuit of Figure 23.25. Using Kirchhoff's voltage law and Ohm's law we obtain

$$v_i = iR + v_o$$

For the capacitor,

$$v_o = \frac{i}{j\omega C}$$

Eliminating $i$ yields

$$v_i = v_o j\omega CR + v_o = v_o(1 + j\omega RC)$$

$$\frac{v_o}{v_i} = \frac{1}{1 + j\omega RC} \qquad (23.10)$$

Equation (23.10) relates the output of the system to the input of the system. Therefore,

$$G(j\omega) = \frac{1}{1 + j\omega RC}$$

It is convenient to convert $G(j\omega)$ into polar form:

$$G(j\omega) = \frac{1\angle 0}{\sqrt{1 + (\omega RC)^2}\angle \tan^{-1}\omega RC}$$

$$= \frac{1}{\sqrt{1 + (\omega RC)^2}}\angle - \tan^{-1}\omega RC$$

Therefore,

$$|G(j\omega)| = \frac{1}{\sqrt{1 + (\omega RC)^2}} \qquad (23.11)$$

$$\angle G(j\omega) = -\tan^{-1}\omega RC \qquad (23.12)$$

The amplitude and phase characteristics for the circuit of Figure 23.25 are shown in Figure 23.26. These show the variation of $|G(j\omega)|$ and $\angle G(j\omega)$ with angular frequency $\omega$.

Note that the circuit is a low-pass filter; it allows low frequencies to pass easily and rejects high frequencies. The cut-off point of the filter, that is the point at which significant frequency attenuation begins to occur, can be varied by changing the values of $R$ and $C$. The quantity $RC$ is usually known as the time constant for the system. Consider the case when $RC = 0.3$. Equations (23.11) and (23.12) reduce to

$$|G(j\omega)| = \frac{1}{\sqrt{1 + 0.09\omega^2}} \qquad (23.13)$$

$$\angle G(j\omega) = -\tan^{-1} 0.3\omega \qquad (23.14)$$

Let us examine the response of this system to a square wave input with fundamental angular frequency 1 and amplitude 1. This waveform is shown in Figure 23.27(a). We

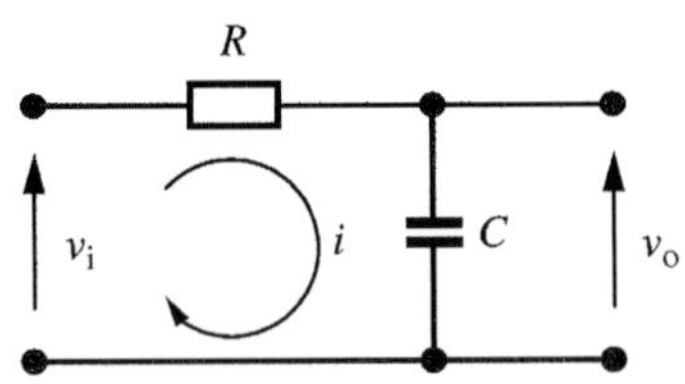


Figure 23.25 Circuit for Example 23.22.

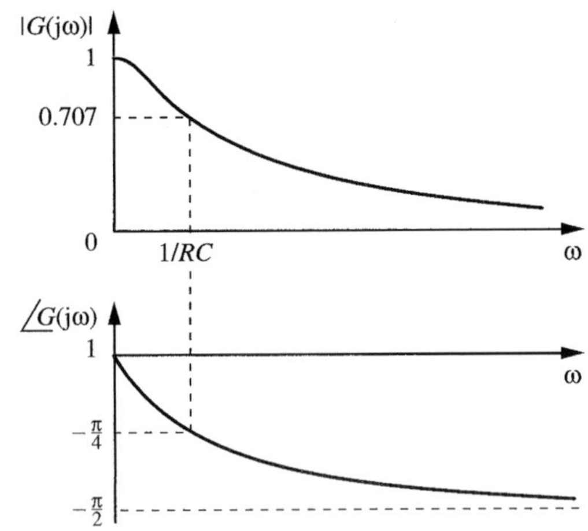


**Figure 23.26** Amplitude and phase characteristics for the circuit of Figure 23.25.

note that $T = 2\pi$. The waveform function is odd and so will not contain any cosine Fourier components. It has an average value of 0 and so will not have a zero frequency component; that is, there will be no d.c. component. Therefore calculating the Fourier components reduces to evaluating

$$f(t) = \sum_{n=1}^{\infty} b_n \sin \frac{2\pi nt}{T}$$

$$b_n = \frac{2}{T} \int_{-T/2}^{T/2} f(t) \sin \frac{2\pi nt}{T}\, dt \qquad \text{for positive integers } n$$

Since $T = 2\pi$, we find

$$\begin{aligned}
b_n &= \frac{1}{\pi}\left(\int_{-\pi}^{0} -1 \sin nt\, dt + \int_{0}^{\pi} \sin nt\, dt\right) \\
&= \frac{1}{\pi}\left(\left[\frac{\cos nt}{n}\right]_{-\pi}^{0} + \left[\frac{-\cos nt}{n}\right]_{0}^{\pi}\right) \\
&= \frac{1}{n\pi}(\cos 0 - \cos \pi n - \cos \pi n + \cos 0) \\
&= \frac{1}{n\pi}(2 - 2\cos \pi n) \\
&= \frac{2}{n\pi}(1 - \cos \pi n)
\end{aligned}$$

The values of the first few coefficients are

$$b_1 = \frac{2}{\pi}(1 - \cos\pi) = \frac{4}{\pi}$$

$$b_2 = \frac{2}{2\pi}(1 - \cos 2\pi) = 0$$

$$b_3 = \frac{2}{3\pi}(1 - \cos 3\pi) = \frac{4}{3\pi}$$

The next stage is to evaluate the gain and phase changes of the Fourier components. Using Equations (23.13) and (23.14):

$\underline{n = 1}$

$$\omega_1 = 1$$

$$|G(j\omega_1)| = \frac{1}{\sqrt{1 + 0.09 \times 1}} = 0.96$$

$$\angle G(j\omega_1) = -\tan^{-1} 0.3 = -16.7^\circ$$

$\underline{n = 3}$

$$\omega_3 = 3$$

$$|G(j\omega_3)| = \frac{1}{\sqrt{1 + 0.09 \times 9}} = 0.74$$

$$\angle G(j\omega_3) = -\tan^{-1} 0.9 = -42.0^\circ$$

$\underline{n = 5}$

$$\omega_5 = 5$$

$$|G(j\omega_5)| = \frac{1}{\sqrt{1 + 0.09 \times 25}} = 0.55$$

$$\angle G(j\omega_5) = -\tan^{-1} 1.5 = -56.3^\circ$$

It is clear that high-frequency Fourier components are attenuated and phase shifted more than low-frequency Fourier components. The effect is to produce a rounding of the rising and falling edges of the square wave input signal. This is illustrated in Figure 23.27(b). The output signal has been obtained by adding together the attenuated and phase-shifted output Fourier components. This is possible because the system is linear.

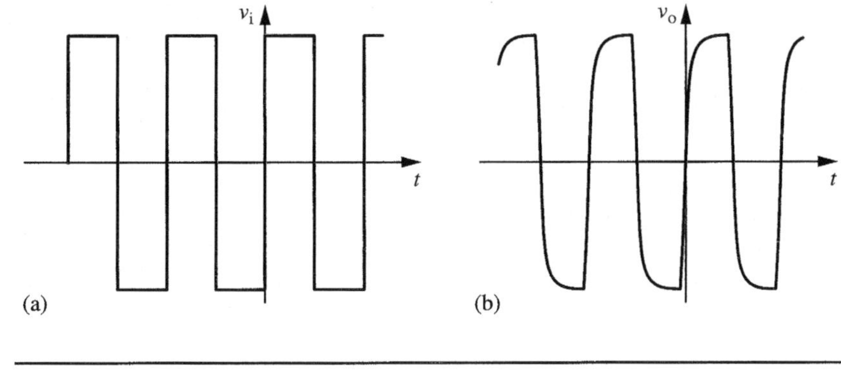


**Figure 23.27**
(a) Input to low-pass filter; (b) output from low-pass filter.

## Review exercises 23

1 Find the half-range Fourier sine series representation of $f(t) = t \sin t, 0 \leqslant t \leqslant \pi$.

2 Find the half-range sine series representation of $f(t) = \cos 2t, 0 \leqslant t \leqslant \pi$.

3 Find (a) the half-range sine series, and (b) the half-range cosine series representation of the function defined in the interval $[0, \tau]$ by

$$f(t) = \begin{cases} \dfrac{4t}{\tau} & 0 \leqslant t \leqslant \dfrac{\tau}{4} \\ \dfrac{4}{3}\left(1 - \dfrac{t}{\tau}\right) & \dfrac{\tau}{4} \leqslant t \leqslant \tau \end{cases}$$

4 Find the Fourier series representation of the function with period $T$ defined by

$$f(t) = \begin{cases} V(\text{constant}) & |t| < T/6 \\ 0 & T/6 \leqslant |t| \leqslant T/2 \end{cases}$$

5 The output from a half-wave rectifier is given by

$$i(t) = \begin{cases} I \sin \omega t & 0 < t < T/2 \\ 0 & T/2 < t < T \end{cases}$$

and is periodic with period $T = \dfrac{2\pi}{\omega}$.

Find its Fourier series representation.

6 Find the complex Fourier series representation of the function with period $T = 0.02$ defined by

$$v(t) = \begin{cases} V(\text{constant}) & 0 \leqslant t < 0.01 \\ 0 & 0.01 \leqslant t < 0.02 \end{cases}$$

7 Find the Fourier series representation of the function with period 8 given by

$$f(t) = \begin{cases} 2 - t & 0 < t < 4 \\ t - 6 & 4 < t < 8 \end{cases}$$

8 The r.m.s. voltage, $v_{\text{r.m.s.}}$, of a periodic waveform, $v(t)$, with period $T$, is given by

$$v_{\text{r.m.s.}} = \sqrt{\frac{1}{T}\int_0^T (v(t))^2 \, dt}$$

If $v(t)$ has Fourier coefficients $a_n$ and $b_n$ show, using Parseval's theorem, that

$$v_{\text{r.m.s.}} = \sqrt{\frac{1}{4}a_0^2 + \frac{1}{2}\sum_{n=1}^{\infty}(a_n^2 + b_n^2)}$$

9 If $f(t)$ has Fourier series

$$f(t) = \frac{a_0}{2} + \sum_{n=1}^{\infty}\left(a_n \cos\frac{2n\pi t}{T} + b_n \sin\frac{2n\pi t}{T}\right)$$

prove Parseval's theorem.

[*Hint:* multiply both sides by $f(t)$ to obtain

$$(f(t))^2 = \frac{a_0 f(t)}{2} + \sum_{n=1}^{\infty}\left(a_n f(t) \cos\frac{2n\pi t}{T} + b_n f(t) \sin\frac{2n\pi t}{T}\right)$$

and integrate both sides over the interval $[0, T]$ using Equations (23.3)–(23.5).]

10 Find the half-range cosine series and the half-range sine series for the function

$$f(t) = \sinh \pi t \qquad 0 < t < 1$$

## Solutions

1 $$\frac{\pi}{2} - \sum_{2}^{\infty}\frac{4n(1 + \cos n\pi)}{\pi(n+1)^2(n-1)^2}\sin(nt)$$

2 $$\frac{2}{\pi}\sum_{1}^{\infty}\frac{n(1 - \cos n\pi)}{(n^2 - 4)}\sin(nt)$$

3 (a) $$\frac{32}{3\pi^2}\sum_{1}^{\infty}\frac{\sin(n\pi/4)\sin(n\pi t/\tau)}{n^2}$$

(b) $$\frac{1}{2} + \frac{8}{\pi^2} \times \sum_{1}^{\infty}\frac{4\cos(n\pi/4) - \cos n\pi - 3}{3n^2}\cos\left(\frac{n\pi t}{\tau}\right)$$

4 $$\frac{v}{3} + \frac{2v}{\pi}\sum_{1}^{\infty}\frac{\sin(n\pi/3)\cos(2n\pi t/T)}{n}$$

5 $\dfrac{I}{\pi} + \dfrac{I}{2}\sin\omega t - \dfrac{I}{\pi}\sum_{2}^{\infty}\dfrac{\cos n\pi + 1}{n^2 - 1}\cos n\omega t$

6 $\dfrac{v}{2\pi}\sum_{-\infty}^{\infty} \mathrm{j}\dfrac{\cos n\pi - 1}{n}\mathrm{e}^{100n\pi \mathrm{j}t}$

7 $\dfrac{8}{\pi^2}\sum_{1}^{\infty}\dfrac{1 - \cos n\pi}{n^2}\cos\left(\dfrac{n\pi t}{4}\right)$

10 cosine series: $\dfrac{1}{\pi}(\cosh\pi - 1)$

$+ \sum_{n=1}^{\infty}\dfrac{2}{\pi(1 + n^2)}((-1)^n\cosh\pi - 1)\cos n\pi t$

sine series:

$- \sum_{n=1}^{\infty}\dfrac{2n}{\pi(1 + n^2)}(-1)^n\sinh\pi\sin n\pi t$

# Tables

# Appendix I Tables

## AI.1 Some useful results

### Algebraic processes

$$(a+b)^2 = a^2 + 2ab + b^2$$

$$(a-b)^2 = a^2 - 2ab + b^2$$

$$a^2 - b^2 = (a+b)(a-b) \qquad \text{'difference of two squares'}$$

$$ax^2 + bx + c = a\left(x + \frac{b}{2a}\right)^2 + c - \frac{b^2}{4a} \qquad \text{'completing the square'}$$

### Quadratic equation

The general form of the quadratic equation is

$$ax^2 + bx + c = 0,\ a \neq 0$$

and its solution is given by

$$x = \frac{-b \pm \sqrt{(b^2 - 4ac)}}{2a}$$

- If $b^2 > 4ac$ the equation has two real roots.
- If $b^2 = 4ac$ the equation has a real root which is repeated.
- If $b^2 < 4ac$ the equation has two complex roots, which are complex conjugates.

### Rules of indices

(1) $a^m a^n = a^{m+n}$ (2) $\dfrac{a^m}{a^n} = a^{m-n}$ (3) $(a^n)^m = a^{nm}$ (4) $a^0 = 1$

(5) $a^{1/n} = {}^n\sqrt{a}$ (6) $a^{-n} = \dfrac{1}{a^n}$ (7) $a^{m/n} = {}^n\sqrt{a^m}$

### Logarithmic formulae

*Definition*

If $y = a^x$ then $x = \log_a y$ expressed verbally as '*x is equal to log to base a of y*'.

### *Rules*

(1) $\log_a(xy) = \log_a x + \log_a y$ *'log of product equal to sum of logs'*

(2) $\log_a(\frac{x}{y}) = \log_a x - \log_a y$ *'log of quotient equal difference of logs'*

(3) $\log_a x^n = n \log_a x$

### *Useful results*

(1) $x = a^{\log_a x}$

(2) $\log_a x = \dfrac{\log_b x}{\log_b a}$ *'change of base'*

When the logarithm of $x$ is to base e then it is denoted by $\ln x$ and called the natural logarithm.

## Hyperbolic functions

### *Definitions*

$\cosh x = \frac{1}{2}(e^x + e^{-x})$ $\sinh x = \frac{1}{2}(e^x - e^{-x})$

$\tanh x = \dfrac{\sinh x}{\cosh x}$ $\mathrm{sech}x = \dfrac{1}{\cosh x}$

$\mathrm{cosech}x = \dfrac{1}{\sinh x}, (x \neq 0)$ $\coth x = \dfrac{1}{\tanh x}, (x \neq 0)$

### *Logarithmic form of inverses*

$\sinh^{-1} x = \ln[x + \sqrt{(x^2 + 1)}]$

$\cosh^{-1} x = \ln[x + \sqrt{(x^2 - 1)}], \quad (x \geq 1)$

$\tanh^{-1} x = \frac{1}{2}\ln\left(\dfrac{1+x}{1-x}\right), \quad (-1 < x < 1)$

## Arithmetic sequence (progression)

- An arithmetic sequence is a sequence of terms of the form

  $a, a + d, a + 2d, a + 3d, \ldots$

  where $a$ is called the first term and $d$ the common difference.
- The *nth* term of the sequence is given by $a + (n - 1)d$.
- The sum of the terms of an arithmetic sequence is called an arithmetic series and the sum of the first $n$ terms is

  $S_n = n[2a + (n - 1)d]/2$

### Geometric sequence (progression)

- A geometric sequence is a sequence of terms of the form

  $$a, ar, ar^2, ar^3, \ldots$$

  where $a$ is called the first term and $r$ the common ratio.
- The *nth* term of the sequence is given by $ar^{n-1}$.
- The sum of the terms of a geometric sequence is called a geometric series and the sum of the first $n$ terms is

  $$S_n = a(1 - r^n)/(1 - r) \text{ if } r \neq 1 \quad \text{and} \quad S_n = an \text{ if } r = 1$$

### The binomial series

- The binomial expansion of the function $(1 + x)^r$, where $r$ is any real number is given by

  $$(1 + x)^r = 1 + rx + \frac{1}{2!}r(r - 1)x^2 + \frac{1}{3!}r(r - 1)(r - 2)x^3 + \ldots$$

- The $(n + 1)^{\text{th}}$ term of the series is $\frac{1}{n!}r(r - 1)(r - 2) \ldots (r - n + 1)x^r$.
- If $r$ is a positive integer then the series terminates after $r + 1$ terms.
- If $r$ is not a positive integer then the expansion is valid only if $|x| < 1$.
- To expand $(a + x)^r$ then first express it in the form $a^r\left(1 + \frac{x}{a}\right)^r$ and then expand as above.

### Taylor and Maclaurin series

The Taylor series expansion of $f(x)$ about $x = a$ is

$$f(x + a) = f(a) + \frac{x}{1!}f'(a) + \frac{x^2}{2!}f''(a) + \ldots = \sum_{n=0}^{\infty} \frac{x^n}{n!} f^{(n)}(a)$$

The expansion is only valid within the region of convergence of the infinite series. In the special case when $a = 0$ we have the Maclaurin series expansion of $f(x)$

$$f(x) = f(0) + \frac{x}{1!}f'(0) + \frac{x^2}{2!}f''(0) + \ldots = \sum_{n=0}^{\infty} \frac{x^n}{n!} f^{(n)}(0)$$

### Some standard Maclaurin series expansions

$$e^x = 1 + \frac{x}{1!} + \frac{x^2}{2!} + \frac{x^3}{3!} + \ldots + \frac{x^n}{n!} + \ldots \quad (\text{all } x)$$

$$\sin x = x - \frac{x^3}{3!} + \frac{x^5}{5!} - \ldots + \frac{(-1)^n x^{2n+1}}{(2n + 1)!} + \ldots \quad (\text{all } x)$$

$$\cos x = 1 - \frac{x^2}{2!} + \frac{x^4}{4!} - \ldots + \frac{(-1)^n x^{2n}}{(2n)!} + \ldots \quad (\text{all } x)$$

$$\ln(1 + x) = x - \frac{x^2}{2} + \frac{x^3}{3} - \frac{x^4}{4} + \ldots + \frac{(-1)^n x^{n+1}}{n + 1} + \ldots \quad (-1 < x \leqslant 1)$$

$$\tan x = x + \frac{x^3}{3} + \frac{2x^5}{15} + \frac{17x^7}{315} + \ldots \quad (-\tfrac{1}{2}\pi < x < \tfrac{1}{2}\pi)$$

$$\sinh x = x + \frac{x^3}{3!} + \frac{x^5}{5!} + \ldots + \frac{x^{2n+1}}{(2n+1)!} + \ldots \quad (\text{all } x)$$

$$\cosh x = 1 + \frac{x^2}{2!} + \frac{x^4}{4!} + \ldots + \frac{x^{2n}}{(2n)!} + \ldots \quad (\text{all } x)$$

## AI.2 Trigonometric identities

$$\cos^2 x + \sin^2 x = 1$$

$$1 + \tan^2 x = \sec^2 x$$

$$1 + \cot^2 x = \operatorname{cosec}^2 x$$

$$\sin(x + y) = \sin x \cos y + \cos x \sin y$$

$$\sin(x - y) = \sin x \cos y - \cos x \sin y$$

$$\cos(x + y) = \cos x \cos y - \sin x \sin y$$

$$\cos(x - y) = \cos x \cos y + \sin x \sin y$$

$$\tan(x + y) = \frac{\tan x + \tan y}{1 - \tan x \tan y}$$

$$\tan(x - y) = \frac{\tan x - \tan y}{1 + \tan x \tan y}$$

$$\sin 2x = 2 \sin x \cos x$$

$$\cos 2x = \cos^2 x - \sin^2 x$$
$$= 1 - 2\sin^2 x$$
$$= 2\cos^2 x - 1$$

$$\sin x + \sin y = 2 \sin \tfrac{1}{2}(x + y) \cos \tfrac{1}{2}(x - y)$$

$$\sin x - \sin y = 2 \cos \tfrac{1}{2}(x + y) \sin \tfrac{1}{2}(x - y)$$

$$\cos x + \cos y = 2 \cos \tfrac{1}{2}(x + y) \cos \tfrac{1}{2}(x - y)$$

$$\cos x - \cos y = -2 \sin \tfrac{1}{2}(x + y) \sin \tfrac{1}{2}(x - y)$$

$$\sin x \cos y = \tfrac{1}{2}[\sin(x + y) + \sin(x - y)]$$

$$\cos x \sin y = \tfrac{1}{2}[\sin(x + y) - \sin(x - y)]$$

$$\cos x \cos y = \tfrac{1}{2}[\cos(x + y) + \cos(x - y)]$$

$$\sin x \sin y = \tfrac{1}{2}[\cos(x - y) - \cos(x + y)]$$

$$\sin 3x = 3 \sin x - 4 \sin^3 x$$

$$\cos 3x = 4 \cos^3 x - 3 \cos x$$

## AI.3 Derivatives and integrals

| $y$ | $dy/dx$ | $\int y\,dx$ |
|---|---|---|
| $x^n$ | $nx^{n-1}$ | $x^{n+1}/(n+1) \quad (n \neq -1)$ |
| $1/x$ | $-1/x^2$ | $\ln\lvert x\rvert$ |
| $\sin x$ | $\cos x$ | $-\cos x$ |
| $\cos x$ | $-\sin x$ | $\sin x$ |
| $\tan x$ | $\sec^2 x$ | $-\ln\lvert\cos x\rvert$ |
| $\sec x$ | $\sec x \tan x$ | $\ln\lvert\sec x + \tan x\rvert$ |
| $\cot x$ | $-\mathrm{cosec}^2 x$ | $\ln\lvert\sin x\rvert$ |
| $\mathrm{cosec}\, x$ | $-\mathrm{cosec}\, x \cot x$ | $-\ln\lvert\mathrm{cosec}\, x + \cot x\rvert$ |
| $\sin^{-1}x$ | $\dfrac{1}{\sqrt{(1-x^2)}}$ | $x\sin^{-1}x + \sqrt{(1-x^2)}$ |
| $\cos^{-1}x$ | $\dfrac{-1}{\sqrt{(1-x^2)}}$ | $x\cos^{-1}x - \sqrt{(1-x^2)}$ |
| $\tan^{-1}x$ | $\dfrac{1}{1+x^2}$ | $x\tan^{-1}x - \frac{1}{2}\ln(1+x^2)$ |
| $\sec^{-1}x$ | $\dfrac{1}{x\sqrt{(x^2-1)}}$ | $x\sec^{-1}x - \ln\lvert x + \sqrt{(x^2-1)}\rvert$ <br> $(0 < \sec^{-1}x < \frac{1}{2}\pi)$ |
| $\mathrm{cosec}^{-1}x$ | $\dfrac{-1}{x\sqrt{(x^2-1)}}$ | $(x\,\mathrm{cosec}^{-1}x + \ln\lvert x + \sqrt{(x^2-1)}\rvert$ <br> $(0 < \mathrm{cosec}^{-1}x < \frac{1}{2}\pi)$ |
| $\cot^{-1}x$ | $\dfrac{-1}{1+x^2}$ | $x\cot^{-1}x + \frac{1}{2}\ln(1+x^2)$ |
| $e^{ax}$ | $ae^{ax}$ | $e^{ax}/a$ |
| $a^x$ | $a^x \ln a$ | $a^x/\ln a$ |
| $\sinh x$ | $\cosh x$ | $\cosh x$ |
| $\cosh x$ | $\sinh x$ | $\sinh x$ |
| $\tanh x$ | $\mathrm{sech}^2 x$ | $\ln\cosh x$ |
| $\mathrm{sech}\, x$ | $-\mathrm{sech}\, x \tanh x$ | $\tan^{-1}(\sinh x)$ |
| $\mathrm{cosech}\, x$ | $-\mathrm{cosech}\, x \coth x$ | $\ln\lvert\tanh\frac{1}{2}x\rvert$ |
| $\coth x$ | $-\mathrm{cosech}^2 x$ | $\ln\lvert\sinh x\rvert$ |
| $\sinh^{-1}x$ | $\dfrac{1}{\sqrt{(1+x^2)}}$ | $x\sinh^{-1}x - \sqrt{(1+x^2)}$ |
| $\cosh^{-1}x$ | $\dfrac{1}{\sqrt{(x^2-1)}}$ | $x\cosh^{-1}x - \sqrt{(x^2-1)}$ |
| $\tanh^{-1}x$ | $\dfrac{1}{1-x^2}$ | $x\tanh^{-1}x + \frac{1}{2}\ln(1-x^2)$ <br> $(\lvert x\rvert < 1)$ |
| $\mathrm{sech}^{-1}x$ | $\dfrac{-1}{x\sqrt{(1-x^2)}}$ | $x\,\mathrm{sech}^{-1}x + \sin^{-1}x$ |
| $\mathrm{cosech}^{-1}x$ | $\dfrac{-1}{x\sqrt{(1+x^2)}}$ | $x\,\mathrm{cosech}^{-1}x + \sinh^{-1}x$ |
| $\coth^{-1}x$ | $\dfrac{1}{1-x^2}$ | $x\coth^{-1}x + \frac{1}{2}\ln(x^2-1)$ <br> $(\lvert x\rvert > 1)$ |
| $\ln x$ | $1/x$ | $x\ln x - x$ |

## AI.4 Some useful standard integrals

| $f(x)$, $(a > 0)$ | $\int f(x)\,\mathrm{d}x$ |
|---|---|
| $\dfrac{1}{a^2 + x^2}$ | $\dfrac{1}{a}\tan^{-1}\left(\dfrac{x}{a}\right)$ |
| $\dfrac{1}{\sqrt{(a^2 - x^2)}}$ | $\sin^{-1}\left(\dfrac{x}{a}\right)$ |
| $\dfrac{1}{\sqrt{(a^2 + x^2)}}$ | $\sinh^{-1}\left(\dfrac{x}{a}\right)$ or $\ln[x + \sqrt{(x^2 + a^2)}]$ |
| $\dfrac{1}{\sqrt{(x^2 - a^2)}}$ | $\cosh^{-1}\left(\dfrac{x}{a}\right)$ or $\ln[x + \sqrt{(x^2 - a^2)}]$ |
| $\dfrac{1}{a^2 - x^2}$ for $\lvert x\rvert < a$ | $\dfrac{1}{2a}\ln\left(\dfrac{a + x}{a - x}\right)$ |
| $\dfrac{1}{x^2 - a^2}$ for $\lvert x\rvert > a$ | $\dfrac{1}{2a}\ln\left(\dfrac{x - a}{x + a}\right)$ |